DEPARTMENT OF CORRECTIONS
STATE OF KANSAS

ILLINOIS CORRECTIONAL INDUSTRIES

NEVADA CORRECTIONS
THE GREAT SEAL OF THE STATE OF NEVADA

ARKANSAS DEPARTMENT OF CORRECTION
HONOR INTEGRITY PUBLIC SERVICE

AMERICAN CORRECTIONAL ASSOCIATION

ALABAMA DEPT. OF CORRECTIONS
ALABAMA GREAT SEAL

ILLINOIS CORRECTIONS

NEW HAMPSHIRE DEPARTMENT OF CORRECTIONS

STATE OF VERMONT DEPARTMENT OF CORRECTIONS

WEST VIRGINIA DIVISION OF CORRECTIONS
STATE OF WEST VIRGINIA MONTANI SEMPER LIBERI

WISCONSIN DEPARTMENT OF CORRECTIONS

Corrections
in the 21st Century

Corrections
in the 21st Century

seventh edition

Frank Schmalleger, PhD
Distinguished Professor Emeritus
University of North Carolina at Pembroke

John Ortiz Smykla, PhD
Distinguished University Professor
University of West Florida

Mc
Graw
Hill
Education

CORRECTIONS IN THE 21ST CENTURY, SEVENTH EDITION

Published by McGraw-Hill Education, 2 Penn Plaza, New York, NY 10121. Copyright © 2015 by McGraw-Hill Education. All rights reserved. Printed in the United States of America. Previous editions © 2013, 2011, and 2009. No part of this publication may be reproduced or distributed in any form or by any means, or stored in a database or retrieval system, without the prior written consent of McGraw-Hill Education, including, but not limited to, in any network or other electronic storage or transmission, or broadcast for distance learning.

Some ancillaries, including electronic and print components, may not be available to customers outside the United States.

This book is printed on acid-free paper.

1 2 3 4 5 6 7 8 9 0 DOW/DOW 1 0 9 8 7 6 5 4

ISBN 978-0-07-814092-1
MHID 0-07-814092-7

Senior Vice President, Products & Markets: *Kurt L. Strand*
Vice President, General Manager, Products & Markets: *Michael Ryan*
Vice President, Content Production & Technology Services: *Kimberly Meriwether David*
Managing Editor: *Penina Braffman*
Marketing Specialist: *Alexandra Schultz*
Director, Content Production: *Terri Schiesl*
Content Project Manager: *Heather Ervolino*
Buyer: *Nichole Birkenholz*
Cover Designer: *Studio Montage, St. Louis, MO*
Cover Image: *Digital Vision/Getty Images*
Media Project Manager: *Jennifer Bartell*
Compositor: *Laserwords Privated Limited*
Typeface: *10.5/Sabon LT Std*
Printer: *R. R. Donnelley*

All credits appearing on page or at the end of the book are considered to be an extension of the copyright page.

Library of Congress Cataloging-in-Publication Data

Schmalleger, Frank.
    Corrections in the 21st century/Frank Schmalleger, John Ortiz Smykla.—Seventh edition.
        pages cm
    ISBN 978-0-07-814092-1 (alk. paper)
    1. Corrections—United States. 2. Corrections—Vocational guidance—United States.
    I. Smykla, John Ortiz. II. Title.
    HV9471.S36 2015
    364.6023'73—dc23

                                                                                    2013042126

The Internet addresses listed in the text were accurate at the time of publication. The inclusion of a website does not indicate an endorsement by the authors or McGraw-Hill Education, and McGraw-Hill Education does not guarantee the accuracy of the information presented at these sites.

dedication }

For my granddaughters, Ava and Malia
—*Frank Schmalleger*

For my wife, Evelyn, and my granddaughter,
Harper Grace
—*John Smykla*

About the Authors

Frank Schmalleger, PhD, is Distinguished Professor Emeritus at the University of North Carolina at Pembroke.

Dr. Schmalleger holds a bachelor's degree from the University of Notre Dame and both a master's and a doctorate in sociology from The Ohio State University with a special emphasis in criminology. From 1976 to 1994, he taught criminal justice courses at the University of North Carolina at Pembroke, serving for many years as a tenured full professor. For the last 16 of those years, he chaired the Department of Sociology, Social Work, and Criminal Justice. As an adjunct professor with Webster University in St. Louis, Missouri, Dr. Schmalleger helped develop a graduate program in security management and loss prevention that is currently offered on U.S. military bases around the world. He taught courses in that curriculum for more than a decade, focusing primarily on computer and information security. Dr. Schmalleger also has taught in the New School for Social Research online graduate program, helping build the world's first electronic classrooms for criminal justice distance learning.

Dr. Schmalleger is the author of numerous articles and many books, including *Criminal Justice Today* (Prentice Hall, 2015), *Criminal Justice: A Brief Introduction* (Prentice Hall, 2014), *Criminology Today* (Prentice Hall, 2015), and *Criminal Law Today* (Prentice Hall, 2014). He is founding editor of the journal *Criminal Justice Studies* (formerly *The Justice Professional*) and has served as imprint advisor for Greenwood Publishing Group's criminal justice reference series.

Dr. Schmalleger is also the creator of a number of award-winning Web sites (including the former cybrary.info and crimenews.info). He is a member of the Academy of Criminal Justice Sciences, the American Society of Criminology, and the Society of Police Futurists International (where he is a founding member). Schmalleger's author website on Amazon.com can be viewed at www.amazon.com/Frank-Schmalleger/e/B001IGFLVI. Follow him on Twitter @schmalleger.

John Ortiz Smykla, PhD, is Distinguished University Professor at the University of West Florida. Previously, he was professor of criminal justice at the University of Alabama where he served as chair of the criminal justice department, and at the University of South Alabama where he also served as department chair of political science and criminal justice. He earned the interdisciplinary social science PhD in criminal justice, sociology, and anthropology from Michigan State University. He holds bachelor's and master's degrees in sociology from California State University at Northridge.

Dr. Smykla has authored or edited five corrections books, including *Probation, Parole, and Community Based Corrections* (2013) and *Offender Reentry: Rethinking Criminology and Criminal Justice* (2014). His coauthored data set *Executions in the United States, 1608–2003: The Espy File,* funded by a grant from the National Science Foundation, is one of the most frequently requested criminal justice data files from the University of Michigan's Inter-University Consortium for Political and Social Research.

Dr. Smykla has published more than 40 research articles on corrections issues, including "The Human Impact of Capital Punishment," "Effects of a Prison Facility on the Regional Economy," "Jail Type and Inmate Behavior," "Juvenile Drug Courts," "Drunk and Alone in a K-Mart Parking Lot: The Pedagogy of Simulations and Contemporary Attitudes Toward Drinking and Driving," "Correctional Privatization and the Myth of Inherent Efficiency," and most recently, "Reentry in the 21st Century: Challenges and Opportunities" and "More than Meets the Eye: Unsettled Issues in Reentry." He is currently engaged in a five-year study of federal reentry court for the U.S. District Court, Northern District of Florida. Dr. Smykla has delivered more than 50 conference papers in the United States and abroad. In 1986, he was a Senior Fulbright Scholar in Argentina and Uruguay.

Dr. Smykla is a member of the Academy of Criminal Justice Sciences and the Southern Criminal Justice Association. In 1996, the Southern Criminal Justice Association named him Educator of the Year. In 1997, he served as program chair for the annual meeting of the Academy of Criminal Justice Sciences. In 2000, he served as president of the Southern Criminal Justice Association. In 2010, the University of West Florida named him a Distinguished University Professor.

Brief Contents

Expanded Contents

CHAPTER 3
SENTENCING
To Punish or to Reform? 54

PART 2 COMMUNITY CORRECTIONS 87

CHAPTER 4
DIVERSION AND PROBATION
How Most Offenders Are Punished 88

CHAPTER 5
INTERMEDIATE SANCTIONS
Between Probation and Incarceration 123

PART 3   INSTITUTIONAL CORRECTIONS   161

PART 4   THE PRISON WORLD   297

PART 5   ISSUES IN CORRECTIONS 413

CHAPTER 13

PRISON ISSUES AND CONCERNS
Overcrowding, Security, Accreditation, Privatization, and Technology 414

CHAPTER 14

THE VICTIM
Helping Those in Need 459

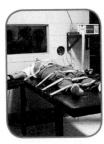

Boxed Features

CAREER PROFILES

ETHICS AND PROFESSIONALISM

PREFACE

Corrections, when seen as the control and punishment of convicted offenders, has been an important part of organized society from the earliest days of civilization. It has not always had a proud past, however. In pre-modern times, atrocious physical punishment, exile, and unspeakable torture were the tools used all too often by those called upon to enforce society's correctional philosophies—especially the strongly felt need for vengeance.

Important changes in correctional practice began around the time of the American Revolution when the purposes of criminal punishments were closely examined by influential reformers. More recently, corrections has become an important field of study in which scientific techniques are valued and reasoned debate is encouraged.

The best, however, is yet to come. Only within the past 30 years have conscientious corrections practitioners begun to embrace the notion of professionalism—wherein ethics, a sense of high purpose, a personal long-term career commitment, a respect for the fundamental humanity of those supervised, and widely agreed-upon principles and standards guide the daily work of correctional personnel. Corrections professionalism, although not yet as well known as police professionalism, has garnered support from policymakers and is winning respect among the public. It serves as this textbook's organizing principle.

Corrections in the 21st Century:

- provides an in-depth look at the past, present, and future of corrections;
- identifies the many *subcomponents* of modern-day corrections;
- highlights the *process* of modern-day corrections;
- focuses on the *issues* facing the correctional enterprise today;
- provides an appreciation for contemporary real-world correctional *practice;*
- examines the opportunities represented by new and developing corrections *technologies;* and
- points students in the direction of the still-emerging ideal of corrections *professionalism.*

It is our belief that a new age of corrections is upon us. It is an age in which the lofty goals of corrections professionalism will take their place alongside the more traditional components of a still-developing field. It is our hope that this textbook will play at least some small part in helping bring about a new and better correctional enterprise—one that is reasonable and equitable to all involved in the justice process.

THE SEVENTH EDITION

The following changes have been made in the Seventh Edition of *Corrections in the 21st Century* to better focus reader attention on the key learning materials in each chapter:

- Correlation of end-of-chapter review questions to the objectives listed at the start of each chapter.
- Enhancement of the photo program to better grab student interest and draw readers into the text.
- Integration of additional evidence-based information throughout the book and frequent citation of the literature relating to such practices.
- Chapter objective numbers placed in the margin near the content to which they relate.
- Placement of Offender Speaks and Staff Speaks boxes on the Online Learning Center to improve readability of the text.
- The addition of Quick Response (QR) scan codes in the margin, leading readers to a wealth of relevant corrections-related materials on the Web (e.g., videos and podcasts) that extend the ideas discussed in the chapter, providing a truly interactive learning experience.
- A number of new stories, many focusing on what's happening internationally in corrections, now open the chapters.
- Incorporation of reviews of the most recent data and literature throughout.
- The addition of a series of Economic Realities and Corrections boxes to the text to illustrate the financial challenges facing correctional agencies and institutions in today's era of budgetary restrictions.
- Updates to statistics and data throughout the book.

Significant chapter-specific content changes include the following:

Chapter 1

- The concept of "sustainable justice."
- New line art depicting the growth in state and federal prison populations.
- Discussion of the Jody Arias case.
- Replacement of the Hurricane Katrina example of social disorganization with the Occupy Wall Street Movement.
- QR codes that direct students to videos and podcasts to extend the ideas discussed in the chapter.
- Discussion of cost-benefit analysis within the enhanced section on evidence-based corrections.

Chapter 2

- A number of Quick Response codes, leading the reader to materials of relevance on the Web.
- Inclusion of historical information on early canon law.

Chapter 3

- New chapter opening story.
- New graphics to improve the chapter's visual appeal.
- Incorporation of updated data and statistics throughout the chapter and inclusion of line art.
- The 2002 U.S. Supreme Court case of *Harris* v. *U.S.*
- QR codes that direct students to videos and podcasts to extend the ideas discussed in the chapter.
- Changes to California's three-strikes law as related to voter approval of that state's Proposition 36.

Chapter 4

- New chapter opening story.
- Latest data on the characteristics of adults on probation.
- Information on the movement to privatize probation.
- Career profile of a federal presentence investigation writer.
- QR codes that direct students to videos and podcasts to extend the ideas discussed in the chapter.
- Coverage on community supervision technology.

- New research on Hawaii's Opportunity Probation Enforcement (HOPE) program.

Chapter 5

- New chapter opening story.
- Revision of coverage on how states are using intermediate sanctions.
- New focus on common elements in states' intermediate sanction reform efforts.
- Evidence-based findings on intermediate sanctions updated.
- QR codes that direct students to videos and podcasts to extend the ideas discussed in the chapter.
- Expanded coverage on the new types of drug courts: veterans treatment court, DWI court, family drug court, reentry court, juvenile drug court, reentry drug court, tribal healing to wellness court, and the Back to TRAC clinical justice model.
- New career profile of a work release program manager.
- New ethics and professionalism insert on the International Community Corrections Association Code of Ethics.
- New coverage on how the fiscal crisis is influencing governors' and legislators' interest in intermediate sanctions.

Chapter 6

- New chapter opening story.
- New learning objective on California's Realignment Act.
- New exhibit of the National Association of Pretrial Service Agencies' Code of Ethics.
- New research from the Justice Policy Institute that discusses the unintended negative consequences of building newer and bigger jails.
- Latest data on the characteristics of jail inmates, staff, and facilities.
- Revised discussion of the most recent data on the decline in the jail suicide rate.
- U.S. Department of Justice updated research on the prevalence of sexual victimization in the nation's jails.
- QR codes that direct students to videos and podcasts to extend the ideas discussed in the chapter.
- Career profile of a jail mental health director.
- Data revision on jails: occupancy, number of public versus private, and size, location, and budgets.

- New discussion of three promising approaches to reentry well suited to the jail setting.
- Revised research on jail industry programs making headlines around the country.
- Major discussion of prisoners confined in jail under California's Realignment Act.

Chapter 7

- New chapter opening story.
- New coverage of the effect of cuts in corrections budgets on personnel, salaries, benefits, overtime, programs, facilities, and services and how states are turning to evidence-based practices, the federal Second Chance Act, drug courts, veterans courts, reentry courts, technology, and assistance from professional associations and advocacy groups for guidance on the effective use of the funds they have.
- Latest data on characteristics of adults under jurisdiction of state and federal prisons.
- Revised discussion of how the movement in EBC and the economic downturn have caused a decline in state prison populations for the first time in four decades.
- QR codes that direct students to videos and podcasts to extend the ideas discussed in the chapter.
- Revised and updated coverage of the federal court order mandating that California reduce its prison population by almost one-fourth.
- New exhibits on the American Correctional Association's Policy on Correctional Health Care, top 10 states with the longest prison sentences, and state prison recidivism rates.
- New detailed analysis of all existing empirical studies on the effectiveness of faith-based prison programs.
- New research on amounts that states are spending on inmate medical care.
- Updated data on the cost of state and federal incarceration.
- Updated discussion of states' use of Justice Reinvestment.
- Revised material on the Federal Bureau of Prisons, UNICOR, and prison security levels.
- Expanded analysis of the important topic of whether incarceration works, citing the latest research by the Pew Center on the States.

Chapter 8

- New chapter opening story.
- Updated material in response to the economic crisis on how states are handling parolees' technical violations.

- Expanded coverage on the needs of prisoners returning to their communities, "ban the box," and the Second Chance Act.
- New research on reentry problems for black women.
- QR codes that direct students to videos and podcasts to extend the ideas discussed in the chapter.
- Career profile of a supervising federal probation officer.
- Revised and expanded analysis of the important topic of what works for parole supervision.
- Latest data on characteristics of adults on parole are included.
- Updated and expanded coverage on the question, "Can parolees vote?"
- New material on reentry court evaluations noting the randomized study being conducted for the U.S. District Court for the Northern District of Florida, the only one of its kind in the United States.
- New exhibit on prisoner reentry and community policing.

Chapter 9

- A new figure that highlights correctional officer pay, showing that it is often higher than commonly believed.
- QR codes that direct students to videos and podcasts to extend the ideas discussed in the chapter.
- Detailed descriptions of custodial and administrative correctional personnel.
- A new exhibit detailing the percentage of women working in corrections.
- Significant revision of the discussion of correctional officer stress.
- Revision of the anti-terrorism material.

Chapter 10

- New chapter opening story.
- Updated and expanded prison argot list.
- Updated and expanded information on sexual victimization within prison.
- Updated statistics and data.
- QR codes that direct students to videos and podcasts to extend the ideas discussed in the chapter.

Chapter 11

- New chapter opening story.
- Removal of some dated material, shortening the chapter slightly.

- Updated information on the impact of California's three strikes law on inmate populations in the state.
- Revised chapter objectives related to material on the doctrine of sovereign immunity and limited court protections of correctional officers facing certain types of civil lawsuits.
- QR codes that direct students to videos and podcasts to extend the ideas discussed in the chapter.
- Three new U.S. Supreme Court cases have been added to the chapter and are now discussed: *Millbrook* v. *U.S.* (2013), *Florence* v. *Burlington County* (2012), and *Howes* v. *Fields* (2012).

Chapter 12

- New chapter opening story.
- Updated coverage on how states are addressing the health care needs of special needs inmates.
- Latest data on the prevalence of HIV in prison.
- Key findings from the American Correctional Association's survey of inmate mental health care.
- Latest data on the characteristics of older inmates (the "silver tsunami" of aging prisoners) and new discussion of why states are not using their compassionate, medical, or geriatric prisoner release laws.
- QR codes that direct students to videos and podcasts to extend the ideas discussed in the chapter.

Chapter 13

- New chapter opening story.
- Updated statistics on the problem of prison crowding, presented new research on overcrowding from the U.S. Government Accountability Office, and addressed new questions about the impact of the recreational use of marijuana on prison overcrowding in two states.
- New material on how states are reducing corrections spending.
- New research findings from interviews with former inmates under active community supervision on the incidence and effects of sexual victimization in state prison.
- Updated statistics on percentage of STGs in prison and jail, and new discussion of the link between STGs in Colorado and the killing of Tom Clements, that state's chief of corrections.
- New material on female gangs.

- New literature from the Colorado DOC arguing that the conditions of supermax confinement do not exacerbate the symptoms of mental illness or create mental illness where none previously existed.
- QR codes that direct students to videos and podcasts to extend the ideas discussed in the chapter.
- Career profile of a federal warden.
- New exhibit on prisoners and detainees held by private prison companies.
- Updated and revised literature on cost comparison of private and public prisons and discussed the ethics of private prison corporations giving campaign contributions and politicians who write laws that favor the private prison industry.
- Updated and expanded coverage on privatizing probation and parole.
- Expanded coverage of inmates' use of cell phones in prison, including new policies to curb their use and new federal legislation making it a felony for inmates to possess them or a wireless device.
- Expanded coverage of the use of security technology to recognize, track, and detect prison offenders and officers and added discussion of the overuse of "virtual visiting."

Chapter 14

- The chapter objectives have been substantially modified along with the summary section and end-of-chapter discussion questions.
- Information about the federal Adam Walsh Child Protection and Safety Act of 2006 was added.
- The timeline on crime victims' rights has been abbreviated.
- QR codes that direct students to videos and podcasts to extend the ideas discussed in the chapter.
- The American Correctional Association correctional policy box has been updated.
- The federally run Dru Sjodin National Sex Offender Public Website is now highlighted.
- The Vision 21 initiative of the federal Office for Victims of Crime is now discussed.

Chapter 15

- New chapter opening story.
- Latest statistics on the number of people whose innocence was established after they were sent to death row, and the trends in capital punishment.

- Latest data on capital punishment around the world and the states that abolished it.
- New coverage of Maryland becoming the 18th state to abolish capital punishment.
- New material on the cost of the death penalty.
- Updated exhibit and text on the number of people executed since 1977 and prisoners under sentence of death.
- New career profile of assistant U.S. attorney.
- New material on "lethal injection firsts" and list of states that (1) have put the death penalty on hold because of legal or legislative action, (2) use only one drug, (3) use more than one drug, and (4) have no death penalty.
- QR codes that direct students to videos and podcasts to extend the ideas discussed in the chapter.
- Advanced discussion of public support for capital punishment.
- Updated coverage and exhibit on compensating people who have been exonerated.
- New text on states' proposal to follow the federal model and create a statewide commission to make the decision as to when to seek the death penalty.

Chapter 16

- New chapter opening story.
- Addition of the U.S. Supreme Court case of *Miller* v. *Alabama* (2012).
- QR codes that direct students to videos and podcasts to extend the ideas discussed in the chapter.
- Statistics and data updated throughout the chapter.
- Ages of juvenile court jurisdiction updated, and Exhibit 16-2 modified to reflect the changes.
- New section on limits of punishment and new U.S. Supreme Court decisions restricting the application of the death penalty in cases involving juveniles.
- Enhanced and updated information on the juvenile court processing of delinquency cases.
- Identification of effective juvenile justice programs through the use of evidence-based research.
- New section on improving the juvenile justice system for girls.

ORGANIZATION

The Seventh Edition of *Corrections in the 21st Century* includes 16 chapters whose organization reflects aspects of the correctional process. Chapters are grouped into five parts, each of which is described in detail in the following paragraphs.

Part One, "Introduction to Corrections," provides an understanding of corrections by explaining the goals underlying the correctional enterprise and by describing the how and why of criminal punishments. Part One identifies professionalism as the key to managing correctional personnel, facilities, and populations successfully. Standard-setting organizations such as the American Correctional Association, the American Jail Association, the American Probation and Parole Association, and the National Commission on Correctional Health Care are identified, and the importance of professional ethics for correctional occupations and correctional administrators is emphasized.

Part Two, "Community Corrections," explains what happens to most convicted offenders, including diversion (the suspension of formal criminal proceedings before conviction in exchange for the defendant's participation in treatment), probation, and intermediate sanctions.

Part Three, "Institutional Corrections," provides a detailed description of jails, prisons, and parole. The reentry challenges facing inmates released from prisons are explained. Education, vocational preparation, and drug treatment programs that are intended to prevent reoffending also are explored.

Part Four, "The Prison World" provides an overview of life inside prison from the points of view of both inmates and staff. Part Four also describes the responsibilities and challenges surrounding the staff role. Chapter 12 focuses attention on special correctional populations, including inmates who are elderly, have HIV/AIDS, are substance abusers, and are mentally and physically challenged. We have chosen to integrate our coverage of women in corrections—including information about the important NIC report titled "Gender Responsive Strategies: Research, Practice, and Guiding Principles for Women Offenders"—throughout the body of the text rather than isolating it in Chapter 12.

Part Five, "Issues in Corrections," explores some of the most controversial topics in contemporary corrections. Prison crowding, capital punishment, the conditional rights of prisoners, and juvenile corrections all can be found in this section of the text. Victims' rights and the role that correctional authorities can play in protecting and advancing those rights also are explored.

PEDAGOGICAL AIDS

Working together, the authors and editor have developed a learning system designed to help students excel in the corrections course. In addition to the many changes already mentioned, we have included a wealth of new photographs to make the book even more inviting and relevant.

To this same end, our real-world chapter-opening vignettes give the material a fresh flavor intended to motivate students to read on; our photo captions, which raise thought-provoking questions, actively engage students in the learning process. Carefully updated tables and figures highlight and amplify the text coverage. And chapter outlines, objectives, and reviews, plus marginal definitions and an end-of-book glossary, all help students master the material.

The Schmalleger/Smykla learning system goes well beyond these essential tools, however. As mentioned, *Corrections in the 21st Century* offers a unique emphasis on corrections professionalism, an emphasis that has prompted us to create a number of innovative learning tools that focus on the real world of corrections:

- A concentration on *Evidence-Based Corrections*—What actually works in correctional settings? that is, what correctional programs are effective in reducing recidivism and in preventing future crimes? Evidence-based corrections is an exciting new development in the corrections field, and a number of agencies, institutions, and organizations now emphasize the use of scientific evidence. Evidence-based policy, which builds on evidence-based corrections, is an approach that helps people make well-informed decisions about policies and programs by putting the best available evidence from research at the heart of policy development and implementation.

- *Career Profiles*—enlightening minibiographies of corrections professionals, such as a parole officer, a victims' advocate, a corrections officer, a youth counselor, and a substance abuse manager.

- Addition of *Economic Realities and Corrections* boxes throughout the text to recognize budgetary constraints affecting correctional agencies nationwide, highlighting innovative evidence-based practices demonstrating "what works."

- *Ethics and Professionalism*—boxes that highlight ethical codes and critical concerns from America's premier corrections-related professional associations. Included are features from the American Correctional Association, the American Jail Association, the American Probation and Parole Association, International Association of Community Corrections, the International Association of Correctional Training Personnel, National Association of Pretrial Services Agencies, and others. Included in each Ethics and Professionalism box are author-created Ethical Dilemmas, which present students with ethical questions from the corrections field and guide them to an insightful resolution. Ethical Dilemmas are supplemented with Web-based resources maintained by the authors and specifically selected to help students navigate particular ethics-related issues.

In addition to the features we have developed to further our goal of creating a uniquely practical, professionally oriented text, we also have included end-of-chapter review material to help students master the concepts and principles developed in the chapter:

- *Chapter Summary*—a valuable learning tool organized into sections that mirror the chapter-opening objectives exactly; the summary restates all of the chapter's most critical points.

- *Key Terms*—a comprehensive list of the terms defined in the margins of the chapter, complete with page references to make it easy for students to go back and review further.

- *Questions for Review*—objective study questions (exactly mirroring the chapter-opening objectives and summary) that allow students to test their knowledge and prepare for exams.

- *Thinking Critically About Corrections*—broad-based questions that challenge students to think critically about chapter concepts and issues.

- *On-the-Job Decision Making*—unique experiential exercises that enable students to apply what they have learned in the chapter to the daily work of correctional personnel.

- *QR Codes*—unique machine-readable codes in every chapter directing students to videos and podcasts that extend the ideas discussed in the chapter, providing a truly interactive learning experience.

SUPPLEMENTS

Visit our Online Learning Center Web site at www.mhhe.com/schmalleger7e for robust student and instructor resources.

For Students

Student resources include features on "Careers in Corrections," "Professionalism in Corrections," "Ethical Dilemmas," corrections-related Internet links, chapter-specific multiple-choice self-quizzes, and exercises.

For Instructors

The password-protected instructor portion of the Web site includes the instructor's manual, a comprehensive computerized test bank, PowerPoint lecture slides, and a variety of additional instructor resources.

Other dynamic instructor resources include:

McGraw-Hill Higher Education and Blackboard have teamed up.

Blackboard, the Web-based course-management system, has partnered with McGraw-Hill to better allow students and faculty to use online materials and activities to complement face-to-face teaching. Blackboard features exciting social learning and teaching tools that foster more logical, visually impactful and active learning opportunities for students. You'll transform your closed-door classrooms into communities where students remain connected to their educational experience 24 hours a day.

This partnership allows you and your students access to McGraw-Hill's Create™ right from within your Blackboard course—all with one single sign-on. McGraw-Hill and Blackboard can now offer you easy access to industry leading technology and content, whether your campus hosts it, or we do. Be sure to ask your local McGraw-Hill representative for details.

Craft your teaching resources to match the way you teach! With McGraw-Hill Create™, www.mcgrawhill-create.com, you can easily rearrange chapters, combine material from other content sources, and quickly upload content you have written such as your course syllabus or teaching notes. Find the content you need in Create by searching through thousands of leading McGraw-Hill textbooks. Arrange your book to fit your teaching style. Create even allows you to personalize your book's appearance by selecting the cover and adding your name, school, and course information. Order a Create book and you'll receive a complimentary print review copy in three to five business days or a complimentary electronic review copy (eComp) via e-mail in minutes. Go to www.create.mcgraw-hill.com today and register to experience how McGraw-Hill Create™ empowers you to teach your students your way.

With the CourseSmart eTextbook version of this title, students can save up to 50 percent off the cost of a print book, reduce their impact on the environment, and access powerful Web tools for learning. Faculty can also review and compare the full text online without having to wait for a print desk copy. CourseSmart is an online eTextbook, which means users need to be connected to the Internet in order to access it. Students can also print sections of the book for maximum portability. For further details, contact your sales representative or go to www.coursesmart.com.

Tegrity Campus is a service that makes your classes available all the time. It automatically captures every lecture in a searchable format, allowing students to review course material when they study and complete assignments. With a simple one-click, start-and-stop process, you capture all computer screens and corresponding audio. Students can replay any part of the class with easy-to-use, browser-based viewing on a PC or Mac.

McGraw-Hill's online courses provide interactive digital content and activities aligned to learning objectives that work with most learning management systems as a true cartridge. Designed to be used in conjunction with a textbook, McGraw-Hill's online course tools combine visual, auditory, and interactive elements to encourage all types of learners to connect and retain knowledge. Course content includes animation, graphics, streaming video, and interactive activities to enliven the content and motivate the learner. Specifically for the area of criminal justice, the McGraw-Hill online course content tools were developed around content areas that have been established by the Academy of Criminal Justice Sciences Minimum Standards of Criminal Justice Education. Preview the *Corrections* course content and more at www.OnlineLearning.com.

Course Management Systems—whether you use WebCT, Blackboard, e-College, or another course management system, McGraw-Hill will provide you with a *Corrections* cartridge that enables you either to conduct your course entirely online or to supplement your lectures with online material. And if your school does not yet have one of these course management systems, we can provide you with PageOut, an easy-to-use tool that allows you to create your own course Web page and access all material on the *Corrections* Online Learning Center.

Please contact your local McGraw-Hill representative for more information on any of the above supplements.

IN APPRECIATION

Writing a textbook requires a great deal of help and support. We would like to acknowledge and thank the many individuals on whom we relied. Special thanks go to William W. Sondervan, Director of Criminal Justice, Investigative Forensics and Legal Studies at the University of Maryland, and Ania Dobrzanska, Program Coordinator with the Moss Group in Washington, DC, for contributing the reading "Professionalism in Corrections" to the Online Learning Center; to Dennis Stevens formerly of Sacred Heart University, Fairfield, Connecticut for his research on special features; to Jody Klein-Saffran at the Federal Bureau of Prisons and Gary Bayens at Washburn University for their contributions to our chapters on parole and juvenile corrections, respectively; to Erika Overall and Major William Hayes of the Kent Division of the King County (Washington) Jail, Regional Justice Center for the photograph and schematic of the fourth-generation jail; to the criminal justice faculty and staff and the dean of the College of Professional Studies at the University of West Florida for their encouragement and for the resources they made available; to Laura Joyce for her help in Web development; and to the many students who suggested ideas for chapter opening stories. We also gratefully acknowledge the contributions of the following individuals who helped in the development of this textbook.

Steve Abrams, Ret.
California Department of Corrections
    and Rehabilitation
Santa Rosa, California

Stanley E. Adelman
University of Arkansas School of Law
Little Rock, Arkansas
University of Tulsa College of Law
Tulsa, Oklahoma

Colleen Andrews
Ozarks Technical Community College
Springfield, Missouri

John Augustine
Triton College
River Grove, Illinois

Tom Austin
Shippensburg University
Shippensburg, Pennsylvania

Ken Barnes
Arizona Western College
Yuma, Arizona

Jeri Barnett
Virginia Western Community College
Roanoke, Virginia

Rose Johnson Bigler
Curry College
Milton, Massachusetts

Kathy J. Black-Dennis
University of Louisville
Louisville, Kentucky

Robert Bohm
University of Central Florida
Orlando, Florida

David A. Bowers Jr.
University of South Alabama
Mobile, Alabama

Greg Brown
Westwood College of Technology
Denver, Colorado

David E. Carter
Southern Oregon University
Ashland, Oregon

Kenneth L. Done
Coahoma Community College
Clarksdale, Mississippi

Vicky Dorworth
Montgomery College
Rockville, Maryland

Carrie L. Dunson
Central Missouri State University
Warrensburg, Missouri

Michael Earll
Western Technical College
La Crosse, Wisconsin

Hilary Estes
Southern Illinois University, Carbondale
Carbondale, Illinois

Robert Figlestahler
Eastern Kentucky University
Richmond, Kentucky

Lynn Fortney
EBSCO Subscription Services
Birmingham, Alabama

Harold A. Frossard
Moraine Valley Community College
Palos Hills, Illinois

Michelle Furlow
Moraine Valley Community College
Palos Hills, Illinois

Don Drennon Gala
Federal Bureau of Prisons
Atlanta, Georgia

Donna Hale
Shippensburg University
Shippensburg, Pennsylvania

Homer C. Hawkins
Michigan State University
East Lansing, Michigan

Nancy L. Hogan
Ferris State University
Big Rapids, Michigan

Ronald G. Iacovetta
Wichita State University
Wichita, Kansas

Connie Ireland
California State University, Long Beach
Long Beach, California

James L. Jengeleski
Shippensburg University
Shippensburg, Pennyslvania

Brad Johnson
Atlanta, Georgia

Kathrine Johnson
University of West Florida
Ft. Walton Beach, Florida

John Calvin Jones
North Carolina A&T State University
Greensboro, North Carolina

Kay King
Johnson County Community College
Overland Park, Kansas

Mike Klemp-North
Ferris State University
Big Rapids, Michigan

Julius Koefoed
Kirkwood Community College
Cedar Rapids, Iowa

Michael Kwan
Salt Lake Community College
Taylorsville, Utah

James Lasley
California State University, Fullerton
Fullerton, California

Walter B. Lewis
St. Louis Community College at Meramec
Kirkwood, Missouri

Shelley Listwan
Kent State University
Kent, Ohio

Jess Maghan
Forum for Comparative Correction
Chester, Connecticut

Preston S. Marks
Keiser University

Laurie A. Michelman
Cayuga Community College
Auburn, New York

Rosie Miller
Coahoma Community College
Clarksdale, Mississippi

Alvin Mitchell
Delgado Community College
New Orleans, Louisiana

Etta Morgan
Pennsylvania State University
Capital College, Pennsylvania

Kathleen Nicolaides
University of North Carolina, Charlotte
Charlotte, North Carolina

Sarah Nordin
Solano Community College
Suisun City, California

Michael F. Perna
Broome Community College
Binghamton, New York

Terry L. Pippin
College of Southern Nevada
Henderson, Nevada

Lisa Pitts
Washburn University
Topeka, Kansas

Scott Plutchak
University of Alabama at Birmingham
Birmingham, Alabama

Bobby B. Polk
Metropolitan Community College
Omaha, Nebraska

Wayne D. Posner
East Los Angeles College
Monterey Park, California

Barbara R. Russo
Wayne Community College
Goldsboro, North Carolina

John Sloan
University of Alabama at Birmingham
Birmingham, Alabama

Larry E. Spencer
Alabama State University
Montgomery, Alabama

Anthony C. Trevelino
Camden County College
Blackwood, New Jersey

Sheryl Van Horne
Radford University
Radford, Virginia

Shela R. Van Ness
University of Tennessee at Chattanooga
Chattanooga, Tennessee

Gennaro F. Vito
University of Louisville
Louisville, Kentucky

Brenda Vos
University of North Florida
Jacksonville, Florida

Kiesha Warren-Gordon
Ball State University
Muncie, Indiana

Anthony White
Illinois Central College
East Peoria, Illinois

Earl White
Illinois Central College
Peoria, Illinois

Ed Whittle
Florida Metropolitan University at Tampa College
Tampa, Florida

Beth Wiersma
University of Nebraska at Kearney
Kearney, Nebraska

Robert R. Wiggins
Cedarville College
Cedarville, Ohio

Jeffrey Zack
Fayetteville Technical Community College
Fayetteville, North Carolina

Kristen M. Zgoba
Rutgers University
Piscataway, New Jersey

Dawn Zobel
Federal Bureau of Prisons
Alderson, West Virginia

Finally, we want to acknowledge the special debt that we owe to the McGraw-Hill team, including managing editor Penina Braffman for keeping the project on track; marketing manager Alexandra Schultz for seeing value in this textbook; the developmental editing team at ansrsource for their attention to the many day-to-day details that a project like this entails; project manager Heather Ervolino; buyer Nichole Birkenholz; full-service project manager Ligo Alex; permissions editor Sheri Gilbert; photo researcher LouAnn Wilson; copy editor JaNoel Lowe; and indexer Judy Lyon Davis. The professional vision, guidance, and support of these dedicated professionals helped bring this project to fruition. A hearty "thank you" to all.

Frank Schmalleger

John Smykla

Introduction to Corrections

Part One develops an understanding of corrections by examining the purposes of correctional punishments and by exploring how offenders have been punished throughout history.

Today, crime rates are falling but the number of people under correctional supervision (on probation or parole or in jail or prison) has only started to decline from historical highs. Get-tough-on-crime attitudes, the War on Drugs, and the reduction in the use of discretionary parole board release explain what some have seen

as the overuse of imprisonment in the past two decades.

Professionalism is the key to effectively managing correctional populations. Standard-setting organizations such as the American Correctional Association, the American Jail Association, the American Probation and Parole Association, and the National Commission on Correctional Health Care offer detailed sets of written principles for correctional occupations and correctional administrators.

Nevertheless, professional credentialing in corrections is new. The seed was planted during the Enlightenment when reformers such as Cesare Beccaria and the Philadelphia Quakers shifted the focus of punishment away from the body and toward the soul and human spirit. Correcting the soul and human spirit required understanding the causes of crime and new reforms. To that end, the National Prison Association (now known as the American Correctional Association) met

in Cincinnati, Ohio, in 1870 to advance correctional theory and practice. The assembly elected then Ohio governor and future U.S. president Rutherford B. Hayes as the first president of the association. Today, the ACA remains the leader in advancing professionalism in corrections through education, training, and skills development.

The professional nature of corrections is also seen in the way sanctions are developed. From a time when theory and practice advocated indeterminate sentences to the legislatively mandated determinate sentences of today, correctional decision makers have had to use their knowledge of human behavior, philosophy, and law to construct sanctions that are fair and just. The correctional goals of retribution, just deserts, deterrence, incapacitation, rehabilitation, and restoration have produced the sanctions of probation, intermediate sanctions, jail, prison, parole, and capital punishment.

What are the consequences of punishment? Choosing the best sanction means understanding the political, social, economic, human, and moral consequences of crime control. For that reason, corrections is a field in which complex decision making requires the skills of professional staff and administrators.

CORRECTIONS

An Overview

CHAPTER OBJECTIVES

After completing this chapter you should be able to do the following:

1 Describe the corrections explosion of the past 20 years, including the recent leveling off of correctional populations.

2 Describe how crime is measured in the United States, and list the kinds of crimes that cause people to enter correctional programs and institutions.

3 List and describe the various components of the criminal justice system, including the major components of the corrections subsystem.

4 Explain the importance of professionalism in the corrections field, and describe the characteristics of a true professional.

5 Define *evidence-based corrections,* and explain the important role that it plays in corrections professionalism today.

6 Understand what is meant by *social diversity,* and explain why issues of race, gender, and ethnicity are important in corrections today.

> " *The use of evidence-based practices in corrections and public policy is now considered the gold standard for policy and program development.*
>
> —Richard Tewksbury and Jill Levenson, "When Evidence Is Ignored: Residential Restrictions for Sex Offenders," *Corrections Today,* December 2007, p. 34 "

In 2013, federal auditors reported that inmates in state prisons and jails had filed more than 173,000 fraudulent income tax returns, claiming refunds totaling $2.5 billion.[1] Another audit found that 29 inmates received $50,000 in federal tax payments for electric vehicles they falsely claimed they had purchased.

Although prisoner tax scams are not new, the number of such cases has grown rapidly in recent years. Inmates typically use stolen social security numbers when filing and have refunds sent to friends and relatives who are not behind bars. Those collaborators then deposit a large portion of the refunds they receive into inmates' accounts.

On a related note, prisoners' use of outlawed cell phones to make calls from inside of correctional institutions has grown exponentially as the number of phones in general circulation has expanded. Recently, for example, California correctional officers seized nearly 6,000 banned cell phones from the state's prisoners, while officials with Maryland's Department of Public Safety and Correctional Services confiscated over 3,600 cell phones in the past three years.[2] In Mississippi, nearly 2,000 contraband phones were confiscated during the first half of 2010 alone. The issue of contraband cell phone use inside of prisons is discussed in a number of places throughout this book.

A corrections officer examines almost 2,000 cell phones that have been confiscated from prisoners at California State Prison Solano over the last few years. How does this photo illustrate at least some of the problems facing correctional personnel today?

Illicit cell phone usage, fraudulent tax return filing, and similar other outlawed[3] activities that occur behind prison bars illustrate the close connection that inmates retain to the outside society, and raise the question, "Do prisons really make us safe?"[4] What about other corrections programs, such as probation, parole, jails, alternative sentencing programs, and institutions for juvenile offenders? If they make our society a safer place in which to live, then the recent and rapid growth in correctional populations that took place between 1980 and 2010—and which is discussed in the next section of this chapter—is understandable. If they don't contribute much to safety and security, however, then we must look elsewhere to understand why such rapid growth occurred.

THE CORRECTIONS EXPLOSION: WHERE DO WE GO NOW?

`CO1-1`

One amazing fact stands out from all the contemporary information about corrections: While serious **crime** in the United States consistently declined throughout much of the 1990s, and while such declines continued into the early years of the 21st century, the number of people under correctional

crime
A violation of a criminal law.

prison

A state or federal confinement facility that has custodial authority over adults sentenced to confinement.

supervision in this country—not just the number of convicted offenders sent to **prison**—continued to climb, and only started to level off after 2010. Crime rates are approximately 20 percent lower today than they were in 1980. They are near their lowest level in 25 years. But the number of people on probation is up almost 300 percent since 1980, the nation's prison population has increased by more than 400 percent, and the number of persons on parole has more than doubled. Exhibit 1–1 illustrates trends in federal and state prison populations.

EXHIBIT 1–1 **The Growth of Imprisonment in the United States**

State prison populations 1925–2012

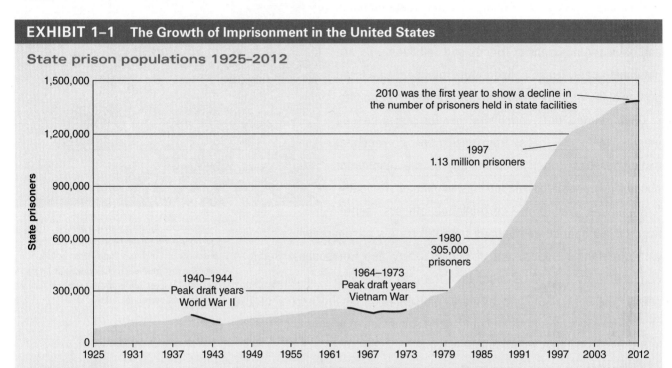

2010 was the first year to show a decline in the number of prisoners held in state facilities

1997
1.13 million prisoners

1980
305,000
prisoners

1940–1944
Peak draft years
World War II

1964–1973
Peak draft years
Vietnam War

Source: Bureau of Justice Statistics, *Crime and Justice Atlas 2000* (Washington, DC: Bureau of Justice Statistics, 2001), pp. 42–43; and E. Ann Carson and Daniela Golinelli, *Prisoners in 2012* (Washington, DC: Bureau of Justice Statistics, 2012); and other years.

Federal prison populations 1925–2012

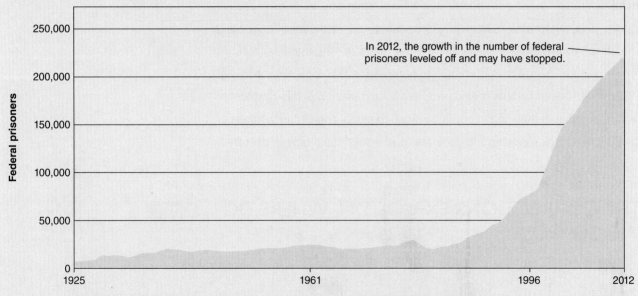

In 2012, the growth in the number of federal prisoners leveled off and may have stopped.

Source: Bureau of Justice Statistics; and E. Ann Carson and Daniela Golinelli, *Prisoners in 2012* (Washington, DC: Bureau of Justice Statistics, 2013); and other years.

EXHIBIT 1–2	Number of State Prisoners by Offense, 2012		
Type of Offense	**All**	**Male**	**Female**
Violent offenses	710,875	678,786	33,695
Property offenses	245,351	220,753	25,486
Drug offenses	225,242	203,080	22,971
Public-order offenses	141,800	134,200	7,950

Source: Adapted from E. Ann Carson and Daniela Golinelli, *Prisoners in 2012* (Washington, DC: Bureau of Justice Statistics, 2013).

The question is, Why? Why did the correctional population increase so dramatically in the face of declining crime rates? The answer to this question, like the answers to most societal enigmas, is far from simple, and it has a number of dimensions.

First, it is important to recognize that get-tough-on-crime laws, such as the three-strikes (and two-strikes) laws that were enacted in many states in the mid-1990s, fueled rapid increases in prison populations. The conservative attitudes that gave birth to those laws are still with us.

A second reason correctional populations have rapidly increased can be found in the nation's War on Drugs. The War on Drugs led to the arrest and conviction of many offenders, resulting in larger correctional populations in nearly every jurisdiction (especially within the federal correctional system). In Exhibit 1–2, compare the total number of individuals incarcerated for drug offenses with, for example, the total incarcerated for property offenses. Although they account for a large portion of the nation's correctional population, drug arrests do not figure into the FBI's calculations of the nation's rate of serious crimes. Hence, the War on Drugs goes a long way toward explaining the growth in correctional populations even while the rate of "serious crime" in the United States appears to be declining.

Third, parole authorities, fearing civil liability and public outcry, became increasingly reluctant to release inmates. This contributed to a further expansion of prison populations.

Fourth, as some observers have noted, the corrections boom created its own growth dynamic.[5] As ever increasing numbers of people are placed on probation, the likelihood of probation violations increases. Prison sentences for more violators result in larger prison populations. When inmates are released from prison, they swell the numbers of those on parole, leading to a larger number of parole violations, which in turn fuels further prison growth. Statistics show that the number of criminals being sent to prison for at least the second time has increased steadily, accounting for approximately 35 percent of the total number of admissions.[6]

Historical Roots of the Corrections Explosion

Seen historically, the growth of correctional populations may be more the continuation of a long-term trend than the result of social conditions prevailing around the start of the twenty-first century. A look at the data shows that correctional populations continued to increase through widely divergent political eras and economic conditions. Census reports show an almost relentless increase in the rate of imprisonment over the past 160 years. In 1850, for example, only 29 people were imprisoned in this country for every 100,000 persons in the population.[7] By 1890, the rate had risen to 131 per 100,000. The rate grew slowly until 1980, when the rate of imprisonment in the United States stood at 153 per 100,000. At that

U.S. correctional populations have grown dramatically over the past 25 years, as this image of inmates living in a modified gymnasium at the Mule Creek State Prison in Ione, California, illustrates. What factors led to a substantial increase in the use of imprisonment in this country beginning in the 1980s?

point, a major shift toward imprisonment began. While crime rates rose sharply in the middle to late 1980s, the rate of imprisonment rose far more dramatically. Today, the rate of imprisonment in this country is around 480 per 100,000 persons. The rate appears to have peaked in 2009 (at over 500 prisoners per every 100,000 people in the country), and now seems to be declining—if only a bit.[8] Exhibit 1–3 illustrates changes in the rate of imprisonment over the past 160 years. Probation statistics—first available in 1935—show an even more amazing rate of growth. Although only 59,530 offenders were placed on probation throughout the United States in 1935, around 4 million people are on probation today.[9] Finally, it is worth noting that although prison populations finally started to decrease around 2011–2012, much of that decrease was due to initiatives such as California's realignment strategy (discussed elsewhere in this text), which repositioned sentenced inmates from state facilities to those at the county level—thus lowering the "official" rate of imprisonment, but not necessarily resulting in a decline in the number of people held behind bars.

Turning the Corner

While get-tough-on-crime attitudes continue to persist in American society today, they have largely been trumped by the economic realities brought on by the Great Recession of the early 21st century. Today's state budgets have been hard pressed to continue funding prison expansion, and the number of people behind bars began to show a decline beginning around 2010. Alternatives to imprisonment, most of which will be discussed in coming chapters, are many and include probation, fines, and community service—to which convicted offenders are being sentenced in increasing numbers. In order to reduce correctional expenditures even further, some states are using forms of early release from prison, shortening time served, reducing the period of probation or parole supervision, and shifting the responsibility of supervising convicted offenders to county-level governments (and away from state responsibility). We will examine these innovations at various

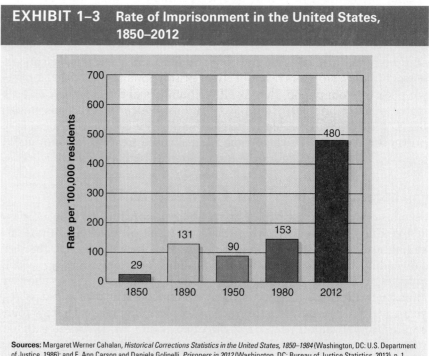

EXHIBIT 1–3 Rate of Imprisonment in the United States, 1850–2012

Rate per 100,000 residents

Year	Rate
1850	29
1890	131
1950	90
1980	153
2012	480

Sources: Margaret Werner Cahalan, *Historical Corrections Statistics in the United States, 1850–1984* (Washington, DC: U.S. Department of Justice, 1986); and E. Ann Carson and Daniela Golinelli, *Prisoners in 2012* (Washington, DC: Bureau of Justice Statistics, 2013), p. 1.

places throughout this text, especially in a number of Economic Realities and Corrections boxes that are found in different chapters.

As states grapple with the economic realities of reduced revenues and constrained budgets, it has become increasingly important to get the most "bang for the buck," so to speak, out of correctional programs. Moreover, responsible legislators and other policy makers are beginning to realize that spending policies of the past will not work in the future. In 2012, in her presidential address to the Academy of Criminal Justice Sciences, Melissa Hickman Barlow outlined a plan for the implementation of **sustainable justice**. Barlow defined sustainable justice as "criminal laws and criminal justice institutions, policies, and practices that achieve justice in the present without compromising the ability of future generations to have the benefits of a just society."[10] Barlow's call for affordable justice, based on principles and operating practices that can be carried into the future without bankrupting generations yet to come, represents an important turning point in our nation's approach to corrections and other justice institutions.

As we will see later in this chapter, the evidence-based movement in corrections, which seeks to evaluate programs and services to see which are the most effective relative to their costs, plays a widening role in correctional administration today—and should contribute much to the call for sustainable justice.

Correctional Employment

Growing correctional populations and increasing budgets have led to a dramatically expanding correctional workforce and enhanced employment opportunities within the field. According to historical reports, persons employed in the corrections field totaled approximately 27,000 in 1950.[11] By 1975, the number had risen to about 75,000. The most current statistics available show that the number of uniformed correctional officers has increased to more than 490,000.[12] When juvenile detention facility personnel, probation and parole officers, correctional administrators, jailers, and other corrections professionals are added, the total number of persons employed in corrections today stands at more than 748,000.[13] Exhibit 1–4 shows some of the employment possibilities in corrections.

sustainable justice

Criminal laws and criminal justice institutions, policies, and practices that achieve justice in the present without compromising the ability of future generations to have the benefits of a just society.

See Sentencing Project Director, Marc Mauer, discuss reducing prison populations in Texas in the face of budget constraints at: http://www.youtube.com/watch?v=956 GuUNWEjc&feature=player_detailpage, or scan this code with the QR app on your smartphone or digital device to watch the video. The transcript of the interview can be read here: http://www.texastribune.org/texas-legislature/82nd-legislative-session/marc-mauer-the-tt-interview/

EXHIBIT 1–4	**Careers in Corrections**

Academic teacher	Field administrator	Psychologist
Activity therapy administrator	Fugitive apprehension officer	Recreation coordinator
Business manager	Human services counselor	Social worker
Case manager	Job placement officer	Statistician
Chaplain	Mental health clinician	Substance abuse counselor
Chemical dependency manager	Parole caseworker	Unit leader
Children's services counselor	Parole officer	Victim advocate
Classification officer	Presentence investigator	Vocational instructor
Clinical social worker	Probation officer	Warden/superintendent
Correctional officer	Program officer	Youth services coordinator
Dietary officer	Program specialist	Youth supervisor
Drug court coordinator	Programmer/analyst	

Note: Consult the Appendix: Careers in Corrections at www.mhhe.com/schmalleger7e for the steps involved in career planning, developing employability and job readiness, and finding the right job.

New prisons mean jobs and can contribute greatly to the health of local economies. Some economically disadvantaged towns—from Tupper Lake, in the Adirondack Mountains of upstate New York, to Edgefield, South Carolina—have cashed in on the prison boom, having successfully competed to become sites for new prisons. Until recently, the competition for new prison facilities is reminiscent of the efforts states made years ago to attract new automobile factories and other industries.

CRIME AND CORRECTIONS

The crimes that bring people into the American correctional system include felonies, misdemeanors, and minor law violations that are sometimes called *infractions*.

Felonies are serious crimes. Murder, rape, aggravated assault, robbery, burglary, and arson are felonies in all jurisdictions within the United States, although the names for these crimes may differ from state to state. A general way to think about felonies is to remember that a **felony** is a serious crime whose commission can result in confinement in a state or federal correctional institution for more than a year.

In some states a felony conviction can result in the loss of certain civil privileges. A few states make conviction of a felony and the resulting incarceration grounds for uncontested divorce. Others prohibit convicted felony offenders from running for public office or owning a firearm, and some exclude them from professions such as medicine, law, and police work.

Huge differences in the treatment of specific crimes exist among states. Some crimes classified as felonies in one part of the country may be misdemeanors in another. In still other states, they may not even be crimes at all! Such is the case with some drug law violations and with social order offenses such as homosexual acts, prostitution, and gambling.

Misdemeanors, which compose the second major crime category, are relatively minor violations of the criminal law. They include crimes such as petty theft (the theft of items of little worth), simple assault (in which the victim suffers no serious injury and in which none was intended), breaking and entering, the possession of burglary tools, disorderly conduct, disturbing the peace, filing a false crime report, and writing bad checks (although the amount for which the check is written may determine the classification of this offense). In general, misdemeanors can be thought of as any crime punishable by a year or less in confinement.

Within felony and misdemeanor categories, most states distinguish among degrees, or levels, of seriousness. Texas law, for example, establishes five felony classes and three classes of misdemeanor—intended to guide judges in assessing the seriousness of particular criminal acts. The Texas penal code then specifies categories into which given offenses fall.

A third category of crime is the **infraction**. The term, which is not used in all jurisdictions, refers to minor violations of the law that are less serious than misdemeanors. Infractions may include such violations of the law as jaywalking, spitting on the sidewalk, littering, and certain traffic violations, including the failure to wear a seat belt. People committing infractions are typically ticketed—that is, given citations—and released, usually upon a promise to appear later in court. Court appearances may be waived upon payment of a fine, which is often mailed in.

felony

A serious criminal offense; specifically, one punishable by death or by incarceration in a prison facility for more than a year.

misdemeanor

A relatively minor violation of the criminal law, such as petty theft or simple assault, punishable by confinement for one year or less.

infraction

A minor violation of state statute or local ordinance punishable by a fine or other penalty, or by a specified, usually very short term of incarceration.

CO1-2   ## Measuring Crime

Two important sources of information on crime for correctional professionals are the FBI's Uniform Crime Reporting Program (UCR) and the

Bureau of Justice Statistics' National Crime Victimization Survey (NCVS). Corrections professionals closely analyze these data to forecast the numbers and types of **correctional clients** to expect in the future. The forecasts can be used to project the need for different types of detention and rehabilitation services and facilities.

correctional clients

Prison inmates, probationers, parolees, offenders assigned to alternative sentencing programs, and those held in jails.

The Crime Funnel

Not all crimes are reported, and not everyone who commits a reported crime is arrested, so relatively few offenders enter the criminal justice system. Of those who do, some are not prosecuted (perhaps because the evidence against them is insufficient), others plead guilty to lesser crimes, and others are found not guilty. Some who are convicted are diverted from further processing by the system or may be fined or ordered to counseling. Hence, the proportion of criminal offenders who eventually enter the correctional system is small, as Exhibit 1–5 shows.[14]

EXHIBIT 1–5   The Crime Funnel

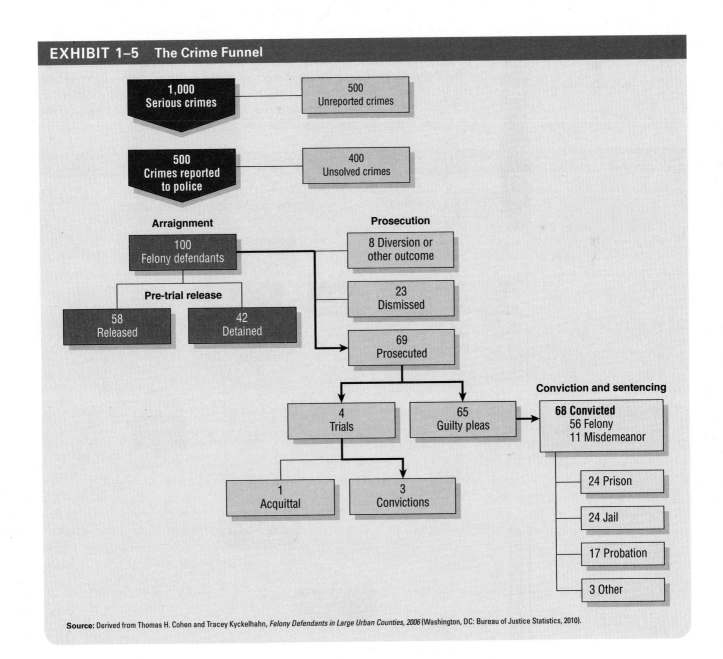

Source: Derived from Thomas H. Cohen and Tracey Kyckelhahn, *Felony Defendants in Large Urban Counties, 2006* (Washington, DC: Bureau of Justice Statistics, 2010).

CO1-3 CORRECTIONS AND THE CRIMINAL JUSTICE SYSTEM

criminal justice

The process of achieving justice through the application of the criminal law and through the workings of the criminal justice system. Also, the study of the field of criminal justice.

criminal justice system

The collection of all the agencies that perform criminal justice functions, whether these are operations or administration or technical support. The basic divisions of the criminal justice system are police, courts, and corrections.

Corrections is generally considered the final stage in the criminal justice process. Some aspects of corrections, however, come into play early in the process. Keep in mind that although the term **criminal justice** can be used to refer to the justice *process*, it can also be used to describe our *system* of justice. Criminal justice agencies, taken as a whole, are said to compose the **criminal justice system**.

The components of the criminal justice system are (1) police, (2) courts, and (3) corrections. Each component, because it contains a variety of organizations and agencies, can be termed a *subsystem*. The subsystem of corrections, for example, includes prisons, agencies of probation and parole, jails, and a variety of alternative programs.

The *process* of criminal justice involves the activities of the agencies that make up the criminal justice system. The process of criminal justice begins when a crime is discovered or reported.

Court decisions based on the due process guarantees of the U.S. Constitution require that specific steps be taken in the justice process. Although the exact nature of those steps varies among jurisdictions, the description that follows portrays the most common sequence of events in response to serious criminal behavior. Exhibit 1–6, which diagrams the American criminal justice system, indicates the relationship among the stages in the criminal justice processing of adult offenders.

EXHIBIT 1–6   The Adult Criminal Justice System

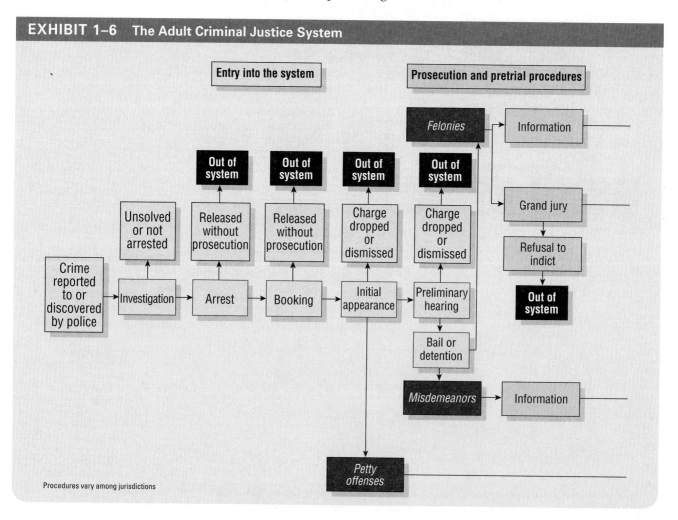

Procedures vary among jurisdictions

Entering the Correctional System

The criminal justice system does not respond to all crime because most crimes are not discovered or reported to the police.[15] Law enforcement agencies learn about crimes from the reports of citizens, through discovery by a police officer in the field, or through investigative and intelligence work. Once a law enforcement agency knows of a crime, the agency must identify and arrest a suspect before the case can proceed. Sometimes a suspect is found at the scene; other times, however, identifying a suspect requires an extensive investigation. Often no one is identified or apprehended—the crime goes unsolved. If an offender is arrested, booked, and jailed to await an initial court appearance, the intake, custody, confinement, and supervision aspects of corrections first come into play at this stage of the criminal justice process.

Prosecution and Pretrial Procedure

After an arrest, law enforcement agencies present information about the case and about the accused to the prosecutor, who decides whether to file formal charges with the court. If no charges are filed, the accused must be released. The prosecutor can also drop charges after filing them. Such a choice is called *nolle prosequi;* and when it happens, a case is said to be "nolled" or "nollied."

A suspect charged with a crime must be taken before a judge or magistrate without unnecessary delay. At the initial appearance, the judge or

EXHIBIT 1–6 *(continued)*

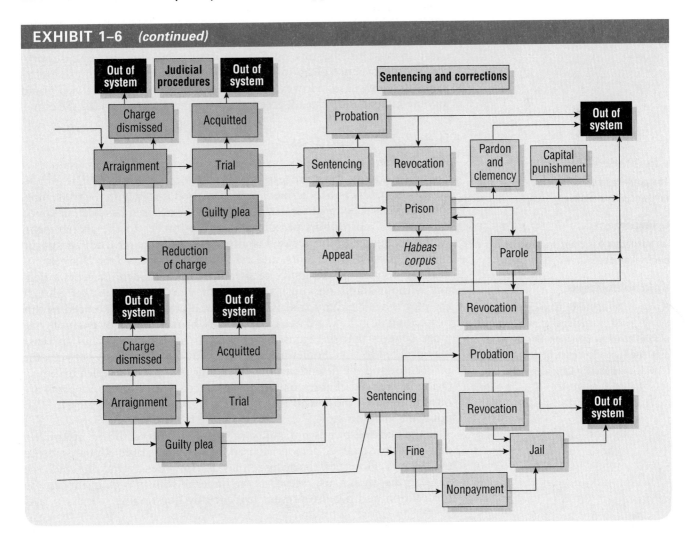

magistrate informs the accused of the charges and decides whether there is probable cause to detain him or her. Often defense counsel is also assigned then. If the offense charged is not very serious, the determination of guilt and the assessment of a penalty may also occur at this stage.

In some jurisdictions, a pretrial-release decision is made at the initial appearance, but this decision may occur at other hearings or at another time during the process. Pretrial release on bail was traditionally intended to ensure appearance at trial. However, many jurisdictions today permit pretrial detention of defendants accused of serious offenses and deemed dangerous, to prevent them from committing crimes in the pretrial period. The court may decide to release the accused on his or her own recognizance, into the custody of a third party, on the promise of satisfying certain conditions, or after posting a financial bond. Conditions of release may be reviewed at any later time while charges are still pending.

In many jurisdictions, the initial appearance may be followed by a preliminary hearing. The main function of this hearing is to determine whether there is probable cause to believe that the accused committed a crime within the jurisdiction of the court. If the judge or magistrate does not find probable cause, the case is dismissed. However, if the judge finds probable cause for such a belief, or if the accused waives the right to a preliminary hearing, the case may be bound over to a grand jury.

A grand jury hears evidence against the accused, presented by the prosecutor, and decides whether there is sufficient evidence to cause the accused to be brought to trial. If the grand jury finds sufficient evidence, it submits an indictment to the court.

Not all jurisdictions use grand juries. Some require, instead, that the prosecutor submit an information (a formal written accusation) to the court. In most jurisdictions, misdemeanor cases and some felony cases proceed by the issuance of an information. Some jurisdictions require indictments in felony cases. However, the accused may choose to waive a grand jury indictment and, instead, accept service of an information for the crime.

Judicial Procedures

Adjudication is the process by which a court arrives at a decision in a case. The adjudication process involves a number of steps. The first is **arraignment**. Once an indictment or information is filed with the trial court, the accused is scheduled for arraignment. If the accused has been detained without bail, corrections personnel take him or her to the arraignment. At the arraignment, the accused is informed of the charges, advised of the rights of criminal defendants, and asked to enter a plea to the charges.

If the accused pleads guilty or pleads **nolo contendere** (accepts a penalty without admitting guilt), the judge may accept or reject the plea. If the plea is accepted, no trial is held and the offender is sentenced at this proceeding or at a later date. The plea may be rejected if, for example, the judge believes that the accused has been coerced. If this occurs, the case may proceed to trial. Sometimes, as the result of negotiations between the prosecutor and the defendant, the defendant enters a guilty plea in expectation of reduced charges or a light sentence. *Nolo contendere* pleas are often entered by those who fear a later civil action and who therefore do not want to admit guilt.

If the accused pleads not guilty or not guilty by reason of insanity, a date is set for trial. A person accused of a serious crime is guaranteed a trial by jury. However, the accused may ask for a bench trial, in which the judge, rather than a jury, serves as the finder of fact. In both instances, the prosecution and defense present evidence by questioning witnesses, and

The Offender Speaks
Visit www.mhhe.com/schmalleger7e to see this feature.

adjudication

The process by which a court arrives at a final decision in a case.

arraignment

An appearance in court prior to trial in a criminal proceeding.

nolo contendere

A plea of "no contest." A no-contest plea may be used by a defendant who does not wish to contest conviction. Because the plea does not admit guilt, however, it cannot provide the basis for later civil suits.

the judge decides issues of law. The trial results in acquittal or conviction of the original charges or of lesser included offenses. A defendant may be convicted at trial only if the government's evidence proves beyond a reasonable doubt that the defendant is guilty, or if the defendant knowingly and voluntarily pleads guilty to the charges.

Sentencing and Sanctions

After a guilty verdict or guilty plea, sentence is imposed. In most cases, the judge decides on the sentence, but in some states, the sentence is decided by the jury, particularly for capital offenses, such as murder.

To arrive at an appropriate sentence, a court may hold a sentencing hearing to consider evidence of aggravating or mitigating circumstances. In assessing the circumstances surrounding a criminal act, courts often rely on presentence investigations by probation agencies or other designated authorities. Courts may also consider victim impact statements.

The sentencing choices available to judges and juries frequently include one or more of the following:

- the death penalty;
- incarceration in a prison, a jail, or another confinement facility;
- community service;
- probation, in which the convicted person is not confined but is subject to certain conditions and restrictions;
- fines, primarily as penalties for minor offenses; and
- restitution, which requires the offender to provide financial compensation to the victim.

In many states, *mandatory minimum* sentencing laws require that persons convicted of certain offenses serve a minimum prison term, which the judge must impose and which may not be reduced by a parole board or by "good-time" deductions.

After the trial, a defendant may request appellate review of the conviction to see whether there was some serious error that affected the defendant's right to a fair trial. In some states, the defendant may also appeal the sentence.

At least one appeal of a conviction is a matter of right. Any further appeal (to a state supreme court or in the case of federal court convictions, to the U.S. Supreme Court) is *discretionary*, which means that the higher court may or may not choose to hear the further appeal. After losing all their available *direct* appeals (also known as *exhaustion of state remedies*), state prisoners may also seek to have their convictions reviewed *collaterally* in the federal courts via a writ of *habeas corpus*. In states that have the death penalty, appeals of death sentences are usually automatic, and extensive federal *habeas corpus* review often takes place before the sentence of death is actually carried out.

The Correctional Subsystem

After conviction and sentencing, most offenders enter the correctional subsystem. Before we proceed with our discussion, it is best to define the term *corrections*. As with most words, a variety of definitions can be found.

In 1967, for example, the President's Commission on Law Enforcement and Administration of Justice wrote that *corrections* means "America's prisons, jails, juvenile training schools, and probation and parole machinery." It is "that part of the criminal justice system," said the commission, "that the public sees least of and knows least about."[16]

Jody Arias on the witness stand in 2013. She was convicted of killing her lover, Travis Alexander. He had been shot in the face, stabbed 29 times, and had his throat slashed. Who decides what happens to defendants after they enter the correctional system?

institutional corrections

That aspect of the correctional enterprise that "involves the incarceration and rehabilitation of adults and juveniles convicted of offenses against the law, and the confinement of persons suspected of a crime awaiting trial and adjudication."

noninstitutional corrections (also *community corrections*)

That aspect of the correctional enterprise that includes "pardon, probation, and parole activities, correctional administration not directly connectable to institutions, and miscellaneous [activities] not directly related to institutional care."

corrections

All the various aspects of the pretrial and postconviction management of individuals accused or convicted of crimes.

Years later, in 1975, the National Advisory Commission on Criminal Justice Standards and Goals said in its lengthy volume on corrections, "*Corrections* is defined here as the community's official reactions to the convicted offender, whether adult or juvenile."[17] The commission noted that "this is a broad definition and it suffers . . . from several shortcomings."

We can distinguish between institutional corrections and noninstitutional corrections. A report by the Bureau of Justice Statistics (BJS) says that **institutional corrections** "involves the confinement and rehabilitation of adults and juveniles convicted of offenses against the law and the confinement of persons suspected of a crime awaiting trial and adjudication."[18] BJS goes on to say that

> correctional institutions are prisons, reformatories, jails, houses of correction, penitentiaries, correctional farms, workhouses, reception centers, diagnostic centers, industrial schools, training schools, detention centers, and a variety of other types of institutions for the confinement and correction of convicted adults or juveniles who are adjudicated delinquent or in need of supervision. [The term] also includes facilities for the detention of adults and juveniles accused of a crime and awaiting trial or hearing.

According to BJS, **noninstitutional corrections**, which is sometimes called **community corrections**, includes "pardon, probation, and parole activities, correctional administration not directly connectable to institutions, and miscellaneous [activities] not directly related to institutional care."

As all these definitions show, in its broadest sense, the term *corrections* encompasses each of the following components, as well as the process of interaction among them:

- the *purpose* and *goals* of the correctional enterprise;
- jails, prisons, correctional institutions, and other *facilities*;
- probation, parole, and alternative and diversionary *programs*;
- federal, state, local, and international correctional offices and *agencies*;
- counseling, educational, health care, nutrition, and many other *services*;
- correctional *clients*;
- corrections *volunteers*;
- corrections *professionals*;
- fiscal appropriations and *funding*;
- various aspects of criminal and civil *law*;
- formal and informal *procedures*;
- effective and responsible *management*;
- community *expectations* regarding correctional practices; and
- the machinery of *capital punishment*.

When we use the word *corrections,* we include all of these elements. Fourteen elements, however, make for an unwieldy definition. Hence, for purposes of discussion, we will say that **corrections** refers to all the various aspects of the pretrial and postconviction management of individuals

> ### EXHIBIT 1–7 American Correctional Association
>
> #### Public Correctional Policy on the Role of Corrections
>
> The overall role of corrections is to enhance public safety and social order. Adult and juvenile correctional systems should:
>
> - implement court-ordered sanctions and provide supervision of those accused of unlawful behavior prior to and after adjudication in a safe and humane manner;
> - offer the widest range of correctional programs that are based on exemplary practices, supported by research and promote pro-social behavior;
> - provide gender- and culturally-responsive programs and services for preadjudicated and adjudicated offenders that will enhance successful reentry to the community and that are administered within the least restrictive environment consistent with public, staff and offender safety;
> - address the needs of victims of crime;
> - routinely review correctional programs and reentry services to ensure that they are addressing the needs of offenders, victims, and the community; and
> - collaborate with other professions to improve and strengthen correctional services and to support the reduction of crime and recidivism.
>
> **Source:** Copyright © American Correctional Association. Reprinted with permission.

Visit http://www.vera.org/faye-taxman-how-corrections-systems-can-deter-future-crime or scan this code with the QR app on your smartphone or digital device and listen to an interview with Faye S. Taxman, director of the Center for Advancing Correctional Excellence at George Mason University, as she speaks about how corrections can deter future crime.

accused or convicted of crimes. Central to this perspective is the recognition that corrections—although it involves a variety of programs, services, facilities, and personnel—is essentially a management activity. Rather than stress the role of institutions or agencies, this definition emphasizes the human dimension of correctional activity—especially the efforts of the corrections professionals who undertake the day-to-day tasks. Like any other managed activity, corrections has goals and purposes. Exhibit 1–7 details the role of corrections as identified by the American Correctional Association (ACA).

The Societal Goals of Corrections

The ACA statement about the purpose of corrections is addressed primarily to corrections professionals. It recognizes, however, that *the* fundamental purpose of corrections "is to enhance social order and public safety." In any society, social order and public safety depend on effective social control. Some forms of social control take the form of customs, norms, and what sociologists refer to as *mores* ('mȯr-,āz). **Mores** are behavioral standards that embody a group's values. Violation of these standards is a serious wrong. They generally forbid such activities as murder, rape, and robbery. **Folkways**, in contrast, are time-honored ways of doing things. Although folkways carry the force of tradition, their violation is unlikely to threaten the survival of the group.

Societal expectations, whatever form they take, are sometimes enacted into law. The **criminal law**, also called *penal law,* is the body of rules and regulations that define public offenses, or wrongs committed against the state or society, and specify punishments for those offenses. Social control, social order, and public safety are the ultimate goals of criminal law.

The correctional subsystem is crucial in enforcing the dictates of the law because the rewards and punishments it carries out play a significant role in society's control of its members.

mores

Cultural restrictions on behavior that forbid serious violations—such as murder, rape, and robbery—of a group's values.

folkways

Time-honored ways of doing things. Although they carry the force of tradition, their violation is unlikely to threaten the survival of the social group.

criminal law (also *penal law*)

That portion of the law that defines crimes and specifies criminal punishments.

Occupy Wall Street demonstrators confront members of the New York Police Department during a demonstration in the city in 2012. What role does the criminal justice system play in the maintenance of social order?

CO1-4 ## PROFESSIONALISM IN CORRECTIONS

Only a few decades ago, some writers bemoaned the fact that the field of corrections had not achieved professional status. Happily, much has changed over the past half century. By 1987, Bob Barrington, who was then the executive director of the International Association of Correctional Officers, was able to proclaim, in a discussion about prisons, that "correctional facilities . . . run smoothly and efficiently for one basic reason: the professional and forward-thinking attitudes and actions of the correctional officers employed."[19]

Some writers on American criminal justice have said that the hallmark of a true profession is "a shared set of principles and customs that transcend self-interest and speak to the essential nature of the particular calling or trade."[20] This definition recognizes the selfless and ethical nature of professional work. Hence, "professionals have a sense of commitment to their professions that is usually not present among those in occupational groups."[21] Work within a profession is viewed more as a "calling" than as a mere way of earning a living. "Professionals have a love for their work that is above that of employment merely to receive a paycheck."[22]

Although it is important to keep formal definitions in mind, for our purposes, we will define a **profession** as an occupation granted high social status by virtue of the personal integrity of its members. We can summarize the *attitude* of a true professional by noting that it is characterized by the following:

- a spirit of public service and interest in the public good;
- the fair application of reason and the use of intellect to solve problems;
- self-regulation through a set of internal guidelines by which professionals hold *themselves* accountable for their actions;
- continual self-appraisal and self-examination;

profession

An occupation granted high social status by virtue of the personal integrity of its members.

Offices of the American Correctional Association (ACA) in Alexandria, Virginia. The ACA is a leading proponent of professionalism in corrections. What does corrections professionalism entail?

- an inner sense of professionalism (i.e., honor, self-discipline, commitment, personal integrity, and self-direction);
- adherence to the recognized ethical principles of one's profession (see the Ethics and Professionalism box in this chapter); and
- a commitment to lifelong learning and lifelong betterment within the profession.

Most professional occupations have developed practices that foster professionalism among their members.

Standards and Training

Historically, professional corrections organizations and their leaders have recognized the importance of training. It was not until the late 1970s, however, that the American Correctional Association (ACA) Commission on Accreditation established the first training standards. The commission did the following:

- specified standards for given positions within corrections;
- identified essential training topics;
- set specific numbers of hours for preservice (120) and annual in-service training (40); and
- specified basic administrative policy support requirements for training programs.[23]

Following ACA's lead, virtually every state now requires at least 120 hours of preservice training for correctional officers working in institutional settings; many states require more. Probation and parole officers are required to undergo similar training in most jurisdictions, and correctional officers working in jails are similarly trained.

Through training, new members of a profession learn the core values and ideals, the basic knowledge, and the accepted practices central to the profession. Setting training standards ensures that the education is

Ethics and Professionalism

American Correctional Association Code of Ethics

1. Members shall respect and protect the civil and legal rights of all individuals.

2. Members shall treat every professional situation with concern for the welfare of the individuals involved and with no intent to gain personally.

3. Members shall maintain relationships with colleagues to promote mutual respect within the profession and improve the quality of service.

4. Members shall make public criticism of their colleagues or their agencies only when warranted, verifiable, and constructive.

5. Members shall respect the importance of all disciplines within the criminal justice system and work to improve cooperation with each segment.

6. Members shall honor the public's right to information and share information with the public to the extent permitted by law subject to individuals' right to privacy.

7. Members shall respect and protect the right of the public to be safeguarded from criminal activity.

8. Members shall refrain from using their positions to secure personal privileges or advantages.

9. Members shall refrain from allowing personal interest to impair objectivity in the performance of duty while acting in an official capacity.

10. Members shall refrain from entering into any formal or informal activity or agreement that presents a conflict of interest or is inconsistent with the conscientious performance of duties.

11. Members shall refrain from accepting any gifts, services, or favors that are or appear to be improper or imply an obligation inconsistent with the free and objective exercise of professional duties.

12. Members shall clearly differentiate between personal views/statements and views/statements/positions made on behalf of the agency or Association.

13. Members shall report to appropriate authorities any corrupt or unethical behaviors for which there is sufficient evidence to justify review.

14. Members shall refrain from discriminating against any individual because of race, gender, creed, national origin, religious affiliation, age, disability, or any other type of prohibited discrimination.

15. Members shall preserve the integrity of private information; they shall refrain from seeking information on individuals beyond that which is necessary to implement responsibilities and perform their duties; members shall refrain from revealing nonpublic information unless expressly authorized to do so.

16. Members shall make all appointments, promotions, and dismissals in accordance with established civil service rules, applicable contract agreements, and individual merit, rather than furtherance of personal interests.

17. Members shall respect, promote, and contribute to a workplace that is safe, healthy, and free of harassment in any form.

Adopted by the Board of Governors and Delegate Assembly in August 1994.

Source: Copyright © American Correctional Association. Reprinted with permission.

Ethical Dilemma 1–1: In light of tight state budgets and overcrowded prisons, should governors use their authority to provide early release to some inmates? If so, under what circumstances? For more information, go to Ethical Dilemma 1–1 at www.justicestudies.com/ethics07.

Ethical Dilemma 1–2: You are the warden of the only medium security prison in your state. Your nephew is sentenced to serve 10 years in your institution. Using the ACA Code of Ethics as a guide, determine what ethical issues you will face. For more information, go to Ethical Dilemma 1–2 at www.justicestudies.com/ethics07.

Ethical Dilemma 1–3: One of your fellow correctional officers accepts candy and snacks from one of the inmates. She doesn't ask for the snacks, nor does she do any favors for the inmate. Should you report this activity? Will you report it? Using the ACA Code of Ethics, determine the ethical issues, if any, involved in this behavior. For more information, go to Ethical Dilemma 1–3 at www.justicestudies.com/ethics07.

Ethical Dilemmas for every chapter are available online.

uniform. Standards also mandate the teaching of specialized knowledge. Standards supplement training by doing the following:

- setting minimum requirements for entry into the profession;
- detailing expectations for those involved in the everyday life of correctional work; and
- establishing basic requirements for facilities, programs, and practices.

From the point of view of corrections professionals, training is a matter of personal responsibility. A lifelong commitment to a career ensures that those who think of themselves as professionals will seek the training needed to enhance their job performance.

The Staff Speaks
Visit www.mhhe.com/schmalleger7e
to see this feature.

Basic Skills and Knowledge

In 1990, the Professional Education Council of the American Correctional Association developed a model entry test for correctional officers. The test was intended to increase professionalism in the field and to provide a standard criminal justice curriculum.[24]

The council suggested that the test could act "as a quality control measure for such education, much as does the bar exam for attorneys." The standard entry test was designed to "reveal the applicant's understanding of the structure, purpose, and method of the police, prosecution, courts, institutions, probation, parole, community service, and extramural programs." It was also designed to "test for knowledge of various kinds of corrections programs, the role of punitive sanctions and incapacitation, and perspective on past experience and current trends."

More recently, Mark S. Fleisher of Illinois State University identified four core traits essential to effective work in corrections.[25] The traits are as follows:

- **Accountability.** "Correctional work demands precision, timeliness, accountability and strong ethics." Students may drift into patterns of irresponsibility during their college years. Once they become correctional officers, however, they need to take their work seriously.

- **Strong writing skill.** Because correctional officers must complete a huge amount of paperwork, they need to be able to write well. They should also be familiar with the "vocabulary of corrections."

- **Effective presentational skills.** "A correctional career requires strong verbal skills and an ability to organize presentations." Effective verbal skills help officers interact with their peers, inmates, and superiors.

- **A logical mind and the ability to solve problems.** Such skills are essential to success in corrections because problems arise daily. Being able to solve them is a sign of an effective officer.

In sum, we can say that a **corrections professional** is a dedicated person of high moral character and personal integrity who is employed in the field of corrections and takes professionalism to heart. He or she understands the importance of standards, training, and education and the need to be proficient in the skills required for success in the correctional enterprise. The corrections professional recognizes that professionalism leads to the betterment of society, to enhanced social order, and to a higher quality of life for all.

corrections professional

A dedicated person of high moral character and personal integrity who is employed in the field of corrections and takes professionalism to heart.

Standard-Setting Organizations

A number of standard-setting **professional associations** in the field of corrections have developed models of professionalism. Among them are the American Correctional Association (ACA), the American Probation and Parole Association (APPA), and the American Jail Association (AJA).

Standard-setting organizations like these offer detailed sets of written principles for correctional occupations and corrections administration. The ACA, the APPA, and the AJA, for example, all have developed standards to guide training and to clarify what is expected of those working

professional associations

Organized groups of like-minded individuals who work to enhance the professional status of members of their occupational group.

Education is an important component of any successful profession. Shown here are three educational institutions offering undergraduate programs in criminal justice—two with a corrections emphasis. What role does the American Correctional Association see for higher education in advancing the corrections profession?

certification

A credentialing process, usually involving testing and career development assessment, through which the skills, knowledge, and abilities of correctional personnel can be formally recognized.

in corrections. Moreover, many professional associations have developed codes of ethics, outlining what is moral and proper conduct. Some of these codes will appear in later chapters.

Correctional associations also offer training, hold meetings and seminars, create and maintain job banks, and produce literature relevant to corrections. They sometimes lobby legislative bodies in an attempt to influence the development of new laws that affect corrections.

Future chapters will present ACA policies. The ACA policies are important because they guide the development of training and because they influence the work environment of many agencies and institutions.

In 1999, the ACA, through its national Commission on Correctional Certification, established a program for certifying correctional staff, from line officers to executive leaders. **Certification** is part of a process called *credentialing* that focuses specifically on the individual. Its counterpart is accreditation, a formal process that highlights the quality of a facility in an effort to ensure that it meets health, safety, and other correctional standards. Accreditation is discussed in more detail in Chapter 13. ACA certification began officially in January 2000 when the first Certified Corrections Executive (CCE) application was accepted by the ACA. The first CCE examination was administered in August 2000.[26]

There are four categories of ACA Certified Corrections Professional (CCP), extending from those who work at the highest organization levels to personnel employed at the line level, working directly with offenders. Those categories are (1) Certified Corrections Executive (CCE), (2) Certified Corrections Manager (CCM), (3) Certified Corrections Supervisor (CCS), and (4) Certified Corrections Officer (CCO). Applicants for certification must pass a 200-item multiple-choice examination, document their corrections experience, show compliance with the ACA's Code of Ethics, and meet minimum requirements for formal education. Educational requirements increase with each certification level. While a high school diploma or equivalent is required of those seeking CCO certification, CCS and CCM certification seekers are required to hold a two-year college degree (or its equivalent), while those applying for certification at the CCE level must hold a four-year college degree (or equivalent). According to the ACA, the organization's certification program creates the *opportunity* for a lifetime of progressive professional achievement. Anyone successfully completing the certification process is designated as a Certified Corrections Professional (CCP).[27] Recertification happens at three-year intervals and requires a specified number of continuing education contact hours.

The purpose of the ACA Professional Certification Program is "to uphold standards for competent practice." Moreover, certification provides an opportunity "for staff to be recognized as qualified correctional practitioners."

Like the ACA, the AJA, through its five-member Jail Manager Certification Commission (JMCC), offers a program for the certification of jail administrators, managers, and supervisory personnel. The first Certified Jail Managers (CJMs) were recognized in 1997.[28]

Education

Education is another component, in addition to basic job skills and job-specific training, of true professionalism. Training, by itself, can never make one a true professional because complex decision-making skills are essential for success in any occupation involving intense interpersonal interaction—and they can be acquired only through general education. Education builds critical-thinking skills, it allows the application of theory and ethical principles to a multitude of situations that are constantly in flux, and it provides insights into on-the-job difficulties.

Correctional education that goes beyond skills training is available primarily from two- and four-year colleges that offer corrections curricula and programs of study (see Exhibit 1–8). Courses in corrections are also typically found in undergraduate and graduate programs in criminal justice. The day will come when at least a two-year degree will be required for entry into the corrections profession.

EVIDENCE-BASED CORRECTIONS (EBC)

Corrections professionalism today includes recognition of the importance of scientific studies of corrections, referred to as **evidence-based corrections (EBC)**. Evidence-based corrections is focused on determining what works

evidence-based corrections (also *evidence-based penology*)

The application of social scientific techniques to the study of everyday corrections procedures for the purpose of increasing effectiveness and enhancing the efficient use of available resources.

EXHIBIT 1–8 American Correctional Association

Public Correctional Policy on Higher Education

The field of corrections, in cooperation with higher education, should contribute to the improvement of the professional practice of corrections. Academic programs concerned with criminal justice, juvenile justice and corrections should:

- provide a pool of qualified candidates for correctional service, and assist in the delineation of dimensions of work responsibilities that may emerge as a result of changing social, economic, political and technological trends;
- promote understanding, both for correctional practitioners and for the public at large, of the complex social, ethical, political and economic factors that influence all areas of corrections;
- challenge assumptions about crime and corrections, and stimulate change when change is needed;
- partner with criminal justice, juvenile justice and corrections organizations to promote and support ethical standards in research, planning and evaluation in all areas;
- engage in public service related to corrections, including informational programs, volunteer programs and opportunities for training, such as internships and practicums to enhance the relationship between the academic community and correctional practitioners;
- encourage colleges and universities to provide opportunities for research and the publication of research findings;
- support, through program and faculty development, the evolution of corrections as a distinct professional discipline;
- implement programs in corrections at the associate degree level that can serve as a minimum requirement for full professional status as a correctional employee; and
- partner with correctional agencies to promote and facilitate learning initiatives for employees.

Source: Copyright © American Correctional Association. Reprinted with permission.

CO1-5

cost-benefit analysis

A systematic process used to calculate the costs of a program relative to its benefits. Programs showing the largest benefit per unit of expenditure are seen as the most effective.

in correctional settings; that is, what correctional programs are effective in reducing recidivism and in preventing future crimes.

One important component of EBC is **cost-benefit analysis**, which seeks to assess the effectiveness of correctional approaches relative to their costs. While evidence-based corrections is a theme of this text, another theme is economic realities in corrections. As you will see, the two themes go hand-in-hand.

In any discussion of evidence-based corrections (also known as *evidence-based penology*), it is important to remember that the word *evidence* refers to scientific evidence, not to criminal evidence. Corrections professionals who adhere to an evidence-based philosophy acknowledge the problem-solving potential of social science research methods, read correctional publications and journals, and keep abreast of the latest findings in their field.

The beginning of the evidence-based movement in corrections can be traced to the 1997 publication of a lengthy report to the U.S. Congress, entitled *Preventing Crime: What Works, What Doesn't, What's Promising*.[29] The report, known as a *meta-analysis* because it assessed more than 500 previously completed studies of various crime prevention programs, looked at the effectiveness of correctional programs in seven different settings: families, police, community, place security, labor markets, schools, and the criminal justice system.

Researchers discovered that a number of the evaluated programs could be declared successful. Successful efforts became known as *what works* programs defined as those that are reasonably certain to reduce recidivism. Other programs were found likely to fail to reduce recidivism and were listed in the category of *what does not work*. Finally, some programs, which fell into a middle ground, were termed *promising*.

Susan Turner, director of the Center for Evidence-Based Corrections at the University of California, Irvine. Turner is shown at the Orange County (California) jail. What is evidence-based corrections?

In 2008, the National Institute of Corrections (NIC) awarded a grant to address evidence-based decision making in local criminal justice agencies to the Center for Effective Public Policy, in partnership with other groups. The goal of the ongoing initiative is to build a systemwide framework that will result in a useful evidence-based decision-making model. The model is intended to help criminal justice policymakers by providing them the information, processes, and tools needed to achieve measurable reductions in pretrial misconduct and in postconviction reoffending.

The principal product of the initial phase of the NIC initiative was the 2010 publication of *A Framework for Evidence-Based Decision Making in Local Criminal Justice Systems.*[30] As the initiative continues to unfold, the NIC and its collaborators are seeking to create and fund pilot projects to demonstrate the value of approaches that are supported by research and that produce positive and measurable outcomes. The NIC is an agency within the federal Bureau of Prisons that provides assistance to federal, state, and local corrections agencies. It has offices in Washington, D.C., and Aurora, Colorado.

Also in 2010, under the direction of Assistant U.S. attorney general Laurie O. Robinson, the Office of Justice Programs (OJP), an arm of the U.S. Department of Justice, announced an agencywide Evidence Integration Initiative, called E2I. Like the NIC partnership, E2I is an ongoing effort to integrate science and research into OJP's programs. The initiative also seeks to generate quality evidence in the form of research and statistical evaluations. Most importantly, according to Robinson, "We are working to move evidence into practice by funding evidence-based programs."[31]

Evidence-based corrections is an exciting new development in the corrections field, and many other agencies, institutions, and organizations are beginning to emphasize the use of scientific evidence. Among them is the Center for Evidence-Based Corrections at the University of California, Irvine. The center stresses the use of scientific studies in corrections as useful in the creation of evidence-based policy. Evidence-based policy, says the center, "is an approach that helps people make well-informed decisions about policies and programs by putting the best available evidence from research at the heart of policy development and implementation."[32] This approach, says the center, "stands in contrast to opinion-based policy, which relies heavily on either the selective use of evidence . . . or on the untested views of individuals or groups, often inspired by ideological views and speculative conjecture."

Finally, in 2005 the University of California, Irvine, announced the creation of its Center for Evidence-Based Corrections. The center seeks "to put science before politics when managing state correctional populations," and to help "corrections officials make policy decisions based on scientific evidence."[33]

Evidence-based corrections helps to inform this book and is discussed in a number of the chapters that follow.

SOCIAL DIVERSITY IN CORRECTIONS

The corrections profession faces a number of social issues that are of special concern to Americans today. Contemporary issues include questions about the purposes and appropriateness of punishment in general and the acceptability of capital punishment in particular; the usefulness of alternative or nontraditional sanctions; the privatization of correctional facilities; and the rights and overall treatment of prisoners. At the forefront of

Visit http://justicestudies.com//qrcodes/ebcp.pdf or scan this code with the QR app on your smartphone or digital device and read *Evidence-Based Correctional Practices,* a paper that introduces some important concepts in the field of evidence-based corrections.

CO1-6

today's issues are those involving concerns about gender, race, ethnicity, and other forms of social diversity.

While a number of these issues are discussed in later chapters, this brief section provides definitions of some of the terms that will be discussed and suggests some structure for what is to follow.

Some terms, such as *race,* are not easy to define. Historical definitions of race have highlighted some supposed biological traits, such as skin color, hair type, or shape of the skull and face. Eighteenth-century European physical anthropologists distinguished between white, black, and Asian (or "yellow") races. The notion of race, however, is now generally recognized as a social construct and is not seen as an objective biological fact. Moreover, racial distinctions have blurred throughout American society, which has long been characterized as a melting pot. Nonetheless, when asked, the majority of Americans today still identify themselves as members of a particular racial group.

To say that race is a social construct means that racial distinctions are culturally defined. It does *not* mean, however, that such distinctions are without consequences. On the contrary, great social significance is often attached to biological or other indicators of race, and race plays a crucial role in social relations. *Racism,* which is also socially constructed, can be the result. **Racism** has been defined as social practices that explicitly or implicitly attribute merits or allocate value to members of racially categorized groups solely because of their race.[34] In the field of corrections, as in other social endeavors, racism (rather than race itself) is the real issue because it can lead to forms of racial discrimination, including inequities in hiring and promotion for those working in corrections, and to unfairness in the handling of inmates or other correctional clients because of their race.

Considerable overlap exists between the concept of race and that of *ethnicity.* In contemporary usage, both terms imply the notion of lineage, or biological and regional as well as cultural background and inheritance. Of the two, however, ethnicity is most closely associated with cultural heritage. Members of an ethnic group generally share a common racial, national, religious, linguistic, and cultural origin. Hence, from an ethnic perspective, a person might identify himself or herself as Hungarian, even though he or she has never lived in Hungary, does not speak Hungarian, and knows little of the history of the Hungarian nation. Ethnic differences can lead to serious consequences as prison gangs built around ethnicity demonstrate.

racism

Social practices that explicitly or implicitly attribute merits or allocate value to individuals solely because of their race.

LaDonna H. Thompson (left), Kentucky Commissioner of Corrections, Colette Peters (middle), Oregon Director of Corrections, and Dora Schriro (right), Director of the Commissioner of Corrections for New York City. In recent years, the number of women working in corrections has increased significantly. Do you think that gender bias exists within the correctional career field today?

At first blush, the term *gender* seems more straightforward than race or ethnicity because it relates to differences between the sexes. In fact, many critical issues that concern correctional administrators today reflect a rapid increase in the number of women entering correctional service.

For many years, corrections was a male-dominated profession. Although the correctional process has always involved some women, historically most women in the profession have attended to the needs of the small number of females held in confinement. It wasn't until the 1970s that women began to enter the corrections professions in significant numbers. Many went to work in facilities that housed males, where they soon found themselves confronting *gender bias* from an entrenched macho culture.

Today, women working in correctional facilities largely have been accepted, as evidenced by the fact their proportion is more than double the proportion of female law enforcement officers: Thirty-five percent of correctional officers in the United States are women, while only 13 percent of police officers are female. As Exhibit 1–9 shows, however, women working in corrections tend to be concentrated in the lower ranks and are underrepresented in supervisory positions. According to the National Center for Women in Policing, women of color hold 12.9 percent of corrections positions, 9.7 percent of top command positions, and 9.1 percent of supervisory positions.[35]

Race, ethnicity, and gender are all aspects of social diversity—although diversity in society extends to many other areas as well, such as economics, religion, education, intellectual ability, and politics. Keep in mind, as you read through this textbook, that in the field of corrections diversity issues can be described from four perspectives: (1) as they impact individual correctional clients, (2) as they determine correctional populations and trends, (3) as they affect the lives and interests of those working in the field of corrections, and (4) as they change the structure and functioning of correctional institutions, facilities, and programs.

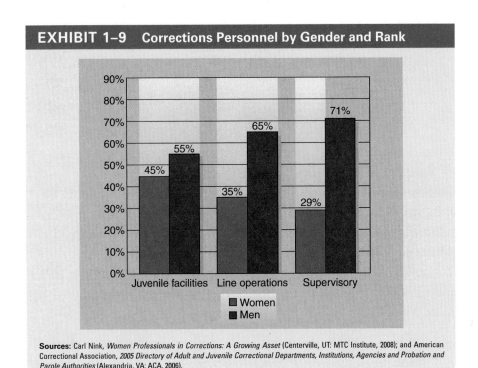

EXHIBIT 1–9   Corrections Personnel by Gender and Rank

Sources: Carl Nink, *Women Professionals in Corrections: A Growing Asset* (Centerville, UT: MTC Institute, 2008); and American Correctional Association, *2005 Directory of Adult and Juvenile Correctional Departments, Institutions, Agencies and Probation and Parole Authorities* (Alexandria, VA: ACA, 2006).

REVIEW AND APPLICATIONS

SUMMARY

1 Although crime rates are at their lowest level in more than 20 years, correctional populations have been increasing because of get-tough-on-crime attitudes, the nation's War on Drugs, and the increasing reluctance of parole authorities, fearing civil liability and public outcry, to release inmates. Moreover, growth in correctional populations and in spending on prisons and jails has led to a dramatically expanding correctional workforce and to enhanced employment opportunities within the field.

2 Two important sources of crime statistics are the FBI's Uniform Crime Reporting Program and the National Crime Victimization Survey, published by the Bureau of Justice Statistics. The crimes that bring people into the American correctional system include felonies, which are relatively serious criminal offenses; misdemeanors, which are less serious crimes; and infractions, which are minor law violations.

3 Criminal justice agencies are said to make up the criminal justice system. The main components of the criminal justice system are police, courts, and corrections. Each can be considered a subsystem of the criminal justice system. The major components of the corrections subsystem are jails, probation, parole, and prisons. Jails and prisons are examples of institutional corrections, while probation and parole are forms of noninstitutional corrections.

4 Professionalism in corrections is important because it can win the respect and admiration of others outside of the field. Moreover, professionals are regarded as trusted participants in any field of endeavor. This chapter also discussed seven aspects of a professional attitude.

5 Evidence-based corrections is the application of social scientific techniques to the study of everyday corrections procedures for the purpose of increasing effectiveness and enhancing the efficient use of available resources. When discussing evidence-based corrections, it is important to remember that the word *evidence* refers to scientific, not criminal, evidence.

6 Social diversity encompasses differences of race, gender, and ethnicity and is important in corrections today because it impacts individual correctional clients, influences correctional populations and trends, affects the lives and interests of those working in the field of corrections, and may help determine the structure and functioning of correctional institutions, facilities, and programs.

KEY TERMS

crime, p. 3
prison, p. 4
sustainable justice, p. 7
felony, p. 8
misdemeanor, p. 8
infraction, p. 8
correctional clients, p. 9
criminal justice, p. 10
criminal justice system, p. 10

adjudication, p. 12
arraignment, p. 12
nolo contendere, p. 12
institutional corrections, p. 14
noninstitutional corrections, p. 14
community corrections, p. 14
corrections, p. 14
mores, p. 15
folkways, p. 15

criminal law, p. 15
penal law, p. 15
profession, p. 16
corrections professional, p. 19
professional associations, p. 19
certification, p. 20
evidence-based corrections, p. 21
cost-benefit analysis, p. 22
racism, p. 24

QUESTIONS FOR REVIEW

1 Why have correctional populations in the United States dramatically increased over the past few decades? How does the rise in correctional populations compare with changes in crime rates over time?

2 What are the kinds of crimes that cause offenders to enter correctional institutions? To enter other kinds of correctional programs?

3 What are the major components of the criminal justice system? What aspects of the corrections subsystem can you identify?

4 Explain the importance of professionalism in corrections and list the seven characteristics of a professional attitude.

5 What is evidence-based corrections? What role does it play in corrections professionalism today?

6 What is meant by the term *social diversity,* and why is the issue of social diversity important in corrections today?

THINKING CRITICALLY ABOUT CORRECTIONS

Vision

Dianne Carter, former president of the National Academy of Corrections, once said, "Too often in corrections, only worker skills are targeted for training, and the organization misses a significant opportunity to communicate its vision and mission."[36] Do you agree or disagree with this statement? Why?

Professionalism

Harold Williamson, a writer in the corrections field, has noted, "Higher levels of professionalization require greater amounts of training and usually involve increased specialization when compared to lesser professionalized activity. Higher levels of professionalization also involve the learning of more abstract knowledge and information."[37] Do you agree? Why or why not?

ON-THE-JOB DECISION MAKING

Training

Today is the first day of your job as a correctional officer. A severe statewide shortage of officers required you to begin work immediately before training, which you are scheduled to attend in three months. When you arrive at the facility, you are ushered into a meeting with the warden. He welcomes you and gives you a brief pep talk. He asks if you have any concerns. You tell him, "Well, I feel a little uneasy. I haven't gone through the academy yet." "Don't worry," he says, "all our new recruits get on-the-job experience before a slot in the academy opens up. You'll do fine!" He shakes your hand and leads you to the door. After you leave the warden's office, you are given a set of keys and a can of mace. The shift supervisor, a sergeant, gives you a brief tour of the prison. Then he tells you that as you learn your job, you will spend most of your time with another officer, though pairing up will not always be possible.

The officer you are assigned to accompany is Harold Gates. At first, you follow Officer Gates across the compound, getting more familiar with the layout of the facility. Then you spend an uneventful afternoon working with Officer Gates in the yard. At 4:30, Officer Gates instructs you to make sure that all inmates have left the classroom building in preparation for a "count." As you enter the building, you encounter a group of six inmates heading toward the door. Before you can move to the side, one of the inmates walks within an inch of you and stares at you. The others crowd in behind him. You can't move. You are pinned to the door by the men. The man directly in front of you is huge—over 6 feet tall and about 280 pounds. His legs look like tree trunks, and his arms are held away from his body by their sheer bulk. You're staring at a chest that could easily pass as a brick wall. With a snarl he growls, "What do you want?"

1. How do you respond? Would you feel more confident responding to a situation like this if you had had some training?

2. If you tell the inmates that it's time for a count and to move along, what will you do next? Will you ask anyone for guidance in similar future situations or just chalk up the encounter to a learning experience? To whom might you talk about it?

3. Suppose you are a manager or supervisor at this facility. How would you handle the training of new recruits?

Leadership

You are a correctional officer at the McClellan Correctional Facility. You and your coworkers have been following, with high interest, the events at Brownley, another correctional facility located approximately 35 miles away. Prisoner rioting at Brownley during the past four days has left 4 correctional officers and 19 prisoners seriously hurt. It now appears, though, that while tensions remain high, the riot has been contained and the prisoners at Brownley are settling back down. The uneasy truce, however, mandates resolution of the issues that led to the riot in the first place.

The main issue leading to the riot was the prisoners' claims of mistreatment at the hands of certain members of the Brownley correctional staff. State correctional administrators have determined that an essential first step in preventing future riots is replacement of certain members of the correctional staff at Brownley. You are called to your supervisor's office, where she informs you that you are being reassigned temporarily to Brownley, with a possibility that the reassignment may become permanent.

This news does not make you happy. The logistical impact alone is irritating because it will mean a significant commute each day. More important, though, is that you will be leaving a cohesive team of skilled and dedicated correctional officers with whom you have developed a close bond. You trust each other, and you trust your leaders. There's no telling what you will encounter at Brownley.

Your worst fears are realized when you report for your first shift and your new sergeant takes you aside. "We can't let them win on this," he says. "You know the drill. Stay on 'em hard, and don't cut 'em any slack. We need to let them know from the get-go that things haven't changed—we're still in charge, whether they like it or not, and we ain't gonna take any guff from the likes of them!"

It is immediately apparent to you that your sergeant has a strong "us-against-them" perspective. Your experience tells you that such an attitude at the leadership level likely induces similar, often stronger attitudes at the correctional officer level, and your common sense tells you that this is probably the root of the problem at Brownley.

1. How do you respond to your new sergeant?

2. If you elect to keep this information to yourself, how will you establish yourself with the Brownley inmates as a CO who does not subscribe to the other CO's practices without appearing weak or exploitable?

3. If you elect to bring this information to the attention of someone higher up in the supervisory chain, how will you deal with potential adverse reactions from your new coworkers?

For additional information, please see: www.mhhe.com/schmalleger7e
Follow the author's tweets about the latest crime and justice news @schmalleger

PUNISHMENTS

A Brief History

[2]

CHAPTER OBJECTIVES

After completing this chapter you should be able to do the following:

1 Describe the types of punishment prevalent in ancient times.

2 List and describe the major criminal punishments used throughout history.

3 Explain the role of torture in the justice systems of times past.

4 Explain the ideas that led to the use of incarceration as a criminal punishment and as an alternative to earlier punishments.

5 Explain the role of correctional reformers in changing the nature of criminal punishment.

> *No man shall be forced by Torture to confesse any Crime against himselfe nor any other unlesse it be in some Capitall case, where he is first fullie convicted by cleare and suffitient evidence to be guilty. After which if the cause be of that nature, That it is very apparent there be other conspiratours, or confederates with him, Then he may be tortured, yet not with such Tortures as be Barbarous and inhumane.*
>
> —Massachusetts Body of Liberties of 1641, Section 45

Before the advent of prisons in the Western world, **corporal punishments** were often imposed for serious crimes. Some, although not regularly administered, were especially gruesome. In 1757, Robert-François Damiens was sentenced to be quartered publicly in Paris for attempting to kill King Louis XV. As the executioners took their places, it was announced that

corporal punishments
Physical punishments, or those involving the body.

> the flesh will be torn from his breasts, arms, thighs and calves with red-hot pincers, his right hand, holding the knife with which he committed said [crime], burnt with sulphur, and, on those places where the flesh will be torn away, poured molten lead, boiling oil, burning resin, wax and sulphur melted together and then his body drawn and quartered by four horses and his limbs and body consumed by fire, reduced to ashes and his ashes thrown to the winds.[1]

As it turned out, Damiens was a very muscular man. He remained conscious throughout the tortures, although a report tells us that he "uttered horrible cries." When it came time for him to be quartered, the four horses were unable to pull him apart—even after repeated attempts. Finally, six horses were used, and when they were still unable to disjoint the prisoner, his muscles had to be "cut through with knives."

Gruesome as this story may be, it illustrates the relative newness of our present system of corrections, which depends largely on the use of fines, probation, imprisonment, and parole. This chapter traces the historical and cultural roots of our present system.

THE STOCKS.

An offender in the stocks in Colonial times. Early punishments were often both physical and public. What purposes did such punishments serve?

PUNISHMENTS IN ANCIENT TIMES

Before the large-scale building of prisons began in 17th-century Europe, a variety of practices, based on the law and justice concepts of certain cultural groups, various practices were used to punish wrongdoers and maintain civil order. We will briefly highlight some of these practices and the traditions that have influenced modern correctional practices.

The Code of Hammurabi

One of the earliest known criminal codes can be traced back to King Hammurabi, who ruled ancient Mesopotamia in an area that today comprises much of modern day Iraq and parts of Iran. Hammurabi, who ruled from 1792–50 B.C., was interested in developing a comprehensive and standardized set of laws that could be applied with consistency to all of his subjects. To that end, he drafted a set of 282 laws, which included specified crimes and the punishments associated with them. It is from the Code of Hammurabi that we get the famous saying "an eye for an eye, and a tooth for a tooth" because his code was largely concerned with fair retribution—meaning that he limited the amount of punishment that could be imposed to what was appropriate for the degree of harm that the offender had inflicted. Although the Hammurabi Code was compassionate in that it limited the degree to which vengeance could be pursued, it was also discriminatory because it distinguished among punishments for wealthy noble men and women, commoners, lower-class individuals, and slaves. The Code of Hammurabi survives today inscribed on a stone pillar that was unearthed in 1901 by French archaeologists who were excavating a site in Iran.

Ancient Greece

CO2-1

In the cultural history of punishments, the Greek city-states provide the earliest evidence that public punishment is part of the Western tradition—and that its roots are in ideas of law and justice. Of all the city-states, the practices of Athens are the best documented. This documentation, which ranges from the writings of orators and philosophers to plays and poetry, tells us that many early crimes were punished by execution, banishment, or exile. Greek poets described stoning the condemned to death, throwing them from high cliffs, binding them to stakes (similar to crucifixion), and cursing them ritually. In many cases, the bodies of executed criminals were regarded as dishonored and were prevented from being buried. Their bodies were left to scavengers and the elements, serving as a warning to anyone contemplating similar crimes.

Other punishments in ancient Athens included "confiscation of property, fines, and the destruction of the condemned offenders' houses."[2] Public denunciation, shaming (*atimia*), imprisonment, and public display of the offender were also used. Criminal punishments in ancient Greece sometimes included civil penalties, such as loss of the ability to transfer property, to vote, and to marry.

Ancient Israel

The chief record of ancient Hebrew history is the Bible. It describes the law and civilization of the ancient Hebrews, including their criminal law and penology. Punishments used by the Hebrews mentioned in the Old Testament included banishment, beating, beheading, blinding, branding and burning, casting down from a high place, crushing, confiscating property, crucifying, cursing, cutting asunder, drowning, exiling, exposing to wild beasts, fining, flaying, hanging, imprisoning, mutilating, plucking of the hair, sawing asunder, scourging with thorns, enslaving, slaying by spear or sword, using the stocks, stoning, strangulating, stripping, and suffocating.[3] Michel Foucault, the French historian, says that the purpose of physical punishments was primarily revenge. "It was as if the punishment was thought to equal, if not to exceed, in savagery the crime itself," he writes.[4]

A stoning in pre-Christian times. How do ancient punishments and the philosophies that influenced them contribute to today's understanding of the role of criminal punishment in society?

Visit http://www.youtube.com/watch?v5oDALXORbtR4 or scan this code with the QR app on your smartphone or digital device to view a YouTube video describing the ancient Code of Hammurabi.

Early Rome

The Twelve Tables, the first written laws of Rome, were issued in 451 B.C. Conviction of some offenses required payment of compensation, but the most frequent penalty was death. Among the forms of capital punishment were burning (for arson), throwing from a cliff (for perjury), clubbing to death (for writing insulting songs about a citizen), hanging (for stealing others' crops), and decapitation. Not mentioned in the Twelve Tables were several other forms of capital punishment in vogue in ancient Rome. For killing a close relative, the offender was subjected to the *culleus*, which consisted of confining the offender in a sack with an ape, a dog, and a serpent, and throwing the sack into the sea. Vestal virgins who had violated their vows of chastity were buried alive. As an alternative to execution, offenders might choose exile. Offenders who went into exile lost their citizenship, freedom, and immovable property. If they returned to Rome, they could be killed by any citizen.[5]

PHYSICAL PUNISHMENTS

In Western societies, the practice of corporal punishment carried over into the Christian era. Physical punishments were imposed for a wide variety of offenses during the Middle Ages. Physical punishments were also used in the American colonies: "The whole baggage of corporal punishments, as they existed in England, were brought to this country, and flourished, especially in New England where the precepts of Calvinism adorned them with pious sanctions."[6] The Puritans, for example, sometimes burned witches and unruly slaves; made wide use of the stocks, the pillory, and the ducking stool; branded criminal offenders; and forced women convicted of adultery to wear "scarlet letters."

As justice historian Pieter Spierenburg notes, many physical punishments during the Middle Ages and in "early modern Europe" were *theatrical punishments*.[7] That is, they were corporal punishments carried out in public. Spierenburg divides punishments that were both physical and public into five degrees of severity: (1) whipping or flogging; (2) burning of the skin; (3) mutilation, or "more serious encroachments on bodily integrity"; (4) a merciful instant death; and (5) a torturous and prolonged death.[8]

CO2-2   ### Flogging

Flogging (or whipping) has been the most common physical punishment through the ages.[9] The code established by Moses, for example, authorized flogging, and Roman law specified flogging as a punishment for

> **The Offender Speaks**
> Visit www.mhhe.com/schmalleger7e to see this feature.

Michael Fay, the American teenager who was caned in Singapore in 1994. Corporal punishments like caning, which involves whipping with a bamboo rod, are still used in more than two dozen countries as criminal sanctions. Fay, who was 18 years old when caned, had spray-painted some parked cars. Can corporal punishment be an effective criminal deterrent?

Arab TV personality, Rosanna Yami. In 2009, Yami, who lives in Saudi Arabia, was sentenced by a Saudi court to receive 60 lashes for her role in a Lebanese TV program that interviewed a Saudi man who boasted of his sex life. The man was sent to prison, and Yami was later pardoned by the Saudi king. Why are physical punishments, like flogging, still used in some parts of the world?

certain forms of theft. Flogging was common in England during the Middle Ages as punishment for a wide variety of crimes. In England, women were flogged in private, but men were whipped publicly.[10]

The construction of flogging whips varied greatly, from simple leather straps or willow branches to heavy, complicated instruments designed to inflict a maximum of pain. A traditional form of whip was the cat-o'-nine-tails, consisting of nine knotted cords fastened to a wooden handle. The "cat" got its name from the marks it left on the body, which were like the scratches of a cat. One especially cruel form of the whip, the Russian knout, was made of leather strips fitted with fishhooks. When a prisoner was whipped, the hooks would dig into the body, ripping away a proverbial "pound of flesh" with each stroke. A thorough whipping with the knout could result in death from blood loss.

Flogging was also widely used in the American colonies to enforce discipline, punish offenders, and make an example of "ne'er-do-wells" (shiftless and irresponsible individuals). As a mechanism for enforcing compliance with prison rules, flogging survived into the 20th century. As late as 1959, Harry Elmer Barnes and Negley K. Teeters were able to write, "Floggings have been prison practice down to our own times, and deaths have occurred due to over-severe whippings in southern prison camps and chain-gangs. Tying prisoners up by their hands and allowing them to hang suspended with their toes barely touching the floor or ground has been a common method of enforcing discipline."[11]

Branding

Branding, a type of mutilation, was practiced by Roman society. Criminals were branded with a mark or letter signifying their crimes. Brands, which were often placed on the forehead or another part of the face, served to warn others of an offender's criminal history.

The last documented incident of facial branding of English criminals occurred in 1699.[12] After that year, offenders were branded on the hand because it was feared that more obvious marks would reduce employment possibilities. Branding was abolished in England during the last half of the 18th century.

The French branded criminals on the shoulder with the royal emblem. They later switched to burning onto the shoulder a letter signifying the crime of which the offender had been convicted.

Branding was also practiced in the early American colonies. The East Jersey Codes of 1668 and 1675, for example, ordered that burglars be branded on the hand with the letter *T* (for *thief*). After a second offense, the letter *R* (for *rogue*) was burned into the forehead. Maryland branded blasphemers with the letter *B* on the forehead. Women offenders were not branded but were forced to wear letters on their clothing.

Mutilation

Mutilation was another type of corporal punishment used in ancient and medieval societies. Archaeological evidence shows that the pharaohs of ancient Egypt and their representatives often ordered mutilation.[13] In ancient Rome, offenders were mutilated according to the law of retaliation, or *lex talionis*. As a punishment philosophy, lex talionis resembles the biblical principle of "an eye for an eye and a tooth for a tooth."

Medieval justice frequently insisted that punishment fit the crime. Hence, "thieves and counterfeiters had their hands cut off, liars and perjurers had their tongues torn out, spies had their eyes gouged out, sex criminals had their genitals removed, and so forth."[14] Blasphemers sometimes had their tongues pierced or cut out and their upper lips cut away.[15]

Mutilation had a deterrent effect; the permanently scarred and disfigured offenders served as warnings to others of what would happen to criminals. Sometimes, mutilation served merely as a prelude to execution. The right hand of a murderer, for example, was sometimes cut off before he was hanged.[16]

Instant Death

According to Spierenburg, beheading, hanging, and garroting (strangulation by a tightened iron collar) were the most common means of merciful or instant death.[17] Instant death was frequently reserved for members of the nobility who had received capital sentences (usually from the king) or for previously honorable men and women who ran afoul of the law. Decapitation, especially when done by the sword, was regarded as the most honorable form of capital punishment—because a sword was a symbol that was both noble and aristocratic. Hanging, says Spierenburg, "was the standard nonhonorable form of the death penalty." For women, however, hanging was considered indecent. Garroting tended to replace hanging as a capital punishment for women.

Lingering Death

The worst fate a criminal offender—especially one convicted of heinous crimes—might meet in medieval Europe was a slow or lingering death, often preceded by torture. Some offenders were burned alive, while others were "broken on the wheel." Breaking on the wheel was a procedure that broke all of the major bones in the body. A person who had been broken on the wheel and was still alive was often killed by an executioner's blow to the heart.

Offenders who were to be hanged sometimes had their arms and legs broken first; others were whipped or burned. Burning alive, a practice used in France until the 18th century, was undoubtedly one of the period's cruelest forms of capital punishment.

A 1786 German woodcut depicts a public execution by burning. What purpose did such public dispensing of justice serve?

The Role of Torture

CO2-3

Various corporal punishments were employed, some of which involved torture. Pain was central to retaliatory punishments, and it was used to extract confessions and get information. "Torture," said one source, "is the twisting (torsion) from its subjects of guilty secrets."[18] The use of torture in medieval England was based on a theory that knowledge of one's own guilt, or of the guilt of others, was an offense in itself. Moreover, the theory went, such knowledge was a kind of property that rightly belonged to the state. Hence, forcing an offender to relinquish such "property," by any means necessary, was a right of the government.

Tortures of all kinds were also used during the Middle Ages in an effort to gain confessions from heretics. Heresy was considered a crime against the church and against God. At the time, there was no separation between church and state in many Western societies, and church courts were free to impose punishment as they saw fit. Believers were sure that the heretic's soul was condemned to eternal damnation and that confession would lead to salvation. As a result, torture flourished as a technique for saving souls. Some saw the suffering induced by corporal punishments as spiritually cleansing. Others compared it to the suffering of Jesus on the cross. They argued that physical pain and suffering might free the soul from the clutches of evil.

A common medieval torture was the rack—a machine that slowly stretched a prisoner until his or her joints separated. In another method of torture, red-hot pincers called *hooks* were used to pull the flesh away. Thumbscrews were used as their name implies. In *cording*, an offender's thumbs were tied tightly together behind the back by a rope that passed through a support in the ceiling. Weights were then tied to the ankles, and the person was hoisted into the air by his or her thumbs.

Stones were used to crush confessions out of offenders: First a convict was covered with boards, and then suffered as one stone after another was placed on top of them.

Exile and Transportation

In a number of early societies exile, or banishment, sometimes took the place of corporal and capital punishment. The ancient Greeks permitted offenders to leave the Greek state and travel to Rome, where they might gain citizenship. Early Roman law also established the punishment of exile. Exile was regarded as akin to a death sentence because the banished person could no longer depend on his or her former community for support and protection. He or she could generally be killed with impunity if attempting to reenter the area.

Exile was practiced in some European communities into the 1800s. One historical study, for example, revealed that, between 1650 and 1750, 97 percent of the noncapital sentences handed down in Amsterdam included banishment.[19] Sentences of banishment drove petty offenders out of a municipality and kept known offenders out of town. But banished criminals resurfaced quickly in neighboring towns, and many communities in Europe confronted a floating population of criminals—especially petty thieves.

Though it was rarely practical to banish offenders from an entire province or nation, England practiced for more than 200 years a form of criminal exile known as *transportation*. An English law authorizing the transportation of convicts to newly discovered lands was passed in 1597. The law was intended primarily to provide galley slaves for a burgeoning English merchant fleet. Soon, however, public support grew for the transportation system as a way of ridding England of felons. As a result, large numbers of convicts were sent to America and other English colonies. One writer estimates that, by the beginning of the American Revolution, 50,000 prisoners had been sent to the New World. Most of them "were sold as indentured servants in the southern colonies, where their market value was greater than in New England."[20]

After the American Revolution, convicted felons began piling up in English jails with no place to go. Legislation was soon passed authorizing prisoners to be housed aboard floating prison ships called *hulks*. Many of these vessels were abandoned merchant ships or broken-down warships. Hulks were anchored in rivers and harbors throughout England. They were unsanitary, rat infested, and unventilated, and the keepers flogged the inmates to force them to work. Disease ran rampant in the hulks, sometimes wiping out all the prisoners on a ship, as well as the crew and nearby citizens. This "temporary" solution lasted about 80 years.

The system of hulks eventually proved impractical, and England soon began shifting its convict population to Australia, which Captain Cook had come upon in 1770. Convict transportation to Australia began in earnest in 1787[21] with English convicts being transported to New South Wales, Norfolk Island, and Van Diemen's Land—now known as Tasmania (see Exhibit 2–1). The journey was long and demanding, and conditions on prison ships were often ghastly. Many convicts did not survive the trip. Those who did were put to work at heavy labor when they reached their destinations, helping develop the growing region.

Visit http://www.youtube.com/watch?v =eOH3Ul2cY8I or scan this code with the QR app on your smartphone or digital device to view an historical YouTube video describing the British system of floating prisons, known as *hulks*.

Devil's Island, the infamous French prison where many political prisoners were held. What role did transportation play in the criminal punishments of times past?

EXHIBIT 2–1 **Van Diemen's Land**

Van Diemen's Land, an island off the southern coast of Australia that is known today as Tasmania, served as a destination in the English system of convict transportation during the early 1800s. The paragraphs that follow, which were written in 1832, give some historical insight into the practice.

Van Diemen's Land was discovered so long ago as the year 1642, by the Dutch navigator Tasman, who gave it the name which it still bears, in honour of his employer Anthony Van Diemen, the then governor of the Dutch possessions in India. It was not, however, till the year 1804 that the country was taken possession of by England. In the early part of that year Colonel David Collins, having been appointed Governor of the projected settlement, arrived on the island with about four hundred prisoners in charge and a force of fifty marines under his command. He was accompanied also by several gentlemen, commissioned to fill the various situations on the new government. They fixed their headquarters on the site of the present capital, to which they gave the name of Hobart Town, after Lord Hobart, the then Secretary for the Colonies. The Colony . . . being thus founded, continued to take root, although at times suffering very great hardships. . . . No sheep or cattle were imported till three years after the settlement of the island. For some time after this, indeed, the colony was looked upon merely as a place of punishment for persons convicted of crimes in New South Wales, numbers of whom accordingly continued to be sent to it every year. Governor Collins died in 1810; and in 1813 Lieutenant-Colonel Davey arrived as his successor.

From about this time the colony began to be considered in a new light. The population consisted no longer merely of the convicts and the garrison; but, besides many persons who, having been originally crown prisoners, had obtained their freedom by servitude or indolence, embraced a considerable number of settlers who had arrived in successive small parties from the neighbouring colony of New South Wales. Hitherto the only places with which Van Diemen's Land was allowed to hold any communication had been New South Wales and England: That restriction was now done away with, and the two colonies were placed, in respect to foreign commerce, on precisely the same footing. . . .

In 1817 Colonel Davey was succeeded in the government by Colonel Sorell. The first object which engaged the attention of the new governor was the suppression of an evil under which the colony had for some years been suffering, the ravages of the bush-rangers, as they were called, or prisoners who had made their escape and roamed at large in the woods. The capture and execution of the principal leaders of these marauders in a short time put an end, for the present, to their destructive inroads.

About 1821 may be said to have begun the emigration from England, which has since proceeded almost with uninterrupted steadiness. . . . In December 1825, Van Diemen's Land was declared entirely independent of New South Wales; and an executive and legislative Council were appointed as advisers to the Governor, the members of both being named by the Crown. In 1827 the island was divided into eight police districts, each of which was placed under the charge of a stipendiary magistrate.

Source: The Society for the Diffusion of Useful Knowledge, *The Penny Magazine*, vol. 1, no. 1, March 31, 1832.

Soon convicts who had served their sentences began to receive land grants. In 1791, the governor of New South Wales initiated a program to give released convicts up to 30 acres of land each, along with enough tools, seeds, and rations to last 18 months.

English transportation of criminals began to wane in 1853, when Parliament abolished transportation for prisoners with sentences of fewer than 14 years. Opposition to transportation was especially strong among the free settlers who had begun to populate Australia and nearby regions. In 1867, the practice of transportation officially ended, although England continued to send inmates from India to its penal colony in the Andaman Islands until World War II.

France also experimented with transportation. Beginning in 1791, French authorities sent prisoners in large numbers to Madagascar, New Caledonia, the Marquesas Islands, and French Guiana. Devil's Island in the Caribbean Sea off the coast of French Guiana continued to function as a prison until 1951. The island was named for the horrors associated with imprisonment there. It was the site of an infamous penal colony that was used mostly for political prisoners. The island was also made famous by the Dreyfus Affair, which began in 1894 when French Captain Alfred Dreyfus (1859–1935) was convicted of treason by a court-martial, sentenced to life imprisonment, and sent to the island. Thirty-six years later, Dreyfus was exonerated after it was demonstrated that the original charges against him were the result of anti-Semitism in the French military and had no factual basis.

The only Western nation to practice transportation into the 1990s was Russia, which sent prisoners to Siberia as late as 1990. Siberia is

In the late 18th century, the English government began turning broken-down war vessels and abandoned transport ships into hulks to house prisoners. What event caused the prison overcrowding that made these hulks necessary?

a cold and formerly desolate region in what is now central and eastern Russia. It stretches from the Ural Mountains to the Pacific Ocean. The extensive area was annexed by Russia in stages during the 16th and 17th centuries. It was used as a place of exile for political prisoners beginning in the early 17th century. In 1741, the Russian Count Biron was found guilty of treason, but his sentence of death by quartering was changed to exile to Siberia.[22] Hard labor in Siberia became a common sentence for criminal offenders in Czarist Russia, and it is estimated that hundreds of thousands of vagrants, felons, political prisoners, and even voluntary exiles were sent to Siberia under the Czars to force settlement of the region and to develop its natural resources. During Joseph Stalin's rule (1928–1953), Siberian prison camps forced tens of millions of victims into a vast labor system. The brutal conditions in these camps resulted in millions of deaths and have been graphically described in the works of Aleksandr Solzhenitsyn.[23] After Stalin's death, the camp population greatly decreased, although some still hold a few criminal offenders. The major industrial cities of today's prosperous Russian Arctic, including Kolyma, Norilsk, and Vorkuta, began as camps constructed by prisoners.

Public Humiliation

Many corporal punishments were carried out in public, primarily to deter other potential lawbreakers. Some other forms of punishment depended on public ridicule for their effect. These included the stocks and the pillory.

Stocks held a prisoner in a sitting position with feet and hands locked in a frame. A prisoner in the pillory was made to stand with his or her head and hands locked in place. Both devices exposed the prisoner to public scorn. While confined in place, prisoners were frequently pelted with eggs and rotten fruit. Sometimes they were whipped or branded. Those confined to the pillory occasionally had their ears nailed to the

Found guilty of the offense of impiety in Athens in 399 B.C., Socrates chose poison over imprisonment. What was the goal of most early penalties for crimes?

wood, and they had to rip them free when released. England abolished the pillory in 1834; according to at least one source, the pillory was still in use in Delaware in 1905.[24]

Confinement

Confinement by chaining or jailing has been a punishment since ancient times. In China, Confucius wrote about prisons being built around 2000 B.C., and the Old Testament describes imprisonment in Babylon and during Egypt's Middle Kingdom (2040–1640 B.C.).[25] At times, confinement served functions other than punishment for crimes. In early Greece, for example, prisons were used to punish convicted offenders, to enforce the payment of debts, to hold those awaiting other punishments, and to detain foreigners who might otherwise flee before their cases could be heard.[26] Until the 1600s and the development of prisons as primary places of punishment, prisons were used to detain people before trial; to hold prisoners awaiting other punishments, such as death or corporal punishment; to force payment of debts and fines; and to hold and punish slaves.

Early European prisons were rarely called *prisons*. They went by such names as *dungeon, tower,* and *gaol* (from which we get the modern term *jail*). Some places used as prisons had been built for other purposes. The Tower of London, for example, was originally a fortified palace that had been used as an arsenal. The French Bastille began as a fortified city gate leading into Paris. Judicial proceedings were not necessary before imprisonment in such places, nor was a formal sentence. As a result, anyone thrown into a dungeon at the behest of authorities was likely to stay there until granted clemency or until death.

INCARCERATION AS PUNISHMENT

CO2-4

Church-run prisons were in place by the 6th century, and they were relatively commonplace by the 9th century. Early Canon (or church) law forbade the drawing of blood as punishment and stressed contrition—principles that were served well by the solitude of imprisonment. Church prisons, which were not under the control of secular society, were built around the extensive system of church-run monasteries that existed throughout Europe during the middle ages.[27]

According to Pieter Spierenburg, a Dutch justice historian, a form of secular punishment that emerged around the year 1500 was *penal bondage,* which included all forms of incarceration.[28] Spierenburg explained, "Courts came to use it almost as frequently as physical sanctions. Instead of being flogged or hanged, some offenders were incarcerated in workhouses or forced to perform labor in some other setting." According to Spierenburg, the word *bondage* means "any punishment that puts severe restrictions on the condemned person's freedom of action and movement, including but not limited to imprisonment."

Among the forms of penal bondage imposed on criminals, vagrants, debtors, social misfits, and others were forced labor on public works projects and forced conscription into military campaigns. Later, houses of correction also subjected inmates to strict routines.

One early form of incarceration developed in France. For at least 200 years, prisoners were regularly assigned to French warships as galley slaves. After the naval importance of galleys had declined, French naval officials continued to have custody of convicted offenders. By the mid-1700s, they had begun to put convicts to work in the shipyards of Toulon, Brest, and Rochefort. At night these prisoners were sheltered in arsenals, where they slept chained to their beds. As Spierenburg notes, "the arsenals were in fact labor camps where convicts had to remain within an enclosed space, so the penalty was more akin to imprisonment than to public works."

The public works penalty, sometimes called *penal servitude,* became especially popular in Germany and Switzerland in the 1600s and 1700s. According to Spierenburg, "convicts dug ore in mines, repaired ramparts, built roads or houses, or went from door to door collecting human waste."[29]

The House of Correction (1550–1700)

Midway between corporal punishments and modern imprisonment stands the workhouse or the house of correction. The development of workhouses was originally a humanitarian move intended to manage the unsettling social conditions of the late 16th and early 17th centuries in England. The feudal system had offered mutual protection for land-owning nobles and for serfs, who were tied to the land. By 1550, that system was breaking down in Europe. Hordes of former serfs roamed the countryside, unable to earn a living. Many flocked to the cities, where they hoped to find work in newly developing industries. The change from an agrarian economy to an industrial one displaced many persons, resulted in growing poverty, and increased the numbers of beggars and vagrants.

Vagrancy became a crime, and soon anyone unable to prove some means of support was imprisoned in a workhouse. The first workhouse in England was called Bridewell because it was located in Bridewell Palace, which was given to London by King Edward III and opened as a prison in 1556.[30] Soon, the word **bridewell** entered the language as a term for a workhouse. English Parliament ordered workhouses to be created throughout England. Parliament intended that those housed in workhouses be taught habits of industry and frugality and that they learn a trade.

At first, prisoners in workhouses were paid for the work they did. Work included spinning, weaving, clothmaking, the milling of grains, and baking. Soon, however, as the numbers of prisoners grew, the workhouse system deteriorated. As workhouses spread through Europe, they became catch-all institutions that held the idle, the unemployed, the poor, debtors, insane persons, and even unruly individuals whose families could not cope with them. According to one writer, imprisonment in a workhouse could serve "as a tool of private discipline. . . . The family drew up a petition explaining why the individual should be imprisoned, and the authorities decided whether or not to consent. Usually, private offenders were confined because of conduct considered immoral."[31]

Hence, workhouses served as informal repositories for people the community regarded as "inconvenient," irresponsible, or deviant—even if their behavior did not violate the criminal law. In the midst of this large population of misfits and unwanted persons could be found a core group of criminal offenders. In 1706 the British Parliament passed legislation "permitting judges to sentence felons to the house of correction for up to two years."[32]

By the end of the 17th century, houses of correction had become mere holding cells with little reformative purpose. Nonetheless, because workhouses relied primarily on incarceration rather than corporal punishments, they provided a model for prison reformers bent on more humanitarian correctional practices.

bridewell

A workhouse. The word came from the name of the first workhouse in England.

Bridewells were penal institutions for social outcasts—ranging from vagrants to petty criminals—who were forced to work under strict discipline. What social conditions prompted governments to establish such houses of correction?

The Emergence of the Prison

Two main elements fueled the development of prisons as we know them today. The first element was a philosophical shift away from punishment of the body toward punishment of the soul or human spirit. By the late 1700s in Europe and America, a powerful movement was under way to replace traditional corporal punishments with deprivation of personal liberty as the main thrust of criminal sentencing. Michel Foucault explains the shift this way:

> The punishment-body relation [was no longer] the same as it was in the torture during public executions. The body now serves as an instrument or intermediary: If one intervenes upon it to imprison it or to make it work, it is in order to deprive the individual of a liberty that is regarded both as a right and as property. The body, according to this penalty, is caught up in a system of constraints and privations, obligations and prohibitions. Physical pain, the pain of the body itself, is no longer the constituent element of the penalty.[33]

The transition from corporal punishments to denial of liberties found its clearest expression in the work of the Philadelphia Society for Alleviating the Miseries of Public Prisons. The society, established by the Pennsylvania Quakers in 1787, had as its purpose the renovation of existing prisons and jails and the establishment of the prison as the basic form of criminal punishment. Thanks largely to the widely publicized works of the society, Pennsylvania became in April 1794 the first state to abolish permanently the death penalty for all crimes except first-degree murder, and it adopted a system of fines and imprisonment in place of corporal punishments.[34] The new Pennsylvania criminal code was important because it "marked the first permanent American break with contemporary juristic savagery, was the forerunner of the reform codes of other American states, and was the essential basis of Pennsylvania criminal jurisprudence until the next systematic revision in 1860."[35]

The second element fueling the development of modern prisons was the passage of laws preventing the imprisonment of anyone except criminals. Civil commitments to prison ended, and a huge class of social misfits were removed from prisons and dealt with elsewhere. Primary among this group were debtors, who historically had been cast into jails as a result of civil rulings against them. John Howard's study of English jails found 2,437 debtors among the 4,084 prisoners he encountered.[36] Many others were vagrants who had committed no "intentional" crime.

According to Pieter Spierenburg, the Dutch were the first Europeans to segregate serious criminals from vagrants and minor delinquents, and Dutch courts were the first European courts to begin substituting imprisonment for corporal punishments.[37] The workhouse in Amsterdam, which opened in 1654, "represented the first criminal prison in Europe," says Spierenburg. By the start of the 1700s, Dutch "courts frequently imposed sentences of imprisonment. During the third quarter of the 17th century, the Amsterdam court did so in one-fifth of its criminal cases; a century later, it did so in three-fifths. By the 1670s, the court of Groningen-City imposed imprisonment in two-fifths of criminal cases." Even so, the imprisonment of debtors persisted in Holland for another 100 years, and Dutch prisons of the period held both criminal and civil "convicts."

These ideas—that "doing time" was often the most appropriate punishment for criminal activity and that incarceration should be imposed only on criminal offenders—soon combined with a burgeoning emphasis on reformation as the primary goal of criminal sentencing. Reformation, argued many prison advocates of the time, could best be achieved by enforced solitude.

The Staff Speaks
Visit www.mhhe.com/schmalleger7e
to see this feature.

In 1776, the British philanthropist Jonas Hanway published a book titled *Solitude in Imprisonment*. Hanway's work appears to have had a significant influence on prison advocates. He argued that the interruption of transportation provided a much-needed opportunity to reexamine prevailing policies for dealing with prisoners. Hanway suggested that reformation should be the primary goal of criminal sentencing and said that it was plainly not being met by sentencing practices then in existence. Solitary confinement, said Hanway, would force the prisoner to face his or her conscience—leading to reformation: "The walls of his prison will preach peace to his soul, and he will confess the goodness of his Maker, and the wisdom of the laws of his country."[38]

CO2-5   THE REFORMERS

Prisons, as institutions in which convicted offenders spend time as punishment for crimes, are relatively modern. They came about largely as a result of growing intellectualism in Europe and America and as a reaction to the barbarities of corporal punishment.

The period of Western social thought that began in the 17th century and lasted until the dawn of the 19th century is known as the Age of Enlightenment. One author explains, "The phrase was frequently employed by writers of the period itself, convinced that they were emerging from centuries of darkness and ignorance into a new age enlightened by reason, science, and a respect for humanity."[39] The Enlightenment, also known as the *Age of Reason*, was more than a set of fixed ideas. Enlightenment thought implied an attitude—a method of knowing based on observation, experience, and reason.

One of the earliest representatives of the Enlightenment was the French social philosopher and jurist Charles de Montesquieu (1689–1755) whose masterwork, *The Spirit of Laws*, was published in 1748. Montesquieu wrote that governmental powers should be separated and balanced in order to guarantee individual rights and freedom. He strongly believed in the rights of individuals. His ideas influenced leaders of both the American Revolution and the French Revolution.[40]

Another celebrated philosopher of the Enlightenment was the French writer Voltaire, who satirized both the government and the religious establishment of France. Voltaire twice served time in the Bastille and chose exile in England over prison for additional offenses. He deeply admired the English atmosphere of political and religious freedom.

A number of important thinkers influenced the justice systems of Western nations and the directions the correctional enterprise would take over the next 200 years. We will now turn our attention to those individuals.

William Penn

William Penn (1644–1718), regarded as the founder of Pennsylvania, was the son of Sir William Penn, a distinguished English admiral. During his youth, Penn traveled widely throughout Europe, served in the Royal Navy, and studied law. In 1667, he converted to the Quaker faith and by the next year found himself confined in the Tower of London as punishment for promoting the faith. While imprisoned, he wrote a paper titled "No Cross, No Crown." After release, he was again imprisoned on a number of occasions, causing him to seek refuge in America. In 1682, Penn obtained a charter creating the Commonwealth of Pennsylvania, and naming him governor. Gathering together hundreds of Quakers, Penn set sail for the New World. The colony he founded promoted religious tolerance, and it was soon attracting persecuted minorities from England, Germany, Holland, and Scandinavia.

Penn's influence on the criminal law of this country and on the coming age of imprisonment was most visible in the "Great Act" of 1682. Through that single piece of legislation, the Pennsylvania Quakers reduced capital offenses to the one crime of premeditated murder and abolished all corporal punishments as they had existed under English code.

John Howard

John Howard (1726–1790) was born to a deeply religious English family. On a trip to Portugal as a young man, Howard was taken prisoner by pirates when the British merchant ship on which he was traveling was captured by a French privateer.[41] He and his fellow passengers were kept below deck in subhuman conditions. When they arrived in France, he was imprisoned in a French dungeon, but he was later released in exchange for a French naval officer.

In 1773, Howard was appointed high sheriff of Bedfordshire. He was shocked at the abysmal conditions that existed in English jails of the time, and he set out on a quest for prison reform. He began arguing for the abolishment of spiked collars and chains, which prisoners were made to wear, and he argued against the common practice of paying jailers for release. Within a few years, Howard had visited almost every county in England, Wales, and Scotland, traveling no fewer than 7,000 miles in 1779 alone. He also inspected prisons in a number of other countries, including France, Belgium, Holland, Italy, Germany, Spain, Portugal, Denmark, Sweden, and Russia.

Although most prisons Howard visited were like those in England, he found one—the Maison de Force in Ghent, Belgium—that embodied the highest standards of its day.

Howard's greatest legacy was his 1777 book, *The State of the Prisons in England and Wales,*[42] in which he described the abysmal state of English prisons. *The State of the Prisons* also contained descriptions of clean and well-run institutions, prisons in which the sexes were separated, and jails in which inmates were kept busy at productive work.

Howard's book promoted the notion that the fundamental business of corrections should be to reform rather than to punish, and he argued that every citizen must accept responsibility for the criminal justice system of the society in which he or she lives. *The State of the Prisons* appealed to policymakers looking for alternatives to existing systems, and it fueled the efforts of prison reformers in both Europe and America. Many of the principles described in Howard's book later became the foundation for the English Penitentiary Act of 1779, which established a decisive shift toward the use of imprisonment rather than transportation and capital punishment.

As Randall McGowen, corrections historian at the University of Oregon, explains, "Howard's contribution was to make the prison the center of focus, shifting all other forms of punishment to the margins. He fostered a vital change of perspective at the very time that judges were sentencing greater numbers of felons to confinement. Howard's book created the impression that the prison was the natural and inevitable shape of punishment."[43]

Howard died of the plague in Russia in 1790. At the time, he was in the midst of his sixth tour of European prisons and was about to leave on a trip to study prisons in Turkey and Asia. On his tomb are engraved these words:

Whosoever Thou Art
Thou Standest at the
Grave of Thy friend

A plaque in Warrington, NW of London honoring John Howard, the great English prison reformer. Howard proposed the idea that the fundamental business of corrections should be to reform rather than to punish. How does his work influence corrections today?

Cesare Beccaria (1738–1794), an Italian jurist and criminologist, was one of the first to argue against capital punishment and inhumane treatment of prisoners. What writing by Beccaria influenced the criminal justice systems of Western Europe?

Visit http://www.ucl.ac.uk/Bentham-Project/who/autoicon/Virtual_Auto_Icon or scan this code with the QR app on your smartphone or digital device to visit Jeremy Bentham's auto-icon at University College London. The auto-icon consists of a wooden cabinet in which is housed Bentham's skeleton dressed in the style of the day, surmounted by a wax head modeled after Bentham. The College also houses Bentham's many private papers and publications, most of which can be accessed through the site.

Cesare Beccaria

Cesare Beccaria (1738–1794) was born in Italy, the eldest son of an aristocratic family. By the time he reached his mid-20s, Beccaria had formed, with his close friends Pietro and Alessandro Verri, an intellectual circle called the Academy of Fists.[44] The academy took as its purpose the reform of the criminal justice system. Through the Verri brothers, Beccaria became acquainted with the work of French and British political writers such as Montesquieu, Thomas Hobbes (1588–1679), Denis Diderot (1713–1784), Claude-Adrien Helvetius (1715–1771), and David Hume (1711–1776).

In 1764 Beccaria published an essay titled *On Crimes and Punishments*. Although the work was brief, it was, perhaps, the most exciting essay on law of the 18th century. In the essay, Beccaria outlined a utilitarian approach to punishment, suggesting that some punishments can never be justified because they are more evil than any "good" they might produce. The use of torture to obtain confessions falls into that category, said Beccaria. Beccaria also protested punishment of the insane, a common practice of the times, saying it could do no good because insane people cannot accurately assess the consequences of their actions. Beccaria said that *ex post facto* laws, or laws passed after the fact, imposed punishment unfairly because a person could not calculate the risk of acting before a law against a specific action was passed. He also argued against the use of secret accusations, the discretionary power of judges, the inconsistency and inequality of sentencing, the use of personal connections to obtain sentencing reductions, and the imposition of capital punishment for minor offenses.

Beccaria proposed that punishment could be justified only if it was imposed to defend the social contract—the tacit allegiance that individuals owe their society, and the obligations of government to individuals. It is the social contract, said Beccaria, that gives society the right to punish its members.

Beccaria also argued that punishment should be swift because swift punishment offers the greatest deterrence. When punishment quickly follows a crime, said Beccaria, the ideas of crime and punishment are more closely associated in a person's mind. He also suggested that the link between crime and punishment would be stronger if the punishment somehow related to the crime.

Finally, said Beccaria, punishments should not be unnecessarily severe. The severity of punishment, he argued, should be proportional to the degree of social damage caused by the crime. Treason, Beccaria said, is the worst crime because it most harms the social contract. Below treason, Beccaria listed crimes in order of declining severity, including violence against a person or his property, public disruption, and crimes against property. Crimes against property, he said, should be punished by fines.

When his essay was translated into French and English, Beccaria became famous throughout much of Europe. Philosophers of the time hailed his ideas, and several European rulers vowed to follow his lead in the reform of their justice systems.

Jeremy Bentham

Philosopher and jurist Jeremy Bentham (1748–1832) was born in London. As a young child, he was considered a prodigy, having been found, at the age of two, sitting at his father's desk reading a multivolume history of England.[45] He began to study Latin at the age of three. When Bentham

ZairaTena

Correctional Officer • New Mexico Women's Correctional Facility • Grants, New Mexico

Zaira Tena is employed by Corrections Corporation of America (CCA) as a correctional officer at the New Mexico Women's Correctional Facility in Grants, New Mexico. This is Tena's first job in corrections. She was attracted to CCA and a career in corrections because of the benefits that CCA offered her.

Tena attended Laramie County Community College in Laramie, Wyoming, before joining CCA. The company provided additional training in interpersonal communication, special-needs inmates, crisis intervention, infectious diseases, suicide prevention, first aid, CPR, and firearms, giving her the skills she needs to ensure the health, welfare, and safety of prison employees and inmates. Because Tena especially enjoys recreation, she also coordinates the institution's recreation activities.

Tena's enthusiasm for her own career and professional development shows in her advice to people thinking about a career in corrections. Wisely, she is taking her own advice. She plans to stay in corrections and hopes one day soon to become assistant shift commander at the Grants women's facility.

> *"I like my job. I like working with people. What I learned and what I'd tell someone is, be very professional, firm, fair, and consistent at all times, and be able to work under a lot of pressure."*

was 12, his father, a wealthy attorney, sent him to Queen's College, Oxford, hoping that he would enter the field of law.

After hearing lectures by the leading legal scholar of the day, Sir William Blackstone (1723–1780), young Bentham became disillusioned with the law. Instead of practicing law, he decided to criticize it, and he spent the rest of his life analyzing the legal practices of the day, writing about them, and suggesting improvements.

Bentham advocated **utilitarianism,** the principle that the highest objective of public policy is the greatest happiness for the largest number of people. Utilitarianism provided the starting point for Bentham's social analysis in which he tried to measure the usefulness of existing institutions, practices, and beliefs against a common standard. Bentham believed that human behavior is determined largely by the amount of pleasure or pain associated with a given activity. Hence, he suggested, the purpose of law should be to make socially undesirable activities painful enough to keep people from engaging in them. In this way, said Bentham, "good" can be achieved.

Bentham's idea, that people are motivated by pleasure and pain and that the proper amount of punishment can deter crime, became known as **hedonistic calculus.** Bentham's hedonistic calculus made four assumptions:

1. People by nature choose pleasure and avoid pain.
2. Each individual, either consciously or intuitively, calculates the degree of pleasure or pain to be derived from a given course of action.
3. Lawmakers can determine the degree of punishment necessary to deter criminal behavior.
4. Such punishment can be effectively and rationally built into a system of criminal sentencing.

Bentham is also known as the inventor of the *panopticon* (from a Greek word meaning "all-seeing")—a type of prison he proposed building in England as early as 1787. The panopticon was intended to put utilitarian ideas to work in the field of penology.

utilitarianism

The principle that the highest objective of public policy is the greatest happiness for the largest number of people.

hedonistic calculus

The idea that people are motivated by pleasure and pain and that the proper amount of punishment can deter crime.

Visit http://www.youtube.com/watch?v=ZCwhKCqdINY&feature=youtu.be or scan this code with the QR app on your smartphone or digital device to view a video of Prof. Philip Schofield of University College London discussing Jeremy Bentham and displaying the auto-icon.

Key to the panopticon was its unique architecture, which consisted of a circular, tiered design with a glass roof and with a window on the outside wall of each cell.[46] The design made it easy for prison staff, in a tower in the center of the structure, to observe each cell (and its occupants). Within the wheel-like structure, walls separated the cells to prevent any communication between prisoners. Speaking tubes linked cells with the observation platform so that officers could listen to inmates.

The panopticon, also called an *inspection house,* was intended to be a progressive and humanitarian penitentiary. Bentham thought of it as a social experiment. The design was touted as being consistent with the ideals of utilitarianism because only a few officers would be subject to the risks and unpleasantness of the inspection role, while many prisoners would benefit from this enlightened means of institutional management.

After years of personally promoting the concept, Bentham saw his idea for an innovative penitentiary die. The panopticon was never built in England, and in 1820, government officials formally disavowed it. The concept may have fallen victim to the growing emphasis on transportation, which delayed all prison construction in England. Another significant factor in the demise of the panopticon ideal, however, was Bentham's insistence that panopticons be built near cities to deter crime among the general population. Although a number of sites were chosen for construction, nearby residents always protested plans to build any sort of prison in their neighborhoods. Despite Bentham's failure ever to construct a facility completely true to his panopticon plan, he will always be remembered for his idea that order and reform could be achieved in a prison through architectural design.

Jeremy Bentham (1748–1832), an English philosopher and social reformer. He spent his life trying to reform the law. His innovative plan for a prison, called the panopticon, consisted of a huge structure covered by a glass roof. A central tower allowed guards to see into the cells, which were arranged in a circle. Although the British government did not use Bentham's plan, several U.S. prisons did, including one in Joliet, Illinois, known as Stateville Correctional Center. What is the name given to Bentham's principle that the highest object of public policy is the greatest happiness for the greatest number of people?

Sir Samuel Romilly

Sir Samuel Romilly (1757–1818) was an English legal reformer who worked ceaselessly to lessen the severity of existing criminal law in his home country. Romilly, once described as "the flower of the English reform movement,"[47] attacked laws that authorized capital punishment for a host of minor felonies and misdemeanors.

Romilly's dedication to his cause drew the admiration from a number of reformers. M. Dumont, once described as "the leading orator of the French Revolution," said of Romilly, "[He is] always tranquil and orderly yet has an incessant activity. He never loses a minute; he applies all his mind to what he is about. Like the hand of three watches, he never stops."[48] Another contemporary said of Romilly that "in the House of Commons he looked like Apollo surrounded by crowds of satyrs and goats. . . . This man it was who led the fight to get the gentleness of the English character expressed in its laws."[49]

Romilly entered Parliament in 1806, and in 1810 proposed a reexamination of the Penitentiary Act of 1779. As a result, the government appointed the Holford Committee to examine issues associated with penal reform. Until his early death in 1818, Romilly fought to reduce the number of English capital crimes. He succeeded in getting passed a bill abolishing the death penalty in cases of "private stealing from the person," and he won the abolition of the death penalty in cases of soldiers and sailors found absent without leave. At the time of his death, 200 offenses were still punishable by sentence of death. The movement he began, however, continued to flower. By 1840, the number of capital crimes in England had been reduced to 14, and by 1861 the number fell to 4 (treason, murder, piracy, and setting fire to arsenals).

Romilly's work and the results it produced led others to recognize the need for alternatives to capital punishment as a means of dealing with the large majority of offenders.

Sir Robert Peel

Sir Robert Peel (1788–1850) was a British parliamentary leader bent on seeing the ideas of Romilly, Bentham, and others incorporated into English law. Peel is best known in the history of criminal justice for establishing a police force that influenced the development of policing throughout much of the rest of the world. His force, the London Metropolitan Police, became known as the Met.

Prior to Peel's time, agents of law enforcement often meted out "justice" as they saw fit, sometimes apprehending the offender and punishing him or her on the spot. Peel and other legal reformers of the day worked to identify the fundamental function of the police as the investigation of crime and the apprehension of criminals. Peel insisted that the police should be responsible for investigation and arrest only, while the trial, defense, and conviction phase of the justice process should reside entirely in the hands of another body, the judiciary.[50] Punishment, he said, should not be imposed by the police but by specialists in the field of penology. In Peel's words, it is necessary for the police "to recognize always the need for strict adherence to police executive functions and to refrain from even seeming to usurp the powers of the judiciary or avenging individuals or the state and of authoritatively judging guilt and punishing the guilty."

In effect, while working to formalize police administration, Peel pointed out the need for other specialists in the administration of justice such as attorneys, magistrates, and correctional personnel. Peel was also primarily

Sir Robert Peel, founder of the London Metropolitan Police. Punishment, said Peel, should not be imposed by the police, but by specialists in penology. In what other ways did Peel influence the field of corrections?

responsible for legislation, Peel's Gaol Act of 1823, aimed at reforming British jails. The Gaol Act required that men and women be segregated while in jail and mandated the supervision of female prisoners by female correctional personnel.[51]

Elizabeth Fry

Elizabeth Fry (1780–1845), a strict Quaker committed to religious and philanthropic work, campaigned during the early 1800s to "expose the plight of women in prison and to promote better conditions for them."[52] While most Enlightenment era thinkers had been influenced by a belief in utilitarian principles, Fry's reformist activities grew out of her religious faith.

Fry had been strongly influenced by a delegation of American Quakers who visited London's notorious Newgate prison in 1813. Their report said that they had been horrified to find "blaspheming, fighting, dram-drinking, half-naked women" occupying part of the facility. A few months later, Fry visited the jail herself and found that women were being held in what she described as "filthy" conditions. From then on, Fry campaigned for reform of the conditions under which women were confined, arguing that women should be treated "tenderly" and "with gentleness and sympathy so that they would submit cheerfully to the rules and cooperate willingly in their own reform."[53]

Fry formed the Ladies Association for the Reformation of Female Prisoners in Newgate and, later, the British Ladies Society for the Reformation of Female Prisoners. Fry's influence was also felt in the United States where concerned women banded together under the banner of prison reform in order to draw attention to the welfare of women prisoners.

Fry and her followers, including American feminist leader Dorothea Dix, believed that women are more likely than men to change and that appeals "to the heart" would be more effective with women offenders than with men. In her 1825 publication, *Observations on the Siting, Superintendence, and Government of Female Prisoners,* Fry provided concrete ideas on how women's prisons should be run. "Especially important for women," she argued, "were cleanliness, plain decent clothing, and warm, orderly surroundings."[54]

Mary Belle Harris

Another American woman reformer who was influenced by Fry was Mary Belle Harris (1874–1957). Harris, who was born in Pennsylvania, eventually became the first warden of the Federal Institution for Women in Alderson, West Virginia, when it opened in 1927. She had turned to a career in corrections only after already having been a teacher, social worker, and archeologist.

Harris came to Alderson after serving as superintendent of the Women's Workhouse on Blackwell Island (New York), as superintendent of the State Reformatory for Women at Clinton, New Jersey, and as assistant director of the section on Reformatories and Detention Homes for the U.S. War Department.

Known as a vocal advocate of correctional reforms and as an avid supporter of the reformation ideal, Harris believed that reformation, not punishment, should be the primary focus of most correctional programs and institutions. Harris also believed that the criminality of women was largely the result of their social roles and specifically their economic dependency upon men. As a result, she advocated training programs that would permit women prisoners to become financially independent upon release. At Alderson, Harris oversaw the development of programs designed to break the cycle of dependency. Her work became widely known and served as a model for women's prisons throughout the nation.

Before retiring in 1941, Harris wrote a number of books describing her experiences in corrections. Among them are *I Knew Them in Prison* (1936) and *The Pathway of Mattie Howard to and from Prison: The Story of the Regeneration of an Ex-Convict and Gangster Woman* (1937).

Sanford Bates

Sanford Bates (1884–1972) was the first director of the Federal Bureau of Prisons (BOP), a position he held from 1930 until 1937. Before becoming the bureau's director, Bates served in the Massachusetts state legislature, was commissioner of Penal Institutions in Boston from 1917 to 1919, and held the position of commissioner of the Massachusetts Department of Corrections. Bates became superintendent of Prisons, U.S. Department of Justice, in 1929. While in that post, he prepared the legislation that established the Federal Bureau of Prisons in 1930.

During his tenure as director of the BOP, Bates authored a number of books including *Prisons and Beyond.*[55] In *Prisons*, Bates wrote that "the perplexing problem confronting the prison administrator of today is how to devise a prison so as to preserve its role of a punitive agency and still reform the individuals who have been sent there." Although the BOP began operations during the Great Depression, Bates believed in rehabilitation and in the value of inmate labor, thinking that work provided both a sense of purpose and a tool for reformation. Consequently, he began Federal Prison Industries (FPI) and served as its chair from 1934 until his death in 1972. Bates created FPI programs involving work on prison farms, public lands, military bases, and highway construction, thereby largely avoiding the ire of labor unions that were seeking jobs for their members. Under Bates's leadership, the U.S. federal prison system became one of the most progressive and adequately financed correctional systems in the world.

Bates believed that prisoner rehabilitation offered the best hope of protecting society from crime.[56] He also became president of the American Correctional Association and, after retiring as director of the BOP, served as executive director of the Boys Clubs of America, parole commissioner for New York State, and New Jersey state commissioner of Institutions and Industries. Today, the Sanford Bates Library, a collection of over 5,000 personal papers, books, and monographs, is housed at Sam Houston State University's George J. Beto Criminal Justice Center.

Mary Belle Harris (1874–1957), the first warden of the Federal Institution for Women at Alderson, West Virginia. What historical role have women played in the development of the field of corrections?

Sanford Bates (1884–1972), first director of the Federal Bureau of Prisons. Why did Bates believe in the value of inmate labor?

George J. Beto

Like Bates, George J. Beto (1916–1991), director of the Texas Department of Corrections from 1962 until 1972, believed in the goal of rehabilitation—promoting it as a goal to be achieved in prisons everywhere. Under Beto's leadership, the Texas prison system became known for its order and stability.

George J. Beto (1916–1991), director of the Texas Department of Corrections from 1962 to 1972. What did Beto mean when he said, "We must blur the line between the institution and the community"?

Beto began his career as a Lutheran minister but became interested in reformation after serving on the Texas Prison Board, a volunteer organization that oversaw the entire state prison system. As a board member, Beto initiated one of the earliest General Education Development (GED) testing programs for prisoners in the nation.[57] He also served for a time on the Illinois Parole Board, frequently visiting the Stateville Prison in Joliet, Illinois.

Beto drew special attention to the importance of preparing inmates for release back into society. On October 11, 1970, as he delivered the presidential address at the Centennial Congress of Correction of the American Correctional Association in Cincinnati, Beto told attendees:

> The future will bring an expanded use of pre-release programs. It is sheer folly to keep a man in prison two or three or four or five years and, at the termination of his sentence or upon parole, release him with a few dollars, a cheap suit, and the perfunctory ministrations of the dismissing officer. To an even greater degree, the future will witness programs which devote themselves to easing the inmate's transition from the most unnatural society known to man—prison society—to the free world. . . . We must blur the line between the institution and the community.[58]

During his tenure as director of the Texas Department of Corrections, Beto earned the nickname "Walking George" for his habit of showing up unannounced at prisons at any hour of the day or night and conducting on-the-spot inspections. He's best known, however, for having developed a program of prisoner management called the *Texas control model*. The control model was built on the belief that inmates were in prison because of a lack of self-control, necessitating the need for strong external controls. The control model depended upon strict rule enforcement, and prisoners were punished for even minor infractions of prison regulations. Beto was convinced that discipline, order, and control were necessary in order to provide a safe environment for inmates to better themselves.[59] Before he left the position of director, Beto convinced the state legislature to enact a law requiring state agencies to buy prison-made goods, thereby greatly expanding opportunities for inmate labor in Texas.

Other correctional reformers, including John Augustus, Alexander Maconochie, Sir Walter Crofton, and Zebulon Brockway, are discussed later in this text.

The George J. Beto Criminal Justice Center at Sam Houston State University in Huntsville, Texas. How can corrections professionals benefit from academic study?

REVIEW AND APPLICATIONS

SUMMARY

1 Corporal, or physical, punishments were the most common response to crime for centuries before criminals began to be incarcerated.

2 Criminal punishments of the past generally consisted of flogging, branding, mutilation, exile, transportation, and public humiliation.

3 Torture of all kinds was used during the Middle Ages in an effort to gain confessions. Torture was justified by the belief that guilty knowledge was properly the property of the king or the state, and that exceptional means could be used to recover it.

4 Many reformers based their ideas on Enlightenment principles, including the use of reason and deductive logic to solve problems. They laid the groundwork for the use of imprisonment as an alternative to traditional punishments.

5 Beginning in the mid-1700s, a number of correctional reformers fought the use of corporal punishments and sought to introduce more humane forms of punishment. Among those reformers were Cesare Beccaria, Jeremy Bentham, and John Howard.

KEY TERMS

corporal punishments, p. 30
bridewell, p. 40

utilitarianism, p. 45

hedonistic calculus, p. 45

QUESTIONS FOR REVIEW

1 What are corporal punishments? What has been the purpose of corporal punishments throughout history? List and describe at least four corporal punishments used in the past for criminal offenders.

2 Describe the major criminal punishments used throughout history. Which ancient civilization provided the earliest evidence that physical punishment is part of Western society tradition?

3 What role did torture play in the application of corporal punishments? How was the use of torture justified?

4 What cultural developments contributed to the creation of prisons as an alternative to corporal punishments?

5 Which important thinkers discussed in this chapter adapted principles born of the Enlightenment and applied them to the field of law and corrections? Describe the contributions each made to the field.

THINKING CRITICALLY ABOUT CORRECTIONS

Corporal Punishment

In 1994 Michael Fay, an American teenager convicted of spray-painting parked cars, was flogged in Singapore. The flogging (called *caning* because it was done with a bamboo rod) sparked an international outcry from opponents of corporal punishment. In this country, however, it also led to a rebirth of interest in physical punishments—especially for teenagers and vandals.

The last official flogging of a criminal offender in the United States took place in Delaware on June 16, 1952, when a burglar was tied to a whipping post in the state's central prison and was given 20 lashes. Since then, no sentencing authority in this country has imposed whipping as a criminal punishment, and most jurisdictions have removed all corporal punishments from their statutes. Moreover, corporal punishment, other than capital punishment, is now forbidden in U.S. prisons under the Eighth Amendment. Amnesty International, however, reports that whipping is still in use in parts of the world for certain kinds of prisoners.

After the Fay flogging, lawmakers in eight states introduced legislation to institute whipping or paddling as a criminal sanction. Mississippi legislators proposed paddling graffitists and petty thieves, Tennessee lawmakers considered punishing vandals and burglars by public caning on courthouse steps, the New Mexico Senate Judiciary Committee examined the feasibility of caning graffiti vandals, and Louisiana looked into the possibility of ordering parents (or a correctional officer if the parents refused) to spank their children in judicial chambers. So far, none of the proposals has become law.

1. Would a return to corporal punishments, in the form of whipping or paddling, be justified for some offenders? Why or why not?
2. Might paddling be appropriate for some juvenile offenders? Why or why not?
3. Do you think that any state legislatures will eventually pass legislation permitting the paddling or whipping of criminal offenders? Why or why not?

Capital Punishment

Proponents frequently cite deterrence as a benefit of the death penalty. Some studies refute this contention. When confronted with such studies, proponents sometimes respond that execution "will definitely deter the executed offender." They also argue that death is the only thing that the offender really "deserves."

1. How would you respond to the proponents' first argument?
2. How would you respond to the proponents' second argument?

ON-THE-JOB DECISION MAKING

Counseling

You are a parole officer for the state corrections system. You are so burdened with paperwork that you rarely get out of the office to see any of your 200 clients—even though you are supposed to make regular home visits.

While you are shuffling papers one day, one of your clients, Bob Boynton, knocks at your door. It is time for him to make his monthly report. You tell him to have a seat, and you ask him the usual questions: "Have you been in trouble with the law since I saw you last?" "Are you still working?" "Are you paying your bills on time?"

Before you finish the interview, Boynton says, "You know, I'm never going to get anywhere this way. I need a better education. The time I spent in prison was wasted. They didn't teach me anything. I need to learn a skill so that I can make more money. If I can't earn better money I won't be able to pay my bills—and I'm afraid that I'll be tempted to get into the drug business again. I don't want to do that!"

You tell Boynton that there are a number of training schools in the area that can teach him a skill. Some of the computer classes offered at the local community college, you've heard, can lead to jobs paying decent wages. Boynton says, "I don't have a high school diploma. I can't get into the college. I'll never learn computers. I'm just too old. Besides, I need to work with my hands."

You go through the list of schools and training centers in the area, but Boynton raises an objection to each one. You

sense that Boynton is trying to transfer responsibility for his success or failure to you. What should you do to get him to take responsibility for himself yet provide support and guidance for his efforts?

Dispute Resolution

As a newly assigned assistant warden, you are responsible for discipline within your correctional facility. During your initial meeting with the warden, he said that your predecessor had a well-earned reputation among the inmate population as one who unfailingly sided with the correctional staff in all disputes between staff and inmates, no matter how egregious the staff member's behavior. Warden Cowen specifically asked you to establish yourself as a fair and impartial arbiter to reduce inmate concerns of injustice in dispute resolution.

An incident on your second day on the job presents you with a dilemma that even Solomon might be at a loss to resolve. Correctional Officer Tim Dashe is a six-year veteran with absolutely no record of abusive behavior toward inmates. In fact, during your transitional briefing into this job, your predecessor cited Dashe as one of the stalwarts on your staff, particularly praising his professionalism, maturity, good judgment, and reliability.

Inmate Deon Kussick has been incarcerated for 13 years without a single blemish on his record. Quiet, mature, and intelligent, Kussick is considered one of the "go-to" inmates when the administration needs cooperation from the prisoners to resolve a problem.

Inexplicably, Dashe and Kussick got into a fight this morning. A real knock-down drag-out, the fight is now the buzz of conversation among both the prisoner population and the correctional staff. Not surprisingly, tension is rising between the prisoners and the staff as both elements back "their" man and claim that the other man was responsible for the fight.

While it is clear that something is amiss, both Dashe and Kussick are closemouthed about the reason or reasons behind the fight. Their vague explanations are of the "it was just one of those things" variety. Obviously, though, there is a significant point of contention between the two men that, unless resolved, might lead to another confrontation. You can't resolve it, however, if you can't figure out what it is.

For you, the situation is particularly delicate, and the stakes are high. The correctional staff is waiting to see if you will back their fellow officer, the inmates are watching to see if you will be impartial in your handling of the incident, and the warden is evaluating your ability to handle a crisis. What you do will establish your reputation for loyalty (among the staff) and fairness (among the inmates) and serve as an indicator (to the warden) of your reliability and judgment.

One of the old-timers among the inmates sidled up a few minutes ago and, with a casualness that belied his intense interest, asked this simple question: "Watcha gonna do, chief?"

1. What are you going to do?
2. Why?

For additional information, please see: www.mhhe.com/schmalleger7e
Follow the author's tweets about the latest crime and justice news @schmalleger

[3]

SENTENCING
To Punish or to Reform?

CHAPTER OBJECTIVES

After completing this chapter you should be able to do the following:

① Describe sentencing philosophy and identify the central purpose of criminal punishment.

② Name the seven goals of criminal sentencing.

③ List and explain the sentencing options in general use today.

④ Explain what a model of criminal sentencing is and identify models in use today.

⑤ Describe three-strikes laws and their impact on the correctional system.

⑥ Identify and explain some major issues related to fair sentencing.

> *We will not punish a man because he hath offended, but that he may offend no more; nor does punishment ever look to the past, but to the future; for it is not the result of a passion, but that the same thing be guarded against in time to come.*
>
> —Seneca, the younger, Roman Philosopher, 3 B.C.–A.D. 65

In 2013, the Washington, D.C.-based Sentencing Project released its annual survey of developments in sentencing policy and practice. Entitled *The State of Sentencing 2012,* the report noted that several states have been reducing services in many areas as they face potential cuts in federal funding and in state tax revenues.[1] "In recent years," the report noted, "reducing prison populations with the goal of controlling correctional costs has been a salient reason" for sentencing reform. State lawmakers in 24 states, said the report, had adopted more than 40 policies designed to "downscale prison populations" and eliminate "barriers to reentry while promoting effective approaches to public safety."

Sentencing is a court's imposition of a penalty on a convicted offender. A **sentence** is the penalty imposed.

This chapter concerns the nature, history, purpose, and philosophy of criminal sentencing. One of the most crucial issues surrounding sentencing is whether to punish or to reform. The punish-or-reform debate has a long history and continues to concern many people today. We turn now to an examination of the history of sentencing philosophy.

sentencing
The imposition of a criminal sanction by a sentencing authority, such as a judge.

sentence
The penalty a court imposes on a person convicted of a crime.

SENTENCING: PHILOSOPHY AND GOALS

`CO3-1`

Philosophy of Criminal Sentencing

Western society has a long tradition of punishing criminal offenders. Historically, offenders were banished, exiled, killed, or tortured. Corporal, or physical, punishments became common during the Middle Ages, replacing executions as the preferred penalty. Physical punishments such as flogging and mutilation, though severe in themselves, deterred rampant use of the death penalty. Eventually, as we shall see in later chapters, imprisonment and a variety of other sentencing alternatives replaced corporal punishments as criminal sanctions.

Contemporary sentencing of offenders is still intimately associated with historical notions of punishment. Crimes are frequently seen as *deserving* of punishment. We often hear it said that the criminal must "pay a debt to society" or that "criminals deserve to be punished." John Conrad puts it another way: "The punishment of the criminal is the collective reaction of the community to the wrong that has been done."[2] Conrad goes on to say, "It is the offender's lot to be punished."

Philosophers have long debated *why* a wrongful act should be punished. Many social scientists suggest that criminal punishment maintains and defends the **social order.** By threatening potential law violators and by making the lives of violators uncomfortable, they say, punishments reduce the likelihood of future or continued criminal behavior.

Still, one might ask, instead of punishing offenders, why not offer them psychological treatment or educate them so that they are less prone

social order
The smooth functioning of social institutions, the existence of positive and productive relations among individual members of society, and the orderly functioning of society as a whole.

55

to future law violation? The answer to this question is far from clear. Although criminal sentencing today has a variety of goals, and educational and treatment programs are more common now in corrections, punishment still takes center stage in society's view. Some writers, such as Conrad, have suggested that society will always *need* to punish criminals because punishment is a natural response to those who break social taboos.[3] Others disagree, arguing that an enlightened society will choose instead to reform lawbreakers through humanitarian means.

CO3-2 The Goals of Sentencing

In 2010, New York state officials refused to let Nushawn Williams out of Erie County's Wende Correctional Facility under the state's civil confinement statute. The law, aimed primarily at predatory sex offenders, permits judges to order certain inmates held after the expiration of their sentences if releasing them would present a danger to the public. Williams was 22 years old in 1999 when he was sentenced to 4 to 12 years in prison for statutory rape and two counts of reckless endangerment. Williams, a convicted drug dealer from Chautauqua County, New York, had been accused of infecting as many as 103 teenage girls and young women with the AIDS virus in a series of drugs-for-sex encounters.[4] At trial, prosecutors were able to show that Williams had sex with the women while knowing he was HIV-positive. Williams, who kept a journal of his many "conquests," was originally charged with one count of reckless endangerment for each sexual encounter and with first-degree assault for each partner who subsequently became infected. The statutory rape conviction stemmed from his having had sex with a 13-year-old girl who later tested positive for the AIDS virus. During trial, prosecutor James Subjack told jurors, "It takes an individual with no regard for human life to do something like this."[5]

The Williams case demonstrates a crucial component of contemporary sentencing philosophy: that people must be held accountable for their actions and for the harm they cause. From this perspective, the purpose of the criminal justice system is to identify persons who have acted in intentionally harmful ways and (where a law is in place) to hold them accountable for their actions by imposing sanctions. Seen this way, our justice system is primarily an instrument of retribution.

A crowded city street. Many social scientists say that criminal punishments help maintain social order. What would a society without order be like?

Sentencing, however, also has a variety of other purposes. As shown in Exhibit 3–1, the goals of sentencing are (1) revenge, (2) retribution, (3) just deserts (or the fact of deserving punishment), (4) deterrence, (5) incapacitation, (6) rehabilitation or reformation, and (7) restoration.

revenge

Punishment as vengeance; an emotional response to real or imagined injury or insult.

Revenge One of the earliest goals of criminal sentencing was revenge. **Revenge** can be described as both an emotion and as an act in response to victimization. Victims sometimes feel as though an injury or insult

EXHIBIT 3–1	Goals of Criminal Sentencing

Goal	Rationale
Revenge	Punishment is equated with vengeance and involves an emotional response to criminal victimization.
Retribution	Punishment involves a "settling of scores" for both society and the victim.
	Victims are entitled to "get even."
Just deserts	Offenders are morally blameworthy and deserving of punishment.
	Punishment restores the moral balance disrupted by crime.
Deterrence	Punishment will prevent future wrongdoing by the offender and by others.
	Punishment must outweigh the benefits gained by wrongdoing.
Incapacitation	Some wrongdoers cannot be changed and need to be segregated from society.
	Society has the responsibility to protect law-abiding citizens from those whose behavior cannot be controlled.
Rehabilitation or Reformation	Society needs to help offenders learn how to behave appropriately.
	Without learning acceptable behavior patterns, offenders will not be able to behave appropriately.
Restoration	Crime is primarily an offense against human relationships and secondarily a violation of a law.
	All those who suffered because of a crime should be restored to their previous sense of well-being.

requires punishment in return. When they act on that feeling, they have taken revenge.

While we think of vengeance as a primitive need, it can still play an important role in contemporary societies and even in modern justice systems. The "tit-for-tat" exchange of terrorist attacks for military incursions between the Palestinians and Israelis that is taking place as this book goes to press is one example of a highly charged emotional situation in which calls for revenge seem to play an important—and sometimes guiding—role. Similarly, had the terrorists who perpetrated the 9/11 attacks been captured (instead of dying in the suicide attacks), there can be little doubt that many Americans would have sought revenge on the perpetrators through our justice system—as was done with Zacarias Moussaoui, the "twelfth highjacker," who was in jail at the time of the 9/11 attacks.

Retribution Retribution involves the payment of a debt to both the victim and society and, thus, atonement for a person's offense. Historically, retribution was couched in terms of "getting even," and it has sometimes been explained as "an eye for an eye, and a tooth for a tooth." *Retribution* literally means "paying back" the offender for what he or she has done. Retribution is predicated on the notion that victims are *entitled* to reprisal.

retribution

A sentencing goal that involves retaliation against a criminal perpetrator.

Because social order suffers when a crime occurs, society is also a victim. Hence, retribution, in a very fundamental way, expresses society's disapproval of criminal behavior and demands the payment of a debt to society. It is not always easy to determine just how much punishment is enough to ensure the debt is paid.

Just Deserts   Retribution is supported by many sentencing schemes today—although the concept is now often couched in terms of **just deserts** even though there is a difference between retribution and just deserts. The concept of just deserts de-emphasizes the emotional component of revenge by claiming that criminal acts are *deserving* of punishment, that offenders are *morally blameworthy,* and that they must be punished. In this way, just deserts restores the moral balance to a society wronged by crime.

Andrew von Hirsch, who identified the rationales underlying criminal punishment, says that when someone "infringes the rights of others . . . he deserves blame [and that is why] the sanctioning authority is entitled to choose a response that expresses moral disapproval: namely, punishment."[6] Hence, from a just deserts point of view, justice *requires* that punishments be imposed on criminal law violators.

Of all the purposes of punishment that are discussed here, only retribution and just deserts are past oriented. That is, they examine what has already occurred (the crime) in an effort to determine the appropriate sentencing response.

Deterrence   A third goal of criminal sentencing is deterrence. **Deterrence** is the discouragement or prevention of crimes similar to the one for which an offender is being sentenced. Unlike retribution and just deserts, deterrence is future oriented in that it seeks to prevent crimes from occurring. Two forms of deterrence can be identified: specific and general.

Specific deterrence is the deterrence of the individual being punished from committing additional crimes. Long ago, specific deterrence was achieved through corporal punishments that maimed offenders in ways that precluded their ability to commit similar crimes in the future. Spies had their eyes gouged out and their tongues removed, rapists were castrated, thieves had their fingers or hands cut off, and so on. Even today, in some countries that follow a strict Islamic code, the hands of habitual thieves are cut off as a form of corporal punishment.

General deterrence occurs when the punishment of an individual serves as an example to others who might be thinking of committing a crime—thereby dissuading them from their planned course of action. The **pleasure-pain principle**, which is central to modern discussions of general deterrence, holds that actions are motivated primarily by the desire to experience pleasure and avoid pain. According to this principle, the threat of loss to anyone convicted of a crime should outweigh the potential pleasure to be gained by committing the crime.

For punishment to be effective as a deterrent, it must be relatively certain, swiftly applied, and sufficiently severe. *Certainty, swiftness,* and *severity* of punishment are not always easy to achieve. The crime funnel, described in Chapter 1, demonstrates that most offenses do not end in arrest, and most arrests do not end in incarceration. Although it may not be easy for all offenders to get away with crime, the likelihood that any individual offender will be arrested, successfully prosecuted, and then punished is far smaller than deterrence advocates would like it to be. When an arrest does occur, an offender is typically released on bail, and, because of an overcrowded court system, the trial, if any, may not happen

---

just deserts

Punishment deserved. A just deserts perspective on criminal sentencing holds that criminal offenders are morally blameworthy and are therefore *deserving* of punishment.

deterrence

The discouragement or prevention of crimes through the fear of punishment.

specific deterrence

The deterrence of the individual being punished from additional crimes.

general deterrence

The use of the example of individual punishment to dissuade others from committing crimes.

pleasure-pain principle

The idea that actions are motivated primarily by a desire to experience pleasure and avoid pain.

until a year or so later. Moreover, although the severity of punishments has increased in recent years, modern punishments are rarely as severe as those of earlier centuries. Arguments over just how much punishment is enough to deter further violations of the criminal law rarely lead to any clear conclusion.

Incapacitation   Many believe that the huge increase in the number of correctional clients has helped lower the crime rate by incapacitating more criminals. Many of these criminals are behind bars, and others are on supervised regimens of probation and parole. **Incapacitation** restrains offenders from committing additional crimes by isolating them from free society. A recent report by the National Center for Policy Analysis, for example, observed that a "major reason for [the] reduction in crime is that crime has become more costly to the perpetrators. The likelihood of going to prison for committing any type of major crime has increased substantially."[7]

The report claims that "the best overall measure of the potential cost to a criminal of committing crimes is *expected punishment*." Expected punishment, says the report, "is the number of days in prison a criminal can expect to serve for committing a crime." The center calculated expected punishment by multiplying the median sentence imposed for each crime by the probabilities of being apprehended, prosecuted, convicted, and sentenced. Crime rates are declining, says the report, because expected prison stays are significantly longer today for every category of serious crime than two decades ago.

The story with which this chapter began says that the handling of correctional clients can stress state budgets. However, a number of studies have claimed to show that incapacitating offenders through incarceration is cost-effective. Such studies conclude that imprisoning certain types of offenders (especially career or habitual offenders) results in savings by eliminating the social costs of the crimes offenders would be likely to commit if they were not imprisoned. Those social costs include monetary loss, medical costs of physical injury, and time lost from work.

One of the most frequently cited studies attempting to quantify the net costs of incarceration was done by Edwin Zedlewski.[8] Zedlewski used a RAND Corporation survey of inmates in three states (Michigan, Texas, and California) to estimate the number of crimes each inmate would commit if not imprisoned. In the survey, the average respondent reported committing anywhere from 187 to 287 crimes annually just before being incarcerated. To calculate the cost associated with each crime, Zedlewski divided the total criminal justice expenditures in the United States by the total number of crimes committed in the United States. From this he concluded that the average crime "costs" $2,300. Multiplying $2,300 by the 187 crimes estimated to be committed annually by a felon, Zedlewski calculated that society saves $430,100 per year for each felon who is incarcerated. Figuring that incarceration costs society about $25,000 per prisoner per year, he concluded that prisons produce a cost-benefit return to society of 17 to 1 ($17 saved for every $1 spent)—leading him to strongly support increased incarceration.

Three years after Zedlewski's work, well-known criminologist John DiIulio performed a cost-benefit analysis using a survey of Wisconsin prisoners. The study, called "Crime and Punishment in Wisconsin," led to the conclusion that prisons saved taxpayers in Wisconsin approximately $2 for every dollar they cost.[9]

Studies such as those by Zedlewski and DiIulio are part of the growing field of correctional econometrics. **Correctional econometrics** is the

incapacitation
The use of imprisonment or other means to reduce an offender's capability to commit future offenses.

The Offender Speaks
Visit www.mhhe.com/schmalleger7e to see this feature.

correctional econometrics
The study of the cost-effectiveness of various correctional programs and related reductions in the incidence of crime.

The Staff Speaks

Visit www.mhhe.com/schmalleger7e to see this feature.

study of the cost-effectiveness of various correctional programs and related reductions in the incidence of crime. Recent studies have identified a decreasing return associated with the expanded use of incarceration. A few years ago, for example, the Washington State Institute for Public Policy conducted an econometric study of how state incarceration rates affect county crime rates in Washington. Institute researchers concluded that "a 10 percent increase (or decrease) in the incarceration rate leads to a statistically significant 3.3 percent decrease (or increase) in crime rates."[10] The study noted, however, that diminishing returns "begin to erode the crime reduction effects as incarceration rates are increased." Other research found that "the effect of prison growth on crime diminishes as the scale of imprisonment increases."[11] In fact, this second study stated that "when the incarceration rate reaches a certain point (the inflection point), a further increase in prison population actually produces an increase in crime."

rehabilitation (also *reformation*)

The changing of criminal lifestyles into law-abiding ones by "correcting" the behavior of offenders through treatment, education, and training.

reintegration

The process of making the offender a productive member of the community.

Rehabilitation or Reformation

The goal of **rehabilitation** or **reformation** is to change criminal lifestyles into law-abiding ones. Rehabilitation has been accomplished when an offender's criminal patterns of thought and behavior have been replaced by allegiance to society's values. Rehabilitation focuses on medical and psychological treatments and on social skills training, all designed to "correct" the problems that led the individual to crime.

A subgoal of rehabilitation is **reintegration** of the offender with the community. Reintegrating the offender with the community means making the offender a productive member of society—one who contributes to the general well-being of the whole.

Rehabilitation, which became the focus of American corrections beginning in the late 1800s, led to implementation of indeterminate sentencing practices (soon to be discussed), probation, parole, and a separate system of juvenile justice. During the 1970s, however, rehabilitation came under harsh criticism. As American society experienced disruptions brought about by economic change, the decline of traditional institutions, and fallout from the war in Vietnam, conservatives blamed the rehabilitative ideal for being too liberal, and liberals condemned it for providing an unfair basis for coercive action against disenfranchised social groups.[12] About

As a goal of sentencing, incapacitation restrains offenders from committing more crimes by isolating them from society. Does this threat of social isolation encourage law-abiding behavior?

the same time, an influential and widely read study by Robert Martinson, which evaluated rehabilitation programs nationwide, reported that few, if any, produced real changes in offender attitudes.[13] Dubbed the "nothing works doctrine," Martinson's critique of rehabilitation as a correctional goal led some states to abandon rehabilitation altogether or to de-emphasize it in favor of the goals of retribution and incapacitation. In other states, attempts at rehabilitation continued but were often muted.

Today, in the face of a difficult economy, many state governments and private organizations are reembracing rehabilitation, emphasizing the cost savings that can result from lowering prison populations and successfully reintegrating past offenders into society. According to Francis T. Cullen and Paul Gendreau, it is time to give the rehabilitative ideal a second chance. They call for *reaffirming rehabilitation.* "Many [rehabilitative] programs fail to work," say Cullen and Gendreau, "because they either are ill-conceived (not based on sound criminological theory) and/or have no therapeutic integrity (are not implemented as designed)." "We would not be surprised," they write, "if young children turned out to be illiterate if their teachers were untrained, had no standardized curriculum, and met the children once a week for half an hour."[14] Until recently, contend Cullen and Gendreau, many correctional treatment programs were in such a state.

Other writers hold that continued efforts at rehabilitation are mandatory for any civilized society as a moral obligation, not merely as an effort to save money. "In order to neutralize the desocializing potential of prisons," says Edgardo Rotman, "a civilized society is forced into rehabilitative undertakings. These become an essential ingredient of its correctional system taken as a whole. A correctional system" with no "interest in treatment," says Rotman, "means . . . de-humanization and regression."[15]

Rehabilitation typically implies the notion of treatment in the belief that offenders who receive appropriate counseling, psychological treatment, psychiatric intervention, or drug therapy will be less prone to repeat criminality. California's Proposition 36, officially known as the Substance Abuse Crime Prevention Act of 2000 (SACPA), is indicative of the return to rehabilitation now occurring. Passed by the state's voters in 2000, it became effective on July 1 of that year. The law's purpose, stated in Section 3(c), is to "enhance public safety by reducing drug-related crime and preserving jails and prison cells for serious and violent offenders, and to improve public health by reducing drug abuse and drug dependence through proven and effective drug treatment strategies." It seeks to accomplish that goal by mandating probation for any person convicted of a nonviolent drug possession offense, and it requires participation in, and completion of, proven and effective community-based treatment programs as a condition of probation.

According to a recent study of the social and financial consequences of Proposition 36 by researchers at UCLA, the initiative had cost California more than $600 million in its first two years.[16] Nonetheless, a net savings resulted from diverting thousands of nonviolent drug offenders from prisons, saving the state $2.50 for every $1 spent on diversion. Researchers found a significant problem, however, in the fact that drug-related rearrest rates for offenders diverted from prison to treatment under the initiative was 48 percent higher than for those who remained in the criminal justice system.[17] According to the researchers, Proposition 36 placed unmanageable burdens on residential drug treatment programs, resulting in relatively ineffective outpatient treatment for many clients who, prior to passage of the Proposition, would have been enrolled in inpatient programs instead.

Erich Parsons
Deputy Sheriff • Palm Beach County, Florida

Erich Parsons is deputy sheriff with the Palm Beach County Sheriff's Department in West Palm Beach, Florida. A 44-year-old Army veteran and grandfather of five, he attended Johnson Bible College in Knoxville, Tennessee, where he received a bachelor of arts degree, and has been an ordained minister since 1986. He has been with the department since 2000, working the midnight to 8 A.M. shift.

Deputy Parsons had no educational background in law enforcement. While working in his family's business in the late 1990s (as a glazier in the family glass factory), he tore his rotator cuff, and he says that during his stay in the hospital he became interested in the job.

"Part of my desire to move on to something of this caliber was the need for significance. I felt that even though I was comfortable where I was and who I was, I like challenges. I'm a kid from the streets—grew up fast. So my penchant was to reach youth, and the training I took in theology was youth ministry–specific. I felt that my greater outreach perhaps would be those individuals in the county level as opposed to the state level, that the street kids needed more than just the church setting."

On a typical day, Deputy Parsons will handle unresolved issues from the previous shift; handle new arrests, fingerprints, and photographs; "and try to maintain order as we're doing all that," he says.

"I love my job," he says. "My satisfaction is to know that I've done my job the best I was able to do, with what was available to me."

"Even though I see the charges as they come in on the rough arrests, I try not to judge them. I know sometimes they're in bad situations. I try to maintain the dignity of an individual. Usually they reciprocate, and say, 'Thank you for treating me human.'"

---

restoration

The process of returning to their previous condition all those involved in or affected by crime—including victims, offenders, and society.

restorative justice

A systematic response to wrongdoing that emphasizes healing the wounds of victims, offenders, and communities caused or revealed by crime.

victim-impact statement

A description of the harm and suffering that a crime has caused victims and survivors.

Restoration Over the past few decades, a new goal of criminal sentencing, known as **restoration,** has developed. **Restorative justice** is based on the belief that criminal sentencing should involve restoration and justice for all involved in or affected by crime.

Advocates of restorative justice (or, as some agencies refer to it, *community justice* or *reparative justice*) believe that crime is committed not just against the state but also against victims and the community. Restorative justice is especially concerned with repairing the harm to the victim and the community. Harm is repaired through negotiation, mediation, and empowerment rather than through retribution, deterrence, and punishment. A restorative justice perspective allows judges and juries to consider **victim-impact statements** in their sentencing decisions. These are descriptions of the harm and suffering that a crime has caused victims and their survivors. Also among the efforts being introduced on behalf of victims and their survivors are victim assistance and victim compensation programs.

Advocates of restorative justice believe not only that the victim should be restored by the justice process but also that the offender and society should participate in the restoration process. To this end, efforts at restoration emphasize the successful reintegration of offenders into the community as well as victims' rights and needs. Another aspect of involving offenders in restoration is having them actively address the harm they have caused. The system strives to accomplish this by holding them directly accountable and by helping them become productive, law-abiding members of their community.[18] Restorative justice programs try to personalize crime by showing offenders the consequences of their behavior.

Restorative justice is based on the premise that because crime occurs in the context of the community, the community should be involved in addressing it. Particular restorative justice or community justice programs might use any of the following: (1) victim–offender mediation, (2) victim–offender reconciliation, (3) victim-impact panels, (4) restorative justice panels, (5) community reparative boards, (6) community-based courts, (7) family group conferences, (8) circle sentencing, (9) court diversion programs, and (10) peer mediation.

Restorative justice seeks to restore the health of the community, repair the harm done, meet victims' needs, and require the offender to contribute to those repairs. Thus, the criminal act is condemned, offenders are held accountable, offenders and victims are involved as participants, and repentant offenders are encouraged to earn their way back into the good graces of society. Restorative justice principles, developed by the Restorative Justice Consortium, are shown in Exhibit 3–2.

Not only is restorative justice having an impact on U.S. sentencing practices (Exhibit 3–3), but also it is becoming influential internationally. A United Nations report on the international acceptance of restorative justice principles in 35 member countries, for example, found that the concept has received considerable international attention by both practitioners and policymakers who view it as an alternative approach to more common criminal justice practices. According to the report, restorative justice is seen as offering promising concepts and options if taken as a supplement to established criminal justice practices. In general, says the report, restorative justice principles are seen as a complement to established justice systems and practices but not as a replacement for existing systems.[19]

SENTENCING OPTIONS AND TYPES OF SENTENCES

CO3-3

Options

Legislatures establish the types of sentences that can be imposed. The U.S. Congress and the 50 state legislatures decide what is against the law and define crimes and their punishments in the jurisdictions in which they have control. Sentencing options in wide use today include the following:

- fines and other monetary sanctions;
- probation;
- alternative or intermediate sanctions such as day fines, community service, electronic monitoring, and day reporting centers;
- incarceration; and
- death penalty.

As punishment for unlawful behavior, fines have a long history. By the 5th century B.C., Greece, for example, had developed an extensive system of fines for a wide variety of offenses.[20] Under our modern system of justice, fines are usually imposed as punishment for misdemeanors and infractions. When imposed on felony offenders, fines are frequently combined with another punishment, such as probation or incarceration.

Fines are only one type of monetary sanction used today. Others include the court-ordered payment of the costs of trial, victim restitution, various fees, forfeitures, donations, and confiscations. **Restitution** consists of payments made by a criminal offender to his or her victim as compensation for

restitution

Payments made by a criminal offender to his or her victim (or to the court, which then turns them over to the victim) as compensation for the harm caused by the offense.

EXHIBIT 3–2   Restorative Justice Principles

The following principles were developed by the Restorative Justice Consortium in order to provide a working basis for particular settings involved in the practice of restorative justice, including adult criminal justice, youthful offenders, schools, the workplace, prisons, and communities.

1. Principles relating to the interests of all participants
   a. Voluntary participation based on informed choice
   b. Avoidance of discrimination, irrespective of the nature of the case
   c. Access to relevant agencies for help and advice
   d. Ongoing access to various established methods of dispute resolution
   e. Processes that do not compromise the rights under the law of the participants
   f. Commitment not to use information in a way that may prejudice the interests of any participant in subsequent proceedings
   g. Protection of personal safety
   h. Protection of and support for vulnerable participants
   i. Respect for civil rights and the dignity of persons

2. Principles relating to those who have sustained harm or loss
   a. Respect for their personal experiences, needs, and feelings
   b. Acknowledgment of their harm or loss
   c. Recognition of their claim for amends
   d. Opportunity to communicate with the person who caused the harm or loss, if that person is willing
   e. Entitlement of victim to be the primary beneficiary of reparation

3. Principles relating to those who caused the harm or loss to others
   a. The opportunity to offer reparation, including before any formal requirement
   b. Reparation appropriate to the harm done and within the person's capacity to fulfill it
   c. Respect for the dignity of the person making amends

4. Principles relating to the interests of local community and society
   a. The promotion of community safety and social harmony by learning from restorative processes and the taking of measures that are conducive to the reduction of crime or harm
   b. The promotion of social harmony through respect for cultural diversity and civil rights, social responsibility, and the rule of law
   c. Opportunity for all to learn mediation and other methods of nonviolent resolution of conflict

5. Principles relating to agencies working alongside the judicial system
   a. Settlement outside the judicial system, except when this is unworkable due to the level of harm done, the risk of further harm, issues of public policy, or disagreement about the critical facts
   b. Avoidance of unfair discrimination by ensuring that rights under the law are not compromised
   c. Provision of a wide and flexible range of opportunities to enable those who have caused loss or harm to make amends

6. Principles relating to the judicial system
   a. A primary goal of repairing harm
   b. Restorative requirements that are fair, appropriate, and workable
   c. Opportunities for community reparation or reparation to others who have suffered harm or loss when a restorative requirement is appropriate but victims decline to participate
   d. Enforcement of community reparation when a restorative requirement is appropriate but those who have caused harm or loss decline to participate
   e. Valuing of voluntary offers to repair harm or loss by those who have caused it
   f. Privileged status of content of restorative meetings, subject to public interest qualifications

7. Principles relating to restorative justice agencies
   a. Commitment to needs-based practice
   b. Safeguarding of legal human rights
   c. The participation of restorative justice practitioners who are seen to be neutral
   d. The participation of restorative justice practitioners who act impartially
   e. Maintenance of neutrality and impartiality by restorative justice practitioners who play no other role in the case
   f. Commitment of restorative justice agencies to keep confidential the content of restorative meetings, subject to the requirements of the law
   g. Participant commitment to confidentiality about the contents of restorative meetings
   h. Facilitation of the engagement of weaker parties in negotiation
   i. Upholding of respectful behavior in restorative processes
   j. Upholding of equality of respect for all participants in restorative processes, separating this from the harm done
   k. Engagement with good practice guidelines within the restorative justice movement
   l. Commitment by the agency to the use of constructive conflict resolution in general and of internal grievance and disciplinary procedures in specific
   m. Commitment to the accreditation of training, services, and practitioners
   n. Commitment to continually improved practice

EXHIBIT 3–3   **American Correctional Association**

Public Correctional Policy on Sentencing

The American Correctional Association actively promotes the development of sentencing policies that should:

- be based on the principle of proportionality. The sentence imposed should be commensurate with the seriousness of the crime and the harm done;
- be impartial with regard to race, ethnicity, and economic status as to the discretion exercised in sentencing;
- include a broad range of options for custody, supervision, and rehabilitation of offenders;
- be purpose-driven. Policies must be based on clearly articulated purposes. They should be grounded in knowledge of the relative effectiveness of the various sanctions imposed in attempts to achieve these purposes;
- encourage the evaluation of sentencing policy on an ongoing basis. The various sanctions should be monitored to determine their relative effectiveness based on the purpose(s) they are intended to have. Likewise, monitoring should take place to ensure that the sanctions are not applied based on race, ethnicity, or economic status;
- recognize that the criminal sentence must be based on multiple criteria, including the harm done to the victim, past criminal history, the need to protect the public, and the

opportunity to provide programs for offenders as a means of reducing the risk for future crime;

- provide the framework to guide and control discretion according to established criteria and within appropriate limits and allow for recognition of individual needs;
- have as a major purpose restorative justice—righting the harm done to the victim and the community. The restorative focus should be both process and substantively oriented. The victim or his or her representative should be included in the "justice" process. The sentencing procedure should address the needs of the victim, including his or her need to be heard and, as much as possible, to be and feel restored to whole again;
- promote the use of community-based programs whenever consistent with public safety; and
- be linked to the resources needed to implement the policy. The consequential cost of various sanctions should be assessed. Sentencing policy should not be enacted without the benefit of a fiscal-impact analysis. Resource allocations should be linked to sentencing policy so as to ensure adequate funding of all sanctions, including total confinement and the broad range of intermediate sanction and community-based programs needed to implement those policies.

Source: Copyright © American Correctional Association. Reprinted with permission.

the harm caused by the offense. While fines are usually paid to the government, restitution may be paid directly to the victim (or paid to the court, which turns it over to the victim). Some innovative courts have ordered offenders to donate specified amounts to specified charities in lieu of a fine.[21] Restitution is an example of a restorative justice sentencing option.

With a sentence of probation, the convicted offender continues to live in the community but must comply with court-imposed restrictions on his or her activity and freedom of movement. Alternative sanctions or intermediate sentencing options (which are discussed in detail in Chapters 4 and 5) usually combine probation with some other punishment, such as community service or house arrest with electronic monitoring. A sentence of incarceration, or total confinement away from the community, is used when the community needs to be protected from further criminal activity by an offender. The death penalty, or capital punishment, is the ultimate sentence. Exhibit 3–4 displays recent trends in four correctional options. Overlaid on the figure in the exhibit is a line showing the rate of change in correctional populations over the past few decades. As the chart shows, correctional populations had been increasing until around 2010, when they finally started to decline.

Types of Sentences

A sentence is generally imposed by a judge. Sentencing responsibility can also be exercised by a jury or a group of judges, or it may be mandated by statute. **Mandatory sentences** are those that are required by law under certain circumstances—such as conviction of a specified crime or of a series of offenses of a specified type. Mandatory sentences may add prison time to sentences for offenders who carried weapons during the commission of

mandatory sentences

Those that are required by law under certain circumstances—such as conviction of a specified crime or of a series of offenses of a specified type.

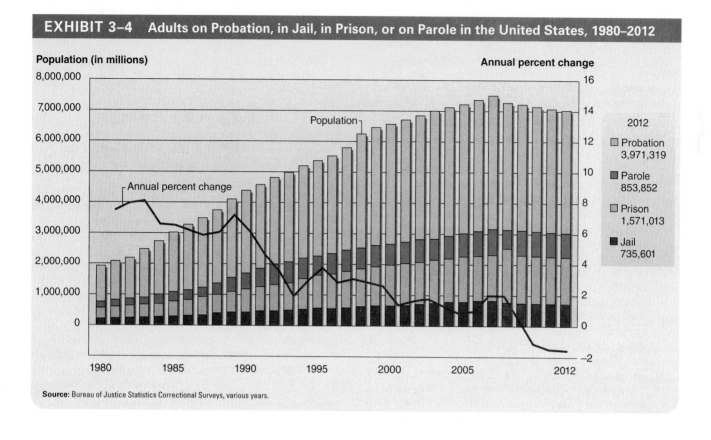

EXHIBIT 3–4   Adults on Probation, in Jail, in Prison, or on Parole in the United States, 1980–2012

2012
- Probation 3,971,319
- Parole 853,852
- Prison 1,571,013
- Jail 735,601

Source: Bureau of Justice Statistics Correctional Surveys, various years.

their crimes, who used or possessed illegal drugs, or who perpetrated crimes against elderly victims. Such sentences allow judges no leeway in sentencing.

Even when there is no mandatory sentence, judges cannot impose just any sentence. They are still limited by statutory provisions. They also are guided by prevailing sentencing goals. A judge usually considers a **presentence report (PSR)**. This report, prepared by the probation department attached to a court, is a social and personal history as well as an evaluation of the offender. Finally, judges' sentencing decisions are influenced by their own personal convictions and characteristics.

Once the sentence is chosen, the judge must decide how it will be served, especially if more than one sentence is being imposed. Sentences can be consecutive or concurrent. **Consecutive sentences** are served one after the other. When a person is convicted of multiple offenses, a judge might impose, for example, a sentence of 10 years for one offense and 20 years for another. If the sentences are to run consecutively, the offender will begin serving the second sentence only after the first one expires. **Concurrent sentences** are served together. If the sentences in the example are to run concurrently, the 10-year sentence will expire when the offender has served one-half of the 20-year sentence. The offender will then need to serve the remainder of the 20-year sentence before being released. When multiple sentences are imposed, most are ordered to be served concurrently.

SENTENCING MODELS

A **model of criminal sentencing** is a strategy or system for imposing criminal sanctions. Sentencing models vary widely (see Exhibit 3–5). Over the past 100 years, a shift has occurred from what might be called a *judicial*

---

presentence report (PSR)

A report prepared by the probation department of a court that provides a social and personal history as well as an evaluation of a defendant as an aid to the court in determining a sentence.

consecutive sentences

Sentences served one after the other.

concurrent sentences

Sentences served together.

model of criminal sentencing

A strategy or system for imposing criminal sanctions.

EXHIBIT 3–5   Sentencing Models

Determinate Sentencing

Sentencing to a fixed term of incarceration may be reduced by good time. Usually, explicit standards specify the amount of punishment and a set release date with no review by a parole board or other administrative agency. Postincarceration supervision may be part of the sentence.

Indeterminate Sentencing

Sentencing in which an administrative agency, generally a parole board, has the authority to release an incarcerated offender and to determine whether an offender's parole will be revoked for violation of the conditions of release. In one form of indeterminate sentencing, the judge specifies only the maximum sentence length (a fixed term); the associated minimum is automatically implied but is not within the judge's discretion. In the more traditional form of indeterminate sentencing, the judge specifies maximum and minimum durations within limits set by statute. The judge has discretion over the minimum and maximum sentences.

Presumptive Guidelines Sentencing

Sentencing meets all the following conditions: (1) the appropriate sentence for an offender in a specific case is presumed to fall within a range authorized by guidelines adopted by a legislatively created sentencing body, usually a sentencing commission; (2) judges are expected to sentence within the range or provide written justification for departure; and (3) the guidelines provide for review of the departure, usually by appeal to a higher court. Presumptive guidelines may employ determinate or indeterminate sentencing structures.

Voluntary/Advisory Guidelines Sentencing

Recommended sentencing policies are not required by law. They serve as a guide and are based on past sentencing practices. The legislature has not mandated their use. Voluntary/advisory guidelines may use determinate or indeterminate sentencing structures.

Mandatory Minimum Sentencing

A minimum sentence is specified by statute for all offenders convicted of a particular crime or a particular crime with special circumstances (e.g., robbery with a firearm or selling drugs to a minor within 1,000 feet of a school). Mandatory minimums can be used in both determinate and indeterminate sentencing structures. Within an indeterminate sentencing structure, the mandatory minimum requires the inmate to serve a fixed amount of time in prison before being eligible for release with the approval of a parole board. Under a determinate sentence, the offender is required to serve a fixed amount of time in prison before being eligible for release.

Visit http://www.npr.org/2013/02/14/171822608/the-drug-laws-that-changed-how-we-punish or scan this code with the QR app on your smartphone or digital device to read or listen to a National Public Radio discussion of how New York's 1970s-era Rockefeller drug laws changed the face of sentencing in America.

model of sentencing to an *administrative model.* Judges generally have far less discretion in sentencing decisions today than they previously had. The majority of sentences imposed in American courts today follow legislative and administrative guidelines.

Sentencing in 19th-century America involved mostly fines, probation, and "flat" prison sentences. **Flat sentences** specify a given amount of time to be served in custody and allow little or no variation from the time specified. A typical flat sentence might be stated as "five years in prison." Flat sentences generally mean that an offender has to complete the sentence imposed and cannot earn an early release.

flat sentences

Those that specify a given amount of time to be served in custody and allow little or no variation from the time specified.

CO3-4 ## Indeterminate Sentencing

By the close of the 19th century, sentencing reform in the United States began replacing the flat sentence with indeterminate sentences.[22] At the time, the criminal justice system was coping with a rapidly expanding and increasingly diverse prison population, increased efficiency of police and courts, and other factors. Overcrowded prisons and the warehousing of inmates resulted.[23]

indeterminate sentence

A sentence in which a judge specifies a maximum length and a minimum length, and an administrative agency, generally a parole board, determines the actual time of release.

In an **indeterminate sentence,** the judge specifies a maximum length and a minimum length within limits set by statute, and a parole board determines the actual time of release. The parole board's determination depends on its judgment of whether the prisoner has been reformed, has been cured, or has simply served enough time. An example of an indeterminate sentence is "5 to 10 years in prison." A second form of indeterminate sentencing requires the judge to specify only the maximum sentence length with the associated minimum set by statute. Some states, for example, require an offender to serve as little as one-quarter of the sentence before becoming eligible for parole.

With an indeterminate sentence, discretion is distributed, not only among the prosecutor, defense counsel, and judge, but also to prison officials and the parole board, who have considerable influence over an offender's length of stay. Prison officials have discretion over the amount of **good time** an inmate earns, which can affect parole eligibility, the discharge date, or both. The parole board decides the actual release date for most inmates. The result is a system of sentencing in which few people understand or can predict who will be imprisoned and for how long.

good time

The number of days or months prison authorities deduct from a sentence for good behavior and for other reasons.

Under indeterminate sentencing, punishments are made to fit the criminal rather than the crime. Proponents of indeterminate sentences assume that crime is a product of individual deviation from the norm and that rehabilitation can be achieved within a prison system designed to punish, not treat, inmates. They also assume that prison personnel have the knowledge to impose treatment or to predict recidivism accurately enough to justify their discretion regarding when an inmate should be released. The use of indeterminate sentences has prompted numerous accusations of disparity in sentencing as well as protests from inmate groups, penologists, and other critics of the penal system. These protests have spurred a movement for sentencing reform.

Determinate Sentencing

determinate sentence (also *fixed sentence*)

A sentence of a fixed term of incarceration, which can be reduced by good time.

A **determinate sentence** (also known as a *fixed sentence*) specifies a fixed period of incarceration, which can be reduced for good time served. The term is generally used to refer to the sentencing reforms of the late 1970s. Determinate sentences are generally based on the incapacitation and deterrence goals of sentencing. The theory behind determinate sentencing is that criminals will be off the streets for longer periods of time. The other advantage, supporters say, is that prisoners know when they will be released. In most determinate sentencing models, parole is limited or is replaced by the use of good-time credits. With good time, inmates are able to reduce their sentences by earning credits. The amount of the reduction depends on the number of credits earned. Good-time credits can be earned by demonstrating good behavior and not being "written up" for violating prison rules. They can also be earned by participating in educational programs, community service projects, or medical experiments. The procedure for earning credits and the number that can be earned vary from state to state. Prison administrators generally favor determinate sentencing and good-time credits because they aid in controlling prison populations.

Guideline Sentencing

As we have seen, the sentences that judges impose are regulated by law. As part of the movement to eliminate sentencing disparities, some states, as well as the federal government, have enacted sentencing guidelines for judges to follow. The guidelines fall into two categories.

Voluntary/Advisory Sentencing Guidelines

Among the earliest guided sentencing innovations in the United States was the experiment with voluntary guidelines, also called *advisory guidelines*. These are recommended sentencing policies that are not required by law. Usually, they are based on past sentencing practices and serve as a guide to judges. Voluntary or advisory guidelines have had disappointing results because they are often not enforced and are sometimes ignored. More importantly, the guidelines are voluntary; judges can simply ignore them. A review of all the major studies conducted on voluntary and advisory guidelines reveals low compliance by judges and, hence, little reduction in disparity.[24]

Presumptive Sentencing Guidelines

By the early 1980s, states had begun to experiment with the use of presumptive sentencing guidelines. These models differ from determinate sentences and voluntary or advisory guidelines in three respects. First, the guidelines are developed, not by the legislature, but by a **sentencing commission** that often represents diverse interests, including private citizens as well as all segments of the criminal justice system. Second, the guidelines are explicit and highly structured, relying on a quantitative scoring instrument. Third, the guidelines are not voluntary or advisory. Judges must adhere to the sentencing system or provide a written rationale for departure.

sentencing commission
A group assigned to create a schedule of sentences that reflect the gravity of the offenses committed and the prior record of the criminal offender.

The forces stimulating presumptive sentencing guidelines were the same as those that had driven the moves to determinate sentencing and voluntary or advisory guidelines: issues of fairness and prison crowding. These concerns provided the impetus for states to adopt guidelines, replace indeterminate sentencing with determinate sentencing, and abolish or reduce discretionary parole release. The first four states to adopt presumptive sentencing guidelines were Minnesota (1980), Washington (1981), Pennsylvania (1982), and Florida (1983).

The state of Washington's Sentencing Reform Act (SRA) of 1981 (as amended), for example, is based on a determinate sentencing model. The law mandated creation of a Sentencing Guidelines Commission, which developed a set of sentencing guidelines "to ensure that offenders who commit similar crimes and have similar criminal histories receive equivalent sentences."[25] The state's presumptive sentencing schedules, which apply to all felonies committed in the state after June 30, 1984, are structured "so that offenses involving greater harm to a victim and to society result in greater punishment." According to the Sentencing Guidelines Commission, "The guidelines apply equally to offenders in all parts of the state, without discrimination as to any element that does not relate to the crime or to a defendant's previous criminal record."

As is typically the case in presumptive sentencing states, Washington's guidelines specify a standard sentence range based on the seriousness of an offense combined with an offender's criminal history "score." In Washington State, a defendant's criminal history includes his or her prior adult felony convictions in any state or federal court or in another country and dispositions in juvenile court. Misdemeanors are not counted except when related to current convictions of felony traffic offenses (e.g., driving under the influence of alcohol or drugs may figure into a defendant's criminal history when felony convictions for crimes such as vehicular assault occur). Judges use forms provided by the state's sentencing commission in calculating an offender's score for sentencing purposes. Crimes representative of each "seriousness level" are shown in Exhibit 3–6.

As in other presumptive sentencing states, in Washington judges may sentence offenders outside the standard ranges found in the state's sentencing grid. Sentences that fall outside established guidelines, however, are not permitted if based solely on determinations of fact made by the sentencing judge—a limitation imposed by the U.S. Supreme Court in the 2004 case of *Blakely* v. *Washington*. In 2005, Washington's sentencing law was changed to require that aggravating circumstances that might lead to sentencing enhancements be proved to a jury.

Federal Sentencing Guidelines In the early 1980s, the U.S. Congress focused its attention on disparity in sentencing.[26] Congress concluded that the sentencing discretion of federal trial judges needed boundaries. The resulting legislation, termed the Sentencing Reform Act (SRA) of 1984,[27] created the United States Sentencing Commission. The nine-member commission, first organized in October 1985, is a permanent body charged with formulating and amending national sentencing guidelines. The commission's guidelines apply to all federal criminal offenses committed on or after November 1, 1987.

Federal sentencing guidelines take into account a defendant's criminal history, the nature of the criminal conduct, and the particular circumstances surrounding the offense. Congress required that all federal trial judges follow the guidelines in their sentencing decisions. Deviations from the guidelines were permitted only when a judge provided a written justification setting forth specific reasons as to why a sentence outside of the range specified by the guidelines was appropriate.

Federal sentencing guidelines have been subject to change, and the commission may submit guideline amendments to Congress each year between the beginning of the regular congressional session and May 1. Suggested amendments automatically take effect 180 days after submission unless Congress rejects them.

Early challenges to the constitutionality of federal sentencing guidelines were resolved by the 1989 case of *Mistretta* v. *United States*, in which the U.S. Supreme Court upheld the 1984 SRA and ruled that Congress had acted properly in delegating authority to the U.S. Sentencing Commission in the creation of sentencing guidelines.

In addition to creating the U.S. Sentencing Commission, the SRA abolished parole for federal offenders sentenced under the guidelines. As a consequence, sentences imposed on convicted federal offenders today are essentially the sentences that will be served. Under federal law, however, inmates may earn up to 54 days of credit (time off their sentences) each year for good behavior.

sentencing enhancements

Legislatively approved provisions that mandate longer prison terms for specific criminal offenses committed under certain circumstances (such as a murder committed because of the victim's race or a drug sale near a school) or because of an offender's past criminal record.

The Legal Environment and Sentencing Guidelines

A number of U.S. Supreme Court cases focused on the authority that judges retain in deciding to depart from sentencing guidelines and on the application of **sentencing enhancements**. In 1994, in the case of *Nichols* v. *United States*, the Court held that "an uncounseled misdemeanor conviction," because no prison term was imposed, is valid when used to enhance punishment at a subsequent conviction. (An "uncounseled conviction" is one in which the defendant was not represented by an attorney.)

EXHIBIT 3–6 State of Washington: Representative Crimes by Level of Seriousness

Level of Seriousness	Representative Offense	Level of Seriousness	Representative Offense
XVI	Aggravated Murder in the First Degree[a]	V	Third Degree Child Molestation First Degree Custodial Sexual Misconduct Domestic Violence Court Order Violation First Degree Extortion Persistent Prison Misbehavior Possession of a Stolen Firearm Stalking
XV	First Degree Murder Homicide by Abuse First Degree Malicious Explosion		
XIV	Second Degree Murder		
XIII	Second Degree Malicious Explosion First Degree Malicious Placement of an Explosive	IV	Second Degree Arson Second Degree Assault Bribing a Witness Counterfeiting Knowingly Trafficking in Stolen Property Threats to Bomb
XII	First Degree Assault First Degree Rape		
XI	First Degree Manslaughter Second Degree Rape		
X	First Degree Child Molestation Indecent Liberties (with Forcible Compulsion) First Degree Kidnapping Leading Organized Crime	III	Third Degree Assault Second Degree Burglary Communication with a Minor for Immoral Purposes Criminal Gang Intimidation Harassment Intimidating a Public Servant Maintaining a Dwelling or Place for Controlled Substances Manufacture, Deliver, or Possess with Intent to Deliver Marijuana Patronizing a Juvenile Prostitute Possession of Incendiary Device Possession of Machine Gun or Short Barreled Shotgun or Rifle Tampering with a Witness
IX	Controlled Substance Homicide Inciting Criminal Profiteering First Degree Robbery/Sexual Exploitation Vehicular Homicide, by Being Under the Influence of Intoxicating Liquor or Any Drug		
VIII	First Degree Arson Deliver or Possess with Intent to Deliver Methamphetamine Hit and Run—Death Second Degree Manslaughter First Degree Promoting Prostitution Vehicular Homicide, by the Operation of Any Vehicle in a Reckless Manner	II	First Degree Computer Trespass Create, Deliver, or Possess a Counterfeit Controlled Substance Health Care False Claims Theft of Rental, Leased, or Lease-Purchased Property (Valued at $1,500 or More) Unlicensed Practice of a Profession or Business
VII	First Degree Burglary Drive-by Shooting Indecent Liberties (without Forcible Compulsion) Involving a Minor in Drug Dealing Use of a Machine Gun in Commission of a Felony	I	Attempting to Elude a Pursuing Police Vehicle False Verification for Welfare Forged Prescription Taking a Motor Vehicle Without Permission Unlawful Use of Food Stamps
VI	First Degree Incest Intimidating a Judge Intimidating a Juror/Witness Theft of a Firearm		

[a] Aggravated murder in the first degree is first-degree murder under certain circumstances. Among them are (a) the victim was a law enforcement officer or firefighter performing his or her official duties; (b) the defendant was serving a term of imprisonment in a state institution at the time of the homicide; (c) the defendant solicited another person to commit the crime for pay, and so on. To learn the statutory elements of each of the offenses listed here, view Title 9 of the Revised Code of Washington (the state's criminal law) online at www.mrsc.org/rcw.htm. Visit the state of Washington Sentencing Guidelines Commission at www.sgc.wa.gov, where you can read the state's online adult sentencing guidelines manual. The manual contains a comprehensive list of all felonies defined by state law along with their location in the sentencing grid.

In the 2002 case of *United States* v. *Cotton,* the Court found that sentences imposed by a federal judge were not improper even though the judge based those sentences on a quantity of drugs that he had estimated and that had not been alleged in the original indictment brought against the defendants. The *Cotton* defendants had been charged with conspiracy to distribute and to possess with intent to distribute a "detectable amount" of cocaine and cocaine base in the city of Baltimore. Under federal law, the penalty for such offenses is "not more than 20 years."[28] After the jury returned a finding of guilty, the judge made an independent finding of drug quantity (more than 500 grams of cocaine base) and then imposed enhanced penalties (up to life) as allowed under federal law. The judge's finding, the Court concluded, was based on "overwhelming and uncontroverted evidence" that the defendants "were involved in a vast drug conspiracy."

In the far-reaching case of *Apprendi* v. *New Jersey* (2000), however, the Supreme Court limited the fact-finding authority of state judges in sentencing decisions. The case involved Charles Apprendi, a New Jersey defendant who had pleaded guilty to unlawfully possessing a firearm—an offense that carried a prison term of 5 to 10 years under state law. Prior to imposing sentence, however, the judge found that Apprendi had fired a number of shots into the home of an African-American family living in his neighborhood. The judge further determined that Apprendi had done so to frighten the family and to convince them to move. Statements made by Apprendi, said the judge, classified the shooting as a hate crime. The judge then applied a sentencing enhancement provision under New Jersey's hate crimes statute and sentenced Apprendi to 12 years in prison—2 years beyond the 10-year maximum authorized by statute for the weapons offense to which he had confessed. Significantly, the sentence was imposed without the benefit of a jury-based fact-finding process and with the judge alone making the determination that a hate crime had taken place. In overturning the state court's finding, the Supreme Court reasoned that Apprendi's due process guarantees were violated when the judge—not a jury—made a factual determination that did not require proof beyond a reasonable doubt. In the words of the Court, "Under the Due Process Clause of the Fifth Amendment and the notice and jury trial guarantees of the Sixth Amendment, any fact (other than prior conviction) that increases the maximum penalty for a crime must be charged in an indictment, submitted to a jury, and proven beyond a reasonable doubt."

In 2002, however, in the case of *Harris* v. *U.S.,* the Court concluded that "a fact increasing the mandatory *minimum* [but not extending the sentence beyond the statutory maximum], need not be alleged in the indictment, submitted to the jury, or proved beyond a reasonable doubt."

Under *Harris,* a judge was permitted to find aggravating factors by a preponderance of evidence and to decide whether they should be used to increase a sentence beyond the minimum specified by law. As long as the judge did not exceed the maximum sentence specified, he or she did not need to treat those factors as elements of the crime that must be proved to a jury. In 2013, however, the *Harris* decision was overruled in *Alleyne* v. *U.S.,* in which the Justices reaffirmed the need to prove to a jury any "element" that increases the penalty for a crime.

Blakely v. *Washington* (2004) built on the Court's holding in *Apprendi.* In *Blakely,* the Court ruled that no criminal sentence in *state* courts can

Ralph Howard Blakely in Grant County (Washington) Superior Court on March 22, 2005. Blakely, made famous for his role in the 2004 U.S. Supreme Court case of Blakely v. Washington, *was sentenced to 35 years in prison for plotting to have his ex-wife and daughter murdered. What did the Court rule in* Blakely v. Washington,?

be enhanced beyond the allowable maximum guideline for an offense unless the facts used to determine the enhanced sentence are found by a jury or the defendant waives the right to a jury or admits the facts in a guilty plea.

In 2007, in the case of *Cunningham* v. *California,* the U.S. Supreme Court found that California's determinate sentencing law (DSL) violated a defendant's right to trial by jury because it placed sentence-elevating fact finding within the province of judges. In that case, a judge following the requirements of the DSL had sentenced John Cunningham to a term of 16 years in prison based on a posttrial sentencing hearing in which he identified six aggravating factors and only one mitigating factor. Cunningham had earlier been found guilty of the continuous sexual abuse of a child younger than 14.

In 2005, in the combined cases of *United States* v. *Booker* and *United States* v. *Fanfan,* the U.S. Supreme Court turned its attention to the constitutionality of *federal* sentencing practices that used what it called "extra-verdict determinations of fact" in the application of sentencing enhancements. The combined cases raised two issues: (1) whether fact finding done by judges under federal sentencing guidelines violates the Sixth Amendment right to trial by jury and (2) if so, whether the guidelines are themselves unconstitutional. Consistent with its findings in *Blakely,* the Court found that, on the first question, defendant Freddie Booker's drug trafficking sentence had been improperly enhanced under federal sentencing guidelines on the basis of facts found solely by a judge. Under a mandatory guidelines system, the Court said, a sentence cannot be increased based on facts found by a judge that were neither admitted by the defendant nor found by a jury. Consequently, Booker's sentence was ruled unconstitutional and invalidated. On the second question, the Court did not strike down the federal guidelines, as some thought might happen. Instead, it held that the guidelines could be taken into consideration by federal judges during sentencing but that they should no longer be regarded as mandatory. In effect, the combined decision in *Booker* and *Fanfan* made the federal sentencing guidelines merely advisory and gave federal judges wide latitude in imposing punishments. The result is that today federal judges must take the guidelines into account when sentencing, but they are no longer required to impose a sentence within the range prescribed by the guidelines.

The Court continues to clarify its decisions in the sentencing arena. In 2007, for example, in the case of *Rita* v. *United States,* the Court held that federal appeals courts hearing challenges from defendants about prison time may presume that federal criminal sentences are reasonable if they fall within U.S. sentencing guidelines.[29] Significantly, the justices wrote, that "even if the presumption increases the likelihood that the judge, not the jury, will find 'sentencing facts,' it does not violate the Sixth Amendment." A 2013 report submitted to Congress by the U.S. Sentencing Commission found that "the sentencing guidelines remain the essential starting point for determining all federal sentences and continue to exert significant influence on federal sentencing trends over time."[30] In a study of actual sentencing practices, the commission found that "the rate at which courts impose sentences within the applicable guideline range [stood] at 53.9% during the most recent time period studied."

Congress has been reconsidering federal sentencing law in light of *Booker.* In the meantime, some expect the federal courts to be flooded with inmates appealing their sentences based on the Court's findings in *Booker.*

The Federal Fair Sentencing Act

In 2010, President Barack Obama signed the federal Fair Sentencing Act (FSA) into law. The act reduced a previous disparity in the amounts of powder cocaine and crack cocaine specified by the federal sentencing guidelines and eliminated what had been a mandatory minimum sentence under federal law for simple possession of crack cocaine. As a result of the FSA, a first conviction for simple possession of any amount of crack cocaine, like simple possession of powder cocaine, is subject to a penalty range of zero to one year of imprisonment regardless of quantity.

Prior to enactment of the FSA, federal sentencing guidelines drew a strong distinction between crack and regular (or powdered) cocaine and typically led to much stiffer sentences for anyone convicted of crack possession. Because many crack users come from the African American community, the disparity in previous law resulted in a disproportionate number of blacks being incarcerated for extended periods. Before passage of the FSA, blacks received longer sentences than whites, not because they received differential treatment by judges but because they comprised the large majority of those convicted of trafficking in crack cocaine.

The FSA's provisions do not apply to people who were sentenced for a federal crack offense prior to August 3, 2010. Consequently, in 2011, 2012, and again in 2013, another bill was introduced in the U.S. House of Representatives to make the FSA's changes to federal crack cocaine sentencing laws retroactive—that is, to apply them to people who had already been sentenced for crack offenses. The new bill is called the Fair Sentencing Clarification Act (FSCA). Under FSCA, which has not yet become law, a motion for a crack sentence reduction would have to be made by the sentencing court, the Bureau of Prisons, or the defendant in order to obtain a sentence reduction for those already serving prison time.

The research arm of the U.S. Sentencing Commission estimates that 12,835 offenders in federal prisons would be eligible to receive a reduced sentence under the FSCA, should it become law.[31]

Even if the FSCA never becomes law, however, the U.S. Sentencing Commission has recognized that "in the sound discretion of the court, a reduction in the term of imprisonment may be appropriate for previously

President Barack Obama signs the Fair Sentencing Act into law on August 3, 2010. What is the purpose of the law?

sentenced, qualified defendants."[32] The Commission also noted that "a reduced guideline range is sufficient to achieve the purposes of sentencing," but that "such a discretionary reduction does not otherwise affect the lawfulness of a previously imposed sentence, does not authorize a reduction in any other component of the sentence, and does not entitle a defendant to a reduced term of imprisonment as a matter of right."[33]

Mandatory Minimum Sentencing

Mandatory minimum sentencing refers to the imposition of sentences required by statute for those convicted of a particular crime or a particular crime with special circumstances, such as robbery with a firearm or selling drugs to a minor within 1,000 feet of a school, or for those with a particular type of criminal history. By 1994, all 50 states had enacted one or more mandatory minimum sentencing laws,[34] and Congress had enacted numerous mandatory sentencing laws for federal offenders. Mandatory minimum sentencing rationales dominated the 1980s and early 1990s.

By the start of the 21st century, many states had adopted sentence enhancements, usually mandating longer prison terms for violent offenders with records of serious crimes. Mandatory sentence enhancements aim to deter known and potentially violent offenders and to incapacitate persistent criminals through long-term incarceration.[35] Such sentence enhancements have come to be known as *three-strikes laws* (and, in some jurisdictions, *two-strikes laws*).

Three-strikes laws vary in breadth. Some stipulate that both the prior convictions and the current offense must be violent felonies; others require only that the prior felonies be violent. Some three-strikes laws count only prior adult convictions; others permit consideration of juvenile adjudications for violent crimes. Under California's three-strikes law, an offender who is convicted of a qualifying felony and has two prior qualifying felony convictions must serve a minimum of 25 years. The law also doubles prison terms for offenders convicted of a second violent felony.[36]

Rationales Mandatory sentences have two goals—deterrence and incapacitation. The primary purposes of modest mandatory prison terms (e.g., three years for armed robbery) are specific deterrence for

mandatory minimum sentencing
The imposition of sentences required by statute for those convicted of a particular crime or a particular crime with special circumstances, such as robbery with a firearm or selling drugs to a minor within 1,000 feet of a school, or for those with a particular type of criminal history.

Many of today's mandatory sentencing laws were passed in reaction to public outcries against especially violent or well-publicized criminal acts. Does mandatory sentencing fulfill the goals of deterrence and incapacitation? How do you think mandatory sentencing laws will fare in an increasingly difficult economic environment?

already-punished offenders, and general deterrence for prospective offenders. If the law increases the imprisonment rate, it also serves the goal of incapacitation, leaving fewer offenders free to victimize the population at large. The intent of three-strikes (and even two-strikes) laws is to incapacitate selected violent offenders with very long terms—25 years or even life.

Mandatory sentencing laws have become highly politicized. By passing mandatory sentencing laws, legislators can convey that they deem certain crimes especially grave and that people who commit these crimes deserve, and can expect, harsh sanctions. Such laws typically represent a rapid and visible response to public outcries following heinous or well-publicized crimes.

Impact Mandatory sentencing has had significant consequences that deserve close attention. Among them are its impact on crime and the operations of the criminal justice system. In today's world of state budget challenges, it remains to be seen whether mandatory sentencing laws will give way to discretionary sentencing schemes that might result in less prison time and increased savings on correctional expenditures.

Crime Evaluations of mandatory minimum sentencing have focused on two types of crimes—those committed with handguns and those related to drugs (the offenses most commonly subject to mandatory minimum penalties in state and federal courts). An evaluation of the Massachusetts law that imposed mandatory jail terms for possession of an unlicensed handgun concluded that the law was an effective deterrent of gun crime, at least in the short term.[37]

However, studies of similar laws in Michigan[38] and Florida[39] found no evidence that crimes committed with firearms had been prevented. An evaluation of mandatory sentence enhancements for gun use in six large cities (Detroit, Jacksonville, Tampa, Miami, Philadelphia, and Pittsburgh) indicated that the laws deterred homicide but not other violent crimes.[40] An assessment of New York's harsh Rockefeller drug laws (which have since been substantially overhauled) was unable to support their claimed efficacy in deterring drug crime in New York City.[41]

The Criminal Justice System Today's busy criminal courts rely on a high rate of guilty pleas to speed case processing and thus avoid logjams. Officials can offer inducements to defendants to enter these pleas. At least in the short term, mandatory sentencing laws may disrupt established plea-bargaining patterns by preventing a prosecutor from offering a short prison term (less than the new minimum) in exchange for a guilty plea. However, unless policymakers enact the same mandatory sentences for several related crimes, prosecutors can usually shift strategies and bargain on charges rather than on sentences.

Most state-level two- and three-strikes laws leave judges no discretion to deviate from the sentences dictated by legislatures. Another central feature of such laws is the extraordinary length of the prison terms they require. Offenders serving life sentences in California and North Carolina under such legislation, for example, become eligible for parole only after serving 25 years, those in New Mexico after 30 years, and those in Colorado after 40 years. Three-strikes laws in some states mandate life without the possibility of parole. Two- and three-strikes laws came about in response to public concerns about crime and the growing belief that many serious offenders were being released from prison too soon.[42] Proponents view such legislation as the best way to deal with the persistent, serious violent offender—the proverbial three-time loser.

Two- and three-strikes laws are a form of **habitual offender statute.** Although habitual offender laws have been on the books in a number of jurisdictions since at least the 1940s, the older laws were often geared to specific types of prior offenses, such as crimes of violence, sex offenses, or crimes perpetrated with guns. Moreover, most early habitual offender laws allowed enhanced sentences but did not make them mandatory as do two- and three-strikes legislation.[43]

habitual offender statute

A law that (1) allows a person's criminal history to be considered at sentencing or (2) makes it possible for a person convicted of a given offense and previously convicted of another specified offense to receive a more severe penalty than that for the current offense alone.

CO3-5

THREE-STRIKES MODELS—WASHINGTON AND CALIFORNIA

During the last decade of the 20th century, 26 states and the federal government enacted new habitual offender laws that fell into the three-strikes category.[44] Washington State was the first of those to do so.[45] California soon followed with a considerably broader version of the three-strikes law. As those laws were being implemented, people debated the impact they would have on the criminal justice systems of those states. Proponents predicted the laws would curb crime and protect society by warehousing the worst offenders for a long time. Opponents argued that defendants facing lengthy mandatory sentences would be more likely to demand trials, slowing the processing of cases, and that more offenders would serve long terms of incarceration, causing prison populations already at crisis levels in many states to rise.[46]

Although they were enacted within months of each other amid the same "three-strikes-and-you're-out" rallying cry and they count many of the same offenses as strikes, the Washington and California laws differ in three important ways. First, in Washington, all three strikes must be for felonies specifically listed in the legislation. Under the California law, only the first two convictions must be from the state's list of "strikeable" crimes (which include most violent offenses and many drug offenses); *any* subsequent felony can count as the third strike. Second, the California law contains a two-strikes provision, by which a person convicted of any felony after one prior conviction for a strikeable offense is to be sentenced to twice the term he or she would otherwise receive. There is no two-strikes provision in the Washington law. Third, the sanctions for a third strike differ. The Washington statute requires a life term in prison without the possibility of parole for a person convicted for the third time of any of the "most serious offenses" listed in the law. In California a "third-striker" has at least the possibility of being released after 25 years.[47]

California's law came under attack for the seeming ease with which offenders who commit relatively minor crimes can be sentenced to prison for a long time. The law, however, found a powerful ally in the Supreme Court. In 2001, for example, the Ninth U.S. Circuit Court of Appeals ruled in *Andrade* v. *Attorney General of the State of California*[48] that two consecutive 25-years-to-life sentences imposed on a California man, Leandro Andrade, who was twice caught shoplifting videotapes from a Kmart, constituted cruel and unusual punishment under the Eighth Amendment to the U.S. Constitution.

On March 5, 2003, however, the U.S. Supreme Court overturned the lower court's finding and ruled that Andrade's two consecutive 25-years-to-life sentences did not violate the Eighth Amendment's proscription against cruel or unusual punishment.[49] In effect, the Court held that it is *not* cruel and unusual punishment to impose a possible life term for a conviction of a nonviolent felony committed by a defendant with a history of serious or violent convictions.

The Staff Speaks
Visit www.mhhe.com/schmalleger7e
to see this feature.

In another 2003 case, *Ewing* v. *California*,[50] the U.S. Supreme Court upheld the conviction and sentence of Gary Ewing under California's three-strikes law. Ewing, who had a lengthy record of prior convictions, had received a 25-years-to-life sentence following his conviction for felony grand theft of three golf clubs. In writing for the Court, Justice Sandra Day O'Connor said that states should be able to decide when repeat offenders "must be isolated from society . . . to protect the public safety," even when nonserious crimes trigger the lengthy sentence.

In November 2012, California voters overwhelmingly approved Proposition 36, which mandated changes in their state's three-strikes law.[51] As a consequence, now only two categories of offenders can be sentenced as three-strikers: (1) those who commit new "serious or violent" felonies as their third offense and (2) previously released murderers, rapists, or child molesters who are convicted of a new third strike, even if it is not a "serious or violent" felony. Under the voter-approved proposition, inmates sentenced under earlier versions of the law are allowed to petition for early release. Estimates are that around 3,000 such inmates may soon be released.

Impact on Local Courts and Jails

When three-strikes laws were first passed in Washington and California, some analysts projected a much greater impact on local criminal justice systems in California because the California law had a much broader scope.[52] They predicted that California courts would be overwhelmed as defendants facing enhanced penalties demanded jury trials. The added time to process cases through trials and the reluctance of courts to grant pretrial release to defendants facing long prison terms, they said, would cause jail populations to explode as the number of jail admissions and the length of jail stays grew.

Early evidence from California supported these predictions. A review of 12,600 two- and three-strikes cases from Los Angeles, for example, showed that two-strikes cases took 16 percent longer to process and three-strikes cases 41 percent longer than nonstrike cases.[53] In addition, strikes cases were three times as likely to go to trial as nonstrike felonies and four times as likely as the same types of cases before the law took effect. This effect led to a 25 percent increase in jury trials as well as an 11 percentage-point rise in the proportion of the jail population awaiting trial, from 59 percent before the law was enacted to 70 percent.

According to more recent data, however, at least some California counties have learned how to handle the changes brought about by the law. A recent survey of eight California counties with populations of more than 1 million identified several that were successfully disposing of two- and three-strikes cases early in the process.[54] In addition, data from the Los Angeles County Sheriff's Department suggest that the pace of strikes cases coming into that system has slowed.[55]

Impact on State Prison Systems

The impact of the Washington and California laws on state corrections departments has not been as severe as projected. Planners in Washington had expected that 40 to 75 persons would be sentenced under three-strikes provisions each year. The actual numbers, however, have been much lower. During the first three years the law was in effect, only 85 offenders—not the 120 to 225 projected—were admitted to the state prison system under the three-strikes law.[56]

A similar overestimate of the impact the California law would have on prisons there was made. According to a 2010 report by the California state auditor, the cost of housing striker inmates "for the additional years they were sentenced to under the three strikes law represents a substantial liability to the State."[57] The auditor estimated that the additional years imposed by the three-strikes law amount to $19.2 billion in additional costs over the duration of the incarceration of the state's current striker inmates. Even though the sheer number of cases affected by the law is significantly higher than that for any other state, the numbers are not as high as originally projected. Still, according to some experts, three-strikes laws have had a real impact on the California prison system. Such laws, they say, funnel increasingly older persons into correctional institutions and ensure that they will remain there for a very long time.[58] The result is an inmate population that is getting older. The aging of America's inmate population is discussed in more detail in Chapter 12. It should be noted, however, that California's recent move toward "realignment" will shift more of the state's sentenced felons into county jails and out of state-funded correctional facilities. The strategy, which began to be implemented in earnest in 2012, is seen as a way of reducing state expenditures on correctional clients. Even so, the cost savings might not be as great as expected because the state has promised to at least partially fund the running of jails throughout the state's 58 counties.

The Current Applicability of Three-Strikes Laws and Habitual Offender Statutes

According to the Washington, D.C.-based Sentencing Project, only a handful of states have convicted more than a hundred individuals using two- and three-strikes statutes—even though more than half of all states have such laws on the books. The Sentencing Project says that only Georgia, South Carolina, Nevada, Washington, and Florida are actually using three-strikes legislation "to any significant extent."[59]

There is also evidence of a movement away from mandatory minimum sentences in a number of jurisdictions where such sentences have been blamed for prison crowding and budgetary problems. In Louisiana, for example, where prison populations increased from 25,260 to 38,000 in the six years following the state's 1995 implementation of mandatory sentences, the legislature eliminated mandatory prison time for crimes such as residential burglary, Medicaid fraud, prostitution, theft of a firearm, and possession of small amounts of controlled substances. "This [was] an attempt to bring under control a system that was bankrupting the state and was not reducing crime," said state senator Donald R. Cravins.[60]

In similar legislative action, other states, including Connecticut, Indiana, and North Dakota, have eliminated some laws that required certain offenders to serve long prison terms without the possibility of parole. Likewise, in 2001, Mississippi passed a law establishing parole eligibility for nonviolent first-time offenders who have served only 25 percent of their sentences—reducing the figure from what had been a required 85 percent under previous law.[61]

The economic problems that have caused some states to use habitual offender statutes less frequently or to release repeat offenders early are present in almost all regions of the country. Some states, however, have moved to release nonviolent and relatively minor drug offenders in order to address budgetary shortfalls in their correctional systems but have refused to shorten the sentences of habitual felons.

In the face of challenging economic conditions a number of states have recently moved to maximize the return on money that they spend on corrections—including jails, prisons, and probation and parole. In 2013, the Washington, D.C.-based Sentencing Project identified five areas that have seen recent legislative action by states wanting to save money while at the same time controlling crime and ensuring public safety. Areas identified by the project, along with related initiatives include:

- *Relaxed mandatory minimums:* In 2012, as discussed elsewhere in this chapter, California voters approved a change in the state's three-strikes law to keep certain offenders from being imprisoned for life following the commission of a third felony. Other states have enacted sentencing reforms to limit the use of incarceration for selected offenders.

- *Sentence modifications and decriminalization:* A few states, like Colorado and Washington, have decriminalized the possession of small amounts of marijuana for personal use, and others have decreased the sentence to be served for other drug offenses. Some have

increased the amount of time by which inmates can reduce their sentences for good behavior. One state—Georgia—has created a system of "accountability courts" which are designed to substitute treatment for imprisonment as a sanction for drug-involved offenders. Still others have raised the dollar amount needed to charge a theft crime as a felony, and have implemented a sentencing structure for such offenses that more closely ties punishment to the value of property stolen.

- *Probation and parole reform:* A number of states, including Delaware, Georgia, and Missouri, have enacted legislation to limit the use of imprisonment for technical violations of parole, and have expanded the use of incarceration alternatives, such as home confinement. Some states, most notably Louisiana, have recently expanded parole eligibility for certain crimes and have provided for the possibility of parole for some offenders sentenced to life in prison.

- *Capital punishment changes:* In 2012, Connecticut eliminated the death penalty as a sentencing option, substituting life without parole in its place. While life in

prison is expensive, it can cost more to prosecute and defend (using public funds) a capital case, than it does to house an inmate sentenced to life in prison.

- *Reforms affecting juvenile justice:* A number of states, including California, Louisiana, and Pennsylvania, have legislatively authorized changes in the handling of individuals who had been sentenced to life without parole as juveniles. Such changes include eliminating life without parole for juveniles who committed offenses other than homicide, and making it possible for those who received such sentences as juveniles to petition the court for a resentencing hearing. Similarly, Colorado has limited the authority of juvenile court judges to transfer cases to adult criminal court.

While many states have sought to curb expenditures in almost all budgetary areas, not all states relaxed their sentencing practices. Massachusetts, for example, recently increased mandatory minimum sentences for certain repeat offenders.

Source: Nicole D. Porter, *The State of Sentencing 2012* (Washington, DC: The Sentencing Project, 2013).

CO3-6 ## ISSUES IN SENTENCING

fair sentencing

Sentencing practices that incorporate fairness for both victims and offenders. *Fairness* is said to be achieved by implementing principles of proportionality, equity, social debt, and truth in sentencing.

Many sentencing reforms have been an attempt to reduce disparity in sentencing and make the process fairer. The term **fair sentencing,** or *fairness in sentencing*, has become popular in recent years. Although fair sentencing today often refers to fairness for *victims*, many suggest that any truly fair sentencing scheme must incorporate fairness for both victims and offenders. These are the issues related to fairness in sentencing:

- proportionality;
- equity;
- social debt; and
- truth in sentencing.

Proportionality

proportionality

The sentencing principle that the severity of punishment should match the seriousness of the crime for which the sentence is imposed.

Proportionality is the sentencing principle that the severity of punishment should match the seriousness of the crime for which the sentence is imposed. To most people today, the death penalty would seem grossly disproportional to the offense of larceny—even if the offender had a history of such violations. However, this was not always the case. Larceny *was* punishable by death in medieval England. On the other hand, probation would seem disproportional to the crime of murder—although it is occasionally imposed in homicide cases.

Equity

Equity is the sentencing principle that similar crimes and similar criminals should be treated alike. The alternative to equity is *disparity,* in which similar crimes are associated with different punishments in different jurisdictions or in which offenders with similar criminal histories receive widely differing sentences. Disparity can also result from judicial discretion when judges hold widely different sentencing philosophies. In a jurisdiction with wide leeway for judges to determine sentences, one judge might treat offenders very harshly while another may be lenient. Under such circumstances, now largely eliminated by sentencing reform, one burglar, for example, might receive a sentence of 30 years in prison upon conviction, but his partner in crime is merely put on probation simply because he appears before a more lenient judge.

Recently, racial and ethnic disparities have become the focus of concern in the sentencing practices of a number of states.[62] In 2008, for example, Connecticut and Iowa both passed legislation requiring minority impact statements to be included in any legislation that changes the current criminal penalty structure.[63] The statements are intended to assess the potential impact of criminal justice-related legislation on racial and ethnic minorities prior to passage. Also in 1988, the Illinois general assembly enacted Senate Bill 2476, which created the Commission to Study Disproportionate Justice Impact. The Committee is charged with studying the degree to which the criminal sentencing structure in Illinois disproportionately affects communities of color.

Wayne Ford, an Iowa state representative, authored that state's Minority Impact Statement Bill and told reporters, "I believe that we need to be tough on crime, but we must also make sure that our laws are fair and equitable."[64] Ford initiated the legislation after the release of a 2007 report by the Washington, D.C.-based Sentencing Project entitled *Uneven Justice: State Rates of Incarceration by Race and Ethnicity.* The report revealed that Iowa imprisons blacks at a rate 13 times that of whites—more than double the national average. The most recent state to implement a minority impact strategy is Colorado. The implementation came at the behest of the state's legislature, which asked the Colorado Commission on Criminal and Juvenile Justice to include minority impact statements in any legislative recommendations that it makes beginning in 2012.[65] In response, the Commission noted that the percentage of minorities "at many stages of the criminal justice system exceeds their proportion of the state population."[66]

Social Debt

Social debt is the sentencing principle that the severity of punishment should take into account the offender's prior criminal behavior. As we have seen, a number of laws designed to recognize social debt have recently been passed. Among them are three-strikes and two-strikes laws. Although there is considerable variation in such laws among states, the primary characteristic of these laws is that they "call for enhanced penalties for offenders with one or more prior felony convictions."[67] They require a repeat offender to serve several years in prison in addition to the penalty imposed for the current offense.

equity
The sentencing principle that similar crimes and similar criminals should be treated alike.

social debt
The sentencing principle that the severity of punishment should take into account the offender's prior criminal behavior.

Truth in Sentencing (TIS)

Until the sentencing reforms of the 1970s, the laws of many states enabled convicted offenders to be released from prison long before they had served their full sentences. Inmates frequently had *good time* deducted from their sentences or time off for good behavior. *Gain time* could be earned for going to school, learning a trade, or doing volunteer work. Moreover, many states mandated routine parole eligibility after inmates had served one-quarter or even one-fifth of their sentences.

Recent truth-in-sentencing laws have changed such practices by requiring offenders to complete sentences very close to the ones they are given. **Truth in sentencing** requires an offender to serve a substantial portion of the sentence and reduces the discrepancy between the sentence imposed and actual time spent in prison (see Exhibit 3–7). The Violent Crime Control and Law Enforcement Act of 1994 includes a truth-in-sentencing provision. To qualify for federal aid under the act, a state must amend its laws so that an imprisoned offender serves at least 85 percent of his or her sentence before being released. Parole eligibility and good-time credits are generally restricted or eliminated in truth-in-sentencing laws.

Today most states have reformed their sentencing practices, moving them in the direction of the 85% federal truth in sentencing requirement.[68] Not all states, however, have fully adopted the 85% standard and are not eligible to receive federal truth-in-sentencing grants.

Broader Issues

Today's two main sentencing initiatives—guideline-based determinate sentencing and restorative justice—represent different attempts to achieve sentencing fairness. The two, however, appear to be inherently at odds with one another. That is because determinate sentencing requires a top-down approach in which an authoritative decision-making body imposes strict limits on the sentencing process, whereas restorative justice emphasizes community involvement at the grassroots level. "All this," say some experts, "suggests that, at its philosophical core, restorative justice appears to be incompatible with sentencing guidelines."[69]

truth in sentencing (TIS)

The sentencing principle that requires an offender to serve a substantial portion of the sentence and reduces the discrepancy between the sentence imposed and actual time spent in prison.

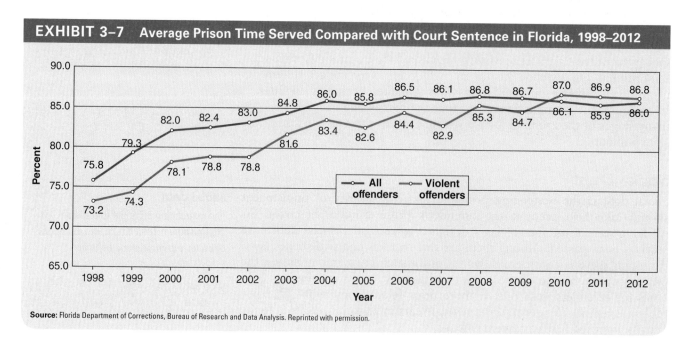

EXHIBIT 3–7   Average Prison Time Served Compared with Court Sentence in Florida, 1998–2012

Source: Florida Department of Corrections, Bureau of Research and Data Analysis. Reprinted with permission.

One way of addressing the differences between these two approaches would be to seek greater community involvement in the development of sentencing guidelines. In fact, many states have encouraged local participation in the guideline-development process. Similarly, some guideline states encourage the use of local sentencing options such as community-based sanctions (which are discussed in more detail in Chapters 4 and 5). For example, North Carolina, a guideline state, assigns county officials the responsibility for developing and recommending local community sentencing options for certain categories of offenders.

Still, community sentencing may be appropriate only for relatively minor offenders, and traditional grid-based guidelines offer little leeway for sentencing offenders convicted of serious crimes. Some authors have suggested creation of a hybrid system of "restorative sentencing guidelines" to resolve the problem. Under the system, a new restorative sentencing option would be created and made applicable to less serious offenders. For such offenders, the traditional guideline grid, based on severity of offense and prior record, would not apply.

REVIEW AND APPLICATIONS

SUMMARY

❶ The philosophy underlying criminal sentencing is that people must be held accountable for their actions and the harm they cause. Western society has a long tradition of sentencing criminal offenders to some form of punishment. Many social scientists suggest that the central purpose of criminal punishment is to maintain social order.

❷ The goals of criminal sentencing today are (1) revenge, (2) retribution, (3) just deserts, (4) deterrence, (5) incapacitation, (6) rehabilitation or reformation, and (7) restoration.

❸ Sentencing options in use today include fines and other monetary sanctions, probation, alternative or intermediate sentences, incarceration, and capital punishment.

❹ A model of criminal sentencing is a strategy or system for imposing criminal sanctions. Sentencing models vary widely among the jurisdictions in the United States. These models include indeterminate sentences, determinate sentences, voluntary or advisory sentencing guidelines, presumptive sentencing guidelines, and mandatory minimum sentencing.

❺ Recent laws have increased penalties for criminal offenses, particularly violent crimes, and for repeat offenders. Many such laws are three-strikes laws. The rationale for such laws is simple: Offenders convicted repeatedly of serious offenses should be removed from society for long periods of time. Many three-strikes laws mandate a life sentence for the third violent felony conviction. Analysts of three-strikes laws predicted that courts would be overwhelmed as more defendants, facing enhanced penalties, demanded jury trials. The added time to process cases and the reluctance to grant pretrial release to defendants facing long prison terms, said analysts, would cause jail populations to explode as the number of admissions and the length of jail stays grew. The actual effects of the laws have been similar to the effects predicted but to a lesser extent. Even so, some states have had difficulties funding increased costs of imprisonment and, like California, are now looking for ways to alleviate the financial burdens that follow from the use of increased imprisonment.

❻ *Fair sentencing* often refers to fairness for *victims.* Fair-sentencing advocates, however, suggest that any truly fair sentencing scheme must incorporate fairness for both victims and offenders. Issues related to fairness in sentencing are proportionality, equity, social debt, and truth in sentencing.

KEY TERMS

QUESTIONS FOR REVIEW

1 Define *sentencing,* describe sentencing philosophy, and name the central purpose of criminal punishment.

2 What are the seven goals of criminal sentencing?

3 What are the major sentencing options in wide use in the United States today?

4 What is a sentencing *model*? How have U.S. models of criminal sentencing changed over the past 100 years?

5 What are three-strikes (and two-strikes) laws? What consequences might three-strikes (and two-strikes) laws have for the criminal justice system and for the corrections subsystem?

6 What is fair sentencing? What are some of the major issues relating to fair sentencing today?

THINKING CRITICALLY ABOUT CORRECTIONS

Rehabilitation

Edgardo Rotman says, in *Beyond Punishment,* "Rehabilitation . . . can be defined tentatively and broadly as a right to an opportunity to return to (or remain in) society with an improved chance of being a useful citizen and staying out of prison."[70] Do you agree that offenders have a right to rehabilitation? Why or why not?

Mandatory Sentencing

Mandatory sentencing laws for drug possession offenses were initially hailed as the best method for toughening the government's response to the growing drug problem. Critics now complain that, in practice, mandatory sentencing rules lead to excessive punishments for many low-level offenders and to unwarranted leniency for the high-volume dealers who were the original targets of the new laws.

Furthermore, critics contend that plea bargaining is the culprit. Faced with lengthy prison terms, many arrested big-time dealers readily provide the names of numerous "little fish" in the drug distribution chain to prosecutors who are too quick to abandon prosecution of a single high-volume dealer in favor of procuring numerous convictions of low-level dealers.

Should mandatory sentencing laws be amended to prohibit plea bargaining in cases in which the accused is charged with trafficking in quantities exceeding an established volume?

In view of the dramatic impact mandatory sentencing has had on prison population growth, should the sentences of current inmates be reviewed with an eye toward reducing, appropriately, the sentences of the previously mentioned little fish?

ON-THE-JOB DECISION MAKING

Recidivism

You have spent the past six years as a counselor at a minimum-security state correctional facility. Your effectiveness has earned you a strong reputation throughout the Department of Corrections as a specialist in prerelease counseling, a program designed to prepare inmates for their return to society upon parole or completion of their sentence.

Lately, a series of highly publicized violent crimes has been committed by former inmates of the state's supermaximum-security facility. All were released recently upon completion of their sentences, and all had moved almost directly from their cell back to the criminal lifestyle that originally landed them in prison.

Hard-line correctional officers insist that because those incarcerated in the "supermax" are the worst of the worst, they cannot be trusted to behave during prerelease counseling. The safety risks such inmates represent, they say, make leaving them in their cells until the law requires they be set free the only sensible course of action. What happens after that, in the hard-liners' opinions, is both the decision and responsibility of the former inmate.

Reformers insist that immediate recidivism is the likely outcome of releasing inmates directly from a harsh, totally controlled lockdown environment. They call for significant transitional counseling as essential for helping inmates adjust to free society and for defusing their angry urge to make society pay for the harsh life from which they are being released.

Both the governor and the commissioner of corrections face daily media demands to explain what the administration is going to do about this problem. In particular, the governor is under the gun because his opponent in the upcoming and hotly contested gubernatorial race has seized on this as an issue that demonstrates "this governor's inability, or unwillingness, to take the tough steps necessary to protect the good citizens of our state."

You have been asked to speak at a meeting to develop potential courses of action to address this problem. The meeting will be chaired by the corrections commissioner, and various wardens, assistant wardens, and senior correctional specialists from throughout the state will attend. It is likely but not yet confirmed that the governor will also attend.

1. What issues will you address?
2. How might you resolve the conflict between the need to protect counselors and staff from the often violent behavior of supermax inmates and the need to provide this critical prerelease counseling to these troubled inmates?
3. How would you respond to hard-line corrections officers who contend that what happens after release is not their problem?

For additional information, please see: www.mhhe.com/schmalleger7e
Follow the author's tweets about the latest crime and justice news @schmalleger

Community Corrections

Part Two examines what happens to convicted offenders, which includes diversion, probation, and intermediate sanctions. *Diversion* is the suspension of formal criminal proceedings before conviction in exchange for the defendant's participation in treatment, counseling, or other programs. Diversion recognizes that not all offenders should be formally prosecuted and subjected to the stigma of formal arrest, trial, and conviction.

As you will learn, diversion has its supporters and critics. Supporters believe diversion is the first opportunity to give offenders individualized assistance before they get too far down the path of crime and to resolve problems that lead to offending behavior. Critics argue that diversion tends to force people to give up some of their freedom without being tried and convicted, it violates the safeguard of due process, and it might actually produce more crime.

If diversion is not warranted or if an offender fails diversion, probation is often the next step in the correctional process. *Probation* is the conditional release of convicted offenders under community supervision. The degree of supervision depends on an offender's risk level. Some offenders pose no risk to the community. For them, checking in monthly at an automated probation kiosk may be all that is necessary. On the other hand, high-risk offenders require intensive face-to-face supervision and sometimes random drug testing, community service, and home confinement with remote-location monitoring.

Sanctions more punitive than probation but not as restrictive as incarceration are called *intermediate sanctions.* Drug court, economic sanctions, community service, day reporting centers, remote-location monitoring, residential centers, and boot camps are some intermediate sanctions.

Today, the current probation and parole workforce of 50,000 investigates and supervises over 5 million adults under probation, parole, and intermediate sanctions. These officers are faced with enormous case investigation and supervision challenges that include increasing caseloads without new resources, deciding on what information to include in a presentence report, figuring out how to structure the report so it is read, and incorporating novel forms of technology into their day-to-day jobs.

Whether supervision is low level or intense, many probationers will violate its technical conditions. Others will commit new crimes. Tightening the offender's supervision without resorting to using an already overburdened system of incarceration is a challenge that probation officers face. The decision to revoke probation and incarcerate the offender is influenced by legal, social, political, and economic issues.

[4]

DIVERSION AND PROBATION

How Most Offenders Are Punished

CHAPTER OBJECTIVES

After completing this chapter you should be able to do the following:

1. Define *diversion* and know its objectives.

2. Explain the rationales for diversion.

3. Give examples of stages at which diversion occurs in the criminal justice process.

4. Discuss diversion policy issues.

5. Define *probation* and know its goals.

6. Explain the reasons for using probation.

7. Describe some of the characteristics of adults on probation.

8. Explain the different ways that probation is administered.

9. Describe the measures used to evaluate probation.

10. Describe the investigation and supervision functions of probation officers.

11. Explain revocation hearings.

> *We won't get true public safety and protection for crime victims until we invest in community corrections—because most offenders are not behind bars, but living as our neighbors.*
>
> —Anne Seymour, national crime victim advocate

On January 7, 2013, Gabriela Cortez, 43, a Spanish teacher at Roosevelt High School in Boyle Heights, Los Angeles, was sentenced to five years probation and barred from teaching for having sex with two of her male students.[1]

Los Angeles Superior Court Judge Edmund W. Clarke Jr. told Cortez that parents have an expectation that "when a child goes off to school he will be treated as if they were there watching" and that Cortez had breached that trust. But the judge said he was persuaded by Cortez's attorney, Edward Robinson, that probation would be "the just sentence." Cortez could have served a maximum sentence of six years and four months behind bars.

The conditions of probation bar Cortez from working in any teaching, coaching, or mentoring position and from being in the presence of minors—other than her own daughter—without other adults present. She is also required to undergo counseling, which the judge said had already begun.

Cortez was arrested February 22, 2012, by Montebello police and released later that day after posting $140,000 bail. Montebello police Lt. Luis Lopez said the investigation began February 15, 2012, after one of the victims came forward to report being molested by a teacher, saying he wanted to get things "off his chest."

The investigation triggered by that victim led to the second victim, who provided information regarding a sexual relationship involving him and Ms. Cortez.

Cortez is one of more than 250 female teachers in the past decade arrested, charged, convicted, and sentenced to probation and/or prison for having sex with students.[2] Arguably, the crime of male and female teacher predator is underreported and the number of such incidences is much larger. What conditions do you think would persuade a judge to sentence a teacher predator to probation?

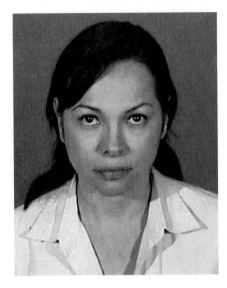

Gabriela Cortez, 43, a Spanish teacher at Roosevelt High School in Boyle Heights, Los Angeles, was sentenced to five years probation and barred from teaching for having sex with two of her male students. The probation conditions bar Cortez from working in any teaching, coaching, or mentoring position and from being in the presence of minors—other than her own daughter—without other adults present. She is also required to undergo counseling. Cortez is one of more than 250 female teachers in the past decade arrested, charged, convicted, and sentenced to probation and/or prison for having sex with students. Arguably, the crime of male and female teacher predator is under-reported and the number of such incidences is much higher. What conditions do you think would persuade a judge to sentence a teacher predator to probation?

OVERVIEW OF DIVERSION AND PROBATION

This chapter introduces you to two areas of corrections that most offenders first experience—diversion and probation. Diversion occurs *before* trial. Probation occurs *after* a person has been convicted. Exhibit 4–1 shows how these two processes can occur in the criminal justice system. Because offenders can be diverted one or more times before they are tried, convicted, and sentenced to probation, we discuss diversion first.

EXHIBIT 4–1   Case Flow Model for Diversion and Probation

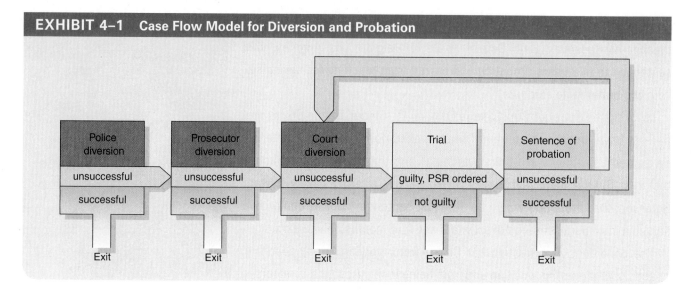

CO4-1   # DIVERSION

Diversion has been defined as "the halting or suspension, before conviction, of formal criminal proceedings against a person, [often] conditioned on some form of counterperformance by the defendant,"[3] and this is the definition we will use. **Counterperformance** is the defendant's participation, in exchange for diversion, in a treatment, counseling, or educational program aimed at changing his or her behavior. The candidate for diversion is a person who has been or could be arrested for an alleged offense and who is or could become the defendant in a criminal prosecution. Suspending the prosecution of a case is the hallmark of the diversion process.

Diversion has its roots in labeling theory, the idea that a person processed through the criminal justice system will be more stigmatized than a person handled informally, as well as the idea that incarceration can do more damage than good.

The overall goal of diversion is to reduce recidivism through rehabilitation. In the criminal justice system, diversion is used in two ways. First, it can be used to keep an offender out of the system and help him or her avoid formal prosecution and labeling. Second, diversion can be used to keep an offender from going further into the system. Drug courts are an example of both methods. Diversion drug courts offer defendants opportunities to obtain employment and avoid the possibility of conviction by changing their drug-using behavior.

Diversion most often includes:

- alternatives to traditional criminal justice proceedings for persons charged with criminal offenses;
- voluntary participation by the accused;
- access to defense counsel prior to a decision to participate;
- strategies—with input from the accused—to address the needs of the accused in avoiding behavior likely to lead to future arrests; and
- dismissal of charges or its equivalent, if the divertee successfully completes the diversion process.

MacKenzie rigorously studied 32 drug court evaluations, 20 of which were diversion drug court programs. Applying the threshold of "evidence-based corrections," meaning the use of scientific evidence to make

Diversion includes access to defense counsel prior to a decision to participate. Do you think diversion invites more law violation by allowing offenders to avoid prosecution?

informed decisions about correctional policy, she concluded that there is very strong evidence that drug courts—including diversion drug courts—reduce the future criminal activities of offenders.[4] We offer a more thorough discussion of drug courts and their effectiveness in reducing criminal activity in Chapter 5.

In 2007, the National Association of Pretrial Services Agencies' (NAPSA) Diversion Committee commissioned a national survey of 253 known pretrial diversion programs nationwide and found that diversion is a successful alternative for eligible defendants. Respondents averaged an 85 percent rate of defendants who complete diversion successfully, and over 80 percent of programs had a rate of 70 percent or higher.[5]

Rationales for Diversion

CO4-2

Diversion has four rationales. First, the experience and the stigma of being formally arrested, tried, and convicted can actually encourage more criminal behavior. For example, having a criminal record might restrict a person's educational, vocational, and social opportunities, making the person more apt to turn to crime to survive. In addition, as a result of time spent in jail or prison, an offender may be more likely to associate with other offenders.

A second rationale for using diversion is that it is less expensive than formally processing an offender through the criminal justice system. The expense of arrest, trial, conviction, and sentence is easily justified for serious crimes. In most cities and counties across the United States today, however, police are overworked, courts are overloaded, jails and prisons are overcrowded, and probation and parole officers have caseloads that are unmanageable. Diversion is a way to reduce or at least contain these burdens, reserving formal criminal justice processing for the cases that need it the most.

A third rationale for diversion is that the public may think formal processing through the criminal justice system is inappropriate for crimes in which the parties to the offense willingly participate even though the offense is committed against the social values and interests represented in and protected by the criminal law. Examples include prostitution, certain

victimless crime

An offense committed against the social values and interests represented in and protected by the criminal law, and in which parties willingly participate.

Visit http://www.discovercorrections.com/ or scan this code with the QR app on your smartphone or digital device and read how *Discover Corrections,* a new and innovative resource on finding a career in corrections, can help you with career resources. How does this information relate to ideas discussed in this chapter?

forms of sexual behavior, gambling, and drug sales. Such offenses are called **victimless crimes** because the participants do not feel they are being harmed. Prosecution is justified on the grounds that these offenses harm society as a whole by threatening the moral fabric of the community. Because formal prosecution of these offenses is costly, offenders are often diverted to health clinics and treatment programs.

A final rationale for using diversion is to give the typical diversion client a better chance in life. Our nation's jails, lockups, prisons, and probation and parole caseloads are filled with people who are economically disadvantaged, belong to minority groups, and are young, undereducated, and chronically unemployed or underemployed. Diversion offers such persons help with some of the challenges they face without adding to their difficulties the stigma of formal arrest, trial, and conviction.

One of the newest diversion programs is for veterans returning from wars in Afghanistan and Iraq.[6] The programs target veterans charged with nonviolent felony offenses. Some of the programs are postplea and administered by specialized veterans courts. (We will return to the concept of veterans courts in the next chapter.) Others are preplea diversion programs. Both programs address the needs of military veterans who are returning and have incidences of substance abuse, domestic violence, post-traumatic stress disorder (PTSD), traumatic brain injury (TBI), unemployment, depression, suicidal ideations, fear of redeployment, and related issues and commit various crimes. Bradley Schaffer administered a 13-week preplea diversion program for veterans having anger and domestic violence problems in Cincinnati, Ohio, from 2002 to 2008. Judges, prosecutors, police, probation officers, substance abuse counselors, therapists, community advocates, mentors, and families worked together toward a holistic outcome focusing on the veterans' recovery and support rather than official processing through the criminal justice system. Veterans who successfully completed the program (almost 57 percent) were less likely to repeat (almost 28 percent) the offense and had their charges reduced, dismissed, or expunged. More than 220,000 service members have been deployed to Afghanistan and Iraq. With over 467,000 persons employed in corrections across the United States, veterans who pursue a career in criminal diversion bring a unique understanding of war and the aftermath of military service and contribute significantly to diversion programming for veterans.

CO4-3 The Process of Diversion

Diversion may occur at any point in the criminal justice process after a criminal complaint has been filed or police have observed a crime. The police, a prosecutor, or a judge may call for diversion. The accused participates voluntarily and has access to defense counsel before deciding whether to participate.

Diversion programs offer a variety of remedial responses to defendants' problems. Such responses can include drug and alcohol treatment, mental health services, employment counseling, and education and training. They may involve agencies in or outside the criminal justice system. The variety of responses often reflects a community's unique criminal justice population.

Diversion is also used for persons who are classified as mentally ill or incompetent and either are not equipped to stand trial or need a form of incarceration and treatment other than imprisonment. Such persons may be referred to an agency for voluntary treatment or civil commitment to an institution in lieu of prosecution and a prison sentence.

Diversion Policy Issues

CO4-4

Diversion has its supporters and critics. Supporters believe diversion is the first opportunity to give offenders individualized assistance before they get too far down the path of crime. Diversion may thus resolve problems that lead to offending behavior. Critics argue that diversion tends to force people to give up some of their freedom without being tried and convicted. They argue that it violates the safeguard of due process. Other critics believe that diversion is "nonpunishment" and might actually produce more crime and jeopardize community safety. And still others contend that diversion programs serve too small a percentage of offenders (mostly less serious crime and low-risk offenders when the real need in criminal justice is to focus on serious crime and high-risk offenders) and spend too many resources on them. To these and other issues about diversion we now turn our attention.

Legal and Ethical Issues There is agreement that a diversion program should protect a defendant's rights. Protections include requiring an informed waiver of the right to a speedy trial, the right to a trial by jury, the right to confront one's accusers, the privilege against self-incrimination, and informed consent to the conditions of a diversion program. For supporters, the risk of violating rights is outweighed by the chance diversion gives defendants to avoid the stigma of a criminal record and by the possibility of resolving problems that might result in future criminal behavior.

Unconditional diversion is the termination of criminal processing at any point before adjudication with no threat of later prosecution. It affords the best protection for a defendant's legal rights because dismissal of charges does not require any counterperformance. In effect, the defendant has everything to gain and nothing to lose. In unconditional diversion, treatment, counseling, and other services are offered on a voluntary basis. Many corrections leaders believe that voluntary treatment is more likely than coerced treatment to have beneficial effects. Whether that is true or not is subject to debate. Research consistently indicates that offenders' motivations for entering correctional programs (voluntary or coerced) are not as important in treatment outcome as their ultimate length of stay in treatment.[7]

Conditional diversion means that charges are dismissed if the defendant satisfactorily completes treatment, counseling, or other programs ordered by the justice system. Conditional diversion at or after arraignment, with judicial participation, affords greater protection against prosecutorial overreach and more assurance of informed voluntary decisions by the defendant than does diversion by the police or the prosecutor. In diversion programs run by the police and prosecutor, some participants may not have been prosecuted at all or might have been exonerated (cleared of blame) if they had been prosecuted. Conditional diversion does not eliminate the possibility of more severe penalties for divertees who fail the program. Judging the success of conditional diversion would mean knowing the percentage of supervised defendants who make all scheduled program and/or judicial appearances as well as the percentage who are not charged with a new offense or technical violation of the conditions of their diversionary period.

Law Enforcement Issues Does diversion weaken law enforcement? Does diversion invite more widespread violation of laws by allowing offenders to avoid conviction? There is no particular evidence one way or the other. Certainly, if unconditional diversion were practiced extensively, there might be increases in violations. However, if unconditional diversion is limited to the first or second charge, then increases in violations are

unconditional diversion

The termination of criminal processing at any point before adjudication with no threat of later prosecution. Treatment, counseling, and other services are offered and use is voluntary.

conditional diversion

Diversion in which charges are dismissed if the defendant satisfactorily completes treatment, counseling, or other programs ordered by the justice system.

less likely. Conditional diversion requiring supervision and counterperformance does not seem more likely to encourage crime than the dispositions it most often replaces—fines, suspended sentences, and probation.

Safety Issues   Some argue that in the long run, diversion can protect the community better than traditional processing can. Traditional methods of managing drug offenders depended on the corrections officer first reporting a violation and then a long time after that passed before a hearing occurred and sanctions were imposed. Diversion drug courts and veterans courts hold regularly scheduled status hearings, monthly or more frequently, with the offender, prosecutor, defense attorney, treatment providers, probation agents, and others. At these hearings, judges monitor the progress of the offender, provide continuing court supervision, keep the offender in treatment, and proscribe sanctions for noncompliance and rewards for compliance. Hence, the court can respond immediately to positive or negative behavior, thereby protecting the community better than traditional criminal processing.

Economic Issues   How cost effective is diversion? What is the least costly method of diversion that will yield acceptable results? What are the trade-offs among different kinds of diversion programs? How does diversion compare in cost and effectiveness with traditional prosecution and sentencing practices?

Presumably, diversion is less conducive to recidivism than is traditional processing. However, efforts to compare diversion with what would have happened without it have been unsuccessful. It seems safe to say that the community protection that diversion affords is at least comparable to the traditional measures that would most likely be used if prosecution were not suspended. The economic question, then, is, which approach costs less?

The costs of both diversion and its alternatives include the costs of arriving at a decision; the costs of implementing decisions; and the costs of undesired consequences of decisions, such as reinstatement of prosecution, leveling of new charges, or revocation of probation or parole because of a new charge or violation.

Diversion is not always the appropriate response to criminal behavior. When diversion fails to bring about the desired changes in an offender's behavior, probation is often the next step in the corrections process.

CO4-5   PROBATION

Probation is the most frequently used form of criminal punishment (see Exhibit 4–2). It is a way to keep the offender at home in the community, avoid incarceration, and carry out sanctions imposed by the court or the probation agency. **Probation** is the conditional release of a convicted offender into the community under the supervision of a probation officer. It is conditional because if the probationer violates the conditions of her or his probation, the judge may either set more restrictive conditions of probation, or revoke probation and sentence the defendant to prison. Later in this chapter, we discuss the impact that revoking even a small percentage of the probation population can have on the prison population.

probation

The conditional release of a convicted offender into the community, under the supervision of a probation officer. It is conditional because it can be revoked if certain conditions are not met.

CO4-6   Reasons for and Goals of Probation

Probation is used for at least four reasons. First, probation permits the offender to remain in the community for reintegration purposes. Offender reintegration is more likely to occur if social and family ties are not broken by incarceration.

EXHIBIT 4–2   Adults on Probation, on Parole, in Jail, or in Prison

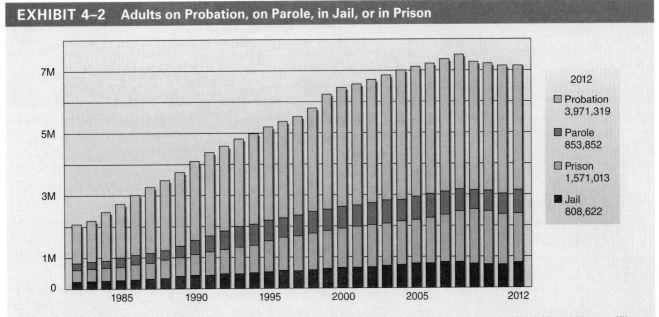

2012
☐ Probation
3,971,319

■ Parole
853,852

☐ Prison
1,571,013

■ Jail
808,622

Sources: Laura M. Maruschak and Erika Parks, Probation and Parole in the United States, 2011 (Washington, DC: Bureau of Justice Statistics, November 2012); Todd D. Minton, Jail Inmates at Mid-year 2012-Statistical Tables (Washington, DC: Bureau of Justice Statistics, May 2013); E. Ann Carson and Daniela Golinelli, Prisoners in 2012—Advance Counts (Washington, DC: Bureau of Justice Statistics, July 2013); and Pew Center on the States, The High Cost of Corrections in America (Washington, DC: Pew Center on the States, June 2012).

Second, probation avoids prison institutionalization and the stigma of incarceration. Prison institutionalization is the process of learning and adopting the norms and culture of institutional living. Living in the artificial environment of an institution does not teach prisoners how to live in the free world. Probationers do not experience prison institutionalization, nor do they have to worry about the negative effects of being treated like a prisoner, which decrease even further their ability to function as a law-abiding citizen when released.

The third reason for probation is that it is less expensive than incarceration, more humanitarian, and at least as effective as incarceration in reducing future criminal activity.

The final reason for probation is that it is fair and appropriate sentencing for offenders whose crimes do not merit incarceration. Furthermore, probation is the base from which more severe punishments can be built. Not all crimes deserve incarceration, nor do all crimes deserve probation. Probation is preferred when the offender poses no threat to community safety, when community correctional resources are available, and when probation does not unduly deprecate the seriousness of the offense. Assessment tools that determine the risk and needs of each offender and statutory sentencing guidelines help identify which offenders deserve community-based punishment and which deserve institutional punishment.

Most probation programs share five goals:

1. Protect the community by preparing the presentence report (PSR) to assist judges in sentencing and supervising offenders. The PSR indicates the degree of risk an offender poses to the community. (We will return to the PSR later in this chapter.)

2. Carry out sanctions imposed by the court. Probation officers (POs) accomplish this by educating offenders about the orders of the court, supervising offenders, and removing them from the community when they violate the conditions of their probation.

Economic Realities and Corrections: Probation

Probation officials across the country increasingly have to do more with less. They oversee agencies that are responsible for record numbers of people under community supervision. Today, 1 in 45 adults in the United States is on probation or parole. Although their budgets are being cut, probation departments are expected to improve the success rates of the increasing numbers of individuals they supervise and to reduce crime in the community by preventing reoffending. These high expectations and the intense public scrutiny that follows a high-profile failure require that probation officials revisit their agency's goals, processes, and measures for success.

The core mission of a probation department is to reduce probationer recidivism. Reviewing a growing body of knowledge and experience, experts point to four evidence-based practices that are essential to probation agencies' success in achieving this mission, especially during tough fiscal times. Based on current best practices, probation departments should

1. Effectively assess probationers' criminogenic risk and need as well as their strengths (also known as "protective factors");

2. Employ smart, tailored supervision strategies;

3. Use incentives and graduated sanctions to respond promptly to probationers' behaviors; and

4. Implement performance-driven personnel management practices that promote and reward recidivism reduction.

From 2005 to 2008, researchers at the Council of State Governments worked with leaders from Travis County (Austin, Texas) to design and integrate each of the four core practices into the department's everyday processes. In spite of the economic recession that started in 2008, when researchers returned to Travis County in 2011 to examine the long-term impact of the department's transformation, they found that implementing the four practices of recidivism reduction is not only possible but also can yield dramatic and positive improvements for the involved agency, the community, and probationers.

- Felony probation revocations declined by 20 percent.

- Felony technical revocations fell by 48 percent—the largest reduction in the five most populous counties in Texas, and nearly 10 times the statewide reduction of 5 percent.

- The decreased number of technical revocations averted $4.8 million in state incarceration costs.

- Reductions in motions to revoke probation averted close to $400,000 in local jail costs in one year (based on costs of $24 per day per person).

- The one-year rearrest rate for probationers fell by 17 percent compared with that of similar probationers before the departmental overhaul.

- Rearrest rates for low-risk offenders declined by 77 percent.

Source: Tony Fabelo, Geraldine Nagy, and Seth Prins, *A Ten-Step Guide to Transforming Probation Departments to Reduce Recidivism* (New York: Council of State Governments Justice Center, 2011).

3. Conduct a risk–needs assessment to identify the level of supervision and the services probationers need.

4. Support crime victims by collecting information that describes the losses, suffering, and trauma experienced by a crime victim or by the victim's survivors. This information is reported to the court in a written document called the *victim-impact statement*. The judge considers it when sentencing the offender. The information is particularly valuable for sentences that include restitution.

5. Coordinate and promote the use of community resources. Probation officers refer offenders to community agencies and programs that serve the offenders' needs. Such programs include drug and alcohol treatment, job training, vocational education, anger management, and life skills training.

Not all probation agencies achieve these objectives in the same way. A probation department's orientation is a function of many things, including department philosophy, leadership, the community served, and the offenders supervised. Some departments lean more toward treating the offender; others lean more toward offender control. It is likely that the majority of probation departments do both, depending on the need and the situation. The American Probation and Parole Association (APPA) policy on probation is found in Exhibit 4–3.

Probation

Purpose

The purpose of probation is to assist in reducing the incidence and impact of crime by probationers in the community. The core services of probation are to provide investigation and reports to the court, to help develop appropriate court dispositions for adult offenders and juvenile delinquents, and to supervise those persons placed on probation. Probation departments in fulfilling their purpose may also provide a broad range of services including, but not limited to, crime and delinquency prevention, victim restitution programs and intern/volunteer programs.

Position

The mission of probation is to protect the public interest and safety by reducing the incidence and impact of crime by probationers. This role is accomplished by:

- assisting the courts in decision making through the probation report and in the enforcement of court orders;
- providing services and programs that afford opportunities for offenders to become more law-abiding;
- providing and cooperating in programs and activities for the prevention of crime and delinquency;
- furthering the administration of fair and individualized justice.

Probation is premised upon the following beliefs:

Society has a right to be protected from persons who cause its members harm, regardless of the reasons for such harm. It is the right of every citizen to be free from fear of harm to person and property. Belief in the necessity of law to an orderly society demands commitment to support it. Probation accepts this responsibility and views itself as an instrument for both control and treatment appropriate to some, but not all offenders. The wise use of authority derived from law adds strength and stability to its efforts.

Offenders have rights deserving of protection. Freedom and democracy require fair and individualized due process of law in adjudicating and sentencing the offender.

Victims of crime have rights deserving of protection. In its humanitarian tradition, probation recognizes that prosecution of the offender is but a part of the responsibility of the criminal justice system. The victim of criminal activity may suffer loss of property, emotional problems, or physical disability. Probation thus commits itself to advocacy for the needs and interests of crime victims.

Human beings are capable of change. Belief in the individual's capability for behavioral change leads probation practitioners to a commitment to the reintegration of the offender into the community. The possibility for constructive change of behavior is based on the recognition and acceptance of the principal of individual responsibility. Much of probation practice focuses on identifying and making available those services and programs that will best afford offenders an opportunity to become responsible, law-abiding citizens.

Not all offenders have the same capacity or willingness to benefit from measures designed to produce law-abiding citizens. Probation practitioners recognize the variations among individuals. The present offense, the degree of risk to the community and the potential for change can be assessed only in the context of the offender's individual history and experience.

Intervention in an offender's life should be the minimal amount needed to protect society and promote law-abiding behavior. Probation subscribes to the principle of intervening in an offender's life only to the extent necessary. Where further intervention appears unwarranted, criminal justice system involvement should be terminated. Where needed intervention can best be provided by an agency outside the system, the offender should be diverted from the system to that agency.

Punishment. Probation philosophy does not accept the concept of retributive punishment. Punishment as a corrective measure is supported and used in those instances in which it is felt that aversive measures may positively alter the offender's behavior when other measures may not. Even corrective punishment, however, should be used cautiously and judiciously in view of its highly unpredictable impact. It can be recognized that a conditional sentence in the community is, in and of itself, a punishment. It is less harsh and drastic than a prison term but more controlling and punitive than release without supervision.

Incarceration may be destructive and should be imposed only when necessary. Probation practitioners acknowledge society's right to protect itself and support the incarceration of offenders whose behavior constitutes a danger to the public through rejection of social or court mandates. Incarceration can also be an appropriate element of a probation program to emphasize the consequences of criminal behavior and thus effect constructive behavioral change. However, institutions should be humane and required to adhere to the highest standards.

Where public safety is not compromised, society and most offenders are best served through community correctional programs. Most offenders should be provided services within the community in which they are expected to demonstrate acceptable behavior. Community correctional programs generally are cost-effective and they allow offenders to remain with their families while paying taxes and, where applicable, restitution to victims.

Source: Reprinted with permission of American Probation and Parole Association.

Probation officer training and development are opportunities to learn new ideas and discuss cases within the context of the agency's goals. Most probation agencies share five goals. What are the goals of probation and what factors influence an agency's decision to emphasize one goal over another?

History of Probation

Probation in America developed during the 19th century. What started as a charitable and volunteer movement took almost 125 years to become available to adults in every state across the country.

Probation Begins in America   It was in the Boston courtroom of municipal court judge Peter Oxenbridge Thatcher, in 1830, that the groundwork for probation was laid. Searching for a new way to exercise leniency and to humanize the criminal law—sentencing goals that still dominate corrections—Judge Thatcher made the first recorded use of *release on recognizance* in America, in sentencing Jerusa Chase.

> The indictment against Jerusa Chase was found at the January term of the court. . . . She pleaded guilty to the same and would have been pronounced at that time, but upon the application of her friends, and with the consent of the attorney of the Commonwealth, she was permitted, upon her recognizance for her appearance in this Court whenever she should be called for, to go at large.[8]

Chase's release had many of the characteristics of present-day probation: suspension of sentence, freedom to stay in the community, conditions on that freedom, and the possibility of revocation of freedom for violation of the conditions.

In 1841, when 57-year-old John Augustus, a wealthy Boston shoemaker, became interested in the operation of the courts, the practice of probation began to emerge. Augustus was particularly sensitive to the problems of persons charged with violating Boston's vice or temperance laws. He was a member of the Washington Total Abstinence Society, an organization devoted to the promotion of temperance. By posting bail in selected cases, he had the offenders released to his care and supervision, and so began the work of the nation's first probation officer, an unpaid volunteer.

By the time of his death in 1859, Augustus had won probation for almost 2,000 adults and several thousand children. Several aspects of his

John Augustus (1785–1859) was a Boston shoemaker who invented probation in 1841 and became the first "unofficial" probation officer. He is called the founder of probation. Which aspects of Augustus's probation system are still in use today?

probation system are still in use. Augustus investigated the age, character, and work habits of each offender. He identified persons he thought redeemable and "whose hearts were not fully depraved, but gave promise of better things." He made probation recommendations to the court. He developed conditions of probation and helped offenders with employment, education, and housing. And he supervised offenders during their probation, which lasted, on the average, about 30 days.

Early Probation Statutes After Augustus's death in 1859, unpaid volunteers continued his work. In 1878, the Massachusetts legislature passed the first statute authorizing probation and provided for the first paid probation officer. The law applied only to Suffolk County (Boston). It required the mayor of Boston to appoint a probation officer from the police department or citizenry and required the probation officer to report to the chief of police; but this was changed three years later so that the probation officer then reported to the state commissioners of prisons.[9] In 1880, a new law authorized probation as an option in all cities and towns in Massachusetts. But because the law remained voluntary and the probation concept was still new, few cities and towns exercised the power. In 1891, the power to appoint probation officers was transferred from the mayor to the court in response to criticism that the mayor's appointments were influenced by political considerations. The second state to pass a probation statute was Vermont, in 1898.

As more and more states passed laws authorizing probation, it became a national institution. On March 4, 1925, President Calvin Coolidge signed the National Probation Act. The act authorized each federal district court to appoint one salaried probation officer with an annual income of $2,600.[10]

The early laws had little in common. Some allowed probation for adults only. Others allowed it for juveniles only. Some laws restricted the crimes for which probation could be granted. Still others provided for hiring probation officers but neglected to provide for paying them. Training for probation officers was brief or nonexistent. Appointments were often based on politics rather than merit, and salaries were typically even lower than those of unskilled laborers. By 1925, probation was available for juveniles in every state; by 1956, it was available for adults in every state.

Characteristics of Adults on Probation

CO4-7

During 2011, for the third consecutive year, the number of adults on probation declined. At 2011 yearend, 3,971,310 were on probation, down 2.0 percent, or almost 82,000 offenders from the beginning of the year. (see Exhibit 4–4).[11] The average length of probation is 37 months for those convicted of one felony to 43 months for those convicted of two or more felonies.[12]

Exhibit 4–5 shows that the majority of adults on probation are in regular caseloads, they have one face-to-face contact with their probation officers per month, and the cost of their supervision is $3.07 per day. By contrast, offenders who pose a higher risk of reoffending or who might otherwise be incarcerated are placed in intensive supervision caseloads. Each caseload averages 29 offenders with 7 face-to-face contacts with their probation officers per month, and costing approximately $8.96 per day. Without probation, the cost of jail incarceration averages $50 to $60 per day, and the cost of prison incarceration averages $60 to $75 per day. Probation is cost-effective providing it can protect the community by matching the level of supervision with the level of risk an offender poses.

EXHIBIT 4–4 **Adults on Probation at Yearend, 1980–2011**

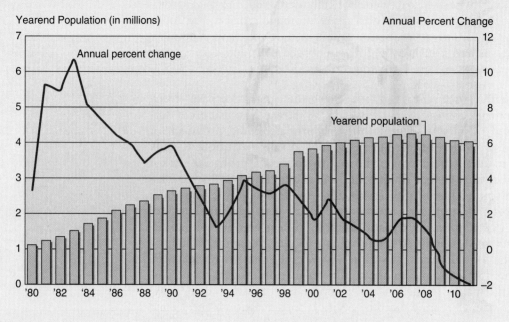

Source: Bureau of Justice Statistics, Annual Probation Survey, 1980–2011.

EXHIBIT 4–5 | **Probation Statistics**

Case Type [1]	Average Caseload per Officer	Average Number of Face-to-Face Contacts Between Probationer and Officer per Month	Average Cost per Day per Probationer
Regular	139	1	$3.07
Intensive	29	7	8.97
Electronic	6	3	8.71
Special	45	4	4.27

[1] **Regular supervision:** Supervision of a probationer according to normal/average number of visits, contacts, or reports with a probation officer. **Intensive supervision:** Supervision of a probationer that includes a greater number of visits, contacts, or reports to or from a probation officer than exists under regular supervision. Offenders who pose a higher risk of reoffending or who might otherwise be incarcerated are candidates for placement under intensive supervision. **Electronic supervision:** Supervision of a probationer that includes the use of an electronic monitoring device such as an ankle bracelet, pager, or voice verification telephone that assists probation officers in ascertaining an offender's whereabouts. **Special supervision:** Supervision of a probationer that includes special programming such as boot camp, substance abuse treatment programs, sex offender treatment, or other programs or services. More about intensive, electronic, and special supervision programming is discussed in Chapter 5.

Source: Adapted from Camille Graham Camp and George W. Camp, *The Corrections Yearbook, 2000,* pp. 170, 172, 176, 177, and 187. Copyright © 2000 Criminal Justice Institute; and Pew Center on the States, *One in 31: The Long Reach of American Corrections* (New York: Pew Charitable Trusts, March 2009).

Exhibit 4–6 presents selected characteristics of the 3.9 million adults on probation at yearend 2011. Most characteristics of adult probationers in 2011 remained stable when compared to those in 2010. Males made up three-quarters (75 percent) of the adult probation population. Over half (54 percent) of probationers were white non-Hispanic, and nearly one-third (31 percent) was black non-Hispanic. Nearly three-quarters (72 percent) were on active status, and about 1 in 5 (18 percent) were being supervised for a violent offense. Fifty-three percent of probationers were being supervised for a felony offense in 2011 compared to 50 percent in 2010.

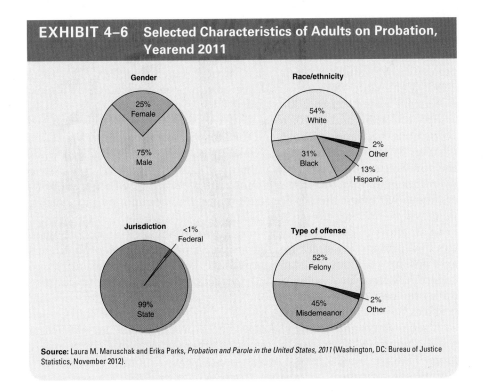

EXHIBIT 4–6 Selected Characteristics of Adults on Probation, Yearend 2011

Gender
- 25% Female
- 75% Male

Race/ethnicity
- 54% White
- 31% Black
- 13% Hispanic
- 2% Other

Jurisdiction
- <1% Federal
- 99% State

Type of offense
- 52% Felony
- 45% Misdemeanor
- 2% Other

Source: Laura M. Maruschak and Erika Parks, *Probation and Parole in the United States, 2011* (Washington, DC: Bureau of Justice Statistics, November 2012).

Recently, researchers at the Department of Justice (DOJ) learned from hour-long interviews with active probationers that 9 percent of male probationers and 28 percent of female probationers had been physically or sexually abused before their sentence and before age 18.[13] (Prevalence estimates of child abuse in the general population are 5 to 8 percent for males and 12 to 17 percent for females.) Abused probationers told DOJ researchers that the abuser was either a family member or someone they knew intimately. Researchers are just beginning to study the link between child abuse and offending.

At 2011 yearend, 1,662 adults were on probation for every 100,000 persons age 18 and older in the United States, down from 1,715 per 100,000 at yearend 2010. Among the states with declining probation populations, California, Florida, Georgia, Michigan, and Texas accounted for 56 percent of the total decrease. California (down 28,600) alone accounted for one-quarter of the total decline. The largest adult probation populations are in Georgia (457,141) and Texas (408,472). The smallest adult probation populations are in New Hampshire (4,121) and North Dakota (4,516). Only 22,668 persons were on federal probation at yearend 2011.

The three states that use probation the most are Georgia (6,205 per 100,000 adult population), Idaho (3,436), and Rhode Island (2,939). The three states that use probation least are New Hampshire (396 per 100,000 adult population), Nevada (563), and West Virginia (583).

Who Administers Probation?

CO4-8

As probation spread throughout the United States in the late 19th and early 20th centuries, its organization and administration depended on local and state customs and politics. Currently, probation in the 50 states is administered by more than 2,000 separate agencies, reflecting the decentralized and fragmented character of contemporary corrections. The agencies have a great deal of common ground, but because they developed

Visit https://modocfees.com/if-static/faq.shtml or scan this code with the QR app on your smartphone or digital device and read about probation intervention fees on the home page of the Missouri Department of Corrections Division of Probation and Parole website. How does this information relate to ideas discussed in this chapter?

in different contexts, they also have a lot of differences in goals, policies, funding, staffing, salaries, budgets, and operation.

In 2000, the average budget for probation agencies across the United States was $56 million, an increase of only 1 percent ($600,000) from 1992. Meanwhile, the number of persons on probation increased almost 37 percent from 1992 to 2000, from 2.8 to 3.8 million.

Between 1982 and 2010, total state expenditures for noninstitutional corrections (probation, parole, and the intermediate sanctions discussed in Chapter 5) increased from approximately $5 billion to $10 billion while the noninstitutional corrections population increased from $1.3 billion to over $3.9 billion, an increase of almost *200 percent*.[14] Probation supporters argue that unless there is adequate funding for community supervision, there will be no reduction in recidivism.

In an effort to offset declining budgets for probation and parole agencies and provide resources for the increased population of probationers and parolees, all but 12 states now have laws allowing authorities to collect fees from probationers and parolees who can afford to contribute to the cost of their supervision.[15] Missouri charges probationers and parolees $60 a month. In Colorado, it's $50 a month. Some states, such as Rhode Island and South Dakota, charge probationers and parolees a token amount ($15 per month), whereas other states charge considerably more. Hawaii charges felony probationers $150 a month. New Mexico law allows probation authorities to collect up to $185 a month from felony probationers. Iowa charges probationers and parolees a one-time enrollment fee of $250. Michigan imposes a fee on a sliding scale of up to 5 percent of monthly income, not to exceed a monthly total fee of $135.

Most states waive or reduce fees for probationers and parolees who are indigent. In Florida, for example, an offender who qualifies for the services of a public defender at trial is presumed to be low income and will be required to pay a fee of $50 a month, which is less than half the amount charged for others on regular probation. In Pennsylvania, offenders who have poverty-level income, are students, or are collecting welfare are entitled to a reduction or a waiver of a $25 monthly supervision fee imposed on those who can afford to pay.

Probation is commonly considered a part of the correctional system, although it is technically a function of the court system. Exhibit 4–7 gives a state-by-state breakdown of how probation is administered.[16]

Kathy Waters, past president of the American Probation and Parole Association, has worked in both executive and judicial branches of government that have the jurisdiction and responsibility for probation. She says there's nothing magical about where probation services are organized and administered.[17]

> There are difficulties in both jurisdictions. . . . Probation and parole continue to change as each matures. . . . Whether under the executive branch of government (which, for some jurisdictions, works well) or under the judiciary (which seems like the only natural place for probation to be in some states), the system will have problems and frustrations that will need to be addressed. . . . Both branches provide leadership, policy establishment and the resources to fulfill their mission.

Privatizing Probation   There is also movement toward privatization in community corrections, including offender assessment, drug testing and treatment, electronic monitoring, halfway house management, and probation field services. There is no census on the number of persons who are under private community supervision. However, a number of states,

EXHIBIT 4–7   **Administration of Adult Probation in the United States**

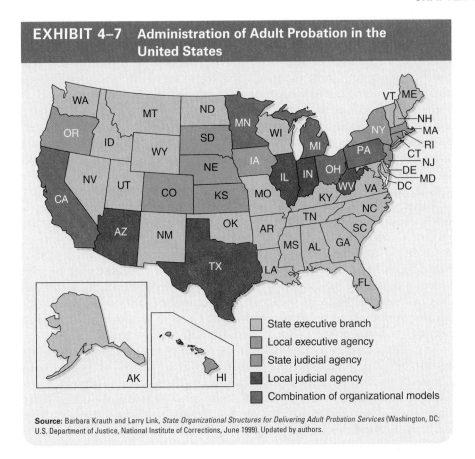

- State executive branch
- Local executive agency
- State judicial agency
- Local judicial agency
- Combination of organizational models

Source: Barbara Krauth and Larry Link, *State Organizational Structures for Delivering Adult Probation Services* (Washington, DC: U.S. Department of Justice, National Institute of Corrections, June 1999). Updated by authors.

including Alabama, Connecticut, Colorado, Georgia, Missouri, Tennessee, and Utah, have privatized community supervision. In most states, the impetus for privatizing community supervision was similar: Staffing and resources were not keeping pace with increasing caseloads. Community supervision officials believed they had exhausted the use of interns and volunteers, and obtaining funding for new staff was not possible. States partnered with the private sector to monitor the low-risk offender population, a group who generally has few needs, whose past records reflect little or no violence, and who successfully completes probation about 90 percent of the time.

However, the debate over privatizing community supervision has its critics. Consider the situation in Georgia. In 2003, Georgia passed SB 474 that transferred supervision of 25,000 convicted misdemeanants from the state Department of Corrections to individual counties and permitted each county to contract with a for-profit probation agency to supervise these misdemeanants. Today, approximately 40 private probation agencies are registered in Georgia; they employ 850 probation officers and serve 640 courts. In Georgia, every person who cannot pay his or her misdemeanor fine on the day of court is placed on probation under the supervision of a private, for-profit

A probation officer involves an offender's family to help with rehabilitation. Probation officers also refer offenders to community agencies to help them overcome the problem that led to their offending behavior. What obstacles might a probation officer face in making referrals to a community agency and involving the family in offender rehabilitation?

company until he or she pays the fine. For example, assume you are ordered to pay $200 for a traffic fine. If you have enough money to pay it on the day you go to court, you can avoid probation. If you cannot, you must pay your fine and a monthly supervision fee in the range of $35–$44 to a private company in weekly or biweekly installments over a period of three months to a year. By the time your probation is over, you may have paid more than two or three times the amount that the judge had ordered. In Americus, Georgia, one high school student convicted of violating the terms of his learner's permit served seven months on probation and paid $505 in court fines and probation fees. Had he been able to pay the fine the day he was sentenced, he would have paid only $155.

Critics argue that for-profit probation is unfair to poor people, needlessly supervises persons who are not a threat to society, and carries the risk of unnecessary incarceration because persons on probation can be arrested for technical violations such as missing a meeting with a probation officer. How often all this happens is unknown because in 2006, the Georgia Assembly passed a law that permits for-profit probation companies to keep their records secret. In the summer of 2008, a reporter with *Mother Jones* visited the offices of Middle Georgia Community Probation Services and was politely told, "We don't talk to reporters."[18]

In Alabama, the situation is similar. A county judge told Judicial Correction Services (JCS), a private probation company based in Atlanta with contracts with more than 180 court systems throughout Alabama, Florida, Georgia, and Mississippi that inability to pay a fine is not a legitimate basis for jail and ordered that everyone be given 30 days to pay a fine without further fines or fees imposed by JCS.[19] The judge issued a scathing opinion against JCS calling the system a "debtor's prison" and a "judicially sanctioned extortion racket."

CO4-9 Does Probation Work?

The most common question asked about probation is, "Does it work?" In other words, do persons granted probation refrain from further crime? **Recidivism**—generally defined as *rearrest*—continues to be the primary outcome measure for probation, as it is for all corrections programs. However, probation is a collection of strategies, some control oriented, some treatment oriented. How these different strategies are measured answers the question "Does probation work?"

recidivism

The repetition of criminal behavior; generally defined as *rearrest*. It is the primary outcome measure for probation as it is for all corrections programs.

Today, the push for evidence-based corrections highlights the importance of using scientific research to study correctional policy. Although the body of scientific evidence to make informed decisions about whether probation strategies reduce criminal activity is not large, we know from sophisticated evaluations in Florida, Maryland, and Washington that control-focused strategies (for example, intensive supervision and remote location monitoring) alone do not reduce criminal activity. However, when control-focused strategies are combined with treatment strategies, there is scientific evidence that probation achieves, on average, a statistically significant 8 to 22 percent reduction in the recidivism rates of program participants compared with a treatment-as-usual group.[20] Still others suggest that if probation agencies adhere to the seven principles of effective rehabilitation—(1) target criminogenic needs; (2) provide intensive services to high-risk rather than low-risk offenders; (3) match styles of service delivery to offender responsivity; (4) adhere to the principles of social and behavioral learning; (5) emphasize positive reinforcers rather than negative ones; (6) develop offender coping skills; and (7) employ staff supportive of offender rehabilitation—criminal activity can be reduced by as much as 50 percent.[21]

Michael Constantakos

U.S. Probation Officer, U.S. District Court,
Northern District of Florida, Pensacola Florida

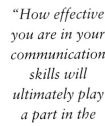

Michael Constantakos is a U.S. probation officer for the U.S. District Courts, Northern District of Florida, Pensacola Division. He is only one of three probation officers dedicated to this investigative unit in the Pensacola Division. In the course of one year, Constantakos averages writing over 40 presentence reports. He has been employed with the U.S. Probation Office for 14 years, 13 of which have been dedicated to the presentence unit. Prior to this assignment, Constantakos was a U.S. Pretrial Services Officer whose duties included writing pretrial bond reports and supervising pretrial defendants. He received his bachelor's of science degree from the College of Architecture, Urban and Public Affairs at Florida Atlantic University. After he received his degree, Constantakos was hired by the Florida Department of Corrections as a probation and parole officer. He served in this capacity for nine years. While employed by the state of Florida, Constantakos furthered his education and received a master of arts degree in public administration at Florida Atlantic University.

Constantakos attributes his love of reading and writing to leading him to his current position as a presentence writer. He notes that this position requires copious hours of reading offense reports as well as current case law regarding sentencing trends. Constantakos added there are also many hours writing "a short story about the defendant's life." As a presentence writer, he must interview the defendant's family members, record the defendant's prior criminal history, and obtain reports concerning the defendant's educational, mental, and/or substance abuse treatment. The position requires the officer to digest the material, condense it, and provide feedback to the court for a fair and just sentence. This is not so easy to do under statutorily imposed deadlines. Constantakos reported, "In some cases, law enforcement has been investigating the suspects for years and we have only 30 days to put all this information together."

Constantakos' desire is to ensure that every defendant sentenced in the federal court system is treated fairly. However, he asserts that "fairly" does not just mean the same sentence for the same crime. The sentence must also take into consideration the defendant's past, present, and possible future behavior. It is this desire that makes him work hard every day to obtain the most information possible about a defendant within the time constraint imposed by federal statute. He strongly believes the more information he obtains about the defendant, the more informed the court will be in rendering a fair and just sentence.

Constantakos advises anyone who seeks a career as a federal probation officer, specifically in the investigative field writing presentence reports, to "fine tune and build on" her or his verbal and written communication skills. The officer is required to communicate with a variety of people, including law enforcement officers, prosecutors, defense attorneys, and judges. "How effective you are in your communication skills will ultimately play a part in the outcome of the case."

> *"How effective you are in your communication skills will ultimately play a part in the outcome of the case."*

We also know that recidivism rates vary from place to place, depending on the seriousness of offenses, population characteristics, average length of probation, and the amount and quality of intervention, surveillance, and enforcement. James Gondles Jr., executive director of the American Correctional Association, argues that, by the time offenders reach probation, other institutions of social control have failed. If the offending behavior could have been controlled, families, neighborhoods, schools, and other social institutions would have controlled it. Offending behavior is not easy to correct and for that reason, Gondles believes that probation systems across the United States need help.

> [Probation officers] are often held accountable for the failures of other elements of the criminal justice community. Therefore, all of us in corrections must help them by doing our own jobs better, to escape the perception that they are ineffective. We must work together to ensure that all elements of the criminal justice system receive adequate funding and that all elements of the criminal justice system work closer together to provide offenders with the services they require.[22]

The APPA, representing U.S. probation officers nationwide, argues that recidivism rates measure just one probation task while ignoring others. The APPA has urged its member agencies to collect data on other outcomes, such as the following:

- amount of restitution collected;
- number of offenders employed;
- amounts of fines and fees collected;
- hours of community service performed;
- number of treatment sessions attended;
- percentage of financial obligations collected;
- rate of enrollment in school;
- number of days of employment;
- educational attainment; and
- number of days drug free.

Advocates of measures other than recidivism tell us that probation should be measured by what offenders do while they are in probation programs, not by what they do after they leave.

CO4-10   WHAT PROBATION OFFICERS DO

Probation officers have two important roles: case investigation and client supervision. Before we explain those roles, let us discuss the danger and stress of probation work.

Probation and parole officer work can be dangerous. In fact, a survey of probation officers in four states found that 39 to 55 percent have been victims of work-related violence or threats. Research in three other states indicated that officers who reported violent and sexual recidivism on their caseload, offender suicide, and threats and/or assaults in the line of duty scored significantly higher on measures of traumatic stress and burnout compared to officers who did not have these experiences.[23] This may explain why 35 states allow probation officers to carry firearms. In North Carolina, for example, all probation officers carry .40-caliber handguns.[24]

However, the physical dangers of the job are not the major sources of a probation officer's stress. It's high caseloads, paperwork overload, and deadline pressure. As reported later in this chapter, the average caseload of a probation officer is very high—139 cases—and computers haven't necessarily reduced the stress. In fact, even with computerized management information systems, officers still deal with hardware and software problems. And the problem with deadlines is that many of them are unexpected and cannot be controlled.

National Institute of Justice (NIJ) researchers found that when they asked probation and parole officers how they deal with stress in a positive way, more officers cited physical exercise than any other technique. Other positive ways include discussing cases with other officers, seeking support through religion, "venting," education, training and stress management programs, and talking to a family member.

On the negative side, many officers reported dealing with stress by taking extra sick days, requesting transfers, or applying for early retirement.

In addition to dealing with stress, building a relationship with the offender and developing rapport are also important. Scholars and practitioners tell us that probation officers must be aware of the cultural differences between themselves and their probationers and understand that diversity if they are to build rapport and help change offending behavior. Recall from our earlier discussion that the majority of probationers are male and almost half are members of minority groups. Slightly more than half of the probation officers are female, and three-fourths of all POs are white. The demographic differences between POs and probationers raise questions on how probation officers can build rapport across gender, race, and ethnicity. Without rapport, experts believe there is more likelihood that probationers will miss scheduled appointments, not follow through on referrals, violate the conditions of probation, reoffend, and end up back in the system. Experts suggest five strategies to build rapport between the probationer and probation officer.[25]

Visit http://media.csosa.gov/video/ dcps15movie.wmv or scan this code with the QR app on your smartphone or digital device and watch the podcast of two Washington, D.C. supervision officers discuss the challenges and rewards of being a community supervision officer. How does this information relate to ideas discussed in this chapter?

1. Sincerity is one thing that allows probationers to forgive probation officers who violate a cultural norm such as saying the wrong thing.

2. High service energy sends a message to probationers that the probation officer is in their corner. The probationers may think that less service energy has something to do with ethnic differences.

3. Knowledge of the probationers' culture increases empathy in the cross-cultural counseling relationship. For example, if the probationer speaks English as a second language, it would be helpful in building rapport for the officer to learn key words and phrases in the probationer's native language.

4. A nonjudgmental attitude increases the officer's credibility.

5. Helping probationers with needed resources facilitates rapport building and officer credibility. The United States Probation and Pretrial Services Charter for Excellence (similar to a code of ethics) shown in the accompanying Ethics and Professionalism box reinforces these rapport-building strategies.

Case Investigation

Case investigation includes the preparation of a *presentence report (PSR)*, which the judge uses in sentencing an offender. The PSR is prepared by the probation department of a court; it provides a social and personal history as well as an evaluation of a defendant as an aid to the court in determining a sentence. In some states, for example, Missouri, the report is called a *sentence assessment report*.[26] As the centerpiece of Missouri's sentencing guidelines, it sets forth the recommended sentence options and the appropriate correctional resources available both in the community and in prison.

case investigation

The first major role of probation officers, consisting of interviewing the defendant and preparing the presentence report (PSR).

Purposes of the Presentence Report
The PSR has two main purposes. First, and most important, the PSR assists the court in reaching a fair sentencing decision. The specific content areas of the PSR vary from jurisdiction to jurisdiction, but common areas include

A probation officer interviews a defendant in preparation of the presentence report (PSR). Case investigation is the first major role of a probation officer. The PSR provides a social and personal history as well as an evaluation of the defendant as an aid to the court in determining a sentence. What questions should a probation officer ask the defendant?

(1) information regarding the current offense; (2) the offender's past adult and juvenile criminal record; (3) family history and background; and (4) personal data about education, health, employment, and substance abuse history. In addition, some state statutes dictate content areas such as victim-impact statements. It is not uncommon for jurisdictions to include a sentencing recommendation in the PSR. However, sentencing reforms are limiting judicial sentencing discretion, so the PSR recommendation is much less important than it once was.

The second purpose of the PSR is to outline a treatment plan for the offender. During the investigation, in addition to determining the degree of risk the offender poses to the community, the probation officer identifies treatment needs so that the offender can receive appropriate services (counseling, treatment, education, community service, restitution, employment, and some form of supervision) during probation or in jail or prison.

In most cases, the court orders the PSR after conviction but before sentencing. The defendant reports to the probation department if released on bond pending sentencing. Otherwise, the probation officer visits the defendant in jail.

Creating a Presentence Report   The PSR starts with an interview between the PO and the defendant. The interview follows a structured format for obtaining information on the offense and the offender.

In the PSR, the PO estimates the offender's degree of risk to the community and need factors (sociological, psychological, and economic) that impact criminal behavior. They administer a comprehensive risk and needs assessment that differentiates between the high-risk offenders, who need multiple face-to-face contacts, drug tests, and other surveillance checks each week, and the low- or reduced-risk offenders who require minimal surveillance to be successful.

The PO summarizes the information gathered and, in most jurisdictions, makes a sentence recommendation. If the sentence recommended is

Ethics and Professionalism

United States Probation and Pretrial Services

Charter for Excellence.

We, the members of Probation and Pretrial Services of the United States Courts, are a national system with shared professional identity, goals, and values. We facilitate the fair administration of justice and provide continuity of services throughout the judicial process. We are outcome driven and strive to make our communities safer and to make a positive difference in the lives of those we serve. We achieve success through interdependence, collaboration, and local innovation. We are committed to excellence as a system and to the principles embodied in this Charter.

We are a unique *profession.*

Our profession is distinguished by the unique combination of:

A multidimensional knowledge base in law and human behavior;

A mix of skills in investigation, communication, and analysis;

A capacity to provide services and interventions from pretrial release through post-conviction supervision;

A position of impartiality within the criminal justice system; and

A responsibility to positively impact the community and the lives of victims, defendants, and offenders.

These *goals* matter most.

Our system strives to achieve the organizational goals of:

Upholding the constitutional principles of the presumption of innocence and the right against excessive bail for pretrial defendants by appropriately balancing community safety and risk of nonappearance with protection of individual liberties;

Providing objective investigations and reports with verified information and recommendations to assist

the court in making fair pretrial release, sentencing, and supervision decisions;

Ensuring defendant and offender compliance with court-ordered conditions through community-based supervision and partnerships;

Protecting the community through the use of controlling and correctional strategies designed to assess and manage risk;

Facilitating long-term, positive changes in defendants and offenders through proactive interventions; and

Promoting fair, impartial, and just treatment of defendants and offenders throughout all phases of the system.

We stand by these *values.*

Our values are mission-critical:

Act with integrity.

Demonstrate commitment to and passion for our mission.

Be effective stewards of public resources.

Treat everyone with dignity and respect.

Promote fairness in process and excellence in service to the courts and the community.

Work together to foster a collegial environment.

Be responsible and accountable.

Ethical Dilemma 4–1: Does gender or celebrity status play a role in who gets probation? For more information, go to Ethical Dilemma 4–1 at www.justicestudies.com/ethics07.

Ethical Dilemma 4–2: Should probation officers be advocates for sentencing reform? Why or why not? What are the issues? For more information, go to Ethical Dilemma 4–2 at www.justicestudies.com/ethics07.

Ethical Dilemmas for every chapter are available online.

incarceration, in most jurisdictions the length must be within guidelines set by statute (see Chapter 3). However, if the sentence recommended is probation or some other intermediate sanction (see Chapter 5), few jurisdictions have guidelines for sentence length. Only recently have some states (e.g., Delaware, Minnesota, North Carolina, and Pennsylvania) begun to design sentencing guidelines for nonprison sentences such as probation. Copies of the PSR are filed with the court and made available to the judge, the prosecutor, and the defense attorney. Exhibit 4–8 is an example of a short-form federal PSR. Space does not allow us to include everything.

EXHIBIT 4–8	**Sample Presentence Report**

IN THE UNITED STATES DISTRICT COURT
FOR THE NORTHERN DISTRICT OF ALABAMA

UNITED STATES OF AMERICA)

v.) PRESENTENCE
) REPORT
)
EDDIE PALMER)

Docket No. CR 09-H-248-S

Prepared For:	Honorable Casandra Phillips
	U.S. District Judge

Prepared By:	Noelle Koval
	U.S. Probation Officer
	Birmingham, AL
	(205)555-0923

Offense: Count One: Possession With Intent to Distribute a Schedule II Controlled Substance (Cocaine Base), not less than 10 Years and not more than Life and/or $4,000,000 Fine. With Enhancement, Mandatory Life and/or $8,000,000 Fine.

Release Status: Released on $25,000 unsecured bond on 8/26/12
Remanded to custody on 12/14/12

Identifying Data
Date of Birth: 1/9/78
Age: 35
Race: B
Sex: M

Charge(s) and Conviction(s)

Eddie Palmer was indicted on two counts by the September 2012 Grand Jury for the Northern District of Alabama. Count One charged that on June 12, 2012, the defendant unlawfully possessed with intent to distribute approximately 500 grams of a mixture or substance containing a detectable amount of cocaine, Schedule II controlled substances, in violation of 21 USC § 841(a)(1). Count Two charged that on June 12, 2012, the defendant carried a firearm during the commission of a drug trafficking crime in violation of 18 USC § 924(c)(1). The October 2012 Grand Jury returned a superseding indictment in which the defendant was charged in two counts. Count One charges that on June 12, 2012, the defendant intentionally possessed with intent to distribute approximately 100 grams of a mixture or substance containing a detectable amount of cocaine base and approximately 240 grains of a mixture or substance containing a detectable amount of cocaine, Schedule II controlled substances, in violation of 21 USC § 841(a)(1). Count Two charges that on June 12, 2012, the defendant carried a firearm during the commission of a drug trafficking crime in violation of 18 USC § 924(c)(1). On December 14, 2012, Palmer pled guilty to Count One, and Count Two was dismissed on motion of the government. Sentencing was continued generally to a later date.

Not shown here is the officer's summary of the defendant's pretrial adjustment, substance abuse history, education and vocational skills, employment record, financial condition, and necessary monthly living expenses.

Disclosure of Presentence Reports One of the most important questions about the PSR is whether the defendant has a constitutional right to see it and challenge the statements contained in it. Some judges and probation officers oppose disclosure for several reasons. First, they fear that persons having knowledge about the offender will refuse to give information if the defendant knows they have given information about him or her. Second, they believe that, if the defendant challenges information in the PSR, court proceedings may be unduly delayed. Third,

| **EXHIBIT 4–8** | **Sample Presentence Report** *(continued)* |

SENTENCING RECOMMENDATION

UNITED STATES DISTRICT COURT

FOR THE NORTHERN DISTRICT OF ALABAMA

UNITED STATES V. EDDIE PALMER   DOCKET NO. CR 09-H-248-S

TOTAL OFFENSE LEVEL: 29

CRIMINAL HISTORY CATEGORY: III

	Statutory Provision	Guideline Provisions	Recommended Sentence
CUSTODY:	Mandatory Life	Mandatory Life	Life
PROBATION:	N/A	N/A	N/A
SUPERVISED RELEASE:	Not Less Than 10 Years	10 Years	10 Years
FINE:	$8,000,000	$15,000 to $8,000,000	$15,000
RESTITUTION:	N/A	N/A	N/A

Justification

The sentence of life is mandatory. Supervised release must be ten years. A $15,000 fine is recommended because it is incumbent upon the defendant to demonstrate that he does not have the financial ability to pay a fine. He and his attorney have not cooperated in providing information, and it appears that he does have the ability to pay the minimum fine based on his purported monthly income from trafficking in illegal drugs.

Voluntary Surrender

The defendant is in custody.

Respectfully submitted,

Noelle Koval

Noelle Koval

U.S. Probation Officer

---

opponents believe that to give the defendant some kinds of information, such as psychological reports, might be harmful to that defendant. And fourth, they argue the PSR is a private and confidential court document.

On the other hand, advocates of disclosure argue that fundamental fairness and due process demand that convicted persons should have access to the information in the PSR on which their sentence is based so they can correct inaccuracies. However, the U.S. Supreme Court has held, in *Williams* v. *Oklahoma* (1959), that unless disclosure is required by state law or court decisions, there is no denial of due process of law when a court considers a PSR without disclosing its contents to the defendant or giving the defendant an opportunity to rebut it.

The trend today is toward limited disclosure of information to the defendant's attorney. The American Bar Association favors disclosure of the factual contents and conclusions of the PSR (not the sources of confidential information) and the defendant's opportunity to rebut them.[27] Federal courts require that the PSR be disclosed to the defendant, his or her counsel, and to the attorney for the government, except in three instances: when disclosure might disrupt rehabilitation of the defendant, when information disclosed in the PSR was obtained on the promise of confidentiality, and when disclosure might result in harm to the defendant or any other person.

The Offender Speaks
Visit www.mhhe.com/schmalleger7e
to see this feature.

Technology and Case Investigations Today, technological innovations are affecting where and how POs do their job. Software packages can generate PSRs from data from official records and interviews

Visit http://www.uscourts.gov/uscourts/
FederalCourts/PPS/Fedprob/2011-09/starr.
html or scan this code with the QR app on
your smartphone or digital device and read
how federal probation officers are using
core correctional skills to change offenders'
behavior and target dynamic risk factors.
How does this information relate to ideas
discussed in this chapter?

supervision

The second major role of probation officers,
consisting of resource mediation, surveillance, and enforcement.

entered by probation officers. The software programs can also calculate risk assessment scores. A PO can edit the report before submitting it to the court.

The trend toward telecommuting is also affecting probation officers' case investigations. Telecommuting (or teleworking) is usually defined as an employee working at home or other telework facility for at least one day a week during regularly scheduled business hours, supported by the necessary hardware and software. Some jurisdictions are finding that pre-sentence officers are successful telecommuters. The U.S. Probation Office in the Middle District of Florida found that presentence officers reported an increase in job satisfaction and a higher level of productivity. They reported to the office to interview defendants, meet with attorneys, attend court hearings, and perform other routine office duties. They spent the remainder of their time at their residences working on their investigations. The officers averaged 2.5 to 3.0 days a week telecommuting. Their work was transmitted electronically through a secure intranet mailing system. Telecommuting was not effective for supervision officers, however, who were needed in the probation office to handle the needs of their offenders and who had to travel in the field to meet their probationers.

Supervision

The second major role of probation officers is client supervision. Proba-tion **supervision** has three main elements: resource mediation, surveillance, and enforcement. *Resource mediation* means providing offenders access to a wide variety of services, such as job development, substance abuse treatment, counseling, and education. *Surveillance* means monitoring the activities of probationers through office meetings, home and work visits, drug and alcohol testing, and contact with family, friends, and employers. *Enforcement* means making probationers accountable for their behavior and making sure they understand the consequences of violating the con-ditions of probation. Client supervision that uses prosocial modeling and rein-forcement, problem solving and cogni-tive techniques are core skills for reducing recidivism in probation supervision.

Caseload The average PO in the United States supervises approximately 139 offenders.[28] Such large caseloads do not allow probation officers time for ade-quate resource mediation, surveillance, or enforcement. A number of jurisdictions are experimenting with Probation Automated Management (PAM). The PAM kiosk is similar to an ATM and allows low-risk probationers to report in 24 hours a day, seven days a week, with their fingerprints as biometric identifiers. The fingerprints are compared to the ones collected when the offender first began probation. Some kiosks also take a digital face photo.

Olmsted County (Rochester, Minnesota) probation officer Bernie Sizer (right), tests Kevin
Rood for alcohol during a visit to Rood's apartment. Case supervision is the second major
role of a probation officer. What are the three
main elements of case supervision?

Once a match is established, the offender can interact with the kiosk by pressing buttons on the touch screen. Data are entered to verify address and employment status and to respond to questions asked by the probation officer. Advocates of probation kiosks argue that they save scarce jail beds for those offenders posing a serious risk to the community and that probation officers can devote more of their face-to-face time with serious offenders. Most departments that use probation kiosks still require the offender to report face-to-face, perhaps once a month.

What is the ideal caseload for probation and parole? The issue has been discussed for as long as there have been professionals in the field. Because probation and parole are pluralistic, highly decentralized, and engaged in by hundreds of departments at the federal, state, county, and municipal levels across the United States, in the early 1990s the APPA adopted the position that a workload model that focused on the amount of time that is required to supervise a particular case up to standards was a sounder, more defensible method of determining the number of staff to supervise an agency's caseload. Yet legislators and policymakers continued to ask, "What is the ideal caseload size?"

Recognizing the need for straightforward caseload standards, in 2006 the APPA consulted experienced practitioners and researchers. It found that with the emergence in the 1990s of the body of research on correctional treatment effectiveness known as evidence-based practices, a robust set of effective strategies of correctional treatment could guide the development of caseload standards. The key is to use evidence-based practices. The APPA believes that "community corrections agencies need to stop wasting time on what does not work or what may even do 'harm' and focus their resources on what does work and does do 'good' in terms of public safety."[29]

Based on current best practices, APPA recommends that probation departments should:

1. Effectively assess probationers' criminogenic risks and needs, as well as assess their strengths;
2. Employ smart and tailored supervision strategies;
3. Use incentives and graduated sanctions to respond promptly to probationers' behaviors;
4. Implement performance-driven personnel management practices that promote and reward recidivism reduction.

The number of cases that can be supervised by a probation or parole officer based on the type of case and level of supervision is shown in

At the entrance to the Olmsted County jail in Rochester, Minnesota, first- and second-time offenders convicted of drunk driving are required to appear before the automated kiosk once a month and check in by handprint to answer questions about their progress. Probation kiosks are used to supervise low-risk offenders who do not require face-to-face contact with a probation officer. What advantages and disadvantages do you see in this approach?

EXHIBIT 4–9	Adult and Juvenile Caseload Standards

ADULT STANDARDS

Case Type	Cases-to-Staff Ratio
Intensive	20:1
Moderate to high risk	50:1
Low risk	200:1
Administrative	No limit? 1,000?

JUVENILE STANDARDS

Case Type	Cases-to-Staff Ratio
Intensive	15:1
Moderate to high risk	30:1
Low risk	100:1
Administrative	Not recommended

Source: American Probation and Parole Association, *Caseload Standards for Probation and Parole* (Lexington, KY: APPA, September, 2006). Reprinted with permission of Mr. William D. Burrell.

EXHIBIT 4–10 **State of Georgia General Conditions of Probation**

The court shall determine the terms and conditions of probation and may provide that the probationer shall:

1. avoid injurious and vicious habits;

2. avoid persons or places of disreputable or harmful character;

3. report to the probation supervisor as directed;

4. permit the supervisor to visit him at his home or elsewhere;

5. work faithfully at suitable employment insofar as may be possible;

6. remain within a specified location;

7. make reparation or restitution to any aggrieved person for the damage or loss caused by his offense, in an amount to be determined by the court. Unless otherwise provided by law, no reparation or restitution to any aggrieved person for the damage or loss caused by his offense shall be made if the amount is in dispute unless the same has been adjudicated;

8. make reparation or restitution as reimbursement to a municipality or county for the payment for medical care furnished the person while incarcerated pursuant to the provisions of Article 3 of Chapter 4 of this title. No reparation or restitution to a local governmental unit for the provision of medical care shall be made if the amount is in dispute unless the same has been adjudicated;

9. repay the costs incurred by any municipality or county for wrongful actions by an inmate covered under the provisions of paragraph (1) of subsection (a) of Code Section 42-4-71;

10. support his legal dependents to the best of his ability;

11. violate no local, state, or federal laws and be of general good behavior; and

12. if permitted to move or travel to another state, agree to waive extradition from any jurisdiction where he may be found and not contest any effort by any jurisdiction to return him to this state.

Source: Georgia Department of Corrections, Probation Division, General Conditions of Probation, Code Section 42-8-35.

Exhibit 4–9. APPA made the caseload size recommendations flexible by stating them in terms of cases-to-staff ratios so agencies that use a team approach can use the recommendations, and framed them as numbers not to be exceeded. Framing the recommendations helps reduce the chance that better staffed agencies will not be forced to allow caseloads to increase.

Regardless of their level of supervision, all probationers are subject to "general" conditions of supervision. These include reporting to a probation officer as directed, paying court-ordered monies, working, obeying all laws, and being "of general good behavior." Exhibit 4–10 presents, as an example, the general conditions for all probationers in Georgia. The court may also order "special conditions" that relate directly to the offender's particular crime or history. For example, a person convicted of cybercrime may be subject to the special conditions shown in Exhibit 4–11.

Technology and Supervision As in case investigation, there is a wide variety of technological tools to help POs in client supervision that only a few years ago did not exist. Computer programs can track fine and probation payments, alert POs when their clients are behind on payments, and help them track whether probationers have satisfied the conditions of their sentences. Kiosk reporting, secure remote alcohol detection, voice verification, facial recognition, and radio-frequency identification chips that are designed to fit under the skin and can be read in a manner similar to a bar code at the grocery store are electronic tools that have the potential to

EXHIBIT 4–11	**Specific Probation Conditions for Computer Crime**		

(A = Internet Access Permitted; B = Limited or 0 Access to Internet)	A	B
You shall consent to your probation officer and/or probation service representative conducting periodic unannounced examinations of your computer(s) equipment which may include retrieval and copying of all memory from hardware/software to ensure compliance with this condition and/or removal of such equipment for the purpose of conducting a more thorough inspection; and consent at the direction of your probation officer to having installed on your computer(s), at your expense, any hardware or software systems to monitor your computer use or prevent access to particular materials. You hereby consent to the periodic inspection of any such installed hardware or software to insure it is functioning properly.	X	X
You shall not possess encryption or steganography software.	X	X
You shall provide your probation officer accurate information about your entire computer system and software; all passwords used by you; and your Internet Service Provider(s).	X	X
You shall possess only computer hardware or software approved by your probation officer. You shall obtain written permission from your probation officer prior to obtaining any additional computer hardware or software or Internet Service Provider(s).	X	X
You shall refrain from using a computer in any manner that relates to the activity in which you were engaged in committing the instant offense or violation behavior, namely _____.	X	X
You shall provide truthful information concerning your identity in all Internet or E-Mail communications and not visit any "chat rooms" or similar Internet locations/sites where minors are known to frequent.	X	
You shall maintain a daily log of all addresses you access via any personal computer (or other computer used by you), other than for authorized employment, and make this log available to your probation officer.	X	
You shall not create or assist directly or indirectly in the creation of any electronic bulletin board, Internet Service Provider, or any other public or private network without the prior written consent of your probation officer. Any approval shall be subject to any conditions set by the U.S. Probation Office of the Court with respect to that approval.	X	X
You shall not possess or use a computer with access to any "on-line" computer service at any location (including employment or education) without prior written approval of the U.S. Probation Office of the Court. This includes any Internet Service Provider, bulletin board system, or any other public or private computer network. Any approval shall be subject to any conditions set by the U.S. Probation Office or the Court with respect to that approval.		X
You shall not purchase, possess, or receive a personal computer which utilizes a modem, and/or an external mode.		X
You will have an occupational condition that you can not be employed directly or indirectly where you are an installer, programmer, or "trouble shooter" for computer equipment.	X	X

Source: Arthur L. Bowker and Gregory B. Thompson, "Computer Crime in the 21st Century and Its Effects on the Probation Officer," *Federal Probation*, vol. 65, no. 2 (September 2001), p. 21.

enhance community supervision. Companies such as ProbationComm and POcheck are hosted web services that save money by hiring fewer officers and that help supervision officers handle more cases in less time, make reporting and payments easier for the offender, save time with a better and faster communication system (for example, e-mail and instant messaging), and focus resources on high and moderate risk offenders.

Another technological innovation, one of the more interesting strategies for managing the three elements of probation supervision, is mapping technology or geographic information systems (GIS). Mapping has helped law enforcement locate hot spots of crime. Police departments used to map with pins on a "point map." Today, mapping is done electronically and affords complex and instant analyses. Probation departments use mapping as a tool for the management of offenders in the community. Mapping helps ensure that probation and parole officers are dispersed in areas with high concentrations of offenders.

For example, the Wisconsin Department of Corrections found through mapping that "if you have an area with a drug usage problem, we would bring drug programming to that area. Really, our experience was we got better attendance and better completion rates with that."[30] The Center for Alternative Sentencing and Employment in New York uses mapping to monitor employment rates in areas where ex-offenders will reside and, with the assistance of community agencies, helps them find a job link upon leaving prison. Learn more about the role of technology in offender supervision, parole hearings, and victim notification in Chapters 5, 8, 11, 13, and 14.

CO4-11

Revocation of Probation

If the offender willfully violates the conditions of his or her probation, a **revocation hearing** is usually the next step. A revocation hearing is a due process hearing that must be conducted by the court or probation authority to determine whether the conditions of probation (or parole as we will see in Chapter 8) have been violated before probation can be revoked and the offender removed from the community. **Revocation** is the formal termination of an offender's conditional freedom.

Revocation is a serious matter for four reasons. First, the offender might lose his or her freedom to remain in the community. Second, the handling of probation violators by supervision agencies and courts consumes a significant portion of the court's time, energy, and resources. One jurisdiction estimated that, in addition to the equivalent of more than two full-time probation officers, the various stages of the probation violation process consume the equivalent of a full-time judge, prosecutor, and courtroom staff.[31] Third, the cost of keeping an offender under probation supervision is much lower than that required for care and treatment in prison or jail. For example, we saw in Exhibit 4–5 that the per day cost of probation ranges from $3.07 to $8.97, depending on the level of supervision and risk an offender poses, but it costs $50 to $60 per day to keep an offender in jail and $60 to $75 per day to keep an offender in prison. And fourth, imprisoning offenders who otherwise would have been placed on probation may force their families to go on welfare or make greater demands on community resources.

Still, revocation is the only way to protect the community from some offenders who refuse to abide by the conditions of probation. A group of

revocation hearing

A due process hearing that must be conducted to determine whether the conditions of probation have been violated before probation can be revoked and the offender removed from the community.

revocation

The formal termination of an offender's conditional freedom.

leading officials in the field of probation and parole, the Reinventing Probation Council, recently concluded that the reason probation has not been able to protect the public is lax enforcement of the probation rules. The council stresses, "All conditions of a probation sentence must be enforced. The response must be swift and sure."[32] Swift and sure is what we are now finding across the United States.

Recently a judge in Hawaii took a group of "high-risk" probationers, gave them "warning hearings," and told them that while the rules of probation were not changing, the old rules would now be strictly enforced.[33] Those who violate the conditions of probation would be arrested. Probationers who fail a morning drug test would be arrested immediately, appear in court within hours, and have the terms of their probation modified to include a short jail stay (usually over a weekend in order to promote ongoing employment). The judge also assured those who needed drug treatment, mental health therapy, or other social services that they would get the treatment they needed and were expected to attend and complete the program. Hawaii's program that requires random drug tests of probationers and, for those who fail, an immediate short stint (typically two days) in jail with no exceptions has been copied in Michigan, South Dakota, Texas, and Washington. All sites report the same results: drastic reductions in illicit-drug and/or alcohol use, reoffending, revocation, and time behind bars.[34] Hawaii's HOPE probationers are longtime criminally active drug users with an average of 17 prior arrests. According to an independent study funded by the National Institute of Justice, when compared to offenders on standard probation, offenders on HOPE Probation were 55 percent less likely to be arrested for a new crime, 72 percent less likely to use drugs, 61 percent less likely to skip appointments with their supervisory officers, and 53 percent less likely to have their probation revoked. That suggests to the researchers that more than mere deterrence is at work; HOPE clients seem to be gaining the ability to control their own behavior.

Violations That Trigger Revocation

Revocation is triggered in one of two ways. Either offenders willfully violate the *technical* conditions of their probation, or they commit *new offenses*.

A **technical violation** is failure to comply with conditions of probation. It is not a criminal act; most revocations are the result of technical violations. According to a report published by the National Institute of Corrections, the most likely reason for prison incarceration of probation (and parole) violators is a technical violation.[35] The most commonly committed technical violations are positive urinalysis, failure to participate in treatment, **absconding** (fleeing without permission of the jurisdiction in which the offender is required to stay), and failure to report to the probation officer. Most probation officers do not ask the court to revoke probation for an occasional technical violation. They understand that technical violations are supervision issues and best handled by program or treatment referrals. One analyst in the NIC report commented, "If our jails and prisons are filled with offenders who are merely noncompliant, there will be no room for the dangerous offender."[36] To ensure compliance, probation officers can tighten the offender's supervision with a reprimand, increase reporting requirements, limit travel or other privileges, increase drug/alcohol testing, make treatment/education referrals, restructure payments (for probationers who demonstrate an inability to pay in accordance with the court-established payment plan), or extend the terms of probation.

A **new offense violation** is the arrest and prosecution for the commission of a new crime. Depending upon the seriousness of the new offense,

technical violation

A failure to comply with the conditions of probation.

absconding

Fleeing without permission of the jurisdiction in which the offender is required to stay.

new offense violation

The arrest and prosecution for the commission of a new crime.

the court may, in response to a violation of probation (or parole, see Chapter 8) based on a new offense, impose a sentence of incarceration upon revocation of probation, *plus* any new sentence of incarceration that may be imposed for the new offense. The two sentences may be imposed to run concurrently or consecutively (see Chapter 3). In the case of parole, a new offense violation may trigger return to prison to serve out the unexpired sentence *plus* the sentence for the new offense. The point to remember is that a substantial percentage of the prison population each year is composed of probation (and parole) violators.

Revocation Hearings Revocation hearings usually begin with a violation report prepared by the probation officer. They are governed by the 1973 U.S. Supreme Court decision known as *Gagnon* v. *Scarpelli*. In this case, the Court said that there was no difference between probation and parole revocation because both of them resulted in loss of liberty. The Court extended the same rights to probationers that it had granted to parolees a year earlier in *Morrissey* v. *Brewer*. The Court ruled that probation cannot be revoked without observing the following elements of due process:

1. written notice of the charge;
2. disclosure of the evidence to the probationer;
3. the opportunity to be heard in person and present evidence as well as witnesses;
4. the right to confront and cross-examine witnesses;
5. the right to judgment by a detached and neutral hearing body;
6. a written statement of the reasons for revoking probation; and
7. the right to counsel under "special circumstances" depending on the offender's competence, case complexity, and mitigating circumstances.

The Scope of Community Supervision We end this chapter by circling back to the beginning. At yearend 2011, 1 in 33 adults in the United States was under community supervision (probation and parole). How equipped are states to handle almost 4 million persons on probation and protect public safety when you evaluate the resources given to probation? Probation receives only 10 percent of the corrections budget but supervises 80 percent of the correctional population. By contrast, prisons receive 90 percent of the corrections budget while supervising only 20 percent of the correctional population.

Exhibit 4–12 ranks the states in terms of the percentage of their adult population on community supervision (probation and parole) in 2007. It also shows the ratio of adults under community supervision to the adult population in each state. For example, Georgia has the largest percentage of its adult population under community supervision (6.5 percent). One in every 15 adults in Georgia is under community supervision. By contrast, New Hampshire has the smallest percentage of its adult population under community supervision (0.64 percent). Only 1 in every 155 adults in New Hampshire is under correctional supervision. Where does your state rank and why?

Visit http://www.oyez.org/cases/1970-1979/1972/1972_71_1225 or scan this code with the QR app on your smartphone or digital device and listen to the oral arguments before the United States Supreme Court in *Gagnon* v. *Scarpelli* on Tuesday, January 9, 1973, and decided May 14, 1973. How does this information relate to ideas discussed in this chapter?

EXHIBIT 4–12 Ratio and Percentage of Adult Population Under Community Supervision by State, 2007

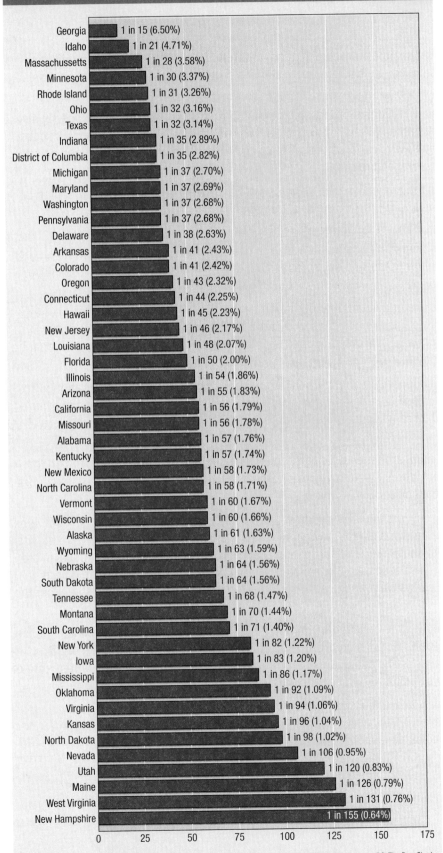

State	Ratio (Percentage)
Georgia	1 in 15 (6.50%)
Idaho	1 in 21 (4.71%)
Massachussetts	1 in 28 (3.58%)
Minnesota	1 in 30 (3.37%)
Rhode Island	1 in 31 (3.26%)
Ohio	1 in 32 (3.16%)
Texas	1 in 32 (3.14%)
Indiana	1 in 35 (2.89%)
District of Columbia	1 in 35 (2.82%)
Michigan	1 in 37 (2.70%)
Maryland	1 in 37 (2.69%)
Washington	1 in 37 (2.68%)
Pennsylvania	1 in 37 (2.68%)
Delaware	1 in 38 (2.63%)
Arkansas	1 in 41 (2.43%)
Colorado	1 in 41 (2.42%)
Oregon	1 in 43 (2.32%)
Connecticut	1 in 44 (2.25%)
Hawaii	1 in 45 (2.23%)
New Jersey	1 in 46 (2.17%)
Louisiana	1 in 48 (2.07%)
Florida	1 in 50 (2.00%)
Illinois	1 in 54 (1.86%)
Arizona	1 in 55 (1.83%)
California	1 in 56 (1.79%)
Missouri	1 in 56 (1.78%)
Alabama	1 in 57 (1.76%)
Kentucky	1 in 57 (1.74%)
New Mexico	1 in 58 (1.73%)
North Carolina	1 in 58 (1.71%)
Vermont	1 in 60 (1.67%)
Wisconsin	1 in 60 (1.66%)
Alaska	1 in 61 (1.63%)
Wyoming	1 in 63 (1.59%)
Nebraska	1 in 64 (1.56%)
South Dakota	1 in 64 (1.56%)
Tennessee	1 in 68 (1.47%)
Montana	1 in 70 (1.44%)
South Carolina	1 in 71 (1.40%)
New York	1 in 82 (1.22%)
Iowa	1 in 83 (1.20%)
Mississippi	1 in 86 (1.17%)
Oklahoma	1 in 92 (1.09%)
Virginia	1 in 94 (1.06%)
Kansas	1 in 96 (1.04%)
North Dakota	1 in 98 (1.02%)
Nevada	1 in 106 (0.95%)
Utah	1 in 120 (0.83%)
Maine	1 in 126 (0.79%)
West Virginia	1 in 131 (0.76%)
New Hampshire	1 in 155 (0.64%)

0   25   50   75   100   125   150   175

Source: Adapted from Pew Center on the States, *One in 31: The Long Reach of American Corrections* (Washington, DC: The Pew Charitable Trusts, March 2009). Table 5-A, "Adult Community Supervision Rates (Probation and Parole)," p. 44.

REVIEW AND APPLICATIONS

SUMMARY

1 Diversion is the official halting or suspension, before conviction, of formal criminal proceedings against a person, often conditioned on some form of counterperformance, such as participation in a treatment, counseling, or educational program.

2 There are four rationales for diversion: (1) Formal processing can encourage more criminal behavior; (2) diversion is cheaper than formally processing an offender through the criminal justice system; (3) formal processing may seem inappropriate for crimes without perceived victims; and (4) formal arrest, trial, and conviction add to the burdens of certain disadvantaged groups.

3 Diversion may occur at any stage in the criminal justice process after a criminal complaint has been filed or police have observed a crime. The police, a prosecutor, or a judge may call for diversion.

4 Issues concerning diversion include (1) the legal and ethical issues of protecting a defendant's rights; (2) the law enforcement question whether diversion encourages violation of the law; (3) the safety question whether diversion protects the community better than traditional processing; and (4) the economic question of diversion's cost-effectiveness.

5 *Probation* is the conditional release of a convicted offender into the community under the supervision of a probation officer. Most probation programs are designed to (1) protect the community by assisting judges in sentencing and supervising offenders, (2) carry out sanctions imposed by the court, (3) help offenders change, (4) support crime victims, and (5) coordinate and promote the use of community resources.

6 Probation is used for four reasons: (1) It permits offenders to remain in the community for reintegration purposes, (2) it avoids institutionalization and the stigma of incarceration, (3) it is less expensive than incarceration and more humanitarian, and (4) it is appropriate for offenders whose crimes do not necessarily merit incarceration.

7 At yearend 2011 federal, state, and local probation agencies supervised slightly more than 4.0 million adult U.S. resident, with misdemeanor convictions accounting for one-half. Twenty-five percent of all probationers were women, and 54 percent of probationers were white.

8 In 29 states, a state or local agency delivers adult probation services. In three states, adult probation services are delivered exclusively through county or multicounty agencies in the executive branch. In eight states, the judicial branch of government is responsible for adult probation services. In five states, local agencies in the judicial branch deliver adult probation services. And in five states, adult probation services are delivered through some combination of state executive branch, local executive agencies, or local agencies in either the judicial or the executive branch.

9 Corrections professionals urge evaluators to collect data on outcomes other than recidivism, such as amount of restitution collected, number of offenders employed, amounts of fines and fees collected, hours of community service, number of treatment sessions completed, percentage of financial obligations collected, rate of enrollment in school, number of days employed, educational attainment, and number of days drug free.

10 Case investigation and client supervision are the two major roles of probation officers. Investigation includes the preparation of a presentence report (PSR), which the judge uses in sentencing an offender. Supervision includes the functions of resource mediation, surveillance, and enforcement.

11 A *revocation hearing* is a due process hearing that must be conducted to determine whether the conditions of probation have been violated before probation can be revoked and the offender is removed from the community. Probation can be revoked when offenders fail to comply with the technical conditions of probation or commit new crimes.

KEY TERMS

QUESTIONS FOR REVIEW

1 Explain diversion.

2 Apply the rationales of diversion to a hypothetical case.

3 Distinguish the stages at which diversion occurs in the criminal justice process.

4 How would you respond to the diversion policy issues?

5 Explain probation and its goals.

6 Defend the reasons for using probation.

7 Construct a profile of the characteristics of adults on probation.

8 Summarize the different ways that probation is administered.

9 Evaluate the measures of probation.

10 Distinguish between the investigation and supervision functions of probation and provide an example of each.

11 Summarize what occurs at a revocation hearing.

THINKING CRITICALLY ABOUT CORRECTIONS

PSRs

Critics of PSRs claim that the information in them is not always verified or reliable and the sentencing recommendation is not disclosed even though the trend today is toward limited disclosure of information to the defendant's attorney. Actually, much of the information in a PSR is hearsay. Although defendants or victims may object to the contents of a PSR or the way it characterizes their behavior, they have no right to have the PSR reflect their views. As a probation officer, how would you respond to these criticisms?

Probation Effectiveness

Recidivism is one current measure of probation effectiveness. Others include the amount of restitution collected, the number of offenders employed, the amounts of fines and

fees collected, the number of hours of community service performed, the number of treatment sessions completed, the percentage of financial obligations collected, the rate of school enrollment, the level of educational attainment, the number of days employed, and the number of days drug free.

1. How important to you, as a taxpayer, is recidivism as a measure of program success?

2. Do you believe probation officers can really keep offenders from committing new crimes or violating the conditions of their probation?

3. If you were a probation officer today, by which outcome measures would you want to be judged? Why?

4. If recidivism is used as a measure of probation's effectiveness, how should it be defined?

ON-THE-JOB DECISION MAKING

Responding to Program Violations

The new diversion program in your county was developed to help first-time misdemeanor drug offenders avoid incarceration and seek help in controlling their dependency. Your job as the new diversion officer is to set the conditions of the diversion program and then monitor and enforce compliance. One of your first clients fails the required weekly drug test.

1. Should you immediately remove that person from the program?
2. Why or why not?

Probation and Recidivism

At a recent staff meeting, the chief PO reported that the department's recidivism rate exceeded the national average by 5 percent. The chief asks what can be done about it. You say, "Look at other measures besides recidivism." The chief asks you to explain. What do you say?

For additional information, please see: www.mhhe.com/schmalleger7e
Follow the author's tweets about the latest crime and justice news @schmalleger

INTERMEDIATE SANCTIONS

Between Probation and Incarceration

CHAPTER OBJECTIVES

After completing this chapter you should be able to do the following:

❶ Define *intermediate sanctions* and describe their purpose.

❷ Describe how intensive supervision probation works.

❸ Explain what drug courts are.

❹ Explain how day fines differ from traditional fines.

❺ Describe what a sentence to community service entails.

❻ Explain what day reporting centers are.

❼ Describe how remote-location monitoring works.

❽ Explain what residential reentry centers are.

❾ Identify the major features of boot camps.

❿ Define *community corrections.*

⓫ Explain what community corrections acts are.

> " *The use of intermediate sanctions is a cost-effective way to keep low-level offenders, such as drug and/or alcohol offenders, in the community, allowing them to avoid the criminogenic effects imprisonment may have.* "
>
> —Michael Tonry, professor of law and public policy, University of Minnesota Law School

Can electronic monitoring keep someone from becoming a criminal in the first place? That is the hope of many college athletic programs across the country.

In February 2012, *The Harvard Crimson* reported that Harvard's head men's basketball coach Tommy Amaker had announced that he had assigned his assistant coaches to monitor what players on the team are saying on their personal Twitter accounts. "Just like we like to monitor their whereabouts, monitor their academics, we need to monitor their Twitter accounts as well," Amaker said to *The Crimson*.[1]

In June 2012, the NCAA criticized University of North Carolina officials for inadequately monitoring student athletes' activity on social networks. That ruling had important implications for all college athletic departments. Across the country, athletic departments have been forced to decide between potentially being cited for "failure to monitor" and upsetting privacy rights groups for monitoring or banning social media use by their players. Yale has a similar monitoring policy. Its basketball coach James Jones has begun visiting the online pages of his athletes to monitor what they are saying. "We've become a cyber society, and more and more, everything is getting online, so we monitor and make sure guys are following the line," Jones said. Some believe that monitoring tweets for curse words, illegal activity, and jokes that go too far can become major issues if left unmonitored. Florida State head coach Jimbo Fisher found his players tweeting things such as "Child support is worse than AIDS."

A cottage industry has cropped up devoted to electronically monitoring players. Kevin Long is the CEO and creator of UDiligence, a service that monitors Facebook and Twitter posts made by college athletes. Once a department signs up for Long's service, athletes are told to install an app on their Facebook and Twitter accounts. A computer program then filters through the players' past and current posts and tweets, searching for over 400 keywords such as "stripper" and "shotgun." When even a photo caption or comment contains one of the keywords, it is added to a list of alerts that is sent daily to the athlete and periodically to the school's athletic department. Big-name schools such as The University of Texas at Austin, Louisiana State University, and the University of Florida have signed up for the service. Long said, "As more and more incidents [occur] where athletes post things that end up in the media, it certainly has increased the interest in making sure athletes are responsible about what they are posting," including keeping them from getting in trouble with the law in the first place.

Expectedly, privacy rights groups are less than thrilled to hear that business is booming. Many have raised concerns that monitoring services such as UDiligence may chill students' speech. According to Bradley Shear, an attorney who writes a blog about social media law, lawyers have at times dissuaded universities from signing up for such services due to liability issues. If a student were to write a post online about committing a crime, the school could be blamed for negligence if it failed to take action after seeing that information via social media monitoring. Nevertheless, UDiligence and companies like it are increasingly popular. Do you think that the threat of **intermediate sanctions** discussed in this chapter is a viable option in preventing illegal or embarrassing tweets?

Visit www.marketplace.org/topics/tech/software-protects-college-athletes-online-no-nos or scan this code with the QR app on your smartphone or digital device and listen to the podcast of American Public Media's Marketplace discuss UDiligence software. How does this information relate to ideas discussed in this chapter?

intermediate sanctions
New punishment options developed to fill the gap between traditional probation and traditional jail or prison sentences and to better match the severity of punishment to the seriousness of the crime.

INTERMEDIATE SANCTIONS

CO5-1

Sanctions less restrictive than prison but more restrictive than probation are not new. Variations of intermediate sanctions like many of those discussed later in this chapter (restitution, fines, and community service) were used as sentences in ancient Israel, Greece, and Rome. Other intermediate sanctions—such as drug court, remote-location monitoring, boot camps, and day fines—started in the 1980s as a way to respond to an increasing number of convicted offenders and widescale prison over-crowding. Prior to this, sentencing options were limited to incarceration or probation. However, there was growing sentiment that some crimes were too severe to be punished by placing the offender on probation, but those same crimes were not severe enough to warrant incarceration. Therefore, states started to develop a series of intermediate sanctions that fell somewhere between probation and incarceration. What is new today is the effort to bring all these sanctions together into a comprehensive sentencing system like the one suggested in Exhibit 5–1, which provides judges an expanded menu of corrections options. Relatively less intrusive interventions proportional to the severity of a violation and the risk of the offender are to the left in Exhibit 5–1; more intrusive ones are to the right. Exhibit 5–1 is also multidimensional, creating depth for each step on the continuum. For example, if an offender on intensive supervision probation (ISP) fails to report as scheduled (whether to an ISP officer or via an automated probation machine as described in Chapter 4) and is relatively low risk, it may be appropriate to require more frequent reporting for a period of time within ISP than to move to the next higher level of intervention.

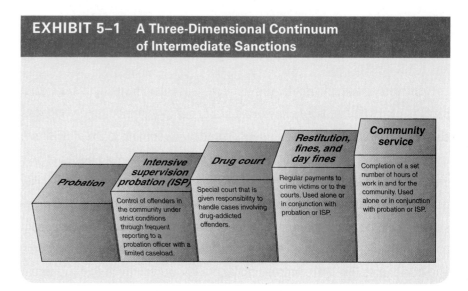

EXHIBIT 5–1   A Three-Dimensional Continuum of Intermediate Sanctions

Intermediate sanctions are most often used for offenders considered nonviolent and low risk. They usually require the offender to lead a productive life in the community by working (finding work if unemployed) or learning new job skills; to perform unpaid community service; to pay restitution to victims; to enroll in a treatment or educational program; or sometimes to do all of these.

Intermediate sanctions are sometimes referred to as *alternatives to incarceration*. They may be used at initial sentencing, after an offender has made progress in compliance and treatment, or as a way to reduce the correctional population.

Value of Intermediate Sanctions

Since January 1, 2002, the nation's jail and prison population has continued to exceed 2 million inmates. This level of increase in the nation's prisons and jails places a heavy economic burden on taxpayers. That burden includes the cost of building, maintaining, and operating prisons and jails as well as the loss of offenders' contributions and the cost of caring for the destabilized families left behind. In addition, overcrowded jails and prisons are hard to manage and staff, and they invite disorder. The fiscal crisis that began in December 2007 is moving many governors and legislators to think "outside the cell" and turn to intermediate sanctions as a way to keep low-level offenders out of prison and in their communities.

Here's a look at how states are using intermediate sanctions[2]:

- Colorado is jailing fewer low-level drug offenders, diverting more offenders to substance abuse treatment centers, sentencing more offenders to intermediate sanctions, increasing the use of parole and reentry for parolees, lessening penalties for persons who violate the conditions of probation or parole, and increasing good time credit.

- Since 2011, at least 13 states have closed prison institutions or are contemplating doing so, potentially reducing prison capacity by more than 13,900 beds.

- Florida eliminated prison sentences for certain third-degree felonies that do not involve the use or threat of violence.

- Indiana and Pennsylvania approved similar legislation that provides a statewide framework for the implementation of problem-solving courts such as drug court, mental health court, family dependency

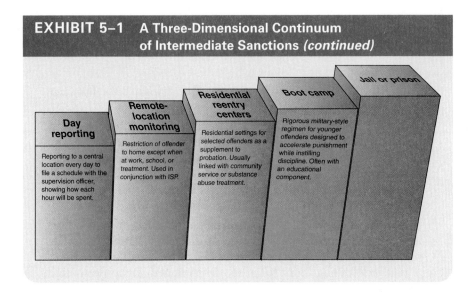

EXHIBIT 5–1 A Three-Dimensional Continuum of Intermediate Sanctions *(continued)*

Day reporting

Reporting to a central location every day to file a schedule with the supervision officer, showing how each hour will be spent.

Remote-location monitoring

Restriction of offender to home except when at work, school, or treatment. Used in conjunction with ISP.

Residential reentry centers

Residential settings for selected offenders as a supplement to probation. Usually linked with community service or substance abuse treatment.

Boot camp

Rigorous military-style regimen for younger offenders designed to accelerate punishment while instilling discipline. Often with an educational component.

Jail or prison

court, community court, reentry court, veterans court, and domestic violence court.

- The Georgia General Assembly is debating a shift in emphasis toward alternatives to prison time for nonviolent offenders.
- The Illinois governor signed laws to increase the use of community alternatives, revise sentencing laws, and implement a rational approach to risk assessment.
- Kansas restored early release for nonviolent inmates, diverted low-level drug cases to treatment, and expanded reentry programs for parolees.
- Kentucky expects to save $422 million and reduce its prison population by more than 3,000 inmates over the next 10 years through the implementation of the 2011 Public Safety and Offender Accountability Act. The law ensures that there is more prison space for violent and career criminals while helping to stop the revolving door for lower-risk, nonviolent offenders.
- Louisiana expanded the use of home arrest and expanded the length of time a felon can be sentenced to house arrest from two to four years.
- Michigan created the Michigan Prisoner Reentry Initiative (MPRI) to plan, support, and sustain local programs providing alternatives and parole supervision.
- Mississippi lawmakers decided in 2008 to cut prison costs by allowing all nonviolent offenders to be considered for parole after serving 25 percent of their sentences instead of 85 percent.
- Missouri judges are provided information on evidence-based practices and what particular sentences would cost the taxpayers.
- Nebraska and three other states (Arkansas, Illinois, and New Jersey) established oversight committees to examine sentencing policies, prison overcrowding, and reentry services.
- New Jersey adopted risk assessment instruments to aid parole boards in considering release issues, expanded drug courts, day reporting, and electronic monitoring statewide; increased the number of persons granted parole; and increased reentry services for parolees.
- New York State invested in intermediate sanctions that focus services on individuals otherwise bound for jail and prison.

- North Carolina developed an evidence-based approach that is expected to reduce prison costs by investing in intermediate sanctions.
- Oklahoma expanded eligibility for community sentencing and the use of parole for nonviolent offenders.
- South Carolina has removed mandatory minimums for first-time offenders.
- Texas avoided the $2 billion cost to build and operate new prisons by spending $241 million on new probation and parole programs, halfway houses, and specialty courts for drug offenders, veterans, drunk drivers, and those with mental illness and now requires all drug possession offenders with less than a gram of drugs be sentenced to probation instead of jail time.
- Vermont legislators made probation standard for misdemeanors and nonviolent felons, gave courts authority to sentence certain offenders to house arrest for up to 180 days instead of prison, and expanded eligibility for adult drug court diversion to include second-time misdemeanants, not just first-time offenders.
- Washington developed the Family and Offender Sentencing Alternative for some nonviolent offenders who have not committed sex offenses and who have custody of children under the age of 18.

The reform efforts in these and other states have common elements:

- In each state, the governor supported reform efforts by appointing department heads authorized to reduce incarceration.
- The state corrections director became an ardent spokesperson for the initiative.
- Initiatives were put under the administrative control of outspoken champions of the broad goal of reducing incarceration.
- Strong research capabilities were directed to improve program design and operations with the objective of reducing incarceration.
- New York and Michigan in particular formed collaborative relationships with stakeholders, politically influential persons, and perhaps most important, local and community groups and agencies.
- Successful states have recognized that no one solution or program—whether it is intermediate sanctions, reentry programming (discussed in Chapter 8) or sentencing reform—will solve the problem of mass incarceration. Multiple and coordinated strategies are important.
- Local and national private nonprofit advocates promoted and explained the value of reform goals to government officials, the media, and the public.
- A developed infrastructure of nonprison programs (intermediate sanctions) provided services necessary to support defendants and former prisoners in the community.

Professional associations too are calling for greater use of intermediate sanctions. The American Jail Association, for example, believes that intermediate sanctions—not prison—should be the backbone of the corrections systems (see Exhibit 5–2). This kind of thinking enables criminal justice officials to give nonviolent offenders intermediate sanctions, thereby teaching them accountability for their actions and heightening their chances for success in the community while reserving expensive prison and jail space for violent offenders. Advocacy of intermediate sanctions by professional organizations such as the American Jail Association, the American Correctional Association, the American Probation and Parole Association, and the International Community Corrections

EXHIBIT 5–2 | **American Jail Association Resolution**

Intermediate Punishments

WHEREAS, the American Jail Association (AJA) recognizes the detrimental impact that crowding places on local jails; and

WHEREAS, many of those who are incarcerated in jails do not pose a known danger to themselves or to society;

THEREFORE BE IT RESOLVED THAT AJA supports the expansion of intermediate punishments in states and localities throughout America for offenders who do not pose a known danger to public safety. AJA believes that intermediate punishments address real concerns of constituents.

Source: Copyright © American Jail Association. Reprinted with permission.

Association can significantly advance career opportunities. Consult the Appendix: Careers in Corrections at the Online Learning Center Web site for the steps involved in career planning, developing employability and job readiness, and finding the right job.

Finally, numerous national and statewide polls tapping public attitudes about preferences for intermediate sanctions with treatment over incarceration give policymakers and legislators breathing room on moves to reduce prison populations during this time of budget crises in states. The public supports intermediate sanctions with treatment over incarceration for low-level drug offenders, and they favor sentencing nonviolent offenders to community service or probation instead of imprisonment.[3] "When the public is made aware of the possible range of punishments, and given information about how and with whom they are used, they support alternatives to incarceration."[4] In 2010 and again in 2012, surveys sponsored by the Pew Center on the states found that a majority of 1,200 registered voters believe that too many people are in prison, a fifth of prisoners could be released without posing a threat to public safety, and there are more effective, less expensive alternatives to prison for nonviolent offenders and that expanding those alternatives is the best way to reduce the crime rate. Furthermore, they supported the "justice reinvestment" concept of using money saved from cutting back on prison expenditures for intermediate sanctions.[5]

Intermediate sanctions are valuable for a number of reasons. First, they provide a means for offenders who are not dangerous to repay their victims and their communities. Second, intermediate sanctions promote rehabilitation—which most citizens want, but most prisons and jails find difficult to provide—and the reintegration of the offender into the community. And third, once the programs are in place, they can do these things at a comparatively low cost. Compare the lower costs of intermediate sanctions with jail and those for prison in Exhibit 5–3.

Intermediate sanctions should not be haphazardly planned or implemented. High-quality intermediate sanctions must be thoughtfully conceived, effectively targeted, well planned, and well staffed. Perhaps the most important lesson learned from 20 years' experience with intermediate sanctions is that "they are seldom likely to achieve their goals unless means can be found to set and enforce policies governing their use. Otherwise, the combination of officials' risk aversion and practitioners' preferences to be guided solely by their judgments about appropriate penalties in individual cases is likely to undermine program goals."[6]

Do some judges go too far in crafting innovative intermediate sanctions? You be the judge. In Cleveland, Ohio, Judge Pinkey Carr sentenced a man for threatening a police officer to stand outside a police station

The Offender Speaks
Visit www.mhhe.com/schmalleger7e to see this feature.

EXHIBIT 5–3	Average Annual Cost of Correctional Options

Correctional Option	Cost per Year per Participant
Boot camp	$32,119
Prison	28,646
Jail	27,237
Halfway house	18,000
Day reporting	10,585
Intensive parole supervision	8,318
Remote-location monitoring	5,400
Drug court	4,333
Parole	3,402
Intensive probation supervision	3,274
Community service	2,759
Probation	1,278
House arrest	402

Sources: Adapted from Linh Vuong, Christopher Hartney, Barry Krisberg, and Susan Marchionna, *The Extravagance of Imprisonment Revisited* (Oakland, CA: NCCD, January 2010); "New Study Reveals Franklin County Day Reporting Center Reaps Rewards for Counties," Franklin County, PA, January 6, 2011, www.co.franklin.pa.us. *Seeking Justice: Crime and Punishment in America* (New York: Edna McConnell Clark Foundation, 1977), p. 34; Camille Graham Camp and George M. Camp, *Adult Corrections* (Middletown, CT: Criminal Justice Institute, 2001), pp. 87, 125, 188, 198; Camille Graham Camp and George M. Camp, *Jails* (Middletown, CT: Criminal Justice Institute, 2001), p. 42; Web site of the National Association of Drug Court Professionals, www.nadcp.org/whatis/; James J. Stephen, *State Prison Expenditures, 2001* (Washington, DC: U.S. Department of Justice, Bureau of Justice Statistics, June 2004); and Pew Center on the States, *One in 31: The Long Reach of American Corrections* (New York: Pew Charitable Trusts, March 2009).

wearing a sign that read, "I apologize to Officer Simone and all police officers for being an idiot calling 911 threatening to kill you. I'm sorry and it will never happen again." The judge gave the sign her personal touch and hand-lettered the sign herself. It may be funny, but is it legal and does it have a rehabilitative purpose? George Washington University law professor Jonathan Turley argues that "stunt" sentences rarely have anything to do with legal justice and are better suited to courtroom reality shows. However in 2004's *United States* v. *Gementera*, the Ninth Circuit ruled that the district court judge who sentenced a mail thief to wear a sign that read, "I stole mail; this is my punishment." imposed the punishment for the stated and legitimate statutory purpose of rehabilitation and to a lesser extent for general deterrence and for protection of the public.

Varieties of Intermediate Sanctions

The specific varieties of intermediate sanctions discussed in the following subsections include intensive supervision probation, drug courts, fines, community service, day reporting centers, remote-location monitoring (formerly known as *house arrest* and *electronic monitoring*), residential reentry centers, and boot camps.

intensive supervision probation (ISP)

CO5-2

Control of offenders in the community under strict conditions by means of frequent reporting to a probation officer whose caseload is generally limited to 30 offenders.

Intensive Supervision Probation Probation with frequent contact between offender and probation officer, strict enforcement of conditions, random drug and alcohol testing, and other requirements is known as **intensive supervision probation (ISP)**. Estimates on the number of persons currently on ISP are not known. However, in 2001, Camp and Camp reported that approximately 5 percent (122,938) of the adult population on probation or parole was on ISP.[7] If we estimated only 5 percent of today's probation and parole population on ISP, we're likely to find more than 200,000 adults on ISP.

As a technique for increasing control over offenders in the community, ISP has gained wide popularity. It allows offenders to live at home but under more severe and more punitive restrictions than those of conventional probation. The primary purpose of such program restrictions and surveillance is to protect the community and deter the offender from breaking the law or violating the conditions of release. Requirements of ISP usually include performing community service, attending school or treatment programs, working or looking for employment, meeting with a probation officer (or team of officers) as often as five times a week, and submitting to curfews, employment checks, and tests for drug and alcohol use. Because of the frequency of contact, subjection to unannounced drug tests, and rigorous enforcement of restitution, community service, and other conditions, ISP is thought more appropriate for higher-risk offenders.

An ISP officer explains court-ordered sanctions to a probationer. Frequent face-to-face contact is a condition of ISP. What other controls are used to monitor offenders on ISP?

ISP was initially the most popular intermediate sanction. It emerged in the 1960s as an effort to improve offender rehabilitation by reducing probation and parole caseloads from 100 or more to 30. However, researchers soon discovered that small caseloads led to enhanced supervision and control (and more violations) but not necessarily to enhanced treatment.[8] It wasn't until ISP combined supervision and control with treatment components and skill development programs and reinforced clearly identified behaviors that it became effective.[9]

Evidence-based research on ISP has produced two main findings. First, restraining offenders in the community by increasing surveillance and control over their activities does *not* reduce their criminal activities.[10] Offenders sentenced to surveillance-oriented ISP programs commit new crimes at about the same rate as comparable offenders receiving different sentences. Also, technical violation and revocation rates are typically higher for ISP surveillance-oriented programs because more frequent contact makes misconduct more likely to be discovered. Early proponents of surveillance-oriented ISP programs argued that ISP would reduce recidivism rates, rehabilitate offenders, and save money and prison resources. However, most evaluations suggest that the combination of high revocation rates and the cost of processing revocations makes savings unlikely.[11]

On the other hand, scientific analysis of 10 treatment-oriented ISP programs indicates, on average, a statistically significant 21.9 percent reduction in the recidivism rates of program participants compared with a treatment-as-usual group[12]—what some call "extremely successful."[13] Two ISP programs that the U.S. Department of Justice says have strong evidence indicating that they achieve their intended outcomes are the Reduced Probation Caseload programs in Iowa and Oklahoma. In Iowa, ISP significantly reduced the likelihood of recidivism by 47 percent for property and violent crime and 20 percent for all offenses. In Oklahoma, the results showed that the treatment group was arrested less often than the control group. At the maximum 1½-year follow-up, the treatment group had a significantly lower probability of recidivism than the control group with a roughly 30 percent lower recidivism rate.[14] According to the editors of the *Criminal Justice Newsletter,* "The lesson from this research is that it is the treatment—not the intensive monitoring—that results in recidivism reduction."[15] Rearrests are reduced when offenders receive treatment in addition to the increased surveillance and control of ISP programs.

CO5-3

drug court

A special court that is given responsibility to treat, sanction, and reward drug offenders with punishment more restrictive than regular probation but less severe than incarceration.

Drug Courts Can you cure addiction by locking it up? Some say it doesn't cure it but makes it worse. Enter drug court, a recent innovation within the American criminal justice system.

Drug court is a special court that is given responsibility to handle cases involving drug-addicted offenders.[16]

Drug courts vary across jurisdictions and no drug court is exactly the same as the next, but there are two general types: deferred prosecution programs (pretrial diversion or "preplea") and postadjudication (postsentencing). People who enter a deferred prosecution program are diverted into the drug court system *before* being convicted, are not required to plead guilty, and are prosecuted only if they fail to complete the program.

Postadjudication (postplea) programs require participants to plead guilty to the charges against them and have their sentences deferred or suspended while they are in the program. The sentence will be waived or reduced, and often the offense will be expunged from their record if they complete the program. The case will be returned to court, and the people will face sentencing on their previously entered guilty plea if they fail to satisfy the program requirements.

Drug court is a new intermediate sanction that uses the power of the court to treat, sanction, and reward drug offenders with punishment more restrictive than regular probation but less severe than incarceration. In 1989, troubled by the devastating impact of drugs and drug-related crime on Dade County (Florida) neighborhoods and the criminal justice system, Miami judge Herbert M. Klein developed the nation's first drug court. Today, the United States and its territories have almost 2,600 drug courts.[17] From 1980 to 2008, the number of people in state prisons for a drug offense increased 1,223 percent.[18] Estimates are about 25 percent of the people in state prison and 5 percent in federal prison were convicted of *drug possession, not selling.*

In addition to the adult drug court that most of us are familiar with, new forms of drug courts are emerging.[19] The different types today include

1. Veterans Treatment Court uses veterans as mentors to help other veterans engage in treatment and counseling to address their unique needs. Since the first veterans court was established in Buffalo, New York, in 2008, 120 such programs have been opened in 35 states, and about 200 others are planned across the nation according to Justice for Vets.[20]

2. DWI Court, a postconviction court, is dedicated to changing the behavior of alcohol-dependent repeat offenders arrested for DWI.

3. Family Drug Court targets parental substance abuse in juvenile abuse, neglect, and dependency cases.

4. Federal Reentry Court is a postadjudication court that provides a blend of treatment and sanction alternatives to address behavior, rehabilitation, and community reentry for nonviolent, substance-abusing federal offenders.

5. Juvenile Drug Court handles selected delinquency cases and in some instances, status offenders who are identified as having problems with alcohol and/or other drugs.

6. Reentry Drug Court facilitates the reintegration of drug-involved offenders into communities upon their release from local or state correctional facilities.

7. Tribal Healing to Wellness Court is a component of the tribal justice system that incorporates and adapts a wellness concept to meet the specific substance abuse needs of each tribal community.

8. The Back on TRAC clinical justice model targets college students whose excessive use of substances has continued despite higher education's best efforts at education, prevention, or treatment and has ultimately created serious consequences for themselves or others.

In comparison with the aims of other types of courts, those of the drug court are much less punitive and more healing and restorative in nature. This new approach integrates substance abuse treatment, sanctions, incentives, and frequent court appearances with case processing to place drug-involved defendants in judicially supervised rehabilitation programs. Successful completion of the treatment program results in dismissal of the charges, reduced or set-aside sentences, lesser penalties, or a combination of these.

Compared to the small number of scientific studies examining the effectiveness of other intermediate sanctions on reducing criminal activity, a relatively large number of evidence-based studies are examining the effectiveness of drug courts. At least *five* independent analyses have concluded that drug treatment courts have achieved success in lowering rates of recidivism among drug offenders. Courts significantly reduce the future criminal activities of offenders an average of approximately 7 to 14 percent.[21] In some evaluations, drug court participants who completed their program had rearrest rates 12 to 58 percent below those of the comparison group. The most influential components of the drug treatment court model are the role of judicial status hearings, drug treatment, and the drug treatment judge.

Judge Sarah Smith congratulates drug court participant Bronco Anderson in her Tulsa, Oklahoma, courtroom for completing phase one and moving to phase two of the drug court program. Drug courts treat, sanction, and reward drug offenders with punishment more restrictive than regular probation but less severe than incarceration. What are the key components of drug court?

Six drug court treatment programs that the U.S. Department of Justice says have strong evidence that they achieve their intended outcomes are the Bronx (NY) Treatment Court, the Brooklyn (NY) Treatment Court, the Jackson County (OR) Community Family Court, the Multnomah County (OR) Sanction Treatment Opportunity Progress (STOP) Drug Program, the Queens (NY) Treatment Court, and the Suffolk County (NY) Drug Treatment Court.[22]

Drug courts are also cost-effective. Evaluations of drug courts nationwide find that they save taxpayers money compared to probation and/or incarceration due to reductions in arrests, case processing, jail occupancy, and victimization costs. The Washington State Institute for Public Policy estimated the annual cost of drug court participation to be $4,300 per person compared to $23,000 per year for incarceration.[23]

Despite the successes of drug courts during the past 20 years, they remain available to less than 10 percent of drug addicted offenders. Although every state has at least one drug court, only a handful of states—like New Jersey and New York—have one in every county.[24] Advocates say the main reason for their scarcity is a lack of money. Drug courts received about $64 million in federal money in 2009. The National Association of Drug Court Professionals says that $1.5 billion over the next six years in federal money—along with matching money from states—could treat all who need it.

Visit http://crimesolutions.gov/TopicDetails.aspx?ID=49 or scan this code with the QR app on your smartphone or digital device and learn about the evaluation outcomes of the six drug court treatment programs that the U.S. Department of Justice says have strong evidence indicating they achieve their intended outcomes. How does this information relate to ideas discussed in this chapter?

However, in spite of the success of the nation's drug courts, there are two problems with relying on the criminal justice system to address substance use that need consideration. First, people who receive treatment through the criminal justice system face the collateral consequences of arrest, prosecution, and conviction; and second, they are not able to address their addiction before being arrested for a drug-related offense due to the lack of community-based treatment options.

CO5-4

fine

A financial penalty used as a criminal sanction.

Fines A **fine** is a financial sanction requiring a convicted person to pay a specified sum of money. The fine is one of the oldest forms of punishment. It is, in practice, the criminal justice tool for punishing minor misdemeanors, traffic offenses, and ordinance violations. In the United States, fines are rarely regarded as a tough criminal sanction. They are not taken seriously for at least four reasons. First, judicial, legislative, and prosecutorial attitudes restrict the use of fines to traffic offenses, minor misdemeanors, and ordinance violations. Second, a judge seldom has enough reliable information on an offender's personal wealth to impose a just fine. Third, mechanisms for collecting fines are often ineffective. Far too often the responsibility for collecting fines has been left to probation officers, who are already overburdened and have no interest in fine collection. As a result, fines are seldom paid. Fourth, many believe that fines work a hardship on the poor while affluent offenders feel no sting.

day fine

A financial penalty scaled both to the defendant's ability to pay and the seriousness of the crime.

A **day fine** is a financial penalty based on the seriousness of the crime and the defendant's ability to pay. It is called a *day fine* because it is based on the offender's daily income. Day fines, also called *structured fines,* have been common in some northern and western European countries for many years. They were introduced in Sweden in the 1920s and were quickly incorporated into the penal codes of other Scandinavian countries. West Germany adopted day fines as a sentencing option in the early 1970s. Today, Sweden and Germany have made day fines the preferred punishment for most criminal cases, including those involving serious crimes. In Germany, for example, day fines are the only punishment for three-quarters of all offenders convicted of property crimes and two-thirds of offenders convicted of assaults.[25] In most Scandinavian countries, day fines are used for punishing traffic offenses. For example, the day fine of an heir to a family-owned sausage business in Finland was caught driving 50 miles per hour (mph) in a 25-mph zone and fined $217,000. With Finnish tax records showing his wealth at $8 million, he was given a world-record speeding fine. His fine more than doubles the existing records of a $96,000 fine given in 2002 to Annssi Vanjoki, a Nokia vice president, for driving his Harley-Davidson 17 miles above the speed limit on a Helsinki street; a $31,200 fine given in 2001 to Pekka Ala-Pietila, Nokia president, for driving through a red light; a $71,000 fine given in 2000 to Jaakko Rysola, dot-com millionaire, for zigzagging through Helsinki in his Ferrari; and a $122,974 fine given in 2009 to the heir of a Norwegian shipping family for drunk driving. If Tiger Woods' car crash had happened in any of these countries, he would have paid a day fine of more than $300,000 rather than a fixed fine of $164 because he makes roughly $10 million each month.[26]

The planning process for introducing day fines is unique for each jurisdiction, depending on its organizational structure, traditions, personalities, and legal culture. Exhibit 5–4 is a sample notification of a structured fine program. The notice may be mailed to a defendant or handed to the defendant when she or he appears in court. Every jurisdiction, however,

| **EXHIBIT 5–4** | **Sample Notification of a Structured Fine Program** |

A PRELIMINARY COMPLAINT
HAS BEEN FILED CHARGING YOU WITH
AN INDICTABLE OFFENSE

IF CONVICTED, THE COURT <u>MAY</u> IMPOSE ONE OR MORE OF THE
FOLLOWING SANCTIONS:

1. JAIL OR PRISON

2. PROBATION

3. A FINE

If a fine is imposed, the Court may structure the level of the fine partly according to the seriousness of the offense and partly in relation to your means or ability to pay the fine. This method of computing the amount of a "structured fine" is an effort by the Court and the Polk County Attorney's Office to equalize the impact of criminal sanctions and to reduce the number of persons who are sentenced to prison, jail, or formal probation.

In order for the County Attorney's Office to consider recommending a structured fine to the Court at the time of sentencing, you or your attorney must schedule an interview with a Structured Fines Officer at 555-1234, IMMEDIATELY. If you intend to secure an attorney to represent you on this charge, please make these arrangements prior to calling the Structured Fines Program.

Your ability to pay a structured fine as well as the length of time needed to pay the fine are based on the information you provide in the attached AFFIDAVIT OF FINANCIAL CONDITION. It is required that you and/or your attorney complete this form prior to meeting with a Structured Fines Officer. It is also required that you take to your meeting with the Structured Fines Officer verification of your income in the form of paycheck stubs, income tax returns, etc.

POLK COUNTY ATTORNEY'S OFFICE
STRUCTURED FINES PROGRAM
POLK COUNTY COURTHOUSE, ROOM B-40
DES MOINES, IOWA 50309
555-1234

Appointments with a Structured Fines Officer are available
Monday through Friday, from 1:30 P.M. to 4:30 P.M.

addresses similar issues: current sentencing patterns, current fine collection operations and their effectiveness, goals and priorities for the day fine program, and potential legal challenges to the program.

Once a system for imposing day fines is put in place, the next step is to develop a structured process for setting fines. This structured process is the feature that distinguishes day fines from traditional fines. The process usually has two parts: (1) a unit scale that ranks offenses by severity and (2) a valuation scale for determining the dollar amount per unit for a given offender.

The first step in setting a day fine is to determine the number of fine units to be imposed. A portion of the unit scale used in a Staten Island, New York, day fine experiment is shown in Exhibit 5–5. The number of units ranges from a low of 5 to a high of 120 for the most serious misdemeanors

EXHIBIT 5–5 Example of a Day Fine Unit Scale

Staten Island Day Fine Unit Scale (Selected Offense Categories)

Penal Law Charge[1]	Type of Offense[2]	Number of Day Fine Units		
		Discount	PRESUMPTIVE	Premium
120.00 AM	Assault 3: Range of 20–95 DF			
	A. Substantial Injury	81	**95**	109
	Stranger-to-stranger; or where victim is known to assailant, he/she is weaker, vulnerable			
	B. Minor Injury	59	**70**	81
	Stranger-to-stranger; or where victim is known to assailant, he/she is weaker, vulnerable; or altercations involving use of a weapon			
	C. Substantial Injury	38	**45**	52
	Altercations among acquaintances; brawls			
	D. Minor Injury	17	**20**	23
	Altercations among acquaintances; brawls			
110/120.00 BM	Attempted Assault 3: Range of 15–45 DF			
	A. Substantial Injury	38	**45**	52
	Stranger-to-stranger; or where victim is known to assailant, he/she is weaker, vulnerable			
	B. Minor Injury	30	**35**	40
	Stranger-to-stranger; or where victim is known to assailant, he/she is weaker, vulnerable; or altercations involving use of a weapon			
	C. Substantial Injury	17	**20**	23
	Altercations among acquaintances; brawls			
	D. Minor Injury	13	**15**	17
	Altercations among acquaintances; brawls			

1. AM = Class A Misdemeanor; BM = Class B Misdemeanor.

2. DF = Day Fines.

Source: Adapted from Bureau of Justice Assistance, *How to Use Structured Fines (Day Fines) as an Intermediate Sanction* (Washington, DC: Bureau of Justice Assistance, 1996), p. 59.

handled by the court. For example, the presumptive number of units for the offense of assault with minor injury and aggravating factors is 70; the range is from 59 to 81 units. The presumptive number is the starting point. Negotiation and consideration of individual circumstances may raise or lower the number. There is no magic in the unit scale established. What is important is to establish a scale broad enough to cover the full range of offenses handled by the courts that will use structured fines.

Once the unit scale is established, the second step is to create a valuation table. The purpose of the valuation table is to establish the dollar amount of each fine. A portion of the valuation table used in the Staten Island experiment is shown in Exhibit 5–6. Net daily incomes run down the left side, and numbers of dependents run across the top. Net daily income is the offender's income (after-tax wages, welfare allowance, unemployment compensation, etc.) divided by the number of days in a payment period. Staten Island planners also adjusted the net daily income downward to account for subsistence needs, family responsibilities, and incomes below the poverty line.

Suppose a defendant convicted of assault, with minor injury and aggravating factors, has a net daily income of $15 and supports four people, including herself. Find the row for her net daily income. Move across the row to the column for the number of dependents. The figure there is the value of one structured fine unit for that defendant. Multiply the number

EXHIBIT 5–6 | **Example of a Day Fine Valuation Table**

Staten Island, New York, Valuation Table Dollar Value of One Day Fine Unit, by Net Daily Income and Number of Dependents

Net Daily Income ($)	Number of Dependents (Including Self)							
	1	2	3	4	5	6	7	8
3		1.05	0.83	0.68	0.53	0.45	0.37	0.30
4	1.70	1.40	1.10	0.90	0.70	0.60	0.50	0.40
5	2.13	1.75	1.38	1.13	0.88	0.75	0.62	0.50
6	2.55	2.10	1.65	1.35	1.05	0.90	0.75	0.60
7	2.98	2.45	1.93	1.58	1.23	1.05	0.87	0.70
8	3.40	2.80	2.20	1.80	1.40	1.20	1.00	0.80
9	3.83	3.15	2.48	2.03	1.58	1.35	1.12	0.90
10	4.25	3.50	2.75	2.25	1.75	1.50	1.25	1.00
11	4.68	3.85	3.03	2.47	1.93	1.65	1.37	1.10
12	5.10	4.20	3.30	2.70	2.10	1.80	1.50	1.20
13	5.53	4.55	3.58	2.93	2.28	1.95	1.62	1.30
14	7.85	4.90	3.85	3.15	2.45	2.10	1.75	1.40
15	8.42	5.25	4.13	3.38	2.63	2.25	1.87	1.50

Source: Adapted from Bureau of Justice Assistance, *How to Use Structured Fines (Day Fines) as an Intermediate Sanction* (Washington, DC: Bureau of Justice Assistance, 1996), p. 64.

of fine units to be imposed (70) by the value of a single fine unit (3.38). The product, $236.60, is the amount of the day fine to be imposed.

The National Institute of Justice (NIJ) sponsored an evaluation of the Staten Island experiment. That evaluation showed that judges used day fines for many offenses for which they had formerly used fixed fine amounts—including some property crimes, drug possession, and assault.[27] Research showed that the average fine increased by 25 percent, from $206 before the experiment to $258 during the year day fines were used. If day fines had not been held low by state law, the average day fine would have been $440. The news on collections was also good. Eighty-five percent of the defendants in the day fine program paid their fines in full, compared with 71 percent in a control program using routine collection processes. Furthermore, when full payment was not made, partial payment was much more likely in the day fine cases than in cases from before the experiment or in the control group. Thus, the higher fines levied in the day fine cases did not make collection more difficult, and the new enforcement procedures independently improved collection rates.

Even though day fines have been tried experimentally in some areas of the United States including Arizona, Connecticut, Iowa, New York, and Oregon, there has been little evidence-based research on the effectiveness of fines in reducing recidivism rates. The Washington State Institute for Public Policy wrote that day fine programs need additional research and development before we can conclude that they do or do not work (i.e., reduce crime outcomes).[28] However, because the use of fines could reduce the costs of courts and corrections and because day fines address problems of inequality, fines are a promising intermediate sanction. At present, most Western justice systems, except the United States, rely heavily on financial penalties. In the 21st century, U.S. jurisdictions are likely to continue their experiments with monetary penalties and to assign them greater importance.

In February 2009, R&B singer Chris Brown pled guilty to felony assault of singer and then-girlfriend, Rihanna, leaving her with visible facial injuries that required hospitalization. Brown was sentenced to five years probation and 180 days of community service. In September 2012, Bryan Norwood, chief of police in Richmond, Virginia, wrote a letter to Brown's sentencing judge in Los Angeles claiming Brown had successfully completed 202 days of community service (although he was required to perform only 180) and attached documents showing that Brown frequently worked at Tappahannock Children's Center (a place where Brown's mother was once a director) performing odd jobs such as painting, washing windows, waxing floors, cutting grass, and picking up trash. This photo shows Brown clearing brush along railroad tracks near the Richmond Police Mounted Patrol stables in September 2009. In January 2013, press reports surfaced suggesting that there were irregularities in the record submitted to the court concerning Brown's community service. Reports alleged that Brown was credited with community service work when in fact he was out of the United States. (In February 2013, police chief Norwood resigned.) In March 2013, the issue of the status of Brown's community service remains unresolved. What do you think? If community service is a criminal sanction and valuable to the community, the victim, and the offender, how should it be supervised?

community service

A sentence to serve a specified number of hours working in unpaid positions with nonprofit or tax-supported agencies.

CO5-5

Community Service Community service is a sentence to serve a specified number of hours working in unpaid positions with nonprofit or tax-supported agencies. Community service is punishment that takes away an offender's time and energy and is sometimes called a "fine of time."

Community service as a criminal sanction began in the United States in 1966 in Alameda County, California. Municipal judges there devised a community service sentencing program for indigent women who violated traffic and parking laws. Too poor to pay fines, these women were likely to be sentenced to jail. But putting them behind bars imposed a hardship on their families. Community service orders (CSOs) increased sentencing options, punished the offenders, lightened the suffering of innocent families, avoided the cost of imprisonment, and provided valuable services to the community. As Alameda judges gained experience with the new sentencing option, they broadened the program to include male offenders, juveniles, and persons convicted of crimes more serious than traffic or parking violations.

The Alameda County community service program received international attention. England and Wales developed pilot projects in the 1970s, using community service as a midlevel sanction between probation and prison and as an alternative to prison sentences up to six months. By 1975, community service had become a central feature of English sentencing. The approach swept throughout Europe, Australia, New Zealand, and Canada.

However, what had begun as an American innovation atrophied in the United States.[29] Today in this country, community service is seldom used as a separate sentence. Instead, it may be one of many conditions of a probation sentence as in the case of Chris Brown. Nor is it viewed as an alternative to imprisonment in the United States, as it is in other countries. Generally speaking, in the United States, public officials do not consider any sanction other than imprisonment punitive enough. Substituting community service for short prison sentences is not accepted. This is unfortunate because community service is a burdensome penalty that meets with widespread public approval,[30] is inexpensive to administer, and produces public value. Also, it can be scaled to the seriousness of the crime. Proponents of community service include the American Correctional Association (see Exhibit 5–7).

Community service can be an intermediate sanction by itself or be used with other penalties and requirements, including substance abuse treatment, restitution, or probation. In the federal courts, community service is not a sentence, but a special condition of probation or supervised release set forth in the presentence report. Offenders sentenced to community service are usually assigned to work for government or private nonprofit agencies. They restore historic buildings; maintain parks and construct campsites; clean roadways and county fairgrounds; remove snow from around public buildings; perform land and river reclamation; and

| **EXHIBIT 5–7** | **American Correctional Association** |

Public Correctional Policy on Community Service and Restorative Justice

Introduction:

Establishing a sense of community is an important part of the rehabilitation process of offenders. Whether within an institution or as part of community corrections, it is beneficial to promote community service for offenders to assist their reentry into society and to promote the positive restoration within the community of the harm that criminal activity has caused.

Policy Statement:

The American Correctional Association supports community service for offenders and urges its use as consistent with correctional management principles and public safety objectives.

While promoting community service, justice systems and institutions must consider factors that contribute to the success of the effort for the offender and the public.

Therefore, when developing criteria for successful community service efforts, criminal justice and rehabilitative programs must:

A. Enhance public safety;

B. Integrate the offender into the community;

C. Contribute to principles of restorative justice;

D. Gain public support for programs and promoting acceptance of offenders;

E. Enhance the self-esteem of offenders by using their time, talents and skills to benefit themselves and others;

F. Provide value to government, the community and nonprofit organizations;

G. Provide valuable, transferable skills to offenders;

H. Balance community service with other responsibilities including family and work, and the availability of transportation;

I. Restore public confidence in offenders; and

J. Maintain public confidence in the justice system.

Source: Copyright © American Correctional Association. Reprinted with permission.

Visit www.corrections.com/news/ article/30116-inside-nic-a-discussion-with-community-services-division-chief-jim-cosby or scan this code with the QR app on your smartphone or digital device and read the interview with Jim Cosby, Community Services Division Chief with the National Institute of Corrections and learn about his philosophy of community service. How does this information relate to ideas discussed in this chapter?

renovate schools and nursing homes. Offenders who are doctors may be ordered to give medical service to persons who might otherwise lack it. Traffic offenders may be ordered to serve in hospital emergency rooms unloading ambulances and helicopters to learn about the injuries they risk for themselves and others. Drug offenders who are prominent sports figures may be ordered to lecture in high schools on the dangers of drugs. The service options are limited only by the imagination of the sentencing judge and the availability of personnel to ensure that the offender fulfills the terms of the sentence. To become and remain a tough criminal sanction, community service must have credible and efficient enforcement mechanisms.

By the late 1980s, some form of community service sanction was in use in all 50 states. When Congress passed the Comprehensive Crime Control Act and Criminal Fine Enforcement Act of 1984, it mandated that felons who receive a sentence (except for class A or B felony—the most serious) must be ordered to pay a fine, make restitution, and/or work in community service. The Bureau of Justice Statistics estimates conservatively that 6 percent of all felons in the United States are sentenced to perform community service, often in conjunction with other sanctions.[31]

Corey Fleetion

Manager of the Escambia County Work Release Program, Pensacola, Florida

Corey Fleetion is the manager of the Escambia County Work Release Program in Pensacola, Florida. He has been employed with the Department of Community Corrections for 20 years. During this period, he has worked in various positions within the department—probation assistant, probation officer, senior probation officer, work release program coordinator/supervisor—and is currently work release program manager. He has worked in pretrial release (PTR), Community Confinement Program (CCP), and the Work Release Program (WRP) and has monitored caseloads of felony and misdemeanor clients as well as inmates on global positioning(GPS)/electronic monitoring system. He was very instrumental in identifying, interviewing, and referring potential inmates in the jail to the Escambia County Drug Court Program. He also assisted circuit and county courts in the first appearance by presenting criminal NCIC/FCIC history. His everyday responsibilities include supervising probation and corrections officers, conducting field visits of inmates and attending violation of probation hearings. Maintaining current policy and procedures for the WRP is vital to ensure that it runs smoothly and effectively.

Fleetion is actively involved in numerous professional and community organizations. He has served more than 15 years with the Florida Council on Crime and Delinquency, serving as vice president, president, and many terms as secretary and treasurer. He is a committee member of the Supervisory Advisory Board of the Florida State Employees Credit Union. As a member of the Workforce Escarosa Youth Development Council, he provides positive input to enhance the opportunities for job training and placement for youth in his community. He also serves as the financial officer of Kingdom Builders Christian Ministries.

Fleetion graduated as class Valedictorian of Coosa County High School in Rockford, Alabama. He continued his education by attending and graduating from the University of Montevallo, Montevallo, Alabama. While a student there, he received an academic scholarship (Talented Minority Undergraduate), and in 1991, he received his bachelor's degree with a major in social work and minor in psychology. He attended the University of Tennessee in Knoxville, Tennessee in 1988 and continued postgraduate education at the University of West Florida in Pensacola, Florida.

Fleetion's involvement with the community and church and his years of working in the Department of Community Corrections have made him an experienced leader in his respective field of study. He contributes his success to his honesty, his desire for continuing education, and his determination for success through hard work, networking, and associating with a diverse group of people. His employment history includes being a certified nursing assistant (CNA) at a nursing home, a receptionist at the Department of Human Resources, and an internship with Child Support and Children and Families. He has also participated in social services with the Community Action Program at Head Start, tutored at Pensacola Junior College, and oversaw senior college interns from the University of West Florida and Pensacola Christian College. His passion in assisting others and for giving individuals an opportunity for a second chance has made him a well-rounded criminal justice professional.

His advice to others is to be aware and learn from your surroundings. Trust yourself and your abilities. There are no short cuts to maturity. He believes that every obstacle is an opportunity and one must never underestimate the value of her or his work as a leader. As you stay in tune with your effects of your leadership, you must always use wisdom, enjoy what you are doing, and have a sense of purpose in fulfilling your destiny.

> *"...every obstacle is an opportunity and one must never underestimate the value of her or his work as a leader."*

States like Washington, Georgia, and Texas are making extensive use of community service. At least one-third of Washington's convicted felons receive sentences that include community service. Washington State sentencing guidelines permit substitution of community service for incarceration at a rate of 8 hours of work for 1 day of incarceration, with a limit of 30 days. Most jurisdictions recognize 240 hours as the upper limit for community service. Washington State also is breaking new ground in sentencing reform with the idea of *interchangeable sentences* for nonviolent or not very violent crimes against strangers. The actual sentence depends on the offender and the purposes to be served. For those with little or no income, community service may substitute for a fine. Before offenders are sentenced to community service in Washington, they complete a community service order questionnaire (see Exhibit 5–8). The questionnaire helps the state department match the offender's abilities and limitations with community service work. A community corrections officer then makes sure the offender performs the required community service.

There is no evidence-based corrections literature examining the effectiveness of community service on reducing criminal activity. What we find instead are descriptions of community service programs in use across the United States. Before it can be concluded that community service does or does not reduce criminal activity, strong research designs are needed. Until then, the jury is still out on community service.

Day Reporting Centers A **day reporting center (DRC)** is a nonresidential community correctional center. Participants are allowed to return home in the evenings, but are required to maintain a strict schedule that is closely monitored.

CO5-6

day reporting center (DRC)

A community correctional center to which an offender reports every day or several days a week for supervision and treatment.

DRCs typically offer numerous services to address offenders' problems, and they strictly supervise offenders in a setting that is more secure than probation but less inhibiting than incarceration. DRCs differ from other intermediate sanctions by a marked concentration on rehabilitation. Staff members assess the offender's needs and offer her or him various types of in-house treatment and referral programs, including substance abuse treatment, education, vocational training, and psychological services. DRCs have an aura of rigor that appeals to those wanting punishment and control of offenders, and it appeals to those advocating more access to treatment for offenders. While DRCs differ in the type of offenders they serve, they all have three common threads: frequent reporting, significant programming to assist offenders, and offender accountability.

DRCs first developed in Great Britain in 1972. British officials noted that many offenders were imprisoned not because they posed a risk to the public but because they lacked basic skills to survive lawfully. Frequently, such offenders were dependent on drugs and alcohol. In 1986, the Hampden County Sheriff's Department in Springfield, Massachusetts, established the first DRC in the United States. Ten years later, a National Institute of Justice survey identified 114 DRCs in 22 states.[32] Since then, however, there has not been an accounting of DRCs across the U.S.

DRCs provide rehabilitation for offenders through intensive programming, while retaining a punishment component by maintaining a highly structured environment. DRCs commonly require offenders to obey a curfew, perform community service, and undergo drug testing. Participants check in at the center in person daily or several times a week and telephone periodically. They are responsible for following a full-time schedule that includes a combination of work, school, and substance abuse or mental health treatment. Programs range in duration from 40 days to 9 months, and program content

EXHIBIT 5–8 Sample Community Service Order Questionnaire

STATE OF WASHINGTON
DEPARTMENT OF CORRECTIONS

COMMUNITY SERVICE WORKER QUESTIONNAIRE
AND RELEASE OF INFORMATION

Name _____

DOC Number _____

By action of the Superior Court, or an administrative Department of Corrections action, you have been ordered to perform community service work. This work must be performed within an approved unit of government or non-profit agency. To help us find the best assignment for you, and ensure reasonable accommodation for any sensory, physical or mental limitations or disabilities that you may have, please supply the following information. You are not obligated to disclose conditions that do not relate to your ability to perform community service.

1. List your job skills.

2. Do you have a preference for a certain agency or a particular type of work that you would like to perform? If yes, describe:

3. List the hours and days you are available for work.

   Monday _____ Wednesday _____ Friday _____ Sunday _____

   Tuesday _____ Thursday _____ Saturday _____

4. What means of transportation do you have to get to and from the work site?

5. Do you wear contacts or glasses? Yes No N/A (circle one)

6. Are you pregnant? Yes No N/A (circle one)

7. Are you currently taking any prescription medications that have side effects that may affect your ability to perform community service work (i.e., drowsiness, slurred speech, etc.)? Yes No (circle one)

   If "Yes," describe side effects:

8. Note whether you have been diagnosed as having any of the following problems:

	Yes	No		Yes	No		Yes	No
Severe Allergy Reactions			Heart Problems			Epilepsy		
Breathing Disorders			Hearing Loss			Uncorrected Vision Problems		
Balance Problems			Diabetes			Other		

   If "Yes," please describe:

9. Is there any activity or motion that is difficult for you to do (i.e., crawling, climbing, bending, lifting, etc.)?

   Yes No (circle one) If "Yes," please describe:

10. Do you have any other sensory, physical and/or mental limitations or disabilities that may affect your ability to do community service? Yes No (circle one) If "Yes," please describe:

11. You are required to provide to your Community Corrections Officer, a clearance from your health care provider, documenting any sensory/physical/mental limitations or disabilities which impact your ability to perform community service hours. This documentation is required within 30 days of today's date, and will be at your expense. Release of information is on the reverse side.

Distributions: ORIGINAL-Community Service Worker, COPY-Worksite, Community Service Coordinator, File

DOC 05-103 (REV 10/97) OCO

COMMUNITY SERVICE PROGRAM

differs. Most programs require a daily schedule of each participant's activities. Some are highly intensive, with 10 or more supervision contacts per day, and a few include 24-hour remote-location or other electronic monitoring.[33] Some centers refer clients to service agencies; others provide services directly. Some focus on monitoring; others emphasize support.

There have been few evaluations of DRCs. Early evaluations were favorable, but they were based on impressions rather than validated findings. The NIJ-sponsored survey showed generally high failure rates, averaging 50 percent. A study conducted on DRCs in North Carolina in 2000 compared the outcome of offenders sentenced to DRCs *plus* intensive supervision probation to that of offenders sentenced to intensive probation alone.[34] The researchers found that the addition of a DRC to ISP did not significantly reduce the rate of rearrest. In fact, they suggested that any rehabilitative effect that DRCs may have is counterbalanced by increased surveillance. "The 'piling up' of sanctions increases the likelihood of the offender's exposure to numerous forms of control and scrutiny culminating in frequent violations of the terms of the sentence."[35] On the positive side, however, the researchers found that DRCs empower the individual offender through literacy courses, a general equivalency diploma (GED), substance abuse counseling, and anger management classes.

BI Incorporated, a private corrections provider with headquarters in Boulder, Colorado, operates day reporting centers in California, Colorado, Illinois, Kansas, New Jersey, New York, and Pennsylvania. One of the services offered at the centers is cognitive skills and behavioral restructuring courses that help offenders identify and change the antisocial beliefs, thoughts, and values that contribute to criminal behavior. Through the use of modeling, role-playing, and reinforcement, cognitive-behavioral interventions assist offenders in developing the positive thinking, judgment, and decision-making skills that promote pro-social behavior. What do we know about DRCs' effectiveness in reducing criminal activity?

Recent studies of DRCs in Vigo County, Indiana,[36] Cook County (Chicago), Illinois,[37] and Franklin County, Pennsylvania,[38] looked at rearrest and reincarceration and which variables were associated with program completion. In Cook County, researchers discovered that almost one-half of the DRC clients who remained in the program for at least 70 days had not been rearrested compared to only one-quarter of the control group (those in the program fewer than 10 days). Similarly, two-thirds of the DRC clients who remained in the program for at least 70 days had not been reincarcerated compared with less than one-half of the control group.

In Vigo County, Indiana, 69 percent of the 179 adult offenders who were placed on DRC during the calendar years 1998 and 1999 successfully completed the program. One-third did not. DRC clients over age 40, married, either living alone or with their spouse, children, or parents, and with little to no history of alcohol and drug abuse were more successful. DRC clients convicted of misdemeanors with only one or two counts who received no charge reduction, who were in DRC as a condition of probation, and whose sentence to DRC did not extend beyond 120 days were also more successful. The researchers showed that the number of subjects who fail to complete the program increases as the sentence to DRC increases.

In 2011, Franklin County, Pennsylvania, published the results of a DRC study conducted by researchers at Shippensburg University. The study followed adult probationers who completed the DRC program from December 16, 2006, to June 1, 2009, and compared them to inmates released to standard probation services from the jail in 2004. Researchers found probationers who completed the DRC program failed probation at a rate of 18.2 percent. In comparison, probationers referred to standard probation services from jail failed at a rate of 47.8 percent. The researchers also said

A probation officer sets up an exclusion zone in red for an offender who is territory-restricted. What are the pros and cons of remote location monitoring as a probationary strategy?

CO5-7

remote-location monitoring

Technologies, including Global Positioning System (GPS) devices and electronic monitoring (EM), that probation and parole officers use to monitor remotely the physical location of an offender.

that because the DRC helped keep down the jail population, the county was able to lease jail space to other jurisdictions, generating $970,285 for the county in 2010.

What we know about the effectiveness of DRC is this: There are simply not enough research studies employing scientific rigor upon which to conclude that DRCs reduce criminal activity. Individual investigations of DRCs like those conducted in Illinois, Indiana, North Carolina, and Pennsylvania that lack randomization of subjects to experimental and control groups and focus only on those who complete the program may show a crime control benefit, but only a systematic review of the body of DRC literature that evaluates the scientific rigor of each study can conclude whether the DRC is an effective crime control strategy for other jurisdictions to adopt. As we said about the effectiveness of community service, the jury is still out.

Remote-Location Monitoring Technologies that probation and parole officers use to monitor remotely the physical location of an offender are known as **remote-location monitoring**. There is no exact accounting on the number of persons under remote-location monitoring. An *Associated Press* investigation published in July 2013 estimated the number at 100,000. *The Prison Legal News*, a publication aimed at inmate leadership, set the estimate at 200,000.

Initially, remote-location monitoring targeted only the traditional clients of house arrest: low-risk probationers, such as those convicted of DUI. More recently, however, it has expanded to include people awaiting trial or sentencing, offenders on probation and parole, and juvenile offenders. Furthermore, whereas electronic house arrest initially gained acceptance as a response to property crimes, advances in remote-location monitoring allow pretrial officers and probation and parole officers to set up exclusion zones (such as schools, parks, and homes) for offenders who are territory-restricted (e.g., stalkers and child molesters). Approximately half the states use Global Positioning System (GPS) to monitor some sex offenders while they are on parole.[39] A minimum of eight states (California, Colorado, Florida, Michigan, Missouri, Ohio, Oklahoma, and Wisconsin) have enacted laws permitting lifetime GPS monitoring of some sex offenders recently, however, the South Carolina Supreme Court declared that lifetime GPS tracking of sex offenders is unconstitutional. It is too early to tell whether the South Carolina ruling will have ripple effects in other states.[40]

Remote-location monitoring uses technological systems such as EM, the GPS, voice verification, and other tracking systems to verify a person's physical location, either periodically or continuously, 24 hours a day. Some GPS ankle bracelets are microphone-equipped. They have the same features as a cellular phone and can record the offender's private conversations without their knowledge and without a court warrant which raises civil liberty issues.

A major benefit of remote-location monitoring is that it costs significantly less than incarceration. The average cost of incarcerating a state or federal inmate has been estimated to range from $36 to $123 per day.[41] In contrast, the daily cost of remote-location monitoring is between $3 and $5, and GPS monitoring is between $5 and $11.[42] Moreover, many courts order program participants to pay all or part of the costs. Another benefit is that it allows defendants and offenders to continue to contribute to the support of their families and pay taxes.

In theory, remote-location monitoring satisfies three correctional goals. First, it incapacitates the offender by restricting him or her to a single location. Second, remote-location monitoring is punitive because it forces the offender to stay home when not at work, school, counseling, or community service. And third, it contributes to rehabilitation by allowing the offender to remain with his or her family and continue employment, education, or vocational training.

It is easy to find evaluations of remote-location monitoring that show positive results. For example, a review of the performance of 17,000 participants in the federal home confinement program found that 89 percent successfully completed the program.[43] And when researchers with the Center for Criminology and Public Policy Research at Florida State University compared the experiences of more than 5,000 medium- and high-risk offenders who were monitored electronically to more than 266,000 offenders not placed on monitoring during a six-year period, they found that electronic monitoring reduced the risk of failure by 31 percent.[44]

However, when researchers examine the body of literature on remote-location monitoring more closely, they find two things. First, the methods used in these studies do not meet the threshold of scientific rigor. Very few employ the gold standard of research—randomly assign subjects to remote-location monitoring programs (the experimental group) and others to programs-as-usual (the control group). And even if randomization is employed, most studies do not focus on the different kinds of remote-location monitoring, meaning what type of monitoring was used, how did it operate, how reliable was the equipment (down time, location failures, errors, tampering), and ways in which remote-location monitoring is linked to other forms of community supervision and treatment. Without scientific rigor, it is questionable whether the available research can be a guide for policymakers on important questions, beginning with "is remote-location monitoring effective?"

And second, the studies focus only on whether remote-location monitoring suppresses an individual's criminal behavior rather than changes it. The positive results noted above in the study of federal home confinement and GPS monitoring in Florida may simply be the result of the extra surveillance offered by remote-location monitoring. The majority of studies on remote-location monitoring do not examine the therapeutic aspects of correctional programs that are known to reduce criminal activity. Changes in an offender's cognitive skills of thinking, reasoning, empathy, and problem solving are seldom subject to the same evaluation that control and surveillance are. After reviewing thousands of studies on correctional interventions, management policies, and treatment and rehabilitation programs, Dr. Doris MacKenzie, professor of criminology and criminal justice at the University of Maryland and former scientist with the U.S. Department of Justice, wrote, "Restraining offenders in the community by increasing surveillance and control over their activities does not reduce their criminal activities."[45] ". . . effective correctional programs must focus on changing the individual."[46] Without a human service component and without measuring its effectiveness on reducing criminal activity, reporting only on control and surveillance leads to the conclusion that remote-location monitoring does not work.

Residential Reentry Centers A **residential reentry center (RRC)** is a medium-security correctional setting that resident offenders are permitted to leave regularly—unaccompanied by staff—for work, CO5-8

residential reentry center (RRC)

A medium-security correctional setting that resident offenders are permitted to leave regularly—unaccompanied by staff—for work, education or vocational programs, or treatment in the community but require them to return to a locked facility each evening.

educational or vocational programs, or treatment in the community but require them to return to a locked facility each evening.

Initially, such centers were called *halfway houses* and were for offenders who either were about to be released from an institution or were in the first stages of return to the community. However, as the number of halfway houses grew and new client groups (divertees, pretrial releasees, and probationers) were added, the umbrella term *residential reentry center* was adopted.

Halfway houses, prerelease and work release centers, and restitution centers are examples of RRCs. Some RRCs specialize in a type of client or treatment—for example, in drug and alcohol abuse, violent and sex offenders, women, abused women, or prerelease federal prisoners. Some are public and some private.

Most scholars attribute the first halfway house in the United States to the Isaac T. Hooper Home in New York City in 1845. For nearly a century, halfway houses were operated by charitable organizations to assist persons leaving prison, and their growth was slow. It wasn't until the 1950s and into the 1960s that the number of halfway houses expanded across the United States as part of a broader movement to deal with offender problems in the community instead of prison. However, when the crime rate did not drop as many had expected, and fueled by the conservative ideology of the 1980s, the growth in halfway houses slowed. Their use was in many cases closer to that of a minimum-security facility instead of a rehabilitative one, and seen as a way to reduce prison crowding.

Unfortunately, it is not possible to know how many RRCs there are today, or how many offenders they serve. "There are no national figures, only educated guesses."[47] Some estimate there may be in excess of 1,000 RRCs serving almost 30,000 residents each year.[48] One difficulty in estimating the number of offenders that RRCs serve is that many residents are already counted in the publications of persons under correctional supervision in jail and prison and on probation and parole published annually by the U.S. Department of Justice, Bureau of Justice Statistics.

The federal Bureau of Prisons (BOP) has the largest number of inmates (9,185) in almost 200 RRCs nationwide representing 4.2 percent of the BOP's total population.[49] Almost 80 percent of eligible federal prisoners are released through RRCs where they spend, on average, three to four months before being released into the community. The primary purpose of the program is to serve as a cost-effective form of punishment. Residents work in the community and return to the center after work. They use their wages to pay for room and board, transportation, court and probation costs, victim restitution, and child support. They also perform community service. On April 11, 2010, Gilbert Arenas, basketball player for the Orlando Magic, started serving a 30-day sentence at the federal Montgomery County (Maryland) halfway house for a gun-related conviction. Arenas was also required to perform 400 hours of community service, donate $5,000 to a fund for victims of violent crimes, and register as a gun offender in Washington, DC.[50]

The objectives of RRCs are community protection and offender reintegration. Community protection is achieved by screening offenders; setting curfews; administering drug or polygraph tests; confirming that when residents leave the center they go directly to work, school, or treatment; and providing a medium-security correctional setting. Reintegration is achieved by giving residents opportunities to learn and use legitimate skills, thereby reducing their reliance on criminal behavior. Staff members determine the obstacles to each resident's reintegration, plan a program to overcome those obstacles, and provide a supportive environment to help the resident test, use, and refine the skills needed.

The benefits of RRCs are many. RRCs benefit offenders by providing them with the basic necessities of food, clothing, and shelter while they find housing and employment. RRCs also offer residents emotional support to deal with the pressures of readjustment and help them obtain community services. Benefits to the community include a moderately secure correctional setting in which residents' behavior is monitored and controlled, as well as an expectation that opportunities for offenders to get on their feet will reduce postrelease adjustment problems and criminal behavior. For the criminal justice system, an RRC offers a low-cost housing alternative to incarceration of nonviolent offenders. An RRC can control offenders in the community at less cost than building and operating more secure facilities. It may also serve as an enhancement to probation and an option for dealing with probation and parole violators.

There has not been much research on the effectiveness of RRCs compared to other intermediate sanctions discussed in this chapter. The state of Colorado conducted a statewide study of recidivism of halfway house clients and analyzed information on all offenders ($n = 3,054$) who terminated from 25 halfway houses.[51] The study tracked cases for 24 months. It reported that 69 percent had no arrest within 24 months. Of the 31 percent who recidivated within 24 months, the majority of cases were drug or alcohol related. Only 3.4 percent were for violent offenses. High-risk, prior criminal history, young age, and lack of postrelease supervision predicted future offending. The report recommended that intensive treatment, therapeutic community models, and multidisciplinary approaches to deal with drug and alcohol addiction should be replicated across the state. The report also called for specific aftercare services to enhance offenders' likelihood of success, maximize public safety, and reduce recidivism.

Recently a study of Ohio's 38 RRCs found that RRCs were most effective with parole violators and higher-risk and proposed using more RRCs and diversion programs as ways to cut prison costs in Ohio.[52] (The average annual cost to incarcerate an inmate in Ohio is $25,000 but only $10,000 to send an offender to an RRC where she or he receives counseling, does household chores, works on job skills, stands by for random room searches, and signs the clipboard as he or she leaves for outside work and returns at a set hour.) Furthermore, the most effective RRC programs provided the greatest number of services targeting criminogenic needs, offered cognitive behavioral treatment, and engaged in role playing and practicing of newly learned skills.

The absence of an adequate body of scientifically rigorous evaluations of RRCs and the current focus on control and suppression instead of individual-level behavioral changes in thinking, reasoning, and problem solving that are known to reduce a person's propensity to commit crime means we cannot say that RRCs reduce criminal activity. Nor can we say that RRCs are ineffective. We can only say that the impact of RRCs is unknown until an adequate body of scientifically rigorous literature becomes available.

Boot Camps In 1983, in an effort to alleviate prison crowding and reduce recidivism, the departments of corrections in Oklahoma and Georgia opened the first adult prison programs modeled after military boot camps. Since then, boot camp (sometimes referred to as *shock incarceration, intensive confinement centers* [ICCs], or *work ethic camps*) has become an increasingly popular intermediate sanction.

CO5-9

boot camp

A short institutional term of confinement that includes a physical regimen designed to develop self-discipline, respect for authority, responsibility, and a sense of accomplishment.

Boot camp is a short institutional term of confinement, usually followed by probation, that includes a physical regimen designed to develop self-discipline, respect for authority, responsibility, and a sense of accomplishment. According to the NIJ, four characteristics distinguish boot camps from other correctional programs:

(1) military drill and ceremony,

(2) a rigorous daily schedule of hard labor and physical training,

(3) separation of boot camp participants from the general prison population, and

(4) the idea that boot camps are an alternative to long-term confinement.

However, as you will learn, the use of correctional boot camps is on the decline, and the evidence-based literature reports that the average boot camp has no effect on recidivism.[53]

However that hasn't stopped some sheriffs from implementing them. David A. Clarke Jr., sheriff of Milwaukee County, Wisconsin, calls his boot camp a "Discipline, Order, Training and Structure" program.[54] Eligibility criteria include low-level offenders who are in physical shape and don't present serious behavioral problems. Inmates wear uniforms, rise early, participate in rigorous physical training by drill instructors (former war veterans from Iraq and Afghanistan), be required to say "yes, sir" and "no, sir," and take classes on job readiness, anger management, and building positive relationships with friends and spouses. Sheriff Clarke is unmoved by those who say such programs do not work. He believes that inmates need to have discipline instilled before other reform efforts at education and job training can work.

Boot camps have progressed through three phases. The first phase stressed military drill and ceremony. The second phase incorporated treatment programs such as anger management and alcohol and drug treatment. In the third phase, some correctional agencies added aftercare such as postrelease supervision, remote-location monitoring, and networking

The military-style training and drill that characterize boot camps are frequently supplemented with substance abuse education and vocational training. What aftercare programs might contribute to the effectiveness of boot camp strategies?

boot camp graduates to community agencies to continue the treatment and services provided in boot camp.

Critics have raised questions about using boot camps as a correctional tool. They note that correctional boot camp programs are built on a model of military basic training that the military itself has found lacking and in some cases has revised. Critics also argue that the military model was designed to produce a cohesive fighting unit and that after military boot camp there is further specialized training and career planning. That is not a goal of corrections. One analyst wrote, "If an offender can't read [or] write and is drug-involved, sending him to a 90-day boot camp that does not address his job or literacy needs will only have a short-term effect, if any, on his behavior."[55]

There is reason for both optimism and skepticism about boot camps. Although boot camps are promoted as a means of reducing recidivism rates, there is no evidence that they significantly reduce recidivism or promote socially desirable activities. A multisite evaluation of boot camps in Texas, South Carolina, and Florida showed no significant differences in reoffending rates among the different groups of offenders.[56] Research on Oklahoma's boot camp program, called the Regimented Inmate Discipline (RID) program, revealed that even when the researchers controlled for type of offense, age, and race on recidivism, boot camp graduates recidivated more frequently than either traditionally incarcerated inmates or probationers.[57] Research published on a county-based boot camp in Florida shows similar results. The likelihood of an offender being rearrested was unaffected by his or her being sent to boot camp. Eighty-one percent of the boot camp graduates were rearrested, averaging 271 days before rearrest. Seventy-three percent of the comparison group was rearrested, averaging 290 days before rearrest.[58]

Some researchers have reported that boot camp graduates have higher self-esteem, have better attitudes toward family, are less likely to see themselves as victims of circumstances, and are more likely to feel in control of their future.[59] However, with limited exceptions, these positive changes didn't translate into reduced recidivism. Research into what boot camp participants say they'll do is less conclusive than research into what they've actually done.

Also disappointing is that the recidivism rates of boot camp graduates are very similar to those of other parolees.[60] One-third to one-half of front-end boot camp participants fail to complete their programs and are sent to prison as a result. In most programs, close surveillance of graduates after release leads to technical violation and revocation rates that are higher than those of comparable offenders in less intensive programs.

Boot camps are also promoted as a means of reducing prison crowding and corrections costs. Here the news is not all bad. Boot camp programs, where imprisoned offenders are transferred by corrections officials, do save money and prison space. Although they often experience high failure, technical violation, and revocation rates, those rates are no higher than those for offenders who have been kept in prison longer. If enough offenders complete boot camp and are released early from prison, the programs can reduce prison crowding. However, a number of researchers have found that most boot camps have not reduced prison crowding because the programs are designed for offenders who would otherwise be on probation, not those who would otherwise have received prison terms.[61] MacKenzie and her colleagues found in a multisite evaluation of boot camps that only two of the five boot camp programs examined appeared to save prison beds. The remaining three boot camp programs appeared to increase the

The Staff Speaks
Visit www.mhhe.com/schmalleger7e to see this feature.

Economic Realities and Corrections: Intermediate Sanctions

Governors, legislatures, and correctional administrators nationwide are coping with budget cutbacks while being under pressure to deliver ever better public safety outcomes.

The governor of Georgia signed legislation to reduce the number of low-level drug possession offenders in prison and expand the use of intermediate sanctions including drug courts, which help treat addicts and hold offenders accountable in the community.

The governor of Pennsylvania signed a law directing low-level nonviolent offenders into community supervision, saving the state $250 million through 2018.

The governor of Texas scrapped plans to build three new prisons, saving his state $2 billion and reinvesting it in treating offenders with mental health and addiction problems.

Why are states pursuing intermediate sanctions that before the economic recession of 2007 would have been called liberal policies on crime and punishment? The first reason is that the economic recession has forced governors, legislators, and correctional administrators to take a hard look at the amount of money being spent on the prison system. Huge prison spending is now viewed as running counter to fiscal conservatism.

Twenty years ago the United States spent $7 billion on its prison population of 970,000 inmates. Today, states are spending more than $63 billion on a prison population of almost 1.4 million inmates. As budgets have tightened, other important functions of government have been squeezed to pay for the escalation in prison spending.

At the same time, many liberals and conservatives have come to recognize that prison is ineffective in rehabilitating offenders. Half of prisoners released are expected to be back in prison within three years. Many have come to see prison as a poor method of achieving prisoner reform. Therefore, the fiscal crisis that began in December 2007 is moving many governors and legislators to think "outside the cell" and turn to intermediate sanctions as a way to keep low-level offenders out of prison and in their communities. Is the public buying it? According to a national public opinion survey conducted in January 2012 and similar surveys in Georgia, Missouri, and Oregon, the answer is a resounding "yes." Three key takeaways from that national survey are these:

1. American voters believe too many people are in prison and the nation spends too much on imprisonment.

2. Voters overwhelmingly support a variety of policy changes that shift non-violent offenders from prison to more effective, less expensive intermediate sanctions like those discussed in this chapter.

3. Support for intermediate sanctions is strong across political parties, regions, age, gender, and racial/ethnic groups.

Specifically, 84 percent of respondents believe that some of the money that we are spending on locking up low-risk, nonviolent inmates should be shifted to strengthening intermediate sanctions. Sixty-nine percent agree that there are more effective, less expensive intermediate sanctions to prison for nonviolent offenders and expanding those alternatives is the best way to reduce the crime rate. And four of five people want to send fewer low-risk, nonviolent offenders to prison and reinvest in intermediate sanctions.

We are seeing significant pieces of legislation favoring intermediate sanctions for nonviolent offenders. Over the past several decades, legislatures passed "tough-on-crime" measures that increased penalties, prison sentences, and skyrocketed the cost of penal incarceration—key reasons why with less than 5 percent of the world's population, the U.S. has almost 25 percent of the world's prisoners.

Without question, voters want a strong public safety system in which criminals are held accountable and illegal activities have consequences. Voters also believe that these goals can be reached while reducing the size and cost of the prison system. Intermediate sanctions can help.

need for prison beds.[62] Crowding can be reduced only if boot camp participants are selected from inmates already incarcerated and only if their participation substantially reduces their overall sentence lengths.

The body of evidence-based corrections literature tells us this about correctional boot camps:

1. There is an adequate body of scientifically rigorous research examining correctional boot camps.

2. The military atmosphere of correctional boot camps does not bring about individual-level changes in thinking, reasoning, and problem solving.

3. An aftercare component to correctional boot camp *may* reduce recidivism, but there is little information about the *type* of aftercare that programs provide. Are individual-level changes the result of drug treatment, employment, or something else? We do not know.

4. To date, it is impossible to say why the recidivism of some correctional boot camp participants is lower than the comparison group.

5. If the goal of correctional boot camp is to reduce recidivism, then there is little reason to continue its use.

6. If there are other goals such as operating as a back-end program or to reduce prison crowding, then we need more research.

COMMUNITY CORRECTIONS

CO5-10

In Chapter 1 you learned that the correctional system can be either institutional or noninstitutional. Institutional corrections (jails and prisons) involves the incarceration and rehabilitation of adults and juveniles. *Noninstitutional corrections* refers to correctional activities not directly related to incarceration. The intermediate sanctions discussed in this chapter, diversion and probation (Chapter 4), and parole (Chapter 8) are examples of correctional activities not directly related to institutional care.

There is no consensus in the field of criminal justice on the definition of **community corrections**. Sometimes the term refers to noninstitutional programs. Sometimes it refers to programs administered by local government rather than the state. Other times, it indicates citizen involvement.

We define *community corrections* as a philosophy of correctional treatment that embraces (1) decentralization of authority from state to local levels; (2) citizen participation in program planning, design, implementation, and evaluation; (3) redefinition of the population of offenders for whom incarceration is most appropriate; and (4) emphasis on rehabilitation through community programs.

Community corrections recognizes the importance of partnership with the community in responding to crime. In short, our communities not only have a *right* to safe streets and homes but also bear *responsibility* for making them safe. All the major components of the criminal justice system have alliances today with the community. The field is experiencing many changes, including the following:

- *community policing*—a law enforcement strategy to get residents involved in making their neighborhoods safer by focusing on crime prevention, nonemergency services, public accountability, and decentralized decision making that includes the public;

- *community-based prosecution*—a prosecution strategy that uses a combination of criminal and civil tactics and the legal expertise, resources, and clout of the prosecuting attorney's office to find innovative solutions to a neighborhood's specific problems;

- *community-based defender services*—a defender strategy that provides continuity in representation of indigent defendants and helps defendants with personal and family problems that can lead to legal troubles; and

- *community courts*—a judicial strategy of hearing a criminal case in the community that is most affected by the case and including that community in case disposition.

Debate and innovation continue to reflect these themes. The Vermont Department of Corrections leads the nation in giving local citizens decision-making authority about punishment and supervision issues that directly affect the offender, the victim, and community safety. In 1995, the Vermont DOC established a network of "community-based reparative boards" (also referred to as *reparative probation*). Today there are 72 reparative boards across Vermont involving more than 350 citizen volunteers. Annually these boards handle more than 1,400 cases. After

community corrections

A philosophy of correctional treatment that embraces (1) decentralization of authority, (2) citizen participation, (3) redefinition of the population of offenders for whom incarceration is most appropriate, and (4) emphasis on rehabilitation through community programs.

conviction and referral by a judge, offenders meet with their local reparative board to review their offense and learn how it harmed the community. They must then accept the terms of what is usually a multifaceted, community-based sanction, including apologies, restitution, and community service. Consider these two examples.

A single mother working in a nursing home stole a ring from a patient. The reparative board built on the woman's interest in crafts and ordered her to make potpourri-filled vases for the senior center.

An artist convicted for a second time for driving under the influence had to paint a mural for the organization whose lawn she drove over. (Coincidentally, it was a substance abuse center.) The reparative boards' solutions are as varied as the crimes they hear.

Research on reparative probation is scarce. Investigators from the University of Vermont looked at over 9,000 cases decided by the reparative boards.[63] They found that offenders sentenced by reparative boards were 23 percent less likely to commit another crime while on reparative probation and 12 percent less likely to commit another crime after probation ended than those sentenced to traditional probation. However, this is only one study. There is not an adequate body of scientifically rigorous evaluations of reparative probation to say that it reduces criminal activity. Nor can we say that, as with many other intermediate sanctions discussed in this chapter, reparative probation is ineffective. We can say only that the impact of reparative probation is unknown until an adequate body of scientifically rigorous literature becomes available. The American Correctional Association has also embraced community corrections. ACA's support of community corrections is shown in Exhibit 5–9.

CO5-11 Community Corrections Acts

community corrections acts (CCAs)

State laws that give economic grants to local communities to establish community corrections goals and policies and to develop and operate community corrections programs.

This spirit of correctional collaboration and community partnership has led 36 states to pass **community corrections acts (CCAs)** (Exhibit 5–10). CCAs are state laws that give economic grants to local communities to establish community corrections goals and policies and to develop and operate community corrections programs. Under a typical CCA, the state provides local agencies the funds to create or expand intermediate sanctions for certain offenders in the community, and in return, the state benefits by avoiding the costs of incarceration. The funding usually supports a spectrum of community-based punishments, including traditional probation supervision to ISP, day reporting centers, RRCs, and other specialized programs and services such as drug courts. These programs usually range from a few hundred dollars to more than $7,000 per offender per year—far less than the annual cost of housing a state prisoner. CCA states that its goal is to save more money on prison. For example, in Kansas, where probation violators had accounted for 36 percent of prison admissions, legislators provided $4 million in grants to local community corrections programs that developed plans to reduce the percentage of violators sent to prison.

Minnesota was one of the first states to enact a CCA. The Minnesota Community Corrections Act of 1973 provides funding to counties or groups of counties to develop community-based sanctions and programs. Funding totaling almost $40 million per year is awarded based on local population, and counties must submit a comprehensive plan every two years indicating how the money will be spent.

The huge success of Minnesota's CCA can be seen in Minnesota's incarceration rate, one of the lowest in the United States today. While the crime rate is not much different from those of other states, the incarceration rate is only 183 persons for every 100,000 residents. The U.S. average

EXHIBIT 5–9 | **American Correctional Association**

Public Correctional Policy on Community Corrections

Introduction:

Community corrections programs are an integral component of a graduated system of sanctions and services. They enable offenders to work and pay taxes, make restitution, meet court obligations, maintain family ties, and develop and/or maintain critical support systems with the community. To be successful, community corrections programs must promote public safety and a continuum of care that responds to the needs of victims, offenders, and the community. These programs should include a collaborative comprehensive planning process for the development of effective policies and services.

Policy Statement:

Community corrections programs include residential and nonresidential programs. Most community corrections programs require offenders to participate in certain activities or special programs that are specifically directed toward reducing their risk to the community. Those responsible for community corrections programs, services, and supervision should:

A. seek statutory authority and adequate funding, both public and private, for community programs and services as part of a comprehensive corrections strategy;

B. develop and ensure access to a wide array of residential and nonresidential services that address the identifiable needs of victims, offenders and the community;

C. inform the public about the benefits of community programs and services; the criteria used to select individuals for these programs; and the requirements for successful completion;

D. recognize that public acceptance of community corrections is enhanced by the provision of victim services, community service and conciliation programs;

E. mobilize the participation of a well-informed constituency, including citizen advisory boards and broad-based coalitions, to address community corrections issues;

F. participate in collaborative, comprehensive planning efforts which provide a framework to assess community needs and develop a systemwide plan for services; and

G. ensure the integrity and accountability of community programs by establishing a reliable system for monitoring and measuring performance and outcomes in accordance with accepted standards of professional practices and sound evaluation methodology.

Source: Copyright © American Correctional Association. Reprinted with permission.

at yearend 2011 was 492 per 100,000 residents. The majority of Minnesota's offenders are handled under the CCA.

Simply having correctional programs in a community does not mean that a community corrections program exists. Consistent goals and consistent approaches to achieving those goals are the backbone of successful community corrections. Community corrections legislation can help accomplish that consistency.

Community Corrections: A Strategy for Safety and Savings in the Future
The current budget crisis the United States is facing has prompted many states to seize the moment and retool their sentencing and corrections options to better manage the 7.3 million Americans under correctional control. Successful reintegration of the

EXHIBIT 5–10   States with Community Corrections Legislation

■ States with legislation

■ States without legislation

Source: Mary Shilton, "Community Corrections Acts by States, 2007," Center for Community Corrections, centerforcommunitycorrections.org. Reprinted with permission.

offender into the community is also the primary goal of the International Community Corrections Association Code of Ethics. The Pew Center on the States wrote in March 2009:

> If we had stronger community corrections, we wouldn't need to lock up so many people at such a great cost. By redirecting a portion of the dollars currently spent on imprisoning the lowest-risk inmates, we could significantly increase the intensity and quality of supervision and services directed at the same type of offender in the community.[64]

To help create a national agenda for stronger and more effective community corrections, the Pew Center brought together leading policymakers, correctional practitioners, and researchers from states such as Arizona, Kansas, and Texas that are already looking at which offenders should be locked up and which ones can be managed effectively in the community. The purpose of the meeting was to identify ways to help correctional agencies adopt the most effective evidence-based practices. The result was publication of the document *Policy Framework to Strengthen Community Corrections*. The framework includes measures that provide incentives for offenders to stay crime and drug free, fiscal incentives for agencies to improve their success rates, and ways to focus treatment and punishment toward one goal—prevent crime—that is more effective than either punishment or treatment alone. Here we briefly detail the six key components of that framework.[65]

1. *Sort offenders by risk to public safety*—Accurately separate those who are more likely to cause great harm from those who may cause relatively little harm. The risk assessment tools discussed in Chapters 4 and 8 can help corrections officials more accurately predict not only how likely a person is to commit a new crime, but also whether that offense will be a violent one. The risk score can then be used to guide decisions about whether a particular offender should go to prison or remain under community control, and which

Ethics and Professionalism

International Community Corrections Association Code of Ethics

Preamble

The International Community Corrections Association, as a private, non-profit, membership organization, acts as a world unifying body and public advocate for the causes and concerns of community-based residential services in the fields of criminal and juvenile justice, substance abuse, mental health, and mental retardation. As such, it expects of its members compassion, belief in the dignity and worth of human beings, respect for individual differences and a commitment to quality care for its clients. It requires of its members the professional background, research, and expertise necessary to ensure performance of effective quality services delivered with integrity and competence. ICCA affirms its primary goal is the successful reintegration of the client into the community.

Basic Precepts

A. General conduct

1. We are committed to contributing time and professional expertise to activities that promote respect for the utility, integrity, and competence of those in the field of community-based residential services.

2. We will not condone dishonesty, fraud, deceit, or misrepresentation.

3. We will distinguish clearly between statements and actions made as private individuals and as representatives of agencies or organizations and IHHA.

4. We will conduct our daily relationships in a dignified, courteous, and professional manner and will not exploit our professional relationships for personal gain.

5. We will work for change and improvement as part of the human service system within the framework of existing policy, procedures, and tradition, respecting all elements of the system and interacting with each in a spirit of cooperation.

6. We will uphold and advocate for the values, knowledge, and need for community-based residential services.

7. We will be committed to the development of sound policies and programs to maintain the quality and effectiveness of or services.

B. Ethical responsibility to clients

1. We do not practice nor condone any form of discrimination on the basis of race, color, sex, age, religion, national origin, mental or physical handicap or any other preference or personal characteristic, condition or status.

2. We will serve clients with the maximum application of professional skill, competence, and dedication to help them assume responsibility for themselves.

3. Exploitation of relationships with clients will not be condoned.

4. We will uphold clients' rights to a relationship of mutual trust, privacy, and confidentiality and to responsible use of information.

5. Adherence to standards essential to the health and safety, as well as to the well being of clients, is fundamental to the quality of life and will be a primary concern.

6. We will assist clients to achieve self-fulfillment and maximum potential within the limits of the equal rights of others and the client's legitimate desires and interests.

7. Toward those whose behavior is unacceptable, we will determine our course between empathy and allowing the client the freedom to take responsibility for his actions.

8. Our goal will be to provide clients with the opportunity for change and self-regulation and the achievement of their maximum potential.

C. Ethical responsibility to colleagues

1. Respecting the training and performance of colleagues and other professionals, we will extend the cooperation necessary to enhance effective quality services to all.

2. We will respect differences of opinion and practice of colleagues and other professionals, expressing criticism in verbal or written communications in a responsible, appropriate, and constructive manner.

3. We will extend to colleagues of other professions the same respect and cooperation that is extended to members of the International Halfway House Association.

D. Ethical responsibilities to employers and contractors

1. We will adhere responsibly to commitments made to our employers and contractors.

2. We will work to improve agencies' and contractors' policies and procedures and the efficiency, effectiveness, and quality of services.

3. We pledge integrity in contracting for the provision of client services, procurement of grants, and purchase of service contracts from any source.

4. We affirm the obligation of contracting agencies to negotiate fairly for the provision of client services and to avoid any practice resulting in unfair advantage to one party over another.

E. Ethical responsibilities to the community

1. We recognize our responsibility to the client without disregarding our responsibility to the community.

2. Believing in man's ability to overcome his problems within the community, we will remain committed to helping clients to return to their communities as productive citizens.

Source: Reprinted by permission of the International Community Corrections Association.

cognitive treatment interventions will change the offender's thinking and reasoning that drive criminal activity. The Pew Center reminds us that risk assessment is risk management, not risk elimination. Risk assessment is an estimate of what a given person might do. The science continues to evolve.

2. *Base intervention programs on science*—Like the Pew Center, this book promotes the application of evidence-based practices. We've seen throughout this book that evidence-based practices result in an average decrease in crime of between 10 percent and 20 percent, whereas programs that are not evidence based tend to see no decrease or may even result in a slight increase in crime. Interventions that follow all evidence-based practices can result in a reduction of criminal activity by as much as 30 percent.

3. *Harness technology*—Today's technology (for example, remote electronic monitoring, the use of GPS technology, portable breathalyzers, and ignition locks) can help community supervision officers monitor an offender's location and compliance, but only if the officers have the tools and resources to do so and respond to violations in ways that don't contribute to further prison crowding. Technological tools cannot by themselves reduce criminal activity, as we pointed out in this chapter. But they offer community supervision officers tools that are more intense than face-to-face supervision alone and are cheaper than incarceration.

4. *Impose swift and certain sanctions for violation*—Today, too many probation and parole agencies are underfunded, understaffed, struggle with high caseloads, and lack legal authority to impose graduated sanctions for violations. Many community supervision officers delay pursuing violations until an offender has committed a new crime or a significant number of technical violations, at which point return to prison is likely. The framework suggested by the Pew Center is to give probation and parole officers authority to impose graduated sanctions on violators without first requiring a time-consuming trip back to court. The framework documents the success of a program in Georgia called *Probation Options Management* that allows chief POs to impose sanctions on violators in certain circumstances. The program reduced the number of days offenders spent in jail awaiting court disposition by 70 percent, saved local jails $1.1 million, and reduced the amount of time that POs spent waiting in courthouses for violation cases to be heard.

5. *Create incentives for success*—The framework also calls for incentives for offenders and community supervision agencies. Arizona is a case in point. In 2008, Arizona adopted the Safe Communities Act. For every month an offender complies with the terms of supervision, the act authorizes the courts to reduce the offender's length of probation by 20 days. And counties that reduce recidivism are awarded 40 percent of the money the state saves by not having to incarcerate rule violators in state prison. This is an example of the community corrections acts discussed earlier. The counties use the money to improve local services for victims and offenders.

6. *Measure progress*—Policymakers, practitioners, and researchers agree that accurate and timely statistics, deployment of resources where they are most needed, effective human service strategies, and ongoing follow-up and assessment are critical to knowing what impact corrections has on reducing criminal activity. Yes, the goal is

to reduce recidivism, but as we reported in Chapter 4, the American Probation and Parole Association urges its members to collect data on other key performance measures such as amount of restitution collected, number of offenders employed, amount of fines and fees collected, hours of community service performed, number of treatment sessions attended, percentage of financial obligations collected, educational attainment, and number of days drug free.

This set of sentencing and correctional principles is offered as a way to meet the challenge of better balancing public safety, offender accountability, and the realities of today's economic crisis. We agree with the Pew Center and its experts that better performance in community corrections can reduce criminal activity and the expensive use of imprisonment for low-risk offenders.

Will the U.S. public support using intermediate sanctions like those discussed in this chapter to respond to nonserious crime? The answer is that a majority will. One month after the Pew Center published its framework for helping correctional agencies adopt the most effective evidence-based practices for making decisions on which offenders should be locked up and which ones can be managed effectively in the community, the National Council on Crime and Delinquency (NCCD) commissioned Zogby International to conduct a national public opinion poll about U.S. voter attitudes toward intermediate sanctions for nonserious offenders.[66] Poll results show that a majority of U.S. adults believes that offenders who commit nonserious crimes do not need incarceration; almost 8 in 10 believe that the appropriate sentence for nonserious offenders are the intermediate sanctions discussed in this chapter; almost 8 in 10 believe intermediate sanctions do not decrease public safety; half believe intermediate sanctions save money; and almost half believe that intermediate sanctions are more effective at reducing recidivism than prison or jail time. NCCD estimates that over $7 billion can be saved if 80 percent of nonviolent, nonserious offenders are sentenced to alternatives instead of incarceration. A savings of this magnitude in the current economic crisis would reduce the economic burden on institutional corrections and fund community corrections and intermediate sanctions that are more appropriate for nonserious, nonviolent offenders.

REVIEW AND APPLICATIONS

SUMMARY

1 *Intermediate sanctions* is the term given to the range of new sentencing options developed to fill the gap between traditional probation and traditional jail or prison sentences, better match the severity of punishment to the seriousness of the crime, reduce institutional crowding, and control correctional costs. Punishments typically identified as intermediate sanctions include intensive supervision probation (ISP), drug courts, fines, community service, day reporting centers, remote-location monitoring, residential reentry centers, and boot camps.

2 Intensive supervision probation (ISP) is control of offenders in the community through strict enforcement of conditions and frequent reporting to a probation officer with a reduced caseload. ISP programs exist in all 50 states. They may be state or county programs and may be administered by parole, probation, or prison departments.

3 Drug courts are special courts that are given responsibility to handle cases involving drug-addicted offenders.

④ A day fine is a financial punishment scaled to the seriousness of the offense and the offender's ability to pay. A traditional fine is based on a fixed amount, without regard to the offender's ability to pay.

⑤ Community service is a sentence to serve a specified number of hours working in unpaid positions with non-profit or tax-supported agencies. Research suggests that, for offenders who do not present unacceptable risks of future violent crimes, community service costs much less than prison, has comparable recidivism rates, and presents negligible risks of violence by those who would otherwise be confined.

⑥ A day reporting center (DRC) is a community correctional center to which an offender reports each day to file a daily schedule with a supervision officer, showing how each hour will be spent. DRCs aim to provide strict surveillance over offenders and, depending on their resources, provide treatment services, refer offenders to community social service agencies, or arrange to have community agencies offer services on site.

⑦ *Remote-location monitoring* refers to technologies that probation and parole officers use to monitor remotely the physical location of an offender. For example, home-based electronic monitoring (EM) is often used by officers to monitor remotely offenders who are restricted to their homes.

⑧ Residential reentry centers (RRCs) are medium-security correctional settings that resident offenders are permitted to leave regularly—unaccompanied by staff—for work, educational or vocational programs, or treatment in the community but require them to return to a locked facility each evening.

⑨ *Boot camp* is a short institutional term, usually followed by probation, that includes a physical regimen designed to develop self-discipline, respect for authority, responsibility, and a sense of accomplishment.

⑩ *Community corrections* is a philosophy of correctional treatment that embraces decentralization of authority from state to local levels; citizen participation in program planning, design, implementation, and evaluation; redefinition of the population of offenders for whom incarceration is most appropriate; and emphasis on rehabilitation through community programs.

⑪ *Community corrections acts (CCAs)* are state laws that give economic grants to local communities to establish community corrections goals and policies and to develop and operate community corrections programs. CCAs decentralize services and engage communities in the process of reintegrating offenders by transferring correctional responsibility from the state to the community and by providing financial incentives for communities to manage more of their own correctional cases.

KEY TERMS

intermediate sanctions, p. 125

intensive supervision probation (ISP), p. 130

drug court, p. 132

fine, p. 134

day fine, p. 134

community service, p. 138

day reporting center (DRC), p. 141

remote-location monitoring, p. 144

residential reentry center (RRC), p. 146

boot camp, p. 148

community corrections, p. 151

community corrections acts (CCAs), p. 152

QUESTIONS FOR REVIEW

1 Explain intermediate sanctions and describe their purpose.

2 Differentiate between intensive supervision probation and regular probation.

3 Distinguish between drug courts and other types of courts.

4 Explain the principles behind day fines.

5 Why is community service sometimes called a "fine of time"?

6 What are the features of a day reporting center?

7 For which offenders do you believe remote-location monitoring is most beneficial?

8 What criteria would you use to assess the effectiveness of residential reentry centers?

9 What would you predict about the future of boot camps from the literature?

10 Discuss the importance of community involvement in community corrections.

11 How do community corrections acts implement the philosophy of community corrections?

THINKING CRITICALLY ABOUT CORRECTIONS

Fines

Summarizing the results of a national survey of judges' attitudes toward fines, researchers noted that "at present, judges do not regard the fine alone as a meaningful alternative to incarceration or probation."[67] What could you tell such judges to convince them that day fines, or structured fines, are a viable sentencing option?

Evidence-Based Corrections

Most of the intermediate sanctions reviewed in this chapter show little, if any, impact on reducing criminal activity. Recognizing that it takes time, money, and talent to build an adequate body of scientifically rigorous research, explain to a group of legislators why they should not pull the plug on intermediate sanctions quite yet. Think about the other goals that intermediate sanctions achieve.

ON-THE-JOB DECISION MAKING

Why Day Fines?

Your state legislature recently passed a bill authorizing day fines as an intermediate sanction. Part of the bill requires each probation department to send one or more probation officers to a workshop to prepare for implementing the bill. The chief probation officer designates you. Before the workshop, you are given two questions: (1) Why are day fines a good idea? (2) What would you do with offenders who don't pay? Write a response to bring to the workshop.

Are Drug Courts Working?

Imagine that you are Herbert M. Klein, founder of the nation's first drug court in Miami, Florida, in 1989. Experience tells you that drug courts provide closer, more comprehensive supervision and much more frequent drug testing and monitoring than other forms of community supervision. Yet some researchers are finding that there is no difference in arrest rates between drug court offenders and comparison group members, and if there is, it's difficult to say why. The media ask you to respond. What do you say? (Recall that in Chapter 4 we talked about outcome measures other than recidivism. You might consider searching the links on the home page of the National Association of Drug Court Professionals at www.nadcp.org/ for additional information.)

For additional information, please see: www.mhhe.com/schmalleger7e
Follow the author's tweets about the latest crime and justice news @schmalleger

Institutional Corrections

Part Three examines jail, prison, and parole. These three correctional components account for 3.2 million offenders daily.

How much have jail inmates, facilities, and staff changed since the country's first jail officially opened in Philadelphia in 1773? As you will learn, many of today's jails are large and some are quickly adapting high technology to their purposes. Even though only 6 percent of the nation's 3,283 locally operated jails are "mega" jails (having 1,000 or more cells), they hold 50 percent of the jail population. And why is it that with only 84 percent of all jail capacity occupied nationwide, jail staff perceive that jails are overcrowded? Staffing has not kept up with the increase in the jail population. Are privatization and accreditation solutions? You will decide.

Prisons also first developed in Pennsylvania. In 1790, a wing of the Walnut Street Jail was devoted to long-term incarceration and served as a model for the world's first prison, the Eastern State Penitentiary, in 1829. The architecture of jails and prisons changed over the years from linear to podular. Prisoner supervision approaches also changed from indirect to direct. Regardless of all the changes, overcrowding remains a problem.

Each day, almost 2,000 people will leave prison. How prepared are they to reenter society? Did they receive the educational and vocational preparation and drug treatment they need to minimize their likelihood of reoffending? Unfortunately, probably not. Prisons simply do not have the resources to rehabilitate all inmates under their care. The federal Second Chance Act, passed by Congress in 2008, now hopes to help offenders make successful transitions from prison or jail back to the community by providing employment assistance, substance abuse treatment, housing, family programming, mentoring, victim support, and other services to reduce reoffending and violating probation and parole.

[6]

JAILS

Way Stations Along the Justice Highway

CHAPTER OBJECTIVES

After completing this chapter you should be able to do the following:

1. Understand how jail populations are different from prison populations.

2. List the purposes of jails.

3. Trace briefly the development of jails in history.

4. Explain how first-, second-, and third-generation jails differ in design and method of inmate management.

5. Outline the characteristics of jail inmates, facilities, and staff.

6. Outline the arguments for and against privatization.

7. Describe how jail vocational and educational programs affect inmate reentry.

8. Discuss how faith-based organizations and a jail chaplain can influence jail inmates and help jail staff.

9. Discuss why jail standards, inspection, and accreditation are important.

10. Discuss what is known about using evidence-based practices to treat substance abuse in jail.

11. Explain California's realignment act.

> *Usually only one factor determines whether a defendant stays in jail before he comes to trial. That factor is not guilt or innocence. It is not the nature of the crime. It is not the character of the defendant. That factor is, simply, money. How much money does the defendant have?*
>
> —U.S. Attorney General Robert F. Kennedy, 1964

Perhaps one of the most watched bail hearings of the decade was that of the "blade runner," Paralympian Oscar Pistorius. On February 22, 2013, at the conclusion of the four-day hearing, Chief Magistrate Desmond Nair spent almost two hours detailing the charges against Pistorius and the origins of bail in the 13th century.

Nair confirmed that Pistorius would be charged with the premeditated murder of his girlfriend Reeva Steenkamp but said that the state had not convinced him that Pistorius was a flight risk or a threat to the community and fixed **bail** at $113,000 (one million South African rand) with $11,300 in cash up front and proof that the rest is available. The 26-year-old track star was also ordered to hand over his passport, turn in any guns he owned and stay away from his upscale home, which is now a crime scene. Pistorius was ordered not to leave his home district without his probation officer's permission and is not allowed to consume drugs or alcohol.

The magistrate questioned whether Pistorius would be a flight risk because he stood to lose a fortune in cash, cars, property, and other assets. He also said that although it had been shown that Pistorius had aggressive tendencies, he did not have a prior record of offenses for violent acts. Therefore, he was not a threat to the community and granted bail for these reasons.

A month later, however, Pistorius's lawyers succeeded in convincing the court to ease the bail restrictions. He is now permitted to leave South Africa to compete in international track meets if he provides an itinerary of his travel plans at least a week before he is due to leave. He must also hand his travel documents back to the court within 24 hours of returning home. He no longer has to be regularly supervised by a probation officer and is allowed to return to his home where he shot Steenkamp. In addition, the condition that he not be allowed to consume alcohol and could be tested at any time for alcohol and "prohibited substances" was also lifted.[1]

Pistorius's story isn't much different from the thousands of men and women who enter our nation's jails each day. Most are not as celebrated or as economically fortunate, but the offense similarities are surprising. As you'll read in this chapter, jails are often disparaged in corrections, but in many places, that image is changing. Today's jails have opportunities that were unheard of just a decade ago. Citizen advocates, community linkages, judicial oversight, and jail professionalism are changing the ways jails are operating. These windows of opportunity can leverage jails to successfully perform their functions.

On February 22, 2013, at the conclusion of a four-day bail hearing, Chief Magistrate Desmond Nair fixed Paralympian Oscar Pistorius's bail at $113,000 (one million South African rand) with $11,300 in cash up front for the premeditated murder of his girlfriend Reeva Steenkamp. What are the alternatives to money bail if one does not have Pistorius's wealth?

bail

A written obligation with or without collateral security, given to a court to guarantee appearance before the court.

BAIL AND PRETRIAL RELEASE IN THE UNITED STATES

The Eighth Amendment of the United States Constitution provides that bail not be excessive for people accused of offenses:

> Excessive bail shall not be required, nor excessive fines imposed, nor cruel and unusual punishments inflicted.

Bail is "excessive" when it is set at a figure higher than an amount reasonably likely to ensure the defendant's presence at the trial. You learned in Chapter 1 that a person's bail can be decided at several stages of the pretrial process (arrest, initial appearance, preliminary hearing, and arraignment). The pretrial process a person goes through and the type of bail available depends on the state and jurisdiction in which she or he is arrested.

A person may be released after their arrest in several ways as they await their court date. The release options that require money to get out of jail pretrial are:

- **Cash bond.** Pay the full bail amount.
- **Deposit bond.** Pay a percentage of the bail amount, usually 10 percent.
- **Property bond.** Submit a deed that allows the court to place a lien on a property.
- **Bail bond.** Pay a nonrefundable fee, usually 10 percent of the bail amount, to a for-profit bail bonding company that enters into an agreement with the court that, in the event the person misses a court appearance, the company would owe the court the full amount of the monetary bail.

The release options that do not involve money up front to get out of jail pretrial are:

- **Release on recognizance.** A promise to return to court.
- **Conditional release.** Release under specific conditions.
- **Release to pretrial services.** Conditions set by a supervising pretrial service agency.
- **Unsecured bond.** The person will be liable for a fee if he or she misses the court hearing.

Concerns over Money for Bail

Until the 1990s, release on recognizance was the most common type of pretrial release. By 2006, however, its use had declined by one-third and the use of financial pretrial release through commercial bail bonding companies increased proportionally.[2]

The judicial system predominantly depends on monetary bail under the assumption that it protects public safety and ensures that the released individual returns to court. However, jurisdictions differ on how they determine what types of bail to set, how much monetary bail is set, and the methods of allowable payments to secure one's release from jail. California alone has 58 different bail schedules to determine monetary amounts as they relate to the alleged offense.[3] When a jurisdiction such as California has so many different bail schedules, the amounts of monetary bail for a charge will vary considerably.

A snapshot of the Baltimore City Jail in Maryland, one of the 20 largest jails in the United States and a detention center that tracks monetary bail amounts, showed that 1 of every 14 people in pretrial detention were held on a total monetary bail of $5,000 or less on February 12, 2012. This means persons are detained because they cannot pay the full monetary bail or the bail bond of $500.[4]

On the next day, February 13, 2012, 62 persons were detained for monetary bail amounts of $1,000 or less and 19 people were held for monetary bail amounts of anywhere between $100 to $250. Too dangerous to be released? Probably not. These individuals were charged with nonviolent offenses such as trespassing, theft, driving on a suspended license, prostitution, failure to pay child support, minor drug charges, and technical violations of supervised release. Considering that keeping someone in jail for a day costs on average $60 ($100 in California and $107 in Florida), the $9 billion financial burden of detaining someone in jail suggests that in cases with low monetary bail amounts, another release option would better use public money.

The practice of paying money for bail is under considerable scrutiny. Research shows that people held in jail pretrial end up with more restrictive sentencing outcomes than people who are free pending trial. People held in jail pretrial are more likely to be convicted of a felony, receive a sentence of incarceration, and be sentenced longer than those released pretrial. Others have found that the interaction between race and other factors such as age, gender, and socioeconomic status can also affect the decision to be released pretrial. Because of a person's race, she or he may have difficulty finding a job and will therefore be seen as a flight risk because of an unstable source of income. Blacks are less likely to be released on their own recognizance than white defendants, and blacks ages 18 to 20 receive significantly higher monetary bail amounts than all other types of defendants.[5]

Persons who are able to post monetary bail may deplete the funds of their family and friends that are needed for rent, food, and bills. If a person is unable to post monetary bail, she or he may lose her or his job, default on financial obligations, and lose property. The American Bar Association's standard relating to pretrial release offered this analysis: "The requirement that virtually every defendant post [monetary] bail . . . imposes personal hardship on them, their families, and on the public which must bear the cost of their detention and frequently support their dependents on welfare."[6] U.S. Attorney General Eric Holder said that the jail system costs 9 billion taxpayer dollars annually, much of which could be saved by using recognized tools to measure the risks that a defendant will not return for required court appearances if released.[7]

Other consequences of being held in jail pretrial aren't always so visible, but researchers and others have noticed them.[8] A person who is in pretrial detention cannot dress as well as someone who comes to trial from home. Jurors who see defendants in shackles and jail uniforms may equate those outward features as signs of dangerousness. Pretrial detention limits a person's ability to work with his or her attorney to prepare a defense, contact witnesses, and help with other activities due to limited telephone use. Pretrial detention may disrupt a medical routine. Children whose parents are held in jail pretrial may have to move and disrupt their education. For these and other reasons, many argue today that the ability to maintain one's job, housing, caregiver responsibilities, and other matters should be available to all people awaiting their court date within the parameters of safety but not requiring they have financial resources to do so.

Visit http://www.npr.org/templates/story/story.php?storyId=122725849 or scan this code with the QR app on your smartphone or digital device and listen to the podcast of the problems of the American money bail system and how the powerful commercial bail bonding lobby blocks pretrial services programs. How does this information relate to ideas discussed in this chapter?

Whether monetary bail increases community safety is also an issue. Some have said that there is no empirical evidence to support this idea.[9] They argue that although a judge may have reason to detain a person out of concern for community safety and thus set a high monetary bail amount, some defendants, such as Bernie Madoff, can post a $10 million bail and remain free until trial and sentencing. The thinking also goes that a for-profit bonding company may recognize that a 10 percent fee from a high bail amount will result in a hefty profit and decide to post the bond to make a profit. On the other hand, bail bondspersons almost never write bail bonds for $1,000 or less because there is only a small profit to be made. They are far more likely to underwrite high bail amounts, which means that defendants charged with serious offenses are more likely to obtain bail than those accused of minor crimes.[10] This also means that bail bondspersons, not prosecutors or judges, are making critical decisions affecting the freedom of those accused of crime.

Commercial bail bonding companies wield considerable financial and political power. They have a strong interest in preserving the practice of monetary bail because it is the source of their income. They oppose release alternatives that do not involve money up front to get out of jail pretrial because it would lower their profits. In Maryland, for example, the for-profit bail bonding industry has been successful in stopping legislation that would more closely regulate the industry. However, four states (Illinois, Kentucky, Oregon, and Washington) have banned the involvement of for-profit bail bonding companies in the judicial process. Other jurisdictions, such as Broward County, Texas, and Philadelphia, Pennsylvania, have also chosen to ban the industry even if their state has not.

Effective Alternatives to Monetary Bail

Researchers estimate that at least 25 percent of the 744,524 inmates confined in local jails could be released pretrial without increasing offenses or failure to appear if effective alternatives to monetary bail are put in place.[11] Other research shows that the American public believes that effective alternatives are better than relying on incarceration for people convicted of low-level, nonviolent offenses. In one study, 60 percent supported the idea of releasing people to pretrial services instead of requiring monetary bail.[12]

Pretrial service agencies typically assist judicial officers in making appropriate release decisions by formulating release recommendations and providing supervision and services to defendants awaiting trial whom the agency can reasonably assure their return to court and no engagement in criminal activity. The U.S. Probation and Pretrial Services System and about one-third of the counties in the United States provide pretrial service functions for their respective courts. They administer evidence-based risk assessment tools to determine a defendant's risk of failing to appear at court and engaging in illegal activity while awaiting trial. They then make recommendations to judicial officers regarding the best release option for the person accused of the offense. If the defendant is released under a condition of pretrial service supervision, the pretrial officer will monitor the services in accordance with the risk assessment and the court's order. Pretrial service or probation and pretrial career opportunities with federal courts are available in 93 of the 94 U.S. district courts. Exhibit 6–1 presents the Code of Ethics of the National Association of Pretrial Services Agencies.

Researchers at Florida State University analyzed data from the Broward County (Florida) Department of Community Control from 2005 through 2010. They found that the use of pretrial release had doubled (1,013 to almost 3,000) during that period. The program decreased the jail population by 1,000 inmates, reduced the average jail stay to 26 days (the lowest in five years), tripled savings from $30 million in 2005 to $104 million in 2010, and reduced the per day client cost from $107.71 in 2005 to only $1.48 in 2010. The researchers suggest that when pretrial release is used with evidence-based practices, significant cost savings are realized.[13]

In addition to the use of pretrial service supervision, a number of other effective alternatives to monetary bail are effective. The use of evidence-based risk assessment can provide insight into the need to detain persons who may pose a risk to public safety or not appear for court. These tools usually classify persons as low risk, moderate risk, or high risk based on a review of their criminal history, education, employment, substance abuse, social networks, cognitions (thinking patterns), housing, finances, and recreation. The level of risk can then set into action the appropriate release option and match the offender with services (responsivity) that increase his or her appearance at court and reduce the threat to public safety. The use of valid risk assessment tools is still in its infancy across the United States, but more jurisdictions are beginning to implement them.

Another effective alternative to monetary bail is the increased use of citations instead of arrest and booking. Maryland, North Carolina and Wisconsin are part of a growing number of states that have passed laws to expand the use of citation releases by law enforcement in lieu of custodial arrests for non-violent offenses. Custodial arrests are enormously expensive and too often result in the unnecessary detention of low-risk individuals. There is public support for citations in lieu of arrest and booking for possession of small amounts of marijuana, driving with no operator's license, reckless driving, driving while license is revoked, and disorderly conduct.[14]

Another option to monetary bail is the use of release on recognizance for low-risk defendants. Low-risk defendants generally appear in court and are not rearrested because they are generally responsible in other areas of their lives.

Technology in the form of automated phone calls, text messages, and e-mails can remind individuals of court dates and reduce failure to appear rates, thereby decreasing reliance on monetary bail after individuals fail to appear in court. These notification programs are used in the Miami County (Ohio) Municipal Court, Los Angeles County Traffic Court, and Multnomah County (Oregon) Circuit Court. All three jurisdictions have seen a reduction in failure to appear rates: 83 percent reduction in Miami County, 20 percent in Los Angeles County, and almost 45 percent in Multnomah County. Multnomah County launched its court notification program in 2005. In 2007, it reported a saving of $1.6 million for the county. Other counties are reaching out more aggressively to pretrial defendants with mailed post cards and personal telephone calls answering defendants' questions.

A final release option is to implement a deposit bond with the court and eliminate the need for commercial bail bonding. Illinois adopted this approach in 1963. Although it still uses monetary bail, the defendant pays 10 percent of her or his bond directly to the court. If she or he appears for all court dates and is not rearrested during the pretrial and trial process, all but a 3 percent administrative fee is returned. Failure to appear results in rearrest and liability for the full bond amount.

PURPOSE OF JAILS

Except for six states that run combined jail/prison systems (Alaska, Connecticut, Delaware, Hawaii, Rhode Island, and Vermont), **jails** are locally operated correctional facilities that confine people before or after

jails
Locally operated correctional facilities that confine people before or after conviction.

EXHIBIT 6–1	**National Association of Pretrial Services Agencies (NAPSA) Code of Ethics**

As a pretrial services professional I will:

- Assist the criminal justice system in its dealings with pretrial defendants to the best of my ability and will conduct myself as a professional at all times;
- Respect the dignity of the individual, be they defendants, victims, or fellow criminal justice professionals;
- Respect the dignity and integrity of the court;
- Respect the presumption of innocence of all defendants, until proven guilty beyond a reasonable doubt, and to uphold the fundamental right of every accused person who has been arrested and is facing prosecution under the U.S. criminal justice system;
- Pledge that the information I provide to the court and the decisions I make are as accurate and objective as possible;
- Treat all people equally regardless of race, national origin, disability, age, gender, sexual orientation or religion;
- Protect the confidentiality of all information obtained, except when necessary to prevent serious, foreseeable, and/or imminent harm to a defendant or other identifiable person(s);
- Avoid impropriety or the appearance of impropriety;
- Avoid any conflicts of interest and will not evaluate, supervise and/or provide services to anyone I have an existing relationship with, nor enter into a personal or business relationship with anyone I evaluate, supervise or provide services to;
- Continue to pursue my own professional development and education to further my expertise in the field;
- Promote the growth of pretrial services, as well as encourage and cooperate with research and development in advancing the field;
- Respect and promote the fundamental principles and professional standards which guide pretrial services and will implement these best practices to the extent I am able;
- Refrain from providing legal advice to any pretrial defendants; and lastly,
- Promise to conduct myself as an individual of good character who will act in good faith in making reliable ethical judgments.

total admission

The total number of people admitted to jail each year.

CO6-1

average daily population (ADP)

Sum of the number of inmates in a jail or prison each day for a year, divided by the total number of days in the year.

conviction. Jails are different from prisons (the subject of Chapter 7) in a number of ways that you will learn about as you read. The fundamental difference between jail and prison is the nature of their populations.[15]

Total admission is the total number of persons admitted to jail each year, which falls between 10 million and 13 million. That translates into about 34,000 people released from jails each day and about 238,000 released each week.

The **average daily population (ADP),** on the other hand, is the sum of the number of inmates in a jail or prison each day for a year divided by the total number of days in the year. Jail ADP at midyear 2012 was 744,524. Prison total admission is estimated at 665,000 a year, and prison ADP at year-end 2012, was 1,571,013 adults (see Chapter 7). The *daily* population of jails is lower than that of prisons, but the *annual* total of people incarcerated in jails is higher. Put another way, it takes almost two years for the nation's state and federal prison population to turn over once; the jail population turns over almost 17 times each year. The jail population is, thus, dynamic, and the prison population is static. The changing nature of jail populations raises significant issues and problems that form the core of this chapter.

At midyear 2012, local jail authorities held or supervised 808,622 offenders.[16] Jail authorities supervised almost 8.0 percent of these offenders (64,098) in alternative programs outside jail facilities (see Exhibit 6–7 later in the chapter). A total of 744,524 were housed in local jails.

Inmates sentenced to jail usually have a sentence of 1 year or less. Seventy percent are released within 3 days; however, an estimated 20 percent will spend at least 1 month, 12 percent at least 2 months, and 4 percent will spend more than 6 months.[17]

At midyear 2012 the majority of the nation's jail population (60 percent) were pretrial detainees.

Jails also incarcerate persons in a wide variety of other categories. Jails are used to do the following:

- Receive persons awaiting court action on their current charge.
- Readmit probation and parole violators and bail-bond absconders.
- Detain juveniles until custody is transferred to juvenile authorities.
- Hold persons with mental illness until they are moved to appropriate health facilities.
- Hold individuals for the military.
- Provide protective custody.
- Confine persons found in contempt.
- Hold witnesses for the courts.
- Hold inmates about to be released after completing a prison sentence.
- Transfer inmates to federal, state, or other authorities.
- House inmates for federal, state, or other authorities because of crowding of their facilities.
- Operate some community-based programs as alternatives to incarceration.
- Hold inmates sentenced to short terms (generally under one year) of incarceration.
- Hold persons for U.S. Immigration and Customs Enforcement.

For all their important roles and responsibilities, jails have been a disgrace to every generation.[18] Many of the nation's 3,283 locally operated jails are old, overcrowded, poorly funded, scantily staffed by underpaid and poorly trained employees, and given low priority in local budgets. Yet a strong groundswell of support is rising for the nation's jails. Tomorrow's jail professionals have tremendous opportunities to continue that momentum. Progress is being made because of new emphases on incorporating evidence-based practices, jail education, staff selection and training, professional associations, standards, technology, accountability, and laws, among other things. Groups such as the American Jail Association (AJA) are advancing jail professionalism through training, information exchange, technical assistance, publications, and conferences. Members of the AJA include sheriffs, jail administrators, judges, attorneys, educators,

CO6-2

Visit http://channel.nationalgeographic.com/channel/videos/county-jail-booking-center/?videoDetect=t%252Cf or scan this code with the QR app on your smartphone or digital device and watch this podcast of jail booking at the Multnomah County (Oregon) detention center. How does this information relate to ideas discussed in this chapter?

Almost 40 percent of the nation's jails like the one pictured are small (less than 50 cells), holding only 3 percent of the jail population. Most small jails were built in the early part of the 20th century. What management style does this jail suggest?

EXHIBIT 6–2   American Jail Association

Mission Statement

To band together all those concerned with or interested in the custody and care of persons awaiting trial, serving sentences, or otherwise locally confined; to improve the conditions and systems under which such persons are detained.

To advance professionalism through training, information exchange, technical assistance, publications, and conferences.

To provide leadership in the development of professional standards, pertinent legislation, management practices, programs, and services.

To present and advance the interests, needs, concerns, and proficiency of the profession as deemed appropriate by the membership and their representatives.

Source: Copyright © American Jail Association. Reprinted with permission.

correctional staff, jail inspection officials, health care providers, and clergy. The AJA mission statement is shown in Exhibit 6–2. This chapter will explore the problems of jails of the past and present and discuss direction for the 21st century.

The Staff Speaks
Visit www.mhhe.com/schmalleger7e to see this feature.

CO6-3   JAILS IN HISTORY

It is believed that King Henry II of England ordered the first jail built in 1166. The purpose of that jail was to detain offenders until they could be brought before a court, tried, and sentenced. From that beginning, jails spread throughout Europe but changed in scope and size over time.

With the development of workhouses and poorhouses in the 15th and 16th centuries in England, sheriffs took on the added responsibility of supervising vagrants, the poor, and the mentally ill. These institutions, despite their distinct names, were indistinguishable from jails. Their squalid, unhealthy conditions and the sheriffs' practice of demanding money from persons under their charge caught the attention of 18th-century Enlightenment reformers. One such reformer was the English sheriff John Howard (see Chapter 2 for a discussion of Howard as a correctional reformer). In 1779, England's Parliament passed the four jail reforms that Howard proposed: secure and sanitary structures, jail inspections, elimination of fees, and an emphasis on reforming prisoners. To this day, the John Howard Association and *Howard Journal* carry Howard's ideas forward.

First Jail in the United States

The first jail in the United States was the Walnut Street Jail in Philadelphia, built in 1773. The jail housed offenders without regard to sex, age, or offense. Following the jail's opening, conditions quickly deteriorated. According to some, the jail became a "promiscuous scene of unrestricted intercourse, universal riot, and debauchery."[19] The Philadelphia Quakers had wanted the Walnut Street Jail to be a place where inmates reformed themselves through reflection and remorse.

In 1790 the Philadelphia Society for Alleviating the Miseries of Public Prisons and the General Assembly of Pennsylvania designated a wing of the Walnut Street Jail a penitentiary. Implementing Quaker beliefs, the penitentiary emphasized prisoner reform through reflection and penitence

© The Library Company of Philadelphia

The Walnut Street Jail, started in Philadelphia in 1773, originally housed offenders without regard to sex, age, or offense. Following its redesignation as a penitentiary in 1790, it housed only convicted felons. Which religious group's principles influenced correctional institutions in Pennsylvania?

and rehabilitation through good conduct. Sixteen solitary cells were added to the facility and workshops were built. Alcohol and prostitution were prohibited; prisoners were segregated by sex, age, and offense; diets were monitored; guardians were appointed to care for minors; and religious, health care, and educational services were provided. Debtors were housed separately from the general inmate population and had no such privileges. Their prison conditions were pitiful, and many debtors starved.[20]

In 1798 a fire destroyed the workshops at Walnut Street. The destruction brought about disillusionment and idleness. Rising costs crippled the jail's budget. Disciplinary problems rose with overcrowding, and escape and violence increased. The number of inmates who were destitute vagrants or debtors soared as did the incidence of disease. There were political conflicts between the religious Quakers and the non-Quaker prison board members. Prisoners rioted on March 27, 1820, and on October 5, 1835, the Walnut Street Jail closed. State prisoners were transferred to the new Eastern State Penitentiary in Philadelphia, the first institution of its kind in the world (see Chapter 7). County inmates and those awaiting trial were transferred to a new county jail.

By the close of the 19th century, most cities across the United States had jails to hold persons awaiting trial and to punish convicted felons. The sheriff became the person in charge of the jail. As crime increased and urban centers expanded, jails grew in importance, as did the sheriffs' control over jails.

United States Jails in the 20th Century

On any given day, America's jails serve a variety of functions. They detain people awaiting arraignment or trial, 60 percent at midyear 2012. They confine offenders serving short sentences for less serious offenses. Jails also serve as surrogate mental hospitals, a topic we return to later in this chapter and in Chapter 12. They frequently detain people with drug or alcohol dependency. They are the first stop on the social services highway for the homeless, street people, and some with extremely poor physical health, especially those with HIV, AIDS, and tuberculosis (TB). We expand on the characteristics of today's jail population later in this chapter.

CO6-4 ## Architecture and Inmate Management

In an attempt to better manage and control inmate behavior, jails have progressed through three phases of architectural design. Each design is based on a particular philosophy of inmate management and control.

First-Generation Jails

First-generation jails were built in a linear design that dates back to the 18th century, when prison and jail design was shifting from single-cell and religious emphasis to congregate housing and secular administration (more on the history of correctional architecture is presented in Chapter 7).

first-generation jail

Jail with multiple-occupancy cells or dormitories that line corridors arranged like spokes. Inmate supervision is intermittent; staff must patrol the corridors to observe inmates in their cells.

In a typical **first-generation jail,** inmates live in multiple-occupancy cells or dormitories. The cells line corridors that are arranged like spokes. Inmate supervision is sporadic or intermittent; staff must patrol the corridors to observe inmates in their cells. Contact between jailers and inmates is minimal unless there is an incident to which jailers must react (see Exhibit 6–3).

The design of such linear jails reflects the assumption that inmates are violent and destructive and will assault staff, destroy jail property, and try to escape. The facility is designed to prevent these behaviors. Heavy metal bars separate staff from inmates. Reinforced metal beds, sinks, and toilets are bolted to the ground or wall. Reinforced concrete and razor wire surround the facility.

The biggest problem with first-generation jails is the inability of an officer to see what is going on in more than one or two cells at a time. That limitation gave rise to the second-generation jails of the 1960s.

Second-Generation Jails

Second-generation jails emerged in the 1960s to replace old, run-down linear jails and provide officers the opportunity to observe as much of the housing area as possible from a single vantage point.

second-generation jail

Jail where staff remain in a secure control booth surrounded by inmate housing areas called *pods* and surveillance is remote.

Second-generation jails adopted a different philosophical approach to construction and inmate management. In a **second-generation jail,** staff remain in a secure control booth overlooking inmate housing areas, called *pods* (see Exhibit 6–4). Although visual surveillance increases in such jails, surveillance is remote, and verbal interaction with inmates is even less

---

EXHIBIT 6–3 **First-Generation Jail—Intermittent Surveillance**

 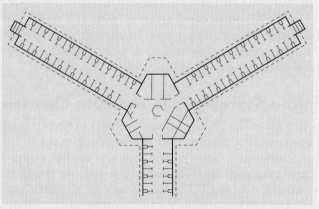

Cells line corridors in first-generation jails. Unable to observe all inmate housing areas from one location, prison and jail staff must patrol inmates' living areas to provide surveillance. What are the consequences of first-generation jails?

EXHIBIT 6-4 *Second-Generation Jail—Remote Surveillance*

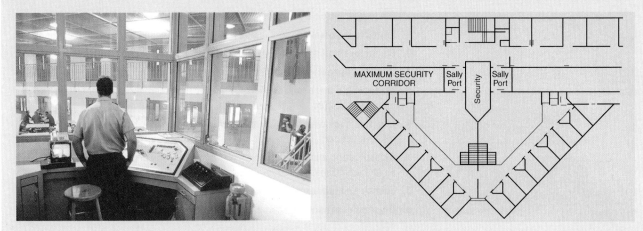

Inmate living areas are divided into pods, or modules, in which cells are clustered around dayrooms that are under remote observation by staff in a secure control room. What are the consequences of second-generation jails?

frequent than in first-generation jails. Property destruction is minimized because steel and cement continue to define the living areas. Outside, fences and razor wire continue to discourage escapes as well as unauthorized entry. Second-generation jails have been termed *podular remote-supervision facilities*.

Although staff can observe activity in common areas, or *dayrooms,* they are unable to respond quickly to problems or even to interact effectively with inmates because of the intervening security control booth. In both the first- and second-generation jails, the biggest problem is that staff and inmates are separated. As David Parrish, former detention commander for the Hillsborough County Sheriff's Department (Tampa, Florida) put it, "Staff managed the hallways and control rooms, generally about 10 percent of the facility, while inmates ran the housing areas, roughly 90 percent."[21]

Third-Generation Jails Third-generation jails, also known as *direct-supervision jails,* emerged in 1974 when the Federal Bureau of Prisons opened three Metropolitan Correctional Centers (MCCs) in three cities: New York, Chicago, and San Diego. These three federal facilities were the first jails planned and designed to be operated under the principles of unit management, which later became known as *direct supervision* (see Exhibit 6–5 for a list of the nine principles of direct supervision). The housing unit design of such jails is podular. Inmates' cells are arranged around a common area, or dayroom. There is no secure control booth for the supervising officer, and there are no physical barriers between the officer and the inmates. Direct supervision places a single deputy directly in a "housing pod" with between 32 and 64 inmates. The officer may have a desk or table for paperwork, but it is in the open dayroom area.

In a third-generation jail, the inmate management style is direct supervision. An officer is stationed in the pod with the inmates, much like a teacher in a classroom. The officer moves about the pod and interacts with the inmates to manage their behavior. Advocates of direct supervision tell us that when correctional officers are in constant and direct contact with inmates, they get to know them and can recognize and respond to trouble before it escalates into violence.

third-generation jail (also *direct-supervision jail*)

A jail where inmates are housed in small groups, or pods, staffed 24 hours a day by specially trained officers. Officers interact with inmates to help change behavior. Bars and metal doors are absent, reducing noise and dehumanization.

EXHIBIT 6–5   Nine Principles of Direct Supervision

1. **Effective control.** The unit officer is the secure perimeter.
2. **Effective supervision.** Continuous supervision is maintained by the unit officers.
3. **Competent staff.** Correctional standards guide recruitment.
4. **Staff and inmate safety.** Performance-based data are collected.
5. **Manageable and cost-effective operations.** There are more architectural choices, commercial-grade furnishings, and equipment options.
6. **Effective communication.** Direct communication exists between inmates and officers, officers and supervisors.
7. **Classification and orientation.** Know with whom you are dealing; intense supervision is maintained for the first 12 to 72 hours.
8. **Justice and fairness.** Unit officers exercise primary informal discipline.
9. **Ownership of operations.** Inmate policy decisions are guided by a team approach.

Visit http://www.youtube.com/watch?v=f44GSsIWbJw or scan this code with the QR app on your smartphone or digital device and watch a podcast on the philosophy of direct supervision. How does this information relate to ideas discussed in this chapter?

The pod contains sleeping areas, dayroom space, all necessary personal hygiene fixtures, and sufficient tables and seats to accommodate unit capacity. Officers are not separated from inmates by a physical barrier. Officers provide frequent, nonscheduled observation of and personal interaction with inmates (see Exhibit 6–6). Due to the close contact, officers are expected to detect signs of tension between inmates and defuse the situation by either talking with inmates or by restricting privileges. They do this by using their communication skills training to maintain a nonviolent environment. Furnishings are used to reduce inmate stress caused by crowding, excessive noise, lack of privacy, and isolation from the outside world. Bars and metal doors are absent, reducing noise and the dehumanization common in first- and second-generation jails.

Direct-supervision jails facilitate staff movement, interaction with inmates, and control and leadership over pods. By supervising inmate activities directly, the staff can help change inmate behavior patterns rather than simply react to them. Staff control inmate behavior through the enforcement of boundaries of acceptable behavior and the administration

EXHIBIT 6–6   Third-Generation Jail—Direct Supervision

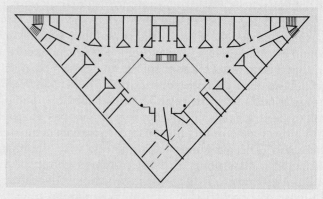

Cells are grouped in housing units, or pods. Each pod has a central dayroom. Prison staff are stationed inside the housing unit to encourage direct interaction between inmates and staff. What are the consequences of direct-supervision jails?

of consequences for violating the boundaries. Observing unacceptable behavior and administering consequences is less likely to occur in first- and second-generation jails where staff supervision is sporadic and remote.

Some researchers tell us that pods and direct supervision provide a safer and more positive environment for inmates and staff than do first- and second-generation jails.[22] But other researchers have found few differences between the perceptions of officers in new generation versus traditional facilities.[23] In one study, new generation officers were no more satisfied with their jobs, did not feel more connected to their coworkers, did not believe communication was improved, did not feel any greater sense of personal involvement in their work, and were just as likely to see their jobs as monotonous and routine as officers working in the more traditional facility. Possible reasons for the lack of difference include the short history of direct supervision, little supporting data, and the belief among sheriffs and jail administrators that direct-supervision facilities are not as "safe" or "strong" as remote-supervision facilities because of distance and physical separation from inmates.[24] Simply put, many agencies are not comfortable removing the "barriers" between "us and them."

The first direct-supervision county jail in the United States was the Martinez Detention Facility in Contra Costa, California. It opened in January 1981. Today, an estimated 349 of the 3,283 local jails use direct supervision, but as one researcher has asked, "Are they really direct-supervision jails?"[25] After receiving surveys from half of the direct-supervision jails, Christine Tartaro, professor of criminal justice at the Richard Stockton College of New Jersey, found that although many jails are being called direct supervision, few of them truly are. Only 40 percent said their facilities operate under a unit management structure, and few offered any inmate services other than recreation on the pod. The majority operated under traditional centralized management and a few used elements of both. Tartaro also found that half of the direct-supervision jails offered correctional officers no more than two days of communication skills training even though the training requirements for learning to communicate with a diverse group of inmates are difficult and need more than one or two days of instruction. The majority of Professor Tartaro's sample (70 percent) also identified their jail's furnishings and fixtures as vandalism resistant and half bolted their furniture to the floor, conveying the message that inmates are expected to misbehave. (The first MCCs outfitted inmate living areas with normalized commercial fixtures, furnishings, and finishes.) Furthermore, because of jail crowding, the majority of the inmates in direct-supervision facilities are no longer housed in single cells. Tartaro believes that jails that are only partially implementing the direct-supervision model are not secure or well-run facilities. This may explain why there are few differences between the perceptions of officers in new generation versus traditional facilities. This risks giving a bad reputation to those that are truly operating under the nine principles of direct supervision as escapes, riots, violence, or no change in the officers' perceptions of their work environments occurs in the partially implemented third-generation jails.

CHARACTERISTICS OF JAIL INMATES, FACILITIES, AND STAFF

CO6-5

Who is in jail? Why are they there? How many jails are there? How many people work in jails? What do we know about the operation and administration of jail facilities? To these and related questions we now turn our attention.

Jail Inmates

The characteristics of jail inmates have changed little over the past decade. Since 2000, almost 9 of 10 jail inmates have been male; 4 of 10 have been white; 4 of 10 have been black; and 1 percent or less have been juveniles.

In June 2012, local jail authorities held or supervised 808,622 offenders. After three consecutive years of decline in the nation's jail population, the number of persons confined in local jails increased by 1.2 percent (or 8,923 inmates) between midyear 2011 and 2012. The majority of the increase occurred in California as a result of public safety realignmnet, a court-ordered public policy to reduce the number of inmates housed in state prisons starting October 1, 2011, and discussed at the end of this Chapter. Excluding the increase in California's jail population, the nationwide jail population would have remained relatively stable during the period.

In 2012, almost 8.0 percent of these offenders (64,098) were supervised outside jail facilities (see Exhibit 6–7). A total of 744,524 were housed in local jails. Jails also held almost 23,000 immigrants (asylum-seekers, people suspected of being in the United States illegally, and legal immigrants convicted of crimes) for the U.S. Immigration and Customs Enforcement, nearly double the number held in 2000.

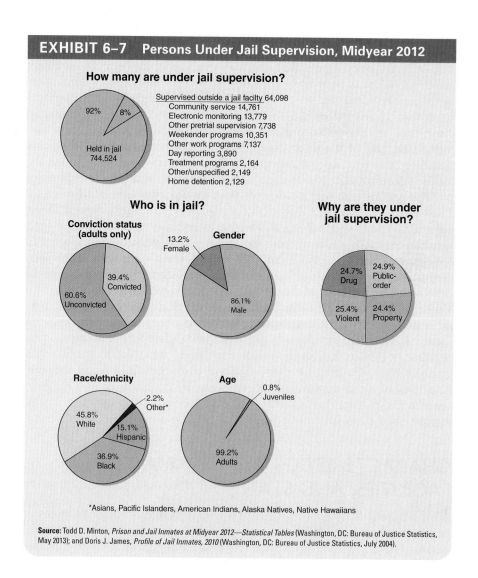

EXHIBIT 6–7   Persons Under Jail Supervision, Midyear 2012

How many are under jail supervision?

92%   8%

Held in jail 744,524

Supervised outside a jail facilty 64,098
Community service 14,761
Electronic monitoring 13,779
Other pretrial supervision 7,738
Weekender programs 10,351
Other work programs 7,137
Day reporting 3,890
Treatment programs 2,164
Other/unspecified 2,149
Home detention 2,129

Who is in jail?

Conviction status (adults only)
39.4% Convicted
60.6% Unconvicted

Gender
13.2% Female
86.1% Male

Why are they under jail supervision?
24.7% Drug
24.9% Public-order
25.4% Violent
24.4% Property

Race/ethnicity
45.8% White
2.2% Other*
15.1% Hispanic
36.9% Black

Age
0.8% Juveniles
99.2% Adults

*Asians, Pacific Islanders, American Indians, Alaska Natives, Native Hawaiians

Source: Todd D. Minton, *Prison and Jail Inmates at Midyear 2012—Statistical Tables* (Washington, DC: Bureau of Justice Statistics, May 2013); and Doris J. James, *Profile of Jail Inmates, 2010* (Washington, DC: Bureau of Justice Statistics, July 2004).

One not-so-promising statistic is the steady percentage in the number of jail inmates who are pretrial detainees (60.6 percent in 2012, up from 56 percent in 2000), leading one of the country's most respected voices in jail issues, Dr. Ken Kerle, to write that "this is another unhappy sign that inmate processing is slowing down."[26] If more jail inmates are not being tried, convicted, or sentenced, jail resources become overburdened, crowding results, and the conditions of confinement worsen.

The Bureau of Justice Statistics and others have compiled a profile of inmates in local jails. At the time of arrest:

- 80 percent earned less than $2,000 a month before they were locked up.
- 75 percent who had mental health problems also had co-occurring substance abuse or dependency issues;
- 68 percent had not seen a health care provider since incarceration;
- 64 percent suffered from some form of mental illness;
- 55 percent of females had been sexually or physically abused;
- 50 percent grew up in homes without both parents;
- 46 percent were not taking their medication at the time of arrest;
- 44 percent had less than a high school education;
- 40 percent had a criminal history;
- 39 percent had a chronic medical condition;
- 33 percent were on probation;
- 33 percent were unemployed at the time of arrest;
- 25 to 87 percent had traumatic brain injury;
- 25 percent had dental problems;
- 14 percent were homeless at the time of arrest;
- 13 percent of males had been sexually or physically abused;
- 12 percent were on parole;
- 5 percent of women were pregnant at the time of arrest; and
- 1.3 percent were HIV positive.

Despite this gloomy picture, jails are in a unique position to help persons leaving jail and resuming life in the community. Today more and more policymakers are recognizing that because jail inmates usually have shorter lengths of stay than state or federal inmates, the community location of most jail facilities means less time away from family, friends, treatment providers, faith institutions, and other social supports. They also realize that jails have opportunities to develop strategies to reduce the criminalization of persons with mental illness and combat this list of problems with interventions and reentry programs prior to release.

Another way to look at the nation's jail population is to consider the rate of incarceration. Confined jail populations give us a count of the total number held in jail (e.g., 744,524 offenders confined in local jails at midyear 2012). Because of differences in total population, however, such counts do not allow for accurate comparison of jurisdictions. Rates of jail incarceration, expressed as the number of jail inmates per 100,000 residents age 18 and older, provide for a more meaningful and useful analysis of trends in incarceration. With rate data, we can compare changes over time. Exhibit 6–8 shows changes in the jail incarceration rate from 2000 through 2012. Note that the incarceration rate increased from 220 jail inmates per 100,000 adults in 2000 to 259 jail inmates per 100,000 adults in 2007, and then declined to 237 in 2012.

EXHIBIT 6–8   Jail Incarceration Rate, 2000–2012

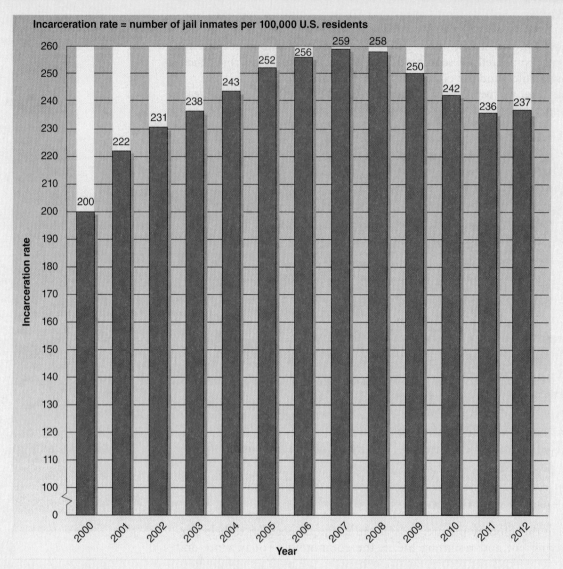

Incarceration rate = number of jail inmates per 100,000 U.S. residents

Source: Adapted from Todd D. Minton, *Prison and Jail Inmates at Midyear 2012—Statistical Tables* (Washington, DC: Bureau of Justice Statistics, May 2013).

Gender and Jail Populations   There has been an upsurge in the number of women incarcerated in the United States, explained, in part, by guideline sentencing under which gender is not regarded as an appropriate consideration. Although females have historically been treated more leniently than men at sentencing, guideline sentencing has tended to limit or end this practice.

The number of women in jail has more than quintupled over the past 25 years, from 19,000 in 1985 to a peak of 100,520 in 2007. Since then the number has declined to 98,600 in 2012. The absolute number of women in jail is much smaller than the absolute number of men. However, their impact on jail operations is significant, raising concerns about the adequacy of jail facilities and the services provided.

The typical female jail inmate is poor, is a high school dropout with low skills, has held mainly low-wage jobs, is young (25 to 29), is unmarried with one to three children, and belongs to a racial minority.

Almost one-half of women and one-third of men in jail are first-time offenders (49 versus 37 percent).[27] Almost half of the women and men in jail were under the influence of alcohol or drugs at the time of the offense. Forty-six percent had members of their immediate families sentenced to prison. Two of every 10 grew up in a home where one or both parents abused drugs, alcohol, or both. And more than one-half of the women (55 percent) and 13 percent of the men had been physically or sexually abused before age 18. Women in jail need targeted interventions that address these issues.

This profile also raises troubling concerns about the children of jailed mothers. Two-thirds of women in jail are mothers with children under age 18 who were living with them prior to detention. When mothers go to jail, children become silent victims. The children may already have been victims if their mothers used drugs during pregnancy. Young children, not yet capable of understanding why their mother is gone, where she has gone, and if or when she will return, may develop depression and feelings of abandonment. Even children who are fortunate enough to be placed with emotionally supportive caregivers must cope with seeing their mother only through a glass barrier and hearing her voice only over the phone. Studies have shown that children of incarcerated mothers have more behavioral problems at home and in school and are four times as likely to become juvenile delinquents as children from similar socioeconomic backgrounds with parents at home. Maintaining bonding with children and family is the most difficult female inmate experience.[28] Recognizing that children should not be made to suffer for the poor choices of their parents and recognizing that support for family maintenance is a societal value, some jails are establishing visitation and parenting programs that accommodate this need. Through such programs, jail administrators have the opportunity to become leaders in preserving families and reducing crime.

Some scholars believe that many women in jail do not pose a threat to public safety but are jailed because they do not have the financial resources to make bail, which makes our discussion of the problems with monetary bail at the beginning of this chapter even more salient for this group of offenders. Seventeen percent are charged with violent offenses.[29] Most are charged with property offenses (32 percent), drug offenses (29 percent), and public-order offenses (21 percent). This suggests some differences are needed in women's facility bed space and program space from men's facility space (for example, there may need to be less high-security bed space and more substance abuse programming space).

The increase in the number of women in jail has required that local officials identify and try to meet the needs of female inmates, yet severe limitations in resources often impede the provision of programs and services for women in jail. Jails are not prepared to house and treat rapidly rising female populations. They have difficulty providing appropriate housing, bed space, programs, jobs, mental health care, and other services. Women in jail have high needs for education, job training, health care, mental health care, alcohol and drug abuse counseling, and parenting skills development. Properly classifying women according to their risks and needs is beyond the scope of most jails in the United States.[30] The National Institute of Justice surveyed 54 jails and found that the same classification instrument was used for both male and female inmates in 50 jails. The survey found no effort to gauge women inmates' different needs, circumstances, and risk profiles.[31]

Ignoring problems relating to women in jail increases a jail's exposure to litigation and liability. The National Institute of Corrections argues against doing nothing: "The 'get tough on inmates' mood, combined with decreasing levels of accountability for maintaining some level of minimum standards, raises the specter of decreased funding for jails, corresponding cutbacks in staff and training, and the rebirth of the sorts of very brutal, barbaric, and often dangerous conditions that led to the initial wave of court intervention in the early 1970s."[32]

Women are normally housed in a "women's unit," often an after-thought built inside facilities designed for men or simply a replica of the men's facility design. Such design fails to take into account the different needs of women. For example, the traditional jail bunks and fixed-seating arrangements in the jail's dayroom or at dining room tables may present safety and comfort issues for women who are pregnant in jail. In Pennsylvania alone, 6 percent of the women who enter jail are pregnant, but the availability of pregnancy tests varies; only 29 of Pennsylvania's 57 county jails that hold women provide the test to every woman admitted. Cost is cited as a reason. A related issue is whether women in jail should be allowed to use contraceptives. Interruptions in birth control use could increase the possibility that they might have unintended pregnancies shortly after release.[33]

Another deficiency affecting women in jail is staffing. Either there are no female correctional officers or there are too few to ensure around-the-clock supervision of women in jail. The result too often is that women inmates are exploited and abused by male staff. Ken Kerle, former managing editor of *American Jails,* argues that the best defense for a jail against female inmates' allegations of sexual harassment by male staff is to have a female officer present at all times.[34]

Recently the National Institute of Corrections released a report to help jail and prison administrators more effectively manage the women in their care.[35] According to the researchers, four factors influence women offenders' behavior. Understanding these factors in combination with each other will help jail administrators consider how to adjust policies and procedures and how to assess and improve services to women in their care. They are:

1. **Pathways perspective.** Women in jail often have histories of sexual and/or physical abuse and substance abuse and are clients of mental health services. These women typically are unskilled, earn low incomes, have sporadic work histories, and are single parents. Thus, understanding how women enter the criminal justice system helps jails improve their responses.

2. **Relational theory and female development.** Relational theory describes the different ways women and men develop. An important difference suggested by the research is that women develop a sense of self and self-worth when their actions arise out of, and lead back into, connections with others even if this means establishing dysfunctional relationships. Many women offenders are drawn into criminal activity because of their relationships with others. Knowing this explains why jail staff often perceive that communicating with female offenders is more difficult and time-consuming than communicating with male inmates.

3. **Trauma theory.** Trauma is the injury done by violence and abuse and it is largely unrecognized by the women offenders themselves. Mental health services that understand past trauma and its effect on current behavior are needed to respond to trauma.

4. **Addiction theory.** When substance abuse treatment programs for women are combined with additional pathway factors (mental illness, trauma, abuse), jail-based treatment is successful.

Minorities comprise approximately 28 percent of the U.S. population but they make up more than 54 percent of the jail population. What are the explanations for the overrepresentation of minorities in jail?

Ethnicity and Jail Populations Whites comprise nearly 70 percent of the U.S. population but only 45.8 percent of the jail population. In the general population, Hispanics make up almost 16 percent, and blacks make up 12.7 percent, but in jail, their populations are 15.1 percent and 36.9 percent, respectively.

Explanations for the overrepresentation of minorities in jail abound. One explanation has to do with the function of jails as pretrial detention centers. The jail population is heavily influenced by bail decisions as we pointed out at the beginning of this chapter. A number of researchers have found that judges impose higher bail—or are more likely to deny bail altogether—if the defendant is a racial minority.[36] Still another reason is the impact of the war on drugs and on law enforcement strategies of racial profiling. Other researchers have argued that the war on drugs has had a particularly detrimental effect on black males.[37] Across the past two decades, more black males than white males have been detained for drug offenses. Researchers at the University of Nebraska argue that police are *reactive* in responding to crimes against persons and property but are *proactive* in dealing with drug offenses. "There is evidence," they write, "to suggest that they [police] target minority communities—where drug dealing is more visible and where it is thus easier to make an arrest—and tend to give less attention to drug activities in other neighborhoods."[38]

Mental Illness and Jail Populations How jails became the institution of choice to manage increasing numbers of people with mental illness and what can be done about it is discussed in more depth in Chapter 12. Here we point out that incarceration—especially jail—has become the nation's default mental health treatment provider and the problems associated with that approach.

Almost two-thirds (64 percent) of all jail inmates have a mental health problem compared to about 11 percent of the general adult population.[39] When researchers investigated the prevalence of "serious" mental illnesses defined as major depressive disorders, bipolar disorders, schizophrenia, and delusional disorders using structured clinical interviews with 20,000 adults entering five jails, they found that almost 15 percent of the men and 31 percent of the women had a serious mental illness.[40] As we will show in

Sixty-four percent of jail inmates have mental health problems compared to about 11 percent of the general population. Why are these individuals not fit subjects for retribution or punishment?

Chapter 12, persons living with mental illness are swept into the criminal justice system because of the failures of the public mental health system and the lack of adequate treatment in most poor communities. Today there may be as many as eight times more people with mental illness in the nation's jails (over 478,000) than there are in mental health hospitals (60,000).[41] The Los Angeles County Jail is the largest psychiatric inpatient facility in the United States with more than 3,400 prisoners suffering with mental health problems.[42] New York's Rikers Island is second with 3,000, and Chicago's Cook County Jail is third with more than 1,500. In six states, jails actually function as quasi-mental health centers. State statutes in Alaska, Kentucky, Mississippi, Montana, New Mexico, and Wyoming authorize jails to hold individuals awaiting transfer to a mental health facility.[43]

Despite the large number of jail inmates with mental illness, these individuals are not often fit subjects for retribution or punishment. James Gondles, executive director of the American Correctional Association, said, "The notion that the prospect of incarceration will deter an individual with a mental illness from committing a crime does not apply to a population that cannot fully comprehend the consequences of its actions, especially in cases where crime is a direct result of illness."[44]

Other experts tell us that the criminal justice system is ill-equipped to meet the special needs of persons with mental illness who are incarcerated or on supervised release in the community. They wind up in jail as a result of behavior linked to their illnesses. And once in jail, mentally ill inmates are more prone to act out in a way that could lead jail officers to use force. In fact, the Los Angeles County Sheriff's Office published a report showing that mentally ill inmates are involved in about one-third of use-of-force incidents by jail officers.[45] LA Sheriff Lee Baca responded to the report by adding more deputies trained in resolving tensions with mentally ill inmates to shifts where specially trained staff were not available.[46]

Over the years, the nation's sheriffs have also said that jails are not equipped to meet the complex needs of persons living with mental illness and asked county and general hospitals to accept them as patients. The sheriffs spelled out six factors as to why jails should not be used for such people:

1. The mentally ill person has usually committed no crime.
2. County jails are overcrowded.
3. Small county sheriffs' officers are not specially trained for the proper handling and care of a mental patient.
4. Many jails do not have proper or adequate detention rooms for the mentally ill.
5. Detention in the county jail is unfair to the patient as well as to the corrections officers.
6. Psychiatrists agree that a patient originally detained in a jail is much more difficult to treat and readjust, and incarceration can contribute to the further decompensation of many people with mental illness.[47]

The nation's sheriffs and others promote the diversion of individuals with mental illness from the nation's jails, collaboration between the justice system and the mental health communities, and treatment and training. Since 2004, 13 states have passed legislation creating or expanding mental health courts to provide alternative sentencing for nonviolent offenders with mental health problems.[48] We complete our discussion of the incarceration of persons who are mentally ill in Chapter 12.

Suicide, Homicide, Sexual Victimization, and Jail Populations

The problems of suicide, homicide, and sexual victimization are challenging ones for jail administrators. In 2011 (the last year for which data are available), 885 persons died in jail, down from 1,100 in 2007.[49] Death from illnesses such as heart disease, AIDs and related conditions, cancer, liver disease, and respiratory disease are the leading causes of deaths in jail (422 in 2010, down from 477 in 2010).

Suicide is the leading cause of jail inmate deaths. Since 2000, an average of 300 jail inmates commit suicide each year. The jail suicide rate is 43 per 100,000 inmates, almost four times what it is for the general U.S. population (11 per 100,000).

The situation for small jails is even worse. The suicide rate for jails with 50 or fewer beds was 169 per 100,000; in the largest jails (those with an ADP of 1,000 or more inmates), the suicide rate was 27 per 100,000 inmates.[50] The reasons are that smaller jails tend to be older and poorly staffed, are less able to provide sight and sound separation for inmates of different ages or genders, are less likely to use volunteers to deliver religious or rehabilitative programs, typically pay lower wages, find it difficult to comply with standards for physical or mental health care, use fewer classifications, and offer less inmate supervision.

Kentucky is one state that successfully reduced its jail suicides from 17 to 4 per year by cross-training jail personnel and mental health providers, developing new screening instruments for arresting and booking officers, establishing a telephonic service that allows jail staff to call a licensed mental health professional for risk management consultation 24 hours a day, and establishing a statewide data collection and analysis system.[51]

The majority of jail inmate suicides typically occur within the first week of incarceration with nearly a quarter occurring within the first two days of admission (time of day is not a factor), are mostly violent offenders (violent offenders who commit suicide outnumber nonviolent offenders by a margin of 3 to 1), and are typically committed by hanging. The majority of inmates who commit suicide have a high school education, are unmarried, white, male, and between the ages of 25 and 44. More than one-third have a history of serious mental illness of the type described earlier, and 8 of 10 had not yet been convicted but were awaiting trial.

The consequences of inmate suicide are lost lives, devastation to families, short- and long-term psychological effects on other inmates and correctional staff, expensive investigations and litigation, and medical care costs.

Suicide, homicide, and sexual victimization are challenging problems for jail administrators. Describe the problem and what jail leadership can do about it.

Homicide in jail is another concern of jail administrators, and here the news is not good. In 2000, 17 jail inmates were murdered. In 2006, the number increased to 36 and decreased to 21 in 2011. The literature on jail homicides offers very few insights other than revealing that kidnapping offenders are the most likely victims of jail homicides, followed by violent offenders, property offenders, and then public-order offenders. Drug offenders have the lowest homicide victimization rate. The majority of jail homicide victims are male, mostly between the ages of 18 and 54, and evenly split between white and black.

In 2003, Congress passed and President Bush signed the Prison Rape Elimination Act. It requires the U.S. Department of Justice to report on the incidence of rape and other forms of sexual victimization in correctional facilities. The Justice Department defines **sexual victimization** as all types of sexual activity, for example, oral, anal, or vaginal penetration; hand-jobs; touching of the inmate's buttocks, thighs, penis, breasts, or vagina in a sexual way; abusive sexual contacts (unwanted contacts with another inmate or any contacts with staff that involved touching of the inmate's buttocks, thigh, penis, breasts, or vagina, in a sexual way); and both willing and unwilling sexual contact. The Justice Department reported that 3.1 percent, approximately 24,000 of all jail inmates nationwide, experienced one or more incidents of sexual victimization in 2008–2009.[52] Most jail inmates reported that the incident involved jail staff. Some said the incident involved another inmate, and some said both other inmates and staff had victimized them. The majority (6,900) who reported that the incident involved jail staff said the sex or sexual contact was unwilling as a result of physical force, pressure, or offers of special favors or privileges. An equally large number of jail inmates (8,400) said they willingly had sex or sexual contact with staff. The Justice Department is clear to note, however, "Regardless of whether an inmate reported being willing or unwilling, any sexual contact between jail inmates and staff is illegal."[53]

In 2012, after conducting a series of public hearings, reviewing the data, conducting site visits, and speaking with correctional staff and inmates, the Prison Rape Elimination Act's review panel concluded that sexual assaults can be reduced by changing attitudes toward potentially vulnerable populations, including female, lesbian, gay, bisexual, transgender, queer (LGBTQ), and physically frail inmates; paying close attention to institutional design and surveillance; providing offender education and staff training; improving operational policies and post orders; and monitoring adherence to established policies. In addition, a reliable inmate-classification system; improved efforts on the part of first responders, investigators, and prosecutors; and timely victim assistance and health care services can help an agency reduce, if not eliminate, inmate sexual victimization.[54]

Juveniles and Jail Populations Over the past 25 years, there has been a dramatic reversal in the theory and practice of punishing juveniles, as Chapter 16 will explain. In the mid-1970s, juvenile offenders were deemed to have special needs, so Congress passed the Juvenile Justice and Delinquency Prevention Act of 1974. It contains four core requirements that participating states must address to receive federal juvenile justice grants:

1. Status offenders may not be held in secure confinement.
2. Juveniles generally may not be held in jails and lockups in which adults are confined.

3. When juveniles are temporarily detained in the same facilities as adults, they must have no "sight or sound" contact with adult inmates.

4. States are required to demonstrate efforts to reduce the disproportionate number of minority youth who come into contact with the juvenile justice system.

By 1996, however, in the face of pressure to increase punishment for juvenile offenders, new legislation allowed cities and states to detain juvenile offenders for up to 12 hours in an adult jail before a court appearance and made it easier to house juveniles in separate wings of adult jails. That shift in philosophy and policy has kept the percentage of juveniles held as adults at about 80 to 85 percent for the past decade even though the number of juveniles in adult jails today is lower today than it was a decade ago (5,400 at midyear 2012 compared to 7.615 at midyear 2000).

The incarceration of juveniles in adult jails is criticized for a number of reasons. Holding juveniles in adult jails places young people at greater risk of being physically, sexually, and mentally abused by adult offenders. Juvenile girls are especially vulnerable to sexual assault. Juveniles in adult jail are almost eight times more likely to commit suicide than are those in juvenile detention centers. One explanation is that juveniles are held in isolated parts of adult jails where they receive less staff support and supervision. Another is that jail staff are not trained to recognize depression in juveniles.

As late as midyear 2008, the U.S. Congress discussed bills that would bar most juveniles charged as adults from being detained in adult jails unless a court finds, after a hearing, that it is in the interest of justice to do so. However, to date the Congress has not acted on any of the proposals.

Jail Facilities

Occupancy Rated capacity is the maximum number of beds allocated to each jail facility by a state or local rating official. The rated capacity for the nation's jails was 866,947 beds at midyear 2012, an increase of 7,225 beds from midyear 2011. However only 84 percent of the jail beds were occupied at midyear 2012, the lowest since 1984 when it was 86 percent. (The other ways to measure capacity are discussed in Chapter 7.)

Public Versus Private Of the nation's 3,283 jails, 37 are privately operating under contract to local governments.[55] Seven states account for most of the contract jail operations: Texas (8), California (5), Pennsylvania (4), and Florida, Missouri, New Mexico, and Tennessee (3 each). Across the country, 254 jails were under one or more court orders either to limit population or to provide specific conditions of confinement. Court orders required about 204 jails to limit population and about 165 to correct specific conditions related to crowding, medical facilities, procedures and policies, programming, inmate classification, exercise, staffing, food service, and religious practices.

Size, Location, and Budget Almost 40 percent of the nation's jails have an average daily population of fewer than 50 inmates and hold less than 3 percent of the jail population.[56] Of all jail jurisdictions holding inmates, the percentage holding 99 or fewer inmates is nearly 59 percent, about 20 percent hold 100 to 249, 10 percent hold 250 to 499, and

rated capacity

The maximum number of beds allocated to each jail facility by a state or local rating official.

Economic Realities and Corrections: Jails

Amid the national budget crises, falling tax revenue, and national unemployment, jails face cutbacks despite the harsh sentencing guidelines passed in the 1980s and 1990s that glutted jail cells. In 1980, about 200,000 persons were confined in the nation's jails. Today that number has soared to more than 735,000.

This chapter establishes the fact that today the United States spends $9 billion a year on the nation's 3,283 jails. At midyear 2011, local jails admitted almost 11.8 million persons, half of whom were admitted to the nation's 50 largest jails.

Five of the nation's 50 largest jails—Los Angeles County; New York City; Harris County, Texas; Cook County, Illinois; and Philadelphia, Pennsylvania—have an average daily population of almost 10,000 or more inmates.

Since 2006 when the Bureau of Justice Statistics began reporting the average daily population and rated the capacity of each of the nation's 50 largest jails, only Harris County (Houston), Texas, has been consistently overcrowded, meaning that it detains anywhere from 2 to 21 percent more inmates than it is rated to have.* Not included in

Harris County jail overcrowding are the inmates who are bused to and from northern Louisiana.

In 2008, John Dyess, chief administrative officer for the Harris County Sheriff's Office, which oversees the jail, said, "This really wasn't built for this. I don't know if we can build our way out of where we are today."† Five years later, the jail remains the most overcrowded large jail in the United States.

The Harris County jail spends more than $1 million a day on its inmates. A shortage of jail corrections officers means the jail spends more than $35 million a year on officer overtime. Doctors write $1 million in prescriptions a month and dentists pull 330 teeth. Washers and dryers handle 170 pounds of laundry a load. Inmates prepare 35,000 meals a day for an average of 88 cents each. Recently, Harris County failed several jail standards tests and was cited for excessive use of force, inmate deaths, and poor medical and mental care. The jail is the biggest mental health facility in Texas.

Instead of letting the economic crisis create jail problems, two jurisdictions larger than Harris County have addressed

the problem and are not using all of their jail bed space. Los Angeles County has the largest daily jail population, almost 19,000 inmates, but uses only 93 percent of its beds. New York City with almost 14,000 persons in jail uses only 66 percent of its beds. These and other jails are investing in pretrial services that are less expensive and protect the community such as the ones discussed in this chapter so that people charged with nonviolent offenses who don't need to be confined can be quickly vetted for community programs and mentally ill persons can receive health care services or, if needed, be placed in a secure health facility.

As we show in this chapter, many people are in jail because they are too poor to post bail. Communities with pretrial programs are in a better position to save money in hard times because they can carefully analyze the individual and figure out better what needs to be done.

*See Bureau of Justice Statistics publications *Jail Inmate Midyear* 2007 through 2011.

†Jesse Bogan, "America's Jail Crisis," *Forbes*, July 13, 2009, www.forbes.com (accessed March 13, 2013).

6 percent hold 500 to 999 inmates. Those housing 1,000 or more (referred to as megajails) inmates account for 5 percent. Typically these large facilities are located in major metropolitan and urban areas. Taxpayers spend $9 billion annually to support the nations' jails. Jail operating budgets are highest in New York (almost $1.1 billion) and lowest in North Dakota ($3.5 million).[57] The average annual cost to incarcerate one jail inmate is approximately $24,000.[58]

Today a number of local jails charge inmates housing fees and medical co-pay fees. It is not known how common this is across the United States, but several states have adopted the practice. Jails in Arkansas, Illinois, Kansas, Kentucky, New Jersey, and Texas now charge inmates an average of $10 for medical services. Dallas County Sheriff Lupe Valdez whose photograph is shown on page 190 said the reason to charge jail inmates for medical services is to cut the cost of transporting inmates to receive medical care. Officials in states that implemented jail medical co-pays as far back as the 1990s reported that such measures cut back on the number of inmates who fake illnesses to get out of their cells.[59]

Some jails are also charging inmates a housing fee. For example, more than half of the 95 jails currently operating in the state of Kansas charge a housing fee ranging from $10 to $70 a day. The most ambitious jurisdiction to charge inmates for their jail stay is Riverside, California, which is facing an $80 million budget shortfall. County Supervisor Jeff Stone believes that about 25 percent of the jail inmates could pay as much as $142.42 housing fee per day.[60] According to the researchers, the overriding reasons that jails assess housing fees are the economic recession, jail crowding, and the need to cover operating costs (e.g., medical, food, utilities, staff, and transportation).[61] However, out of concern for gender-responsive services for females, some are asking what impact medical co-pays will have on female offenders who statistically enter correctional facilities with more medical problems than do males and who will have to pay extra for something that is a result of being female.[62] Others believe that jail medical co-pays and housing fees are a tax on inmates' families, who are responsible for putting money into inmate commissary accounts to pay for such services.[63]

Will policies charging inmates close budget gaps, or is it more symbolic? We pointed out earlier in this Chapter that 80 percent of jail inmates earned less than $2,000 a month before they were locked up, 44 percent had less than a high school diploma, and, at the time of their arrest, 33 percent were unemployed and 14 percent were homeless. So it is very unlikely that counties are going to collect any money from them. Jail fees, along with assessed court costs and possibly child support and restitution, can create more debt for inmates after they are released and make successful reentry more difficult.

Almost 80 jails in the United States are also generating new revenue by allowing well-behaved inmates a chance to receive meatball subs, cheeseburgers, pizza, and wings complete with celery, blue cheese, and a Pepsi ordered through companies like Aramark's "iCare" and Sendapackage. Aramark tailors its menus to each jail's rules. Prices generally run from $7 to $14 for a hot meal and $20 to $100 for a junk-food box. Jails receive revenue on every dollar. For example, the Bexar County Jail in San Antonio, Texas, makes 45 cents on every dollar in sales.

Sendapackage operates only in New York. It sells only items that corrections regulations will allow including soft drinks, cigarettes, canned ravioli, cotton hoodies, baseball caps, cans of Beefaroni, watches, gummi

Nicole Brockett, a 22-year-old bartender in Los Angeles, served 21 days for DUI at the Santa Ana City Jail, one of a dozen pay-to-stay jails in California, instead of incarceration at the nearby county jail. Brockett paid $82 per day for living conditions that the jail says are "a world away from cement and steel bars." What are the advantages and disadvantages of pay-to-stay jail?

bears, stereo headphones, and music on cassettes since CDs are not allowed because they can be broken into sharp objects. Sendapackage sends about 40 orders to inmates every day. Each order averages about $110. Inmates and their relatives and friends place orders online or by telephone or mail. Will programs like this create envy, violence, and extortion among inmates? Will overindulgence in junk food lead to health problems and potentially raise taxpayer costs for inmate health care? It's too early to tell what impact Aramark's "iCare" food service for jails will have. Jail staff including Captain Richard Fisher of the Rock Island County Jail, Illinois, say, "Jails are always run better when your inmates are happy." But others cringe. Sheriff Joe Arpaio of Maricopa County, Arizona, who serves his jail inmates only "nutraloaf," a brick-hard concoction made from blending together dry milk, vegetables and bread dough, says pepperoni pizza is not his idea of jail food. "Instead of calling it a jail, let's call it the Hilton," he said.[64]

pay-to-stay jail
(also *self-pay jails*)

An alternative to serving time in a county jail. Offenders convicted of minor offenses are offered privileges for a fee from $75 to $127 per day.

Pay-to-Stay Jail In addition to charging inmates housing, food, and medical co-pay fees as a way to offset jail operations, some jurisdictions have added **pay-to-stay jails**, also referred to as *self-pay jails*. The concept of pay-to-stay is surging after actors such as Keifer Sutherland, star of *24*, and Gary Collins, star of countless TV shows, served their sentences for DUI at the Glendale, California, city jail. The Beverly Hills Police Department, California, opened its pay-to-stay jail in late 2009.

Pay-to-stay jails are an alternative to serving time in a county jail and offer privileges to offenders (sometimes called *clients*) convicted of minor offenses such as DUI and non-drug-related offenses who pay $75 to $127 per day. Estimates are that there are approximately 13 pay-to-stay jails in California.[65] Exhibit 6–9 compares six pay-to-stay jails in southern California in terms of cost per day, number of beds available, amenities, what inmates are allowed to bring in, and eligibility criteria. For example, persons convicted of DUI and sentenced to 21 days in the Santa Ana City Jail will pay more than $1,700 for extra privileges. Recently, an assistant sheriff of Orange County (California) was convicted of perjury and misuse of public funds. He served his sentence of 243 days at the Fullerton City Jail and paid $18,000 for a private cell, bathroom, and shower stall; use of his cell phone; and food brought by his visitors and even pizza delivery.

Offenders normally petition the court at their sentencing proceedings to serve their sentence at a pay-to-stay jail. If the court agrees and the city accepts the offender's application, he or she is housed separately from other inmates but may have minimal contact with the general inmate population during meal service. Most pay-to-stay jail inmates are required to work several hours a day outside their cells in food preparation, laundry, facility sanitation, vehicle washing, and so on, even if they work elsewhere in the community or attend school. The accommodations are usually cleaner and safer.

Supporters of the self-pay model argue that pay-to-stay jails benefit everyone: Paying inmates generate cash for the community (the Pasadena, California, city jail collected $234,000 from pay-to-stay clients at the rate of $127 a night in 2008, and the Burbank, California, city jail collected $109,000 at the rate of $85 a night[66]); taxpayers pay less to house offenders in city rather than county jails; offenders can serve their time in a smaller, nonviolent facility; and paying inmates are generally easier to deal with.

On the other hand, critics charge that pay-to-stay jails create inherent injustices, offering cleaner, safer alternatives to those who can afford

EXHIBIT 6–9 **Comparison of Six Pay-to-Stay Jails**

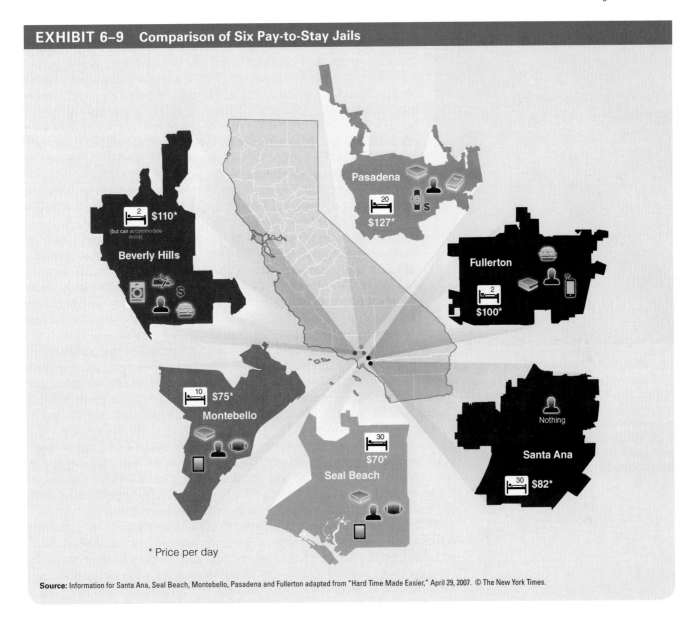

* Price per day

it. The concept of offering a cleaner, safer jail is valid, they say, but the criterion of inmates paying for it is not. To date, there is no research to support the claims of self-pay jails or whether offenders who pay for their own jail stay are less likely to recidivate.

Jail Staff and Workforce Development

Twenty years ago, staffing was cited as the number-one concern in a survey of 2,452 jails.[67] Dr. Ken Kerle says this is still a major problem.[68] Today, an estimated 234,000 people work in the nation's jails.[69] Women comprise one-third of all jail employees (one-fourth of all corrections officers). Sixty-six percent of all jail corrections officers are white, 24 percent are black, 8 percent are Hispanic, and 2 percent are of other races. Minority employees are underrepresented relative to their proportion among inmates. Consult the Appendix: Careers in Corrections at the Online Learning Center Web site for the steps involved in career planning, developing employability and job readiness, and finding the right job.

Lupe Valdez is sheriff of Dallas County, Texas. She is the only female sheriff in Texas, the only Hispanic female sheriff in the United States, and she is openly gay. Her department has an operating budget of $132 million, employs 2,250 personnel, and operates the seventh largest jail in the United States. Why are staffing issues a major concern of most jails today?

Visit http://www.youtube.com/watch?v=yKvjW06MF_k or scan this code with the QR app on your smartphone or digital device and watch this podcast of the recruiting video for County Sheriff's Office (Kansas). How does this information relate to ideas discussed in this chapter?

In spite of the fact that there are more beds than inmates, as noted earlier, jail staff perceive that jails are overcrowded because there are not enough staff on shifts to handle the workload properly. Jail staff think of a jail as overcrowded if, due to staff shortages, inmate counts, bed checks, and cell searches are not performed and inmate programs such as visitation and outdoor recreation are postponed.[70] Because most jails are locally funded, local politics determines how much staff a county government allocates to operate the county jail. How much is the county willing to spend on the jail compared to other county agencies such as roads, police, and fire?

Most jails spend 75 to 90 percent of their budgets on salaries. One jail post operating 24 hours a day, seven days a week requires five officers when sick time, vacation, and other leaves are factored in. This partially explains why county officials are reluctant to increase staffing to correspond with an increase in inmate population. Yet understaffing poses a threat to inmate and staff security and safety. Too often inadequate staffing leads to inmate lockdowns to prevent escape and ease the handling of prisoners. Furthermore, without appropriate staff supervision, little can be done to protect inmates from one another in multiple-occupancy cells.

Other problems of jail staff include substandard pay compared to that of other employees in the criminal justice system, low job prestige, high turnover, and inadequate systems for recruitment, selection, and training. The National Sheriff's Association (NSA) believes that too often "warm bodies are taken off the street, put into uniform, given a set of keys, and told to go to work."[71] Concerning salaries, the NSA wrote, "Jail officer careers will never achieve the status they deserve so long as counties continue to pay jail officers less money than the officers assigned to law enforcement. . . . No person wants to make a career where the reward is lousy wages. You can't attract the people who have the potential to be the best officers by paying them wages in the poverty range."[72]

Although the Palm Beach County Florida Sheriff's Department starts certified jail corrections officers at $47,220, not all jails can do this. Nevertheless, most jails can help officers find satisfaction in their work by setting clearly defined goals, identifying the officer's job obligations and performance expectations, and providing jail officers adequate organizational resources to perform their jobs. Attracting and retaining jail employees depends on engaging in effective recruitment, providing meaningful preservice and inservice training and career development, and developing responsive management and leadership.

Jail human resource specialists argue that to recruit exceptional candidates to work as jail corrections officers, jails should do more than outline only the minimum qualifications for an officer position. Instead of listing menial and basic job descriptions of feeding inmates, logging information, and so on, a different approach is to create catchy job descriptions. Examples are writing criminal and internal jail reports, qualifying for advancement in classification and transport, monitoring, evaluating, making recommendations on technology equipment, joining special response teams, becoming instructors in firearms, conducting energy devices (CEDs), using OC (oleoresin capsicum) spray, investigating the introduction of contraband into the facility, and becoming a security threat group specialist (STGs), the latter only for jails in very large jurisdictions such as Chicago, Los Angeles, Miami, and New York (see Chapter 13 for description of STGs).[73]

Those same jail human resource specialists also tell us that agencies can easily promote career opportunities to the public by revamping the jail's website and other marketing materials; creating a presence on Facebook, Twitter, and other social media; creating a job-shadowing program such as a "ride-along" offering open house tours; and emphasizing, promoting, and supporting professional development.

In 1999, the American Correctional Association (ACA) embarked on a major effort to support professional development in corrections by developing a national Commission on Correctional Certification (CCC) and an online corrections academy. Just as accreditation provides an opportunity for facilities to be recognized, certification is an opportunity for jail staff to be recognized as qualified correctional practitioners. The ACA certification process requires applicants to meet the educational requirements of the category within which they seek certification (for example, the correctional executive position requires a college degree, correctional managers and supervisors require an associate degree, and correctional officers require a high school diploma). Then applicants must pass a national examination developed by the National Institute of Corrections pertaining to the job tasks and related competencies associated with the job category. Finally, applicants enter into "candidacy status," a two-year period during which they must pass a certification examination. Those who pass the certification exam become Certified Corrections Professionals for three years. Maintaining that status involves becoming recertified and obtaining a specified number of continuing education credits. Through the efforts of the ACA's Commission on Correctional Certification, jail personnel are in the process of upgrading their public image and professional stature and achieving the status of other professions that rely on universal compliance with a self-imposed credentialing process. The American Jail Association's Code of Ethics for Jail Officers is shown in the Ethics and Professionalism box.

JAIL ISSUES

In May and June 2007, 45 sheriffs and jail administrators from across the United States met to discuss the most important issues facing jails today and make recommendations to the Justice Department.[74] The jail managers cited inmate medical and mental health as their top concern and recommended that the government give jails more support in that area. (We discuss the impact of the Affordable Care Act on corrections in Chapter 7.)

Five years later, jail leaders who attended the National Jail Leadership Command Academy at Sam Houston State University in Huntsville, Texas, said that inmate medical and mental health services was a continuing acute problem and argued that local governments should collaborate more with jails to provide an inpatient mental health program, help manage medical costs, assist with housing for inmates who are acutely mentally ill/suicidal, and develop more community diversion programs.[75]

All jail managers agreed that inmates are arriving in jail with more serious and costly mental health problems that they (the jail managers) are responsible for treating. They said they need other agencies and resources in the community to help share the burden of the treatment. Jails may be able to do a relatively good job of stabilizing a mentally ill person while he or she is in jail but are incapable of dealing with long-term needs. As a result, once released, the inmates reoffend and come back to jail.

We conclude this chapter by elaborating on other concerns of jail managers: privatization, reentry, accreditation, and evidence-based practices.

CO6-6

Privatization

privatization

A contract process that shifts public functions, responsibilities, and capital assets, in whole or in part, from the public sector to the private sector.

Privatization is defined as a contract process that shifts public functions, responsibilities, and capital assets, in whole or in part, from the public sector to the private sector.

Jails can be privatized in one of three ways: through private management, private sector development, or private services provision. With private management, private firms have total responsibility for the operation of a facility. This is the most common application of the term *privatization* and the most controversial aspect of the private sector's involvement in corrections.

With private sector development, the private sector develops, designs, and finances or arranges for the financing of jails. This often involves owning the jail and leasing it back to the jurisdiction through a lease/purchase contract, which serves as an alternative to a public bond issue or tax increase.

For private services provision, jails contract with private vendors to run services such as health and dental care, alcohol and drug treatment, mental health services, food service, training, and programming. This is the most familiar privatization model and the least controversial.

The debate between proponents and opponents of jail privatization surfaced early and continues today. Pressures for privatization come from escalating costs and crowded jails as well as from general dissatisfaction with county government. Jail privatization is sometimes seen as a practical option when a jurisdiction needs to update facilities quickly in response to a court order for additional capacity. Advocates of privatization claim that private organizations can operate facilities more efficiently and cost-effectively.

Opponents of jail privatization dispute cost comparisons or dismiss them altogether. Some insist that the fundamental point is that it is the responsibility of local governments to operate jails, not to delegate power and liability. Opponents believe that the administration of justice is a basic function of government and a symbol of state authority and should not be delegated. From this perspective, jails are, as John J. DiIulio Jr., University of Pennsylvania professor of politics, religion, and civil society, put it, "a public trust to be administered on behalf of the community and in the name of civility and justice."[76]

Opponents also fear that if we privatize jails, we risk enabling private corporations to use their political influence to continue programs not in the public interest. For example, would private contractors keep jail occupancy rates high to maintain profit? Might private contractors accept only the best inmates, leaving the most troublesome for public facilities to handle?

Turning a jail over to a private corporation also raises questions about accountability. Who is responsible for monitoring the performance of the private contractor? Who will see that local laws and regulations are followed? As jail incarceration rates continue to rise, the debate over privatizing jails and the competition for new contracts will continue.

Professional associations have addressed jail privatization through policy statements that range from cautious (American Correctional Association) to negative (American Jail Association and the National Sheriff's Association). The American Federation of State, County and Municipal Employees has been opposed from the beginning, and the American Bar Association has urged a moratorium until more information is available.

Jail Reentry (Begins at Entry)

reentry

The transition offenders make from prison or jail to the community.

Another solution to jail crowding is jail **reentry**, the process of transition that offenders make from prison or jail to the community. (We return to a discussion of reentry in Chapter 8.) It seems only natural to add jail reentry to the list of strategies so that fewer people, once released, return to jail.

Bradley Lord, Psy.D.

Director of Mental Health, Escambia County Sheriff's Office, Pensacola, Florida

Dr. Lord is the director of Mental Health for the Escambia County Sheriff's Office (ECSO) in Pensacola, Florida. He operates a mental health department for the Escambia County Jail, which includes supervising case managers, licensed therapists, and psychiatrists. He is second in command of the Health Services Section of the ECSO and supervises 70 employees. He also completes mental health evaluations for ECSO for newly hired patrol and canine deputies. Over the past 15 years, he has worked in drug rehabilitation settings, inpatient psychiatric settings, outpatient settings, and private practice.

Lord received his B.A. degree in psychology from the University of West Florida, his master of science degree in counseling and psychology from Troy University, and his Psy.D. in clinical psychology from California Southern University. His doctoral project focused on leadership development within the adolescent population. He is a licensed therapist and a certified addictions professional in the state of Florida. He attributes his leadership style to his military experiences, diverse professional experiences, and course curriculum provided by his varied academic experiences.

Lord avidly enjoys teaching as an adjunct instructor at the University of West Florida. He encourages students and colleagues to further their education and become lifelong learners because new information, not only in the psychology field but also the forensics field, is always available. Being current with data and trends when working within the professional fields of forensics and psychology is necessary to provide the best care and guidance for clients and employees. It is simply not enough to earn a degree and work in forensics or psychology because of their dynamic and ever-changing fields. Individuals who do not keep up with the new information and trends associated with these professions simply become antiquated and fail their clients and organizations they represent.

"It is simply not enough to earn a degree and work in forensics or psychology because of their dynamic and ever-changing fields. Individuals who do not keep up with the new information and trends associated with these professions simply become antiquated and fail their clients and organizations they represent."

Evidence suggests that improving inmate job skills, helping inmates find jobs upon release, and increasing inmate wage potential all have a significant impact on recidivism.[77] We find success stories in small rural jails and in large urban jails. Jim Parsons, director of the Vera Institute of Justice Substance Use and Mental Health Programs, describes three promising approaches to reentry that are particularly well suited to jail settings: (1) the use of administrative records as a way to target scarce resources to frequent service users (FSU), those who are likely to benefit the most from receiving reentry services, (2) the APIC model, and (3) strengths-based approaches to jail reentry programming and family-based service models.[78]

Targeting Frequent Service Users and Using Jail Data to Assess the Risk of Recidivism
The Frequent Users Service Enhancement (FUSE) initiative uses cross-system data to provide housing services for chronic users of both jail and shelter systems. FUSE providers in New York City conduct a quarterly data match between the city's jail and shelter records to identify people who meet the program's criteria of at least four jail and four shelter stays during the preceding five-year period. Preliminary results from an evaluation of the FUSE model in Connecticut found that the first 30 recruits to the program had incurred an estimated $12 million in lifetime jail and shelter system costs.

Once the list of the names has been produced, service providers match them against jail and shelter rosters to identify those who are eligible for FUSE's targeted housing supports.

Visit www.youtube.com/watch?v= jBkz0X3s6pl or scan this code with the QR app on your smartphone or digital device and watch this 2013 podcast of New York City Mayor Bloomberg announcing the New Jail-Based Community Re-Entry Program, Part of State of the City Promise to Further Reduce Recidivism. How does this information relate to ideas discussed in this chapter?

Another approach to targeting reentry services uses assessments to determine the risk of recidivism as a way to identify those who are repeatedly cycling through jails. Two of the most commonly used offender assessment tools developed to assess an offender's level of risk are the Level of Services Inventory—Revised and the Correctional Offender Management Profiling for Alternative Sanctions. However, the training requirements to administer these tools, their high licensing costs, and the need for a private environment in which to conduct assessment interviews act as obstacles to the use of these tools by jails. Competing each assessment can take up to an hour. In the country's largest jails, assessing every person entering the jail would require a dedicated, trained staff of dozens.

An alternative to these assessments is the Vera Institute of Justice's Service Priority Indicator (SPI). It uses four pieces of data that significantly predict readmission to department of corrections (DOC) custody within one year of release: people who (1) were younger than 20 at admission, (2) had a current charge for either a property or drug offense, (3) had a specified number of prior DOC admissions, and (4) had a DOC admission within the previous eight weeks.

Based on these factors, the SPI classifies people as having "low," "medium," "high," or "very high" risk of recidivism. The SPI significantly differentiates between the four groups and has found that 24 percent of the "low"-risk group readmitted to DOC custody within one year of release compared with 84 percent of the "very high"-risk group.

The SPI addresses the limited resources available to conduct lengthy risk assessment interviews by providing an instrument for recidivism risk that can be automatically generated for every person as part of the standard jail intake system. Although the SPI is not designed to replace more detailed, in-person risk and needs assessments, it provides a method for directing available resources to individuals with an elevated risk of recidivism who may benefit from a more in-depth assessment.

APIC The APIC acronym summarizes the four essential stages of reentry service provision: *a*ssessing risks and needs, *p*lanning for treatment based on the assessment, *i*dentifying appropriate providers in the jail and in the community to address the inmate's needs, and *c*oordinating the transition back to the community and ensuring continuity of care. The APIC model also identifies a variety of commonly occurring reentry service needs, including housing, inpatient and outpatient treatment for mental health and substance abuse disorders, medication, counseling and other behavioral health services, medical care, income support and benefits, food and clothing, child care, and transportation.

Building upon Family and Peer Networks
Families are often the primary source of financial and emotional support when people return from jail or prison. In addition, family contacts can be instrumental in helping former inmates identify employment opportunities and find housing. Helping people maintain contact with their families and intimate partners while they are incarcerated has been shown to improve both short- and long-term outcomes, buffering returning inmates from the damaging effects of incarceration.

Reentry strategies that support families are also important for the children and partners of people who were formerly incarcerated. The Bureau of Justice Statistics estimates that approximately 1.7 million children under the age of 18 in the United States have at least one parent in state or federal prison. An equivalent national figure is not available for jails, but a survey of 311 people interviewed while they were held in jail in Maryland and Wisconsin found that 67 percent of respondents were parents. Estimates based on prison parenthood data suggest that there are between 700,000 and 800,000 children with at least one parent in jail on any given day.

Services that build on peer and family support networks are particularly suited to jails where families often live close by and tend to have relatively easy access to their incarcerated relatives. The Family Justice Program of the Vera Institute of Justice develops correctional interventions designed to capitalize on the existing strengths and supports found within families. One such program is the Children of Incarcerated Parents Program (CHIPP), a partnership between the New York City Administration for Children's Service (ACS) and the jail. The program's goal is to maintain and strengthen bonds between children in foster care and their incarcerated parents. One component of CHIPP, the Riker's Island Family Visitation Program, provides dedicated visiting days when children who are in foster care custody can visit their incarcerated parents. On these designated days, ACS transports children to the jail for extended two-hour visits, provides children's toys and games in the jail visiting area, and relaxes the usual rules limiting physical contact between inmates and their visiting relatives.

Exhibit 6–10 shows what some of the jails across the United States are doing in jail reentry.

EXHIBIT 6–10 **Jail Reentry**

To date, reentry policies and programs have primarily targeted people released from state and federal prisons. However, jail reentry has at least as much of an impact on public safety, if not more. Although the nation's jail capacity is lower than its prison capacity—there are approximately 691,000 jail beds, compared to 1.4 million prison beds—admissions and releases from jails far exceed those from prisons. According to the Bureau of Justice Statistics 2004 Survey of Large Jails, 20 percent of jail inmates serve at least one month, and only 4 percent serve more than six months. As a result, the jail population is continuously turning over, resulting in approximately 12 million admissions and releases per year.

The short sentences served in jail and the proximity of jails to inmates' home communities have important implications—both positive and negative—for the role of local jails in addressing the challenges of prisoner reentry, highlighted as follows:

- **Mental illness.** Sixteen percent of both jail inmates and state prisoners report a mental condition or overnight stay in a mental hospital. However, only 41 percent of jail inmates with mental illness receive mental health services compared to 61 percent of state prisoners with mental illness.
- **Substance abuse and dependence.** More than two-thirds (68 percent) of jail inmates are dependent on or abuse drugs or alcohol, but only 18 percent receive treatment or participate in other substance abuse programs after entering jail. Sixty-nine percent of jail inmates are regular drug users, and 29 percent of convicted jail inmates report drug use at the time of their offense.
- **Limited employability.** Fifty-seven percent of jail inmates were working full-time the month prior to their arrest. Thirty percent of all jail inmates reported personal earnings totaling less than $300 per month.
- **Extensive criminal histories.** Three-fourths of jail inmates have served a prior probation or incarceration sentence, and nearly a quarter (24 percent) have served three or more prior sentences to incarceration. More than half of all jail inmates have a current criminal justice status at the time of arrest.

Source: Adapted from Nancy G. La Vigne, Amy L. Solomon, Karen A. Beckman, and Kelly Dedel, *Prisoner Reentry and Community Policing: Strategies for Enhancing Public Safety* (Washington, DC: U.S. Department of Justice, Office of Community Oriented Policing Services, March 2006).

The Offender Speaks
Visit www.mhhe.com/schmalleger7e to see this feature.

CO6-7

Educational, Vocational, and Inmate Work Programs

Many jail inmates have poor reading skills. National studies show that more than 40 percent of all jail inmates have less than a ninth-grade education.[79] They also have substance abuse problems and few job skills. They frequently cannot find jobs after they are released or can find only low-paid or temporary work. As a result, in part, they often return to a life of crime.

Too many jails simply warehouse inmates and care little about education or job skills. It costs taxpayers money to provide educational services to jail inmates—the same people who already have financially and psychologically burdened society through their crimes. Education does not guarantee that an offender will remain free of crime upon release. However, consider the alternative: More than 40 percent of defendants on pretrial release have one or more prior convictions. The cost of keeping one inmate in jail for one year ranges from $20,000 to $40,000. Studies also show that inmates who earn their GEDs while incarcerated are far less likely to return to crime. Educational and vocational programs help offenders help themselves, they boost self-esteem, and they encourage legitimate occupations upon release. Overall, it costs less to educate offenders and teach them job skills than to do nothing to change their attitudes, abilities, and outlooks. Ignoring an offender's educational and vocational deficiencies leaves the offender with fewer marketable skills or qualifications when released, increasing the chance of a return to crime.

On an average day, nearly 20 percent of all jail inmates work at least six hours a day. Some jails go further, creating opportunities for inmates to learn work habits and skills that are in demand in the community, earn wages that apply to their fines, court costs, and family obligations, provide quality goods to consumers, and reduce inmate idleness. Jail industries making headlines include:[80]

- **Lewis County Jail, Chehalis, Washington.** Inmates who meet certain criteria are able to obtain certification in commercial baking and basic kitchen safety for employment in restaurants, cafes, hotels, cafeterias, delis, catering, and institutional operations. The program is sponsored by the Consolidated Food Management.

- **Lafayette Parish, Louisiana.** Inmates manufacture and deliver can liners for trash and garbage use to government or nonprofit agencies in the state of Louisiana. In 2009, total sales reached over $200,000.
- **Two Bridges Regional Jail, Maine.** Inmates in one of the newest jail industries programs in the country design and fabricate wood items.
- **Franklin County Jail, Pennsylvania.** Inmates produce the newsletter for the Council for the Arts and wash, dry, and deliver uniforms for the Chambersburg Cardinals, a minor league football team.
- **Los Angeles Sheriff's Department Jail Enterprise Unit, California.** Inmates produce lunch and trash bags for the sheriff's food service unit, saving the sheriff's office over $100,000 annually instead of purchasing the bags. The Unit is expanding to market the bags to other government agencies within Los Angeles County.
- **Arapahoe County, Colorado.** Inmates are involved in a wide array of recycling initiatives. In 2007, the program earned almost $300,000, and about one-fourth of the revenues were paid to inmates as wages.
- **Hampden County Jail, Massachusetts.** Inmates enroll in a Culinary Arts Program at Springfield Technical Community College and operate the Olde Armory Grille. They gain experience in food preparation and delivery.

Elsewhere across the country, jail inmates are involved in animal grooming, auto repair, body work and detailing, events setup and breakdown, computer data entry, digital imaging, furniture assembly and repair, graphics, laundry, silk-screening, telephone marketing, and welding.

Jail Ministry

CO6-8

Very little is written about the use and effects of jail ministry and faith-based programming in jail. Too often the topic is looked at skeptically by outsiders who believe that inmates pretend to "find God" as a convenient way to obtain release or forgiveness. However, getting into trouble and then turning to religion is supported by the "coping" literature, which links major life events to a greater tendency to turn to spirituality or religion. What we will explore here, however, is not the research supporting the veracity of inmates' claims of conversion but the partnership between government and faith-based organizations to meet the nation's corrections needs. We will also consider the experiences of those who minister to jail inmates.

Religious belief can make a difference in people's lives and can assist in tackling social problems. Much crime is the result of people making the wrong moral choices. Churches and religious organizations can provide the moral and spiritual aspects to correctional programs. There are not enough correctional officers, probation or parole officers, or police to prevent every ex-offender from committing another crime, so help from other partners is needed. Pat Nolan, vice president of Prison Fellowship Ministries writes, "The way society will be able to reduce crime is if during their time of incarceration, offenders have been transformed and internalized a moral code that allows them to exercise self-restraint and be good citizens after they are released. . . . It will be helpful to look upon local churches as partners to help teach inmates these important lessons during their incarceration and to act as mentors as they re-enter their communities."[81]

Recently, researchers conducted a study to investigate the impact of religious programs on two matched groups of adult male prisoners in New York.[82] They found that inmates most actively involved in Bible studies (meaning they attended 10 or more classes over the course of one year) were less likely than inmates who attended fewer classes (or none) to commit institutional infractions or, if they did, the infractions were not as serious as the infractions of those who attended fewer classes (or none); and inmates most actively involved in Bible studies were less likely than inmates who attended fewer classes (or none) to be arrested during a one-year follow-up. Subsequent research found that differences in rearrest peaked at two and three years after release. The average time to rearrest for the inmates who were most actively involved in Bible studies was 3.8 years versus 2.3 years for inmates who attended fewer classes (or none). However, differences between the two groups diminished after that and were not statistically significant in years four through eight. Over time, the effects of Bible study attendance are diminished in importance. Risk for arrest in years four through eight was explained by other factors such as prior record, race, and age.

Those who minister to jail inmates tell us there are at least five benefits of jail chaplaincy. First, most jail chaplains believe that the cycle of crime can be broken only one life at a time. Jail inmates must experience an inner conversion before they change their behavior. Jail chaplains can assist in that conversion. Second, jail chaplains can help jail staff with their emotional and family problems. An on-site chaplain can help staff deal with problems daily as they develop. Third, jail chaplains are in a unique position to mediate and moderate tensions and conflicts between inmates and staff before they get serious. Pleading for nonviolence is a chaplain's strong tool. Inmates usually see a jail chaplain as being neutral. The chaplain has the unique opportunity to speak his or her mind and be seen as someone who cares enough to confront and comfort. Fourth, the public perceives ministering to the disadvantaged as legitimate, so such ministry helps the community remember those they would just as soon forget. In the role as community liaisons, chaplains help raise the awareness about and sensitivity to jail issues and interests. The ability of chaplains to involve the public as jail volunteers is an added benefit. And fifth, jail chaplains can help inmates confront the truth about themselves and reverse the "everything is relative" attitude that offenders develop to justify their crimes.

In the following excerpt, a chaplain shares some thoughts about his two years on the job:[83]

> A chaplain occupies a unique place in an inmate's thinking. She or he is not seen as "one of them"; we are not associated so much with the institution or judicial system. That gives us unique opportunities to speak openly and be viewed not as someone who has a sinister hidden agenda, but as someone who cares enough to confront.

Jail Standards, Inspection, and Accreditation

CO6-9

Dr. Ken Kerle, probably the most known advocate today for improving our nation's jails, wrote recently, ". . . jail inspection is about as popular in many places as a skunk in the living room and many county officials, including sheriffs, would just as soon avoid it altogether. It is no accident that 12 states today have no jail inspections and 8 states with inspection standards have no enforcement agency to compel compliance."[84] Florida is one example. According to the *Orlando Sentinel*, "When it comes to grading Central Florida's jails, no bell curve exists. Every facility generates near-perfect grades and glowing reviews."[85] Florida's Model Jail Standards inspection is a voluntary, peer-accreditation system of part-time inspectors, people usually employed as corrections managers, law enforcement officers, or fire inspectors somewhere else in Florida. Many Florida jails are also inspected through another peer-based system administered by the Florida Corrections Accreditation Commission, but accreditation is optional. Such oversight raises questions about the state's ability to oversee its jails. Members from the Florida Corrections Accreditation Commission and inspectors measuring the Florida Model Jail Standards recently each gave the Osceola County Jail nothing but praise just before two inmates escaped, another incident in which an inmate was accidentally released, and failure to note that razor wire had been incorrectly installed—issues that led to the disciplining of 30 officers, demotions of two captains, resignation of the jail director, and firing of the county manager. "If almost every jail is reaccredited by meeting 100 percent of the standards reviewed and if every facility meets an overwhelming majority of the Florida Model Jail Standards, then are these detention facilities truly being tested?" asked the *Orlando Sentinel*.

On the other hand, other populous states such as Illinois, New York, Pennsylvania, Ohio, and Texas mandate state oversight of county jails. Texas, for example, has the Commission on Jail Standards, an independent state agency with the authority to develop standards, conduct inspections, and fine or close jails if they fail to comply. New York state statute allows the Commission of Corrections' jail investigators to visit any of the state's prisons or county jails at any time and may view any records they deem necessary to complete their duties. The Commission has a $3 million budget and a full-time nine-member board appointed by the governor. They may close any correctional facility if it is unsafe, unsanitary, or inadequate. Any person who does not obey its orders is guilty of a misdemeanor. The American Bar Association agrees with independent oversight and authority to act. It recommends that all federal, state, tribal, and territorial governments create independent bodies with broad authority and access to corrections facilities.[86]

Code of Ethics for Jail Officers

As an officer employed in a detention/correctional capacity, I swear (or affirm) to be a good citizen and a credit to my community, state, and nation at all times. I will abstain from questionable behavior which might bring disrepute to the agency for which I work, my family, my community, and my associates. My lifestyle will be above and beyond reproach, and I will constantly strive to set an example of a professional who performs his/her duties according to the laws of our country, state, and community and the policies, procedures, written and verbal orders, and regulations of the agency for which I work.

On the job I promise to

KEEP the institution secure so as to safeguard my community and the lives of the staff, inmates, and visitors on the premises.

WORK with each individual firmly and fairly without regard to rank, status, or condition.

MAINTAIN a positive demeanor when confronted with stressful situations of scorn, ridicule, danger, and/or chaos.

REPORT either in writing or by word of mouth to the proper authorities those things which should be reported and keep silent about matters which are to remain confidential according to the laws and rules of the agency and government.

MANAGE and supervise the inmates in an evenhanded and courteous manner.

REFRAIN at all times from becoming personally involved in the lives of the inmates and their families.

TREAT all visitors to the jail with politeness and respect and do my utmost to ensure that they observe the jail regulations.

TAKE advantage of all education and training opportunities designed to assist me to become a more competent officer.

COMMUNICATE with people in or outside of the jail, whether by phone, written word, or word of mouth, in such a way so as not to reflect in a negative manner upon my agency.

CONTRIBUTE to a jail environment which will keep the inmate involved in activities designed to improve his/her attitude and character.

SUPPORT all activities of a professional nature through membership and participation that will continue to elevate the status of those who operate our nation's jails. Do my best through word and deed to present an image to the public at large of a jail professional, committed to progress for an improved and enlightened criminal justice system.

Adopted by the American Jail Association Board of Directors on November 10, 1991, Revised May 19, 1993.

Ethical Dilemma 6–1: Female offenders have an average of 2.5 children. Increasing numbers of incarcerated, pregnant, and/or parenting women being sentenced to jail have resulted in many more children being separated from their mothers. Should jail administrators concern themselves with providing services for families of jail inmates? For more information, go to Ethical Dilemma 6–1 at www.justicestudies.com/ethics06.

Ethical Dilemma 6–2: Sometimes administrators must make hard decisions when faced with budget cuts. As a jail administrator, you must cut one position, either a correctional officer or a teacher. Which position will you cut? Why? For more information, go to Ethical Dilemma 6–2 at www.justicestudies.com/ethics06.

Ethical Dilemmas for every chapter are available online.

Jail standards now govern inmate health care; the use of force; protection of inmates from violence; provision of services including food, clothing, shelter, protection from fires, and exercise; searches of all types; access to mail and reading materials; practice of one's faith; and inmate discipline. The task for jail managers is to translate jail standards into understandable and objective guidelines. For example, a court ruling that lighting in an inmate's cell may not be so low as to present an unreasonable risk of serious harm to inmates may leave a jail manager guessing as to how much light to have in the jail. However, a standard stating that lighting in inmate cells must be "at least 20 foot-candles at desk level" turns the vague statement into a measurable objective.

Today, jail compliance with standards set forth by the American Correctional Association (ACA) has become the best defense to ensure that jails are operating properly and highlight where improvements are needed. Two ACA publications, *Standards for Adult Local Detention Facilities* and *Standards for Small Jail Facilities*, cover the standards for the services, programs, and operations they consider essential to good jail management. Jails that comply with 100 percent of the mandatory standards and 90 percent of the nonmandatory ones are awarded accreditation.

Jail accreditation is a process through which correctional facilities and agencies can measure themselves against nationally adopted standards and through which they can receive formal recognition and accredited status. We will expand on the issue of correctional accreditation in Chapter 13.

Although jails were slow to respond to the standards movement, their response has increased in recent years. Approximately 131 adult local detention facilities were ACA accredited. ACA acts on agency requests for accreditation at its annual Winter Conference and Summer Congress of Correction.[87]

There are several reasons jails have been slow to adopt national standards or seek national accreditation. First, accreditation is expensive and time-consuming. Many jails do not have the resources to commit to it. This is especially true of small jails that are already overburdened. Second, jails hold relatively few long-term inmates. Few inmates are in a jail long enough to file a successful legal action regarding poor conditions in the jail. Knowing this, some jail administrators may not be willing to undergo the expense and burden of seeking accreditation. Third, some states have their own standards that jails must meet.

There are, however, at least five reasons for jails to have national accreditation:

1. Accreditation by the ACA indicates that a jail adheres to strict standards to protect the health and safety of staff and inmates.
2. Being accredited may help a jail defend itself against lawsuits over conditions of incarceration.
3. In preparing for the accreditation review, the sheriff's office may evaluate all operations, procedures, and policies, leading to better management practices.
4. With accreditation come professional recognition and status, greater appreciation by the community, and a sense of pride in the achievement and in the hard work that went into it.
5. And recently, ACA in conjunction with the American Jail Association, National Sheriff's Association, National Institute of Corrections, and the Federal Bureau of Prisons developed a set of core jail standards to establish minimum practices for small- and medium-size facilities. This new option makes certification easier now for small- and medium-size jails.

jail accreditation
Process through which correctional facilities and agencies can measure themselves against nationally adopted standards and through which they can receive formal recognition and accredited status.

Evidence-Based Practices

The final priority identified by the group of sheriffs and jail administrators in 2007 and reiterated in 2012 at the National Jail Leadership Command Academy in Hunstville, Texas, relates to evidence-based practices. The body of jail-related research is very small compared to what is known about prisons, yet the sheriffs and jail administrators agreed that if more was known about what works in jails, they would be able to improve everything from efficiency and cost-effectiveness to public safety, agency accountability, and proactive planning.

CO6-10   Also in 2007, researchers reported on what evidence-based practices are used in the nation's jails to treat substance abuse. Of 13 key evidence-based practices recommended by the National Institute on Drug Abuse, the researchers found that jail administrators reported implementing an average of only 1.6 (see Exhibit 6–11).[88] Only four best practices are used in more than half of all jails: (1) comprehensive treatment methods to address offenders' multiple needs, (2) engagement with community agencies to provide services for drug-involved offenders, (3) use of positive incentives to encourage inmate behavior, and (4) use of standardized substance abuse assessment tools to understand the extent and impact of drug usage.

In spite of the fact that half of the jails use these four evidence-based practices, however, the jails have not conducted the rigorous evaluations that are necessary to show the impact the practices have on reduced criminal activity.

EXHIBIT 6–11   Percentage of Jails That Use Evidence-Based Practices to Treat Substance Abuse

Practice	Percentage
Comprehensive treatment to address multiple needs of offenders	90%
Engagement with other agencies to provide services	73%
Incentives to encourage positive behavior	54%
Standardized substance abuse assessment	51%
Treatment programs are 90 days or more	49%
Drug testing	34%
Addressing co-occuring disorders	32%
Continuing care/aftercare	32%
Use of graduated sanctions	27%
Techniques to engage offender in treatment (e.g. motivational enhancements)	24%
Treatments that are evidence-based (e.g. cognitive behavior therapy)	12%
Standardized risk assessment tool	12%
Involvement of family in treatment	10%

0%   10%   20%   30%   40%   50%   60%   70%   80%   90%   100%

Source: Adapted from Peter D. Friedman, Faye S. Taxman, and Craig E. Henderson, *"Evidence-Based Treatment Practices for Drug-Involved Adults in the Criminal Justice System,"* Journal of Substance Abuse Treatment, vol. 32, no. 3 (2007), pp. 267–277.

PRISONERS CONFINED IN JAIL AND CALIFORNIA'S REALIGNMENT

CO6-11

If a judge sentences an offender to a state or federal prison and the prison is overcrowded, the inmate is held in a local jail until prison space becomes available. A decade ago, almost 70,000 state and federal prisoners were held in local jails because prisons were overcrowded. Today, the number is more than 82,000 even though the number of persons sentenced to prison declined for the second consecutive year.

Today California is experiencing a seismic shift in corrections policy that is likely to change the national landscape in the number of persons sentenced to prison and to jail. In November 2006, plaintiffs in two class action lawsuits, *Plata* v. *Brown* (involving inmate medical care) and *Coleman* v. *Brown* (involving inmate mental health care), argued that persistent overcrowding in the state's prison system was preventing the California Department of Corrections and Rehabilitation (CDCR) from delivering constitutionally adequate health care to inmates.

In August 2009, a three-judge panel declared that overcrowding in the state's 33 prisons was the primary reason that CDCR was unable to provide inmates with constitutionally adequate health care. The court ruled that in order for CDCR to provide such care, it would have to reduce the prisoner population by 33,000 in the state's 33 prisons within two years.

On May 23, 2011, the U.S. Supreme Court upheld the ruling by the lower three-judge panel and ordered the state of California to reduce its prison population by 33,000 within two years to alleviate overcrowding. In response, the California State Legislature and governor enacted a series of bills, most notably Assembly Bill 109—the 2011 Public Safety Realignment. The most significant policy change created by the 2011 realignment is the shift of responsibility for adult offenders and parolees from the state to the counties. The new law took effect on October 1, 2011. It mandates that individuals sentenced for nonserious, nonviolent, or nonsex offenses serve their sentences in county jails instead of state prison and jails be supervised by county probation departments rather than state parole officers. The bill is funded through vehicle license fees and a portion of the state sales tax. Counties can use the new funding to create more jail beds or fund intermediate sanctions like those discussed in Chapter 5. Supporters of realignment are hoping that although the U.S. Supreme However, the original bill did not include funds for data collection. Only now are legislators and policymakers pushing for funding for data that can provide an assessment of realignment and guide the state in building safer communities and better systems for aiding reentering offenders.[89]

The shift in responsibilities can be divided into three parts: the shift of lower-level offenders, the shift of parolees, and the shift of parole violators.

design capacity

The number of inmates that planners or architects intend for the facility

Lower-Level Offenders

The 2011 realignment limited which felons can be sent to state prison, thereby requiring that counties manage more felons. Sentences to state prison are now limited to registered sex offenders, individuals with a current or prior serious or violent offense, and individuals that commit certain other specified offenses. Thus, counties are now responsible for housing and supervising all felons who do not meet those criteria. The shift occurred on a prospective basis effective October 1, 2011, meaning that no inmates under state jurisdiction prior to that date were transferred to the counties. Only lower-level offenders convicted after that date came under county jurisdiction.

Parolees

Before realignment, state parole agents supervised individuals released from state prison in the community. Following realignment, however, state parole agents supervise only individuals released from prison whose current offense is serious or violent as well as certain other individuals including those assessed to be mentally disordered or high-risk sex offenders. The remaining individuals—those whose current offense is nonserious and nonviolent, and who otherwise are not required to be on state parole—are released from prison to community supervision under county jurisdiction. This shift was also done on a prospective basis, so that only individuals released from state prison after October 1, 2011 became a county responsibility. County supervision of offenders released from state prison is referred to as Post-Release Community Supervision and will generally be conducted by county probation departments.

Parole Violators

Prior to realignment, individuals released from prison could be returned to state prison for violating a term of their supervision. Following realignment, however, those offenders released from prison—whether supervised by the state or counties—must generally serve their revocation term in county jail. In addition, individuals realigned to county supervision will not appear before the Board of Parole Hearings (BPH) for revocation hearings, and will instead have these proceedings in a trial court. These changes were also made effective on a prospective basis, effective October 1, 2011.

By 2016–2017, the CDCR estimates that the prison population will be lower by nearly 40,000 inmates, or 24 percent, than it otherwise would have been absent the 2011 realignment. However, even assuming no increase in the California offender population, the reduction in the state prison population means an increase in the county jail population.

REVIEW AND APPLICATIONS

SUMMARY

1 There are 3,283 locally operated jails in the United States. Besides incarcerating people who have sentences of a year or less, jails serve a number of purposes. They hold people awaiting trial, probation and parole violators, adults and juveniles awaiting transfer, and prison inmates about to be released. Sometimes they operate community-based programs. The jail population is different from the prison population in terms of total admissions and average daily population.

2 The *daily* population of jails is lower than that of prisons, but the *annual* total of people incarcerated in jails is higher.

3 Jails emerged in Europe in the 12th century to detain offenders for trial. In the 15th and 16th centuries, the poor and unemployed were detained alongside criminals. The first jail in America was the Walnut Street Jail. Quakers designed it according to their principles of religious reflection and penance. It fell short of reaching its goals and closed in 1835.

4 American jails have progressed through three phases of architecture and inmate management: first-generation jails (linear design and sporadic supervision), second-generation jails (pod design and remote supervision), and third-generation jails (pod design and direct supervision).

5 By mid-2011, jails held or supervised 808,622 offenders. An estimated 39 percent of jail inmates are convicted offenders. Women represent 13.2 percent of the jail population; nonwhites, 54.2 percent; and juveniles, 0.7 percent. Almost two-thirds of all jail inmates have a mental health problem, and there are more people with mental illness in jail than there are in mental health hospitals. Jail suicide is almost four times what it is for the general U.S. population, jail homicides are up, and 3.1 percent of all jail inmates experienced one or more incidents of sexual victimization involving another inmate or staff. By mid-2012, 84 percent of jail capacity was occupied. Thirty-seven jails are privatized. The most (eight) are in Texas. Approximately 234,000 people work in jails. The increase in the jail population is outpacing the growth in jail staff. The problems of jail staff include low pay and prestige, high turnover, and inadequate systems for recruitment, selection, and training.

6 Advocates of privatization claim they can build and operate jails more efficiently than can government. Opponents argue they cannot, or they dismiss the cost issues altogether. For them, operating a jail is a basic function of government and a symbol of state authority and should not be delegated.

7 Jail vocational and educational programs are important avenues for managing inmates, reducing recidivism, and successful reentry. They keep inmates occupied, boost self-esteem, and help inmates find jobs after release.

8 Jails are partnering with faith-based organizations to meet the needs of jail inmates. Jail chaplaincy can influence jail inmates in five ways. First, chaplains can help inmates with the inner conversion needed to break the cycle of crime. Second, a jail chaplain can help staff deal with day-to-day problems. Third, a jail chaplain can mediate and moderate tensions and conflicts between inmates and staff. Fourth, jail chaplaincy can involve the public as jail volunteers and remind people that inmates exist. And fifth, chaplains can help inmates confront the truth about themselves.

9 Jail standards, inspection, and accreditation are important for five reasons. First, inspection and accreditation indicate that a jail adheres to strict standards. Second, accreditation may help a jail defend itself against lawsuits over conditions of incarceration. Third, through inspection and accreditation, the sheriff's office may evaluate all jail operations, procedures, and policies, leading to better management practices. Fourth, accreditation generates professional recognition and status, greater appreciation by the community, and a sense of pride. And fifth, the ACA in conjunction with the American Jail Association, National Sheriff's Association, National Institute of Corrections, and the Federal Bureau of Prisons now has a set of core jail standards to establish minimum practices for small- and medium-size facilities. This new option makes certification easier for small- and medium-size jails.

10 The National Institute on Drug Abuse recommends 13 key evidence-based practices to treat substance abuse. Jails implement an average of only 1.6. Four evidence-based practices are used in more than one-half of all jails. However, jails have not conducted scientific evaluations to show the impact the practices have on reduced criminal activity.

11 California's realignment act is the shift of responsibility for adult offenders and parolees from the state to the counties. The new law mandates that individuals sentenced for nonserious, nonviolent, or nonsex offenses will serve their sentences in county jails instead of state prison and will be supervised by county probation departments rather than state parole officers.

KEY TERMS

bail, p. 163

jails, p. 167

total admission, p. 168

average daily population (ADP), p. 168

first-generation jail, p. 172

second-generation jail, p. 172

third-generation jail, p. 173

direct-supervision jail, p. 173

rated capacity, p. 185

pay-to-stay jail, p. 188

self-pay jails, p. 188

privatization, p. 192

reentry, p. 192

jail accreditation, p. 201

design capacity, p. 203

QUESTIONS FOR REVIEW

1 Jails serve a number of purposes. Which do you believe is the most important and why?

2 Describe how jail populations are different from prison populations.

3 Summarize the history of jails.

4 Explain how first-, second-, and third-generation jails differ.

5 What can you infer from the characteristics of jail inmates, facilities, and staff?

6 What ideas can you add to the arguments for and against jail privatization?

7 How do jail vocational and educational programs affect inmate behavior, recidivism, and reentry?

8 What criteria would you use to assess the impact that faith-based organizations and jail chaplains have on jail inmates and staff?

9 What ideas can you add to the arguments for and against jail standards, inspection, and accreditation?

10 Explain how jails could do more to implement evidence-based practices to treat substance abuse and demonstrate their impact on reduced criminal activity.

11 Explain the impact of California's realignment act on local jails and probation departments.

THINKING CRITICALLY ABOUT CORRECTIONS

Mentally Ill Inmates

Explain why mentally ill jail inmates should not be subjects for incarceration as some suggest, and why jails are ill-equipped to meet their needs.

Evidence-Based Practices

Why are evidence-based practices necessary for jails?

ON-THE-JOB DECISION MAKING

Promoting Direct Supervision

You are the administrator of a new county jail with the architecture and philosophy of direct supervision. The new jail replaced a jail built in 1912. Some of the senior staff have begun complaining to you about direct supervision. They say they don't like to interact with inmates. They talk about "the good old days" when inmates were "on the other side" of the reinforced glass and steel bars. There's even been a letter to the editor in the local newspaper complaining that the new jail doesn't "look like a jail."

1. What could you tell the senior staff about direct-supervision philosophy that might ease their concerns?

2. What strategies might you use to educate the public about the benefits of direct supervision?

Jail Standards, Inspection, and Accreditation

Imagine that you have just been elected as the first college-educated sheriff of a large county with a megajail (more than 1,000 beds). Your state has jail standards but inspection is done by a jail committee from another county and there is no enforcement agency to compel compliance. At the annual state sheriffs' meeting, you give a talk on the issues you see with neighboring counties inspecting each other's jails and the lack of enforcement to compel compliance. What will you say?

For additional information, please see: www.mhhe.com/schmalleger7e
Follow the author's tweets about the latest crime and justice news @schmalleger

PRISONS TODAY

Change Stations or Warehouses?

CHAPTER OBJECTIVES

After completing this chapter you should be able to do the following:

❶ Explain the differences between the Pennsylvania and Auburn prison systems.

❷ Outline the nine eras of prison development.

❸ Describe the characteristics of today's prisoners and discuss reasons for the incarceration of women and minority prisoners.

❹ Explain prisoner classification and its purposes.

❺ Discuss the arguments for and against faith-based correctional institutions.

❻ Explain what the evidence-based literature says about prison industries.

❼ Report on the availability of education and health care programs for prisoners.

❽ Compare state and federal prison organization and administration.

❾ Discuss the question "Does incarceration work?"

> *If you had a dollar to spend on reducing crime, and you looked at the science instead of the politics, you would never spend it on the prison system.*
>
> —Michael Jacobson, honorary trustee and former president, Vera Institute of Justice, and former Commissioner, New York City Corrections and Probation

In 1969, Jerry Sandusky joined Joe Paterno's coaching staff at Penn State University as the defensive line coach. Eight years later, Sandusky established Second Mile, a nonprofit foundation to help underprivileged and at-risk children in Pennsylvania. Beginning in 1994, seven boys as young as 7 years who had met Sandusky through Second Mile became victims of his sexual abuse.[1]

On May 3, 1998, Sandusky assaulted victim 6, then 11 years old, in the locker rooms and showers at Penn State. The victim's mother reported to university police that Sandusky showered with her son.

For the next month, university officials investigated. During the course of the investigation, police listened in on a conversation between the victim's mother and Sandusky, who admitted to showering with the boy, and said, "I was wrong. I wish I could get forgiveness. I know I won't get it from you. I wish I were dead."

University Police Chief Harmon e-mailed University Vice President Gary C. Schultz, saying, "We're going to hold off on making any crime log entry. At this point I can justify that decision because of the lack of clear evidence of a crime." Tim Curley, the athletic director, notified Schultz that he had told Paterno about the incident, but he maintained that he didn't know about the incident.

A university police detective and a state public welfare caseworker interviewed Sandusky, who admitted hugging victim 6 in the shower but said there was nothing "sexual about it." He said he has done this with other children. District Attorney Ray Gricar decided not to file charges.

A year later, from July through December 2001, victim 3 was assaulted in the athletic department's building and other places several times.

On December 28, 1999, victim 4 was listed as a member of the Sandusky family party at the 1999 Alamo Bowl. Sandusky is said to have threatened to send the boy home after he resisted Sandusky's sexual advances. He reportedly told the boy that he could walk on the field with Penn State's football team at the bowl game. The boy is in a photograph with Sandusky that appears in *Sports Illustrated.*

In Fall 2000, Jim Calhoun, a janitor, found Sandusky in the showers of the football building performing oral sex on a boy pinned against a wall. The boy is identified as victim 8 in the grand jury report.

On November 5, 2011, Jerry Sandusky, former Penn State University defensive line coach, was arrested on charges of sexually abusing eight boys over a 15-year period. A week later, he told Bob Costas in a telephone interview broadcast on national television that he was innocent of the charges against him and declared that he was not a pedophile. He said, "I shouldn't have showered with those kids." Seven months later, prosecutors opened their sexual abuse case against Sandusky. He was charged with more than 50 criminal counts of abusing 10 boys over a number of years. On June 22, 2012, Sandusky was convicted of sexually abusing 10 boys. He was found guilty of 45 of the 48 counts against him. On October 9, 2012, Sandusky was sentenced to 30 to 60 years in prison. He is serving his sentence at the State Correctional Institution in Greene County, a maximum-security prison. His inmate number is KT2386. What is a maximum-security prison, what types of offenders are confined there, and do you believe a maximum-security facility is appropriate for Sandusky?

On February 9, 2001, Mike McQueary, a graduate assistant, entered the Penn State locker room and heard "rhythmic, slapping sounds" that he believed were related to sexual activity. He later said under oath that he saw Sandusky raping a boy who appeared to be 10 years old. He said he reported the incident to Paterno the next day. But Paterno insisted that McQueary did not tell him the extent of the assault but that McQueary had said only that he had witnessed something inappropriate involving Sandusky and a child.

Paterno waited one day to report the incident to university President Graham Spanier and Vice President Gary Schultz. Two weeks later, Spanier, Schultz, and Curley decided to report the shower incident to the Pennsylvania Department of Public Welfare.

Two days later, Curley informed Shultz and Spanier that he had changed his mind after talking about the situation with Paterno. Instead of reporting the incident, Curley said they should offer Sandusky professional help and tell him to stop bringing guests to the locker room. They did not report the incident.

Six months later, Sandusky assaulted victim 5 in the showers at Penn State.

Seven years later, victim 1 was a freshman in high school where Sandusky was a volunteer coach. The boy's mother called the school to report a sexual assault, and Sandusky was barred from the school district. The school reported the incident to the authorities and an investigation by the Pennsylvania attorney general began.

On November 5, 2011, Sandusky was arrested on charges of sexually abusing eight boys over a 15-year period. He was arraigned and released on $100,000 bail after being charged with 40 counts. Curley and Schultz were charged with perjury and failure to report what they knew of the allegations.

Four days later, the university's Board of Trustees fired Paterno and Spanier.

On November 14, 2011, Sandusky made his first extended public comments since his arrest. In a telephone interview with Bob Costas that was broadcast on the television program "Rock Center," Sandusky said he was innocent of the charges against him and declared that he was not a pedophile. He said, "I shouldn't have showered with those kids."

On January 22, 2012, Joe Paterno died of lung cancer. He was 85 years old.

Six months later, prosecutors opened their sexual abuse case against Sandusky. He was charged with more than 50 criminal counts of abusing 10 boys over a number of years.

On June 22, 2012, Sandusky was convicted of sexually abusing 10 boys. He was found guilty of 45 of the 48 counts against him.

On October 9, 2012, Sandusky was sentenced to 30 to 60 years in prison. He is serving his sentence at the State Correctional Institution in Greene County, a maximum-security prison. His inmate number is KT2386.

Later in this chapter, you will learn more about state and federal prison systems. We begin the chapter with a look at the history of American prisons. Then we discuss the composition of the prison population, programs for prisoners, and the way America's prisons are organized and administered. We conclude with the question "Does incarceration work?"

Visit http://www.youtube.com/ watch?v=0ikUWU3cbq8 or scan this code with the QR app on your smartphone or digital device and watch the podcast of Philadelphia's Eastern State Penitentiary illustrated with period lithographs, engravings, and photographs and understand the history of the prison from its initial practice of total solitary confinement through its transformation into an overcrowded "Big House" to its replacement with a modern facility in 1970. How does this information relate to ideas discussed in this chapter?

penitentiary

The earliest form of large-scale incarceration. It punished criminals by isolating them so that they could reflect on their misdeeds, repent, and reform.

Pennsylvania system (also separate system)

The first historical phase of prison discipline, involving solitary confinement in silence instead of corporal punishment; conceived by the American Quakers in 1790 and implemented at the Walnut Street Jail.

Auburn system

The second historical phase of prison discipline, implemented at New York's Auburn prison in 1815. It followed the Pennsylvania system and allowed inmates to work silently together during the day, but they were isolated at night. Eventually sleeping cells became congregate and restrictions against talking were removed.

CO7-1 HISTORY OF PRISONS IN AMERICA

Prisons are relatively modern social institutions, and their development is distinctly American. Until the mid-18th century, fines, banishment from the community, corporal punishment, and execution were the primary forms of punishing offenders. By the latter part of the century, incarceration was championed as a more humane form of punishment. It reflected and fueled a shift from the assumption that offenders were inherently criminal to a belief that they were simply not properly trained to resist temptation and corruption. The two prison systems that emerged in the United States—the Pennsylvania system and the Auburn system—were copied throughout the world.

The Pennsylvania and Auburn prison systems developed in the United States at the turn of the 19th century. Pennsylvania Quakers advocated a method of punishment more humane than the public corporal punishment used at the time. The Quakers shifted the emphasis from punishing the body to reforming the mind and soul. Together with an elite group of 18th-century Philadelphians, they ushered in the first **penitentiary**, a place for reform of offenders through repentance and rehabilitation. They believed prisoners needed to be isolated from each other in silence to repent, to accept God's guidance, and to avoid having a harmful influence on each other. Known as the **Pennsylvania system** or the *separate system*, this method was first used at the Walnut Street Jail, which the Quakers reorganized in 1790 as the country's first penitentiary. The Eastern State Penitentiary, constructed in 1829, was also based on these principles. The prison was designed for solitary confinement and labor with instruction in labor, morals, and religion. To make the isolation less severe and to help inmates prepare for employment after release, prison officials permitted inmates to work by themselves in their cells at various occupations, such as shoemaking, weaving, tailoring, and polishing marble. For the first time in American history, rehabilitation and deterrence emerged as goals of corrections.

The solitary confinement of the Pennsylvania system was expensive, and it reportedly drove prisoners insane and further hardened criminal tendencies. Reformers responded with what has been termed the **Auburn system**: regimentation, military-style drill, silence unless conversation was required in workshops, congregate working and eating, separation of prisoners into small individual cells at night, harsh discipline, shaved heads, black-and-white striped uniforms, and industrial workshops that contracted with private businesses to help pay for the institution. Prison factories in the 19th century produced shoes, barrels, carpets, engines, boilers, harnesses, clothing, and furniture—goods that could not be produced under the "solitary" system of Pennsylvania or not in quantities sufficient to make a profit. This merchandise was sold on the open market to American consumers or exported to Canada and Latin America, and the proceeds helped support prison operations. The first prison to use this system opened in Auburn, New York, in 1819. The Auburn system, congregate by day and separate by night, eventually gave way to congregate cells at night and removal of the restrictions against talking.

Prison reform in the United States caught the attention of prison officials around the world. The Pennsylvania system of isolation and silence became popular in Europe. In the United States, the two competing philosophies of prison life clashed, and the debate over which system was superior raged on for decades. Supporters of the Pennsylvania system argued that it was easier to control prisoners and prevented prisoners from learning bad habits from each other. Supporters of the Auburn system claimed that prisoners' spirits needed to be broken before true reform could begin and that their system of harsh discipline and congregate but silent labor accomplished that. Auburn supporters also argued that their prison system was cheaper to build and that the use of contract labor would keep down costs.

A system that was congregate by day (and eventually by night as well) seemed more compatible with the political and economic tone of the time. The Pennsylvania system represented a traditional approach to production: handcrafted labor in solitary cells. In contrast, the Auburn system reflected the emerging developments of the Industrial Revolution: power machinery, factory production, and division of labor. The attractiveness of the Auburn system's perceived economic benefits as well as a belief in the rehabilitative value of hard work settled the debate. Thus, the congregate system became the preferred model of incarceration in the United States. In 1913, Eastern State Penitentiary, the epitome of the Pennsylvania system, converted to the Auburn system, ending the great debate. Congregate prisons have been the mode ever since. Today, however, new voices are calling for a return to long-term solitary confinement in supermax prisons (one of several topics discussed in Chapter 13).

The Eastern State Penitentiary, completed in 1829, was designed on the Quakers' principle of solitary confinement in silence with instruction in labor, morals, and religion. What name was given to this separate system of prisoner management?

EXHIBIT 7–I	Stages of Prison History in the United States			
Stage	**Penitentiary Era**	**Mass Prison Era**	**Reformatory Era**	**Industrial Era**
Years	1790–1825	1825–1876	1876–1890	1890–1935
Goal	Rehabilitation and deterrence	Incapacitation and deterrence	Rehabilitation	Incapacitation
Characteristics	Separate and silent Congregate and silent	Congregate labor and living spaces without silence Contract prison labor	Indeterminate sentencing Parole	Public accounts industries Contract labor State-use labor Convict lease Public works labor
Examples of Institutions	Walnut Street Penitentiary, Philadelphia, PA Eastern State Penitentiary, Cherry Hill, PA Auburn Prison, Auburn, NY	Sing Sing Prison, Ossining, NY San Quentin State Prison, San Quentin, CA	Elmira, NY Indiana Reformatory for Women and Girls, Indianapolis, IN	Most major prisons
Related Events	1819 Auburn Penitentiary, New York, implements congregate, silent system. 1829 Eastern State Penitentiary opens under the Pennsylvania prison model.	1841 John Augustus begins the practice of probation in Massachusetts. 1871 *Ruffin* v. *Commonwealth* establishes that convicted felons not only forfeit liberty but also are slaves of the state; this provides the legal justification for courts to maintain a "hands-off doctrine." 1913 Eastern State Penitentiary converts to the Auburn prison model.	1876 The first women's prison, the Indiana Reformatory for Women and Girls, opens. 1876 Zebulon Brockway is appointed warden at Elmira Reformatory and initiates first parole system in the United States. 1878 First probation law is passed in Massachusetts.	1899 First juvenile court established in Cook County (Chicago), Illinois. 1914–1918 World War. 1929 Hawes-Cooper Act is passed to regulate interstate sale of prison-made goods. 1929 Great Depression begins. 1930 Federal Bureau of Prisons is established.

Stages of Development

Prisons in America have progressed through nine stages of development (see Exhibit 7–1). Many of these changes were influenced by cultural movements in society. As you review the historical stages, think about how the goals of imprisonment changed in each era as society changed. Remember

EXHIBIT 7–1	Stages of Prison History in the United States *(continued)*			
Punitive Era	**Treatment Era**	**Community-Based Era**	**Warehousing Era**	**Just Deserts Era**
1935–1945	1945–1967	1967–1980	1980–1995	1985–Present
Retribution	Rehabilitation	Reintegration	Incapacitation	Retribution
Strict punishment and custody	Medical model Emerging prisoner unrest	Intermediate sanction: halfway houses, work release centers, group homes, fines, restitution, community service	Sentencing guidelines End of discretionary parole release Serious crowding More prison riots	Just deserts Determinate sentencing Truth in sentencing Three-strikes law Serious crowding
U.S. Penitentiary, Alcatraz, CA	Patuxent Institution, Jessup, MD	Major prison riots (Attica, NY; Santa Fe, NM)	Most major prisons	Spreading through the United States
1934 Alcatraz ("Hellcatraz") opens. 1939 Great Depression ends. 1939–1945 World War II begins and ends. 1942–1945 Japanese and Japanese American relocation centers open and close.	1950 Federal Youth Corrections Act is passed to create treatment for offenders under the age of 22 in the federal system. 1964 *Cooper* v. *Pate* formally recognizes the constitutional rights of prisoners. 1967 *In re Gault,* U.S. Supreme Court rules that juvenile offenders are entitled to state-provided counsel and due process guarantees. 1967 President Johnson's Commission on Law Enforcement and Administration of Justice recommends changing the criminal justice system.	1970 Massachusetts becomes first state to close all of its juvenile reform schools. 1974 Robert Martinson's "What Works" is published and is used by politicians as reason to pull resources from prisons. 1976 Maine is first state to abolish discretionary parole board release. 1979 Prison Industry Enhancement (PIE) certification program repeals limitations on interstate commerce in prison-made goods.	1980s President Reagan declares "war on drugs." 1984 Federal Sentencing Reform Act imposes mandatory sentences for specific crimes. 1993 Three-strikes-and-you're-out laws spread across the United States. 1994 Congress passes the Violent Crime Control and Law Enforcement Act, which increases financial incentives for states to put more violent criminals in prison.	1994 Federal Bureau of Prisons opens its supermax prison. 1995 Eight states reinstate chain gangs. 1999 Number of people incarcerated in the United States exceeds 2 million for the first time. 2004 Abuse of prisoners at Abu Ghraib prison in Baghdad, Iraq, by U.S. military personnel becomes public. 2007 Evidence-based research and economic recession shape correctional practice.

too that old ways did not disappear when new ways emerged. Rather, new thinking challenged the thinking of previous eras and facilitated the development of new correctional policy, including the shift toward professionalism in corrections. Most often, new ideas simply developed alongside existing ones.

CO7-2 **Penitentiary Era (1790–1825)** The first era in prison history was the penitentiary era. In 1790, the renovated Walnut Street Jail opened with a penitentiary wing that emphasized the Quakers' religious belief in prisoner reform through reflection, penitance, and rehabilitation through good conduct. From that beginning, two competing prison systems merged, the Pennsylvania system of separate and silent confinement and the Auburn system of harsh discipline and congregate but silent labor. The era witnessed the demise of the Pennsylvania system and the building of 30 state prisons on the Auburn pattern of congregate by day and separate by night. This pattern eventually changed to congregate both day and night.

Mass Prison Era (1825–1876) The second era was the mass prison era. During that period, the idea of prison as a place for punishment flourished across the United States. As a result, 35 more Auburn-system prisons were built, including Sing Sing in New York State in 1825, San Quentin in California in 1852, and Joliet in Illinois in 1858. Most were built by prisoners who quarried the stones on-site.

Interior view of a cellblock at Eastern State Penitentiary. Linear design and sporadic inmate supervision characterized Eastern State. What problems emerged at Eastern State that caused the demise of the Pennsylvania system?

Reformatory Era (1876–1890) The third era was the reformatory era. Influenced by progressive beliefs that education and science were vehicles for controlling crime, the first reformatory for young men opened at Elmira, New York, in 1876. The reformatory, whose prisoners had indeterminate sentences (a sentence for which a judge specifies a maximum length and a minimum length and for which an administrative agency, generally a parole board, determines the actual time of release), used a grading system that led to early release on parole and offered academic education, vocational training, individual rehabilitation, and military instruction and discipline. During this era, 20 reformatories opened for men in addition to the first prison for women Mount Pleasant in Reformatory for Women and Girls in Indianapolis. Massachusetts passed the first probation law in 1878, extending progressive belief into community supervision as well.

public accounts system

The earliest form of prison industry in which the warden was responsible for purchasing materials and equipment and for overseeing the manufacture, marketing, and sale of prison-made items.

contract system

A system of prison industry in which the prison advertised for bids for the employment of prisoners whose labor was sold to the highest bidder.

convict lease system

A system of prison industry in which a prison temporarily relinquished supervision of its prisoners to a lessee. The lessee either employed the prisoners within the institution or transported them to work elsewhere in the state.

Industrial Era (1890–1935) Fourth was the industrial era. During this time, inmates worked in prison industries. The first prisons had used the **public accounts system** for work. The warden at the Walnut Street Jail determined the product, purchased materials and equipment, and oversaw the manufacture, marketing, and sale of prison-made items. At Auburn, prison industries expanded to include copper, weaving, tailor, blacksmith, and shoemaking shops. However, as more states adopted the Auburn model, the **contract system** replaced the public accounts system. Under the contract system, the prison advertised for bids for the employment of prisoners whose labor was sold to the highest bidder. The desire to increase profits for the prison and the private contractor often led to exploitation of the prisoners under this system.

During the industrial era, prisons progressed from the public accounts and contract systems of the Pennsylvania and Auburn prisons to *convict lease, state use,* and *public works* systems. Which system was used in a state depended on the region the state was in and the period in which the transition was made.

The **convict lease system** was prevalent in the post–Civil War South and functioned as a replacement for the institution of slavery. Many southern prisons had been destroyed during the war. Southern states found it easier to relinquish supervision of their prisoners to a lessee. The lessee either employed prisoners as slave labor for private businesses within a state institution or transported them to work elsewhere in the state. Railway, lumber, and coal mining companies leased the highest numbers of inmates. Lessees housed, fed, clothed, and disciplined inmates. The convict lease system generated income for the prison and reduced overhead because the contractors were responsible for feeding and sheltering the convicts they leased. Left to the mercy of the contractors, however, leased convicts were subjected to terrible abuses of nearly unimaginable brutality.

From attempts to deal with this problem emerged the state use system. Under the **state use system,** prisoners manufactured products for use by state governments and their agencies, departments, and institutions. By putting inmates to work manufacturing products for sale exclusively to government agencies, prisons were better able to keep inmates occupied while reducing direct competition with the private sector and avoiding the exploitative character of inmate leasing. As the western states developed, a **public works system** emerged. This system used inmates to build public buildings, roads, and parks.

In time, national labor organizations saw prison industries as unfair competition and lobbied Congress to regulate prison industry. In 1929, the Hawes-Cooper Act banned the interstate shipment of prison-made goods. The Ashurst-Sumners Act of 1935 prohibited carriers from accepting prison-made goods for transportation. Ashurst-Sumners also mandated the labeling of prison-made goods. In 1940, Congress passed the Sumners-Ashurst Act, forbidding the interstate transportation of prison-made goods for private use, regardless of whether a state banned importation of prison goods (products manufactured for the federal government or other state governments were exempt). Thus, much of the private market was closed to goods made by inmates. Today, it is a violation of federal law for state prisons to sell their products in interstate commerce unless they are certified by a federal program known as Prison Industry Enhancement (PIE). Under provisions of the PIE program, inmates must be paid the same wages as free workers engaged in similar work. They must also be allowed to keep 20 percent of what they earn. The rest of their wages can be withheld to pay income taxes, child support obligations, room and board charges, and restitution to victims and to victim assistance funds. We return to a discussion of PIE later in this chapter.

It was also during the industrial era that the federal Bureau of Prisons (BOP) was established in 1930. We return to a discussion of the BOP later in this chapter.

Punitive Era (1935–1945) The closing of prison industries ushered in the punitive era with its emphasis on strict punishment and custody. The holding of prisoners in the Big House, in complete idleness, monotony, and frustration, characterized this era. The "escape-proof" federal prison on the island of Alcatraz in San Francisco Bay opened on the

The Industrial Revolution ushered in the era of the industrial prison. The era had good intentions. What were they and what happened?

state use system

A system of prison industry that employs prisoners to manufacture products consumed by state governments and their agencies, departments, and institutions.

public works system

A system of prison industry in which prisoners were employed in the construction of public buildings, roads, and parks.

eve of this era. It became the prototype of the latter-day supermax prisons that we will discuss in Chapter 13. It was retrofitted with the latest security hardware then available and staffed with an elite corps of officers. It opened in 1934 to receive the toughest prisoners in the federal BOP.

Treatment Era (1945–1967)

The sixth era, treatment, emerged in response to prison riots across the United States. After World War II, the prison population exploded. Overcrowding, idleness, poor food, and other deprivations led prisoners to take matters into their own hands. Prison riots erupted in California, Colorado, Georgia, Illinois, Louisiana, Massachusetts, Michigan, Minnesota, New Jersey, New Mexico, Ohio, Oregon, Pennsylvania, Utah, and Washington. The riots aroused public support for prisoner rehabilitation.

Reform through classification, therapy, and increased use of the indeterminate sentence was the focus of the **medical model**, in which criminal behavior was regarded as a disease to be treated. If the diagnosis showed poor socialization and inadequate work skills as the factors that caused a person to turn to crime, the prescription could involve a combination of social skills counseling and vocational training. Maryland's Patuxent Institution with legions of mental health experts promised to predict dangerousness accurately and to release only those prisoners who were no longer a threat to the community. However, Patuxent failed to keep that promise. Scholars and advocacy groups also began finding fault with the medical model. They argued that it did not have as favorable an effect on recidivism as supporters argued it would have. They also argued that the medical model encouraged inmates to give the false impression that they were rehabilitated and suitable for early release. Above all was the view that the medical model was a form of coercion and that genuine changes in human behavior could not be coerced. In addition, the social and political unrest of the 1960s had found its way into the nation's prisons. A race riot broke out at San Quentin in 1967, and protests, riots, and killings occurred in other prisons. Corrections experts believed that a new approach was needed—one in which offenders were supervised in the community rather than imprisoned in fortresslike institutions.

Community-Based Era (1967–1980)

Community-based corrections mostly developed after the 1960s although some community-based programs had begun a century earlier. New York City Quakers opened the Isaac T. Hopper Home in 1845 as a shelter for released inmates; Zebulon Brockway opened the Detroit House of Corrections in 1861 as a shelter for released women; the Philadelphia House of Industry opened in 1889; and Maude Ballington Booth opened Hope Hall, a refuge for ex-inmates in New York, in the 1890s. After that, the community-based concept lay dormant until the 1950s when church groups founded more halfway houses (St. Leonard's House in Chicago and Crenshaw House in Los Angeles) and then until 1967 when President Lyndon Johnson's crime commission came to the conclusion that the community was a source of offenders' problems. The commission recommended that offenders be rehabilitated by using community resources. More halfway houses, community corrections centers, intensive supervision probation programs, work release centers, and the like quickly spread across the United States. By the end of the 20th century, halfway houses—which were practically unknown a century earlier—were an indispensable part of corrections.

Observers soon discovered that the community-based approach did not lower the crime rate, reduce the prison population, or make the

---

medical model

A philosophy of prisoner reform in which criminal behavior is regarded as a disease to be treated with appropriate therapy.

community safer. With the goals of community corrections unmet, the community-based era gave way, and President Nixon ushered in the country's attitude of "get tough on crime."

Warehousing Era (1980–1995) During the warehousing era, indeterminate sentencing was replaced by determinate sentencing in all states. Discretionary parole board release was abolished in a number of states and the federal government, and the pendulum swung from rehabilitation to incapacitation. President Reagan declared "war on drugs," federal sentencing reform mandated sentences for specific crimes, and three-strikes-and-you're-out and truth-in-sentencing laws swept across the United States. Within 15 years, the number of people under correctional supervision jumped from 1.8 million to almost 6 million. Prisons were operating over capacity, and controlling prisoners in such an environment was difficult. For staff and inmates alike, the nation's prisons were dangerous places to be. Extreme crowding resulted in violent outbreaks, which further hardened the attitudes of correctional policymakers and caused them to crack down even more.

Just Deserts Era (1985–present) Along with the get-tough policies of the warehousing era emerged a distinct but parallel vision of corrections. The just deserts philosophy focuses on punishment and provides a philosophy that supports the practice of warehousing. Chain gangs, striped uniforms, and boot camps have been resuscitated, parole has been cut back to 19th-century levels, and corrections has become as much of a political football as at any time in its history. Under the philosophy of just deserts, offenders are punished because they deserve it. The sanction used depending on the seriousness of the offense. Just deserts is not concerned with inmate rehabilitation, treatment, or reform. It separates treatment from punishment. Prisons today provide opportunities for inmates to improve themselves, but participation is not mandatory, nor is it a condition of release as it was for most of the 20th century. Change is facilitated, not coerced. Determinate sentencing, capital punishment, truth in sentencing, and three-strikes laws have grown in popularity. As we move into the 21st century, supermax and "no-frills" prisons are becoming the trend. Economic realities and evidence-based practices are also beginning to influence this era as pointed out in every Chapter of the book.

WHO IS IN PRISON TODAY?

In July 2013, the Bureau of Justice Statistics (BJS) reported that the U.S. prison population declined for the third consecutive year, falling to an estimated 1,571,013 prisoners at yearend 2012.[2] Upon deeper inspection, however, we find that the decline was driven almost entirely by California. Its prison population fell by 15,035 individuals in part due to the state's Public Safety Realignment policy. No other state had its prison population change in either direction by more than 1,500 people over that period.

In 1990 and 2001, two class action lawsuits were filed against the state of California, challenging the constitutionality of its prison conditions as a result of chronic overcrowding in its 33 prisons. A three-judge federal district court panel reviewed extensive evidence and heard testimony related to the subject of these lawsuits. In August 2009, the panel ordered the state to reduce its prison population by more than 33,000 persons over two years. In May 2011, the U.S. Supreme Court's *Brown* v. *Plata* upheld

Visit http://www.ted.com/talks/philip_zimbardo_on_the_psychology_of_evil.html or scan this code with the QR app on your smartphone or digital device and watch the podcast of Dr. Philip Zimbardo, past president of the American Psychological Association, and well-known for his controversial Stanford Prison Experiment, explains the psychology of prison evil and basing his presentation on his insights and graphic unseen photos from the Abu Ghraib prison trials. How does this information relate to ideas discussed in this chapter?

this ruling, finding that the court-mandated population cap is necessary to remedy the violation of prisoners' constitutional rights.

As the lawsuits wound their way through the federal court system, the California legislature took steps to reduce the prison population. Recognizing that parole revocation was a key driver of the prison population, lawmakers in 2009 enacted Senate Bill (SB) 18, which established a new type of "nonrevocable" parole (NRP is discussed in further detail in Chapter 8) for individuals, who, according to the validated risk assessment tool used by the California Department of Corrections and Rehabilitation (CDCR), did not pose a high risk to reoffend. Additional criteria were included in the statute that a person had to meet to be placed under NRP.

Parole for people under NRP cannot be revoked for any reason; they can be incarcerated again only for a new crime. Also enacted in 2009, SB 678 created the California Community Corrections Performance Incentive Program (discussed in Chapter 5), which promoted the use of evidence-based strategies for reducing the rate of failure during probation. SB 678 also developed a mechanism for providing additional funding to probation departments via corrections expenditure savings realized through fewer revocations to prison.

When the U.S. Supreme Court's decision in *Brown* v. *Plata* in 2011 made clear that the federal district court's earlier rulings would not be vacated, the California legislature passed Assembly Bill (AB) 109 and AB 117. Known collectively as the 2011 realignment legislation, this law realigned custody responsibilities for a particular class of offenders—those identified as nonviolent, nonserious, and nonsex offenders—from state to local jurisdictions and transferred postrelease supervision responsibilities for this population from state parole officers to county probation officers.

Starting October 1, 2011, eligible offenders began serving their sentences at the local level rather than in state prisons, which affected the national total in the number of persons in prison in 2012. The legislation also stipulated that any parolee whose parole is revoked will serve a term no longer than 180 days in the county jail (this provision excludes people sentenced to life), and parolees who do not incur any infractions will be released from parole after six months.

What the realignment plan is actually realigning is the division of correctional labor between state and local government. So while the overall downward trend in California's prison population looks promising on the surface, it is important to recognize the impact of realignment on California's local jails (Chapter 6) to fully comprehend the nature and magnitude of the changes that have taken place.

Today 1 in every 143 U.S. persons is under the jurisdiction of a state or federal prison. If we include all correctional populations (probation, parole, jail, and prison), 1 in every 32 adults is under correctional control. Twenty-five years ago it was 1 in every 77. This explosion in the correctional population presents enormous challenges for public safety and public spending as this and other chapters explain.

The imprisonment rate—the number of sentenced prisoners per 100,000 U.S. residents—declined for the third straight year, falling to 480 from 492 in 2011. The rate of imprisoned people per 100,000 ranged from 62 in the federal prison system (the lowest) to 893 in Louisiana (the highest). Prison statistics among the states and the federal government are shown in Exhibit 7–2.

When prison and jail incarceration rates are combined, the United States imprisons 717 people per 100,000 population, up from 684 in 2000 and

EXHIBIT 7–2	Prison Statistics Among the States and the Federal Government, Yearend 2012

Number of Prisoners Under Jurisdiction		Incarceration Rate per 100,000 Population of Sentenced Prisoners		Number of Female Prisoners Under Jurisdiction	
5 Highest					
Federal	217,815	Louisiana	893	Federal	14,049
Texas	166,372	Mississippi	717	Texas	13,549
California	134,584	Alabama	650	California	6,098
Florida	101,930	Oklahoma	632	Florida	6,985
Georgia	55,457	Texas	601	Ohio	3,868
5 Lowest					
North Dakota	1,512	Federal	62	Vermont	127
Vermont	2,053	Maine	145	Maine	164
Maine	2,108	Minnesota	184	North Dakota	171
Wyoming	2,204	Rhode Island	190	Rhode Island	186
New Hampshire	2,790	Massachusetts	199	New Hampshire	207

Source: Adapted from E. Ann Carson and Daniela Golinelli, *Prisoners in 2012 - Advance Counts* (Washington, DC: U.S. Department of Justice, Bureau of Justice Statistics, July 2013).

601 in 1995. In terms of prisoners per 100,000 people, that's more than any other country in the world. Russia is second with 629, followed by Rwanda (604), St. Kitts and Nevis (588), Cuba (531), U.S. Virgin Islands (512), British Virgin Islands (488), Palau (478), Belarus (468), Belize (455), Bahamas (422), Georgia (415), American Samoa (410), Grenada (408), and Anguilla (401).[3] Almost three-fifths of countries (59 percent) have rates below 150 per 100,000. *With less than 5 percent of the world's population, the United States has almost a quarter of the world's prisoners.*

States with almost identical populations and crime rates have widely different rates of incarceration. For example, in 2011 Wisconsin had a population of 5.7 million residents, a crime rate per 100,000 population of 2,670 offenses, and an incarceration rate of 359.[4] Minnesota had 5.3 million residents, a crime rate of 2,770 offenses, and an incarceration rate of only 183. With similar population and crime rates, Wisconsin's incarceration rate was almost twice as much as Minnesota's. What causes these disparities among states and their prison use? An interesting answer to this question was provided by Bowers and Waltman. Their investigation of felony sentencing in the United States found that the preferences of the public weigh heavily on the sentencing of violent offenders. More recently, world leaders of the prison administrations of the 45 member countries of the Council of Europe concluded that levels of imprisonment are usually influenced more by political decisions than by levels of crime or rates of detection of crime. They also concluded that jurisdictions can choose to have high or low rates of imprisonment, and this choice is reflected in the sentencing patterns adopted by legislatures.[5] Today as states grapple with the economic downturn, we can see how political decisions about what constitutes dangerousness or seriousness impact prison populations. A decade ago nonviolent offenders and parole violators would have been incarcerated. Today's economic problems find legislators and policymakers reducing prison time for nonviolent offenders and establishing programs like California's nonrevocable parole.

State and Federal Inmates Held in Privately Operated Facilities and Local Jails

The issue of correctional privatization, including the pros and cons of building and operating private prisons, is discussed in depth in Chapter 13. The focus here is on the current use of privately operated correctional facilities.

At year end 2011 (the last year for which the data are available), 31 states and the federal system held 130,941 prisoners (8.2 percent of their prisoner population) in 107 privately operated prisons, up from 77,854 inmates in 101 private prisons in 2000.[6] The federal system (38,546) Texas (18,603) Florida (11,827) Arizona (6,457) Oklahoma (6,025) Georgia (5,615) Tennessee (5,147), Mississippi (4,669), and Colorado (4,303) reported the largest number of inmates in private facilities at year end 2011.

Also at yearend 2011, 36 states and the federal system housed 5.1 percent (80,058) of their prisoner populations in local jails. Over the next few years, the number of state prisoners confined in local jails will increase as California's public safety realignment policy places new nonviolent, nonserious, nonsexual offenders under county jurisdiction for incarceration in local jail facilities. Because it incarcerates more individuals than any other state except Texas, California's prison population will have national implications.

CO7-3 ## Gender

Women have historically represented a modest share of the prison population. In 1980, about 13,000 women were in prison, representing 4 percent of the prison population. Today, almost 109,000 women are in state and federal prisons, representing 7 percent of the U.S. prison population (see Exhibit 7–3). If current trends continue, 1 of every 18 black females, 1 of every 45 Hispanic females, and 1 of every 111 white females can expect to spend time in prison.[7]

At yearend 2012, California, Texas, and the federal system held almost 31 percent of all female inmates. See Exhibit 7–2 for the jurisdictions with the highest and lowest female prison populations.

At yearend 2012, almost 109,000 adult women were under state or federal prison jurisdiction, almost 31 percent of them in California, Texas, and federal prisons. Why are women in prison, and what will it take to reduce their incarceration?

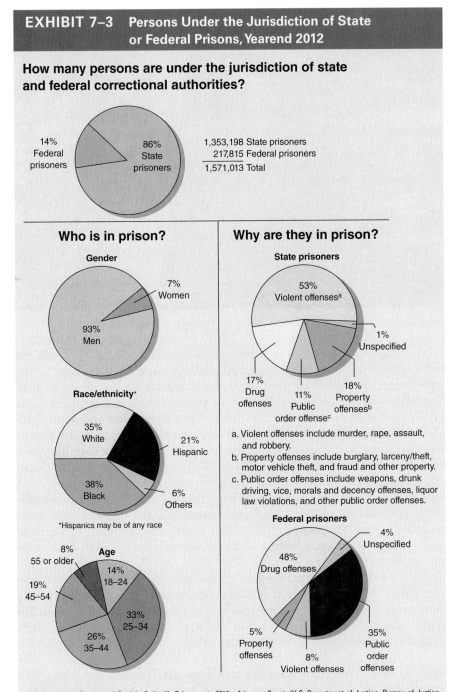

EXHIBIT 7–3 Persons Under the Jurisdiction of State or Federal Prisons, Yearend 2012

How many persons are under the jurisdiction of state and federal correctional authorities?

14% Federal prisoners
86% State prisoners

1,353,198 State prisoners
217,815 Federal prisoners
1,571,013 Total

Who is in prison?

Gender

7% Women
93% Men

Race/ethnicity*

35% White
21% Hispanic
38% Black
6% Others

*Hispanics may be of any race

Age

8% 55 or older
19% 45–54
14% 18–24
33% 25–34
26% 35–44

Why are they in prison?

State prisoners

53% Violent offenses[a]
1% Unspecified
17% Drug offenses
11% Public order offense[c]
18% Property offenses[b]

a. Violent offenses include murder, rape, assault, and robbery.
b. Property offenses include burglary, larceny/theft, motor vehicle theft, and fraud and other property.
c. Public order offenses include weapons, drunk driving, vice, morals and decency offenses, liquor law violations, and other public order offenses.

Federal prisoners

4% Unspecified
48% Drug offenses
5% Property offenses
8% Violent offenses
35% Public order offenses

Source: E. Ann Carson and Daniela Golinelli, *Prisoners in 2012 - Advance Counts* (U.S. Department of Justice, Bureau of Justice Statistics, July 2013) and E. Ann Carson and William J. Sabol, *Prisoners in 2011* (Washington, DC: U.S. Department of Justice, Bureau of Justice Statistics, December 2012).

Beth Richie, a professor of criminal justice and women's studies at the University of Illinois at Chicago, and Elaine Lord, former superintendent of the Bedford Hills Correctional Facility (New York's maximum-security prison for women), describe the racial/ethnic profile of women in prison as one of the most vivid examples of racial disparity in the United States and prison as the worst environment possible for mothers and women with mental illness.[8] Lord quit her job after 20 years because she stopped believing in the confinement of mentally ill women.

The number of state, federal, and private confinement correctional facilities in the United States is 1,292. Minorities make up two-thirds of the prison population. Why is that so?

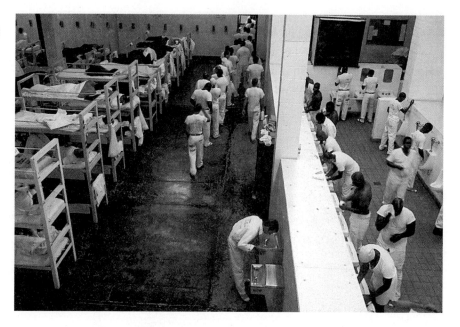

The majority of women in prison are women of color. Two-thirds are black, Hispanic, or of other nonwhite ethnic groups. They are also young and poor. Only one-third graduated from high school or earned a GED. Two-thirds have a history of physical or sexual abuse, and 3.5 percent are HIV positive. Three-fourths suffer from major depression and manic psychotic disorders. Sadly, the corrections literature suggests that, despite the fact that some women do quite well putting their lives back together when they are released from prison, most are likely to return to the same disenfranchised neighborhoods and difficult situations without having received any services to address their underlying problems. If it is true, as the corrections literature suggests, that prior arrest history predicts postprison recidivism, then the outlook for women prisoners is bleak: 65 percent of women in prison have a history of prior convictions. One-half have three or more convictions.

Scholars debate the reasons for the increase in women's incarceration over men's. Some suggest that as women moved into jobs from which they were formerly excluded, they gained the opportunities and skills to commit criminal acts for which incarceration was appropriate punishment. Others disagree, saying that poverty of young, female, single heads of households has contributed to the increase in women's crime and incarceration, particularly for property and drug offenses. One scholar put it this way: "The war on drugs has translated into a war on women."[9] Others think the criminal justice system is becoming more "gender blind" due to the emergence of "get-tough" attitudes and sentencing policies. Instead of seeing women offenders as weaker and giving them differential, if not preferential, treatment, judges and juries now sentence women more harshly whether they are first-time drug offenders or they have committed crimes against persons or property. The combined effects of harsh drug laws, changing patterns of drug use, and mandatory sentencing policies have lead to a significant increase in women's incarceration. Almost one-third of women in state prisons and more than one-half of women in federal prisons are serving time for nonviolent, drug-related offenses. Quite likely, the reason for the increase in women's incarceration is a product of all these theories. To reduce women's incarceration is to understand and implement programs about women's development, trauma, and addiction discussed in Chapter 6.

Race

The primary observation to be made about the prison population in the United States is that minorities are strikingly overrepresented. Although minorities comprise only 20 percent of the U.S. population, they make up almost two-thirds of all incarcerated offenders. Conversely, whites are underrepresented: more than 80 percent of the general population but only 35 percent of the prison population.

Research conducted by The Sentencing Project on state rates of incarceration show us that:[10]

- Blacks are incarcerated at nearly six times the rate of whites.
- Hispanics are incarcerated at nearly double the rate of whites.
- States exhibit substantial variation in the ratio of black to white incarceration, ranging from a high of 13.6:1 in Iowa to a low of 1.9:1 in Hawaii.
- States with the highest black to white ratio are disproportionately in the Northeast and Midwest, including Iowa, Vermont, New Jersey, Connecticut, and Wisconsin.
- States with the highest Hispanic to white ratio are also disproportionately in the Northeast and Midwest, including Massachusetts, Pennsylvania, New York, New Hampshire, and New Jersey.

If current trends continue, 1 of every 3 black males born today can expect to go to prison in his lifetime as can 1 of every 6 Latino males compared to 1 in 17 white males.[11]

As is the case with so many other criminological controversies, there is a debate over the relationship between race and crime. Official prison data suggest that the reason more minorities are disproportionately in prison, and for longer terms, is differential crime offending. Fifty-six percent of the persons in prison for violent offenses at yearend 2012 were minority. Recently, two Washington State Supreme Court justices stunned audiences when they said they didn't believe that anyone was in prison because of age, race, disability, and other factors. One of the Justices referred to those who represent the poor as "poverty pimps" and used the words "you people" when stating that black people commit crimes in their own communities. Shirley Bondon, manager of Washington State's Administrative Office of Courts who oversees programs to remove barriers in the legal system, said she couldn't believe a justice of the Supreme Court would make comments like that in her presence. Brandon said she took the comments personally as though the justices were saying that she and all blacks had a predisposition for criminality. "I was offended," she added.[12]

Others argue that the higher arrest rates, convictions, and sentences to prison of blacks are a function of racial profiling and racism in the criminal justice system. After reviewing 32 state-level studies of the decision to incarcerate and length of sentence imposed, Cassia Spohn, professor of criminology and criminal justice at Arizona State University, concluded there is ample evidence among these studies that, controlling for other relevant factors, blacks and Hispanics are more likely to be incarcerated than whites and, in some jurisdictions, receive longer sentences. And others have found gross racial disparities when arrest and incarceration for drug dependence and abuse are examined at the city and county levels.[13] Although government statistics indicate that blacks and whites use and sell drugs at similar rates, blacks are admitted to prison for drug offenses at 10 times the rate of whites in the 198 largest counties in the United States. The rate of admission to prison for drug offenses is 25 per 100,000 for whites and 262 per 100,000 for blacks, suggesting there are differences in the way counties construct policies concerning drug offenses. What are those practices that arrest and incarcerate more black drug offenders? One factor is that 51 percent of blacks live in metropolitan areas, compared with 21 percent of whites. Generally speaking, drug use is higher in urban areas, there are more law enforcement resources in urban areas, and there are more drug arrests in urban areas. Law enforcement practices are also a factor. Drug transactions in low-income, minority areas are more likely to be in public and between strangers, making it easier for police to make arrests whereas drug dealing by whites is more likely to occur in clubs, bars, and private homes. Prosecutorial discretion in deciding which cases to bring to trial and which pleas to accept and the ability of blacks to afford private attorneys are other reasons.

Still others argue that although discriminatory practices exist, it is improbable that criminal justice bias alone could account for the disproportionate arrest rates of blacks. They suggest the social problems of unemployment, economic deprivation, social disorganization, and social isolation of the nation's inner cities as additional causes. The inner city, the residence of most of the nation's poor, experiences by far the highest violence rates. Middle-class communities have more resources to deal with offenders, especially drug offenders, and get them into treatment. In low-income communities, those resources are not available, so a drug problem is more likely to develop into a criminal justice problem.

These levels of racial disparity are causing some states to implement racial impact statements. Policymakers routinely require analysis of the fiscal or environmental impact of proposed new laws, and it has been proposed that legislators do the same before implementing new sentencing laws. In 2008, Iowa and Connecticut (two states with some of the highest black-to-white ratios of incarceration) took the lead among the states and enacted racial impact statements. The analysis of crime and sentencing data will project relative racial composition of new prison sentences.

Age

The nation's population is aging, and this is reflected in the prison population. Middle-aged and older inmates make up a growing portion of the prison population. In 2000, 56 percent of the nation's prisoners were between 18 and 34 years old, 40 percent were between 35 and 54, and 4 percent were over 55. Today, for the fourth straight year, the representation of 18- to 34-year-olds had decreased to 47 percent, the presence of 35- to 54-year-olds had increased to 45 percent, and the presence of inmates 55 and older had increased to 8 percent (see Exhibit 7–3). In Chapter 12, we'll discuss the issues surrounding older prisoners in more detail.

Most Serious Offense

Another characteristic to compare is the most serious offense of which a prisoner was convicted. At yearend 2012, 53 percent of state prisoners were held for violent offenses, up from 46 percent in 1995. The percentage of state prisoners held for property offenses dropped from 23 percent in 1995 to 18 percent in 2012 and the percentage held for drug offenses dropped from 22 to 17 percent across the same time period. Still, the number of inmates doing time for drug violations in state and federal prison is triple what it was a decade ago. Convictions for public order offenses stayed the same at about 11 percent.

Among federal inmates, persons sentenced for drug offenses constituted the largest group (48 percent), similar to what it was in 1995. Immigration, weapon, and other public order offenders made up approximately

35 percent of the federal prison population up from 18 percent in 1995. The percentage of violent offenders in federal prison was 8 percent, similar to what it was in 1995. And property offenders constituted 5 percent, paralleling what it was in 1995 (see Exhibit 7–3).

PROGRAMS FOR PRISONERS

Among the most important elements of an inmate's institutional experience are the programs and services available. Today there is evidence-based research supporting the success rates against recidivism for correctional programs and services in education (academic and vocational), drug and alcohol, mental health, anger management, faith-based interventions, job readiness, and other programs. Some programs and services such as recreation and personal wellness do not directly indicate a reduction in recidivism, but, as you will read later in this chapter, experts tell us that personal wellness and recreation are vehicles to promote health and prevent disease, a goal for all of us.

But what does success mean? According to one of the best reviews of the current evidence of the effectiveness of adult correctional programming by Aos and his colleagues at the Washington State Institute for Public Policy, it means reducing recidivism by 5 to 15 percent.[14]

Classification

Researchers with the Pennsylvania Department of Corrections use the following analogy to make the point that criminal justice agencies often attempt to determine what is wrong with offenders by relying on subjective assessments of offenders' likelihood of reoffending:

> Imagine that a couple goes to the grocery store, fills a cart with their desired items, walks to the checkout lane, and the clerk simply eyeballs their selections and says, "looks like about $200 worth to me." They probably would not be too happy with this approach. Of course, if they felt it was an underestimate, they might be willing to let it go, but most people would expect a more systematic means of tallying the bill. Indeed, the widespread use of bar-coded scanners is yet the latest attempt to take human error out of the cashier process.[15]

The analogy demonstrates the importance of classification, the principal management tool for allocating scarce prison resources efficiently and minimizing the potential for escape or violence. Prisoner **classification** is the process of subdividing the inmate population into meaningful categories to match offender needs with correctional resources.

Classification is based on the premise that there are wide differences among prisoners. Its purpose is to assign inmates to appropriate prison housing and to help staff understand, treat, predict, and manage prisoner behavior.

One hundred years ago, the Elmira Reformatory in Elmira, New York, classified offenders as "specimens" and labeled them either "Mathematical Dullards," "Those Deficient in Self-Control," or "Stupid."[16] Today, the classifications are more sophisticated. The belief is that "somewhere between the extremes of 'all offenders are alike' and 'each offender is unique' lies a system (or systems) of categorization along pertinent dimensions that will prove to be of value in reaching correctional goals."[17]

The American Correctional Association believes that classification is one of the most important features of an effective correctional treatment system.

classification
The process of subdividing the inmate population into meaningful categories to match offender needs with correctional resources.

CO7-4

Classification is one of the most important features of an effective correctional treatment system. What is its purpose?

EXHIBIT 7–4 American Correctional Association

Public Correctional Policy on Classification

Introduction

Proper classification of offenders promotes public, staff, and offender safety. It is a continuing process basic to identifying and matching offender needs to correctional resources. Classification also serves as a tool for identifying gaps in correctional services. This continuing process involves all phases of correctional management.

Policy Statement

Classification should balance the public's need for protection, the needs of offenders, and the efficient and effective operation of the correctional system. In developing and administering its classification system, a correctional agency should:

A. develop written classification policies that establish criteria specifying different levels of security, supervision, and program involvement; establish procedures for documenting and reviewing all classification decisions and actions; describe the appeal process to be used by individuals subject to classification; and specify the time frames for monitoring and reclassifying cases;

B. develop the appropriate range of resources and services to meet the identified risk and program needs of the population served;

C. base classification decisions on rational assessment of objective and valid information, including background material (criminal history, nature of offense, age, gender, social history, educational needs, medical/mental health needs, etc.) as well as information regarding the individual's current situation, adjustment, and program achievement;

D. train all personnel in the classification process and require specialized training for those directly involved in classification functions;

E. use the classification process to assign individuals to different levels of control on the basis of valid criteria regarding risk (to self and others) and individual needs, matching these characteristics with appropriate security, level of supervision, and program services;

F. involve the offender directly in the classification process;

G. assign appropriately trained staff to monitor individual classification plans for progress made and reclassification needs;

H. objectively validate the classification process and instruments, assess on a planned basis the degree to which results meet written goals, and, as needed, refine the process and instruments; and

I. provide for regular dissemination of classification information to all levels of correctional staff and ensure that all staff understand the nature and purpose of proper classification of offenders.

Source: Copyright © American Correctional Association. Reprinted with permission.

ACA's policy statement on classification is presented in Exhibit 7–4. What does ACA recommend a correctional agency do to balance the public's need for protection, the needs of offenders, and the efficient and effective operation of the correctional system?

Types of Classification There are two types of prisoner classification: external and internal. **External classification** determines an inmate's security level (maximum, close, medium, minimum, or community) for *interinstitutional* placement. External classification answers the question "Where should I put this inmate?"

external classification

Interinstitutional placement of an inmate that determines an inmate's security level.

Internal classification is *intrainstitutional* placement. Once an inmate arrives at the institution, she or he undergoes a classification review. Classification staff review an inmate's behavior, personality, and educational, chemical dependency, medical, and mental health needs. Staff then assign inmates to housing units or cellblocks, work, and programming based on their risk, needs, and time to serve. The Pennsylvania Department of Corrections develops a unique correctional plan for each prisoner that identifies problem areas and treatment needs to be addressed by the prisoner during incarceration (see Exhibit 7–5). In approximately two-thirds of the states, the processes of internal and external classification are done at the same time.[18] Classification staff recommend both an inmate's security level and housing assignments and programming. The remaining states defer internal classification to the facility to which the prisoner is transferred.

A survey by the National Council on Crime and Delinquency (NCCD) found that only nine states had a formal internal classification system that used structured scoring instruments, staff specialists who were formally trained to use them, and a reclassification process to update previously classified prisoners. NCCD found that some kind of internal classification process exists in all prison systems to assign newly arrived inmates to housing units, work assignments, and programs, but these processes are usually informal and rely on subjective criteria.[19] Most state correctional agencies use the same classification assessment criteria for both males and females.[20] However, a few states—including Idaho, Massachusetts, New York, and Ohio—have developed gender-specific classification instruments that acknowledge that the nature and extent of women's criminal behavior and the ways in which they respond to supervision and incarceration make a difference.

Advantages of Classification Good internal classification systems offer a number of advantages. First, separating inmates by risk level and program needs puts extremely aggressive inmates in high security while those who require less or are at risk of being victimized are kept in low security. Within those levels of security, prisoners' needs may also be considered. Does the facility offer drug and alcohol treatment? Sex offender treatment? Anger management training? GED preparation? Such classification offers prisoners a chance for counseling, education, or vocational training, and it may keep aggressive inmates from assaulting passive inmates.

Second, a good classification system minimizes misclassification, thus promoting a safe environment for inmates and staff. When prisons are over capacity, as they are today, staff feel pressure to classify inmates quickly, which often results in misclassification. A good classification system will include safeguards against misclassification. For example, when there is not enough space in maximum-security facilities, a good system will direct staff to house only the lowest-risk high-security inmates in medium-security facilities.

Third, a good classification system more accurately places inmates and more effectively deploys staff. Without good classification, the tendency is to place inmates in more secure, more expensive prisons than necessary. Good classification controls the inmate population, assigns inmates to appropriate security levels, and better deploys staff.

Fourth, a good classification system enhances prison security by reducing tension in prison. Misclassification can jeopardize a prison's security and increase violence and escapes. A review of the major developments and trends in prisoner classification over a recent 20-year period found significant

internal classification

Intrainstitutional placement that determines, through review of an inmate's background, assignment to housing units or cellblocks, work, and programming based on the inmate's risk, needs, and time to serve.

The Staff Speaks
Visit www.mhhe.com/schmalleger7e
to see this feature.

The Offender Speaks
Visit www.mhhe.com/schmalleger7e
to see this feature.

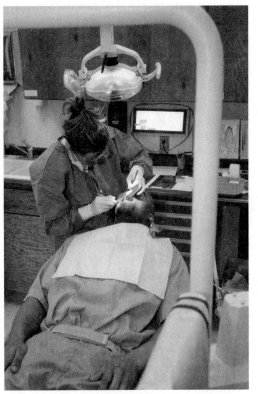

Classification of incoming inmates is based on many factors, including medical, dental, and mental health care needs; custody needs; institutional risk; work skills; and educational needs. Classification serves the custody goals of a prison but tends to label prisoners. Is such labeling appropriate?

EXHIBIT 7–5 Pennsylvania's Prisoner Intake Process

The Intake Process

The PA DOC intake process is designed to be completed in two weeks, as shown in the following table. However, it can take up to four to six weeks to establish medical, mental health, initial custody, and programming requirements for the prisoners.

Identifying the Prisoner

During day 1, the prisoner's identification is verified and he/she is strip searched, photographed, and fingerprinted; court documents are reviewed; and the prisoner's property is inventoried. Each prisoner bathes and receives baseline drug tests for illicit substances and medical and mental health screens. Additionally, the prisoner is interviewed by custody staff to identify potential security threat group membership and by a counselor to determine the need for separating the prisoner from other prisoners or staff members. Each prisoner also is issued a prisoner handbook in English, Spanish, or Braille. At the end of the first day, the prisoner has been identified, assigned to a cell, and has received institutional clothing and toiletries.

On day 2, a counselor provides formal orientation during which basic institutional rules and procedures are explained.

During the next 7 business days, the prisoner receives a full medical examination and takes a series of academic achievement, psychological, and substance abuse tests. As indicated by the results from the written tests, the psychologist and drug and alcohol treatment specialist conducts clinical interviews with the prisoner. In addition, the medical staff interview the prisoner about his/her medical history. DNA samples are collected from prisoners convicted of murder, stalking, and/or a sex-related offense. By the end of the 10th day at the intake center, prisoners have medical, mental health, education, and substance abuse ratings that indicate their level of need for services and/or treatment. These ratings are forwarded to classification staff for custody, facility, work, and programming assignments.

Classification

Classification staff use PACT [Pennsylvania Assessment and Classification Tool]—a fully automated classification system that synthesizes data collected throughout the intake process to establish a prisoner's custody level and to recommend housing, work detail, treatment, and programming assignments—to classify and assess the needs of prisoners. They also develop electronically a classification summary that is used by staff at the long-term facility to plan with the prisoner his/her institutional program and work assignments. The facility placement recommendation considers the prisoner's custody level, separation and regionalization issues, program needs, and bed space availability. Because PACT and the classification summary are automated, the counselor simply reviews the preliminary custody assessment, annotates any applicable administrative or discretionary overrides, recommends a preliminary custody level, and generates a form for recording the custody assessment and facility placement recommendations and decisions.

Initial Classification

Classification staff use PACT to determine the prisoner's custody level and facility placement. The initial custody level is based on seven discrete items: severity of current offense, severity of criminal history, escape history, institutional adjustment, number of prior institutional commitments, time to expected release, and stability factors (e.g., current age, marital status, and employment at arrest). A facility placement recommendation also is made during the initial classification process. It addresses custody, program, medical, and mental health needs; case management/case planning; and other specific prisoner or institution needs (e.g., electrician, maintenance technician, plumber).

Administrative overrides—based on the prisoner's legal status, current offense, and sentence—can change classification recommendations. Discretionary overrides by the case manager are permitted based on the prisoner's security threat group affiliation; escape history; nature of current offense; and behavior, mental health, medical, dental, and program needs. Information about cases for which discretionary overrides are recommended is forwarded electronically to the appropriate staff for approval. Multiple levels of review by classification supervisory staff and the central office are required for all overrides.

Reclassification

The reclassification process parallels the initial classification process. Regularly scheduled custody reassessments are conducted as part of the prisoner's annual review. Reassessments are also conducted following major misconduct reports and select minor violations, significant changes in the prisoner's program needs, time credits, escape time, sentence continuations, detainers, prerelease applications, unusual incident reports, transfer requests, and as needed to ensure the safety and security of the facility.

Reclassification is based on the severity of current offense, severity of criminal history, escape history, history of institutional violence, number and severity of misconduct reports during the previous 18 months, current age, program participation, work performance, and housing performance. As with the initial classification, these items are tallied on the PACT to create the total score. Again, mandatory and discretionary override factors are considered and reviewed.

EXHIBIT 7–5 Pennsylvania's Prisoner Intake Process *(continued)*

Overview of Pennsylvania's Prisoner Intake Process

Tasks	Conducted	Who Is Tested?	Personnel Responsible for Task	Instrument(s) and/or Process(es) Used
Day 1				
Identification	Yes; mandatory	All prisoners	Records staff	Court orders, AFIS, and LiveScan
Medical screen within 24 hours	Yes; mandatory	All prisoners	Health care staff	Medical screen
Mental health screen	Yes; mandatory	All prisoners	Intake office and mental health staff	Mental health screen
Drug testing	Yes; mandatory	All prisoners	Health care	Urine test
Prisoner separation	Yes; mandatory	All prisoners	Security staff and counselors	Interview and court documents
Gang membership	Yes; mandatory	All prisoners		Tattoos, criminal and institutional records, and interview
Days 2–10				
Academic achievement	Yes; mandatory	All prisoners	Education staff	TABE and WRAT
IQ tests	Yes; mandatory	All prisoners	Psychology staff	Beta III and WAIS
Vocational aptitude	No; not required			
Substance abuse	Yes; mandatory	All prisoners	Drug treatment staff	TCUDDS
Psychological	Yes; mandatory	All prisoners	Psychology staff	PAI, GBA, and clinical interview
Physical exam	Yes; mandatory	All prisoners	Health care staff	Physical exam, blood work, and interview
DNA testing	Yes; not required	Prisoners convicted of murder, stalking, and/or a sex-related crime	Lab technicians	Blood work
Days 11–15				
Criminal history	Yes; mandatory	All prisoners	Records staff	NCIC, presentence investigation, DOC MIS, and court orders
Social history	Yes; mandatory	All prisoners	Classification staff	Interview and presentence investigation
Institutional adjustment	Yes; mandatory	All prisoners	Classification staff	Jail documents and DOC MIS
Custody level	Yes; mandatory	All prisoners	Classification staff	PACT
Internal classification	Yes; mandatory	All prisoners	Classification staff	Custody and needs assessments
Security level/facility	Yes; mandatory	All prisoners	Classification staff	PACT
Prisoner separation	Yes; mandatory	All prisoners	Classification and security staff	Self-reports and court documents
Victim notification	Yes; not required	Only prisoners with a victim	District attorney's office	Offense type

Source: Adapted from Patricia L. Hardyman, James Austin, and Johnette Peyton, *Prisoner Intake Systems: Assessing Needs and Classifying Prisoners* (Washington, DC: U.S. Department of Justice, National Institute of Corrections, February, 2004).

improvement in classification technology (e.g., computer software to help collect, store, and manage the data) and more sophisticated assessment of risk and of medical, mental health treatment, and education needs.[21]

Orientation to the Institution

While the process of internal classification is being conducted, state and federal prison systems provide inmates an orientation to the institution. For several weeks, as shown in Pennsylvania's prisoner intake process (Exhibit 7–5), inmates participate in an admission and orientation program. It provides an introduction to all aspects of the institution and includes screening by staff from the case management, medical, and mental health units. Inmates receive copies of the institution's rules and regulations, including the inmate discipline policy, and they are introduced to the programs, services, policies, and procedures of the facility. Increasingly, prison systems such as the Louisiana State Penitentiary at Angola use inmates to orient new arrivals to prison life. According to some researchers, North Carolina conducts one of the most detailed orientations, which includes videos about the facility, prisoner responsibilities, and diseases as well as questionnaires about drug use, potential visitors, and family background.[22]

Unit Management: Faith-Based and Veterans Dorms

Unit management is based on the idea that cooperation is most likely in small groups that have lengthy interactions.[23] A unit is a self-contained living area for 50 to 200 inmates that is managed semiautonomously within the larger institution. Third-generation jails discussed in Chapter 6 are unit management systems.

unit management system

A method of controlling prisoners in self-contained living areas and making inmates and staff (unit manager, correctional counselor, and unit secretary) accessible to each other.

In the federal system and in a number of states, prisons and jails use a **unit management system.** The purpose of dividing correctional facilities into functional units, each with its own permanently assigned staff and a unit manager who serves as a "mini warden," was largely to improve program delivery. Many units—drug treatment units, in particular—were established to focus on specific program needs. The unit team—typically composed of the unit manager, one or more case managers, two or more correctional counselors, and a unit secretary—is directly responsible for the inmates living in that unit. Unit staff receive input from other employees involved in an inmate's progress (such as work supervisors, teachers, and psychologists) and meet with the inmate on a regular basis to develop, review, and discuss the work assignments and programs the inmate should be involved in as well as any other needs or concerns.

Traditional correctional institutions make decisions through a centralized and hierarchical management structure whereas unit management strives to decentralize decision making. When decisions are made at the unit level, they are made with better information and by staff who know the inmates better. Unit management gives inmates direct daily contact with the staff who make most of the decisions about their daily lives. It results in improved inmate access to staff and greater staff access to inmates, providing staff with an awareness of significant inmate concerns and potential problems. Unit management also means that not all units will be managed in the same way. Having different management methods is a strength because different inmates require different management approaches.

The success of unit management is affected by internal classification. Inmates who are assigned to a given institution are then assigned to a specific unit based on their risks and needs. After the processes of internal classification and initial orientation, each inmate meets with the unit team to formulate a program plan, which may include drug treatment, education, and vocational training as well as institution maintenance jobs or other work assignments. The unit team reviews the inmate's progress and makes changes in the program plan as needed. Unit management emphasizes candid, open communication between staff and inmates. Direct and frequent communication helps staff know inmates, understand their needs, and respond appropriately to those needs. Two types of unit management discussed here are faith-based and veterans dorms.

In faith-based dorms, inmates volunteer to be housed in facilities that provide special activities and classes, religious and secular, aimed at character development and personal growth.[24] Today, nearly half of state and federal prison systems are operating or developing at least one residential faith-based program.[25]

CO7-5

Supporters of faith-based initiatives argue that such programs *may* reduce recidivism and improve other postrelease outcomes, are generally free or low cost because they are provided by volunteer groups, may improve in-prison behavior (such as more compliance with rules, participation in treatment, and physical and mental health among inmates), and lessen the dehumanization of incarceration and are unlikely to harm anyone.

On the other hand, opponents argue that faith-based prison programs may not be effective; may actually cost taxpayers; promote a religious orientation and hence may be unconstitutional as reported in a recent legal challenge to a taxpayer-supported prison program in Iowa run by Charles Colson's Prison Fellowship; may actually lessen offender accountability for their crimes; and may coerce some inmates into certain kinds of religious activity.

The only detailed analysis of every existing empirical study on the effectiveness of faith-based prison programs was published in 2011 by Emory University law school professor Alexander Volokh.[26] His 50-page analysis can be summed up as:

> Most studies cannot be taken seriously because they are tainted by the "self-selection problem." It is hard to determine the effect of faith-based prison programs because they are voluntary, and volunteers are more likely to be motivated to change and are therefore already less likely to commit infractions or be re-arrested. . . .
>
> The only credible studies done so far compare participants with non-participants who volunteered for the program but were rejected. Some studies in this category find no effect, but some do find a modest effect. But even those that find an effect are subject to additional critiques: for instance, participants may have benefitted from being exposed to treatment resources that non-participants were denied.
>
> Thus, based on current research, there is no strong reason to believe that faith-based prisons work. However, there is no strong reason to believe that they do not work.

Professor Volokh goes on to tell us that the weak evidence supporting faith-based correctional institutions reflects the state of our research. Faith-based prison programs are not evidence-based correctional interventions. What we need, he says, is more experimentation with faith-based facilities, not less.

However the experimentation Professor Volokh recommends requires a *randomized* experimental design, something that criminal justice practitioners (judges, wardens, chiefs of police) rarely agree to because *randomization,* not police chiefs, wardens, or judges, decides which subjects are assigned to experimental and control groups.

Others tell us that faith-based programming in prison should not be contingent on the issue of program effectiveness for several reasons. "First, regardless of social science findings, prisoners have a right to express their religious views. . . . Second . . . the real outcome or purpose of religion in prison is not only to reduce anti-social behavior/criminal behavior or relapse into criminal activity, but also to counteract the tendency of prisons to dehumanize people and help prisoners prevent a further decline in their humanity. . . . Finally . . . [researchers] question whether we can accurately tap into the deeper religious dimensions of that person's motivations and thereby assess whether a particular individual has changed."[27]

Aside from the methodological critique of the literature on faith-based prison programs, Professor Volokh tells us that there are five additional facts we should know:[28]

1. There are a lot of faith-based prison programs. As mentioned earlier, nearly half of state and federal prison systems are operating or developing at least one residential faith-based program.

2. One faith-based prison program in Iowa, the InnerChange Freedom Initiative run by Charles Colson's Prison Fellowship (PF), was struck down by a federal district court as unconstitutional for advancing religion, however other InnerChange programs still exist in other state prisons. Professor Volokh believes that faith-based programs that ". . . are explicitly motivated by Christian and Biblical principles are probably more vulnerable to unconstitutional challenges; programs that are more interfaith and have less explicitly religious content. . . are probably less so."[29]

3. Faith-based prison programs are promoted on the grounds that they *may* improve in-prison behavior (such as compliance with rules, participation in treatment, and physical and mental health among inmates) and reduce recidivism and other post-release outcomes.

4. The body of literature examining faith-based prison programs suffers from serious methodological limitations that make it impossible

One of the most recent types of unit management housing to appear in prison and jail is veterans-only facilities to house and assist the 9 percent of prisoners who are war veterans. What makes these prison housing units unique?

to know if they produce intended outcomes such as small and non-representative samples, a reliance on anecdotal evidence, limited statistical analysis, and questionable evaluator bias.

5. The few empirical studies with methodological rigor that produced positive results only had a weak effect. Furthermore, it is still not known if the participants in those studies benefitted from resources they received *after* release from prison that non-participants did not have, or the faith-based prison program itself.

One of the most recent types of unit management housing to appear in prison and jail is veterans-only facilities to house and assist the growing number of Iraq and Afghanistan war veterans who are incarcerated. One estimate is that about 9 percent of the prison and jail population in the U.S. is made up of veterans.[30]

Veterans-only facilities are springing up in communities across the U.S. near military bases in Florida, Georgia, and Virginia to address post-traumatic stress disorder, addiction, depression, and other common issues faced by veterans that may have influenced their offending behavior.

Oftentimes the walls of these special housing units are painted with the logos of every service branch. The inmates are usually supervised by corrections officers with military backgrounds, and sometimes the corrections counselors are also former service members.

In some of the veterans-only housing units, even the job assignments carry a military-themed title. For example, at the Creek Correctional Center in Chesapeake, Virginia, the "mess crew" works in the kitchen, the "hazmat" team cleans up spills, and the "intel coordinator" gathers information on veterans programs in the community.[31]

Only time will tell if veterans-only facilities in jails and prison are effective. To date, there is no empirical research examining the effectiveness of veterans-only housing units on reducing criminal activity. What we find instead are descriptions of veterans-only programs in use across the U.S. and anecdotal evidence and testimonials that they work. Before it can be concluded that veterans-only jail and prison housing units do or do not reduce criminal activity, strong research designs are needed. Until then, the jury is out on veterans-only housing units.

Work Assignments

Work is a very important part of institutional management and offender programs. Meaningful work programs are the most powerful tool prison administrators have in managing crowding and idleness, which can lead to disorder and violence. And now the news on prisoner work assignments is even better. The evidence-based reviews introduced in Chapter 1 and mentioned throughout the text show that the average prison industry program reduces the recidivism rate of participants by almost 6 percent. Some prison industries achieve better results, some worse. On average, however, researchers find that the typical prison industry can be expected to reduce recidivism by 6 percent.[32]

Prison work is generally of one of three types: operational assignments within the institution, community projects, or prison industry.

Operational Assignments

In operational assignments within the institution, inmates perform tasks necessary to the functioning of the facility or larger corrections system. Institutional maintenance assignments including farm and other agricultural activities are the largest single option for inmate work. Forty-five states, the District of Columbia, and the BOP pay inmates a wage for services rendered to the institution. The average wage range for institutional maintenance work is $0.99 to $3.98 per day. Inmates working in institutional maintenance perform the following types of work: laundry, heating and air conditioning repair, building maintenance and custodial service, landscaping and grounds maintenance, and food preparation and service. Most of the 763 inmates serving time at the Federal Prison Camp in Pensacola, Florida, leave the prison every day to perform institutional maintenance on the community's many military bases.

Community Projects Many correctional institutions allow inmates to gain work experience through community projects. Through them offenders contribute their labor to benefit the community while developing job skills in a practical, nonprison setting. Community work usually takes the form of construction, landscaping, horticulture, and agriculture activities. Construction/repair of public property and parks development and maintenance are by far the most common types of community work activities. Examples of other community projects include building houses for low-income persons, painting municipal swimming pools, providing snow removal services, providing backup firefighting services, and delivering antidrug programs in schools. In South Carolina, inmates who meet the criteria for community work build playground equipment, pick up trash on state highways, maintain and clean up state parks, aid flood victims, clean up debris after storm damage, and provide skilled labor for Habitat for Humanity. Inmate work organizations also raise money for the Special Olympics and other charities.

CO7-6

State Prison Industries and the Prison Industry Enhancement Certification Program (PIECP) PIECP allows inmates to work for a private employer in a "free-world" occupation and earn the prevailing wage. Created by Congress in 1979, PIECP encourages states and local correctional agencies to form partnerships with private companies to give inmates real work opportunities.

How much does the electorate support PIECP? Eighty-two percent of U.S. voters said that job training is very important for a person to reintegrate successfully into society after incarceration.[33] Their faith in prison

Inmates at the Snake River Correctional Institution, Ontario, Oregon, make calls arranging business meetings for the consulting firm Perry Johnson. What are the benefits of prison industry for inmates, their families, and victims while in prison and after release, the institution, the business community, and taxpayers?

industry programs is supported by the what-works literature introduced in Chapter 1. Of the 30 rigorous evaluations of prison industries examined by the Washington State Institute for Public Policy, an agency created by the state legislature to conduct research on policy issues, the studies showed an average 6 percent reduction in recidivism due to prison industry.

The PIE certification program has two primary objectives: First, to generate products and services that enable prisoners to make a contribution to society, help offset the cost of their incarceration, compensate crime victims, and provide inmate family support. And second, to provide a means of reducing prison idleness, increasing inmate job skills, and improving the prospects for successful inmate transition to the community upon release.

Currently, PIE certification programs operate in 37 states and 4 counties in the United States. These programs manage more than 175 business partnerships with private industry.[34] Offender salaries generate millions of dollars for victims' programs, inmate family support, for correctional institution room and board costs, state and federal taxes, and mandatory inmate savings.

In addition to PIE certification programs, there are hundreds of innovative prison industry programs across the United States. Inmates in many states train guide dogs to aid visually impaired persons, hearing dogs to assist those who are deaf and hearing impaired, and service dogs to assist individuals suffering from various physical needs. Some Nevada inmates learn building construction while others learn to employ resistance-free training methods to tame and train wild horses in order to improve their adoptability. Women inmates at the Belfair Mission Creek Corrections Center in Washington are taken to the rivers and canals around Hood Canal and are paid $1 an hour to spray pesticides in order to save salmon habitats. Inmates at the Washington State Penitentiary in Walla Walla work as research assistants for a professor of entomology at Washington State University to raise and tag Monarch butterflies to track their migratory path. They earn 42 cents an hour. At the Louisiana State Penitentiary in Angola, a maximum-security prison, inmates built Prison View, a nine-hole golf course that is on prison property and open to the public. Although inmates cannot play, they learned landscape design, horticulture, and groundskeeping. Inmates in Nebraska and 34 other states volunteer for a one-year-long rigorous Braille translation program certified by the Library of Congress. They earn between 38 cents and $1.08 an hour with at least half making 54 cents or less.

One of the best-known prison industry programs operates at the Eastern Oregon Correctional Institution in Pendleton, Oregon, the famous mill town known for Pendleton fabrics. There prisoners make a line of T-shirts, jackets, and jeans known as Prison Blues®. All 50 inmates working in the factory are paid prevailing industry wages, which range from a base of $7.80 to $9.58 per hour. They can also earn bonus incentives for quality and productivity.

What Impact Does PIECP Have? In June 2006, researchers at the University of Baltimore asked whether PIECP inmates return to prison less frequently or enter more successful employment than inmates in traditional prison industries and those who did not work at all.[35] The researchers found that PIECP inmates became tax-paying citizens more quickly and remained in that status longer than inmates who worked in traditional prison industries or not at all. Furthermore, 82 percent of PIECP inmates were not arrested in their first year following release, compared to

Many state correctional systems channel prison labor into industrial and commercial programs. One such program is the Prison Blues® brand of jeans, T-shirts, work shirts, and yard coats manufactured by Oregon Corrections Enterprises, a division of the Oregon Department of Corrections. What benefits to inmates do such work programs provide?

Federal Prison Industries (FPI)

A federal, paid inmate work program and self-supporting corporation.

UNICOR

The trade name of Federal Prison Industries. UNICOR provides such products as U.S. military uniforms, electronic cable assemblies, and modular furniture.

77 percent of inmates who worked in traditional prison industry jobs, and 76 percent of those who were not employed at all while in prison.

Although the results of the PIECP study are positive, they are not conclusive because participants in the three groups were not randomly assigned to groups. Prisoners volunteered to participate in the PIECP and traditional prison industries. Therefore, inmates who worked either in PIECP or traditional prison industries were "self-selected" and may have had different motivations and backgrounds than other inmates, which may have led to better outcomes.

Federal Prison Industries and UNICOR In the federal system, legislation authorizing the establishment of paid inmate work programs was introduced in Congress during the Great Depression in 1934. The American Federation of Labor (AFL) voiced its opposition, arguing that federal prison industries would have an unfair advantage over the public sector because they would pay their inmates less than a private company worker would be paid for carrying out similar assignments and that it would take away jobs from the private sector at a time when working people needed every job they could get.

President Franklin Roosevelt took a personal interest in the matter and called AFL president William Green and BOP director Sanford Bates to the Oval Office. Together, the three men were able to draw out Green's objections to the proposed legislation and his suggestions for improvement, and ultimately the AFL withdrew its opposition. On June 23, 1934, President Roosevelt signed the law that authorized the establishment of **Federal Prison Industries (FPI)**. FPI is a federal work program in which inmates are paid. Better known by its trade name, **UNICOR**, FPI is a self-supporting corporation owned by the federal government and overseen by a governing board appointed by the president.

Since 1934, FPI has operated factories and employed inmates in America's federal prisons. When the United States entered World War II in December 1941, FPI manufactured bomb fins and casings, TNT cases, parachutes, cargo nets, and wooden pallets for the military. It also handled the military's laundry and built, remodeled, and repaired military patrol boats, tugboats, and barges. FPI also contributed in another way to the war effort. It trained inmates to move directly into jobs in defense industries after release from prison.

The mission of FPI is to employ and provide job skills training to the greatest practical number of inmates confined within the federal Bureau of Prisons; contribute to the safety and security of federal correctional facilities by keeping inmates constructively occupied; produce market-priced quality goods for sale to the federal government; operate in a self-sustaining manner; and minimize FPI's impact on private business and labor. FPI has traditionally relied on manufacturing office furniture, electronics, and clothing for the bulk of its business, but it has begun to enter new industries such as renewable energy (making solar panels, energy-efficient lighting, and small wind turbines). Federal agencies are required to purchase items when possible from UNICOR. This chapter's Economic Realities and Corrections: Prisons discusses the controversy surrounding UNICOR: Is it siphoning jobs at much lower wages that could be filled by those who need them during the nation's toughest period of unemployment in decades?

What Impact Does UNICOR Have? There is very little independent research on whether UNICOR reduces criminal activity. More than 10 years ago, the federal BOP released a study that compared the postrelease activities of a group of inmates who had participated in

Economic Realities and Corrections: Prisons

UNICOR, the trade name for Federal Prison Industries, Inc. (FPI), has not been immune to the nation's economic pinch. Since 2007, a tight economy, dwindling agency budgets, and Congressional moves to weaken its preferential status as the supplier of manufactured goods for federal agencies (UNICOR isn't allowed to sell to the private sector) have reduced the company's size.

The sluggish economy and tight budgets have reduced government orders, forcing the Bureau of Prisons to close or downsize 43 UNICOR factories; only 66 remain today. They manufacture clothing and textiles, electronics, fleet management and vehicular components, industrial products, office furniture, recycling activities, and data entry and encoding services. Under current practice—governed by intricate laws, regulations, and policies—federal agencies must buy prisoner-made goods if they are comparable in price, quality, and time of delivery to private sector goods with certain exceptions.

UNICOR's overall sales of approximately $885 million in 2009 fell to $772 million in 2010 and to $745 million in 2011. UNICOR uses the revenue it generates to purchase raw materials and equipment (approximately 80 percent), to pay staff salaries (17 percent), and to pay inmate salaries (4 percent).

Under current law, all physically able federal inmates who are not a security risk are required to work. Inmates who are not employed by FPI have other labor assignments in prison. FPI work assignments are usually considered more desirable because their wages are higher (23 cents to $1.15 an hour) and allow inmates to learn a trade.

However, the economic recession caused layoffs in the number of FPI employees. From a high of approximately 23,200 inmates in 2007, the number of inmates employed by FCI dropped to approximately 15,900 in 2010. Federal corrections officials worry that FPI workforce cuts could spark unrest in already overcrowded federal facilities where industry jobs have kept prisoners occupied and out of recreation yards and housing units.

But it is not only the economic recession that is impacting FPI. Private industry and Congress want FPI to scale back. They use arguments similar to the ones they used in 1934 when the FPI was first introduced: With much lower wages, FPI is taking away jobs from law-abiding citizens who need them during the nation's toughest period of unemployment in decades.

Private manufacturers in rural Alabama, Mississippi, and Tennessee have had to lay off employees after losing clothing contracts for the Defense Department to UNICOR. Its lower operating costs and laws that require federal agencies to use inmate-made products when available enables UNICOR to undercut private manufacturers.

After losing a $45 million contract to UNICOR, Steven Eisen, CEO of Tennier Industries, a military clothing manufacturer in rural Tennessee, told reporters, "Our government screams, howls and yells how the rest of the world is using prisoners or slave labor to manufacture items, and here we take the items right out of the mouths of people who need it."* Representative Bill Huizenga, a Michigan Republican agreed, saying "If China did this—having their prisoners work at subpar wages in prisons—we would be screaming bloody murder."†

UNICOR supporters say it has not taken large numbers of jobs away from private industry. They documented only 300 layoffs directly linked to private companies losing work to federal prisoners at four textile plants in Alabama and Tennessee. Advocates also say that UNICOR faces challenges that private industry does not: Many convicted felons don't know how to work.

In recent years, support for Congressional critics of UNICOR has increased as jobs, competition, and the role of government have become potent political issues. Several members of the U.S. House of Representatives proposed overhaul legislation to limit UNICOR's preferential status as the supplier of manufactured goods to federal agencies by putting a limit on FPI's sales to the federal government. This would open more product areas to private companies and strengthen requirements that prices for prisoner-made products be competitive. Some proposed legislation would impose federal work-safety standards and higher wages, starting at $2.50 an hour. However, the bills have always stalled in the Senate.

Under current practice — governed by intricate laws, regulations, and policies — a federal agency must buy prisoner-made goods if FPI offers an item that is comparable in price, quality and time of delivery to that of the private sector, with certain exceptions. The company's prices are not always the lowest, but it frequently has been able to underbid private companies, Congressional aides say.

FPI supporters argue that there is a high correlation between prisoners who work in prison industries and a higher-than-average success rate of not being rearrested, not being reconvicted, and not returning to prison. However, as we pointed out in this chapter and as stated by an analyst in crime policy with the Congressional Research Service,‡ the limited number of rigorous evaluations of correctional industry programs makes it impossible to draw any definitive conclusions about the programs' ability to reduce recidivism. Another analysis that summarized the results of four evaluations of correctional industry programs also found that inmates who participated in correctional industry programs were less likely to recidivate. However, the researchers reported that they could not rule out sampling error as a possible explanation for the positive effect. The researchers also reported that many of the studies included in the analysis lacked stringent methodological rigor, thereby preventing the researchers from concluding that the programs lead directly to less reoffending. One wonders whether the economic recession that started in 2007 will produce any changes in the FPI program.

*As quoted in Diane Cardwell, "Private Businesses Fight Federal Prisons for Contracts," *The New York Times,* March 4, 2012, www.nytimes.com (accessed March 15, 2012).
†Ibid.
‡Nathan James, *Federal Prison Industries* (Washington, DC: Congressional Research Service, December, 2011), pp. 4–5.

UNICOR programs with those of another group of inmates who had not. The study found that inmates employed by UNICOR were 24 percent more likely, upon release, to become employed and remain crime free for as long as 12 years after release than those who were not involved in UNICOR programs. Another study showed that inmates employed in federal prison industries had survival times (measured by the number of days before recommitment) that were 20 percent longer than those of the comparison group.[36] However, independent evaluations have concluded that the results are not conclusive. Without independent evaluations, we do not know whether, and how much, UNICOR reduces criminal activity.

CO7-7 ## Education and Recreation Programs

The majority of prisoners cannot read or write well enough to function in society. Among federal and state inmates, about 37 percent do not have a high school diploma or a GED compared to 19 percent of the general population.[37]

A survey of inmate education programs conducted by the American Correctional Association found that only 283,000 were participating in educational programs.[38] This may be due in part to the higher rate of learning disabilities found among inmates.[39] An estimated 30 to 50 percent of inmates have a learning disability compared with 5 to 15 percent of the general adult population.

However, can prison education programs rehabilitate prisoners so that they eventually contribute constructively to society upon reentry and cost less than incarceration? The answer is a resounding, "Yes, they can."

Research analysts with the Fortune Society, a prisoner reform advocacy group, found that it cost $44,000 per year to incarcerate one prisoner in New Jersey, whereas the cost to attend Princeton University is $37,000 per year.[40] A report by the Correctional Association of New York found lopsided spending on prison versus college education. Specifically, it cost $44,000 per year to house a prisoner in New York versus $7,645 tuition per year for a full-time in-state student within the State University of New York system.[41] Exhibit 7–6 in this chapter shows that five states spent as much or more on corrections than they did on higher education!

In 2013, the Rand Corporation published the results of the largest study to date measuring the effectiveness of correctional education on recidivism and employment.[42] It found that inmates who participated in correctional education programs – remedial education to develop reading and math skills, GED preparation, postsecondary education or vocational training - were 43 percent less likely to return to prison within three years of release in comparison to those who did not participate. The researchers also found that prisoners who participated in academic or vocational education programs had a 13 percent better chance of finding employment than those who did not. And prisoners who participated specifically in vocational training programs (including welding, computing, culinary arts, construction trades and auto mechanics) were 28 percent more likely to be employed after release from prison than those who did not participate.

The Rand findings show that not only does correctional education reduce postrelease recidivism and increase the odds of employment, but it does so cost-effectively. Focusing only on the direct costs of correctional education programs and laying aside for the moment the indirect costs such as the financial and emotional costs to the victim and the criminal justice system as a whole, the researchers estimate that the three year reincarceration costs for those who did not receive correctional education

Visit http://www.youtube.com/watch?v =KJYGvxiiCrk or scan this code with the QR app on your smartphone or digital device and watch the podcast of Jody Lewen, winner of the University of California at Berkley 2006 Peter E. Haas Public Service Award and director of the Patten University extension site, discuss her experiences teaching at San Quentin State Prison, and the inmates' reactions to the program. How does this information relate to ideas discussed in this chapter?

EXHIBIT 7–6 American Correctional Association Public Correctional Policy on Correctional Health Care

Introduction

Incarcerated individuals, or those in the custody of criminal justice and juvenile justice agencies, have a legal right to adequate health care in accordance with generally recognized professional standards utilizing a comprehensive holistic approach that is sensitive to the cultural, age and gender responsive needs of a growing and diverse population. To ensure accountability and professional responsibility, these services should follow the policy guidelines below, as well as the health care standards of the American Correctional Association.

Policy Statement

Health care programs for offenders include comprehensive medical, dental and mental health services. Such programs should:

A. Be delivered by qualified and appropriately credentialed health care professionals;

B. Include a comprehensive health promotion and disease prevention program designed to meet the specific health maintenance needs of the specific residential population, which includes health, nutrition, and safety education programs;

C. Employ a stratified system of service delivery to maximize the efficient use of medical and mental health care resources;

D. Include correctional officers who work in health care units as active participants in the multidisciplinary treatment team;

E. Create community linkages, which will facilitate the continuation of the treatment plans by community health care agencies for persons being released from incarceration;

F. Establish appropriate classification, programs and housing assignments for juvenile, elderly, female and other identified classes of special needs offenders;

G. Establish hospice services for terminally ill offenders supported by a compassionate release program for those who qualify;

H. Provide all offenders with language-appropriate verbal and written information concerning access to health care services during intake screening, followed by more formal instruction during the admission and orientation program;

I. Provide continuous, comprehensive services commencing at admission, including effective and timely screening, assessment and treatment, and appropriate referral to alternate health care resources where warranted;

J. Establish a system to provide access to emergency treatment 24 hours per day;

K. Establish a formal process to screen for, identify, treat and manage offenders with infectious diseases;

L. Provide appropriate health care training programs that are cognizant of cultural, age and gender issues for all correctional and health care staff, and allow for continuing professional and medical education programs;

M. Provide a medical records system to document diagnosis and treatment programs to facilitate treatment continuity and cooperation between health care professionals, consistent with privacy, confidentiality and security requirements;

N. Provide a pharmaceutical distribution system that conforms to applicable state and federal laws and established formularies;

O. Provide a continuing quality improvement program, including risk management programs and peer review activities to monitor and evaluate the health care services delivered;

P. Establish a patient bill of rights;

Q. Provide a system for medical and administrative review of grievances relating to health care offered, provided or denied;

R. Provide screening for co-occurring disorders;

S. Provide all offenders given new prescriptions with verbal counseling and written information about their medications, which should be provided by a health care practitioner;

T. Provide a sufficient supply of prescription medication upon release to ensure continuity of care; and

U. Provide the opportunity to establish living will and/or advanced directive.

Source: Copyright © American Correctional Association. Reprinted with permission.

would be between $2.94 million and $3.25 million. In comparison, for those who did receive correctional education, the three year reincarceration costs would be between $2.07 million and $2.28 million. This means that reincarceration costs are $0.87 million to $0.97 million *less* for those who receive correctional education.

In announcing the findings, U.S. Attorney General Eric Holder said "These findings reinforce the need to become smarter on crime by

Inmates at the Fremont Correctional Facility in Cañon City, Colorado, learn new career skills in renewable energy fields. They attend class five hours a day and do homework from a textbook in their cells. Inmates who pass the program earn certificates and 20 college credits. What is the illiteracy rate among prisoners compared to that of the general population? Why are there so few prisoners enrolled in education classes?

expanding proven strategies for keeping our communities safe, and ensuring that those who have paid their debt to society have the chance to become productive citizens. WE have an opportunity and an obligation to use smart methods – and to advance innovative new programs – that can improve public safety while reducing costs. As it stands, too many individuals and communities are harmed, rather than helped, by a criminal justice system that does not serve the American people as well as it should. This important research is part of our broader effort to change that."[43]

Education is also an opportunity for prisoners to earn good time credits (also called *earned time*), first introduced in Chapter 3. In at least 21 states, inmates can earn time off their sentences by participating in or completing educational courses. In Nevada, for example, an inmate can earn 10 days per month for participation in an education program, and an additional 60, 90, or 120 days for obtaining a certificate, diploma, or degree, respectively.

So if corrections-based educational programs are effective in reducing recidivism, why are only 283,000 inmates enrolled? There are a number of reasons. First, correctional educators face substantial hurdles in delivering effective instruction. Inmates do not enter prison or jail to attend classes. They often do not see the importance of gaining an education, and many have a history of educational failure. They do not enroll in programs or participate in classes with the same enthusiasm as the noninstitutionalized population. Even negative peer pressure can discourage inmates from joining programs. Correctional educators face the challenge of motivating inmates to involve themselves in educational programming because they know that programming inside correctional facilities greatly influences what happens once inmates are released. Emphasizing the relevance of education to inmates, helping inmates experience success in learning, and developing an institutional culture that endorses the importance of education are vital components as correctional facilities work to achieve rehabilitation through education. Second, educational programming has not been a high priority in correctional budgeting, particularly because the beginning of the warehousing era. The bulk of correctional spending has been on security. Third, educational programming cannot be delivered given the present state of overcrowding. Today, almost 24 states and the federal system are operating their prisons at or more than 100 percent of capacity.[44] California's prisons were operating at 175 percent of their lowest capacity. And fourth, many states, such as California, Florida, Illinois, Iowa, and Kentucky are slashing correctional education budgets because of the current budget crisis.[45] What we know, though, is that states have a responsibility to ensure public safety and cannot abandon this duty in times of budgetary crisis. Prison education programs prevent more crimes than increasing incarceration rates and lengthening sentences—and cost far less. They even save states money on correctional budgets by reducing the number of offenders who return to prison in the future, as the Rand findings show.

Recreation is another important prison program, and here the courts have made numerous rulings that guarantee prisoners some minimal amount of time in recreational activities. However, the specifics about the nature and extent of recreation programming in prison and inmates' participation in such programs are not known. What is known is that recreation and organized sports can make doing time more bearable and, as a result, make the jobs of correctional officers easier. Recreation programs can also be used as an incentive for good behavior, and by reducing tension, they can cut the number of prison assaults. Physical and mental health experts tell us that recreation programs can be a vehicle for teaching ways to promote health and prevent disease. Inmates who play hard are more likely to stay fit, possibly reducing health costs. Nutrition experts know that eating healthful food, participating in a regular exercise program, and stopping smoking are central to maintaining good health in prison. They also reduce the cost of prison health care.

On May 21, 2009, Eduardo Barba, who is serving 30 years for two second-degree felonies at the Utah State Prison, received his Associate of Arts degree in architectural technology from Utah State University. Barba was one of three students chosen to speak during the ceremony. Why is prisoner education important?

Physical and Mental Health Care

Good health care plays an important role in the day-to-day operations of a correctional facility. Investments in prisoner health care mean fewer correctional disturbances, disciplinary actions, and inmate injuries and less negative publicity for the institution. For the nation's one-half million correctional employees and thousands of daily visitors to prisons and jails, good health care also reduces their risk of becoming infected from inmates with communicable diseases.

Many people in prison and jail face significant barriers to obtaining needed health care services in the community either prior to their incarceration or upon their release. In 2011, the Office of National Drug Control Policy found that one-third to three-quarters of offenders in jails in 10 major cities were not covered by any type of health insurance because of unemployment and restrictions by Medicaid (the federal-state health insurance partnership for the poor).[46]

However, because of the Affordable Care Act (ACA) signed by President Obama in 2011, ex-felons will start receiving health coverage in January 2014. Expansion of Medicaid (the federal-state health insurance partnership for the poor) is the vehicle for delivering health insurance to former prisoners. The "inmate exclusion" as it is called allows for the use of federal Medicaid funding to pay for the care provided to an incarcerated individual when that individual is a patient in a medical institution such as in a hospital, nursing facility, juvenile psychiatric facility, or intermediate care facility for at least 24 hours. Because community-based inpatient medical care represents a sizable portion of the cost provided to incarcerated individuals, a state can realize considerable cost savings if it effectively uses Medicaid funding. Using the "inmate exclusion" rule,

California saved almost $31 million in 2013 and North Carolina saved $10 million.[47]

Extending benefits to ex-offenders may not be the most popular aspect of the ACA, but it is significant because the health of ex-offenders is worse than that of the general population. They have higher rates of chronic and infectious diseases such as asthma, TB, diabetes, hepatitis, HIV/AIDS, addiction, and mental illness.[48]

Prison and jail systems are obligated to provide health care to inmates. However, the U.S. Supreme Court ruled in 1976 in *Estelle v. Gamble* that inmates do not have *unqualified* access to health care. Lower courts have held that the Constitution does not require the medical care provided prisoners to be perfect, the best obtainable, or even very good.[49] According to an excellent review of legal health care standards and the legal remedies available to prisoners, the courts support the **principle of least eligibility:** that prison conditions—including the delivery of health care—must be a step below those of the working class and people on welfare. As a result, prisoners are denied access to medical specialists, second opinions, prompt delivery of medical services, technologically advanced diagnostic techniques, the latest medications, and up-to-date medical procedures.

principle of least eligibility

The requirement that prison conditions— including the delivery of health care—must be a step below those of the working class and people on welfare.

CO7-8

PRISON ORGANIZATION AND ADMINISTRATION

All 50 states and the BOP operate prisons. In addition, four local jurisdictions in the United States operate prison systems: Cook County (Chicago), Illinois; Philadelphia; New York City; and Washington, DC. It is estimated that there are 1,292 state, federal, and private confinement facilities: 102 federal and 1,190 state.[50] (Private confinement facilities operate under contract to state or federal correctional authorities and are included in those counts.)

Jurisdictions use a variety of capacity measures to reflect both the space available to house inmates and the ability to staff and operate an institution. Some use rated capacity (first introduced in Chapter 6), which is the number of beds or inmates a state official assigns to an institution. Some use **operational capacity,** the number of inmates that a facility's staff, existing programs, and services can accommodate. Others use **design capacity,** the number of inmates that planners or architects intend for the facility. For instance, an architect might design a prison for 1,100 inmates. Administrators might add more staff, programs, and services to be able to confine 1,300 in the same space. The design capacity was 1,100, but the operational and rated capacities are 1,300. The institution is operating 18 percent above design capacity.

operational capacity

The number of inmates that a facility's staff, existing programs, and services can accommodate.

design capacity

The number of inmates that planners or architects intend for the facility.

Overall, state prisons are operating between 46 percent below capacity (New Mexico) to 44 percent over capacity (Illinois) and the federal prison system is operating at 38 percent over capacity, leading U.S. Attorney General Eric Holder to argue that some prison terms are too long, especially the mandatory ones that federal and state governments require judges to impose for certain offenses. On Thursday, April 4, 2013, the Attorney General addressed the 15th annual National Action Network Convention and told the audience, "It is time to ask ourselves some fundamental questions about our criminal justice system. Statutes passed by legislatures that mandate sentences, irrespective of the unique facts of an individual case, too often bear no relation to the conduct at issue, breed disrespect for the system, and are ultimately counterproductive. It is time

EXHIBIT 7–7	Top Ten States With the Longest Prison Sentences

State	Average Time Served		Cost to State for Keeping Prisoners Longer	Quick Facts
	1990	2009		
1. Michigan	2.4 years	4.3 years	$471.9 million	$53,247 per prisoner per year kept 4.3 years instead of 2.4 years.
2. Pennsylvania	2.9 years	3.8 years	$316.6 million	Increase in time served a result of changes in how prisoners received parole. In 1994 required one out of five votes to grant parole. By 1996, changed to five out of nine.
3. New York	3.5 years	3.6 years	$65.6 million	$60,072 per prisoner per year kept 3.6 years instead of 3.5 years.
4. Virginia	1.7 years	3.3 years	$518.8 million	Second-highest percentage increase in the U.S.
5. Georgia	1.8 years	3.2 years	$536.1 million	$28,563 per prisoner per year kept 3.8 years instead of 1.8 years.
6. Arkansas	1.9 years	3.2 years	$305.1 million	Toughest sentences for drug offenders; average prisoner serves 3 years.
7. Oregon	2.4 years	3.2 years	$121.5 million	Lowest recidivism rate in U.S.—22 percent compared to 43 percent nationally.
8. Oklahoma	1.7 years	3.1 years	$203.9 million	$25,636 per prisoner per year kept 3.1 years instead of 1.7 years.
9. West Virginia	2.1 years	3.1 years	$74.8 million	$27,708 per prisoner per year kept 3.1 years instead of 2.1 years.
10. New Hampshire	2.4 years	3.1 years	$14.5 million	Tenth highest recidivism rate in the U.S. (44.2 percent).

Source: Adapted from Pew Center on the States, *Time Served: The High Cost, Low Return of Longer Prison Terms* (Washington, DC: The Pew Charitable Trusts, 2012).

to examine our systems and determine what truly works. We need to ensure that incarceration is used to punish, to rehabilitate, and to deter—and not simply to warehouse and forget."[51] See Exhibit 7–7 for the top 10 states with the longest prison sentences and some quick facts about each one of them. We return to the issue of prison capacity and overcrowding in Chapter 13.

State Prison Systems

Organization The administration of state prisons is a function of the executive branch of government. The governor appoints the director of corrections, who in turn appoints the wardens of the state prisons. A change in governors often means a change in state prison leadership and administration.

The organization of most state prison systems involves a central authority, based in the state capital. Local communities, private contractors, or the state itself may provide prison services (from treatment and education to maintenance and repair). This method of organizational structure and delivery of services across wide geographic areas is often criticized for its fragmentation; duplication of structure, effort, and services; lack of coordination; and ambiguous goals. Still, for legal control and for maintaining an equitable distribution of resources, a centralized model has been maintained while in other areas of corrections (e.g., community corrections and probation), services are often decentralized.

As we explained about the organization and administration of probation in Chapter 4, there is no correct way to organize corrections. Any arrangement that helps corrections reach its goals is appropriate. The organizational styles found across the United States developed over time and are the result of political interaction and accommodation among government agencies and interest groups.

Size and Costs State departments of corrections vary in size. The smallest is South Dakota's with more than 900 employees working in juvenile and adult institutions and community services and an annual operating budget of $108 million. The largest is California's with 66,800 authorized positions and an annual operating budget of $9.5 billion.[52]

An estimated 455,000 people work in adult correctional facilities: 66 percent are correctional officers; 12 percent are clerical, maintenance, and food service workers; 10 percent are professional/technical staff; 3 percent are educators; 2 percent are administrator; and 7 percent are other.[53] Male employees outnumber female employees by a ratio of 2 to 1. Nineteen percent of all correctional facility staff are black, and 7 percent are Hispanic. In the summer of 2010, a survey conducted by the American Correctional Association reported on correctional officer wages while in training, entry level after training, and after the first year of employment. The highest wages for training are $45,166 in Massachusetts, $40,000 in New Jersey, and $36,600 in California. For entry level after training, highest wages are $45,288 in California, $45,166 in Massachusetts, and $40,000 in New Jersey. After one year of employment, highest wages are $60,660 in California, $53,674 in New Jersey, and $48,653 in Massachusetts.[54]

Twenty years ago, the United States spent about $7 billion on corrections. Today our epidemic of incarceration costs taxpayers $63.4 *billion* a year.[55] Corrections is the fourth-largest category of states' spending following education, Medicaid, and transportation. The vast majority of funds that go to state corrections systems—9 of every 10 dollars—goes to prisons.[56] Some ask if the money spent on state corrections encroaches on funds for higher education because the money has to come from somewhere. Is there discussion about this kind of trade-off? Jennifer Gonnerman, a reporter for the *Village Voice,* writes, "When parents get a tuition bill for their kids' college education, I always think they should get a little note that says tuition went up $200 last year because we decided to build two new prisons. Then we can all decide whether we think that's a good use of our money or not."[57] Others have said, "Every additional dollar spent on prisons, of course is one dollar less that can go to preparing for the next Hurricane Katrina, educating young people, providing health care to the elderly, or repairing roads and bridges."[58] Exhibit 7–8 shows the ratio of corrections to higher education spending in 2007. Vermont, Michigan, Oregon, Connecticut, and Delaware spend as much money or more on corrections as they do on higher education.

States spend, on average, approximately $27,180 a year to incarcerate one offender.[59] "In states like Connecticut, Maine, Massachusetts, and Rhode Island, it's anywhere from $46,000 to $51,000."[60] And depending on the prison security level, the capital costs of building one prison cell can be as much as $100,000.[61] States with the highest and lowest reported average annual operating costs per inmate are shown in Exhibit 7–9.

However, amounts that states are spending today on corrections have been significantly reduced. A combination of falling crime rates; a policy

Visit http://www.cbsnews.com/8301-3445_162-57418495/the-cost-of-a-nation-of-incarceration/ or scan this code with the QR app on your smartphone or digital device and watch the CBS NEWS Sunday Morning podcast detailing cost and other problems with the U.S. epidemic of incarceration. How does this information relate to ideas discussed in this chapter?

EXHIBIT 7–8   Ratio of Corrections Spending to Higher Education Spending, 2007

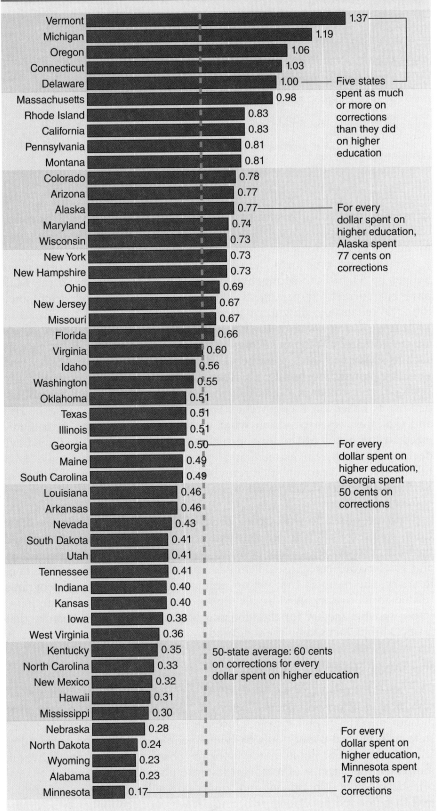

Vermont	1.37
Michigan	1.19
Oregon	1.06
Connecticut	1.03
Delaware	1.00
Massachusetts	0.98
Rhode Island	0.83
California	0.83
Pennsylvania	0.81
Montana	0.81
Colorado	0.78
Arizona	0.77
Alaska	0.77
Maryland	0.74
Wisconsin	0.73
New York	0.73
New Hampshire	0.73
Ohio	0.69
New Jersey	0.67
Missouri	0.67
Florida	0.66
Virginia	0.60
Idaho	0.56
Washington	0.55
Oklahoma	0.51
Texas	0.51
Illinois	0.51
Georgia	0.50
Maine	0.49
South Carolina	0.49
Louisiana	0.46
Arkansas	0.46
Nevada	0.43
South Dakota	0.41
Utah	0.41
Tennessee	0.41
Indiana	0.40
Kansas	0.40
Iowa	0.38
West Virginia	0.36
Kentucky	0.35
North Carolina	0.33
New Mexico	0.32
Hawaii	0.31
Mississippi	0.30
Nebraska	0.28
North Dakota	0.24
Wyoming	0.23
Alabama	0.23
Minnesota	0.17

Five states spent as much or more on corrections than they did on higher education

For every dollar spent on higher education, Alaska spent 77 cents on corrections

For every dollar spent on higher education, Georgia spent 50 cents on corrections

50-state average: 60 cents on corrections for every dollar spent on higher education

For every dollar spent on higher education, Minnesota spent 17 cents on corrections

Source: Jennifer Warren, *One in 100: Behind Bars in America 2008*. Published by The Pew Charitable Trusts, 2009. Reprinted with permission of The Pew Charitable Trusts.

EXHIBIT 7–9	States with the Highest and Lowest Reported Average Annual Operating Costs per Inmate		
Highest		**Lowest**	
Massachusetts	$51,277	Alabama	$14,111
Maine	$48,005	Kentucky	$14,364
Connecticut	$45,662	Texas	$15,012
Rhode Island	$45,477	Louisiana	$15,487
Oregon	$40,690	South Dakota	$16,895

Source: Vera Institute of Justice, *The Potential of Community Corrections to Improve Safety and Reduce Incarceration* (New York: Vera Institute of Justice, July 2013).

shift from lock-'em-up justice to rehabilitation and community sanctions for nonviolent, nonserious, and nonsex offenders; and a dwindling appetite for hefty prison budgets has lowered the number of people behind bars.

For the first time in a decade, California may cut its corrections budget by $1 billion. More than two-thirds of the states and the BOP have cut corrections personnel, salaries, benefits, and overtime since the 2007 economic downturn began.[62] In 2011 and 2012, this led to 17 states closing some of their prisons and investing a portion of the estimated $337 million in savings in infrastructure and civic institutions such as substance abuse treatment, housing, education, and jobs located in high-risk neighborhoods, a practice known as **justice reinvestment**.[63] Justice reinvestment is a data-driven approach that ensures that policymaking is based on a comprehensive analysis of criminal justice data and the latest research about what works to reduce crime, and is tailored to the needs of the local jurisdiction. Since 2007, 17 states have developed justice reinvestment strategies and are projected to save $3.3 billion over 10 years. Justice reinvestment in Texas alone resulted in $1.5 billion in construction savings and $340 million in averted annual construction costs.[64]

What do states do with closed prisons? New York Governor Andrew Cuomo closed 7 of its 67 prisons and proposed using some of the closed facilities for new retail development, wildlife sanctuary, manufacturing, and solar power enterprises. Pennsylvania repurposed Eastern State Penitentiary, the nation's first prison, into a museum that offers programs related to its history. And Texas repurposed the old Central State Farm into a satellite facility for the Houston Museum of Natural History that hosts exhibits focused on the surrounding county's ecosystems.

justice reinvestment

The practice of reducing spending on prisons and investing a portion of the savings into infrastructure and civic institutions located in high-risk neighborhoods.

Federal Bureau of Prisons

The federal Bureau of Prisons (BOP) is an entirely separate system from state and local prison systems. Before the 1890s, the federal government did not operate its own prisons. Instead, the Department of Justice paid state prisons and county jails to house people convicted of committing federal crimes. The public outcry over the convict lease system, however, motivated the passage of a federal law prohibiting the leasing of federal offenders. Many state prisons and county jails subsequently became reluctant to house federal offenders because it was not economically advantageous to incarcerate inmates they could not lease. Moreover, the expansion of federal law enforcement activities and the enactment of new federal laws in the late 19th century led to an increase in the prosecution of federal lawbreakers and to overcrowding in the prisons where they were held. With a growing population of federal prisoners and the growing reluctance of nonfederal prisons to house them, the federal government had no choice but to build prisons of its own. Congress authorized the establishment of three federal penitentiaries in 1891: at Atlanta (Georgia), Leavenworth (Kansas), and McNeil Island (Washington). The BOP was formally established in 1930. Today the BOP houses over 216,000 inmates in 117 federal institutions, 15 privately managed prisons, 185 residential reentry centers, and home detention.

The BOP employs more than 38,000 people nationwide. Twenty-seven percent of the BOP workforce is female and one-third is minority. Thirty percent of BOP personnel have completed some college. Another 30 percent have a bachelor's degree or further education.

The starting salary of a federal correctional officer is approximately $30,000. Starting federal salaries are slightly higher in areas where prevailing local pay levels are higher. Other employment opportunities with the BOP include accountant, attorney, chaplain, clinical psychologist, contract specialist, correctional treatment specialist, dental hygienist, dentist, drug treatment specialist, employee services specialist, health system administrator, information technology specialist, legal instruments examiner, medical records technician, physician, recreation specialist, registered nurse, nurse practitioner, pharmacist, physical therapist, physician assistant, safety specialist, secretary, teacher, and training instructor. Consult the Appendix: Careers in Corrections at the Online Learning Center Web site for the steps involved in career planning, developing employability and job readiness, and finding the right job. Exhibit 7–10 shows the mission statement of the BOP.

The President's 2013 budget request for the BOP totals $6.9 billion which accounts for over 25 percent of the entire Department of Justice (DOJ) budget.[65] If present trends continue, the share of the DOJ budget consumed by the BOP will approach 30 percent in 2020.

The largest portion of the BOP budget is for institution security and administration, including the costs of facility maintenance, motor pool operations, and other administrative functions. The second highest cost is for inmate care and programs. This includes the cost of all food, medical supplies, clothing, welfare services, transportation, staff salaries, academic courses, social and occupational education courses, religious programs, psychological services, and drug abuse treatment.

Bureau of Prisons Thirty years ago, the number of inmates under BOP jurisdiction was 25,000. Today the number stands at 217,815.[66]

Changes in federal sentencing and correctional policy since the early 1980s have contributed to the rapid growth in the federal prison population. These changes include increasing the number of federal offenses

---

EXHIBIT 7–10	**Federal Bureau of Prisons' Mission Statement**

It is the mission of the Federal Bureau of Prisons to protect society by confining offenders in the controlled environments of prison and community-based facilities that are safe, humane, and appropriately secure and that provide work and other self-improvement opportunities to assist offenders in becoming law-abiding citizens.

Source: Federal Bureau of Prisons, July 1998.

Deborah B. Brown

Circuit Administrator—Circuit 1
Florida Department of Corrections

Deborah B. Brown is the circuit administrator for Circuit 1 of the Florida Department of Corrections composed of Escambia, Santa Rosa, Okaloosa, and Walton counties. She oversees the operations of seven field offices with a total of 131 staff members. Since 1980, she has been an employee of the Department of Corrections. She began her career as a correctional probation officer in Jacksonville and has held supervisory and management positions in Tallahassee, Lake City, and Pensacola. She relocated to Pensacola in 2003 as the deputy circuit administrator and has been the circuit administrator since 2004. Brown is affiliated with various colleges as the internship coordinator for her circuit.

Brown attended the University of Alabama and was selected to attend the Correctional Leadership Conference in Longmont, Colorado. She obtained her Supervisory Certificate in the Certified Public Managers (CPM) program from Florida State University.

Brown has excellent interpersonal skills, which she has used in coordinating various programs in all of the circuits for which she has worked. She is a strong advocate for continued learning and achievement and inspires others to reach their highest potential. Her goal is to involve herself in areas where she can be most effective in assisting others to establish proactive implementations in their lives to obtain positive results.

Various community entities of which Brown is a member have recognized her partnership, participation, and leadership within her community. She steadfastly volunteers and mentors in the public school system wherever she resides. Students who are considering pursuing a career in corrections should complete an internship with a corrections agency, become a volunteer, and advocate for offenders.

> *"My advice to students interested in a career in corrections is to internship with a corrections agency, become a volunteer, and advocate for offenders."*

subject to mandatory minimum sentences, changes to the federal criminal code that have made more crimes federal offenses (We discuss the movement to abolish parole in Chapter 8.)

While the number of state inmates has decreased, the federal prison population has continued to increase causing serious overcrowding. For more than a decade, the BOP has been operating at 30 percent or more over rated capacity, and the problem is worse in high- and medium-security facilities. Today, overcrowding averages 38 percent across all BOP facilities, 47 percent in medium-security facilities, and 51 percent in high-security prisons.[67] The negative consequences of overcrowding include:

- increases in serious assaults (16 per 5,000 inmates in 2009, the most recent year data are available)
- triple and sometimes quadruple bunking
- crowded bathroom facilities
- reduced shower times
- shortened and/or staggered meal times
- longer waits for food service
- limited recreational activities
- a decrease in program opportunities which, if an inmate has access to and completes, allows them to earn the maximum amount of good time credit in order to reduce their sentences
- increases in inmate idleness

- waiting lists for rehabilitative services such as education, vocational training, substance abuse treatment, faith-based reentry programs
- visitor accommodations
- and fewer opportunities for an inmate to work in a FPI factory

Overcrowding also taxes the infrastructure that was designed for a smaller inmate population, affecting use of toilets, showers, water, electricity, wear and tear on food service equipment, general usage and upkeep of a facility, all of which affects the facility itself, the environment, and the local community.

Data show that a growing proportion of federal inmates are incarcerated for immigration- and weapons-related offenses, but the largest portion of newly admitted inmates are incarcerated for drug offenses.[72] The vast majority of drug offenders (more than 95 percent) were sent to federal prison for trafficking offenses (trafficking offenses include an offense where an offender knowingly and intentionally imported, exported, manufactured, distributed, dispensed, sold, possessed, or had intent to traffic any controlled substance listed in the U.S. criminal code). More than a quarter of the federal prison population are noncitizens imprisoned for immigration crimes (crimes committed by illegal immigrants) because some countries such as Cuba and Vietnam refuse to take back their convicted citizens, leaving the BOP to hold the foreigners indefinitely.

The cost of incarceration in the federal prison system also varies by security level. Across all security levels, the average is $29,027. By security levels, the average costs are as follows:[69]

High security	$34,046
Medium security	$26,686
Low security	$27,166
Minimum security	$21,694

In January 2013, the Congressional Research Service prepared a report for Members and Committees of Congress. That report recommended that Congress revise some of its policies that were adopted over the past three decades that have contributed to the steadily increasing number of offenders being incarcerated. Specifically, it advocated modifying mandatory minimum penalties, expanding the use of residential reentry centers, placing more offenders on probation, reinstating parole for federal inmates, expanding the amount of good time credit an inmate can earn, and repealing federal criminal statutes for some offenses.[70]

Prison Security Levels

Prisons are classified by the level of security they provide. Most jurisdictions use maximum-, medium-, and minimum-security classifications. A **maximum- or close/high-security prison** is designed, organized, and staffed to confine the most violent and dangerous offenders for long periods. It imposes strict controls on the movement of inmates and their visitors, and custody and security are constant concerns. The prison has a highly secure perimeter with watchtowers and high walls. Inmates live in single- or multiple-occupancy barred cells. The staff-to-inmate ratio is high, routines are highly regimented, and prisoner counts are frequent. Programs, amenities, and privileges are few. The cost to incarcerate an inmate in maximum-security prison averages more than $34,000 per year.[71]

Inmates in a **medium-security prison** are considered less dangerous than those in maximum-security prisons and may serve short or long sentences.

maximum- or close/high-security prison

A prison designed, organized, and staffed to confine the most dangerous offenders for long periods. It has a highly secure perimeter, barred cells, and a high staff-to-inmate ratio. It imposes strict controls on the movement of inmates and visitors, and it offers few programs, amenities, or privileges.

medium-security prison

A prison that confines offenders considered less dangerous than those in maximum security, for both short and long periods. It places fewer controls on inmates' and visitors' freedom of movement than does a maximum-security facility. It, too, has barred cells and a fortified perimeter. The staff-to-inmate ratio is generally lower than that in a maximum-security facility, and the level of amenities and privileges is slightly higher.

Maximum-security prisons confine the most violent and dangerous offenders for long periods. They are surrounded by high walls and gun towers. On average, how much does it cost to incarcerate one offender per year in a maximum-security prison?

Medium-security prisons impose fewer controls on inmates' and visitors' freedom of movement than do maximum-security facilities. Outwardly, medium-security prisons often resemble maximum-security institutions, and they, too, have barred cells. The staff-to-inmate ratio is generally lower than in a maximum-security facility. Medium-security prisons place more emphasis on treatment and work programs than do maximum-security prisons, and the level of amenities and privileges is slightly higher. The cost to incarcerate an inmate in medium-security averages more than $26,000 per year.

A **minimum-security prison** confines the least dangerous offenders for both short and long periods. It allows as much freedom of movement and as many privileges and amenities as are consistent with the facility's goals while following procedures to avoid escape, violence, and disturbance. The staff-to-inmate ratio is low, and inmates live in dormitory housing or private rooms. Some leave the institution for programming in the community.

minimum-security prison

A prison that confines the least dangerous offenders for both short and long periods. It allows as much freedom of movement and as many privileges and amenities as are consistent with the goals of the facility. It may have dormitory housing, and the staff-to-inmate ratio is relatively low.

Medium-security prisons incarcerate less dangerous inmates than maximum-security prisons. They impose fewer controls on inmates' freedom of movement and place more emphasis on treatment and work programs. On average, how much does it cost to incarcerate one offender per year in a medium-security prison?

These institutions are sometimes referred to as **open institutions** because no fences or walls surround them. The cost to incarcerate an inmate in minimum-security averages approximately $22,000 per year.

open institution

A minimum-security facility that has no fences or walls surrounding it.

DOES INCARCERATION WORK?

CO7-9

In June 2002, the Bureau of Justice Statistics reported on the recidivism of 272,111 prisoners discharged from 15 states and tracked for three years after their release in 1994.[72] Overall, 68 percent were rearrested within three years, and a little more than half were back in prison for committing a new crime or for violating the rules of their supervision.

In April 2011, the Pew Center on the States reported on the results of its survey that asked all states to report their three-year return-to-prison rates for all inmates released in 1999 and 2004. The survey addressed the issue of whether incarceration works. The results indicated that 45 percent of people released in 1999 and 43 percent of those sent home in 2004 were reincarcerated within three years for either committing a new crime or violating conditions governing their release. Exhibit 7–11 compares the BJS and Pew data on recidivism.

Recidivism rates between 1994 and 2007 have consistently remained around 40 percent, suggesting that despite the massive increase in corrections spending, the system has had little success in preventing recidivism. According to the Pew Center, "If more than four out of 10 adult American offenders still return to prison within three years of their release, the system designed to deter them from continued criminal behavior clearly is falling short. That is an unhappy reality, not just for offenders, but for the safety of American communities."[73]

After reading statistics like these, you might wonder whether incarceration works. The answer depends on whom you ask and how he or she interprets the question. What does "work" mean? Does it refer to the prevention of rearrest, reconviction, or reincarceration? Should a new offense be related to previous ones? What if a new offense occurs 5 or 10 years after release from prison? Should the prison experience deter potential *and* actual offenders? Should it lower the crime rate? If so, by how much,

EXHIBIT 7–11	State Prison Recidivism Rates, 1999–2002 and 2004–2007	
State	**1999–2002 Recidivism**	**2004–2007 Recidivism**
Alabama	36%	35%
Alaska	N/A	N/A
Arizona	40	39
Arkansas	49	44
California	61	58
Colorado	N/A	N/A
Connecticut	46	44
Delaware	N/A	N/A
Florida	N/A	N/A
Georgia	38	35
Hawaii	N/A	N/A
Idaho	33	34
Illinois	52	52
Indiana	N/A	38
Iowa	32	34
Kansas	55	43
Kentucky	39	41
Louisiana	44	39
Maine	N/A	N/A
Maryland	N/A	N/A
Massachusetts	38	42
Michigan	38	31
Minnesota	55	61
Mississippi	27	33
Missouri	49	54
Montana	42	42
Nebraska	29	32
Nevada	N/A	N/A
New Hampshire	N/A	N/A
New Jersey	48	43
New Mexico	N/A	44
New York	40	40
North Carolina	44	41
North Dakota	N/A	40
Ohio	39	40
Oklahoma	24	26
Oregon	33	23
Pennsylvania	37	40
Rhode Island	N/A	31
South Carolina	27	32
South Dakota	34	46
Tennessee	N/A	N/A
Texas	32	32
Utah	66	54
Vermont	N/A	N/A
Virginia	29	28
Washington	33	43
West Virginia	N/A	27
Wisconsin	46	46
Wyoming	N/A	25
TOTAL	45	43

Source: Adapted from Pew Center on the States, *State of Recidivism: The Revolving Door of America's Prisons* (Washington, DC: The Pew Charitable Trusts, 2011), pp. 10–11.

how fast, and at what cost? What about criminological theories that link crime to forces outside the individual and over which the offender has little or no control such as his or her biological or psychological makeup, social structures, and even the more radical explanations that link crime to economic development, race, class, and gender? Politicians and researchers see the question differently. Governors and directors of corrections see the question straightforwardly: Were it not for prison, there would be more crime. Removing convicted offenders from the community ensures public safety, and the cost of incarceration is the price tag for ensuring that safety.

Researchers feel the effectiveness question can be answered only with randomly designed experiments in which identically matched offenders are randomly assigned to prison or to other punishments. Even if such experiments were possible, there are differences between prisoners and people not sent to prison, and these differences will influence future offending.

The common expectation is that crime rates will decline as the number of persons incarcerated increases and that crime will increase if incarceration rates fall. If you look at the relationship between the crime index and the prison population over the past 10 years, you might reach the conclusion that as the nation's prison population grew, crime fell and, therefore, the experiment in locking up more people lowered the nation's volume of crime. For example, David Muhlhausen, a policy analyst at the Heritage Foundation, argues that increasing incarceration decreases crime. "Considering that there are still about 12 million crimes a year," Muhlhausen concludes, then "maybe we're not incarcerating enough people."[74] Unfortunately, if you look at the past quarter century of prison buildup, you find that as the prison population increased, crime increased, decreased, increased, and decreased. There is simply no strong or consistent relationship between incarceration rate and crime rate.[75] Bruce Western of Harvard University estimated that only 10 percent of the decline in crime in recent years was due to increased incarceration. The rest resulted from other factors, including the ebbing of the crack cocaine epidemic, changes in policing strategies, changes in policy and practice such as treatment diversion programs, sentence reduction incentives for participation in prison programming, enhanced reentry support, reduced technical violation of parole, and the strong economy of the 1990s.[76]

University of Maryland criminologist Dr. Doris MacKenzie answers the question "Does incarceration work?" this way:

> In summary, there is evidence that incapacitation has the potential for reducing crime in the community. The difficulty lies in determining the amount of crime prevented and how much should be considered a large reduction in crime. Questions also revolve around the costs of such policies in terms of money and impact on future generations in inner cities.[77]

Questions such as whether one can determine the amount of crime prevented through incarceration; whether that reduction is large enough; whether the amount spent on that reduction is worth it; and whether the impact of incarceration on families and communities left behind is acceptable, speak to the importance of justice reinvestment to project the consequences of incarceration. Until then, there is no indication that we have come any closer in reaching consensus on the question of whether incarceration works.

Visit http://www.doc.ri.gov/documents/ reentry/Pew_Reducing_Recidivism.pdf or scan this code with the QR app on your smartphone or digital device and read what five state corrections directors say about their strategies for reducing recidivism and the barriers that complicate the job. How does this information relate to ideas discussed in this chapter?

REVIEW AND APPLICATIONS

SUMMARY

1 The Pennsylvania and Auburn prison systems emerged in the United States at the turn of the 19th century. The Pennsylvania system isolated prisoners from each other to avoid harmful influences and to give prisoners reflection time so they might repent. The Auburn system allowed inmates to work together during the day under strict silence. At night, however, prisoners were isolated in small sleeping cells. With time, sleeping cells became congregate and restrictions against talking were removed.

2 There have been nine eras in U.S. prison history:

- Penitentiary era (1790–1825)
- Mass prison era (1825–1876)
- Reformatory era (1876–1890)
- Industrial era (1890–1935)
- Punitive era (1935–1945)
- Treatment era (1945–1967)
- Community-based era (1967–1980)
- Warehousing era (1980–1995)
- Just deserts era (1985–present)

3 At yearend 2012, 1,353,198 people were under the jurisdiction of state correctional authorities, and 217,815 people were under the jurisdiction of the federal prison system. Of these state and federal inmates, 7 percent were female, 35 percent were white, 38 percent were black, and 21 percent were Hispanic. Reasons for the increase in women prisoners include women's presence in the U.S. labor market, which has brought about increased opportunities for crime; the increased poverty of young, female, single heads of households, which means that more women are turning to crime to support themselves and their families; changes in the criminal justice system, which no longer affords women differential treatment; and the combined effects of harsh drug laws, changing patterns of drug use, and mandatory sentencing policies. Reasons for the increase in minority prisoners include an increase in serious criminal activity that results in incarceration; racial profiling and racism by the criminal justice system; and the prevalence of social conditions that exist in the nation's inner cities, which is where most minorities in the United States regardless of race live, and the fact that large urban areas have the highest violence rates.

4 Classification is the principal management tool for allocating scarce prison resources efficiently and minimizing the potential for escape or violence. The purpose is to assign inmates to appropriate prison housing and to help staff understand, treat, predict, and manage prisoner behavior. There are two types of classification, external and internal. External classification determines an inmate's security level (maximum, close, medium, minimum, or community). Internal classification determines an inmate's assignment to housing units or cellblocks, work, and programming based on the inmate's risk, needs, and time to serve.

5 Today, state and federal prison systems are operating or developing faith-based and veterans-only housing units. Supporters of faith-based initiatives argue that such programs may reduce recidivism and improve other postrelease outcomes; are generally free or low cost because they are provided by volunteer groups; may improve in-prison behavior; lessen the dehumanization of incarceration; and are unlikely to harm anyone. Opponents argue that faith-based programs may not be effective; may actually cost taxpayers; promote a religious orientation and hence could be unconstitutional; may lessen offender accountability for their crimes; and may coerce some inmates into certain kinds of religious activity. Veterans-only facilities house and assist the growing number of war veterans who are incarcerated to address post-traumatic stress disorder, addiction, depression, and other common issues that may have influenced their offending behavior. To date, veterans-only and faith-based housing units are not evidence-based.

6 The evidence-based literature on prison industries shows that the average prison industry program reduces the recidivism rate of participants by almost 6 percent.

7 Among federal and state inmates, about 37 percent do not have a high school diploma or a GED compared to 19 percent of the general population. Only 283,000 inmates participate in educational programs. Evidence-based literature shows that corrections-based educational programs are effective in reducing crime. Specifics about the nature and extent of recreation programming in prison and inmates' participation in them is not known, but recreation and organized sports can make doing time easier, be used as an incentive, reduce tension, promote health, prevent disease, and reduce prison health care costs. In 1976, the U.S. Supreme Court ruled in *Estelle* v. *Gamble* that inmates have a constitutional right to reasonable, adequate health care for serious medical needs. However, the Court also made clear that such a right did not mean that prisoners have unqualified access to health care.

8 All 50 states, the Federal Bureau of Prisons (BOP), and four local jurisdictions operate correctional institutions. State prison administration, a function of the executive branch of government, is most often organized around a central authority operating from the state capital. There are three levels of state prison security: maximum, for the most dangerous offenders serving long sentences; medium, for less dangerous offenders serving long or short sentences; and minimum, for the least dangerous offenders.

9 Whether incarceration works depends on whom you ask and how he or she interprets the question. Politicians and researchers see the question differently. Governors and directors of corrections see the question straightforwardly: Were it not for prison, there would be more crime. Researchers feel the question can be answered only with randomly designed experiments. There is no indication that we have come any closer to reaching consensus on the question of whether incarceration works.

KEY TERMS

penitentiary, p. 210
Pennsylvania system, p. 210
Auburn system, p. 210
public accounts system, p. 214
contract system, p. 214
convict lease system, p. 214
state use system, p. 215
public works system, p. 215

medical model, p. 216
classification, p. 225
external classification, p. 226
internal classification, p. 227
unit management system, p. 230
Federal Prison Industries (FPI), p. 236
UNICOR, p. 236
principle of least eligibility, p. 242

operational capacity, p. 242
design capacity, p. 242
justice reinvestment, p. 246
maximum- or close/high-security prison, p. 249
medium-security prison, p. 249
minimum-security prison, p. 250
open institution, p. 251

QUESTIONS FOR REVIEW

1 Explain the differences between the Pennsylvania and Auburn prison systems.

2 Summarize the eras of prison development.

3 What can you infer from the characteristics of today's prisoners and the reasons for the incarceration of women and minority inmates?

4 Are there criteria you would add to prisoner classification schemes?

5 Summarize the literature and the issues on the program effectiveness of faith-based institutions.

6 Discuss the impact of the evidence-based literature on prison industries.

7 What ideas can you add to the reasons for including education, recreation, and health care programs for prisoners?

8 Evaluate the strengths and limitations of the various ways prisons are organized and administered.

9 What ideas can you add to the question "Does incarceration work?"

THINKING CRITICALLY ABOUT CORRECTIONS

What Does Incarceration Costs Taxpayers?

In August 2011, the Vera Institute of Justice distributed a survey to the department of corrections in every state to collect the information necessary to calculate the total cost of prisons in fiscal year 2010: direct department expenditures and associated costs paid by budgets other than that of the department. Corrections departments from 40 states completed and returned the survey.

Download the document The Price of Prisons: What Incarceration Costs Taxpayers at vera.org/priceofprisons and examine the prison-related costs paid by budgets other than that of the department. How might those outside costs be spent elsewhere if nonviolent, nonserious, and nonsex offenders were given less expensive intermediate sanctions such as those discussed in Chapter 5 and currently used in California's realignment program?

Does Incarceration Work?

This chapter concludes with the statement, "Thus, there is no indication that we have come any closer in reaching consensus on the question of whether incarceration works." After more than 200 years of prison history, what is it about the question "Does incarceration work?" that makes it so difficult to reach consensus? Do you think there's a model muddle in corrections, meaning that adult prisons set more goals than their resources can accomplish? Do you see areas where the goals of adult prisons conflict with one another and thus make it difficult to answer the question "Does incarceration work?" If you had the ability to remove the confusion, what goal(s) would you set for adult prisons and which measures of effectiveness would you employ?

ON-THE-JOB DECISION MAKING

High-Tech Recruiting

Imagine that you are the recruiting manager for your state's department of corrections. You know that recruiting for corrections has never been easy, but you are very tech savvy and excited to unveil your department's new and cutting-edge recruitment strategy. Forget the pen and paper—you now have keyboards and Web sites, search engines and aggregators, tweets, friending, and fan pages. How will you update your department's image? What kind of "branding" will you use that focuses on your state's unique opportunities? What will your "splash" page look like? What digital, online, print, out-of-home (posters, postcards, radio, TV), and internal (employee referral program, new hire surveys, climate surveys, and exit interview) strategies will you use? How can you use Google's Adwords? What about banner ads and where? What about aggregators such as Indeed.com and SimplyHired.com? What about a fan page on Facebook? What about a careers page on Twitter to tweet about upcoming testing dates, new job openings, and other important events? And what about a channel on YouTube? What will you expect to get out of this, and how will you know you have achieved it?

Advancing Prison Education Programming

As the newly appointed director of prison education programming, you remember two things from your undergraduate corrections course: first, few inmates participate in prison education programs; second, while literacy alone will not prevent crime, it is one of the many skills needed to function well as a responsible and law-abiding adult in our society.

Your warden would like to create a model prison education program and asks you (1) what can be done with little or no budget increase to encourage more inmates to participate in prison education and (2) how will you know whether your strategies have been effective? What will you tell the warden?

For additional information, please see: www.mhhe.com/schmalleger7e
Follow the author's tweets about the latest crime and justice news @schmalleger

PAROLE

Early Release and Reentry

[8]

CHAPTER OBJECTIVES

After completing this chapter you should be able to do the following:

1. Present a brief history of American parole development.

2. Understand the function of parole in the criminal justice system.

3. Define *parole* and explain the parole decision-making process.

4. Describe the characteristics of the parole population.

5. Explain what works in parole supervision.

6. Summarize current issues in parole.

> *We must create a pathway for people coming out of prison to get the jobs, skills, and education they need to leave a life of crime. That means supporting effective training and mentoring programs to help people transition into jobs. That means reevaluating the laws against hiring people with a criminal record so that we don't foreclose legal and effective ways out of poverty and crime. That also means giving former prisoners parenting skills so they can give their children the sense of hope and opportunity that so many of them were denied.*
>
> —President Barack Obama

Offender reentry is a "hot-button" topic around the world. Recently Singapore, an island country off the southern tip of the Malay Peninsula, announced a new plan to help offenders stay crime free after release from prison.[1]

Singapore is composed of 63 islands and is the world's fourth leading financial center. Of its almost 5.4 million population, 12,504 adults were under the jurisdiction of the Singapore Prison Service at yearend 2012. The rate of incarceration then was 230 per 100,000 adult population, and the return rate to prison was 27 percent.

Minnesota is one U.S. state that has similar statistics: a population of 5.4 million, almost 10,000 adults in prison, and an incarceration rate of 183 per 100,000 adult population. However, as was shown in the previous chapter's Exhibit 7-11, Minnesota's return to prison rate averages 58 percent.

Known as the Mandatory Aftercare Scheme (MAS), Singapore's reentry program targets offenders assessed to be at high risk of reoffending. Almost one-half of Singapore's prison population has been incarcerated five times or more. Teo Chee Hean, Singapore's deputy prime minister said, "Given that multiple repeat offenders now form the majority of the prison population, more focus needs to be provided in the period after their release when they are most vulnerable. This [MAS] will help these ex-inmates break the cycle of reoffending and transit from imprisonment to reintegration within the community."

MAS consists of three phases: the halfway house, the home detention phase, and the community reintegration phase. Prisoners in Singapore are released after serving two-thirds of their prison sentence as long as their prison behavior was positive, even if they are assessed to be a threat to society.

Ten months before they are released offenders participate in pre-MAS planning where authorities perform a risk and needs assessment. For those with families, pre-MAS planning involves the family.

When offenders are released from prison they will be sent to a halfway house where they will participate in counseling, employment skills training, and either seek employment or enroll in vocational training. Offenders in this phase will also wear an electronic monitor.

In the home detention phase offenders will be required to observe daily curfews, continue electronic monitoring, be subject to urine testing, and maintain either their employment or vocational training.

In the final community reintegration phase, the curfew is removed but the other conditions may continue.

The Singapore Prison Service announced plans to implement a reentry program to help offenders stay crime-free. Called the Mandatory Aftercare Scheme, the program took effect in April 2013. Prisoners will prepare for the program 10 months before their release from prison and continue through three postrelease phases: the halfway house phase, the home detention phase, and the community reintegration phase. According to officials, why is the program needed, and what is involved in each of the three phases?

The Singapore government is also reviewing its policy on awarding inmates good time, a practice they call remission (the number of days or months authorities deduct from a sentence for good behavior and for other reasons). Currently, most inmates are granted one-third remission of their prison sentences without any conditions imposed on them after release. Authorities are studying remission practices in other countries before deciding what is suitable for Singapore.

Although it was once politically taboo to speak of providing resources for prisoners, these startling statistics have brought many lawmakers across the world, both liberal and conservative, to the same conclusion: The nation's correctional system is correcting very little. That reality has sparked a movement to improve prisoner "reentry," a buzzword that's on the lips of politicians everywhere.

Visit http://www.youtube.com/watch?v=vGYDE8IV-c8 or scan this code with the QR app on your smartphone or digital device and watch the podcast of Singapore's Mandatory Aftercare Scheme explained by Deputy Prime Minister Teo Chee Hean. How does this information relate to ideas discussed in this chapter?

PAROLE AS PART OF THE CRIMINAL JUSTICE SYSTEM

Parole is the conditional release of a prisoner prior to completion of the imposed sentence under the supervision of a parole officer (responsibility for offenders' passes from the courts to the corrections system upon imprisonment). Parole is usually granted by authorities in the correctional system.

Release on parole may be mandatory or discretionary. **Discretionary release** is at the paroling authority's discretion within boundaries established by the sentence and the law. **Mandatory release** is early release after a specific period of time as specified by law. In those states that permit discretionary release, state laws give correctional officials the authority to change, within certain limits, the *length* of a sentence. Correctional officials may also change the *conditions* under which convicted offenders are supervised—for example, they may release offenders from prison to supervision in the community or to an outside facility. The American Probation and Parole Association (APPA), the nation's largest association of probation and parole professionals, supports discretionary parole (see Exhibit 8–1).

parole
The conditional release of a prisoner, prior to completion of the imposed sentence, under the supervision of a parole officer.

discretionary release
Early release based on the paroling authority's assessment of eligibility.

mandatory release
Early release after a time period specified by law.

Historical Overview

CO8-1

The parole concept has its roots in an 18th-century English penal practice—indentured servitude. Judges transferred custody of physically fit condemned felons to independent contractors, paying those contractors a fee to transport the prisoners to the American colonies and sell their services for the duration of their sentences to the highest bidder. This practice was similar to today's parole in that the indentured servant had to comply with certain conditions to remain in supervised "freedom." This practice was discontinued with the beginning of the American Revolutionary War in 1775 because English offenders were joining colonial forces against England.

EXHIBIT 8–I American Probation and Parole Association

Policy Statement on Discretionary Parole

Definition

Parole can refer to both a guidelines process and a discretionary decision. Both of these methods of parole have merit. This position statement addresses only discretionary parole. Discretionary parole is a decision to release an offender from incarceration whose sentence has not expired, on condition of sustained lawful behavior that is subject to supervision and monitoring in the community by parole personnel who ensure compliance with the terms of release.

APPA Position

The American Probation and Parole Association supports discretionary parole as an integral and important part of a criminal justice system that is committed to public safety, victim and community restoration and the reintegration of offenders as law-abiding and productive citizens.

Discretionary parole decisions are based on a number of factors that weigh the need for punishment, successful community reintegration and victim and community restoration. These factors include the nature of the crime; the offender's criminal history, behavior in prison, social background and risk posed to the community; and information from crime victims and affected communities. Discretionary parole decisions enhance public safety by working to keep dangerous offenders incarcerated and that other offenders carefully selected for release receive the necessary structure and assistance to become law-abiding citizens in the community in which they reside.

Discussion

Parole is rooted in the fundamental belief that offenders can be motivated to make positive changes in their lives. Offenders are more likely to cooperate with correctional authorities if release is conditioned on good behavior, and after release the likelihood of their becoming law abiding is increased when offered assistance. The result is enhanced public safety.

Discretion is inherent at every level of the criminal justice system. Police exercise discretion when determining whom to arrest and charge. The court system uses discretion to decide whom to indict, whom to release pre-trial, whether to go to trial, and what criminal penalties to recommend. Judges use their discretion to determine the appropriate level of punishment given the circumstances of the crime and the offender's criminal history. They may sentence one offender to probation and another to prison for the same offense.

Parole boards closely examine and consider each offender's entire record, recognizing that correctional authorities can better manage inmates who have an incentive to follow institutional rules. The possibility of parole also provides inmates with an incentive to participate in programs that build competency skills. Parole boards know that the great majority of offenders sent to prison will eventually be released.

Parole boards are in a unique position to listen to and address the needs and concerns of crime victims and communities. Parole board control over offenders and communication with victims provides the framework for victim assistance and community restoration from the damage of crime.

During periods when there are an inadequate number of correctional beds, parole boards apply a rational process, targeting for release those inmates who pose the least risk to community safety. Parole boards are the only component of the criminal justice system that can weigh all of the factors and release only those offenders who can be best managed under community supervision, thus providing a powerful enhancement to public safety.

The core services offered by parole—investigations, victim advocacy, release planning, community supervision, immediate response to violations, and treatment services—provide optimum public protection. Parole is a powerful partner to both the courts and to victims. Parole boards ensure that the victim's voice is both heard and heeded, creating a natural and valuable ally for victims and victim advocacy groups.

The American Probation and Parole Association is committed to promoting discretionary parole as an integral and important part of the criminal justice system, designed to enhance the protection of victims and promotion of community safety.

Source: Reprinted with permission of American Probation and Parole Association.

Visit http://video.pbs.org/video/1290027448/ or scan this code with the QR app on your smartphone or digital device and watch the PBS podcast of transporting female convicts to Australia in 1789. How does this information relate to ideas discussed in this chapter?

From 1775 through 1856, English offenders were sent to Australia as punishment. Those who committed more felonies in Australia were transported to England's most punitive prison on Norfolk Island, 1,000 miles off the east coast of Australia. In 1840, British Navy Captain Alexander Maconochie was appointed superintendent of the penal colony. Maconochie favored indeterminate sentences rather than fixed sentences. He recommended and in part implemented a marks system to measure the prisoner's progress toward release from prison, and he urged a system of graduated release and aftercare of prisoners to resettle them in the community. He developed a "ticket of leave" system, which moved inmates through stages: imprisonment, conditional release, and complete restoration of liberty. Inmates moved from one stage to the next by earning "marks" for improved conduct, frugality, and good work habits.

Although Maconochie had control over island tickets of leave, he could not control a graduated return to society in England. Maconochie's ideas did not blend well with the official English position on punishment, which was rooted in deterrence and relied on the infliction of suffering. He was removed in 1844 and the penal colony at Norfolk Island lapsed into a period of extraordinary brutality before it closed in 1856. Maconochie is referred to as the founder of parole.

In 1854, Sir Walter Crofton, director of the Irish prison system, implemented a system that was based on Maconochie's ticket of leave system. Crofton's version required that upon conditional release, a former inmate do the following:

1. Report immediately to the constabulary on arrival and once a week thereafter.
2. Abstain from any violation of the law.
3. Refrain from habitually associating with notoriously bad characters.
4. Refrain from leading an idle and dissolute life without means of obtaining an honest living.
5. Produce the ticket of leave when asked to do so by a magistrate or police officer.
6. Not change locality without reporting to the constabulary.[2]

The former inmate who did not comply with the conditions of release was reimprisoned. Crofton's system of conditional release is considered the forerunner of modern American parole.

Use of the term *parole* for early release from prison began with a letter from Dr. Samuel G. Howe of Boston to the Prison Association of New York in 1846. Howe wrote, "I believe there are many [prisoners] who might be so trained as to be left upon their parole (a promise made with or confirmed by a pledge of one's honor) during the last period of their imprisonment with safety."[3]

Early American Parole Development The first legislation authorizing parole in the United States was enacted in Massachusetts in 1837. The Elmira Reformatory in New York, which opened in 1876, was the first U.S. correctional institution to implement an extensive parole program.

By 1889, 12 states had implemented parole programs; by 1944, all 48 states had enacted parole legislation.

Parole Development in the Early 20th Century The 1920s and early 1930s were a turbulent period in the United States. During Prohibition, organized crime increased, street gang warfare escalated, and the media provided obsessive coverage of criminals and their activities. Prison riots erupted in response to prisoner idleness and arbitrary rules and punishment. Prisons and the parole system failed to rehabilitate offenders.

The Wickersham Commission, a commission on law enforcement and observance appointed by President Herbert Hoover, issued a report in 1931 that advocated uniformity in state parole practices by recommending that states establish centralized policymaking boards to write standards and guidelines for parole practices.[4] This report included a list of the "essential elements" of a good parole system:

1. indeterminate sentence law permitting the offender to be released (conditionally) at the time when he or she is most likely to make a successful transition back to society;

Captain Alexander Maconochie, who became superintendent of the British penal colony on Norfolk Island, Australia, in 1840, implemented a "ticket of leave" system to ease inmate transition from custody to freedom. Later, Sir Walter Crofton, director of the Irish prison system, implemented a system based on Maconochie's ideas. How did their systems influence current parole procedures?

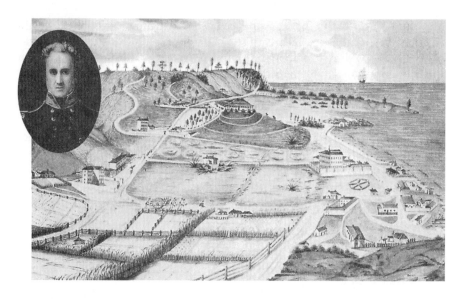

2. provision of quality release preparation—in the institution—for the offender who is reentering the community;

3. familiarity by the parole officer with the home and environmental conditions of the offender before he or she leaves the institution; and

4. sufficient staffing levels to ensure an adequate number of parole officers to supervise parolees.[5]

The Wickersham Commission reported that parole was logical because it was an inexpensive way to supervise offenders. Moreover, the commission reported, the parolee earns money whereas the prisoner cannot support himself or herself and cannot contribute financially to his or her family. By 1944, all of the states had passed parole legislation.[6]

Despite the fact that all states had enacted parole legislation, by the mid-1940s, opposition to it was strong. The attitude that parole boards were turning hardened criminals loose on society sparked a series of angry attacks through national and state commissions, investigatory hearings, editorials and cartoons, press releases, and books.[7] Opponents claimed that parole had a dismal performance record, its goals were never realized, parole board members and parole officers were poorly trained, and parole hearings were little more than hastily conducted, almost unthinking interviews.

In spite of the gap between its goals and reality, parole fulfilled important functions for officials in the criminal justice system. Wardens supported parole because the possibility of earning parole served as an incentive for offenders, making it easier to keep peace. Wardens also used parole to control prison overcrowding by keeping the number of people being released on parole about equal to the number of new prisoner admissions. Legislators supported parole because it cost less than incarceration. District attorneys supported parole because they felt it helped with plea bargaining. Without parole, district attorneys argued, there was little motivation for defendants, particularly those facing long prison sentences, to plead guilty to lesser crimes. District attorneys also supported parole because parolees could be returned to prison without new trial proceedings.

Together, these groups made a claim to the public that parole actually extended state control over offenders because parolees were supervised.

Eventually, the public accepted the claim that parole was tough on criminals and that abolishing parole would end state control over dangerous persons.

Parole Development in the Late 20th Century Opposition to parole resurfaced in the 1960s and 1970s, this time as part of a larger political debate about crime, the purposes of sanctioning, and the appropriateness of the unlimited discretion afforded various sectors of the criminal justice system (paroling authorities in particular). During this period, the debate on correctional policy addressed both the assumptions of the rehabilitative ideal and the results of indeterminate sentencing and parole.

In the 1970s, research indicated that prison rehabilitation programs had few positive benefits. Parolees were not rehabilitated, as parole advocates had claimed.[8] This position was supported on all sides of the political spectrum, including by those who believed that prisons "coddled" dangerous criminals and by those who questioned the ethics of coercing offenders into submitting to unwanted treatment as a condition of release.[9] These research findings led to many of the sentencing reforms of the 1970s and 1980s and helped usher in the warehousing and just deserts eras discussed in Chapter 7. During a time when supporting parole represented a "soft" stance on crime and when crime rates and recidivism were up, the public did not want prisoners released on parole.

In 1987, the American Probation and Parole Association voiced its support of parole and objected to efforts to abolish it. Nevertheless, in that same year, six states abolished discretionary parole board release. By the year 2000, 16 states and the federal government had abolished it, and another four states had abolished discretionary parole release for certain violent offenses or other crimes against a person, a topic we return to later in this chapter. The APPA position statement on parole is presented in Exhibit 8–2.

Reentry

Reentry is the use of programs targeted at promoting the effective reintegration of offenders back to communities upon release from prison and jail. Reentry has occurred since the Walnut Street Jail opened in 1773. However, the scale of offender reentry is larger today than ever before,

EXHIBIT 8–2	**American Probation and Parole Association**

Position Statement on Parole

The mission of parole is to prepare, select, and assist offenders who, after a reasonable period of incarceration, could benefit from an early release while, at the same time, ensuring an appropriate level of public protection through conditions of parole and provision of supervision services. This is accomplished by:

- assisting the parole authority in decision making and the enforcement of parole conditions;
- providing prerelease and postrelease services and programs that will support offenders in successfully reintegrating into the community; and
- working cooperatively with all sectors of the criminal justice system to ensure the development and attainment of mutual objectives.

Source: Reprinted with permission of American Probation and Parole Association.

and we face enormous challenges in managing the reentry of persons leaving prison and jail. Ninety-five percent of all prisoners will be released prior to the expiration of their sentences. In just 20 years, the number of inmates being released from prison has quadrupled. Almost 2,000 offenders leave state and federal prison every day and as we noted in Chapter 7, almost one-half are reincarcerated within three years for either committing a new crime or for violating conditions governing their release.[10]

Why is corrections not correcting? There are many reasons. Among them are the following:

- **Parole supervision:** Most parole officers manage large caseloads and typically meet with offenders for about 15 minutes once or twice a month. Why should we expect such a small amount of contact to make a large difference?

- **Shift in parole function:** Parole has shifted from a service orientation to a surveillance-oriented, control-based strategy centered on monitoring behavior, detecting violations, and enforcing rules. Surveillance technologies such as the Global Positioning System, remote-control monitoring, and drug testing make it easier to monitor behavior and detect violations. However, what academics and practitioners have been telling us for years—that surveillance alone does not change criminal behavior—is in fact a reality. To reduce a parolee's criminal activity, parole agencies and officers must employ evidence-based practices that focus on individual-level change and are shown to work such as academic and vocational education, cognitive-behavioral treatment, and drug courts.

- **Responses to technical violations:** Violators of probation and parole represent the fastest-growing category of admissions to jail and prison, one-third nationally, and 60 to 70 percent in some states such as California.[11] Legislators are beginning to realize that as the correctional populations swell, so do corrections budgets. American taxpayers spent almost $30 billion for corrections in 2001. Today it's more than $52 billion.

The current budget crisis has changed the way that several states now respond to probation and parole violators. Kansas allows probation and parole officers to decide whether those who violate early release conditions for nonviolent offenses should go back to prison. Tennessee accelerates prison releases for probation and parole violators who are sent back to prison and complete drug abuse and other counseling programs. Arizona lets probation and parole violators end their community supervision early by applying "good time" (time that is subtracted from a person's sentence for positive behavior, program completion, etc.) against their sentences, thereby reducing the chances they could be sent back to prison for condition violations. Other changes are taking place across the country.

Offender Problems Research shows that when people are released from jail and prison, their job prospects are dim, their chances of finding a place to live are bleak, and their health is poor. Fewer than half have a job lined up before leaving prison. Three-fourths still have a substance abuse problem. More than one-third have a physical or mental disability. Almost one in five has hepatitis C. More than half have dependent children who rely on these reentering adults for financial support. Only one-third participated in educational programs while incarcerated, and even fewer participated in vocational training.[12] (See Exhibit 8–3.) These former inmates will work fewer weeks each year and earn less money as

| EXHIBIT 8-3 | Service Needs of State and Federal Prisoners |

Area of Need	Prevalence (Percentage of All Prisoners)
Substance abuse	75
Physical or mental disability	83
No high school diploma	86
No diploma or GED	40
Earned less than $600/month prior to incarceration	50
Homeless before or after incarceration	10

Source: The Council of State Governments, *The Report of the Re-Entry Policy Council: Charting the Safe and Successful Return of Prisoners to the Community* (Lexington, KY: The Council of State Governments, 2005), p. 49. Reprinted with permission.

well as have limited upward mobility than if they had never been incarcerated. Research also shows that returning prisoners are increasingly concentrated in communities that are often crime ridden and lack services and support systems.[13] For example, in Illinois, 51 percent of prisoners released from state correctional institutions in 2001 returned to Chicago, and 34 percent of them returned in just 6 of Chicago's 77 neighborhoods. And, no services were located in two of those six neighborhoods. Regrettably, parole violations and new crimes are often committed because offenders reentering the community lack the skills and support to adapt to community life. But as we will discuss later, now that we know that there are geographic concentrations of returning prisoners to a handful of neighborhoods in most large cities, we have an opportunity to place our reentry efforts in those areas.

Prisoner reentry problems are magnified for women leaving prison, especially minority women. Nearly two-thirds of the women confined in jails and state and federal prisons are black, Hispanic, or of other non-white ethnic groups. As reported in Chapters 6 and 7, women in prison have a high rate of prior sexual or physical abuse, high rates of positive-HIV status and other sexually transmitted diseases, and high alcohol, drug use, and addiction rates at the time of arrest. "In most of their communities," writes Beth Richie of the University of Illinois at Chicago, "there are few services and very limited resources available to assist women in the process of reentry."[14]

The situation is even more grim when we look at the reentry problems for black women.[15] These women leaving prison have unique needs in the areas of family and health care that current reentry systems do not consider. Black children are more likely than white or Hispanic children to have a parent who is incarcerated. They are also more likely to be in foster care and remain there longer than white or Hispanic children. Due to their time in poverty, jail, and prison, black women are more vulnerable to becoming HIV positive. Compounding the problem is a generation of black men who are not present in the community to assist with childcare and provide an income for the home. Reentry services have not accounted for the additional challenges that black women face but that white and Hispanic women do not. Although the challenges facing black women leaving prison are daunting, in recent years the United States has witnessed a surge of policy interest and innovation in response to these realities that we point out shortly.

Reentry Programs to Help Ex-Offenders

With so many problems and such high rearrest rates, it has become clear to many that simply placing an offender in prison does not deter future criminal behavior. The U.S. prison and parole systems have become a revolving door that cities and towns across the nation were not prepared to handle.

Researchers have found that individuals returning home from prison or jail have complex needs and must address a number of issues, which may include:[16]

- **Mental health.** The incidence of serious mental illnesses is two to four times higher among prisoners than it is among the general population.
- **Substance abuse.** Three-quarters of those returning from prison have a history of substance use. More than 70 percent of prisoners with serious mental illnesses also have a substance use disorder.
- **Housing and homelessness.** More than 10 percent of people entering prisons and jails are homeless in the months before their incarceration. For those with mental illness, the rate is even higher: about 20 percent.
- **Education and employment.** Two of every five prisoners and jail inmates lack a high school diploma or its equivalent. Employment rates and earnings histories of people in prisons and jails are often low before incarceration as a result of limited education experiences, low skill levels, and the prevalence of physical and mental health problems. Incarceration only exacerbates these challenges.
- **Children and families.** Approximately 2 million children in the United States have parents who are currently incarcerated, and more than 10 million minor children have parents who at some point have been under some form of criminal justice supervision.
- **Women.** Women parolees on reentry have gender-specific needs with respect to childcare, protection from sexual harassment and abusive relationships, reproductive health problems, few job-related skills or experiences to support themselves or their children, and housing that is safe, secure, and affordable.

Recently, the Legal Action Center (LAC) published the results of an exhaustive two-year study of legal obstacles that people with criminal records face when they attempt to reenter society and become productive, law-abiding citizens. LAC developed a report card to "grade" how states deal with seven roadblocks that criminals face upon reentry: employment, public assistance and food stamps, housing benefits, voting, access to criminal records, parenting, and driving. States were graded from 1 (being the best) to 10 (the worst). Scores ranged from 10 to 48. States with the lowest overall scores have the fewest barriers to reentry. State scores are shown in Exhibit 8–4.

In response to the roadblocks, we see policymakers at all levels of government showing unprecedented interest in the record number of people coming out of prisons and jails.

The national Second Chance Act (SCA) was signed into law on April 9, 2008. It had received bipartisan support in both houses of Congress and from a broad spectrum of leaders representing state and local government, law enforcement, corrections, courts, service providers, and community organizations. This first-of-its-kind federal legislation authorizes making grants to government agencies and nonprofit organizations to provide

EXHIBIT 8–4   Report Card on How States Deal with the Legal Obstacles Prisoners Face on Reentry

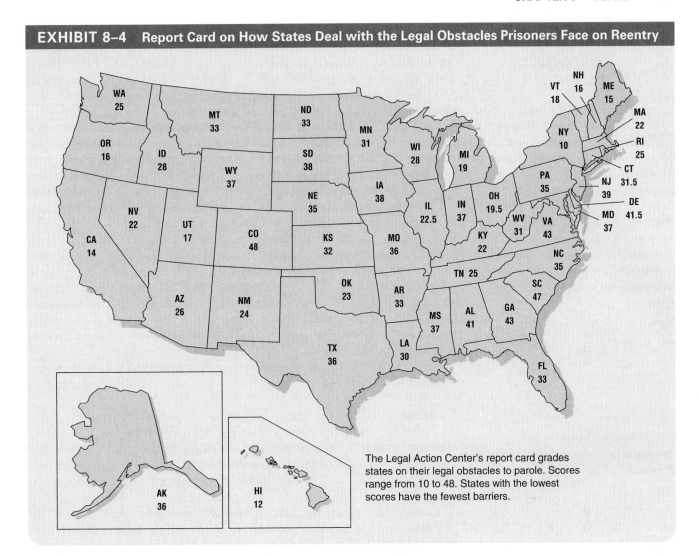

The Legal Action Center's report card grades states on their legal obstacles to parole. Scores range from 10 to 48. States with the lowest scores have the fewest barriers.

employment assistance, substance abuse treatment, housing, family programming, mentoring, victim support, and other services that can make a person's transition from prison or jail safer and more successful. Since 2009, more than 300 local, state, and tribal governments and nonprofit organizations have received SCA grants for reentry programs serving juveniles and adults. Examples of SCA awards include:

- Reentry agencies in San Mateo, California, use screening and assessment tools to develop individualized reentry plans that include peer mentoring support, education and employment services, mental health and substance abuse treatment, life skills training, and housing services.

- The Illinois Department of Corrections uses its SCA grant to expand its Moms & Babies Program, a prison-based nursery program that allows mothers to keep their newborn babies with them in prison for up to 24 months.

- The United States Probation and Pretrial Services for the Northern District of Florida uses its SCA grant to help qualified offenders under supervision with transportation, employment, housing, and other reentry needs.

Visit http://www.youtube.com/watch?
v=Xm8XoWwkfHA or scan this code with
the QR app on your smartphone or digital
device and watch the podcast of "Boxed
Out: Criminal Records & the 'Ban the
Box' movement in Philadelphia." In 2011,
Philadelphia passed an ordinance that bars
employers from inquiring about the criminal
histories or doing background checks of job
applicants until after the initial interview.
How does this information relate to ideas
discussed in this chapter?

parole eligibility date

The earliest date on which an inmate might
be paroled.

However, the economic downturn has also affected congressional fund-ing for SCA. It was first funded in 2009 with $25 million. In 2010, Congress signaled its support for such strategy by appropriating $100 million but in 2011 reduced funding to $83 million. And in 2012, funding was only to $63 million. At a time when Congress is increasingly focused on reducing spending, future allocations may not be so robust.

State and local governments have been equally busy in addressing reentry issues. Recognizing that 65 million Americans—or one in four adults—have a criminal record that a routine background check may identify, at least ten states and over 50 cities and counties have taken steps to remove barriers to employment for qualified workers with crimi-nal records, specifically by removing conviction history questions from job applications—a reform commonly known as "ban the box."[17] The new laws remove unfair barriers to employment of people with criminal records by prohibiting employers from requiring disclosure of past con-victions on initial applications, information that often ends any realistic job prospects for ex-offenders. Employers can ask about criminal back-grounds and run background checks after determining that an applicant meets minimum job qualifications. However the new reforms do not apply to police, schoolteachers or other government jobs working with children, the elderly, or the disabled.

American Correctional Association's policy statement favoring reentry is shown in Exhibit 8–5.

Eligibility for Reentry An inmate's eligibility for parole is deter-mined by the sentence received from the court as set by law. The **parole eligibility date** is the earliest date on which an inmate might be released. State statutes usually dictate parole eligibility dates and specify what por-tion of a sentence an offender must serve before being considered for release.

An offender's parole eligibility date is also affected by good time credit first discussed in Chapter 3. At least 31 states and the federal government provide some type of good time incentives. Many states such as Califor-nia, Michigan, and Washington have either already increased time off for good behavior from one-third to as much as one-half of sentence time or are considering doing so in order to reduce overcrowding and the correc-tions budget.[18]

CO8-2

paroling authority

A person or correctional agency (often
called a *parole board* or *parole commission*) that has the authority to grant parole,
revoke parole, and discharge from parole.

Granting Parole—The Paroling Authority

Every jurisdiction in the United States has a paroling authority. In most states, a **paroling authority** is a correctional agency (often called a *parole board* or *parole commission*) that has statutory authority to grant parole, set conditions of parole, supervise parolees, revoke parole, and discharge from parole. For jurisdictions with determinate sentencing and no discre-tion for the timing of release, the paroling authority still may determine conditions of release.

Parole boards vary in size from 3 members (Alabama, Hawaii, Mon-tana, North Dakota, Washington, and West Virginia) to 10 or more (Michigan, 10; Connecticut, 11; Ohio, 11; Illinois, 12; Texas, 18; and New York, 19). Of the 52 jurisdictions—the 50 states, the District of Columbia, and the federal government—only 34 have full-time salaried parole board members.

Parole board members accustomed to relying on experience and intu-ition in parole rulings must now take computerized inmate risk assessments

---

EXHIBIT 8–5 | **American Correctional Association**

Public Correctional Policy on Reentry of Offenders

Introduction:

Successful reentry of offenders in the community is in the best interest of society. Reentry programs enhance public safety, help prepare offenders for transition to responsible citizenship, can help reduce future criminal behavior, remove the barriers that make it difficult for offenders to reenter their communities, and develop necessary community support.

Policy Statement:

The American Correctional Association fully supports evidence-based practices and reentry programs, and encourages the elimination of any local, state and federal laws and policies that place barriers on the offender's successful reentry. Therefore, public and private agencies at the federal, state and local levels should:

A. Advocate for the review and revision of existing laws and regulations that inhibit the successful reentry of offenders;

B. Initiate individualized transitional planning during intake to a facility.

C. Provide recidivism-risk and reentry-needs assessments and associated services and programs during incarceration;

D. Provide an expedited process to obtain appropriate legal identification prior to or upon release;

E. Assist the offender in accessing appropriate housing upon release;

F. Provide sufficient staff trained to supervise and motivate offenders released to the community;

G. Encourage institution and community supervision staff to integrate work efforts to assure a comprehensive continuum of supervision and services;

H. Develop community partnerships and support networks for providing to provide a seamless and timely connection between pre- and post-release programs and services;

I. Provide information and assistance to address health care needs following release such as obtaining Medicaid, medical and substance abuse treatment, and other health and psychological services. Provide a sufficient supply of prescription medication upon release;

J. Provide information and assistance to offenders to gain employment upon release, such as pre-employment readiness training, job identification and retention skills training, and job placement services;

K. Ensure that offenders who have served in the U.S. military are provided with information regarding the benefits and services to which they may be entitled, and are referred at discharge, to the Department of Veterans' Affairs or local veteran service organizations; and

L. Provide services to facilitate successful family and community reunification.

Source: Copyright © American Correctional Association. Reprinted with permission.

---

and personality tests into account.[19] At least 15 states have begun requiring some type of risk assessment tool to calculate an inmate's odds of recidivism, while helping prisons cut down on their costs of operations.[20] Previously (and still in some states) parole board members considered factors like the severity of a crime or whether an offender showed signs of remorse. By contrast, data- and evidence-based methods based on inmate

The Staff Speaks
Visit www.mhhe.com/schmalleger7e
to see this feature.

interviews and biographical data such as age at first arrest are designed to recognize patterns that may predict future crime and make release decisions more objective.

However, computerized risk assessments are not without their critics. Bernard Harcourt, University of Chicago professor of law and political science, tells us that relying on statistics can result in unintended racial bias.[21] Age at first incarceration and the number of total incarcerations can speak indirectly to a person's race, even if the computerized software is not directly considering it. Data show that there is link between race and prior criminal history, and a link between prior criminal history and prediction of recidivism. Others, such as Chris Baird, former head of the National Council on Crime and Delinquency, remind us that it is extremely important to recognize that computerized risk assessment tools have limitations.[22] They may be better tools for setting supervision guidelines for parolees rather than determining prison sentences or deciding who should be realeased.[23] The problem with implicit racial bias and the fact that murderers and sex offenders are often much less likely to commit another offense than someone guilty of a lesser crime are things a computerized risk-assessment tool may or may not predict but public opinion and advocacy groups would not allow.

In the 1970s, the United States Parole Commission developed the **salient factor score (SFS)**, a risk assessment instrument to estimate an inmate's likelihood of recidivating following his or her release from prison. The SFS has been revised several times since the pilot project in 1972.

Today, the SFS is a series of six static factors based on an objective scale through empirically validated research. Static factors are ones that do not change over time and are known to be related to recidivism, such as age at first conviction, prior incarcerations, number and severity of previous arrests or convictions, and supervision failures. The primary benefits of using the SFS are that the items are objective, easily scored, few in number, and unable to be manipulated by offenders.

The salient factor score used today by the U.S. Parole Commission is shown in Exhibit 8–6. Each of the six items' responses is weighted. The

salient factor score (SFS)

Scale, developed from a risk-screening instrument, used to predict parole outcome.

A parole board meets to consider a release candidate. While discretionary release by parole boards was at one time very common, it has been eliminated in many jurisdictions. Does parole provide offenders with an effective opportunity to reintegrate into society?

total score (a range from 0 to 10) is then calculated. The higher the total score, the lower the likelihood of recidivism. The total score is then placed into one of four risk categories (Poor, 0–3; Fair, 4–5; Good, 6–7; and Very Good, 8–10). Where the SFS intersects with the offense characteristics shown in the first vertical column (category one represents the least serious offenses; category eight represents the most severe) gives the range (in months) of incarceration judges may order at sentencing. Parole boards in jurisdictions across the United States use various types of risk assessments as shown in Exhibit 8–7.

Granting Parole—The Hearing

In general, parole hearings are attended by victims, the applicant, the institutional representative, and hearing examiners or parole board members. A two-year study of 5,000 parole hearings in Colorado found that the parole board heard too many cases to allow for individualized treatment.[24] The time for a typical parole hearing was 10 to 15 minutes. Unusual cases take longer.

In today's high-tech environment, a number of states are experimenting with video conferencing. The surge in virtual hearings is also a way for cash-strapped communities to boost efficiency and cut costs. So far, reported annual savings are $600,000 in Georgia, $30 million in Pennsylvania, and $50,000 in transportation costs in Ohio.[25]

The final decision to grant or deny parole is based on both eligibility guidelines and the interview. If parole is granted, a contract that defines the release plan is executed and the inmate is given a release date. The inmate who is conditionally released to community supervision is called a **parolee.**

The trend among parole authorities is to grant or deny parole on the basis of risk to the community. If parole is denied, the common reasons are "not enough time served," "poor disciplinary record," "need to see movement to lower security and success there," and "lack of satisfactory parole program" (proposed home, work, or treatment in the community). In that case, the inmate remains in prison, and a date is set for the next review. The waiting period between hearings depends on the jurisdiction and the inmate's offense.

For example, on Thursday, August 23, 2012, the New York State Parole Board virtually interviewed Mark David Chapman, the man who shot and killed John Lennon in 1980. Chapman was sentenced to 20 years to life in 1980 and became eligible for parole on December 4, 2000. For the seventh time, the parole board denied parole and wrote to Chapman, "You shot and killed an innocent victim, an international music star. Your actions clearly demonstrated a callous disregard for the sanctity of human life."[26] The parole board noted that Chapman had no prior convictions and that they had considered his good conduct in prison, educational accomplishments, remorse, letters of support, and "significant" opposition to his release. But the board decided, however, that "parole shall not be granted for good conduct and program completions alone. Therefore, despite your positive efforts while incarcerated, your release at this time would greatly undermine respect for the law and tend to trivialize the tragic loss of life which you caused as a result of this heinous, unprovoked, violent, cold and calculated crime," the board wrote. According to New York law, Chapman is entitled to a parole hearing every two years. His next scheduled parole hearing will be in August 2014. Yoko Ono, the wife of the late musician, said in 2010 that she opposed paroling

parolee

A person who is conditionally released from prison to community supervision.

EXHIBIT 8–6	**United States Parole Commission Salient Factor Score**

Item A. Prior Convictions/Adjudications (*Adult or Juvenile*) .... ☐
  None = 3; One = 2; Two or three = 1; Four or more = 0

Item B. Prior Commitment(s) of More than 30 Days (*Adult/Juvenile*) ...... ☐
  None = 2; One or two = 1; Three or more = 0

Item C. Age at Current Offense/Prior Commitments .... ☐

26 years or older	Three or fewer prior commitments = 3
	Four prior commitments = 2
	Five or more commitments = 1
22-25 years	Three or fewer prior commitments = 2
	Four prior commitments = 1
	Five or more commitments = 0
20-21 years	Three or fewer prior commitments = 1
	Four prior commitments = 0
19 years or younger	Any number of prior commitments = 0

Item D. Recent Commitment Free Period (three years)............................ ☐
No prior commitment of more than 30 days (adult or juvenile) or released to the community from last such commitment at least 3 years prior to the commencement of the current offense = 1; Otherwise = 0

Item E. Probation/Parole/Confinement/Escape Status Violator This Time ... ☐

Neither on probation, parole, confinement, or escape status at the time of the current offense; nor committed as a probation, parole, confinement, or escape status violator this time = 1; Otherwise = 0

Item F. Older Offenders... ☐
If the offender was 41 years of age or older at the commencement of the current offense (and the total score from Items A-E above is 9 or less) = 1; Otherwise = 0

Total Score .... ☐

Chapman and believed he could be a danger to her, Lennon's two sons, the public, and even to himself.

Conditions of Parole Paroling authorities set specific conditions for parole on a case-by-case basis (see Exhibit 8–8). Parolees must comply with these conditions, averaging three years, which may include restitution, substance abuse aftercare, remote-electronic monitoring, and/or house arrest, among others.

Parolees are technically in state or federal custody; they have merely been granted the privilege of living in the community instead of prison. Parole officers, who work closely with the parolee and the paroling authority, carry out the supervision of parolees. They can initiate parole revocation hearings and return parolees to prison if they threaten community

EXHIBIT 8–6	United States Parole Commission Salient Factor Score (continued)

Offense Characteristics	Offender Chracterisistics: Parole Prognosis			
Severity of Offense Behavior	Very Good Risk (10–8)	Good Risk (7–6)	Fair Risk (5–4)	Poor Risk (3–0)
Category One	≤ 4 months	≤ 8 months	8–12 months	12–16 months
Category Two	≤ 6 months	≤ 10 months	12–16 months	16–22 months
Category Three	≤ 10 months	12–16 months	18–24 months	24–32 months
Category Four	12–18 months	20–26 months	26–34 months	34–44 months
Category Five	24–36 months	36–48 months	48–60 months	60–72 months
Category Six	40–52 months	52–64 months	64–78 months	78–100 months
Category Seven	52–80 months	64–92 months	78–110 months	100–148 months
Category Eight*	100 + months	120 + months	150 + months	180 + months

*Note: For category eight, no upper limits are specified due to the extreme variability of the cases within this category. For decisions exceeding the lower limit of the applicable guideline category by more than 48 months, the commission will specify the pertinent case factors upon which it relied.

safety or otherwise violate the conditions of release. Depending on the severity of the crime and the risk presented by the offender, parole supervision can incorporate several types of contact with and "examination" of the parolee, including drug testing, setting of a curfew, remote-location monitoring, and employment verification.

The conditions under which parolees must live are very similar in form and structure to those for probationers. Sometimes the rules are established by law, but more often they are established by the paroling authority. The paroling authority can require any of the following forms of release: standard parole supervision, parole with enhanced treatment and programming conditions, halfway house placement, intensive supervision, parole with remote-electronic monitoring or voice and location tracking, or release with follow-up drug testing and payment of supervision fees and restitution.

EXHIBIT 8–7	Risk Assessment Instruments Used by Other Jurisdictions Across the United States

Jurisdiction	Use a Risk Instrument?	Description of Instrument
Alabama	Yes	A 12-item instrument that consists of 11 static factors and 1 dynamic factor.
Alaska	No	
Arizona	No	
Arkansas	Yes	A 14-item instrument that examines 4 categories of predictors; all items are static.
California	No	
Colorado	Yes	An 8-item instrument that consists of 1 dynamic factor and 7 static factors.
Connecticut	Yes	A 5-item instrument consisting of static factors.
Delaware	No	
Florida	No Response	
Georgia	Yes	There are 10 risk factors examined, 6 static factors and 4 dynamic factors.
Hawaii	No	
Idaho	No Response	
Illinois	No	
Indiana	No Response	
Iowa	No Response	
Kansas	No Response	
Kentucky	Yes	A 9-item instrument that consists of 5 static items and 4 dynamic items.
Louisiana	No	
Maine	No Response	
Maryland	Yes	A 9-item risk instrument that has 5 static risk factors and 4 dynamic risk factors.
Massachusetts	No	
Michigan	Yes	This instrument consists of 34 items with a combination of static and dynamic factors.
Minnesota	Yes	
Mississippi	No	
Missouri	No Response	
Montana	Yes	A 7-item instrument that consists of 6 static factors and 1 dynamic factor.
Nebraska	Yes	A 9-item instrument that consists of 8 static factors and 1 dynamic factor.
Nevada	No	
New Hampshire	No	

EXHIBIT 8–7	Risk Assessment Instruments Used by Other Jurisdictions Across the United States *(continued)*

Jurisdiction	Use a Risk Instrument?	Description of Instrument
New Jersey	Yes	A 54-item instrument that contains both static and dynamic factors.
New Mexico	No	
New York	Yes	A 17-item instrument that consists of static factors.
North Carolina	No	
North Dakota	No Response	
Ohio	Yes	A 6-item instrument that consists of static factors.
Oklahoma	No Response	
Oregon	No	
Pennsylvania	Yes	A 54-item instrument that contains both static and dynamic factors.
Rhode Island	No Response	
South Carolina	Yes	A 10-item instrument that consists of 7 static factors and 3 dynamic factors.
South Dakota	Yes	The instrument contains 6-items on static factors for the risk assessment and 3 items for the needs assessment.
Tennessee	Yes	A 10-item instrument consisting of static risk factors.
Texas	Yes	An instrument consisting of static factors; used for sex offender risk assessment.
Utah	Yes	A 7-item instrument that consists of static risk factors.
Vermont	Yes	A 13-item instrument that consists of 7 static risk factors and 6 dynamic risk factors.
Virginia	No	
Washington	Yes	A 54-item instrument that contains both static and dynamic factors.
West Virginia	Yes	A 10-item instrument that contains 5 static factors and 5 dynamic factors.
Wisconsin	No	
Wyoming	No	
U.S. Parole Commission	Yes	A 6-item instrument that consists of static factors.

Source: Shamir Ratansi and Stephen M. Cox, *State of Connecticut Assessment and Validation of Connecticut's Salient Factor Score.* New Britain, CT: Connecticut Statistical Analysis Center. Central Connecticut State University, Department of Criminology and Criminal Justice. October 2007. Reprinted by permission of the authors.

Brian S. Davis

Supervising U.S. Probation Officer, U.S. District Court,
Northern District of Florida, Pensacola, Florida

Brian S. Davis is a supervising U.S. probation officer for the U.S. District Courts, Pensacola Division. He currently oversees the operations of the supervision unit composed of five U.S. probation officers in addition to maintaining an intensive supervision caseload of approximately 35 federal offenders. Davis is a 16-year veteran of the U.S. Probation Office. He had seven years of prior probation experience with the Florida Department of Corrections. Davis has spent several years as a team member of the Robert A. Dennis, Jr. (RAD) Reentry Court Program in the Northern District of Florida. He is trained in and teaches cognitive behavioral therapy. He is also trained in other cognitive programs that seek to provide offenders an opportunity to change during their term of supervision. Davis has also supervised internship placements for a local university. He routinely provides training in evidence-based practices to U.S. District Court judges from around the country. Additionally, Davis is an assistant firearms instructor in the Northern District of Florida.

Davis received his bachelor of science degree from Troy University. He attributes his professional leadership style to the quality and relevance of the course curriculum and his experiences with collegiate athletic programs. Davis' leadership and management skills allow for effective supervision with limited resources. His desire is to continue to exhibit a balanced style of law enforcement and programming leadership and management that will inspire officers to pursue personal achievement and satisfaction with their career choices. Davis works at strengthening ties within the community to reach the common goal of providing support and opportunities for offenders who exhibit the desire to change.

Davis' desire is to use evidence-based programs to promote cognitive self-change for offenders and effective supervision for the community in a joint effort with the court family to reduce recidivism and accomplish his department's mission.

Davis' advice to anyone seeking a career in the probation field is to understand how much influence people in the profession have on individuals' futures. A new officer should find the balance between complying with techniques while providing opportunities for people to change for the long term and always remaining firm but showing empathy to any offender's personal situations.

> *"A new officer should find the balance between complying with techniques while providing opportunities for people to change for the long term and always remaining firm but showing empathy to any offender's personal situations."*

Types of Parole Release on parole may be mandatory or discretionary. Discretionary parole decisions are made by a paroling authority such as a parole board or parole commission after its members review a case to determine whether they believe the prisoner is ready to be returned to the community. The criteria used to reach the decision vary from state to state, as discussed earlier. Discretionary parole decisions occur in jurisdictions using indeterminate sentencing.

Mandatory parole release is set by law and occurs in jurisdictions using determinate sentencing. It requires the correctional authority to grant parole after the inmate serves a specific period of time as required by law. Exhibit 8–9 compares discretionary and mandatory parole release.

Historically, most states have used discretionary parole release. But over the past few decades, the balance between the two methods of parole release has shifted. In 1977, 69 percent of parolees received discretionary parole board release. States began moving away from discretionary prison release policies in the 1980s in favor of determinate sentences and

EXHIBIT 8–8	**Sample State Conditions of Parole**

State of Alaska

Standard Conditions of Parole

The following standard conditions of parole apply to all prisoners released on mandatory or discretionary parole, in accordance with AS 33.16.150(a).

1. REPORT UPON RELEASE: I will report in person no later than the next working day after my release to the parole officer located at the PAROLE OFFICE and receive further reporting instructions. I will reside at _____.

2. MAINTAIN EMPLOYMENT/TRAINING/TREATMENT: I will make a diligent effort to maintain steady employment and support my legal dependents. I will not voluntarily change or terminate employment without receiving permission from my parole officer to do so. If discharged or if employment is terminated (temporarily or permanently) for any reason, I will notify my parole officer the next working day. If I am involved in an education, training, or treatment program, I will continue active participation in the program unless I receive permission from my parole officer to quit. If I am released, removed, or terminated from the program for any reason, I will notify my parole officer the next working day.

3. REPORT MONTHLY: I will report to my parole officer at least monthly in the manner prescribed by my parole officer. I will follow any other reporting instructions established by my parole officer.

4. OBEY LAWS/ORDERS: I will obey all state, federal, and local laws, ordinances, orders, and court orders.

5. PERMISSION BEFORE CHANGING RESIDENCE: I will obtain permission from my parole officer before changing my residence. Remaining away from my approved residence for 24 hours or more constitutes a change in residence for the purpose of this condition.

6. TRAVEL PERMIT BEFORE TRAVEL OUTSIDE ALASKA: I will obtain the prior written permission of my parole officer in the form of an interstate travel agreement before leaving the state of Alaska. Failure to abide by the conditions of the travel agreement is a violation of my order of parole.

7. NO FIREARMS/WEAPONS: I will not own, possess, have in my custody, handle, purchase, or transport any firearm, ammunition, or explosives. I may not carry any deadly weapon on my person except a pocket knife with a 3 " or shorter blade. Carrying any other weapon on my person such as a hunting knife, axe, club, etc. is a violation of my order of parole. I will contact the Alaska Board of Parole if I have any questions about the use of firearms, ammunition, or weapons.

8. NO DRUGS: I will not use, possess, handle, purchase, give, or administer any narcotic, hallucinogenic, (including marijuana/THC), stimulant, depressant, amphetamine, barbiturate, or prescription drug not specifically prescribed by a licensed medical person.

9. REPORT POLICE CONTACT: I will report to my parole officer, no later than the next working day, any contact with a law enforcement officer.

10. DO NOT WORK AS AN INFORMANT: I will not enter into any agreement or other arrangement with any law enforcement agency which will place me in the position of violating any law or any condition of my parole. I understand the Department of Corrections and Parole Board policy prohibits me from working as an informant.

11. NO CONTACT WITH PRISONERS OR FELONS: I may not telephone, correspond with, or visit any person confined in a prison, penitentiary, correctional institution or camp, jail, halfway house, work release center, community residential center, restitution center, juvenile correctional center, etc. Contact with a felon during the course of employment or during corrections-related treatment is not prohibited if approved by my parole officer. Any other knowing contact with a felon is prohibited unless approved by my parole officer. I will notify my parole officer the next working day if I have contact with a prisoner or felon.

12. CANNOT LEAVE AREA: I will receive permission from my parole officer before leaving the area of the state to which my case is assigned. My parole officer will advise me in writing of limits of the area to which I have been assigned.

13. OBEY ALL ORDERS/SPECIAL CONDITIONS: I will obey any special instructions, rules, or order given to me by the Alaska Board of Parole or by my parole officer. I will follow any special conditions imposed by the Alaska Board of Parole or my parole officer.

Source: State of Alaska Board of Parole, *Parole Handbook, Appendix II: Conditions of Parole*, June 1998.

mandatory prison release. (We will return to a discussion of this trend later in this chapter.) Consistent with the adoption of truth in sentencing and other mandatory release statutes, mandatory prison release is increasing, while discretionary parole release is decreasing. Exhibit 8–10 shows how much the share of prison releases by type changed from 1977 to 2011.

EXHIBIT 8–9	Comparing Discretionary Release and Mandatory Release	
	Discretionary Release	**Mandatory Release**
Release date	Decided by parole board	Determined by law
Criteria	Based on parole board guidelines	None[1]
Postrelease supervision	Yes	Maybe

1. Corrections authorities may have discretion to grant or deny good-time credits in mandatory release cases.

Source: Adapted from Jeremy Travis and Sarah Lawrence, *Beyond the Prison Gates: The State of Parole in America* (Washington, DC: Urban Institute, 2002). Copyright © 2002 The Urban Institute. Reprinted with permission.

Mandatory release is the most common method of release from prison today. Some argue that abandonment of discretionary release in favor of mandatory release has detrimental effects. Proponents of discretionary parole board release argue that parole boards serve a salutary function by requiring inmates to focus their efforts on successful reentry from prison to the community. Without the prospect of discretionary release, inmates have fewer incentives for engaging in good behavior or participating in rehabilitative programs, and prison administrators have fewer mechanisms for relieving institutional crowding.

Exhibit 8–11 shows the amount of discretion that state parole boards have to release inmates. Parole boards in 24 states have nearly full discretion

EXHIBIT 8–10   Percentage of All Prison Releases, 1977 and 2011

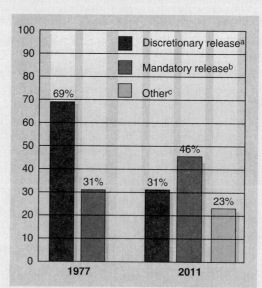

a. Discretionary release applies to persons who entered parole as the result of a parole board decision.
b. Mandatory release applies to persons who entered parole because of determinate sentencing statutes, good time provisions, or emergency release.
c. Other includes reinstatements (persons returned to parole after serving time in prison because of a parole violation), term of supervised release (persons sentenced by a judge to a fixed period of incarceration), other (parolees who were transferred from another state, placed on supervised release from jail, released to a drug transition program, released from a boot camp, conditional medical or mental health release to parole, absconders, and others), and unknown. Similar data not available in 1977.

Source: Adapted from Laura M. Maruschak and Erika Parks, *Probation and Parole in the United States, 2011* (Washington, DC: U.S. Department of Justice, Bureau of Justice Statistics, November 2012), pp. 7–8.

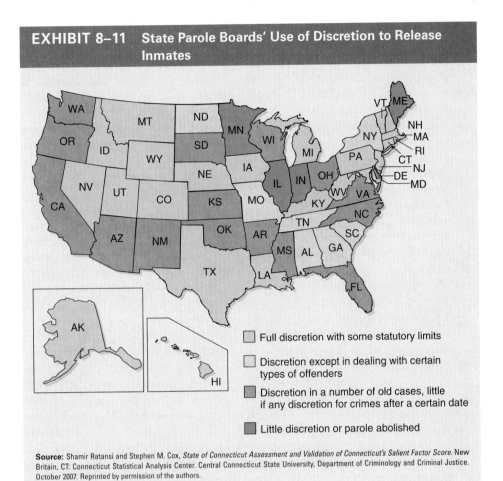

EXHIBIT 8–11   State Parole Boards' Use of Discretion to Release Inmates

☐ Full discretion with some statutory limits

☐ Discretion except in dealing with certain types of offenders

▨ Discretion in a number of old cases, little if any discretion for crimes after a certain date

■ Little discretion or parole abolished

Source: Shamir Ratansi and Stephen M. Cox, *State of Connecticut Assessment and Validation of Connecticut's Salient Factor Score.* New Britain, CT: Connecticut Statistical Analysis Center. Central Connecticut State University, Department of Criminology and Criminal Justice. October 2007. Reprinted by permission of the authors.

within statutory limits. In six states, parole boards have discretion except in cases involving certain violent offenses. Sixteen states have either abolished parole boards or the parole boards have discretion only in a small number of cases that occurred before a certain date but no discretion or limited discretion with cases after a specific date. And four states have either completely abolished parole or have very limited discretion. Later in the chapter we return to a discussion of the "abolish parole" movement.

In January 2010, the California legislature introduced a new type of release from prison called **nonrevocable parole (NRP).**[27] NRP is a type of unsupervised parole that, unlike regular parole, cannot be revoked for technical violations. Persons allowed NRP are no longer under the jurisdiction of the California Department of Corrections and Rehabilitation, and they do not report to a parole officer. Persons are discharged from NRP after one year. Only offenders convicted of nonviolent, nonsexual, low-level crimes who have been assessed and determined not to be a serious risk to the public are eligible for NRP. In addition, the offenders must have demonstrated acceptable behavior in prison and must have made progress with any substance abuse issues. In the first year of operation, some 6,500 prisoners received NRP at an estimated cost savings of $100 million. They will be returned to prison only if they are arrested for a new offense, convicted, and sentenced to a term of incarceration in the same manner as any other criminal defendant.

Proponents of NRP argue that it removes low-level offenders from parole supervision, reduces the average parole officer caseload from 70

nonrevocable parole (NRP)

A type of unsupervised parole that cannot be revoked for technical violations; the person does not report to a parole officer.

Economic Realities and Corrections: Parole and Reentry

In 2011, at least 40 states made cuts to correctional expenditures by reducing labor costs, eliminating prison programs, and making food service changes. Twenty-nine states adopted policy reforms in the areas of sentencing, probation and parole, collateral consequences, and juvenile justice. Nine states in particular enacted policies designed to reduce parole revocations. According to the National Governors Association, the salient reason for making these changes was the reduction in state revenues caused by the recession. The following were among the policy reforms affecting parole revocations.

Alabama—Limited Incarceration for Parole Violators

Lawmakers broadened the range of administrative penalties through Senate Bill 267 for parole violations to reduce the use of incarceration for persons who violate the conditions of parole. The measure authorized sentencing options including short-term confinement in county jail facilities and eliminated incarceration in state prison facilities in specified circumstances.

Louisiana—Expanded Parole Eligibility for Certain Prisoners and Adopted Alternative Sanctions for Technical Parole Violators

House Bill 415 authorized alternative sanctions for persons with nonviolent offenses who commit technical parole violations. Prior to reform, an individual whose parole was revoked for a first technical violation was required to serve up to 90 days in custody or a maximum sentence of six months in a drug diversion program. HB 415 authorizes a parole officer to impose administrative sanctions for a technical violation of parole conditions. According to the Department of Corrections, 4,258 individuals violated the conditions of their parole in 2010. The new measure is expected to save the state more than $3.9 million by reducing the length of confinement for certain prisoners.

North Carolina—Limited Use of Prison as a Sentencing Option for Certain Probationers

Lawmakers enacted several provisions through HB 642, known as the Justice Reinvestment Act, to reduce spending on incarceration and to redirect the savings into community-based treatment alternatives. Additionally, the bill expands the authority of probation officers to sanction persons on community supervision such as requiring probationers to comply with a variety of additional conditions, including jail confinement, without returning to court for a modification. Under the jail confinement provision, the probationer is given an opportunity to waive a hearing and submit to short periods of incarceration of not more than six days per month rather than appear before a judge and face a complete revocation.

Texas—Established New Standard to Reduce Probation Revocationers Admitted to Prison

HB 1205 entitles defendants to time credits applied to the completion of their community supervision if certain conditions are met. Time credits are awarded for meeting various conditions and participating in programs to earn a high school diploma or equivalency certificate, to pay associated fines and fees, and to successfully complete parenting classes or anger management programs. The bill requires the court to review the defendant's record and determine the time when he or she will be eligible for a sentence reduction.

SB 1055 requires county probation departments across Texas to submit a community reduction plan, which establishes a targeted reduction in the number of probation violators in the state prison system. During 2010, a small number of probation violators—630 individuals, or 0.4 percent—were admitted to Texas prisons. The measure further authorizes county probation departments to receive additional state funding appropriated from estimated savings from the reduction of probationers being revoked to prison. This approach is consistent with the justice reinvestment framework adopted in other states.

parolees to 45, allows the state to focus parole supervision on the most serious and violent parolees, allows law enforcement to continue to conduct warrantless searches on these parolees, reduces the number of parolees returned to custody for parole violations, and reduces the need for bed space in county jails and state prisons. Critics note that they recognize the need to reduce crowding and cut costs but not at the expense of public safety. It is too early to tell what impact NRP will have, but if it costs less than regular parole and does not contribute to an increase in serious and violent crime, chances are other states will consider adopting it.

CO8-4 ## CHARACTERISTICS OF PAROLEES

The tremendous increase in the prison population discussed in Chapter 7 has given many people a sense of safety and security. However, the majority of the population is also unconcerned—or unaware—that at least 95 percent of those who enter prisons eventually return to the community, and most do so in about two and one-half years. Some have put it this way: More prisoners in results in more prisoners out!

Almost 2,000 prisoners each day leave prison. About one in five leaves prison with no postrelease supervision because of changes in sentencing legislation that allow some prisoners to "max out" (serve their full sentences) and leave prison with no postcustody supervision as discussed previously.

After declining in 2009, the U.S. parole population increased for the second consecutive year by nearly 13,300 offenders (from about 840,600 at yearend 2010 to 853,900 at yearend 2011). One in every 280 U.S. adults is on parole.[28] Eighty-seven percent of those adults were state parolees; the rest were federal. In midyear 2006, the Bureau of Justice Statistics estimated that 14,000 full-time parole officers were supervising the nation's parole population, each with a caseload of about 38 active parolees.[29] (Some agencies supervise both parolees and probationers.) Men and women made up nearly equal percentages of full-time employees. Consult the Appendix Careers in Corrections at the Online Learning Center Web site for the steps involved in career planning, developing employability and job readiness, and finding the right job.

The basic demographics of parolees have not changed much over the past 20 years. The typical adult parolee is a white, non-Hispanic male on mandatory parole and under active parole supervision for more than one year. The median age is 34, with an 11th-grade education. Women make up 11 percent of the parole population (see Exhibit 8–12). The region with the highest number of parolees is the South, followed by the West, Northeast, and Midwest.

Not all who are sent to prison are released on parole. Those who are the most serious offenders (those who have life sentences or who face the death penalty) or who have disciplinary problems while incarcerated generally are not paroled. Instead, they live out their lives in prison or are released when they have served their entire sentences.

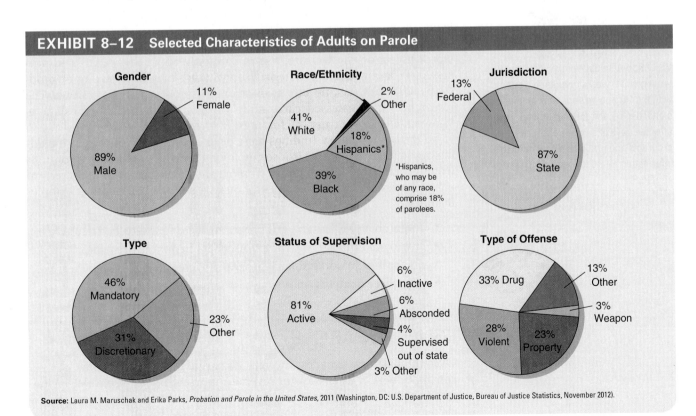

EXHIBIT 8–12 Selected Characteristics of Adults on Parole

Source: Laura M. Maruschak and Erika Parks, *Probation and Parole in the United States,* 2011 (Washington, DC: U.S. Department of Justice, Bureau of Justice Statistics, November 2012).

EXHIBIT 8–13	Selected Parole Populations Among the States, Yearend 2011				
Five Jurisdictions with the Largest Parole Populations	Number Supervised	Five Jurisdictions with the Highest Rates of Supervision	People Supervised per 100,000 Adult U.S. Residents	Five Jurisdictions with the Lowest Rates of Supervision	People Supervised per 100,000 Adult U.S. Residents
California	111,063	District of Columbia	1,178	Maine	2
Texas	106,518	Arkansas	1,015	Florida	28
Pennsylvania	94,581	Pennsylvania	944	Virginia	36
New York	47,243	Louisiana	796	Massachusetts	44
Louisiana	27,640	Oregon	749	North Carolina	51

Source: Adapted from Laura M. Maruschak and Erika Parks, *Probation and Parole in the United States, 2011* (Washington, DC: U.S. Department of Justice, Bureau of Justice Statistics, November 2012).

Exhibit 8–13 defines parole populations among the states at yearend 2011. California had the largest number of adults on parole, followed by Texas and Pennsylvania. The District of Columbia and Pennsylvania also had the highest rates of parole supervision, which means they used parole more than any other jurisdiction Maine used parole the least.

CO8-5 Parole Supervision: What Works?

In 2012, researchers at the Urban Institute, the Council of State Governments, and the John Jay College of Criminal Justice Prisoner Reentry Institute launched a clearinghouse to identify and analyze all research on the subject of prisoner reentry. Its purpose is to provide government agencies and criminal justice practitioners a scientifically solid basis for deciding which reentry programs work for the more than 700,000 people released from prison each year.

Approximately 1,000 studies have been identified as potentially being worth listing on the website, but to date only about 300 have been processed. Programs are characterized by whether they have strong or modest beneficial effects, no effect, or strong or modest harmful effects. The researchers also assessed each study's "rigor," which they translate as "how much can we trust the findings."

To date, preliminary findings have been compiled in four areas including brand name programs (those employing a variety of treatment options from mental health treatment to employment assistance to address returning prisoners' needs), employment, housing, and mental health. Examples include:

- comprehensive "aftercare" programs were found to be effective,
- employment programs for ex-offenders had mixed results,
- one-half of prison industry programs were rated as being effective,
- only three analyses on housing issues were available.

Visit http://nationalreentryresourcecenter.org/what_works or scan this code with the QR app on your smartphone or digital device and read what works on the effectiveness of a wide variety of reentry programs and practices. How does this information relate to ideas discussed in this chapter?

CO8-6 ISSUES IN PAROLE

Over the past few decades, the face of parole has changed. This chapter concludes with a discussion of several important issues in parole, including voting rights, reentry courts, successful reintegration programs involving victims, the abolition of discretionary parole board release, prisoner reentry and community policing, and community-focused parole.

Ethics and Professionalism

American Probation and Parole Association Code of Ethics

- I will render professional service to the justice system and the community at large in effecting the social adjustment of the offender.
- I will uphold the law with dignity, displaying an awareness of my responsibility to offenders while recognizing the right of the public to be safeguarded from criminal activity.
- I will strive to be objective in the performance of my duties, recognizing the inalienable right of all persons, appreciating the inherent worth of the individual, and respecting those confidences which can be reposed in me.
- I will conduct my personal life with decorum, neither accepting nor granting favors in connection with my office.
- I will cooperate with my co-workers and related agencies and will continually strive to improve my professional competence through the seeking and sharing of knowledge and understanding.
- I will distinguish clearly, in public, between my statements and actions as an individual and as a representative of my profession.
- I will encourage policy, procedures, and personnel practices, which will enable others to conduct themselves in accordance with the values, goals, and objectives of the American Probation and Parole Association.
- I recognize my office as a symbol of public faith and I accept it as a public trust to be held as long as I am true to the ethics of the American Probation and Parole Association.
- I will constantly strive to achieve these objectives and ideals, dedicating myself to my chosen profession.

Source: Reprinted with permission of American Probation and Parole Association.

Ethical Dilemma 8–1:

Offenders often leave prison without job skills, money, or personal coping skills. Should they be released on parole? Is parole working? What can agencies do to assist parolees? For more information, go to Ethical Dilemma 8–1 at www.justicestudies.com/ethics07.

Ethical Dilemma 8–2:

A woman with young children is a repeat offender who has again violated her parole. Should she remain in the community, or should she return to prison? What are the issues? Should a parolee's gender make a difference in treatment? For more information, go to Ethical Dilemma 8–2 at www.justicestudies.com/ethics07.

Ethical Dilemmas for every chapter are available online.

Can Parolees Vote?

Currently, an estimated 5.9 million people in the United States have lost their voting rights as the result of a felony conviction, including some 2.6 million citizens who have served their sentences.[30]

A parole officer questions one of his parolees about a suspected new offense violation. Which jurisdictions use parole the most? The least?

Racial disparities in the criminal justice system also translate into diversities in the disenfranchised population as well—meaning that felons are restricted from voting. An estimated 38 percent (roughly 2 million persons) of the total disenfranchised population is black, far more than their percent in the general populations. This suggests to some that racial disparities in disenfranchisement reflects not only increased involvement in criminal behavior but also biased policy and decision making.[31]

The U.S. Constitution, Article 1, Section 2, gives the matter of voting rights to the states. Only two states—Maine and Vermont—do not deny persons the right to vote based on a criminal conviction; even prisoners may vote by absentee ballot. People with felony convictions in Florida, Iowa, Kentucky, and Virginia are disenfranchised for life, unless they are granted clemency by the governor. The rest of the country falls somewhere in between. In some cities there are efforts to register jail inmates who have not yet been convicted and do not have a past felony conviction. Jails in the District of Columbia, Los Angeles, San Francisco, and elsewhere help inmates vote by absentee ballot. However most counties do not actively help jail inmates vote.

In addition to disenfranchisement by law, there is confusion among election officials about their state's felony disenfranchisement policies. For example, a study by the Sentencing Project found that 37 percent of public officials surveyed in 10 states either misstated a central provision of the voter eligibility law or were unsure about what it said.[32] Almost one-fourth of Ohio's boards of elections misinformed callers posing as people with felony convictions, telling them that they could not vote while under community supervision, although Ohio state law denies voting rights to felons only while they are incarcerated. During the research, 13 of Ohio's 88 boards of elections said they did not know the state's law on whether people on probation or parole could vote.[33]

We present the arguments for and against felon disenfranchisement next. As you read them, remember that they have not been scientifically proved. They sound rational on the surface, but social science research has yet to validate them.

Only Maine and Vermont do not place any restrictions on the right to vote for people with felony convictions. Missy Shea of the Vermont Secretary of State's office helps at Marble Valley Regional Correctional Facility in Rutland with the voter registration process. An estimated 5.9 million people in the United States have lost their voting rights as a result of a felony conviction. What are the arguments for and against felon disenfranchisement?

There are at least four arguments in support of felon disenfranchisement. First, inmates should be denied the right to vote as a matter of principle because they committed a felony. Second, states have the right to deny felons the right to vote as added punishment, just as they have the right to restrict felons from certain occupations. Third, denying felons the right to vote sends a message about respect for the law and acts as a deterrent to crime. And fourth, felons should be denied the right to vote because they cannot be trusted to make politically informed decisions.

On the other hand, there are five arguments against felon disenfranchisement. First, voting is not a privilege but a right guaranteed by the Constitution, and states don't have the right to take it away. Second, felon disenfranchisement laws are unfair to minorities who are treated unfairly by the criminal justice system—one of every eight adult black males is ineligible to vote. Third, felon disenfranchisement laws are not an effective form of punishment because most ex-felons did not vote before incarceration. Fourth, removal of an inmate's right to vote is inconsistent with reentry. Offenders should be encouraged to accept more responsibility for their future roles in the community, not less. John Timoney, former Miami police chief and president of the Police Executive Research Forum, put it this way: "I do not think we should give criminals an excuse for not reforming themselves because they are bitter about having had one of their most important rights—the right to vote—taken away. I think it is better to remove any obstacles that stand in the way of offenders resuming a healthy, full, productive life . . . my sense is, once you've cleared the four walls of the jail, your right to vote should be restored."[34] And fifth, once we open the door by declaring that a certain group of people does not deserve the basic right to vote, then which group of people might be the next we attempt to restrict?

Reentry Courts

It is incumbent on criminal justice policymakers who are interested in greater public safety and more efficient use of public tax dollars to consider how we might better handle the challenges of the almost 2,000 offenders who leave prison each day. Because of the potential threats that parolees pose to victims, families, children, and communities, investing in effective parole programs may be one of the best investments we make.

One of the latest innovations in helping offenders released from prison make a successful adjustment to the community is the reentry court. A **reentry court** manages the return to the community of individuals released from prison, using the authority of the court to apply graduated sanctions and positive reinforcement and to marshal resources to support the prisoner's reintegration.

Los Angeles County Superior Court Judge Michael Tynan congratulates Melanie Hightower for graduating from the Second Chance Women's Reentry Court. Reentry courts manage the return to the community of individuals released from prison. What are the core elements of reentry court that facilitate an individual's successful return to the community?

reentry court

A court that manages the return to the community of individuals released from prison.

The U.S. Department of Justice proposes that a reentry court have six core elements:

- **Assessment and planning.** Correctional administrators and the reentry judge meet with inmates who are near release to explain the reentry process, assess inmates' needs, and begin building links to a range of social services, family counseling, health and mental health services, housing, job training, and work opportunities that support reintegration.

- **Active judicial oversight.** The reentry court sees all prisoners released into the community with a high degree of frequency, maybe once or twice a month. Also involved are the parole officer and others responsible for assessing the parolee's progress. In court, offender progress is praised, and offender setbacks are discussed.

- **Case management of support services.** The reentry court acts as a service broker and advocates on behalf of parolees for "wraparound services" such as substance abuse treatment, job training, employment, faith instruction, family member support, housing, and community services.

- **Accountability to the community.** Reentry courts appoint broad-based community advisory boards to develop and maintain accountability to the community. Advisory boards also help courts negotiate the sometimes difficult task of brokering services for parolees and advocate on their behalf.

- **Graduated sanctions.** Reentry courts establish a predetermined range of graduated sanctions for violations of the conditions of release that do not automatically require return to prison.

- **Rewarding success.** Reentry courts incorporate positive judicial reinforcement actions after goals are achieved. Examples include negotiating early release from parole or conducting graduation ceremonies similar to those used in drug courts.

According to the U.S. Department of Justice, "The successful completion of parole should be seen as an important life event for an offender, and the court can help acknowledge that accomplishment. Courts provide powerful public forums for encouraging positive behavior and for acknowledging the individual effort in achieving reentry goals."[35] The U.S. Department of Justice is promoting the idea and asking communities to experiment with it, depending upon statutory framework, caseload considerations, administrative flexibility, and levels of collaboration among the judiciary, corrections officers, parole officers, police, business community, religious institutions, community organizations, and the like. Whichever form a reentry court takes, developing new ways that communities can manage and support offenders after release from prison with assistance in securing employment, housing, substance abuse treatment, family counseling, and other services is essential to our ability to reduce crime and keep communities safe.

In March 2013, the U.S. Department of Justice's National Institute of Justice reported that "little is known about the challenges associated with reentry court implementation and the effectiveness and cost-effectiveness of these programs. Furthermore, a well-established reentry court model has not been clearly documented."[36]

Some jurisdictions are evaluating the policies, practices, community context, and implementation barriers related to reentry programs as well as their process and impact. In comparing active and postprogram recidivism outcomes with other individual-level outcomes (e.g., regarding employment, substance use, and housing). In addition, researchers are matching—rather than randomly assigning—reentry participants with offenders who do not participate in reentry programs. Assigning individuals to experimental and control groups through matching raises the issue of selection bias and lessens our confidence that any difference between the two groups is the result of reentry, not selection.

The Robert A. Dennis, Jr. (RAD) Reentry Court program in the United States District Court of Northern District of Florida, however, has embarked on what may be the nation's only court evaluating reentry programs that randomly assign offenders to reentry and nonreentry programs. When the program started in 2010, participants were interviewed and selected by the reentry team (judge, U.S. attorney, federal public defender, and probation officer). Recognizing the problem of selection bias and desiring to know whether reentry court works, random selection was introduced in January 2012.

Every six months, eligible offenders are randomly assigned to either reentry court or supervision as usual. Eligibility criteria for the RAD reentry court include medium- to high-risk individuals (as measured by the federal postconviction risk assessment) and a minimum of 24 months remaining on supervision; no sex offenders are allowed. Participants progress through four phases, each of which lasts a minimum of 12 weeks (see Exhibit 8–14). Once participants complete the reentry court program, their term of supervision is reduced by 12 months. The impact evaluation will track all offenders for 36 months following release from prison. Evaluation results are expected in 2017.

Reintegration Involving Victims

Successful reintegration programs also involve victims.[37] Victims and victim organizations can assist in the reintegration of parolees by providing parole board members and parole officers with relevant information, offering their experience and expertise, and encouraging offender accountability.

Each year, about 30 million people in America become victims of crime. Most states give victims the right to (1) be notified about parole proceedings, (2) be heard on matters relating to the offender's parole, (3) be present at parole proceedings, and (4) receive restitution as a condition of parole. These rights are designed to ensure that the views of victims are taken into account before decisions about parole are made and to help victims prepare themselves for the offender's release. Victim input can highlight the need for strict supervision or special conditions such as restitution orders, order of protection, or mandated treatment in order to discourage reoffending and encourage reintegration.

Graduates of the Robert A. Dennis, Jr. Reentry Court, United States District Court, Northern District of Florida. What are the criteria for participating in the Robert A. Dennis, Jr. federal reentry court?

Programs involving victims operate in a number of ways. Some encourage victims to volunteer relevant information to parole officers. For example, in stalking cases, victims can tell parole officers whether offenders are in areas where they are not supposed to be. Other programs encourage victim–offender communication. In these programs, victims educate offenders about the impact of the crime and generate remorse in the hope that they can change offender behavior in the future. Whether the program features one-on-one conversation or a victim talking to an audience of imprisoned or paroled offenders, the aim is to convey to offenders the consequences of their actions in terms of the victims' pain and suffering. We return to a discussion of how corrections agencies participate in meeting victims' needs in Chapter 14.

Abolition of Discretionary Parole Board Release

Earlier in this chapter we discussed the strong opposition to parole in the 1930s and that opponents wanted to abolish it. They argued that parole boards were turning hardened criminals loose on society, parole had a dismal performance record, its goals were never realized, parole board members and parole officers were poorly trained, and parole hearings were little more than hastily conducted, almost unthinking interviews. In spite of the gap between goals and this 1930s reality, parole fulfilled important functions for wardens, legislators, and district attorneys.

The movement to abolish discretionary parole boards resurfaced in the 1970s when the concept of "just deserts"—the idea that offenders deserve punishment for what they do to society—was being discussed.[38]

The Offender Speaks
Visit www.mhhe.com/schmalleger7e to see this feature.

EXHIBIT 8–14 **Robert A. Dennis, Jr. Reentry Court Phases**

PHASE 1 (Minimum of 12 Weeks)

Program Components of Phase 1

- Attend a cognitive behavioral treatment (CBT) program as directed
- Attend monthly reentry court sessions
- Submit to random urinalysis through code-a-phone or as directed
- Maintain crime-free lifestyle
- Comply with all supervision conditions, including but not limited to substance and mental health treatment as ordered
- Be current with any court-ordered financial obligations or must be abiding by a payment plan that addresses the obligation
- Participate in outreach project, as directed

Additional Phase 1 Components

- Meet with vocational rehabilitation, complete preliminary assessment report, and maintain follow-up
- Begin an educational program as directed (GED, college, adult literacy, technical)
- Begin employment program or secure and maintain employment, and submit verification
- Begin developing relapse prevention plan
- Meet and establish relationship with mentor

Criteria for Advancing

- No unexcused absences from scheduled services (vocational rehabilitation; mental health services; educational program; drug treatment; etc.) for 60 days prior to advancing
- No positive drug/alcohol tests for 60 days prior to advancing
- Have made progress toward employment as determined by the Reentry Court team *or*
- Have made progress toward enrollment in educational program (GED, college, adult literacy, technical)
- Have no new arrests or technical violations for duration of phase (arrest or violation results in sanctions imposed by Reentry Court; if allowed to return to Reentry Court following sanctions, participant must begin Phase 1 from start)
- Be current with any court-ordered financial obligations or must be abiding by a payment plan that addresses the obligation
- Approval to advance by Reentry Court team

PHASE 2 (Minimum of 12 Weeks after Completing Phase 1)

Program Components of Phase 2

- Attend a cognitive behavioral treatment (CBT) program as directed
- Attend monthly Reentry Court sessions
- Submit to random urinalysis through code-a-phone or as directed
- Maintain crime-free lifestyle

- Comply with all supervision conditions, including but not limited to substance and mental health treatment as ordered
- Be current with any court-ordered financial obligations or must be abiding by a payment plan that addresses the obligation
- Participate in outreach project, as directed

Additional Phase 2 Components

- Maintain/progress in educational program, as directed
- Maintain employment
- Continue developing relapse prevention plan
- Maintain relationship with mentor

Criteria for Advancing

- No unexcused absences from scheduled services for 75 days prior to advancing
- No positive drug/alcohol tests for 75 days prior to advancing.
- Consistent gainful employment as verified and approved by the Reentry Court team *or*
- Consistent full-time enrollment in educational program
- Obtain GED certification if applicable
- No new arrests or technical violations for duration of phase (arrest or violation results in sanctions imposed by Reentry Court; if participant allowed to return to Reentry Court following sanctions, return to Phase 1)
- Be current with any court-ordered financial obligations or must be abiding by a payment plan that addresses the obligation
- Approval to advance by Reentry Court team

PHASE 3 (Minimum of 12 Weeks after Completing Phase 2)

Program Components of Phase 3

- Attend a cognitive behavioral treatment (CBT) program as directed
- Attend monthly Reentry Court sessions
- Submit to random urinalysis through code-a-phone or as directed
- Maintain crime-free lifestyle
- Comply with all supervision conditions, including but not limited to substance and mental health treatment as ordered
- Be current with any court-ordered financial obligations or must be abiding by a payment plan that addresses the obligation
- Participate in outreach project, as directed

Additional Phase 3 Components

- Maintain/progress in educational program, as directed
- Maintain employment
- Continue developing relapse prevention plan
- Maintain relationship with mentor
- Fully integrated into and contributing to Reentry Court program

EXHIBIT 8–14   Robert A. Dennis, Jr. Reentry Court Reentry Court Phases *(continued)*

Criteria for Advancing

- No unexcused absences from scheduled services for 90 days prior to advancing
- No positive drug/alcohol tests for 90 days prior to advancing.
- Consistent employment with no disciplinary write-ups at work *or*
- Consistent full-time enrollment with satisfactory progress in educational program
- No new arrests or technical violations for duration of phase (arrest or violation results in sanctions imposed by Reentry Court; if participant allowed to return to Reentry Court following sanctions, return to Phase 1 or Phase 2 as determined by Reentry Court team)
- Be current with any court-ordered financial obligations or must be abiding by a payment plan that addresses the obligation
- Actively participate in Reentry Court sessions
- Approval to advance by Reentry Court team

PHASE 4 (Minimum of 4 Weeks after Completing Phase 3)

Program Components of Phase 4

- Attend a cognitive behavioral treatment (CBT) program as directed
- Attend monthly Reentry Court sessions
- Submit to random urinalysis through code-a-phone or as directed
- Maintain crime-free lifestyle
- Comply with all supervision conditions, including but not limited to substance and mental health treatment as ordered
- Be current with any court-ordered financial obligations or must be abiding by a payment plan that addresses the obligation
- Participate in outreach project, as directed

Additional Phase 4 Components

- Maintain/progress in educational program, as directed
- Maintain employment
- Complete an approved, written relapse prevention plan and present relapse prevention plan to group
- Maintain relationship with mentor
- Actively facilitating positive and negative reinforcement in Reentry Court sessions

Criteria for Graduation

- Completion of CBT
- No positive drug/alcohol tests for duration of phase
- Consistent employment; OR
- Consistent full-time enrollment in educational program
- No new arrests or technical violations for duration of phase (arrest or violation results in sanctions imposed by Reentry Court; if participant allowed to return to Reentry Court following sanctions, return to Phase 1, Phase 2, or Phase 3 as determined by Reentry Court team)
- Present relapse prevention plan to group
- Demonstrate leadership in group
- Approval to graduate by Reentry Court team

POSTREENTRY COURT PHASE (24 weeks)

Components of Postreentry Court Phase

- Return to traditional supervision
- Maintain crime-free lifestyle
- Comply with all supervision conditions, including but not limited to substance and mental health treatment as ordered

Criteria for Early Termination (up to one year prior to the original expiration date) from the Term of Supervision

- No violations for duration of phase
- No arrests for duration of phase

However, states did not do away with parole altogether; they restructured it. As the data in Exhibit 8–15 show, by the end of 2000, 16 states and the federal government had abolished discretionary release from prison by a parole board for all offenders. Another four states had abolished discretionary parole release for certain violent offenses or other crimes against a person. In these states, postrelease supervision still exists and is referred to as "mandatory supervised release," "controlled release," or "community control." Parole boards still have discretion over inmates who were sentenced for crimes committed prior to the effective date of the law that eliminated parole board release and the responsibility to place offenders under either conditional or supervised release, the authority to return an offender to prison for violating the conditions of parole or supervised release, and the power to grant parole for medical reasons.

EXHIBIT 8–15	**States That Have Abolished Discretionary Release, 2000**

For All Offenders	**For Certain Violent Offenders**
Arizona	Alaska
California[1]	Louisiana
Delaware	New York
Florida[2]	Tennessee
Illinois	
Indiana	
Kansas[3]	
Maine	
Minnesota	
Mississippi	
North Carolina	
Ohio[4]	
Oregon	
Virginia	
Washington	
Wisconsin	

1. In 1976 the Uniform Determinate Sentencing Act abolished discretionary parole for all offenses except some violent crimes with a long sentence or a sentence to life.
2. In 1995 parole eligibility was abolished for offenses with a life sentence and a 25-year mandatory term.
3. Excludes a few offenses, primarily first-degree murder and intentional second-degree murder.
4. Excludes murder and aggravated murder.

Source: Adapted from Timothy A. Hughes, Doris James Wilson, and Allen J. Beck, *Trends in State Parole, 1999–2000* (Washington, DC: U.S. Department of Justice, Bureau of Justice Statistics, October 2001).

Visit http://www.theiacp.org/Publications-Guides/Projects/ViolenceReductionStrategies/TargetingCriminalityVideo/tabid/254/Default.aspx or scan this code with the QR app on your smartphone or digital device and watch the podcast of successful police-corrections partnerships. How does this information relate to ideas discussed in this chapter?

Why did some states abolish discretionary release from prison by a parole board? There are at least four reasons.

First, scholars concluded that indeterminate sentencing and discretionary parole did not achieve offender rehabilitation, which was unfair because it was based solely on parole board judgment without explicit standards of fairness and equity in sentencing. Studies showed that wide disparities resulted when the characteristics of the crime and the offender were taken into account, and decisions were influenced by the offender's race, socioeconomic status, and place of conviction. Second, eliminating discretionary parole appeared to be tough on crime. Third, parole boards' lack of openness in the decision-making process, in which boards made their parole decisions on a case-by-case basis without benefit of a written set of policies and procedures, prompted criticism. Today only 30 states make their parole board votes public. The rest are kept secret.[39] Fourth, state politicians were able to convince the public that parole was the cause of the rising crime problem and that abolition was the solution.

Prisoner Reentry and Community Policing

Reentry isn't just for corrections anymore for two reasons. First, the fourfold increase in the number of persons being released each year from state and federal prisons over the past two decades into crime-ridden neighborhoods that lack services and support systems is more than community corrections officers can handle. There has not been a fourfold increase in the number of community supervision officers as Chapter 4 pointed out, and for that reason probation and parole agencies are experimenting with privatization in community corrections (see Chapter 13).

Second, in spite of all the efforts being made at prisoner reform, offenders are still leaving prison unprepared for successful reentry as this chapter has pointed out. Not enough prisoners are receiving education or vocational training. Not enough prisoners are receiving alcohol and drug treatment. Not enough prisoners are receiving life skills. These challenges not only impact prisoners but also threaten public safety. Prisoners who are not prepared to lead productive, law-abiding lives will reoffend. Communities that provide prisoners the services and environment to transition successfully into the community will also protect themselves from further harm.

One way some communities are responding to the problems of prisoner reentry is to involve community policing with reentry initiatives. The argument for involving community policing in reentry is this: Because the majority of ex-offenders are rearrested within three years, making contact with former prisoners is part of the everyday business of law enforcement. In fact, researchers at the Urban Institute say that "arrest frequencies for returning prisoners are 30 to 45 times higher than for the general population. Police agencies stand to benefit from their involvement in reentry because successful efforts to reduce reoffending among released prisoners can, by definition, prevent future crimes and help improve community relations with police."[40] In places where we find corrections and law enforcement officers as partners in reentry, the chief executives of these agencies can ensure that collaborative efforts are publicly framed in terms of safety issues, effectively combatting any allegations that reentry is "soft on crime." They can attest that when police and corrections do not collaborate, officers on the street encounter the same men and women. Law enforcement agencies are also able to send an important message to people leaving prison. They inform ex-offenders that through collaboration with corrections they are willing to help them find the supports and services they need while holding ex-prisoners accountable for their actions.[41]

The community policing approach is to analyze and understand the reasons behind repeat offending and create partnerships with local businesses, residents, government agencies, and other stakeholders to solve underlying crime problems and prevent future offending.

Joint supervision of parolees by teams of police and parole officers is the most common way that police currently contribute to prisoner reentry efforts. Team supervision usually takes the form of police accompaniment on parole home visits, parole ride-alongs on police patrols, and parole involvement in policing activities, such as attending community meetings and staffing neighborhood substations. The team approach sends the message that community corrections is not soft on crime. It also contributes additional eyes and ears to enhance surveillance and assistance to community supervision. Exhibit 8–16 offers a brief summary of four law enforcement agencies' challenges and their progress in establishing prisoner reentry programs.

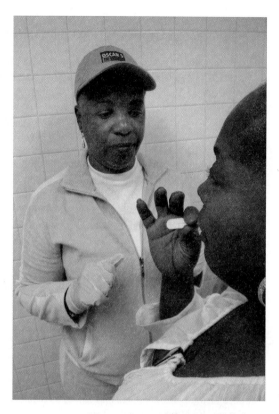

A parolee blows into a disposable plastic mouthpiece. The parole officer then attaches the mouthpiece to a portable handheld breath-testing machine that digitally registers the parolee's blood-alcohol level. Other portable alcohol technology tests urine, skin, and hair. What are the advantages of such technology in supervising parolees?

Community-Focused Parole

Earlier we said that communities that provide prisoners the services and environment to transition successfully into the community will also protect themselves from further harm. Community policing and prisoner reentry is one strategy.

Another is community-focused parole, a process of engaging the community so the community engages parole.[42] The process requires at least three changes to current parole practice.

The first is to capture a mission statement that the public understands. Some parole agencies are adopting public safety in addition to offender reform as a definition of their services. By raising their profile in the community as agencies that deliver public safety and highlighting that in their mission statement, parole agencies could decentralize parole officers into local neighborhoods (perhaps utilizing neighborhood police substations) and form collaborative partnerships with police and others similar to what community police do with local businesses, residents, government agencies, and other stakeholders to solve underlying crime problems and prevent future offending.

A second change is visibility. Unless the work of parole is made visible to the community, it will not result in the service being valued or supported. For many citizens, the issue of prisoners and their return to society is met with fear. However, scientifically conducted public opinion polls show that the public supports offender job training, treatment, and

EXHIBIT 8–16   Prisoner Reentry and Community Policing

Las Vegas (Nevada) Metropolitan Police Department (LVMPD) identified homelessness as a major issue in one of its largest police districts, and found that individuals in need of services were not being connected with existing resources available to them. In response, LVMPD staff designed and implemented a pilot reentry initiative that focuses on people booked into the county jail who have no home where they can return upon release. During the period of this project, LVMPD staff gathered and coordinated relevant stakeholders, implemented a screening process during booking at the jail, and arranged a collaborative reentry process that places program participants in housing and connects them to necessary services.

"I am proud that our department worked collaboratively to address the challenge of homelessness in a compassionate way through better coordination of services with community stakeholders. This approach has resulted in connecting those individuals in need with the right people, at the right time, and with the right services, said LVMPD Sheriff Douglas C. Gillespie.

Washington D.C. Metropolitan Police Department (MPD) coordinated with officers from CSOSA (Court Services & Offender Supervision Agency) to conduct home visits to people under CSOSA supervision. Building on this effort, specific police districts extended this practice to include people recently released from the metropolitan area correctional facilities and identified as most at risk of reoffending. In one particular district, MPD staff formalized an existing relationship with a local social service provider, and leveraged this relationship to connect this high-risk population to services.

Muskegon County (Michigan) Sheriff's Department (MCSD) struggled with an overpopulated jail, much like many other communities throughout the country. A significant portion of the jail population comprises people incarcerated for their first offense. To decrease the jail population and increase public safety, MCSD staff worked on designing a reentry program for first-time offenders, which they hoped would limit the time served in the facility and connect them to community-based services upon release.

White Plains (New York) Police Department (WPPD) implemented the White Plains Reentry Initiative in 2004. This program focused on people leaving the Westchester County Penitentiary (WCP), and helped them reenter the White Plains community and develop an ongoing support system in the community. The initiative coordinated with a variety of partners—including professionals from the public school district, community mental health providers, and other service providers—who attended monthly panel meetings in WCP, meeting with people scheduled to be released in the next 30 days to the City of White Plains. At these sessions, the reentry partners provided overviews of each agency's services and a WPPD officer discussed possible repercussions for reoffending. As a learning site, WPPD focused its efforts on improving communication among stakeholders through monthly case conference meetings and the development of a web-based database of reentry participants.

"I am proud that during my time as Police Commissioner, our department was able to launch this program, as it has been successful in helping individuals scheduled for release transition back into the community as well as ensuring they are able to contribute positively once they get out of prison, said former White Plains Police Commissioner and CSG Justice Center Board Member Frank Straub.

Source: Excerpted from Laura Draper and Blake Norton, *Lessons Learned: Planning and Assessing a Law Enforcement Reentry Strategy* (Washington, DC: U.S. Department of Justice, Office of Community Oriented Policing Services, March 2013).

education. Media relations can help create a positive image and increase visibility regarding the work of parole. Other examples are participating in local events and using a highly visible offender community service work program that involves nonprofit organizations.

The Robert A. Dennis, Jr. Reentry Court—discussed earlier—reconnects with the community of Pensacola, Florida, in a prosocial, positive way through the Re-Entry Alliance Pensacola (REAP) What You Sow Community Garden. It is a collaborative effort among various stakeholders in the community, including the federal court, the mayor of Pensacola, the Federal Bureau of Prisons, the Pensacola Chapter of the American Inns of Court, Richards Memorial United Methodist Church, Pensacola United Methodist Community Ministries, master gardeners from the Escambia County Extension agricultural programs, research professors from the University of West Florida, and an impressive number of caring, community-minded citizens who donate their time and labor to the project, all of whom are committed to evidence-based practices to reduce recidivism rates.

The idea for the REAP Community Garden came in response to social science research that supports the need for strong prosocial influences and activities for moderate- to high-risk offenders on community supervision.

The garden accomplishes this by providing regular occasions for offenders to work with their attorney mentors on a worthwhile community project that breathes new life into the community. The garden assists an ongoing local community ministry by providing fresh produce for weekly meals to the homeless and groceries to needy families in the area each month. Additionally, the Federal Prison Camp at Pensacola supported the project by permitting inmates to provide the labor to build more than 40 raised garden beds. This example of community-focused parole activity demonstrates that participating in such a community project can be transformative for everyone involved.

The third change—building partnerships—is central to any community-oriented initiative. Strategies that raise an agency's profile and elicit support are critical to the development of a community-focused parole service. Appearances on local news shows, articles in local newspapers, meetings with neighborhood associations, and sponsoring of local events such as Relay for Life are ways that parole agencies show they care about the community and can educate it about strategies in place to support and supervise returning prisoners.

The literature on community-oriented policing has found that proactive crime prevention strategies can yield long-term crime reduction benefits. It stands to reason then that community-focused parole can also have a positive impact on community safety.

REVIEW AND APPLICATIONS

SUMMARY

❶ Early English judges spared the lives of condemned felons by exiling them first to the American Colonies and then to Australia as indentured servants. Captain Alexander Maconochie, superintendent of the British penal colony on Norfolk Island, devised a "ticket of leave" system that moved inmates through stages. Sir Walter Crofton used some of Maconochie's ideas for his early release system in Ireland. In the United States, Zebulon Brockway implemented a system of upward classification.

❷ Paroling authorities play powerful roles in the criminal justice system. They determine the length of incarceration for many offenders and can revoke parole. The paroling authority's policies have a direct impact on an institution's population. Paroling authorities use state laws and information from courts and other criminal justice agencies to make release decisions.

❸ *Parole* is the conditional release of a prison inmate prior to sentence expiration with supervision in the community. The parole process of release begins in the courtroom when the judge sentences an offender to either a determinate or an indeterminate sentence. After serving a certain portion of his or her sentence, an offender is eligible for parole release. That aspect varies from state to state. If an inmate maintains good conduct for a certain amount of time preceding the parole hearing and is granted parole, he or she must live in accordance with specified rules and regulations in the community. If a parolee either violates the technical conditions of parole or commits a new crime, he or she may have parole revoked.

❹ After declining in 2009, the U.S. parole population increased for the second consecutive year by nearly 13,300 offenders (from about 840,600 at yearend 2010 to 853,900 at yearend 2011). One in every 280 U.S. adults is on parole. Eighty-seven percent are state parolees. The typical adult parolee is a white, non-Hispanic male, on mandatory parole and under active parole supervision for more than one year. His median age is 34, and he has an 11th-grade education. Women make up 11 percent of the parole population. The region with the highest number of parolees is the South, followed by the West, Northeast, and Midwest.

5 Researchers at the Urban Institute, the Council of State Governments, and the John Jay College of Criminal Justice Prisoner Reentry Institute launched a clearinghouse to identify and analyze all research done on the subject of prisoner reentry. It found that comprehensive "aftercare" programs were found to be effective, employment programs for ex-offenders had mixed results, and one-half of prison industries programs were rated as effective.

6 This chapter discussed six current issues in parole: inmate voting, reentry court, reintegration involving victims, abolition of parole, community policing and reentry, and community-focused parole. Only Maine and Vermont do not place any restrictions on the right to vote for people with felony convictions. Reentry court requires the parolee make regular court appearances for progress assessment. Reintegration involving victims encourages victims to educate offenders about the impact of the crime and generate remorse in the hope that they can change offender behavior in the future. Today, 16 states and the federal government have abolished discretionary release from prison by a parole board for all offenders. Another four states have abolished discretionary parole release for certain violent offenses or other crimes against a person. In community policing and reentry we find joint supervision of parolees by teams of police and parole officers. The goal of community-focused parole is to engage the community so the community engages parole.

KEY TERMS

parole, p. 259

discretionary release, p. 259

mandatory release, p. 259

parole eligibility date, p. 268

paroling authority, p. 268

salient factor score (SFS), p. 270

parolee, p. 271

nonrevocable parole (NRP), p. 279

reentry court, p. 285

QUESTIONS FOR REVIEW

1 Explain the history of parole development in the United States.

2 Outline how parole functions in the criminal justice system.

3 Describe parole and the parole decision-making process.

4 What can you infer from the characteristics of the parole population?

5 What do you think about what works in parole supervision?

6 Critique the current issues in parole.

THINKING CRITICALLY ABOUT CORRECTIONS

Reentry and Cognitive Transformation

Individual-level change is required before opportunities for work, reuniting families, and providing housing make a difference in a parolee's life. Others refer to this change as cognitive transformation. How can parole agencies help offenders achieve cognitive transformation and successful reentry?

Abolish Parole?

Sixteen states and the federal government have abolished discretionary parole board release from prison in favor of mandatory release. Another four states abolished it for certain violent offenses or other crimes against a person. Proponents of discretionary prison release argue that abandonment of discretionary release has a detrimental effect. They believe that parole boards serve a salutary function by requiring inmates to focus their efforts on successful reentry from prison to the community. They argue that without the prospect of discretionary prison release, inmates have fewer incentives for cognitive transformation and opportunities for work, reuniting with families, and housing. Critically examine the issues of this debate.

ON-THE-JOB DECISION MAKING

Nonrevocable Parole

To help your state reduce prison crowding and the money it spends on prisons, your parole agency decides it is going to study California's nonrevocable parole law and urge your state legislature to adopt something similar. Go to the California Department of Corrections and Rehabilitation Web site http://www.cdcr.ca.gov/. Click first Parole and then Non-Revocable Parole tabs. Study the eligibility criteria. Are there criteria you believe should be added to the list or possibly deleted? Defend your position to a legislative subcommittee on criminal justice.

Mentors and Offender Reentry

As chief parole officer in your area, write a two-page proposal recommending the involvement of mentors in offender reentry. Include what you believe are the advantages of mentoring for offender reentry and strategies for recruiting, training, and matching mentors with parolees.

For additional information, please see: www.mhhe.com/schmalleger7e
Follow the author's tweets about the latest crime and justice news @schmalleger

The Prison World

Part Four explores life inside prison for inmates and staff, the legal challenges surrounding their roles and responsibilities, and the special needs of inmates who are elderly, infected with HIV or AIDS, or mentally or physically challenged.

Custodial staff are most directly involved in the daily work of managing the inmate population. The extent to which correctional officers share beliefs, values, and behaviors is largely a function of the correctional

officer subculture and each individual's personality.

Prisoners, too, develop a subculture that helps them adjust to the self-doubt, reduced self-esteem, and deprivations they experience as a result of confinement. Inmate subculture is also based on the life experiences that prisoners bring with them when they enter confinement. One question that we try to answer concerns why men's prisoner subculture encourages isolation but women's prisoner subculture encourages relationships.

For a century, prisoners were considered civilly dead, and prisons operated entirely without court intervention. However, in 1970, the U.S. Supreme Court declared that, if states were going to operate prisons, they would have to do so according to the dictates of the Constitution. Since then, prisoners have reclaimed many of their conditional rights under the

U.S. Constitution. But today, changes in state and federal statutes have slowed the pace of prisoners' rights cases, and the U.S. Supreme Court seems to have become less sympathetic to prisoners' civil rights claims.

Inmates with special needs—those who are elderly, suffer from HIV, AIDS, or other chronic diseases, or are mentally or physically challenged—present significant problems for correctional managers. Special needs inmates may be more prone to violence and disruption. They frequently require close monitoring to reduce the risk of suicide, and they may tax scarce medical resources and become targets of abuse by other inmates.

The preprison drug use and sexual activity of many prisoners has brought HIV, AIDS, and tuberculosis into jails and prisons. Managing these problems requires training in early detection, treatment, classification, staff education, and adequate funding. These problems are compounded by the fact that many prisoners have co-occurring physical and mental health problems.

[9] THE STAFF WORLD

Managing the Prison Population

CHAPTER OBJECTIVES

After completing this chapter you should be able to do the following:

1. List the staff roles within the organizational hierarchy of correctional institutions.

2. Identify the types of power available to correctional officers and list and describe the most common correctional officer personality types.

3. List and describe the seven correctional officer job assignments.

4. Identify five significant correctional staff issues.

5. Detail the nature of workplace corruption among correctional personnel and explain its causes.

6. Explain the impact that terrorism is having on prisons and on the operation of correctional institutions today.

> *Corrections is not a business where only one sex, race, religion, or type of person can succeed. It takes men and women of all races, religions, and color to create a dynamic and effective workforce to manage diverse inmates and solve the problems we face.*
>
> —Dora Schriro, former Missouri director of corrections

Recently, American Correctional Association (ACA) executive director James A. Gondles Jr. issued a special media statement titled "*Guard* Must Go."[1] Gondles was objecting to the use of the word *guard* by the media to describe correctional officers. "The role of correctional officers," said Gondles, "is to ensure that offenders complete their sentences in a way that sufficiently addresses the wide range of problems they often bring with them, while maintaining corrections' paramount duty—public safety."

Gondles pointed to the fact that the ACA had taken action to eliminate the word *guard* from its publications, advertisements, and announcements more than 20 years earlier and that doing so had now become official policy. Rejecting the term *guard,* Gondles said, was necessary "because it implies that the job is inherently passive and demands nothing more than watching locked-up inmates. Nothing could be further from the truth."

In contrast, said Gondles, the term *correctional officer* "embodies the diverse skills officers employ each day—communication skills, cultural awareness, first aid, suicide prevention, emergency response preparedness, program and service delivery, and the proper use of force."

James A. Gondles Jr., American Correctional Association executive director. Why does Director Gondles reject use of the word "guard" in describing today's correctional officers?

THE STAFF HIERARCHY

CO9-1

Practically speaking, a prison of any size has a number of different staff roles—each with its own unique set of tasks. **Roles** are the normal patterns of behavior expected of those holding particular social positions. **Staff roles** are the patterns of behavior expected of correctional staff members in particular jobs. Eventually, many people internalize the expectations others have of them, and such expectations can play an important part in their self-perceptions.

Ideally, today's correctional staff members have four main goals:

1. to provide for the security of the community by incarcerating those who break the law;
2. to promote the smooth and effective functioning of the institution;
3. to ensure that incarceration is secure but humane; and
4. to give inmates the opportunity to develop a positive lifestyle while incarcerated and to gain the personal and employment skills they need for a positive lifestyle after release.[2]

Prison staff are organized into a hierarchy, or multilevel categorization, according to responsibilities. An institution's hierarchy generally has a warden or superintendent at the top and correctional officers at a lower level. A typical correctional staff hierarchy includes the following:

- administrative staff (wardens, superintendents, assistant superintendents, and others charged with operating the institution and its programs and with setting policy);

roles

The normal patterns of behavior expected of those holding particular social positions.

staff roles

The patterns of behavior expected of correctional staff members in particular jobs.

- clerical personnel (record keepers and administrative assistants);
- program staff (psychologists, psychiatrists, medical doctors, nurses, medical aides, teachers, counselors, caseworkers, and ministers—many of whom contract with the institution to provide services);
- custodial staff (majors, captains, lieutenants, sergeants, and correctional officers charged primarily with maintaining order and security);
- service and maintenance staff (kitchen supervisors, physical plant personnel, and many outside contractors); and
- volunteers (prison ministry, speakers, and other volunteers in corrections).

custodial staff

Those staff members most directly involved in managing the inmate population.

program staff

Those staff members concerned with encouraging prisoners to participate in educational, vocational, and treatment programs.

Organizational charts graphically represent the staff structure and the chain of command within an institution. An organizational chart for a typical medium-to-large correctional institution is shown in Exhibit 9–1. **Custodial staff** are most directly involved in managing the inmate population through daily contact with inmates. Their role is to control prisoners within the institution. **Program staff,** on the other hand, are concerned with encouraging prisoners to participate in educational, vocational, and treatment programs. Custodial staff, who make up more than 60 percent

EXHIBIT 9–1   Organizational Chart of a Typical Midsize or Large Correctional Institution

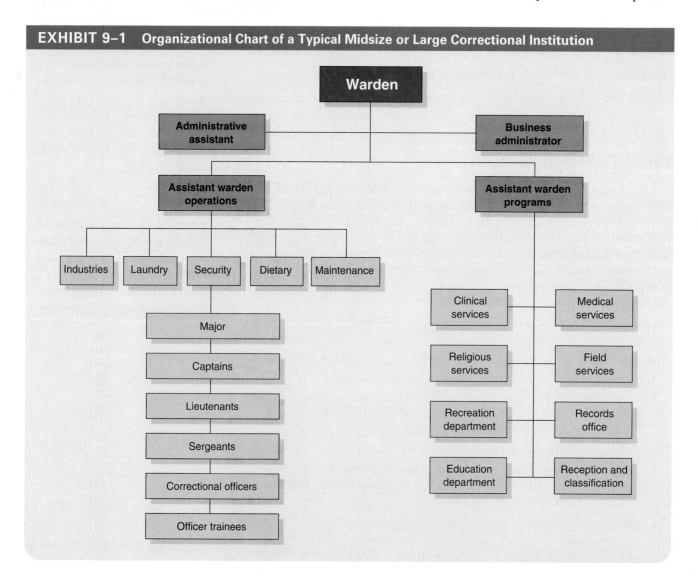

of prison personnel, are generally organized in a military-style hierarchy, from assistant or deputy warden down to correctional officer. Program staff generally operate through a separate organizational structure and have little in common with custodial staff.

To a great extent, prison management involves managing relationships—among employees, between employees and inmates, and among inmates. Prisons are unique in that most of the people in them (the inmates) are forced to live there according to the terms of their sentence; they really do not want to be there. Such a situation presents tremendous challenges. The people on the front lines dealing around the clock with such challenges are the correctional officers.

THE CORRECTIONAL OFFICER— THE CRUCIAL PROFESSIONAL

Although security is still the major concern, correctional officers today are expected to perform a variety of other tasks. As one commentator has said,

> Correctional officers have more responsibilities [now] than in the past and their duty is no longer to merely watch over the prisoners. They now have to play several roles in keeping prisoners in line. They have to be "psychiatrists" when prisoners come to them with their problems, and they have to be "arbitrators and protectors" when inmates have complaints or problems with each other, while still watching out for their own safety. In these situations, the wrong decision could offend someone and start a riot. This makes correctional officers "prisoners" of the daily emotional and physical moods of the inmates.[3]

Don Josi and Dale Sechrest explain it this way: "Correctional officers today must find a balance between their security role and their responsibility to use relationships with inmates to change their behavior constructively. They routinely assume numerous essential yet sometimes contradictory roles (e.g., counselor, diplomat, caretaker, disciplinarian, supervisor, crisis manager), often under stressful and dangerous conditions."[4]

Josi and Sechrest then go on to say, "These divergent and often incompatible goals can prove problematic; role conflict, role diffusion, and role ambiguity may be difficult if not impossible to avoid."[5]

Bases of Power

`CO9-2`

Correctional officers rely on a variety of strategies to manage inmate behavior. After surveying correctional officers in five prisons, John Hepburn identified five types of officers' power, according to the bases on which they rest: legitimate power, coercive power, reward power, expert power, and referent power.

Legitimate Power   Correctional officers have power by virtue of their positions within the organization. That is, they have formal authority to command. As Hepburn says, "The prison guard has the right to exercise control over prisoners by virtue of the structural relationship between the position of the guard and the position of the prisoner."[6]

Coercive Power   Inmates' beliefs that a correctional officer can and will punish disobedience give the officer coercive power. Many correctional officers use coercive power as a primary method of control.

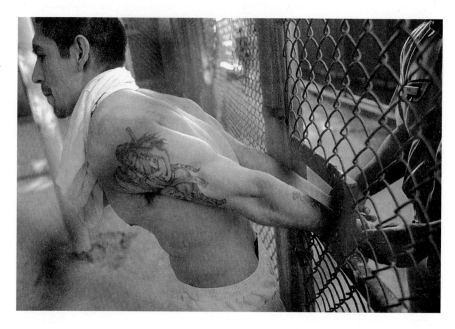

Securing an inmate in preparation for a trip back to his cell. Correctional officers need to elicit inmates' cooperation to effectively carry out their custodial duties. What are some techniques officers might use?

gain time

Time taken off an inmate's sentence for participating in certain positive activities such as going to school, learning a trade, and working in prison.

Reward Power Correctional officers dispense both formal and informal rewards to induce cooperation among inmates. Formal rewards include assignment of desirable jobs, housing, and other inmate privileges. Correctional officers are also in a position to influence parole decisions and to assign good-time credit and **gain time** to inmates. Informal rewards correctional officers use include granting special favors and overlooking minor infractions of rules.

Expert Power Expert power results from inmates' perceptions that certain correctional officers have valuable skills. For example, inmates seeking treatment may value treatment-oriented officers. Inmates who need help with ongoing interpersonal conflicts may value officers who have conflict-resolution skills. Such officers may be able to exert influence on inmates who want their help.

Referent Power Referent power flows from "persuasive diplomacy." Officers who win the respect and admiration of prisoners—officers who are fair and not abusive—may achieve a kind of natural leadership position over inmates.

Some years before Hepburn's study, Gresham Sykes wrote that correctional officers' power can be corrupted through inappropriate relationships with inmates.[7] Friendships with prisoners as well as indebtedness to them can corrupt. According to Sykes, staff members who get too close to inmates and establish friendships are likely to find their "friends" asking for special favors. Similarly, officers who accept help from inmates may one day find that it is "payback time." In difficult or dangerous situations, help may be difficult to decline. In such cases, staff members must be careful not to let any perceived indebtedness to inmates influence their future behavior.

The Staff Subculture

Prison life is characterized by duality. An enormous gap separates those who work in prisons from those who live in them. This gap has a number of dimensions. One is that staff members officially control the institution

A correctional officer talks with an inmate. Effective communication is one way of overcoming the differences in beliefs, values, and behaviors between inmates and prison staff. What barriers to communication might such differences create?

and enforce the rules by which inmates live. Other formal and informal differences exist, including differences in background, values, and culture. Primarily, however, the relationship between correctional officers and inmates can be described as one of structured conflict.[8]

Structured conflict is a term that highlights the tensions between prison staff members and inmates that arise out of the correctional setting. In one sense, the prison is one large society in which the worlds of inmates and staff bump up against one another. In another sense, however, the two groups keep their distance from each other—a distance imposed by both formal and informal rules. Conflict arises because staff members have control over the lives of inmates, and inmates often have little say over important aspects of their own lives. The conflict is structured because it occurs within the confines of an organized institution and because, to some extent, it follows the rules—formal and informal—that govern institutional life.

Both worlds—inmate and staff—have their own cultures. Those cultures are generally called *subcultures* to indicate that both are contained within and surrounded by a larger culture. One writer has defined **subculture** as the beliefs, values, behavior, and material objects shared by a particular group of people within a larger society.[9] That is the definition we will use. The subcultures of inmates and correctional officers exist simultaneously in any prison institution. The beliefs, values, and behavior that make up the **staff subculture** differ greatly from those of the inmate subculture. Additionally, staff members possess material objects of control, such as keys, vehicles, weapons, and security systems.

Kauffman has identified a distinct correctional officer subculture within prisons.[10] Those beliefs, values, and behaviors set correctional officers apart from other prison staff and from inmates. Their beliefs and values form an "officer code," which includes the following:

- Always go to the aid of an officer in distress.
- Do not "lug" (bring in for inmate use) drugs or other contraband.

structured conflict

The tensions between prison staff members and inmates that arise out of the correctional setting.

subculture

The beliefs, values, behavior, and material objects shared by a particular group of people within a larger society.

staff subculture

The beliefs, values, and behavior of staff. They differ greatly from those of the inmate subculture.

- Do not rat on other officers.
- Never make a fellow officer look bad in front of inmates.
- Always support an officer in a dispute with an inmate.
- Always support officer sanctions against inmates.
- Do not be a "white hat" or a "goody two-shoes."
- Maintain officer solidarity in dealings with all outside groups.
- Show positive concern for fellow officers.

Correctional Officers' Characteristics and Pay

Many people believe that working in corrections is not financially rewarding unless an employee can rise to supervisory positions. In an example to the contrary, the highest paid employee at the State Correctional Institution in Pittsburg, Pennsylvania, in 2011 was a corrections officer who earned $139,000.[11] The officer held the lowest rank in the institution—just above trainee—but earned more than the prison's superintendent because of the amount of overtime he worked. According to published reports, many officers in Pennsylvania's correctional institutions earn six-figure incomes because of the number of hours they work. Exhibit 9–2 shows what correctional officers and supervisors earned in 2011 in Pennsylvania.

In terms of ethnicity, the American Correctional Association (ACA) says that most correctional personnel at state and local levels are white males. Two-thirds of female custodial and administrative staff members are white. Thirty-two percent of corrections personnel at the state level are members of minority groups.[12] Of these, most are black. See Exhibit 9–3 for the demographic characteristics of staff members working for the Federal Bureau of Prisons in 2013.

Although blacks comprise only 12.6 percent of the U.S. population, they account for 21 percent of the correctional workforce. Hispanics are underrepresented (accounting for 16.3 percent of the country's population and just 8 percent of the correctional workforce), as are other minorities

EXHIBIT 9–2 Correctional Officer Pay in the State of Pennsylvania, 2011

RANK	NUMBER	TOP EARNER	TOP OVERTIME	MEDIAN OVERTIME		MEDIAN EARNER
Captains	8	$87,861	$12,620	$2,291 →		$77,962
Lieutenants	18	$73,817	$9,646	$2,789 →		$63,706
Sergeants	42	$129,597	$62,554	$20,314 →		$84,916
Corrections Officer	271	$139,571	$76,056	$11,495 →		$54,905
Officer Trainee	26	$34,584	$10,699	$1,434 →		$19,287
Other professionals						
Counselor II	16	$71,395	$9,170	$1,239 →		$48,566
Registered Nurse	18	$94,128	$19,627	$3,618 →		$69,521
Licensed Practical Nurse	10	$74,951	$16,811	$6,214 →		$61,946
Food Service Instructor	18	$72,069	$8,313	$2,960 →		$42,843
Clerk Typist II	18	$33,121	$5,032	$0 →		$23,161

Source: Rich Lord, "It Doesn't Pay to Get Promoted in Pa. Prisons," *Pittsburgh Post-Gazette*, Feb. 26, 2012. Copyright © Pittsburgh Post-Gazette, all rights reserved. Reprinted with permission.

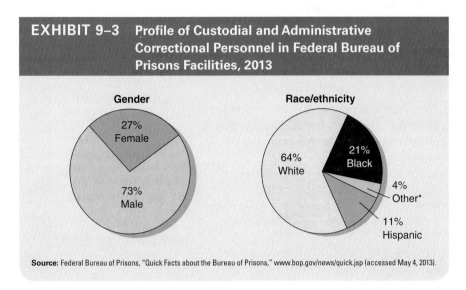

EXHIBIT 9–3   Profile of Custodial and Administrative Correctional Personnel in Federal Bureau of Prisons Facilities, 2013

Gender

27% Female

73% Male

Race/ethnicity

64% White

21% Black

4% Other*

11% Hispanic

Source: Federal Bureau of Prisons, "Quick Facts about the Bureau of Prisons," www.bop.gov/news/quick.jsp (accessed May 4, 2013).

(5 percent of the population, 3 percent of correctional staff). Whites, on the other hand, are slightly underrepresented.

The Federal Bureau of Prisons employs approximately 38,000 personnel in its prisons, and about 27 percent of them are women.[13] About 21 percent of correctional staff members in federal institutions are black. In juvenile facilities, females make up slightly more than 42 percent of the correctional workforce.

The American Correctional Association also says that approximately 13 percent of all correctional staff positions are supervisory (i.e., above the level of sergeant). Females hold 16 percent of all supervisory positions but fewer positions at the level of warden or superintendent.[14] Consult the Appendix: Careers in Corrections at the Online Learning Center Web site for the steps involved in career planning, developing employability and job readiness, and finding a job in corrections.

Correctional Officer Personalities

The staff subculture contributes to the development of **correctional officer personalities.** Those personalities reflect the personal characteristics of the officers as well as their modes of adaptation to their jobs and institutional conditions, the requirements of staff subculture, and institutional expectations.[15] We will next explore the common personality types that have been identified.[16]

correctional officer personalities
The distinctive personal characteristics of correctional officers, including behavioral, emotional, and social traits.

The Dictator The dictator likes to give orders and seems to enjoy the feeling of power that comes from ordering inmates around. Correctional officers with dictator personalities are often strongly disliked by prisoners and may face special difficulties if taken hostage during a prison uprising. Some dictator officers cross the line by personally degrading inmates under their charge through the use of profanity or racist language or by displays of religious and ethnic intolerance. Certain aspects of the dictator personality may lead to illicit and illegal activities by forcing inmates to provide sexual and other favors.

The Friend The correctional officer who tries to befriend inmates is often a quiet, retiring, but kind individual who believes that close friendships with inmates will make it easier to control the inmates and the work

First Lieutenant Gary F. Cornelius

Programs Director • Fairfax County Adult Detention Center •
Fairfax County Office of the Sheriff • Fairfax, Virginia

First Lieutenant Gary Cornelius is programs director with the Fairfax County Adult Detention Center in Fairfax, Virginia. He has held this position since October 1995 but has been with the sheriff's department since 1978.

He earned his bachelor of arts and social sciences with a focus in criminal justice from Edinboro State College in Pennsylvania in 1974. He later completed specialized police courses at the Northern Virginia Criminal Justice Academy Basic Police School as well as the U.S. Secret Service. He is a former officer of the Uniformed Division of the Secret Service.

Lieutenant Cornelius is also the author of five books, including *The Twenty Minute Trainer, The Correctional Officer: A Practical Guide,* and *The Art of the Con: Avoiding Offender Manipulation.* "Writing gives me a chance to share what I have learned and to learn new concepts through research," he says.

His duties include the development and oversight of inmate programs, ranging from recreation to rehabilitation and substance abuse. He oversees inmate education, manages volunteers and college interns, and supervises other staff members in charge of inmate recreation.

Cornelius says he enjoys watching his efforts—and the efforts of his teammates—result in positive changes. "Probably the best thing about my job is working with good people who care about both jail security and making programs work for the betterment of inmates," he says. "The most difficult aspect is convincing staff of the need for programs, rehabilitative efforts, and volunteers. And trying to get through the old-fashioned 'jailhouse mentality.'"

What are the skills that serve him best in his day-to-day affairs? "Tolerance for others' points of view, patience, not giving up, and diplomatic people skills when dealing with both civilians and sworn staff," he says.

> *"Having staff work together on an idea and watching operations improve is one of the best parts of this job."*

environment. Inmates, however, usually try to capitalize on friendships by asking for special treatment, contraband, and the like.

The Merchant Merchant-personality correctional officers (also called *rogue officers* or *rotten apples*) set themselves up as commodity providers to the inmate population. If an inmate needs something not easily obtained in prison, the merchant will usually procure it—at a cost. Often such behavior is a violation of institutional rules, and it can lead to serious violations of the law as the merchant correctional officer smuggles contraband into the institution for the "right price." We will discuss correctional officer corruption in more detail later in this chapter.

The Turnkey Turnkey officers do little beyond the basic requirements of their position. A turnkey usually interacts little with other officers and does the minimum necessary to get through the workday. Unmotivated and bored, the turnkey may be seeking other employment. Some turnkey officers have become disillusioned with their jobs. Others are close to retirement.

The Climber The correctional officer who is a climber is set on advancement. He or she may want to be warden or superintendent one day and is probably seeking rapid promotion. Climbers are often diligent officers who perform their jobs well and respect the corrections profession. Climbers who look down on other officers, however, or attempt to look good by making coworkers look bad, can cause many problems within the institution.

The Reformer The reformer constantly finds problems with the way the institution is run or with existing policies and rules. He or she always seems to know better than anyone else and frequently complains about working conditions or supervisors.

The Do-Gooder The do-gooder is another type of reformer—one with a personal agenda. A devoutly religious do-gooder may try to convert other correctional officers and inmates to his or her faith. Other do-gooders actively seek to counsel inmates, using personal techniques and philosophies that are not integrated into the prison's official treatment program.

Tom Hanks as a correctional officer in The Green Mile. *This chapter describes a variety of correctional officer personality types. Which do you think is the most common? The least?*

Although the personalities described here may be exaggerated, their variety suggests that correctional officer personalities result from many influences, including the following:

- general life experiences;
- biological propensities;
- upbringing;
- staff subculture;
- working conditions; and
- institutional expectations and rules.

CORRECTIONAL OFFICER JOB ASSIGNMENTS

CO9-3

Seven different correctional officer roles or job assignments have been identified.[17] They are classified by their location within the institution, the duties required, and the nature of the contact with inmates. The seven types are as follows:

1. **Block officers** are responsible for supervising inmates in housing areas. Housing areas include dormitories, cell blocks, modular living units, and even tents in some overcrowded prisons. Safety and security are the primary concerns of block officers. Conducting counts, ensuring the orderly movement of prisoners, inspecting personal property, overseeing inmate activity, and searching prisoners are all part of the block officer's job. Block officers also lock and unlock cells and handle problems that arise within the living area. Block officers are greatly outnumbered by the inmates they supervise. Hence, if disturbances occur, block officers usually withdraw quickly to defensible positions within the institution.

2. **Work detail supervisors** oversee the work of individual inmates and inmate work crews assigned to jobs within the institution or outside it. Jobs assigned to inmates may include laundry, kitchen, and farm

block officers
Those responsible for supervising inmates in housing areas.

work detail supervisors
Those who oversee the work of individual inmates and inmate work crews.

The Offender Speaks
Visit www.mhhe.com/schmalleger7e
to see this feature.

industrial shop and school officers

Those who ensure efficient use of training and educational resources within the prison.

yard officers

Those who supervise inmates in the prison yard.

administrative officers

Those who control keys and weapons and sometimes oversee visitation.

perimeter security officers

Those assigned to security (or gun) towers, wall posts, and perimeter patrols. These officers are charged with preventing escapes and detecting and preventing intrusions.

relief officers

Experienced correctional officers who know and can perform almost any custody role within the institution, used to temporarily replace officers who are sick or on vacation or to meet staffing shortages.

duties as well as yard work and building maintenance. Work detail supervisors must also keep track of supplies and tools and maintain inventories of materials. Prison buildings are sometimes constructed almost exclusively with the use of inmate labor—creating the need for large inmate work details. On such large projects, supervising officers usually work in conjunction with outside contractors.

3. **Industrial shop and school officers** work to ensure efficient use of training and educational resources within the prison. Such resources include workshops, schools, classroom facilities, and associated equipment and tools. These officers oversee inmates who are learning trades, such as welding, woodworking, or automobile mechanics or who are attending academic classes. Ensuring that students are present and on time for classes to begin, protecting the school and vocational instructors, and securing the tools and facilities used in instruction are all part of the job of these officers. The officers work with civilian instructors, teachers, and counselors.

4. **Yard officers** supervise inmates in the prison yard. They also take charge of inmates who are (1) moving from place to place, (2) eating, or (3) involved in recreational activities. Like other officers, yard officers are primarily concerned with security and order maintenance.

5. **Administrative officers** are assigned to staff activities within the institution's management center. They control keys and weapons. Some administrative officers oversee visitation. As a result, they have more contact with the public than other officers do. Many administrative officers have little, if any, contact with inmates.

6. **Perimeter security officers** (also called *wall post officers*) are assigned to security (or gun) towers, wall posts, and perimeter patrols. They are charged with preventing escapes and detecting and preventing intrusions (such as packages of drugs or weapons thrown over fences or walls from outside). Perimeter security can become a routine job because it involves little interaction with other officers or inmates and because relatively few escape attempts occur. Newer institutions depend more heavily on technological innovations to maintain secure perimeters, requiring fewer officers for day-long perimeter observation.

7. **Relief officers** are experienced correctional officers who know and can perform almost any custody role in the institution. They are used to temporarily replace officers who are sick or on vacation or to meet staffing shortages.

CO9-4 # CORRECTIONAL STAFF ISSUES

Gender and Staffing

On a pleasant Sunday morning a few years ago, a high-custody female inmate at the Chillicothe (Missouri) Correctional Center was sitting in a dormitory, drinking her morning coffee. Having a good time, surrounded by friends, the inmate began laughing. Soon, however, the laughter turned to choking. Unable to breathe, she turned blue. Correctional officer Lisa Albin rushed to her side and found her hanging onto her bed, unable to speak. Albin remained calm as she applied the Heimlich maneuver to the inmate. After three attempts, the trapped coffee cleared the inmate's windpipe and she began breathing again. After the incident, the inmate wrote a

EXHIBIT 9–4 | **American Correctional Association**

Public Correctional Policy on Employment of Women in Corrections

The American Correctional Association affirms the value of women employees and supports equal employment opportunities for women in adult and juvenile correctional agencies. To encourage the employment of women in corrections, correctional agencies should:

- ensure that recruitment, selection, and promotional opportunities for women are open and fair;
- assign female employees duties and responsibilities that provide career development and promotional opportunities equivalent to those provided to other employees;
- provide all levels of staff with appropriate training on developing effective and cooperative working relationships between male and female correctional personnel;
- provide all levels of staff with appropriate education and training in cross-gender supervision; and
- conduct regular monitoring and evaluation of affirmative action practices and be proactive in achieving corrective actions.

letter of thanks to the superintendent, saying, "If it had not been for Mrs. Albin I could have very well died in that room. She literally saved my life and I will be forever grateful to her and for the training she received."[18]

Literature and films almost invariably portray correctional officers as "tobacco-chewin', reflective sunglasses-wearin', chain-gang-runnin', good ol' boys."[19] Today's officer generally defies this stereotype, and women working in corrections have helped erode this otherwise persistent myth. See Exhibit 9–4 for the ACA policy on women in corrections and Exhibit 9–5 for a map of the percentage of women working in adult correctional facilities throughout the United States in 2007.

Like most women working in male-dominated professions, female correctional officers face special problems and barriers—many of which are rooted in sexism. Prisons are nontraditional workplaces for women. As a consequence, female correctional officers—especially those working in men's prisons—often find themselves in a confusing situation. As one author explains it, "On the one hand, to be female is to be different, an outsider. On the other hand, female guards have much in common with and are sympathetic to their male peers as a result of their shared job experience."[20]

According to studies, female correctional officers typically say that they perform their job with a less aggressive style than men.[21] This difference in style seems due mostly to differences in life experiences and to physical limitations associated with women's size and strength. Life experiences prepare most women for helping roles rather than aggressive ones. As a consequence, women are more likely to rely heavily on verbal skills and intuition. Female correctional officers use communication rather than threats or force to gain inmate cooperation. They tend to talk

A female corrections officer watches inmates playing a game of checkers. Female correctional officers competently perform day-to-day custodial tasks. Are there any areas of a male prison that female correctional officers should be barred from supervising?

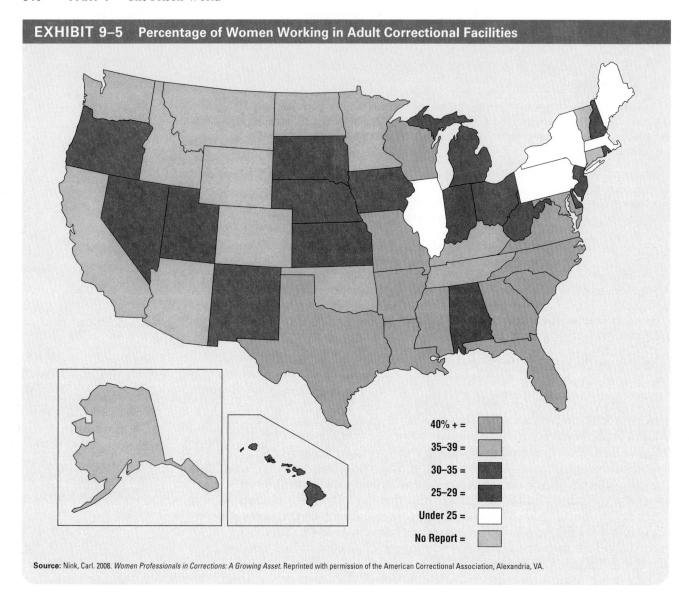

EXHIBIT 9–5   Percentage of Women Working in Adult Correctional Facilities

40% + =
35–39 =
30–35 =
25–29 =
Under 25 =
No Report =

Source: Nink, Carl. 2008. *Women Professionals in Corrections: A Growing Asset.* Reprinted with permission of the American Correctional Association, Alexandria, VA.

out problems. Studies have also found that female correctional officers rely more heavily than male correctional officers on established disciplinary rules when problems arise. Male staff members, on the other hand, are more likely to bully or threaten inmates to resolve problems.

According to research, 55 percent of female officers indicate that their primary reason for taking a job in corrections is an interest in human service work or in inmate rehabilitation.[22] In striking contrast, only 20 percent of male officers give this as their primary reason for working in corrections.

Perhaps as a result of such attitudes, gender makes a dramatic difference in the number of assaults on correctional officers. One national survey of maximum-security prisons in 48 states, the District of Columbia, and the Federal Bureau of Prisons showed that female officers were assaulted only about one-fourth as often as male officers.[23]

Although female correctional officers may take a different approach to their work, the skills they use complement those of male staff members. As one expert writes, "Women may humanize the workplace in small ways by establishing less aggressive relationships with inmates."[24]

Studies also show that male officers, by and large, believe that female officers competently perform day-to-day custodial tasks. Most male staff members are "pro-woman," meaning that they applaud the entry of women into the corrections profession.[25] Many male correctional officers do express concerns about women's ability to provide adequate backup in a crisis, however. It is important to note that the need to use force in prison is relatively rare and that officers generally do not respond to dangerous situations alone. Nonetheless, some female correctional officers report that in emergencies, some male officers adopt a protective, chivalrous attitude toward them. Women generally report that they resent such "special treatment" because it makes them feel more like a liability than an asset in an emergency.

Another issue concerning women in today's workplace is personal and sexual harassment. Studies show that few female correctional officers personally experience unwanted touching or other forms of sexual harassment. The forms of harassment women most commonly experience are physical (nonsexual) assaults, threats, unfounded graphic sexual rumors about them, and demeaning remarks from peers, inmates, and supervisors.[26]

A fair amount of harassment is tolerated in the correctional officer subculture. It is viewed as customary and is often accorded little significance. The response to any form of harassment, however, is determined by the officer experiencing it. He or she can tolerate it, resist it, or report it. Female correctional officers, however, express fear of being ostracized if they complain.

One writer has made the following recommendations for improving the acceptance of women as correctional officers:[27]

1. Require managers and guards to undergo training to sensitize them to the concerns of women working in prisons.

2. Establish a strong policy prohibiting sexual and personal harassment with significant consequences for harassers.

3. Screen male job candidates for their ability and willingness to develop relationships of mutual respect with female colleagues.

Stress

In all occupational categories, employers estimate that more than 25 percent of all reported sick time is due to stress.[28] Stress—tension in a person's body or mind resulting from physical, chemical, or emotional factors—appears to be more commonplace in prison work than in many other jobs. Nonetheless, it is often denied. As one early writer on correctional officers' stress observed, "Most officers . . . try to disguise the toll taken by the job and make the best of what is often a frustrating situation. Though not immune to the pressures of the workplace, these officers project a tough, steady image that precludes sharing frustrations with other coworkers or family members. Some of these officers may be particularly vulnerable to stress."[29]

Correctional officers frequently deny that they are under stress, fearing that admitting to feelings of stress might be interpreted unfavorably. One correctional lieutenant, an 11-year veteran, reported repeatedly observing new correctional employees succumbing to the effects of stress by becoming depressed or turning to alcohol for relief. Although she wanted to intervene, she said she "couldn't" because "no one in law enforcement is allowed to show any emotion or signs of weakness."[30]

In misguided attempts to deal with the effects of stress, many COs resort to self-medication or other tactics to deal with feelings that they

stress

Tension in a person's body or mind, resulting from physical, chemical, or emotional factors.

The Staff Speaks
Visit www.mhhe.com/schmalleger7e
to see this feature.

may not readily admit, even to themselves. Unfortunately, such ineffective methods do not alleviate the pressure and may instead make it worse.

Stress among correctional officers has a number of sources. Feelings of powerlessness, meaninglessness, social isolation, and self-estrangement all contribute to stress. Some authors have identified job alienation as the major source of stress among COs.[31] Correctional officers rarely participate in setting the rules they work under and the policies they enforce; as a result, they may feel alienated from those policies and rules and from those who create them.

One 2011 report found that the most significant stressors faced by correctional officers include (in order of declining significance):[32]

- Job Dangerousness
- Job Pay
- Conflict with Supervisors
- Conflict with Peers
- Role Conflict
- Job Satisfaction
- Pressure due to Gender

Exhibit 9–6 shows this list graphically.

Symptoms of stress can be psychological, behavioral, or physical. Psychological symptoms of stress include anxiety, irritability, mood swings, sadness or depression, low self-esteem, emotional withdrawal, and hypersensitivity (to others and to what others say). Behavioral symptoms of stress include an inability to make decisions, increased interpersonal conflict, blocked creativity and judgment, poor memory, lowered productivity, and difficulty concentrating. The physical symptoms of stress include insomnia, headaches, backaches, gastrointestinal disturbances, fatigue, high blood pressure, and frequent illnesses.

Poorer job performance and exhaustion are the results of stress. When stress reaches an unbearable level, burnout can occur. Burnout, a severe

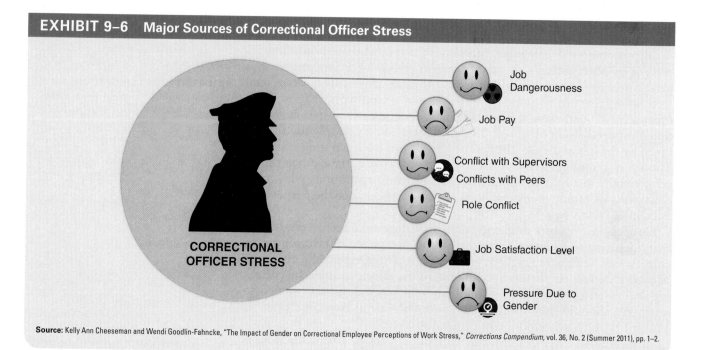

EXHIBIT 9–6   **Major Sources of Correctional Officer Stress**

CORRECTIONAL OFFICER STRESS

Job Dangerousness

Job Pay

Conflict with Supervisors

Conflicts with Peers

Role Conflict

Job Satisfaction Level

Pressure Due to Gender

Source: Kelly Ann Cheeseman and Wendi Goodlin-Fahncke, "The Impact of Gender on Correctional Employee Perceptions of Work Stress," *Corrections Compendium,* vol. 36, No. 2 (Summer 2011), pp. 1–2.

reaction to stress, is "a state of physical and emotional depletion that results from the conditions of one's occupation."[33]

Studies have shown that a person's ability to tolerate stress depends on the frequency, severity, and types of stressors confronted.[34] Stress tolerance also depends on a number of personal aspects, including past experiences, personal values and attitudes, sense of control, personality, residual stress level, and general state of health.

Authorities suggest a number of techniques for avoiding or reducing job stress. Among them are the following:[35]

1. Communicate openly. Tell people how you feel.
2. Learn not to harbor resentment, not to gossip, and to complain less often.
3. Learn to feel confident in your skills, your values and beliefs, and yourself.
4. Develop a support system. Close friends, pets, social activities, and a happy extended family can all help alleviate stress.
5. Be a good and conscientious worker, but don't become a workaholic.
6. Learn to manage your time and do not procrastinate.
7. Make it a habit to get a good night's sleep.
8. Exercise regularly.
9. Watch your diet. Avoid excessive fat, sugars, salt, red meat, and caffeine.
10. Learn some relaxation exercises such as self-affirmation, mental imaging, deep breathing, stretching, massage, or yoga.
11. Try to have fun. Laughter can combat stress quite effectively.
12. Spend time cultivating self-understanding. Analyze your feelings and your problems—and recognize your accomplishments.
13. Set goals and make plans. Both bring order and direction to your life.

One especially effective strategy for coping with job stress is to develop clear and favorable role definitions. According to J. T. Dignam and colleagues, "Officers who have more opportunities for receiving assistance and goal clarification from supervisors and coworkers [are] less likely to experience role ambiguity than those for whom such support is not available or. Further, the risk of burnout or other deleterious consequences of occupational stress may be reduced for those who are 'insulated' by social support."[36]

Stress is an unhappy outcome of the correctional officer's job. How does on-the-job stress arise in the correctional officer's role? How might it be reduced?

Similarly, another group of researchers found that "support from colleagues or supervisors may be one of the most important factors ameliorating stress in the workplace."[37] The same researchers also found that when correctional officers felt "rewarding companionship" with fellow correctional officers, they reported fewer stressful events (even when objective measures showed an actual rise in such events). Most researchers agree that candidates need more extensive and thorough training to prepare them for the psychological and sociological consequences of becoming correctional officers.

Staff Safety

Staff safety is a major stressor for individual correctional officers and a primary management concern for correctional administrators. Safety planning must include consideration of the following elements (adapted, in part, from studies of staff safety needs in both juvenile[38] and adult[39] institutions):

- a functionally designed physical plant that limits inmate movement and incorporates technologically advanced security systems, perimeter barriers, and rooms, doors, and locks;
- a behavior management system that establishes clear guidelines for acceptable behavior, reward systems to reinforce expected behavior, and disciplinary systems to discourage unacceptable behavior;
- appropriate staff and inmate relationships (in particular, staff must be aware of, and prepared to respond to, the dangers posed by prison gangs);
- policies and procedures, published in a manual and distributed to staff and supervisors, that support consistent implementation of rules and regulations and prevent the risk of staff letdowns resulting from excessive routine;
- shift scheduling that ensures a mutually supportive balance of senior and junior staff because a sound mix of age and experience facilitates the achievement of inmate control while providing opportunities for on-the-job development of junior officers by senior officers;
- effective supervision at every level;
- comprehensive staff training that ensures all correctional officers and their supervisors know every rule, regulation, policy, and procedure that affects their particular job (if, as the saying goes, knowledge is power, such training is key to empowering the staff to maintain a controlled, safe environment); and
- development of, and training for, a sound action plan that addresses all contingencies.

In addition to advocating thorough planning as just outlined, Stewart and Brown[40] urge continuing research to identify what works, what doesn't work, and emerging trends in staff safety. In particular, they recommend development of a safety program tailored to the needs of correctional officers nationwide. It should be modeled, they suggest, on safety programs designed for police officers, probation officers, and other officers in law enforcement.

Job Satisfaction

High levels of stress reduce the satisfaction correctional officers get from their jobs. In a sad indictment of the corrections field, a 1996 study found that correctional officers were significantly different from most other groups of correctional employees. "They showed the lowest levels of organizational commitment, possessed the highest levels of skepticism about organizational change, were the least positive about careers in corrections and the rehabilitation of offenders, possessed the lowest levels of job satisfaction, were the least involved in their jobs, and were described as having the poorest work habits and overall job performance."[41] In a separate study, correctional supervisors and managers were found to have much higher levels of job satisfaction and professionalism.[42]

One reason for the difference in job satisfaction between supervisory personnel and those on the front lines of corrections work is that correctional officers often feel alienated from policymaking.[43] As one writer puts it, "when looking at the atmosphere and environment of a state or federal prison, it would seem obvious what correction personnel like least about working there: surveys of personnel who resign or quit show that their biggest problems are with supervisory personnel rather than inmates."[44]

Correctional officers' job satisfaction appears to be tied to the amount of influence they feel they have over administrative decisions and policies. Officers who feel they have some control over the institution and over their jobs seem much more satisfied than officers who believe they have no control. Hence, it appears that correctional officers' job satisfaction can be greatly enhanced by caring administrators who involve the officers in policymaking.

For some correctional officers, the perception that their profession suffers a generally poor public image[45] further reduces their job satisfaction. Compared to local and state police officers and agents of the various federal law enforcement organizations, correctional officers may be viewed as the "poor relations" of the law enforcement family. As one researcher wrote, "Most people do not know of a child who says, I want to be a correctional officer when I grow up."[46]

Media portrayals of correctional officers exacerbate the situation. Movies and television often depict COs as lowly qualified "guards" (considered a derogatory title; "guards work at Macy's and banks")[47] whose primary function seems to be abusing prisoners. Correctional officers "believe they are seen as brutes, only a shade better than the people behind bars."[48] Consequently, COs have a difficult time overcoming these images as they attempt to convey the significance and professional demands of their positions to civic leaders and the public.[49]

There is evidence, however, that job satisfaction among correctional officers is rising. The rise may be partly due to increasing awareness of what correctional officers find most important in the work environment. Recent studies have identified the most important determinants of job satisfaction among correctional officers as (1) working conditions, (2) the level of work-related stress, (3) the quality of working relationships with fellow officers, and (4) length of service.[50]

In one of the most significant studies to date, treatment-oriented correctional staff reported far higher levels of job satisfaction than did custody-oriented staff.[51] The study was of survey data collected from 428 Arizona correctional service officers (CSOs) and 118 correctional program officers (CPOs). Job satisfaction was significantly greater among the human-services-oriented CPOs than among the traditional-custody-oriented CSOs. The findings suggest that additional attention should be given to enhancing and enriching the duties of correctional officers, extending their control over and involvement in prisoners' activities, and redefining their roles more as service workers than as control agents.

Determinants of job satisfaction appear to differ for male and female correctional officers. One study found that the quality of working relationships with other officers, the amount of stress experienced at work, the length of service as a correctional officer, and educational level were all positively related to job satisfaction for males.[52] Women officers, on

Visit ccajob.com or scan this code with the QR app on your SmartPhone or digital device to watch two videos showing why a career in corrections can be enjoyable.

the other hand, appeared to place more emphasis on the quality of working relationships with all other correctional officers (not just the ones with whom they worked) and tended to be happier in prisons at lower security levels. Other studies have related higher job satisfaction among white female officers to the officers' positive evaluation of the quality of supervision. In other words, white female correctional officers tend to be happier in prisons that they believe are well run.[53]

Professionalism

A common difference between a professional and a nonprofessional is that a professional learns every aspect of the job whereas a nonprofessional avoids the learning process and often considers it a waste of time. Professionals seek to prevent mistakes at all costs, but if they occur, the professional does not let them slide; nonprofessionals tend to ignore or hide them. A professional tries to be great, whereas a nonprofessional just tries to get by at what he or she does.

Professionalism is commitment to a set of agreed-upon values aimed at improving the organization while maintaining the highest standards of excellence and dissemination of knowledge.[54] In addition to having knowledge and skills, professionals must present humanistic qualities: selflessness, responsibility and accountability, leadership, excellence, integrity, honesty, empathy, and respect for coworkers and prisoners.

Professional correctional organizations that operate at the national level, such as the American Correctional Association (discussed in Chapter 1, and mentioned elsewhere in this chapter), have qualified and well-trained employees, well-run professional development departments, and well-developed standards of conduct. Such organizations provide the support needed for operating agencies and individual correctional facilities to achieve fairness in handling inmates and correctional personnel while documenting and addressing issues that may arise in inmate and employee conduct. These organizations also help to define common sets of values that establish the tone and climate for day-to-day operations in correctional facilities.

The vision provided by professional organizations helps build confidence that employees will be professional and will have integrity, respect,

Visit www.youtube.com/watch?v=RTlm-Ham_es or scan this code with the QR app on your SmartPhone or digital device to watch a video showing a day in the life of a correctional officer.

Training can enhance professionalism. As more and more prison staff develop a professional perspective, the structural organization of prisons and interactions among staff and inmates may significantly change. What kinds of training may help correctional officers adjust to a changing environment?

Ethics and Professionalism

International Association of Correctional Officers: The Correctional Officer's Creed

To speak sparingly . . . to act, not argue . . . to be in authority through personal presence . . . to correct without nagging . . . to speak with the calm voice of certainty . . . to see everything and to know what is significant and what not to notice . . . to be neither insensitive to distress nor so distracted by pity as to miss what must elsewhere be seen. . . .

To do neither that which is unkind nor self-indulgent in its misplaced charity . . . never to obey the impulse to tongue lash that silent insolence which in time past could receive the lash . . . to be both firm and fair . . . to know I cannot be fair simply by being firm, nor firm simply by being fair. . . .

To support the reputations of associates and confront them without anger should they stand short of professional conduct . . . to reach for knowledge of the continuing mysteries of human motivation . . . to think; always to think . . . to be dependable . . . to be dependable first to my charges and associates and thereafter to my duty as employee and citizen . . . to keep fit . . . to keep forever alert . . . to listen to what is meant as well as what is said with words and with silences.

To expect respect from my charges and my superiors yet never to abuse the one for abuses from the other . . . for eight hours each working day to be an example of the person I could be at all times . . . to acquiesce in no dishonest act . . . to cultivate patience under boredom and calm during confusion . . . to understand the why of every order I take or give. . . .

To hold freedom among the highest values though I deny it to those I guard . . . to deny it with dignity that in my example they find no reason to lose their dignity . . . to be prompt . . . to be honest with all who practice deceit that they not find in me excuse for themselves . . . to privately face down my fear that I not signal it . . . to privately cool my anger that I not displace it on others . . . to hold in confidence what I see and hear, which by telling could harm or humiliate to no good purpose . . . to keep my outside problems outside . . . to leave inside that which should stay inside . . . to do my duty.

Source: Copyright © 2000 Bob Barrington. Used by permission of the International Association of Correctional Officers.

Ethical Dilemma 9–1:
There are reports that find sexual misconduct is a problem in prisons for women. These reports state that male staff victimize women inmates. Should only female staff work in prisons for women? What are the issues? For more information go to Ethical Dilemma 9–1 at www.justicestudies.com/ethics06.

Ethical Dilemma 9–2:
Stress among correctional staff is widespread, and your facility has a stress-reduction program. You are feeling very stressed, but you are afraid to take advantage of the program, thinking it may reflect poorly on you at promotion time. Do you participate in the program anyway? For more information go to Ethical Dilemma 9–2 at www.justicestudies.com/ethics06.

Ethical Dilemmas for every chapter are available online.

---

the ability to engage in teamwork, the motivation for continued learning, and commitment to the profession.

According to William Sondervan, former commissioner of the Maryland Division of Corrections and previous director of professional development for the American Correctional Association, professionalism in corrections is vitally important to the integrity, safety, and security of correctional agencies and institutions.[55] Corrections professionalism, says Sondervan, requires that any correctional organization establish or clarify the following three elements:

- **purpose**—the reason for an organization's existence;
- **mission**—what is done to support the organization's purpose; and
- **vision**—the planned future direction of the organization.

Together, says Sondervan, purpose, mission, and vision provide a roadmap for the development of professionalism within an organization.

Exhibit 9–7 depicts the formal mission, vision, and goals of the Maryland Department of Public Safety and Correctional Services, and Exhibit 9–8 lists the values and beliefs that support the department's mission and vision statements.

purpose
The reason for an organization's existence.

mission
That which is done to support an organization's purpose.

vision
The planned future direction of an organization.

EXHIBIT 9–7 | **Maryland Department of Public Safety and Correctional Services, Mission and Vision Statement**

Mission

The Department of Public Safety and Correctional Services protects the public, its employees, and detainees and offenders under its supervision.

Vision

The Maryland Department of Public Safety and Correctional Services will be nationally recognized as a department that believes its own employees are its greatest strength, and values the development of their talents, skills, and leadership.

We will be known for dealing with tough issues like gang violence, by capitalizing on the strength of interagency collaboration.

We will be nationally known as the department that takes responsibility for the greatest of problems, and moves quickly and quietly to bring about successful change.

The Department of Public Safety and Correctional Services will be known as one of the national leaders in the development and use of technology through system interoperability.

Others will look to this department for its effective leadership and evidence-based practices.

We will be known for our belief in the value of the human being, and the way we protect those individuals, whether they are members of the public, our own employees, those we are obligated to keep safe and in custody, or victims of crime.

The Maryland Department of Public Safety and Correctional Services will be known as an organization that focuses on its mission and takes care of its people.

Source: Reprinted with permission of the Maryland Department of Public Safety and Correctional Services.

EXHIBIT 9–8 | **Maryland Division of Correction Values**

Integrity	We are a principle-based organization. We recognize and respect the dignity of all individuals. We strive for and expect honesty, truth and respect in our service to customers and stakeholders.
Dedication	We are committed to fulfilling our mission by serving our customers and stakeholders with concern and sensitivity under challenging circumstances.
Teamwork and Communication	We value results-oriented teamwork as an essential tool to accomplish our mission. We encourage open, effective communication throughout the Division to efficiently integrate our internal and external partnerships.
Public Trust and Confidence	We value public trust and confidence. We strive to assure our citizens that we are good stewards of the public's resources entrusted to us. Through community outreach, we hope to inspire public confidence in the **P**rofessional **R**esults **I**n **D**aily **E**fforts **(PRIDE)** we take in our duties.
Professionalism	We value effective leadership and strive for impartiality and fairness in the workplace. We encourage personal and professional development. We recognize and reward dedication and commitment to competence and the highest standards of achievement.

Source: Reprinted with permission of the Maryland Department of Public Safety and Correctional Services.

Although the development of an appropriate mission statement is vital at the organizational level, the development of a sense of personal ethics is crucial to daily on-the-job success. In support of personal ethics, the International Association of Correctional Officers has published a Correctional Officer's Creed (see the Ethics and Professionalism box), which summarizes the duties and responsibilities of a correctional officer.

Officer Corruption

CO9-5

A few years ago, 24 members of the violent Black Guerrilla Family prison gang were arrested in Maryland following a seven-month long investigation into the smuggling of contraband into Baltimore-area prisons.[56] Four of those arrested were state correctional officers. Using bribes, threats, and promised favors, leaders of the gang were able to coerce the officers into smuggling contraband to imprisoned associates and extorting money from other inmates. The favored prisoners feasted on salmon, shrimp, and other delicacies while smoking expensive cigars and drinking premium vodka. Using smuggled cell phones, they were able to arrange for attacks on witnesses and rival gang members living outside the prison. One of the corrupt officers, a woman who played a central role in facilitating the gang's illegal activities, is reported to have provided sexual favors for inmates in return for money.

In another incident that apparently stemmed from correctional officer corruption, 76-year-old convicted mass murderer Charles Manson was caught with a mobile phone in his prison cell at California's Corcoran State Prison in February 2011. It was the second time in two years that officers had confiscated a phone from Manson during a cell search. Manson, who is serving a life sentence, was convicted in the 1969 murders of seven people, including pregnant actress Sharon Tate.

Legislative analysts for the state of California estimate that more than 10,000 cell phones made their way into California prisons in 2010.[57] According to those same analysts, prison employees are the main source of smuggled phones that end up in the hands of prisoners. A recent California state inspector general's report detailed the story of how a single corrections officer made $150,000 a year smuggling phones to inmates. Although his activities were eventually discovered and he was fired, he was not criminally prosecuted because it is not against the law in California to take cell phones into prisons—even though it is a violation of prison rules for inmates to possess them. Following the incident involving Manson, state senator Alex Padilla called on California Governor Jerry Brown to mandate the periodic searching of correctional officers reporting for work.

Other forms of correctional officer corruption and job malfeasance include the misuse of confidential information, drinking and abusing drugs while on duty, sleeping on duty, unnecessary roughness or brutality against inmates, racism, and filing false disciplinary reports on inmates. A small number of sadistic people may even be attracted to working in corrections because they think it will provide them the opportunity to physically abuse others. Pre-employment personality inventories, background checks, and face-to-face pre-employment interviews are all crucial in preventing such people from obtaining positions of authority in correctional facilities.

Contributing to the problem of corruption among correctional staff is low pay—especially in some jurisdictions. "If someone is desperate to make ends meet and someone offers them $2,100 to smuggle in a cell phone, it's a hell of a temptation," says Brian Olsen, executive director of a Texas labor union that represents Texas correctional officers.[58]

While all examples used in this chapter come from state correctional agencies, a look at statistics seems to show that corruption among federal correctional personnel is relatively rare. A recent Congressional report by the U.S. Department of Justice's (DOJ) Office of the Inspector General (OIG), for example, found only 238 likely cases of criminal misconduct by BOP employees.[59] Given that the number of persons employed by the BOP is approximately 39,000 BOP misconduct levels appear to be among the lowest in government.

CO9-6   THE IMPACT OF TERRORISM ON CORRECTIONS

In 2009, convicted terrorist Kevin James, 32, was sentenced in federal court in Santa Ana, California, to 16 years in prison. James had pleaded guilty in 2007 to conspiracy to wage war against the United States[60] and had been accused of plotting terrorist attacks on Jewish and military targets throughout California. Among those targets were Los Angeles International Airport, the Israeli Consulate, and Army recruiting centers.

Those who investigated James's background found that he had formed an Islamic terrorist group in California's Tehachapi Prison in 1997. While serving a 10-year sentence for robbery, James joined the Nation of Islam—a traditional American Islamic faith. Soon, however, he became engaged with a fringe group of Sunni Muslims at Tehachapi. The group, known as *Jamiyyat Ui Islam Is Saheeh* (the Assembly of Authentic Islam, or JIS), operates today throughout prisons in California where it is known as a radical Islamist prison gang, or STG. JIS advocates attacks on enemies of the Islamic faith, the U.S. government, Jews, "infidels," and supporters of Israel.

Eventually, James took control of JIS and began distributing a handwritten manifesto known as the JIS Protocol in which he justified the killing of infidels. Following transfer to the maximum-security California State Prison in Sacramento, James recruited more inmates to join JIS and used soon-to-be paroled inmates to recruit additional members outside of prison. Using smuggled letters and phone calls, James communicated his plans for terrorist attacks to recruits on the outside.

Mark Hamm, a criminal justice professor who studied the case of Kevin James, notes that "prisoner radicalization grows in the secretive underground of inmate subcultures through prison gangs and extremist interpretations of religious doctrines that inspire ideologies of intolerance, hatred and violence."[61] Hamm also learned that "prisoners are radicalized through a process of one-on-one proselytizing by charismatic leaders." Especially vulnerable, says Hamm, are those inmates who no longer have contact with their families and are angry and embittered by their circumstances. "I discovered," says Hamm, "that charismatic leadership was more important than other commonly cited factors associated with prisoner radicalization."[62]

Because of their marginal social status, inmates may be particularly vulnerable to recruitment by terrorist organizations. According to Chip Ellis, research and program coordinator for the National Memorial Institute for the Prevention of Terrorism, "Prisoners are a captive audience, and they usually have a diminished sense of self or a need for identity and protection. They're usually a disenchanted or disenfranchised group of people, [and] terrorists can sometimes capitalize on that situation."[63] Ellis points out that inmates can be radicalized in a variety of ways, including exposure to extremist literature and other radical inmates as well as through anti-U.S. sermons delivered during religious services.

Convicted terrorist Kevin James answers questions put to him during an exclusive TV interview with producer and investigative journalist Eric Longabardi. James is the founder of Jamiyyat Ui Islam Is Saheeh (the Assembly of Authentic Islam). Does terrorist recruiting take place in prison?

The FBI says that al-Qaeda continues to actively recruit followers inside American correctional institutions. Islamic terrorists are keenly aware of the 9,600 Muslims held in the federal prison system and see them as potential converts. "These terrorists seek to exploit our freedom to exercise religion to their advantage by using radical forms of Islam to recruit operatives," says FBI counterterrorism chief John Pistole.[64] "Unfortunately," notes Pistole, "U.S. correctional institutions are a valuable venue for such radicalization and recruitment."

Anti-Terrorism Planning

Not only must today's prison administrators be concerned about inmate involvement in terrorist activities, they must also think about and plan for the impact of the terrorism event within their facilities and within the communities in which their facilities are located. Moreover, incarcerating those who have been convicted of acts of terrorism presents new challenges for correctional administrators. For example, Sheik Omar Abdel-Rahman, spiritual leader for many terrorists, including Osama bin Laden, is now serving a life sentence in a U.S. federal penitentiary for conspiring to assassinate former Egyptian President Hosni Mubarak and blow up five New York City landmarks in the 1990s. Speculation that the sheik continues to motivate terrorist acts against the United States gained credibility when his attorney was sentenced to 28 months in prison in 2006 for passing illegal communications between Abdel-Rahman and an Egyptian-based terrorist organization known as the Islamic Group.[65] Another convicted terrorist, September 11 conspirator Zacarias Moussaoui, also known as the 20th hijacker, is serving a life sentence at the federal administrative maximum facility in Florence, Colorado. Moussaoui's fellow prisoners, housed on what has come to be known as "Bomber's Row," include al-Qaeda shoe bomber Richard Reid; Ramzi Yousef, mastermind of the 1993 World Trade Center bombing; seven of Yousef's accomplices; Ahmed Ressam, who was arrested at the Canadian border with explosives he intended to use to bomb Los Angeles International Airport; four men convicted in the 1998 bombing of U.S. embassies in Africa; and Abdul Hakim Murad, convicted in a 1995 al-Qaeda plan to bomb 12 airplanes during a two-day period.

Muslim prisoners at prayer in a Virginia correctional facility. Radicalized inmates of any faith can represent a threat to facility security. What connection might exist between radicalized inmates and criminals or terrorist groups on the outside?

Jess Maghan, former training director for the New York City Department of Corrections and now the director of the Forum for Comparative Corrections and professor of criminal justice at the University of Illinois at Chicago, points out that "the interaction of all people in a prison (staff, officers, and inmates) can become important intelligence sources."[66] Moreover, says Maghan, the flow of information between inmates and the outside world needs to be monitored in order to detect attack plans—especially when prisons house known terrorist leaders or group members. Covert information, says Maghan, can be passed through legal visits (where people conveying information may have no idea of its significance), sub rosa communications networks in prisons that can support communications between inmates and the outside world, and prison transportation systems.

In 2005, the Institute for the Study of Violent Groups at Sam Houston State University charged that Wahhabism—the most radical form of Islam—was being spread in American prisons by clerics approved by the Islamic Society of North America (ISNA). ISNA is one of two organizations

Indonesian terrorist Imam Samudra in prison in Bali awaiting execution. Samudra was convicted of masterminding terrorist bombings that killed 202 people in 2002 and was sentenced to death by firing squad. While imprisoned, Samudra wrote a jailhouse manifesto on the funding of terrorism through cyberfraud. He was executed by firing squad in 2008. How might incarcerated terrorists constitute a threat to the facilities in which they are housed? To the rest of society?

that the Federal Bureau of Prisons uses to select prison chaplains to serve inmates in its facilities.[67] "Proselytizing in prisons," said the institute, "can produce new recruits with American citizenship." An example might be Chicago thug Jose Padilla, aka Abdulla al-Mujahir, who converted to Islam after exposure to Wahhabism while serving time in a Florida jail. Authorities claim Padilla intended to contaminate a U.S. city with a radiological dirty bomb. In 2007, Padilla was convicted of federal terrorism charges. Similarly, convicted shoe bomber Richard Reid converted to radical Islam while in an English prison before planning his attack on an American Airlines flight from Paris to Miami.[68]

A few years after the attacks of 9/11, the Office of the Inspector General of the U.S. Department of Justice released a review of the practices used by the Federal Bureau of Prisons in selecting Muslim clergy to minister to inmates in the bureau's facilities. The report concluded that the primary threat of radicalization came not from chaplains, contractors, or volunteers but from inmates. According to the report, "Inmates from foreign countries politicize Islam and radicalize inmates, who in turn radicalize more inmates when they transfer to other prisons."[69] The report also identified a form of Islam unique to the prison environment called "Prison Islam."[70] The report said that Prison Islam is a form of Islam that is used by gangs and radical inmates to further unlawful goals. It adapts itself easily to prison values and promotes the interests of the incarcerated. Prison Islam was found to be especially common in institutions where religious services are led by lay *Mullahs* (spiritual leaders, who are often inmates)—a practice made necessary by a lack of Muslim chaplains. The report recommended that "the BOP can and should improve its process for selecting, screening, and supervising Muslim religious services providers. We recommend," said the report, that "the BOP take steps to examine all chaplains', religious contractors', and religious volunteers' doctrinal beliefs to screen out anyone who poses a threat to security." Echoing those sentiments is Mark Hamm, who says that the most significant thing that prison administrators can do to undercut terrorist recruitment in prison is to hire chaplains who have been properly vetted. "Without them," says Hamm, "radicalized prisoners are free to operate on their own, independent of religious authority to ensure moderation and tolerance."[71]

In 2006, the U.S. Justice Department's Office of the Inspector General released another report—this one critical of BOP inmate mail monitoring procedures, saying that "the threat remains that terrorist and other high-risk inmates can use mail and verbal communications to conduct terrorist or criminal activities while incarcerated." The report was based on findings that three convicted terrorists had been able to send 90 letters to Islamic extremists in the Middle East in 2005, praising Osama bin Laden. The report noted the fact that the BOP does not have the needed number of translators proficient in Arabic who are able to read inmate mail and said that budget restrictions do not allow for the reading of all incoming and outgoing mail.[72]

The threat of a terrorist act being carried out by inmates within a prison or jail can be an important consideration in facility planning and management. Of particular concern is the possibility of bioterrorism. A concentrated population such as exists within a prison or jail would be highly susceptible to rapid transmission of the ill effects from such an attack.[73]

Significant recommendations for addressing the terrorist threat within correctional institutions come from Y. N. Baykan, a management specialist with the Maryland Division of Correction. Baykan says that no successful strategies are being used today to control radical Islamist influences in American prisons and suggests the following:[74]

- Prison administrators must realize that the threat of transnational terrorism in American facilities is real.
- Radical Islamic groups should be seen as sophisticated social networks rather than gangs.
- Prison authorities must evaluate existing policies and strategies, looking closely at the roles and backgrounds of chaplains and volunteers and the rules governing religious conversions.
- Meetings of radicals should be closely monitored as should incoming propaganda.
- Prison staff should be taught to understand political Islam and should use information-management solutions that involve cutting-edge collection, storage, and analysis of data.
- Prison authorities must follow what is happening in other countries and learn from it.
- Threat information should be shared by all stakeholders, including state and federal systems and other law enforcement agencies.

As the United States faces more and more threats of terrorism, it is likely that the issues identified here will take on greater significance for correctional facilities throughout the nation and around the world.

REVIEW AND APPLICATIONS

SUMMARY

1 There is a hierarchy of staff positions from warden (or superintendent) at the top down to correctional officer and correctional officer trainee. A typical correctional staff includes (1) administrative staff, (2) clerical personnel, (3) program staff, (4) custodial staff, (5) service and maintenance staff, and (6) volunteers.

2 The types of power available to correctional officers are legitimate power, coercive power, reward power, expert power, and referent power. Correctional officer personality types discussed in this chapter are (1) the dictator, (2) the friend, (3) the merchant, (4) the turnkey, (5) the climber, (6) the reformer, and (7) the do-gooder.

3 The seven correctional officer assignments are (1) block officers, (2) work detail supervisors, (3) industrial shop and school officers, (4) yard officers, (5) administrative officers, (6) perimeter security officers (also called *wall post officers*), and (7) relief officers.

4 The five significant correctional staff issues discussed in this chapter are (1) gender-related concerns, (2) correctional officer stress, (3) staff safety, (4) job satisfaction among those working in corrections, and (5) professionalism.

5 Some correctional officers become corrupt, and serious corruption can threaten the security of the institution. Greed, the desire for sexual gratification, and a lack of professionalism can all contribute to corruption among corrections personnel.

6 Today's prison administrators and corrections personnel must be vigilant against the threat of terrorism and must guard against terrorist activities from within the institution and from outside.

KEY TERMS

roles, p. 299

staff roles, p. 299

custodial staff, p. 300

program staff, p. 300

gain time, p. 302

structured conflict, p. 303

subculture, p. 303

staff subculture, p. 303

correctional officer personalities, p. 305

block officers, p. 307

work detail supervisors, p. 307

industrial shop and school officers, p. 308

yard officers, p. 308

administrative officers, p. 308

perimeter security officers, p. 308

relief officers, p. 308

stress, p. 311

purpose, p. 317

mission, p. 317

vision, p. 317

QUESTIONS FOR REVIEW

1 What staff roles does the hierarchy of a typical correctional institution include?

2 According to John Hepburn, what are five bases of the power that correctional officers use to gain inmate compliance?

3 What are the seven correctional officer job assignments?

4 What are the five significant correctional staff issues discussed in this chapter?

5 How might correctional officers become corrupt? What kinds of activities might corrupt officers engage in?

6 Briefly explain the impact that terrorism is having on prisons and prison administration.

THINKING CRITICALLY ABOUT CORRECTIONS

Prison Rape

James Gilligan, MD, contends that rape in prisons is "an intrinsic and universal part of the punishments that our government metes out to those whom it labels as 'criminal.'"[75] In essence, Gilligan suggests, prison administrators passively employ inmate-on-inmate rape as a management tool to control the prisoner population.

Dr. Gilligan bases his charge on three contentions:

First, the relevant legal authorities, from judges to prosecutors who send people to prison, to the prison officials who administer them, are all aware of the existence, the reality, and the near-universality of rape in the prisons. Indeed, this is one reason that many conscientious judges are extremely reluctant to send anyone to prison except when they feel compelled to, either by the violence of the crime or, as is increasingly true, by laws mandating prison sentences even for nonviolent crimes, such as drug offenses.

Second, the conditions that stimulate such rapes (the enforced deprivation of other sources of self-esteem, respect, power, and sexual gratification) are consciously and deliberately imposed upon the prison population by the legal authorities.

Third, all these authorities tacitly and knowingly tolerate this form of sexual violence, passively delegating to the dominant and most violent inmates the power and authority to deliver this form of punishment to the more submissive and nonviolent ones, so that the rapists in this situation are acting as the vicarious enforcers of a form of punishment that the legal system does not itself enforce formally or directly.

Given that rape is universally acknowledged as a crime, Dr. Gilligan's charge is tantamount to an accusation of criminal conspiracy of monumental proportions.

1. Do you believe there is merit to Gilligan's claims?

2. If so, how would you propose addressing this issue?

The Staff Subculture

The staff culture is generally instilled in correctional officer trainees by more experienced officers and by work experiences. Socialization into the staff subculture begins on the first day of academy training or the first day of work (whichever comes first). One of the most important beliefs of the staff subculture is that officers should support one another.

Some people argue that the staff subculture is dangerous because it can sustain improper and even illegal behavior while forcing correctional officers to keep to themselves what they know about such behavior. Others, however, suggest that the staff subculture is a positive element in the correctional world. It is important to correctional officer morale, they claim. They also suggest that it "fills the gaps" in formal training by establishing informal rules to guide staff behavior and decision making in difficult situations. The staff subculture can provide informal "workarounds" when the formal requirements of a correctional officer's position seem unrealistic.

1. Do you think the staff subculture contributes to or detracts from meeting the goals of institutional corrections? Why?
2. Do you think the staff subculture benefits or harms the lives and working environment of correctional officers? Explain.
3. What functions of the staff subculture can you identify? Rate each of those functions as positive or negative for its role in meeting the goals of institutional corrections.

ON-THE-JOB DECISION MAKING

Use of Force

You are an experienced correctional officer assigned to yard duty. As you patrol the prison yard, watching inmates milling around and talking, a fellow officer named Renée approaches you. Renée was hired only a week ago, and she has gained a reputation for being inquisitive—asking experienced correctional officers about prison work. Renée walks up and says, "You know, I'm wondering what I should do. Yesterday I saw an officer push an inmate around because the guy didn't do what he asked. I don't know if the inmate didn't hear what was being said, or if he was just ignoring the officer." Renée looks at the ground. "What am I supposed to do in a situation like that? Should I have said something right then? Should I talk to the officer privately? Should I suggest to the officer that maybe the inmate didn't hear him? He knows we aren't supposed to use force on inmates unless it's really necessary. If I see him do this kind of thing again, should I report him?" Looking up, Renée says, "I know we're supposed to support each other in here. But what would you do?" How would you respond to Renée's questions?

Former CO Inmate

For about four years, Alex Kaminsky was one of your fellow correctional officers at the McClellan Correctional Facility. During your service together, you developed a friendship close enough to include social occasions outside the job, and your wives became good friends.

Two years ago, Kaminsky was convicted of dealing controlled substances to inmates and received a 12- to 20-year sentence. Upon your recent transfer to the Brownley Correctional Facility, you discover that Kaminsky is one of the inmates incarcerated there. He resides in one of the cell blocks that falls in your area of responsibility and works on the maintenance crew that you supervise.

1. Should you seek assignment to another area of the prison or seek to have Kaminsky transferred out, to prevent the necessity of having contact with him? Explain.
2. If Kaminsky approaches you, should you permit the reestablishment of a relationship that might (or might not) prove beneficial to his rehabilitation?

For additional information, please see: www.mhhe.com/schmalleger7e
Follow the author's tweets about the latest crime and justice news @schmalleger

THE INMATE WORLD

Living Behind Bars

CHAPTER OBJECTIVES

After completing this chapter you should be able to do the following:

1 Explain what *inmate subculture* is and explain how it forms.

2 Know what is meant by the *prison code,* and be able to list some elements of it.

3 Explain what is meant by *prison argot.*

4 List some common roles that male inmates assume.

5 Describe some major differences between women's and men's prisons.

6 Compare some of the characteristics of female inmates with those of male inmates.

7 Explain how the social structure in women's prisons differs from that in men's prisons.

In prison, those things withheld from and denied to the prisoner become precisely what he wants most of all.

—Eldridge Cleaver, African-American author and activist

In 2012, the reigning Miss America, twenty-three-year-old Laura Kaeppeler, dedicated the year of her reign to the theme "Circles of Support: Mentoring Children of Incarcerated Parents."[1] Kaeppeler said, "It's everyday life for millions of children, and it allows me to connect with people on a level they don't expect a pageant contestant to connect with them. This is a real problem people can relate to." Kaeppeler's father had been imprisoned when she was 17 for a white-collar crime.

This chapter will examine prison life, the inmate subculture, and the prison experience in general by looking first at men in prison and then at imprisoned women.

Laura Kaeppeler, Miss America 2012. Kaeppeler dedicated the year of her reign to the support of children of incarcerated parents. What other issues do inmates face?

MEN IN PRISON

As we have already seen, most state inmates are male, belong to racial or ethnic minority groups, are relatively young, and have been incarcerated for a violent offense. A recent Bureau of Justice Statistics study examined social, economic, and other characteristics of state inmates nationwide.[2] Highlights of that study are shown in Exhibit 10–1.

Prisons and other total institutions are small, self-contained societies with their own social structures, norms, and rules. Although not entirely isolated, prison inmates are physically, emotionally, and socially restricted from anything more than minor participation in the surrounding society. As a consequence, they develop their own distinctive lifestyles, roles, and behavioral norms.

In his classic work *Asylums,* Erving Goffman used the phrase **total institution** to describe a place where the same people work, eat, sleep, and engage in recreation together day after day.[3] Life within total institutions is closely planned by those in control, and activities are strictly scheduled. Prisons, concentration camps, mental hospitals, and seminaries are all total institutions, said Goffman. They share many of the same characteristics—even though they exist for different purposes and house different kinds of populations. His words were echoed years later by Hans Toch, who noted that "prisons are 24-hour-a-day, year-in-and-year-out environments in which people are sequestered with little outside contact."[4]

Goffman also identified a number of modes of adaptation to prison life by which inmates attempt to adjust to the conditions around them. Some inmates, said Goffman, *convert* to life within institutions, taking on the staff's view of themselves and of institutional society. Others *withdraw.* Still others make attempts at *colonization*—meaning that they strike a balance between values and habits brought from home and those dictated by the social environment of the prison. Finally, some inmates *rebel,* rejecting the demands of their surroundings and often ending up in trouble with authorities. As Victoria R. Derosia of Castleton State College points

total institution

A place where the same people work, play, eat, sleep, and recreate together on a continuous basis. The term was developed by the sociologist Erving Goffman to describe prisons and other similar facilities.

EXHIBIT 10–1   National Profile of State Prison Inmates

57%
had a high school diploma or its equivalent

55%
had never married

43%
had lived with both parents most of the time while growing up

67%
were employed during the month before their arrest for their current crime

37%
had an immediate family member who had served time

38%
had not been incarcerated before

32%
committed their offense under the influence of alcohol

32%
committed their offense under the influence of drugs

96%
were U.S. citizens

Sources: E. Ann Carson and William J. Sabol, *Prisoners in 2011* (Washington, DC: Bureau of Justice Statistics, December 2012); Bureau of Justice Statistics, *Characteristics of State Prison Inmates,* retrieved February 27, 2013 from www.ojp.usdoj.gov/bjs/crimoff.htm#inmates; Allen Beck et al., *Survey of State Prison Inmates, 1991* (Washington, DC: U.S. Department of Justice, March 1993); and Christopher J. Mumola and Jennifer C. Karberg, "Drug Use and Dependence, State and Federal Prisoners, 2004" (Washington, DC: Bureau of Justice Statistics, 2006).

out in her book *Living Inside Prison Walls*, some people "will make it through incarceration relatively unscathed and move on to a better life as a rehabilitated (or habilitated) citizen, while others will repeatedly fail at life outside prison. Offenders will successfully or poorly adjust to prison because of, or in spite of, who they were before incarceration, who they were while in prison, what they chose to do or not to do in prison, and who they want to become once released."[5]

What Is the Inmate Subculture?

Although any prison has its own unique way of life or culture, it is possible to describe a general inmate subculture that characterizes the lives of inmates in correctional institutions nationwide. The **inmate subculture**

inmate subculture (also *prisoner subculture*)

The habits, customs, mores, values, beliefs, or superstitions of the body of inmates incarcerated in correctional institutions; also, the inmate social world.

(also called the *prisoner subculture*) can be defined as "the habits, customs, mores, values, beliefs, or superstitions of the body of inmates incarcerated in correctional institutions."[6]

Prisoners are socialized into the inmate subculture through a process known as *prisonization*. The concept of **prisonization** was identified by Donald Clemmer in his book *The Prison Community*.[7] Clemmer defined *prisonization* as the process by which inmates adapt to prison society, and he described it as "the taking on of the ways, mores, customs, and general culture of the penitentiary." When the process of prisonization is complete, Clemmer noted, prisoners have become "cons."

In a further study of prisonization, Stanton Wheeler examined how prisoners adapted to life at the Washington State Reformatory.[8] Wheeler found that prisonization has greater impact with the passage of time. The prisonization of inmates, said Wheeler, can be described by a *U-shaped* curve. When an inmate first enters prison, the conventional values of the outside society still hold sway in his life. As time passes, however, he increasingly adopts the prison lifestyle. Wheeler also found that within the half-year before release, most inmates begin to demonstrate a renewed appreciation for conventional values.

In *The Society of Captives*,[9] Gresham Sykes described what he called the **pains of imprisonment**. According to Sykes, new inmates face major problems including the loss of liberty, a lack of material possessions, deprivation of goods and services, the loss of heterosexual relationships, the loss of personal autonomy, and a reduction in personal security. These deficits, Sykes noted, lead to self-doubts and reduced self-esteem. Prison society compensates for such feelings and reduces the pains of imprisonment for the prison population as a whole. It also meets the personal and social needs induced in inmates by the pains of imprisonment. In short, said Sykes, inmate society compensates for the losses caused by imprisonment, and it offers varying degrees of comfort to those who successfully adjust to it.

The inmate subculture can vary from one institution to another. Variations are due to differences in the organizational structure of prisons. Maximum-security institutions, for example, are decidedly more painful for inmates because security considerations require greater restriction of inmate freedoms and access to material items. As a result, the subcultures in maximum-security institutions may be much more rigid in their demands on prisoners than those in less secure institutions.

How Does an Inmate Subculture Form?

Early students of inmate subcultures, particularly Clemmer and Sykes, believed that such subcultures developed in response to the deprivations in prison life. This perspective is called **deprivation theory**. Shared deprivation gives inmates a basis for solidarity.[10]

A more recent perspective is that an inmate subculture does not develop in prison but is brought into prison from the outside world. Known as **importation theory**, this point of view was popularized by John Irwin and Donald R. Cressey.[11] It was further supported by the work of James Jacobs.[12] Importation theory holds that inmate society is shaped by factors outside prison—specifically, preprison life experiences and socialization patterns. Inmates who lived violent lives outside tend to associate with other violent inmates and often engage in similar behavior in prison.[13]

More realistic is the **integration model**, which acknowledges that both theories have some validity. According to the integration model, people

---

prisonization

The process by which inmates adapt to prison society; the taking on of the ways, mores, customs, and general culture of the penitentiary.

pains of imprisonment

Major problems that inmates face, such as loss of liberty and personal autonomy, lack of material possessions, loss of heterosexual relationships, and reduced personal security.

CO10-1

deprivation theory

The belief that inmate subcultures develop in response to the deprivations in prison life.

importation theory

The belief that inmate subcultures are brought into prisons from the outside world.

integration model

A combination of importation theory and deprivation theory. The belief that, in childhood, some inmates acquired, usually from peers, values that support law-violating behavior but that the norms and standards in prison also affect inmates.

In some prisons, inmate subculture is fragmented as inmates form competing gangs and other groups along ethnic, racial, and geographic lines. How could the differences among such groups affect the order and stability of a prison?

undergo early socialization experiences. In childhood, some people develop leanings toward delinquent and criminal activity, acquiring—from peer groups, parents and other significant adults, television, movies, other mass media, and even computer and video games—values that support law-violating behavior. Those who become inmates are also likely to have experienced juvenile court proceedings and may have been institutionalized as juveniles. As a consequence, such people are likely to have acquired many of the values, much of the language, and the general behavioral patterns of deviant or criminal subcultures before entering adult prison.

The integration model also recognizes, however, the effects that the norms and behavioral standards of inmates in a particular prison have on those who are imprisoned. If a new inmate has already been socialized into a criminal lifestyle, the transition into the inmate subculture is likely to be easy. For some people, however—especially white-collar offenders with little previous exposure to criminal subcultures—the transition can be very difficult. The language, social expectations, and norms of prison society are likely to be foreign to them.

CO10-2

Norms and Values of Prison Society

Central to prison society is a code of behavior for all inmates. The **prison code** is a set of inmate rules antagonistic to the official administration and rehabilitation programs.[14] Violations of the code result in inmate-imposed sanctions, ranging from ostracism to homicide. Sykes and Messinger have identified five main elements of the prison code:[15]

prison code

A set of norms and values among prison inmates. It is generally antagonistic to the official administration and rehabilitation programs of the prison.

1. Don't interfere with the interests of other inmates. Never rat on a con. Don't have loose lips.
2. Don't lose your head. Don't quarrel with other inmates. Play it cool. Do your own time.
3. Don't exploit other inmates. Don't steal. Don't break your word. Pay your debts.
4. Don't whine. Be tough. Be a man.
5. Don't be a sucker. Don't trust the guards or staff. Remember that prison officials are wrong and inmates are right.

Prison Argot—The Language of Confinement

CO10-3

Prison argot is the special language of the inmate subculture. *Argot* is a French word meaning "slang." Prison society has always had its own unique language illustrated by the following argot-laden paragraph:

> The new con, considered fresh meat by the screws and other prisoners, was sent to the cross-bar hotel to do his bit. He soon picked up the reputation through the yard grapevine as a canary-bird. While he was at the big house, the goon squad put him in the freezer for his protection. Eventually, he was released from the ice-box and ordered to make little ones out of big ones until he was released to the free world. Upon release he received $100 in gate money, vowing never to be thrown in the hole or be thought of as a stool-pigeon again.[16]

prison argot

The special language of the inmate subculture.

Prison argot originated partly as a form of secret communication. Gresham Sykes, however, believed that it serves primarily as "an illustrative symbol of the prison community"—or as a way for inmates to mark themselves as outlaws and social outcasts.[17] Sykes's work brought prison argot to the attention of sociologists and criminologists. Since Sykes's time other authors have identified a number of words, terms, and acronyms in prison argot. Some of these terms are presented in Exhibit 10–2. Interestingly, rap musicians, many of whom have spent time in prison or deal with prison-related themes, have brought prison argot to a wider audience.

Social Structure in Men's Prisons

Inmate societies, like other societies, have a hierarchy of positions. Inmates assume or are forced into specific social roles, and some inmates—by virtue of the roles they assume—have more status and power than others.

Early writers often classified prisoners by the crimes they had committed or their criminal histories. Irwin, for example, divided prisoners into such categories as thieves (those with a culture of criminal values), convicts (time doers), square johns (inmates unfamiliar with criminal subcultures), and dope fiends (drug-involved inmates).[18]

Other writers have identified **inmate roles,** defining them as prison lifestyles or as forms of ongoing social accommodation to prison life. Each role has a position in the pecking order, indicating its status in the prison society.

inmate roles

Prison lifestyles; also, forms of ongoing social accommodation to prison life.

About a decade ago, Frank Schmalleger developed a typology of male inmate roles.[19] It is based on actual social roles found among inmates in prison, and it uses the prison argot in existence when it was created to name or describe each type. Each type can be viewed as a prison lifestyle either chosen by inmates or forced on them. Some of the types were previously identified by other writers. Although the terminology used in the typology sounds dated, the types of inmates it identifies are still characteristic of prison populations today. The 13 inmate types are discussed in the following paragraphs.

The Real Man Real men do their own time, do not complain, and do not cause problems for other inmates. They see confinement as a natural consequence of criminal activity and view time spent in prison as an unfortunate cost of doing business. Real men know the inmate code and abide by it. They are well regarded within the institution and rarely run into problems with other inmates. If they do, they solve their problems on their own. They never seek the help of correctional officers or the prison administration. Although they generally avoid trouble within the institution, they usually continue a life of crime once released.

CO10-4

EXHIBIT 10–2 Prison Argot: The Language of Confinement

Argot in Men's Prisons

ace duce: best friend

back door parole: to die in prison

badge (or bull, hack, "the man," or screw): a correctional officer

ball busters: violent inmates

banger (or burner, shank, sticker): a knife

billys: white men

boneyard: conjugal visiting area

booty bandit: an imprisoned sexual predator who preys on weaker inmates

bug juice: antidepressant or antipsychotic medications provided by the medical staff

cantones: gang term for prisons

catch cold: to be killed

cat-J (or J-cat): a prisoner in need of psychological or psychiatric therapy or medication

cellie: cell mate

center men: inmates who are close to the staff

chester: child molester

chota: a correctional officer

croaker: a physician or a doctor

dancing on the blacktop: being stabbed

diaper sniper: child molester

diddler: a child molester or pedophile

dog: homeboy or friend

fag: a male inmate believed to be a natural (preprison) homosexual

fish: a newly arrived inmate

gorilla: an inmate who uses force to take what he wants from others

got stretched: became angry

grandma's: gang headquarters

hacks: correctional officers

hipsters: young, drug-involved inmates

homeboy: a prisoner from one's hometown or neighborhood

in the car: circle of friends

ink: tattoos

jointman: a prison inmate who behaves like a correctional officer

kite: a contraband letter

lemon squeezer: an inmate who has an unattractive "girlfriend"

lugger: an inmate who smuggles contraband into the facility

man walking: phrase used to signal that a guard is coming

merchant (or peddler): one who sells when he should give; or one who sells goods and services to other inmates illegally

nimby: not in my back yard

ninja turtles: correctional officers dressed in riot gear

punk: a male inmate who is forced into a submissive role during homosexual relations

rat (or snitch): an inmate who squeals (provides information about other inmates to the prison administration)

real men: inmates respected by other inmates

seed: the inmate's child

shank: a knife

schooled: knowledgeable in the ways of prison life

shakedown: search of a cell or a work area

shu (pronounced *shoe*): special housing unit

sleeved: covered with tatoos

slinging rock: selling crack

soda: cocaine

stainless-steel ride: lethal injection

toughs: those with a preprison history of violent crimes

tree jumper: rapist

turn out: to rape or make into a punk

veterano: a long-time gang member

wolf: a male inmate who assumes an aggressive role during homosexual relations

Argot in Women's Prisons

cherry (or cherrie): an inmate not yet introduced to lesbian activities

fay broad: a white inmate

femme (or mommy): an inmate who plays a female role during a lesbian relationship

lark: a woman who talks with the staff

safe: the vagina, especially when used for hiding contraband

stud broad (or daddy): an inmate who assumes a male role in a lesbian relationship

Sources: Gresham Sykes, *The Society of Captives* (Princeton, NJ; Princeton University Press, 1958); Rose Giallombardo, *Society of Women: A Study of Women's Prison* (New York: John Wiley, 1966); Richard A. Cloward et al., *Theoretical Studies in Social Organization of the Prison* (New York: Social Science Research Council, 1960). For a more contemporary listing of prison slang terms, see Reinhold Aman, *Hillary Clinton's Pen Pal: A Guide to Life and Lingo in Federal Prison* (Santa Rosa, CA: Maledicta Press, 1996); Jerome Washington, *Iron House: Stories from the Yard* (Ann Arbor, MI: QED Press, 1994); Morrie Camhi, *The Prison Experience* (Boston: Charles Tuttle, 1989); Harold Long, *Survival in Prison* (Port Townsend, WA: Loompanics Unlimited, 1990); insideprison.com (accessed March 24, 2009); Mother Jones, "A Glossary of Prison Slang" (July/August 2008), http://motherjones.com/politics/2008/07/glossary-prison-slang (accessed March 10, 2011).

The Mean Dude Some inmates are notorious for resorting quickly to physical power. They are quick to fight and, when fighting, give no quarter. They are callous, cold, and uncaring. Mean dudes control those around them through force or the threat of force. The fear they inspire usually gives them a great deal of power in inmate society. At the very least, other inmates are likely to leave the mean dude alone.

The Bully A variation of the mean dude is the bully. Bullies use intimidation to get what they want. Unlike mean dudes, they are far more likely to use threats than to use actual physical force. A bully may make his threats in public so that others see the victim's compliance.

The Agitator The agitator, sometimes called a *wise guy,* is constantly trying to stir things up. He responds to the boredom of prison life by causing problems for others. An agitator may point out, for example, how a powerful inmate has been wronged by another inmate or that an inmate seen talking to a "rat" must be a snitch himself.

The Hedonist The hedonist adapts to prison by exploiting the minimal pleasures it offers. Hedonists always seek the easy path, and they plot to win the "cushiest" jobs. They may also stockpile goods to barter for services of various kinds. Hedonists live only in the now with little concern for the future. Their lives revolve around such activities as gambling, drug running, smuggling contraband, and exploiting homosexual opportunities.

The Opportunist The opportunist sees prison as an opportunity for personal advancement. He takes advantage of the formal self-improvement opportunities of the prison, such as schooling, trade training, and counseling. Other inmates generally dislike opportunists, seeing them as selfish *do-gooders.* Staff members, however, often see opportunists as model prisoners.

The Retreatist Some inmates, unable to cope with the realities of prison life, withdraw psychologically from the world around them. Depression, neurosis, and even psychosis may result. Some retreatists attempt to lose themselves in drugs or alcohol. Others attempt suicide. Isolation from the general prison population combined with counseling or psychiatric treatment may offer the best hope for retreatists to survive the prison experience.

The Legalist Legalists are known as *jailhouse lawyers,* or simply *lawyers,* in prison argot. They are usually among the better-educated prisoners, although some legalists have little formal education. Legalists fight confinement through the system of laws, rules, and court precedent. Legalists file writs with the courts, seeking hearings on a wide variety of issues. Although many legalists work to better the conditions of their own confinement or to achieve early release, most also file pleas on behalf of other prisoners.

The Radical Radicals see themselves as political prisoners of an unfair society. They believe that a discriminatory world has denied them the education and skills needed to succeed in a socially acceptable way. Most of the beliefs held by radical inmates are rationalizations that shift the blame for personal failure onto society. The radical inmate is likely to be familiar with contemporary countercultural figures.

The Offender Speaks
Visit www.mhhe.com/schmalleger7e
to see this feature.

Visit http://www.youtube.com/watch?v
=Y8NMLu5oNLo or scan this QR code with
the QR app on your SmartPhone or digital
device to view a video on women inmates in
Maryland.

The Colonist Colonists, also referred to as *convicts,* turn prison into home. Colonists know the ropes of prison, have many "friends" on the inside, and often feel more comfortable in prison than outside it. They may not look forward to leaving prison. Some may even commit additional offenses to extend their stay. Colonists are generally well regarded by other prisoners. Many are old-timers. Colonists have learned to take advantage of the informal opportunity structure in prisons, and they are well versed in the inmate code.

The Religious Inmate Religious inmates profess a strong religious faith and may attempt to convert both inmates and staff. Religious inmates frequently form prayer groups, request special meeting facilities and special diets, and may ask for frequent visits from religious leaders. Religious inmates are often under a great deal of suspicion from inmates and staff, who tend to think they are faking religious commitment to gain special treatment. Those judged sincere in their faith may win early release, removal from death row, or any number of other special considerations.

The Punk The punk is a young inmate, often small, who has been forced into a sexual relationship with an aggressive, well-respected prisoner. Punks are generally "turned out" through homosexual rape. A punk usually finds a protector among the more powerful inmates. Punks keep their protectors happy by providing them with sexual services.

The Gang-Banger Gang-bangers, or those affiliated with prison gangs, know that there is power in numbers. They depend upon the gang for defense and protection as well as for the procurement of desired goods and services. Gang-bangers are known by their tattoos and hand signs, which indicate gang affiliation and can be read by anyone familiar with prison society. Prison gangs, which are discussed in more detail in Chapter 13, often have links outside prison—leading to continued involvement in crime by those directing them from inside prison and to the creation of channels for the importation of banned items into correctional facilities.

Former Florida prison inmate Joe Murphy, who served time for murder, leads a prayer at the Okaloosa Correctional Institution in Crestview, Florida. What different kinds of inmates does this chapter identify?

Sexuality in Men's Prisons

Violence and victimization occur in men's prisons, and a good deal of prison violence has sexual overtones. The top of the sexual hierarchy in male prisons is occupied by inmates engaged in situational homosexuality who are called, quite simply, *Men*. They are heterosexual inmates who feel compelled to engage in homosexual behavior by the conditions of confinement.[20] Men with the power to own and control their own "punk" rise to the top of the inmate sexual hierarchy.

Punks are "owned" by powerful inmates who provide them protection from sexual violence and from other inmates. Many punks are forced to fill the traditional role of a wife and can often be found doing their Man's laundry, ironing, and making up the Man's bed. Although punks are usually seen as totally powerless and dependent upon their Man, punks can influence their "owners" in various ways. As one inmate observer[21] describes it, "There are punk wiles just as there are feminine wiles. A contented punk is much more desirable than a sullen and reluctant one, so there is a definite incentive for the Men to back off from a confrontation with their punks on an issue which they don't consider essential, though no Man will tolerate a rebellious punk." He adds, "A Man has a social obligation to share his wealth with his punk, much as a rich man on the outside is expected to keep his wife in furs and take her out to eat. As one Man put it: 'You punks have got it made; you don't have to fight, and you get all the dope and commissary from the men with the most money.'"[22]

The most powerful Men in prison society, cell block leaders, gang leaders, and so on, will "own" the most desirable punks. Punks, however, can be sold or given away. Once a person has become a punk, he can never again become a Man—at least not while still in prison. Not all punks, however, are outcasts. Punks belonging to Men who have high social status within the institution are treated with deference by other inmates. One rule of inmate society demands that Men must share what comforts they have accumulated in prison with their punks.

It is not uncommon for affectionate relationships to develop between Men and their punks. Some couples even "marry" in imitation ceremonies—many of which are followed by "parties" and attended by inmate "guests." As one writer explains it, "Imprisoned long enough, men can transfer any emotion they feel for women to their punks."[23]

One person who has contributed significantly to the study of sexual violence in men's prisons is Daniel Lockwood.[24] Using interviews and background data from prison files, Lockwood identified and studied 107 "targets" of aggressive sexual threats and 45 inmate "aggressors" in New York state male prisons. He also conducted a general survey that revealed that 28 percent of all male prisoners had been targets of sexual aggressors in prison at least once. Lockwood found that only one of the inmates he interviewed had actually been raped—an indication that the incidence of prison rape is quite low relative to other types of harm that may accompany sexual incidents, such as physical abuse, verbal abuse, threatening gestures, and threatening propositions.

Targets, when compared with nontargets, were found to be physically slight, young, white, nonviolent offenders from nonurban areas. They generally had a higher rate of psychological disturbance than other inmates

Texas prison inmate Roderick Johnson, who claims that he was raped hundreds of times after his return to prison on charges of bouncing a $300 check while on parole for breaking and entering. In 2004, a federal lawsuit filed by Johnson, 33, an admitted homosexual, was allowed to go to trial. It names the head of the Texas Department of Criminal Justice, along with more than a dozen other officials at the James V. Allred Unit in Iowa Park, claiming that they failed to protect him from violent sexual attacks. What will the 2003 Prison Rape Elimination Act do for inmates like Johnson? Use the Internet to learn what happened to the civil suit filed on Johnson's behalf.

EXHIBIT 10–3   Inmate Note

> Yo S
> Check this out if you don't give me a peace
> of your ass I am going to take you off the
> count and that is my word.
> I be down a very long time So I need it Very
> Bad I will give you 5 Pack's of Smokes if
> you do it OK That is my word So if you
> Want to live you Better do it and get it over
> with there are Three of us who need it.
> OK . . .

---

and were more apt to attempt suicide while in prison. Exhibit 10–3 shows a note found by a new inmate in his cell at a New York state prison unit. The new inmate was young and not prison-wise. After discovering the note, the inmate asked to be moved to the prison's isolation area. His request was granted.[25]

The typical incident of sexual aggression, Lockwood found, is carried out by a group. About half the incidents Lockwood identified included physical violence, and another third involved threats. The incidents studied showed patterns of escalation from verbal abuse to physical violence.

Lockwood also found that prison rapes generally occur when gangs of aggressors circumvent security arrangements to physically control their victims. Fear, anxiety, suicidal thoughts, social disruption, and attitude changes develop in many victims of homosexual rape.

In 2003, in an effort to learn more about prison rape, Congress mandated the collection of prison rape statistics under the Prison Rape Elimination Act (PREA).[26] The PREA, which also established the federal Prison Rape Commission, calls for an evaluation of issues related to prison rape as well as for the development of national standards to help prevent prison rape.

Tasked by the PREA to gather data on prison rape, the Bureau of Justice Statistics completed the first-ever national survey of the prevalence of sexual victimizations based on reports of former state prison inmates in 2012. The survey included information from completed interviews with 18,526 former inmates who were still under parole supervision. It found:

- An estimated 9.6 percent of former state prisoners reported one or more incidents of sexual victimization during their most recent period of incarceration.

- Among all former state prisoners, 1.8 percent reported experiencing one or more incidents while in a local jail, 7.5 percent while in a state prison, and 0.1 percent while in a postrelease community treatment facility.

- About 5.4 percent of former state prisoners reported an incident involving another inmate, and 5.3 percent reported an incident involving facility staff.

- An estimated 1.2 percent of former prisoners reported that they unwillingly had sex or sexual contact with facility staff, and 4.6 percent reported that they "willingly" had sex or sexual contact with staff.

- More than three-quarters of all reported staff sexual misconduct involved a male inmate with female staff.
- Among former state prisoners, the rate of inmate-on-inmate sexual victimization was at least three times higher for females (13.7 percent) than males (4.2 percent).
- Among heterosexual males, an estimated 3.5 percent reported being sexually victimized by another inmate. In comparison, among males who were bisexual, 34 percent reported being sexually victimized by another inmate. Among males who were homosexual or gay, 39 percent reported being victimized by another inmate.
- Rates of sexual victimization did not vary based on commonly cited characteristics of facilities, including size or age of facility, crowding, inmate-to-staff ratios, or gender composition of staff.
- Following their release from prison, 72 percent of victims of inmate-on-inmate sexual victimization indicated they felt shame or humiliation, and 56 percent said they felt guilt.
- Seventy-nine percent of unwilling victims of staff sexual misconduct said they felt shame or humiliation, and 72 percent said they felt guilt.[27]

Finally, injuries were reported in about 18 percent of incidents of inmate-on-inmate sexual victimizations and in less than 1 percent of incidents of staff-on-inmate sexual victimizations.[28]

Official reports by correctional administrators are unlikely to reflect the true incident of sexual violence. As BJS notes, "due to fear of reprisal from perpetrators, a code of silence among inmates, personal embarrassment, and lack of trust in staff, victims are often reluctant to report incidents to correctional authorities."[29] To circumvent such issues and to gather more reliable information, BJS has implemented a system of self-reports in which data are collected from incarcerated individuals as well as those recently released. The data reported here are from the *National Former Prisoner Survey* (NFPS), published in 2012.

WOMEN IN PRISON

CO10-5

In America today, there are far fewer women's prisons than men's prisons, and men in prison outnumber women in prison 12 to 1.[30] As noted in Chapter 7, however, the number of women in prison has grown faster than that of men.

A state usually has one women's prison housing a few hundred women. The size of a women's prison generally depends on the population of the state. Some small states house women prisoners in special areas of what are otherwise institutions for men.

Women's prisons are generally quite different from men's. Here's how one writer describes them:

> Often, there are no gun towers, no armed guards, and no stone walls or fences strung on top with concertina wire. Neatly pruned hedges, well-kept flower gardens, attractive brick buildings, and wide paved walkways greet the visitor's eye at women's prisons in many states. Often these institutions are located in rural, pastoral settings that may suggest tranquility and well-being to the casual observer.[31]

Such rural settings, however, make it hard for female inmates to maintain contact with their families who may live far from the correctional facility.

Although there are far fewer women in prison than men, the number of women behind bars is growing steadily. What might account for the increasing number of imprisoned women?

Although there are far fewer women in prison than men, the number of women behind bars is growing steadily. What might account for the increasing number of imprisoned women?

Many prisons for women are built on a cottage plan. Cottages dot the grounds of such institutions, often arranged in pods. A group of six or so cottages constitutes a pod. Each cottage is much like a traditional house, with individual bedrooms; a day room with a television, chairs, couches, and tables; and small personal or shared bathrooms.

Security in women's prisons is generally more relaxed than in men's, and female inmates may have more freedom within the institution than their male counterparts. Practically speaking, women—even those in prison—are seen as less dangerous than men and less prone to violence or escape.

Treatment, education, recreation, and other programs in women's prisons have often been criticized as inferior to those in men's prisons. Recent research has uncovered continuing disparities in many areas.[32] For example, men's institutions often have a much wider range of vocational and educational training programs and services and larger and better-equipped law libraries. Similarly, exercise facilities—including weight rooms, jogging areas, and basketball courts—are often better equipped and larger in men's institutions today than in women's.

Prison administrators have often found it impractical to develop and fund programs at the same level in women's and men's prisons because of differences in interest, participation, and space and the fact that relatively low numbers of women prisoners don't allow for the same economies of scale found in men's institutions. Nonetheless, it is important to strive for parity of opportunity as an ideal. The American Correctional Association, for example, through its Guidelines for Women's Prison Construction and Programming,[33] insists that the same level of services and opportunities be available in women's prisons as in men's prisons in the same jurisdiction.

In some instances, women may be placed in an institution housing inmates with a range of security levels. Consequently, women who are low security risks may have less personal freedom than their male counterparts. Women may also not have the opportunity to transfer to a less secure institution as their risk level drops.

Overcrowding, violence, and poor conditions are not unknown in prisons for women. By 2002, the Julia Tutwiler Prison for Women in Wetumpka, Alabama, for example, was home to more than 1,000 women.

Jack Osborn

Custody Utility Officer • Jefferson City Correctional Center • Jefferson City, MO

Jack Osborn is a custody utility officer at the Jefferson City Correctional Center in Missouri. As a utility officer, he may be assigned to any area or department that needs an additional staff member.

Osborn advises knowing the inmates and being able to interpret behavioral changes. "Know what silence means. Communicate—listen," he says. "Learn who runs drugs and gambling, who the punks are. That's where your trouble will come from." Osborn believes that if you follow this advice and know the mechanics of the job, you should have a great career in corrections.

"What makes a good custody officer? Being honest goes far. If you don't know the answer, say so. If you say you will find out, do it. Learn to say no, too. You can change it to a yes easier than changing a yes to a no."

Built in 1942 with a capacity of only 364 inmates, it became the focus of a federal lawsuit brought by inmates to address extreme crowding.

Due largely to overcrowded conditions, the facility did not have the ability to separate dangerous prisoners from one another when its population was at its peak, nor did it have the resources to safely care for and separately house prisoners with mental illness and those with serious diseases. Meaningful programs for inmates were practically nonexistent, and most of the female prisoners spent endless idle hours in terribly hot dormitories crammed full of beds, sleeping pallets, and bunks.

The severe beating of a correctional officer in July 2002 brought problems with understaffing and crowded dorms into the spotlight. At the time there were, on average, only 12 officers at any given time responsible for supervising more than 1,000 prisoners—and at one point, there were as few as 9 officers on duty. Ninety-one assaults were recorded within the institution in 2002, making Alabama's only women's prison the most violent institution in the state.

The prisoner-brought lawsuit asked for, among other things, a reduction in crowding and the hiring of more corrections officers. Finally, under pressure from a federal judge, the state reduced the population at Tutwiler, sending hundreds of women to prisons out of state through contracts for prison space. Today, the Tutwiler prison has been expanded to a design capacity of 417 inmates but contains 743 beds. It's inmate population had fallen to 655 by the end of 2010—meaning that it was operating at 155 percent of its capacity.[34]

Characteristics of Women Inmates

CO10-6

Many of our conceptions of female inmates derive more from myth than reality. Recent BJS surveys provide a more realistic picture of female inmates.[35] At the start of 2012, women comprised 7.0 percent of sentenced prisoners in the nation. Since 2000, the female prison population

An imprisoned woman. How do men's and women's prisons differ?

has grown 28 percent,[36] a noticeably higher rate of growth than experienced in the male prison population, which had a 20 percent increase during the same period. As of January 1, 2012, there were 111,387 women under the jurisdiction of state and federal prison authorities.[37]

Female prisoners largely resemble male prisoners in race, ethnic background, and age. However, they are substantially more likely to be serving time for a drug offense and less likely to have been sentenced for a violent crime. Women are also more likely than men to be serving time for larceny or fraud.

Female inmates have shorter criminal records than male inmates. They generally have shorter maximum sentences than men. Half of all women receive a maximum sentence of 60 months or less, and half of all men are sentenced to 120 months or less.

Significantly, more than 4 in 10 of the women prisoners responding to BJS surveys reported prior physical or sexual abuse. One of the major factors distinguishing male inmates from female inmates is that the women have experienced far more sexual and physical abuse than had the men. Interviews with incarcerated women have found that 70 percent of them report the occurrence of sexual molestation or severe physical abuse in childhood at the hands of parents or adolescent caregivers.[38] Fifty-nine percent report some form of sexual abuse in childhood or adolescence, and 75 percent of those interviewed report having been severely abused by an intimate partner as adults.

A report by the National Institute of Corrections found that women enter correctional institutions through different "pathways" than men. According to the report, most women offenders are typically nonviolent and their crimes are less threatening to community safety than those committed by male offenders. "Women's most common pathways to crime," said the report, "result from abuse, poverty, and substance abuse"—all of which, according to the report, are interconnected.[39] Exhibit 10–4 is a comparison of selected characteristics of female and male state prisoners.

Offenses of Incarcerated Women

Drug offenses account for the incarceration of a high percentage of the women behind bars. Twenty-five percent of all women in state prisons are serving time on drug charges.[40] Some sources estimate that drug crimes and other crimes indirectly related to drug activities together account for the imprisonment of around 95 percent of today's women inmates. In short, drug use and abuse, or crimes stimulated by the desire for drugs and drug money, are what send most women to prison. This has been true for more than a decade. According to an ACA report, the primary reasons incarcerated women most frequently give for their arrest are (1) trying to pay for drugs, (2) attempts to relieve economic pressures, and (3) poor judgment.[41]

According to the BJS, before arrest, women in prison use more drugs than men and use those drugs more frequently.[42] About 54 percent of imprisoned women have used drugs in the month before the offense for which they were arrested compared with 50 percent of the men. Female inmates are also more likely than male inmates to have used drugs regularly (65 percent vs. 62 percent), to have used drugs daily in the month preceding their offense (41 percent vs. 36 percent), and to have been under

| **EXHIBIT 10–4** | **Characteristics of Women and Men in State Prisons** |

Women in Prison

Criminal Offense

37% are in prison for violent offenses

25% are in prison for drug offenses

29% are in prison for property offenses

8% are in prison for public-order offenses

1% or less are in prison for other offenses

Criminal History

46% are nonviolent recidivists

28% have no previous sentence

26% are violent recidivists

Family Characteristics

78% have children

42% lived with both parents most of time growing up

33% had a parent/guardian who abused alcohol or drugs

17% were married at the time they committed the offense for which they were incarcerated

45% have never married

47% have a family member who had been incarcerated

Drug and Alcohol Use

59% used drugs daily in the month before the current offense

36% were under the influence of drugs at the time of the offense

12% were under the influence of alcohol at the time of the offense

Men in Prison

Criminal Offense

54% are in prison for violent offenses

18% are in prison for property offenses

17% are in prison for drug offenses

11% are in prison for public-order offenses

1% or less are in prison for other offenses

Criminal History

50% are violent recidivists

31% are nonviolent recidivists

19% have no previous sentence

Family Characteristics

64% have children

43% lived with both parents most of time growing up

26% had a parent/guardian who abused alcohol or drugs

18% were married at the time they committed the offense for which they were incarcerated

56% have never married

37% have a family member who had been incarcerated

Drug and Alcohol Use

56% used drugs daily in the month before the current offense

31% were under the influence of drugs at the time of the offense

18% were under the influence of alcohol at the time of the offense

Sources: E. Ann Carson and William J. Sabol, *Prisoners in 2011* (Washington, DC: Bureau of Justice Statistics, 2012); Allen Beck et al., *Survey of State Prison Inmates, 1991* (Washington, DC: U.S. Department of Justice, March 1993); and Christopher J. Mumola and Jennifer C. Karberg, "Drug Use and Dependence, State and Federal Prisoners, 2004" (Washington, DC: Bureau of Justice Statistics, 2006).

the influence at the time of the offense (36 percent vs. 31 percent). Nearly one in four female inmates surveyed reported committing the offense to get money to buy drugs compared with one in six males.

Female inmates who used drugs differed from those who did not in the types of crimes they committed. Regardless of the amount of drug use, users were less likely than nonusers to be serving a sentence for a violent offense.

Social Structure in Women's Prisons

CO10-7

As might be expected, the social structure and the subcultural norms and expectations in women's prisons are quite different from those in men's prisons. Unfortunately, however, relatively few studies of inmate life have been conducted in institutions for women.

One early study of women at the Federal Reformatory for Women in Alderson, West Virginia, was an effort to compare subcultural aspects of women's prisons with those of men's. Rose Giallombardo reached the conclusion that "many of the subcultural features of the institution are imported from the larger society."[43] Giallombardo believed that male and female inmate subcultures are actually quite similar except that women's prisons develop "a substitute universe," a world "in which inmates may preserve an identity which is relevant to life outside the prison."

Giallombardo was unable to find in the women's prison some of the values inherent in a male inmate subculture, such as "Do your own time." The inmate subculture in a women's prison, she said, tends to encourage relationships rather than isolation. Hence, women are expected to share their problems with other inmates and to offer at least some support and encouragement to others. On the other hand, she observed, women prisoners tend to see each other as conniving, self-centered, and scheming. Hence, a basic tenet of the inmate subculture in a women's prison is "You can't trust other women." As Giallombardo put it, women prisoners tend to believe that "every woman is a sneaking, lying bitch."

Giallombardo concluded that the social structure of women's prisons and the social role assumed by each inmate are based on three elements:

1. the individual woman's level of personal dependence and her status needs (which are said to be based upon cultural expectations of the female role);
2. the individual's needs arising from incarceration combined with the institution's inability to meet female inmates' emotional needs; and
3. needs related to the individual's personality.

A more recent study was of inmates in the District of Columbia Women's Reformatory at Occoquan, Virginia.[44] Esther Heffernan identified three roles that women commonly adopt when adjusting to prison. According to Heffernan, women's roles evolve partly from the characteristics the women bring with them to prison and depend partly on the ways the women choose to adapt to prison life. The roles she described are discussed in the following paragraphs.

The Cool Inmate Cool women usually have previous records, are in the know, are streetwise, and do not cause trouble for other inmates while in prison. Cool women are seen as professional or semiprofessional criminals who work to win the maximum number of prison amenities without endangering their parole or release dates.

The Square Inmate Square women are not familiar with criminal lifestyles and have few, if any, criminal experiences other than the one for which they were imprisoned. They tend to hold the values and roles of conventional society.

The Life Inmate Life inmates are habitual or career offenders and are generally well socialized into lives of crime. They support inmate values and subculture. Life inmates typically have been in and out of prison from an early age and have developed criminal lifestyles dedicated to meeting their political, economic, familial, and social needs outside conventional society.

Recently, California State University (Fresno) criminologist Barbara Owens studied the culture of imprisoned women at Central California Women's Facility in Chowchilla, California, and found a "prison culture that is itself complex and diverse across numerous dimensions."[45] Owens identified a central component of that culture that she refers to as "the mix."

The mix, according to Owens, "is any behavior that can bring trouble and conflict with staff and other prisoners." It consists of fighting, doing drugs, prison-based lesbian activity ("homo-secting," in Owens's terms), and making trouble for the staff. It also involves continuing the kinds of behaviors that brought women to prison. Consequently, the mix is to be avoided by those who want to leave prison and not return. New women coming into the institution, Owens found, were advised to "stay out of the mix." The mix, says Owens, is also a state of mind, a way of thinking like a troublemaker.

One writer, summarizing the results of studies such as those discussed here, found that two primary features distinguish women's prisons from men's prisons:[46]

1. The social roles in women's prisons place greater emphasis on homosexual relations as a mode of adaptation to prison life.
2. The mode of adaptation a female inmate selects is best assessed by studying the inmate's preinstitutional experiences.

Pseudofamilies and Sexual Liaisons

A unique feature of women's prisons is pseudofamilies. **Pseudofamilies** are family-like structures, common in women's prisons, in which inmates assume roles similar to those of family members in free society. Pseudofamilies appear to provide emotional and social support for the women who belong to them. Courtship, marriage, and kinship ties formed with other women inmates provide a means of coping with the rigors of imprisonment. One inmate has explained pseudofamilies this way: "It just happens. Just like on the outside, you get close to certain people. It's the same in here—but we probably get even closer than a lot of families because of how lonely it is otherwise."[47]

Some authors suggest that pseudofamilies are to women's prisons what gangs are to men's.[48] Men establish social relationships largely through power, and gang structure effectively expresses such relationships. Women relate to one another more expressively and emotionally. Hence, family structures are one of the most effective reflections of women's relationships in prison, just as they are in the wider society. At least one study of prison coping behavior found that new female inmates, especially those most in need of support, advice, and assistance in adjusting to the conditions of incarceration, are the women most likely to become members of prison pseudofamilies.[49]

To a large extent, the social and behavioral patterns of family relationships in prison mirror their traditional counterparts in the community. Families in women's prisons come in all sizes and colors. They can be virtual melting pots of ethnicity and age. A member of a family may be young or old and may be black, white, or Hispanic. As in families in free society, there are roles for husbands and wives, sisters, brothers, grandmothers, and children. Roles for aunts and uncles do not exist, however.

"Stud broads," in prison argot, assume any male role, including that of husband and brother. Other inmates think of them as men. "Men" often assume traditional roles in women's prisons, ordering women around, demanding to be waited on, expecting to have their rooms cleaned and their laundry done, and so forth. Most women who assume masculine roles within prison are said to be "playing" and are sometimes called *players*. Once they leave, they usually revert to female roles. A "femme" or "mommy" is a woman who assumes a female role in a family and during homosexual activity.

pseudofamilies

Family-like structures, common in women's prisons, in which inmates assume roles similar to those of family members in free society.

The kinship of substitute families plays a major role in the lives of many female inmates, who take the relationships very seriously. How might these relationships supplant values such as "do your own time" commonly found in the subculture of men's prisons?

Most women in prison, including those playing masculine roles, were generally not lesbians before entering prison. They resort to lesbian relations within prison because relationships with men are unavailable.

Although gender roles and family relationships within women's prisons appear to have an enduring quality, women can and sometimes do change role genders. When a woman playing a male role, for example, reverts to a female one, she is said to have "dropped her belt." A stud broad who drops her belt may wreak havoc on relationships within her own family and in families related to it.

Special Needs of Female Inmates

Rarely are the special needs of imprisoned women fully recognized—and even less frequently are they addressed. Many of today's prison administrators and correctional officers still treat women as if they were men. Nicole Hahn Rafter, for example, says that many prisons have an attitude akin to "just add women and stir."[50]

A recent report by the National Institute of Corrections (NIC) called for criminal justice agencies to acknowledge the "many differences between male and female offenders," and for the implementation of gender-responsive programming for treating the problems of imprisoned women.[51] *Gender-responsiveness* can be defined as "creating an environment . . . that reflects an understanding of the realities of women's lives and addresses the issues of the women."[52] Gender-responsive programming might, for example, strengthen policies against staff sexual misconduct in institutions that house women; provide more "safe and nurturing" drug treatment programs; and help inmate mothers to maintain strong relationships with their children. The NIC report concluded that " gender-responsive practice can improve outcomes for women offenders by considering their histories, behaviors, and life circumstances."[53]

Susan Cranford is division director of the Community Justice Assistance Division of the Texas Department of Criminal Justice. Rose Williams is warden of Pulaski State Prison in Hawkinsville, Georgia. Recently, Cranford and Williams suggested that "correctional staff should keep the unique needs of women offenders in mind."[54] They say that the effective running of a women's prison requires consideration of those needs.

A critical difference between male and female prisoners, say Cranford and Williams, is "the manner in which they communicate." Female offenders, they note, are usually much more open, more verbal, more emotional, and more willing to share the intimacies of their lives than men are. Male prisoners, like most men in free society, are guarded about the information they share and the manner in which they share it. "For men, information is power. For women, talking helps establish a common ground, a way to relate to others."

Gender-specific training is vital for COs who work in women's prisons, say Cranford and Williams. Proper training, they write, can head off the development of inappropriate relationships (especially initiated by male staff members), which could lead to sexual misconduct. Moreover, staff members who work with women should receive additional training in negotiating and listening skills.

An example of effective gender-specific training is the task-oriented curriculum titled *Working with the Female Offender* developed by Florida's Department of Corrections.[55] The program addresses unique aspects of managing female inmates and provides correctional staff training in the behaviors, actions, needs, and backgrounds presented by female offenders. A special segment examines how female offenders relate to supervision in various institutional or community corrections settings.

Moreover, say Cranford and Williams, it is important to realize that a woman's children are usually very important to her and that many imprisoned women have children on the outside. Hence, parenting skills should be taught to imprisoned mothers because most will rejoin and be with their children during critical stages in the children's development.

There are, however, those who feel that gender-responsive strategies won't work. The reason, they say, is because more and more women are being "convicted of crimes for which they would not previously have received a custodial sentence," and are being sent to prison "not because of the seriousness of their crimes, but mainly to receive psychological programming and reintegration training when, in fact, their main problems have stemmed from inadequate housing, poverty, and abusive men."[56] In other words, gender-responsive strategies assume that imprisonment can make a positive difference in women's lives, something that may not be true because such strategies often do little to address the problems women will again face upon release.

Mothers in Prison

According to one BJS study,[57] an estimated 6.7 percent of black women, 5.9 percent of Hispanic women, and 5.2 percent of white women are pregnant at the time of incarceration.

An estimated 4,000 women prisoners give birth each year, even though most women's prisons have no special facilities for pregnant inmates.[58] Some experts recommend that women's prisons should routinely make counseling available to pregnant inmates and that they should fully inform these women of the options available to them, including abortion and adoption.[59]

The ACA[60] recommends that institutions provide counseling for pregnant inmates, that "prenatal care" should be offered, and that deliveries should be made at community hospitals.[61] Similarly, the American Public Health Association's standards for health services in correctional

The Staff Speaks
Visit www.mhhe.com/schmalleger7e to see this feature.

institutions say that pregnant inmates should be provided with prenatal care, including medical exams and treatment, and that pregnant prisoners should be allowed a special program of housing, diet, vitamin supplements, and exercise.

Once inmates give birth, other problems arise—including the critical issue of child placement. Some states still have partial civil death statutes, which mean that prisoners lose many of their civil rights upon incarceration. In such states, women may lose legal custody of their children. Children either become wards of the state or are placed for adoption.

Although there is some historical precedent for allowing women inmates to keep newborns with them in the institutional setting, very few women's prisons permit this practice. Overcrowded prisons lack space for children, and the prison environment is a decidedly undesirable environment for children. A few women's prisons allow women to keep newborns for a brief period. Most, however, arrange for foster care until the mother is able to find relatives to care for the child or is released. Others work with services that put prison-born infants up for adoption. Some facilities make a special effort to keep mother and child together. Even relatively progressive prisons that allow mother–child contact usually do so only for the first year.

Many women are already mothers when they come to prison. BJS statistics[62] show that more than three-quarters of all women in prison in the United States have young children (i.e., under the age of 18). Black (69 percent) and Hispanic (72 percent) female inmates are more likely than white (62 percent) female inmates to have young children. Also, black women are more likely than other women to have lived with their young children before being imprisoned.

The children of 25 percent of women inmates with children under age 18 live with the other parent. More than a third of white female inmates report that their children are living with the children's fathers compared to a quarter of Hispanic women and less than a fifth of black women. Regardless of race, grandparents are the most common caregivers: 57 percent of imprisoned black mothers look to grandparents for child care as do 55 percent of imprisoned Hispanic mothers and 41 percent of imprisoned white mothers. Nearly 10 percent of the inmate mothers reported that their children are in a foster home, agency, or institution.

Worry about children affects female inmates' physical and emotional well-being. Although 78 percent of mothers (and 62 percent of fathers) report having at least monthly contact with their children, only 24 percent of mothers (and 21 percent of fathers) report personal visits from their children at least monthly.[63] A majority of both mothers (54 percent) and fathers (57 percent) report never having had a personal visit with their children since their imprisonment began.

According to BJS, nearly 90 percent of women with children under age 18 have had contact with their children since entering prison. Half of all women inmates surveyed have been visited by their children, four-fifths have corresponded by mail, and three-quarters have talked with children on the telephone. Female inmates with children under age 18 are more likely than those with adult children to make daily telephone calls to their children.

Understandably, inmate mothers frequently express concern about possible alienation from their children due to the passage of time associated with incarceration. They often worry that their children will develop strong bonds with new caretakers and be unwilling to return to them upon release.[64]

Incarcerated fathers and their daughters at the Richmond City Jail during a "Date with Dad Night" in 2013. Officials say that the dance offers a rare chance for fathers and daughters to bond. What are the problems faced by imprisoned parents? By their children?

Finally, it is important to note that a number of women's prisons operate programs designed to develop parenting skills among inmates. Included are the Program for Caring Parents at the Louisiana Correctional Institute for Women; Project HIP (Helping Incarcerated Parents) at the Maine Correctional Center; and Neil J. Houston House, a program for nonviolent female offenders in Massachusetts.[65]

One 2011 study found that 1.7 million American children had a parent in prison.[66] Statistically speaking, 1 of every 43 American children has a parent in prison today, and ethnic variation in the numbers are striking. Although only 1 of every 111 white children has experienced the imprisonment of a parent, 1 of every 15 black children has had that experience. Moreover, between 1991 and 2007, the number of incarcerated fathers rose 76 percent while the number of incarcerated mothers increased by 122 percent.

The effects of parental incarceration on children can be significant. A number of studies show that the children of incarcerated mothers experience alienation, hostility, anger, significant feelings of abandonment, and overall dysfunction. They are much less likely to succeed in school than their peers and far more likely to involve themselves in gangs, sexual misconduct, sexual abuse, and overall delinquency.[67]

In the federal population, 63.4 percent of male prisoners and 58.8 percent of female prisoners have minor children. The state data reverse this distribution, with 65.3 percent of female inmates and 54.7 percent of male inmates having minor children.

It is noteworthy that male inmates are, for the most part, rarely provided any special assistance for maintaining contact with their children during their incarceration. During the past decade, however, administrators in women's institutions across the country have implemented measures to foster stronger bonds between incarcerated mothers and their children. Ranging from the establishment of prison nurseries to the development of special visitation areas, these measures seek to facilitate the continued family contact that appears to be so important to female offenders.[68]

With 1 in 12 inmates pregnant at the time of admission[69] and 22 percent of all minor children with a parent in prison being under 5 years old,[70] correctional administrators need to address the unique problems presented by pregnant offenders and those with very young children. Some institutions have opted to create nurseries on site. At Nebraska's Correctional Center for Women, for example, inmates due for release before their children are 18 months old may keep the children with them in a specially designated floor of a standard prison building. The mothers are provided parenting and child-care classes, and they work only part-time. While they work, other trained inmates provide child care.

Another example of programs designed to facilitate family bonding is the Ohio Reformatory for Women's annual three-day weekend camp, which brings children ages 6 to 12 from all over the state to spend days with their inmate mothers. Originally pioneered at Bedford Hills Correctional Facility, New York's maximum-security prison for women, such camping visits have become more common in other facilities as well. Some states even allow overnight camping trips, both on and off the prison grounds.

Inmates apply for the program in January each year. Local churches and other community service groups support the program.[71] Selection criteria include a review of inmates' disciplinary records during incarceration, and those whose crimes involved their children are prohibited from participating. During the weekend, activities such as storytelling, softball, crafts, and meals facilitate bonding between mother and child. The inmates return to the prison to sleep at night, but the children "camp out" in sleeping bags at a local church.

Another innovative effort is Florida's "Reading Family Ties: Face to Face" program.[72] Begun in February 2000, it uses high-speed videoconferencing technology to permit weekly family visits between incarcerated mothers in two rural institutions and their children in the Miami area. Inmate mothers may sit before an Internet-linked camera to read to their children. Logistical limitations, of course, are significant, but administrators plan to expand the program to other major cities in Florida.

Perhaps the most family-centered efforts are being tried in California and Illinois. Oakland's Project Pride[73] permits mothers convicted of nonviolent offenses to serve the last portion of their sentences in residential community settings with their preschool-age children. Under the Family Foundations Program in Santa Fe Springs (CA), sentencing of convicted mothers with substance abuse histories can include treatment in residential centers where they can live with their children. Similarly, at Illinois's Decatur Correctional Center, infants live in separate rooms with their mothers. Books and toys are plentiful in the unit, and large day rooms are decorated with colorful murals. The program is intended to serve women whose children will be two years old or younger by the time they are released from prison.[74]

Prison programs to help fathers learn better parenting are also on the increase. The National Fatherhood Initiative, for example, started Inside Out Dad in 2004, and it now operates in more than 400 prisons and jails nationwide. The program's goal is to reduce recidivism through better fathering.[75]

Some hard-liners might decry such programs as unjustified coddling of convicted offenders. Few, however, can argue the benefits such programs provide to the children of incarcerated parents. Meanwhile, it remains to be seen whether the programs will serve to sustain family relationships, ease prisoners' return to the family environment after release, and, ultimately, reduce recidivism rates.

Cocorrectional Facilities

In 1971, a disturbance at the federal women's prison at Alderson, West Virginia, led to calls for ways to expand incarceration options for women. The Federal Bureau of Prisons responded by moving low-security female prisoners from the crowded Alderson institution to a federal minimum-security prison at Morgantown, West Virginia. The Morgantown facility had been built for young men but had not reached its design capacity. With this move, the modern era of coed prisons, or cocorrections, was born.

A **coed prison** is a facility housing both men and women, and **cocorrections** is the incarceration and interaction of female and male offenders under a single institutional administration.[76] It is estimated that as many as 52 adult correctional institutions in the United States are coed and that they confine almost 23,000 men and 7,000 women.[77]

Since its inception, cocorrections has been cited as a potential solution to a wide variety of corrections problems. The rationales in support of cocorrections are that it:

1. reduces the dehumanizing and destructive aspects of incarceration by permitting heterosocial relationships;
2. reduces problems of institutional control;
3. creates a more "normal" atmosphere, reducing privation;

coed prison

A prison housing both female and male offenders.

cocorrections

The incarceration and interaction of female and male offenders under a single institutional administration.

4. allows positive heterosocial skills to emerge;

5. cushions the shock of release;

6. increases the number of program offerings and improves program access for all prisoners; and

7. expands career opportunities for women.

An examination of the cocorrections literature from 1970 to 1990, however, found no evidence that cocorrections benefits female prisoners.[78] A former warden of a coed prison contends that "going coed" has often been done to appease male egos and smooth the running of men's prisons. Warden Jacqueline Crawford tells us that most women in prison have generally been exploited by the men in their lives. A coed prison, she says, furthers this experience because male prisoners continue the abuse women have come to expect from men.[79]

Others have found that some women's prisons have been turned into coed prisons, thus limiting correctional options for women. Overall, researchers have concluded, "Cocorrections offers women prisoners few, if any, economic, educational, vocational, and social advantages."[80] Whether prisoners released from coed prisons adjust better to the community or experience less recidivism has not been sufficiently studied.

Although literature related to single-sex prisons[81] has repeatedly shown poor overall performance in prisoner rehabilitation and public safety, correctional decision makers, policymakers, legislators, and the public are not calling for an end to one-sex imprisonment. If cocorrections is to become more than window dressing, however, it requires more attention to planning, implementation, and evaluation. Despite some early claims of success, coed prisons are not a quick fix for problems of prison administration.

REVIEW AND APPLICATIONS

SUMMARY

1 Prison inmates live their daily lives in accordance with the dictates of the inmate subculture. The inmate subculture consists of the customs and beliefs of those incarcerated in correctional institutions. *Deprivation theory* holds that prisoner subcultures develop in response to the pains of imprisonment. *Importation theory* claims that inmate subcultures are brought into prisons from the outside world. The integration model uses both theories to explain prisoner subcultures.

2 An important aspect of the male inmate subculture is the prison code. The prison code is a set of norms for the behavior of inmates. Central elements of the code include notions of loyalty (to prison society), control of anger, toughness, and distrust of prison officials. Because the prison code is a part of the inmate subculture, it is mostly opposed to official policies.

3 The inmate subculture also has its own language, called *prison argot*. Examples of prison argot are "fish" (a new inmate), "cellie" (cell mate), and "homeboy" (a prisoner from one's hometown).

4 Inmate roles are different prison lifestyle choices. They include the real man, the mean dude, the bully, the agitator, the hedonist, the opportunist, the retreatist, the legalist, the radical, the colonist, the religious inmate, the punk, and the gang-banger.

5 There are far fewer women's prisons than men's in the United States. Women's prisons often have no gun towers or armed guards and no stone walls or fences topped by barbed wire. They tend to be more attractive and are often built on a cottage plan. Security in most women's prisons is more relaxed than in institutions for men, and female inmates may have more freedom within the institution than do their male counterparts in their institutions. Other gender-based disparities favoring male prisoners exist. A lack of funding and inadequate training have been cited to explain why programs available to women inmates are often not on a par with those available to male prisoners.

6 Female prisoners largely resemble male prisoners in race, ethnic background, and age. However, they are substantially more likely to be serving time for drug offenses and less likely to have been sentenced for violent crimes.

7 Although there are many similarities between men's and women's prisons, the social structure and the subcultural norms and expectations of women's prisons differ from those of men's prisons in a number of important ways. One important difference is that the prisoner subculture in a women's prison tends to encourage relationships rather than isolation. As a consequence, pseudofamilies arise, with fully developed familial relationships and roles.

KEY TERMS

total institution, p. 327

inmate subculture, p. 328

prisoner subculture, p. 328

prisonization, p. 329

pains of imprisonment, p. 329

deprivation theory, p. 329

importation theory, p. 329

integration model, p. 329

prison code, p. 330

prison argot, p. 331

inmate roles, p. 331

pseudofamilies, p. 343

coed prison, p. 348

cocorrections, p. 348

QUESTIONS FOR REVIEW

1 What is *inmate subculture,* and how is it central to understanding society in men's prisons?

2 What is the *prison code?* What are some of its key features? How does it influence behavior in men's prisons?

3 What is *prison argot?* Give some examples.

4 Explain what is meant by *inmate roles,* and give some examples.

5 In what ways do women's prisons differ from men's prisons?

6 Compare female and male inmates by their criminal histories, their family characteristics, and the offenses for which they are incarcerated.

7 How does the social structure of women's prisons differ from that in men's prisons? What are *pseudofamilies,* and why are they important to the society of women's prisons?

THINKING CRITICALLY ABOUT CORRECTIONS

Prison Birth

A woman who gives birth in prison may lose her child to state authorities or may have her parental rights severely restricted. In most cases, the child is removed from the inmate mother shortly after birth. Do you think this is fair? Why or why not?

Housing Assignments

Not surprisingly, state policies differ significantly on the question of housing assignments for prisoners. Some permit inmates to choose their cell mates while others enforce random cell assignments. What are the advantages and disadvantages of each policy style? Which style do you think is best?

ON-THE-JOB DECISION MAKING

Male Officers in Women's Prisons

You are a correctional officer assigned to a women's prison. Six months ago, the superintendent of your institution ordered an investigation to determine the proper role of male officers within the facility. The investigation centered on charges by a handful of inmates that they had been sexually harassed by male COs. The alleged harassment included requests for sexual favors in return for special privileges, observation of female inmates in various states of undress while in their rooms and in shower facilities, and inappropriate touching during cell and facility searches (policy allows only female COs to conduct body searches).

Although the investigation was inconclusive, the activities of male COs have been restricted. They are no longer permitted to have any physical contact with inmates unless an emergency demands that they restrain or search inmates. They have been reassigned to areas of the facility where they cannot view shower and toilet facilities. They are expected to announce their presence in living areas, and they have been ordered to take special classes on staff-inmate interaction.

Unfortunately, however, there are not enough female COs for all of the reassignments required by the recent shift in policy. As a result, the routines of female officers are being significantly disrupted. Female officers are being asked to work shifts that are inconvenient for their personal lives (many are mothers or college students and had come to count on predictable shift work). Most female COs also feel that their workload has increased because they have to cover areas of the institution and assume tasks that male officers would previously have handled.

A few female COs have already left for jobs elsewhere, citing difficulties created in the work environment by the new policies. The talk among the correctional staff is that many of the remaining female staff members might also soon leave. If more female COs leave the facility, it will be impossible for those who remain to keep the facility running under the new rules.

1. Did the superintendent make the right decision in limiting the activities of male COs? Why or why not?
2. Might there be other ways to resolve the issues raised by the investigation into sexual harassment? If so, what might they be?

Same-Sex Relationships

You are a chaplain working in a large state-run correctional facility. You take pride in your reputation among the inmates as a fair and reasonable counselor who treats them with courtesy and respect and never judges them for past transgressions or present problems.

Ronald, an inmate whom you know well, comes to you with a special request. He wants to marry Lawrence, another inmate, and he wants you to perform the ceremony in private. He also tells you that he knows that the "marriage" will have no legitimacy on the outside but says that the ceremony will be deeply moving for him and for Lawrence. Ronald's incarceration record is sterling. His disciplinary record shows no infractions, and there are numerous positive annotations regarding the obvious sincerity of his efforts to rehabilitate himself in preparation for his return to free society.

You are concerned that Ronald may actually be straight, and that his relationship with Lawrence may arise more from the pains of imprisonment than from any innate sexual orientation. You are uncertain what prison regulations might say about such a ceremony, but you suspect that, were you to inquire, the ceremony would be officially disallowed. Additionally, church elders in your denomination have condemned same-sex marriages like the one you are being asked to perform. Still, you think that Ronald is well-meaning in his efforts to form a more stable relationship with Lawrence, and you believe that such a relationship can help him adjust to the stresses of prison life.

1. What do you do? Is this an issue that you need time to think about, or do you answer right away?
2. Would you consider counseling Ronald in order to better assess his "true" sexual orientation?
3. Is his "true" sexual orientation an important consideration?
4. Would you further consider counseling Ronald and Lawrence, individually and jointly, regarding their desire to formalize their relationship?
5. Would you take the issue to the prison superintendent?

For additional information, please see: www.mhhe.com/schmalleger7e
Follow the author's tweets about the latest crime and justice news @schmalleger

[11]

THE LEGAL WORLD

Prisoners' Rights

CHAPTER OBJECTIVES

After completing this chapter you should be able to do the following:

1 Explain what is meant by the *hands-off doctrine.*

2 Identify the key legal sources of prisoners' rights.

3 List the five ways in which inmates can challenge their conditions of confinement.

4 Describe the major changes that took place during the prisoners' rights era.

5 List and explain the four amendments to the U.S. Constitution on which most prisoners' claims are based.

6 Explain how the development of rights for female prisoners has differed from that of rights for male prisoners.

7 Describe the doctrine of sovereign immunity and explain how some limited court protections shield correctional officers today from certain types of civil lawsuits.

> *All persons under any form of detention or imprisonment shall be treated in a humane manner and with respect for the inherent dignity of the human person.*
> —United Nations General Assembly Resolution 43/173, December 9, 1988

In 2011, the U.S. Supreme Court, in the case of *Brown* v. *Plata,* ordered the state of California to aggressively reduce its prison population by releasing as many as 58,000 inmates over the next two years.[1] The Justices held that overcrowded conditions throughout the state's prisons had significantly deprived inmates of their right to adequate health care and thereby violated the Eighth Amendment's ban on cruel and unusual punishment. The high Court's ruling upheld an earlier order by a three-judge federal panel intended to reduce the number of inmates supervised by the California Department of Corrections and Rehabilitation (CDCR) to around 120,000. At the time of the ruling, the CDCR was supervising around 160,000 inmates in 33 facilities originally designed to hold only 84,000. The rest of the state's prisoners were housed under contract in correctional facilities outside of the state, but the Supreme Court determined that the policy of transferring inmates was inadequate to address California's overcrowding problem. In rendering the *Plata* ruling the Justices were drawing upon a legal tradition recognizing the rights of inmates that began in the United States more than 40 years earlier.

California's Folsom prison. In 2011, the U.S. Supreme Court ruled that California officials had to release as many as 58,000 inmates because of prison overcrowding. How did inmate rights figure into that decision?

THE HANDS-OFF DOCTRINE

CO11-1

In 1871, almost 140 years before the California order was issued, a Virginia judge declared the following: "A convicted felon . . . punished by confinement in the penitentiary instead of with death . . . is in a state of penal servitude to the State. He has, as a consequence of his crime, not only forfeited his liberty, but all his personal rights except those which the law in its humanity accords to him. He is for the time being the slave of the State. He is *civiliter mortuus;* and his estate, if he has any, is administered like that of a dead man. The Bill of Rights is a declaration of general principles to govern a society of freemen, and not of convicted felons and men civilly dead."[2]

In the case of *Ruffin* v. *Commonwealth,* the judge was voicing what had long been believed: that prisoners had no rights. It was this kind of thinking that long supported a "hands-off" approach to prisoners' rights. If inmates were really civilly dead, the federal government and the federal courts certainly had no cause to tell the states how to run their prisons.

hands-off doctrine

A historical policy of American courts not to intervene in prison management. Courts tended to follow the doctrine until the late 1960s.

Under the **hands-off doctrine,** U.S. courts for many decades avoided intervening in prison management. The doctrine was based on two rationales: (1) that under the *separation of powers* inherent in the U.S. Constitution, the judicial branch of government should not interfere with the running of correctional facilities by the executive branch and (2) that judges should leave correctional administration to correctional experts. For a very long time in our nation's history, states ran their prisons as they saw fit. Prison inmates were thought of as "nonpersons," and rights pertained only to persons. Pleas from prisoners based on allegations of deprivations of their rights were ignored.

The hands-off doctrine and the philosophy of the prisoner as a slave of the state began to change in the mid-1900s. Public attitudes about punishment versus rehabilitation changed, and more and more people became aware that inmates had *no* rights. As a result, the courts began to scrutinize the correctional enterprise in America.

Decline of the Hands-Off Doctrine

The 1941 case of *Ex parte Hull* began a dismantling of the hands-off doctrine. Prior to *Hull*, it had been common for corrections personnel to screen inmate mail, including prisoner petitions for writs of *habeas corpus.* Corrections officials often confiscated the petitions, claiming they were improperly prepared and not fit to submit to court. In *Hull,* the Supreme Court ruled that no state or its officers may interfere with a prisoner's right to apply to a federal court for a writ of *habeas corpus.* Thus, court officials, not corrections officials, have the authority to decide whether such petitions are prepared correctly.

Although this seemed like a small step at the time, it would facilitate a major leap in prisoners' rights. Three years later, in *Coffin* v. *Reichard* (1944), the Sixth Circuit Court of Appeals extended *habeas corpus* hearings to consider the conditions of confinement. Even more important, the *Coffin* case was the first in which a federal appellate court ruled that prisoners do not automatically lose their civil rights when in prison.[3] In the words of the Court, a prisoner "retains all the rights of an ordinary citizen except those expressly, or by necessary implication, taken from him by law."

San Quentin State Prison in Marin County, California. Opened in 1852, it is one of the state's oldest and best-known correctional institutions. Under the hands-off doctrine, American courts long refused to intervene in prison management. When did the hands-off doctrine end?

Another important development occurred in 1961 with the Supreme Court's ruling in *Monroe* v. *Pape*. Prior to *Pape*, it was believed that the phrase "under color of state law" in the Civil Rights Act of 1871 meant that a Section 1983 suit (explained in more detail on page 358) could involve only actions authorized by state law. In *Pape*, however, the Court held that for activities to take place *under color* of state law, they did not have to be *authorized* by state law. The statute, said the Court, had been intended to protect against "misuse of power, possessed by virtue of state law and made possible only because the wrongdoer is clothed with the authority of state law."

Officials "clothed with the authority of state law" seemed to include state corrections officials. Thus, state corrections officials who violated an inmate's constitutional rights while performing their duties could be held liable for their actions in federal court regardless of whether state law or policy supported those actions.[4]

A third important case establishing inmates' rights to access the courts was *Cooper* v. *Pate* (1964). In *Cooper*, a federal circuit court clarified the *Pape* decision, indicating that prisoners could sue a warden or another correctional official under Title 42 of the U.S. Code, Section 1983, based on the protections of the Civil Rights Act of 1871.

Commenting on the importance of *Cooper*, one observer noted,

> Just by opening a forum in which prisoners' grievances could be heard, the federal courts destroyed the custodian's absolute power and the prisoners' isolation from the larger society. The litigation itself heightened prisoners' consciousness and politicized them.[5]

With prisoners' access to the courts now established, cases challenging nearly every aspect of corrections were soon filed. The courts, primarily the federal district courts, began to review prisoners' complaints and intervene on prisoners' behalf.

The hands-off era is said to have ended in 1970 when a federal district court declared in *Holt* v. *Sarver* the entire Arkansas prison system "so inhumane as to be a violation of the Eighth Amendment bar on cruel and unusual punishment."[6] Robert Sarver, the Arkansas commissioner of corrections, admitted that "the physical facilities at both [prison units named in the suit] were inadequate and in a total state of disrepair that could only be described as deplorable." Additionally, he testified that inmates with trustee status, some of them serving life or long-term sentences, constituted 99 percent of the security force of the state's prison system.

Commissioner Sarver continued, testifying that "trustees sell desirable jobs to prisoners and also traffic in food, liquor, and drugs. Prisoners frequently become intoxicated and unruly. The prisoners sleep in dormitories. Prisoners are frequently attacked and raped in the dormitories, and injuries and deaths have resulted. Sleep and rest are seriously disrupted. No adequate means exist to protect the prisoners from assaults. There is no satisfactory means of keeping guns, knives, and other weapons away from the prison population."[7]

The *Holt* court declared in 1970,

> The obligation . . . to eliminate existing unconstitutionalities does not depend upon what the Legislature may do or upon what the Governor may do. . . . If Arkansas is going to operate a Penitentiary System, it is going to have to be a system that is countenanced by the Constitution of the United States.[8]

Prisoner litigation had brought sad conditions to light, and the court had intervened to institute reforms for the prisoners in Arkansas.

The case of Holt v. Sarver *brought the hands-off era to a close and opened a new era of prisoners' rights. What were the issues involved in that case?*

CO11-2 PRISONERS' RIGHTS

Legal Foundations

prisoners' rights

Constitutional guarantees of free speech, religious practice, due process, and other private and personal rights as well as constitutional protections against cruel and unusual punishments made applicable to prison inmates by the federal courts.

Prisoners' rights have four legal foundations: the U.S. Constitution, federal statutes, state constitutions, and state statutes. Most court cases involving prisoners' rights have involved rights claimed under the U.S. Constitution, even though state constitutions generally parallel the U.S. Constitution and sometimes confer additional rights. State legislatures and Congress can also confer additional prisoners' rights.

The U.S. Constitution The U.S. Constitution is the supreme law of our land. At the heart of any discussion of prisoners' rights lies one question: What does the Constitution have to say? As scholars began to search the Constitution, they could find no requirement that prisoners give up all of their rights as U.S. citizens (and human beings) after conviction.

constitutional rights

The personal and due process rights guaranteed to individuals by the U.S. Constitution and its amendments, especially the first 10 amendments, known as the *Bill of Rights*. Constitutional rights are the basis of most inmate rights.

It is important to remember, however, that **constitutional rights** are not absolute. Does freedom of speech mean that you have a protected right to stand up in a crowded theater and yell "fire"? It does not (at least not unless there *is* a fire). That is because the panic that would follow such an exclamation would probably cause injuries and would needlessly put members of the public at risk of harm. Hence, the courts have held that, although freedom of speech is guaranteed by the Constitution, it is not an absolute right; in other words, there are limits to it (*Schenck* v. *United States,* 1919).

So, the central issue raised by those interested in prisoners' rights seems to be the degree to which a person retains constitutional rights when convicted of a criminal offense and sentenced to prison. Addressing that issue has become a job of the courts. The positions on it dependent upon the courts' interpretation of the U.S. Constitution, state constitutions, and federal and state laws. Generally speaking, the courts have recognized four legitimate **institutional needs** that justify some restrictions on the constitutional rights of prisoners:

institutional needs

Prison administration interests recognized by the courts as justifying some restrictions on the constitutional rights of prisoners. Those interests are maintenance of institutional *order,* maintenance of institutional *security, safety* of prison inmates and staff, and *rehabilitation* of inmates.

1. maintenance of institutional *order;*
2. maintenance of institutional *security;*
3. *safety* of prison inmates and staff; and
4. *rehabilitation* of inmates.

According to the courts, *order* refers to calm and discipline within the institution, *security* is the control of individuals and objects entering or leaving the institution, *safety* means avoidance of physical harm, and *rehabilitation* refers to practices necessary for the health, well-being, and treatment of inmates.[9]

Federal Statutes Laws passed by Congress can confer certain rights on inmates in federal prisons. In addition, Congress has passed a number of laws that affect the running of state prisons. The Civil Rights Act of 1871, for example, was enacted after the Civil War to discourage lawless activities by state officials. Section 1983 reads as follows:

> Every person who, under color of any statute, ordinance, regulation, custom, or usage, of any State or Territory, subjects, or causes to be subjected, any citizen of the United States or other person within the jurisdiction thereof to the deprivation of any rights, privileges, or immunities secured by the Constitution and laws, shall be liable to the party injured in an action at law, suit in equity, or other proper proceeding for redress.

This section imposes **civil liability** (but not criminal blame) on any person who deprives another of rights guaranteed by the U.S. Constitution. The Civil Rights Act of 1871 allows state prisoners to challenge conditions of their imprisonment in federal court. Most prisoner suits brought under this act allege deprivation of constitutional rights. Another important piece of legislation is the Civil Rights of Institutionalized Persons Act (CRIPA),[10] which is discussed in more detail in Chapter 12.

civil liability

A legal obligation to another person to do, pay, or make good something.

State Constitutions Most state constitutions are patterned after the U.S. Constitution. However, state constitutions tend to be longer and more detailed than the U.S. Constitution and may contain specific provisions regarding corrections. State constitutions generally do not give prisoners more rights than are granted by the U.S. Constitution except in a few states such as California and Oregon. Inmates in such states may challenge the conditions of their confinement in state court under the state's constitutional provision.

State Statutes Unlike the federal government, state governments all have inherent police power, which allows them to pass laws to protect the health, safety, and welfare of their citizens. A state legislature can pass statutes to grant specific rights beyond those conferred by the state constitution. Often such legislation specifies duties of corrections officials or standards of treatment for prisoners. Prisoners who can show failure of officials to fulfill state statutory obligations may collect money damages or obtain a court order compelling officials to comply with the law.

CO11-3

Mechanisms for Securing Prisoners' Rights

Inmates today have five ways to challenge the legality of their confinement, associated prison conditions, and the practices of correctional officials: (1) a state *habeas corpus* action, (2) a federal *habeas corpus* action after state remedies have been exhausted, (3) a state tort lawsuit, (4) a federal civil rights lawsuit, and (5) a petition for injunctive relief.[11]

Writ of Habeas Corpus A **writ of** *habeas corpus* is an order from a court to produce a prisoner in court so that the court can determine whether the prisoner is being legally detained. *Habeas corpus* is Latin for "you have the body." A prisoner, or someone acting for a prisoner, files a *habeas corpus* petition asking a court to determine the lawfulness of the imprisonment. The petition for the writ is merely a procedural tool. If a writ is issued, it has no bearing on any issues to be reviewed. It guarantees only a hearing on those issues.

Federal and state prisoners may file *habeas corpus* petitions in federal courts. State prisoners must first, however, exhaust available state *habeas corpus* remedies. In 2000, of 11,880 petitions that inmates filed in *federal* courts, 3,870 (33 percent) were *habeas corpus* actions; of 46,371 petitions that inmates filed in *state* courts, 21,345 (46 percent) were *habeas corpus* actions.[12]

A writ of habeas corpus *is a court order requiring that a prisoner be brought before the court so that the court can determine whether the person is being legally detained. What is required of a state prisoner who wants to bring a* habeas corpus *action in federal court?*

writ of *habeas corpus*

An order that directs the person detaining a prisoner to bring him or her before a judge, who will determine the lawfulness of the imprisonment.

tort

A civil wrong, a wrongful act, or a wrongful breach of duty, other than a breach of contract, whether intentional or accidental, from which injury to another occurs.

Tort Action in State Court State inmates can file a tort action in state court. A **tort** is a civil wrong, a wrongful act, or a wrongful breach of duty, other than a breach of contract, whether intentional or accidental, from which injury to another occurs. In tort actions, inmates commonly claim that a correctional employee, such as the warden or a correctional officer, or the correctional facility itself failed to perform a duty required by law regarding the inmate. Compensation for damages is the most common objective. Tort suits often allege such deficiencies as negligence, gross or wanton negligence, or intentional wrong.

Federal Civil Rights Lawsuit Federal and state inmates can file suit in federal court alleging civil rights violations by corrections officials. Most of these suits challenge the conditions of confinement, under Section 1983 of the Civil Rights Act of 1871, which is now part of Title 42 of the U.S. Code. Lawsuits may claim that officials have deprived inmates of their constitutional rights, such as adequate medical treatment, protection against excessive force by correctional officers or violence from other inmates, due process in disciplinary hearings, and access to law libraries. According to the Bureau of Justice Statistics, 1 of 10 civil cases filed in U.S. district courts is *Section 1983 litigation* as it is commonly called.

When such suits seek monetary damages from federal agents for violation of constitutional rights, they are often referred to as *Bivens* actions, recalling the 1971 case in which the U.S. Supreme Court articulated inmates' entitlement to sue. In subsequent rulings (e.g., *FDIC* v. *Meyer*, 1994), the Court specified that "a *Bivens* action may only be maintained against an individual," not the federal agency by which he or she is employed, and it declined to extend the damage action authority of *Bivens* to permit suits against private entities operating correctional facilities under federal contract (*Correctional Services Corporation, Petitioner* v. *John E. Malesko*, 2001).

nominal damages

Small amounts of money a court may award when inmates have sustained no actual damages, but there is clear evidence that their rights have been violated.

If inmates are successful in their civil suits, in state or federal courts, the courts can award three types of damages. **Nominal damages** are small amounts of money that may be awarded when inmates have sustained no actual damages, but there is clear evidence that their rights have been violated.

compensatory damages

Money a court may award as payment for actual losses suffered by a plaintiff, including out-of-pocket expenses incurred in filing the suit, other forms of monetary or material loss, and pain, suffering, and mental anguish.

Compensatory damages are payments for actual losses, which may include out-of-pocket expenses the inmate incurred in filing the suit, other forms of monetary or material loss, and pain, suffering, and mental anguish. Some years ago, for example, a federal appeals court sustained an award of $9,300 against a warden and a correctional commissioner. The amount was calculated by awarding each inmate $25 for each day he had spent in solitary confinement (a total of 372 days for all the inmates) under conditions the court found cruel and unusual (*Sostre* v. *McGinnis*, 1971).

punitive damages

Money a court may award to punish a wrongdoer when a wrongful act was intentional and malicious or was done with reckless disregard for the rights of the victim.

Punitive damages are awarded to punish the wrongdoer when the wrongful act was intentional and malicious or was done with reckless disregard for the rights of the inmate.

injunction

A judicial order to do or refrain from doing a particular act.

Request for Injunctive Relief An **injunction** is a judicial order to do or refrain from doing a particular act. A request for an injunction might claim adverse effects of a health, safety, or sanitation procedure and might involve the entire correctional facility. It is important for anyone working in corrections to realize that a lack of funds cannot justify failure to comply with an injunction (*Smith* v. *Sullivan*, 1977).

EXHIBIT 11–1   Criminal Court Structure in the United States

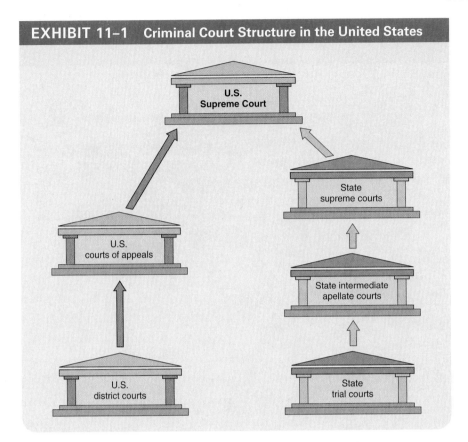

The Criminal Court System There is a dual court system in the United States; the federal and state court systems coexist (see Exhibit 11–1). The federal court system is nationwide with one or more federal courts in each state. These courts coexist with state court systems. Whether a defendant is tried in a federal court or a state court depends on which court has jurisdiction over the particular case.

The **jurisdiction** of a court is the power or authority of the court to act with respect to a case before it. The acts involved in the case must have taken place or had an effect in the geographic territory of the court, or a statute must give the court jurisdiction.

District courts are the trial courts of the federal system. They have original jurisdiction over cases charging defendants with violations of federal criminal laws. Each state has at least one U.S. district court, and some, like New York and California, have as many as four. There are also federal district courts in Puerto Rico, the District of Columbia, and the U.S. territories. There are currently 11 U.S. courts of appeals arranged by circuit, a District of Columbia circuit, and one federal circuit (see Exhibit 11–2).

Each state has its own court system. Most state court structures are similar to the federal court structure—with trial courts, intermediate appellate courts, and a top appellate court. In most states, the trial courts are organized by county.

Although federal offenses are prosecuted in federal court and state offenses are prosecuted in state courts, the federal courts have supervisory jurisdiction over the administration of criminal justice in the state courts. The U.S. Supreme Court has ruled that constitutional requirements for criminal procedure in federal courts also apply to the states. Violation of these constitutional requirements can be the subject of both state appeals and federal suits by prisoners.

jurisdiction

The power, right, or authority of a court to interpret and apply the law.

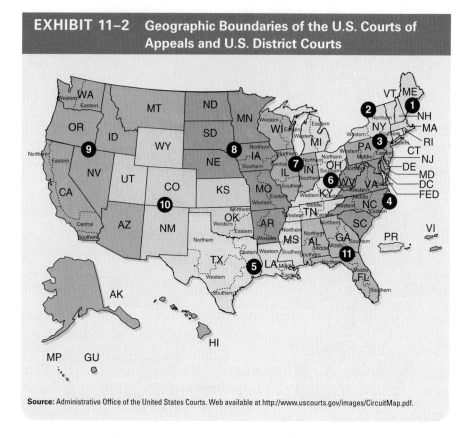

EXHIBIT 11–2 Geographic Boundaries of the U.S. Courts of Appeals and U.S. District Courts

Source: Administrative Office of the United States Courts. Web available at http://www.uscourts.gov/images/CircuitMap.pdf.

Inmate Grievance Procedures

Inmate grievance procedures are formal institutional processes for hearing inmate complaints. Grievance procedures, which typically employ internal hearing boards, are the method most frequently used by inmates to enforce the protections afforded to them by law.[13] Most inmate grievances concern discipline, program assignments, medical issues, personal property, and complaints against staff members. Only about 1 in 12 inmate grievances is approved or results in some action being taken by prison administrators to correct the problem.

The creation of formal mechanisms for the hearing of inmate grievances was encouraged by the comptroller general of the United States following the riot at New York's Attica Prison. The comptroller's report published in 1977[14] listed a number of reasons for establishing grievance mechanisms, including (1) promoting justice and fairness, (2) providing opportunities for inmates to voice complaints, (3) reducing the number of court cases filed by inmates, (4) assisting correctional administrators in the identification of institutional problems, and (5) reducing violence.

Today most correctional systems use a three-step process for resolving grievances. First, a staff member or committee in each institution receives complaints, investigates them, and makes decisions. Second, if a prisoner is dissatisfied with that decision, the case may be appealed to the warden. Third, if the prisoner is still dissatisfied, the complaint may be given to the state's commissioner of corrections or the state's corrections board. This three-step procedure satisfies the requirements for U.S. Department of Justice certification.

THE PRISONERS' RIGHTS ERA (1970–1991)

CO11-4

Many refer to the era following *Holt* v. *Sarver* (1970) as the *prisoners' rights era*. As some have observed, "The prisoners' rights movement must be understood in the context of a 'fundamental democratization' that has transformed American society since World War II, and particularly since 1960."[15] Over the past 40 years, an increasing number of once-marginal groups, including blacks, Hispanics, gays, and those who are economically disenfranchised and physically and mentally challenged, have acquired social recognition and legal rights that were previously unavailable to those outside the American social mainstream. Seen in this context, the prisoners' rights era was but a natural outgrowth of an encompassing social movement that recognized the existence and potential legitimacy of a wide number of group grievances.

Although the phrase *prisoners' rights era* might give the impression that prisoners won virtually every case brought during that period, such is not the case. Although prisoners did win some significant court battles, it was the turnaround in legal attitudes toward prisoners that was most remarkable. As we shall see, courts went from practically ignoring prison systems to practically running those systems. It might be more appropriate to refer to the period as the "court involvement era." We will now review some of the most important cases won *and* lost by inmates, presented in order of the constitutional amendments on which they were based.

When we speak of prisoners' rights, we are generally speaking of the rights found in four of the amendments to the U.S. Constitution. Three of these—the First (free expression), Fourth (privacy), and Eighth Amendments (cruel and unusual punishment)—are part of the Bill of Rights (the first 10 amendments to the Constitution). The fourth is the Fourteenth Amendment (deprivation of life, liberty, and property). Keep in mind that what we call *inmates' rights* today are largely the result of federal court decisions that have interpreted constitutional guarantees and applied them to prisons and prison conditions. Often such a case sets a **precedent**, serving as an example or authority for future cases. Rulings in cases that find violations of inmates' rights must be implemented by the administrators of affected correctional systems and institutions. (See Exhibit 11–3 for more U.S. Supreme Court cases involving prisoners' rights.)

CO11-5

precedent

A previous judicial decision that judges should consider in deciding future cases.

First Amendment

> Congress shall make no law respecting an establishment of religion, or prohibiting the free exercise thereof; or abridging the freedom of speech, or of the press; or the right of the people peaceably to assemble, and to petition the government for a redress of grievances.

First Amendment guarantees are important to members of a free society. It is no surprise, then, that some of the early prisoners' rights cases concerned those rights. For example, in 1974, in *Pell* v. *Procunier*, four California prison inmates and three journalists challenged the constitutionality of regulation 415.071 of the California Department of Corrections and Rehabilitation (CDCR). That regulation specified that "press and other media interviews with specific individual inmates will not be permitted." The rule had been imposed after a violent prison episode that corrections authorities attributed at least in part to a former policy of free face-to-face prisoner-press interviews. Such interviews had apparently resulted in a relatively small number of inmates gaining disproportionate notoriety and influence with other prisoners.

EXHIBIT 11–3	Selected U.S. Supreme Court Cases Involving Prisoners' Rights

Case Name	Year	Decision
Millbrook v. *U.S.*	2013	Federal correctional agencies are generally shielded against civil lawsuits seeking monetary damages for the acts or omissions of their employees.
Florence v. *Burlington County*	2012	Officials may strip-search persons who have been arrested and taken to a detention facility even though the arrest is for a minor offense, in order to insure the safety and security of the jail or detention.
Howes v. *Fields*	2012	Inmates who are facing questioning by law enforcement officers while incarcerated need not be advised of their *Miranda* rights.
Brown v. *Plata* (Eighth Amendment)	2011	Found that seriously overcrowded conditions in California prisons are a violation of the Eighth Amendment's ban on cruel and unusual punishment.
U.S. v. *Georgia*	2006	Under the Americans with Disabilities Act, a state may be liable for rights deprivations suffered by inmates held in its prisons who are disabled.
Johnson v. *California*	2005	The decision invalidated the California Department of Corrections and Rehabilitation's unwritten policy of racially segregating prisoners in double cells each time they entered a new correctional facility.
Wilkinson v. *Austin*	2005	The Court upheld an Ohio policy allowing the most dangerous offenders to be held in "supermax" cells following several levels of review prior to transfer.
Overton v. *Bazzetta*	2003	The decision upheld the Michigan Department of Corrections' visitation regulation that denies most visits to prisoners who commit two substance abuse violations while incarcerated.
Porter v. *Nussle* (Eighth Amendment)	2002	The "exhaustion requirement" of the Prison Litigation Reform Act of 1995 (PLRA) applies to all inmate suits about prison life, whether they involve general circumstances or particular episodes and whether they allege excessive force or some other wrong.
Hope v. *Pelzer* (Eighth Amendment)	2002	The Court found an Eighth Amendment violation in the case of a prisoner who was subjected to unnecessary pain, humiliation, and risk of physical harm.
Booth v. *Churner* (Eighth Amendment)	2001	The decision upheld a requirement under the PLRA that state inmates must "exhaust such administrative remedies as are available" before filing a suit over prison conditions.
Lewis v. *Casey*	1996	Earlier cases do not guarantee inmates the wherewithal to file any and every type of legal claim. All that is required is "that they be provided with the tools to attack their sentences."
Sandin v. *Conner* (Fourteenth Amendment)	1995	Perhaps signaling an end to the prisoners' rights era, this case rejected the argument that disciplining inmates is a deprivation of constitutional due process rights.
Wilson v. *Seiter* (Eighth Amendment)	1991	The case clarified the totality of conditions notion, saying that some conditions of confinement "in combination" may violate prisoners' rights when each would not do so alone.
Washington v. *Harper* (Eighth Amendment)	1990	An inmate who is a danger to self or others as a result of mental illness may be treated with psychoactive drugs against his or her will.

EXHIBIT 11–3	**Selected U.S. Supreme Court Cases Involving Prisoners' Rights** *(continued)*	

Case Name	Year	Decision
Turner v. *Safley* (First Amendment)	1987	A Missouri ban on correspondence between inmates was upheld as "reasonably related to legitimate penological interests."
O'Lone v. *Estate of Shabazz* (First Amendment)	1987	An inmate's right to practice religion was not violated by prison officials who refused to alter his work schedule so that he could attend Friday afternoon services.
Whitley v. *Albers* (Eighth Amendment)	1986	The shooting and wounding of an inmate was not a violation of that inmate's rights, because "the shooting was part and parcel of a good-faith effort to restore prison security."
Ponte v. *Real*	1985	Inmates have certain rights in disciplinary hearings.
Hudson v. *Palmer* (Fourth Amendment)	1984	A prisoner has no reasonable expectation of privacy in his prison cell that entitles him to protections against "unreasonable searches."
Block v. *Rutherford* (First Amendment)	1984	State regulations may prohibit inmate union meetings and use of mail to deliver union information within the prison. Prisoners do not have a right to be present during searches of cells.
Rhodes v. *Chapman* (Eighth Amendment)	1981	Double-celling of inmates is not cruel and unusual punishment unless it involves the wanton and unnecessary infliction of pain or conditions grossly disproportionate to the severity of the crime committed.
Ruiz v. *Estelle* (Eighth Amendment)	1980	The Court found unconstitutional conditions in the Texas prison system—including overcrowding, understaffing, brutality, and substandard medical care.
Cooper v. *Morin*	1980	Neither inconvenience nor cost is an acceptable excuse for treating female inmates differently from male inmates.
Jones v. *North Carolina Prisoners' Labor Union, Inc.* (First Amendment)	1977	Inmates have no inherent right to publish newspapers or newsletters for use by other inmates.
Bounds v. *Smith*	1977	The case resulted in the creation of law libraries in many prisons.
Estelle v. *Gamble* (Eighth Amendment)	1976	Prison officials have a duty to provide proper inmate medical care.
Wolff v. *McDonnell* (Fourteenth Amendment)	1974	Sanctions cannot be levied against inmates without appropriate due process.
Procunier v. *Martinez* (First Amendment)	1974	Censorship of inmate mail is acceptable only when necessary to protect legitimate governmental interests.
Pell v. *Procunier* (First Amendment)	1974	Inmates retain First Amendment rights that are not inconsistent with their status as prisoners or with the legitimate penological objectives of the corrections system.
Cruz v. *Beto* (First Amendment)	1972	Inmates have to be given a "reasonable opportunity" to pursue their religious faiths. Also, visits can be banned if such visits constitute threats to security.
Johnson v. *Avery*	1968	Inmates have a right to consult "jailhouse lawyers" when trained legal assistance is not available.
Monroe v. *Pape*	1961	Individuals deprived of their rights by state officers acting under color of state law have a right to bring action in federal court.

Tammy Waldrop

Inspector of Correctional Facilities • Palm Beach County, Florida

Tammy Waldrop is an inspector with the Palm Beach County (Florida) Sheriff's Office, assigned to Corrections Administration. Quarterly, Waldrop inspects all four correctional facilities in Palm Beach County to verify that each one complies with agency, local, state, and American Correctional Association standards. She investigates staff and inmate grievances and works with the Legal Advisors' office to resolve conflicts.

Waldrop received her bachelor's degree in criminal justice from Florida Atlantic University in Boca Raton. She remembers that the undergraduate course that influenced her the most was a sociology course titled "Social Conflict." She says, "This course changed my perspective on life and my views on crime. It was the best preparation for my current job. It helped me understand the importance of changing conflict into occasions for problem solving."

In the future, Waldrop would like to build on her present career, attend law school, concentrate on corrections law, and work in the Legal Advisors' office.

> *"In corrections, the words care, custody, and control are repeatedly stated as your primary tasks. But remember three additional words in your interactions with inmates: fair, firm, and consistent. And never, never lie to an inmate."*

---

legitimate penological objectives

The realistic concerns that correctional officers and administrators have for the integrity and security of the correctional institution and the safety of staff and inmates.

balancing test

A method the U.S. Supreme Court uses to decide prisoners' rights cases, weighing the rights claimed by inmates against the legitimate needs of prisons.

The U.S. Supreme Court held that "in light of the alternative channels of communication that are open to the inmate appellees, [regulation] 415.071 does not constitute a violation of their rights of free speech." Significantly, the Court went on to say, "A prison inmate retains those first amendment rights that are not inconsistent with his status as prisoner or with the *legitimate penological objectives* of the corrections system" (emphasis added). **Legitimate penological objectives** are the permissible aims of a correctional institution. They include the realistic concerns that correctional officers and administrators have for the integrity and security of the correctional institution and the safety of staff and inmates. The *Pell* ruling established a **balancing test** that the Supreme Court would continue to use, weighing the rights claimed by inmates against the legitimate needs of prisons.

Freedom of Speech and Expression Visits to inmates by friends and loved ones are forms of expression. But prison visits are not an absolute right. In *Cruz* v. *Beto* (1972), the Supreme Court ruled that all visits can be banned if they threaten security. Although *Cruz* involved short-term confinement facilities, the ruling has also been applied to prisons.

Another form of expression is correspondence. As a result of various court cases, prison officials can (and generally do) impose restrictions on inmate mail. Inmates receive mail not directly from the hands of postal carriers but from correctional officers. They place their outgoing mail not in U.S. Postal Service mailboxes but in containers provided by the correctional institution.

Corrections officials often read inmate mail—both incoming and outgoing—in an effort to uncover escape plans. Reading inmate mail, however, is different from censoring it. In 1974, in *Procunier* v. *Martinez,* the U.S. Supreme Court held that the censoring of inmate mail is acceptable only when necessary to protect legitimate government interests. The case turned upon First Amendment guarantees of free speech.

Under a 1979 federal appeals court decision, in *McNamara* v. *Moody,* prison officials may not prohibit inmates from writing vulgar letters or those that make disparaging remarks about the prison staff. Similarly, although correctional administrators have a legitimate interest in curbing inmates' deviant sexual behavior, courts have held that viewing nudity is not deviant sexual behavior. Hence, prison officials may not ban mailed nude pictures of inmates' wives or girlfriends (*Peppering* v. *Crist,* 1981) although restrictions against posting them on cell walls have generally been upheld. Similarly, officials may not prevent inmates from receiving, by mail direct from publishers, publications depicting nudity unless those publications depict deviant sexual behavior (*Mallery* v. *Lewis,* 1983).

In 1989, in the case of *Thornburgh* v. *Abbott,* in an effort to clear up questions raised by lower court rulings concerning mailed publications, the U.S. Supreme Court ruled as follows:

> Publications which may be rejected by a warden include but are not limited to publications which meet one of the following criteria: (1) it depicts or describes procedures for the construction or use of weapons, ammunition, bombs, or incendiary devices; (2) it depicts, encourages, or describes methods of escape from correctional facilities or contains blueprints, drawings, or similar descriptions of Bureau of Prisons institutions; (3) it depicts or describes procedures for the brewing of alcoholic beverages or the manufacture of drugs; (4) it is written in code; (5) it depicts, describes, or encourages activities which may lead to the use of physical violence or group disruption; (6) it encourages or instructs in the commission of criminal activities; (7) it is sexually explicit material which by its nature or content poses a threat to the security, good order, or discipline of the institution or facilitates criminal activity.

Unless at least one of these standards is met, restrictions on the receipt of published materials—especially magazines and newspapers that do not threaten prison security—are generally not allowed. In the 2006 U.S. Supreme Court case of *Beard* v. *Banks,* however, the justices held that Pennsylvania prison officials could legitimately prohibit the state's most violent inmates from having access to newspapers, magazines, and photographs. Prison officials had argued that the policy helped motivate better behavior on the part of particularly difficult prisoners. The Court agreed, noting that "prison officials have imposed the deprivation only upon those with serious prison-behavior problems; and those officials, relying on their professional judgment, reached an experience-based conclusion that the policies help to further legitimate prison objectives."

Similarly, in the case of *Turner* v. *Safley* (1987), the Supreme Court upheld a Missouri ban on correspondence among inmates. Such a regulation is valid, the Court said, if it is "reasonably related to legitimate penological interests." *Turner* established that officials had to show only that a regulation was reasonably *related* to a legitimate penological interest. No clear-cut damage to legitimate penological interests had to be shown.

The U.S. Supreme Court sided with corrections officials in its 1977 decision in *Jones* v. *North Carolina Prisoners' Labor Union, Inc.* In *Jones,* the Court upheld regulations established by the North Carolina Department of Correction that prohibited prisoners from soliciting other inmates to join the union and barred union meetings and bulk mailings concerning the union from outside sources. Citing *Pell* v. *Procunier,* the Court went on to say, "The prohibition on inmate-to-inmate solicitation does not

Inmate rights are not absolute but are limited by legitimate penological objectives. What does the phrase "legitimate penological objectives" mean?

unduly abridge inmates' free speech rights. If the prison officials are otherwise entitled to control organized union activity within the confines of a prison, the solicitation ban is not impermissible under the First Amendment, for such a prohibition is both reasonable and necessary."

Freedom of Religion Lawsuits involving religious practices in prison have been numerous for at least 40 years. In 1962, for example, in *Fulwood* v. *Clemmer*, the court of appeals for the District of Columbia ruled that the Black Muslim faith must be recognized as a religion and held that officials may not restrict members of that faith from holding services.

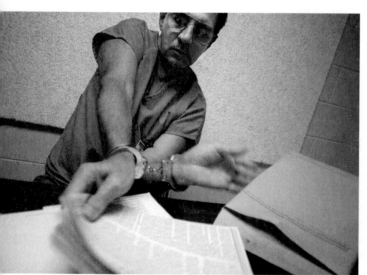

Inmates have limited rights to send and receive mail. Restrictions on inmates' mail focus on maintaining institutional security. Judicial interpretations of which constitutional amendment have led to inmates' rights to send and receive mail?

In 1970, the U.S. Supreme Court refused to hear an appeal from inmate Jack Gittlemacker, who wanted the state of Pennsylvania to provide him with a clergyman of his faith. The Court held that although states must give inmates the opportunity to practice their religions, they are not required to provide clergy for that purpose.

In *Cruz* v. *Beto* (mentioned earlier), the Supreme Court also decided that inmates had to be given a "reasonable opportunity" to pursue their religious faiths. Later federal court decisions expanded this decision, requiring officials to provide such a "reasonable opportunity" even to inmates whose religious faiths were not traditional.

In 1975, the U.S. Court of Appeals for the Second Circuit ruled in *Kahane* v. *Carlson* that an Orthodox Jewish inmate has the right to a kosher diet unless the government can show good cause for not providing it. Similarly, the courts have held that "Muslims' request for one full-course pork-free meal once a day and coffee three times daily is essentially a plea for a modest degree of official deference to their religious obligations" (*Barnett* v. *Rodgers*, 1969).

On the other hand, courts have determined that some inmate religious demands need not be met. In the 1986 Fifth Circuit Court of Appeals case

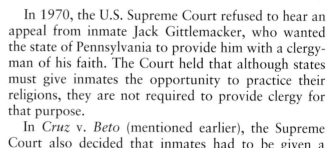

of *Udey* v. *Kastner,* for example, Muslim prisoners had requested raw milk, distilled water, and organic fruits, juices, vegetables, and meats. The special diet was so costly that a federal court allowed the prison to deny the inmates' request.

In 2000, the Religious Land Use and Institutionalized Persons Act (RLUIPA) became law. RLUIPA says, "No government shall impose a substantial burden on the religious exercise of a person residing in or confined to an institution even if the burden results from a rule of general applicability unless the government demonstrates that imposition of the burden on that person (1) is in furtherance of a compelling governmental interest; and (2) is the least restrictive means of furthering that compelling governmental interest." Because RLUIPA is a federal law, it is especially relevant to prison programs and activities that are at least partially supported with federal monies. In 2005, in the case of *Benning* v. *State,* the Eleventh Circuit Court of Appeals found in favor of a Georgia state prison inmate who claimed that RLUIPA supported his right as a "Torah observant Jew" to eat only kosher food and wear a yarmulke (or skullcap) at all times. Also in 2005, in the case of *Cutter* v. *Wilkinson,* the U.S. Supreme Court ruled in favor of past and present Ohio inmates who claimed that the state's correctional system failed to accommodate their nonmainstream religious practices.

Fourth Amendment

The right of the people to be secure in their persons, houses, papers, and effects, against unreasonable searches and seizures, shall not be violated, and no Warrants shall issue, but upon probable cause, supported by Oath or affirmation, and particularly describing the place to be searched, and the persons or things to be seized.

The right to privacy is at the heart of the Fourth Amendment. Clearly, unreasonable searches without warrants are unconstitutional. Does this mean that an inmate has a right to privacy in his or her cell? When is it reasonable to search a cell without a warrant? Some suggest that the

Correctional officers preparing for a cell search at Rikers Island Jail in New York City. One of the officers is carrying an electric stun shield for protection from aggressive inmates. Prisoners do not retain the right to privacy in their cells or possessions because institutional interests of safety and security supersede constitutional guarantees of privacy. Under which amendment to the Constitution does the right to be free from unreasonable searches and seizures fall?

The Offender Speaks
Visit www.mhhe.com/schmalleger7e
to see this feature.

needs of institutional security prohibit privacy for inmates. Others argue that a prison cell is the equivalent of an inmate's house. Over the years, the courts have been fairly consistent in deciding that the privacy rights implied in this amendment must be greatly reduced in prisons to maintain institutional security.

In *United States* v. *Hitchcock* (1972), an inmate claimed that his Fourth Amendment rights had been violated by a warrantless search and seizure of documents in his prison cell. Previously, courts had generally held that "constitutionally protected" places—such as homes, motel rooms, safe-deposit boxes, and certain places of business—could not be searched without a warrant. In *Hitchcock*, however, the U.S. Court of Appeals for the Ninth Circuit created a new standard: "first, that a person have exhibited an actual (subjective) expectation of privacy and second, that the expectation be one that society is prepared to recognize as reasonable." The court concluded that, although Hitchcock plainly expected to keep his documents private, his expectation was not reasonable. In the words of the court,

> It is obvious that a jail shares none of the attributes of privacy of a home, an automobile, an office, or a hotel room. In prison, official surveillance has traditionally been the order of the day. . . . [Hence], we do not feel that it is reasonable for a prisoner to consider his cell private.

In *Hudson* v. *Palmer* (1984), a Virginia inmate claimed a correctional officer had unreasonably destroyed some of his permitted personal property during a search of his cell. The inmate also claimed that under the Fourth Amendment, the cell search was illegal. Echoing *Hitchcock*, the U.S. Supreme Court ruled that "a prisoner has no reasonable expectation of privacy in his prison cell entitling him to the protection of the Fourth Amendment against unreasonable searches." Similarly, in *Block* v. *Rutherford* (1984), the Court ruled that prisoners do not have the right to be present during searches of their cells.

In 1985, the Ninth Circuit Court of Appeals decided a case involving inmates at San Quentin State Prison (*Grummett* v. *Rushen*). The inmates had brought a class action lawsuit against prison administrators, objecting to the policy of allowing female correctional officers to view nude or partly clothed male inmates. Women officers, complained the inmates, could see male inmates while they were dressing, showering, being strip-searched, or using toilet facilities. Such viewing, said the inmates, violated privacy rights guaranteed by the U.S. Constitution.

At the time of the suit, approximately 113 of the 720 correctional officers at San Quentin were female. Both female and male correctional officers were assigned to patrol the cell block tiers and gun rails. Both were also assigned to supervise showering from the tiers and from the gun rails, but only male officers were permitted to accompany inmates to the shower cells and lock them inside to disrobe and shower. Female officers were allowed to conduct pat-down searches that included the groin area.

The court found that prison officials had "struck an acceptable balance among the inmates' privacy interests, the institution's security requirements, and the female guards' employment rights." According to the court,

> The female guards are restricted in their contact with the inmates, and the record clearly demonstrates that at all times they have conducted themselves in a professional manner, and have treated the inmates with respect and dignity. . . . Routine pat-down searches, which include the groin area, and which are otherwise justified by security needs, do not violate the Fourteenth Amendment because a correctional officer of the opposite gender conducts such a search.

Eighth Amendment

Excessive bail shall not be required, nor excessive fines imposed, nor cruel and unusual punishments inflicted.

Many prisoners' rights cases turn upon the issue of **cruel and unusual punishment**. Defining such punishment is not easy. A working definition, however, might be "punishments that are grossly disproportionate to the offense as well as those that transgress today's broad and idealistic concepts of dignity, civilized standards, humanity, and decency."[16] Cases concerning constitutional prohibition of cruel and unusual punishment have centered on prisoners' need for decent conditions of confinement. In the case that began this chapter, *Brown* v. *Plata* (2011), for example, overcrowded conditions in California prisons were found to have violated the Eighth Amendment by making it impossible for adequate health care to be delivered to most inmates. Inmates' rights cases involving the Eighth Amendment cover areas as diverse as medical care, prison conditions, physical insecurity, psychological stress, and capital punishment.

Medical Care In 2012, federal Judge Mark Wolf of the District of Massachusetts ordered the Massachusetts Department of Correction to provide a male inmate, Michelle Kosilek, with sex change surgery.[17] Kosilek, the judge noted, had twice tried to kill himself and even attempted to castrate himself—proving, in the judge's opinion, a need for immediate medical intervention. Kosilek is serving a life sentence for the murder of his wife.

The history of inmates' rights in the health care area can be traced to the 1970 case of *Holt* v. *Sarver* in which a federal district court declared the entire Arkansas prison system inhumane and found that it was in violation of the Constitution's Eighth Amendment's ban on cruel and unusual punishment.

In a related case, medical personnel in state prisons had given inmates injections of apomorphine without their consent in a program of "aversive stimuli." The drug caused vomiting, which lasted from 15 minutes to an hour. The state justified it as "Pavlovian conditioning." The federal courts, however, soon prohibited the practice (*Knecht* v. *Gillman*, 1973).

Another decision, that of *Estelle* v. *Gamble* (1976), spelled out the duty of prison officials to provide inmates with medical care. The Court held that prison officials could not lawfully demonstrate **deliberate indifference** to the medical needs of prisoners. In the words of the Court, "Deliberate indifference to serious medical needs of prisoners constitutes the 'unnecessary and wanton infliction of pain' proscribed by the Eighth Amendment." A serious medical condition is one that "causes pain, discomfort, or threat to good health" (*Rufo* v. *Inmates of Suffolk County Jail*, 1992). The mental health needs of prisoners are governed by the same constitutional standard of deliberate indifference as those described in court opinions dealing with the physical health of inmates.[18]

Prison Conditions The 1976 federal court case of *Pugh* v. *Locke* introduced the **totality of conditions** standard. That standard, said the court, is to be used in evaluating whether prison conditions are cruel and unusual. The *Pugh* court held that "prison conditions [in Alabama] are so debilitating that they necessarily deprive inmates of any opportunity to rehabilitate themselves or even maintain skills already possessed." The totality of conditions approach was also applied in a 1977 federal case, *Battle* v. *Anderson*, in which officials in overcrowded Oklahoma prisons

cruel and unusual punishment

A penalty that is grossly disproportionate to the offense or that violates today's broad and idealistic concepts of dignity, civilized standards, humanity, and decency (*Estelle* v. *Gamble*, 1976, and *Hutto* v. *Finney*, 1978). In the area of capital punishment, cruel and unusual punishments are those that involve torture, a lingering death, or unnecessary pain.

deliberate indifference

Intentional and willful indifference. Within the field of correctional practice, the term refers to calculated inattention to unconstitutional conditions of confinement.

totality of conditions

A standard to be used in evaluating whether prison conditions are cruel and unusual.

A Newark, NJ, prison inmate takes tuberculosis medication as a nurse watches. A number of Eighth Amendment cases have established that prison officials have a duty to provide adequate medical care to inmates in their charge. How does the concept of "deliberate indifference" relate to that requirement?

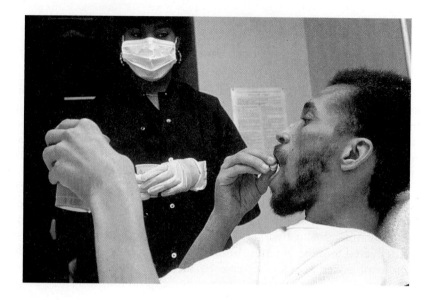

had forced inmates to sleep in garages, barbershops, libraries, and stairwells. Oklahoma prison administrators were found to be in violation of the cruel and unusual punishment clause of the U.S. Constitution.

The U.S. Supreme Court ruled on the use of solitary confinement in *Hutto* v. *Finney* (1978). The Court held that confinement in Arkansas's segregation (solitary confinement) cells for more than 30 days was cruel and unusual punishment. It then went on to exhort lower courts to consider the totality of the conditions of confinement in future Eighth Amendment cases. Where appropriate, it said, a court should specify the changes needed to remedy the constitutional violation.

In the 1991 case of *Wilson* v. *Seiter,* the U.S. Supreme Court clarified the totality of conditions standard. The Court noted,

> Some conditions of confinement may establish an Eighth Amendment violation "in combination" when each would not do so alone, but only when they have a mutually enforcing effect that produces the deprivation of a single, identifiable human need such as food, warmth, or exercise—for example, a low cell temperature at night combined with a failure to issue blankets. . . . To say that some prison conditions may interact in this fashion is a far cry from saying that all prison conditions are a seamless web for Eighth Amendment purposes. Nothing so [shapeless] as "overall conditions" can rise to the level of cruel and unusual punishment when no specific deprivation of a single human need exists.

Several rulings have addressed inmate claims that overcrowding was cruel and unusual punishment. A U.S. Supreme Court case, *Rhodes* v. *Chapman* (1981), decided the issue of double-celling (housing two inmates in a cell designed for one) in long-term correctional facilities. In response to rising prison populations, Ohio authorities had begun double-celling. There was no evidence that Ohio authorities had wantonly inflicted pain through the practice, and double-celling had not resulted in food deprivation, a lower quality of medical care, or a decrease in sanitation standards. For those reasons, the Court denied the inmates' claims.

In *Rhodes,* the Court also emphasized that the Eighth Amendment prohibition of cruel and unusual punishment is a fluid concept that "must draw its meaning from the evolving standards of decency that mark the progress of a maturing society." In other words, what is considered cruel and unusual changes as society evolves.

In 1982, the U.S. Court of Appeals for the Seventh Circuit ruled, in *Smith* v. *Fairman*, that double-celling in a short-term facility (a jail) was not cruel and unusual punishment. The court said that government officials did not intend to punish inmates by double-celling. The double-celling was innocent overcrowding required by circumstances.

Many conditions of confinement that violate prisoners' Eighth Amendment rights can be remedied by changes in prison rules, by special training for correctional personnel, or by educational programs for prisoners. The remedies can be implemented through everyday administrative policies in the prison once prisoners' court petitions have brought violations to light. Relief of overcrowding, however, is not always within the power of prison administrators. Prison officials have little control over the sizes of their prisons or the numbers of inmates the courts assign to them. New prison facilities are expensive and take time to build.

The Eighth Amendment's prohibition of cruel and unusual punishment has been tied to prisoners' need for decent conditions of confinement. In determining whether conditions such as overcrowding and inadequate diet constitute a denial of such protection, courts have used the concept of totality of conditions. What is meant by the totality of conditions?

Fourteenth Amendment

No State shall make or enforce any law which shall abridge the privileges or immunities of citizens of the United States; nor shall any State deprive any person of life, liberty, or property, without due process of law; nor deny to any person within its jurisdiction the equal protection of the laws.

When the Constitution and the Bill of Rights became law, the people of many states thought the document applied only to federal courts and to federal law. This attitude prevailed at least until the end of the Civil War. After the war, to clarify the status of the newly freed slaves and to apply the Bill of Rights to state actions, the Fourteenth Amendment was passed. The just-quoted portion of the Fourteenth Amendment is relevant to our discussion.

Most cases involving prisoners' rights and the Fourteenth Amendment deal with issues of **due process**. Due process requires that laws and legal procedures be reasonable and that they be applied fairly and equally. The right to due process is a right to be fairly heard before being deprived of life or liberty.

By 1987, long after the hands-off doctrine had eroded, U.S. Supreme Court justice Sandra Day O'Connor summarized the thrust of earlier opinions, holding that "prison walls do not form a barrier separating prison inmates from the protections of the Constitution" (*Turner* v. *Safley*). Without access to the courts, O'Connor said, inmates have no due process opportunities.

To bring their cases to court, however, prisoners need access to legal materials, and many of them need legal assistance. What if one inmate understands how to file cases with the court, but a second inmate does not? Does the second inmate have a right to enlist the aid of the first? "Yes," said the U.S. Supreme Court in *Johnson* v. *Avery* (1968). Inmates have a right to consult "jailhouse lawyers" (other inmates knowledgeable in the law) when trained legal advisers are not available.

The case of *Wolff* v. *McDonnell* (1974) expanded the concept of due process by applying it to disciplinary actions within prisons. Prior to *Wolff*, prison administrators had the discretion to discipline inmates who broke prison rules. Disciplinary procedures were often tied to vague or nonexistent rules of conduct and were exercised without challenge. A prisoner might be assigned to solitary confinement or might have good-time

due process

A right guaranteed by the Fifth, Sixth, and Fourteenth Amendments to the U.S. Constitution and generally understood, in legal contexts, to mean the expected course of legal proceedings according to the rules and forms established for the protection of persons' rights.

credits reduced because of misconduct. Because the prisoner was physically confined and lacked outside communication, there was no opportunity for the prisoner to challenge the charge. The *Wolff* Court concluded that sanctions (disciplinary actions) could not be levied against inmates without appropriate due process, saying,

> [The state of Nebraska] asserts that the procedure for disciplining prison inmates for serious misconduct is a matter of policy raising no constitutional issue. If the position implies that prisoners in state institutions are wholly without the protection of the Constitution and the Due Process Clause, it is plainly untenable. Lawful imprisonment necessarily makes unavailable many rights and privileges of the ordinary citizen, a retraction justified by the consideration underlying our penal system. . . . But though his rights may be diminished by the needs and exigencies of the institutional environment, a prisoner is not wholly stripped of constitutional protections when he is imprisoned for a crime.

The *Wolff* Court imposed minimal due process requirements on prison disciplinary proceedings that could lead to solitary confinement or reduction of good-time credits. The requirements included (1) advance notice by means of a written statement of the claimed violation, (2) a written statement by an impartial fact finder of the evidence relied on and the reasons for imposing punishment, and (3) an opportunity to testify and call witnesses unless the fact finder concluded such proceedings would undermine institutional security.

In 1976, inmates lost three due process appeals. First, in *Baxter* v. *Palmigiano,* the Supreme Court decided that due process for an inmate in a disciplinary hearing does not include a right to counsel even when the consequences are potentially "serious." In a second opinion issued that year (*Meacham* v. *Fano*), the Court held that prisoners have no right to be in any particular prison and therefore have no due process protections before being transferred from one prison to another. A third case (*Stone* v. *Powell*) denied prisoners the right in most instances to seek federal review of state court Fourth Amendment search-and-seizure decisions.

Inmates' right to legal materials was formally recognized in 1977 in the U.S. Supreme Court decision in *Bounds* v. *Smith*. In *Bounds,* the Court held,

Inmates must be allowed access to the courts and assistance in preparing their cases. To meet that requirement, most states stock law libraries in each correctional institution. Under which clause of the Fourteenth Amendment does inmates' access to the courts fall?

> The fundamental constitutional right of access to the courts requires prison authorities to assist inmates in the preparation and filing of meaningful legal papers by providing prisoners with adequate law libraries or adequate assistance from persons trained in the law.

As a result of the *Bounds* decision, law libraries were created in prisons across the nation.

As we saw in Chapter 9, one challenge facing corrections personnel is to find safe, humane ways to manage inmate populations. Inmates often have grievances regarding conditions of confinement or disciplinary actions for infractions. Those grievances must be dealt with to maintain the safety and security of the institution. The Supreme Court's decision in *Jones* v. *North Carolina Prisoners' Labor Union, Inc.*

(1977) required prisons to establish and maintain formal opportunities for the airing of inmate grievances. *Ponte* v. *Real* (1985) required prison officials to explain to inmates why their requests to have witnesses appear on their behalf at disciplinary hearings were denied.

The due process clause protects against unlawful deprivation of life or liberty. When a prisoner sued for damages for injuries (*Daniels* v. *Williams,* 1986), the Supreme Court ruled that prisoners could sue for damages in federal court only if officials had inflicted injury intentionally. According to the Court, "The due process clause is simply not implicated by a negligent act of an official causing unintended loss or injury to life, liberty, or property."

A 2001 ruling by a panel of federal judges in the case of *Gerber* v. *Hickman* addressed a unique claim of unlawful deprivation of life. Gerber wanted to impregnate his wife. He was, however, serving a life sentence in a California Department of Corrections and Rehabilitation (CDCR) prison, and CDCR regulations prohibit conjugal visits for life-term prisoners. Consequently, the Gerbers could not employ the usual method for creating the child they desired.

Undeterred, Gerber sought permission to artificially inseminate his wife. CDCR officials denied his request, citing the facts that (1) impregnating his wife was not medically necessary for Gerber's physical well-being and (2) Gerber had failed to show that denial of the request would violate his constitutional rights.

In a civil suit, however, Gerber alleged that the CDCR regulation violated the due process clause by denying him his constitutional right to procreate. On a defendant's motion, the suit was dismissed in federal district court. Gerber appealed to the U.S. Court of Appeals for the Ninth Circuit where a three-judge panel initially held "that the right to procreate survives incarceration." The panel reversed the district court's dismissal and reinstated Gerber's claim, mandating further review of the case. Upon review, however, the full Ninth Circuit Court of Appeals ruled that prison inmates do not have a constitutional right to fatherhood. The appellate court's majority opinion cited the 1984 U.S. Supreme Court case of *Hudson* v. *Palmer* (mentioned earlier in this chapter), which held that "while persons imprisoned . . . enjoy many protections of the Constitution, it is also clear that imprisonment carries with it the . . . loss of many significant rights."

As we have seen, federal and state inmates can file suits in federal court alleging civil rights violations by corrections officials. In 1988, the U.S. Supreme Court (in *West* v. *Atkins*) decided that private citizens who contracted to do work for prisons could be sued for civil rights violations against inmates. The Court found that such contractors were acting "under color of state law," as required by Section 1983 of the Civil Rights Act of 1871.

As a result of Supreme Court decisions, most prisons now have rules that provide for necessary due process when prisoners appear before disciplinary committees. The makeup of disciplinary committees varies among institutions. The committees may include both inmates and free citizens.

End of the Prisoners' Rights Era

By the late 1980s, the prisoners' rights era was drawing to a close. Following a change in the composition of the Supreme Court, the justices sitting on the Court had become less sympathetic to prisoners' civil rights claims. As discussed earlier, the 1986 case of *Daniels* v. *Williams* helped establish the notion that due process requirements were intended to prevent abuses

frivolous lawsuits

Lawsuits with no foundation in fact. They are generally brought for publicity, political, or other reasons not related to law.

of power by correctional officials, not to protect against mere carelessness. Furthermore, judicial and legislative officials began to realize that inmates frequently abused what had previously been seen as their right of access to the courts. As state costs of defending against **frivolous lawsuits** by inmates began to grow, federal courts began to take a new look at prisoners' rights.

Examples of abuse of the court system by prison inmates abound. One inmate sued the state of Florida because he got only one bread roll with dinner. He sued two more times because he did not get a salad with lunch and because prison-provided TV dinners did not come with drinks. He sued yet again because his cell was not equipped with a television. Another inmate claimed prison officials were denying him freedom of religion. His religion, he said, required him to attend prison chapel services in the nude. Still another inmate, afraid that he could get pregnant through homosexual relations, sued because prison officials would not give him birth control pills.

As early as 1977, the U.S. Supreme Court refused to hear an appeal from Henry William Theriault, founder of the Church of the New Song (or CONS).[19] Theriault, an inmate at the federal penitentiary in Atlanta, had a mail-order divinity degree. Members of CONS celebrated communion every Friday night. They claimed that prison officials must supply them with steak and Harvey's Bristol Cream sherry for the practice. Although "Bishop Theriault" admitted that he had originally created CONS to mock other religions, he claimed that he became a serious believer as the religion developed and acquired more followers. The U.S. Supreme Court dismissed that argument and held that the First Amendment does not protect so-called religions that are obvious shams.

The Cases   One of the important cases setting the stage for a review of prisoners' claimed rights was that of *Turner* v. *Safley,* decided in 1987. In *Turner,* the U.S. Supreme Court established a four-pronged test for determining the reasonableness of prison regulations. In order for a prison regulation to be acceptable, said the Court, there must first be a "valid, rational connection" between the prison regulation and the "legitimate governmental interest" offered to justify it. A second factor relevant in determining the reasonableness of a prison restriction, especially one that limits otherwise established rights, is whether alternative means of exercising that right remain available to prison inmates. If they do, then the restriction is more acceptable. A third consideration is the impact that accommodating an asserted constitutional right would have on officers and other inmates and on the allocation of scarce prison resources. If accommodation makes the job of correctional officers more dangerous or if it is unduly expensive, then it need not be granted. Finally, the fourth prong holds that prisoners have no recourse if there are no readily available alternatives that might permit exercise of claimed rights without compromising penological goals. In other words, if inmates or their attorneys cannot suggest a workable alternative to meet an asserted right, then accommodations need not be made.

In *Wilson* v. *Seiter* (1991), the U.S. Supreme Court sided with prison officials in a way uncharacteristic of the previous two decades. In *Wilson,* the Court found that overcrowding, excessive noise, insufficient locker space, and similar conditions did not violate the Constitution if the intent of prison officials was not malicious. The Court ruled that the actions of officials did not meet the "deliberate indifference" standard defined in *Estelle* v. *Gamble* (1976).

After *Wilson,* inmates won very few new cases. The courts either reversed themselves or tightened the conditions under which inmates could win favorable decisions. Decisions supporting freedom of religion had been among the earliest and most complete victories during the prisoners' rights era. Even in that area, however, things began to change. The courts held that crucifixes and rosaries could legally be denied to inmates because of their possible use as weapons (*Mark* v. *Nix,* 1993, and *Escobar* v. *Landwehr,* 1993). Although some jurisdictions had previously allowed certain Native American religious items within prisons (*Sample* v. *Borg,* 1987), the courts now ruled that prohibiting ceremonial pipes, medicine bags, and eagle claws did *not* violate the First Amendment rights of Native American inmates (*Bettis* v. *Delo,* 1994).

In the 1992 Supreme Court case of *Hudson* v. *McMillan,* the "deliberate indifference" standard was interpreted as requiring both actual knowledge *and* disregard of the risk of harm to inmates or others. This tighter definition allowed federal courts to side more easily with state prison officials in cases in which prisoners claimed there was deliberate indifference. In 1994, in the case of *Farmer* v. *Brennan,* the Supreme Court ruled that even when a prisoner is harmed and even when prison officials knew that the risk of harm existed, officials cannot be held liable if they took appropriate steps to mitigate that risk.

If there was any question that the prisoners' rights era had ended, that question was settled in 1995 by the case of *Sandin* v. *Conner.* In *Sandin,* the Supreme Court rejected the argument that, by disciplining inmates, a state deprived prisoners of their constitutional right not to be deprived of liberty without due process. "The time has come to return to those due process principles that were correctly established and applied in earlier times," said the Court. A year later, the decision in *Lewis* v. *Casey* overturned portions of *Bounds* v. *Smith.* The *Bounds* case had been instrumental in establishing law libraries in prisons. The Court in *Lewis* held, however, that "*Bounds* does not guarantee inmates the wherewithal to file any and every type of legal claim but requires only that they be provided with the tools to attack their sentences."

In *Edwards* v. *Balisok* (1997), the Supreme Court made it even harder to successfully challenge prison disciplinary convictions. The Court held that prisoners cannot sue for monetary damages under Section 1983 of the U.S. Code for loss of good-time credits until they are able to sue successfully in state court to have their disciplinary conviction set aside.

In 2003, in the case of *Overton* v. *Bazzetta,* the Court upheld visitation regulations established by the Michigan Department of Corrections that denied most visits to prisoners who had committed two substance abuse violations while incarcerated. In its ruling, the Court said that "the regulations bear a rational relation to legitimate penological interests [sufficient] to sustain them." Wording taken directly from the Court's opinion is shown in Exhibit 11–4. It provides a summary of the factors used by the courts to decide whether prison regulations meet constitutional requirements.

In a somewhat different kind of case, the U.S. Supreme Court found that federal correctional officers are "law enforcement officers" within the meaning of federal law—and that they are therefore immune from claims alleging injury or loss of property "caused by negligence or a wrongful act or omission" when acting within their scope of employment. The case, *Ali* v. *Federal Bureau of Prisons,*[20] involved a federal prisoner who claimed that some of his personal belongings had disappeared when he was transferred between prisons.

EXHIBIT 11–4 *Overton v. Bazzetta (2003)*

Responding to concerns about prison security problems caused by the increasing number of visitors to Michigan's prisons and about substance abuse among inmates, the Michigan Department of Corrections (MDOC) promulgated new regulations limiting prison visitation. . . .

The fact that the regulations bear a rational relation to legitimate penological interests suffices to sustain them regardless of whether respondents have a constitutional right of association that has survived incarceration. This Court accords substantial deference to the professional judgment of prison administrators, who bear a significant responsibility for defining a corrections system's legitimate goals and determining the most appropriate means to accomplish them. The regulations satisfy each of four factors used to decide whether a prison regulation affecting a constitutional right that survives incarceration withstands constitutional challenge.

First, the regulations bear a rational relationship to a legitimate penological interest. The restrictions on children's visitation are related to MDOC's valid interests in maintaining internal security and protecting child visitors from exposure to sexual or other misconduct or from accidental injury. They promote internal security, perhaps the most legitimate penological goal, by reducing the total number of visitors and by limiting disruption caused by children. It is also reasonable to ensure that the visiting child is accompanied and supervised by adults charged with protecting the child's best interests. Prohibiting visitation by former inmates bears a self-evident connection to the State's interest in maintaining prison security and preventing future crime. Restricting visitation for inmates with two substance-abuse violations serves the legitimate goal of deterring drug and alcohol use within prison.

Second, respondents have alternative means of exercising their asserted right of association with those prohibited from visiting. They can send messages through those who are permitted to visit, and can communicate by letter and telephone. Visitation alternatives need not be ideal; they need only be available.

Third, accommodating the associational right would have a considerable impact on guards, other inmates, the allocation of prison resources, and the safety of visitors by causing a significant reallocation of the prison system's financial resources and by impairing corrections officers ability to protect all those inside a prison's walls.

Finally, [complainants] have suggested no alternatives that fully accommodate the asserted right while not imposing more than a [minimum] cost to the valid penological goals.

Source: *Overton* v. *Bazzetta,* 539 U.S. 126 (2003), Syllabus.

Finally, in two cases from 2012, the Supreme Court sided with correctional officials in limiting the rights of inmates. In the first case, *Howes* v. *Fields* (2012), the Court found that inmates who face questioning by law enforcement officers while they are incarcerated need not be advised of their *Miranda* rights prior to the start of interrogation. In the second case, *Florence* v. *Burlington County* (2012), the Court ruled that officials had the power to strip-search persons who had been arrested prior to admission to a jail or other detention facility even if the offense for which they were arrested was a minor one. In that case, Justice Kennedy, writing for the majority, noted that "maintaining safety and order at detention centers requires the expertise of correctional officials, who must have substantial discretion to devise reasonable solutions to problems." He went on to write that "the term 'jail' is used here in a broad sense to include prisons and other detention facilities."

The Legal Mechanisms Changes in state and federal statutes have also slowed the pace of prisoners' rights cases. In 1980, Congress modified the Civil Rights of Institutionalized Persons Act.[21] It now requires a state inmate to exhaust all state remedies before filing a petition for a writ of *habeas corpus* in federal court. In effect, a state prisoner must give the state an opportunity to correct alleged violations of its prisoners' federal rights (*Duncan* v. *Henry*, 1995). Inmates in federal prisons may still file *habeas corpus* petitions directly in federal court. In their petitions, federal inmates are now required to show (1) that they were deprived of some right to which they were entitled despite the confinement and (2) that the deprivation of this right made the imprisonment more burdensome.

The Prison Litigation Reform Act of 1995[22] (PLRA) was another legislative response to the ballooning number of civil rights lawsuits filed by prisoners. It restricts the filing of lawsuits in federal courts by:

1. requiring state prisoners to exhaust all local administrative remedies prior to filing suit in federal court;
2. requiring inmates to pay federal filing fees unless they can claim pauper status;[23]
3. limiting awards of attorneys' fees in successful lawsuits;
4. requiring judges to screen all inmate lawsuits and immediately dismiss those they find frivolous;
5. revoking good-time credit toward early release if inmates file malicious lawsuits;
6. barring prisoners from suing the federal government for mental or emotional injury unless there is an accompanying physical injury;
7. allowing court orders to go no further than necessary to correct the particular inmate's civil rights problem;
8. requiring some court orders to be renewed every two years or be lifted; and
9. ensuring that no single judge can order the release of federal inmates for overcrowding.

In May 2001, the U.S. Supreme Court further restricted inmate options under the PLRA. The ruling mandates that inmates must complete prison administrative processes that could provide some relief before suing over prison conditions even if that relief would *not include a monetary payment* (*Booth* v. *Churner*, 2001).

A 2005 study of the PLRA's effectiveness conducted by the National Council for State Courts (NCSC), found that the PLRA "achieved its intended effects" and significantly lowered the number of frivolous filings by inmates in federal courts.[24]

FEMALE INMATES AND THE COURTS

CO11-6

The prisoners' rights movement has been largely a male phenomenon. While male inmates were petitioning the courts for expansion of their rights, female inmates frequently had to resort to the courts simply to gain rights that male inmates already had.

The Cases

One early state case, *Barefield* v. *Leach* (1974), demonstrated that the opportunities and programs for female inmates were clearly inferior to those for male inmates. In that case, a court in New Mexico spelled out one standard for equal treatment of male and female inmates. The court

Many claims of female inmates have focused on the failure of correctional institutions to provide them with educational opportunities and medical care comparable to those provided male inmates. The equal-protection clause of which amendment guarantees female inmates conditions of confinement comparable to those of male inmates?

said that the equal-protection clause of the Constitution requires equal treatment of male and female inmates but not identical treatment. *Barefield,* however, was a state case—not binding on other states or the federal government.

In 1977, in *State, ex rel. Olson* v. *Maxwell,* the Supreme Court of North Dakota ruled that a lack of funds was not an acceptable justification for unequal treatment of male and female prisoners. Although this decision also came in a state court case, it would later be cited as a legal authority in a similar federal court case.

In *Glover* v. *Johnson* (1979), a U.S. district court case, a group of female prisoners in the Michigan system filed a class action lawsuit claiming that they were denied access to the courts and constitutional rights to equal protection. The prisoners demanded educational and vocational opportunities comparable to those for male inmates. At trial, a prison teacher testified that, although men were allowed to take shop courses, women were taught remedial courses at a junior high school level because the attitude of those in charge was "Keep it simple, these are only women." The court found that "the educational opportunities available to women prisoners in Michigan were substantially inferior to those available to male prisoners." Consequently, the court ordered a plan to provide higher education and vocational training for female prisoners in the Michigan prison system. *Glover* was a turning point in equal treatment for imprisoned women. Since 1979, female inmates have continued to win the majority of cases seeking equal treatment and the elimination of gender bias.

In the 1980 case of *Cooper* v. *Morin,* the U.S. Supreme Court accepted neither inconvenience nor cost as an excuse for treating female jail inmates differently from male inmates. Female inmates at a county jail in New York had alleged that inadequate medical attention in jail violated their civil rights. Later that same year, a federal district court rejected Virginia's claims that services for female prison inmates could not be provided at the same level as those for male inmates because of cost-effectiveness issues (*Bukhari* v. *Hutto,* 1980). Virginia authorities said that the much smaller number of women in prison raised the cost of providing each woman with services. The appellate court ordered the state of Virginia to provide equitable services for inmates, regardless of gender.

An action challenging the denial of equal protection and the conditions of confinement in the Kentucky Correctional Institution for Women was the basis of *Canterino* v. *Wilson,* decided in U.S. district court in 1982. The district court held that the "levels system" used to allocate privileges to female prisoners, a system not applied to male prisoners, violated both the equal-protection rights and the due process rights of female inmates. The court also held that female inmates in Kentucky's prisons must have the same opportunities as men for vocational education, training, recreation, and outdoor activity.

In 1982, in *McMurray* v. *Phelps,* a district court in Louisiana ordered an end to the unequal treatment of female inmates in that state's jails. (Recall that the federal courts have supervisory jurisdiction over state courts.) The next year, the Seventh Circuit Court of Appeals found that strip searches of female misdemeanor offenders awaiting bond in a Chicago lockup were unreasonable under the Fourth Amendment (*Mary Beth G.* v. *City of Chicago,* 1983). In addition, the court found that a policy of subjecting female arrestees to strip searches while subjecting similarly situated males only to hand searches violated the equal-protection clause of the Constitution.

In 1994, in a class action suit by female inmates, a federal district court held the District of Columbia Department of Corrections liable under the Eighth Amendment for inadequate gynecological examinations and testing, inadequate testing for sexually transmitted diseases, inadequate health education, inadequate prenatal care, and an inadequate overall prenatal protocol (*Women Prisoners of the District of Columbia Department of Corrections* v. *District of Columbia,* 1994).

Court oversight of OB-GYN services at the District of Columbia Department of Corrections ended in 2004, following an agreement in which the department promised to continue to provide adequate services for women inmates. The agreement ended 33 years of court oversight of the DC department—involving a total of 15 class action lawsuits filed by inmate groups or their representatives during that time.[25]

Also in 2004, U.S. district judge Myron Thompson approved a settlement in a class action lawsuit centered on concerns about medical care and general conditions at three Alabama women's prisons. Thompson said that the settlement, which required lowering the number of prisoners held at three locations, would not make the facilities "comfortable or pleasant" but would "afford class members the basic necessities mandated by the United States Constitution."[26] Affected were the Julia Tutwiler Prison for Women, the Tutwiler Annex, and the Birmingham Work Release Facility—all operated by the Alabama Department of Corrections. The lawsuit, filed by the Southern Center for Human Rights, had complained of "intensely overcrowded" and "unbearably hot and poorly ventilated dormitories." Tutwiler Prison had been built in the 1940s to hold no more than 364 inmates but was filled with more than 1,000 inmates at the time of the lawsuit. Under the agreement, the population was lowered to 700 by sending some inmates to prisons in Louisiana and by releasing others under community supervision.

CO11-7 CORRECTIONAL OFFICER CIVIL LIABILITY AND INMATE LAWSUITS

doctrine of sovereign immunity

A historical legal doctrine that held that a governing body or its representatives could not be sued because it made the law and therefore could not be bound by it.

Until recently, the **doctrine of sovereign immunity** barred legal actions against state and local governments. The doctrine of sovereign immunity held that a governing body or its representatives could not be sued because it made the law and therefore could not be bound by it. Consequently, federal and state correctional facilities and their officers, acting in their official capacity, were generally held to be immune from lawsuits.

Today, however, immunity is a much more complex issue. Some states have officially abandoned any claims of immunity through legislative action. New York State, for example, has declared that public agencies are equally as liable as private agencies for violations of constitutional rights. Other states, such as California, have enacted statutory provisions that define and limit governmental liability.[27] A number of state immunity statutes have been struck down by court decision. In general, states are moving in the direction of setting dollar limits on liability and adopting federal immunity principles, including "good faith" and "reasonable belief" rules, to protect individual officers.

At the federal level, the concept of sovereign immunity is embodied in the Federal Tort Claims Act (FTCA),[28] which grants broad immunity to certain federal government agencies—especially law enforcement agencies—when their employees act negligently within the scope of their employment. In the 2008 U.S. Supreme Court case of *Ali* v. *Federal Bureau of Prisons*, the Court held that federal correctional officers are law enforcement officers for purposes of civil litigation and found that the BOP was immune to the type of suit that had been brought against it. In *Ali,* a federal prison inmate filed suit against the BOP under the Federal Tort Claims Act (FTCA),[29] which authorizes "claims against the United States for money damages . . . for injury or loss of property . . . caused by the negligent or wrongful act or omission of any employee in the government while acting within the scope of his office or employment." In denying Ali's claim, the Court found that the law specifically provides immunity for federal law enforcement officers and determined that federal corrections personnel are "law enforcement officers" within the meaning of the law. In the 2013 case of *Millbrook* v. *U.S.,*[30] the Court reaffirmed its earlier finding that federal correctional officers are law enforcement officers whose agencies are protected against suits under the FTCA for acts or omissions that arise within the scope of their employment.

Individual officers (as opposed to the agencies for which they work), however, are not necessarily protected under federal or state law. Nonetheless, federal courts have generally shielded correctional officers from "constitutional lawsuits if reasonable officers believe their actions to be lawful in light of clearly established law and the information the officers possess." In doing so, the Court has recognized a form of qualified immunity as a defense "which shields public officials from actions for damages unless their conduct was unreasonable in light of clearly established law."[31] According to the Court, "[T]he qualified immunity doctrine's central objective is to protect public officials from undue interference with their duties and from potentially disabling threats of liability."[32]

REVIEW AND APPLICATIONS

SUMMARY

1 The hands-off doctrine was a working philosophy of the courts in this country until 1970. It allowed corrections officials to run prisons without court intervention. The hands-off doctrine existed because courts were reluctant to interfere with activities of the executive branch and because judges realized that they were not experts in corrections.

2 The key legal sources of prisoners' rights are the U.S. Constitution, federal statutes, state constitutions, and state statutes.

3 Inmates can challenge the legality of their confinement, associated prison conditions, and the practices of correctional officials through (1) a state *habeas corpus* action, (2) a federal *habeas corpus* action, (3) a state tort lawsuit, (4) a federal civil rights lawsuit, and (5) an injunction to obtain relief.

4 During the prisoners' rights era (1970–1991), inmates won many court cases based on claims that conditions of their confinement violated their constitutional rights. Court decisions affected inmate rights to freedom of expression, including free speech; personal communications; access to the courts and legal services; religion; assembly and association; the voicing of grievances about disciplinary procedures; protection from personal and cell searches; health care, including diet and exercise; protection from violence; adequate physical conditions of confinement; and rehabilitation.

5 Most prisoners' claims focus on denial of constitutional rights guaranteed by the First (freedom of expression and religion), Fourth (freedom from unlawful search and seizure), Eighth (freedom from cruel and unusual punishment), and Fourteenth (due process and equal protection of the law) Amendments.

6 The prisoners' rights movement has been largely a male phenomenon. More recently, female inmates have had to petition the courts to gain rights that male inmates already had.

7 In times past, the doctrine of sovereign immunity shielded federal, state, and local governments from lawsuits. More recently, however, correctional agencies—at least on the federal level—have been protected by federal law from certain civil suits stemming from the negligent actions of their employees. Individual officers are also shielded by court precedent to the extent that their actions are reasonable in light of clearly established law.

KEY TERMS

hands-off doctrine, p. 354
prisoners' rights, p. 356
constitutional rights, p. 356
institutional needs, p. 356
civil liability, p. 357
writ of *habeas corpus,* p. 357
tort, p. 358
nominal damages, p. 358

compensatory damages, p. 358
punitive damages, p. 358
injunction, p. 358
jurisdiction, p. 359
precedent, p. 361
legitimate penological objectives,
p. 364
balancing test, p. 364

cruel and unusual punishment,
p. 369
deliberate indifference, p. 369
totality of conditions, p. 369
due process, p. 371
frivolous lawsuits, p. 374
doctrine of sovereign immunity,
p. 380

QUESTIONS FOR REVIEW

1 Why was the hands-off doctrine so named? What was the basis for the doctrine?

2 What are the key legal sources of prisoners' rights?

3 What are the legal mechanisms through which inmates can challenge the legality of their confinement and associated prison conditions?

4 What rights were won by inmates during what the book calls the *prisoners' rights era?*

5 What constitutional amendments are most often cited by prisoners claiming rights? What claimed rights are associated with each of these amendments?

6 Do the rights accorded male inmates correspond to the rights of female inmates? Why or why not?

7. What is the doctrine of sovereign immunity? To what extent are today's correctional officers shielded from civil lawsuits brought by inmates?

THINKING CRITICALLY ABOUT CORRECTIONS

Freedom of Nonverbal Expression

The right to freedom of nonverbal expression is said to be implied in the First Amendment. Hence, how people wear their hair and how they dress are expressions that some believe are protected by the First Amendment.

1. Might there be modes of dress that interfere with a correctional institution's legitimate goals?

2. If so, what might they be?

Checks and Balance

On January 11, 2003, in a dramatic legal move shortly before leaving office, former Illinois governor George Ryan commuted the sentences of every one of the state's 167 death row inmates. Four of the sentences were reduced to 40-year terms; the remaining 163 sentences were commuted to life in prison. Governor Ryan based his action on his determination of inherent arbitrariness and unfairness in the application of capital punishment and on the high risk of executing an innocent person.

Although the scope of his action is unusual, the commutations typify the power placed in the hands of each state's chief executive. Essentially, this means that, within the respective states and based solely on personal opinion, a single individual is empowered to overturn sentencing decisions and attendant legal rulings on those decisions made at any level up to and including the nation's most powerful court, the U.S. Supreme Court.

1. Should this be the case?

2. Does the lack of a legal mechanism to counter a governor's decision regarding a pardon or a commutation violate the principle of checks and balances so intricately woven into America's state and federal governmental structures?

ON-THE-JOB DECISION MAKING

Inmate Communications

You are a prison administrator. The prison where you work has a rule that inmates may write letters in English only. This rule seems sensible. After all, if inmates could write in languages not understood by correctional officers, they could discuss plans to escape, riot, or smuggle drugs or weapons into the prison. The courts allow the censoring of outgoing inmate mail; what good is that power if corrections personnel cannot read the mail?

You realize, however, that inmates who cannot write in English will have difficulty communicating with the outside world and with their families. Inmates unable to write in English will not even be able to write to their attorneys. You also wonder what might happen if an inmate can write in English but his parents can read only a foreign language. If the inmate and his parents cannot afford long-distance phone calls, they will not be able to communicate with each other at all. You begin to consider how the English-only rule might be changed to facilitate wholesome communications while still preventing communications that might endanger the safety of the institution and the inmate population.

1. Can the English-only rule be amended to meet the inmate needs discussed here while still being consistent with legitimate institutional concerns? If so, how?

2. Does an inmate have a constitutionally protected right to communicate with his or her parents?

3. What if that right conflicts with prison policy?

Law Libraries

The Supreme Court's ruling in *Bounds* v. *Smith* (1977) led to the establishment of law libraries for prisoner use in correctional facilities throughout the nation. Numerous subsequent prisoner civil suits resulted in follow-on rulings mandating the need to maintain these libraries with up-to-date reference materials in serviceable condition.

You are an advisor on correctional issues on the staff of your state's attorney general. In the past few weeks, she has repeatedly complained that these rulings impose excessive financial demands on the state's already nearly impoverished correctional system. In particular, she says, routine vandalism by inmates who tear pages from law books and take the pages back to their cells—or simply discard them—is especially costly. It also creates a circumstance in which another inmate could threaten another civil suit upon finding a book to be "unserviceable" when attempting to use it, a threat to which the system can respond only by immediately purchasing a replacement book.

This, the attorney general says, typifies a cycle that causes an extraordinary drain on limited financial resources. She rants about the "ludicrous" fact that the reference material in her own office is so out of date as to be virtually unusable, but she cannot fix the problem because she spends that portion of her budget on repeatedly restoring the prisoners' law libraries in the various institutions throughout the state.

The attorney general has tasked you to resolve this issue.

1. What will you do?
2. Might advances in information technology be the key to a solution?

**For additional information, please see: www.mhhe.com/schmalleger7e
Follow the author's tweets about the latest crime and justice news @schmalleger**

SPECIAL PRISON POPULATIONS

Prisoners Who Are Substance Abusers, Who Have HIV/AIDS, Who Are Mentally Challenged, and Who Are Elderly

CHAPTER OBJECTIVES

After completing this chapter you should be able to do the following:

1 Define the term *inmate with special needs.*

2 Report on the management needs of special population inmates.

3 Report on the impact of substance abusers on the corrections system.

4 Discuss why treating HIV in prison is difficult.

5 Discuss the five essential elements of cost-effective management of HIV/AIDS inmates.

6 Explain why so many inmates have mental illnesses.

7 Describe ways to divert persons with mental illness from the criminal justice system.

8 List the cost and health issues associated with older inmates.

9 Review the legal issues surrounding special population inmates.

I cannot think of a more challenging or needful segment of our work than our involvement with special populations.

—Thomas E. Patterson, Executive Director, Utah Department of Corrections

Tuberculosis, a contagious and potentially fatal disease, is a major health problem in prisons and jails. March 24 of every year is World Tuberculosis Day when the International Committee of the Red Cross (ICRC) calls on prison and jail managers, public health authorities, and the international community at large to pay increased attention to the dangers posed by the ongoing development of multidrug-resistant TB (MDR-TB) in prisons and jails and its spread outside detention walls.

Russian prisoners suffering from tuberculosis and the more fatal resistant TB strain known as "multi-drug-resistant tuberculosis (MDR-TB)" take their medicine at a prison camp outside the Siberian city of Kemerovo. The International Committee of the Red Cross works with prison health authorities and non-governmental agencies around the world to treat prisoners suffering from TB and MDR TB. What are the implications for housing prisoners with special needs?

TB can be more than 100 times more prevalent inside than outside prisons and jails. This is often due to overcrowding, insufficient ventilation, ignorance of preventive measures, and failure to supervise treatment and ensure adherence to proper medical programs. Inadequate medical care not only fails to cure TB patients but also contributes to the emergence of resistant strains that infect patients, other prisoners, and the community at large.

"More and more patients are developing highly resistant strains of TB in prisons and jails. When this happens, TB, a previously curable disease, can become extremely difficult to treat; some patients cannot be cured with existing drug regimens. The association of MDR-TB with HIV/AIDS or hepatitis C further complicates the problem,"[1] explained Abu Rabi, ICRC medical doctor.

The ICRC has been fighting TB in prisons in Eastern Europe, Southwest and Central Asia, and Uganda for many years. It is also currently cooperating with the authorities in Kyrgyzstan and the Philippines in an effort to combat the disease.

The terms "multiresistant" or "MDR TB" are used when the disease no longer responds to the combination of two or more of the drugs commonly used to treat TB. MDR TB is spreading at an alarming pace in prisons and jails. The ICRC completed a multiyear program in Azerbaijan, Georgia, and Armenia in cooperation with prison health authorities for treating prisoners suffering from the MDR TB form of tuberculosis.

The ICRC closely monitors individual prisoners suffering from MDR TB individually—from diagnosis to cure. The process can take up to two years. The key to the program's success lies in the ICRC's collaboration with nongovernmental organizations (NGOs) that provide appropriate medical supervision for prisoners who are released before the end of their treatment.

CO12-1

INMATES WITH SPECIAL NEEDS

inmates with special needs

Those prisoners who exhibit unique physical, mental, social, and programmatic needs that distinguish them from other prisoners and to whom jail and prison management and staff have to respond in nontraditional and innovative ways.

Increasingly, prisons and jails are dealing with a growing population of inmates with special needs. **Inmates with special needs** are "those prisoners who exhibit unique physical, mental, social, and programmatic needs that distinguish them from other prisoners and for whom jail and prison management and staff have to respond to in nontraditional and innovative ways."[2] These special populations suffer from mental illness; chemical dependency (drug or alcohol); communicable diseases (especially HIV/AIDS and tuberculosis); chronic diseases (e.g., diabetes, heart disease, seizures, and detoxification); the general problems of people who are elderly; the special concern of managing young female offenders in correctional settings; the problems that arise when youthful offenders are housed in adult institutions; and the issues arising from sexual identity, prisoner victimization, transgender prisoners, and the management of sex offenders within correctional settings.

Such inmates present operational and administrative problems for correctional staff—it is often difficult for the staff to know what they are observing or, once they recognize an inmate's special needs, how to address the situation. Thomas Patterson, executive director of the Utah Department of Corrections, recently said that more and more special populations are the norm rather than the exception.[3] He went on to say that if we add sex offenders and substance abusers to the mix of special populations, upward of 80 percent of offenders would require attention to the challenges they present inside prisons and jails.[4] "To turn a blind eye on special populations is to neglect ethical and humane obligations and more rapidly spin the turnstile of recidivism."[5]

CO12-2

A statewide research study on jail management in New Mexico found that inmates with special needs require extra attention from jail staff.[6] For example, they must be watched closely for possible suicide. Almost 9 of 10 such inmates disrupt normal jail activities; 7 of 10 require an excess of scarce medical resources; 4 of 10 engage in acts of violence; and almost 3 of 10 are abused by other inmates. The characteristics of inmates with special needs, the treatment programs offered, and the policies for dealing with those inmates depend on the type of special need.

The American Correctional Association urges correctional agencies to develop and adopt procedures for the early identification of inmates with special needs, to provide the services that respond to those needs, and to monitor and evaluate the delivery of services in both community and institutional settings (see Exhibit 12–1). This chapter reviews the management and treatment of the five largest groups of inmates with special needs: substance-abusing inmates, HIV-positive and AIDS inmates, inmates with mental illness, inmates with tuberculosis, and older inmates.

Substance-Abusing Inmates

substance-abusing inmate

An incarcerated individual suffering from dependency on one or more substances including alcohol and a wide range of drugs.

Alcohol and other drug problems are the common denominator for most offenders in the criminal justice system, and untreated substance-abusing offenders are more likely to relapse to drug abuse and return to criminal behavior. A **substance-abusing inmate** is an incarcerated person suffering from dependency on one or more substances including alcohol and a wide range of drugs.

Substance abuse takes a toll on users, the community, and the criminal justice system. Today, between 60 and 80 percent of individuals under supervision of the criminal justice system have a substance use-related issue. This includes individuals who committed a crime to support a substance

EXHIBIT 12–1 **American Correctional Association**

Public Correctional Policy on Offenders with Special Needs

Introduction:

The provision of humane and gender-responsive programs and services for the accused and adjudicated requires addressing the special needs of juvenile, youthful and adult offenders. To meet this goal, correctional agencies should develop and adopt procedures for the early identification of offenders with special needs. Agencies should provide the services that respond to these needs and monitor and evaluate the delivery of services in both confined and community settings.

Policy Statement:

Correctional systems must assure provision of specialized services, programs and conditions of confinement to meet the special needs of offenders. To achieve this, correctional systems should:

A. Identify the juvenile, youthful and adult offenders who require special care or programs including:

- Offenders with psychological needs, developmental disabilities, psychiatric disorders, behavioral disorders, disabling conditions, neurological impairments, and substance abuse disorders;
- Offenders who have acute or chronic medical conditions, are physically disabled or terminally ill;
- Older offenders;
- Offenders with social and/or educational deficiencies, learning disabilities, or language barriers;
- Offenders with special security or supervision needs;
- Sex offenders; and
- Female offenders.

B. Provide services and programs in a manner consistent with professional standards and nationally-accepted exemplary practices. Such services and programs may be provided within the correctional agency itself, by referral to another agency that has the necessary specialized resources, or by contracting with private or volunteer agencies or individuals that meet professional standards;

C. Provide appropriately trained, licensed and/or certified, staff, contractors and volunteers for the delivery of, care, programs, and services and provide incentives to attend the continuing education and training necessary to maintain credentials and state-of-the-art, knowledge and mastery-level skills;

D. Maintain professionally appropriate records of all delivered services and programs;

E. Conduct evaluations of service delivery adherence to program standards, while also evaluating the effectiveness of the services, with regular feedback to administrators and service providers for continuous quality improvement; and

F. Provide leadership and advocacy for legislative and public support to obtain the resources needed to meet these special needs.

Source: Copyright © American Correctional Association. Reprinted with permission.

use disorder, those charged with a drug-related crime, and others who simply use drugs illegally or abuse alcohol regularly. However, only 11 percent receives any treatment while incarcerated.[7] Another 458,000, although not meeting the strict medical criteria for alcohol and drug abuse and addiction nevertheless were either under the influence of alcohol or other drugs at the time of their offense, stole money to buy drugs, are substance abusers, violated the alcohol or drug laws, or share some combination of these characteristics. Consider these startling statistics reported by the national Center on Addiction and Substance Abuse (CASA) at Columbia University. Alcohol and drugs are involved in

- 78 percent of violent crimes;
- 83 percent of property crimes; and
- 77 percent of public order, immigration or weapons offenses, and probation/parole violations.

As this chapter points out, we know how to reduce the costs of incarceration and the crimes committed by substance-involved offenders.

CO12-3

However, the barriers to action include the setting of mandatory sentences that eliminate the possibilities of alternative sentencing such as drug courts or parole, the lack of a clear mandate to provide treatment, the economic interests in prison expansion, politicians who are more concerned with being reelected and fear being labeled "soft on crime" by opponents, and the failure of public policy to reflect the science of addiction and changing public attitudes about addiction and justice. But there is some good news. A number of states (and the federal government) have either reversed mandatory sentencing or are considering doing so. There are more examples of evidence-based practices informing correctional policy today as evidenced across these chapters. And the public doesn't think treatment is bad. An ABC news poll found that two-thirds of Americans support state laws requiring treatment—not jail time for first- and second-time drug offenders.[8]

Drug Use and Dependence If inmates are any indication, the war on drugs is not affecting persons who commit prison-bound offenses. The U.S. Department of Justice reported its findings on drug use and dependence among state and federal prisoners in 1997 and 2004.[9] That survey found that nearly one-third of state inmates and one-fourth of federal inmates committed their offenses under the influence of drugs. Drug use in the month before the offense by state prisoners remained unchanged from 1997 (stable at 56–57 percent), but drug use in the month before the offense by federal prisoners rose from 45 to 50 percent. Today 17 percent of state prisoners are incarcerated for drug offenses, down from 21 percent a decade ago. At the federal level, it's 48 percent, down from 56 percent a decade ago. Clearly, the number of state and federal inmates in prison for drug offenses is cause to rethink our policies and ask whether what we as a country are doing is smart on our budget. If we are releasing inmates with as little as $50, no treatment (as documented by CASA), a bus ticket, and a "good luck" wish, why is it difficult to understand why they are committing new crimes and reentering the system?

Almost two-thirds of all U.S. jail and prison inmates (some 1.5 million) meet the medical criteria for substance abuse addiction but only 11 percent receive any treatment while incarcerated. What should jails and prisons do to control the revolving door of drug and alcohol abusers and addicts in and out of prison?

Drug Treatment Programs Why should prisoners receive drug treatment? According to Jeremy Travis, president of John Jay College of Criminal Justice and former director of the National Institute of Justice, there are two powerful reasons.[10]

First, drug offenders consume a staggering volume of illegal drugs, and any reduction in their drug use represents a significant reduction in the nation's demand for illegal drugs. About 60 percent of the cocaine and heroin consumed by the entire nation in a year is consumed by individuals arrested in that year. Drug treatment has the potential for significantly reducing the nation's demand for illegal drugs.

Second, we now know from the evidence-based literature that we can reduce drug use in the offender population. Drug abuse treatment improves outcomes for drug-abusing offenders and has beneficial effects for public health and safety. There is ample, consistent, and cumulative evidence that cognitive behavioral treatment for incarcerated populations is an effective intervention for drug abusers even if the motivation for entering treatment is coerced.[11] The National Treatment Improvement Evaluation Study found that cognitive-based treatment programs in prison produced reductions in criminal behavior and in arrests.[12] Participation in correctional substance abuse treatment is also associated with enhanced mental health and physical health. Ideally, treatment programs should begin the moment a person enters prison. Research shows that treatment programs that start nine months to a year before prison release, provide community-based aftercare services (housing, education, employment, and health care), attract and retain staff who demonstrate concern for the offender's welfare, and give offenders a clear understanding of the program's rules and the penalties for breaking them provide the greatest chances for success.[13] Community aftercare services are particularly important for substance abusers because they tend to have medical problems such as cirrhosis of the liver, diabetes, and HIV/AIDS.

The criminal justice system has become the largest source of mandated, or coerced, drug treatment in the United States.[14] Contrary to what some believe, research consistently indicates that offenders' motivations for entering drug treatment (voluntary or coerced) are not as important in

Many inmates enter prison addicted to illegal drugs. Although there's evidence that cognitive-based drug and alcohol treatment in prison reduces recidivism, only 11 percent of inmates who need substance abuse treatment actually receive it. Should correctional facilities be required to provide cognitive-based substance abuse treatment? What are the benefits of cognitive-based substance abuse treatment?

treatment outcome as their ultimate length of stay in treatment. The longer inmates participate in treatment, the more likely they are to adopt prosocial attitudes and overcome their initial resistance. (Generally, better outcomes are associated with treatment that lasts longer than 90 days with the greatest reductions in drug abuse and criminal behavior occurring to those who complete treatment.) This point is important because treatment in a prison always involves an element of coercion.

With 2,000 inmates returning to the general population every day, correctional health and public health are becoming increasingly intertwined. Health care and disease prevention in correctional facilities must become a top priority for correctional managers and all correctional personnel.

Drug treatment programs provide evidence that rehabilitation is more likely to succeed for those offenders who complete drug treatment programs, and reducing drug-seeking behavior aids in management of jail facilities. A NIJ-sponsored research study found that the greatest benefit of drug treatment programs in jails was that they provided a "behavioral management tool" that controlled inmates' behavior and helped lower the incidence of inmate violence.[15]

The study evaluated five drug treatment programs in California and New York. At all five sites, substance abuse inmates in drug treatment programs had lower rates of serious physical violence and other behavioral problems (e.g., insubordination and possession of nondrug contraband) than those not in the programs. During a one-year follow-up, 83 percent of the inmates in drug treatment and 77 percent of the control group were not convicted of another offense.

Therapeutic Community One successful prison-based substance treatment program is the therapeutic community. A **therapeutic community (TC)** is a residential treatment program in which inmates are housed in a separate unit within a prison or jail facility and is characterized by highly structured treatment involving resocialization, intensive counseling, and an increasing level of responsibility as the inmate progresses through the program. TC relies on interactions within the peer group to help members confront their addictions and to commit to lifestyle changes that will enable them to remain drug free and crime free.[16]

Postrelease Outcomes Evaluations of prison-based TC programs conducted in several states and the federal prison system have provided empirical support for the effectiveness of these programs in reducing recidivism and relapse to drug use, especially when combined with continuity of care in the community following release from prison to parole.

The federal BOP published the results of a three-year evaluation of its residential drug abuse treatment programs that are designed for inmates with moderate to severe substance abuse problems.[17] The study assessed the postrelease outcomes of 1,842 men and 473 women released from 20 different federal prisons with residential drug treatment programs. The evaluation revealed that male inmates who completed residential drug abuse treatment were 16 percent less likely to be rearrested or have their supervision revoked than were inmates who did not receive such treatment; the comparable figure for female inmates was 18 percent. This reduction in recidivism was coupled with a 15 percent reduction in drug use by male participants and an 18 percent reduction in drug use by female participants. The study also found improved employment for women after release. The research strongly suggests that residential drug abuse treatment can make a significant difference in the lives of inmates following

therapeutic community (TC)

A residential treatment program in which substance abuse inmates are housed in a separate unit within a prison or jail facility.

their release from prison and return to the community. Similar results have been reported in Delaware where researchers conducted a longitudinal study of inmates who completed in-prison and work-release TC treatment.[18] They were more drug free and arrest free than their control groups at 18-month and three- and five-year follow-up periods. The Delaware research demonstrates the importance of treatment continuing during the transition stage to work and the free community.

Drug abuse treatment is cost-effective in reducing drug abuse and bringing about associated health care, crime, and incarceration cost savings. Positive net economic benefits are consistently found for drug abuse treatment across various settings and populations. Arizona led the way in drug reform by passing the Drug Medicalization, Prevention and Control Act in 1996. The act requires drug users to be placed on probation and to participate in appropriate drug treatment. Based on prison costs of almost $53 per day, Arizona saved an estimated $6.7 million in incarceration costs.[19] In 2000, 61 percent of California voters passed Proposition 36—the Substance Abuse and Crime Prevention Act. It requires that first- and second-time nonviolent drug offenders convicted of drug possession, use, or transportation be offered substance abuse treatment instead of incarceration. However, the legislation authorized $120 million per year for only five years, and as the state's budget crisis worsened, the legislature declined to fund Prop 36 past 2011. Many have questioned why the law guaranteed only five years of funding for a mandate that would continue indefinitely. At its peak, Prop 36 was helping 36,000 people a year, and a UCLA study said that every $1 invested in Prop 36 treatment saved the state between $2.50 and $4 in incarceration costs—some $2 billion in savings—enough some say that should have won more budget support.[20]

California Proposition 36 requires that first- and second-time nonviolent simple drug possession offenders be placed on probation instead of being sentenced to time behind bars. On Wednesday, June 27, 2001, California state senate president pro tem John Burton held a news conference on the Lindesmith Center Drug Policy Foundation's grading of how 11 counties plan to implement Proposition 36. How do such new laws save taxpayers' money and rehabilitate drug offenders?

What Works? Principles of Drug Abuse Treatment for Criminal Justice Populations

Controlling the revolving door of drug and alcohol abusers and addicts in the criminal justice population is an important aspect of management for corrections officials. The National Institute on Drug Abuse (NIDA) looked at all the research that had been published on drug abuse treatment for the last 40 years and discovered 13 principles that constitute effective drug treatment.[21] They are:

1. Drug addiction is a brain disease that affects behavior and the brain's anatomy and chemistry, and these changes can last for months or years after the individual has stopped using drugs.

2. Effective drug abuse treatment engages participants in a therapeutic process, retains them in treatment for an appropriate length of time, and helps them learn to maintain abstinence over time.

3. Effective drug abuse treatment must last long enough to produce stable behavioral changes.

4. A comprehensive assessment of the nature and extent of an individual's drug problems and mental health evaluation is the first step in effective drug abuse treatment.

5. Tailoring services to fit the needs of the individual is an important part of effective drug abuse treatment because individuals differ in terms of age, gender, ethnicity, problem severity, recovery stage, and level of supervision needed.

6. Effective drug abuse treatment programs carefully monitor drug use through urinalysis or other objective methods because individuals trying to recover from drug addiction may experience a relapse, or return, to drug use.

7. Effective drug abuse treatment programs target cognitions (thoughts and feelings that are associated with criminal behavior). These include believing that one is entitled to have things one's own way; feeling that one's criminal behavior is justified; failing to be responsible for one's actions; and constantly failing to anticipate or appreciate the consequences of one's behavior.

8. Effective drug abuse treatment programs incorporate treatment planning for drug-abusing offenders, and treatment providers are aware of correctional supervision requirements as treatment goals.

9. Effective drug abuse treatment programs recognize that continuity of care helps offenders deal with problems at reentry such as learning to handle situations that could lead to relapse, learning how to live drug free in the community, and developing a drug-free peer support network.

10. Effective drug abuse treatment programs recognize that a balance of rewards and sanctions encourages prosocial behavior and treatment participation.

11. Effective drug abuse treatment programs recognize that offenders with co-occurring drug abuse and mental health problems require an integrated approach that combines drug abuse treatment with psychiatric treatment, including the use of medication to address depression, anxiety, and other mental health problems.

12. Effective drug abuse treatment programs recognize that medications are an important part of treatment for many drug-abusing offenders and can be instrumental in enabling offenders with co-occurring mental health problems to function successfully in society.

13. Effective drug abuse treatment programs understand that rates of infectious diseases such as tuberculosis and HIV/AIDS are higher in drug abusers, incarcerated offenders, and those under community correctional supervision than in the general population.

HIV-Positive and AIDS Inmates

HIV/AIDS is the fourth leading cause of death worldwide. **HIV** is the acronym for **human immunodeficiency virus,** which is any of a group of retroviruses that infect and destroy helper T cells of the immune system. When enough of a person's T cells have been destroyed by HIV, he or she is diagnosed with **AIDS,** or **acquired immunodeficiency syndrome.** The AIDS virus attacks the body's natural immune system, making it unable to fight off diseases. In this state, a person is highly vulnerable to life-threatening conditions, which people with healthy immune systems can fight off easily.

Corrections professionals should be concerned with treating communicable diseases in the inmate population for at least four reasons:

1. Sexually transmitted diseases, HIV/AIDS, hepatitis B and C, and tuberculosis can be transmitted to other inmates.

2. Correctional employees and prison visitors are at risk of becoming infected from inmates with communicable diseases if appropriate precautions are not implemented.

HIV (human immunodeficiency virus)

A group of retroviruses that infect and destroy helper T cells of the immune system, causing the marked reduction in their numbers that is diagnostic of AIDS.

AIDS (acquired immunodeficiency syndrome)

A disease of the human immune system that is characterized cytologically, especially by reduction in the numbers of CD4-bearing helper T cells to 20 percent or less of normal, rendering a person highly vulnerable to life-threatening conditions. The disease is caused by infection with HIV commonly transmitted in infected blood and bodily secretions (as semen), especially during sexual intercourse and intravenous drug use.

3. Almost 2,000 prisoners are released every day from prison. Unless they are effectively treated, they may transmit their diseases into the community, threatening public health.

4. Unless prisoners are treated in prison, they become a financial burden on community health care systems.[22]

Recently, the Bureau of Justice Statistics reported on HIV in prison.[23] The major finding is that the number of HIV-positive state and federal inmates continues to decline as shown in Exhibit 12–2.

EXHIBIT 12–2 **HIV and AIDS in Correctional Institutions, 1995, 2000–2010**

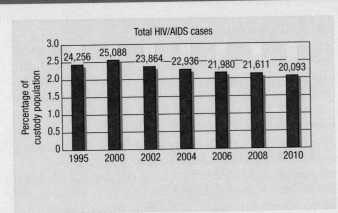

Total HIV/AIDS cases

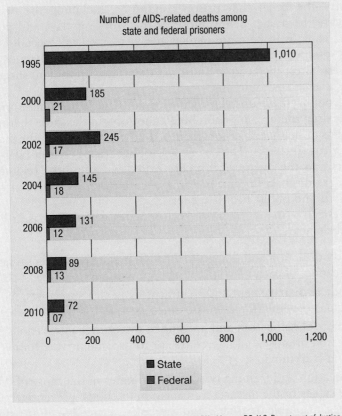

Number of AIDS-related deaths among state and federal prisoners

■ State
■ Federal

Sources: Adapted from Laura M. Maruschak, *HIV in Prisons, 2001–2010* (Washington, DC: U.S. Department of Justice, Bureau of Justice Statistics, September 2012).

CO12-4

Treating HIV in prison is difficult for at least five reasons.[24] The first is the issue of privacy. People infected with HIV usually do not want to disclose their condition. The therapeutic regimen often involves taking multiple drugs several times a day, and going to the prison medication line often compromises a prisoner's privacy and increases the risk of stigmatization by other inmates and staff. Stigmatization can range from isolation and shunning to more overt forms of abuse. This is true even when high-quality health care is available. Anti-retroviral therapies (ART) can effectively treat HIV but only if corrections officials help inmates overcome the obstacles to obtaining the treatment.

A second reason involves the frequency of taking medication and the prison routine. Some drugs must be taken with food and others in a fasting state. As the therapeutic regimen increases to five or six times a day, it strains the routine of most prisons to dispense medication frequently and to provide food as required.

The third reason is distrust of the medical and legal system. Not surprisingly, many inmates do not trust the legal and health care systems. This may be especially true for women and minorities who have a documented history of being experimented on without consent and being denied appropriate legal and medical care.

The fourth reason is fear of side effects. The HIV drug regimen is known to make patients feel worse than they already do. Consequently, inmates will be less likely to adhere to the strict dosages and timing.

The final reason is that the courts have rejected the idea that the level and quality of health care available to prisoners must be the same as is available to society at large.[25] This falls under the principle of least eligibility—the belief that prison conditions, including the delivery of health care, be a step below those of the working class and people on welfare. Thus, prisoners are denied access to medical specialists, timely delivery of medical services, technologically advanced diagnostic techniques, the latest medication and drug therapies, up-to-date surgical procedures, and second opinions.

Overcoming these obstacles will not be easy. If an inmate undergoes complex drug therapy in prison but cannot obtain the same therapy upon release, his or her health is compromised. In addition, he or she may transmit the virus to others. The key is developing trust between HIV-infected prisoners and the prison health care team, extending the regimen when inmates are discharged, and building collaboration between correctional institutions and public health agencies.

Cost-effective management of such inmates with HIV has at least five essential elements:

CO12-5

1. early detection and diagnosis through medical and mental health screening of each new jail inmate upon admission;

2. medical management and treatment by health specialists, including regular reevaluation and assessment;

3. inmate classification and housing to discourage intravenous drug use and homosexual intercourse or to provide private rooms for terminally ill inmates;

4. education and training of staff and inmates in the cause of AIDS, the stages of the disease, transmission methods, preventive measures, available treatment and therapies, testing issues and policies, confidentiality issues and policies, classification and program

The Offender Speaks
Visit www.mhhe.com/schmalleger7e to see this feature.

assignment policies, and supervision issues, including transportation and inmate movement; and

5. adequate funds to provide increasingly costly treatment to inmates with HIV or AIDS.

Dealing with HIV/AIDS Inmates Most correctional systems test their inmates for HIV, but testing policies vary widely:

- All states (except Kentucky, Missouri, New Hampshire, and Utah) and the federal BOP test inmates if the inmates request a test.
- All states (except Georgia, Massachusetts, Michigan, Oregon, and West Virginia) and the federal BOP test inmates if they have HIV-related symptoms.
- 42 states and the federal BOP test inmates after they are involved in an incident.
- 23 states test all inmates who enter their facilities.
- 18 states and the federal BOP test inmates who belong to specific "high-risk groups."
- 6 states (Alabama, Arkansas, Delaware, Missouri, Nevada, and Texas) test inmates upon their release.
- 3 states (Alabama, Arkansas, and New York) test inmates selected at random.
- 5 states (Idaho, Iowa, Missouri, Nevada, and North Dakota) test all inmates currently in custody.[26]

Today's corrections professionals need a network of medical experts—university medical school faculty, state health department staff, federal health officials, and local health care providers—to consult about HIV and AIDS. Such consultation will give corrections professionals reliable information and familiarize the noncorrectional medical community with the problems facing jails. The American Correctional Association (ACA) recommends that all correctional staff adopt universal precautions when dealing with inmates. This means the staff should assume that all inmates are carrying the virus because, without testing, there is no way to know who is infected and who is not.[27]

Education and Prevention HIV education and prevention programs are becoming more common in correctional facilities. Incarceration offers opportunities for high-risk inmates to learn basic disease information, safer sex practices, tattooing risks, and triggers for behavior relapse, and they may develop more accurate risk self-perceptions. Such programs benefit not only the inmate but also the health and well-being of the community to which the inmate returns. (Canadian officials estimate that 45 percent of inmates acquire a tattoo while in prison. Believing that stopping tattooing isn't going to happen, Canadian correctional officials set up safe tattoo studios in 6 of its 51 federal prisons.[28])

The types of education and prevention programs provided vary among correctional systems but may include instructor-led programs, pretest/posttest counseling, multisession prevention counseling, and audiovisual and written materials.

Another method of reducing high-risk behavior among incarcerated populations is peer-led counseling. In addition to providing information

HIV/AIDS is a serious problem for our nation's correctional facilities. To overcome the taboo that prevents at-risk people from testing themselves for HIV, the Reverend Jesse Jackson took an HIV test with Cook County (Chicago) jail inmates. Should HIV-positive inmates be treated any differently then other inmates? Should they be isolated?

about HIV/AIDS in formal settings, the informal interactions that incarcerated peer educators have with other inmates in the yard or other locations around the institution offer opportunities for ongoing dialogue about HIV/AIDS. Peer-led counseling is also cost-effective because most peer educators are volunteers and therefore provide HIV/AIDS education to others at no additional cost to the correctional facility.

Research on peer-led counseling has shown that peer educators report significant improvement in their self-esteem, may become paid employees of community-based organizations following release from prison as a result of the skills acquired in peer education training, and are influential in encouraging other inmates to volunteer for HIV testing. However, only 13 percent of state and federal prisons and 3 percent of jails in the United States offer peer-led HIV/AIDS education programs.

A little bit of charm and persuasion also works. When the Reverend Jesse Jackson visited the Cook County Jail in Chicago, he along with 177 jail inmates and 25 ministers, took a two-minute HIV test.[29] "We're here to save your lives," Reverend Jackson told the inmates. He talked with them about the psychological barrier, the "taboo," that prevents at-risk people from testing themselves for HIV infection. He told the inmates, "Regardless of the results, people who take the test can't lose. Those who test negative should view themselves as lucky—they can get out of the way of AIDS through their knowledge, behavior, and commitment. HIV-positive detainees, on the other hand, can take solace in the fact that early detection leads to correction." Results were reported within two weeks, and only two tests came back positive. Those persons received counseling and referrals.

However, what is done in prison may be undone in the community if ex-prisoners do not continue their treatment after they leave prison. A Texas study found that only about 30 percent of former inmates had filled a prescription for their medication within two months of release.[30] Halting treatment and reverting to dangerous behaviors such as drug use and unprotected sex diminishes the benefits inmates received while they were under direct prison supervision, which poses a public health challenge for all of us. Some states such as New York focus on educating prisoners about their treatment and aftercare options. When inmates are near their release, they are connected with community organizations that help them plan for their continued HIV care. Appointments are arranged for inmates to visit a clinic or doctor upon release, and each inmate leaves prison with a 30-day supply of medications and necessary prescriptions. Researchers don't know how well community groups and clinics follow through with former inmates or how well former prisoners follow through with their care. Roberto Potter, director of research at the University of Central Florida's department of criminal justice and former senior health scientist with the Centers for Disease Control and Prevention in Atlanta, believes that early intervention—making HIV/AIDS care and education available to those on probation—is the key and not waiting until offenders progress all the way to prison.[31]

Inmates with Mental Illness

Mental illness does not have to be a life sentence. Mental health is fundamental to a person's overall health, indispensable to personal well-being, and instrumental in leading a balanced and productive life. Every day, our nation's jails face the challenge of dealing with offenders who are not only suffering from schizophrenia, bipolar disorders, and major depression, among other illnesses but also from co-occurring substance abuse and dependence disorders and require close monitoring, medication, and other services.

The estimated prevalence of serious mental illness in U.S. prisons ranges from 7 to 16 percent.[32] Of people with mental illness in the general population, men are four times more likely to be incarcerated, and women have an eightfold higher risk. The reasons are associated with specific sociodemographic characteristics such as male gender, younger age, and nonwhite race. Other reasons are high rates of substance abuse, insufficient community resources, a national drug policy that emphasizes interdiction over treatment, delays in release from prison and jail to the community, insufficient inmate access to evidence-based mental health therapies, and insufficient planning for reentry of mental health inmates into the community.

CO12-6

Recently, ACA conducted a statewide survey of inmate mental health care.[33] It found that of the 47 states that responded, mental health testing is completed at intake. "Such screening is completed within 24 hours in Indiana, Louisiana, Massachusetts, and Pennsylvania; within seven days in Maryland; within 14 days in both Florida and Kentucky; and within 72 hours in New Jersey."[34]

As special needs inmates, people who are mentally ill do not do well in prison. They are perceived as disruptive, unpredictable, and sometimes dangerous. They are stigmatized, neglected, and easy prey for inmate assaults and robberies. The stress of incarceration can worsen their symptoms, leading to acute psychiatric disturbances, including harm to self or others, and adjustment and disciplinary problems such as refusal to leave one's cell or destruction of property. Behaviors that are characteristic of mental illness such as neglecting personal hygiene, ignoring orders, screaming, and banging against walls oftentimes are met with discipline, which can mean being placed in isolation where the conditions worsen.

Is corrections being asked to shoulder the burden of the nation's failure to diagnose properly and care for those with mental or emotional disorders? You be the judge: It is estimated that there are nearly eight times more people who are mentally ill in the nation's jails and prisons (nearly 478,000) than there are in mental hospitals (60,000).[35] Six to 8 percent of the 10 to 12 million people who enter the nation's jails annually have severe mental illness. The three largest de facto psychiatric hospitals in the United States are now the Los Angeles County Jail, Rikers Island Jail in New York City, and Cook County Jail in Chicago. The L.A. County Jail spends $10 million a year on psychiatric medication![36]

Suggesting that these facilities replace mental hospitals altogether overstates their treatment capacity and the function of these facilities—the

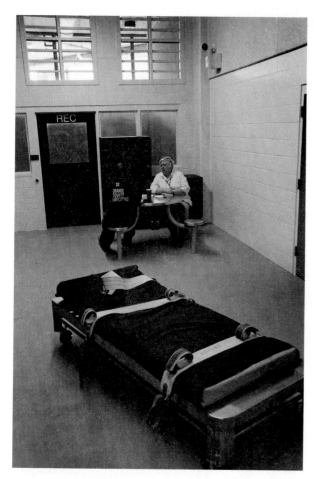

There are more people who are mentally ill in U.S. jails and prisons than there are in mental hospitals, but correctional officers are not therapists and correctional facilities are not mental hospitals. Why are there so many people who are mentally ill in U.S. jails and prisons and what are the innovative strategies for keeping people with mental illness out of correctional facilities?

mental health care required is far beyond what most correctional facilities are equipped to offer. Correctional officers are not therapists and correctional facilities are not mental hospitals. Corrections personnel are not trained to facilitate mental health treatment and, according to Dr. David Satcher, U.S. surgeon general from 1998 to 2002, "they should not have to."[37]

Why So Many? Why are there so many people who are mentally ill in the nation's jails and prisons? The reasons include failure to differentiate who should be in jail and who shouldn't, failure to treat people before they enter the criminal justice system, deinstitutionalization (moving the mentally ill from hospitals to nonsecure residential community settings), stricter commitment laws, less stringent discharge criteria, reductions or curtailment of public funding, lack of adequate insurance coverage, and three-strikes laws because those with mental illness may, when the illness is not effectively treated, be less able to follow the rule of law.[38] Former mental patients as well as people whose bizarre behavior might have landed them in a hospital bed a few years ago are now being arrested and are ending up in jail. Although 40 state mental hospitals have closed in the last decade, more than 400 new prisons have opened,[39] state spending for treatment of people who are mentally ill is one-third less today than it was in 1950,[40] and changes in mental health laws have made involuntary commitment more difficult. As a result, jails and prisons have become the institutions most likely to house those with mental illness.

In addition, offenders often live as transients or in crowded conditions, increasing their levels of stress, which can precipitate mental illness. Offenders also tend to be economically disadvantaged, meaning they are less likely to get mental health treatment. Finally, they have high rates of substance abuse, which is correlated with mental illness.

Correctional facilities have an opportunity to provide prevention and treatment interventions to a seriously underserved and needy population. Policies and programs for prisoners help them return to our communities as better citizens, in better health, under treatment for their medical and mental health conditions, and better equipped and motivated to protect themselves and others, while possibly reducing the cost to taxpayers of future health care and reincarceration. Good health care is also an integral part of institutional security. Investments in prisoner health care result in fewer correctional disturbances, disciplinary actions, and inmate injuries and in less negative publicity for the institution.[41]

Given that a significant expansion of resources for state mental health care systems is highly unlikely, the key to curbing recidivism of people who are mentally ill is to expand public health services into the jails and prisons so that inmates can begin therapy the moment they walk into custody. When that happens, correctional institutions can provide offenders a better "hand off" from the institution to the community. Unless correctional policy moves in this direction, mental illness will continue to worsen in isolation and, for some inmates, lead to suicide.

What will it take for corrections policy to shift in that direction? Dean Aufderheide, director of Mental Health Services for the Florida

Department of Corrections, believes we need to think of mental illness as a chronic illness. When we do that, we'll develop new strategies for dealing with it in prison and after release. He wrote, "By conceptualizing mental illness as a chronic illness, one that waxes and wanes, and like diabetes, is the manifestation of dynamic combinations of genetic and congenital vulnerabilities, environmental influences, and individual behavior, public health and safety officials can collaborate in seizing the opportunity to develop more and effective and efficient strategies for managing inmates with mental illness in prison and after release."[42]

The Staff Speaks
Visit www.mhhe.com/schmalleger7e to see this feature.

Innovative Alternatives There are many successful and innovative ways to divert persons with mental illnesses from the criminal justice system, including the creation of law enforcement–mental health liaison programs, increased training of law enforcement personnel, and a general improvement in the funding and effectiveness of community mental health services. Three innovative strategies are presented next.

CO12-7

The Memphis Police Crisis Intervention Team (CIT) has won widespread national acclaim for the cooperative relationships that developed between the police and the mental health system. CIT officers, dispatchers, and other key police personnel receive intensive training about the signs and symptoms of serious mental illnesses, crisis intervention and deescalation techniques, and community mental health resources and options. A specialized mental health triage unit at the University of Memphis medical center was created to respond specifically to individuals referred by the police. Memphis police now know they have options available to them other than arrest and incarceration. So far there have been fewer arrests, better treatment outcomes, and reduced officer injuries.[43] CIT has been emulated in more than 50 communities across the United States, and other communities have developed alternative law enforcement–mental health triage capabilities.

A second innovative strategy for keeping people with mental illness out of jail and prison is mental health court, an extremely recent phenomenon. The term *mental health court* is most often used to refer to a specialized docket for defendants with mental illness that provides the opportunity to participate in court-supervised treatment. A court team, composed of a judge, court personnel, and treatment providers, defines the terms of participation, provides ongoing status assessments with individualized sanctions and rewards, and determines resolution of cases upon successful completion of court-ordered treatment plans. In 1997, there were four mental health courts in the United States. Today more than 150 have been established and dozens more are being planned.[44] Two rationales underlie mental health courts: (1) to protect the public by addressing the mental illness that contributed to the criminal act, thereby reducing recidivism, and (2) to recognize that criminal sanctions, whether intended as punishments or deterrents, are neither effective nor morally appropriate when mental illness is a significant cause of the criminal act. Very little research is available on the effectiveness of mental health courts, but early findings on such courts in Broward County, Florida, point to relative success. Defendants were twice as likely to receive services for their mental illness and were no more likely to commit a new crime despite spending 75 percent fewer days in jail than did comparable defendants.[45] Congress has promoted the development of mental health courts with the passage of the Law Enforcement and Mental Health Project Act in 2000, which makes federal funds available to local jurisdictions seeking to establish or expand mental health courts and diversion

Jon Wood

Family Counselor • Kandiyohi County Community Corrections • Kandiyohi, Minnesota

Jon Wood is a family counselor with the Kandiyohi County Community Corrections office in Kandiyohi, Minnesota. He has held that position for the past 11 years, after working in a similar position as a contractor for two years. Prior to that he received a master's degree in community counseling and a bachelor's degree in applied psychology from St. Cloud State University in St. Cloud, Minnesota.

Wood says the bulk of his time is spent providing counseling to first-time offenders, either in a one-on-one capacity or in a family setting. He specializes in dealing with juveniles with mental health issues, many of which are just emerging or have not even been diagnosed yet. He also works with schools, collaborates with other mental health professionals who might be dealing with the same individuals, and deals with social service agencies and probation agents.

Most of his clients are very young—according to Wood, the problems start to show up around age 10. "They're showing some behaviors at school, and I try to coordinate treatment with psychologists and psychiatrists, so we can figure out what to do for them," he says. "And a big challenge is trying to talk parents into making it happen, given the stigma that is attached to mental health issues."

Wood says his goal is to help both parents and children understand the illnesses that they are facing and help them develop methods of dealing with them. This means developing new cognitive skills and learning problem-solving and negotiation skills. "It's trying to help them find other ways to think," he says, "so they don't have to always be fighting each other or some authority figure.

"About once every two years I'll get a letter from a parent saying thanks. It doesn't happen very often but once in a while. And every now and then I'll run into an old client in a grocery store, and he tells me that he's going to college. So I know that something that we talked about made sense to him."

> "So often parents who are dealing with the juvenile justice system get to a point where they freak out, they don't want to have anything to do with it, and they throw their hands up in the air and give up."

programs, and the Mentally Ill Offender Treatment and Crime Reduction Act of 2004, which authorizes federal funds for jail diversion, mental health treatment for inmates with mental illnesses, community reentry services, and training. The acts recognize that states and communities are

There are eight times more people with mental illness in jail and prison than there are in mental hospitals. What are some ways the needs of women correctional clients with mental disorders can be met?

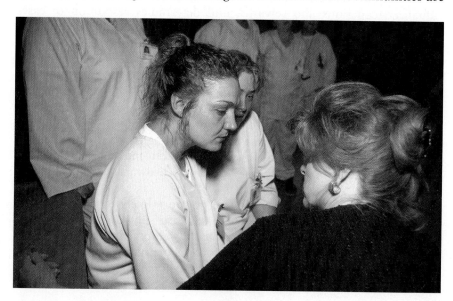

Economic Realities and Corrections: Special Prison Populations

Spending for corrections across all sectors of government has risen 36 percent since 1986, reaching an estimated $68 billion a year. However, most spending has been devoted to capital construction and infrastructure development for jails and prisons. In contrast, fewer new resources are available to help individuals who are elderly or who have mental and substance use disorders or HIV/AIDS. In challenging economic times when states face the grim reality of substantial budget shortfalls, it is increasingly difficult to secure adequate resources to fund effective prison and community programs for special prison populations. Although some progress can be claimed in meeting the needs of special prison populations, as this chapter shows, the unmet need for inmates who are elderly, are mentally challenged, abuse substances, and have HIV/AIDS persists unabated. These deficits place offenders at greater than average risk for reincarceration, and put at risk the communities in which the offenders are released and are likely to reoffend. The success of prison programs for special populations who in increasing numbers need these services hinges on the availability of effective and readily available treatment programs. As noted by Thomas Patterson, executive director of the Utah Department of Corrections, more and more special populations are the norm rather than the exception in prison. How ready are we to provide the prison services that manage their needs to reduce their reliance on postrelease criminal activities when two-thirds are rearrested and one-half is reincarcerated?

best able to develop their own innovative approaches to reduce the criminalization of people with mental illnesses.

A third strategy to keep people who are mentally ill out of jail and prison is the Assertive Community Treatment (ACT) Program. ACT programs are teams of social service professionals who provide a broad and integrated range of services to individuals diverted from jails or reentering communities following incarceration with severe and persistent mental illnesses. The services include medication and medication management, housing assistance, case management, substance abuse treatment, vocational supports, and mobile crisis management. ACT teams emphasize preventing people in crisis from "falling through the cracks." Today there are approximately 15 ACT programs in the United States, 3 of them in the Ohio Department of Rehabilitation and Corrections, for individuals with severe and persistent mental illnesses reentering their communities after completing prison sentences.

The American Association for Community Psychiatrists Committee on the Mentally Ill Behind Bars developed a list of recommendations to keep people with mental illness out of jail:[46]

1. Address the lack of access to community mental health and other diagnostic services in order to improve early diagnosis and treatment.

2. Create alternatives to incarceration for as many nonviolent offenders with mental illness as possible. For example, have a center to which police can take people who are experiencing a mental crisis.

3. Improve jail conditions that have negative effects on the mental health of inmates. For example, researchers are finding that serious bullying is a cause of suicide.[47] Suicide is the leading cause of death in jail and ranks fifth in prison behind cancer, heart disease, respiratory disease, and liver disease.[48]

4. Establish vigorous programs designed to reintegrate inmates with mental illness into the community, with specific attention paid to their housing needs.

5. Create oversight boards to prevent human rights abuses and to guarantee that adequate physical and mental health services are available upon release.

Developing innovative alternatives for keeping people with mental illness out of jail and prison requires staff who are educated and trained in multidisciplinary perspectives. Consult the Appendix: Careers in Corrections at the Online Learning Center Web site www.mhhe.com/schmalleger7e for the steps involved in career planning, developing employability and job readiness, and finding the right job.

Inmates with Tuberculosis

tuberculosis (TB)

A highly variable communicable disease that is characterized by toxic symptoms or allergic manifestations that in humans primarily affect the lungs.

Visit http://www.icrc.org/eng/resources/documents/film/av003a-azerbaijan-combating-mdr-tb-detention.htm or scan this code with the QR app on your smartphone or digital device and watch this podcast showing how Azerbaijan has become a model for combating TB in prisons with the combination of individual attention in Azerbaijan's central treatment facility, specialist follow-up care, and solid political commitment. How does this information relate to ideas discussed in this chapter?

Although not extremely common among the general U.S. population, **tuberculosis** has traditionally been more common in correctional facilities.[49] It is estimated that the risk of incurring a tuberculosis infection is 4 to 17 times higher for those incarcerated than for those who live in the general population because of very close living quarters, overcrowding, poor sanitation, ignorance of preventive measures, failure to supervise and ensure adherence to treatment, and the large number of inmates with a high risk of having TB, such as HIV-positive detainees, intravenous drug users, and immigrants.[50] TB is considered to be the most common cause of death among the world's prisoners.[51]

When a person who has TB coughs, sneezes, or laughs, tiny droplets of fluid containing TB bacteria are released into the air, which are then inhaled by others. The TB germ becomes active in people when their immune system becomes weak. It multiplies and causes active TB. If left untreated, active TB can cause the infected person to literally waste away.

In 2009, all states reported testing their inmates for TB at intake and tracking identified cases. States also report using more than one testing policy.

- 31 states test inmates annually.
- 29 states test inmates upon a physician's request.
- 11 states test inmates upon their request.[52]

Experts concerned about TB in correctional facilities have indicated that the most important issues for corrections professionals are to understand the causes and control of TB, to implement appropriate and cost-effective screening programs, and to develop close working relationships with local health authorities. Public health departments can provide correctional facilities access to expert TB medical consultation and laboratory services. Health department staff can also train correctional personnel in performing, interpreting, and recording tuberculin skin tests, identifying signs and symptoms of tuberculosis disease, initiating and observing therapy, monitoring medication side effects, collecting specimens, educating inmates, and maintaining record systems.

Older Inmates

The special circumstances surrounding the incarceration of older inmates also create new challenges for correctional institutions. With more than 2.3 million adults in jail and prison today, problems that were manageable two decades ago now threaten to overwhelm state and federal corrections systems. One issue that is being addressed by administrators across the nation is the rising tide of older prisoners, what some are calling the "silver tsunami" of aging prisoners, the issue we turn to next in this chapter.

The Aging of the Prison Population

Most of us imagine prisoners as young and aggressive. However, *people who are elderly* and *passive* describe a significant portion of the prison population. The definition of *elderly* is subject to debate. Some define *elderly* as 65 years of age and older, some suggest 60 years, others suggest 55, and still others 50. There are some who do not consider chronological age at all. Rather, they believe that, because of the impact of prison lifestyle, including lower socioeconomic status and limited access to medical care, a prisoner's physiological age may be higher than his or her chronological age. In addition, some say that a lengthy prison stay can age an inmate 10 years beyond her or his chronological age.

Despite the differences among definitions of *elderly*, it is possible to establish a common chronological starting point to define *older* inmates for purposes of comprehensive planning, programming, evaluation, and research within and among prison systems. After careful study of the issue, the National Institute of Corrections recommended that correctional agencies nationwide adopt age 50 as the chronological starting point for defining *older inmates*.[53] Using that definition, there are 246,600 elderly prisoners behind bars in the United States—enough to fill the Louisiana Superdome more than three times.[54] Corrections experts predict that by 2030, there will be upward of 400,000 elderly prisoners, nearly a third of the total prison population.[55] This number does not even include prisoners ages 50–54.[56]

Serving a sentence for aggravated murder, Betty Tewell, 75, ties her shoes on her bunk at the Ohio Reformatory for Women in Marysville, Ohio. The Ohio Department of Rehabilitation and Correction predicts that by 2025, a quarter of its population will be older offenders. Currently, they make up nearly 10 percent of the state's 44,700 inmates. What are the options states are looking at to save money and respond to the needs of older inmates who pose no threat outside prison?

CO12-8

Geriatric Prison Facilities Recently, a number of scholars and policymakers have argued in favor of age-segregated prisons for four reasons.[57] First, age segregation allows correctional authorities to relocate older prisoners from institutions that are largely oriented toward the care and needs of younger inmates to institutions designed to care for the specific and specialized health care needs of older prisoners. Second, the financial costs of making physical and program changes in every prison in the United States in order to comply with the Americans with Disabilities Act of 1990 would be prohibitive. Advocates of age-segregated prisons argue that age-segregated prisons could reduce a correctional system's civil liabilities if they centralize disability services in age-segregated institutions that fully comply with ADA requirements. Third, age-segregated prisons advance prisoner safety. Kerbs and Jolley report four key findings from studies of older prisoners' safety in non-age-segregated prisons: Older prisoners are victimized by younger prisoners; they feel vulnerable to attack by younger prisoners; they prefer to live with inmates in their own age bracket; and at times they choose to live in age-segregated protective custody units. Why not then, they ask, provide age-segregated correctional institutions to enhance the safety of older inmates while decreasing the risk of civil liabilities when older inmates are mainstreamed with younger inmates? And fourth, age-segregated facilities can promote rehabilitation by advancing age-specific treatment opportunities.

Today we find age-segregated prisons in Alabama, Arizona, Georgia, Illinois, Kansas, Kentucky, Maryland, Michigan, Minnesota, Mississippi,

North Carolina, New Jersey, Ohio, Pennsylvania, South Carolina, Tennessee, Texas, Virginia, West Virginia, and Wisconsin. Few stairs, reduced distances, geriatric chairs and beds, walkers, wheelchairs, handrails, more crafts and leisure activities, and staff trained in gerontological issues make these facilities unique. The majority confine only male prisoners who are elderly. Older female prisoners, who constitute 7 percent of the total population of prisoners who are elderly, are generally kept in a state's only women's prison.

Prison Hospice Programs Before the onset of AIDS and the increased numbers of prisoners who are elderly, few prisoners died while incarcerated. Inmate deaths occur more frequently now, and correctional administrators have taken measures to address the unique problems associated with helping prisoners who are terminally ill through their passing. A **hospice** is an interdisciplinary, comfort-oriented care facility that helps patients who are seriously ill die with dignity and humanity in an environment that facilitates mental and spiritual preparation for the natural process of dying. Hospice programs provide a wide array of services, including pain management, spiritual support, and psychological counseling as well as grief counseling for bereaved families. In 2007, the American Correctional Association reported that hospice care or similar services were offered in nearly all state prison systems.[58]

Often one of the challenges in starting a prison hospice is educating the prison staff in caring for prisoners who are terminally ill and making a psychological adjustment to overcome the resentment that prisoners are getting this level of care. According to Elizabeth Craig, executive director of the National Prison Hospice Association (NPHA) in Boulder, Colorado, "In my view, inmates are being punished by being incarcerated; we don't need to create more suffering for them."[59]

One of the nation's best-known prison hospice program is the one at the Louisiana State Penitentiary (LSP) at Angola. Angola's hospice unit opened in 1998, and two years later it was honored for the program with the American Hospital Association's Circle of Life Award. Of its nearly 5,200 inmates, more than 90 percent are expected to die while incarcerated.[60]

LSP Angola's hospice program has five core goals:

1. Provide quality end-of-life care regardless of a patient's criminal charge or personal history.
2. Honor the patient's support system, including his family (as defined by him).
3. Address the patient's needs holistically with emphasis on palliation of physical, social, spiritual, and emotional suffering.
4. Assist the patient with activities that he considers life affirming.
5. Maintain an end-of-life care system consistent with "free-world" standards.

A fundamental part of hospice care at LSP Angola is the emphasis on family. Each inmate patient is allowed to designate two inmates from Angola's general prisoner population as "family," and within the constraints of security, these inmates are treated like the inmate's biological family members. Angola's staff provides whatever considerations are possible within the constraints of security to ensure that the patient's final days are as meaningful as possible for all involved.

---

hospice

An interdisciplinary, comfort-oriented care facility that helps seriously ill patients die with dignity and humanity in an environment that facilitates mental and spiritual preparation for the natural process of dying.

Visit http://www.youtube.com/watch?v=DzPzmeieXPE or scan this code with the QR app on your SmartPhone or digital device and watch the trailer of the documentary *Serving Life* about the hospice program at Louisiana State Penitentiary at Angola where the average sentence is more than 90 years. How does this information relate to ideas discussed in this chapter?

Other options states are looking at to save money and respond to the needs of prisoners who are terminally ill include releasing terminally ill, disabled, and dying inmates (sometimes called *compassionate release*) who pose no threat outside prison, providing volunteer inmate aides as in the program at Angola, and increasing family visitation.

Compassionate, medical, or geriatric prisoner release laws exist in 41 states, but some argue they are rarely if ever used because of "political considerations" related to public safety policy and a length review process. From 2001 until 2008, Colorado released just three prisoners under its compassionate release policy. In 2011, 106 requests for compassionate release were filed in New York, but only 5 were granted. Twenty-nine persons died prior to their release. Oregon has never released more than two prisoners per year; as of 2009, Maryland and Oklahoma have never released a single prisoner under their geriatric release provisions; and the federal Bureau of Prisons, the largest prison system in the United States with over 217,00 inmates, has filed less than 24 motions for compassionate release per year since 1992.[61] However, in December 2013, the U.S. Department of Justice said it would withdraw regulations proposed under the Bush administration that limited compassionate release to inmates with serious medical conditions and would issue a new policy to cover elderly prisoners who served significant portions of their sentences for non-violent crimes.

Absent research to explain these findings, Tina Maschi, a Fellow with the Op-Ed Project (a social venture founded to increase the range of voices and quality of ideas in the world) believes that the reason behind the sparing use of compassionate release is simply politics. She wrote, "Public opinion is often against such programs and their narrow eligibility criteria and complicated bureaucratic procedures (including a lengthy referral and review process) often deter prisoners from applying in the first place."[62]

These forms of release are not without their critics, however. Some argue it's like a shell game and there is no real cost savings: You shift the expense of medical care from one state agency to another, mostly Medicaid, which is funded partly by federal money. Even though the expense of medical care transfers from one state agency to another, hospitals, community health centers, nursing homes, and hospices are equipped to assist the elderly. Most prisons generally lack the long-term care we associate with geriatric facilities. Still others are troubled by the fact that convicted criminals are released into adult care homes in the community used by the rest of the population. North Carolina state senator Debbie Clary asked, "Do you want your grandmother in the same room beside a convicted felon?"[63]

Visit http://www.youtube.com/watch?v=7fZmt02bmaU or scan this code with the QR app on your SmartPhone or digital device and watch this podcast on elderly inmates dying in prison. How does this information relate to ideas discussed in this chapter?

Health Issues The physical, mental, and medical health care needs of older inmates have implications for prison policymakers, administrators, and staff. Older, sicker inmates challenge health care systems.

It is estimated that a prisoner who is elderly suffers from an average of three chronic illnesses. Additionally, men and women who are elderly require screening for colon cancer, prostate cancer, breast cancer, and many other conditions that become more prevalent as people age.

Researchers in California found that almost 70 percent of the women prisoners who are geriatric said that at least one prison activity was very difficult for them: 59 percent reported difficulties hearing orders, 57

Get-tough-on-crime policies have led to an increased number of inmates serving longer periods of time behind bars. The Colorado Territorial Correctional Facility in Cañon City includes a 32-bed infirmary for prisoners who are elderly with cancer, heart disease, diabetes, and respiratory problems and highlights the public health costs associated with prisoners who are elderly. What are some of the special needs of inmates who are geriatric?

percent said it was very difficult for them to drop to the floor for alarms, 35 percent said it was very difficult for them to stand in line for head counts, 14 of the 35 women who were assigned to upper bunks said it was very difficult for them to climb on and off a top bunk, and 61 percent said they had been given jobs that were too difficult to perform, including janitorial and yard crew work.[64] Incarcerating older prisoners with impaired eyesight, physical disabilities, cancer, arthritis, diabetes, heart disease, hypertension, or Alzheimer's disease and treating these illnesses raise many concerns. For example, how ethical is it for prisons to provide surgery, physical therapy, and daily medication to prisoners who are elderly when people outside prison are unable to afford similar medical treatment? However, if left untreated, might these inmates be less likely to provide for themselves upon release and more likely to become a health care burden to society?

Another issue that must be considered is the effect of health-related legislation. For example, the Americans with Disabilities Act (ADA) affects not only mainstream society but also prisons and jails. Designing prison spaces that are accessible for prisoners who are elderly with ramps, handrails, good lighting, and subtle grades, is now law under ADA. In *Goodman & U.S.* v. *Georgia* (2006), the Supreme Court ruled that prisoners with disabilities may sue for monetary damages if the violation of ADA is so serious as to also constitute a violation of civil rights.[65]

Cost and Recidivism Issues

The economic consequences of incarcerating older prisoners are huge. The estimated national cost per year to confine a prisoner age 50 and older is $68,270.[66] If a 50-year-old inmate lives to 80, this figure is projected to be $2,048,100. The annual cost in New York is considerably more: $93,000. In California it's $138,000 for an elderly female prisoner, and because prisons are not eligible for Medicaid and Medicare funding, states must pick up the tab.

It is doubtful that, when mandatory sentencing laws, three-strikes laws, and truth-in-sentencing laws were enacted, the economic impact of incarcerating prisoners who are elderly for long periods of time was actually considered. Unless legislatures give courts and prison administrators more leeway to interchange prison sentences with community sentences, states will continue to find themselves in economic crises as they attempt to provide for the 33 percent of the inmate population that is projected to be elderly by the year 2030.

It is also likely that when laws regarding mandatory sentencing, three strikes, and truth in sentencing were enacted, legislatures ignored the evidence-based literature in two arenas. First, the data show that the increasing population of aging prisoners is not due to any "elderly crime wave" but to individuals entering prison at a younger age and staying there until they are old—often for not so serious crimes. These people are caught in the net of the newer habitual offender and mandatory minimum laws and are given punishments of 20 years or more for low-level and drug offenses. In Texas, 65 percent of prisoners age 50 and older are incarcerated for nonviolent drug, property, and other crimes.[67]

Second, recidivism drops dramatically with age. For example, in New York, only 7 percent of prisoners who were released from prison at ages 50 to 64 returned for new convictions within three years. That number drops to 4 percent for prisoners age 65 and older. The driver of reimprisonment for this older age group seems to be parole violations—which could result from missing a meeting with a parole officer, having a positive drug test, or having contact with a victim—and can return individuals to prison without a conviction for a new crime.

SEXUALLY TRANSMITTED DISEASES IN JAIL

Most studies on infectious diseases in correctional facilities focus on prison. The problem of sexually transmitted diseases (STDs) in jail is addressed less frequently even though some believe that STDs are more common in jail than in prison.[68] However, rapid turnover and frequent movement of inmates make jails difficult settings in which to study the prevalence of various diseases. But recently, the Society of Correctional Physicians published a report by Dr. Karl Brown, infectious disease supervisor at New York City's Rikers Island Jail, on the increase of STDs in jail and the difficulties diagnosing and treating four of the most common STDs found in jail today: syphilis, gonorrhea, chlamydia, and genital herpes. **Syphilis** is caused by the bacteria *Treponema pallidum*. Syphilis is passed from person to person through direct contact with a syphilis sore. Transmission of the bacteria occurs during sexual contact. **Gonorrhea** is caused by *Neisseria gonorrhea*, a bacteria that grows and multiplies in mucous membranes of the body. Gonorrhea bacteria grows in the warm, moist areas of the reproductive tract, including the cervix, uterus, and fallopian tubes in women and in the urethra (urine canal) in women and men. The bacteria can also grow in the mouth, throat, and anus. Gonorrhea is spread through sexual contact. **Chlamydia** is the most frequently reported STD in the United States. It is caused by the bacteria *Chlamydia trachomatis*. Chlamydia is transmitted through sexual contact. **Genital herpes** is a lifelong infection caused by the herpes simplex viruses type 1 (HSV-1) and type 2 (HSV-2). A person can get HSV-1 by coming into contact with the saliva of an infected person. HSV-1 causes infections of the mouth and lips, so-called fever blisters. A person almost always gets HSV-2 infection during sexual contact with someone who has a genital HSV-2 infection. According to Brown, after declining for many years, the rates of syphilis, gonorrhea, and chlamydia began increasing in jails and juvenile detention centers in 2000, especially among female prisoners.

The jail environment may be the key to controlling STDs, but less than half of the nation's jails have a policy of routine screening, and even in those jails with routine screening, less than half of the inmates were tested for syphilis, gonorrhea, or chlamydia. Brown also found another problem: Approximately half of arrestees were released within 48 hours, but most jails received the inmates' test results more than 48 hours after admission.

The type of screening for STDs in jail should be based on the prevalence of STDs as measured by the population served. For example, gonorrhea and chlamydia are four times higher in northern Florida than they are in northern California. The key to controlling STDs is to continuously collect, monitor, and analyze information and then to discuss the results with public health officials. Diagnosis also requires a thorough nonjudgmental sexual history and a careful genital exam.

syphilis

A sexually transmitted disease caused by the bacteria *Treponema pallidum*. If left untreated, syphilis can cause serious heart abnormalities, mental disorders, blindness, other neurological problems, and death. Syphilis is transmitted when an infected lesion comes in contact with the soft skin of the mucous membrane.

gonorrhea

The second most common sexually transmitted disease. Often called *the clap*, gonorrhea is caused by the *Neisseria gonorrhea* bacteria found in moist areas of the body. Infection occurs with contact to any of these areas.

chlamydia

The most common sexually transmitted disease. Caused by the bacteria *Chlamydia trachomatis*, it can affect the eyes, lungs, or urogenital (urinary-genital) area, depending on the age of the person infected and how the infection is transmitted.

genital herpes

A sexually transmitted disease caused by the herpes simplex virus, or HSV. It is one of the most common STDs in the United States.

CO12-9

LEGAL ISSUES

Providing inmates adequate health care is of concern to the courts and professional associations. As we discussed in Chapter 7, in 1976, the U.S. Supreme Court ruled in *Estelle* v. *Gamble*[69] that inmates have a constitutional right to reasonable, adequate health services for serious medical needs. However, the Court also made clear that such a right did not mean that prisoners have unqualified access to health care. Lower courts have held that the Constitution does not require that medical care provided to prisoners be perfect, the best obtainable, or even very good.[70] Nevertheless, health care professionals and inmate advocates—such as the American Medical Association, the American Correctional Health Services Association, and the National Commission on Correctional Health Care—insist on alleviating the pain and suffering of all persons, regardless of their status. They believe that no distinction should be made between inmates and free citizens.

Another important piece of legislation affecting inmate health care is the Civil Rights of Institutionalized Persons Act (CRIPA).[71] This law places prisoners in a class with others confined in government institutions, such as people with disabilities and elderly people in government-run nursing homes.

Inmates with Disabilities

Inmates with special needs face numerous difficulties. Consider the case of Ronald Yeskey. Yeskey was sentenced to 18 to 36 months in a Pennsylvania correctional facility. He was recommended for a motivational boot camp, which would have shortened his sentence to six months. He was, however, refused admission to the boot camp because of a physical disability—hypertension. He sued, claiming that the **Americans with Disabilities Act (ADA)** of 1990 prohibits any "public entity" from discriminating against a "qualified individual with a disability" because of that disability.

In 1998 in a unanimous opinion, the U.S. Supreme Court held that state prisons fall squarely within the ADA's definition of a "public entity."[72] Reacting to the decision, Yeskey's attorney noted, "The court's ruling means that prison officials cannot discriminate against prisoners with disabilities and must make reasonable modifications to prison operations so that these prisoners will have reasonable access to most prison programs";[73] otherwise, prisoners can sue for monetary damages.

Inmates with HIV/AIDS

Most suits by prisoners with HIV/AIDS are claims that officials have violated a prisoner's rights by revealing the condition or by segregating the prisoner because of the condition. In 1988, officials in Erie County, New York, placed an HIV-positive female prisoner in a segregated prison wing reserved for inmates with mental illness. They also placed on her possessions red stickers revealing her HIV-positive status. The inmate sued, claiming denial of her rights to privacy and due process. The district court agreed (*Nolley* v. *County of Erie*, 1991). In the same year, however, the Eleventh Circuit Court of Appeals held that an Alabama policy of isolating all HIV-positive inmates did not violate the Fourth or Eighth Amendments (*Harris* v. *Thigpen* and *Austin* v. *Pennsylvania Dept. of Corr.*).

Americans with Disabilities Act (ADA)

Public Law 101-336, enacted July 26, 1990, which prohibits discrimination and ensures equal opportunity for people with disabilities in employment, state and local government services, public accommodations, commercial facilities, and transportation. It also mandates the establishment of TDD/telephone relay services.

Prisoners in wheelchairs and others with special needs place an extraordinary strain on prison resources. Inmates with disabilities are protected under the federal Americans with Disabilities Act (ADA) of 1990. What does the act require of correctional facilities? What are the alternatives to incarceration for inmates with disabilities?

Other legal issues relate to the work assignments of HIV/AIDS inmates. In 1994 in *Gates* v. *Rowland*, the Ninth Circuit Court of Appeals ruled that California correctional officials could continue to bar HIV-positive inmates from working in prison kitchens. The court made it clear that its decision was based more on the anticipated reactions of prisoners receiving the food than on any actual risk of infection. The court agreed that food service "has often been the source of violence or riots" because inmates "are not necessarily motivated by rational thought and frequently have irrational suspicions or phobias that education will not modify" and because prisoners "have no choice of where they eat." Correctional officials had based their policy, the court said, on "legitimate penological concerns."

Inmates with Mental Illness

The federal courts have recognized the right of inmates who are mentally ill to treatment. According to a district court in Illinois, this right is triggered when it becomes reasonably certain that (1) the prisoner's symptoms demonstrate a serious mental disease or brain injury, (2) the disease or injury is curable or at least treatable, and (3) delaying or denying care would cause substantially more harm to the inmate (*Parte* v. *Lane*, 1981). In 1990, in *Washington* v. *Harper*, the U.S. Supreme Court ruled that inmates who are dangerous to themselves or others as a result of mental illness may be treated with psychoactive drugs against their will. Such involuntary drug treatment, however, has to be in the best interest of the inmate's mental health, not just for the convenience of the correctional institution.

REVIEW AND APPLICATIONS

SUMMARY

① Some inmates require special treatment or care because they suffer from mental illness, chemical dependency, a communicable disease, or typical problems associated with people who are elderly. These inmates present unique problems for correctional staff and administrators.

② Inmates with special needs present significant management problems because they are typically more violent and prone to be disruptive, require close monitoring as suicide risks, tax scarce medical resources, and are often targets of abuse by other inmates.

③ A tenfold increase in prison populations over the past 25 years caused a commensurate increase in the number of inmates with substance abuse problems. These inmates tremendously drain finite resources, are disruptive to daily life within the walls, and create unique management problems in all areas of prison life.

④ Special difficulties related to HIV/AIDS among prison populations include privacy issues, disruption of the prison routine due to the frequency of taking medication, inmate distrust of the medical and legal systems, fear of side effects, and the legal dilemma embodied in the principle of least eligibility.

⑤ The five essential elements of cost-effective management of HIV/AIDS inmates are early detection and diagnosis, medical management and treatment, inmate classification and housing, education and training of staff and inmates, and funding.

6 The increase in the number of inmates with mental illness is attributable to several factors: the deinstitutional-ization of persons who are mentally ill to nonsecure residential environments; stricter commitment laws; failure to know who should and should not be in jail; failure to treat them before they enter the criminal justice system; less stringent discharge criteria; reduction or elimination of public funding; lack of adequate insurance cover-age; and three-strikes laws because those with mental illness may, when the illness is not effectively treated, be less able to follow the rule of law.

7 Ways to divert persons with mental illnesses from the criminal justice system include the creation of law enforcement–mental health liaison programs, increased training of law enforcement personnel, and a general improvement in the funding and effectiveness of community health services.

8 Estimates are that, on average, each older inmate is afflicted with three chronic illnesses that require ongoing and expensive medical treatment. Some question the equity of providing such free treatment to criminal offend-ers when the same free treatment is not provided to the public at large. The annual cost of incarcerating an inmate who is elderly is significantly higher than the average per inmate cost of incarceration.

9 In 1976, the U.S. Supreme Court ruled in *Estelle* v. *Gamble* that inmates have a constitutional right to reasonable, adequate health services for serious medical needs. However, the Court also made clear that such a right did not mean that prisoners have unqualified access to health care. The Civil Rights of Institutionalized Persons Act (CRIPA) places prisoners in a class with others confined in government institutions. In 1998, the U.S. Supreme Court held that state prisons fall squarely within the ADA's definition of a "public entity" and prohibits them from discriminating against a "qualified individual with a disability" because of that disability. Federal courts have ruled differently on whether segregation of inmates with HIV violates the inmate's rights to privacy and due pro-cess. A district court agreed, a circuit court of appeals disagreed. The federal courts have also recognized the right of inmates who are mentally ill to treatment.

KEY TERMS

inmates with special needs, p. 386

substance-abusing inmate, p. 386

therapeutic community (TC), p. 390

HIV (human immunodeficiency virus), p. 392

AIDS (acquired immunodeficiency syndrome), p. 392

tuberculosis (TB), p. 402

hospice, p. 404

syphilis, p. 407

gonorrhea, p. 407

chlamydia, p. 407

genital herpes, p. 407

Americans with Disabilities Act (ADA), p. 408

QUESTIONS FOR REVIEW

1 What defines an inmate with special needs?

2 Summarize the management problems that special-needs inmates pose for corrections officials.

3 What criteria would you use to assess the impact that substance abusers have on the corrections system?

4 How would you design a system that makes it easier to treat HIV in prison?

5 What ideas can you add to the five essential ele-ments of providing cost-effective management of HIV/AIDS inmates?

6 What evidence explains why there are so many inmates with mental illness in prison?

7 Suggest additional strategies for diverting persons with mental illness from the criminal justice system.

8 What should corrections do about the cost and health issues associated with older inmates?

9 Why is it important to understand the legal issues surrounding special population inmates?

THINKING CRITICALLY ABOUT CORRECTIONS

Aging Prison Population and Costs

As the prison population ages, the costs of incarcerating large numbers of older inmates will skyrocket. This, in turn, will strain correctional budgets and adversely impact correctional administrators' ability to provide essential services to the general prisoner population. Should inmates who are elderly be released from incarceration? Could services provided by other public agencies be tapped to meet the needs of inmates who are elderly? If so, which services might be invoked?

The Principle of Least Eligibility

Discussions of the principle of least eligibility invariably fire emotions. Should inmates rate free medical care that is not available to law-abiding citizens? Why or why not? Would you support a ballot proposal to formalize the principle of least eligibility as law in your state? Why or why not? If such a law were adopted, do you think it would withstand challenge through the state and federal court systems? Why or why not?

ON-THE-JOB DECISION MAKING

How to Use Personal Experience to Advance Correctional Training in HIV/AIDS

You are the warden of a state prison and on record as a supporter of the principle of least eligibility. Walter Edmunds is one of your most dependable correctional officers. Mature, calm, and unfailingly professional, Edmunds can be counted on in every crisis. You have come to rely on his leadership as a positive element among the correctional staff. Unfortunately, Edmunds has a young son dying of AIDS, which he contracted through a blood transfusion during an appendectomy.

Yesterday your medical staff conducted training for your correctional officers on procedures for handling inmates suffering from HIV and AIDS. About 10 minutes into the training session, Edmunds apologized for interrupting and then asked why the prisoners received top-notch medical treatment for free treatment that ordinary law-abiding citizens can't afford.

From that single question, things quickly deteriorated, and Edmunds became increasingly agitated. Before long, the training room was in turmoil as Edmunds's questions and angry comments whipped up the sympathy and anger of his fellow correctional officers.

Clearly out of his depth, the medical officer canceled the remainder of the training session and then bolted to your office. By the time he finished relating the incident, one of your correctional lieutenants appeared to report that the unionized correctional staff was in an uproar and threatening to walk off the job. What would you do to defuse this situation? Once you contained the crisis, how would you handle Edmunds?

Deciding Legitimate Penological Concerns

You are a correctional lieutenant at a state prison that has a conjugal visitation program. Carl Packard, one of your inmates, was recently diagnosed as HIV-positive. During an interview with a member of the medical staff, Packard acknowledged recent illicit drug use during which he shared a needle with other inmates. He and the medic believe this needle sharing to be the source of Packard's HIV infection.

Yesterday, Packard applied for a conjugal visit with his wife. You summoned him to your office and asked if he had advised his wife of his infection. Packard stated he had not and that he had no intention of "tellin' that bitch nothin'." This morning, you sought guidance from the prison's legal advisor and the warden. They informed you that infection with HIV did not prohibit an inmate's participation in the conjugal visitation program and that privacy policies prohibit you from informing Mrs. Packard of her husband's physical condition. You strongly believe that the threat to Mrs. Packard's health and safety outweighs what you consider to be ill-advised rules and policies.

1. What do you do?
2. What is your reasoning?

For additional information, please see: www.mhhe.com/schmalleger7e
Follow the author's tweets about the latest crime and justice news @schmalleger

Issues in Corrections

Part Five focuses on some of the most controversial debates in contemporary corrections. Prison overcrowding became a problem shortly after a wing of the Walnut Street Jail was converted into the world's first prison in 1790, and it continues to be a problem today. When prisons are overcrowded, safety is compromised and conditions for disturbances and riots ripen.

One way to control prison overcrowding is to build more prisons. Today, the federal government and some states are building supermax prisons to deal with inmates whose violent behavior makes it impossible for them to live among the general prison population. Other options to control prison overcrowding are accreditation, which mandates acceptable staff-inmate ratios; privatization, the goal of which is to turn institutions into cost-effective private businesses; and technology, which can reduce the number of people required to supervise a given inmate population.

The increase in attention to victims' rights has also changed the corrections landscape. Today, all states and the federal government have laws that establish, protect, and enforce victims' rights. However, as you will learn, victims' rights laws are unevenly applied and sometimes partially ignored. Would a constitutional amendment, as recommended by Congress and the president, result in more even application and enforcement?

Possibly no other corrections issue has received more attention than capital punishment. The watershed U.S. Supreme Court case *Furman* v. *Georgia* (1972) changed the way judges and juries impose the death penalty. New research on defendant–victim racial characteristics, execution of the innocent, and social consensus is sharpening the debate over capital punishment.

The face of juvenile corrections is also changing. The first juvenile court established in Cook County (Chicago, Illinois) in 1899 had high hopes for controlling and preventing delinquency. However, today society's response to rare yet high-profile juvenile offending means that the needs of the vast majority of juveniles who are arrested for nonviolent offenses are virtually ignored. There is no magic bullet to prevent delinquency, but there are correctional strategies and "best practices" that work. Implementing them will be up to you, the next generation of correctional professionals.

[13]

PRISON ISSUES AND CONCERNS

Overcrowding, Security, Accreditation, Privatization, and Technology

CHAPTER OBJECTIVES

After completing this chapter you should be able to do the following:

1. List the four main reasons prisons are overcrowded.

2. Identify six methods of controlling prison overcrowding.

3. Explain how prisons control the influence of security threat groups (STGs).

4. Identify five causes of prison riots.

5. Describe what can be done to prevent prison riots.

6. Outline the emergence of supermax housing and its impact on prisoners and staff.

7. Describe "no-frills" jails and prisons and their impact on corrections.

8. List the reasons that correctional agencies and facilities should be accredited.

9. List the arguments for and against privatization.

10. Discuss the impact of technology on corrections.

When the door is locked against the prisoner, we do not think about what is behind it. [But] were we to enter the hidden world of punishment, we should be startled by what we see. One day in prison is longer than almost any day you and I have had to endure.

—Supreme Court Associate Justice Anthony Kennedy, address to the American Bar Association,

August 2003

The vast majority of public jails and prisons in the United States have contracts with the private sector to provide services such as medical and mental health care, educational and/or vocational programming, food preparation, and facility maintenance. Most of the time, there is no controversy about those arrangements. However, as you will learn later in this chapter, the idea of having governments transfer complete management of jails and prisons to private correctional agencies is highly controversial.

In the fall of 2012, David Cameron, Prime Minister of the United Kingdom, shocked the private prison industry by announcing that owners of private prisons who fail to stop prisoners from reoffending will be fined.[1] He went on to say that the private prison industry will receive full fees only if reconviction rates fall by 5 percent within one year of release. So far, "payment by results" has not been a criterion in the United States. It may be on the horizon, however, because governments are strapped for cash and pressured to show the public that the $63 billion spent on corrections each year is lowering the rates of rearrest and reconviction. So far, private prison lobbyists in the United States have been able to stave off the payments by results movement, claiming it is unethical to require more of the private sector than the public sector. If government agencies aren't held to the same standard, the argument goes, why should the private sector be held to a higher standard? The economic realties impacting corrections and discussed in every chapter of this book will shape the privatization debate and perhaps require both the public sector *and* the private sector to produce better results. Weigh what will happen to rates of rearrest and reconviction if payment by results is not on the horizon as you explore six other important aspects of the prison environment: overcrowding, riots and violence, supermax housing, "no-frills" prisons and jails, accreditation, and technocorrections.

In the fall of 2012, David Cameron, Prime Minister of the United Kingdom, shocked the private prison industry by announcing that private prison owners who fail to stop prisoners from reoffending will be fined. "Payment by results" has not been a criterion used in the United States. Do you think it should be? Why?

OVERCROWDING

In the past, a prison was often referred to as "the big house." Today, however, a more appropriate description is "the full house." Over the past 25 years, prison population has increased sixfold—from 240,000 to almost 1.6 million. Some say that prisons are "capacity driven"; that is, if you cut the ribbon, they are full. Saying exactly how full, though, is difficult because each state has its own method for measuring prison capacity. Four states and the federal BOP use rated capacity only (the number of beds in a facility), 9 states use operational capacity only (the number of inmates that can be accommodated based on a facility's staff and existing programs and services), and 4 use design capacity only (the number of inmates that planners intended the facility to house).[2] The problem is compounded because 32 jurisdictions use more than one definition, and some have their own definitions. In spite of the differences, by any measure today's prisons are overcrowded. At yearend 2012, 18 states and the BOP were operating prison systems above 100 percent of their maximum reported facility capacity.[3]

CO13-1 Why Are Prisons Overcrowded?

Prisons are overcrowded for four main reasons. The first is a continuous increase in the number of people sent to prison. In 2000, 1,391,261 persons were in state and federal prisons. At yearend 2012, that number had increased to almost 1.6 million, an average annual increase of 1.8 percent.

The second reason is that offenders now serve a larger portion of their sentences. The amount of time served has increased from an average of 22 months for prisoners released in 1990 to 57 months for those released in 2004.[4] Sentencing laws changed, reducing the difference between the sentence imposed and the actual time served and restricting the possibility of early release from prison. Jurisdictions began to depart from the prevailing approach, known as *indeterminate sentencing* (broad authorized sentencing ranges, parole release, and case-by-case decision making), in the mid-1970s (see Chapter 3). Today the trend in many jurisdictions is toward determinate sentencing—a fixed term of incarceration and no possibility of parole. In addition, most jurisdictions have adopted one or more of the following sentencing approaches: mandatory minimum sentences, three-strikes laws, or truth-in-sentencing laws requiring offenders to serve mandated percentages of imposed sentences (see Chapter 3).

The third reason prisons are overcrowded is that many incoming prisoners are drug users, not the drug dealers the tougher drug laws were designed to capture. The goal of tougher drug laws was to arrest and convict drug dealers, thereby reducing drug use and the drug-related crime rate. This goal has not been achieved. As we pointed out in Chapter 12, the majority of persons sentenced to prison for drug offenses are low-level, nonviolent offenders, primarily street-level dealers and couriers, not the kingpins or major traffickers the laws were written for. One in four drug offenders sentenced to prison in New York has been convicted of simple possession.[5]

However, as a sign of how far and how fast attitudes about the recreational use of drugs such as marijuana are changing, citizens in Colorado and Washington voted in November 2012 to legalize the sale and possession of marijuana for recreational use by adults. When Seattle interim police chief Jim Pugel addressed the annual Cannabis Freedom March on Saturday, May 11, 2013, he told the crowd, "We are not here to condemn it. We are not here to endorse it. We are here to make sure it is all done legally."[6] Later he told a *Seattle Times* reporter that he could never have imagined addressing such a gathering in his career. In fact, earlier in Pugel's career, he worked as an undercover police officer arresting people for buying marijuana that then carried a one- to three-year sentence. Time will tell what impact such new laws will have on prison crowding.

The fourth reason prisons are overcrowded is a trend some people call the "prison industrial complex." Private corporations have a real estate investment in the prisons they build and operate. Correctional officers' unions are expanding in many states and securing the use of incarceration into the future. Rural communities such as Del Norte, California—a remote, impoverished county in the northwest corner of the state with an unemployment rate of more than 20 percent and all of its industries severely depressed since the 1980s—negotiated successfully with the California Department of Corrections to build Pelican Bay State Prison, one of the nation's largest state prisons. States have had an incentive to incarcerate because the 1994 crime bill provided matching funds to states to keep violent offenders in prison longer by denying them parole and requiring that they serve at least 85 percent of their sentence. However as we reported in Chapter 7, the prison industrial complex has also been affected by today's economic realities, and today states are spending less on corrections and more on justice reinvestment. Since 2011, at least 33 states have either reported prison closures and reduced prison capacity or are contemplating doing so.

What Are the Consequences of Prison Overcrowding?

Researchers and prison administrators routinely observe the consequences of prison overcrowding. In September 2012, the U.S. Government Accountability Office (GAO) published a report focusing on the impact of overcrowding on inmates, staff, infrastructure, and safety and security in the nation's 117 federal prisons.[7] In brief, the report found:

1. The BOP uses double and triple bunking in excess, bringing together inmates for longer periods of time, increasing the risk of violence and of potential victims.

2. In addition to overcrowding in the prisons' housing and common areas (e.g., television rooms), inmates experience overcrowded bathroom facilities, reductions in shower times, and shortened meal times in addition to longer waits for food service and more limited recreational activities.

3. 11 to 12 percent of federal inmates are on waiting lists to enter literacy programs.

4. Some 7,000 federal inmates are on a waiting list to enter a substance abuse program (depending on a person's security level, the wait may be anywhere from 80 to 205 days).

5. Overcrowding in federal prisons means fewer opportunities to engage in meaningful work, resulting in inmate idleness, additional tension, and fighting; that discord then affects the security and safety of other inmates and staff; the decline in the number of UNICOR jobs noted first in Chapter 7 has also resulted in waiting lists.

6. Overcrowded visiting rooms make it difficult for inmates to visit with their families, and a facility's infrastructure and staff resources may not support the increase in visitors as a result of the expanded prison population. Limited visiting capacity and larger numbers of inmates lead to frustrations for inmates and visitors.

7. Overcrowding limits inmate access to telephone calls and computer emails.

The Staff Speaks
Visit www.mhhe.com/schmalleger7e to see this feature.

Visit http://video.pbs.org/video/1945093979 or scan this code with the QR app on your SmartPhone or digital device and watch the PBS documentary discuss the United Supreme Court's decision that ordered California to reduce its overcrowded prisons. How does this information relate to ideas discussed in this chapter?

Although new prison facilities are being built, crowding continues to be an issue in many places. The auditorium of the Deuel Vocational Institution in Tracy, California, is converted into a dormitory to house prisoners. The prison has a design capacity of 1,681 but an operating capacity of 3,748. How is realignment affecting California's prison overcrowding?

8. Because of overcrowding, correctional officers don't have time to use core correctional skills with inmates who choose not to discuss personal problems in front of other inmates.

9. An increase in inmates results in heightened water usage for heating, laundry, showers, toilets, sanitation, and food service; the BOP is the *largest* energy and water consumer in the entire Department of Justice. Its energy bill alone jumped from $79 million in 2005 to more than $107 million in 2011.

10. Overcrowding affects inmate conduct and the imposition of discipline, thereby affecting security and safety; the most frequently imposed sanctions are loss of privileges, disallowance of good time credit, and segregation.

11. Overcrowding may also result in a critical incident (e.g., assaults on staff by several inmates or a food or work strike), which could lead to a facility lockdown—a temporary situation in which all inmates are confined to their cells. Almost 4,000 lockdowns were reported from 2006 through 2011; the number increased from 2006 through 2009, peaking at 1,042 that year and then declining to 824 in 2011.

Prisons Under Court Order Every five to seven years, the U.S. Department of Justice's Bureau of Justice Statistics conducts a census of state and federal adult correctional facilities. The census provides detailed information on the types of inmates housed, facility age and type, building plans, security level, court orders, programs, facility operations and security conditions, confinement space, and staff characteristics. The last census, published in 2008, found that there were fewer public and private prisons under federal court order than there had been in 2000. The number of prisons under federal court order or consent decree to limit the size of their inmate population declined from 145 in 2000 to 44 in 2005, from 119 public and 26 private prisons in 2000 to 21 public and 23 private in 2005. Prisons under federal court order or consent decree for specific conditions also declined from 320 to 218, from 303 public and 17 private prisons in 2000 to 190 public and 28 private prisons in 2005.[8] Among the reasons prisons are under federal court order are to reduce crowding; improve inmate visiting, mail, and telephone privileges; accommodate prisoners who are physically challenged; permit religious expression; and offer mental health treatment.

One court order in particular has all state departments of corrections on alert. As discussed in Chapter 6, after almost two decades of litigation in lower state and federal courts, the U.S. Supreme Court ruled in 2011 that serious overcrowding in California's prisons violated the Constitution's ban on cruel and unusual punishment. It ordered California to reduce its prison population by more than 30,000 inmates. Is this a wake-up call for other states with serious prison overcrowding? Some say that Justice

Anthony Kennedy's 52-page Supreme Court opinion was fact specific and may be narrower than prisoner advocates hoped. However, others, including David Fathi, director of the American Civil Liberties Union's National Prison Project, believe that the Court's opinion is a helpful precedent and signals that the federal courts will step in when necessary to enforce essential rights of prisoners.[9] California has responded to the Court's order with realignment legislation discussed in Chapter 6. Under realignment, newly convicted low-level offenders without current or prior serious violent offenses stay in county jail to serve their sentence.

Prison Sexual Violence Another serious consequence of prison overcrowding is sexual violence, which includes nonconsensual sexual acts (considered the most serious form of sexual assault), abusive sexual assault, staff sexual misconduct, and staff sexual harassment.

The Prison Rape Elimination Act (PREA) of 2003 discussed in Chapter 10 requires the Bureau of Justice Statistics to perform a comprehensive statistical review and analysis of the incidents and effects of sexual victimization for each calendar year.

In June 2012, the BJS released its annual report based on 18,526 completed interviews with former inmates under active community supervision.[10]

Among the findings are these:

- An estimated 9.6 percent of former state prisoners reported one or more incidents of sexual victimization during their most recent period of incarceration in a jail, prison, and post-release community treatment facility.

- Among all former state prisoners, 1.8 percent reported experiencing one or more incidents while in a local jail, 7.5 percent while in a state prison, and 0.1 percent while in a postrelease community treatment facility.

- About 5.4 percent of former state prisoners reported an incident involving another inmate, and 5.3 percent reported an incident involving facility staff.

- An estimated 1.2 percent of former prisoners reported that they unwillingly had sex or sexual contact with facility staff, and 4.6 percent reported that they "willingly" had sex or sexual contact with staff.

- More than three-quarters of all reported staff sexual misconduct involved a male inmate with female staff. Among former state prisoners, the rate of inmate-on-inmate sexual victimization was at least three times higher for females (13.7 percent) than males (4.2 percent).

- Among heterosexual males, an estimated 3.5 percent reported being sexually victimized by another inmate. In comparison, among males who were bisexual, 34 percent reported being sexually victimized by another inmate. Among males who were homosexual or gay, 39 percent reported being victimized by another inmate.

- Rates of sexual victimization did not vary based on commonly cited characteristics of facilities, including size or age of facility, crowding, inmate-to-staff ratios, or gender composition of staff.

- Among male former inmates, inmate-on-inmate and staff-on-inmate victimization rates were higher in facilities under a court order or consent decree, in facilities reporting a major disturbance in the 12 months prior to the most recent facility census, in facilities with medium or greater security levels, and in facilities with a primary function of housing general population than rates in facilities without these characteristics.

- Among female former inmates, rates of inmate-on-inmate victimization were lower in community corrections centers, in facilities that permitted 50 percent or more of their inmates to leave unaccompanied during the day, in minimum or low security facilities, and in privately operated facilities than in facilities without these characteristics.

- Following their release from prison, 72 percent of victims of inmate-on-inmate sexual victimization indicated they felt shame or humiliation, and 56 percent said they felt guilt. Seventy-nine percent of unwilling victims of staff sexual misconduct said they felt shame or humiliation, and 72 percent said they felt guilt.

In September 2008, after nine days of public hearings, a federal review panel released a list of 32 best practices for preventing sexual assaults in correctional facilities.[11] Among the recommendations are:

1. Make prevention of sexual assault a high and unequivocal priority and institute a zero tolerance policy conveyed from the top down.

2. Consider the risk of sexual predation or victimization of inmates when making inmate housing assignments.

3. Install video cameras in places where assaults are likely to occur.

4. Have independent investigators conduct or at least oversee any investigation of sexual victimization.

5. Limit those who participate in or observe strip searches of inmates to correctional officers of the same sex as the inmate.

6. Train staff members in how childhood abuse, sexual abuse, and other trauma affect and ultimately surface among male and female inmates.

7. Train staff in the requirements of the PREA and the prison system's sexual assault policies.

8. Offer higher pay to prison staff in order to better attract and retain recruits and to retain experienced staff.

9. Establish a telephone hotline for inmates to report threats and sexual victimization confidentially and directly to the office of prosecutor or system inspector general.

10. Implement a peer training program in which appropriately selected and trained inmates teach new inmates about how to avoid sexual victimization and how to report threats and assaults.

11. Ban pornography, especially for those inmates who have a history of sexual assault or are assessed as being at a high risk of becoming sexual predators.

12. Reduce prison overcrowding.

13. Replace inmate idleness with work and programming.

CO13-2 How Can Prison Overcrowding Be Controlled?

In most jurisdictions across the United States today, we find at least six methods of controlling prison overcrowding:

1. Reduce the number of people going to prison.

2. Release the less dangerous to make room for the more dangerous.

3. Change prison or jail sentences to community-related sentences.

4. Increase the number of releases.

5. Expand existing prison capacity or build new prisons.

6. Implement an overall program of structured sentencing.

The first four methods are referred to as *front-end, trap-door, side-door,* and *back-end* strategies, respectively (see Chapter 5).

The fifth method of controlling prison overcrowding is the most commonly considered—build more prisons. For the past 25 years, political leaders have addressed public concerns about crime by devoting unprecedented financial resources to the construction of prisons. The number of prisons increased from 1,160 in 1995 to 2,236 today. In 1990, the nation's prisons cost \$12 billion.[12] Today it's more than \$63 billion.[13]

However, the fiscal crisis that began in 2007 is changing the face of corrections. To balance their budgets, we've pointed out previously that governors are looking at corrections—the fastest-growing segment of state budgets, second only to Medicaid. Ten years ago, it would have been unthinkable for governors to propose slowing prison growth, closing institutions, or putting a moratorium on building new ones, but today all areas of public spending are being looked at for possible savings. Many people today are echoing what Ryan Sherman, a spokesperson for the powerful California corrections officer union said on January 3, 2011, "The state cannot build its way out of the overcrowding prison problem. If they build more beds, we will fill up more beds and continue to be overcrowded. Until we figure out how to reform and reorganize the department so it's efficient and accountable, and take into consideration the limited budget and what's best for the state, I don't anticipate anything improving a great deal."[14]

Instead of new construction, the majority of states today are engaged with one or more of the following ways to reduce corrections spending:

- making more use of use evidence-based corrections;
- applying justice reinvestment (an approach to reduce corrections spending and reinvest savings in strategies that can decrease crime and strengthen neighborhoods);
- sentencing reform;
- creating alternatives for "prison bound" offenders;
- reducing time served in prison;
- speeding early release;
- adopting risk assessment instruments to aid parole boards in considering release issues;
- reducing revocations;
- reducing personnel costs;
- downsizing or eliminating programs;
- closing and/or selling facilities;
- changing food services;
- implementing new technology;
- exploring strategies to save on energy costs;
- diverting more offenders to drug courts;
- establishing medical parole for terminally ill prisoners;
- considering parole for aging people;
- instituting more "good time" policies;
- implementing or expanding work release, intermediate sanctions, and community corrections; and
- reducing barriers to successful reentry.

Many states are looking closely at what Texas—a state known for its "tough-on-crime" approach and its "lock-'em-up-and-throw-away-the-key" attitude—has done to reduce its prison population and halt plans for prison expansion. Texas addressed three key areas:

1. **In prison.** Knowing that many prison sentences and repeat offenses result from drug crimes, Texas offered substance-abuse treatment in jail and prison and put some prisoners in treatment after being released.

2. **During parole and probation.** Many inmates who commit minor infractions while on parole end up back in prison. Texas created detention centers to provide supervised housing to punish those offenders without sending them to prison.

3. **After prison.** Many former inmates fail to adjust successfully to life outside and end up committing more crimes. Texas built residential treatment centers and halfway houses to help former prisoners with the transition.

Texas spent several hundred million dollars to develop these programs initially. The changes are expected to avoid the costs of building more prisons, reduce the correctional budget by $210 million, and result in an additional savings of $233 million.[15]

The sixth method of controlling prison overcrowding is the use of sentencing guidelines that are designed to save prison beds for more serious crimes and violent offenses. Structured sentencing is a compromise between indeterminate sentencing and mandatory determinate sentencing (see Chapter 3). Guidelines were conceived as a way to guide judicial discretion in sentencing.

structured sentencing

A set of guidelines for determining an offender's sentence.

Under **structured sentencing,** a commission creates a set of guidelines that consider both the severity of a current offense and a few personal characteristics of the offender (notably, a prior criminal record). Sentencing commissions take a wide range of forms from mere advisory panels to bodies that have the full, legislatively delegated force of law to establish a state's sentencing guidelines. The commissions gather facts and figures on whom their states are incarcerating, why, and for how long. The stronger commissions use the information to develop guidelines and grid charts that seek to prioritize prison bed space for the most serious offenders and require judges to spell out their reasons if they depart from the sentencing recommendations. Today 21 states, the federal government, and the District of Columbia have sentencing commissions.[16]

A jurisdiction establishing structured sentencing might consider implementing nonprison options such as interchangeability of punishments, also called **exchange rates.** A sentencing commission might, for example, decide that three days under house arrest or 40 community service hours is equivalent to one day of incarceration or that three years under intensive supervision is equivalent to one year in prison.[17]

exchange rates

An approach to sentencing that emphasizes interchangeability of punishments; for example, three days under house arrest might be considered equal to one day of incarceration.

PRISON SECURITY

For prisoners, staff, and their families on the outside, nothing is more frightening than a prison gang confrontation, a prison riot, or a natural disaster involving a prison.

Prison Gangs—Security Threat Groups

Prison gangs are among the most significant developments in American prisons since the existence of the Gypsy Jokers Motorcycle Club was first recorded at the Walla Walla, Washington, penitentiary in 1950.

To eliminate any publicity that gang members may draw about their gang or its activities and to describe accurately how these gangs negatively impact the security of prison operations, experts refer to them as **security threat groups (STGs)**. An STG is an inmate group, gang, organization, or association that has a name or identifying signs, colors, clothing, shoes, hair, tatoos, hand signs, associations, scars, language/codes, or symbols and whose members or associates engage in a pattern of gang activity or departmental rule violation to pose a threat to the staff, to public safety, to the secure and orderly operation of a correctional institution, or to other inmates. Most STGs were founded along racial and ethnic lines to offer inmates protection, but today many of them have joined alliances with other STGs to conduct organized criminal activity such as drug trafficking, prostitution, assault, or extortion. Research shows that STG members are five times more likely to incite or be involved in prison violence than are nonmembers and twice as likely to perpetuate assault within the first three years of incarceration when compared to inmates not affiliated with an STG. STG activity is a reflection of the intricacies that corrections professionals must contend with on a daily basis.[18]

Recently, Mark Pitcavage, a historian and expert on race-based STGs, conducted a study of contemporary prison STGs. His interview with the Southern Poverty Law Center's *Intelligence Report* is presented in Exhibit 13–1.

In 2002, the National Major Gang Task Force (NMGTF) surveyed all adult prison systems in the United States, Guam, Puerto Rico, the U.S. Virgin Islands, and Canada. With almost 80 percent responding, NMGTF identified more than 1,600 STGs with a total estimated membership of almost 114,000 inmates. By 2009, the percentage of known STG membership had spiked to more than 356,000 inmates. Montana reports the lowest percentage of STGs (less than 1 percent), and Oklahoma reports the highest (70 percent). On average, 14 percent of a state's prison population is STG.[19]

Six major STGs in the United States are recognized nationally for their participation in organized crime and violence. They are:[20]

1. *Aryan Brotherhood:* Originated in 1967 in California's San Quentin Prison, its racial makeup is white.
2. *Black Guerilla Family:* Founded in 1966 at San Quentin Prison and considered the most politically oriented of the major state prison STGs, its racial makeup is black.
3. *Mexican Mafia:* Formed in the late 1950s in California's youth facility at Duel, its racial makeup is Mexican American/Hispanic.
4. *La Nuestra Familia:* Originated in the California state prison at Soledad in the mid-1960s, its racial makeup is Mexican American/Hispanic.
5. *Neta:* Established in 1970 in the Rio Piedras Prison, Puerto Rico, its racial makeup is Puerto Rican American/Hispanic.
6. *Texas Syndicate:* Originated in California's Folsom prison in the early 1970s in direct response to the other California prison gangs (notably the Aryan Brotherhood and the Mexican Mafia), which were attempting to prey on native Texas inmates, its racial makeup is Mexican American/Hispanic.

New among the STGs is an influx of street gangs, such as Mara Salvatrucha 13 (MS-13) composed mostly of Salvadorans, Hondurans, Guatemalans, and Nicaraguans, Miami's "112 Avenue Boys," and Boston's "Franklin Field Pistons," that have less national organization than

security threat groups (STGs)
The current term for prison gangs that describes how they negatively impact the security of prison operations.

Visit http://www.youtube.com/watch?v=_9Ll5hCFnVk or scan this code with the QR app on your SmartPhone or digital device and watch the podcast of the top ten prison gangs in the United States. How does this information relate to ideas discussed in this chapter?

EXHIBIT 13–1   "Behind the Walls: An Expert Discusses the Role of Race-Based Gangs in America's Prisons"

An Interview with Mark Pitcavage

Intelligence Report (IR): Why do prisoners join gangs?
Mark Pitcavage (MP): Prison gangs offer protection—and money and drugs. Some offer ideology, racial or otherwise, but protection is the key.

IR: Is virtually every prisoner affiliated?
MP: No, no. A lot of prisoners never become affiliated. It all depends on the prison. If you're talking about a minimum security prison, you're not going to see much of that. In maximum security prisons, you see much more gang activity.

In state prisons, where many inmates are serving long sentences, there is a great deal of gang activity. There are gangs in federal prisons, too. Some gangs even have federal and state prison chapters. But even in state prison, where there is generally more activity, a minority of prisoners will belong.

IR: What are the largest prison gangs?
MP: The most prominent white supremacist gangs are the Aryan Brotherhood, the Aryan Circle, the Nazi Low Riders, and the Peckerwoods. There are racist black groups, like the Black Guerilla Family, the Five Percenters, and the Moorish Science Temple. And major Hispanic gangs include the Mexican Mafia (known as "la eme," for its first letter) and La Nuestra Familia. And basically apolitical street gangs like the Crips and the Bloods are inside the prisons, too.

IR: Did something occur to help promote these gangs' growth?
MP: Many prison populations were desegregated during the 1960s, and one result was that many inmates felt they had to join a race-based gang for protection. If white prisoners and black prisoners were separated, then that would not be an issue. [*IR Editor's note: Some states have actually resegregated certain cell blocks as a security measure meant to weaken race-based gangs.*]

But the key to the Aryan Brotherhood—and the key to understanding virtually all prison gangs—is that ideology often takes a back seat to organized criminal activity. The Aryan Brotherhood is an organized crime group—that is the primary dynamic behind it. It's all about drugs, protection rackets, prostitution, extortion, witness intimidation, assaults, etc.

In many prisons, the Aryan Brotherhood actually makes alliances with gangs of other races. If they were ideological white supremacists, they wouldn't do that. That is why a lot of people who join race-based prison gangs while in prison don't stay with them once they're out or join other white supremacist groups. They just aren't primarily ideologically motivated.

IR: There was a major federal bust of 40 members of the Aryan Brotherhood, 30 in prison and 10 on the outside, in October 2002. A central allegation was that members killed or attempted to kill people inside and outside the prisons in order to control drug trafficking, gambling, and extortion. How do prisoners reach outside the walls to control or influence activity that involves the free world?
MP: There are a lot of ways you can pass on information from the prisons. Wives and girlfriends of prisoners often play an important role. The Aryan Circle, for example, uses its female supporters on the outside, who they call *sisters,* to conduct business operations and spread racist propaganda. And you can always meet privately with your attorney, who may be willing to carry messages to someone else on the outside. There are ways. If you are in a maximum-security prison or in administrative isolation, it obviously is more difficult.

IR: You note in your report that the men who murdered James Byrd Jr. in the Jasper, Texas, truck-dragging incident had developed their racial beliefs while behind bars. What is the link between incarceration and politicization?
MP: Exactly what dynamic occurs varies with each particular individual, but there are some universals. Prisoners have a lot of time on their hands, and as a result they are desperate for reading materials. They are desperate for stimulation. Some of them are just fine with pumping weights, but others aren't and seek out extremist publications as well as nonextremist publications. You see prisoners asking for free subscriptions, for correspondence, for people to send them materials, anything. They may not be ideological at that point, but they want something—and the material they get can lead to their politicization.

Another thing is that many prisoners want to justify or rationalize what they have done or what has happened to them. They don't want to say they did something wrong or deserved what they got. This is true whether you are black or white. By adopting a particular ideological slant, you can rationalize that you are not a simple criminal, that you are in jail for political reasons.

Left-wing extremists have rationalized bank robberies as expropriations from the state. A right-wing prisoner rationalizes his crime as fighting back against ZOG [or "Zionist Occupied

---

traditional STGs and do not easily fit into standard prison gang categories because of their smaller numbers, fewer cohesive ties, and less organized methods of operation.

CO13-3   STGs have a profound impact on prison security, and many prisons today have a security threat group unit that is responsible for the identification and overall coordination of all STG-related information at their facilities. In an attempt to control STG influence, some prison administrators have transferred known STG members from one institution to another only to find that this practice actually increased STG organization and activity—it extended the STG's influence throughout a state's prison

EXHIBIT 13–1	**"Behind the Walls: An Expert Discusses the Role of Race-Based Gangs in America's Prisons"** *(continued)*

Government," a term used by many neo-Nazis]—and he will be backed up morally by white supremacist publications.

The ideologies offer an excuse and a sense of empowerment that allows someone in jail to be transformed from a criminal into a "prisoner of war" or "political prisoner."

IR: Are there other benefits for prisoners?

MP: If you join a movement, you can receive all kinds of benefits from outside people in the movement. A lot of left-wing groups do serious prisoner support, sending you gifts or money, raising funds for your defense. They may write you letters, put up Web pages about you, and so on. Many right-wing groups do the same, setting up "prison ministries." Often young women are encouraged to write to male prisoners, something that is seen as a terrifically important benefit.

This can play out well for prisoners who get out. They enter a world where they are heroes. They are ex-"POWS," liberated "political prisoners" who can tell the youngsters outside what it's all about. As such, they have access to women, drugs, all kinds of things.

IR: How do outside groups recruit in the prisons?

MP: Sending materials and writing letters are the most common ways. Sometimes visits are used. Prisoners are lonely and have often been abandoned by their friends and family. Extremists capitalize on those feelings.

IR: Who decides what literature gets into prison?

MP: They're called security threat group analysts. The federal level has a whole bunch of them. On the state level, they may be substantial or sometimes just a few who monitor activities in all the prisons in a given state. They look at all the materials coming in and out of prison to see if they are allowable or if they are linked to extremism, street gangs, organized crime, violence and so on. If they identify a prisoner as a member of one of these groups, they may be able to take additional measures against him, such as placing him in administrative segregation. They have fairly wide latitude.

IR: Is there a relationship between getting recruited into these racist groups and then committing hate crimes or other violence after leaving prison?

MP: My suspicion is that there is probably not a huge link, because a lot of these people just join the gangs while they are in prison, and then leave them when they get out. But the fact is that some prisoners do get genuinely politicized, and on top of that, prison gives them an education in violence. It's a mess. I think that is what happened in Texas (with the murderers of James Byrd Jr.), and the result was one of the most inhumane acts ever perpetrated in modern America.

IR: Is there a significant distinction between those who come into prison without much racial awareness, like the men who killed James Byrd, and extremists who enter prison already highly politicized?

MP: People who are already ideologically extreme don't stop their activities in prison—some of them see prison as a great opportunity for recruiting. Take Leroy Schweitzer, the Montana Freeman (a form of "sovereign citizen") leader who's in federal prison in South Carolina serving a 22-year sentence for various financial scams. He's teaching prisoners how to engage in "paper terrorism," how to file bogus liens against public officials, attorneys, and others. He even showed one jewel dealer serving a 40-year sentence on money laundering charges how to file a (bogus) $1.5 billion lien against the judge in his case.

Other imprisoned ideologues try to influence followers outside of prison. Craig "Critter" Marshall, environmental extremist serving a five-year sentence for conspiracy to commit arson, told *Earth First!* readers last year that the only form of solidarity he wants is more arsons. He wrote something like, "When someone picks up a bomb, instead of a pen, is when my spirits really soar."

IR: How much of a threat do these gangs pose to prison staff?

MP: Prisons are dangerous. I don't know whether the violence from gang members is greater than that of nongang members, although obviously there is a greater potential for planned or organized violence. But there is a lot of training for this sort of thing now—prisons in general have better control mechanisms, whether it is cameras, doors that can automatically shut, or special training. But that doesn't stop prisoners from killing each other all the time—and it doesn't stop guards from being assaulted. Let's face it, prisons are nasty places.

Source: Excerpt from Mark Pitcavage, "Behind the Walls: An Expert Discusses the Role of Race-Based Gangs in America's Prisons," *Intelligence Report,* Winter 2002, Vol. 108, pp. 24–27. Copyright © 2002 Southern Poverty Law Center. Used with permission.

system. Other states enacted "gang enhancement" statutes that imposed severe sentences on STG activity. Today, many states are adopting a new strategy, segregating known STG members to highly restrictive supermax housing, correctional facilities that are designed to house the "worst of the worst" prisoners under complete lockdown and total isolation. Advocates of this approach contend that removing STG leaders from the general prison population reduces the amount of control that STG leaders exert.

However, blunting the power base of an STG by dispersing its members to other prison facilities may come at a high cost. On March 19, 2013, Tom Clements, Colorado's chief of corrections, was shot and killed when he opened the front door of his home. The investigation into the shooting continues, but evidence is mounting that the gunman was believed to be Evan Ebel, a member of the STG "211 Crew." Ebel had been released on January 28, 2013, directly into the streets after almost six years in solitary confinement. Investigators are trying to sort out whether Clements' death was ordered by an in-prison "shot caller" (a 211 crew superior who can order gang-sanctioned hits from inside prison) or the act of a lone gunman whose years in solitary confinement may have nurtured paranoia and a hatred of prison officials.

Two explanations for STG development are deprivation and importation. As noted in Chapter 10, the basic premise of deprivation theory is that inmates develop a social system as a way to adapt to the pains of imprisonment. Because inmates are deprived of liberty, autonomy, goods and services, sexual relations, and security, they develop a culture that helps them get back what imprisonment has taken away. Importation theory, on the other hand, emphasizes that inmates' preprison attitudes and values guide their reactions and responses to the internal conditions of prison. Both theories are valid; most major STGs can be traced to preprison attitudes and values, but prison conditions influence when and to what extent STG activity and violence occur.

Besides STGs, there is another kind of threat to prison security today. It's the threat posed by radicalized prisoners. For example, Sheikh Omar Abdel Rahman, the blind sheikh who is serving a life sentence in New York for conspiring to bomb a number of New York landmarks, was accused of sending messages from prison through visiting attorneys to members of Gama'a al-Islamiyya, Egypt's largest militant group.

Mark Hamm, professor of criminology at Indiana State University, recently completed a study for the National Institute of Justice on prisoner radicalization and profiled the case of Kevin Lamar James.[21] James and three other men pleaded guilty to conspiracy to wage war against the United States for plotting to attack U.S. military facilities, Israeli government facilities, and Jewish synagogues in Los Angeles. As a teenager, James was a member of the 76th Street Crips in Los Angeles. When he was 21, he was sentenced to 10 years in prison for robbery. In prison, he followed the beliefs of the Nation of Islam. Finding those beliefs uninteresting, he embraced the teachings of Jam'iyyat UI-Islam Is-Saheed (the Assembly of Authentic Islam), or JIS, whose message says it is the duty of Muslims to violently attack enemies of Islam, including the U.S. government.

By 2004, James had several dozen followers. One of those, Levar Washington, was ready for parole. James directed Washington to recruit five people without felony records from the community, acquire firearms, and find people with explosives expertise. James's plan was to attack a target of the Iraq war—a U.S. Army recruiting office—on September 11, 2005, four years to the day after the 9/11 attacks. James directed the attack from his prison cell even though the outside group lived in an apartment in Los Angeles. However, when

Our knowledge of female gang members lags behind what we know about male gang members. What are the reasons for this lack of attention?

one of the outside members dropped his cell phone at a gas station robbery, it led to the indictment of James and the three men.

Professor Hamm found that moving from religious radicalization to terrorism can be prevented by hiring prison chaplains, diversifying corrections personnel, training staff on the recruitment activities of gangs, and increasing our research base on prison culture that leads to radicalization and terrorist recruitment. "When there is a shortage of chaplains to provide religious guidance, into that void comes inmates with exotic religious messages," says Hamm.[22]

Can gang members change? Gabriel Morales, founder of Gang Prevention Services in Seattle, says "yes." In November 2008, he told a reporter with the *Seattle Post-Intelligencer* that his brother, a former gang member, changed at age 40.[23] "He was a gang member," Morales told the reporter. "He had no teeth—his bones were brittle. He looked a lot older than me though he was younger. He got tired of it. He had a kid, and he got tired of his kid seeing him when he was locked up and crying and missing Daddy. It broke his heart. He had to change his heart before he changed his mind."

The evidence-based literature confirms Morales's point. Researchers James Byrne and Don Hummer remind us that "changing" inmate behavior rather than simply "controlling" it is key.[24] Classification systems that are control based may predict STG involvement, but they will not reduce criminal activity. Classification systems that focus on offenders' participation in prison programming and cognitive behavioral treatment are the most effective prison violence reduction strategies. Finding the optimal "tipping point" in oneself is the key. For Morales's brother, it happened when he saw his kid unhappy at seeing his dad locked up. That changed his heart and his thinking about criminal gang activity.

Female Gangs—Security Threat Groups

Male gang offenders have received most of the attention in the corrections literature, but acknowledging that female offenders also become involved in gangs is also important. Female participation in STGs creates a set of challenges similar to those of their male counterparts. Because women represent only 7 percent of the prison population, they have been relegated to the periphery of correctional research. This lack of attention occurs for several possible reasons.[25] First, relatively few gangs have an exclusive female membership (most women belong to blended or coed STGs). Second, women's roles may be temporary or on the periphery (as associates rather than full members). And third, given the low number of female STG members, correctional and law enforcement officials could place a high priority on the investigation of male STG members.

In 2011, Canadian researchers analyzed a database of 337 female inmates that the Correctional Service of Canada identified as gang members. The researchers matched the gang members with 337 female inmates who were not gang members to understand whether gang members were more likely to violate institutional rules than their nonaffiliated counterparts. Among their findings are the following:[26]

1. About half of both groups were single.
2. Most of the offenders were white.
3. 4 of 10 gang members and almost 3 of 10 nongang members were Canadian aboriginals.
4. Almost one-half of STG members were full members.

5. Of the one-half of STG members classified as associates, those who have less formal attachments may be more likely to renounce or leave the gang.

6. Convictions for drug-related crimes were the main offense for both gang members and nonaffiliated women.

7. Gang members were more likely to have a prior conviction as a youth or adult.

8. More female gang inmates than nongang inmates had previously been incarcerated (65 percent and 49 percent, respectively).

9. Gang members had a higher rate of prior convictions than nongang members for homicide or attempted homicide, sexual offenses, robbery, drug offenses, and organized crime.

10. The number of incidents of institutional misconduct was almost twice as high for gang members than for nongang member (18 incidents compared to 10 incidents, respectively).

11. In comparison to nonaffiliated members, gang members were more involved in conduct that posed a significant threat to institutional safety, including fighting, assaulting, and threatening; provoking violence; creating or participating in a disturbance; jeopardizing security; and possessing or dealing in contraband.

12. Three times as many gang members than nongang members refused to provide a urine sample.

13. More gang members than nonaffiliated women offenders disobeyed rules, were disrespectful or abusive to staff members, and destroyed property.

14. STG members were placed in segregation at a higher rate than nonaffiliated women offenders.

What do these findings mean? They tell us that female gang members are more involved with the underground prison economy and drug distribution than nonaffiliated women offenders. Gang members' conduct also undermines the activities of correctional officers and rehabilitative programming.

Earlier we identified the ways prison administrators respond to STG activity (known STG members are transferred from one institution to another, subjected to "gang enhancement" statutes that impose severe sentences, or segregated to highly restrictive to supermax housing). One of the problems is that they are seldom formally evaluated and there is little empirical evidence of their success. Furthermore, an approach that is successful in one prison could fail in another, and what works for male STG members may or may not work for women members. Recall from Chapter 6 the discussion of the four factors (the pathways perspective, relational theory and female development, trauma theory, and addiction theory) that explain why women offenders behave the way they do. Understanding these factors in combination with each other will help prison administrators consider how to adjust their policies and procedures and how to assess and improve services to female STG members in their care.

Jail Gangs—Security Threat Groups

Most of our knowledge about STGs is based on research conducted in state or federal prisons. Comparatively little is known about the extent of STGs in jails and for that reason we report on it here.

In 2004, researchers from California State University, Chino; the University of Missouri, St. Louis; and the National Youth Gang Center examined the perceptions of jail administrators about the problems that STG members cause in their facilities, the prevalence of these populations, methods of classifying gang membership, and approaches that may reduce the disruption or violence associated with these groups.[27] In spite of the methodological limitations of the study (e.g., jails in the northeast and small jails were underrepresented), the results shed some light on the influence of STGs in jails.

Jail administrators said designation of gang membership by another law enforcement agency along with tattoos, clothing/gang colors, hand signs, and an individual's self-declaration was commonly used to define STG membership. They estimated STG membership at 13.2 percent. Extrapolating this estimate to the June 2011 population of offenders confined in jail (735,601), for example, would result in 97,099 STG members held in jail on any given day.

When asked about the problems that STG members cause in their facilities, jail administrators reported that gang members are less disruptive than inmates with severe mental illnesses but are more likely to assault other inmates. Their most important tools to control STG harm were the gathering and dissemination of gang intelligence within the facility and to other law enforcement agencies. Segregation of STG members was also effective in large jails, but small jails were unlikely to have the ability or resources to segregate inmates. A prime example of jail monitoring of STGs is the Broward County Sheriff's Department (Ft. Lauderdale, Florida, the second most populous county in Florida) where persons suspected of being involved with an STG are interviewed, information is collected, activity documented, and paraphernalia managed.

According to researchers from California State University, the University of Missouri, and the National Youth Gang Center study, the benefits of controlling STGs in jails are twofold. First, jails will be safer and as a result there will be less need for inmates to join gangs in search of safety. And second, information sharing may enhance the effectiveness of prison-based STG intervention.

Prison Riots and Disturbances

Each prison disturbance and riot is unique. The precipitating conditions, resolutions, and aftermath are shaped by the characteristics of the institution, its staff, its administration, and its inmate population as well as the state or federal agency to which it belongs. No amount of comprehensive planning can prevent all disturbances and riots because, as one expert contends, some have no root causes.[28] It is impossible to predict where and when they will occur. Still, understanding prison disturbances and riots can help correctional administrators avoid some problems, take steps to prevent certain events from launching into full-fledged riots, limit the extent of damage, and terminate disturbances and riots in the least costly way.

In May 2002 and again in July/August 2006, the American Correctional Association (ACA) published the results of a survey of prison disturbances, riots, assaults, and escapes. ACA defined **disturbance** as an altercation involving three or more inmates, resulting in official action beyond summary sanctions, and for which there is an institutional record. Most prison disturbances were fights, stabbings, assaults, shouting obscenities at staff, refusal to follow orders (e.g., clean cell area and return to cell), hostage taking, and cell extraction. A **riot** is any action by a group of inmates that constitutes a forcible attempt to gain control of a facility or area within a facility.

The ACA recorded a decrease in prison disturbances from 2,674 in 2000 to 405 in 2006 and reported a similar decrease in riots from 2000 to

disturbance

An altercation involving three or more inmates, resulting in official action beyond summary sanctions and for which there is an institutional record.

riot

Any action by a group of inmates that constitutes a forcible attempt to gain control of a facility or area within a facility.

2006. In 2000, there were two riots. In 2006, there were no riots.[29] From 2000 to 2006, there were also decreases in the number of inmates killed by inmates and staff, staff and officers assaulted, inmate suicide attempts and deaths, inmates injured by staff, and escapees and walkaways.

What some states call a *riot*, others downplay and call a *disturbance*. For example, in 1993 there were more than 186 disturbances in 21 corrections systems—but only 7 were classified as riots.[30] In Connecticut, a gang fight involving more than 300 inmates and causing more than $100,000 in damage was called a *riot*. At Leavenworth, a racial fight involving 427 inmates that caused significant damage to the prison's auditorium, chapel, and industry buildings was called a *disturbance*. Correctional administrators label most incidents *disturbances* because the term is less sensational.

How many prison riots have there been in the United States? Nobody knows for sure. Not only do we have different opinions as to what constitutes a riot, but wardens and state officials are also reluctant to publicize loss of control. Scholars estimate that almost 500 prison riots have taken place in the United States since 1855.[31]

The New Mexico Penitentiary riot, which took place on February 2 and 3, 1980, is considered one of the world's five largest prison riots. Thirty-three inmates died and hundreds more were treated for injuries. None of the 12 corrections officers taken hostage were killed, but seven were treated for injuries caused by beatings and rapes. What are some of the causes of prison riots, and how can they be prevented?

Despite reformers' appeals for overhauls of prison programs and management, violence-provoking conditions continue to exist in many prisons. Three of the bloodiest and most violent prison riots in the United States occurred in severely overcrowded prisons in New York in 1971, in New Mexico in 1980, and in Ohio in 1993.

In the 1971 riot at the Attica Correctional Facility, New York where 2,225 inmates were incarcerated in a prison designed for 1,200, 43 lives were lost: Four inmates were killed during the riot as part of inmate "justice," and when police stormed in to retake the prison, they killed 10 civilian hostages and 29 prisoners. The New York State Special Commission that investigated the riot wrote, "With the exception of Indian massacres in the late 19th century, the State Police assault which ended the four-day prison uprising was the bloodiest one-day encounter between Americans since the Civil War."[32]

In the 1980 riot at the Penitentiary of New Mexico in Santa Fe where 1,136 inmates were confined in a space designed for 900 inmates, the taking of human life was brutal. Thirty-three inmates were tortured, dismembered, decapitated, burned alive, and killed by fellow inmates. Although staff were held hostage, none were killed.

The longest prison riot in U.S. history occurred at the Southern Ohio Correctional Facility in Lucasville in 1993 where 1,820 inmates were held in a prison built for 1,540. Inmates killed nine of their fellow inmates and one correctional officer in the 11-day siege.

The riot at Lucasville cost an estimated $15 million in property damage. At Santa Fe, the estimate was $28.5 million. At Attica, the cost was more than $3 million. A new chapter in the cost of prison riots was written on August 28, 2000, when, after three decades of waiting, federal district court judge Michael A. Telesca accepted New York State's agreement to set aside $12 million (the largest amount ever in a prisoners' rights case) to compensate more than 500 inmates and relatives for the abuse that the prisoners suffered. After hearing the inmates' stories, Judge Telesca described the aftermath as littered with "brutal beatings and acts of torture" and unlimited racial epithets.

Causes of Prison Riots According to sociology professor Burt Useem at Purdue University, there are five theoretical explanations for the causes of prison riots.[33]

CO13-4

The first is random chance. Useem says that some prison riots have no root causes. It is impossible to predict where and when they will occur.

The second explanation is bad conditions. This explanation tells us that overcrowding, antiquated facilities, low staffing levels, insufficient staff training, lack of programs for inmates, lack of funding, and poor implementation of correctional policy account for prison riots. Overcrowding is the most important of these. It causes heightened prison tension and potential violent disruption. Overcrowding is responsible for curtailing or even eliminating opportunities for education, vocational training, and recreation as discussed earlier in this chapter. When the ratio of correctional officers to inmates becomes too low, something has to give. At Attica, Santa Fe, and Lucasville, overcrowding raised tensions, interfered with prisoner classification, reduced living space, and restricted access to programs. Restlessness and boredom grew.

The third explanation involves rebellious inmates and racial antagonism. This includes gang members and violent or aggressive inmates. Riots tend to occur in higher-security facilities. Outside prison, the ratio of racial minorities to whites is about one to five. In prison, however, whites are the minority. That different ratio, in addition to overcrowding, close living quarters, and lack of space, adds to racial antagonism. Antagonism is heightened when inmates separate themselves along racial or ethnic lines for self-protection. Researchers have discovered that as inmates' perception of overcrowding increases, their antagonism toward other racial and ethnic groups also increases. Prisoners at Attica, Santa Fe, and Lucasville were young, violence prone, and poorly classified. Most were undereducated, underemployed, and uncommitted to society's means for achieving social goals. The racial and ethnic minority imbalance together with these individual factors prompted many inmates to adopt tough attitudes and join STGs for self-protection.

The fourth explanation focuses on institutional structure and readiness. Riots occur when a prison's infrastructure wears thin and authorities fail to plan and prepare. At Attica, a faulty weld joint in a metal gate gave way and allowed prisoners access to most areas of the institution. At Santa Fe, inmates pounded on "shatterproof" glass with a fire extinguisher until the glass fell out of the frame. At Lucasville, inmates collected master keys from staff hostages and opened cell doors.

The fifth explanation focuses on administrative factors. Poor prison management and administration are linked to prison riots. Poor management can result from frequent staff turnover, low correctional officer qualifications, inadequate training, poor staff–inmate communication, and low staff pay. At Attica, Santa Fe, and Lucasville, inmates' complaints about living conditions, lack of programs, and officers' excessive use of force and harassment went unheard by administration. Rumors of riots were not taken seriously.

Preventing Prison Riots Prison violence provokes more violence. Measures to prevent prison riots must become a national priority, and change must occur. Three years before the Attica riot, the U.S. National Advisory Commission on Civil Disorders (the Kerner Commission) warned that the only effective way to prevent riots, whether in or out of prison, was to eliminate sources of tension by making good "the promises of American democracy to all citizens, urban and rural,

CO13-5

white and black, Spanish surname, American Indian, and every minority group."[34] While that change is long range, corrections officials can implement immediate measures to reduce the likelihood of inmate aggression, including the following:

- formal inmate grievance procedures;
- ombudsmen to mediate disputes;
- an improved classification system;
- smaller institutions;
- meaningful prison school and work programs;
- alternatives to incarceration;
- professional corrections staff who are trained and well paid;
- administrators who are visible and available to staff and inmates; and
- clearly written and understood policies on the use of force when necessary.

To ensure that the use of force is appropriate and justifiable, the ACA recommends establishing policies and procedures that govern its use (see Exhibit 13–2).

SUPERMAX HOUSING AND "NO-FRILLS" PRISONS AND JAILS

In an effort to control the behavior of violence-prone inmates, two new types of prisons are emerging—supermax housing and "no-frills" prisons and jails. Both alter the conditions of confinement for thousands of U.S. prisoners, raising important issues for the prisoners and staff who must live and work in them and the society that must accept the prisoners when they are released.

CO13-6 Supermax Housing

Prison systems have always needed a way to deal with inmates whose violent behavior makes it impossible for them to live with the general prison population. Generally such measures involve separating such inmates and are called *segregation* or *solitary confinement*. Prisoners who are dangerous or chronically violent, have escaped or attempted to escape from a high-security correctional facility, have incited or attempted to incite disruption in a correctional facility, or who have preyed on weaker inmates are removed from the general population. You may recall from Chapter 7 that, in 1829, the Eastern State Penitentiary in Cherry Hill, Pennsylvania, was built on the principle of solitary confinement. However, in 1913 the Pennsylvania legislature dropped "solitary" from sentencing statutes, and housing arrangements at Eastern State became congregate. From that point forward, specialized housing units were developed for management and control of troublesome inmates.

The Federal Bureau of Prisons (BOP) returned to the idea of controlling the most violent and disruptive inmates in indefinite solitary confinement when it opened Alcatraz in 1934. Alcatraz, which had a capacity of 275, did not offer any treatment program; its sole purpose was to incarcerate and punish the federal prison system's most desperate criminals and worst troublemakers. Alcatraz was "America's Devil's Island, 'Hellcatraz'—a place where convicts slowly went insane from the tedium and hopelessness

EXHIBIT 13–2	Public Correctional Policy on Use of Force

Introduction:

Correctional agencies are responsible for ensuring the safety in correctional programs. To achieve this goal, it may be necessary for correctional staff to use legally authorized force to respond to resistance and other situations.

Policy Statement:

Correctional agencies are committed to exercising an appropriate use of force consistent with statutory requirements and the needs of the situation. Use of force consists of intervention with an offender to promote safety, control behavior and enforce order. Use of force includes use of restraints (other than for routine transportation and movement), chemical agents, electronic devices and weapons. Force is justified only in instances of self-defense, protection of others, protection of property, prevention of escapes, and maintaining or regaining control, and then only as a last resort and in accordance with appropriate statutory authority.

To ensure that the use of force is appropriate and justifiable, correctional agencies should establish and maintain policies and procedures that:

A. Prohibit the use of force as a retaliatory or disciplinary measure; establish strategies to reduce and prevent the need to use force; authorize force only when no reasonable alternative is possible; and advocate that force used be the minimum amount necessary;

B. Define the range of methods for and alternatives to physical response, and that specify the conditions under which each is permitted. These policies must assign responsibility for authorizing the use of physical force; outline the steps for appropriate implementation of the use of physical force; provide for close monitoring of the person while in restraints; and require proper documentation, administrative review, investigation and remedial action;

C. Provide ongoing specialized staff training designed to teach staff to anticipate, stabilize and diffuse situations that might give rise to conflict, confrontation and violence and that ensures staff's competency in the use of all methods and equipment in the use of force;

D. Establish and maintain procedures that limit the use of deadly force to those instances where it is legally authorized and where there is an imminent threat to human life or to public safety;

E. Prohibit restraint techniques that cause or could cause partial or complete impairment of respiratory exchange (positional asphyxia) such as the hogtie position or certain restraints on the neck, or those that cause or could cause partial or complete paralysis;

F. In consultation with health care staff, limit the use of physical restraints on pregnant offenders in the last trimester of pregnancy and/or during labor and delivery to occurrences when the offender is a risk for escape, harming herself or harming others, or poses a significant and known safety and security risk for other reasons; and

G. Whenever possible, assure that age, gender, health and mental health status are considered prior to initiating the use of force and that the least restrictive and/or least likely type to cause impairment/harm is utilized. Medical conditions such as pregnancy, respiratory ailments, advanced age, or physically debilitating diseases create an increased risk of serious injury and should be factored into the decision regarding which response is appropriate for the situation.

Source: Copyright © American Correctional Association. Reprinted with permission.

of endless years on 'the Rock.' "[35] By 1963, Alcatraz was judged an expensive failure; it symbolized a penal philosophy that was outdated in an era that espoused rehabilitation, not punishment, as the goal of incarceration. Alcatraz closed on March 21, 1963. During the era of rehabilitation

At the federal supermax prison in Florence, Colorado, three mirrored-glass gun towers define the maximum-security level of heightened confinement. Officially known as the United States Penitentiary Florence Administrative Maximum (ADMAX), 25 percent of the 400 prisoners there will remain in confinement for the rest of their lives. What are the pros and cons of such facilities?

supermax housing

A freestanding facility, or a distinct unit within a facility, that provides for management and secure control of inmates who have been officially designated as exhibiting violent or serious and disruptive behavior while incarcerated.

that followed the Alcatraz closing, prison officials used the *dispersal model*—problem prisoners were distributed to a number of prisons. Prison officials hoped that dispersal among populations of generally law-abiding inmates would dilute the influence of problem prisoners, but they soon learned that dispersing problem inmates across dozens of prisons led to having dozens of problem facilities.

By the 1970s, the goal of incarceration had shifted back to punishment. Disturbances, violence, and riots at state and federal prisons convinced the BOP to try again to control the most troublesome federal inmates in one location. The BOP reverted to the *concentration model*—all problem prisoners would be housed together in a separate facility. The federal prison at Marion, Illinois, was chosen for this purpose. The construction features at Marion, however, made it difficult for staff to maintain complete control over recalcitrant inmates. Open cell fronts were a major limitation in Marion's design to control the toughest prisoners. Through their cell bars, inmates threw trash, urine, and feces at corrections officers; passed contraband; set fires; and verbally harassed and lunged at staff and other prisoners as they walked by. Tension, hostility, violence, and murder were all too common. On October 23, 1983, a state of emergency was declared after two corrections officers and one prisoner were murdered by inmates, and two other officers were seriously injured. The Marion prison went into lockdown for the next 23 years, setting the model for dozens of state and federal supermaxes to crack down on prison violence. Over the next few years, the BOP conceived plans to build a supermax facility that would implement construction features for controlling difficult inmates.

In 1994, the BOP opened its first **supermax housing** facility at Florence, Colorado, a rural community of about 3,800 residents 110 miles south of Denver. Officially known as United States Penitentiary Florence Administrative Maximum (ADMAX), the prison houses the 450 most dangerous, violent, escape prone, and STG federal inmate leaders. More than 25 percent will never be released from federal custody and will remain in confinement for the rest of their lives. Among the prisoners at ADX are Zacarias Moussaoui, confessed 9/11 conspirator; Olympic Park bomber Eric Rudolph; "Unabomber" Ted Kaczynski; Robert Hanssen, American FBI agent-turned Soviet spy; Oklahoma City bombing conspirator Terry Nichols; would-be "shoe bomber" Richard Reid; and 1993 World Trade Center bombing conspirator Ramzi Yousef.

Construction cost for the federal supermax prison in Florence, Colorado, totaled $60 million ($150,000 per cell). Annual operating cost per cell per year is another $40,000, or $19.2 million total annually. According to Mears and Watson, a low-end estimate of the typical life course of a supermax prison (35 years) is close to $1 billion.[36]

Supermax prisons are significantly more expensive to build than traditional prisons due in part to the enhanced and extensive high-security features on locks, doors, and perimeters; heavily reinforced concrete walls, ceilings, and floors; and incorporation of advanced electronic systems and technology. Providing meals and other services at individual cell fronts, having multiple-officer escorts, and maintaining elaborate electronic systems contribute to the high cost.

Cell design at the federal supermax prison in Florence, Colorado, resists vandalism. Each prisoner's bed, desk, stool, and bookcase are made of reinforced concrete and anchored in place. Each 7 by 12-foot cell has a shower stall with flood-proof plumbing and a 12-inch black-and-white television set. Cell windows deny prisoners all views of the outside except the sky above. A simple hole-in-the-wall apparatus for lighting cigarettes has replaced matches and cigarette lighters. Meals are dispensed through cell slots in separate heated trays from airline-style carts pulled by small tractors. Cells are staggered so that inmates cannot make eye contact with other inmates. There are no congregate activities of any kind. Each cell has a double-entry door: an interior barred cage door backed up by a windowed steel door that prevents voice contact among prisoners. Visits are noncontact, and inmates are allowed out of their cells for an hour a day of solitary exercise.

The prison has 1,400 electronically controlled gates, 168 television monitors, and three mirror-glass gun towers. The 400 cells are subdivided among nine units—each unit is self-contained and includes a sick-call room, law library, and barber chair. "What puts a man in is his behavior, and what gets a man out is his behavior," said John M. Vanyur, former associate warden.[37] The average stay in supermax in California is 6.8 years, and research on Colorado found that 4 of 10 offenders go straight from supermax cells where they were confined 23 hours a day to the streets. As noted earlier, one reason that Evan Ebel is suspected of shooting and killing Tom Clements, Colorado's chief of corrections, was Ebel's years spent in solitary confinement that nurtured his paranoia and hatred of prison officials. Ebel was released directly to the streets after almost six years in solitary confinement.

This type of supercontrolled environment took hold across the United States in the 1990s and first half of the 21st century as politicians promoted supermaxes to a crime-fatigued nation after decades of rising crime rates, prison riots, and hostage taking. Today, 44 states, the District of Columbia, and the BOP now operate one or more supermax prisons that collectively house more than 80,000 inmates.[38] Despite the fact that supermax prisons typically cost two to three times more to build and operate than traditional maximum-security prisons, the facilities were politically and publicly attractive until the economic recession began in December 2007. Read this chapter's feature "Economic Realities and Corrections: Supermax Prisons" and learn what governors in several states are doing to downsize supermaxes and save money. "Supermax prisons have become political symbols of how 'tough' a jurisdiction has become."[39]

The National Institute of Corrections (NIC) studied supermax prisons nationwide and described the supermax prison as "a highly restrictive, high-custody housing unit within a secure facility, or an entire secure facility, that isolates inmates from the general population and from each other due to grievous crimes, repetitive assaultive or violent institutional behavior, the threat of escape or actual escape from high-custody facility(s), or inciting or threatening to incite disturbances in a correctional institution."[40] Supermax housing does not include maximum or close custody facilities that are designated for routine housing of inmates with high-custody needs, inmates in disciplinary segregation or protective custody, or other inmates requiring segregation or separation for other routine purposes. In fact, NIC opined that as comforting as it might be to prison staff to send nuisance inmates who continuously test the limits, frequently break minor rules, consume an inordinate amount of staff time, are situationally assaultive, or cannot control their behavior due to mental illness to supermax facilities, it is inappropriate to do so. Use of extended control housing for nuisance inmates is inefficient, consumes expensive high-security beds, has little overall operational impact, and is arguably overkill. And according to some, use of supermax for nonviolent inmates happens all too often. Marianne McNabb, former regional administrator for the Washington State Department of Corrections said, "People have a notion that behind the supermax facilities are all psychopathic serial killers. But many are low-level criminals who, because of the inability to manage their behavior in the open institutional population, and how they are dealt with by staff, are kept in virtual lockdown."[41]

NIC found that a universal definition of supermax housing is problematic and states vary considerably in their criteria for the placement in and release of inmates from these facilities. The many states that provided information had different reasons and needs for supermax housing. Some supermax prisons house inmates who could not be controlled in traditional administrative segregation units, including prisoners who are uncontrollable due to mental illness. Others are an extension or expansion of segregation and house protective custody and/or disciplinary segregation inmates. Still others house inmates who would reside in close custody among the general population in most other jurisdictions. As these prisons have increased in number, been reported on by the media, and gained popularity with the public, a variety of names have emerged to describe them: *restrictive housing, special housing unit, extended control unit, maxi-maxi, maximum control facility, secured housing unit, intensive housing unit, intensive management unit,* and *administrative maximum penitentiary.* The term *supermax* is the one heard most frequently in the media and in the field of corrections. Yet, as the NIC survey indicates, the term is applied to a wide variety of facilities and programs handling an equally wide variety of inmate populations. NIC's conclusion is, "Supermax as defined in the survey may exist in relatively few agencies."[42]

To date, research on super-maximum-security prisons is minimal despite the rapid increase in and costs of such facilities nationally. Criminologists, psychiatrists, lawyers, and the courts who have studied the

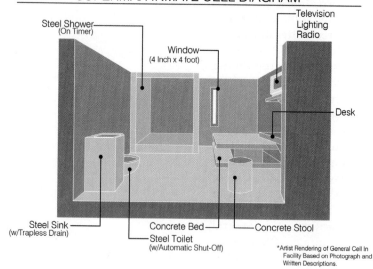

SUPERMAX INMATE CELL DIAGRAM

Steel Shower
(On Timer)

Window
(4 Inch x 4 foot)

Television
Lighting
Radio

Desk

Steel Sink
(w/Trapless Drain)

Concrete Bed

Steel Toilet
(w/Automatic Shut-Off)

Concrete Stool

*Artist Rendering of General Cell In Facility Based on Photograph and Written Descriptions.

Each prisoner's bed, desk, stool, and bookcase at the federal supermax prison in Florence, Colorado, are made of reinforced concrete and anchored in place. Each 7 by 12-foot cell has a shower stall with flood-proof plumbing. Cells are staggered so that inmates cannot make eye contact with other inmates. Each cell has a double-entry door: an interior barred cage door backed up by a windowed steel door that prevents voice contact among prisoners. What kind of inmates should/should not be held in such facilities?

effects of long-term solitary confinement report evidence of acute sensory deprivation, paranoid delusion belief systems, irrational fears of violence, resentment, little ability to control rage, and mental breakdowns. Forty-five percent of prisoners in Washington's supermax units were diagnosed as seriously mentally ill.[43]

The vast majority of inmates in long-term solitary confinement remain anxious, angry, depressed, insecure, and confused. Some commit suicide. For example, although isolated prisoners make up less than 2 percent of the total inmate population in California, they accounted for 42 percent of the suicides from 2006 to 2010.[44] The situation in federal prison is even worse. After U.S. Senator Richard Durbin (D-IL) held the first-ever congressional hearing on the use of solitary confinement in the federal prison system and learned that one-half of all prison suicides are committed by prisoners held in supermax prisons, the federal BOP agreed to a comprehensive review of the use of solitary confinement by an independent analyst.[45]

The impact of supermax facilities on staff is also a subject of much discussion. Having to deal on a daily basis with inmates who have proven to be the most troublesome—in an environment that prioritizes human control and isolation—presents staff with extraordinary challenges. Correctional administrators with experience in operating supermax prisons talk about the potential for creating a "we/they syndrome" between staff and inmates. The nature and reputation of the inmate and frequently the inmate's behavior, combined with ultracontrol and rigidity, magnify the tension between inmates and staff. When there is little interaction except in control situations, the adversarial nature of the relationships tends to be one of dominance and, in return, resistance on both sides. Stuart Grassian, a physician and expert on prison control units, believes that people who work in supermax facilities lose their capacity to be shocked by the kinds of things they see. "It may put money in your pocket," Dr. Grassian notes, "but over time it destroys you psychologically and brings out rage and sadism and violence and brutality."[46]

One piece of academic research that examined what the goals of supermax prison are, how they ought to be assessed, what the unintended effects are, and what political, moral, and economic factors enter the decision to build or not was published in 2006.[47] Mears and Watson reviewed the literature; visited three supermax prisons where they conducted focus groups and interviews with corrections policymakers, officials, and practitioners; and interviewed similar individuals in eight other states. They concluded, "no solid empirical foundation exists to say with confidence that they [supermax prisons] are either effective or ineffective."[48] The fact that Mears and Watson found a wide range of goals and impacts from increasing prison safety and order to controlling and improving prisoners' behavior, reducing the influence of gangs, increasing public safety, and increasing efficiencies throughout correctional systems makes cross-state evaluations of supermax prisons a challenge, and how goals should be measured remains unclear.

Mears and Watson's analysis also pointed to a wide range of potential unintended impacts, some positive (for example, increasing the quality of life among general population prison staff and inmates and improving the economy in the communities where supermax prisons are located) and some negative (for example, decreasing the quality of inmate–staff relations and increasing mental illness among supermax-confined inmates). But how common these unintended impacts are, nobody knows; and until we do know, we can't conclude that supermax prisons merit support.

So far, only one study used a powerful type of research design to assess whether supermax prisons contribute to a decrease in prison violence, and the results are at best mixed. The study focused on four states, three of which had supermax prisons (Arizona, Illinois, and Minnesota) and one that did not (Utah). Researchers studied inmate-on-inmate and inmate-on-staff assaults and found that the opening of a supermax prison did not reduce the level of inmate-on-inmate violence although in Illinois there was a reduction in assaults on staff. The finding in Illinois suggested support for supermax prisons, but it raised this question: Why would a supermax prison reduce inmate-on-staff assaults but not inmate-on-inmate assaults?[49]

In 1995, inmates at Pelican Bay's supermax unit challenged the constitutionality of extreme isolation and environmental deprivation. They claimed that the degree of segregation was so extreme and the restrictions so severe that the inmates confined there were psychologically traumatized and, in some cases, deprived of sanity. The federal court agreed. The court ruled in *Madrid* v. *Gomez* (1995) that "conditions in security housing unit did impose cruel and unusual punishment on mentally ill prisoners" and "those who were at particularly high risk for suffering very serious or severe injury to their mental health."[50] The court declared that the state of California could not continue to confine inmates who were already mentally ill or those who were at an unreasonably high risk of suffering serious mental illness in the supermax unit. The court also appointed a **special master** (a person appointed to act as the representative of the court) to work with the state of California to develop a satisfactory remedial plan and provide a progress report to the court.

In 2005, the U.S. Supreme Court ruled on a case from Ohio that challenged the constitutionality of the "process" by which inmates were sent to supermax prisons. The Court said in *Wilkinson* v. *Austin* that Ohio's revised classification process that gave the inmate advanced notice of the impending action, an informal administrative hearing in which the inmate speaks on his or her behalf, and a statement of reasons after the decision is made provided the basic elements of due process that were sufficient to protect inmates against arbitrary or erroneous placement in supermax conditions.[51] What the Supreme Court said in *Wilkinson* is that because supermax conditions are so much more stringent than those in more "typical" prisons, inmates have a liberty interest in not being sent there and must, therefore, be afforded procedural protections before that decision is made.

However, not everyone agrees that the conditions of supermax confinement exacerbate symptoms of mental illness and create mental illness where none previously existed, and these findings may impact future court decisions. In January 2011, the U.S. Department of Justice released the results of a one-year longitudinal study of the psychological effects of supermax confinement conducted by the Colorado Department of Corrections.[52] Colorado houses 6.2 percent (1,413) of its 23,000-inmate population in supermax confinement. The researchers found that psychological disturbances were not unique to prisoners in supermax confinement. Elevated psychological disturbances were present among prisoners in the general population as well. The researchers also noted that there was initial improvement in psychological well-being for both groups at the first two testing sessions followed by relative stability for the remainder of the year. They also reported that contrary to expected findings, offenders with mental illness did not deteriorate over time in supermax

special master

A person appointed by the court to act as its representative to oversee remedy of a violation and provide regular progress reports.

confinement at a rate more rapid and more extreme than those without mental illness. They conclude that although inmates in supermax confinement possessed traits believed to be associated with long-term segregation, those features could not be attributed to supermax confinement alone because they were present at the time of placement and occurred in the comparison study group.

As you can imagine, however, the study has its critics. Among them is Dr. Stuart Grassian, Boston psychiatrist who is internationally recognized for describing the crippling effects of supermax confinement. Dr. Grassian described the report as "garbage in, garbage out. Their approach and methodology are fatally flawed."[53] Grassian and others argue that the research was flawed from the start because the researchers started with inmates experiencing mental health crises at the beginning of their study. Hence, their baseline data were slanted. They also question the truthfulness of the inmates' responses. Will inmates, they ask, admit to mental health problems if they are trying to earn their way out of supermax confinement? They also question the results of the study by raising the issue of the so-called Hawthorne Effect, a form of reactivity whereby subjects improve or modify an aspect of their behavior being experimentally measured simply in response to the fact that they are being studied, not in response to any particular experimental manipulation. The critics point out that two inmates were thrown out of the study because they made sexual advances to one of the female graduate students conducting the interviews.

No-Frills Prisons and Jails

CO13-7

No-frills prisons and jails that take away prisoner amenities and privileges are part of the corrections landscape. New policies are designed to make jail and prison life as unpleasant as possible in the belief that such conditions deter even the most hardened criminals.

no-frills prisons and jails
Correctional institutions that take away prisoner amenities and privileges.

Proponents of no-frills jails and prisons argue that the only incentives offenders should have is the opportunity to straighten out their lives. They further argue that incentives such as smoking, use of weight equipment and electronic equipment, and wearing personal clothing encourage offenders to fake their way through incarceration to get the privileges. Pleasures of any kind, proponents claim, contribute to the crime rate by making prison a tolerable way of life. Reducing or eliminating amenities and privileges is what inmates deserve. Those favoring this argue that this is not vindictive revenge—the offender committed a serious crime that warrants incarceration, and incarceration is meant to be punitive.

From Alaska to Mississippi to Massachusetts, states are gearing up to pass no-frills legislation. Alaska passed the No-Frills Prison Act in 1997, which removed or prohibited premium cable television, cassette tape players, tobacco use, pornographic material, and weight-lifting equipment. Former Alaska senator Dave Donley sponsored the bill and defended the legislation by observing that "this law will make people think twice before committing a crime in Alaska."[54] In Mississippi, former representative Mark McInnis said it clearly: "The people who run the prisons want happy prisoners. I want prisoners to be so miserable that they won't even think of coming back."[55] And former Massachusetts governor William Weld said that life in prison should be "akin to a walk through the fires of hell," where inmates should learn only the joys of busting rocks.[56] At

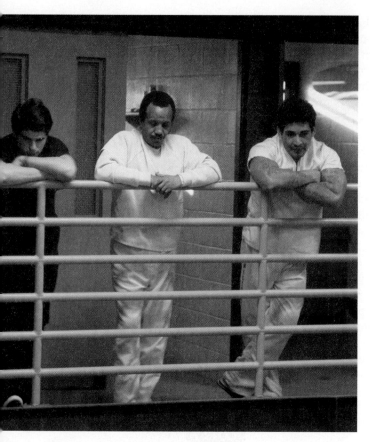

No-frills prisons and jails take away prisoner amenities and privileges. What are the arguments for and against no-frills prisons and jails?

the federal level, the No-Frills Prison Act was enacted in 1996. It prohibits in-cell television viewing (except for prisoners who are segregated from the general population for their own safety), coffee pot, hot plate, or heating element; R-, X-, or NC-17 rated movies; boxing, wrestling, judo, Karate, or any other martial art; any bodybuilding or weight-lifting equipment; and use or possession of any electric or electronic musical instrument in all federal prisons.

Often the public favors taking away prison amenities because it assumes they are paid for by tax dollars. States that permit in-cell television and electric equipment do not pay for them. They are purchased by the inmates or their families. Political rhetoric contributes to the public misconception regarding who pays for prison amenities. Would the public be more supportive of prison amenities if it knew the inmates paid for them? According to a citizens' survey in Tampa Bay, Florida, the answer is yes. "Respondents who were informed that prisoners pay for their privileges were more likely to support inmate access to all of the amenities except air-conditioning than were those who were told tax dollars are used to finance inmate privileges. . . . It is only when citizens are informed that taxpayers absorb the cost that they become unsupportive. . . . This finding suggests that educating people that inmates pay for the more 'luxurious' items will result in higher levels of support for them."[57]

Arguably, proponents of no-frills jails and prisons have a point. Privileges, if not handled properly, can undermine rehabilitation. On the other hand, without privileges, offenders may not take advantage of the opportunity for rehabilitation in the first place. In a perfect world, prison would make offenders realize that their mistakes have caused them pain and deprived them of their freedom, and they would gratefully volunteer for rehabilitation programs to gain back their freedom. However, in a perfect world, these people would most likely not be incarcerated to start with because they would have realized that their behaviors were causing them unwanted consequences and would have taken corrective measures outside prison. Most offenders do not think this way; they do not think about the consequences beforehand. They think they will never get caught. The eventual consequences for their lack of responsibility are arrest and incarceration.

In August 2002, *Corrections Compendium*, the peer-reviewed journal of the American Correctional Association, published the results of a survey on inmate privileges in U.S. prison systems.[58] Comparing the results of that survey with one taken four years earlier, the *Compendium* concluded, "The trend for decreased privileges has continued for a variety of reasons [to reduce the coddling of inmates, to control the problems of overcrowding and lack of resources, or for practical reasons such as elimination of secondhand smoke] . . . and will likely continue in the future."[59] Some of the results of the survey follow:

1. Smoking is prohibited in 53 percent of U.S. prisons.
2. Free weights are prohibited in 38 percent of U.S. prisons.
3. Electronic equipment (for example, television, radio, CD or cassette players, calculators, electric shavers, typewriters, coffee/hot pots,

Charles L. Lockett

Warden, Federal Correctional Complex, United States
Penitentiary 2, Coleman, Florida

Charles L. Lockett is a native of Alabama. He received a bachelor of arts degree in political science from Texas Southern University and completed graduate studies in business administration at the University of Dallas. Lockett assumed the duties of warden at the Federal Correctional Complex (FCC), United States Penitentiary 2, Coleman, Florida, in 2012. The FCC is the largest of its type in the nation, with five separate components: an administrative (shared services) facility, a male low-level security structure, a male medium-level security facility with a female satellite camp, and two high-level security facilities.

Lockett began his career with the Federal Bureau of Prisons in 1987 as a correctional officer at the Federal Correctional Institution (FCI) in Fort Worth, Texas. Since then, he has held various positions of increasing authority, including contracting officer at the FCI in Tallahassee, Florida; supervisory contract specialist/assistant controller at the Metropolitan Correctional Center (MCC) in Miami, Florida, and the FCI in Fort Worth, Texas; controller at the MCC in Chicago, Illinois; executive assistant and camp administrator at the FCI in Manchester, Kentucky; associate warden at the FCIs in Morgantown, West Virginia, and Petersburg, Virginia; deputy warden at the FCC in Coleman, Florida; senior deputy regional director for the North Central Region, Kansas City, Kansas; warden at the FCC in Terre Haute, Indiana, and subsequently returning to the FCC in Coleman as warden. Lockett's single most noteworthy endeavor is being a good husband to his wife and a father to his four kids.

I would suggest to students entering the field to remember the acronym *C.A.R.* *Communication:* If you learn to be an effective communicator, which requires listening, you will be successful in making things happen. *Attitude:* If you have a great attitude it will become infectious and liberating to the people you serve. *Responsiveness:* if you are responsive to the needs of the organization, everyone will want you on their team.

> *"Public service is a higher calling. It starts with personal leadership. Leadership requires being a good follower. And the best leadership style is that of the Servant Leader because they realize their influence is so much broader and purposeful."*

clocks, musical instruments, fans, desk lamps, hair dryers/curlers, and video games) is prohibited in the District of Columbia. All other facilities attach restrictions to their use.

4. R-rated movies are prohibited in 58 percent of U.S. facilities.

5. Books and magazines are restricted everywhere by content, quantity, space considerations, who sends them, and custody level.

To date, no court case has been heard on no-frills prisons and jails. Unless the eliminated or reduced amenity or privilege results in serious harm to the inmate, the no-frills movement will continue.

At present, there is no evidence that making prisons and jails more unpleasant has any effect on crime. Legislators claim that inmates will not want to be incarcerated or reincarcerated under such harsh conditions. However, more than 200 years of prison history has not proved that making a prison austere deters offenders. State wardens, corrections experts, and attorneys do not believe that eliminating privileges will reduce crime.[60] They cringe at the idea of trying to maintain civility without amenities and privileges. "What some outside the corrections profession perceive as privileges, we in the profession see as vital prison and jail management tools to insure the safety of the facility," said Bobbie Huskey, former president of the ACA.[61]

Others have wondered what impact no-frills incarceration may have on institutional security. Eliminating frills might "increase disturbances, either in the short term if inmates react violently to the loss or in the long term if inmates have more idle time, resent the perceived vindictiveness of corrections managers, or conclude they have nothing more to lose by misbehaving."[62] A corrections official in Florida concluded, "From a correctional administrator's standpoint, there is a point at which further reductions create an undue risk to a safe and orderly operation." A 27-year veteran corrections administrator in the New Jersey Department of Corrections fears that the "take-back trend," as he calls it, might result in inmate retaliation on staff.[63] Sufficient time has not passed to study the long-term impact of no-frills incarceration. However, there is concern that eliminating privileges (such as weight lifting, television, and recreation) that keep inmates busy may encourage inmates to spend more time planning or causing trouble.

If privileges are eliminated, what positive incentives will correctional staff have with which to motivate appropriate inmate behavior? A survey of 823 wardens of state adult prisons indicates that programs and amenities serve a critical control function.[64] Correctional officers can grant access to privileges and amenities in exchange for adherence to rules and restrict access as punishment for rule violation. "The entire prison disciplinary structure is founded on punishments that amount to restriction of privileges," report the survey's authors. Chances are that prison administrators will not completely eliminate or abolish privileges or amenities; they will curtail availability and offer the privileges or amenities as a reward for good behavior.

ACCREDITATION

We introduced the issue of accreditation in Chapter 6. Here we expand on that discussion. *Accreditation* is a process through which correctional facilities and agencies can measure themselves against nationally adopted standards and through which they can receive formal recognition and accredited status. Besides accreditation, some correctional agencies use the evidence-based standards introduced throughout this text. However, here the focus is on accreditation.

ACA standards are the national benchmark for the effective operation of correctional systems throughout the United States and are necessary to ensure that correctional agencies and facilities operate professionally. The ACA administers the only national accreditation program for all components of adult and juvenile corrections. For that reason, the federal courts have increasingly relied on ACA's standards to decide whether correctional agencies and facilities meet constitutional standards. The ACA's policy on accreditation is shown in Exhibit 13–3.

CO13-8 ## Why Should Correctional Agencies and Facilities Be Accredited?

There are at least eight reasons that correctional agencies and facilities should be accredited:[65]

1. Accreditation Improves Staff Training and Development Accreditation requires having written policy and procedures to establish a training and staff development program for all categories of personnel. The professional growth of employees is developed through training plans that annually identify current job-related training needs in relation to position requirements, current correctional issues, new theories, techniques, and technologies.

EXHIBIT 13–3   **American Correctional Association**

Public Correctional Policy on Standards and Accreditation

Introduction

Adult and juvenile correctional agencies should provide community and institutional programs and services that offer a full range of effective, just, humane, and safe dispositions and sanctions for accused and adjudicated offenders. To assure accountability and professional responsibility, these programs and services should meet accepted professional and performance-based standards and obtain accreditation. The use of standards and the accreditation process provides a valuable mechanism for self-evaluation, stimulates improvement of correctional management and practice, and provides recognition of acceptable programs and facilities. The American Correctional Association and the Commission on Accreditation for Corrections have promulgated national standards and a voluntary system of national accreditation for correctional agencies. The beneficiaries of such a process are the staff of correctional agencies, offenders, and the public.

Policy Statement

All adult and juvenile detention and correctional facilities, institutional services, and community programs should be operated in accordance with the standards established by the American Correctional Association. These facilities and programs should be accredited through the Commission on Accreditation for Corrections. To fulfill this objective, correctional agencies should:

- A. implement improvement to comply with appropriate correctional standards;
- B. seek and maintain accreditation through the process developed by the Commission on Accreditation for Corrections in order that, through self-evaluation and peer review, necessary improvements are made, programs and services come into compliance with appropriate standards, and professional recognition is obtained.

Source: Copyright © American Correctional Association. Reprinted with permission.

2. Accreditation Assesses Program Strengths and Weaknesses

Accreditation assesses issues and concerns that affect the quality of life at a facility such as staff training, adequacy of medical services, sanitation, use of segregation and detention, incidents of violence, crowding, offender activity levels, programs, and provisions of basic services that may impact the life, safety, and health of inmates and staff.

3. Accreditation Is a Defense Against Lawsuits

Accredited agencies and facilities have a stronger defense against litigation through documentation and the demonstration of a "good faith" effort to improve conditions of confinement. For example, in *Grayson v. Peed* (1999), the U.S. Supreme Court said, "The appellant's own expert penologist conceded that [Sheriff] Peed's policies met the standards of both the Virginia Board of Corrections and the American Correctional Association. . . . Appellant's claims that [Sheriff] Peed provided inadequate training for his employees must also fail. At the time of the incident, the jail had been accredited for more than ten years . . . by the American Correctional Association . . . whose training requirements often surpass minimal constitutional standards."

4. Accreditation Establishes Measurable Criteria for Upgrading Operations Through the standards and accreditation process, agencies continuously review their policies and procedures and have the ability to make necessary improvements when deficiencies are recognized.

5. Accreditation Improves Staff Morale and Professionalism Accreditation is awarded to the "best of the best" in the corrections field. Staff have a better understanding of policies and procedures, and this contributes to improved working conditions for staff.

6. Accreditation Offers a Safer Environment for Staff and Offenders Staff and offenders benefit from increased accountability and attention to physical plant issues and security procedures. Whether for an agency or facility, the accreditation process ensures assessment of strengths and weaknesses.

7. Accreditation Reduces Liability Insurance Costs Insurance companies offer a reduction on liability insurance premiums to accredited agencies and facilities. Adherence to nationally recognized standards for fire, safety, health, and training reduces claim expenses, allowing up to a 10 percent credit on liability insurance premiums.

8. Accreditation Offers Performance-Based Benefits Performance-based standards provide data that can be used to gauge the day-to-day management of the facility, thereby providing agencies with a cost-effective, proactive approach to offender care. They can also be used to justify requests for additional funding.

Traditionally, correctional agencies have sought accreditation for one of three reasons: first, to ensure that the organization is in compliance with national standards; second, to demonstrate to interested parties that the organization is operating at acceptable professional levels; and third, to comply with court orders. Consult the Appendix Careers in Corrections at the Online Learning Center Web site for the steps involved in career planning, developing employability and job readiness, and finding the right job.

PRIVATIZATION

More than 128,000 state and federal inmates are held in private prison facilities in 30 states across the United States. Still the debate over privatization continues. Why do state governments contract with for-profit companies for such services?

According to Malcolm Feeler, the involvement of the private sector in corrections began shortly after the first English colonists arrived in Virginia in 1607.[66] Convicted felons were transported by private entrepreneurs to America, as a condition of pardon, to be sold into servitude. During the 18th century, jails and prisons emerged in the American colonies as alternatives to servitude or the death penalty. Privately operated facilities copied from English custom became popular. Private contractors claimed they could both manage prisons and employ convicts in labor, arguing that the practice would be both rehabilitative and financially rewarding. San Quentin was the first U.S. prison constructed and operated by a private provider in the 1850s. However, after a number of major scandals surfaced surrounding the mismanagement of the facility by the private provider, California turned San Quentin prison over to the control of state government. By 1885, 13 states had contracts with private enterprises to lease out prison labor.

As discussed in Chapter 6, *privatization* is defined as a contract process that shifts public functions, responsibilities, and capital assets, in whole or in part, from the public sector to the private sector. In corrections, privatization is generally one of three types: contracting out, private sector development, or private management.

Contracting out of specific services entails a competition among private bidders to perform governmental activities such as providing medical and mental health services, educational and vocational programming, food preparation, maintenance, work, and industry. Contracts for specialized services generate little controversy.

Private sector development refers to the private sector developing, designing, and financing or arranging for the financing of correctional facilities. This often involves owning the facility and leasing it back to the jurisdiction through a lease/purchase contract, which serves as an alternative to a public bond or tax increase.

The third type of privatization is full-scale *private management* of jails and prisons. Because it involves government transfer of assets, commercial enterprises, and management responsibilities to the private sector, this option is controversial.

The most recent data show that in 2010, of almost 1.6 million state and federal inmates, 128,195 were held in private prison facilities in 30 states (33,830 in private federal facilities and 94,365 in private state facilities).[67] The percentage of U.S. prisoners held in private facilities increased from just over 3 percent a decade ago to 8 percent in 2010.

However, the number of privately held Immigration and Customs Enforcement (ICE) and U.S. Marshals Service (USMS) detainees increased more rapidly than did privately held state or federal prisoners in the past decade (Exhibit 13-4). Unlike prisoners, federal detainees are generally waiting to have their case decided in court rather than serving time because they were convicted of a crime. The combined population of privately held ICE and USMS detainees nearly equaled the number of federal prisoners in private prisons in 2010. ICE detainees include those who (1) violate administrative laws by being in the United States without proper documentation, (2) overstay their visas, (3) are charged or convicted of crimes that subject them to deportation, (4) were previously deported or ordered to leave the country but have returned to or remained in the United States, and (5) are refugees seeking political asylum. USMS responsibilities include apprehending fugitives and housing and transporting all federal detainees from the time they enter federal custody until they are either acquitted or convicted and delivered to a federal prison facility.

Visit http://www.cnbc.com/id/44762286/ Billions_Behind_Bars_Inside_America039s_Prison_Industry or scan this code with the QR app on your SmartPhone or digital device and watch several CNBC podcasts on private prisons. How does this information relate to ideas discussed in this chapter?

EXHIBIT 13–4	**Prisoners and Detainees Held by Private Prison Companies, 2002 and 2010**		
	2002	**2010**	**Change (2002–2010)**
Prisoners			
State prisons	73,497	94,365	+28%
Federal prisons	20,274	33,830	+67%
Detainees			
Immigration and Customs Enforcement	4,841	14,814	+206%
U.S. Marshals Service	4,061	17,154	+322%

Source: Cody Mason, *Dollars and Detainees: The Growth of For-Profit Detention* (Washington, DC: The Sentencing Project, July 2012), p. 4. Reprinted with permission.

The catalyst for privatizing correctional institutions goes back to the public policies adopted during the 1970s and 1980s. The War on Drugs and harsh sentencing policies, including mandatory minimum sentences, fueled a rapid expansion in the nation's prison population. In 1976, RCA Services assumed control of the Weaversville Intensive Treatment Unit in North Hampton, Pennsylvania, marking the modern beginning of privatization in corrections. Other private companies followed suit and bid for contracts to operate halfway houses. In the 1980s, these companies extended their reach by contracting with the Immigration and Naturalization Service (restructured and renamed ICE following the terrorist attacks of 9/11) to detain undocumented immigrants. Shortly thereafter, for-profit prison privatization expanded rapidly. Today, the Corrections Corporation of America (CCA) and the GEP Group collectively manage more than half of the private prison contracts in the United States. Their combined revenues exceeded $2.9 billion in 2010.[68]

Other reasons for the growth in private corrections are the public's lack of confidence in the ability of correctional services provided by federal, state, and local governments to rehabilitate offenders and a reluctance to provide more funding for rising correctional costs. The enthusiasm for privatization is fueled by the prospect for more innovative, cost-effective prison management, including the involvement of the private sector in the financing of new prison construction. This enthusiasm is not shared by all, however.

The Debate

Largely because there has been no conclusive research, arguments continue to rage over the merits of privately run correctional facilities. The overriding reason supporting privatization in corrections is the desire of state and local governments to rapidly increase bed space, and save taxpayers money by providing correctional services traditionally supplied by government at less cost. Proponents also argue that for-profit private prisons can improve the quality of correctional services, and reduce crime and recidivism, and be an economic boom for the areas in which they are located, providing many jobs and feeding public coffers with increased tax revenue. Time and space do not allow us to report all of these arguments, but let's review what we know from the literature about the most central argument: Does for-profit private prison cost less than publicly run prisons?

The U.S. General Accounting Office (GAO) reviewed cost comparisons in four state-funded studies and one commissioned by the federal government and concluded "these studies do not offer substantial evidence that savings have occurred" through privatization.[69]

Researchers at the University of Cincinnati studied 33 cost-effectiveness evaluations of public and private prisons and concluded that prison size, age, and security level, not prison ownership (public vs. private), predict prison costs: "Relinquishing the responsibility of managing prisons to the private sphere is unlikely to alleviate much of the financial burden on state correctional budgets."[70]

The National Council on Crime and Delinquency (NCCD) conducted a national survey of private correctional management firms and found that, rather than the projected 20 percent savings, the firms provided an average savings of only about 1 percent, and most of that was achieved through lower labor costs. "In summary," wrote NCCD, "the cost benefits of privatization have not materialized to the extent promised by the private sector."[71]

In 2004, researchers found that state-run prisons accept a disproportionate number of expensive and high-risk inmates. Those with minimum or medium levels of security classification made up 90 percent of the private sector's population compared with only 69 percent in the public sector.[72] "It's cherry-picking," one state representative said. "They leave the most expensive prisoners with taxpayers and take the easy prisoners."[73]

In 2009, researchers at the University of Utah reviewed eight cost comparison studies resulting in vastly different conclusions. Half of the eight studies found private prisons to be more cost-efficient. The other four were evenly split and found both types of prisons statistically even. This information led the researchers to conclude that "prison privatization provides neither a clear advantage nor disadvantage compared to publicly managed prisons" and that "cost savings from privatization are not guaranteed and appear minimal." The report concluded that the value of moving toward prison privatization is "questionable."[74]

In 2010, research conducted by the Arizona State Department of Corrections found that despite a state law stipulating that private prisons must create "cost savings," the state had not saved money by contracting out minimum-security beds. Inmates in private prisons cost as much as $1,600 more per year.[75] A spokesman for Arizona Governor Jan Brewer did not dispute the findings. He said that state officials have "pretty wide lends" to interpret the cost-savings mandate. "It is a significant advantage to have a private firm be able to come in and front the costs," he said.[76] A spokesman for CCA, the largest for-profit private prison operator in the United States, echoed the governor's position saying, "There is a mixed bag of research out there. It's not as black and white and cut and dried as we would like."[77] Nothing in the U.S. Constitution says that prisoners must be held in government-owned or operated facilities. Recall the history of privatization in America presented earlier: The involvement of the private sector in corrections began shortly after the first English colonists arrived in Virginia in 1607. Is it oversell to argue for cost-savings? Should publicly-run prisons be held to the same standard?

Most advocates of privatization also suggest that allowing facilities to be operated by the private sector could result in cost reductions of 20 percent. Most studies, however, report more modest savings. In fact, researchers at the University of Cincinnati looked at 33 cost-effectiveness evaluations of public and private prisons and concluded that prison size, age, and security level, not prison ownership (public vs. private), predict prison costs: "Relinquishing the responsibility of managing prisons to the private sphere is unlikely to alleviate much of the financial burden on state correctional budgets."[78] There are very few studies comparing the quality of inmate confinement between public and privately operated correctional institutions. Some report that private prisons outperform their public counterparts. Others do not.

Proponents also argue that public prisons are not without their problems, and unlike state and federal governments, private firms are free from politics, cumbersome bureaucracies, and costly union contracts. Proponents also suggest that privately run correctional facilities can be economic boons for the areas in which they are located, providing many jobs and feeding public coffers with increased tax revenues.

Opponents of privatization, on the other hand, build their arguments on mostly philosophical grounds. One writer says that the fundamental issue is a moral one: Should private prisons companies lobby and contribute to campaigns that support policies—harsher prison sentences and increased reliance on incarceration than on probation and parole—that serve those companies? Since 2000, the three largest private prison companies have contributed more than $6 million to state politicans.[79] No clear quid pro quo (something given or received for something else) exists between these corporations' campaign contributions and the politicians writing laws that favor the private prison industry. The link is thin and ambiguous at best. Yet the question remains: Will private prisons, in their pursuit for profits, find ways to keep cells filled, prison construction booming, and more offenders under private supervision? For private prison corporations to do well and reward their shareholders, people have to go to prison. Most opponents of privatization argue that the practice is inherently flawed by the profit motive of private corporations. The corporate interest in maximizing profits, they claim, can have numerous negative consequences for inmates, correctional employees, and society. Some claim, for example, that the need to maintain healthy profit margins may preclude the cost of rehabilitation and recreational programs for inmates. Other opponents of privatization say that privately run companies save money by paying lower wages and benefits than states do. In fact, when Gary Mohr, director of Ohio's Department of Rehabilitation and Corrections and former consultant with the Corrections Corporation of America, proposed privatizing two Ohio prisons to save the state money, a state representative asked him how privatization would save the state money. He answered that private companies pay less and allow less vacation, sick, and personal time." It takes two state employees to staff a position for a week," he said, "but only requires 1.7 private employees to do the same job. We are paying more people to be off more often than they are."[80] The bottom line, he said, is that private prisons require 45 fewer people to fill 150 spots than the state. If Mohr is right, shouldn't efficiency trump politics?

The debate over prison privatization is healthy but begs the question of why the United States has mass incarceration—especially when crime rates are falling—in the first place. During the recent fiscal crisis, a slight reduction in the prison population has occurred, as noted in Chapter 7; the use of probation and parole has increased, as discussed in Chapters 4 and 8; and new solutions to reduce prison populations such as California's non-revocable parole and realignment have been employed. We must prioritize human prison conditions, rehabilitation, and low recidivism with the spirit of free competition, not settle for an either/or in the debate over prison privatization. Exhibit 13-5 summarizes the arguments for and against private prisons.

Visit http://www.vera.org/ernest-drucker-plague-prisons or scan this code with the QR app on your SmartPhone or digital device to watch the podcast of Michael Jacobson, director of the Vera Institute of Justice, discuss the impact of 40 years of domestic drug policy on U.S. incarceration rates with Ernest Drucker, professor emeritus in the Department of Family and Social Medicine, Montefiore Medical Center/Albert Einstein College of Medicine and adjunct professor of epidemiology at Columbia University's Mailman School of Public Health. How does this information relate to ideas discussed in this chapter?

CO13-9   Privatizing Probation and Parole

Other correctional areas experiencing privatization include probation and parole. In most states, the impetus for privatizing probation and parole was similar: Staffing and resources were not keeping pace with increasing caseloads. Community supervision officials felt they had exhausted the use of interns and volunteers, and obtaining funding for new staff was not possible. States partnered with the private sector to monitor the low-risk offender population, a group that generally has few needs, whose past records reflect little or no violence, and that successfully completes

EXHIBIT 13–5	Arguments For and Against Private Prisons

For Private Prisons

1. Private operators can provide construction financing options that allow the government client to pay only for capacity as needed in lieu of accumulating long-term debt.

2. Private companies offer modern state-of-the-art correctional facility designs that are efficient to operate and that are built according to value-engineering specifications.

3. Private operators typically design and construct a new correctional facility in half the time required for a comparable government construction project.

4. Private vendors provide government clients with the convenience and accountability of one entity for all compliance issues.

5. Private corrections management companies are able to mobilize rapidly and to specialize in unique facility missions.

6. Private corrections management companies provide economic development opportunities by hiring locally and, to the extent possible, purchasing locally.

7. Government can reduce or share its liability exposure by contracting with private corrections companies.

8. The government can retain flexibility by limiting the contract function and by specifying facility mission.

9. Adding other service providers injects competition among both public and private organizations.

Against Private Prisons

1. There are certain responsibilities that only the government should meet, such as safety and environmental protection. To provide incarceration, the government has legal, political, and moral obligations. Major constitutional competition among both public and private issues revolves around the deprivation of liberty, discipline, and preserving the constitutional rights of inmates. Related issues include the use of force, loss of time credit, and segregation.

2. Few private companies are available from which to choose.

3. Private operators may be inexperienced with key correctional issues.

4. Operators may become monopolies through political ingratiation, favoritism, and so on.

5. Government may lose the capability to perform the function over time.

6. The profit motive will inhibit the proper performance of duties. Private prisons have financial incentives to cut corners and offer lower wages, pensions, benefits, and staffing levels.

7. The procurement process is slow, inefficient, and open to risks.

8. Creating a good, clear contract is a daunting task.

9. Lack of enforcement remedies in contracts leaves only termination or lawsuits as recourse.

Source: From Dennis Cunningham, *"Public Strategies for Private Prisons."* Paper presented at the Private Prison Workshop, January 29–30, 1999, Institute on Criminal Justice, University of Minnesota Law School. Reprinted with permission of the author.

community supervision about 90 percent of the time. In 2007, about 10 states had contracts with private agencies to provide supervision for an estimated 300,000 offenders on court-ordered community supervision, typically for misdemeanor, low-risk offenses.[81]

In Connecticut, for example, the privatization initiative to monitor low-risk offender populations by the private sector allowed scarce resources to be used to better monitor offenders with higher levels of risk. Private case management responsibilities in Connecticut included sending an introductory letter to the probationer, monitoring restitution payments and compliance with conditions of probation, responding to probationer's inquiries, preparing standardized reports for probation officers, providing verification of conditional compliance, and providing statistical reports.

The situation in Colorado was similar. When Colorado officials adopted risk management and looked at how treatment and supervision were matched with levels of risk, they found more probation officers were needed than the Colorado General Assembly would fund. The result was a directive that allowed probation departments to contract with private agencies for the supervision of low-risk probationers. Thirteen of Colorado's 22 judicial districts have entered into such contracts. The private agencies directly bill the probationers for their supervision services, eliminating public expenditures for community supervision.

However, the debate over privatizing community supervision has its critics because unlike government agencies, private entities make a profit by collecting fees and fines from offenders. Without standards in contracting, oversight and monitoring, private agency supervision officers' compensation can be directly tied to the fees he or she collects.

The Salvation Army—the organization best known for ringing holiday bells and donating clothes—has been in the probation business in Florida since 1970. In 1975, the Florida legislature passed the Salvation Army Act, which allowed the church to run probation programs for counties. By 1979, judges in nearly one-half of Florida's 67 counties were sending probationers to the Salvation Army, but today the number has dwindled to 11 counties.[82] More than 50 counties dropped contracts with the Salvation Army for various reasons. Some judges did not like the mix of church and state and chose to use a private company. Other counties contended that the Salvation Army wasn't motivated enough to compel offenders to pay fines and fees. But what seemed to displease other counties was the fact that the Salvation Army used offender fees to pay itself even before it paid restitution to victims. In Hillsborough County (Tampa), Florida, the Salvation Army took its $55 monthly cost of supervision fee before a probationer paid any other costs, which made it harder for an offender to pay other amounts owed and ultimately get off probation. Other counties complained that when offenders were referred to court-ordered programs such as anger management and personal money management (classes typically offered by the Salvation Army), it charged offenders for them: $25 for a class in personal money management, $45 for anger management, $75 for shoplifters anonymous, and $80 for alternatives to violence through education. Officials in some counties believed that private companies offered better deals. Consider what has happened in Georgia.

In 2003, the Georgia legislature passed SB 474 that transferred supervision of 25,000 convicted misdemeanants from the state Department of Corrections to individual counties and permitted each county to contract with a for-profit probation agency to supervise these misdemeanants. Today, approximately 40 private probation agencies are registered in Georgia; they employ 850 probation officers and serve 640 courts.[83]

In Georgia, every person who cannot pay his or her misdemeanor fine on the day of court is placed on probation under the supervision of a private, for-profit company until he or she pays the fine. For example, assume you are ordered to pay $200 for a traffic fine. If you have enough money to pay it on the day you go to court, you can avoid probation. If you can't you must pay your fine and a monthly supervision fee in the range of $35–$44 to a private company in weekly or biweekly installments over a period of three months to a year. By the time your probation is over, you may have paid more than twice or three times the amount that the judge had ordered. In Americus, Georgia, just 10 miles from where President Jimmy Carter was raised, one high school student convicted of violating the terms of his learner's permit served seven months on probation and paid $505 in court fines and probation fees. Had he been able to pay the fine the day he was sentenced, he would have paid only $155.[84]

Critics argue that for-profit probation is unfair to poor people, needlessly supervises persons who are not a threat to society, and carries the risk of unnecessary incarceration because persons on probation can be arrested for technical violations such as missing a meeting with a probation officer. How often all this happens is unknown because in 2006, the

Georgia Assembly passed a law that permits for-profit probation companies to keep their records secret. In the summer of 2008, a reporter with *Mother Jones* visited the offices of Middle Georgia Community Probation Services and was politely told, "We don't talk to reporters."[85]

In 2007, the Private Probation Association of Georgia (PPAG) attempted to expand the reach of private probation and lobbied the General Assembly to allow it to supervise people convicted of more than 90 types of felonies ranging in seriousness from child molestation to shoplifting to credit card fraud and for a new law that would allow it to charge every misdemeanor probation a minimum monthly fee of $50 (in contrast, felony probationers were paying the state $23 per month for probation supervision). A coalition of Georgia judges, sheriffs, and others strongly opposed the bill, and it was defeated. PPAG pledged it would continue its efforts to enter the business of felony probation supervision.

The absence of systematic research on for-profit probation supervision means that we don't know how private community supervision is working elsewhere. In the meantime, however, several recommendations for improving the selection, performance, and accountability of private community supervision officers have been made. These include developing more rigorous statewide requirements for the private supervision of offenders under community control, increasing training and educational standards for private agency staff, strengthening agency reporting obligations, evaluating whether private community supervision officers have achieved performance goals, and establishing procedures for working with indigent offenders.[86]

TECHNOCORRECTIONS

CO13-10

The technological forces that made the use of cell phones commonplace is converging with corrections to create "technocorrections." Technological changes have impacted communication, offender and officer tracking and recognition, and detection.

Communication

Information is crucial to a well-run correctional system. Knowing what is happening gives correctional administrators the power not only to react to problems promptly but also to anticipate and prevent them.

Several years ago, the Federal Bureau of Prisons set up e-mail programs that allow inmates to send and receive e-mails.[87] According to the BOP, the program cuts down on the amount of paper mail (which can conceal drugs and other contraband), helps prisoners connect regularly with their families, and helps inmates build computer skills they can use when they return to the community. The BOP uses proceeds from prison commissaries and charges inmates 5 cents a minute to compose and read e-mails. Messages are screened for key words, are read by correctional officers before they are sent, and can be sent only to contacts who agree beforehand to receive e-mail from specific inmates.

Technology has also produced the newest prison **contraband**: cell phones.[88] We used to think of prison contraband as a file inside a cake. Now it's a smartphone hidden under a mattress. Visitors smuggle them in. Inmates returning from work release smuggle them in. And staff sell them to inmates for as much as $1,000. The number of cell phones confiscated in California prisons increased from 261 in 2006 to more than 15,000 in 2011.[89] California prison authorities twice found an LG flip phone under Charles

contraband

Any item that represents a serious threat to the safety and security of the institution.

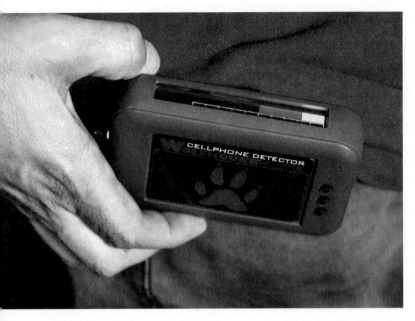

New technology similar to the Wolfhound contraband cell phone detection device can detect when cell phones are turned on or transmitting data. A directional antenna then helps locate the phone. New Jersey is experimenting with 24 of these detection devices. Why is inmate access to cell phones a threat to public safety? Are there any advantages in allowing inmates to have cell phones? Is it possible for corrections to control the disadvantages while allowing the advantages?

The Offender Speaks
Visit www.mhhe.com/schmalleger7e to see this feature.

Visit www.govtech.com/public-safety/ Video-Visitation-Bus-Connects-Jail-Inmates.html or scan this code with the QR app on your SmartPhone or digital device and watch the podcast of Pinellas County (Florida) Sheriff Jim Coats talking about the video visitation bus, which travels to four cities in Pinellas County to facilitate communication between inmates and their families. How does this information relate to ideas discussed in this chapter?

Manson's mattress. Inmates are using smuggled cell phones to threaten victims, conduct drug deals, order killings, and plot escapes. In December 2010, Georgia prisoners used cell phones to coordinate work stoppages with inmates at other prisons. They sent text messages, created e-mail distribution lists, and publicized their complaints about visitation, food, and living conditions on Facebook and Twitter. In response, some states have passed new laws making inmate phone possession a felony, have trained dogs to detect cell phones, and have added high-tech security equipment, much like machines used at airports. In August 2010, President Obama signed a bill making inmate possession of a cellphone or a wireless device in federal prison a felony punishable by up to a year of additional sentence.

The solution may be a new system introduced in California and Mississippi. Called *managed access,* cell towers at each prison accept communication only from approved phones that prison officials control. The cost to install the system at all 33 California prisons was between $16 million and $33 million. A one-day test at a single California prison intercepted more than 4,000 attempts to place calls, send text messages, or access the Internet.[90] The payoff for the company installing the towers comes from inmates' use of prison pay phones. Their use at the test site went up by 64 percent in the days after the test. Other states would like the Federal Communications Commission to grant them authority to overpower the signal with a stronger one (called *jamming*) or "trick" the cell phone to react as if a "no service" signal is received (called *spoofing*). However, the Communications Act of 1934 prohibits the manufacture, importation, marketing, sale, or operation of jamming or spoofing devices because they would "bleed" over into the public broadcast area.

Videoconferencing Prison systems across the country are using videoconferencing for arraignments, interrogations, and visitation. Until Connecticut installed videoconferencing in all of its 18 prisons, it sometimes cost as much as $1,800 to transport an inmate from prison to a courtroom. Connecticut and other states report using videoconferencing between judges and inmates to improve public safety and save money.[91]

The advantages of video conferencing include:

- increasing the number of visitations conducted each day;
- reducing staff time in checking in visitors;
- reducing the staff time previously needed to escort inmates to a centralized visitation area or courtroom for arraignments and other preliminary proceedings;
- reducing inmate movement, thereby increasing safety for staff and inmates;
- reducing space requirements and construction and operating costs on visitation areas; and
- eliminating contraband that was formerly passed by visitors in face-to-face contact.

Videoconferencing can also be especially helpful in high-profile cases for which security is tighter and exposure to the public needs to be minimized.

Virtual visiting has become the latest trend in prisons; at least 20 states now have some type of video conferencing system in place.[92] Because most prisoners are housed in facilities far removed from their homes, frequent visits sometimes are impossible, and video calls offer the opportunity for virtual face time.

However, we are beginning to see virtual visiting replacing face-to-face visiting altogether even when it is not necessary. In July 2012, the District of Columbia eliminated all face-to-face visitation and switched completely to video visiting.[93] Even a prisoner's family who lives nearby must go to a video conference center to chat with the inmate. Although the District of Columbia department of corrections will save money by avoiding the costs and problems of escorting inmates and their families and friends to the visiting room, prisoners who now get no face time with families and friends are not enthusiastic about the change. Although the District of Columbia does not charge families and friends, other jurisdictions see virtual visiting as a cash cow and charge widely varying fees.

The Ada County Jail in Idaho allows visitors to register for two free 25-minute video visits per week. Thereafter, families must pay for videos at the rate of $15 for 30 minutes or $30 for 60 minutes. The sheriff projected that virtual visiting would generate more than $2 million in two years.[94]

In contrast, Indiana's Rockville Correctional Facility charges families $12.50 for 30 minutes of virtual visitation, which is only slightly less than the $15 charge for a 30-minute local phone call. The Virtual Visitation Program in Pennsylvania allows one 55-minute virtual visit a month for $15 with the fee going to the not-for-profit hosting the program. Priority for virtual visitation is given to inmates who participate in parenting skills classes and other family-oriented programs. Virginia's Department of Corrections recently expanded its virtual visitation program and charges at the rate of $15 for 30 minutes and $30 for 60 minutes. The fees go to community churches that host visiting sites.[95]

However, not all agencies charge. The Pinellas County, Florida, Sheriff's Office outfitted a handicapped accessible bus with video visitation equipment, which travels to four cities.[96]

The fact is that if families were calling a family member who was not incarcerated using Skype or some other voice-over Internet protocol, the call would cost them nothing. Strengthening family bonds is an important ingredient in reducing recidivism, and virtual visiting can be a helpful way for inmates to stay connected to their families—but at what cost?

Telemedicine   Telemedicine, one of the newest advances in medicine, is providing prisoners cost-effective health care. Taking a prisoner to a specialist outside the prison poses a danger to correctional officers and the community by giving the prisoner an opportunity to escape or to have contact with other people in a less-controlled environment. Telemedicine allows physicians to consult with on-site medical personnel through video-conferencing and compatible medical devices, such as medical microcameras. Health care in correctional settings is improved, and the substantial savings on in-prison consultations and on trips to local providers can offset the costs of introducing this technology. Arizona, for example, saved $237,000 in 2008 by using telemedicine in nine correctional facilities.[97] Those states that have implemented telemedicine use it for medical and mental health services as well as for staff training and education.[98] However, some critics question the quality of medicine inmates receive via telemedicine, and point out that inmates need practice interacting effectively with people outside of prison.

biometrics

The automated identification or verification of human identity through measurable physiological and behavioral traits.

Offender and Officer Tracking and Recognition

Automated kiosks, also discussed in Chapter 5, are on the way to replacing routine visits to probation and parole officers. Offenders are instructed to report to a kiosk at a specified location. There they are electronically interviewed and in some cases tested for alcohol by means of a breath analysis attachment. Using the kiosks, offenders can also e-mail their parole officers to schedule personal meetings. The system identifies the offender by reading a magnetic card and using a biometric fingerprint scanner. **Biometrics** is the automated identification or verification of human identity through measurable physiological and behavioral traits such as iris, retinal, and facial recognition; hand and finger geometry; fingerprint and voice identification; and dynamic signature. The biometrics of the future are body odor, ear shape, facial thermography, and thermal imagery.

Remote-location monitoring of offenders, also discussed in Chapter 5, is steadily improving and is likely to be used far more in the future. However, remote-location monitoring is not just for inmates. Correctional officers can also wear personal alarm and location units that allow a computer to track their locations and respond to distress signals by sending the closest officers to the site of the emergency.

Fairly new in the field of corrections is the Global Positioning System (GPS). Already used in airplanes, automobiles, and SmartPhones, GPS is now also used for monitoring offenders under community supervision. The GPS tracking unit worn by an offender allows computers to pinpoint the offender's location at any time to the precise street address. The device can be programmed to send a signal if an offender enters a forbidden zone or even a spoken warning emanating from the device itself instructing the offender to leave the area or face the consequences. In the field of inmate monitoring, there is also some discussion about implanting chips in offenders' bodies that would alert officials to unacceptable behavior. In some cases, when criminal activity was detected, the chip might give an electric shock that would temporarily shut down the offender's central nervous system.

A new technological tool designed to track an offender's alcohol consumption is the continuous transdermal alcohol monitoring device. An electrostatic pad presses against the offender's upper arm, chemically "tasting" sweat for signs of alcohol. A continuous transdermal alcohol monitor was used on Lindsay Lohan after she violated her probation stemming from DUI charges.[99]

Administrators are also relying on new telecommunications technology to help track inmates and former inmates. Speaker ID technology identifies a speaker even if he or she has a cold, just woke from a deep sleep, or has a poor telephone connection. Systems using speaker ID can be used to keep track of who calls inmates in prison and to monitor criminal activity such as escape plans, gang activity, and smuggling contraband. Speaker ID can also be used for low-risk offenders granted early parole as an alternative to incarceration. The system can make random calls and positively identify the speaker from his or her response. The offenders never know when or how they will receive calls. When no one answers the phone or the speaker is not identified, the system alerts authorities to a possible violation.

Prison medical staff videoconference with an offsite physician about a prisoner's physical health. Advances in technology have helped make prisons and jails safer and more secure, while facilitating innovations such as telemedicine. What promises might tomorrow's technologies hold for correctional institutions?

To increase the efficiency of inmate monitoring and cut administrative costs, a smart card, a plastic card embedded with a computer chip, can be used to store all types of information about the inmate—from medical care to meals eaten.

The use of facial recognition technology is also on the increase in corrections. All 300 employees of the Prince George County Correctional Center in Upper Marlboro, Maryland, swipe picture-image ID cards across a scanner. The swipe alerts the system that an employee is entering the facility. The system verifies the image from a database and using the biometrics of the employee's face, compares it to the one captured by the camera. Eventually, Prince George County will use biometric-based access control technology to screen visitors to determine whether they are ex-inmates.

The principles of geographic information systems (GISs) are also changing corrections.[100] GIS links graphics with tabular information to produce a graphical, layered, spatial interface or map that can help prison management in many ways.

Proponents foresee a time when corrections mapping can be used to do the following:

1. track and display inmate location and movement;
2. indicate whether a housing unit is balanced with regard to religion, group affiliation, age, race, and ethnicity;
3. pinpoint the locations of gang members and link them to each inmate's behavioral and criminal history as well as the inmate's rank in the hierarchy of the group;
4. pinpoint areas in a prison that are potentially dangerous such as hallways or blind corners where a number of assaults may have occurred;
5. incorporate aerial photos of a facility to check for possible security breaches and potential escape routes;
6. provide a basis for proactive investigation and enforcement, for example, mapping the flow of money in and out of prison and then linking it to data about visitation, telephone calls, and correspondence addresses to show a potential drug problem; and
7. link inmate data to the names, telephone numbers, and addresses of all the people the inmate had contact with during incarceration, in case of an escape.

Detection

To maintain prison security, researchers have developed new detection technologies. One is ground-penetrating radar (GPR), which can be used to locate underground escape tunnels. Another is heartbeat monitoring. Using the same technology employed by geologists to detect earthquakes, geophone machines can detect the heartbeat of an inmate trying to escape in a laundry or trash truck leaving the prison. In 1999, heartbeat monitoring prevented the escape of a prisoner in Tennessee. X-rays and magnetic resonance imaging scan the body for concealed weapons, eliminating the necessity for a physical search. Noninvasive drug detection technology places a swab or patch on the skin, which absorbs perspiration and signals the presence of illegal drugs. Pupillometry (a binocular-like device that flashes a light to stimulate pupil contraction) can also measure drug or alcohol use. Another technological tool for drug testing has inmates look through a viewfinder. Ion scans can also detect drug particles on visitors to correctional facilities. In addition, correctional officers can now control prison riots and disturbances using a joystick and monitor that directs an "assault intervention device," a 6-foot robot to blast millimeter waves that simulate intense heat under the skin where pain receptacles are located.

Implementation

Despite the increase in such technology, obstacles must still be overcome. Corrections personnel have been slow to embrace new technology, in part because new systems can be unreliable and difficult to maintain and have high life cycle costs. Ethical concerns about the rights of offenders might be another barrier to implementing new technology. Through a program sponsored by the Department of Justice—Staff and Inmate Monitoring (SAINT)—the Navy's Space and Naval Warfare System Center in Charleston, South Carolina, is systematically addressing biometric and smart card technology through development, testing, and evaluation of a prototype system in the Navy Consolidated Brig in Charleston.[101] There is no question, however, that new technologies are playing an increasingly important role in correctional institutions as a means to address critical health, safety, and security issues.

REVIEW AND APPLICATIONS

SUMMARY

1 Prisons are overcrowded for four main reasons. First, over the past decade, there has been an increase in imprisonment. Second, changes in federal and state sentencing laws require more offenders to serve longer periods. Third, there has been an increase in imprisonment for drug and violent offenses. Fourth, a prison industrial complex has emerged.

2 This chapter examined six methods of controlling prison overcrowding. First, reduce the number of people who go to prison by making more use of *front-end strategies* such as diversion, community corrections, and intermediate sanctions. Second, put a cap or ceiling on the prison population, sometimes called a *trap-door strategy.* Third, use what are called *side-door strategies,* such as giving sentenced offenders the opportunity to apply to the sentencing court for release to intensive community corrections programs, usually six months after imprisonment. Fourth, use more parole and halfway houses, called *back-door strategies.* Fifth, build more prisons and/ or expand existing facilities. Sixth, use structured sentencing guidelines that are designed to save prison space for serious crimes and violent offenses, while using community corrections and intermediate sanctions for lesser offenses.

3 Prisons control the influence of security threat groups by referring to them as STGs rather than "gangs." Some prisons have security threat group units that are responsible for the identification and overall coordination of all STG-related information at their facilities. Some prisons transfer known STG members from one institution to another. Some states have enacted "gang enhancement" statutes that impose severe sentences on STG activity. And some states have built supermax prisons that house STG members in complete lockdown and isolation.

4 Prison riots occur for a number of reasons. Sometimes they result from spontaneous outburst. Most experts believe that the primary causes of prison riots are bad conditions (overcrowding, antiquated facilities, low staffing levels, insufficient staff training, lack of programs for inmates, lack of funding, and poor implementation of correctional policy), rebellious inmates and racial antagonism, institutional structure and readiness, and administrative factors (for example, frequent staff turnover, low correctional officer qualifications, inadequate training, poor staff–inmate communication, and low staff pay).

⑤ Preventing prison riots requires changes both outside and inside the prison. Outside prison it is important for other social institutions to reduce sources of tension that contribute to crime. Inside prison experts recommend implementing formal inmate grievance procedures, ombudsmen, improved classification systems, smaller institutions, meaningful educational and work programs, alternatives to incarceration, professional prison staff who are well trained and well paid, and clearly written and well-understood policies on the use of force.

⑥ A supermax housing facility is a freestanding facility or a distinct unit within a facility that provides for management and secure control of inmates who have been officially designated as violent or who exhibit serious and disruptive behavior while incarcerated. Some experts who have studied the effects of long-term solitary confinement report evidence of acute sensory deprivation, paranoid delusion belief systems, irrational fears of violence, resentment, little ability to control rage, and mental breakdowns. Others believe the conditions of supermax confinement do not exacerbate symptoms of mental illness or create mental illness where none previously existed. They tell us that psychological disturbances are present among prisoners in the general population as well. Supermax prisons also present extraordinary challenges for staff, possibly creating a "we/they syndrome" and magnifying tensions between inmates and staff.

⑦ No-frills prisons and jails eliminate prisoner privileges and amenities in the belief that this process will deter criminals from future criminal activity. It appears, however, that no-frills correctional facilities may actually produce the results they were designed to avert, thereby increasing the number of prison disturbances and making it difficult for corrections staff to motivate appropriate inmate behavior. Corrections professionals tell us that they consider what outsiders perceive as privileges and amenities to be important management tools. Research from Florida shows that public views on prison amenities are not as harsh as many assume. The public is willing to provide and retain amenities if they are useful for inmate management and rehabilitation.

⑧ Correctional facilities and agencies should be accredited for eight reasons. Accreditation improves staff training and development, assesses program strengths and weaknesses, is a defense against lawsuits, establishes measurable criteria for upgrading operations, improves staff morale and professionalism, offers a safer environment for staff and offenders, reduces liability insurance costs, and offers performance-based benefits.

⑨ Arguments in favor of privatization include construction financing options that allow government clients to pay only for capacity as needed in lieu of accumulating long-term debt; modern state-of-the-art correctional facility designs that are efficient to operate; less time to build than comparable government construction projects; convenience and accountability of one entity for all compliance issues; rapid mobilization and specialization in unique facility missions; and economic development opportunities from hiring and purchasing locally. Reasons not to privatize include the moral issue of the government's responsibility for public safety; a lack of private companies from which to choose; private contractor inexperience with corrections issues; the potential for private vendors to become a monopoly through political ingratiation and favoritism; the potential for government to lose the capability to perform the function over time; the potential for the profit motive to inhibit proper performance of duties; slow procurement processes that are open to risks; the difficulty of creating a contract with a private vendor; and the potential for a lack of enforcement to result in termination or expensive lawsuits as the only recourse.

⑩ Technology has affected corrections in the areas of communication, offender and officer tracking and recognition, and detection.

KEY TERMS

structured sentencing, p. 422

exchange rates, p. 422

security threat groups (STGs), p. 423

disturbance, p. 429

riot, p. 429

supermax housing, p. 434

special master, p. 438

no-frills prisons and jails, p. 439

contraband, p. 451

biometrics, p. 454

QUESTIONS FOR REVIEW

1 Debate the four reasons that prisons are overcrowded.

2 Which method of controlling prison crowding do you believe is most important?

3 What do you believe is the most effective solution for controlling the influence of security threat groups (STGs)?

4 Rank the five causes of prison riots in order from most to least important.

5 Speculate what can be done to prevent prison riots.

6 Summarize the emergence of supermax housing and its impact on prisoners and staff.

7 What do you think about no-frills jails and prisons and their impact on corrections?

8 What ideas can you add to the reasons correctional agencies and facilities should be accredited?

9 Critique the arguments for and against privatization.

10 Debate the pros and cons of using technology in corrections.

THINKING CRITICALLY ABOUT CORRECTIONS

The Politics of Defining Prison Overcrowding

Think about the three ways to discuss prison overcrowding. Which definition of *capacity* is the most conservative? Which one is the most liberal? Explain. If you were a warden of a prison operating at 40 percent over capacity but you didn't believe your prison was overcrowded in the strict sense of the word, and a reporter asked you if your facility was overcrowded, which definition would you offer and why? How do the politics of corrections, your job, and the definition of *overcrowding* influence your response and shape the public debate on prison overcrowding?

No-Frills Jails and Prisons and the Politics of Misinformation

The public favors taking away prison amenities in part because it believes they are paid for by tax dollars. However, in this chapter you learned that a survey of Orlando, Florida, residents indicates that they supported inmate access to prison amenities when they learned that the prisoners, not the taxpayers, paid for their privileges. If most jurisdictions require inmates to pay for their amenities, why is the public misinformed? Can the politics of misinformation both harm and help corrections? Explain.

ON-THE-JOB DECISION MAKING

Overcoming Opposition to Privatization

It is 2020 and you are the director of your state's Department of Corrections and Rehabilitation. Your predecessors contracted with several private vendors to perform government activities such as food preparation and inmate programming. You signed contracts for full-scale private management of two state prisons. So far, your experience with privatization has been successful. Predictions from a decade ago that your state would not privatize the entire state department of corrections might be wrong. Your prisons continue to operate above capacity, and you believe that you spend more time in court than you do in your office. You need more bed space, but the public refuses to spend more on prisons. You are thinking seriously about a proposal that would turn over the management of all your state's adult prisons to the public sector. How will you overcome the opposition of your state's correctional officer association?

What Inmates Need to Know to Work Their Way out of Supermax Prison

Morris Thigpen, former director of the National Institute of Corrections, tells us, "It is imperative that all inmates placed in supermax be fully aware of how they can work their way out." Assume that your state is planning a supermax prison. You remember Thigpen's words. What will you propose as opportunities for inmates to demonstrate positive behavior to work their way out?

For additional information, please see: www.mhhe.com/schmalleger7e
Follow the author's tweets about the latest crime and justice news @schmalleger

THE VICTIM

Helping Those in Need

CHAPTER OBJECTIVES

After completing this chapter you should be able to do the following:

❶ Briefly summarize the history of America's victims' rights movement including important federal victims' rights legislation.

❷ List and describe the costs and consequences of criminal victimization.

❸ Understand how corrections agencies participate in meeting victims' needs, and identify the kinds of victim services provided by correctional agencies.

❹ Explain how crime victim compensation programs work.

❺ Describe the official mission of the federal Office for Victims of Crime and identify its various operating divisions.

❻ Understand the nature of victim impact statements, and explain why they are important.

❼ Anticipate the future of victims' rights by identifying the five global challenges now facing victims' rights advocates.

> *As a victim you're amazed that no one will ask you about the crime, or the effect that it has on you and your family. You took the . . . defendant's blows, heard his threats, listened to him brag that he'd 'beat the rap' or 'con the judge.' No one ever hears these things. They never give you a chance to tell them.*
>
> —A victim

Thirty-years ago, 15-year-old Mary Vincent became the surviving victim of one of the most gruesome crimes of the 20th century.[1] Vincent, who had been hitchhiking on a trip to her grandfather's house in Corona, California, was attacked and raped by Larry Singleton—an innocuous-looking 51-year-old man who offered her a ride. In an act of sadistic violation, Singleton hacked off Vincent's forearms with a hatchet and left her for dead on a hillside. She survived, and was found the next morning wandering near a road holding the stubs of her arms in the air to prevent blood loss.

Although victims' advocates argued for a lengthy prison term for Vincent's attacker, an apparently unrepentant Singleton was paroled after serving only eight years in prison. He took up residence in Florida, and Vincent lived in constant fear that he would attack her again. Vincent's concern finally abated in 1997 when Singleton was arrested and charged with the murder of 31-year-old Roxanne Hayes, a supposed prostitute. A year later he was convicted of first-degree murder. Singleton died of cancer in 2001 while on death row at Florida's Union Correctional Institution. Today a recovered Vincent leads a full and active life in the Pacific Northwest.

Violent-crime survivor Mary Vincent throws the first pitch during the Giants "Resolve to Stop the Violence Project Day" in 1999 at 3Com Park, in San Francisco. Vincent was brutally raped by Larry Singleton—who cut off her forearms with a hatchet when she was 15 years old. Singleton's release, after only eight years in prison, came to symbolize the lack of attention to the plight of crime victims that had once been characteristic of the U.S. criminal justice system. How has the situation of crime victims changed?

(CO14-1) A BRIEF HISTORY OF AMERICA'S VICTIMS' RIGHTS MOVEMENT

victim

A person who suffers direct or threatened physical, psychological, or financial harm as a result of the commission or attempted commission of a crime or delinquent act.

According to the state of California's Constitution, a **victim** is "a person who suffers direct or threatened physical, psychological, or financial harm as a result of the commission or attempted commission of a crime or delinquent act."[2] The word *victim* also includes the person's spouse, parents, children, siblings, guardian, and a lawful representative of a crime victim who is deceased, a minor, or physically or psychologically incapacitated. The term *victim* does not include a person in custody for an offense, the accused, or a person whom the court finds would not act in the best interests of a minor victim.

Victims were rarely recognized in the laws and policies that govern our nation until the 1970s. From a legal perspective, crimes were considered offenses against the state (because the state made the law), not against the individual. Victims merely set the wheels of justice in motion (by filing charges) and, if necessary, helped carry out justice (by testifying in court). The victim had little or no status within the justice system, and victims' rights were virtually nonexistent.[3]

Tremendous strides have since been made in **victims' rights** legislation and the introduction of victims' services. Few movements in American history have achieved as much success in prompting legislative response as did victims' rights activists' campaigns through the 1980s and 1990s.

The 1980 enactment of Wisconsin's victims' Bill of Rights, the nation's first state bill of rights for crime victims, launched an era of dramatic progress in the victims' rights movement.[4] Passage of the federal Victim and Witness Protection Act of 1982[5] (VWPA) and release of the *Final Report* by the President's Task Force on Victims of Crime in the same year brought national visibility to crime victims' concerns.

The VWPA and the *Final Report* were catalysts for a decade of significant advances in victims' rights. By the date of release of the *Final Report,* four states had legislated victims' basic rights.[6] Today, all states have laws modeled after the VWPA that establish, protect, and enforce victims' rights. There are now more than 27,000 victim-related state statutes and 30 state victims' rights constitutional amendments.

Most states' victims' bills of rights include basic provisions for treatment with dignity and compassion, ongoing access to information about the status of the case and the offender, notification of hearing and trial dates, permission to attend related judicial proceedings, input at sentencing and parole hearings (through victim impact statements), and restitution.

Today, all states have legislated victims' rights to notification of events and proceedings at various stages of the judicial process; 40 have legislated victims' rights to attend criminal justice proceedings[7]; and 32 constitutionally protect these rights.[8] All states permit consideration of victim impact information at sentencing with most permitting victim presentation of the information during the sentencing hearing. The majority of states require that victim impact information be included in the presentencing report, and at least half require that the court consider this information in its sentencing decision.

According to the National Victims' Constitutional Amendment Passage network (NVCAP), California Proposition 9, or the Victims' Rights and Protection Act of 2008 (also known as *Marsy's Law*), is the most comprehensive victims' bill of rights of any state in the nation.[9] Proposition 9 appeared on the November 4, 2008, statewide ballot in California and passed with 53.8 precent of the vote. It amended the California Constitution by adding new provisions regarding victims of crimes. Proposition 9 provides victims in California a number of specifically enforceable rights, as enumerated in Exhibit 14–1.

Despite the advances in victims' rights legislation, there remain serious deficiencies in those laws and in their implementation. Crime victims' rights, which vary significantly at the state level, are often ignored, and many victims are still denied the right to participate in the justice process. Implementation of state-enacted constitutional victims' rights is often arbitrary and based on judicial preference. Many states make no provision for victims' rights in cases involving juvenile offenders.

victims' rights
The fundamental rights of victims to be represented equitably throughout the criminal justice process.

Visit www.ncjrs.gov/ovc_archives/ncvrw/ 2010/multimedia/videoFiles/2010_NCVRW_ Theme.mov or scan this code with the QR app on your SmartPhone or digital device and watch a video prepared by the national Office for Victims of Crime discussing victims' rights.

| EXHIBIT 14-1 | Victims' Rights in California |

In order to preserve and protect a victim's rights to justice and due process, a victim shall be entitled to the following rights:

1. To be treated with fairness and respect for his or her privacy and dignity, and to be free from intimidation, harassment, and abuse, throughout the criminal or juvenile justice process.

2. To be reasonably protected from the defendant and persons acting on behalf of the defendant.

3. To have the safety of the victim and the victim's family considered in fixing the amount of bail and release conditions for the defendant.

4. To prevent the disclosure of confidential information or records to the defendant, the defendant's attorney, or any other person acting on behalf of the defendant, which could be used to locate or harass the victim or the victim's family or which disclose confidential communications made in the course of medical or counseling treatment, or which are otherwise privileged or confidential by law.

5. To refuse an interview, deposition, or discovery request by the defendant, the defendant's attorney, or any other person acting on behalf of the defendant, and to set reasonable conditions on the conduct of any such interview to which the victim consents.

6. To reasonable notice of and to reasonably confer with the prosecuting agency, upon request, regarding the arrest of the defendant if known by the prosecutor, the charges filed, the determination whether to extradite the defendant, and, upon request, to be notified of and informed before any pretrial disposition of the case.

7. To reasonable notice of all public proceedings, including delinquency proceedings, upon request, at which the defendant and the prosecutor are entitled to be present and of all parole or other post-conviction release proceedings, and to be present at all such proceedings.

8. To be heard, upon request, at any proceeding, including any delinquency proceeding, involving a post-arrest release decision, plea, sentencing, post-conviction release decision, or any proceeding in which a right of the victim is at issue.

9. To a speedy trial and a prompt and final conclusion of the case and any related post-judgment proceedings.

10. To provide information to a probation department official conducting a pre-sentence investigation concerning the impact of the offense on the victim and the victim's family and any sentencing recommendations before the sentencing of the defendant.

11. To receive, upon request, the pre-sentence report when available to the defendant, except for those portions made confidential by law.

12. To be informed, upon request, of the conviction, sentence, place and time of incarceration, or other disposition of the defendant, the scheduled release date of the defendant, and the release of or the escape by the defendant from custody.

13. To restitution.

14. To the prompt return of property when no longer needed as evidence.

15. To be informed of all parole procedures, to participate in the parole process, to provide information to the parole authority to be considered before the parole of the offender, and to be notified, upon request, of the parole or other release of the offender.

16. To have the safety of the victim, the victim's family, and the general public considered before any parole or other post-judgment release decision is made.

17. To be informed of the rights enumerated in paragraphs (1) through (16).

Source: Section 28(e) of Article I of the California Constitution.

Federal Legislation

Congressional concern for crime victims was evident in the VWPA; its stated purpose was "to enhance and protect the necessary role of crime victims and witnesses in the criminal justice process; to ensure that the federal government does all that is possible to assist victims and witnesses of crime, within the limits of available resources, without infringing on the constitutional rights of the defendant; and to provide model legislation for state and local governments."[10]

A subsection of the Crime Control Act of 1990,[11] known as the *Victims' Rights and Restitution Act of 1990 (Victims' Rights Act)*, established a Bill of Rights for federal crime victims.[12] The Victims' Rights Act requires that federal law enforcement officials use their "best efforts" to ensure that victims receive basic rights and services. The **best efforts standard**

best efforts standard

A requirement of the federal Victims' Rights and Restitution Act of 1990 (also known as the *Victims' Rights Act*) that mandates that federal law enforcement officers, prosecutors, and corrections officials use their best efforts to ensure that victims receive basic rights and services during their encounter with the criminal justice system.

An assault victim arriving at the Macomb County, Michigan, Prosecutor's Office Crime Victims Rights Unit is greeted by victim advocate Kay McGuire. The unit's staff assists victims of violent crimes during the investigation, trial, presentencing, and postsentencing phases of their victimization and advises victims regarding compensation entitlements under Michigan's Crime Victim Compensation Act. What other kinds of agencies have traditionally provided help to crime victims?

made the federal law weaker than many state victims' rights laws in which provision for victims' rights and services is mandatory. The basic rights and services that officials must use their best efforts to provide include the following:

- fair and respectful treatment by authorities;
- reasonable protection from the accused;
- notification of court proceedings;
- presence at public court proceedings unless the court specifies otherwise;
- conference with the prosecutor;
- restitution; and
- updates to information about the offender, including conviction, sentencing, imprisonment, and release.

The Violent Crime Control and Law Enforcement Act,[13] passed in 1994, established new rights for victims of sexual assault, domestic violence, sexual exploitation, child abuse, and telemarketing fraud. This legislation also designated significant funding for combating domestic violence and sexual assault, placed more than 100,000 community police officers on the street, and launched a number of other crime prevention initiatives.

In 1996, the federal Community Notification Act, known as *Megan's Law*, was enacted to ensure community notification of the locations of convicted sex offenders.[14]

In the Victims' Rights Clarification Act of 1997, Congress asserted victims' rights to attend proceedings and deliver victim impact statements within the federal system. This act was passed to ensure that victims and survivors of the Alfred P. Murrah Federal Building bombing in Oklahoma City, Oklahoma, could observe the trial and provide input at sentencing. Exhibit 14–2 summarizes federal victims' rights legislation.

On October 9, 2004, the U.S. Senate passed the Crime Victims' Rights Act[15] as part of the Justice for All Act of 2004. The act establishes statutory rights for victims of federal crimes and gives them the necessary legal

EXHIBIT 14–2 | Federal Victims' Rights Legislation

Legislation	Provisions
Adam Walsh Child Protection and Safety Act, 2006	Established a national sex offender registry and extended the civil remedies for child sex crime victims to persons victimized as children, even if their injuries did not surface until the person became an adult.
Crime Victims' Rights Act, 2004	Established statutory rights for victims of federal crimes and gave them the necessary legal authority to assert those rights in federal court.
Unborn Victims of Violence Act (also known as *Laci and Conner's Law*), 2004	Made it a separate federal crime to "kill or attempt to kill" a fetus "at any stage of development" during an assault on a pregnant woman.
Victims' Rights Clarification Act, 1997	Ensured that victims of federal crimes had the right both to attend proceedings and to deliver or submit a victim impact statement.
Mandatory Victim Restitution Act, 1996	Made restitution mandatory on the federal level in all violent crime cases and in certain other cases.
Community Notification Act (also known as *Megan's Law*), 1996	Ensured that communities are notified of the release and location of convicted sex offenders.
Violent Crime Control and Law Enforcement Act, 1994	Created new rights for victims of sexual assault, domestic violence, sexual exploitation, child abuse, and telemarketing fraud.
Victims' Rights and Restitution Act (also called the *Victims' Rights Act*), 1990	Created the first federal bill of rights for victims of crime and required federal law enforcement officers, prosecutors, and corrections officials to use their *best efforts* to ensure that victims receive basic rights and services.
Victims of Crime Act (VOCA), 1984	Established the federal Office for Victims of Crime (OVC) to provide federal funds in support of victim assistance and compensation programs around the country and to advocate for the fair treatment of crime victims. Also established the federal Crime Victims' Fund to assist states in paying for support services to crime victims.
Victim and Witness Protection Act (VWPA), 1982	Enacted a set of basic rights for crime victims and became a national model for state victims' rights laws.

authority to assert those rights in federal court. The act grants the following rights to victims of federal crimes:

1. to be reasonably protected from the accused;
2. to reasonable, accurate, and timely notice of any public proceeding involving the crime or of any release or escape of the accused;

3. to be included in any such public proceeding;

4. to be reasonably heard at any public proceeding involving release, plea, or sentencing;

5. to confer with the federal prosecutor handling the case;

6. to full and timely restitution as provided by law;

7. to proceedings free from unreasonable delay; and

8. to be treated with fairness and with respect for the victim's dignity and privacy.

The legislation also requires federal courts to ensure that these enumerated rights are afforded to victims. Similarly, federal law enforcement officials are required to make their "best efforts to see that crime victims are notified of, and accorded," these rights. To teach citizens about the rights of victims of crime, the federal government created a Web site that can be accessed via **www.crimevictims.gov.** It includes a directory of crime victims' services that can be searched locally, nationally, and internationally. A user-friendly database of victims' rights laws is available online at **www.victimlaw.info.**

The Proposal for a Federal Victims' Rights Constitutional Amendment

The 1982 President's Task Force on Victims of Crime made 68 recommendations for protection of victims' rights, including a recommendation that the Sixth Amendment to the U.S. Constitution be amended to guarantee specific rights to crime victims. Although the recommendation has not yet been implemented, the National Organization for Victim Assistance (NOVA), Mothers Against Drunk Driving (MADD), the National Center for Victims of Crime (NVC—formerly the National Victim Center), and other national victims' organizations joined together in 1987 to create the National Victims' Constitutional Amendment Network (NVCAN).[16] NVCAN spent the next decade assisting state legislators in their efforts to pass amendments. Efforts to pass state constitutional amendments produced impressive results. Each of the 33 state victims' rights amendments passed by an overwhelming majority—80 to 90 percent in most states.[17]

The proposal to adopt a federal constitutional amendment gained momentum in April 2002 when President George W. Bush announced his support of the bipartisan Crime Victims' Rights Amendment authored by Senators Feinstein and Kyl.[18] Although that initiative failed, a federal victims' rights amendment has been proposed a number of times since; Reps. Trent Franks, R-AZ; Jim Costa, D-CA; and Ed Royce, R-CA, offered a modified version in 2013. As proposed, the amendment would provide specific constitutionally protected rights to crime victims but could not be used as grounds for a new trial or in support of a claim for damages. Exhibit 14–3 documents advances in victims' rights and services since 1965. Keep up-to-date on the status of the proposed victims' rights constitutional amendment via the National Victims' Constitutional Amendment Passage (NVCAP) network at www.nvcap.org.

THE COSTS AND CONSEQUENCES OF VICTIMIZATION

`CO14-2`

According to a two-year National Institute of Justice (NIJ) study,[19] personal crimes result in costs of about $105 billion annually for medical expenses, lost earnings, and public victim assistance programs. For

EXHIBIT 14–3	Crime Victims' Rights in America: A Timeline

2008
- California voters approve Proposition 9, amending the state's constitution to recognize the rights of crime victims.

2006
- President George W. Bush signs into law the Violence Against Women Act of 2005.

2005
- The U.S. Department of Justice launches its National Sex Offender Public Registry Web site (www.nsopw.gov). The site has since been renamed the Dru Sjodin National Sex Offender Public Web site.

2004
- Congress passes the Justice for All Act of 2004, which includes the Crime Victims' Rights Act of 2004, providing substantive rights for crime victims and mechanisms to enforce them.

2003
- Congress passes the PROTECT Act of 2003—also known as the *Amber Alert Law*—which creates a national AMBER network (America's Missing: Broadcast Emergency Response) to facilitate rapid law enforcement and community response to kidnapped or abducted children.
- Congress passes the Prison Rape Elimination Act, designed to track and address the issue of rape in correctional institutions and develop national standards aimed at reducing prison rape.

2002
- By the end of 2002, all 50 states, the District of Columbia, U.S. Virgin Islands, Puerto Rico, and Guam had established crime victim compensation programs.

2001
- Congress responds to the terrorist acts of September 11 with a host of new laws, providing funding for victim assistance, tax relief for victims, and other accommodations and protections for victims.

2000
- In October, Congress extended VAWA through 2005 and authorized funding at $3.3 billion over the five-year period.
- In October, Congress passes the Trafficking Victims Protection Act of 2000 to combat *trafficking* in persons and to protect such victims.

1999
- On January 19, 1999, the federal victims' rights constitutional amendment (Senate Joint Resolution 3, identical to SJR 44) is introduced in the 106th Congress.

1998
- Senators Jon Kyl and Dianne Feinstein introduce Senate Joint Resolution 44, a new bipartisan version of the federal victims' rights constitutional amendment, in the Senate.
- Four new states pass state victims' rights constitutional amendments, bringing the total to 33.
- Congress enacts the Child Protection and Sexual Predator Punishment Act of 1998, providing for numerous sentencing enhancements and other initiatives addressing sex crimes against children.
- In October, the Identity Theft and Deterrence Act of 1998 is signed into law.

1997
- A federal victims' rights constitutional amendment is reintroduced in the opening days of the 105th Congress with strong bipartisan support.
- In March, Congress passes at historic speed the Victims' Rights Clarification Act of 1997 to clarify existing federal law allowing victims to attend a trial and to appear as "impact witnesses" during the sentencing phase of both capital and noncapital cases. President Clinton immediately signs the act.
- Congress enacts a federal antistalking law.
- The Office for Victims of Crime publishes *New Directions from the Field: Victims' Rights and Services for the 21st Century.*

1996
- Federal victims' rights constitutional amendments are introduced in both houses of Congress with bipartisan support.
- The Community Notification Act, known as *Megan's Law,* provides for notifying communities of the location of convicted sex offenders by amendment to the national Child Sexual Abuse Registry law.
- President Clinton signs the Antiterrorism and Effective Death Penalty Act, making restitution mandatory in violent crime cases and expanding compensation and assistance services for victims of terrorism both at home and abroad, including victims in the military.
- The Mandatory Victims' Restitution Act makes restitution in federal cases mandatory, regardless of the defendant's ability to pay.
- The National Domestic Violence Hotline is established.

1995
- The National Victims' Constitutional Amendment Network (NVCAN) proposes the first draft of language for a federal victims' rights constitutional amendment.

1994
- President Clinton signs a comprehensive package of federal victims' rights legislation as part of the Violent Crime Control and Law Enforcement Act. The act includes the Violence Against Women Act (VAWA) and establishes a National Child Sex Offender Registry.

1993
- Congress passes the Child Sexual Abuse Registry Act, establishing a national repository for information about child sex offenders.
- Twenty-two states pass antistalking statutes, bringing the total number of states with antistalking laws to 50 plus the District of Columbia.

1992
- The National Crime Victims Research and Treatment and Center and the National Victim Center publish *Rape in America: A Report to the Nation.*
- Congress reauthorizes the Higher Education Bill, which includes the Campus Sexual Assault Victims' Bill of Rights.

| EXHIBIT 14–3 | Crime Victims' Rights in America: A Timeline *(continued)* |

1991
- Representative Ilena Ros-Lehtinen (R-FL) files the first Congressional Joint Resolution to place victims' rights in the U.S. Constitution.
- The American Probation and Parole Association (APPA) establishes a Victim Issues Committee to examine victims' issues and concerns related to community corrections.
- The New Jersey legislature passes a victims' rights constitutional amendment, which is ratified by voters in November. By the end of 1991, seven states had incorporated victims' rights into their constitutions.

1990
- The U.S. Congress passes the Hate Crime Statistics Act requiring the U.S. attorney general to collect data of incidence of crimes motivated by prejudice based on race, religion, sexual orientation, or ethnicity.
- President George H. W. Bush signs into law the Student Right-to-Know and Campus Security Act, requiring institutions of higher education to disclose murder, rape, robbery, and other crimes on campus.
- Congress passes the Victims of Child Abuse Act, which features reforms to make the federal criminal justice system less traumatic for child victims and witnesses.
- The Victims' Rights and Restitution Act of 1990 incorporates a Bill of Rights for federal crime victims and codifies services that should be available to victims of crime.

1987
- The National Victims' Constitutional Amendment Network (NVCAN) is formed.
- The American Correctional Association establishes a Task Force on Victims of Crime.

1985
- The National Victim Center (renamed the National Center for Victims of Crime in 1998) is founded to promote the rights and needs of crime victims.
- The United Nations General Assembly adopts the Declaration of Basic Principles of Justice for Victims of Crime and Abuse of Power that serves as the basis for victim service reform throughout the world.

1984
- The passage of the Victims of Crime Act (VOCA) establishes the Crime Victims Fund, made up of federal criminal fines, penalties, and bond forfeitures, to support state victim compensation and victim service programs.
- President Reagan signs the Justice Assistance Act, which establishes a financial assistance program for state and local government and funds 200 new victim service programs.
- The National Center for Missing and Exploited Children (NCMEC) is created.
- Congress passes the Family Violence Prevention and Services Act, which earmarks federal funding for programs serving victims of domestic violence.
- Victim-witness coordinator positions are established in the U.S. attorneys' offices within the U.S. Department of Justice.

1983
- The U.S. Department of Justice creates the Office for Victims of Crime (OVC) within the Office of Justice Programs to implement recommendations from the President's Task Force on Victims of Crime.
- The International Association of Chiefs of Police adopts a Crime Victims' Bill of Rights and establishes a Victims' Rights Committee to emphasize the needs of crime victims by law enforcement officials nationwide.

1982
- President Reagan appoints the Task Force on Victims of Crime. The Task Force's *Final Report* offers 68 recommendations that become the framework for the advancement of new programs and policies.
- The federal Victim and Witness Protection Act of 1982 brings "fair treatment standards" to victims and witnesses in the federal criminal justice system.
- California voters overwhelmingly pass Proposition 8, which guarantees restitution and other statutory reforms to crime victims.

1980
- Mothers Against Drunk Driving (MADD) is founded.
- Wisconsin passes the first Crime Victims' Bill of Rights.

1979
- Frank G. Carrington, considered by many to be the founder of the victims' rights movement, creates the Crime Victims' Legal Advocacy Institute, Inc. The nonprofit organization was renamed the Victims' Assistance Legal Organization (VALOR), in 1981.
- The World Society of Victimology is formed to promote research of victims and victim assistance.

1976
- The National Organization for Women (NOW) forms a task force to examine the problem of battering.

1975
- Citizen activists from across the country unite to expand victim services and increase recognition of victims' rights through the formation of the National Organization for Victim Assistance (NOVA).

1974
- The federal Law Enforcement Assistance Administration (LEAA) funds its first victim-witness programs.

1972
- The first three victim assistance programs are created in St. Louis, Missouri; San Francisco, California; and Washington, DC.

1965
- The first crime victim compensation program is established in California.

Source: Adapted from Office for Victims of Crime, "Crime Victims' Rights in America: A Historical Overview" (Washington, DC: Office of Justice Programs, 2011), http://ovc.ncjrs.gov/ncvrw2011/pdf/landmarks.pdf (accessed March 5, 2013).

tangible losses

Costs such as medical expenses, lost wages, and property losses that accrue to crime victims as a result of their victimization.

intangible losses

Costs such as fear, pain, suffering, and reduced quality of life that accrue to crime victims as a result of their victimization.

victims, crime costs may include (1) out-of-pocket expenses, such as for medical bills and property replacement, (2) reduced productivity at work, home, or school, and (3) nonmonetary losses, such as fear, pain, suffering, and reduced quality of life.

Unlike **tangible losses** (such as medical expenses or lost wages), **intangible losses** (such as pain, suffering, and reduced quality of life) do not have a market price and cannot be bought or sold. Nevertheless, these losses are real and can be valued in dollars—victims would pay dearly to avoid them.

The true cost of victimization includes intangible losses, the annual cost of which is estimated at $644 billion in the United States (see Exhibit 14–4). Violent crime (including drunk driving) accounts for $610 billion of this total; property crime, $34 billion. These estimates exclude several other types of crime such as white collar crime, personal fraud, and drug crime.

The cost of crime victimization is far higher when its impact on society is considered. Such costs include (1) monies spent by the criminal justice system to find, prosecute, and confine offenders, (2) social costs associated with fear of crime (e.g., changed behavior, the fear of being outside at night, moving to a safer neighborhood), (3) mental health costs associated with healing "wounds" from victimization, (4) private security expenditures by the general population concerned about crime, (5) monies spent by employers to train temporary or new employees, (6) the costs of lost productivity borne by employers, (7) insurance claims processing costs (for example, life insurance claims for fatalities and workers' compensation claims), (8) workers' compensation and disability payments, especially those made to workers victimized while on the job, and (9) legal expenses incurred in recovering productivity losses from offenders and insurance companies (e.g., drunk drivers and their insurers). The National Crime Victimization Survey (NCVS) data include estimates of the number of hours of work and earnings lost due to medically related problems associated with victimization. Some specifics from the NIJ study follow:

Marsy Nicholas, the young murder victim whose death in 1983 later became the catalyst for California's Proposition 9: Marsy's Law, shown with her brother, Dr. Henry Nicholas, whom former California Gov. Pete Wilson called the "driving force" (http://en.wikipedia.org/wiki/Henry_Nicholas#cite_note-6) behind the constitutional Amendment. Dr. Nicholas cofounded and served as cochairman, president and CEO of Broadcom Corp. Marsy, a University of California Santa Barbara student, was stalked and killed by her ex-boyfriend in 1983. What is the thrust of the California legislation?

- Violent crime is associated with 3 percent of all U.S. medical spending and 14 percent of all injury-related medical spending.
- Violent crime results in wage losses equivalent to 1 percent of U.S. earnings.
- Violent crime is a significant factor in the need for mental health care. As much as 10 to 20 percent of mental health care expenditures in the United States may be attributable to crime, primarily for victims treated as a result of their victimization.
- Personal crime reduces the average American's quality of life by 1.8 percent. Violence alone causes a 1.7 percent loss through homicide and personal injury. These estimates apply only to victimized households, not the broader impact of crime-induced fear on our society.

An even more recent study provides insight into tangible and intangible victim costs associated with specific types of offenses.[20] That study, authored by Kathryn E. McCollister, Michael T. French (both of the University of Miami), and Hal Fang (at the University of Colorado at

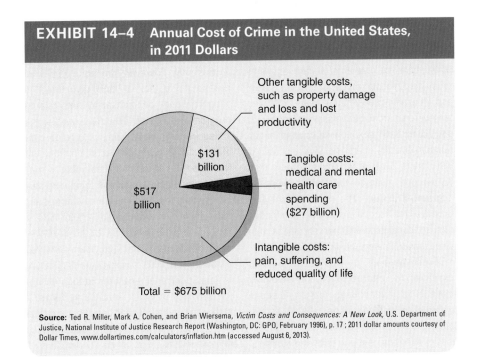

EXHIBIT 14–4　Annual Cost of Crime in the United States, in 2011 Dollars

Other tangible costs, such as property damage and loss and lost productivity

$131 billion

$517 billion

Tangible costs: medical and mental health care spending ($27 billion)

Intangible costs: pain, suffering, and reduced quality of life

Total = $675 billion

Source: Ted R. Miller, Mark A. Cohen, and Brian Wiersema, *Victim Costs and Consequences: A New Look,* U.S. Department of Justice, National Institute of Justice Research Report (Washington, DC: GPO, February 1996), p. 17 ; 2011 dollar amounts courtesy of Dollar Times, www.dollartimes.com/calculators/inflation.htm (accessed August 6, 2013).

Denver), found that tangible costs associated with an incident of murder, for example, total $737,517; intangible costs reach $8,442,000 per homicide. Similarly, the average rape victim, according to the authors, incurs $5,556 in tangible costs; intangibles amount to $199,642 per incident. The study estimated intangible costs by weighing, among other things, jury-compensation awards associated with typical victimizations and related civil court proceedings. Crime victimization cost estimates, like those discussed here, can help government agencies and other organizations create effective policies and shape substance abuse treatment or other interventions that can reduce crime.

Who Pays the Bill?

Victims and their families pay the bill for some crimes, and the public largely pays the bill for others. Insurers pay $45 billion in crime-related claims annually.[21] That is $265 per U.S. adult. The government pays $8 billion annually for restorative and emergency services to victims in addition to about one-fourth of the $11 billion in health insurance claim payments.

Taxpayers and insurance purchasers cover almost all the tangible victim costs of arson and drunk driving. They cover $9 billion of the $19 billion in tangible nonservice costs of larceny, burglary, and motor vehicle theft.

Victims pay about $44 billion of the $57 billion in tangible nonservice expenses for violent crimes—murder, rape, robbery, assault, and abuse and neglect. Employers pay almost $5 billion because of these crimes, primarily in health insurance bills. (This estimate excludes sick leave and disability insurance costs other than workers' compensation.) Government bears the remaining costs, in the form of lost tax revenues and Medicare/Medicaid payments. Crime victim compensation accounts for 38 percent of homeowner insurance premium costs and 29 percent of automobile insurance premium costs.

Criminologists and public policy researchers are now using crime cost estimates to help assess the desirability of various policy options. Reported costs can be used to assess the wisdom of early offender release and diversion programs.

Economic Realities and Corrections: Victim Services

In 2013, declining tax revenue, inaccurate financial forecasting, and a redirection of funds by the Texas legislature combined to produce a $16 million shortfall in the budget of the state's Compensation to Victims of Crime Fund. The Crime Victim Services Division (CVSD), which manages the fund, operates from the Texas attorney general's office. CVSD's mission is to assist in compassionately and effectively delivering crime victim services by offering information, resources, and education to victims and the organizations that assist them.

The Crime Victims' Compensation (CVC) program is supported through a legislative appropriation from the Compensation to Victims of Crime Fund, which also provides grants to domestic violence, rape crisis, and other victim programs throughout the state.

Victims' services in Texas began with the 1979 passage of the state's Crime Victims' Compensation Act, which created the fund to encourage increased victim participation in the apprehension and prosecution of criminals and reimbursement to victims for certain out-of-pocket expenses incurred as a result of violent crime.

In 2011, the crime victims' fund distributed more than $36 million in grants to organizations that provide victim-related advocacy work such as emergency shelters, crisis counseling, and accompaniment to court.

In 2011, the fund received 37,528 individual requests for compensation, including 29,573 applications from victims of crime and 7,955 applications by law enforcement agencies requesting reimbursement of fees for sexual assault examinations. In that year, 15,121 victims were awarded benefits, averaging $4,752 per victim; 8,091 sexual assault examination reimbursements, averaging $474 per award, were made. Most of the awards (more than 52 percent) made to the victims were for aggravated assault. The sexual abuse of a child was the second most commonly funded offense, consuming 14.8 percent of the individual award money paid in 2011.

Expenses paid to victims help cover expenses for attorney fees, bereavement leave, child or dependent care, crime scene cleanup, replacement of items taken as evidence, funerals and burials, loss of support, loss of earnings, rent and relocation, travels, and medical and mental health. The largest single expense, totaling more than $38 million in 2011, was for acute hospital care for victims of violent crime.

As budget shortfalls impinge on victim services programs in Texas, both grants to individual crime victims and programs that offer services to victims have been threatened with severe cutbacks. Moneys available for crime victim compensation, for example, dropped from a peak of $138 million in 2007 to $87 million in 2013.

A significant factor contributing to this deficit is declining revenue from court fees imposed upon defendants in criminal case, which have constituted approximately 86 percent of the crime victim fund's state revenue.

Recently, however, the state of Texas has begun to look at innovative ways to support victim compensation and related programs. In March 2009, for example, the Texas Department of Criminal Justice initiated a pilot program in selected confinement facilities through which inmate labor is contracted to telemarketers and telephone survey companies to generate revenue. Calls made by inmates generated $4,509,686.15 in revenue in 2010 and $6,057,132.261 in 2011—much of which helps to fund victim services.

During its 2009 session, the legislature enacted additional measures to help ensure the solvency of victim services in Texas. It authorized counties to sell unclaimed criminal trial exhibits with 50 percent of the proceeds to be deposited in the victims of crime fund.

Although Texas appears to have found innovative ways to keep both victim services and victim compensation alive, similar programs in other jurisdictions are also facing cuts. Local officials in other states may be able to benefit by looking at some of the efforts Texas has made to save its victims' programs.

Sources: Brandi Grissom, "Crime Victim Services Bracing for Big Cuts," *The Texas Tribune,* February 16, 2012, www.texastribune.org/2012/02/16/crime-victims-services-bracing-big-cuts/ (accessed June 5, 2013); Texas Crime Victim Compensation Fund, "Crime Victims' Compensation," www.oag.state.tx.us/victims/about_comp.shtml (accessed June 5, 2013); Office of the Texas Attorney General, *Appreciation for Dedication: Crime Victim Services Annual Report 2011,* www.oag.state.tx.us/AG_Publications/pdfs/cvs_annual2011.pdf (accessed June 5, 2013).

CO14-3 THE ROLE OF CORRECTIONS

In the past, correctional agencies were viewed only as facilities for punishing and rehabilitating offenders. Today, they also serve crime victims—protecting them from intimidation and harassment, notifying them of offender status, providing avenues for victim input into release decisions, and collecting restitution.[22] Public safety consultant Anne Seymour calls corrections-based victim services a "specialized discipline" within the field of victims' rights and services.[23]

Correctional agencies are also beginning to recognize the important role that victims can play in helping them develop policies, procedures, and programs that consider victims as well as correctional staff and offenders. Across the nation, crime victims are being asked to join advisory committees and agency boards, become official members of parole commissions, and serve as teachers in innovative classes that sensitize offenders to the impact of their offenses.

Correctional agencies are beginning to acknowledge victims' needs in their mission statements. In Oregon, for example, the state board of parole recently issued the following statement: "The Board's mission is to work in partnership with the Department of Corrections and local supervisory authorities to protect the public and reduce the risk of repeat criminal behavior through incarceration and community supervision decisions based on applicable laws, victims' interests, public safety, and recognized principles of offender behavioral change."[24] Many state corrections departments have now issued similar mission statements (see Exhibit 14–5 for the American Correctional Association's Policy Statement on Crime Victims).

Crime victims' involvement with correctional agencies helps ensure priority for victim safety and services within correctional agencies (see Exhibit 14–6). Victim advisory committees now exist in a number of correctional agencies for that purpose.

Samantha Alexander, sister of murder victim Travis Alexander, makes a victim impact statement to the court in the 2013 Jodi Arias trial. Arias was convicted of first degree murder in the brutal killing of the 29-year-old Alexander in his Colorado home after he ended their romance. His sister told the court about what his loss meant to her. What is the purpose of a victim impact statement?

Victim Notification

Victim notification of the release or pending release of convicted offenders is an important service. Without notification, victims are denied an opportunity to take precautions to ensure their own safety.

The importance of providing offender release information to crime victims has long been recognized. In 1982, it was one of the primary recommendations of the President's Task Force on Victims of Crime. In the *Final Report*, the Task Force recommended that parole boards notify victims and their families in advance of parole hearings if victims provide the paroling authority with their names and addresses. In addition, the task force called on parole boards to allow victims of crime, their families, or their representatives to attend parole hearings and to provide information about the impact of the crime. According to the National Victim Services Survey, marked improvements have occurred in this area since 1985.[25]

There is, however, no consistent victim notification procedure. Some correctional agencies notify victims of only certain types of inmate releases (such as the release of sex offenders). Others notify victims of changes in offender classification. Some notify victims of an inmate's escape, and others notify victims of an inmate's clemency or death. At the federal level, the BOP has created one of the nation's first comprehensive victim notification programs, which has served as a model to the states for more than a decade. The BOP notifies victims of any major change in an inmate's status.

Innovative technologies have emerged in recent years that augment victim access to notification and information. At least 10 state correctional agencies utilize automated voice notification systems that place telephone calls to victims, if requested, and inform them of offenders' pending release or release hearings. Victims can also contact a centralized call center 24 hours a day, seven days a week. Call center operators confirm offender status and provide referrals to community-based victim services. Many state correctional agencies are following the example of the Illinois Department of Corrections, which provides current updates on inmate status and location and relevant upcoming hearings to victims and the general public via the Internet.[26]

In most jurisdictions, victims must request certain types of notification. Many victims do not request notification simply because they have not been informed that they have a right to do so.

victim notification

Notification to victims of the release or pending release of convicted offenders who have harmed them.

| EXHIBIT 14–5 | American Correctional Association |

Public Correctional Policy on Victims of Crime

Victims have the right to be treated with respect and compassion, to be informed about and involved in the criminal and juvenile justice process as it affects their lives, to be protected from harm and intimidation, and to be provided necessary financial and support services that attempt to restore a sense of justice to them. Although many components of the criminal justice and juvenile justice systems share in the responsibility of providing services to victims of crime, the corrections community has an important role in this process and should:

- support activities that advocate for the rights of the victims;
- promote local, state, and federal legislation that emphasizes victims' rights and the development of victim services;
- support efforts by federal, state, and local units of government to increase funding and improve use of existing resources to support victim services and programs;
- advocate for programs in which offenders provide restitution to victims, compensation and service to the community and, whenever possible, hold offenders financially responsible for their crimes;
- promote active participation of victims in the criminal justice and juvenile justice processes, including the opportunity to attend and be heard and/or to participate in juvenile and adult institutional release and/or parole release hearings; provide separate waiting areas for victims and their families where offenders and victims may be present at the same hearing;
- provide advance notification of institutional release when safe and consistent with applicable law or expeditious notification of an escape to victims;
- educate, with sensitivity to culture, language and disability needs, victims and victim service providers about correctional practices and involve correctional personnel in victim advocacy activities;
- educate justice officials regarding victims' services, the impact of crime on victims, and promote sensitivity to victims' rights;
- operate victims' assistance programs that appropriately fall within the responsibility of the field of corrections. Correctional agencies should, at a minimum but not limited to:
  - designate personnel in each agency to respond to questions and concerns of victims and to ensure that appropriate victim notification and assistance procedures are implemented;
  - develop and distribute materials describing the correctional system and specific victims' rights within that system;
  - support and facilitate the use of victim impact statements in sentencing, post-conviction reviews, and programming processes; and
  - provide appropriate victims' services to staff who are assaulted, held hostage or otherwise victimized.
- promote the use of community resources and volunteers to serve the needs of victims.

Source: Copyright © American Correctional Association. Reprinted with permission.

Victim and Witness Protection

Every day in the United States, victims and witnesses are harassed, intimidated, and retaliated against by incarcerated offenders through intimidating phone calls, mail, or threatened visits from friends and associates. Many correctional agencies have responded creatively to this problem. Today when such problems occur, 37 states revoke an offending inmate's privileges, 36 transfer the inmate to a more restrictive level, 28 allow the filing of a new criminal charge, and 21 allow enhancement of the inmate's sentence. In addition, 40 state correctional agencies document

The Offender Speaks
Visit www.mhhe.com/schmalleger7e to see this feature.

> **EXHIBIT 14–6**   Department of Justice
>
> ### Crime Victim Treatment Improvement Plan
>
> Many people believe that much more needs to be done to involve victims and the community in the correctional process. A plan proposed by the Department of Justice to improve the treatment of crime victims recommended these specific steps:
>
> - Every state department of corrections and every parole authority should establish an advisory committee of victims and service providers to guide and support victim-related policies, programs, and services.
> - Correctional agencies should designate staff to provide information, assistance, and referrals to victims of crime.
> - Mission statements of correctional agencies should recognize victims as an important constituency and should address victims' rights and services.
> - A correctional agency should notify victims of any change in the offender's status that would allow the offender access to the community or to the victims.
> - A correctional agency should place a high priority on ensuring victims' safety from intimidation, threats, or harm by offenders.
> - Information about offender status and victims' rights should be accessible in several languages through toll-free numbers and printed materials.
> - Correctional agencies should collect and distribute restitution payments as ordered by the court, and wage-earning opportunities should be increased for inmates, wards, and parolees who owe restitution.
> - Victims' input should be sought for all decisions affecting the release of adult and juvenile offenders.
> - Victim-impact awareness should be a basic component of the education and treatment programs of correctional agencies.
> - Protected, supported, mediated dialogue between victim and offender should be available upon the victim's request.
> - A crime victim should be notified of any violation of the conditions of the offender's probation or parole and should be allowed to comment before or during the violation hearing.
> - Uniform practices should be developed and implemented for notification of a sex offender's release.
>
> **Source:** Adapted from Office of Justice Programs, *New Directions from the Field: Victims' Rights and Services for the 21st Century* (Washington, DC: U.S. Department of Justice, 1998).

such harassment and threats in the offender's case file, 35 recommend investigation for additional prosecution, and 31 recommend revocation of parole when a parolee harasses, intimidates, or attempts retaliation.[27] California authorities are using an innovative method to stop the increasing number of instances in which inmates use telephones or letters to threaten and harass victims. The California Department of Corrections and Rehabilitation has created a program to block victims' phone numbers from inmate access and check inmates' outgoing mail.

In managing offenders who are ordered by the court to community supervision or released early from prison with supervision, probation and parole officers need to ensure the safety of victims and the public. Officers generally use surveillance to identify offenders who pose a continued threat and make monitoring efforts such as checking with contacts at the offender's home and place of employment and with neighbors to ensure that the offender is meeting the conditions of probation or parole.

Just as there are special units in law enforcement and prosecutors' offices, probation and parole departments have begun to establish special units such as those for sex offender and domestic violence to provide intensive probation or parole to reduce the safety risks to victims and society as a whole. Agents in these units have smaller caseloads than agents in other units and have received specialized training in intensive supervision.

Correctional agencies also use intermediate sanctions to ensure victim safety. Such sanctions include electronic monitoring, house arrest, random alcohol and drug testing, parole to a location other than the victim's community, mandatory restitution, and increased surveillance.

Community Notification

Most states have passed laws that either provide for community notification of sexual offender releases or authorize the general public or certain individuals or organizations to access sexual offender registries. Often referred to as *Megan's Laws*, in memory of seven-year-old Megan Kanka, who was murdered by a twice-convicted sex offender paroled to her New Jersey neighborhood, community notification laws recognize that a community has a compelling interest in being informed of offenders' whereabouts. In 1996, a federal Megan's Law was enacted that requires states to release relevant registration information when necessary to protect the public.[28] In the mid-1990s, in rapid succession, every state enacted a Megan's Law of its own. In 2006, the federal government established a public national sex offender Web site (Exhibit 14–7).

Most state community notification laws impose a registration requirement on a sex offender at the time he or she is released on parole or probation, and the requirement typically remains in force for the duration of the parole or probation period.[29] A few states, including Alaska, California, Michigan, Montana, and South Carolina, impose a lifetime registration requirement for sex offenders against children, and other states have established a fixed registration period of 15 or 25 years. Approximately 30 states have provisions for some type of DNA testing or registration for genetic identification purposes.

To be truly effective, **community notification** laws require coordination among law enforcement officials, courts, correctional agencies, victim service providers, the news media, and other key stakeholders.

community notification

Notification to the community of the release or pending release of convicted offenders.

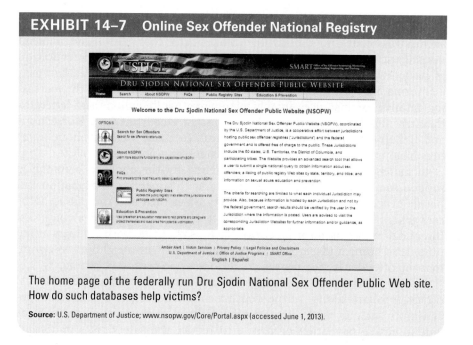

EXHIBIT 14–7   Online Sex Offender National Registry

The home page of the federally run Dru Sjodin National Sex Offender Public Web site. How do such databases help victims?

Source: U.S. Department of Justice; www.nsopw.gov/Core/Portal.aspx (accessed June 1, 2013).

Mary Achilles

Victim Advocate • Commonwealth of Pennsylvania

Mary Achilles heads the Office of the Victim Advocate for the Commonwealth of Pennsylvania, where she supervises a staff of 16. The office was formed in 1995 as an independent agency to provide services to both corrections and parole.

She began her career in 1979 as a prosecution assistant in the district attorney's office in Philadelphia where she worked for 14 years. She moved to the department of corrections in 1993 and worked to establish the state's victim notification program. She holds a bachelor's degree in criminal justice and a master's degree in public administration.

On a daily basis, Achilles deals with victims and allows them to provide input into the release process. Her office files petitions to the board of probation and parole on behalf of victims to deny release or set supervision conditions and selects victims to view executions if they desire to do so.

Achilles says she was drawn to her current role while working in the district attorney's office. "Helping prepare cases for trial, I started to see the inconvenience and the draw that they had on the victim," she says.

"Our philosophy is that we have to work with victims to prepare them for the fact that the offender will be released," she adds. "We'll petition the board to deny their release, but the reality is that 90 percent of all offenders will be released again."

"The challenge for us is that we work in agencies that are about the managing of offenders. Those agencies by design are about the movement of offenders through the process, and to get those agencies to be sensitive to the individual victim is always a battle."

Despite the challenges, Achilles is enthusiastic about her job. "It is incredible to see the strength of the human spirit. Since we mostly deal with state-level offenders, we're talking murders and rapes and serial rapes, the horrible stuff people don't want to talk about. It's amazing to me how people can triumph over tragedy—how much stronger they can be as a result of it."

> *"Victims raise a variety of issues—'I don't want him near my child's school or in my community.' I'm always engaging decision makers about what's best for the victim, the offender, and the community at large."*

Correctional agencies play a major role in providing this service by determining when and to where sex offenders will be paroled and by conducting community outreach and public education projects. Concerns, however, have been expressed over reported vigilantism (threats and acts of violence) in connection with community notification provisions and with the inability of released offenders to find housing and to live peacefully in the community.

A promising practice in planning and implementing community notification programs emerged in 1990 in the state of Washington.[30] The Washington approach considers the rights and interests of victims, the community, and offenders. The strategy incorporates the following elements: establishing requirements for registration, requiring registration information for offenders, implementing guidelines for failure to register, implementing guidelines for a preliminary offender risk assessment, compiling offender information packets for distribution to the prosecutor of the county where the offender plans to reside, distributing special bulletins to law enforcement agencies, developing notification policies, creating guidelines concerning who should have access to sex offender registry information, and conducting community outreach efforts that involve victims and address their rights and needs.

Crime Impact Classes

Over the past decade, the number of educational programs in correctional institutions that involve both offenders and victims has greatly increased. The purpose of such programs is to help offenders understand the devastating impact their crimes have on victims and their families and friends, on their communities, and on themselves and their own families. For victims, participation in programs with offenders is useful because, although the harm they have suffered cannot be undone, they may prevent others from being victimized. Studies also show that participation in impact panels helps heal victims' emotional wounds.[31]

Notable among victim–offender programs is the Impact of Crime on Victims (IOC) program initiated by the California Youth Authority in 1986. The program has been replicated in more than 20 juvenile and adult correctional agencies and numerous diversion programs. IOC programs include a 40-hour curriculum that is designed to educate offenders about how different crimes affect victims and society.[32]

The U.S. Department of the Navy's Corrections and Programs Division took an important step in integrating victims into its corrections process when it issued guidelines in 1996 instructing U.S. Naval correctional facilities to implement impact-of-crime classes for prisoners before releasing them from custody. Information from inmates and correctional staff indicate that, after completing the classes, offenders have a greater understanding of the impact of their criminal conduct.

The passage of protective legislation represents a meaningful first step. But National Center for Victims of Crime surveys indicate that enforcement is generally lacking.[33] The NCVC reports that less than 40 percent of surveyed local criminal justice professionals knew their states had such legislation and that rates of required victim notifications range as low as 30 percent. Criminal justice officials cite lack of funding as the most common reason for their inability to meet these responsibilities.[34]

Victim–Offender Dialogue

During the past two decades, a number of victim–offender dialogue programs have been developed in juvenile and criminal justice agencies, predominantly in juvenile probation agencies. These programs, primarily used in property crime cases, give victims an opportunity to engage in a structured dialogue with their offenders, who have already admitted their guilt or been convicted/adjudicated. When conducted with sensitivity to the victim and with care to ensure that participation by both victim and offender is voluntary, the victim–offender dialogue process can be very effective in helping victims overcome feelings of trauma and loss.[35] The program, which is closely linked to restorative justice initiatives discussed in earlier chapters, gives victims more satisfaction with the justice system, increases their likelihood of being compensated, and reduces fear of future victimization.

In recent years, correctional agencies have begun to experiment with victim–offender dialogue in violent crime cases. In 1995, for example, the Texas Department of Criminal Justice initiated a victim–offender mediation/dialogue program for victims of severe violence and their incarcerated offenders. Under this program, the victim initiates the contact.

The Victimization of Correctional Staff

Correctional agencies have begun to recognize the impact of victimization on their employees. Correctional professionals are exposed to a wide

The entrance to the federal Office for Victims of Crime (OVC). OVC has developed model programs for assisting crime victims—including victimized correctional staff. What forms of criminal victimization might correctional staff experience?

range of victimization, including verbal harassment by inmates, sexual harassment by inmates or colleagues, physical or sexual assaults, hostage situations, and murder. To lessen the acute and chronic trauma this violence has on employees, many adult correctional agencies have developed written policies and procedures to respond to staff victimization and critical incidents.[36]

Most institutions have standard procedures for dealing with correctional staff victimization that focus on prevention. Many prison management departments, including those in California, South Carolina, and Texas, have developed procedures for helping victimized staff. Guidelines for response to employee victimization have also been developed under a national training and technical project funded by the OVC.[37] The OVC project provides a comprehensive model for correctional agencies that is based on victims' rights laws, either state or federal.

VICTIM COMPENSATION

CO14-4

Victims generally have three options for recovering crime-related financial losses: (1) state-sponsored compensation programs, (2) court-ordered restitution, and (3) civil remedies, or lawsuits against offenders. **Victim compensation** programs, which exist in every state, may pay for medical care, mental health counseling, lost wages or loss of support, funeral and burial expenses, and/or crime scene cleanup.[38]

Restitution, the subject of the next section in this chapter, can be ordered in juvenile and criminal courts as a way to hold offenders financially accountable for their crimes.[39] The financial as well as preventative remedies that crime victims can seek through the civil justice system are not discussed in this text, but you should know that they represent one more avenue that victims can pursue to be compensated financially for their injuries. At the very least, correctional offices should consider implementing a policy of informing victims and victim service providers of the legal rights of crime victims to pursue reparations through the civil justice system.

The first victim compensation programs were established in New Zealand and Great Britain in 1964. These programs were based on a concept suggested by British Magistrate Margery Fry in the late 1950s. The first victim compensation program established in the United States was California's, created in 1965. By the time the President's Task Force on Victims of Crime released its *Final Report* in 1982, 36 states had victim compensation programs.[40] Today, all 50 states, the District of Columbia, the U.S. Virgin Islands, Guam, and Puerto Rico operate victim compensation programs.[41]

Victim compensation programs provide assistance to victims of almost all types of violent crime: rape, robbery, assault, sexual abuse, drunk driving, and domestic violence. These programs, as a rule, pay expenses but do not pay for lost, stolen, or damaged property. Eligibility and specific benefits vary from state to state.

In a typical year, state compensation programs pay approximately $240 million to more than 110,000 victims.[42] The amounts paid by each state vary considerably. Ten states pay less than $500,000 annually, and about 15 pay more than $3 million. The two states with the largest programs, California and Texas, pay nearly one-half of the total benefits paid in the United States.

Benefit maximums, which also vary from state to state, generally range from $10,000 to $25,000, although maximums are lower or higher for a few states. For example, California, Maryland, Minnesota, Ohio, Texas,

victim compensation

A form of victim assistance in which state-funded payments are made to victims to help them recover financial losses due to crime.

and Wisconsin allow benefits of $40,000 to $50,000. Some states, such as New York, set no limit on payment of medical expenses; other states, such as Washington, pay medical expenses up to a predetermined maximum. Many states also set limits for other types of expenses, such as funerals and mental health counseling. Nationally, the average amount paid to each victim applying for compensation is about $2,000.

President's Task Force on Victims of Crime

In 1982, the President's Task Force recommended federal funding to help support state victim compensation programs. It also documented problems in several state victim compensation programs: absence of a system for emergency compensation to cover immediate need for food, shelter, and/or medical assistance; insufficient maximum reimbursement levels; lack of coverage for domestic violence; and differences in residency requirements for eligible crime victims. Many of these problems have since been remedied through federal and state legislation and increased federal and state funding.

State-operated victim compensation programs have improved dramatically since 1982, in benefits provided and in recipients. However, some of the concerns raised by the President's Task Force, such as emergency compensation and insufficient maximums, have not been fully addressed by all states.

Victims of Crime Act

The task force's recommendation for federal support of state victim compensation programs was implemented through the Victims of Crime Act (VOCA),[43] passed in 1984. VOCA established the federal Office for Victims of Crime, which administers the federal Crime Victims' Fund, reimbursing states for up to 40 percent of victim compensation payments and providing technical assistance to state compensation programs.

All 50 states and the U.S. territories also receive annual VOCA victim assistance grants to support their victim assistance programs. A $500,000 base allocation is awarded to each state, the District of Columbia, the U.S. Virgin Islands, and Puerto Rico. The Northern Mariana Islands, Guam, and American Samoa each receive a $200,000 base allocation. Additional awards beyond the base allocation are distributed based on population. These awards support approximately 6,100 annual grants for crisis intervention, counseling, emergency shelter, criminal justice advocacy, and emergency transportation programs.[44] More than $2.3 billion in VOCA victim assistance grants was awarded between FY 1986 and FY 2001.[45]

Victims must apply for compensation in the state where the crime occurs. Prior to VOCA, many states' programs provided compensation only to residents unless a reciprocal agreement had been made with a victim's previous state of residence. States are now required, by federal law, to cover residents, nonresidents, and victims of federal crimes. Two states still restrict eligibility to U.S. citizens.

Recent Trends

Due to increases in publicity concerning victim compensation programs and new laws mandating that rights, services, and information be provided to victims, the number of victims applying for financial assistance has increased. As a result, many victim compensation program budgets were inadequate, and victims did not receive the compensation that they should have. Today, although a few states are still unable to pay all eligible claims, most do.

The Staff Speaks
Visit www.mhhe.com/schmalleger7e to see this feature.

Eligibility Requirements

Each state has victim eligibility requirements for compensation benefits. Although states' requirements vary, most programs require that the victim do the following:

- Report the crime promptly, usually within 72 hours. A few states allow more time or less, but most have "good cause exceptions" that apply to children, incapacitated victims, and others with special circumstances.
- Cooperate with law enforcement agencies in investigation and prosecution of the crime.
- Submit a timely application for compensation, generally within one year. Again, a few states allow more time or less, and most may waive the deadline under certain circumstances.
- Provide other information as needed by the program.
- Not file claims for compensation of victimization that resulted from claimant criminal activity or misconduct.

The VOCA Victim Compensation Final Program Guidelines encourage state compensation program staff members to meet with victims and victim service providers; to review state statutes, program guidelines, and policies for responsiveness to crime victims' needs; and to identify potential barriers to victim cooperation with law enforcement agencies, such as apprehension about personal safety and fear of offender retaliation. Victims tend to be reluctant to cooperate if offenders threaten violence or death. Age and psychological, cultural, or linguistic barriers may also influence the amount of victim cooperation. For instance, a young child, senior citizen, or foreign national may have difficulty communicating. Embarrassment or shame may delay or prevent reporting of a sexual assault.

Compensation programs are the victim's last resort. All other potential sources, such as the offender's insurance or public benefits, must be exhausted before state victims' compensation may be paid. If, however, payment from another source is delayed, the program may provide funds to the victim, which must be repaid if and when the victim receives that other payment.

The victim cannot have been engaged in criminal activity. Dependents' eligibility depends largely on the victim's eligibility. Dependents or relatives of a homicide victim, for example, who was committing a crime at the time of death are generally not eligible for benefits.

Benefit Criteria

All compensation programs cover the same major expenses, although limits vary. The primary costs covered by all states are medical expenses, mental health counseling, wages lost as a result of a crime-related injury, lost support (for dependents of homicide victims), and funeral expenses. Nationwide, medical fees represent well over half of all compensation awards, with lost wage and support payments comprising the next highest payment percentage. In a few states, 20 to 40 percent of awards are for counseling; compensation payment in this area is increasing rapidly throughout the country. Of claim payment recipients, 25 to 30 percent are children age 17 and under.[46]

Many compensation programs also may pay for the following:

- moving or relocation expenses, when a victim may be in danger or relocation becomes medically necessary as a result of victimization;

- transportation for medical services when the provider is located far from the victim's residence or when other special circumstances exist;
- services, such as child care and/or housekeeping, that the victim cannot perform due to a crime-related injury;
- essential lost or damaged personal possessions (11 states pay for medically necessary equipment, such as eyeglasses or hearing aids, but only a few cover other such items);
- crime-scene cleanup—securing or restoring a home to its precrime condition; and
- rehabilitation—physical or job therapy, ramps, wheelchairs, and/or home or vehicle modification and/or driving instruction.

Restitution

Restitution is repayment to the victim, by the offender, for losses, damages, or expenses that result from a crime. Restitution is a form of victim compensation that holds the offender liable for the victim's financial losses. Restitution is generally seen not as a punishment or an alternative to fines or sanctions but as a debt owed.[47]

Criminal courts often order restitution to compensate victims for expenses that are the direct result of a crime. It is most often ordered in cases of property crime, such as a burglary. It may also be ordered to reimburse victims for expenses related to physical and/or mental health recovery and, for survivors of homicide victims, to make up for loss of support. Restitution is also common for cases of theft of services (e.g., restaurant bills), fraud, forgery, and traffic or vehicle law violation. Judges have also begun to order community restitution in which convicted offenders pay back the community through service.

Restitution as a significant remedy for crime victims was first imposed on the federal level in 1982 when the VWPA required federal judges to order full restitution in criminal cases or state on the record their reasons for not doing so.[48] That same year, the *Final Report* of the President's Task Force on Victims of Crime reinforced the VWPA by recommending that judges order restitution in all cases in which the victim suffered financial loss or state compelling reasons for a contrary ruling in the case record.[49]

The importance of restitution was emphasized in 1994, with enactment of the federal Violent Crime Control and Law Enforcement Act, which made restitution mandatory in cases of sexual assault or domestic violence. In 1996, the Mandatory Victim Restitution Act made restitution mandatory in all violent crime cases and in certain other cases on the federal level.[50]

In the decade that followed VWPA, every state enacted statutes that addressed restitution, most following the lead of the federal model. However, states continue to amend their statutes, creating a patchwork of financial reparations for victims across the country. Today, some states mandate restitution only in cases involving violent crimes, and others mandate restitution only in cases involving property crimes. A number of states require that offenders be on probation or parole before victims may collect restitution, and many do not require restitution from juvenile offenders. Probationers who fail to make restitution payments may have their probation revoked.

Despite developments in legislation, restitution remains one of the most underenforced of victims' rights in terms of ordering and monitoring, collecting, and dispersing payments. A recent DOJ study of recidivism among probationers reported of 32 counties surveyed,[51] only half required restitution in at least one-third of all felony probation cases. Of felony probationers who had completed their sentences, only 54 percent had fully satisfied restitution orders.[52]

All in all, the NCVC reports a poor record nationwide for ordering and collecting restitution from convicted offenders.[53] Even so, national research studies indicate that restitution is one of the most significant factors affecting the satisfaction of victims with the criminal justice process.[54]

Collecting Restitution in Institutions Many correctional agencies encourage inmates to fulfill restitution obligations. These agencies increase collections by offering incentives (such as increased visitation and prison commissary services or priority enrollment in education programs) for compliance and by denying privileges for failure or refusal to participate.

The California Department of Corrections and Rehabilitation (CDCR) has implemented an Inmate Restitution Fine Collections System, supported by state law, that allows deduction of up to 50 percent of inmate wages for payment of court-ordered restitution. These funds are transferred to the State Restitution Fund for disbursement. The system, which started operation in November 1992, was modified by statute in 2008 to collect half of every dollar earned or received by inmates from outside sources and deposit it into the Restitution Fund. CDCR's Victim Services Program staff coordinate voluntary inmate and parolee restitution payments as well.

Community Restitution Offenders who are truly indigent may be given the option to perform community service in lieu of monetary restitution. According to OVC, however, this option should be offered only with victim consent. Some victims prefer that the monetary restitution order stand until such time, if any, the offender is able to fulfill it. Other victims may feel somewhat compensated if they participate in the decision about the type and location of the service to be performed. Payment of victim restitution does not necessarily preclude an order for community restitution. In many instances, the offender has done damage not only to the victim but also to the community.

THE OFFICE FOR VICTIMS OF CRIME

CO14-5

Established by VOCA, OVC's official mission is to enhance the nation's capacity for assisting crime victims and to provide leadership in changing attitudes, policies, and practices to promote justice and healing for all victims.[55] OVC has five divisions that manage specific program areas, as follows:

- **Federal Assistance Division (FAD):** This division, which includes American Indian and Alaska Native initiatives, works to enable victims of federal crimes to fully participate in the criminal justice process. FAD distributes funds to nonprofit organizations, federal and military criminal justice agencies, and American Indians and Alaska Natives to support both training for service providers and direct services for victims, including crisis counseling, temporary shelter, and travel expenses incurred in going to court. FAD also supports services for U.S. citizens who are victims of federal crimes in foreign countries. In addition, the Children's Justice Act allows FAD to sponsor programs to improve the investigation and prosecution of child abuse in Indian country. These include establishing and training multidisciplinary teams to handle child sexual abuse cases.

- **Program Development and Dissemination Division (PDD):** PDD develops national-scope training and technical assistance, demonstration programs, and initiatives to respond to emerging issues in the victim assistance field. It is also responsible for coordinating public outreach and awareness. PDD provides information and assistance on highly technical victims' issues, including services for trafficking victims, victims with disabilities, and victims who are mentally ill.

- **State Compensation and Assistance Division (SCAD):** SCAD administers federal grant programs for state crime victim compensation and state-administered local **victim assistance programs.**

- **Training and Information Dissemination Division (TID):** TID oversees the design, development, and dissemination of training and technical assistance on program development and implementation issues. The division coordinates the dissemination of training and technical assistance efforts with OVC divisions, manages the OVC professional development and state scholarship programs, and manages educational and training initiatives—such as the National Victim Assistance Academy and the State Victim Assistance Academies (SVAAs).

- **Terrorism and International Victim Assistance Services Division (TIVAS):** TIVAS was created to address emerging issues related to serving victims of violent crime, mass victimization, and terrorism both in the United States and abroad. TIVAS develops programs and initiatives to respond to victims of terrorism, mass violence, commercial exploitation, international trafficking of women and children, and other crimes involving U.S. and foreign nationals. TIVAS also coordinates OVC resources and funding for victims of terrorism and transnational crimes and administers the Antiterrorism and Emergency Assistance Program.

victim assistance program

An organized program that offers services to victims of crime in the areas of crisis intervention and follow-up counseling and that helps victims secure their rights under the law.

The OVC has emerged as an invaluable support agency for state and territorial agencies as well as for crime victims themselves. Its effective administration of victim compensation and assistance grant programs enables states and territories to provide greatly improved services to crime victims. Meanwhile, its *Fact Sheet* and *Help Series* publications provide crime victims timely and comprehensive informational materials. A typical example[56] includes guidance to victims on their fundamental rights and an up-to-date listing of compensation and assistance program contact points within each state and U.S. territory. OVC makes these materials readily available through its well-designed and superbly maintained Web site at www.ojp.usdoj.gov/ovc.

CO14-6 VICTIM IMPACT STATEMENTS

Victim impact statements are assertions—by a victim and/or friends or relatives of the victim—about the crime's impact on the victim and the victim's family. Victim impact statements, now permitted at all sentencing

> ### EXHIBIT 14–8   Sample Victim Impact Statement
>
> ## VICTIM IMPACT STATEMENT
>
> If you need more space to answer any of the following questions, please feel free to use as much paper as you need, and simply attach these sheets of paper to this impact statement. Thank you.
>
> ### Your Name
>
> ### Defendant's Name(s)
>
> 1. How has the crime affected you and those close to you? Please feel free to discuss your feelings about what has happened and how it has affected your general well-being. Has this crime affected your relationship with any family members, friends, co-workers, and other people? As a result of this crime, if you or others close to you have sought any type of victim services, such as counseling by either a licensed professional, member of the clergy, or a community-sponsored support group, you may wish to mention this.
>
> 2. What physical injuries or symptoms have you or others close to you suffered as a result of this crime? You may want to write about how long the injuries lasted or how long they are expected to last and whether if you sought medical treatment for these injuries. You may also want to discuss what changes you have made in your life as a result of these injuries.
>
> 3. Has the crime affected your ability to perform your work, make a living, run a household, go to school, or enjoy any other activities you previously performed or enjoyed? If so, please explain how these activities have been affected by this crime.

hearings,[57] may be verbal or written, depending on the jurisdiction. Many states and the federal government now require that victim impact statements be included in presentencing reports (see Exhibit 14–8). The Crime Control and Law Enforcement Act of 1994 gave federal victims of violent crime or sexual assault a federal **right of allocation**—the right to make a statement at sentencing. Another federal law, the Child Protection Act of 1990, provides that victim impact statements from young children be allowed to take the form of drawings or models.

Victim impact statements typically include a tally of the physical, financial, psychological, and emotional impact of crime. As such, they provide information for courts to use in assessing the human and social cost of crime. Of equal significance, they also provide a way for victims to take part in the justice process. In most states, the right to make an impact statement is available to the direct victim, to family members of homicide victims, to the parents or guardians of a victimized minor, and to the guardian or legal representative of an incompetent or incapacitated victim.

According to OVC, the first victim impact statement was made in 1976 in Fresno County, California, by James Rowland,[58] who was then the county's chief probation officer. Rowland's contributions, which detailed the harm suffered by victims in that case, led Fresno County to make victim impact statements a part of all presentence reports.

In 1991, the U.S. Supreme Court case of *Payne v. Tennessee*[59] upheld the constitutionality of victim impact statements. Additionally, the Payne decision specifically permitted victim impact statements in cases involving potential application of the death penalty.

Victim impact statements are also frequently provided by victims or their survivors to parole hearing bodies. Statements are sometimes made

right of allocution

A statutory provision permitting crime victims to speak at the sentencing of convicted offenders. A federal right of allocution was established for victims of federal violent and sex crimes under the Violent Crime Control and Law Enforcement Act of 1994.

in person; at other times, they are submitted on audiotape or videotape, by teleconferencing, via computerized forms of communication, or in writing. Such statements give the paroling authority crucial information about the financial, physical, and emotional impact of crime upon the individuals most affected by it. In the past two decades, the passage of laws requiring victim input at parole has been seen as one of the greatest advances in victims' rights. Forty-three states now provide this right.[60] This right loses its meaning, however, if paroling authorities do not notify victims of crime and their families of hearings in advance or do not schedule time during the hearing to allow them to describe the impact of crime on their lives.

THE FUTURE OF VICTIMS' RIGHTS

CO14-7

Visit www.ncjrs.gov/ovc_archives/ncvrw/ 2011/multimedia/video_files/2011_NCVRW_ Theme.mov or scan this code with the QR app on your SmartPhone or digital device to watch an Office for Victims of Crime video discussing possible future trends in victims' services.

In 2010, the federal Office for Victims of Crime announced its Vision 21 initiative, which was intended to "expand the vision and impact of the crime victim services field by designing a philosophical and strategic framework for defining the role of the field in the country's response to crime."[61] The initiative was also designed to "move the field of victim services forward into the future." Vision 21 involves a comprehensive national analysis of the current state of the field of crime victims and the development of a comprehensive report, which will include a battery of recommendations. According to OVC, those recommendations will provide "a blueprint for a demonstration project" to enhance victim services nationwide. Vision 21 recommendations won't be compiled until after this book goes to press, but they are scheduled to be available on the Web at http://ovc.ncjrs.gov/vision21.

An earlier OVC report, *New Directions from the Field*,[62] summarized hundreds of recommendations from the field and from listening to victims, their advocates, and allied professionals who work with crime victims throughout the nation. In the course of compiling those recommendations, certain key ideas emerged. The following five global challenges for responding to victims of crime in the 21st century form the core of the ideas and recommendations presented in the report:

1. enact and enforce consistent, fundamental rights for crime victims in federal, state, juvenile, military, and tribal justice systems and administrative proceedings;
2. provide crime victims with access to comprehensive, quality services regardless of the nature of their victimization, age, race, religion, gender, ethnicity, sexual orientation, capability, or geographic location;
3. integrate crime victims' issues into all levels of the nation's educational system to ensure that justice and allied professionals and other service providers receive comprehensive training on victims' issues as part of their academic education and continuing training in the field;
4. support, improve, and replicate promising practices in victims' rights and services built upon sound research, advanced technology, and multidisciplinary partnerships; and
5. ensure that the voices of crime victims play a central role in the nation's response to violence and those victimized by crime.

REVIEW AND APPLICATIONS

SUMMARY

1 Victims were rarely recognized in the laws and policies that govern our nation until the 1970s. Since then, tremendous strides have been made in victims' rights legislation and victim services. Passage of the federal Victim and Witness Protection Act (VWPA) of 1982 brought national visibility to crime victims' concerns. In 1990, the Victims' Rights and Restitution Act (Victims' Rights Act) established a bill of rights for federal crime victims. The Violent Crime Control and Law Enforcement Act of 1994 established new rights for victims of sexual assault, domestic violence, sexual exploitation, child abuse, and telemarketing fraud. In 1996, the Community Notification Act, known as *Megan's Law,* was enacted to ensure community notification of the locations of convicted sex offenders. In 1997, the Victims' Rights Clarification Act of 1997 asserted victims' rights to attend proceedings and deliver victim impact statements.

2 The costs that crime victims suffer can be divided into two major categories: (1) tangible losses, including medical bills, property, and wages and (2) intangible losses, such as lost quality of life as well as fear, pain, and suffering.

3 Correctional agencies play an important role in meeting victims' needs. Services provided by correctional agencies include (1) victim and community notification of offender release or change in status, (2) victim and witness protection services, (3) classes for offenders on the impact of crime, and (4) opportunities for victim–offender dialogue.

4 Crime victim compensation provide options to assist victims recover crime-related financial losses. Such programs typically pay for medical and mental health care, lost wages, funeral expenses, and crime-scene cleanup.

5 OVC's official mission is to enhance the nation's capacity for assisting crime victims and to provide leadership in changing attitudes, policies, and practices to promote justice and healing for all victims. OVC's five operating divisions consist of (1) the Federal Assistance Division, (2) the Program Development and Dissemination Division, (3) the State Compensation and Assistance Division, (4) the Training and Information Dissemination Division, and (5) the Terrorism and International Victim Assistance Services Division.

6 Victim impact statements are assertions by victims and/or friends or relatives of victims about the crime's impact on the victim and the victim's family. These statements are important because judicial authorities consider them in making decisions regarding sentencing and parole.

7 The five global challenges now facing victims' rights advocates are to (1) enact and enforce consistent, fundamental rights for crime victims; (2) provide crime victims access to comprehensive, quality services regardless of the nature of their victimization, age, race, religion, gender, ethnicity, sexual orientation, capability, or geographic location; (3) integrate crime victims' issues into all levels of the nation's educational system; (4) support, improve, and replicate promising practices in victims' rights and services built upon sound research, advanced technology, and multidisciplinary partnerships; and (5) ensure that the voices of crime victims play a central role in the nation's response to violence and those victimized by crime.

KEY TERMS

victim, p. 460
victims' rights, p. 461
best efforts standard, p. 462
tangible losses, p. 468

intangible losses, p. 468
victim notification, p. 471
community notification, p. 474
victim compensation, p. 477

victim assistance program, p. 482
right of allocution, p. 483

QUESTIONS FOR REVIEW

1 Briefly outline the history of the American victims' rights movement including important federal victims' rights legislation.

2 What costs do crime victims suffer as a result of their victimization?

3 What can correctional agencies do to assist crime victims?

4 What are crime victim compensation programs, and what do they do?

5 What is the official mission of the federal Office for Victims of Crime, and what are its five operating divisions?

6 Describe victim impact statements. In what ways are they important?

7 What are the five global challenges now facing victims' rights advocates.

THINKING CRITICALLY ABOUT CORRECTIONS

Constitutional Amendment

In 1996, resolutions to amend the Constitution to include crime victims' rights were introduced in the U.S. House and Senate. A proposed federal constitutional amendment was reintroduced in modified form in 1999 with bipartisan support. In 2002, President George W. Bush announced his support for such an amendment. A federal constitutional amendment for victims' rights, say supporters, is needed for many different reasons, including to establish consistency in the rights of crime victims in every state and at the federal level; to ensure that courts engage in careful balancing of the rights of victims and defendants; to guarantee crime victims the opportunity to participate in criminal justice proceedings; and to further enhance the participation of victims in the criminal justice process. Do you agree or disagree that the U.S. Constitution should be amended to include victims' rights? Why?

The Focus of Correctional Agencies

Although correctional services for victims exist today in many correctional agencies and institutions across the country, some people believe that correctional agencies have enough to do without worrying about victims. Dealing with offenders is a full-time job, say such critics, and the time and expense required to meet the needs of victims are just not available. In addition, they say, corrections is about controlling and rehabilitating offenders, not about making victims "whole again."

1. Should correctional agencies and correctional personnel be involved in victims' support programs? Why or why not?

2. If you were a corrections professional, how would you feel about being called upon to assist crime victims?

ON-THE-JOB DECISION MAKING

Restitution

You are director of a victim's advocacy program in your community. A criminal justice professor at a local university has asked you to participate in a public forum panel discussion addressing programs for restitution to crime victims. You decide to accept the invitation.

Upon arriving at the meeting the following week, you are surprised to find a significant turnout. The audience is larger than you expected, and the local news media are out in force. You did not anticipate this much interest.

As the meeting begins, it quickly becomes apparent that much of the audience consists of former offenders or offenders' family members. To your discomfort, you find yourself repeatedly faced with answering the same question over and over: How am I supposed to succeed in my efforts to live a noncriminal life when the bulk of my earnings get seized to repay my victim?

One particularly articulate offender conveys his dilemma: I am genuinely sorry, he says, for the suffering I caused. And while I know that nothing I do can erase my victim's painful memories of my crime, I truly want to repay her for the losses I caused, if only as a token of my genuine remorse.

But the reality, he says, is this: An unskilled ex-con's employment opportunities are limited. They are not going to get a "position" at the upper end of the pay scale. The work they find will be just "a job." It won't pay much, and it is unlikely that they will earn benefits. As a result, their weekly net pay will probably be insufficient to cover housing, feeding, and clothing themselves and their families.

When a significant percentage of that net pay is diverted to a restitution payment, he says, former offenders simply will not have enough left to meet their basic needs. It will not take long for the pressure to build. Under those circumstances, that pressure may generate a willingness to consider returning to the "easy money" available through crime. He says that makes the restitution program counterproductive because it contributes to defeating a primary aim of the rehabilitation effort: to encourage rejection of the criminal lifestyle.

1. How would you respond to the points this former offender has presented?

2. How do you answer the offender's question "How am I supposed to succeed in my efforts to live a noncriminal life when the bulk of my earnings get seized to repay my victim?"

Offenders Meet Victims

You work in a state correctional facility. A month ago you were promoted from yard supervisory work to implement a program in which you will conduct classes for offenders and their victims. Classes are held within the institution, and usually about five or six victims show up at each session to confront inmates. Many of the victims come from a local victims' rights group and, although they have all been victims of violent crime, they are not the people who have been victimized by the inmates participating in the class. Classes usually involve victims telling about the impact of their personal crime experience on them and the particular burdens crime places upon victims everywhere.

What strategies could you implement to ensure that inmates express true remorse for what they have done and that victims do not use the class as an opportunity to demean inmates?

For additional information, please see: www.mhhe.com/schmalleger7e
Follow the author's tweets about the latest crime and justice news @schmalleger

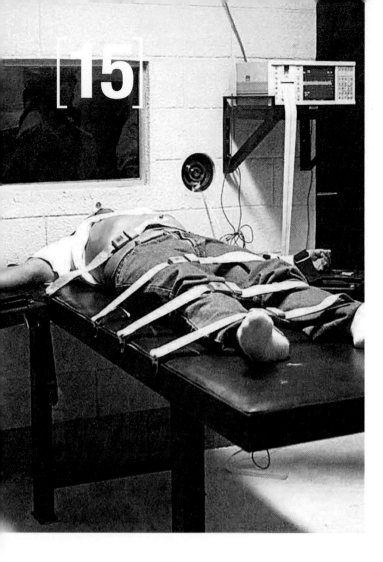

DEATH

The Ultimate Sanction

CHAPTER OBJECTIVES

After completing this chapter you should be able to do the following:

1. Discuss the history of capital punishment.

2. Describe the characteristics of people executed in the United States since 1977 and on death row today.

3. Discuss the politics influencing capital punishment.

4. Summarize the arguments for and against the death penalty.

5. List and summarize the major U.S. Supreme Court decisions that influenced capital punishment legislation.

6. Describe the death penalty appeals process.

7. Summarize Liebman's findings on the frequency of errors in capital punishment cases.

8. Discuss the Supreme Court's reasoning for banning the execution of offenders with mental retardation and juveniles.

> *Whatever you think about the death penalty, a system that will take life must first give justice.*
>
> —John J. Curtin Jr., president, American Bar Association, 1990–1991

Do innocent people get sentenced to die?

That is the fundamental question being asked in places such as the Center for Wrongful Convictions at Northwestern University, the Innocence Project at Yeshiva University's Benjamin N. Cardozo School of Law, and the U.S. Congress. Northwestern's Center for Wrongful Convictions and Yeshiva's Innocence Project are dedicated to identifying and rectifying wrongful convictions and other serious miscarriages of justice. Congress aided the effort in 2004 by passing the Justice for All Act. Among the provisions of the act is Title IV, the Innocence Protection Act, which provides access to postconviction DNA testing in federal cases, helps states improve the quality of legal representation in capital cases, and increases compensation in federal cases of wrongful convictions from a flat $5,000 to $50,000 per year in noncapital cases and $100,000 per year in capital cases. The Innocence Protection Act also established the Kirk Bloodsworth (the first person in the United States cleared by DNA testing) Post-Conviction DNA Testing Program, which authorizes $25 million over five years to defray the costs of postconviction DNA testing.

Kirk Bloodsworth spent nine years on death row before he was pardoned by the governor of Maryland for a crime he did not commit. He was the first person in the United States cleared by DNA testing. How is it possible that innocent people can be convicted—and even sentenced to die—under our system of justice?

DNA testing is now a major factor in changing the criminal justice system. It provides scientific proof that our system convicts and sentences innocent people—and that wrongful convictions are not isolated or rare events. According to the Death Penalty Information Center,[1] of the 143 people in 26 states whose innocence has been established after they were sent to death row since 1973, DNA testing played a substantial role in establishing the innocence and freedom of 18 of them. Exhibit 15–1 lists the **exonerations** by year and state. Each exoneree served an average of 10.1 years on death row before exoneration.

exonerate

To clear of blame and release from death row.

The first person in the United States cleared by DNA testing was Kirk Bloodsworth.[2] In 1984, he was 24 years old and a former marine with neither a criminal history nor a deviant past. Like his father, he was a waterman on the Eastern Shore of Maryland. Bloodsworth's neighbor saw on television a police sketch of the suspect in the rape and murder of 9-year-old Dawn Hamilton. The girl had been found in the woods stripped of clothing from the waist down and her head crushed with a piece of concrete. The neighbor thought it looked like Bloodsworth and called the police. With the police and prosecutor under intense pressure to solve the crime, it was a short route to trial, conviction, and a death sentence. It took the jury only two and one-half hours to decide to send Bloodsworth to the gas chamber.

EXHIBIT 15–1   Exonerations from Death Row, 1973–2013, and by State

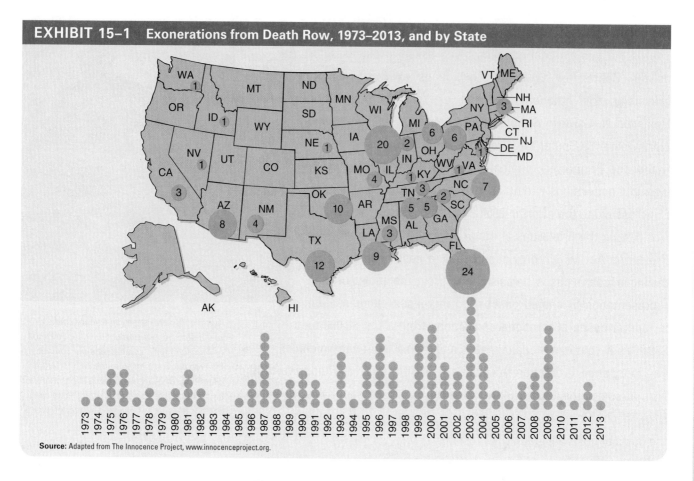

Source: Adapted from The Innocence Project, www.innocenceproject.org.

After reading a book by crime novelist Joseph Wambaugh about genetic fingerprinting, Bloodsworth asked his attorney to have DNA experts analyze semen stains that had been found on the victim's underwear. The new analysis, undertaken independently by a private company and the FBI, conclusively cleared Bloodsworth of the crime. In 1993, he was released from prison. A few months later, the governor of Maryland granted him a pardon.[3] Not until 2004 was the real killer identified by DNA tests. He bore little resemblance to the description that the police had compiled from eyewitnesses.

Bloodsworth, who had served almost nine years behind bars, thought that his nightmare had ended when he was released from prison. Far from it. His reentry into free society has been difficult and painful. After his release, people telephoned him in the night shouting, "They never should have let you out." He once found the words "child killer" scrawled across his windshield. His first night off death row, sleeping in his father's house, he relieved himself in the corner of the bedroom—thinking in the darkness that he was standing in front of his urinal in his death row cell. He suffers from recurring dreams of execution, and that dream still haunts him—still grabs him in the night and drags him down the long hallway toward death. Right before the end, he says, he wakes up, drenched in sweat and choking to breathe.

HISTORY OF CAPITAL PUNISHMENT

CO15-1

Capital punishment was once common throughout the world and imposed for many crimes, including murder, rape, stealing, witchcraft, piracy, desertion, sodomy, adultery, concealing the birth or death of an infant, aiding runaway slaves, counterfeiting, and forgery. Death, however, was not the harshest punishment—torture was. Torture, so cruel that death came as a relief, sometimes lasted for days. Death was a form of leniency. Criminals were boiled, burned, roasted on spits, drawn and quartered, broken on wheels, disemboweled, torn apart by animals, gibbeted (hung from a post with a projecting arm and left to die), bludgeoned (beaten to death with sticks, clubs, or rocks), or pressed (crushed under a board and stones).

Capital punishment began changing in the 18th century during the Enlightenment. This philosophical movement led to many new theories on crime and punishment. One of these theories proposed that punishment should fit the crime. Penalties involving torture began to disappear, and the use of the death penalty diminished.

At the turn of the 20th century, some states began to ban capital punishment and others began to limit its use. After World War I, as socialists challenged capitalism, a number of states reinstated the death penalty in order to deter threats of revolution. Around the same time, criminologists argued that capital punishment was a necessary social measure, and as the United States suffered through Prohibition and the Great Depression in the 1930s, there were more executions, an average of 167 per year, than in any other decade in American history.

By 1950, as prosperity followed World War II, public sentiment for capital punishment faded. The number of executions dropped. Support for capital punishment was at its lowest in 1966 (42 percent), and constitutional challenges were starting to surface. In the late 1960s, the U.S. Supreme Court began "fine-tuning" the way the death penalty was administered. In 1968 in *U.S.* v. *Jackson*,[4] the Court held that the provision of the federal kidnapping statute requiring that the death penalty be

capital punishment

Lawful imposition of the death penalty.

On September 30, 1283, Dafydd ap Gruffydd, the last native prince of Wales, was condemned to die for plotting the death of King Edward I. On October 3, 1283, Dafydd was dragged through the streets behind a horse, hanged and then revived, disemboweled (his stomach was cut open, and his intestines were removed and thrown into a fire as he watched), beheaded, and then drawn and quartered. Drawing-and-quartering was officially abolished as a method of execution in Britain in 1870. Why did penalties involving torture disappear?

Amir Karbalaei (right), Payam Amini (center), and Majid Qasemi (left), are seen hanging with ropes around their necks in the northeastern Lavizan district of Tehran, Iran, on Sunday, September 29, 2006, five days after their death verdict was approved by the Iranian Supreme Court. The men were convicted of abducting, raping, and robbing women. How would you describe the international use of capital punishment?

imposed only upon the recommendation of a jury was unconstitutional because it encouraged defendants to waive their right to a jury trial to ensure they would not receive a death sentence. Later that year in *Witherspoon* v. *Illinois*,[5] the Court held that a potential juror's mere reservations about the death penalty were insufficient grounds to prevent that person from serving on the jury in a death penalty case. Jurors could be disqualified only if the prosecutors showed that the juror's attitude toward capital punishment would prevent him or her from making an impartial decision about punishment. The watershed case in capital punishment took place in 1972 when the Court decided *Furman* v. *Georgia*.[6] In brief, the Court held that Georgia's death penalty statute, which gave the sentencing authority (judge or trial jury) complete sentencing discretion without any guidance as to how to exercise that discretion, could result in arbitrary sentencing and was therefore in violation of the Eighth Amendment's ban against cruel and unusual punishment.

On June 29, 1972, the Court voided 40 death penalty statutes because they were no longer valid. Four years later, in *Gregg* v. *Georgia*, the Supreme Court upheld guided discretionary capital statutes, opining that "such standards do provide guidance to the sentencing authority and thereby reduce the likelihood that it will impose a sentence that fairly can be called capricious and arbitrary." Almost 40 years later, the trends in capital punishment are these: Death sentences are down, executions are down, and public support for capital punishment is falling. This chapter will explore these issues.

Capital Punishment Around the World

In 2012 Amnesty International documented 682 executions in 21 countries, but the total did not include figures from China, which executes more people than the rest of the world combined. The five countries that reported the most executions in 2012 were China (1,000s), Iran (314+), Iraq (129+), Saudi Arabia (79+), and the United States (43).[7]

At yearend 2013, the majority of countries (140) had abolished the death penalty in law or in practice.[8] Fifty-eight countries still retain it. Retentionist and abolitionist countries are shown in Exhibit 15–2.

CAPITAL PUNISHMENT IN THE UNITED STATES

The face of capital punishment is changing in the United States. On May 2, 2013, Maryland became the sixth state in six years to abolish capital punishment, bringing to 18 the number of states without the death penalty. When Maryland Governor Martin O'Malley signed the bill that ended capital punishment he said, "With the legislation signed today, Maryland has effectively eliminated a policy that is proven not to work."[9]

Economic Realities and Corrections: Capital Punishment

The death penalty is under attack today because it costs too much. New Jersey and New Mexico abolished it in 2007 and 2009, respectively, citing cost as a primary reason. Consider the following costs:

- **$32,000.** In Kansas for a nondeath penalty trial (2003).

- **$55,772.** Average for legal representation in federal cases to which the death penalty applied but in which it was not sought (1998).

- **$192,333.** Average for legal representation in federal death penalty cases that resulted in a plea bargain (1998).

- **$508,000.** In Kansas for a death penalty trial (2003).

- **$620,932.** Average for the defense in a federal death penalty case (2008).

- **$1.6 million.** For Utah taxpayers to take a capital case from trial to execution (2012).

- **$2.16 million.** Estimate per execution in North Carolina (1993).

- **$51 million.** For Florida taxpayers per year to keep inmates on death row more than holding them for life without parole.

- **$71 million.** In Maryland for all capital cases that did not result in a death sentence (2008).

- **$186 million.** For Maryland taxpayers for pursuing five capital cases between 1978 and 1999.

- **$308 million.** Estimate per execution in California (2012).

- **$4 billion.** For California's capital punishment since its reinstatement in 1978.

The high cost of crime scene investigations, pretrial preparations and motions, expert witness investigations, jury selection, the necessity for two trials—one on guilt and one on sentencing—appeals, and heightened death row security and maintenance costs are pushing officials to limit the number of capital murder cases that can be prosecuted to hopefully reduce costs.

Source: Ron Sylvester, "From a Budget Standpoint, Is Death Row Worth It?" *The Wichita Eagle* (Kansas), October 20, 2009, www.kansas.com (accessed March 1, 2013); George Skelton, "It's Time to Dump California's Death Penalty by Passing Prop. 34," *Capitol Journal,* September 12, 2012, www.latimes.com (accessed September 17, 2012); Carol J. Williams, "Death Penalty Costs California $184 million a Year, Study Says," *Los Angeles Times,* June 20, 2011, http://articles.latimes.com/2011/jun/20/local/la-me-adv-death-penalty-costs-20110620 (accessed June 20, 2011); Brooke Adams, "Utah's Death Penalty Costs $1.6 Million More Per Inmate," November 15, 2012, www.sltrib.com/sltrib/politics/55277767-90/death-penalty-utah-watson.html.csp (accessed November 21, 2012).

EXHIBIT 15–2 Abolitionist and Retentionist Countries

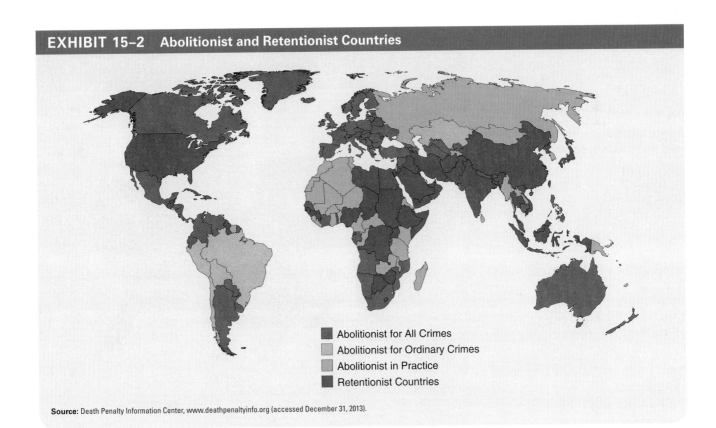

- Abolitionist for All Crimes
- Abolitionist for Ordinary Crimes
- Abolitionist in Practice
- Retentionist Countries

Source: Death Penalty Information Center, www.deathpenaltyinfo.org (accessed December 31, 2013).

On May 2, 2013, Maryland Governor Martin O'Malley signed legislation that abolished capital punishment and replaced it with the sentence of life in prison without the possibility of parole. Do you think the six states that abolished capital punishment since 2007 (New York and New Jersey in 2007; New Mexico in 2009; Illinois in 2011; Connecticut in 2012; and Maryland in 2013) will be the "bellwether" of the American death penalty?

capital crime

A crime for which the death penalty may but need not necessarily be imposed.

Today, 32 states, the U.S. military, and the federal government allow capital punishment and 18 states and the District of Columbia do not (see Exhibit 15–3). Public opinion, grassroots lobbying, political and legislative changes, judicial rulings, and the current economic crisis are reshaping the capital punishment debate.

Although research on executions in the United States has been hampered by a lack of official records, more than 15,000 executions, beginning in the 1600s, have been confirmed.[10]

Executions were halted in 1968 pending a U.S. Supreme Court decision on the constitutionality of certain aspects of capital punishment. By 1977, the Court had ruled that capital punishment itself was not unconstitutional and did not violate the Eighth Amendment to the U.S. Constitution, thus paving the way for executions to resume. The first person to be executed after the moratorium ended was Gary Gilmore, who gave up his right to appeal and was executed by firing squad on January 17, 1977, by the state of Utah. See Exhibit 15–4 for the number of executions from 1976 through 2013.

Today in the United States, what constitutes a **capital crime**—a crime that is punishable by death—is defined by law. This definition varies among jurisdictions. In Delaware, for example, first-degree murder with at least one statutory aggravating circumstance is a capital crime. In Nevada,

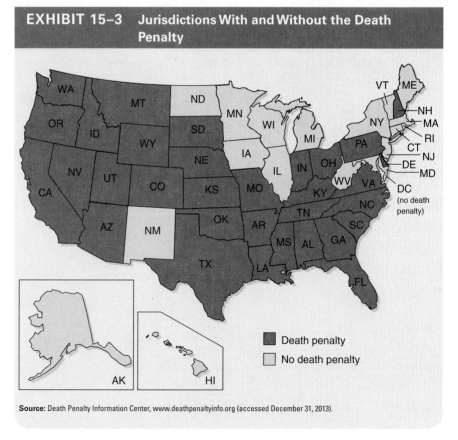

EXHIBIT 15–3   Jurisdictions With and Without the Death Penalty

■ Death penalty
□ No death penalty

Source: Death Penalty Information Center, www.deathpenaltyinfo.org (accessed December 31, 2013).

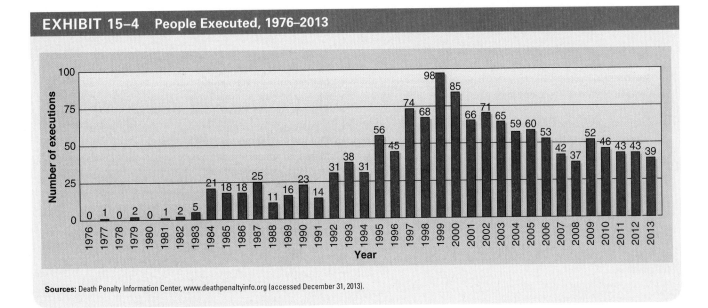

EXHIBIT 15–4   People Executed, 1976–2013

Sources: Death Penalty Information Center, www.deathpenaltyinfo.org (accessed December 31, 2013).

first-degree murder with at least 1 of 15 aggravating circumstances is a capital crime. In Texas, criminal homicide with one of nine aggravating circumstances is a capital offense.[11]

The Federal Death Penalty

The Constitution of the United States does not mention the death penalty, but it does permit the federal government to deprive citizens of life after giving due process. In 1790, the first Congress mandated the death penalty for several offenses, including treason, willful murder on federal property, forgery, piracy, counterfeiting, and several crimes on the high seas; the first federal death penalty was used on June 25, 1790, when Thomas Bird was hanged for murder in Maine. By the end of the 19th century, the number of federal capital crimes had expanded to include kidnapping, spying, all murders, and arson of a dwelling or a fort.

Since 1790, the federal government has executed 336 men and 4 women. Of these, 134 (39 percent) were white, 118 (35 percent) were black, 63 (19 percent) were Native American, and 25 (7 percent) were Hispanic or of unknown origin. Methods of execution in federal cases have included hanging, electrocution, and the gas chamber. Today the federal government uses lethal injection.

From 1972, the year of the Supreme Court's *Furman* decision (discussed later in this chapter), until the late 1980s, federal capital prosecutions were rare. In 1988, President Reagan signed the Anti–Drug Abuse Act, which authorized capital punishment for murder committed by people involved in certain drug trafficking activities.

In 1994, President Clinton signed into law the Violent Crime Control and Law Enforcement Act. Title VI is the Federal Death Penalty Act. It dramatically expanded the number of federal offenses punishable by death (see Exhibit 15–5).

In addition to incorporating the Supreme Court law ban on execution of offenders with mental retardation and juveniles, the Federal Death Penalty Act also exempts women while they are pregnant. The act permits federal employees who oppose the death penalty to opt out of participating in executions, and it restricts the federal government's ability to seek

Visit http://www.deathpenaltyinfo.org/state_by_state or scan this code with the QR app on your SmartPhone or digital device. There you will find state-by-state information concerning many aspects of the death penalty. It discussed whether it is a death penalty state and life without parole is an option, the number of executions before and after 1976, the current death row population, the number of women on death row, the murder rate, the number of innocent persons freed, the number of clemencies granted, the method of execution, and the location of death row. How does this information relate to ideas discussed in this chapter?

EXHIBIT 15–5   **Federal Laws Providing for the Death Penalty**

- Assassination or kidnapping resulting in the death of the president or vice president
- Bank-robbery-related murder or kidnapping
- Civil rights offenses resulting in death
- Death resulting from aircraft hijacking
- Death resulting from offenses involving transportation of explosives, destruction of government property, or destruction of property related to foreign or interstate commerce
- Destruction of aircraft, motor vehicles, or related facilities resulting in death
- Espionage
- First-degree murder
- Genocide
- Mailing of injurious articles with intent to kill or resulting in death
- Murder by a federal prisoner
- Murder by an escaped federal prisoner already sentenced to life imprisonment
- Murder by the use of a weapon of mass destruction
- Murder committed at an airport serving international civil aviation
- Murder committed by the use of a firearm during a crime of violence or a drug-trafficking crime
- Murder committed during a drug-related drive-by shooting
- Murder committed during an offense against maritime navigation
- Murder committed during an offense against a maritime fixed platform

- Murder committed in a federal government facility
- Murder during a hostage taking
- Murder during a kidnapping
- Murder for hire
- Murder involved in a racketeering offense
- Murder involving torture
- Murder of a court officer or juror
- Murder of a federal judge or law enforcement official
- Murder of a foreign official
- Murder of a member of Congress, an important executive official, or a Supreme Court Justice
- Murder of a state correctional officer
- Murder of a state or local law enforcement official or other person aiding in a federal investigation
- Murder of a U.S. national in a foreign country
- Murder related to a carjacking
- Murder related to rape or child molestation
- Murder related to sexual exploitation of children
- Murder related to the smuggling of aliens
- Murder related to a continuing criminal enterprise or related murder of a federal, state, or local law enforcement officer
- Murder with the intent of preventing testimony by a witness, victim, or informant
- Retaliatory murder of a member of the immediate family of law enforcement officials
- Retaliatory murder of a witness, victim, or informant
- Terrorist murder of a U.S. national in another country
- Treason
- Willful wrecking of a train resulting in death

Source: Adapted from Tracy L. Snell, *Capital Punishment, 2011–Statistical Tables* (Washington, DC: U.S. Department of Justice, July 2013).

---

the death penalty for Native Americans whose offense occurred within the boundaries of Indian country.

The last three federal executions were:

- Timothy McVeigh, white, executed June 11, 2001.
- Juan Raul Garza, Hispanic, executed June 19, 2001.
- Louis Jones Jr., black, executed March 18, 2003.

Procedures in Federal Capital Cases Federal prosecutors who wish to file capital charges are required by the Department of Justice to first obtain authorization from the attorney general. The request is reviewed by the assistant attorney general, by the deputy attorney general, and ultimately by the attorney general.

For example, on Monday, November 17, 2003, lawyers for serial bomber Eric Rudolph met with then attorney general John Ashcroft's death penalty committee. The committee's job was to listen, review evidence, and recommend to the attorney general whether Rudolph should be added to the list of 124 people tried under the federal death law since it was reinstated in 1988. On Friday, December 13, 2003, the attorney general authorized prosecutors to seek the death penalty against Rudolph. However, in April 2005, Rudolph pleaded guilty and was sentenced to four life terms in exchange for avoiding a trial and a potential death sentence. Rudolph is confined at the federal supermax prison in Florence, Colorado (read more about supermax confinement in Chapter 13).

The new Federal Death Penalty Act changes an offender's right to counsel in three ways. First, it requires that a minimum of two lawyers be appointed to represent federal capital defendants. Second, at least one of the two lawyers must have experience in capital work. And third, the federal court must consider the federal public defender's recommendation regarding which counsel are qualified for appointment in capital cases.

Federal Death Row The federal death row is at the U.S. Penitentiary, Terre Haute, Indiana. It is called the Special Confinement Unit (SCU). It opened in 1999 because of the increasing number of federal defendants sentenced to death. At yearend 2013, 59 people—57 males and 2 females—were on federal death row in Terre Haute.

SCU is a two-story renovated housing unit. It includes 120 single cells, upper-tier and lower-tier corridors, an industrial workshop, indoor and outdoor recreation areas, a property room, a food preparation area, attorney and family visiting areas, and a video-teleconferencing area that is used to facilitate inmate access to the courts and to their attorneys.

When Timothy McVeigh was executed in 2001 for the murder of 168 people in the Oklahoma City bombing, the U.S. Department of Justice instituted an elaborate process to handle any last-minute legal interruptions that might prevent or delay his execution. Two hours before McVeigh's execution, prison officials ended his visiting privileges to give him one final opportunity to seek a stay from the courts or President Bush. Forty-five minutes before the execution—and again at 10 minutes before the execution—the White House was contacted by telephone. In the event of a delay, a U.S. marshal was ready to instruct the executioner to step away from the execution equipment and to notify McVeigh and everyone present that the execution had been delayed or stayed. McVeigh received no stays.

Race and the Federal Death Penalty In 2000, the Justice Department released its findings on the question of racial and geographic disparities in federal death penalty prosecutions forwarded to the Justice Department for review between 1995 and 2000. It reported that 80 percent of the defendants were from minorities.[12] The study found that minorities are overrepresented in the federal death penalty system as both victims and defendants relative to the general population. Then attorney general Janet Reno said, "This should be of concern to all of us."[13]

The study confirmed an internal Justice Department report on racial disparities that found that between 1988, when President Reagan signed the Anti–Drug Abuse Act into law, and October 1993, the attorney general authorized federal prosecutors to seek the death penalty against 30 defendants. More than 70 percent were black, and one-half of the remaining defendants were Mexican American.[14] Later in this chapter, we will examine the debate over such statistics.

DEATH ROW TODAY

CO15-2

Characteristics of People Executed Since 1977

At yearend 2013, 1,359 people had been executed in the United States since Gary Gilmore's execution in January 1977. Like Gilmore, 141 other death row inmates asked the court to drop their appeals and carry out the death sentence. Each time, the inmate either fired the defense lawyer or told him or her to stop filing appeals. Their reasons are similar—mainly remorse, a desire for atonement, and not wanting to spend their lives in prison.[15]

The peak year for executions in the United States since they resumed in 1977 was 1999, when 98 people were executed. By 2012, the number of

Few issues generate more public controversy than that of the death penalty. In some states there are movements to end the death penalty, but in others, the move is to speed up death row appeals and complete the sentence of execution. Do demonstrations such as these influence the public policy implemented by state legislatures?

executions had declined to 43. Thirty-seven percent (508) of all executions have taken place in Texas. Has the death penalty affected the murder rate in Texas? You be the judge: From 2001 through 2012 (the last year for which complete *Uniform Crime Reports* data are available), the annual murder rate in the United States per 100,000 population averaged 5.32. In Texas, the average was 5.61. In 2012, in states with the death penalty, the murder rate was 4.7, but the average in states without it was 3.7.

From the time of Gary Gilmore's execution in 1977 through yearend 2013 the South led the United States in executions with 1,111. In 2012, 36 (84 percent) of the 39 executions took place in the South. Since 1977, only 0.01 percent of all the people executed have been female; 56 percent were white, 35 percent black, 7 percent Hispanic, and 2 percent of other backgrounds.[16] Inmates executed in 2013 had been on death row an average of 15 years. In 1990, by comparison, the average time to execution was about 7 years.

Characteristics of Prisoners Under Sentence of Death

At yearend 2013 3,108 persons were awaiting execution, a decrease of almost 300 from one decade earlier. At the time of Gary Gilmore's execution on January 17, 1977, there were 423 people on death row. Ten years later, the number was 1,984. After more than 20 years of continued increase in the number of people sentenced to die in the United States, the number on death row peaked in 2000 to 3,593 and has been decreasing ever since.

Today, U.S. juries are imposing fewer death sentences than they did on average during the 1990s. In the 1990s, an average of almost 300 people were sentenced to death each year. Since 2000, the average has been 118, a decrease of more than 60 percent.

Forty-six percent of the nation's death row population is in three states: California (731), Florida (412), and Texas (298). Exhibit 15–6 shows additional characteristics of inmates under sentence of death.

Victim Race, Gender, Geography, and the Death Penalty

Defendant–victim racial combinations have been the subject of considerable debate.[17] Recognizing that whites and minorities are murder victims in approximately equal numbers, why is it that 78 percent of the victims

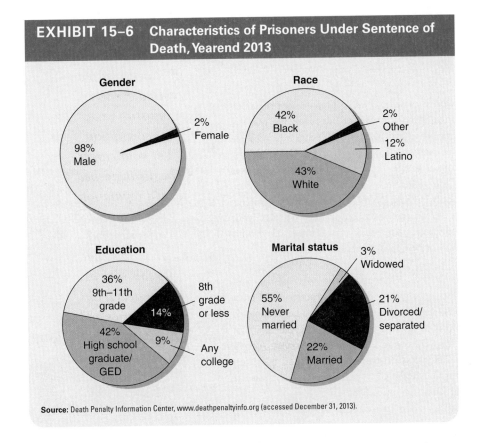

EXHIBIT 15–6   Characteristics of Prisoners Under Sentence of Death, Yearend 2013

Gender
- 98% Male
- 2% Female

Race
- 42% Black
- 2% Other
- 12% Latino
- 43% White

Education
- 36% 9th–11th grade
- 8th grade or less
- 14%
- 42% High school graduate/GED
- 9% Any college

Marital status
- 3% Widowed
- 55% Never married
- 21% Divorced/separated
- 22% Married

Source: Death Penalty Information Center, www.deathpenaltyinfo.org (accessed December 31, 2013).

in cases resulting in executions since 1977 have been white? This disparity is confirmed even in studies that control for similar crimes by comparing defendants with similar backgrounds. Does it imply that white victims are considered more important by the criminal justice system? Some have argued that blacks and Hispanics are more likely than whites to be sentenced to death and executed because they are more likely to be arrested on facts that can support a capital charge and because whites are more likely to negotiate plea bargains that spare their lives. Others disagree, citing consistent patterns of racial bias.[18] A study of more than 1,500 homicide cases in North Carolina between 1990 and 2009 found that defendants of all races were more than twice as likely to be sentenced to death if at least one of their alleged victims was white. Another study concluded that in the cases of the 159 people then on death row in North Carolina, prosecutors had removed blacks from juries at more than twice the rate that they struck prospective nonblack jurors. A new law in North Carolina might change that, however. In 2009, North Carolina lawmakers passed the Racial Justice Act. For the first time, the law allows judges to consider statistical evidence that suggests that race was a significant factor in the prosecutor's seeking or the court's imposing the death sentence on a disproportionate number of people from a minority group. A similar bill passed in Kentucky and is being considered by lawmakers in California, Pennsylvania, and other states.

Researchers have also asked if location is related to whether or not someone is sentenced to die. All things considered, how can a capital murder on one side of a county or city line result in a death sentence and, on the other side, life in prison? But according to a review of Virginia's system of capital punishment by the Virginia General Assembly, "Location, more than any other factor impacted the probability that prosecutors would actually seek the death penalty for capital murder cases."[19] The lawmakers studied 215 capital punishment-eligible cases in Virginia from 1995 to 1999 and found

Len Register

Assistant U.S. Attorney, U.S. Department of Justice, U.S. District Court, Northern District of Florida, Pensacola, Florida

Len Register, a career prosecutor with the U.S. Department of Justice (DOJ) in Pensacola, Florida, is an assistant U.S. attorney. He was the managing assistant U.S. attorney for 10 of his 21 years with DOJ in Jackson, Tennessee, and Pensacola. Prior to joining the DOJ, Register was a state prosecutor for 12 years and spent 3 years in private practice. During his state tenure, he was a member of the trial team who prosecuted Ted Bundy for kidnapping and murdering a 12-year-old school girl from Lake City, Florida. Following his appointment by Florida's governor to serve as the chief prosecutor for Florida's Eighth Judicial Circuit, Register supervised the investigation and indictment of Danny Rolling, who later pled guilty to the murder of five University of Florida students in August 1990.

As a faculty advisor for the National College of District Attorneys in 1990, Register appeared several times on the Court TV network as a panelist on the death penalty and high-profile capital cases in Florida. Having previously served as a Correctional Officer I at Florida State Prison while waiting to begin law school, Register obtained his bachelor's and doctor of law degrees at the University of Florida in Gainesville. He is a recipient of the Florida Council on Crime & Delinquency's Statewide Distinguished Service Award for Criminal Justice. Register has witnessed Florida's death penalty imposed on three occasions, including the executions of Bundy and Rolling. He is an adjunct professor at the University of West Florida in the Department of Justice Studies.

Register's advice to those seeking a career in corrections or the criminal justice arena is never to turn a blind eye to an injustice or act of corruption. "Let your career be distinguished by a reputation for personal integrity and a commitment to fair play as you deal with adversaries and offenders."

> *"...never turn a blind eye to an injustice or act of corruption. Let your career be distinguished by a reputation for personal integrity and a commitment to fair play as you deal with adversaries and offenders."*

that statewide, prosecutors in high-density, urban areas sought the death penalty for only 16 percent of their capital-eligible cases. In comparison, prosecutors in medium-density, mostly suburban areas sought the death penalty in approximately 45 percent of the cases and prosecutors in low-density, mostly rural areas sought execution in 34 percent of the cases. Some argue that differences among communities is a positive factor. Jury pools are different, and they speak for the community. Others disagree, pointing to the U.S. Supreme Court mandate that the death penalty be reserved for the worst crimes committed by the worst offenders. If a rural county has few murders, then a relatively unaggravated homicide may appear to be the worst of the worst. If the crime is put on a continuum in an urban area, it may not be considered this way. The issue the Virginia lawmakers asked of themselves is whether these disparate outcomes are acceptable in a system in which the ultimate sanction is death and prosecutors are vested with discretionary authority to prosecute difficult and troubling cases.

Location can also change the outcome in federal death penalty prosecutions.[20] Whereas a state homicide is prosecuted in the county of offense, a federal homicide is prosecuted in one of 94 federal districts. Consider the federal Eastern District of Louisiana, for example. It consists of 12 parishes (counties) including Orleans Parish (New Orleans). If a federal homicide happens in New Orleans, a jury pool is chosen from the federal district pool of all 12 parishes, not just Orleans Parish. The outcome can be affected by incorporating more white and more conservative jurors from other areas than the predominant minority and more liberal community members of Orleans Parish who may be unfazed by the murder. Critics of this approach, including conservative Supreme Court Justice

Antonin Scalia, have called for the abolition of the federal death penalty and the selection of the jury from the county of offense to prosecute federally.[21]

More recently, researchers at Bowling Green State University examined the data on almost 6,000 homicides in Ohio that occurred between 1981 and 1997. They found that even after controlling for several legally relevant factors, analyses revealed that homicides with white female victims were more likely to result in a death sentence than others. "In fact," the researchers wrote, "homicides with white female victims are the only statistically distinct victim dyad. This is consistent with the view that black female victims do not have the same status as white female victims. In other words, it appears that decision making in homicides is not influenced by the same factors in all cases, and that white female victim homicides may be substantively unique."[22]

Reporters observe the execution chair in which Gary Gilmore sat when facing a Utah firing squad on January 17, 1977. Upper right on the chair back are the bullet holes. Draped over the back of the chair is the corduroy material hood that Gilmore wore during the execution. On March 15, 2004, Utah repealed its use of the firing squad, leaving lethal injection as the only option. Should condemned inmates be permitted to choose the method of their execution if, when they were sentenced to die, state law allowed the choice?

Methods of Execution

Five methods of execution are used in the United States: (1) lethal injection, (2) electrocution, (3) lethal gas, (4) hanging, and (5) firing squad. As you can see in Exhibit 15–7, lethal injection is the predominant method of execution, used in 35 states. (Remember that although Connecticut, Maryland, and New Mexico abolished capital punishment, the laws were not retroactive, leaving 2 persons on death row in New Mexico, 5 in Maryland, and 11 in Connecticut.) In 1977, Oklahoma became the first state to adopt lethal injection as a means of execution. Today nine states authorize electrocution; five states, lethal gas; two states, hanging; three states, firing squad should lethal injection ever be held unconstitutional. See Exhibit 15–8 for the first state to use lethal injection and changes in the number of drugs that states use. The federal government authorizes a different method of execution under each of two different laws; the method of execution for federal prisoners prosecuted under the *Code of Federal Regulations*, Volume 28, Part 26, is lethal injection; for those offenses prosecuted under the Violent Crime Control and Law Enforcement Act of 1994, the method used is that in the state in which the person was convicted. If the state has no death penalty, the inmate is transferred to another state that has one.

When lethal injection is used, the condemned person is strapped to a gurney, and several heart monitors are positioned on his or her chest. Two needles (one is a backup) are inserted into arm veins. Long tubes connect the needle through a hole in a wall to several intravenous drips. A saline solution is started immediately. At the warden's signal, a curtain is raised, exposing the inmate to the witnesses in an adjoining room.

Most states use a three-drug combination for lethal injections: anesthetic (either pentobarbital or, formerly, sodium thiopental), pancuronium bromide (a paralytic agent, also called Pavulon), and potassium chloride (stops the heart and causes death). The inmate is injected with the three drugs administered over a five-minute period. The first is 60 cc of sodium thiopental or pentothal to kill pain and cause unconsciousness. Next flows 60 cc of pavulon or pancuronium bromide, which paralyzes the entire muscle system and stops the inmate's breathing. Finally, the flow of 60 cc of potassium chloride stops the heart. Death results from anesthetic overdose

EXHIBIT 15–7 Method of Execution

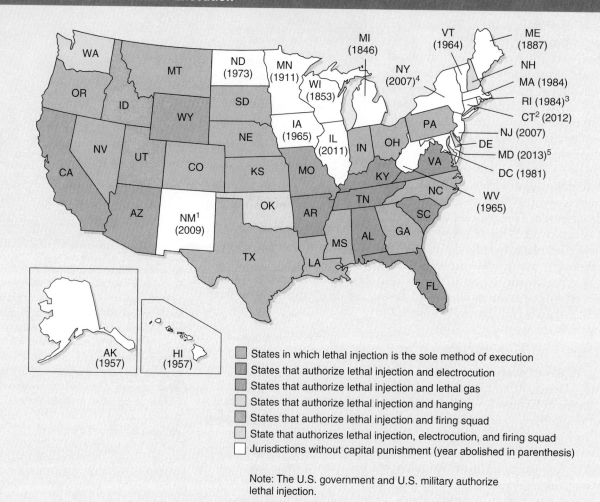

States in which lethal injection is the sole method of execution

States that authorize lethal injection and electrocution

States that authorize lethal injection and lethal gas

States that authorize lethal injection and hanging

States that authorize lethal injection and firing squad

State that authorizes lethal injection, electrocution, and firing squad

Jurisdictions without capital punishment (year abolished in parenthesis)

Note: The U.S. government and U.S. military authorize lethal injection.

Note: The U.S. government and U.S. military authorize lethal injection.

1. New Mexico voted to abolish the death penalty in March 2009. However, the repeal was not retroactive, leaving two people on the state's death row.
2. Connecticut voted to abolish the death penalty in April 2012. However, the repeal was not retroactive, leaving 11 people on the state's death row.
3. In 1979, the Supreme Court of Rhode Island held that a statute making a death sentence mandatory for someone who killed a fellow prisoner was unconstitutional. The legislature removed the statute in 1984.
4. In 2004, the New York Court of Appeals held that a portion of the state's death penalty law was unconstitutional. In 2007, it ruled that its prior holding applied to the last remaining person on the state's death row. The legislature has rejected attempts to restore the statute.
5. Maryland abolished the death penalty in May 2013. However, the repeal was not retroactive, leaving five people on the state's death row.

Source: Death Penalty Information, www.deathpenaltyinfo.org (accessed December 31, 2013); and Tracy L. Snell, *Capital Punishment 2011—Statistical Tables* (Washington, DC: U.S. Department of Justice, Bureau of Justice Statistics, July 2013).

and respiratory and cardiac arrest while the condemned person is unconscious. However, legal challenges in many states have raised concerns that condemned inmates are being inadequately anesthetized before being executed. Manufacturers of anesthetics are refusing to provide departments of corrections drugs for executions which explains, in part, the reason why executions have stalled. Refer to Exhibit 15–9 for the states in which the death penalty is on hold because the state has pending legal or legislative action, uses one drug, uses more than one drug, and has no death penalty.[23]

What Is Death Row Like?

death row

A prison area housing inmates who have been sentenced to death.

Prisoners who are sentenced to death are held on **death row,** a prison within a prison. All states except Missouri and Tennessee segregate death row inmates from the general prison population. According to

EXHIBIT 15–8 Lethal Injection "Firsts"

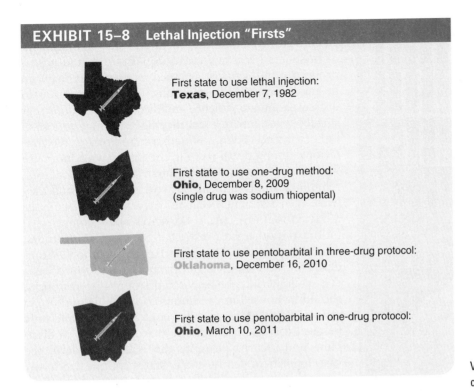

First state to use lethal injection:
Texas, December 7, 1982

First state to use one-drug method:
Ohio, December 8, 2009
(single drug was sodium thiopental)

First state to use pentobarbital in three-drug protocol:
Oklahoma, December 16, 2010

First state to use pentobarbital in one-drug protocol:
Ohio, March 10, 2011

Visit http://doc.mo.gov/OD/ or scan this code with the QR app on your SmartPhone or digital device and read comments by George Lombardi, director of Missouri's Department of Corrections, on the benefits of mainstreaming death-sentenced inmates. How does this information relate to ideas discussed in this chapter?

George Lombardi, director of the Missouri Department of Corrections, mainstreaming death row prisoners with the general population saves money; provides death row inmates more access to recreation, visitation, and prison programs and services; benefits non-death-row inmates because, before mainstreaming, even non-death-row prisoner movement

EXHIBIT 15–9 Jurisdictions Where Death Penalty Is On Hold Because of Legal or Legislative Action, Uses One or More Drugs, No Death Penalty

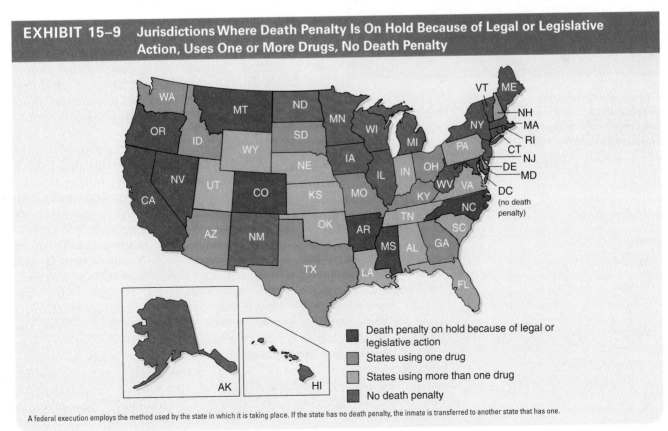

- Death penalty on hold because of legal or legislative action
- States using one drug
- States using more than one drug
- No death penalty

A federal execution employs the method used by the state in which it is taking place. If the state has no death penalty, the inmate is transferred to another state that has one.

Prisoners who are sentenced to death are held on death row. Do most death-sentenced prisoners need to be separated from the general prison population? Why or why not?

was restricted due to security concerns over the segregated death row unit; and facilitates staff management of prisoners because recreation, visitation, and prison programs and services are seen as privileges that can be taken away. Mainstreaming in Missouri has also decreased inmate violence and disciplinary actions that surface when inmates feel they have nothing to lose.[24] Otherwise, according to Lombardi and others, the conditions among death rows in the majority of states are virtually indistinguishable. Inmates receive few, if any, rehabilitation, treatment, or work programs, and they leave their individual cells for an average of one hour a day. About one-half of the states allow contact visitation; the other half restrict it to inmates' attorneys. According to the American Bar Association's Standards for the Treatment of Prisoners, death row prisoners, while permissibly separated from other prisoners, should be housed in conditions comparable to those in general population. Solitary confinement should only be used for brief periods for reasons related to discipline and security. Despite the ABA's standard, the vast majority of death penalty states confine death row prisoners in solitary confinement based solely on their death sentences. For that reason, death row existence has been called "living death" to convey a prisoner's loneliness, isolation, boredom, and loss of privacy.[25]

What many people forget is that a death row inmate's living environment is a correctional officer's workplace. Prison is a loud place, and sound can cause the most torment. The concrete and steel construction materials and furnishings that guarantee security and durability in death row amplify normal sounds within its hard walls. It takes little effort to imagine what effect shouting, flushing toilets, opening and closing steel doors, janitorial work, the blaring of televisions and radios, and voices wailing has not only on those who live there but also on those who work there. In summer the oppressive heat and in winter the freezing cold are trapped by walls of steel and concrete. The quality of life experienced by inmates depends on the work environment created by the corrections officers who guard them, but even the corrections officers are affected by the surroundings. Consult the Appendix: Careers in Corrections at the Online Learning Center Web site for the steps involved in career planning, developing employability and job readiness, and finding the right job.

Death row cells usually have steel bunks, toilets, and sinks. These are bolted to concrete floors and cinder block walls. Small lockers or wall shelves hold prisoners' personal property, which may include toiletries, books, pictures, a clock, and usually a television. The television is the death row inmate's most valued possession, not only because of its entertainment value but also because it makes available the world that the death row inmate has lost. Sometimes correctional officers use the threat of revoking television or telephone privileges to control behavior on death row. However, corrections officers say that death row inmates seldom exhibit disciplinary problems. One death row warden described death row inmates as "the group who causes the least trouble."[26] Researchers in Indiana examined the disciplinary records of 39 death row inmates who were transferred to the general prison population following modification of their sentences from death to capital life. The researchers found that, despite the heinousness of their capital offenses, the majority of these former death row inmates did not commit acts of serious violence on death row or after their transfer to the general prison population. Most presented little persistent disciplinary management difficulty in the general prison population.[27] The reasons, researchers suggest, are aging, prior adjustment to institutionalization while on death row, restrictive death row conditions, and higher levels of supervision.

Most death row inmates spend 22 to 23 hours a day in five-by-eight- or six-by-nine-foot cells, about the size of a bathroom. They are counted once an hour. They receive their meals through slots in the cell doors. Generally twice a week, they are handcuffed, escorted to, and locked in shower stalls for 5- or 10-minute showers. In some jurisdictions, death row inmates may visit the prison library; in others, books are taken to them. In Florida, death row inmates may receive mail every day except holidays and weekends. They may have cigarettes, snacks, radios, and a 13-inch television in their cells. They do not have cable television or air-conditioning and they are not allowed to be with each other in a common room. They can watch religious services on closed-circuit television. They wear orange T-shirts and blue pants.

Most death row inmates slowly lose their ties with the outside world. Although some states permit contact visits, most allow only noncontact visits. Every time death row inmates leave death row for visits—whether contact or noncontact—they are strip-searched before and after. Over the years, visitors and mail come less frequently, and they sometimes cease altogether. Corrections officers assigned to death row are instructed not to establish relationships with inmates because it may make it more difficult to carry out their duties. Pennsylvania's policy manual for death row corrections officers reads, "Employees must not be too familiar or discuss personal items of interest with the inmates."[28]

Preparing for an execution is a correctional officer's toughest job. "We begin to dread electrocutions weeks before they take place," says former corrections officer Lynch Alford Sr. "We're almost glad when someone is commuted, regardless of what crime he committed. We just sit around and wait. We drink coffee. We don't talk about anything. We don't talk about the electrocution. We just get it over with as soon as possible and then go home immediately." A death row inmate who refuses to walk to the death chamber is carried by corrections officers, sometimes screaming and kicking. "Guards have been known to go all to pieces during episodes such as these. Their nerves just don't hold up. In my opinion it is something you never become accustomed to. It's the most gruesome job I've come in contact with during my 35 years with the department. The more you see, the more you hate it."[29] Texas law governing execution is presented in Exhibit 15–10. At one time, Texas death row inmates had more freedom, worked in a prison garment factory, enjoyed group recreation, participated in education programs, and had an occasional contact visit. But in 1999, seven condemned prisoners escaped. After they were captured, prison officials moved death row from Huntsville to Livingston, eliminated the work and education programs, put inmates in permanent solitary confinement, and eliminated television.

Public Opinion, Politics, and Capital Punishment

CO15-3

Sixty percent of Americans say they favor the death penalty for convicted murderers, the lowest level of support the Gallup Poll has measured since November 1972, when 57 percent were in favor. Death penalty support peaked at 80 percent in 1994, but it has gradually declined since then.

The Offender Speaks
Visit www.mhhe.com/schmalleger7e to see this feature.

Visit http://www.deathpenaltyinfo.org/death-row or scan this code with the QR app on your SmartPhone or digital device and read about the conditions of death row such as whether television is permitted, contact with family and lawyer is allowed, educational and vocational opportunities are offered, and single cells and group recreation are provided. How does this information relate to ideas discussed in this chapter?

EXHIBIT 15–10	Capital Punishment in Texas

Execution of Convict

Whenever the sentence of death is pronounced against a convict, the sentence shall be executed at any time after the hour of 6 P.M. on the day set for the execution, by intravenous injection of a substance or substances in a lethal quantity sufficient to cause death and until such convict is dead, such execution procedure to be determined and supervised by the Director of the institutional division of the Texas Department of Criminal Justice.

Warrant of Execution

Whenever any person is sentenced to death, the clerk of the court in which the sentence is pronounced, shall within ten days after the court enters its order setting the date for execution, issue a warrant under the seal of the court for the execution of the sentence of death, which shall recite the fact of conviction, setting forth specifically the offense, the judgment of the court, the time fixed for his or her execution, and directed to the Director of the Department of Corrections at Huntsville, Texas, commanding him to proceed, at the time and place named in the order of execution, to carry the same into execution, as provided in the preceding Article, and shall deliver such warrant to the sheriff of the county in which such judgment of conviction was had, to be by him delivered to the said Director of the Department of Corrections, together with the condemned person if he or she has not previously been so delivered.

Taken to Department of Corrections

Immediately upon the receipt of such warrant, the sheriff shall transport such condemned person to the Director of the Department of Corrections, if he or she has not already been so delivered, and shall deliver him or her and the warrant aforesaid into the hands of the Director of the Department of Corrections and shall take from the Director of the Department of Corrections his receipt for such person and such warrant, which receipt the sheriff shall return to the office of the clerk of the court where the judgment of death was rendered. For his services, the sheriff shall be entitled to the same compensation as is now allowed by law to sheriffs for removing or conveying prisoners under the provisions of Section 4 of Article 1029 or 1030 of the Code of Criminal Procedure of 1925, as amended.

Upon the receipt of such condemned person by the Director of the Department of Corrections, the condemned person shall be confined therein until the time for his or her execution arrives, and while so confined, all persons outside of said prison shall be denied access to him or her, except his or her physician, lawyer, and clergyperson, who shall be admitted to see him or her when necessary for his or her health or for the transaction of business, and the relatives and friends of the condemned person, who shall be admitted to see and converse with him or her at all proper times, under such reasonable rules and regulations as may be made by the Board of Directors of the Department of Corrections.

Executioner

The Director of the Texas Department of Corrections shall designate an executioner to carry out the death penalty provided by law.

Place of Execution

The execution shall take place at a location designated by the Texas Department of Corrections in a room arranged for that purpose.

Present at Execution

The following persons may be present at the execution: the executioner, and such persons as may be necessary to assist him in conducting the execution; the Board of Directors of the Department of Corrections; two physicians, including the prison physician; the spiritual advisor of the condemned; the chaplains of the Department of Corrections; the county judge and sheriff of the county in which the Department of Corrections is situated; and any of the relatives or friends of the condemned person that he or she may request, not exceeding five in number, shall be admitted. No convict shall be permitted by the prison authorities to witness the execution.

Body of Convict

The body of a convict who has been legally executed shall be embalmed immediately and so directed by the Director of the Department of Corrections. If the body is not demanded or requested by a relative or bona fide friend within forty-eight hours after execution then it shall be delivered to the Anatomical Board of the State of Texas, if requested by the Board. If the body is requested by a relative, bona fide friend, or the Anatomical Board of the State of Texas, such recipient shall pay a fee not to exceed twenty-five dollars to the mortician for his or her services in embalming the body for which the mortician shall issue to the recipient a written receipt. When such receipt is delivered to the Director of the Department of Corrections, the body of the deceased shall be delivered to the party named in the receipt or his or her authorized agent. If the body is not delivered to a relative, bona fide friend, or the Anatomical Board of the State of Texas, the Director of the Department of Corrections shall cause the body to be decently buried, and the fee for embalming shall be paid by the county in which the indictment which resulted in conviction was found.

Source: Excerpted from Texas Code of Criminal Procedure, Chapter 43, Articles 43.15–43.26.

Death penalty researchers across the country are finding that although the public may accept the use of capital punishment, it may actually prefer other punishment options such as life without the possibility of parole (LWOP) when given the opportunity. There is now a significant body of research showing that support for the death penalty drops considerably when it is compared with alternatives such as a sentence of life in prison with no parole. In a national poll of 1,500 registered voters, Lake Research Partners found a clear majority of voters (61 percent) would choose a punishment other than the death penalty for murder, including life with no possibility of parole and with restitution to the victim's family (39 percent), life with no possibility of parole (13 percent), or life with the possibility of parole (9 percent).[30] The future of public support for the death penalty may depend as much on the impact of unforeseen tragedies such as the Oklahoma City bombing or the shootings at the Sandy Hook Elementary School as it does on political campaigns by death penalty supporters and opponents. However, for now, views on the death penalty appear to be stable with just over 6 in 10 Americans in favor of it since 2010.

Similar shifts are taking place in the judicial and political arenas. Jurors and judges are now imposing fewer death penalties. The number of persons sentenced to die dropped by more than two-thirds in the past decade, from 224 in 2000 to 77 in 2012.

Professional organizations and the judiciary are also weighing in on the question of capital punishment. The American Medical Association's Code of Ethics prohibits physicians from participating in a lethal injection and recently, the 40,000-member American Board of Anesthesiologists decided to revoke the certification of any member who participates in executing a prisoner by lethal injection. Mark Rockoff, the board's secretary said, "We are healers, not executioners."[31]

In 1997, the American Bar Association called for a death penalty moratorium until jurisdictions implement policies and procedures that ensure that death penalty cases are administered fairly and impartially, in accordance with due process, and with minimum risk of executing innocent people. The ABA reiterated that call in 2000 and again in 2003. And a survey of the world's leading criminologists published in 2009 that asked their expert opinions on whether the empirical research supports the contention that the death penalty is a superior deterrent concluded that the death penalty does not add deterrent effects above those already achieved by long-term imprisonment.[32]

Voices from the bench are also speaking out. In rare public statements, four past and present U.S. Supreme Court Justices have spoken out against the death penalty. "If statistics are any indication," said former U.S. Supreme Court Justice Sandra Day O'Connor, "the system may well be allowing some innocent defendants to be executed." She suggested that "perhaps it's time to look at minimum standards for appointed counsel in death cases and adequate compensation for appointed counsel when they are used."[33] Justice Ruth Bader Ginsburg added that she has "yet to see a death penalty case among the dozens coming to the Supreme Court

Tani Cantil-Sakauye, chief justice of the California Supreme Court, told reporters that the death penalty is no longer effective in California and suggested that she would welcome a public debate on its merits and costs. What is the estimated cost per execution in California, and what has been the cost to California taxpayers for capital punishment since its reinstatement in 1978?

The Staff Speaks
Visit www.mhhe.com/schmalleger7e to see this feature.

Six months after his appointment to the U.S. Supreme Court, John Paul Stevens joined the conservative majority of Justices and allowed the use of the death penalty in the United States. At the time, he wrote it is possible to ensure "evenhanded, rational and consistent imposition of death sentences under law" with careful and narrow use. Thirty-two years later, Justice Stevens reversed course. He said personnel changes on the court, coupled with "regrettable judicial activism," had created a system of capital punishment that is shot through with racism, skewed toward conviction, infected with politics, tinged with hysteria, hopelessly flawed, and unconstitutional. If you were a U.S. Supreme Court Justice, what would you say?

CO15-4

on eve-of-execution stay applications in which the defendant was well-represented at trial" and that "people who are well represented at trial do not get the death penalty."[34] In 1994, when the U.S. Supreme Court denied review in the Texas death penalty case of Bruce Edwin Callins, Justice Harry A. Blackmun wrote in his dissent opinion, "From this day forward, I no longer shall tinker with the machinery of death. For more than 20 years I have endeavored to develop rules that would lend more than the mere appearance of fairness to the death penalty endeavor. Rather than continue to coddle the court's delusions that the desired level of fairness has been achieved, I feel obligated simply to concede that the death penalty experiment has failed."[35]

In 1976, just six months after being appointed to the U.S. Supreme Court by President Gerald Ford, Justice John Paul Stevens voted to reinstate capital punishment. He did not join the most liberal Justices at the time—William Brennan and Thurgood Marshall—who insisted that any execution violated the Eighth Amendment ban on cruel and unusual punishment. Instead, he joined the conservative majority and wrote that it is possible to ensure "evenhanded, rational and consistent imposition of death sentences under law." Thirty-two years and 1,100 executions later, Justice Stevens reversed course and said the death penalty is hopelessly flawed and unconstitutional. He framed the question this way: It's not whether you believe in a death penalty, it's whether you believe in *this* death penalty, the one the U.S. is currently using. He wrote that personnel changes on the Court, coupled with "regrettable judicial activism," had created a system of capital punishment that is shot with racism, skewed toward conviction, infected with politics, and tinged with hysteria. He added, "That the murder of black victims is treated as less culpable than the murder of white victims provides a haunting reminder of once-prevalent Southern lynchings." Justice Stevens said that he and the other Justices voted to continue capital punishment in 1976, arguing for a careful and narrow use of capital punishment, but since then, the Supreme Court has made its use increasingly less careful and less narrow. He also commented on the unreliability of capital punishment, pointing out that more than 130 people have been exonerated and released from death row since 1973.[36]

There are many arguments favoring capital punishment and many arguments opposing it. Some of the arguments—pro and con—are summarized in Exhibit 15–11. Where do you stand?

CO15-5   THE COURTS AND THE DEATH PENALTY

"Death is different [from other punishments]," said U.S. Supreme Court Justice William Brennan. For that reason, every phase of a capital crime proceeding, from jury selection to sentencing instructions, has been influenced by court rulings. The legal history of today's death penalty can be traced through several landmark cases. In the June 29, 1972, decision in *Furman v. Georgia*,[37] the U.S. Supreme Court ruled by a vote of five to four that the death penalty, as imposed and carried out under the laws of Georgia, was cruel and unusual punishment in violation of the Eighth and Fourteenth Amendments. According to the Court, Georgia's death penalty statute gave the sentencing authority (judge or trial jury) complete freedom to impose a death or life imprisonment sentence without standards or guidelines; the death penalty had been imposed arbitrarily, discriminatorily, and selectively against minorities. The Supreme Court voided 40 death penalty statutes, thereby commuting the death sentences of all 629

EXHIBIT 15–11	Arguments Favoring and Opposing the Death Penalty

PRO

- It deters people from crime through fear of punishment; it exerts a positive moral influence by stigmatizing crimes of murder and manslaughter.
- It is a just punishment for murder; it fulfills the "just deserts" principle of a fitting punishment; life in prison is not a tough enough punishment for a capital crime.
- It is constitutionally appropriate; the Eighth Amendment prohibits cruel and unusual punishment, yet the Fifth Amendment implies that, with due process of law, one may be deprived of life, liberty, or property.
- It reduces time spent on death row to reduce costs of capital punishment and the attendant costs of postconviction appeals, investigations, and searches for new evidence and witnesses.
- It protects society from the most serious and feared offenders; it prevents the reoccurrence of violence.
- It is more humane than life imprisonment because it is quick; making the prisoner suffer by remaining in prison for the rest of his or her life is more torturous and inhumane than execution.
- It is almost impossible for an innocent person to be executed; the slow execution rate results from the process of appeals, from sentencing to execution.

CON

- It does not deter crime; no evidence exists that the death penalty is more effective than other punishments.
- It violates human rights; it is a barbaric remnant of an uncivilized society; it is immoral in principle; and it ensures the execution of some innocent people.
- It falls disproportionately on racial minorities; those who murdered whites are more likely to be sentenced to death than are those who murdered blacks.
- It costs too much; $2 million to $5 million are poured into each execution while other criminal justice components such as police, courts, and community corrections lack funding.
- It boosts the murder rate; this is known as the *brutalizing effect;* the state is a role model, and when the state carries out an execution, it shows that killing is a way to solve problems.
- Not everyone wants vengeance; many people favor alternative sentences such as life without parole.
- It is arbitrary and unfair; offenders who commit similar crimes under similar circumstances receive widely differing sentences; race, social and economic status, location of crime, and pure chance influence sentencing.

death row inmates around the United States, and suspended the death penalty because existing statutes were no longer valid. It is important to note that the Court majority did *not* rule that the death penalty itself was unconstitutional but that only the way in which it was administered at that time.

States responded to the *Furman* decision by rewriting their capital punishment statutes to limit discretion and avoid arbitrary and inconsistent results. The new death penalty laws took two forms. Some states imposed a **mandatory death penalty** for certain crimes, and others permitted **guided discretion,** which sets standards for judges and juries to use when deciding whether to impose the death penalty.

In 1976, the U.S. Supreme Court rejected mandatory death penalty statutes in *Woodson* v. *North Carolina* and *Roberts* v. *Louisiana,* but it approved guided discretion statutes in *Gregg* v. *Georgia* and two companion cases.[38]

mandatory death penalty

A death sentence that the legislature has required to be imposed upon people convicted of certain offenses.

guided discretion

Decision making bounded by general guidelines, rules, or laws.

EXHIBIT 15-12 The Florida Death Penalty Statute

921.141 Sentence of death or life imprisonment for capital felonies; further proceedings to determine sentence.

(1) SEPARATE PROCEEDINGS ON ISSUE OF PENALTY. Upon conviction or adjudication of guilt of a defendant of a capital felony, the court shall conduct a separate sentencing proceeding to determine whether the defendant should be sentenced to death or life imprisonment as authorized by s. 775.082. The proceeding shall be conducted by the trial judge before the trial jury as soon as practicable. If, through impossibility or inability, the trial jury is unable to reconvene for a hearing on the issue of penalty, having determined the guilt of the accused, the trial judge may summon a special juror or jurors as provided in chapter 913 to determine the issue of the imposition of the penalty. If the trial jury has been waived or if the defendant pleaded guilty, the sentencing proceeding shall be conducted before a jury impaneled for that purpose, unless waived by the defendant. In the proceeding, evidence may be presented as to any matter that the court deems relevant to the nature of the crime and the character of the defendant and shall include matters relating to any of the aggravating or mitigating circumstances enumerated in subsections (5) and (6). Any such evidence that the court deems to have probative value may be received, regardless of its admissibility under the exclusionary rules of evidence, provided the defendant is accorded a fair opportunity to rebut any hearsay statements. However, this subsection shall not be construed to authorize the introduction of any evidence secured in violation of the Constitution of the United States or the Constitution of the State of Florida. The state and the defendant or his counsel shall be permitted to present argument for or against sentence of death.

(2) ADVISORY SENTENCE BY THE JURY. After hearing all the evidence, the jury shall deliberate and render an advisory sentence to the court, based upon the following matters:

(a) whether sufficient aggravating circumstances exist as enumerated in subsection (5);

(b) whether sufficient mitigating circumstances exist that outweigh the aggravating circumstances found to exist; and

(c) based on these considerations, whether the defendant should be sentenced to life imprisonment or death.

(3) FINDINGS IN SUPPORT OF SENTENCE OF DEATH. Notwithstanding the recommendation of a majority of the jury, the court, after weighing the aggravating and mitigating circumstances, shall enter a sentence of life imprisonment or death, but if the court imposes a sentence of death, it shall set forth in writing its findings upon which the sentence of death is based as to the facts:

(a) that sufficient aggravating circumstances exist as enumerated in subsection (5), and

(b) that there are insufficient mitigating circumstances to outweigh the aggravating circumstances.

In each case in which the court imposes the death sentence, the determination of the court shall be supported by specific written findings of fact based upon the circumstances in subsections (5) and (6) and upon the records of the trial and the sentencing proceedings. If the court does not make the findings requiring the death sentence, the court shall impose sentence of life imprisonment in accordance with s. 775.082.

(4) REVIEW OF JUDGMENT AND SENTENCE. The judgment of conviction and sentence of death shall be subject to automatic review by the Supreme Court of Florida within 60 days after certification by the sentencing court of the entire record, unless the time is extended for an additional period not to exceed 30 days by the Supreme Court for good cause shown. Such review by the Supreme Court shall have priority over all other cases and shall be heard in accordance with rules promulgated by the Supreme Court.

(5) AGGRAVATING CIRCUMSTANCES. Aggravating circumstances shall be limited to the following:

bifurcated trial

Two separate hearings for different issues in a trial, one for guilt and the other for punishment.

mitigating circumstances

Factors that, although not justifying or excusing an action, may reduce the culpability of the offender.

aggravating circumstances

Factors that may increase the culpability of the offender.

In *Gregg*, the Court approved automatic appellate review, a proportionality review whereby state appellate courts compare a sentence with those of similar cases, and a **bifurcated trial,** or special two-part trial. The first part of a bifurcated trial, the *guilt phase*, decides the issue of guilt. If the defendant is found guilty, the second part of the trial, the *penalty phase*, takes place. The penalty phase includes presentation of facts that mitigate or aggravate the circumstances of the crime. **Mitigating circumstances** are factors that may reduce the culpability of the offender (make the defendant less deserving of the death penalty). **Aggravating circumstances** are factors that may increase the offender's culpability (make the defendant more deserving of death). Florida's death penalty statute, including its list of mitigating and aggravating circumstances (subsections 5 and 6), is shown in Exhibit 15–12.

In 2002, the U.S. Supreme Court handed down another decision that shaped capital sentencing. In *Ring* v. *Arizona*,[39] the Court held that only juries, not judges, can determine the presence of "aggravating factors" to be

EXHIBIT 15–12 **The Florida Death Penalty Statute** *(continued)*

(a) The capital felony was committed by a person under sentence of imprisonment or placed on community control.

(b) The defendant was previously convicted of another capital felony or of a felony involving the use or threat of violence to the person.

(c) The defendant knowingly created a great risk of death to many people.

(d) The capital felony was committed while the defendant was engaged, or was an accomplice, in the commission of, or an attempt to commit, or flight after committing or attempting to commit, any robbery, sexual battery, arson, burglary, kidnapping, or aircraft piracy or the unlawful throwing, placing, or discharging of a destructive device or bomb.

(e) The capital felony was committed for the purpose of avoiding or preventing a lawful arrest or effecting an escape from custody.

(f) The capital felony was committed for pecuniary gain.

(g) The capital felony was committed to disrupt or hinder the lawful exercise of any governmental function or the enforcement of laws.

(h) The capital felony was especially heinous, atrocious, or cruel.

(i) The capital felony was a homicide and was committed in a cold, calculated, and premeditated manner without any pretense of moral or legal justification.

(j) The victim of the capital felony was a law enforcement officer engaged in the performance of his official duties.

(k) The victim of the capital felony was an elected or appointed public official engaged in the performance of his official duties if the motive for the capital felony was related, in whole or in part, to the victim's official capacity.

Source: Florida Statute 921.141.

(6) MITIGATING CIRCUMSTANCES. Mitigating circumstances shall be the following:

(a) The defendant has no significant history of prior criminal activity.

(b) The capital felony was committed while the defendant was under the influence of extreme mental or emotional disturbance.

(c) The victim was a participant in the defendant's conduct or consented to the act.

(d) The defendant was an accomplice in the capital felony committed by another person and his participation was relatively minor.

(e) The defendant acted under extreme duress or under the substantial domination of another person.

(f) The capacity of the defendant to appreciate the criminality of his conduct or to conform his conduct to the requirements of law was substantially impaired.

(g) The age of the defendant at the time of the crime.

(7) VICTIM IMPACT EVIDENCE. Once the prosecution has provided evidence of the existence of one or more aggravating circumstances as described in subsection (5), the prosecution may introduce, and subsequently argue, victim impact evidence. Such evidence shall be designed to demonstrate the victim's uniqueness as an individual human being and the resultant loss to the community's members by the victim's death. Characterizations and opinions about the crime, the defendant, and the appropriate sentence shall not be permitted as a part of victim impact evidence.

(8) APPLICABILITY. This section does not apply to a person convicted or adjudicated guilty of a capital drug trafficking felony under s. 893.135.

weighed in the capital sentencing process. Although judges may still reduce sentences, the Court held that a defendant may not receive a penalty that exceeds the maximum penalty that he or she would have received if punished according to the facts in the jury verdict. Two years later in *Schriro* v. *Summerlin*,[40] the U.S. Supreme Court determined that its 2002 decision in *Ring* v. *Arizona* was not retroactive, thereby denying new sentencing hearings for dozens of death row inmates in Arizona, Idaho, Montana, and Nebraska whose sentences were originally handed down by judges. With their decision in *Summerlin*, the Justices decided that their original decision in *Ring* was a procedural rule and thus was not retroactive.

Appealing the Death Penalty

CO15-6

Death penalty cases may pass through as many as 10 courts across 3 stages: trial and direct review, state postconviction appeals, and federal *habeas corpus* appeals (see Exhibit 15–13).

EXHIBIT 15–13 The Capital Criminal Process: Trial Through State and Federal Postconvictions

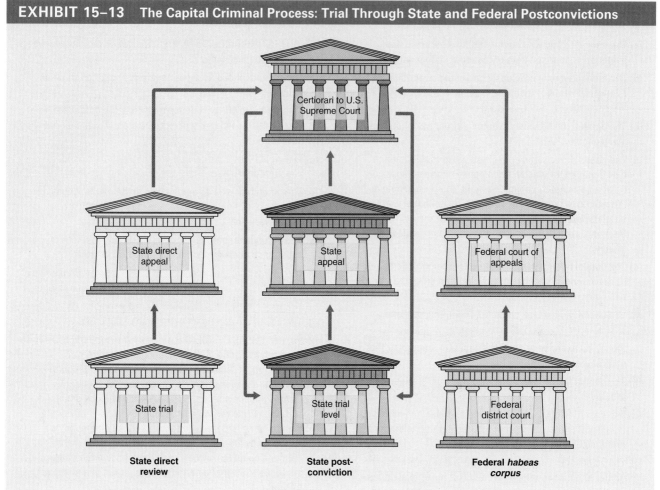

Source: James S. Liebman, Jeffrey Fagan, and Valerie West, *A Broken System: Error Rates in Capital Punishment Cases, 1973–1995.* (New York: Columbia University School of Law, 2000), p. 23. Reprinted with permission.

serious error

Error that substantially undermines the reliability of the guilt finding or death sentence imposed at trial.

In stage one, trial and direct review, a death sentence is imposed. As a consequence of the *Furman* decision, the laws of all states require that legal issues about the trial and sentence automatically be appealed to the state appellate courts. Alabama and Ohio have two rounds of appeals in the direct review process; this means that the legal issues may be heard first in the state court of criminal appeals (court 1) before reaching the state supreme court (court 2). These courts evaluate the trial for legal or constitutional errors and determine whether the death sentence is consistent with sentences imposed in similar cases. State appellate courts seldom overturn a conviction or change a death sentence. The defendant then petitions the U.S. Supreme Court (court 3) to grant a petition for a writ of *certiorari*—a written order to the lower court whose decision is being appealed to send the records of the case forward for review. Stage one, direct review, consumes about five years—half of the time required for the entire appeals process. Nationally, the rate of **serious error** (error that substantially undermines the reliability of the guilt finding or death sentence imposed at trial) discovered on direct review is 41 percent. States with the highest rate of serious error found on direct review are Wyoming (67 percent), Mississippi (61 percent), North Carolina (61 percent), Alabama (55 percent), and South Carolina (54 percent).[41]

If the defendant's direct appeals are unsuccessful and the Supreme Court denies review, stage two—state postconviction appeals—begins.

At this point, many death row inmates allege ineffective or incompetent trial counsel, and new counsel is engaged or appointed. The new counsel petitions the trial court (court 4) with newly discovered evidence; questions about the fairness of the trial; and allegations of jury bias, tainted evidence, incompetence of defense counsel, and prosecutorial or police misconduct. If the trial court denies the appeals, they may be filed with the state's appellate courts (either directly to the state supreme court or, if there exists a dual level of appellate review, through a petition first to the state court of criminal appeals (court 5) followed by a petition to the state supreme court (court 6). Most often, the state appellate courts deny the petition. Defendant's counsel then petitions the U.S. Supreme Court (court 7). If the U.S. Supreme Court denies the petition for a writ of *certiorari*, stage two ends and stage three begins. The rate of serious error found on state postconviction appeals is 10 percent. State postconviction reversals are highest in Maryland (52 percent), Wyoming (33 percent), Indiana (25 percent), Utah (23 percent), and Mississippi (20 percent).

In stage three, the federal *habeas corpus* stage, a defendant files a petition in U.S. district court (court 8) in the state in which the defendant was convicted and is incarcerated and alleging violations of constitutional rights. Such rights include the right to due process (Fourteenth Amendment), prohibition against cruel and unusual punishment (Eighth Amendment), and effective assistance of counsel (Sixth Amendment). If the district court denies the petition, defense counsel submits it to the U.S. court of appeals (court 9) for the circuit representing the jurisdiction. If the court of appeals denies the petition, defense counsel asks the U.S. Supreme Court (court 10) to grant a writ of *certiorari*. If the U.S. Supreme Court denies *certiorari*, the office of the state attorney general asks the state supreme court to set a date for execution. Federal courts find serious error in 40 percent of the capital cases they review. The highest rate of serious error is found in California (80 percent), Montana (75 percent), Mississippi (71 percent), Idaho (67 percent), and Georgia (65 percent). The Eleventh Circuit—the nation's most active capital appeals circuit with jurisdiction over Alabama, Georgia, and Florida—finds serious error in 50 percent of the death cases it reviews.

In 1996, in an effort to reduce the time people spend on death row and the number of federal appeals, the U.S. Congress passed the Antiterrorism and Effective Death Penalty Act (AEDPA). The AEDPA defines filing deadlines and limits reasons for second, or successive, federal appellate reviews to (1) new constitutional law, (2) new evidence that could not have been discovered at the time of the original trial, or (3) new facts that, if proven, would be sufficient to establish the applicant's innocence. Under the AEDPA, if the U.S. Supreme Court denies the petition for a writ of *certiorari* in the final federal *habeas corpus* appeal, defense counsel may once again petition the federal courts; however, before a second, or successive, application for a writ of *habeas corpus* may be filed in a U.S. district court, defense counsel must petition the appropriate U.S. court of appeals for an order authorizing the district court to consider the application. The petition to the U.S. court of appeals is decided by a three-judge panel; the panel must grant or deny the authorization to file the second, or successive, application within 30 days after the petition is filed. If the panel approves the petition, the district court must render a decision regarding the application within 180 days. If the motion is appealed to the court of appeals representing the jurisdiction, the court must render its decision within 120 days. If the petition is filed with the U.S. Supreme Court, the Court may grant the petition for *certiorari* or let the lower court's decision stand.

DEATH PENALTY ISSUES IN THE 21ST CENTURY

Of all the reforms that capital punishment has gone through since *Furman*, perhaps none has been as significant as those that have occurred in the 21st century. We have already discussed how the cost of capital punishment, the current budget crisis, and public opinion and politics are shaping the debate on capital punishment. We add three more issues for you to consider: wrongful convictions, the banning of executions of offenders who have mental retardation, and juveniles.

CO15-7

Visit http://www.washingtonpost.com/local/crime/dc-plans-changes-in-police-lineups-informants-to-stop-errors/2013/02/13/315673d4-7617-11e2-8f84-3e4b513b1a13_story.html?hpid=z3 or scan this code with the QR app on your SmartPhone or digital device and watch the podcast of the changes taking place in Washington, D.C., in response to wrongful convictions discovered in recent years. How does this information relate to ideas discussed in this chapter?

Wrongful Convictions: The Liebman Study

According to some scholars, Americans seem to be of two minds about the death penalty. One is the fear that capital trials put people on death row who do not belong there. The other is that capital appeals take too long. The two sides are not as oppositional as it might appear, however. It may be that capital sentences spend too much time under appellate review and they are fraught with unacceptable levels of error. At least that is the conclusion of one of the most controversial studies of appellate reviews of capital sentences ever undertaken in the United States, known as the *Liebman study*.

Possibly because four times as many people had their death sentences overturned or received clemency than were executed since 1977, the Judiciary Committee of the U.S. Senate asked Columbia law professor James Liebman to calculate the frequency of error in capital cases.[42] Liebman and his colleagues studied what happened when 4,578 capital cases were appealed. Their conclusion is powerful: The overall rate of prejudicial error in the U.S. capital punishment system is 68 percent. More than two of every three capital judgments reviewed by the courts were found to be seriously flawed. Ten states (Alabama, Arizona, California, Georgia, Indiana, Maryland, Mississippi, Montana, Oklahoma, and Wyoming) have overall error rates of 75 percent or higher. Almost 1,000 of the cases sent back for retrial ended in sentences less than death, and 87 ended in *not guilty* verdicts.

On Friday, January 19, 2003, former Illinois death row inmate LeRoy Orange was pardoned by Governor George Ryan after spending 19 years on death row for a crime he did not commit. Since 1983, 143 persons have been released from death row, and news of their innocence has set off a new debate over capital punishment in the United States. How has the Liebman report shaped the debate?

Liebman and his colleagues found two types of serious error. The first is incompetent defense lawyering (accounting for one-third of all state postconviction appeals). A review of death penalty cases in Pennsylvania spanning three decades found that lawyers who handle such cases—typically at taxpayers' expense because the defendants are indigent—are often overworked and underpaid and present only the barest defense.[43] These lawyers neglect basic steps, including interviewing defendants, seeking witnesses, and investigating a defendant's background. Such attorneys receive $2,000 for court preparation and $400 a day in court to handle a case that veteran defense lawyers say requires a minimum outlay of $35,000 to $40,000. Ronald Greenblatt, chair of the Philadelphia chapter of the Pennsylvania Association of Criminal Defense Lawyers, told a Philadelphia reporter, "The attorneys who are doing this work, because of the low pay, are not doing it the right way. We really need to stop it."[44] Philadelphia has more than 11,000 lawyers, but fewer than 30 are willing to take court appointments in capital trials.

The second is prosecutorial suppression of evidence that the defendant is innocent or does not deserve the death penalty (accounting for almost 20 percent). When the errors were corrected through the stages already discussed, 8 of 10 people on retrial were found to deserve a sentence less than death and 7 percent were found innocent of the capital crime. Exhibit 15–14 shows that for every 100 death sentences imposed, 41 were turned back at the trial and direct review phase because of serious error. Of the 59 that passed to the state postconviction stage, 10 percent—6 of the original 100—were turned back due to serious flaws. Of the 53 that passed to the next stage of federal *habeas corpus*, 40 percent—an additional 21 of the original 100—were turned back because of serious error. Together, 68 of the original 100 were thrown out after 9 to 10 years had passed because of serious flaws. Of the 68 individuals whose death sentences were overturned for serious error, 82 percent (56)

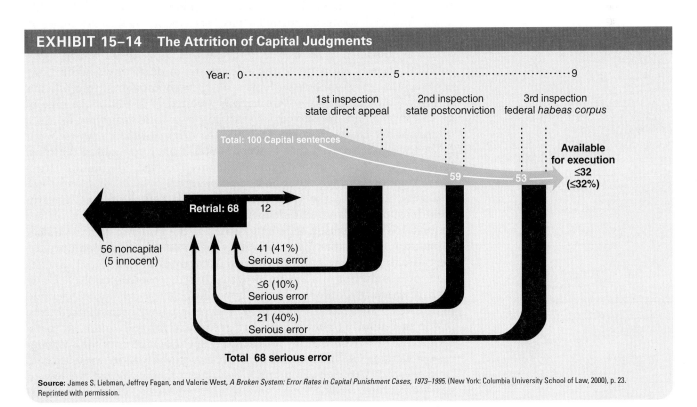

EXHIBIT 15–14   The Attrition of Capital Judgments

Source: James S. Liebman, Jeffrey Fagan, and Valerie West, *A Broken System: Error Rates in Capital Punishment Cases, 1973–1995.* (New York: Columbia University School of Law, 2000), p. 23. Reprinted with permission.

Steve Manning, a former Chicago police officer, was sentenced to death for murder and kidnapping but his case was overturned in 1998. After his release, Manning sued the FBI for framing him because he wouldn't help them by working as an undercover informant. He won a $6.5 million judgment but the civil award was overturned.

were found on retrial not to deserve the death penalty, including 5 who were found innocent of the offense. Each one had spent an average of nine years and two months on death row.

What if a death sentence is imposed today in the United States? What could the defendant, relative, lawyer, or judge expect? Liebman and his colleagues answer this way: "The capital conviction or sentence will probably be overturned due to serious error. It'll take 9 or 10 years to find out, given how many other capital cases being reviewed for likely error are lined up ahead of this one. If the judgment is overturned, a lesser conviction or sentence will probably be imposed."[45]

If death sentences are not reliable and persons are wrongfully convicted and sentenced, the error has serious consequences for the wrongly convicted, for the family of the victim whose search for justice is incomplete, for the family of the person wrongly convicted in terms of the prolonged and distorted grief they suffer, for subsequent victims of the real offender still at large, and for the public in terms of lost confidence in the criminal justice system. A report in the *Chicago Tribune* revealed that police and prosecutors rarely pursue new leads and suspects after a wrongly convicted defendant has been released from death row.[46] The actual perpetrators remain in society to commit additional crimes, and many death row exonerees remain under a cloud of police suspicion because law enforcement failed to find the true offender.

Another consequence of wrongful convictions not often discussed is the cost of serious errors. On January 25, 2005, a federal jury in Chicago found two FBI agents liable for framing Steve Manning, former Chicago police officer and awarded Manning $6.5 million.[47] Jurors said the FBI agents induced witnesses to make false statements against Manning in the murder investigation of trucking firm owner James Pellegrino. Manning was convicted of the murder and sent to Illinois' death row in 1993. In 2000, he was exonerated and released from death row. Eddie Lowery received a $7.5 million settlement along with apologies from officials in Riley County, Kansas, where he was arrested in 1981 for the rape of an elderly woman. He served 10 years in prison and registered as a sex offender after he was paroled. In 2003, the original rape kit was sent for DNA testing. It showed that Lowery couldn't have committed the rape. Illinois death row inmate Dennis Williams received $13 million from Cook County (Chicago) after he was exonerated.

Today, 26 states, the District of Columbia, and the federal government have passed laws that compensate people wrongfully convicted (see Exhibit 15–15). Texas, a state best known as the leader in capital punishment, now has another distinction: It is the most generous in compensating those who were wrongfully convicted. Between 1992 and 2013, Texas paid more than $65 million to 89 wrongfully convicted people.[48] However, research in California shows how difficult it is for the exonerated to receive compensation. Since 2000, 132 people have been released from prison in California after a court declared them factually innocent. California can award $100 a day for each day spent behind bars for a wrongful conviction. Of the 132 claims, 7 were withdrawn, 56 were rejected by the Victim Compensation and Government Claims Board, 14 have a hearing pending, and of the 55 who went to a hearing, 11 were approved

EXHIBIT 15-15   **When Justice Fails: Exonerated Compensation by State**

Compensation by State

- Alabama has a minimum of $50,000 for each year of wrongful incarceration.
- California has a maximum of $100 per day (or $36,500 per year) for wrongful incarceration.
- Connecticut bases compensation on claims for loss of liberty, loss of earning capacity, physical and mental pain, attorney's fees, and other expenses related to such person's wrongful conviction.
- The District of Columbia asks the court to determine what amount fairly and reasonably compensates the exonerated person.
- Florida provides for $50,000 annually for wrongful incarceration with a maximum of $2 million.
- Illinois allows for $85,350 for those who served up to 5 years, $170,000 for those who served between 5 and 14 years, and $199,150 for those who served more than 14 years.
- Iowa provides $50 per day (or $18,250 per year) of wrongful incarceration plus lost wages up to $25,000 a year plus attorney's fees.
- Louisiana provides $15,000 per year of wrongful incarceration with a maximum of $150,000.
- Maine has a maximum of $300,000.
- Maryland's Board of Public Works determines compensation packages for pardoned persons who were wrongfully convicted and may grant a reasonable amount for any financial or other appropriate counseling for the individual.
- Massachusetts has a maximum of $500,000.
- Mississippi allows $50,000 for each year of wrongful incarceration with a maximum of $500,000.
- Missouri provides $50 per day (or $18,250 per year) of postconviction confinement.
- Nebraska allows $25,000 per year with a maximum of $500,000.
- New Hampshire provides a maximum of $20,000 for the entirety of the wrongful incarceration.
- New Jersey allows twice the amount of the exoneree's income in the year prior to incarceration or $20,000 per year of incarceration, whichever is greater.
- New York, whose Court of Claims determines what amount will fairly and reasonably compensate the wrongfully convicted person, has no maximum amount.
- North Carolina provides $50,000 for each year of wrongful incarceration with a maximum of $750,000.
- Ohio allows $40,330 per year in addition to lost wages, costs, and attorney's fees.
- Oklahoma provides $175,000 for the entirety of the wrongful incarceration.
- Tennessee has a maximum of $1,000,000 for the entirety of a wrongful incarceration.
- Texas allows $80,000 per year of a wrongful incarceration, as well as $25,000 per year spent on parole or as a registered sex offender, plus an annuity.
- United States (federal) allows $50,000 per year in noncapital cases and $100,000 per year in capital cases.
- Utah provides the monetary equivalent of the nonagricultural payroll wage in the state to a wrongfully convicted person for each year of incarceration up to a maximum of 15 years.
- Vermont gives between $30,000 and $60,000 per year the person was incarcerated if a request is filed within 3 years of exoneration.
- Virginia provides 90% of the Virginia per capita personal income for up to 20 years.
- West Virginia does not specify a maximum amount.
- Wisconsin provides $5,000 for each year in prison with a maximum of $25,000 plus attorney's fees.

Source: Innocence Project, *Making Up For Lost Time: What the Wrongfully Convicted Endure and How to Provide Fair Compensation* (New York: Benjamin N. Cardozo School of Law, Yeshiva University, 2010).

for compensation. Critics charge that exonerees are asked to prove things far beyond what is reasonable. For example, one exoneree who had been declared factually innocent by a Santa Clara County Superior Court judge was told by the three-member board that his claim was rejected because the victim of the robbery still believed he was guilty. The claimant filed a civil lawsuit and was eventually awarded $1 million, not from the Victim Compensation and Government Claims Board, but from Santa Clara county.[49] Nobody knows the exact amount that has been paid out, but it is reasonable to believe that prejudicial error is costly. It includes money lost on education, health and human services, community protection, and economic growth and development.

How can we reduce serious capital error? Liebman identifies two options. The first is to end the death penalty entirely. The second is to curb the scope of the death penalty to reach only the small number of

Visit http://www.law.virginia.edu/html/news/2009_spr/garrett.htm or scan this code with the QR app on your SmartPhone or digital device and watch the podcast of University of Virginia Law School Professor Brandon Garrett explain his research on why some people are induced to confess. How does this information relate to ideas discussed in this chapter?

offenses on which there is broad social consensus that only the death penalty will serve. The reforms he suggests follow:[50]

1. Require proof beyond any doubt that the defendant committed the capital crime.
2. Require that aggravating factors substantially outweigh mitigating ones before a death sentence may be imposed.
3. Bar the death penalty for people with extenuating circumstances.
4. Make life imprisonment without parole an alternative to the death penalty and clearly inform juries of the option.
5. Abolish judge overrides of jury verdicts imposing life sentences.
6. Use comparative review of murder sentences to identify what counts as the "worst of the worst."
7. Base charging decisions in potentially capital cases on full and informed deliberations.
8. Make all police and prosecution evidence bearing on guilt versus evidence and on aggravation versus mitigation available to the jury at trial.
9. Insulate capital sentencing and appellate judges from political pressure.
10. Identify, appoint, and compensate capital defense counsel in ways that attract an adequate number of well-qualified lawyers to do the work.

Another option is to follow the federal model or what is being proposed in Ohio and elsewhere. You'll recall from earlier in this chapter that federal prosecutors who wish to file capital charges are required to first obtain authorization from the U.S. attorney general. The request is reviewed by the assistant attorney general, the deputy attorney general, and ultimately the attorney general. The goal is to cure geographical unfairness across the United States.

Ohio and a few other states are considering creating a statewide commission to replace local prosecutors in making the decision as to when to seek the death penalty. James Brogan, a retired appeals court judge from Dayton, told the Ohio Supreme Court that "As [Ohio Supreme Court] Justice Paul Pfeifer said, it's a lottery whether or not you get the death penalty depending on where you live."[51] In Tennessee, county prosecutors submit murder cases to a statewide commission, which has the ultimate authority to decide whether a death sentence should be pursued.

Today 10 states require videotaping of at least some interrogations such as those in crimes that carry the death penalty, and seven state supreme courts have required or strongly encouraged recording.[52]

CO15-8   ## Banning the Juvenile Death Penalty

The first recognized juvenile execution in the United States occurred in 1642 when Thomas Graunger was hanged in Plymouth, Massachusetts, for committing the crime of buggery (having sex with an animal) when he was 16 years old.[53] Since then, the United States has executed 365 people for offenses they committed when children. In the current era of capital punishment, 22 people were executed for offenses they committed as juveniles.[54] The last was Scott Allen Hain on April 3, 2003, by lethal injection in Oklahoma. Four months after his 17th birthday, Hain and an accomplice committed murder. He was sentenced to die in May 1988.

The U.S. Supreme Court first addressed the constitutionality of applying the death penalty to juvenile offenders in 1988 in *Thompson* v. *Oklahoma*.[55] The Court ruled in a 5–4 opinion that it was unconstitutional to sentence a 15-year-old to death. The following year, in *Stanford* v. *Kentucky*[56] and *Wilkins* v. *Missouri*,[57] the Court held that the Eighth Amendment's prohibition against cruel and unusual punishment did not forbid imposition of the death penalty for crimes committed by people at 16 and 17 years of age. Justice Antonin Scalia's majority opinion reasoned that, because a majority of the 37 states that had death penalty statutes at the time allowed capital punishment for juveniles, the practice did not violate evolving standards of decency.

However on March 2, 2005, the U.S. Supreme Court, by a narrow 5–4 vote in *Roper* v. *Simmons*,[58] reversed itself and said that it was unconstitutional and in violation of the Eighth Amendment's ban on cruel and unusual punishment to execute people for crimes they committed before turning age 18. The Court's ruling vacated the death sentences of 72 people on death rows across the United States. Most of these offenders will wind up with life sentences, many without parole.

In deciding *Roper* v. *Simmons*, the justices reasoned several things. First, since their 1987 decisions in *Stanford* v. *Kentucky* and *Wilkins* v. *Missouri*, 5 states had banned capital punishment for juveniles, making the practice illegal in 30 states. The justices said that the trend toward banning capital punishment for juveniles reflected "evolving standards of decency that mark the progress of a maturing society."

Second, the justices cited scientific literature from the American Academy of Child and Adolescent Psychiatry, the American Medical Association, and the American Psychological Association showing that adolescents lack mature judgment, are less aware of the consequences of their decisions and actions, are more vulnerable than adults to peer pressure, and have a greater tendency toward impulsiveness and lesser reasoning skills, regardless of how big they are or how tough they talk. Or, as one person put it, "They may look like, talk like, act like and even shoot like adults, but they think like kids. . . . Juveniles are not the same as adults even though the crimes might be the same."[59]

Third, the justices cited overseas legal practices and pointed out that the death penalty for juvenile offenders has become a uniquely American practice. The death penalty for juveniles has been abandoned by nations everywhere else in large part due to the express provisions of the United Nations Convention on the Rights of the Child and of several other international treaties and agreements. Since 1990, juvenile offenders are known to have been executed in only eight countries: China, Democratic Republic of Congo, Iran, Nigeria, Pakistan, Yemen, Saudi Arabia, and the United States. The justices said that the United States' practice of executing juvenile criminals was out of line with other developed countries.

On March 2, 2005, Christopher Simmons's case led the U.S. Supreme Court to bar the execution of juveniles for crimes they committed before turning age 18 as cruel and unusual punishment prohibited by the Eighth Amendment. What were the court's rationales in deciding Atkins *and* Simmons?

Banning the Execution of People with Mental Retardation

In 1989, the U.S. Supreme Court held that executing people with mental retardation was not a violation of the Eighth Amendment. But on June 19, 2002, the Court held in *Atkins* v. *Virginia* that execution of offenders with mental retardation is cruel and unusual punishment prohibited by the Eighth Amendment. The Court argued that a national consensus has developed against executing this group of people. At that time, 12 states banned executions altogether. However, beginning in 1988 Arizona, Arkansas, Colorado, Connecticut, Florida, Georgia, Indiana, Kansas, Kentucky, Maryland, Missouri, Nebraska, New Mexico, New York, North Carolina, South Dakota, Tennessee, Washington, and the federal government passed statutes banning the execution of offenders with mental retardation. The Court argued that it was not so much the number of states that

Daryl Atkins, whose case led the U.S. Supreme Court on June 19, 2002, to bar the execution of people with mental retardation as cruel and unusual punishment prohibited by the Eighth Amendment, sits in a York-Poquoson Courtroom in Yorktown, Virginia. In 2008, his sentence was commuted to life in prison. Should states be required to adopt the three-pronged clinical definition of intellectual disability?

had passed similar statutes but the consistency of the direction of change. In the words of the Court, "Given the well-known fact that anticrime legislation is far more popular than legislation providing protections for persons guilty of violent crime, the large number of states prohibiting the execution of people with mental retardation (and the complete absence of states passing legislation reinstating the power to conduct such executions) provides powerful evidence that today our society views these offenders as categorically less culpable than the average criminal. The evidence carries even greater force when it is noted that the legislatures that have addressed the issue have voted overwhelmingly in favor of the prohibition."[60]

School records and the results of an IQ test confirmed that Daryl Renard Atkins, the Virginia inmate whose case persuaded the U.S. Supreme Court to exclude murderers with mental retardation from executions, had an IQ of 59 (a score of 70 or below is generally considered an indicator of mental retardation). Mental retardation (or intellectual disability as it is refereed to by clinicians) is defined as substantial limitations in intellectual functions of reasoning or problem-solving, limitations in adaptive behavior or "street smarts." and evidence of the condition before age 18. However, in its 2002 ruling, the Supreme Court did not set a clear standard for mental disability and left it to the states to define mental retardation. Since the Court's ruling, most states adopted the three-pronged clinical definition, but Florida, Georgia, Mississippi, and Texas set their own standards. For example, under Florida's law, if you have an IQ over 70, you are eligible for execution regardless of intellectual function or adaptive behavior. In fall 2013 the Supreme Court granted judicial review to clarify the legal standard for mental disability in the case of a Florida death row inmate who is illiterate and was once judged to be severely mentally disabled. Oral arguments are scheduled for March 2014.

In July 2005, a jury decided that Atkins was intelligent enough to be executed on the basis that the constant contact he had with his lawyers had intellectually stimulated him and raised his IQ above 70, making him competent to be put to death under Virginia law. However, two and one-half years later, evidence of prosecutorial misconduct surfaced that would have stricken the testimony of Atkins' codefendant William Jones. Without Jones' testimony being admissible the judge ruled to commute Atkins sentence to life and the Virginia Supreme Court agreed.

REVIEW AND APPLICATIONS

SUMMARY

1 Capital punishment has been imposed throughout history for crimes ranging from horse stealing and witchcraft to crimes against humanity and murder. Before the 18th century, torture often preceded death. In the 18th century, use of the death penalty diminished as philosophers argued that punishment should fit the crime. After World War I, states reinstated use of the death penalty to deter threats to capitalism, and criminologists argued that capital punishment was a necessary social measure. After World War II, however, sentiment for capital punishment faded, and constitutional challenges surfaced, culminating in the Supreme Court decision of *Furman* v. *Georgia* in 1972.

2 At yearend 2013, 1,359 people had been executed in the United States since Gary Gilmore's execution in January 1977. The peak year was 1999, when 98 people were executed. Thirty-seven percent (508) of all executions have taken place in Texas. The South leads the United States with 1,111 executions. Only 0.01 percent of all the people executed since 1977 were female; 56 percent were white, 35 percent black, and 7 percent Hispanic. Today, 3,108 prisoners are on death row. Forty-six percent of the nation's death row population is in three states: California (731), Florida (412), and Texas (298). Ninety-eight percent of all prisoners on death row are male, with whites predominating (43 percent). Inmates executed in 2013 had been on death row an average of 15 years.

3 Among the influences on capital punishment are public opinion; executive, legislative, and judicial changes; and professional organizations. Public opinion continues to support capital punishment with more people choosing life imprisonment as an option. Professional organizations and legislatures across the country are calling for death penalty moratoriums, funding studies of capital punishment, granting death row inmates access to DNA testing, affording extra assistance to lawyers handling capital cases, raising the amount of financial compensation that states provide innocent people found to have been erroneously convicted, allowing prosecutors to seek life without parole instead of the death penalty, and barring the execution of juveniles and offenders with mental retardation.

4 Arguments in favor of the death penalty include the following: It deters rational people from becoming habitual killers; it is "just" punishment for taking someone's life; it is constitutional as long as it is achieved with due process of law; it reduces the amount of time a person spends on death row; it protects society from feared offenders; it is more humane than life imprisonment; and it is almost impossible for an innocent person to be executed. Arguments against the death penalty include the following: It violates human rights; it does not deter violent crime; it is implemented arbitrarily and unfairly; it falls disproportionately on racial minorities; it actually boosts the murder rate by promoting homicides in the months following an execution; not everyone wants vengeance; and it costs too much to support a capital trial, appeals, and execution.

5 The landmark cases that influenced capital punishment were *Furman* v. *Georgia* (1972), *Gregg* v. *Georgia* (1976), *Ring* v. *Arizona* (2002), *Atkins* v. *Virginia* (2002), and *Roper* v. *Simmons* (2005). In *Furman* v. *Georgia,* the U.S. Supreme Court ruled that capital punishment, as imposed by Georgia, constituted cruel and unusual punishment—Georgia's death penalty statute gave the sentencing authority (judge or trial jury) complete freedom to impose a death sentence without standards or guidelines. As a result of the *Furman* ruling, state death penalty statutes took two forms—mandatory death penalty or sentencing based on guided discretion. In *Woodson* v. *North Carolina* and *Roberts* v. *Louisiana,* the Court rejected mandatory statutes. However, in *Gregg* v. *Georgia,* the Court ruled that Georgia's new guided discretion death penalty legislation was not unconstitutional. In *Ring* v. *Arizona,* the Court held that only juries, not judges, can determine the presence of aggravating factors to be weighed in the capital sentencing process. The Court held that a defendant may not receive a penalty that exceeds the maximum penalty that he or she would have received if punished according to the facts in the jury verdict. In *Atkins* v. *Virginia* (2002) and *Roper* v. *Simmons* (2005), the Court ruled that it was unconstitutional to execute persons with mental retardation or who commit capital crimes before turning age 18.

6 Death penalty cases may pass through as many as 10 courts and across 3 stages: trial and direct review, state postconviction appeals, and federal *habeas corpus* appeals.

7 Liebman found that the frequency of errors in capital punishment cases is 68 percent. More than two of every three capital judgments reviewed by the courts were found to be seriously flawed. Ten states (Alabama, Arizona, California, Georgia, Indiana, Maryland, Mississippi, Montana, Oklahoma, and Wyoming) had overall error rates of 75 percent or higher. Almost 1,000 of the cases sent back for retrial ended in sentences less than death, and 87 ended in *not guilty* verdicts.

8 In 2002, the Court held in *Atkins* v. *Virginia* that execution of offenders with mental retardation is cruel and unusual punishment prohibited by the Eighth Amendment because a national consensus has developed against executing these offenders. In 2005, the Court held in *Roper* v. *Simmons* that execution of persons for crimes they committed before turning age 18 was also unconstitutional and in violation of the Eighth Amendment. The Court's reasoning in both cases was similar: The large number of states banning the execution of people with mental retardation and of persons who committed capital crimes before turning age 18 provided evidence that our society views offenders with mental retardation and juveniles as categorically less culpable than the average criminal.

KEY TERMS

QUESTIONS FOR REVIEW

1 Trace the history of capital punishment inside and outside the United States noting, in particular, the number of U.S. jurisdictions with and without the death penalty, the Supreme Court rulings that first halted and then resumed executions, the number of persons executed since 1977, and what constitutes a capital crime.

2 What are the characteristics of people executed in the United States since 1977 and on death row today?

3 Illustrate the politics influencing capital punishment.

4 Prioritize the arguments for and against the death penalty.

5 What major U.S. Supreme Court decisions influenced capital punishment legislation?

6 Evaluate the death penalty process.

7 Debate Liebman's findings on the frequency of errors in capital punishment cases.

8 What is the Supreme Court's reasoning for banning the execution of juveniles and offenders with mental retardation?

THINKING CRITICALLY ABOUT CORRECTIONS

Murder Rates and the Death Penalty

According to the Death Penalty Information Center, in 2012 death penalty states recorded higher murder rates than non-death-penalty states. The average murder rate among death penalty states was 4.7 per 100,000 population; for non-death-penalty states, the rate was 3.7. The South executes the largest percentage of offenders who are convicted of a capital crime (84 percent) and records the highest murder rate (5.5 murders per 100,000 people); the Northeast executes the fewest (0.3 percent) and records the lowest murder rate, 3.9. What conclusions might you draw from these data? How might we prevent geographical unfairness?

Cost of Execution

Research shows that execution costs more than life imprisonment. Do you think there is a point at which the economic consequence of execution outweighs its value to the public? Explain.

ON-THE-JOB DECISION MAKING

Should the Cost of a Capital Trial Be a Factor in a Prosecutor's Decision to Seek the Death Penalty?

Capital murder trials are longer and more expensive at every step than other murder trials. The irreversibility of the death sentence requires courts to follow heightened due process in the preparation and course of the trial. Defendants are much more likely to insist on a trial when they are facing a possible death sentence. Crime investigations, pretrial preparations and motions, expert witness investigations, jury selection, and the necessity for two trials—one on guilt and one on sentencing—make capital cases extremely costly even before the appeals process begins. After conviction, there are constitutionally mandated appeals that involve both prosecution and defense costs. Even if a jury recommends life over death or ends as a hung jury or if the condemned person's sentence is commuted after he or she has served time on death row, the state has already paid the cost of a capital trial. Assume that you are the prosecuting attorney in a rural county of 7,500 people in a southern state. A capital case is coming up for trial. Estimates of costs for the case begin at $500,000. How will you justify paying for the prosecution of the case?

Does Maintaining Innocence Put Innocent People at Risk?

Why would a person confess to a crime he or she didn't commit and possibly face the death penalty? Professor Saul Kassin wrote an interesting article on the psychology of confessions. His thesis is innocence puts people at risk. Innocence does not protect people in a number of critical stages in criminal justice. In interrogation, police presume suspects are guilty. However, innocent people believe that everyone can see the transparency of their innocence and will naively waive their rights. Because their resistance to admitting guilt is seen as resistance and further evidence of their guilt, interrogations become more confrontational. Torture techniques like those used in the Abu Ghraib prisoner torture scandal show, for example, that extreme tactics such as excessive interrogation time and no rest is accompanied by the suspect's stress, fatigue, and feeling of helplessness. A similar study was conducted by Brandon Garrett, University of Virginia professor of law.

Read Kassin's article "On the Psychology of Confessions: Does Innocence Put Innocents at Risk?" *American Psychologist*, vol. 60, no. 3, pages 215–228. (If you're not sure how to access *American Psychologist* online at your library, consult your librarian.)

How can we prevent these harms to innocent people?

For additional information, please see: www.mhhe.com/schmalleger7e
Follow the author's tweets about the latest crime and justice news @schmalleger

[16]

JUVENILE CORRECTIONS

End of an Era?

CHAPTER OBJECTIVES

After completing this chapter you should be able to do the following:

❶ Explain *parens patriae* and describe the historical origins of the U.S. system of juvenile justice.

❷ Summarize six U.S. Supreme Court cases that changed modern-day juvenile court proceedings.

❸ Discuss the two types of juvenile crime and explain the nature of juvenile court jurisdiction.

❹ List and explain the three stages of the juvenile justice process.

❺ Explain how youth gangs affect juvenile correctional institutions.

❻ Elaborate upon changes now taking place in the area of juvenile corrections.

" *The vast majority of youth are good citizens who have never been arrested for any type of crime.* "

—Shay Bilchik, director, Center for Juvenile Justice Reform at Georgetown University

In 2012, Pennsylvania juvenile court judge John Hodge found 14-year-old Jordan Brown delinquent in the murder of Kenzie Houk and her unborn child.[1] Houk, the 26-year-old girlfriend of Brown's father, had been killed by a shotgun blast fired by Brown in 2009 when he was 11 years old. Houk's two daughters, ages 4 and 7, were in the house when she was killed but were physically unharmed. The judge ordered Brown to a juvenile detention facility where he could stay until he turns 21, at which time the juvenile court's jurisdiction over him will end.[2] Had Brown been transferred to adult criminal court and tried there—as some wanted—he could have faced life in prison without the possibility of parole.

Although most juvenile offenders are charged with property offenses rather than violent offenses, the majority of juvenile offenses reported by the media involve violent crime, which overstates the violence issue and unduly alarms the public. During the closing years of the 20th century, high-profile juvenile violence—such as juvenile-perpetrated high school shootings—changed juvenile corrections from an emphasis on treatment to a focus on punishment. As a result, attention and scarce resources highlighted a small portion of juvenile offenders, neglecting the vast majority. This chapter will show, however, that the rehabilitative ideal, in concert with evidence-based initiatives, is beginning to reestablish itself in the handling of juveniles who have been adjudicated delinquent.[3]

The farmhouse where 11-year-old Jordan Brown killed 26-year-old Kenzie Marie Houk in 2009 in Wampum, Pennsylvania. Brown was adjudicated delinquent after shooting the pregnant mother of two. Can juveniles be more easily reformed than adults?

HISTORY OF THE JUVENILE JUSTICE SYSTEM   `CO16-1`

The historical origins of America's juvenile justice system can be traced to early England where the English Poor Laws, beginning with the Statute of Laborers in 1349, regulated the lives of the working and nonworking poor. A law passed in 1536 said that children older than 5, but less than 14, who lived in idleness and had taken to begging "may be put to service" under government authority.

By 1601, the English Poor Laws had evolved so that a child whose parents were unable to provide for his or her care could be taken away from them and sent to a facility where they would be made an apprentice to a craftsperson and provided with work. Under English law, abandoned and neglected children became the responsibility of the monarch, and the Commonwealth became their guardian.

Bridewells (the first houses of corrections) confined both children and adults until 1704 when John Howard brought to England a model of a Roman institution for juvenile offenders (see Chapter 2). Colonists took these ideas with them to America, and reformers tailored the ideas to their

parens patriae

A Latin term that refers to the state as guardian for minors and for people who are mentally incompetent.

experiences, creating houses of refuge, reform schools, and industrial schools for juveniles. Both the English and American juvenile justice systems utilize the doctrine of *parens patriae,* which means literally "parent of his country." According to *parens patriae,* the state has the power to act as guardian for minors and for people who are mentally incompetent.

The first known application of *parens patriae* in America occurred in 1636 when Bridget Fuller was ordered by the governor of Plymouth Colony to take Benjamen Eaton, keep him in school for two years, and keep him employed.[4] By the end of the 19th century, every U.S. state had affirmed its right to act as guardian of minors.

Houses of Refuge

The New York House of Refuge, the first legally chartered U.S. custodial institution for juvenile offenders, was founded in 1825 by penal reformer Thomas Eddy, educational reformer John Griscom, and the Society for the Prevention of Pauperism. Its purpose was to provide poor, abused, and orphaned youths with food, clothing, and lodging in exchange for hard work, discipline, and study. The concept spread, and houses of refuge were established throughout the United States.

Living conditions in houses of refuge were not as generous as the term *refuge* might imply. Administrators of these institutions subjected juveniles to hard physical labor and were known to use corporal punishment. Residents were expected to earn their keep and comply with strict institutional rules. Guards and superintendents, substitutes for parents or guardians, exhibited little tolerance or understanding.

Despite the path-breaking role the house of refuge played in the development of the U.S. juvenile justice system, such institutions were short-lived. The movement as a whole died out by the middle of the 19th century.

Reform Schools

reform school

A penal institution to which especially young or first-time offenders are committed for training and reformation.

The nation's first state-sponsored **reform school** opened in Massachusetts in 1848. Named the Lyman School for Theodore Lyman, a former mayor of Boston, the institution resembled a prison. The school was designed to house 300 boys. Because of liberal admissions policies and unregulated commitment procedures, the reformatory was filled within a few years. The Massachusetts legislature authorized an addition, doubling the structure's capacity.

In the late 1800s, with the school again becoming overcrowded, a ship in Boston Harbor was designated an annex to it. Any boy under age 14 could be committed to either Lyman School or its Nautical Branch. Boys who were housed at the Nautical Branch were trained in navigation and the duties of seamen and then transferred to passing vessels that needed cabin boys or young laborers.

Because the Lyman School housed only boys, the Massachusetts legislature voted to create a separate institution for girls. Belief that the physical and emotional makeup of girls was inherently more delicate than that of boys led reformers to focus on a new European model for the girls school.

European-style reform schools introduced a small residential arrangement, breaking down structural barriers so that staff and inmates could interact, providing a more intimate setting for treatment. Advocates of the European-style reform school believed that personal contact with youth was the cornerstone of the rehabilitative effort. Under the new design, as many as 30 inmates with similar personality traits were placed in separate small homes or cottages and supervised by paid "cottage parents."

Residents of each house or cottage lived, worked, and attended school together, meeting with inmates in other living quarters only infrequently.

The first of the European-style reform schools was the Lancaster Industrial School for Girls in Massachusetts, established in 1854. The Lancaster cottages had features associated with both school and home and provided academic classes and domestic training programs. Lancaster's cottage plan gained national attention as prison reform advocates encouraged adoption of this system for youthful offenders throughout the United States.

Industrial Schools

After the Civil War, state welfare services expanded and began to require that juvenile reform schools and adult penal institutions help pay operating costs by contracting inmate labor to local manufacturers. The use of juvenile contract labor hindered the growth of reform schools. Manufacturers controlled the children during working hours, and exploitation and brutality were common. Some reform schools were converted into housing units to better serve manufacturers' labor needs.

Concerned citizens and elected officials recognized the inadequacies of reform schools. Public efforts were made to improve institutional life and to reduce the number of children being incarcerated. Special state committees investigated abuses in contract labor systems, and reform schools were added to the list of public institutions that were subject to annual inspection by regulatory agencies.

The Linn County Juvenile Justice Center in Cedar Rapids, Iowa. The juvenile court movement of the late 1800s gave rise to the juvenile justice system that we know today. Why are juveniles held separately from adult prisoners?

The First Juvenile Court

The movement toward establishing a separate juvenile court began in 1870 when the Illinois Supreme Court heard *People ex rel. O'Connell* v. *Turner*.[5] Daniel O'Connell was committed to the Chicago Reform School for vagrancy. His parents protested the confinement and petitioned the court for Daniel's release. In its decision, which ordered Daniel's release, the Illinois Supreme Court:

- recognized that Daniel's parents genuinely wanted to care for their son;
- held that vagrancy was a matter of misfortune, not a criminal act;
- viewed Daniel's commitment to the Chicago Reform School as a punishment, not merely as a placement in a school for troubled children; and
- deemed Daniel's incarceration to be imprisonment, meaning that the doctrine of *parens patriae* did not apply and formal due process protections were required.

By the end of the 19th century, debate about juvenile facilities had established the need for differentiating between juveniles and adults in court procedures. Some states had even established children's aid societies to represent juveniles in court and to supervise them in the community.

The first completely separate juvenile court was established in Illinois in 1899. The Illinois legislature passed the law An Act to Regulate the Treatment and Control of Dependent, Neglected and Delinquent Children, which established a juvenile court in Cook County that had jurisdiction over any youth who committed an act that would be a crime if committed by an adult. However, young criminal offenders were not the only juveniles who needed help or supervision—the legislation was revised also to give the juvenile court jurisdiction over

> any child who for any reason is destitute or homeless or abandoned; or dependent on the public for support; or has not proper parental care or guardianship; or who habitually begs or receives alms; or who is found living in any house of ill fame or with any vicious or disreputable person; or whose home, by reason of neglect, cruelty or depravity on part of its parents, guardian or other person in whose care it may be, is an unfit place for such a child; and any child under the age of eight years who is found peddling or selling any article or singing or playing any musical instrument upon the street or giving any public entertainment.[6]

The intent of the new legislation was to give the juvenile court jurisdiction when the child's best interests would be served.

The Illinois act was a prototype for legislation in other states, and juvenile courts were quickly established in Wisconsin (1901), New York (1901), Ohio (1902), Maryland (1902), and Colorado (1903). By 1945, all states had established separate juvenile courts. New terminology accompanied the establishment of the juvenile court, to differentiate it from adult criminal court. Juvenile offenders are "delinquents" rather than "criminals"; they are "taken into custody" rather than "arrested"; a "petition" rather than a "charge" is filed; juveniles are "held on petition" rather than "indicted"; there is an "adjudicatory hearing" rather than a "trial"; the court returns a "finding" rather than a "verdict" and imposes a "disposition" rather than a "sentence"; and the offender is "adjudicated" rather than "convicted," sent to a "training school" rather than a "prison," and put on "aftercare" rather than "parole."

CO16-2 THE U.S. SUPREME COURT AND THE JUVENILE JUSTICE SYSTEM

For most of the 20th century, all juvenile hearings were considered civil proceedings—rules of criminal procedure did not apply. Juveniles had no constitutional protections, and there were no challenges to the admissibility of evidence or the validity of testimony. Six landmark U.S. Supreme Court decisions dramatically changed the juvenile justice system, establishing due process rights for juvenile offenders. These and other significant cases affecting juvenile justice are shown in Exhibit 16–1.

Kent v. United States (1966)

In 1959, Morris A. Kent Jr., age 14, was taken into custody in Washington, D.C., on a petition alleging burglary and attempted purse snatching. He was placed on juvenile probation and returned to his mother's custody. In September 1961, an intruder entered a woman's apartment, raped her, and stole her wallet. Police found Kent's fingerprints at the crime scene. Kent, now age 16 and still on probation, was taken into custody and charged with rape and robbery. He confessed to these offenses and several similar incidents. Kent's mother retained an attorney, who, anticipating that the case would be transferred to an adult criminal court, filed a motion to oppose the transfer.

The juvenile court judge did not rule on this motion; instead, he waived jurisdiction and remanded Kent to the jurisdiction of the adult criminal

EXHIBIT 16–1 Significant U.S. Supreme Court Decisions Affecting Juvenile Justice

2012 — *Miller* v. *Alabama* (2012)

Mandatory life without parole sentences for individuals 17 or younger convicted of homicide violate the Eighth Amendment.

2010 — *Graham* v. *Florida* (2010)

The imprisonment of juveniles for life without the possibility of parole as punishment for nonhomicide offenses is unconstitutional under the Eighth Amendment's ban on cruel and unusual punishments.

2005 — *Roper* v. *Simmons* (2005)

Minimum age for the death penalty raised to age 18 (i.e., offenders who were younger than 18 when they committed their crimes may not be punished by death).

Illinois v. *Montanez* (1996)

1995 — Voluntary confessions made by juvenile suspects may be admissible in court even when not made in the presence of a parent or another "concerned adult."

1990 —

Stanford v. *Kentucky* (1989)

Thompson v. *Oklahoma* (1988)

Minimum age for death penalty is set at 16.

1985 —

Schall v. *Martin* (1984)

Preventive "pretrial" detention of juveniles is allowable under certain circumstances.

Eddings v. *Oklahoma* (1982)

Defendant's youthful age should be considered a mitigating factor in deciding

1980 — whether to apply the death penalty.

Smith v. *Daily Mail Publishing Co.* (1979)

Oklahoma Publishing Co. v. *District Court* (1977)

The press may report juvenile court proceedings under certain circumstances.

1975 — *Breed* v. *Jones* (1975)

Waiver of a juvenile to criminal court following adjudication in juvenile court constitutes double jeopardy.

McKeiver v. *Pennsylvania* (1971)

Jury trials are not constitutionally required in juvenile court hearings.

1970 — *In re Winship* (1970)

In delinquency matters, the state must prove its case beyond a reasonable doubt.

In re Gault (1967)

In hearings that could result in commitment to an institution, juveniles have four basic constitutional rights.

1965 — *Kent* v. *United States* (1966)

Courts must provide the "essentials of due process" in transferring juveniles to the adult system.

court system. Kent was tried in U.S. district court, found guilty of six counts of housebreaking, and found "not guilty by reason of insanity" on the rape charge. He received indeterminate sentences of 5 to 15 years on each count of housebreaking.

Kent's lawyer appealed the conviction, citing that the juvenile court judge failed to hear motions filed on Kent's behalf before waiving the case to adult criminal court and that Kent's due process rights had been denied. The U.S. Supreme Court heard the case, and Kent's conviction was reversed.

In *Kent*,[7] the Court ruled that, in a case involving transfer of jurisdiction, the juvenile defendant is entitled to certain essential due process rights: (1) a hearing, (2) representation by an attorney, (3) access to records involved in the transfer, and (4) a written statement of reasons for the transfer.

In re Gault (1967)

On June 8, 1964, Gerald F. Gault, age 15, was taken into custody for making a crank telephone call to an adult neighbor and taken to a detention home by the sheriff of Gila County, Arizona. At the time, Gault was on juvenile probation for involvement in the theft of a woman's wallet in February 1964.

The complainant was not present at the juvenile court hearing on the following day. No one was sworn at the hearing, no transcript or recording of the proceedings was made, and no decision was issued. Gault was returned to the detention home—where he remained for several days— and then released. At a second hearing, on June 15, the judge committed Gault to the Arizona State Industrial School "for the period of his minority." Gault's attorney filed a petition for a writ of *habeas corpus* that was heard by the U.S. Supreme Court in December 1966.

In its May 1967 *Gault*[8] decision, the U.S. Supreme Court ruled that, in proceedings that might result in commitment to an institution, juveniles have the right to (1) reasonable notice of charges, (2) counsel, (3) question witnesses, and (4) protection against self-incrimination.

In re Winship (1970)

Samuel Winship, age 12, was charged with stealing $112 from a woman's purse. Winship's attorney argued that there was "reasonable doubt" of Winship's guilt. The court agreed, but, because New York juvenile courts operated under the civil court standard of "preponderance of the evidence," it adjudicated Winship delinquent and committed him to a training school for 18 months.

The U.S. Supreme Court in *Winship*[9] ruled that the reasonable doubt standard should be required in all delinquency adjudications.

McKeiver v. Pennsylvania (1971)

Joseph McKeiver, age 16, was charged with robbery, larceny, and receiving stolen property in Philadelphia, when he and 20 or 30 other juveniles took 25 cents from three boys. McKeiver had no prior arrests, was doing well in school, and was employed. McKeiver's attorney requested a jury trial; his request was denied, and McKeiver was adjudicated and put on probation.

McKeiver's attorney appealed to the state supreme court on the grounds that the juvenile court violated the Sixth Amendment's guarantee of the right to an impartial jury and the Seventh Amendment's guarantee of the right to a trial by jury. The state supreme court affirmed the lower court, arguing that, of all due process rights, a trial by jury is the one most likely to destroy the traditional nonadversarial character of juvenile court proceedings.

The U.S. Supreme Court in *McKeiver*[10] held that the due process clause of the Fourteenth Amendment did not require jury trials in juvenile court (although a state could provide a jury trial if it wished), that juries are not necessarily more accurate than judges, and that juries could be disruptive and therefore adversarial to the informal atmosphere of the juvenile court.

Breed v. Jones (1975)

In February 1971, Gary S. Jones, age 17, was charged with armed robbery and adjudicated delinquent in a Los Angeles juvenile court. The judge deferred disposition, pending receipt of a predisposition report and a recommendation from the probation department. Jones was returned to detention. When the court reconvened for the disposition hearing, the judge waived jurisdiction to adult criminal court. Counsel for Jones filed a petition for a writ of *habeas corpus,* arguing that waiver to criminal court violated the double jeopardy clause of the Fifth Amendment. The U.S. district court denied the petition, saying that Jones had not been tried twice because juvenile adjudication is not a trial. Jones was tried in adult criminal court, convicted of robbery, and committed to the California Youth Authority for an indeterminate period.

The U.S. Supreme Court in *Breed*[11] ruled that juvenile adjudication for violation of a criminal statute is equivalent to a criminal court trial; therefore, the double jeopardy clause applied. The Court ordered that Jones be released or remanded to the original juvenile court for a disposition hearing. Jones, now over 18, was released.

Schall v. Martin (1984)

Gregory Martin, age 14, was arrested and charged with robbery, assault, and possession of a weapon. Facts in the case showed that he and two other teenagers hit a boy on the head with a loaded gun and stole the boy's jacket and sneakers. Martin was held pending adjudication under a New York preventive detention statute because the court found there was a "serious risk" that he would commit another crime if released. Martin's attorney challenged the fairness of preventive detention, arguing that pretrial detention is essentially punishment and that many juveniles detained before trial are released before, or immediately after, adjudication. Martin was adjudicated delinquent, and his case eventually reached the U.S. Supreme Court, which upheld the constitutionality of the preventive detention statute. The Court ruled that preventive detention serves a legitimate government objective in protecting both the juvenile and society from pretrial crime and is not intended to punish the juvenile.

Limits on Punishment

Beginning in 2005 with the case of *Roper* v. *Simmons,* the Supreme Court turned its attention to juvenile punishments. In *Roper,* the Court held that no one under the age of 18 at the time of the crime could be sentenced to death, effectively raising the minimum age for the death penalty in the United States to 18. Then, in 2010, in the case of *Graham* v. *Florida,* the Court ruled that sentencing a juvenile to life in prison without the possibility of parole for nonhomicide offenses is unconstitutional under the Eighth Amendment's ban on cruel and unusual punishment. The decision in *Graham* was based in part on scientific evidence that the Court considered showing that children's brains are not mature, indicating the possibility for rehabilitation among youthful offenders. Finally, in 2012, in the case of *Miller* v. *Alabama,* the Court found that mandatory life sentence without parole for individuals who had not yet reached their 18th birthday at the time of their conviction for homicide violates the Eighth Amendment. In *Miller,* the key word is *mandatory,* meaning that state laws requiring such a penalty for these offenses are invalid.

Impact of Decisions on Juvenile Court

The U.S. Supreme Court's decisions in these cases affirmed juvenile due process rights. As a result, the "best interest of the child" is no longer the only concern for juvenile courts; they also are required to protect the juvenile's constitutional rights.

THE CONTEMPORARY JUVENILE JUSTICE SYSTEM

Every state has at least one court with juvenile jurisdiction. In most states, however, it is not actually called "juvenile court."[12] The names of the courts with juvenile jurisdiction vary by state—district, superior, circuit, county, family, or probate court, to name a few. Often the court of juvenile jurisdiction has a separate division for juvenile matters. Courts with juvenile jurisdiction generally have jurisdiction over delinquency, status offenses, and abuse/neglect matters and possibly other matters such as adoption, termination of parental rights, and emancipation. Whatever their name, courts with juvenile jurisdiction are generically referred to as *juvenile courts.*

State statutes define age limits for juvenile court jurisdiction. In most states, the juvenile court has original jurisdiction over all youths under age 18 at the time of offense (see Exhibit 16–2).[13]

Juvenile Crime

Annually, U.S. law enforcement agencies take approximately 1.0 million juveniles into custody.[14] According to the Federal Bureau of Investigation (FBI), juveniles accounted for 10.8 percent of all 2012 arrests and 11.7 percent of all 2012 violent crime arrests. Most juvenile arrests were for property crime offenses (see Exhibit 16–3).

More than 90 percent of the cases handled by juvenile courts are for **delinquent offenses**—acts committed by a juvenile that, if committed by an adult, could result in criminal prosecution. The remaining cases are for **status offenses**—acts that are considered offenses only when they are committed by juveniles (e.g., running away, truancy, curfew violations ungovernability, and liquor law violations). Liquor law violations account for 22 percent of status offense cases; truancy, 38 percent; curfew, 9 percent; running away, 12 percent; ungovernability, 13 percent; and miscellaneous other status offenses, 6 percent.[15]

Bullying

Bullying is another area of concern for those involved with juvenile justice. According to a recent survey of more than 43,000 school-age children, 45 percent of boys and 50 percent of girls said that they had

delinquent offenses

Acts committed by juveniles that, if committed by adults, could result in criminal prosecution.

status offenses

Acts that are law violations only for juveniles, such as running away, truancy, or ungovernability (sometimes referred to as *incorrigibility* or *being beyond parental control*).

EXHIBIT 16–2 Oldest Age for Original Juvenile Court Jurisdiction in Delinquency Cases by State

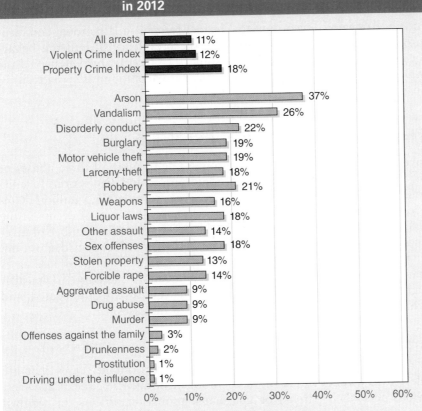

- 16th birthday
- 17th birthday
- 18th birthday

Note: Illinois and Wisconsin place 17-year-olds in juvenile courts for misdemeanor charges but in adult criminal courts for felony charges.

EXHIBIT 16–3 Percentage of Arrests Involving Juveniles in 2012

CO16-3

All arrests	11%
Violent Crime Index	12%
Property Crime Index	18%
Arson	37%
Vandalism	26%
Disorderly conduct	22%
Burglary	19%
Motor vehicle theft	19%
Larceny-theft	18%
Robbery	21%
Weapons	16%
Liquor laws	18%
Other assault	14%
Sex offenses	18%
Stolen property	13%
Forcible rape	14%
Aggravated assault	9%
Drug abuse	9%
Murder	9%
Offenses against the family	3%
Drunkenness	2%
Prostitution	1%
Driving under the influence	1%

Source: Adapted from Federal Bureau of Investigation, *Crime in the United States 2012* (Washington, DC: Federal Bureau of Investigation, 2013).

Two teenage males bully another boy. Why is bullying so prevalent today?

been bullied, teased, or taunted in a way that seriously upset them at least once during the past 12 months.[16] Perhaps more surprisingly, 56 percent of boys and 43 percent of girls admit to having bullied, teased, or taunted someone at least once within the past year. The study, conducted by the Los Angeles-based Josephson Institute of Ethics, also found that one-third of all high school students said that violence was a big problem at their school, and one in four said that they do not feel very safe at school. More than half admitted that within the past year, they had hit a person because they were angry. Ten percent of surveyed students said that they had taken a weapon to school at least once in the past 12 months, and 16 percent admitted that they had been intoxicated at school.

According to the U.S. Department of Education, bullying can have a number of negative consequences for those who are bullied, including:

- lowered academic achievement and aspirations;
- increased anxiety;
- loss of self-esteem and confidence;
- depression and post-traumatic stress;
- general deterioration in physical health;
- self-harm and suicidal thinking;
- feelings of alienation in the school environment, such as fear of other children; and
- absenteeism from school.[17]

Bullying that occurs on the Internet and through social media can be equally damaging. According to Michael Josephson, a national commentator on ethical issues, "It's not only the prevalence of bullying behavior and victimization that's troublesome. The Internet has intensified the injury. What's posted on the Internet is permanent, and it spreads like a virus—there is no refuge."[18]

CO16-4 THE JUVENILE JUSTICE PROCESS

Juvenile offenders are processed through one or more of three phases of the juvenile justice process: intake, adjudication, and disposition. Juvenile courts throughout the United States process more than 1.5 million delinquency cases every year.[19] Exhibit 16–4 shows the flow of events in the U.S. juvenile justice system, and Exhibit 16–5 shows the number of juveniles who were adjudicated delinquent and their subsequent disposition. Juvenile courts also process approximately 142,300 status offense cases annually, none of which fall into the "delinquency" category.[20] Typically, slightly more than 60 percent of status offense cases are adjudicated, and probation is ordered in almost 50 percent of the cases.

Intake

In the first phase of the juvenile justice process, **intake,** cases that are referred to juvenile court (by law enforcement agencies, social agencies, school personnel, parents or guardians, probation officers, or victims) are reviewed by a court-appointed officer (usually a prosecutor or probation officer), who recommends a course of action. The intake officer

intake

The first stage of the juvenile justice process. A court-appointed officer reviews the case and recommends a course of action—dismissal, informal disposition, formal disposition, or transfer to adult criminal court.

EXHIBIT 16–4 The Flow of Events in the Juvenile Justice System

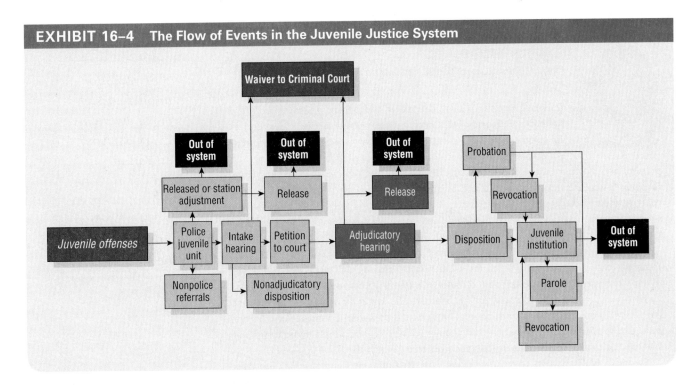

recommends that the case be (1) dismissed, (2) resolved informally (no petition is filed with the court), (3) resolved formally (a petition for an adjudication hearing is filed with the court), or (4) transferred to adult criminal court. The juvenile court establishes guidelines for the intake officer. Criteria considered in the decision in many jurisdictions include

EXHIBIT 16–5 Juvenile Court Processing of Delinquency Cases, 2009

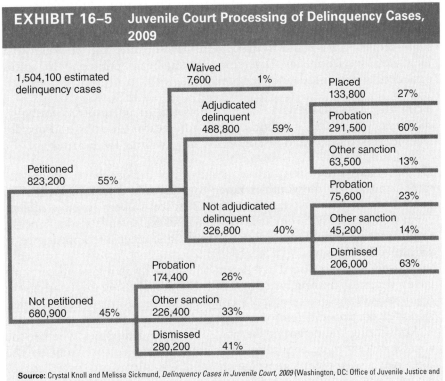

Source: Crystal Knoll and Melissa Sickmund, *Delinquency Cases in Juvenile Court, 2009* (Washington, DC: Office of Juvenile Justice and Delinquency Prevention, 2012), p. 4.

Sophia Nelson

Drug Counselor and Parent Educator • West Palm Beach, Florida

Sophia Nelson is a drug counselor and parent educator in West Palm Beach, Florida. As a drug counselor, she carries a caseload of 55 clients and conducts intake assessments and provides treatment.

As a parent educator, Nelson facilitates group counseling for children and single mothers and assists the children in her groups in improving their communication and interaction skills and building confidence. She helps single mothers improve their life skills and develop and acquire the knowledge, skills, and attitudes they need to maintain strong family ties, find and keep good jobs, manage their finances, and lead productive lives.

Nelson graduated from Bethune-Cookman College in Daytona Beach, Florida, with a degree in criminal justice. The courses she recalls enjoying the most were those in which there was significant classroom discussion, especially courses in prisoners' rights, correctional counseling, and social policy. She says she knew from these courses that she wanted a career working with people. Now that she's a drug counselor and parent educator, she feels she contributes to her community by helping people avoid drugs and develop healthier lifestyles. She says, "I see lives change each day."

For now, Nelson wants to keep working with drug offenders and teaching life skills to parents and children. But one day she hopes to be a prison warden and influence correctional policy on a large scale.

> *"Be ready for a roller-coaster ride of emotions. Every day your clients are up and down. Your personality has to be able to adjust to that for you to be successful."*

severity of the alleged offense, any prior history of delinquent behavior, attitude, age, and emotional stability.

Informal Disposition In cases that are resolved informally, disposition is decided by the intake officer, and the case goes no further. The disposition imposed is usually informal probation or some form of diversion—requiring the youth to make restitution or referring the youth to a local social service agency. Diversion is generally an option only for status offenders or low-risk delinquent offenders.

Formal Disposition In cases that are to be resolved formally, the intake officer files a petition for an adjudicatory hearing and decides whether the youth should be confined while awaiting the hearing.

Detention Hearing If the intake officer decides that secure placement is advisable, the youth is taken to a **juvenile detention facility.** In general terms, a juvenile detention facility serves to keep juvenile offenders in secure custody through various stages of the juvenile justice process, to protect the community and the juvenile, and to ensure appearance at scheduled hearings.

A juvenile who is placed in a detention facility by an intake officer must have a **detention hearing,** usually within 48 hours. During this hearing, the court reviews the intake officer's confinement decision and orders either release or continued detention pending adjudication and disposition.

Also during the detention hearing, the court determines whether the youth has legal representation and, if not, appoints defense counsel. The court may also appoint a **guardian *ad litem,*** who serves as a special guardian for the youth throughout the court proceedings. In many jurisdictions, defense counsel also serves as guardian.

---

juvenile detention facility

A facility for keeping juvenile offenders in secure custody, as necessary, through various stages of the juvenile justice process.

detention hearing

A judicial review of the intake officer's detention decision.

guardian *ad litem*

A person appointed by the juvenile court, often defense counsel, to serve as a special guardian for the youth being processed through the juvenile justice system.

Adjudication

In the second phase of the juvenile justice process, adjudication, a juvenile court hears the case. A **juvenile court** is any court that has original jurisdiction over matters involving juveniles.

Adjudicatory Hearing During the adjudicatory hearing, attorneys typically present physical evidence, examine and cross-examine witnesses, and argue on behalf of their clients. If, after hearing arguments, the court rules that the evidence supports the allegations, a predisposition report is ordered and a disposition hearing scheduled.

Disposition

In the third phase of the juvenile justice process, the juvenile court decides on a **disposition.**

Predisposition Report The court's disposition decision is based on its review of the intake report (information regarding the current offense and any previous delinquent behavior; crime severity and prior adjudication greatly influence the decision) and the **predisposition report,** a document usually prepared by a probation officer, similar to the presentence report (PSR) discussed in Chapter 4. A predisposition report typically includes (1) medical and psychological background, (2) educational history, (3) information gathered from interviews with the juvenile, family members, and other people who know the youth, (4) availability of appropriate placement options, and (5) recommendations for suitable disposition. Any treatment "needs" of the youth are also considered.

Disposition Hearing At the disposition hearing, the court imposes the appropriate sanction. In some jurisdictions, the youth is remanded either to the state correctional system or to a social service agency. Many juvenile courts ensure that adjudicated juveniles receive an appropriate disposition by establishing predefined sanctions based on type of offense, past delinquency, effectiveness of previous interventions, and assessment of special treatment, counseling, or training needs. Some of the more widely used sanctions are juvenile probation and commitment to group homes, residential treatment centers, boot camps, and juvenile correctional institutions. If the sanction imposed is probation, the youth is permitted to remain in the community under the supervision of a court services officer.

If a youth poses a threat to public safety but incarceration is not warranted, the court may impose intensive supervised probation (ISP). The major differences between regular probation and ISP are that the ISP involves (1) more rigid conditions and (2) more frequent contact between the probation officer and the probationer—more face-to-face interaction, closer monitoring of the juvenile's activities, and more frequent evaluation of the juvenile's progress.

juvenile court

Any court that has jurisdiction over matters involving juveniles.

disposition

The third stage of the juvenile justice process in which the court decides the disposition (sentence) for a juvenile case.

predisposition report

A report that documents (1) the juvenile's background; (2) his or her educational history; (3) information gathered from interviews with the juvenile, family members, and others; (4) available placement options; and (5) recommended dispositions.

The Staff Speaks
Visit www.mhhe.com/schmalleger7e to see this feature.

Juvenile probation officers play an important role in the juvenile justice process, beginning with intake and continuing through the period in which a juvenile is under court supervision. Why is writing the predisposition report such an important part of the probation officer's responsibilities?

group home

A nonsecure residential facility for juveniles.

residential treatment center

A residential facility that provides intensive treatment services to juveniles.

blended sentencing

A two-part (juvenile and adult) sentence in which the adult sentence may be waived if the offender complies with all provisions of the juvenile sentence.

Another sanction that may be imposed is referral to a **group home.** Group homes are operated by private agencies under contract with local or state government or by the public corrections unit under direction of the juvenile court. Typically, group homes accommodate 15 to 30 residents. They provide living quarters, recreational and leisure areas, kitchen and dining room, and meeting room space. Youths attend school in the community, participate in field trips, and may be granted special passes to visit family, attend religious services, or participate in activities. The range of services provided by the group home often depends on the type of offender usually referred. Some group homes are treatment oriented, providing individual and/or group counseling to youths with problems such as substance abuse or lack of self-control.

Another community-based program is the **residential treatment center.** Residential treatment centers often provide long-term care and intensive treatment services.

Today, most states have juvenile boot camps. Boot camp programs vary in size, requirements, and structure. For the most part, juvenile corrections officials have been slow to accept the boot camp concept; they consider the amount of time devoted to military drill, ceremony, and exercise an encroachment on the time available for education or rehabilitation programs.

A few states have responded to violent juvenile crime by enacting **blended sentencing** legislation in which the juvenile court may impose both a juvenile sentence and an adult criminal sentence. In 1996, for example, the Kansas legislature passed a blended sentencing law that created a new category referred to as "extended jurisdiction juvenile prosecution" for serious and violent offenders.[21] Under this legislation, two sentences are imposed, but the adult criminal sentence is waived if the juvenile offender does not violate any of the provisions of the juvenile sentence.

Juvenile Correctional Facilities

Recently, the Council of Juvenile Correctional Administrators (CJCA) reported the results of its survey of juvenile corrections throughout the United States.[22] The survey, which includes information from 45 state and territorial (including Puerto Rico) youth correctional agencies, found that 18 states operate free-standing juvenile correction agencies, 12 place the responsibility for juvenile corrections within a child welfare/social service system, 11 operate distinct youth correction agencies under a human services umbrella, and 10 (including Puerto Rico) place the responsibility for juvenile corrections within an adult corrections agency. Five state agencies were responsible for all juvenile services, and three (including Puerto Rico) were responsible only for juveniles confined in facilities. Three-quarters of the responding agencies were charged with the responsibility for juvenile corrections to include postrelease community-based reentry programs.

Operating budgets for the agencies surveyed ranged from $642 million (Florida) to about $10 million (North Dakota). On average, more than 80 percent of operating budgets were allocated to residential placements— including institutions, training schools, detention centers, assessment centers, group homes, camps, and shelters.

Nationwide, according to OJJDP-funded research, the number of delinquency cases involving detention increased 29 percent between 1985 and 2009, from 246,300 to 318,000. The largest relative increase was for person cases (114 percent), followed by public order cases (71 percent) and drug offense cases (67 percent). In contrast, the number of property offense cases declined 25 percent during this same period.[23]

Consistent with those data, the CJCA survey determined that a total of 219,335 youths were under correctional supervision in 2006, including those housed in secure institutional treatment facilities, non-secure residential facilities, and nonresidential community programs such as probation and parole. Of this number, 38 percent were white; 38 percent were black; 20 percent were Hispanic; less than 1 percent were Alaskan Native/Pacific Islander; 1 percent were American Indian; 1 percent were Asian; and 2 percent of the youths weren't classified by ethnicity (see Exhibit 16–6).

Of the more than 200,000 youths under correction supervision throughout the nation, 14 percent were placed in the most restrictive settings, such as training schools and detention centers, and 66 percent were placed in community-based programs such as probation, day treatment, and outreach programs. The remainder were served in nonsecure residential settings and reception/diagnostic centers or were placed out of state. Medical, mental health, education, life skills, and recreation programs were offered to all supervised juveniles in all jurisdictions—and some jurisdictions also offered specialized vocational, sex offender treatment, family therapy, substance abuse treatment, and other programs. Twenty-seven of the jurisdictions included in the survey results reported having at least one specialized unit designated for youths with identifiable mental health problems.

When speaking of youths in custody, a distinction should be made between *detained* and *committed* youths. Detained youths are those held prior to adjudication or disposition awaiting a hearing in juvenile or criminal court or after disposition awaiting placement elsewhere. Committed offenders are those who have been adjudicated delinquent and who have been ordered held under correctional supervision by a judicial authority as a result of case disposition.

Youths who have either been adjudicated delinquent or been taken into custody because of alleged delinquent behavior account for approximately 95 percent of both detained and committed offenders. Compared with the detained population, however, the committed juvenile population shows a greater proportion of youths held for sexual assault, burglary, and theft; and fewer youths held for technical violations of probation or parole. The committed population also demonstrates proportionally more youths held for being ungovernable, and fewer youths held for running away from home.

A correctional officer congratulates a member of a graduating class at California's Jack B. Clarke High School, part of a state youth correctional facility in Norwalk, California. How can educational opportunities benefit youth held in detention centers?

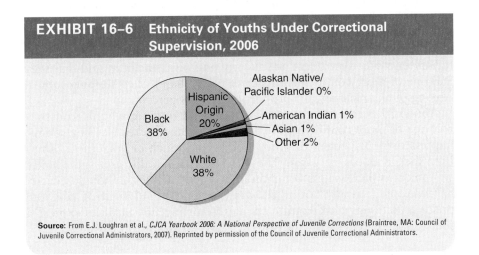

EXHIBIT 16–6   **Ethnicity of Youths Under Correctional Supervision, 2006**

- Black 38%
- Hispanic Origin 20%
- Alaskan Native/Pacific Islander 0%
- American Indian 1%
- Asian 1%
- Other 2%
- White 38%

The number of committed delinquents held in public or private facilities as part of a court-ordered disposition was 28 percent higher in 2003 than in 1991. The public facility committed population was 11 percent greater in 2003 than in 1991; and the private facility committed population was 77 percent greater.[24]

The latest data on juvenile correctional facilities gathered through the OJJDP's second Juvenile Residential Facility Census (JRFC) and published in 2011 identified 2,860 juvenile facilities throughout the United States, 2,458 of which held a total of 81,015 offenders younger than 21 years of age.[25]

The JRFC survey found that group homes or halfway houses made up 27 percent of all facilities and held 10 percent of all committed or detained juvenile offenders. Facilities identifying themselves as detention centers (30 percent) were the second most common type of facility, and detention centers held 40 percent of all juvenile offenders in residential facilities.

The survey also found that most residential facilities were small with fewer than 50 residents but that most offenders were in large facilities. Large facilities were most likely to be state operated, and very few state-operated facilities held 10 or fewer residents. In contrast, the JRFC survey found that 43 percent of private facilities were that small.

Although state-operated facilities made up just 19 percent of all facilities surveyed, they accounted for 66 percent of facilities holding more than 200 residents. Private facilities, on the other hand, made up 53 percent of all facilities, but they accounted for 80 percent of facilities holding 10 or fewer residents.

Security in Juvenile Facilities   One-third of all juvenile detention facilities reported that they lock youths in their sleeping rooms to confine them. Very few private facilities locked youths in sleeping rooms at least some of the time. Among public facilities, 73 percent of local facilities and 58 percent of state facilities reported locking youths in sleeping rooms. Of those, three-quarters said that they took such action when youths were out of control, and one-quarter did so when youths were thought to be suicidal. Locking youths in their rooms during shift changes was found to be fairly common (in 43 percent of facilities). More than half (54 percent) said they locked sleeping rooms whenever youths were in them. Locking sleeping rooms at night was more common (87 percent). Just more than one-quarter said youths were locked in their sleeping rooms part of each day, and a few facilities said they locked youths in their rooms most of each day (1 percent) or all of each day (1 percent). Six percent said they rarely locked youths in sleeping rooms and had no set schedule for doing so.

Facilities participating in the JRFC survey were asked whether they used various types of locked doors or gates to confine youths within the facility or to keep intruders out. Nearly half of all facilities said that they had one or more confinement features other than locked sleeping rooms. Among public facilities, the proportion was 78 percent.

About 90 percent of detention centers and training schools said they had one or more confinement features other than locked sleeping rooms, but less than 20 percent of group homes and ranch or wilderness camps used locked doors or gates. The use of fences, walls, and surveillance equipment is increasingly common in juvenile facilities, although security hardware is generally not as elaborate as that found in adult jails and prisons. National accreditation standards for juvenile facilities express a preference for relying on staff rather than hardware to provide security.

The guiding principle is to house juvenile offenders in the "least restrictive placement alternative." Staff security measures include periodically taking counts of the youths held, using classification and separation procedures, and maintaining an adequate ratio of security staff to juveniles.

Facilities responding to the JRFC survey reported that daytime locks confined 8 in 10 juvenile offenders at least some of the time. This represents an increase from 1997, when 7 in 10 offenders were housed in facilities with locked arrangements. Most youths in facilities with daytime locks were in facilities that held all youths under the same security arrangements. Overall, a larger proportion of committed juveniles than detained juveniles were determined to be held in facilities that relied primarily on staff security.

Juveniles in residential placement for homicide, sexual assault, robbery, aggravated assault, arson, and technical violations were the most likely to be held behind locked doors or gates. Compared with juveniles held for delinquency offenses, those in residential placement for status offenses were more likely to be confined under staff-secure arrangements (19 versus 32 percent). Facilities indicated whether they had various types of locked doors or gates intended to confine youths within the facility. Nearly half of all facilities that reported security information said they had one or more confinement features (other than locked sleeping rooms).

Among group homes and ranch or wilderness camps, fewer than 2 in 10 facilities said they had locked doors or gates to confine youths. A facility's staff, of course, also provides security. In some facilities, remote location is a security feature that also helps keep youths from leaving. Overall, 16 percent of facilities reported external gates in fences or walls with razor wire. This arrangement was most common among detention centers (39 percent), training schools (37 percent), and boot camps (32 percent).

Crowding JRFC data show that crowding is a problem in a significant number of residential facilities, and in 2008, 22 percent of the facilities reported residential populations at the limit of available beds, and 3 percent had more residents than standard beds.

Twenty-five percent of facilities said that the number of residents they held on the 2008 census date put them at or over the capacity of their standard beds or that they relied on some makeshift beds. Overall, these facilities held more than 17,291 residents, the vast majority of whom were offenders younger than 21. A large proportion of private facilities (30 percent) said they were operating at 100 percent capacity.

Females in Custody Male offenders dominate the juvenile system. This is especially true of the custody population. Females account for a small proportion of the juvenile custody population, but their numbers have increased recently. The 14,590 female offenders held in 2003 accounted for 15 percent of offenders in residential placement, an increase of 2 percent since 1991. The female proportion was higher among status offenders held (40 percent) than among delinquents (14 percent) and higher for detained (18 percent) than for committed (12 percent) delinquents.

Detention centers held the largest proportion of female offenders, and long-term secure facilities (e.g., training schools) held about one-quarter of female offenders, and group homes and halfway houses held about one-tenth.

Melanie Estes

Day Youth Counselor • United Methodist Family Services • Richmond, Virginia

Melanie Estes has been with the agency for only a few years and is currently one of two senior counselors. She completed a four-year degree in criminal justice in 1997 and is planning to attend graduate school in social work at Virginia Commonwealth University.

As a youth counselor, Estes assists in developing, implementing, evaluating, and modifying individual and group treatment plans. She ensures that daily routine and expectations are followed in the residential home. It is also her responsibility to plan, oversee, and evaluate daily and weekly schedules of agency program activities. She is the liaison between the agency and the residents' social workers, probation officers, parents, and any others who may be involved in the youths' treatment. She keeps all parties informed of residents' progress.

As a staff member, Estes's foremost duty is to act as a change agent for clients in the program. She believes that it is important that staffers learn that their interactions and interventions with one another are as crucial to the habilitative process as their interactions and interventions with youth. As a team member, she is asked to evaluate her coworkers' performance and to provide support, feedback, and training for other team members. Once a month, she is the chairperson and recorder for the weekly team meeting.

"Working with troubled juveniles is challenging and rewarding, especially with abandoned and abused children. I'm not kidding anyone when I say that it is hard to maintain a healthy balance between friend and caretaker. But one of the greatest experiences I ever had is to help at-risk youth."

Visit www.ojjdp.gov/mpg or scan this code with the QR app on your SmartPhone or digital device to visit OJJDP's Model Program Guide.

Visit www.nc4yc.org or scan this code with the QR app on your SmartPhone or digital device to visit the National Center for Youth in Custody.

Staff in Juvenile Correctional Facilities The CJCA survey found that 35,598 direct care staff members served the needs of the juvenile correctional population in the jurisdictions surveyed. *Direct care staff* was defined to include staff members at secure and nonsecure residential facilities who have routine contact with youths under correctional supervision—including youth care staff, teachers, counselors, nurses, chaplains, food care workers, and temporary or contractual employees who supervise youths.

Almost three-quarters of all jurisdictions reported having education prerequisites for staff members to include high school or GED-level completion, and three jurisdictions (Colorado, Rhode Island, and the state of Washington) require an associate's degree, and two (Missouri and North Dakota) require a bachelor's degree or its equivalent.

Evidence-Based Practice and Juvenile Corrections

The identification of effective programs through evidence-based research has been in the forefront of the national agenda on violence prevention for the last decade. In support of that agenda, federal agencies that distribute grant funds have increasingly emphasized the need to implement programs that have been demonstrated to be effective.

Two of the best-known evidence-based initiatives in the area of juvenile justice are the Blueprints for Violence Prevention program developed by the Center for the Study and Prevention of Violence (CSPV) at the University of Colorado–Boulder and the Office of Juvenile Justice and Delinquency Prevention's (OJJDP) Model Programs Guide (MPG). The

Blueprints study, one of the earliest research efforts to focus on evidence-based delinquency programs, began as an effort to identify model violence prevention initiatives and implement them within the state of Colorado.[26] OJJDP soon became an active supporter of the Blueprints project and provided additional funding to CSPV to sponsor and evaluate program replications in sites across the United States. As a result, Blueprints has evolved into a large-scale prevention initiative, identifying model programs and providing technical support to help sites choose and implement those programs that have been proven to be effective. After reviewing more than 600 programs to date, the Blueprints study has identified 11 model and 21 promising programs that prevent violence and drug use and treat youth with problem behaviors.[27]

The MPG, also developed with support from OJJDP, is intended to assist communities in implementing evidence-based prevention and intervention programs that can make a difference in the lives of children.[28] The MPG database consists of more than 200 evidence-based programs that cover the continuum of youth services from prevention through sanctions to reentry. Juvenile justice practitioners, administrators, and researchers use it to initiate programs that have already been proven to enhance accountability, ensure public safety, and reduce recidivism. OJJDP offers the MPG in the form of an easy-to-use online database that addresses a range of issues, including substance abuse, mental health, and education. The MPG database contains summary information on many evidence-based delinquency programs categorized into exemplary, effective, and promising based on an established set of methodological criteria and the strength of the findings. The MPG database can be queried through an online search tool at www.ojjdp.gov/mpg/search.aspx.

A number of other programs also work to disseminate information on evidence-based programs in the area of juvenile corrections. One of the newest such programs launched in 2010 by OJJDP is run by the National Center for Youth in Custody (NC4YC). It was a response to the call from the field for assistance to improve youth detention and correction facilities and adult facilities housing youthful offenders. NC4YC is co-directed by the Council of Juvenile Correctional Administrators (CJCA) and the National Partnership of Juvenile Services (NJPS). NC4YC's stated objectives are to:[29]

- Deliver strategic, targeted, and measurable training and technical assistance directly to facilities that detain or confine youth.
- Identify, document, and promote effective evidence-based approaches to working with youth in custody.
- Expand the knowledge base and research on juvenile justice and best practices in detaining and confining youth.
- Create a resource community for juvenile justice practitioners, youth in custody, and families.

The Washington, D.C.-based Justice Policy Institute (JPI) has singled out one state—Connecticut—as a leader in evidence-based innovations. The state has moved quickly to embrace the evidence-based movement in juvenile justice. According to JPI, "By 2012, Connecticut had a strong commitment to invest in alternatives to detention and incarceration, improve conditions of confinement, examine the research, and focus on treatment strategies with evidence of effectiveness."[30] Exhibit 16–7, taken from a JPI report, highlights the evidence-based interventions now being employed by the state of Connecticut in an effort to reduce the state's population of institutionalized juveniles.

EXHIBIT 16–7 **Connecticut's Array of Evidence-Based Family Interventions**

BRIEF STRATEGIC FAMILY THERAPY®

Brief Strategic Family Therapy (BSFT) is designed for medium-risk children and adolescents between the ages of 6 and 17 who display symptoms of or are at risk for substance abuse, conduct problems, delinquency, and other behavior problems. BSFT is typically delivered in 12 to 16 family sessions at home or other locations convenient to the family. The treatment seeks to correct maladaptive family interactions, inappropriate family alliances, and parents' tendency to unfairly blame all problems on a single individual (usually the adolescent). The expectation of the treatment is that transforming how the family functions will help improve the youth's behavior. BSFT has demonstrated significantly better outcomes than other adolescent treatment methods in several evaluation studies dating back to 1988.

FUNCTIONAL FAMILY THERAPY

Functional Family Therapy (FFT) is a highly structured family therapy treatment model program for youth ages 11–18 who exhibit characteristics of or are at high risk for delinquency, violence, substance use, conduct disorder, oppositional defiant disorder, or disruptive behavior disorder. FFT usually requires 8 to 15 sessions for referred youth and their families and up to 26 sessions for severe cases. FFT therapy is typically conducted in an office setting but can be delivered in the home or at school and other community settings. FFT's effectiveness has been demonstrated in a long series of clinical studies dating back 40 years. In one evaluation, 40 percent of youth randomly assigned to FFT avoided subsequent arrests following treatment compared with just 7 percent of youth assigned to other treatments.

INTENSIVE IN-HOME CHILD AND ADOLESCENT PSYCHIATRIC SERVICES

Intensive In-Home Child and Adolescent Psychiatric Services (IICAPS) is a rigorous home-based intervention model for children with serious psychiatric disorders who are at high risk for placement in psychiatric or correctional facilities and whose families need assistance in managing them safely in the home and community. The IICAPS model was designed by adolescent treatment experts at the Yale Child Study Center to address and maintain high-needs youth at home rather than removing them from their families and placing them in expensive (and often ineffective) residential programs. The IICAPS model is currently being evaluated in a random assignment study, but results will not be available until 2015.

MULTIDIMENSIONAL FAMILY THERAPY

MultiDimensional Family Therapy (MDFT) is a family-based treatment developed for adolescents with drug and behavior problems and for substance abuse prevention with early adolescents. It has a heavy emphasis on family therapy. The treatment seeks to curb the adolescent's substance abuse and other problem behavior as well as to improve overall family functioning. MDFT has proved significantly more effective than group therapy, family discussion groups, and other treatment approaches in several random assignment studies.

MULTIDIMENSIONAL TREATMENT FOSTER CARE

Multidimensional Treatment Foster Care (MDFT) targets children at the highest risk for out-of-home placement. In MDFT, youth are assigned to live with a foster family and receive counseling for up to a year while their parents (or guardians) simultaneously receive counseling and parenting skills training. At the end of the therapy process, youth are reunited with their biological families. MDFT has been evaluated extensively with excellent results.

MULTISYSTEMIC THERAPY

Multisystemic Therapy (MST) is an intensive family- and community-based treatment program that focuses on addressing all environmental systems that impact chronic and violent juvenile offenders: their homes and families, schools and teachers, and neighborhoods and friends. MST works with youth ages 12 through 17, including those with a long and serious offending history. MST clinicians go where the child is and are on call 24 hours a day, seven days a week. MST is an evidence-based "Blueprint" program endorsed by OJJDP, the U.S. Surgeon General, and other national leaders in juvenile justice.

Source: Justice Policy Institute, *Juvenile Justice Reform in Connecticut,* (2013) p. 22. Reprinted with permission.

waiver provisions

Provisions under which the juvenile court orders transfer of the case to adult criminal court.

direct file provisions

Provisions under which the prosecutor determines whether to initiate a case against a juvenile in juvenile court or in adult criminal court.

Transfer to Adult Criminal Court

All states and the District of Columbia allow adult criminal prosecution of juveniles under certain circumstances. Juveniles may be transferred to adult criminal court under one of three provisions: waiver, direct file, or statutory exclusion. Under discretionary judicial **waiver provisions,** the juvenile court orders transfer of the case to adult criminal court. In all but four states (Massachusetts, Nebraska, New Mexico, and New York), a juvenile court judge is authorized to waive the juvenile court's original jurisdiction over cases that meet certain criteria and to refer them to criminal court for prosecution. Under **direct file provisions,** the prosecutor determines whether to initiate a case against a juvenile in juvenile court or in adult criminal court. Fifteen states have statutes that specify circumstances in which the prosecutor may make the transfer decision. Under **statutory exclusion provisions,** also known as *mandatory waiver,* state law specifies adult criminal court jurisdiction for certain juvenile cases. An increasing number of states automatically exclude from juvenile court any cases that meet specific age and offense criteria. Fifteen states mandate that certain juvenile cases be filed directly in criminal court. In 2009, 7,600 juvenile cases were transferred to adult criminal court. Of these, 46 percent involved a crime against a person, 31 percent involved property crime, 13 percent involved a drug law violation, and 10 percent involved a public-order offense.[31]

statutory exclusion provisions

Provisions under which adult criminal court jurisdiction for certain juvenile cases is established by state law.

Teen Courts

Teen courts, also called *peer* and *youth courts,* have become a popular alternative to the traditional juvenile court for relatively young or first-time offenders. The teen court was first used in Grand Prairie, Texas, in 1976.[32] Since then the number of teen courts has increased to an estimated 1,150 nationwide.[33] Teen courts handled approximately 125,000 cases in 2005.[34]

teen courts

Courts in which youths adjudicate and impose disposition for a juvenile offense.

In youth court, youth volunteers work with adults to conduct sentencing hearings and trials for young offenders. The primary purpose of youth courts is to effectively divert juvenile delinquents from the formal juvenile or criminal justice system. Adults and youth volunteers work as colleagues to achieve the goals of restoring justice to the victims, the respondents, and the community. Most important, young offenders learn that their peers will work with them to ensure that justice is served and that there are consequences for their delinquent behavior.

All teen courts are diversion processes. These programs may handle crimes and offenses that would otherwise be eligible for prosecution in juvenile court, adult court, traffic court, or a school's disciplinary process. Without a youth court, juvenile offenders in some cases would not be held accountable for their antisocial, delinquent, and criminal behavior because of the backlog in the juvenile system. Youth courts provide a measured response for youths who violate the law.

Depending on which of the many teen court models is followed, young people may take on the roles of judge, prosecutor, defense attorney, community or victim advocate, respondent or youth advocate, juror, presiding juror, bailiff, or clerk.

Teen courts generally use one of four models: Adult Judge, Youth Judge, Youth Tribunal, or Peer Jury. In the Adult Judge model, an adult serves as judge, ruling on legal terminology and courtroom procedure, and youths serve as attorneys, jurors, clerks, bailiffs, and so on. The Youth Judge model parallels the Adult Judge model, with the exception that a youth serves as judge. In the Youth Tribunal model, youth attorneys present the case to a panel of three youth judges. The Peer Jury model uses no attorneys—the case is presented to a youth jury by a youth or adult and the jury questions the defendant directly. Forty percent of teen courts use the Adult Judge model, 26 percent the Peer Jury, 8 percent the Youth Tribunal, and 17 percent the Youth Judge. The remaining 9 percent use a combination of two or more of these models.[35]

In the majority of cases, young defendants admit their wrongdoing or plead no contest to be eligible for teen court. A few teen courts (less than 8 percent) allow a youth to plead not guilty. In those programs, the teen court can conduct a trial to determine guilt or innocence. If the young

Teen courts allow youths to adjudicate peers accused of minor law violations and to impose a reasoned disposition on juveniles who come before them. Why might such courts be more effective than "traditional" juvenile courts?

person is found guilty, the youth court sentences him or her. Young people must give informed consent to participate in all youth courts. In most teen courts, parents or guardians must also give consent.

Teen courts turn peer pressure into a positive tool: Youth volunteers tell respondents clearly that their behavior is wrong. However, the underlying philosophy of youth courts is not merely to punish respondents. Instead, youth volunteers work through creative ways to make respondents understand in concrete terms that their behavior has harmed specific individuals and the community. This balanced and restorative approach provides respondents opportunities to repair the harm that they caused and to give back to their community in a meaningful way. Specific needs of the respondents are identified, and the sentence (or disposition) is directed at building strengths and skills in the respondents.

Quite commonly, a teen court disposition requires a respondent to serve on the youth court as a juror or bailiff in a subsequent youth court case. This means that respondents are not excluded from the circle of their law-abiding peers but are included once more within the community and have a chance to see the law from both sides. This requirement also helps ensure that the youth court reflects the diversity of the community.

Failure to complete the disposition imposed by the youth court generally results in referral back to the original agency. For example, youths failing to complete their disposition for crimes are referred back to the referring agency; youths failing to complete their disposition for violating school rules are referred back to the school disciplinary process.

Youth courts have quietly emerged as the most replicated—and fastest growing—juvenile intervention program in the United States. Estimates are that teen courts will be handling as many as 25 percent of all juvenile arrests by 2015.

According to the OJJDP, community service was the most common disposition imposed in teen court cases in the year 2000.[36] Other dispositions included victim apology letters, apology essays, teen court jury duty, drug/alcohol classes, and monetary restitution.

Tammy Hawkins, teen court coordinator for Odessa, Texas, says that teen court makes quite an impact when you give a teenaged jury sole discretion in handing down sentences. "The juvenile defendant receives this sentence from his peers and sees that they are saying, 'We as your peers do not agree with your actions and breaking the law is not acceptable.' A child is more likely to listen to one of their own, as opposed to an adult or the system. After all, as one defendant put it, 'Your peers are the ones that you want to accept you.'"[37]

CO16-5   YOUTH GANGS

The proliferation of gang problems in large and small cities, suburbs, and even rural areas over the last two decades led to the development of a comprehensive, coordinated response to America's gang problem by OJJDP. One aspect of the OJJDP response involves the implementation and operation of the National Gang Center (NGC).

The NGC helps policymakers, practitioners, and researchers in their efforts to reduce youth gang involvement and crime. A central component of these efforts is the annual National Youth Gang Survey (NYGS). The most recently available NYGS includes responses from around

2,150 police agencies across the country, and departments serving cities and towns across the country.[38]

Survey participants are asked to report information only for youth gangs, which the researchers define as "a group of youths or young adults in your jurisdiction that you or other responsible persons in your agency or community are willing to identify as a 'gang.'" Motorcycle gangs, hate or ideology groups, prison gangs, and exclusively adult gangs are excluded from the survey. Respondents provide information regarding the presence or absence of active youth gangs in their jurisdictions and detail the type of activity in which gangs are involved. According to findings from the most recent survey:

- Thirty-four percent of the city and county law enforcement agencies experienced youth gang problems.
- Approximately 756,000 gang members and 29,400 gangs are estimated to have been active in the United States in 2010.
- Gang problems are highly prevalent in larger cities where 99 percent of law enforcement agencies have reported multiple years of gang problems.
- Among very large cities, the number of reported gang-related homicides increased 13 percent from 2009 to 2010.
- Larger cities have a much longer, more extensive history of gang problems, and nearly half have experienced ongoing gang problems since before the 1990s (see Exhibit 16–8).
- Very few rural counties have long-standing gang problems.[39]

The youth gang problem is one of the most important issues for juvenile corrections today. Many of the youths confined for serious crimes committed violent acts as gang members. For some correctional institutions, a primary housing consideration is a youth's gang affiliation—rival gang members must be housed separately. Juvenile correctional personnel

The Offender Speaks
Visit www.mhhe.com/schmalleger7e to see this feature.

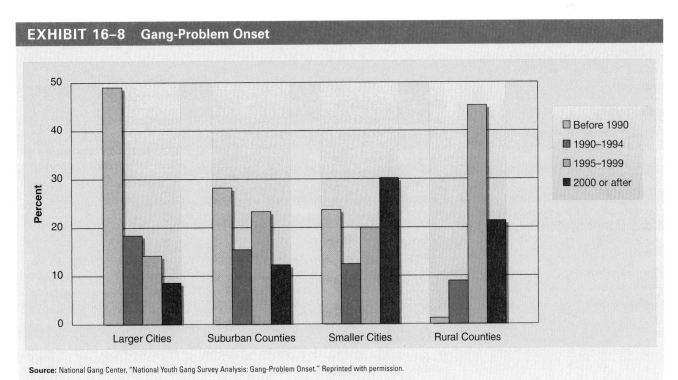

EXHIBIT 16–8   Gang-Problem Onset

Legend: Before 1990 | 1990–1994 | 1995–1999 | 2000 or after

Source: National Gang Center, "National Youth Gang Survey Analysis: Gang-Problem Onset." Reprinted with permission.

A member of the infamous Mara Salvatrucha 13 gang. Mara Salvatrucha, which has been called "America's most deadly gang," is made up predominately of Salvadorans. It originated in the Los Angeles area, not El Salvador, but the gang was later exported back to that country. What can be done to stop the spread of street gangs?

gang

A criminal enterprise having an organizational structure, acting as a continuing criminal conspiracy, that employs violence and any other criminal activity to sustain itself.

youth gang

A gang whose membership generally comprises people between the ages of 12 and 24.

street gang

An organized group of people on the street often engaged in significant illegitimate or criminal activity.

regularly deal with problems that stem from gang-related activity within the institution: extortion, violence, and attempts to smuggle in contraband.

One of the more pressing gang-related issues facing today's juvenile corrections agencies is identification of youth gangs. According to the FBI, a **gang** is "a criminal enterprise having an organizational structure, acting as a continuing criminal conspiracy, which employs violence and any other criminal activity to sustain the enterprise."[40] Members of the group need not wear similar clothing ("colors") or tattoos or use hand signs (called "throwing") or initiation rituals, and the group might not even have a specific name (e.g., "Crips" or "Bloods"). Participation in criminal activity is what distinguishes community groups or social clubs from gangs. Other terms that have been used to distinguish among types of gangs are *street gang* and *youth gang*. The term **youth gang** tends to emphasize the age of a gang's members and is usually applied to gangs consisting of members between the ages of 12 and 24. According to the OJJDP, the phrase **street gang** refers to an organized group of people on the street, often engaged in significant illegitimate or criminal activity.[41] The membership age of street gangs varies, says OJJDP, while some youth gangs are more street based than others.[42]

Police departments tend to view gangs somewhat differently than our definitions might indicate. According to a recent survey of police agencies nationwide, the most important distinguishing characteristic of a youth gang is that its members commit crimes together.[43] The fact that the gang has a name and that its members "hang out together" is somewhat less important. See Exhibit 16–9 for additional information on the criteria used by law enforcement agencies to distinguish youth gangs from other types of organizations.

Graffiti is a common method of communication for gangs.[44] It serves as the gang "newspaper" or "bulletin board," communicating many messages, including challenges, warnings, and pronouncements. Juvenile corrections professionals must become familiar with gang language, graffiti, and symbols to be able to deal with gang power and control. The names of some of the gangs currently operating in the United States are given in Exhibit 16–10.

EXHIBIT 16–9	Criteria Used by Law Enforcement Agencies to Define a Youth Gang	
	Agencies Selecting as Most Important Criterion	
Gang Characteristic	*Number*	*Percentage*
Commits crimes together	613	50%
Has a name	228	19
Hangs out together	119	10
Claims a turf or territory of some sort	104	9
Displays/wears common colors or other insignia	101	8
Has a leader or several leaders	89	7

Note: Number of observations was 1,221.

Source: Office of Juvenile Justice and Delinquency Prevention, *National Youth Gang Survey* (Washington, DC: U.S. Department of Justice, November 2000), Table 45.

EXHIBIT 16–10	Names of Some Youth Gangs Operating in the United States

3-D Kings	Insane Gangster Disciples
10th Street Thugs	Latin Counts
Asian Boyz	Latin Disciples
Asian Family	Latin Eagles
Asian Gangsters	Latin Force
Baby Demons	Latin Kings
Bad Boys	Locos
Black Angels	Maniac Latin Disciples
Black Gangster Disciples	Mara Salvatrucha
Bloods	Masters of Destruction
Born to Kill	Mexican Mafia
Brown Mexican Pride	Midnight Crypts
Crips	Natoma
Devil Boys	Nazi Low Riders
Dogg Pound	Playboy Gangster Crips
Fourth World Mafia	T-Dogs
Gangster Disciples	Toy Soldiers
Gaylords	Vice Lords
Hmong Nation	Young Bloods
Hollywood Criminals	West Side Crips
Imperial Vice Lords	Wetback Power
Insane Cobras	

Note: Some of the groups listed here also contain adult members, although youth "branches" consist primarily of members ages 12 to 24.

Sources: Adapted from Florida Department of Corrections, "Security Threat Groups in Florida," www.dc.state.fi.us/pub/gangs/fi.html (accessed June 20, 2005); Massachusetts Department of Corrections, "Gang Security Threat Group Information," www.state.ma.us/doc/gang/Ganglist.htm (accessed June 20, 2005); and Robert Walker, "Gangs in the United States," www.gangsorus.com/usgangs.html (accessed June 20, 2005).

One reason that gangs successfully recruit members within the correctional setting is that the transition to a confined existence can be traumatic. Residents often challenge new arrivals, usually within the first few days, threatening physical harm to intimidate and exploit the youth. A youth who is the object of such an encounter may believe that joining a gang is the only way to survive.

Another reason that incarcerated juveniles join gangs is boredom. Their typical daily routine includes eating meals, exercise, and schoolwork. Leisure activities, family visitation, social programs, and other special services are intermittent and are permitted only if the juvenile complies with institutional rules. Involvement in gang activity may represent excitement and adventure for confined juveniles.

JUVENILE JUSTICE REFORM

CO16-6

A comprehensive overview of recent changes in U.S. juvenile justice policy published by the Washington, D.C.-based Urban Institute a few years ago found that over the past several decades, state governments have enacted "sweeping changes in law and policy that have profoundly affected the juvenile justice landscape in the United States."[45] Among those changes are new laws intended to reduce the confidentiality of juvenile hearings and records, increased efforts to target drug and weapons offenses among youth, enhanced laws for transferring seriously delinquent youth into the adult criminal justice system, broader information-sharing among juvenile and adult justice agencies, and new sentencing guidelines to encourage consistency in juvenile dispositions. Although many recent changes, including some mandatory minimum sentencing statutes specifically applicable to juvenile offenders, amount to "get-tough" efforts designed to target serious and violent crime committed by juveniles, many states have simultaneously moved to improve the administration of juvenile justice by creating specialized juvenile drug courts, truancy court programs, mental health initiatives targeting troubled youth, and enhancing diversion programs, utilizing evidence-based approaches in policy decisions, and increasing treatment options for youth. The Urban Institute also found that California, Florida, New York, and New Jersey were among the most "legislatively active states" and had introduced many new measures focused on juvenile justice reform.

In 2011, the New York-based Vera Institute of Justice's Center on Youth Justice released a report on juvenile correctional reform. The report noted that "a growing body of research conducted over several decades has persuaded most experts and many practitioners that punitive responses to juvenile offenders—particularly those placed in secure facilities—yield poor results for the youth involved and for public safety."[46] Reflecting a national movement toward the deinstitutionalization of juvenile offenders, the report's authors proposed the Missouri model as an alternative model of juvenile justice confinement for national emulation. The Missouri model of youth confinement, established by the Missouri Division of Youth Services in the early 1980s, stresses small cottagelike residences, individualized and group treatment, and positive relationships between youth and staff. More importantly, the Missouri model is built around a philosophy known as *positive youth development* (PYD), which emphasizes relationships and activities intended to build on the positive qualities that juveniles bring with them when they enter the program.

A juvenile corrections officer moves furniture out of Sacramento County Boy's Ranch following the closing of two of the three juvenile detention facilities in the county in 2010. How do the closings reflect a change in the handling of juveniles that is occurring nationwide?

The nature of juvenile corrections has changed along with other aspects of the juvenile justice system over the last 20 years.

According to Ania Dobrzansak, the juvenile justice grant manager for the Professional Development Department of the American Correctional Association (ACA), "The public image of juvenile corrections has evolved considerably. What was once viewed as a punitive warehousing operation is now recognized as a multifaceted specialization that involves in-depth knowledge of the juvenile offender's personality and behavior; and on the part of the juvenile corrections worker, interpersonal communication skills, motivation, commitment to teamwork and integrity."[47]

Since it was founded in 1870, the ACA has advocated juvenile justice reform (see Exhibit 16–11). In a recent campaign for juvenile justice reform, the ACA called for:

- legislative and community action to fund and operate early intervention strategies;
- support of continued research and responsible action based on the results of research already available on prevention programs that work;
- support of system reforms that allow juvenile justice officials, family, social, educational, and other agencies and institutions to relate to a specific child and to work together for the best interests of the child, including accountability or shared use of confidential information about children at risk;
- support of programs that address the causes of violent and delinquent activity in communities;
- opposition to efforts to establish automatic certification of juvenile offenders to adult status for certain offenses;
- opposition to determinate sentencing for juvenile offenders; and
- support of the use of confidential systems for information sharing about juvenile offenders.[48]

Improving the Juvenile Justice System for Girls

In 2012, the Georgetown Center on Poverty, Inequality and Public Policy released a report on improving the juvenile justice system for girls.[49] The report noted that the existing juvenile justice system was originally designed for delinquent boys and doesn't adequately recognize the needs of girls. The Center also examined the challenges facing girls in the juvenile justice system and offered suggestions for gender-responsive reform at the local, state, and federal levels. In the report's words:

> The typical girl in the system is a non-violent offender, who is very often low-risk, but high-need, meaning the girl poses little risk to the public but she enters the system with significant and pressing personal needs. The set of challenges that girls often face as they enter the juvenile justice system include trauma, violence, neglect, mental and physical problems, family conflict, pregnancy, residential and academic instability, and school failure. The juvenile justice system only exacerbates these problems by failing to provide girls with services at the time when they need them most.[50]

The Center concluded its report with a number of policy recommendations that it hopes will be enacted at the federal level, including:

- Conduct research on programs for girls, particularly regarding best practices in gender-responsive programming and conditions of confinement for girls.

EXHIBIT 16–11   American Correctional Association

Public Correctional Policy on Juvenile Justice

Introduction

The juvenile justice system must provide a continuum of services, programs, and facilities that ensure maximum opportunity for rehabilitation and are consistent with public safety. These should place a high priority on providing individualized care and rehabilitative services to juvenile offenders throughout the juvenile justice system. To implement this policy, juvenile justice officials and agencies should:

- increase public awareness as to why it is in their best interest to promote, support, participate in, and fund those programs that have proven effective in preventing delinquency and producing healthy, positive, and socially responsible children and adolescents;
- establish and maintain effective working relationships with those who can have an impact on the juvenile to achieve the fullest possible cooperation in making appropriate decisions in individual cases and in providing and using services and resources;
- provide a range of non-residential and residential programs and services in the least restrictive manner, consistent with the needs of individual offenders and the protection of the public;
- engage the family, whenever practical, appropriate, and therapeutic to the youth, in the development and implementation of his or her treatment plan;
- use a juvenile classification system to identify the risk and needs of the juvenile offender, and develop and implement an individualized treatment plan based on this assessment;
- advocate for the separation of status offenders from adjudicated delinquent offenders in the same facilities;
- provide a range of non-secure and secure short-term detention options pending adjudication;
- advocate for the separation of adjudicated from pre-adjudicated youths in the same housing units;
- with the involvement of the youth and prior to release from custody, develop a transition plan that includes educational and/or vocational programs for aftercare/reentry and ensure that these reentry services are available and provided when the youth returns from residential placement;
- establish written policies and procedures that will protect the rights and safety of the juvenile, the victim, and the public in as balanced a manner as possible;
- establish procedures to safeguard the accuracy and use of juvenile records and support limitations on their use according to approved national standards, recognizing that the need to safeguard the privacy and rehabilitative goals of the juvenile should be balanced with concern for the protection of the public, including victims;
- develop performance outcome measures from which program effectiveness and system operations can be assessed and adjusted when needed; and
- implement research and evaluation initiatives that will measure the effectiveness of juvenile justice programs and disseminate findings to the field.

Source: Copyright © American Correctional Association. Reprinted with permission.

- Mandate a comprehensive effort by the U.S. Department of Justice to improve training and technical assistance for judges as well as law enforcement and juvenile justice staff for better recognition of the unique needs of marginalized girls.
- Allocate federal funding and encourage states to apply for federal funding for gender-specific programming.

A young girl prepares to play cards at the T. Don Hutto Residential Center in Taylor, Texas. What special problems face girls in the juvenile justice system?

- Close the loophole that currently allows states to detain youths for technical violations of court orders—a practice that has a disproportionate impact on girls.
- Encourage the development of national standards for gender-responsive programming.
- Promote policies to keep girls out of the adult criminal justice system.

REVIEW AND APPLICATIONS

SUMMARY

1 *Parens patriae* is a legal philosophy that is used to justify intervention in children's lives when their parents are unwilling or unable to care for them. Historically, houses of refuge, the first legally chartered custodial institutions for juvenile offenders, were established in the early 19th century. Reform schools, which were established in the middle of the 19th century, sought to reform rather than punish young offenders through vocational (especially trade and industrial), physical, and military education. Reform schools for girls used "cottagelike" residential units. Industrial schools emerged in the latter part of the 19th century and emphasized vocational training for youthful offenders.

2 Six U.S. Supreme Court decisions established due process rights for juvenile offenders:

- *Kent* v. *United States* (1966)—a juvenile who is to be transferred to adult criminal court is entitled to a hearing, representation by an attorney, access to records being considered by the juvenile court, and a statement of reasons for the transfer.

- *In re Gault* (1967)—in a proceeding that might result in commitment to an institution, a juvenile is entitled to reasonable notice of charges, counsel, questioning of witnesses, and protection against self-incrimination.

- *In re Winship* (1970)—proof beyond a reasonable doubt, not simply a preponderance of the evidence, is required during the adjudicatory stage for a delinquent offense.

- *McKeiver* v. *Pennsylvania* (1971)—trial by jury is not a constitutional requirement for juvenile adjudication.

- *Breed* v. *Jones* (1975)—transfer to adult criminal court after juvenile court adjudication constitutes double jeopardy.

- *Schall* v. *Martin* (1984)—preventive pretrial detention of juveniles is allowable under certain circumstances.

❸ Most cases handled by the juvenile courts are for delinquent offenses—acts committed by a juvenile that if committed by an adult could result in criminal prosecution. The remaining cases are for status offenses—acts that are offenses only when committed by juveniles. Such offenses include running away, truancy, ungovernability, and liquor law violations. Juvenile courts have original jurisdiction over juvenile delinquents and status offenders, usually under age 18.

❹ The three stages of the juvenile justice process are intake, adjudication, and disposition. During the intake stage, a court-appointed officer recommends a course of action—dismissal, informal disposition, formal disposition, or, in some instances, transfer to adult criminal court—for a juvenile who has been referred to the juvenile court. Adjudication is judicial determination of guilt or innocence. Disposition is judicial imposition of the most appropriate sanction.

❺ A *gang* is a group of individuals involved in continuing criminal activity. Youth gangs are a serious problem for juvenile correctional professionals. For some juvenile institutions, gang affiliation is an important consideration in housing arrangements.

❻ Changes that have recently taken place in the area of juvenile justice include both new get-tough efforts intended to punish serious juvenile offenders more severely and improvements in the administration of juvenile justice. Mandatory minimum sentences and enhanced laws for transferring seriously delinquent youth into the adult justice system provide examples of the former, and newly created specialized courts and initiatives intended to help troubled youths provide examples of the latter. More recently, a focus on the special needs of delinquent girls has been added to the agenda of both researchers and policy makers.

KEY TERMS

parens patriae, p. 526
reform school, p. 526
delinquent offenses, p. 532
status offenses, p. 532
intake, p. 534
juvenile detention facility, p. 536
detention hearing, p. 536
guardian *ad litem,* p. 536

juvenile court, p. 537
disposition, p. 537
predisposition report, p. 537
group home, p. 538
residential treatment center, p. 538
blended sentencing, p. 538
waiver provisions, p. 544
direct file provisions, p. 544

statutory exclusion provisions, p. 545
teen courts, p. 545
gang, p. 548
youth gang, p. 548
street gang, p. 548

QUESTIONS FOR REVIEW

1 Explain the principle of *parens patriae,* and review the historical development of juvenile justice in the United States.

2 What significant U.S. Supreme Court rulings established due process rights for juveniles? What impact did each have on juvenile court proceedings?

3 What is a *delinquent offense?* A *status offense?* What is the nature of juvenile court jurisdiction?

4 Identify and explain the three stages of the juvenile justice process.

5 How do youth gangs impact correctional facilities for juveniles?

6 What changes are now taking place in the area of juvenile corrections that will likely determine how juvenile offenders are handled in the future?

THINKING CRITICALLY ABOUT CORRECTIONS

Sentencing Project

The Sentencing Project reports that abuse (physical and sexual) and suicide rates are higher for children who serve time in adult correctional institutions than for those held in juvenile correctional institutions—youths held in adult institutions are 7.7 times more likely to commit suicide, 5 times more likely to be sexually assaulted, twice as likely to be beaten by staff, and 50 percent more likely to be attacked with a weapon.[51] What conclusions might you draw from this report?

Public Access to Juvenile Court Proceedings

Juvenile court proceedings are becoming more accessible to the public. At least 21 states now permit open juvenile court proceedings for serious or violent crime charges or repeat offenses. In 1995, Georgia passed a law allowing the public admission to adjudicatory hearings for youths who have been charged with delinquent offenses.

1. Do you think juvenile court proceedings should be open to the public?
2. Why or why not?

ON-THE-JOB DECISION MAKING

Youth Violence

In recent months, there has been a spate of violent crimes committed by youthful offenders in your community, including numerous murders, assaults, rapes, and armed robberies. Gang violence, in particular, seems to be escalating.

Josh McFadden, a crusading journalist in your town, has been whipping up public sentiment for the inclusion of a "get-tough" referendum on the upcoming ballot. In daily newspaper articles and during frequent guest appearances on local television programs, McFadden beats the same old drum: It's time to treat all criminals as criminals, no matter what their age, he says. His strident calls for abolition of delinquency laws and automatic waiver to adult court of all juveniles who commit violent felonies seem to be touching a nerve.

You are a juvenile probation officer. You and your coworkers truly believe juveniles need special handling that is different from what they would receive in the adult criminal justice system.

In recent weeks, you have been flooded with requests to appear on various discussion panels. Your supervisor has been reluctant to enter the fray but authorizes you to participate in an upcoming panel discussion to be televised within the community. Josh McFadden will be on the panel.

1. What issues would you present to support retention of the current procedures for handling juvenile offenders?
2. How would you address the waiver of jurisdiction to adult court question?

Teen Court

Read the following case:

IN THE MATTER OF: Beth Leonard
CHARGES: Three (3) counts of retail theft.

Hoover police were summoned to the Hoover Mall branch store of Fancy This on March 17, 2013, at 11:20 A.M. regarding a shoplifter. Beth Leonard, a 16-year-old high school honor student, was arrested at 11:52 A.M. for three (3) counts of retail theft.

An employee noticed Beth entering the dressing room with a blue short outfit and a swimsuit. Beth exited the dressing room carrying only her purse. After a quick scan of the room, the attendant, unable to locate the clothes, called security. Beth was led to the manager's office, where she confessed to putting the items on under her clothing and attempting to leave.

When the police arrived, they asked for identification and discovered a bottle of Spring Musk Perfume bearing a new, undamaged sales sticker in Beth's purse. Upon prompting, Beth admitted that she had taken this item from the Perfumeria, a mall perfume store.

A further search of Beth's purse revealed two pairs of earrings with sales stickers from Carter's, a mall accessory shop. Beth admitted to taking these items without purchasing them.

While searching Beth's purse, the officer located her wallet and found $85 in cash. When asked why she didn't just pay for the items, Beth stated she was planning to purchase a gift for her parents' wedding anniversary.

A conference was later held between Beth, her parents, and the arresting officer. During this conference, Beth stated that all her girlfriends did this and they never got caught. She was dared by one to bring certain items to her with the sales tags still intact to prove that she had not paid for them. It was dumb, but she did it, and she was sorry.

1. If you were the intake officer handling this case, would you recommend that a teen court handle it?
2. Why or why not?

For additional information, please see: www.mhhe.com/schmalleger7e
Follow the author's tweets about the latest crime and justice news @schmalleger

ENDNOTES

Chapter 1

1. Stephen Ohlemacher, "2 Prison Inmates Claim $1.1 Billion in Tax Refunds; 173,000 Fraudulent Prison Tax Returns Uncovered," *Huffington Post*, January 17, 2013, www.huffingtonpost.com/2013/01/18/prison-tax-fraud-billion-refund-inmates_n_2502137.html (accessed January 30, 2013).

2. "The New Wolfhound-PRO Contraband Cell Phone Detector to be 'Unleashed' at the American Correctional Association Winter Conference," PRNewswire, January 25, 2011, www.prnewswire.com/news-releases/the-new-wolfhound-pro-contraband-cell-phone-detector-to-be-unleashed-at-the-american-correctional-association-winter-conference-114559409.html (accessed March 15, 2011).

3. The word *outlawed* is used loosely. Although some states have outlawed inmate possession of working cell phones and some others are moving in that direction, such possession is more often a violation of administrative regulations.

4. For an in-depth discussion of this issue, see Steven Raphael and Michael A. Stoll (eds.), *Do Prisons Make Us Safer? The Benefits and Costs of the Prison Boom* (New York: Russell Sage Foundation, 2010).

5. Fox Butterfield, "Crime Keeps on Falling, but Prisons Keep on Filling," *New York Times* News Service, September 28, 1997.

6. See, for example, Jory Farr, "A Growth Enterprise," www.press-enterprise.com/focus/prison/html/agrowthindustry.html (accessed March 28, 2002).

7. Margaret Werner Cahalan, *Historical Corrections Statistics in the United States, 1850–1984* (Washington, DC: U.S. Department of Justice, 1986).

8. E. Ann Carson and Daniela Golinelli, *Prisoners in 2012* (Washington, DC: Bureau of Justice Statistics, 2013).

9. Laura M. Maruschak and Thomas P. Bonczar, *Probation and Parole in the United States, 2012* (Washington, DC: Bureau of Justice Statistics, 2013).

10. Melissa Hickman Barlow, "Sustainable Justice: 2012 Presidential Address to the Academy of Criminal Justice Sciences," *Justice Quarterly*, 2012, pp. 1–17, 1First Article.

11. Cahalan, *Historical Corrections Statistics.*

12. Bureau of Labor Statistics, "Correctional Officers," *Occupational Outlook Handbook*, www.bls.gov/ooh/protective-service/correctional-officers.htm (accessed January 30, 2013).

13. Kristen A. Hughes, *Justice Expenditure and Employment in the United States, 2003* (Washington, DC: Bureau of Justice Statistics, 2006), p. 6.

14. The figure may be somewhat misleading, however, because an offender who commits a number of crimes may be prosecuted for only one.

15. Much of the following material is adapted from Bureau of Justice Statistics, *Report to the Nation on Crime and Justice*, 2nd ed. (Washington, DC: Bureau of Justice Statistics, 1988), pp. 56–58.

16. President's Commission on Law Enforcement and Administration of Justice, *The Challenge of Crime in a Free Society* (Washington, DC: U.S. Government Printing Office, 1967), p. 159.

17. National Advisory Commission on Criminal Justice Standards and Goals, *Corrections* (Washington, DC: U.S. Government Printing Office, 1975), p. 2.

18. Bureau of Justice Statistics, *Correctional Populations in the United States, 1995* (Washington, DC: U.S. Government Printing Office, 1997).

19. Bob Barrington, "Corrections: Defining the Profession and the Roles of Staff," *Corrections Today*, August 1987, pp. 116–120.

20. Arlin Adams, *The Legal Profession: A Critical Evaluation*, 93 Dick. L. Rev. 643 (1989).

21. Harold E. Williamson, *The Corrections Profession* (Newbury Park, CA: Sage, 1990), p. 79.

22. Adams, *The Legal Profession.*

23. Williamson, *The Corrections Profession*, p. 20.

24. P. P. Lejins, "ACA Education Council Proposes Correctional Officer Entry Tests," *Corrections Today*, vol. 52, no. 1 (February 1990), pp. 56, 58, 60.

25. Mark S. Fleisher, "Teaching Correctional Management to Criminal Justice Majors," *Journal of Criminal Justice Education*, vol. 8, no. 1 (Spring 1997), pp. 59–73.

26. See Robert B. Levinson, Jeanne B. Stinchcomb, and John J. Greene III, "Corrections Certification: First Steps Toward Professionalism," www.aca.org/development/doc_certification firststeps.pdf (accessed March 23, 2003).

27. See the ACA's Professional Certification Program Web page at www.corrections.com/aca/development/certification.htm (accessed September 10, 2013) for more information.

28. The AJA defines a jail manager as "a person (sworn or civilian) who directs, administers, and/or is in charge of the operations of an adult jail facility, division, bureau, department, program, and/or shift; and/or a person (sworn or civilian) who supervises the work and performance of an employee or employees in an adult jail facility." See AJA, *CJM: Handbook for Candidates*, www.corrections.com/aja/cjm_handbook.pdf (accessed March 25, 2007).

29. Lawrence W. Sherman et al., *Preventing Crime: What Works, What Doesn't, What's Promising* (Washington, DC: National Institute of Justice, 1997).

30. National Institute of Corrections, "A Framework for Evidence-Based Decision Making in Local Criminal Justice Systems" (Center for Effective Public Policy, 2010), www.cepp.com/documents/EBDM Framework.pdf (accessed September 10, 2011).

31. Office of Justice Programs, "Justice Resource Update" (Washington, DC: U.S. Department of Justice, 2010).

32. The University of California, Irvine, Center for Evidence-Based Corrections, http://ucicorrections.seweb.uci.edu (accessed June 6, 2009).

33. Center for Evidence-Based Corrections, University of California, Irvine, http://ucicorrections.seweb.uci.edu (accessed January 30, 2013).

34. Michale Omi and Howard Winant, *Racial Formation in the United States: From the 1960s to the 1980s* (New York: Routledge and Kegan Paul, 1986), p. 145.

35. National Center for Women and Policing, *Equality Denied: The Status of Women in Policing, 2001* (Beverly Hills, CA: NCWP, 2002), p. 11.

36. Dianne Carter, "The Status of Education and Training in Corrections," *Federal Probation*, vol. 55, no. 2 (June 1991), pp. 17–23.

37. Williamson, *The Corrections Profession.*

Chapter 2

1. *Gazette d'Amsterdam,* April 1, 1757. Cited by Michel Foucault, *Discipline & Punish: The Birth of the Prison,* trans. Alan Sheridan (New York: Vintage Books, 1995).

2. Edward M. Peters, "Prison Before the Prison: The Ancient and Medieval Worlds," in Norval Morris and David J. Rothman (eds.), *The Oxford History of the Prison* (New York: Oxford University Press, 1995), p. 6.

3. James Hastings et al., *Dictionary of the Bible,* vol. 1 (New York: Scribner; 1905), pp. 523 ff. Cited in Arthur Evans Wood and John Barker Waite, *Crime and Its Treatment: Social and Legal Aspects of Criminology* (New York: American Book Company, 1941), p. 462.

4. *Gazette d'Amsterdam,* p. 8.

5. See Peters, "Prison Before the Prison," pp. 14–15.

6. Wood and Waite, *Crime and Its Treatment,* p. 462.

7. Pieter Spierenburg, "The Body and the State: Early Modern Europe," in Norval Morris and David J. Rothman (eds.), *The Oxford History of the Prison* (New York: Oxford University Press, 1995), pp. 52–53.

8. Ibid., p. 53.

9. Harry Elmer Barnes and Negley K. Teeters, *New Horizons in Criminology,* 3rd ed. (Englewood Cliffs, NJ: Prentice Hall, 1959), p. 290.

10. Some of the information in this section comes from Harry Elmer Barnes, *Story of Punishment* (Montclair, NJ: Patterson Smith, 1930); and George Ives, *A History of Penal Methods* (London: Stanley Paul, 1914).

11. Barnes and Teeters, *New Horizons,* p. 349.

12. Ives, *A History of Penal Methods,* p. 53.

13. Henry Burns Jr., *Corrections: Organization and Administration* (St. Paul, MN: West, 1975), p. 86.

14. Barnes and Teeters, *New Horizons,* p. 292.

15. Ives, *A History of Penal Methods,* p. 56.

16. John Howard, *The State of the Prisons* (London: J. M. Dent, 1929).

17. Spierenburg, "The Body and the State," p. 53.

18. Burns, *Corrections,* p. 87.

19. Spierenburg, "The Body and the State," p. 62.

20. See Abbott Emerson Smith, *Colonists in Bondage* (Chapel Hill: University of North Carolina Press, 1947).

21. For a good account of the practice, see Robert Hughes, *The Fatal Shore: The Epic of Australia's Founding* (New York: Vintage Books, 1988).

22. James Trager, *The People's Chronology* (New York Henry Holt, 1994).

23. See Aleksandr Solzhenitsyn, *The Gulag Archipelago, 1918–1956* (1974) and *The Gulag Archipelago* 2 and 3 (1975, 1978).

24. Barnes and Teeters, *New Horizons,* p. 293.

25. Norman Johnson, "Evolving Function: Early Use of Imprisonment as Punishment," *The Prison Journal,* Supplement to vol. 89, no. 1 (March 2009), pp. 10S–34S.

26. Peters, "Prison Before the Prison," p. 7.

27. Johnson, "Evolving Function: Early Use of Imprisonment as Punishment," p. 14S.

28. Spierenburg, pp. 49–77.

29. Ibid., p. 67.

30. Johnson, "Evolving Function: Early Use of Imprisonment as Punishment," p. 14S.

31. Ibid., p. 72.

32. Randall McGowen, "The Well-Ordered Prison," in Norval Morris and David J. Rothman (eds.), *The Oxford History of the Prison* (New York: Oxford University Press, 1995), p. 83.

33. *Gazette d'Amsterdam,* p. 11.

34. See Wood and Waite, *Crime and Its Treatment,* p. 463.

35. Harry Elmer Barnes, *The Repression of Crime* (New York: Doran, 1926), p. 101.

36. John Howard, *The State of the Prisons in England and Wales* (London: William Eyres, 1777).

37. Spierenburg, "The Body and the State," pp. 49–77.

38. McGowen, "The Well-Ordered Prison," p. 86.

39. "Enlightenment, Age of," *Microsoft Encarta 96, CD-ROM* (Redmond, WA: Microsoft Corporation, 1995).

40. Ibid.

41. Some of the information in this section comes from The Nanaimo Region John Howard Society (of Canada) at http://jhsnr.org (accessed October 30, 2011).

42. Howard, *The State of the Prisons.*

43. Randall McGowen, "The Well-Ordered Prison: England 1780–1865," in Norval Morris and David J. Rothman (eds.), *The Oxford History of the Prison* (New York: Oxford University Press, 1995), p. 87.

44. Some of the information in this section comes from *The Internet Encyclopedia of Philosophy,* www.utm.edu/research/iep/ (accessed June 26, 2012).

45. Some of the information in this section comes from the Bentham Project at University College, London, www.ucl.ac.uk/Bentham–Project (accessed October 30, 2011).

46. For further information, see Frank E. Hagan, "Panopticon," in Marilyn D. McShane and Frank P. Williams III (eds.), *Encyclopedia of American Prisons* (New York: Garland, 1996), pp. 341–342.

47. Wood and Waite, *Crime and Its Treatment,* p. 456.

48. From "The Secret of Great Workers," *The Penny Magazine,* vol. 1, no. 1 (March 31, 1832), citing M. Dumont, "Recollections of Mirabeau."

49. See Margaret Wilson, *The Crime of Punishment* (New York: Harcourt Brace, 1931), p. 165.

50. See the All Saints Project, www.klis.com/allsaints/pnotes.htm (accessed October 30, 2011). This site includes input from the Royal Canadian Mounted Police and the Nova Scotia Crime Prevention Association.

51. See Lucia Zedner, "Wayward Sisters: The Prison for Women," in Norval Morris and David J. Rothman (eds.), *The Oxford History of the Prison* (New York: Oxford University Press, 1995).

52. Ibid., p. 333.

53. Ibid., p. 336.

54. Ibid.

55. Sanford Bates, *Prisons and Beyond* (New York: Macmillan, 1936).

56. Rodney Henningson, "Sanford Bates," in Marilyn D. McShane and Frank P. Williams (eds.), *Encyclopedia of American Prisons* (New York: Garland, 1996), pp. 51–53.

57. David M. Horton and George R. Nielsen, *Walking George: The Life of George John Beto and the Rise of the Modern Texas Prison System* (Denton: University of North Texas Press, 2006).

58. Dan Richard Beto, review of Jeremy Travis and Michelle Waul (eds.), *Prisoners Once Removed: The Impact of Incarceration and Reentry on Children, Families, and Communities* (Washington, DC: Urban Institute Press, 2003), in *Federal Probation,* vol. 68, no. 2 (2004), www.uscourts.gov/fedprob/September_2004/bookshelf.html (accessed January 10, 2007).

59. Charles Jeffords and Jan Lindsey, "George J. Beto," in Marilyn D. McShane and Frank P. Williams (eds.), *Encyclopedia of American Prisons* (New York: Garland, 1996), pp. 58–61.

Chapter 3

1. Nicole D. Porter, *The State of Sentencing 2012* (Washington, DC: The Sentencing Project, 2013).

2. John P. Conrad, "The Pessimistic Reflections of a Chronic Optimist," *Federal Probation*, vol. 55, no. 2 (1991), p. 7.

3. Sigmund Freud, *Totem and Taboo*, trans. and ed. by James Strachey (New York: Norton, 1990).

4. Lisa Kennedy, "The Miseducation of Nushawn Williams," *POZ online*, August 2000, www.poz.com/archive/august2000/inside/nushawnwilliams.html (accessed June 20, 2002); Jackie Cooperman, "AIDS Scare Triples in Scope," ABCNEWS.com, October 28, 1997.

5. "'AIDS Monster' Denied Parole in New York," *Austin Chronicle*, August 31, 2001, www.austinchronicle.com/issues/dispatch/2001-08-31/cols_aboutaids.html (accessed June 20, 2002).

6. Andrew von Hirsch, *Doing Justice: The Choice of Punishments* (New York: Hill and Wang, 1976), pp. 48–49.

7. Morgan O. Reynolds, *The Reynolds Report: Crime and Punishment in the U.S.*, NCPA Policy Report No. 209 (Dallas, TX: National Center for Policy Analysis, 1997), www.public-policy.org/~ncpa/studies/s209/s209.html (accessed August 30, 2007).

8. Edwin Zedlewski, *Making Confinement Decisions*, Research in Brief (Washington, DC: National Institute of Justice, 1987).

9. John J. DiIulio, "Crime and Punishment in Wisconsin," *Wisconsin Policy Research Institute Report*, vol. 3, no. 7 (1990), pp. 1–56; see also William Barr, *The Case for More Incarceration* (Washington, DC: U.S. Department of Justice, Office of Policy Development, 1992).

10. Washington State Institute for Public Policy, *Evidence-Based Public Policy Options to Reduce Future Prison Construction, Criminal Justice Costs, and Crime Rates* (Olympia, WA: The Institute, October 2006), p. 10. For a national overview of such data, see William Spelman, "What Recent Studies Do (and Don't) Tell Us About Imprisonment and Crime," in Michael Tonry (ed.), *Crime and Justice: A Review of Research*, vol. 27 (Chicago: University of Chicago Press, 2002), p. 422.

11. R. A. Liedka and B. Useem, "The Crime-Control Effect of Incarceration: Does Scale Matter?" *Criminology and Public Policy*, vol. 5, no. 2 (2006), pp. 245–276. Cited in Howard N. Snyder and Jeanne B. Stinchcomb, "Do Higher Incarceration Rates Mean Lower Crime Rates?" *Corrections Today*, vol. 68 (October 2006), p. 92.

12. Francis T. Cullen and Paul Gendreau, "Assessing Correctional Rehabilitation: Policy, Practice, and Prospects," in Julie Horney (ed.), *Criminal Justice 2000*, vol. 3 (Washington, DC: National Institute of Justice, 2000).

13. Robert Martinson, "What Works? Questions and Answers About Prison Reform," *Public Interest*, vol. 35 (Spring 1974), pp. 22–54.

14. Cullen and Gendreau, "Assessing Correctional Rehabilitation."

15. Edgardo Rotman, *Beyond Punishment: A New View on the Rehabilitation of Criminal Offenders* (Westport, CT: Greenwood, 1990), p. 11.

16. Jack Leonard and Megan Garvey, "Users Kicking Prop. 36, Not Drugs," *Los Angeles Times*, April 01, 2007, page A-1.

17. Christie Gardiner, "Diverted, or Not? A Preliminary Analysis of California's Proposition 36," paper presented at the annual meeting of the American Society of Criminology (ASC), Los Angeles Convention Center, Los Angeles, CA, November 01, 2006.

18. Marty Price, "Crime and Punishment: Can Mediation Produce Restorative Justice for Victims and Offenders?" www.vorp.com/articles/crime.html (accessed February 9, 1999).

19. United Nations, *Restorative Justice: Report of the Secretary-General* (Vienna, Austria: United Nations Commission on Crime Prevention and Criminal Justice, 2002).

20. Graeme Newman, *The Punishment Response* (Philadelphia: Lippincott, 1978), p. 104.

21. See, for example, Andrew R. Klein, *Alternative Sentencing: A Practitioner's Guide* (Cincinnati, OH: Anderson, 1988).

22. Much of what follows is derived from Bureau of Justice Assistance, *National Assessment of Structured Sentencing* (Washington, DC: Bureau of Justice Assistance, 1996).

23. S. A. Shane-DuBow, A. P. Brown, and E. Olsen, *Sentencing Reform in the U.S.: History, Content and Effect* (Washington, DC: U.S. Department of Justice, 1985).

24. J. Cohen and M. H. Tonry, "Sentencing Reforms and Their Impacts," in A. Blumstein et al. (eds.), *Research on Sentencing: The Search for Reform* (Washington, DC: National Academy Press, 1983), pp. 305–459.

25. State of Washington, Sentencing Guidelines Commission, *Adult Sentencing Manual 2000*, www.sgc.wa.gov/adult_sentencing_manual_2000.htm (accessed October 30, 2011).

26. The materials in this section are derived from the website of the United States Sentencing Commission, www.ussc.gov.

27. Title II of the Comprehensive Crime Control Act of 1984; 18 U.S.C. § 3551–3626 and 28 U.S.C. § 991–998.

28. 21 U.S.C. 841(b)(1)(C).

29. *Rita* v. *United States*, U.S. Supreme Court, 551 U.S. 338 (2007).

30. U.S. Sentencing Commission, News Release, "Sentencing Commission Issues Comprehensive Report on the Continuing Impact of *United States* v. *Booker* on Federal Sentencing," January 30, 2013.

31. United States Sentencing Commission, Office of Research and Data, "Memorandum: Analysis of the Impact of Amendment to the Statutory Penalties for Crack Cocaine Offenses Made by the Fair Sentencing Act of 2010," January 28, 2011.

32. USSG §1B1.10, comment.

33. Ibid., p. 15.

34. M. Tonry, *Sentencing Matters* (Oxford, UK: Oxford University Press, 1995).

35. U.S. Department of Justice, *Mandatory Sentencing* (Washington, DC: Office of Justice Programs, 1997).

36. In 1999, California's three-strikes law was upheld by the U.S. Supreme Court in the case of *Riggs* v. *California*, 525 U.S. 1114 (1999) cert. denied.

37. G. L. Pierce and W. J. Bowers, "The Bartley-Fox Gun Law's Short-Term Impact on Crime in Boston," *Annals of the American Academy of Political and Social Science*, vol. 455 (1981), pp. 120–132.

38. C. Loftin, M. Heumann, and D. McDowall, "Mandatory Sentencing and Firearms Violence: Evaluating an Alternative to Gun Control," *Law and Society Review*, vol. 17 (1983), pp. 287–318.

39. C. Loftin and D. McDowall, "The Deterrent Effects of the Florida Felony Firearm Law," *Journal of Criminal Law and Criminology*, vol. 75 (1984), pp. 250–259.

40. D. McDowall, C. Loftin, and B. Wierseman, "A Comparative Study of the Preventive Effects of Mandatory Sentencing Laws for Gun Crimes," *Journal of Criminal Law and Criminology*, vol. 83, no. 2 (Summer 1992), pp. 378–394.

41. Joint Committee on New York Drug Law Evaluation, *The Nation's Toughest Drug Law: Evaluating the New York Experience*, a project of the Association of the Bar of the City of New York, the City of New York, and the Drug Abuse Council, Inc. (Washington, DC: Government Printing Office, 1978).

42. Much of what follows is taken from John Clark, James Austin, and D. Alan Henry, *Three Strikes and You're Out: A Review of State Legislation* (Washington, DC: National Institute of Justice, 1997).

43. Bureau of Justice Assistance, *National Assessment of Structured Sentencing* (Washington, DC: U.S. Department of Justice, February 1996).

44. Elizabeth A. King, "Inter Alia," *Corrections Compendium*, April 2002, p. 22.

45. Several states have had such laws on the books for many years. For example, South Dakota has had three-strikes–type legislation since 1877.

46. James Austin, "'Three Strikes and You're Out': The Likely Consequences on the Courts, Prisons, and Crime in California and Washington State," *St. Louis University Public Law Review,* vol. 14, no. 1 (1994).

47. The Washington law does permit the governor to grant a pardon or clemency, but it also recommends that no person sentenced under this law to life in prison without parole be granted clemency until he or she has reached 60 years of age and is judged no longer a threat to society.

48. *Andrade v. Attorney General of the State of California,* 270 F.3d 743 (2001).

49. *Lockyer v. Andrade,* 538 U.S. 63 (2003).

50. *Ewing v. California,* 538 U.S. 11 (2003).

51. Tracey Kaplan, "Proposition 36: Voters Overwhelmingly Ease Three Strikes Law," *Mercury News,* November 7, 2012.

52. Austin, "'Three Strikes and You're Out.'"

53. Countywide Criminal Justice Coordination Committee, *Impact of the "Three Strikes Law" on the Criminal Justice System in Los Angeles County* (Los Angeles: CCJCC, November 15, 1995).

54. Center for Urban Analysis, Santa Clara County Office of the County Executive, *Comparing Administration of the "Three-Strikes Law" in the County of Los Angeles with Other Large California Counties* (Santa Clara, CA: Center for Urban Analysis, Santa Clara County Office of the County Executive, May 1996).

55. Los Angeles County Sheriff's Department, *"Three Strikes" Law— Impact on Jail: Summary Analysis* (Los Angeles: Los Angeles County Sheriff's Department, August 31, 1996).

56. John Clark et al., *Three Strikes and You're Out: A Review of State Legislation* (Washington, DC: National Institute of Justice, 1997).

57. The California State Auditor, *California Department of Corrections and Rehabilitation: Inmates Sentenced Under the Three Strikes Law and a Small Number of Inmates Receiving Specialty Health Care Represent Significant Costs* (Sacramento, CA: May 2010), p. 1.

58. Ryan S. King and Marc Mauer, *Aging Behind Bars: "Three Strikes" Seven Years Later* (Washington, DC: Sentencing Project, 2001).

59. Ibid.

60. Fox Butterfield, "States Ease Laws on Time in Prison," *The New York Times,* Sept. 2, 2001, www.nytimes.com/2001/09/02/us/states-ease-laws-on-time-in-prison.html (accessed June 25, 2011).

61. Ibid.

62. Ryan S. King, *The State of Sentencing 2008: Developments in Policy and Practice* (Washington: The Sentencing Project, 2009).

63. Connecticut House Bill 5933 (2008); Iowa HF 2393 (2008).

64. The Sentencing Project, "Iowa Governor Signs Nation's First Racial Impact Sentencing Bill" (Washington: The Sentencing Project, 2007), p. 2.

65. Colorado Commission on Criminal and Juvenile Justice, *Annual Report 2012* (Denver, CO: The Commission, 2012).

66. Ibid., p. 8.

67. Edith E. Flynn et al., "Three-Strikes Legislation: Prevalence and Definitions," in National Institute of Justice, *Task Force Reports From the American Society of Criminology* (Washington, DC: National Institute of Justice, 1997).

68. Katherine J. Rosich and Kamala Mallik Kane, "Truth in Sentencing and State Sentencing Practices," *NIJ Journal,* No. 252 (July 2005), http://www.nij.gov/journals/252/sentencing.html (accessed May 1, 2013).

69. Robin I. Lubitz and Thomas W. Ross, "Sentencing Guidelines: Reflections on the Future," *Sentencing and Corrections: Issues for the 21st Century,* no. 10 (Washington, DC: National Institute of Justice, 2001).

70. Edgardo Rotman, *Beyond Punishment: A New View on the Rehabilitation of Criminal Offenders* (Westport, CT: Greenwood Press, 1990), p. 3.

Chapter 4

1. "Gabriela Cortes, Teacher at Roosevelt High School, Arrested for Sexual Relationships With Students," *Huffington Post,* February 23, 2012, www.huffingtonpost.com; "Female High School Teacher Gets 5 Years Probation for Sex With Students," *Daily News* (Los Angeles), January 7, 2013, www.dailynews.com (accessed January 8, 2013).

2. "The Big List: Female Teachers With Students," *WorldNetDaily,* November 26, 2012, www.wnd.com (accessed January 8, 2013).

3. B. J. George, "Screening, Diversion and Mediation in the United States," *New York Law School Law Review,* vol. 29 (1984), pp. 1–38.

4. Doris Layton MacKenzie, *What Works in Corrections: Reducing the Criminal Activities of Offenders and Delinquents* (New York: Cambridge University Press, 2006).

5. National Association of Pretrial Services Agencies, *Pretrial Diversion in the 21st Century: A National Survey of Pretrial Diversion Programs and Practices* (Washington, DC: National Association of Pretrial Services Agencies, 2009).

6. Bradley Schaffer, "Veterans Courts and Diversion Alternatives," *American Jails,* vol. 23, no. 6 (February 2010), pp. 21–24.

7. M. D. Anglin and Y. Hser, "Treatment of Drug Abuse," in Michael Tonry and James Q. Wilson (eds.), *Drugs and Crime: Crime and Justice: A Review of Research,* vol. 13 (Chicago: University of Chicago Press, 1990), pp. 393–460; D. N. Nurco, T. W. Kinlock, and T. E. Hanlon, "The Nature and Status of Drug Abuse Treatment," *Maryland Medical Journal,* vol. 43 (January, 1994), pp. 51–57; D. D. Simpson et al., "A National Evaluation of Treatment Outcomes for Cocaine Dependence," *Archives of General Psychiatry,* vol. 56, no. 6 (1999), pp. 507–514.

8. John Augustus, *A Report of the Labors of John Augustus, for the Last Ten Years, in Aid of the Unfortunate* (Boston: Wright and Hasty, 1852); reprinted as *John Augustus, First Probation Officer* (New York: National Probation Association, 1939), p. 26.

9. Robert Panzarella, "Theory and Practice of Probation on Bail in the Report of John Augustus," *Federal Probation,* vol. 66, no. 3 (December 2002), pp. 38–43.

10. Sanford Bates, "The Establishment and Early Years of the Federal Probation System," *Federal Probation,* vol. 14 (1950), pp. 16–21; Joel R. Moore, "Early Reminiscences," *Federal Probation,* vol. 14 (1950), pp. 21–29; Richard A. Chappell, "The Federal Probation System Today," *Federal Probation,* vol. 14 (1950), pp. 30–40.

11. Laura M. Maruschak and Erika Parks, *Probation and Parole in the United States, 2011* (Washington, DC: Bureau of Justice Statistics, November 2012).

12. Sean Rosenmerkel, Matthew Durose, and Donald Farole, *Felony Sentences in State Courts, 2006—Statistical Tables* (Washington, DC: U.S. Department of Justice, Bureau of Justice Statistics, December 2009), Table 2.4, p. 14.

13. Caroline Wolf Harlow, *Prior Abuse Reported by Inmates and Probationers* (Washington, DC: Department of Justice, Bureau of Justice Statistics, April 1999).

14. Tracey Kyckelhahn, *State Corrections Expenditures, FY 1982-2010* (Washington, DC: Bureau of Justice Statistics, December 2012).

15. "States Imposing More Fees on Inmates and Probationers," *Corrections Journal,* January 23, 2006, p. 7.

16. Barbara Krauth and Larry Link, *State Organizational Structures for Delivering Adult Probation Services* (Washington, DC: U.S. Department of Justice, National Institute of Corrections, June 1999), pp. 3–5.

17. Kathy L. Waters, "Probation, Parole and Community Corrections: A Difficult Topic to Understand?" *Corrections Today*, vol. 65, no. 1 (February 2003), p. 10.

18. Celia Perry, "Probation Profiteers," *Mother Jones*, July/August 2008, www.motherjones.com (accessed February 23, 2013).

19. Ethan Bonner, "Judge in Alabama Halts Private Probation," *The New York Times*, July 13, 2012, www.nytimes.com (accessed February 23, 2013).

20. Steve Aos, Marna Miller, and Elizabeth Drake, *Evidence-Based Adult Corrections Programs: What Works and What Does Not* (Olympia, WA: Washington State Institute for Public Policy, 2006); and Jennifer L. Sheem and Sarah Monchak, "Back to the Future: From Klocklar's Model of Effective Supervision to Evidence-Based Practice in Probation," *Journal of Offender Rehabilitation*, vol. 47, no. 3 (2008), pp. 220–247.

21. Mario Paparozzi and Matthew DeMichele, "Probation and Parole: Overworked, Misunderstood, and Under-Appreciated: But Why?" *The Howard Journal*, vol. 47, no. 3 (July 2008), pp. 275–296.

22. James A. Gondles Jr., "The Probation and Parole System Needs Our Help to Succeed," *Corrections Today*, vol. 65, no. 1 (February 2003), p. 8.

23. Peter Finn and Sarah Kuck, *Stress Among Probation and Parole Officers and What Can Be Done About It* (Washington, DC: U.S. Department of Justice, National Institute of Justice, 2005); see also Kristen R. Lewis, Ladonna S. Lewis, and Tina M. Garby, "Surviving the Trenches: The Personal Impact of the Job on Probation Officers," *American Journal of Criminal Justice*, vol. 38, no. 1 (2013), pp. 67–84.

24. Jeff Holcomb, "The Carrying of Firearms by Probation Officers," paper presented at the annual meeting of the Academy of Criminal Justice Sciences, Cincinnati, Ohio, March 2008; see also Brian Freskos, "Probation Officers' Role Evolving as Law Has Shifted Parole's Focus," *Star News Online* (Wilmington, North Carolina), November 17, 2010, www.starnewsonline.com (accessed February 23, 2013).

25. Mark Sanders, "Building Bridges Instead of Walls: Effective Cross-Cultural Counseling," *Corrections Today*, vol. 65, no. 1 (February 2003), pp. 58–59.

26. "Missouri Considers New Sentencing System," *Corrections Compendium*, vol. 29, no. 6 (November/December 2004), p. 39.

27. American Bar Association, *Standards Relating to Sentencing Alternatives and Procedures* (Chicago: American Bar Association, n.d.).

28. Finn and Kuck, *Stress Among Probation and Parole Officers.*

29. American Probation and Parole Association, *Caseload Standards for Probation and Parole* (Lexington, KY: APPA, September 2006), www.appa-net.org (accessed February 23, 2013).

30. Michelle Gaseau, *Mapping to Improve Supervision and Community Corrections*, October 23, 2000, www.corrections.com (accessed October 10, 2011); Jaishankar Karuppannan, "Mapping and Corrections: Management of Offenders with Geographic Information Systems," *Corrections Compendium*, vol. 30, no. 1 (January/February 2005), pp. 7–9, 31–33.

31. Peggy Burke, "Probation and Parole Violations: An Overview of Critical Issues," in Madeline M. Carter (ed.), *Responding to Probation and Parole Violators* (Washington, DC: National Institute of Corrections, April 2001), p. 6.

32. "Leading Officials Issue Plan for 'Reinventing' Probation," *Criminal Justice Newsletter*, vol. 30, no. 7 (April 1, 1999), pp. 1–2.

33. *HOPE in Hawaii: Swift and Sure Changes in Probation* (Washington, DC: National Institute of Justice, June 2008); see also Angela Hawken and Mark Kleiman, *Managing Drug-Involved Probationers with Swift and Certain Sanctions: Evaluating Hawaii's HOPE* (Washington, DC: U.S. Department of Justice, National Institute of Justice, December 2009).

34. Mark Kleiman, "African Americans Suffer from High Rates of Incarceration and Crime: Here's How to Drastically Reduce Both," *Washington Monthly*, January/February 2013, www.washingtonmonthly.com (accessed January 19, 2013).

35. Burke, "Probation and Parole Violations," pp. 5–6.

36. Ibid., p. 5.

Chapter 5

1. Jacob D. H. Feldman, "Coaches Monitor Athletes Online in the Age of Twitter," *The Harvard Crimson*, February 3, 2012, www.thecrimson.com (accessed February 20, 2012).

2. Malcom Young, "Getting Prison Numbers Down—For Good," *The Crime Report*, January 1, 2012, www.thecrimereport.org (accessed January 3, 2012); *On the Chopping Block*, The Sentencing Project (Washington, DC: The Sentencing Project, August 2011); William T. (Bill) Robinson III, "Time Is Right for Criminal Justice Reform," *The Hill's Congress Blog*, October 25, 2011, http://thehill.com/blogs (accessed January 2, 2012); and Carrie Teegardin and Bill Rankin, "Georgia Rethinks Its Prison Stance," *Atlantic Journal-Constitution*, January 3, 2012, www.ajc.com (accessed January 3, 2012).

3. See, for example, "Changing Public Attitudes Toward the Criminal Justice System" www.soros.org/initiatives/usprograms/focus/justice/articles_publications/publications/hartpoll_20020201 (accessed February 17, 2013); Marc Mauer, *Race to Incarcerate* (New York: Free Press, 2006), p. 13; Frank T. Cullen and Brenda A. Vose, "Public Support for Early Intervention: Is Child Saving a Habit of the Heart?" *Victims and Offenders*, vol. 2, no. 2 (2007), pp. 109–124; "The UConnPoll: Prison Crowding," University of Connecticut, Center for Survey Research and Analysis, March 8, 2004.

4. William H. DiMascio, *Seeking Justice: Crime and Punishment in America* (New York: Edna McConnell Clark Foundation, 1997), p. 43.

5. Pew Center on the States, "Public Attitudes on Crime and Punishment," www.pewcenteronthestates.org, September 2010 (accessed January 5, 2011); Pew Center on the States, "Public Opinion on Sentencing and Corrections Policy in America," www.pewcenteronthestates.org, March 2012 (accessed February 18, 2013).

6. Michael Tonry and Mary Lynch, "Intermediate Sanctions," in Michael Tonry (ed.), *Crime and Justice: A Review of Research*, vol. 20 (Chicago: University of Chicago Press, 1996), pp. 102–103.

7. Camille Graham Camp and George M. Camp, *Adult Corrections Yearbook* (Middletown, CT: Criminal Justice Institute, 2001), p. 170.

8. Betsy A. Fulton, Susan Stone, and Paul Gendreau, *Restructuring Intensive Supervision Programs: Applying What Works* (Lexington, KY: American Probation and Parole Association, 1994).

9. Doris Layton MacKenzie, "Evidence-Based Corrections: Identifying What Works," *Crime & Delinquency*, vol. 46, no. 4 (October 2000), pp. 457–472.

10. Doris Layton MacKenzie, *What Works in Corrections: Reducing the Criminal Activities of Offenders and Delinquents* (New York: Cambridge University Press, 2006), p. 322; and Steve Aos, Marna Miller, and Elizabeth Drake, *Evidence-Based Public Policy Options to Reduce Future Prison Construction, Criminal Justice*

Costs, and Crime Rates (Olympia, WA: State Institute for Public Policy, 2006), p. 6.

11. Joan Petersilia, Arthur J. Lurigio, and James M. Byrne, "Introduction," in James M. Byrne, Arthur J. Lurigio, and Joan Petersilia (eds.), *Smart Sentencing: The Emergence of Intermediate Sanctions* (Newbury Park, CA: Sage, 1992), pp. ix–x; Elizabeth Deschenes, Susan Turner, and Joan Petersilia, *Intensive Community Supervision in Minnesota: A Dual Experiment in Prison Diversion and Enhanced Supervised Release* (Washington, DC: National Institute of Justice, 1995); Joan Petersilia and Susan Turner, *Evaluating Intensive Supervision Probation/Parole: Results of a Nationwide Experiment* (Washington, DC: National Institute of Justice, May 1993).

12. Aos, Miller, and Drake, *Evidence-Based Public Policy Options.*

13. "Washington State Researchers Rates What Works in Treatment," *Criminal Justice Newsletter*, September 1, 2006, p. 2.

14. See http://crimesolutions.gov (accessed February 19, 2013).

15. "Washington State Researchers Rates What Works in Treatment," *Criminal Justice Newsletter.*

16. National Association of Drug Court Professionals, www.nadcp.org/whatis/ (accessed January 15, 2011).

17. Nastassia Walsh, *Addicted to Courts: How a Growing Dependence on Drug Courts Impacts People and Communities* (Washington, DC: Justice Policy Institute, March 2011), p. 2.

18. Ibid., p. 4.

19. "Types of Drug Courts," National Association of Drug Court Professionals, www.nadcp.org (accessed February 19, 2013).

20. Oralandar Brand-Williams, "Specialized Court Helps Out Troubled Veterans," *Detroit News*, November 27, 2012, www.detroitnews.com (accessed November 28, 2012).

21. Aos, Miller, and Drake, *Evidence-Based Public Policy Options*; Christopher T. Lowenkamp, Alexander M. Holsinger, and Edward J. Latessa, "Are Drug Courts Effective: A Meta-Analytic Review," *Journal of Community Corrections*, vol. 28 (Fall 2005), pp. 5–10; Deborah Koetzle Shaffer, *Reconsidering Drug Court Effectiveness: A Meta-Analytic Review* (Las Vegas, NV: Department of Criminal Justice, University of Nevada, 2006); David B. Wilson, Ojmarrh Mitchell, and Doris Layton MacKenzie, "A Systematic Review of Drug Court Effects on Recidivism," *Journal of Experimental Criminology*, vol. 2, no. 4 (November 2006), pp. 459–487; Doris Layton MacKenzie, *What Works in Corrections: Reducing the Criminal Activities of Offenders and Delinquents*, pp. 221–240.

22. See http://crimesolutions.gov/TopicDetails.aspx?ID=49 (accessed February 18, 2013).

23. Aos, Miller, and Drake, *Evidence-Based Public Policy Options.*

24. "Drug Courts Unavailable to Most," *Corrections Today*, vol. 71, no. 6 (December 2009), p. 16; and Sam Hananel, "Drug Courts Successful for Few Who Get It," *The Washington Post*, November 30, 2009, www.washingtonpost.com (accessed February 18, 2013).

25. Bureau of Justice Assistance, *How to Use Structured Fines (Day Fines) as an Intermediate Sanction* (Washington, DC: Department of Justice, November 1996).

26. "Finn's Speed Fine Is a Bit Rich," MSNBC online, http://news.bbc.co.uk/2/hi/business/3477285.stm (accessed January 6, 2011); "Sentencing Law and Policy," May 12, 2009 and December 1, 2009, sentencing.typepad.com (accessed February 18, 2013).

27. Bureau of Justice Assistance, *How to Use Structured Fines.*

28. Aos, Miller, and Drake, *Evidence-Based Public Policy Options*, p. 9.

29. Michael Tonry, "Parochialism in U.S. Sentencing Policy," *Crime & Delinquency*, vol. 45, no. 1 (1999), p. 58.

30. DiMascio, *Seeking Justice*, pp. 43–45.

31. Ibid., p. 37.

32. Dale G. Parent et al., *Day Reporting Centers* (Washington, DC: National Institute of Justice, 1995).

33. Dale Parent, "Day Reporting Centers: An Emerging Intermediate Sanction," *Overcrowded Times*, vol. 2 (1991), pp. 6, 8; Jack McDevitt and Robyn Miliano, "Day Reporting Centers: An Innovative Concept in Intermediate Sanctions," in James M. Byrne, Arthur J. Lurigio, and Joan Petersilia (eds.), *Smart Sentencing: The Emergence of Intermediate Sanctions* (Newbury Park, CA: Sage, 1992).

34. Liz Marie Marciniak, "The Addition of Day Reporting to Intensive Supervision Probation: A Comparison of Recidivism Rates," *Federal Probation*, vol. 64, no. 1 (June 2000), pp. 34–39.

35. Ibid., p. 37.

36. Roy Sudipto, "Adult Offenders in a Day Reporting Center—A Preliminary Study," *Federal Probation*, vol. 66, no. 1 (June 2002), pp. 44–51.

37. Christine Martin, Arthur J. Lurigio, and David E. Olson, "An Examination of Rearrests and Reincarcerations Among Discharged Day Reporting Center Clients," *Federal Probation*, vol. 67, no. 1 (June 2003), pp. 24–31.

38. "New Study Reveals Franklin County Day Reporting Center Reaps Rewards for Counties," Franklin County, PA, January 6, 2011, www.co.franklin.pa.us (accessed February 15, 2011).

39. Kathrine Johnson, "States' Use of GPS Offender Tracking Systems," *Journal of Offender Monitoring*, vol. 15, no. 2 (Summer/Fall 2002), pp. 15, 21–22, 26; Katharine Mieszkowski, "Tracking Sex Offenders with GPS," www.salon.com/news/feature/2006/12/19/offenders/index_np.htm (accessed February 20, 2013).

40. Robert S. Gable and Kirkland R. Gable, "The Practical Limitations and Positive Potential of Electronic Monitoring, *Corrections Compendium*, vol. 32, no. 5 (September/October 2007); *SC v. Dykes*, No. 27124 (S.C. May 9, 2012). p. 6.

41. Pew Charitable Trusts, *Public Safety, Public Spending: Forecasting America's Prison Population 2007–2011* (Philadelphia, PA: Pew Charitable Trusts, 2007).

42. Robert S. Gable and Kirkland R. Gable, "The Practical Limitations and Positive Potential of Electronic Monitoring," p. 6.

43. Darren Gowen, "Overview of the Federal Home Confinement Program, 1988–1996," *Federal Probation*, vol. 64, no. 2 (December 2000), pp. 11–18; see also Brian K. Payne and Randy R. Gainey, "The Electronic Monitoring of Offenders Released from Jail or Prison: Safety, Control, and Comparisons to the Incarceration Experience," *The Prison Journal*, vol. 84, no. 4 (December 2004), pp. 413–435.

44. William Bales, Karen Mann, Thomas Blomberg, Gerry Gaes, Kelle Barrick, Karla Dhungana, and Brian McManus, *A Quantitative and Qualitative Assessment of Electronic Monitoring* (Washington, DC: U.S. Department of Justice, National Institute of Justice, January 2011).

45. Layton MacKenzie, *What Works in Corrections*, p. 322.

46. Ibid., p. 335; see also William D. Burrell and Robert S. Gable, "From B.F. Skinner to Spiderman to Martha Stewart: The Past, Present and Future of Electronic Monitoring of Offenders," *Journal of Offender Rehabilitation*, vol. 46, no. 3/4 (2008), pp. 101–118.

47. Nancy Hicks, "A New Relationship: Halfway Houses and Corrections," *Corrections Compendium*, vol. 12, no. 4 (October 1987), pp. 1, 5–8.

48. Camp and Camp, *Adult Corrections Yearbook*, p. 124.

49. "Weekly Population Report," www.bop.gov (accessed February 20, 2013)

50. Dan Morse, "Arenas Arrives at Halfway House to Serve Sentence," *The Washington Post*, April 11, 2010, www.washingtonpost.com (accessed January 7, 2011); and A. J. Perez, "Gilbert Arenas Sentenced to 30 days in Halfway House," *NBA Fanhouse*, March 29, 2010, nba.fanhouse.com (accessed January 7, 2011).

51. Division of Criminal Justice, Office of Research and Statistics, *Executive Summary: 2000 Community Corrections Study Results* (Denver: State of Colorado, Division of Criminal Justice, Office of Research and Statistics, March 22, 2001), www.cdpsweb.state .co.us/ors/docs.htm (accessed February 20, 2013).

52. Christopher T. Lowenkamp and Edward J. Latessa, "Developing Successful Reentry Programs: Lessons Learned from the 'What Works' Research," *Corrections Today*, vol. 67, no. 2 (April 2005), pp. 72–77; and "Halfway Houses Seen as Way to Cut Prison Costs in Ohio," www.cleveland.com/metro (accessed February 20, 2013).

53. Aos, Miller, and Drake, *Evidence-Based Public Policy Options*.

54. Steve Schultze, "Clarke Drops Plan for Early Prisoner Release," *Journal Sentinel* (Milwaukee, WI), January 27, 2010, www.json-line.com; and Steve Schultze, "Milwaukee County's Inmate Training Program Raising Concerns," *Journal Sentinel* (Milwaukee, WI), December 5, 2010, www.jsonline.com (accessed February 21, 2013).

55. Merry Morash and Lila Rucker, "Critical Look at the Ideal of Boot Camp as Correctional Reform," *Crime & Delinquency*, vol. 36 (1990), pp. 204–222; DiMascio, *Seeking Justice*, p. 41.

56. Doris L. MacKenzie and J. W. Shaw, "The Impact of Shock Incarceration on Technical Violations and New Criminal Activities," *Justice Quarterly*, vol. 10, no. 3 (1993), pp. 463–486.

57. Dionne T. Wright and G. Larry Mays, "Correctional Boot Camps, Attitudes, and Recidivism: The Oklahoma Experience," *Journal of Offender Rehabilitation*, vol. 28, no. 1/2 (1998), pp. 71–87.

58. Jeanne B. Stinchcomb and W. Clinton Terry III, "Predicting the Likelihood of Rearrest Among Shock Incarceration Graduates: Moving Beyond Another Nail in the Boot Camp Coffin," *Crime & Delinquency*, vol. 47, no. 2 (April 2001), pp. 221–242.

59. See, for example Cheryl L. Clark and David W. Aziz, "Shock Incarceration in New York State: Philosophy, Results, and Limitations," in Doris L. MacKenzie and Eugene E. Hebert (eds.), *Correctional Boot Camps: A Tough Intermediate Sanction* (Washington, DC: National Institute of Justice, 1996), pp. 38–68; MacKenzie and Hebert, *Correctional Boot Camps*; Parent, *Correctional Boot Camps*.

60. Dale Parent, "Boot Camps Failing to Achieve Goals," *Over-crowded Times*, vol. 5 (1994), pp. 8–11; Doris Layton MacKenzie, "Boot Camps: A National Assessment," *Overcrowded Times*, vol. 5 (1994), pp. 14–18; Philip A. Ethridge and Jonathan R. Sorensen, "An Analysis of Attitudinal Change and Community Adjustment Among Probationers in a County Boot Camp," *Journal of Contemporary Criminal Justice*, vol. 13, no. 2 (May 1992), pp. 139–154.

61. W. J. Dickey, *Evaluating Boot Camp Prisons* (Washington, DC: National Institute of Justice, 1994); Peter Katel and Melinda Liu, "The Bust in Boot Camps," *Newsweek*, February 21, 1994, p. 26; Parent, "Boot Camps Failing to Achieve Goals."

62. Doris L. MacKenzie and Claire Souryal, *Multi-Site Evaluation of Shock Incarceration: Executive Summary* (Washington, DC: National Institute of Justice, 1994); see also Doris L. MacKenzie and A. Piquero, "The Impact of Shock Incarceration Programs on Prison Crowding," *Crime & Delinquency*, vol. 40 (1994), pp. 222–249.

63. Wilson Ring, "Study: Novel Sentencing Program Really Works," www.rulandherald.com (accessed February 21, 2013).

64. Pew Center on the States, *One in 31: The Long Reach of American Corrections* (New York: Pew Charitable Trusts, March 2009), p. 3.

65. Ibid., pp. 23–30.

66. Christopher Hartney and Susan Marchionna, *Attitudes of U.S. Voters Toward Nonserious Offenders and Alternatives to Incarceration* (Oakland, CA: National Council on Crime and Delinquency, June 2009).

67. George F. Cole et al., *The Practice and Attitudes of Trial Court Judges Regarding Fines as a Criminal Sanction* (Washington, DC: National Institute of Justice, 1987).

Chapter 6

1. Jon Gambrell and Christopher Torchia, "Oscar Pistorius Free on Bail Ahead of Murder Trial; Questions in Girlfriend's Death Linger," *StarTribune*, February 22, 2013, http://www.startribune. com/world/192486001.html (accessed February 22, 2013); "Oscar Pistorius Freed on Bail in Murder Case," *CBS News*, February 22, 2013, www.cbsnews.com (accessed February 22, 2013).

2. Melissa Neal, *Bail Fail: Why the U.S. Should End the Practice of Using Money for Bail* (Washington, DC: Justice Policy Institute, 2012), p. 10.

3. Ibid., p. 23.

4. Ibid., p. 17.

5. Ibid., p. 15.

6. American Bar Association, *ABA Standards for Criminal Justice: Pretrial Release, 3rd Edition* (Chicago, IL: 2007).

7. Ted Gest, "A Call for Reforming the Nation's Costly Pretrial Detention System," *The Crime Report*, www.thecrimereport.com (accessed June 21, 2011).

8. Melissa Neal, *Bail Fail*, p. 13.

9. Ibid., p. 21.

10. Jonathan Lippman, *2013 State of the Judiciary, Let Justice Be Done* (Albany, NY: Court of Appeals Hall, 2013), pp. 5–6.

11. Shima Baradaran and Frank McIntyre, "Predicting Violence," *Texas Law Review*, vol. 90 (2012): 497–570.

12. As cited in Neal, *Bail Fail*, p. 27.

13. Alex Piquero, "Cost-Benefit Analysis for Jail Alternatives and Jail." Prepared for the Broward Sheriff's Office, Department of Community Control (Tallahassee, FL: Florida State University, College of Criminology and Criminal Justice, October 2010).

14. As cited in Melissa Neal, *Bail Fail*, p. 31.

15. Michael O'Toole, "Jails and Prisons: The Numbers Say They Are More Different Than Generally Assumed," *American Jails*, www. corrections.com/aja/mags/articles/toole.html (accessed March 7, 2013); see also Daron Hall, "Jails vs. Prisons," *Corrections Today*, vol. 68, no. 1 (February 2006) p. 8.

16. Todd D. Minton, *Jail Inmates at Midyear 2012—Statistical Tables* (Washington, DC: Bureau of Justice Statistics, May 2013).

17. Doris J. James, *Profile of Jail Inmates, 2002* (Washington, DC: U.S. Department of Justice, Bureau of Justice Statistics, July 2004); and Allen J. Beck, "What Do We Know About Jails at the National Level?" Presentation at the Jail Reentry Roundtable, Urban Institute, Washington, DC, June 27, 2006.

18. National Advisory Commission on Criminal Justice Standards and Goals, *Corrections* (Washington, DC: U.S. Government Printing Office, 1973), p. 273.

19. Marilyn D. McShane and Frank P. Williams III (eds.), *Encyclopedia of American Prisons* (New York: Garland, 1996), p. 494.

20. Ibid., p. 496.

21. David M. Parrish, "The Evolution of Direct Supervision in the Design and Operation of Jails," *Corrections Today*, www .corrections.com/aca/cortoday/october00/parrish.html (accessed March 7, 2013).

22. Linda Zupan, *Jails: Reform and the New Generation Philosophy* (Cincinnati, OH: Anderson, 1991); see also Richard Wener, "The Invention of Direct Supervision," *Corrections Compendium*, vol. 30, no. 2 (March/April, 2005), pp. 4–7, 32–34.

23. Brandon K. Applegate and Eugene A. Paoline III, "Jail Officers' Perceptions of the Work Environment in Traditional Versus New Generation Facilities," *American Journal of Criminal Justice,* vol. 31 (2007), pp. 64–80.

24. Dennis McCave, "Testing the Seams: When the Limits Are Pushed in Direct Supervision," *American Jails,* vol. 16, no. 1 (2002), pp. 51–56.

25. Peter Perroncello, "Direct Supervision: A 2001 Odyssey," *American Jails,* vol. 15, no. 6 (2001), p. 25. See also Constance Clem et al., *Direct Supervision Jails: 2006 Sourcebook* (Longmont, CO: National Institute of Corrections Information Center, September 2006); Christine Tartaro, "Are They Really Direct Supervision Jails? A National Study," *American Jails,* vol. 20, no. 5 (November/December 2006), pp. 9–17.

26. Ken Kerle, "Jail Statistics: The Need for Public Education," *American Jails* (September/October 2006), p. 5.

27. Doris J. James, *Profile of Jail Inmates, 2002* (Washington, DC: U.S. Department of Justice, Bureau of Justice Statistics, July 2004).

28. James Austin, Luiza Chan, and Williams Elms, *Women Classification Study—Indiana Department of Corrections* (San Francisco, CA: National Council on Crime and Delinquency, 1993).

29. James, *Profile of Jail Inmates, 2002;* see also Gail Elias and Kenneth Ricci, *Women in Jail: Facility Planning Issues* (Washington, DC: U.S. Department of Justice, National Institute of Corrections, March 1997).

30. Tim Brennan and James Austin, *Women in Jail: Classification Issues* (Washington, DC: U.S. Department of Justice, National Institute of Corrections, March 1997).

31. Merry Morash, Timothy S. Bynum, and Barbara A. Koons, *Women Offenders: Programming Needs and Promising Approaches* (Washington, DC: U.S. Department of Justice, National Institute of Justice, August 1998).

32. William C. Collins and Andrew W. Collins, *Women in Jail: Legal Issues* (Washington, DC: U.S. Department of Justice, National Institute of Corrections, December 1996).

33. Rich Lord, "ACLU Study Faults Jails on Women's Health Care," *Pittsburgh Post-Gazette,* February 16, 2012, www.post-gazette.com (accessed February 22, 2012).

34. Kenneth Kerle, "Women in the American World of Jails: Inmates and Staff," *Margins: Maryland's Law Journal on Race, Religion, Gender, and Class,* vol. 2, no. 1 (Spring 2002), pp. 41–61.

35. Barbara Bloom, Barbara Owen, and Stephanie Covington, *Gender-Responsiveness Strategies Research, Practice, and Guiding Principles for Women Offenders* (Washington, DC: U.S. Department of Justice, National Institute of Corrections, June 2003); Tara Gray, G. Larry Mays, and Mary K. Stohr, "Inmate Needs and Programming in Exclusively Women's Jails," *Prison Journal,* vol. 75, no. 2 (1995), pp. 186–195.

36. Samuel Walker, Cassia Spohn, and Miriam DeLone, "Corrections: A Picture in Black and White," in Tara Gray (ed.), *Exploring Corrections* (Boston: Allyn & Bacon, 2002), pp. 13–24.

37. Michael Tonry, *Malign Neglect* (New York: Oxford University Press, 1995); *Targeting Blacks: Drug Law Enforcement and Race in the United States* (New York: Human Rights Watch, 2008); and Ryan S. King, *Disparity by Geography : The War on Drugs in America's Cities* (Washington, DC: The Sentencing Project, 2008).

38. Walker, Spohn, and DeLone, "Corrections," p. 16.

39. Doris J. James and Lauren E. Glaze, *Mental Health Problems of Prison and Jail Inmates* (Washington, DC: U.S. Department of Justice, Bureau of Justice Statistics, September 2006).

40. Henry J. Steadman, Fred C. Osher, Pamela Clark Robbins, Brian Case, and Steven Samuels, "Prevalence of Serious Mental Illness Among Jail Inmates," *Psychiatric Services,* vol. 60, no. 6 (June 2009), pp. 761–765.

41. Ibid.; see also Liz Lipton, "Few Safeguards Govern Elimination of Psychiatric Beds," *Psychiatric News,* vol. 36, no. 15 (August 3, 2001), p. 9, http://pn.psychiatriconline.org/cgi/content/full/36/15/9 (accessed January 13, 2011).

42. Sally Satel, "Out of the Asylum, Into the Cell," *The New York Times,* November 1, 2003, www.psychlaws.org/GeneralResources/article199.htm (accessed January 13, 2007); Bazelon Center for Mental Health Law, "Lawsuit Alleges Civil Rights Violations in Cook County Jail," August 12, 2003, www.bazelon.org/newsroom/archive/2003/8-12-03cookcounty (accessed January 13, 2011).

43. Amanda Petterati and Nastassia Walsh, *Moving Target: A Decade of Resistance to the Prison Industrial Complex* (Washington, DC: Justice Policy Institute, 2008), p. 4.

44. James A. Gondles, "The Mentally Ill Don't Belong in Jail," *Corrections Today,* vol. 67, no. 2 (April 2005), p. 6.

45. Lance Couturier, Frederick Maue, and Catherine McVey, "Releasing Inmates with Mental Illness and Co-occurring Disorders into the Community," *Corrections Today,* vol. 67, no. 2 (April 2005).

46. Jack Leonard and Robert Faturechi, "L. A. County Jailers More Likely to Use Force on Mentally Ill Inmates," *Los Angeles Times,* January 11, 2012, latimes.com (accessed January 20, 2012).

47. Kenneth E. Kerle, *Exploring Jail Operations* (Hagerstown, MD: American Jail Association, 2003), p. 31.

48. Ray Bynum, Gerald Milan, Daniel W. Phillips III, and Barbara Weber, "Mental Health Education and Corrections," *American Jails,* vol. 22, no. 4 (September/October, 2008), pp. 23–29.

49. Margaret Noonan, *Mortality in Local Jails and State Prisons, 2000–2011, Statistical Tables* (Washington, DC: Bureau of Justice Statistics, December 2012).

50. Margaret Noonan, *Mortality in Local Jails, 2000–2006* (Washington, DC: U.S. Department of Justice, Bureau of Justice Statistics, July 2010). Christina Tartaro and Rick Ruddell, "Trouble in Mayberry: A National Analysis of Suicides and Attempts in Small Jails," *American Journal of Criminal Justice,* vol. 31, no. 1 (2006), pp. 81–100; see also Rick Ruddell and G. Larry Mays "Expand or Expire: Jails in Rural America," *Corrections Compendium,* vol. 31, no. 6 (November/December 2006) pp. 1–2, 4–5, 20–21, 27.

51. Connie Milligan and Ray Sabbatine, "From Public Crisis to Innovation—The Mental Health Crisis Network," *American Jails,* vol. 21, no. 6 (January/February 2008), pp. 9–14.

52. Allen J. Beck and Paige M. Harrison, *Sexual Victimization in Prisons and Jails Reported by Inmates, 2008–09* (Washington, DC: U.S. Department of Justice, Bureau of Justice Statistics, August 2010).

53. Allen J. Beck and Paige M. Harrison, *Sexual Victimization in Local Jails Reported by Inmates, 2007* (Washington, DC: U.S. Department of Justice, Bureau of Justice Statistics, June 2008), p. 2.

54. G.J. Mazza, *Report on Sexual Victimization in Prisons and Jails: Review Panel on Prison Rape* (Washington, DC: Department of Justice, April 2012).

55. James J. Stephan and Georgette Walsh, *Census of Jails, 2006* (Washington, DC: U.S. Department of Justice, Bureau of Justice Statistics, December 2011).

56. Ibid., p. 14.

57. American Correctional Association, *Vital Statistics in Corrections,* p. 26.

58. Niyi Awofeso, "Measuring and Evaluating Quality of Health Care Services in Prisons and Jails," *American Jails,* vol. 22, no. 3 (July/August, 2008), pp. 35–38.

59. Kevin Krause, "Dallas County to Begin Charging Jail Inmates for Medical Care," *The Dallas Morning News,* February 21, 2012, www.dallasnews.com (accessed February 23, 2012).

60. Jennifer Medina, "In California, A Plan to Charge Inmates for Their Stay," *The New York Times,* December 11, 2011, www.nytimes.com (accessed December 13, 2011).

61. Michael L. Birzer and Delores Craig-Moreland, "Why Do Jails Charge Housing Fees?" *American Jails*, vol. 20, no. 1 (March/April 2006), pp. 63–68; Laura Bauer, "Some Inmates Pay for Their Crimes and Jail Stays," www.kansascity.com (accessed February 23, 2012); Tracy Loew, "Debt to Society Costs Some Inmates $60 a Night," www.usatoday.com (accessed February 22, 2012).

62. Joann Brown Morton, "Providing Gender-Responsiveness Services for Women and Girls," *Corrections Today*, vol. 69, no. 4 (August 2007), pp. 6, 12.

63. Kevin Krause, "Dallas County to Begin Charging Jail Inmates for Medical Care."

64. Stephanie Simon, "Jailbirds Order Up Hot Wings," *Wall Street Journal*, April 27, 2010, http://online.wsj.com (accessed March 11, 2013); see also, Alan Feuer, "The Cellblocks Amazon.com," *The New York Times*, November 1, 2013, www.nytimes.com (accessed November 2, 2013).

65. Jennifer Steinhauer, "For $82 a Day, Booking a Cell in a 5-Star Jail," *The New York Times*, April 29, 2007, www.nytimes.com (accessed March 11, 2013); Jennifer Steinhauer, "Some Jails Let Prisoners Pay to Stay in Nicer Surroundings," *The San Diego Union-Tribune*, April 29, 2007, www.signonsandiego.com (accessed March 11, 2013); Larry Welborn and Eric Carpenter, "Jaramillo Wants to Pay for Jail," *The Orange County Register*, March 3, 2007, www.ocregister.com (accessed March 11, 2013). See also the Web sites of the Huntington Beach (CA) police department, Torrence (CA) police department, and Santa Ana (CA) police department. Beverly Hills Police Department opened its pay to stay jail in late 2009.

66. Alex Doobuzinskis, "$85-a-Night Jail a Hit With L.A.'s Celebrity Convicts," www.prisonlegalnews.org (accessed March 11, 2013).

67. National Sheriff's Association, *The State of Our Nation's Jails, 1982* (Washington, DC: National Sheriff's Association, 1982).

68. Kerle, "Women in the American World of Jails."

69. Stephan and Walsh, *Census of Jails, 2006.*

70. National Sheriff's Association, *The State of Our Nation's Jails.*

71. Ibid., p. 231.

72. Ibid., p. 151.

73. Jason L. Shofner, "5 Tactical Approaches for Recruiting," *American Jails*, vol. 26, no. 2 (May/June 2012), pp. 12–15).

74. Jeanne B. Stinchcomb and Susan W. Campbell, *Jail Leaders Speak: Current and Future Challenges to Jail Operations and Administration* (Washington, DC: U.S. Department of Justice, Bureau of Justice Statistics, 2008).

75. Susan W. McCampbell, "Priorities of the Day," *American Jails*, vol. 26, no. 6 (January/February 2013), pp. 15–19.

76. As cited in National Institute of Corrections, *Briefing Paper: Trends in Jail Privatization* (Boulder, CO: National Institute of Corrections Information Center, February 1992).

77. Christine Tartaro and Marissa P. Levy, "Factors Associated with Recidivism among Reentry Program Participants in the Jail Setting: Results and Recommendations," in Matthew S. Crow and John Ortiz Smykla, *Offender Reentry: Rethinking Criminology and Criminal Justice* (Boston, MA: Jones & Bartlett, 2014), pp. 125–146.

78. James Parsons, "Addressing the Unique Challenges of Jail Reentry," in Matthew S. Crow and John Ortiz Smykla, *Offender Reentry: Rethinking Criminology and Criminal Justice* (Boston, MA: 2014), pp. 104–123.

79. Doris J. James, *Profile of Jail Inmates, 2002* (Washington, DC: Bureau of Justice Statistics, October 2004), p. 2.

80. Rod Miller, "When Jail Inmates Work Everyone Wins," *American Jails*, vol. 24, no 3 (July/August 2010), pp. 8–16.

81. Pat Nolan, "Prison Fellowship and Faith-Based Initiatives," *On the Line*, vol. 25, no. 5 (November 2002), p. 2.

82. Bryon R. Johnson, David B. Larson, and Timothy C. Pitts, "Religious Programs, Institutional Adjustment, and Recidivism Among Former Inmates in Prison Fellowship Programs," *Justice Quarterly*, vol. 14, no. 1 (March 1997), pp. 145–166; Bryon R. Johnson, "Religious Programs and Recidivism Among Former Inmates in Prison Fellowship Programs: A Long-Term Follow-Up Study," *Justice Quarterly*, vol. 21, no. 2 (June 2004), pp. 329–354.

83. Sheldon Crapo, "Breaking the Cycle of Crime . . . One Life at a Time," *American Jails*, vol. 11, no. 1 (March/April 1997), p. 24.

84. Kenneth E. Kerle, *Exploring Jail Operations*, p. 128.

85. Anthony Colarossi and Willoughby Mariano, "If All Central Florida Jails Rate an A, Is It Deserved?" *Orlando Sentinel*, May 15, 2010, www.orlandosentinel.com (accessed May 20, 2011).

86. American Bar Association, Criminal Justice Section, Report to the House of Delegates, August 21, 2008, www.abanet.org/crimjust/policy/am08104b.pdf-2008-08-21 (accessed January 20, 2011).

87. Kathy Black-Dennis, director of Standards and Accreditation, American Correctional Association (personal communication, February 25, 2011).

88. Peter D. Friedman, Faye S. Taxman, and Craig E. Handerson, "Evidence-Based Treatment Practices for Drug-Involved Adults in the Criminal Justices System," *Journal of Substance Abuse Treatment*, vol. 32, no. 3 (April 2007), pp. 267–277.

89. Ryken Grattet, "Realignment in California: The Story So Far," *The Crime Report*, July 22, 2013, www.thecrimereport.com (accessed July 22, 2013).

Chapter 7

1. Justin Sablich, Ford Fessenden, and Alan McLean, "Timeline: The Penn State Scandal," *The New York Times*, November 11, 2011, www.nytimes.com (accessed April 4, 2013); Bill Chappell, "Penn State Abuse Scandal: Guide and Timeline," *National Public Radio*, June 21, 2012, www.npr.org (accessed April 4, 2013); Associated Press, "Penn State Scandal Timeline: Key Dates in the Jerry Sandusky Sex Abuse Case," *The Huffington Post*, April 4, 2013 (accessed April 4, 2013).

2. E. Ann Carson and Daniela Golinelli, *Prisoners in 2012—Advance Counts* (Washington, DC: U.S. Department of Justice, Bureau of Justice Statistics, July 2013).

3. Roy Walmsley, *World Prison Population List*, 8th ed. (London: Kings College, University of London, January 2009), www.risonstudies.org (accessed April 5, 2013); and Adam Liptak, "Inmate Court in U.S. Dwarfs Other Nations," www.nytimes.com (accessed April 23, 2011).

4. Federal Bureau of Investigation, "Crime in the United States 2011," www.fbi.gov (accessed April 6, 2013); Carson and Sabol, *Prisoners in 2011.*

5. Andrew Coyle, "The Use and Abuse of Prison Around the World," *Corrections Today* (December 2004), pp. 64–67; see also David A. Bowers and Jerold L. Waltman, "Do More Conservative States Impose Harsher Felony Sentences? An Exploratory Analysis of 32 States," *Criminal Justice Review*, vol. 18, no.1 (Spring 1993), pp. 61–70.

6. E. Ann Carson and William J. Sabol, *Prisoners in 2011* (Washington, DC: U.S. Department of Justice, Bureau of Justice Statistics, December 2012); James J. Stephan and Jennifer C. Karberg, *Census of State and Federal Facilities, 2000* (Washington, DC: U.S. Department of Justice, Bureau of Justice Statistics, October 2003); and James J. Stephen, *Census of State and Federal Correctional Facilities, 2005* (Washington, DC: U.S. Department of Justice, Bureau of Justice Statistics, October 2008).

7. Marc Mauer, "Addressing Racial Disparities in Incarceration," *The Prison Journal,* vol. 91, no. 3 (2011), pp. 87–101.

8. Beth R. Richie, "Challenges Incarcerated Women Face as They Return to Their Communities: Findings from Life History Interviews," *Crime & Delinquency,* vol. 47, no. 3 (July 2001), pp. 368–389; and Elaine A. Lord, "The Challenges of Mentally Ill Offenders in Prison," *Criminal Justice and Behavior,* vol. 35, no. 8 (August 2008), pp. 928–942.

9. Meda Chesney-Lind, "Putting the Breaks on the Building Binge," *Corrections Today,* vol. 54, no. 6 (August 1992), p. 30.

10. Marc Mauer and Ryan S. King, *Uneven Justice: State Rates of Incarceration by Race and Ethnicity* (Washington, DC: The Sentencing Project, July 2007), p. 3.

11. Marc Mauer, "Addressing Racial Disparities in Incarceration."

12. Steve Miletich, "Two State Supreme Court Justices Stun Some Listeners with Race Comments," *The Seattle Times,* October 22, 2010, seattletimes.nwsource.com (accessed October 27, 2011).

13. Cassia Spohn, *Thirty Years of Sentencing Reform: The Quest for a Racially Neutral Sentencing Process* (Washington, DC: U.S. Department of Justice, National Institute of Justice, 2000); Phillip Beatty, Amanda Petteruti, and Jason Ziedenberg, *The Vortex: The Concentrated Racial Impact of Drug Imprisonment and the Characteristics of Punitive Counties* (Washington, DC: Justice Policy Institute, 2007); and Ryan S. King, *Disparity by Geography: The War on Drugs in America's Cities* (Washington, DC: The Sentencing Project, May 2008).

14. Steve Aos, Marna Miller, and Elizabeth Drake, *Evidence-Based Public Policy Options to Reduce Future Prison Construction, Criminal Justice Costs, and Crime Rates* (Olympia, WA: State Institute for Public Policy, 2006).

15. Kathleen A. Gnall and Gary Zajac, "Assessing for Success in Offender Reentry," *Corrections Today,* vol. 67, no. 2 (April 2005), p. 94.

16. Carl B. Clements, "The Future of Offender Classification: Some Cautions and Prospects," *Criminal Justice and Behavior,* vol. 8 (1981), pp. 15–16.

17. Carl B. Clements, "Offender Classification: Two Decades of Progress," *Criminal Justice and Behavior,* vol. 23 (1996), p. 123.

18. Patricia L. Hardyman, James Austin, and Johnette Peyton, *Prisoner Intake Systems: Assessing Needs and Classifying Prisoners* (Washington, DC: U.S. Department of Justice, National Institute of Corrections, February 2004), p. viii.

19. J. Alexander et al., *Internal Prison Classification Systems: A Field Test of Three Approaches* (San Francisco, CA: National Council on Crime and Delinquency, 1997).

20. Ibid., p. ix.

21. Hardyman, Austin, and Peyton, *Prisoner Intake Systems: Assessing Needs and Classifying Prisoners, p.* ix.

22. Ibid.

23. Robert B. Levinson, *Unit Management in Prisons and Jails* (Lanham, MD: American Correctional Association, 1999).

24. Melvina Sumter, "Editorial Introduction: Faith Based Prison Programs," *Criminology & Public Policy,* vol. 5, no. 3 (August 2006), pp. 523–528.

25. National Institute of Corrections, *Report of the National Institute of Corrections Advisory Board Hearings: Faith-Based Approach to Correctional Issues* (Washington DC: U.S. Department of Justice, National Institute of Corrections, June 2005).

26. Alexander Volokh, "Do Faith-Based Prisons Work?" *Alabama Law Review,* vol. 63, no. 1 (2011), pp. 48–95.

27. As discussed in Sumter, "Editorial Introduction."

28. Alexander Volokh, "Do Faith-Based Prisons Work?" pp. 44–45.

29. Ibid., p. 45.

30. Elizabeth Prann, "First Veteran Exclusive Jail Dorm Opens," *Fox News,* May 5, 2012, www.foxnews.com (accessed April 7, 2013).

31. Mike Hixenbaugh, "Chesapeake Prison Opens Wing for Military Veterans," *The Virginian Pilot,* December 27, 2012, www.hamptonroads.com (accessed December 29, 2012).

32. Aos, Miller, and Drake, *Evidence-Based Public Policy Options.*

33. Barry Krisberg and Susan Marchionna, *Attitudes of U.S. Voters Toward Prisoner Rehabilitation and Reentry Policies* (San Francisco CA: National Council on Crime and Delinquency, April 2006), www.nccd-crc.org (accessed February 11, 2007).

34. Bureau of Justice Assistance, *Prison Industry Enhancement Certification Program,* www.ojp.usdoj.gov/BJA/grant/piecp.html (accessed April 9, 2013).

35. Cindy J. Smith et al., *Correctional Industries Preparing Inmates for Re-entry: Recidivism and Post-Release Employment* (Washington, DC: U.S. Department of Justice, June 2006).

36. W. Saylor and G. Gaes, *Study of "Rehabilitating" Inmates Through Industrial Work Participation, and Vocational and Apprenticeship Training* (Washington, DC: Federal Bureau of Prisons, 1996); Joseph Summerill, "Congress Continues to Dismantle UNICOR," *Corrections Today,* vol. 67, no. 4 (July 2005) pp. 26–27, 30.

37. "Pathways from Prison to Postsecondary Education Project," A project announcement by the Vera Institute of Justice, New York, 2013.

38. "Inmate Education Programs," *Corrections Compendium,* vol. 33, no. 3 (May/June 2008), p. 9.

39. Anne F. Parkinson and Stephen J. Steurer, "Overcoming the Obstacles in Effective Correctional Instruction," *Corrections Today,* vol. 66, no. 2 (April 2004), pp. 88–91.

40. Jamaal Abdul-Alim, "Exploring the Use of Pell Grants to Go From Prison to College," *Juvenile Justice Information Exchange,* December 10, 2012, www.jjie.org (accessed January 16, 2013).

41. Ibid.

42. Lois M. Davis, Robert Bozick, Jennifer L. Steele, Jessica Saunders, and Jeremy N. V. Miles, *Evaluating the Effectiveness of Correctional Education* (Santa Monica, CA: Rand Corporation, 2013).

43. As quoted in "Justice and Education Departments Announce New Research Showing Prison Education Reduces Recidivism, Saves Money, Improves Employment," U. S. Department of Justice, Office of Public Affairs, Thursday, August 22, 2013.

44. E. Ann Carson and William J. Sabol, *Prisoners in 2011.*

45. Ryan S. King and Marc Mauer, *State Sentencing and Corrections Policy in an Era of Fiscal Constraint* (Washington, DC: The Sentencing Project, 2002).

46. Office of National Drug Control Policy, 2011 Annual Report: Arrestee Drug Abuse Monitoring Program II (Washington, DC: Office of National Drug Control Policy, 2011).

47. The Council of State Governments, *Medicaid and Financing Health Care for Individuals Involved with the Criminal Justice System* (Lexington, KY: The Council of State Governments, December 2013).

48. Michael Ollove, "Ex-Felons Are About to Get Health Coverage," *The Huffington Post,* April 5, 2013, www.huffingtonpost.com (accessed April 5, 2013).

49. Michael S. Vaughn and Leo Carroll, "Separate and Unequal: Prison Versus Free-World Medical Care," *Justice Quarterly,* vol. 15 (1998), pp. 3–40.

50. James J. Stephan, *Census of State and Federal Correctional Facilities, 2005* (Washington, DC: U.S. Department of Justice, Bureau of Justice Statistics, October 2008).

51. "Attorney General Eric Holder Speaks at the 15th Annual National Action Network Convention," April 5, 2013,

www.justice.gov/iso/opa/ag/speeches/2013/ag-speech-130404.
html (accessed April 5, 2013).

52. Excerpted from California and South Dakota's departments of corrections Web sites (accessed April 14, 2013).

53. Stephan, *Census of State and Federal Correctional Facilities 2005*, p. 12; Jon Ortiz, "Fiscal Changes Hit Prison Officers Union Hard," *The Sacramento Bee*, June 28, 2009, www.sacbee.com (accessed April 12, 2013).

54. American Correctional Association, "Correctional Officer Wages and Benefits," *Corrections Compendium*, vol. 35, no. 2 (Summer 2010), pp. 21–39.

55. "The Cost of a Nation of Incarceration," *CBS NEWS Sunday Morning*, www.cbsnews.com, April 22, 2012 (accessed April 24, 2012).

56. *The Continuing Fiscal Crisis in Corrections: Setting a New Course* (New York: Vera Institute of Justice, October 2010), p. 7.

57. Jennifer Gonnerman, "An Expert Analyzes the Prison Population Boom" *Village Voice*, February 22, 2000, p. 56; and Pew Center on the States, *One in 31: The Long Reach in American Corrections* (New York: Pew Charitable Trusts, March 2009), p. 20.

58. Pew Charitable Trusts, *Public Safety, Public Spending: Forecasting America's Prison Population 2007–2011* (Philadelphia: Pew Charitable Trusts, 2007).

59. Vera Institute of Justice, *The Potential of Community Corrections to Improve Safety and Reduce Incarceration* (New York: Vera Institute of Justice, July 2013).

60. Ibid.

61. Pew Charitable Trusts, *Public Safety, Public Spending*.

62. Sources consulted include "States Reduce Prison Spending," *Corrections Compendium*, vol. 34, no. 3 (Fall 2009), p. 32; Judith Greene and Marc Mauer, *Downscaling Prisons: Lessons from Four States* (Washington, DC: The Sentencing Project, 2010); Len Engel, John Larivee, and Richard Luedman, "Reentry and the Economic Crisis: An Examination of Four States and Their Budget Efforts," *Corrections Today*, vol. 71, no. 6 (December 2009), pp. 42–45; *The Continuing Fiscal Crisis in Corrections: Setting a New Course*; Les Zaitz, "Oregon to Close Prison, Lay off 63 Workers in $2.5 Million Budget Cut," www.oregonlive.com, September 30, 2010 (accessed April 15, 2013); Mark Hornbeck, "Michigan Prisons Focus on Released Inmates: Curb Inmate Count, Help Inmates Return to Society, Leader Urges," *Detroit News*, April 27, 2010, www.detnews.com (accessed April 15, 2013); and Tom Beyerlein, "Probation, Parole for Nonviolent Crime Could Save States $15B," *Dayton Daily News*, June 10, 2010, www.daytondailynews.com (accessed April 15, 2013).

63. Nicole D. Porter, *On the Chopping Block 2012: State Prison Closings* (Washington, DC: The Sentencing Project, December 2012) and The Sentencing Project, *Life Goes On: The Historic Rise in Life Sentences in America* (Washington, DC: The Sentencing Project, September 2013).

64. Urban Institute, *The Justice Reinvestment Initiative: Experience from the States* (Washington, DC: Urban Institute, 2012).

65. Nancy LaVigne and Julie Samuels, *The Growth and Increasing Costs of the Federal Prison System: Drivers and Potential Solutions* (Washington, DC: Urban Institute, December 2012), p. 2.

66. E. Ann Carson and Daniella Golinellil, *Prisoners in 2012—Advance Counts*, p. 3.

67. Nathan James, *The Federal Prison Population Buildup: Overview, Policy Changes, Issues, and Options* (Washington, DC: Congressional Research Service, January 22, 2013), p. 22

68. Ibid., p. 4.

69. Nathan James, *The Federal Prison Population Buildup: Overview, Policy Changes, Issues, and Options*, p. 15.

70. Ibid., pp. 36-51.

71. Annual incarceration costs vary by jurisdiction. Federal estimates are provided here. See Nathan James, *The Federal Prison Population Buildup: Overview, Policy Changes, Issues, and Options*, p. 15.

72. Patrick A. Langan and David J. Levin, *Recidivism of Prisoners Released in 1994* (Washington, DC: Bureau of Justice Statistics, June 2002).

73. Pew Center on the States, *State of Recidivism: The Revolving Door of America's Prisons* (Washington, DC: The Pew Charitable Trusts, April 2011), p. 2.

74. Scott Shane, "U.S. Tops World in Prison Population; Overtakes Russia for Dubious Honor," *Arizona Republic*, June 8, 2003, p. A 14.

75. See, for example, series of three articles in *Criminology & Public Policy*, vol. 5, no. 2 (2006), pp. 213–298.

76. Bruce Western, *Punishment and Inequality in America* (New York: Russell Sage Foundation, 2006).

77. Layton MacKenzie, *What Works in Corrections: Reducing the Criminal Activities of Offenders and Delinquents*, p. 340.

Chapter 8

1. Sources consulted include Wayne Chan, "Mandatory Aftercare Scheme to Help Offenders Stay Crime-Free," April 17, 2012, www.channelnewsasia.com (accessed April 21, 2012); International Centre for Prison Studies, www.prisonstudies.org (accessed April 23, 2013); "Mandatory Aftercare Scheme to Help Offenders Stay Crime-Free," www.youtube.com, (accessed April 23, 2013); "Singapore's Crime Rate Drops in First Half," *Yahoo! News*, August 14, 2012, sg.news.yahoo.com (accessed April 23, 2013); and "Singapore—The CIA World Factbook," www.cia.gov (accessed April 23, 2013).

2. Charles L. Newman, *Sourcebook on Probation, Parole and Pardons*, 3rd ed. (Springfield, IL: Charles C. Thomas, 1970), pp. 30–31; see also Norval Morris, *Maconochie's Gentlemen: The Story of Norfolk Island and the Roots of Modern Prison Reform* (New York: Oxford University Press, 2002).

3. Philip Klein, *Prison Methods in New York State* (New York: Columbia University Press, 1920), p. 417. Cited in U.S. Department of Justice, *Attorney General's Survey of Release Procedures*, vol. 4 (Washington, DC: U.S. Government Printing Office, 1939–1940), p. 5. For an excellent history of parole supervision and its relationship to reentry, see Mario Paparozzi and Roger Guy, "Reentry: Parole by Any Other Name" in Matthew S. Crow and John Ortiz Smykla (eds.), *Offender Reentry: Rethinking Criminology and Criminal Justice* (Boston, MA: Jones & Bartlett, 2014), pp. 7–22.

4. G. W. Wickersham, *Reports of the United States National Commission on Law Observance and Enforcement: Wickersham Commission, Report on Penal Institutions, Probation and Parole* (Washington, DC: U.S. Government Printing Office, 1930–1931), p. 324.

5. Ibid., p. 325.

6. Edwin H. Sutherland and Donald R. Cressey, *Principles of Criminology* (Chicago: Lippincott, 1955), p. 568.

7. David J. Rothman, *Conscience and Convenience: The Asylum and Its Alternatives in Progressive America* (Boston: Little Brown, 1980), pp. 159–161.

8. Douglas R. Lipton, Robert Martinson, and Judith Wilks, *The Effectiveness of Correctional Treatment: A Survey of Treatment Evaluation Studies* (New York: Praeger, 1975).

9. Peggy McGarry, *Handbook for New Parole Board Members* (Philadelphia: Center for Effective Public Policy, 1989), p. 4.

10. Patrick A. Langan and David J. Levin, *Recidivism of Prisoners Released in 1994* (Washington, DC: U.S. Department of Justice, Bureau of Justice Statistics, July 2002); see also Pew Charitable Trusts, *Public Safety, Public Spending: Forecasting America's Prison Population 2007–2011* (Philadelphia: Pew Charitable Trusts, 2007); Pew Center on the States, *State of Recidivism: The Revolving Door of America's Prisons* (Washington, DC: The Pew Charitable Trusts, April 2011), p. 2.

11. Heather West and William J. Sabol, *Prisoners in 2007* (Washington, DC: U.S. Department of Justice, Bureau of Justice Statistics, December 2008), Appendix Table 5, p. 17.

12. The Council of State Governments, *The Report of the Re-Entry Policy Council: Charting the Safe and Successful Return of Prisoners to the Community* (Lexington, KY: The Council of State Governments, 2005).

13. Nancy G. La Vigne et al., *Prisoner Reentry and Community Policing Strategies for Enhancing Public Safety* (Washington, DC: Urban Institute, 2006); Marc Mauer and Meda Chesney-Lind (eds.), *Invisible Punishment: The Collateral Consequences of Mass Imprisonment* (New York: The New Press, 2002).

14. Beth E. Richie, "Challenges Incarcerated Women Face as They Return to Their Communities: Findings from Life History Interviews," *Crime & Delinquency,* vol. 47, no. 3 (July 2001), p. 370.

15. Geneva Brown, *The Intersectionality of Race, Gender, and Reentry: Challenges for African-American Women* (Washington, DC: American Constitution Society, November 2010).

16. Theodire M. Hammett, Cheryl Roberts, and Sofia Kennedy, "Health-Realted Issues in Prisoner Reentry," *Crime & Delinquency,* vol. 47, no. 3 (2001), pp. 390-409; U.S. Department of Justice, Office of Justice Programs, Bureau of Justice Statistics, and United States Department of Justice, Federal Bureau of Prisons, *Survey of Inmates in State and Federal Correctional Facilities, 1997* (Ann Arbor, MI: Inter-university Consortium for Political and Social Research, 2001). doi:10.3886/ICPSR02598.v1; Paula M. Ditton, *Mental Health and Treatment of Inmates and Probationers* (Washington, DC: U.S. Department of Justice, Bureau of Justice Statistics, 1999); Caroline Wolf Harlow, *Education and Correctional Populations* (Washington, DC: U.S. Department of Justice, Bureau of Justice Statistics, 2003); Harry J. Holzer, Steven Raphael, and Michael A. Stoll, *Employment Barriers Facing Ex-Offenders* (Washington, DC: The Urban Institute, 2003); *Children with Incarcerated Parents,* Annie E. Casey Foundation, www.aecf.org (accessed May 5, 2013); and Cheryl G. Swanson, Courtney W. Schnippert, and Amanda L. Tryling, "Reentry and Employment: Employers' Willingness to Hire Formerly Convicted Felons in Northwest Florida," in Matthew S. Crow and John Ortiz Smykla (eds.), *Offender Reentry: Rethinking Criminology and Criminal Justice* (Boston, MA: Jones & Bartlett, 2014), pp. 203–224.

17. *Ban the Box: Resource Guide* (New York: National Employment Law Project, August 2013), www.nelp.org (accessed December 17, 2013).

18. The Pew Charitable Trusts, *Collateral Costs: Incarceration's Effect on Economic Mobility* (Washington, DC: The Pew Charitable Trusts, 2010), p. 25; and Josh Farley, "Will the State Bring Back Half-Off Sentences for Good Behavior?" *Kitsap Sun* (Bremerton, WA), October 9, 2010, www.kitsapsun.com (accessed May 7, 2013).

19. "More States Use Risk-Assessment Software in Making Parole Decisions," *The Crime Report,* October 12, 2013, www.thecrimereport.org (accessed October 13, 2013).

20. Jacob Kastrenakes, "Prisons Turn to Computer Algorithms for Deciding Who to Parole," *The Verge,* October 14, 2013, www.theverge.com (accessed October 15, 2013).

21. As quoted in Joseph Walker, "State Parole Boards Use Software to Decide Which Inmates to Release," *The Wall Street Journal,* October 13, 2013, www.wsj.com (accesses October 15, 2013).

22. Ibid.

23. Ibid.

24. Mary West-Smith, Mark R. Pogrebin, and Eric D. Poole, "Denial of Parole: An Inmate Perspective," *Federal Probation,* vol. 63, no. 2 (December 2000).

25. Colleen Long, "Courts Nationwide Hold Hearings With Video," *The Denver Post,* May 8, 2011, www.denverpost.com (accesses May 12, 2011).

26. Alyssa Newcomb, "John Lennon's Killer Mark David Chapman Denied Parole for Seventh Time," *ABC News,* August 23, 2012, abcnews.go.com (accessed August 25, 2012).

27. "Non-Revocable Parole," California Department of Corrections and Rehabilitation, www.cdcr.ca.gov/Parole/Non_Revocable_Parole/index.html (accessed May 8, 2013); Sam Stanton, "Critics Say New California Parole Policy Is Costly, Dangerous," *The Sacramento Bee,* April 12, 2010, www.sacbee.com (accessed May 8, 2013); and John Wilkens, "Inmates Released Under New Law," *The San Diego Union Tribune,* January 26, 2010, www.signonsandiego.com (accessed May 8, 2013).

28. Laura M. Maruschak and Erika Parks, *Probation and Parole in the United States, 2011* (Washington, DC: U.S. Department of Justice, Bureau of Justice Statistics, November 2012).

29. Thomas P. Bonczar, *Characteristics of State Parole Supervising Agencies, 2006* (Washington, DC: U.S. Department of Justice, Bureau of Justice Statistics, August 2008).

30. "Disenfranchisement News," *The Sentencing Project,* November 14, 2012, www.sentencingproject.org (accessed November 14, 2012).

31. Marc Mauer, "Voting Behind Bars: An Argument for Voting by Prisoners," *Howard Law Journal,* vol. 54, no. 3 (2011), pp. 549–566.

32. "Wrongly Turning Away Ex-Offenders," *The New York Times,* November 3, 2012, www.nytimes.com (accessed February 6, 2013).

33. Erika Wood and Rachel Bloom, *DeFacto Disenfranchisement* (Washington, DC: The Sentencing Project, 2008).

34. John F. Timoney, "Two More Issues for President Obama, With Implications for Justice and Race," *Subject to Debate: A Newsletter of the Police Executive Research Forum,* vol. 22, no. 11 (November 2008), p. 2.

35. *Reentry Courts: Managing the Transition from Prison to Community* (Washington, DC: Office of Justice Programs, September, 1999), p. 9.

36. Christine Lindquist, Jennifer Hardison Walters, Michael Rempel, and Shannon M. Carey, *The National Institute of Justice's Evaluation of Second Chance Act Adult Reentry Courts: Program Characteristics and Preliminary Themes from Year 1* (Washington, DC: U. S. Department of Justice, National Institute of Justice, March 2013), p. 2.

37. Susan Herman and Cressida Wasserman, "A Role for Victims in Offender Reentry," *Crime & Delinquency,* vol. 47, no. 3 (July 2001), pp. 428–445.

38. Andrew von Hirsch, *Doing Justice: The Choice of Punishments, Report of the Committee for the Study of Incarceration* (New York: Hill and Wang, 1976).

39. Jessica Fargan, "Herald Eyes Parole Votes, Turns to Court for Records' Release," *Boston Herald,* November 13, 2008 www.bostonherald.com (accessed May 7, 2013).

40. La Vigne et al., *Prisoner Reentry and Community Policing, Strategies for Enhancing Public Safety,* p. 16.

41. Justin Jones and Edward Flynn, "Cops and Corrections: Reentry Collaborations for Public Safety," *Corrections Today,* vol. 70, no. 2 (April 2008), pp. 26–29; and Ashbel T. Wall II and Tracy Z. Poole, "Partnerships with Local Law Enforcement and Community Agencies: A Critical Component to Successful Prison Reentry Initiatives," *Corrections Today,* vol. 70, no. 2 (April 2008), pp. 30–37.
42. Donald G. Evans, "Community-Focused Parole," *Corrections Today,* vol. 68, no. 7 (December 2006), pp. 90–91.

Chapter 9

1. James A. Gondles Jr., "*Guard* Must Go," *Corrections Today,* August 2006, p. 9.
2. See Sylvia G. McCollum, "Excellence or Mediocrity: Training Correctional Officers and Administrators," *The Keeper's Voice,* vol. 17, no. 4 (Fall 1996).
3. Anthony R. Martinez, "Corrections Officer: The 'Other' Prisoner," *The Keeper's Voice,* vol. 18, no. 1 (Spring 1997).
4. Don A. Josi and Dale K. Sechrest, *The Changing Career of the Correctional Officer: Policy Implications for the 21st Century* (Boston: Butterworth-Heinemann, 1998), p. 11.
5. Ibid., p. 12.
6. John Hepburn, "The Exercise of Power in Coercive Organizations: A Study of Prison Guards," *Criminology,* vol. 23, no. 1 (1985), pp. 145–164.
7. Gresham Sykes, *The Society of Captives* (Princeton, NJ: Princeton University Press, 1958).
8. See, for example, James B. Jacobs and Lawrence J. Kraft, "Integrating the Keepers: A Comparison of Black and White Prison Guards in Illinois," *Social Problems,* vol. 25, no. 3 (1978), pp. 304–318.
9. Adapted from John J. Macionis, *Society: The Basics,* 2nd ed. (Englewood Cliffs, NJ: Prentice Hall, 1994), p. 405.
10. Kelsey Kauffman, *Prison Officers and Their World* (Cambridge, MA: Harvard University Press, 1988), pp. 85–86.
11. Rich Lord, "It Doesn't Pay to Get Promoted in Pa. Prisons," *Pittsburgh Post-Gazette,* February 26, 2012.
12. American Correctional Association, *Vital Statistics in Corrections* (Lanham, MD: ACA, 2000), p. 143; James J. Stephan and Jennifer C. Karberg, *Census of State and Federal Correctional Facilities, 2000* (Washington, DC: Bureau of Justice Statistics, 2003).
13. ACA, *Vital Statistics in Corrections.*
14. Ibid.
15. See, for example, E. Poole and R. M. Regoli, "Work Relations and Cynicism Among Prison Guards," *Criminal Justice and Behavior,* vol. 7 (1980), pp. 303–314.
16. Adapted from Frank Schmalleger, *Criminal Justice Today: An Introductory Text for the 21st Century,* 9th ed. (Upper Saddle River, NJ: Prentice Hall, 2007).
17. Lucien X. Lombardo, *Guards Imprisoned: Correctional Officers at Work,* 2nd ed. (Cincinnati, OH: Anderson, 1989).
18. Adapted from Dora B. Schriro, "Women in Prison: Keeping the Peace," *The Keeper's Voice,* vol. 16, no. 2 (Spring 1995).
19. Ibid.
20. M. I. Cadwaladr, "Women Working in a Men's Jail," *FORUM,* vol. 6, no. 1 (1994).
21. Ibid.
22. N. C. Jurik and J. Halemba, "Gender, Working Conditions, and the Job Satisfaction of Women in a Non-Traditional Occupation: Female Correctional Officers in Men's Prisons," *Sociological Quarterly,* vol. 25 (1984), pp. 551–566.
23. Joseph R. Rowan, "Who Is Safer in Male Maximum Security Prisons?" *The Keeper's Voice,* vol. 17, no. 3 (Summer 1996).

24. Ibid.
25. See, for example, Stephen Walters, "Changing the Guard: Male Correctional Officers' Attitudes Toward Women as Co-workers," *Journal of Offender Rehabilitation,* vol. 20, no. 1 (1993), pp. 47–60.
26. Cadwaladr, "Women Working in a Men's Jail."
27. Ibid.
28. Public Service Commission (of Canada), "Stress and Executive Burnout," *FORUM,* vol. 4, no. 1 (1992). Much of the material in this section is taken from this work.
29. B. M. Crouch, "The Guard in a Changing Prison World," in B. M. Crouch (ed.), *The Keepers: Prison Guards and Contemporary Corrections* (Springfield, IL: Charles C. Thomas, 1980).
30. Shannon Black, "Correctional Employee Stress & Strain," *Corrections Today,* October 2001, p. 99.
31. Lombardo, *Guards Imprisoned.*
32. Kelly Ann Cheeseman and Wendi Goodin-Fahncke, "The Impact of Gender on Correctional Employee Perceptions of Work Stress," *Corrections Compendium,* Vol. 36, No. 2 (Summer 2011), p. 1–2.
33. Public Service Commission, "Stress and Executive Burnout."
34. For an excellent overview of the literature on correctional officer stress, see Tammy L. Castle and Jamie S. Martin, "Occupational Hazard: Predictors of Stress Among Jail Correctional Officers," *American Journal of Criminal Justice,* vol. 31, no. 1 (Fall 2006), pp. 65–80.
35. "Not Stressed Enough?" *FORUM,* vol. 4, no. 1 (1992). Adapted from C. C. W. Hines and W. C. Wilson, "A No-Nonsense Guide to Being Stressed," *Management Solutions,* October 1986, pp. 27–29.
36. J. T. Dignam, M. Barrera, and S. G. West, "Occupational Stress, Social Support, and Burnout Among Correctional Officers," *American Journal of Community Psychology,* vol. 14, no. 2 (1986), pp. 177–193.
37. M. C. W. Peeters, B. P. Buunk, and W. B. Schaufeli, "Social Interactions and Feelings of Inferiority Among Correctional Officers: A Daily Event-Recording Approach," *Journal of Applied Social Psychology,* vol. 25, no. 12 (1995), pp. 1073–1089.
38. Jessie W. Doyle, "6 Elements That Form a Context for Staff Safety," *Corrections Today,* October 2001, pp. 101–104.
39. Terry L. Stewart and Donald W. Brown, "Focusing on Correctional Staff Safety," *Corrections Today,* October 2001, pp. 90–93.
40. Ibid.
41. David Robinson, Frank Porporino, and Linda Simourd, "Do Different Occupational Groups Vary on Attitudes and Work Adjustment in Corrections?" *Federal Probation,* vol. 60, no. 3 (1996), pp. 45–53. See also Francis T. Cullen et al., "How Satisfying Is Prison Work? A Comparative Occupational Approach," *The Journal of Offender Counseling Services and Rehabilitation,* vol. 14, no. 2 (1989), pp. 89–108.
42. Timothy J. Flanagan, Wesley Johnson, and Katherine Bennett, "Job Satisfaction Among Correctional Executives: A Contemporary Portrait of Wardens of State Prisons for Adults," *Prison Journal,* vol. 76, no. 4 (1996), pp. 385–397.
43. Lombardo, *Guards Imprisoned.*
44. Martinez, "Corrections Officer."
45. Thomas Gillan, "The Correctional Officer: One of Law Enforcement's Toughest Positions," *Corrections Today,* October 2001, p. 113.
46. Black, "Correctional Employee Stress & Strain," p. 99.
47. Andrew Metz, "Life on the Inside: The Jailers," in Tara Gray (ed.), *Exploring Corrections* (Boston: Allyn & Bacon, 2002), p. 65.

48. Ibid., p. 64.
49. Black, "Correctional Employee Stress & Strain," p. 99.
50. Stephen Walters, "The Determinants of Job Satisfaction Among Canadian and American Correctional Officers," *Journal of Crime and Justice,* vol. 19, no. 2 (1996), pp. 145–158.
51. John R. Hepburn and Paul E. Knepper, "Correctional Officers as Human Services Workers: The Effect on Job Satisfaction," *Justice Quarterly,* vol. 10, no. 2 (1993), pp. 315–337.
52. Stephen Walters, "Gender, Job Satisfaction, and Correctional Officers: A Comparative Analysis," *The Justice Professional,* vol. 7, no. 2 (1993), pp. 23–33.
53. Dana M. Britton, "Perceptions of the Work Environment Among Correctional Officers: Do Race and Sex Matter?" *Criminology,* vol. 35, no. 1 (1997), pp. 85–105.
54. Adapted from William Sondervan, "Professionalism in Corrections," in Frank Schmalleger and John Smykla (eds.), *Corrections in the Twenty-First Century,* 5e (New York: McGraw-Hill, 2011), p. 572.
55. Ibid.
56. Justin Fenton, "Indictments Reveal Prison Crime World," *Baltimore Sun,* April 18, 2009.
57. Jack Dolan, "California Prison Guards Union Called Main Obstacle to Keeping Cell Phones Away from Inmate," *Los Angeles Times,* February 4, 2011. Web posted at http://www.latimes.com/news/local/la-me-prison-guards-20110204,0,2785860.story (accessed February 21, 2011).
58. Mike Ward, "Low Pay May Make Prison Guards Ripe for Smugglers," *American Statesman,* October 24, 2008.
59. U.S. Department of Justice, Office of the Inspector General, *Semiannual Report to Congress: April 1, 2008–September 30, 2008* (Washington, DC: USGPO, 2008).
60. International Herald Tribune, "Man Behind U.S. Terrorism Plot Gets 16 Years," March 6, 2009. Web posted at http://www.iht.com/articles/ap/2009/03/06/america/NA-US-Terrorism-Probe.php (accessed March 27, 2009).
61. Mark S. Hamm, "Prisoner Radicalization: Assessing the Threat in U.S. Correctional Institutions," *NIJ Journal* (No. 261), p. 17.
62. Ibid., p. 18.
63. Quoted in Meghan Mandeville, "Information Sharing Becomes Crucial to Battling Terrorism Behind Bars," Corrections.com, December 8, 2003, http://database.corrections.com/news/results2.asp?ID_8988 (accessed August 1, 2005).
64. "FBI: Al-Qaida Recruiting in U.S. Prisons," United Press International wire service, January 7, 2004, http://database.corrections.com/news/results2.asp?ID_9148 (accessed August 1, 2005).
65. "Lawyer Sentenced to 28 Months in Prison on Terrorism Charge," Court TV News, October 16, 2006, www.courttv.com/news/2006/1016/cynne_Stewart_ap.html.
66. Jess Maghan, *Intelligence-Led Penology: Management of Crime Information Obtained from Incarcerated Persons,* paper presented at the Investigation of Crime World Conference, 2001, p. 6.
67. Institute for the Study of Violent Groups, "Land of Wahhabism," *Crime and Justice International,* March/April 2005, p. 43.
68. Office of the Inspector General, *A Review of the Federal Bureau of Prisons' Selection of Muslim Religious Services Providers* (Washington, DC: U.S. Department of Justice, 2004).
69. Ibid., p. 8.
70. Ibid.
71. Mark S. Hamm, "Terrorist Recruitment in American Correctional Institutions: An Exploratory Study of Non-Traditional Faith Groups," nonpublished paper, December 2007.
72. U.S. Department of Justice, Office of the Inspector General, *The Federal Bureau of Prisons' Monitoring of Mail for High-Risk Inmates* (Washington, DC: U.S. Government Printing Office, 2006).
73. Keith Martin, "Corrections Prepares for Terrorism," Corrections Connection News Network, January 21, 2002, www.corrections.com (accessed July 10, 2005).
74. Y. N. Baykan, "The Emergence of Sunni Islam in America's Prisons," *Corrections Today,* February 2007, pp. 49–51.
75. James Gilligan, *Violence: Reflections on a National Epidemic* (New York: Vintage Books, 1997), p. 165.

Chapter 10

1. "Miss Wisconsin Makes Father's Prison Time a Miss America Platform," CBS News, January 15, 2012, www.cbsnews.com/8301-31749_162-57359505-10391698/miss-wisconsin-makes-fathers-prison-time-a-miss-america-platform (accessed May 18, 2012).
2. Allen Beck et al., *Survey of State Prison Inmates, 1991* (Washington, DC: U.S. Department of Justice, March 1993), www.ojp.usdoj.gov/bjs/pub/ascii/sospi91.txt.
3. Erving Goffman, *Asylums: Essays on the Social Situation of Mental Patients and Other Inmates* (Garden City, NY: Anchor Books, 1961).
4. Hans Toch, *Living in Prison: The Ecology of Survival,* reprint ed. (Washington, DC: American Psychological Association, 1996), p. xv.
5. Victoria R. DeRosia, *Living Inside Prison Walls: Adjustment Behavior* (Westport, CT: Praeger, 1998).
6. "Inmate Subculture," in Virgil L. Williams (ed.), *Dictionary of American Penology: An Introductory Guide* (Westport, CT: Greenwood, 1979).
7. Donald Clemmer, *The Prison Community* (Boston: Holt, Rinehart & Winston, 1940).
8. Stanton Wheeler, "Socialization in Correctional Communities," *American Sociological Review,* vol. 26 (October 1961), pp. 697–712.
9. Gresham M. Sykes, *The Society of Captives: A Study of a Maximum Security Prison* (Princeton, NJ: Princeton University Press, 1958).
10. Stephen C. Light, *Inmate Assaults on Staff: Challenges to Authority in a Large State Prison System,* dissertation, State University of New York at Albany (Ann Arbor, MI: University Microfilms International, 1987).
11. John Irwin and Donald R. Cressey, "Thieves, Convicts and the Inmate Culture," *Social Problems,* vol. 10 (Fall 1962), pp. 142–155.
12. James Jacobs, *Stateville: The Penitentiary in Mass Society* (Chicago: University of Chicago Press, 1977).
13. Miles D. Harer and Darrell J. Steffensmeier, "Race and Prison Violence," *Criminology,* vol. 34, no. 3 (1996), pp. 323–355.
14. John M. Wilson and Jon D. Snodgrass, "The Prison Code in a Therapeutic Community," *Journal of Criminal Law, Criminology, and Police Science,* vol. 60, no. 4 (1969), pp. 472–478.
15. Gresham M. Sykes and Sheldon L. Messinger, "The Inmate Social System," in Richard A. Cloward et al. (eds.), *Theoretical Studies in Social Organization of the Prison* (New York: Social Science Research Council, 1960), pp. 5–19.
16. Peter M. Wittenberg, "Language and Communication in Prison," *Federal Probation,* vol. 60, no. 4 (1996), pp. 45–50.
17. Sykes, *The Society of Captives.*
18. John Irwin, *The Felon* (Englewood Cliffs, NJ: Prentice Hall, 1970).
19. Adapted from Frank Schmalleger, *Criminal Justice Today,* 7th ed. (Upper Saddle River, NJ: Prentice Hall, 2003).
20. See, for example, Donald Tucker, *A Punk's Song: View from the Inside* (AMS Press, 1981), from which some of the information here is adapted.
21. Ibid.

22. Ibid.

23. Ibid.

24. Daniel Lockwood, *Sexual Aggression Among Male Prisoners*, dissertation, State University of New York at Albany (Ann Arbor, MI: University Microfilms International, 1978); Daniel Lockwood, "Issues in Prison Sexual Violence," *The Prison Journal*, vol. 58, no. 1 (1983), pp. 73–79.

25. Adapted from Toch, *Living in Prison*, p. 274.

26. Pub. L. No. 108–79.

27. Bureau of Justice Statistics, *PREA Data Collection Activities, 2012* (Washington, DC: US Dept. of Justice, 2012).

28. Allen J. Beck and Paige M. Harrison, *Sexual Victimization in Prisons and Jails Reported by Inmates, 2008–09* (Washington, DC: Bureau of Justice Statistics, 2010).

29. Allen J. Beck and Timothy A. Hughes, *Sexual Violence Reported by Correctional Authorities, 2004* (Washington, DC: Bureau of Justice Statistics, 2005).

30. E. Ann Carson and Daniela Golinelli, *Prisoners in 2012* (Washington, DC: Bureau of Justice Statistics, December 2013).

31. Phyllis J. Baunach, "Critical Problems of Women in Prison," in Imogene L. Moyer (ed.), *The Changing Roles of Women in the Criminal Justice System* (Prospect Heights, IL: Waveland Press, 1985), pp. 95–110.

32. See John W. Palmer and Stephen E. Palmer, *Constitutional Rights of Prisoners*, 6th ed. (Cincinnati, OH: Anderson, 1999).

33. American Correctional Association, *Standards for Adult Correctional Institutions* (Lanham, MD: ACA, 1990).

34. Alabama Department of Corrections, *Monthly Statistical Report for November 2010* (Montgomery, Alabama; Alabama Department of Corrections, 2011), p. 3.

35. Lawrence A. Greenfeld and Tracy L. Snell, *Women Offenders*, Bureau of Justice Statistics Special Report (Washington, DC: Bureau of Justice Statistics, December 1999, revised October 3, 2000); Carson and Golinelli, *Prisoners in 2012*.

36. Carson and Golinelli, *Prisoners in 2012*.

37. Ibid.

38. Angela Browne, Brenda Miller, and Eugene Maguin, "Prevalence and Severity of Lifetime Physical and Sexual Victimization Among Incarcerated Women," *International Journal of Law and Psychiatry*, vol. 22, no. 3–4 (1999), pp. 301–322.

39. Bloom et al., *Gender-Responsive Strategies: Research, Practice, and Guiding Principles for Women Offenders* (Washington, DC: National Institute of Corrections, 2003).

40. Carson and Golinelli, *Prisoners in 2011*.

41. American Correctional Association, *Female Offenders: Meeting Needs of a Neglected Population* (Laurel, MD: ACA, 1993).

42. Tracy Snell, *Women in Prison* (Washington, DC: Bureau of Justice Statistics, 1994).

43. Rose Giallombardo, *Society of Women: A Study of a Women's Prison* (New York: John Wiley, 1966).

44. Esther Heffernan, *Making It in Prison: The Square, the Cool, and the Life* (New York: Wiley-Interscience, 1972).

45. Barbara Owens, "The Mix: The Culture of Imprisoned Women," in Mary K. Stohr and Craig Hemmens (eds.), *The Inmate Prison Experience* (Upper Saddle River, NJ: Prentice Hall, 2004), pp. 152–172.

46. Williams, "Inmate Subculture," p. 109.

47. Kathryn Watterson, *Women in Prison: Inside the Concrete Tomb*, 2nd ed. (Boston: Northeastern University Press, 1996), p. 291.

48. For example, see John Gagnon and William Simon, "The Social Meaning of Prison Homosexuality," in David M. Petersen and Charles W. Thomas (eds.), *Corrections: Problems and Prospects* (Englewood Cliffs, NJ: Prentice Hall, 1980).

49. Doris Layton MacKenzie, James Robinson, and Carol Campbell, "Long-Term Incarceration of Female Offenders: Prison Adjustment and Coping," *Criminal Justice and Behavior*, vol. 16, no. 2 (1989), pp. 223–238.

50. Nicole Hahn Rafter, *Partial Justice: Women, Prisons and Social Control* (New Brunswick, NJ: Transaction, 1990).

51. Bloom et al., *Gender-Responsive Strategies*.

52. Barbara Bloom and Stephanie Covington, *Gendered Justice: Programming for Women in Correctional Settings*, paper presented at the American Society of Criminology annual meeting, San Francisco, November 2000, p. 11.

53. Bloom et al., *Gender-Responsive Strategies*.

54. Susan Cranford and Rose Williams, "Critical Issues in Managing Female Offenders," *Corrections Today*, vol. 60, no. 7 (December 1998), pp. 130–135.

55. John DeBell, "The Female Offender: Different . . . Not Difficult," *Corrections Today*, vol. 63, no. 1 (February 2001), pp. 56–61.

56. Pat Carlen, "Analyzing Women's Imprisonment: Abolition and Its Enemies," *Women, Girls & Criminal Justice*, vol. 7, no. 6 (October/November 2006), p. 85.

57. Tracy L. Snell, "Women in Prison," *Bureau of Justice Statistics Bulletin* (Washington, DC: Bureau of Justice Statistics, March 1994).

58. As estimated by Vesna Markovic, "Pregnant Women in Prison: A Correctional Dilemma?" *The Keepers' Voice*, Summer 1995.

59. Ibid.

60. American Correctional Association, *Standards for Adult Correctional Institutions*, 3rd ed. (ACA, January 1990).

61. Gerald Austin McHugh, "Protection of the Rights of Pregnant Women in Prison and Detention Facilities," *New England Journal of Prison Law*, vol. 6, no. 2 (Summer 1980), pp. 231–263.

62. Snell, "Women in Prison."

63. National Institute of Corrections, *Services for Families of Prison Inmates* (Washington, DC: NIC, 2002), p. 3.

64. Phyllis Jo Baunach, "Critical Problems of Women in Prison," in Imogene L. Moyer (ed.), *The Changing Roles of Women in the Criminal Justice System* (Prospect Heights, IL: Waveland Press, 1985), p. 16.

65. John J. Sheridan, "Inmates May Be Parents, Too," *Corrections Today*, vol. 58, no. 5 (August 1996), p. 100.

66. Patricia Allard and Judith Greene, *Children on the Outside: Voicing the Pain and Human Costs of Parental Incarceration* (New York; Justice Strategies, 2011).

67. L. Wright and C. Seymour, *Working with Children and Families Separated by Incarceration: A Handbook for Child Welfare Agencies* (Washington, DC: Child Welfare League of America, 2000).

68. Kelsey Kauffman, "Mothers in Prison," *Corrections Today* (February 2001), pp. 62–65.

69. Harrison and Beck, *Prisoners in 2006*.

70. Christopher J. Mumola, *Incarcerated Parents and Their Children*, Bureau of Justice Statistics Special Report (Washington, DC: Bureau of Justice Statistics, August 2000), p. 1.

71. Suzanne Hoholik, "Weekend Camp Lets Mother, Kids Bond," *The Columbus Dispatch*, July 22, 2000, pp. A1–A2.

72. Rini Bartlett, "Helping Inmate Moms Keep in Touch," *Correctional Compass* (Tallahassee, FL: Department of Corrections, February 2001), www.dc.state.fl.us/pub/compass/0102/page07.html (accessed June 2, 2007).

73. Kauffman, "Mothers in Prison," p. 62.

74. Huey Freeman, "Illinois Prison Program Guides New Mothers," Pantagraph.com, www.pantagraph.com/news/state-and-regional/illinois/article_ab1d5106-4631-11df-97d4-001cc4c002e0.html (accessed March 12, 2011).

75. Rick Jervis, "Prison Dads Learn Meaning of 'Father,'" *USA Today,* June 18, 2010, www.usatoday.com/news/nation/2010-06-17-prison-dads_N.htm (accessed March 15, 2011).

76. John Ortiz Smykla, "Coed Prison: Should We Try It (Again)?" in Charles B. Fields (ed.), *Controversial Issues in Corrections* (Boston: Allyn & Bacon, 1999), pp. 203–218.

77. John Ortiz Smykla and Jimmy J. Williams, "Co-Corrections in the United States of America, 1970–1990: Two Decades of Disadvantages for Women Prisoners," *Women & Criminal Justice,* vol. 8, no. 1 (1996), pp. 61–76.

78. Ibid.

79. Jacqueline K. Crawford, "Two Losers Don't Make a Winner: The Case Against the Co-correctional Institution," in John Ortiz Smykla (ed.), *Coed Prison* (New York: Human Sciences Press, 1980), pp. 263–268.

80. Smykla and Williams, "Co-corrections in the United States," p. 61.

81. Lawrence W. Sherman et al., *Preventing Crime: What Works, What Doesn't, What's Promising* (Washington, DC: NIJ, 1997).

Chapter 11

1. Rich Pedroncelli, "Judges Back a One-Third Reduction in State Prison Population," *Los Angeles Times,* February 10, 2009.

2. *Ruffin* v. *Commonwealth,* 62, Va. 790, 1871.

3. Frances Cole, "The Impact of *Bell* v. *Wolfish* Upon Prisoners' Rights," *Journal of Crime and Justice,* vol. 10 (1987), pp. 47–70.

4. D. J. Gottlieb, "The Legacy of *Wolfish* and *Chapman*: Some Thoughts About 'Big Prison Case' Litigation in the 1980s," in I. D. Robbins (ed.), *Prisoners and the Law* (New York: Clark Boardman, 1985).

5. James B. Jacobs, *New Perspectives on Prisons and Imprisonment* (Ithaca, NY: Cornell University Press, 1983).

6. *Holt* v. *Sarver,* 442 F.2d 304 (1971).

7. Ibid.

8. *Holt* v. *Sarver,* 309 F.Supp. 362 (E.D.Ark.1970), aff'd, 442 F.2d 304 (8th Cir. 1971).

9. Todd Clear and George F. Cole, *American Corrections,* 4th ed. (New York: Wadsworth, 1997).

10. Civil Rights of Institutionalized Persons Act, 42 U.S.C. § 1997 et seq. (1976 ed., Supp. IV), as modified 1980. (Current through P.L. 104-150, approved June 3, 1996.)

11. R. Hawkins and G. P. Alpert, *American Prison Systems: Punishment and Justice* (Englewood Cliffs, NJ: Prentice Hall, 1989).

12. John Scalia, *Prisoner Petitions Filed in U.S. District Courts, 2000, with Trends 1980–2000* (Washington, DC: U.S. Department of Justice, December 2001).

13. Florida Department of Corrections, Office of the Inspector General, *Annual Report* 1994–1995, www.dc.state.fl.us/pub/IGannual/19941995/page6.html (accessed May 30, 2002).

14. *Report of the Comptroller General of the United States: Grievance Mechanisms in State Correctional Institutions and Large-City Jails* (Washington, DC: U.S. Government Printing Office, June 17, 1977), Appendix I.

15. James B. Jacobs, "The Prisoners' Rights Movement and Its Impacts," in Edward J. Latessa, Alexander Holsinger, James W. Marquart, and Jonathan R. Sorensen, *Correctional Contexts: Contemporary and Classical Readings,* 2nd ed. (Los Angeles: Roxbury, 2001), p. 211. Reprinted from James B. Jacobs, *Crime and Justice,* vol. II (Chicago: University of Chicago Press, 1980).

16. See *Estelle* v. *Gamble,* 429 U.S. 97 (1976), and *Hutto* v. *Finney,* 437 U.S. 678 (1978).

17. Sheri Qualters, "Federal Judge Orders Sex-Reassignment Surgery for Mass. Prisoner," *Law Journal,* September 4, 2012.

18. American Civil Liberties Union, *ACLU Position Paper: Prisoners' Rights* (Fall 1999), www.aclu.org/library/PrisonerRights.pdf (accessed March 2, 2011).

19. In 1977, Theriault's appeal to the U.S. Supreme Court was denied (see 434 U.S. 953, November 14, 1977).

20. *Ali* v. *Federal Bureau of Prisons,* 552 U.S. 214 (2008).

21. In Section 1997e, Congress created a specific, limited exhaustion requirement for adult prisoners bringing actions pursuant to section 1983.

22. Prison Litigation Reform Act, Pub. L. No. 104-134, § 801-10, 110 Stat. 1321 (1995).

23. If a prisoner wishes to proceed as an indigent on appeal, the prisoner must file in the district court, with the notice of appeal, a motion for leave to proceed as an indigent, a certified copy of a prison trust account statement, and Form 4 from the Appendix of Forms found in the *Federal Rules of Appellate Procedure.*

24. Fred L. Cheesman, Brian J. Ostrom, and Roger A. Hanson, *A Tale of Two Laws Revisited: Investigating the Impact of the Prison Litigation Reform Act and the Antiterrorism and Effective Death Penalty Act* (Williamsburg, VA: National Center for State Courts, 2005).

25. "Court Intervention Ends for D.C. DOC," *Corrections Today,* December 2004, p. 12.

26. "Judge Approves Settlement in Alabama Prison Lawsuit," *Corrections Journal,* August 9, 2004, p. 1.

27. California Government Code, Section 818.

28. Federal Tort Claims Act, U.S. Code, Title 28, Section 1346(b), 2671-2680.

29. U.S.C. Section 1346(b)(1).

30. *Milbrook* v. *U.S.,* U.S. Supreme Court, No. 11-10362 (decided March 27, 2013).

31. *Elder* v. *Holloway,* 114 S.Ct. 1019, 127 L.Ed.2d 344 (1994).

32. Ibid.

Chapter 12

1. "Tuberculosis in Prisons: A Major Health Problem," *International Committee of the Red Cross,* March 22, 2013, www.icrc.org (accessed March 27, 2013)

2. Stan Stojkovic (ed.), *Managing Special Populations in Jails and Prisons* (Kingston, NJ: Civic Research Institute, 2005), p. xv.

3. Thomas E. Patterson, "Addressing Special Populations in Corrections," *Corrections Today,* vol. 74, no. 4 (August/September, 2012), p. 10.

4. Ibid., p. 10.

5. Ibid., p. 10.

6. G. Larry Mays and Daniel L. Judiscak, "Special Needs Inmates in New Mexico Jails," *American Jails,* vol. 10, no. 2 (1996), pp. 32–41.

7. National Center on Addiction and Substance Abuse, *Behind Bars II: Substance Abuse and America's Prison Population* (New York: National Center on Addiction and Substance Abuse, Columbia University, February 2010).

8. Kate Miltner, "Treatment over Jail Time Poll: Most Favor Efforts to Combat Addiction over Punishment," http://abcnews.go.com/sections/politics/dailynews/poll010606.html (accessed March 18, 2013).

9. Christopher J. Mumola and Jennifer C. Karberg, *Drug Use and Dependence, State and Federal Prisoners, 2004* (Washington, DC: U.S. Department of Justice, Bureau of Justice Statistics, October 2006).

10. Jeremy Travis, *Framing the National Agenda: A Research and Policy Perspective.* Speech to National Corrections Conference on Substance Abuse, April 23, 1997.

11. M. D. Anglin and Y. Haer, "Treatment of Drug Abuse," in Michael Tonry and James Q. Wilson (eds.), *Drugs and Crime: Crime and Justice: A Review of Research,* vol. 13 (Chicago: University of Chicago Press, 1990), pp. 393–460; D. N. Nurco, T. W. Kislock, and T. E. Hanlon, "The Nature and Status of Drug Abuse Treatment," *Maryland Medical Journal,* vol. 43 (January 1994), pp. 51–57; D. D. Simpson et al., "A National Evaluation of Treatment Outcomes for Cocaine Dependence," *Archives of General Psychiatry,* vol. 56, no. 6 (1999), pp. 507–514; and Doris Layton MacKenzie, *What Works in Corrections: Reducing the Criminal Activities of Criminals and Delinquents* (NewYork: Cambridge University Press, 2006).

12. Center for Substance Abuse Treatment, *NTIES: The National Treatment Improvement Study—Final Report* (Rockville, MD: U.S. Department of Health and Human Services, Substance Abuse and Mental Health Services Administration, 1997).

13. Marcia R. Chaiken, *Prison Programs for Drug-Involved Offenders* (Washington, DC: National Institute of Justice, October 1989); D. A. Andrews et al., "Does Correctional Treatment Work? A Clinically Relevant and Psychologically Informed Meta-Analysis," *Criminology,* vol. 28, no. 3 (1990), pp. 369–404; Donald Lipton and Frank Pearson, *The CDATE Project: Reviewing Research on the Effectiveness of Treatment Programs for Adults and Juvenile Offenders,* paper presented at the annual meeting of the American Society of Criminology, Chicago, IL, 1996.

14. Lana D. Harrison, "The Revolving Prison Door for Drug-Involved Offenders: Challenges and Opportunities," *Crime & Delinquency,* vol. 47, no. 3 (July 2001), pp. 462–485.

15. Sandra Tunis et al., *Evaluation of Drug Treatment in Local Corrections* (Washington, DC: U.S. Department of Justice, 1997).

16. Steven S. Martin, James A. Inciardi, and Daniel J. O'Connell, "Treatment Research in *Oz*—Is Randomization the Ideal or Just Somewhere Over the Rainbow?" *Federal Probation,* vol. 67, no. 2 (September 2003), pp. 53–60.

17. Bernadette Pelissier et al., *TRIAD Drug Treatment Evaluation Project Final Report of Three-Year Outcomes: Part I* (Washington, DC: Federal Bureau of Prisons, Office of Research and Evaluation, September 2000).

18. James A. Inciardi et al., "An Effective Model of Prison-Based Treatment for Drug-Involved Offenders," *Journal of Drug Issues,* vol. 27, no. 2 (Spring 1997), pp. 261–278; James A. Inciardi, Steven S. Martin, and Clifford A. Butzin, "Five-Year Outcomes of Therapeutic Community Treatment of Drug-Involved Offenders After Release from Prison," *Crime & Delinquency ,* vol. 50, no. 1 (January 2004), pp. 88–107.

19. *Administrative Office of Courts, Drug Treatment and Education Fund, Annual Report, Fiscal Year 1999,* Arizona Supreme Court, November 2001.

20. Josh Richman, "Money Is Gone, But Proposition 36's Drug-Treatment Mandate Remains," *Oakland Tribune* (Oakland, CA), February 22, 2013, www.contracostatimes.com (accessed February 22, 2013); and Scott Ehlers and Jason Ziedenberg, *Proposition 36: Five Years Later* (Washington, DC: Justice Policy Institute, April 2006).

21. National Institute on Drug Abuse, *Principles of Drug Abuse Treatment for Criminal Justice Populations—A Research-Based Guide* (Washington, DC: U.S. Department of Health and Human Services, 2006).

22. National Commission on Correctional Health Care, *The Health Status of Soon-to-Be-Released Inmates: A Report to Congress,* Vol. I (Washington, DC: U.S. Department of Justice, September 2004), p. ix.

23. Laura M. Maruschak, *HIV in Prisons, 2001–2010* (Washington, DC: U.S. Department of Justice, Bureau of Justice Statistics, September 2012).

24. *Management of the HIV-Positive Prisoner* (New York: World Health CME, n.d.).

25. Michael S. Vaughn and Leo Carroll, "Separate and Unequal: Prison Versus Free-World Medical Care," *Justice Quarterly,* vol. 15, no. 1 (March 1998), pp. 3–40.

26. Laura M. Maruschak, *HIV in Prisons, 2007–08* (Washington, DC: U.S. Department of Justice, Bureau of Justice Statistics, December 2009).

27. American Correctional Association, *Managing Special Needs Offenders* (Lanham, MD: American Correctional Association, 2004).

28. Theodore M. Hammett, Cheryl Roberts, and Sofia Kennedy, "Health-Related Issues in Prisoner Reentry," *Crime & Delinquency,* vol. 47, no. 3 (July 2001), pp. 390–409; Abe Macher, "Clinical Management of HIV Disease in Correctional Facilities," in Stan Stojkovic (ed.), *Managing Special Populations in Jails and Prisons,* pp. 4–1 to 4–57; "Jailhouse Tatooing" (New York: Civic Reaserch Institute, 2006), *American Jails,* vol. 20, no. 4 (September/October 2006), pp. 96–98.

29. Jaime Shimkus, "Side by Side, Ministers and Detainees Test for HIV Infection," *CorrectCare,* Fall 2001, p. 16.

30. Christina Hernandez, "HIV Prisoners: What Happens When They Get Out?" *The Crime Report,* October 29, 2009, www.thecrimereport.com (accessed October 26, 2011).

31. Ibid.

32. "Inmate Mental Health Care," *Corrections Compendium,* Summer 2011, pp. 20–39; Neil Osterweil, "Severe Mental Disorders Highly Prevalent in Jails, Prisons" *Clinical Psychiatry News,* November 17, 2011, www.clinicalpsychiatrynews.com (accessed November 23, 2011).

33. "Inmate Mental Health Care," *Corrections Compendium.*

34. Ibid., p. 20.

35. Thomas N. Faust, "Shift the Responsibility of Untreated Mental Illness out of the Criminal Justice System," *Corrections Today,* April 2003, pp. 6–7; see also Liz Lipton, "Few Safeguards Govern Elimination of Psychiatric Beds," *Psychiatric News,* vol. 36, no. 15 (August 3, 2001), p. 9, http://pn.psychiatriconline.org/cgi/content/full/36/15/9 (accessed January 13, 2011); James and Glaze, *Mental Health Problems of Prison and Jail Inmates.*

36. Michael P. Maloney, Michael P. Ward, and Charles M. Jackson, "Study Reveals That More Mentally Ill Offenders Are Entering Jail," *Corrections Today,* April 2003, pp. 100–103.

37. As quoted in Phillip Comey, "Health Care and Prisons: Considering the Connection," *On the Line* (Lanham: MD. American Correctional Association, November 2005), p. 1.

38. Risdon N. Slate et al., "Doing Justice for Mental Illness and Society: Federal Probation and Pretrial Service Officers as Mental Health Specialists," *Federal Probation,* vol. 67, no. 3 (December 2003).

39. Maloney, Ward, and Jackson, "Study Reveals."

40. The Bazelon Center for Mental Health Law, *Position Statement on Involuntary Commitment, 1999.* As cited in The Sentencing Project, *Mentally Ill Offenders in the Criminal Justice System: An Analysis and Prescription* (Washington, DC: The Sentencing Project, January 2002), p. 4.

41. John M. Greacen, "Then & Now: Reflections on 25 Years of Correctional Health Care," *CorrectCare,* vol. 16, no. 1 (Winter 2002), pp. 9, 22.

42. Dean H. Aufderheide, "The Mentally Ill in America's Prisons," *Corrections Today,* vol. 67, no. 1 (2005), pp. 30–33.

43. Randy M. Bourn et al., "Police Perspectives on Responding to Mentally Ill People in Crisis: Perceptions of Program Effectiveness," *Behavioral Sciences and the Law,* vol. 16, no. 4 (1998), pp. 393–402.

44. Michael Thompson, Fred Osher, and Denise Tomasini-Joshi, *Improving Responses to People with Mental Illness: The Essential Elements of a Mental Health Court* (Washington, DC: U.S. Department of Justice, Bureau of Justice Assistance, 2007).

45. Roger A. Boothroyd et al., "The Broward Mental Health Court: Process, Outcomes and Service Utilization," *International Journal of Law and Psychiatry*, vol. 26 (2003), pp. 55–71.

46. American Association for Community Psychiatrists, *Position Statement on Persons with Mental Illness Behind Bars, 1999*, www.wpic.pitt.edu/aacp/finds/mibb.html (accessed March 23, 2013). See also Arthur J. Lurigio, "Effective Services for Parolees with Mental Illnesses," *Crime & Delinquency*, vol. 47, no. 3 (July 2001), pp. 446–461; other recommendations can be found in Elaine A. Lord, "The Challenges of Mentally Ill Female Offenders in Prison," *Criminal Justice and Behavior*, vol. 35, no. 8 (August 2008), pp. 928–942, and Kenneth Adams and Joseph Ferrandino, "Managing Mentally Ill Inmates in Prison," *Criminal Justice and Behavior*, vol. 35, no. 8 (August 2008), pp. 913–927.

47. Eric Blaauw, Frans Willem Winkel, and Ad J. F. M. Kerkhof, "Bullying and Suicidal Behavior in Jails," *Criminal Justice and Behavior*, vol. 28, no. 3 (June 2001), pp. 279–299.

48. Margaret E. Noonan, *Mortality in Local Jails and State Prisons, 2000–2010—Statistical Tables* (Washington, DC: U.S. Department of Justice, Bureau of Justice Statistics, December 2012).

49. Mason R. Goodman, "An Overview of Tuberculosis in Jails in the United States for Health Care and Administrative Corrections Professionals," *American Jails*, vol. 10, no. 4 (1996), pp. 45–50.

50. Paula J. Moynihan, "The Role of Diet and Nutrition in the Etiology and Prevention of Oral Disease," *Bulletin of the World Health Organization*, vol. 83, no. 9 (2005), pp. 641–720.

51. American Correctional Association, *Managing Special Needs Offenders*; Abe Macher, "Tuberculosis in Correctional Facilities," in Stan Stojkovic (ed.), *Managing Special Populations in Jails and Prisons* (New York: Civic Research Institute, 2006), pp. 6–1 to 6–55.

52. "Inmate Health Care and Communicable Diseases," *Corrections Compendium*, vol. 32, no. 5 (September/October 2007), pp. 9–31.

53. Joann B. Morton, *An Administrative Overview of the Older Inmate* (Washington, DC: National Institute of Corrections, August 1992), www.nicic.org.

54. *At America's Expense: The Mass Incarceration of the Elderly* (New York: American Civil Liberties Union, June 2012).

55. Ibid.

56. Ibid.

57. Ryan S. King and Marc Mauer, *Aging Behind Bars: "Three Strikes" Seven Years Later* (Washington, DC: The Sentencing Project, August 2001).

58. "Inmate Health Care and Communicable Diseases," p. 9.

59. Anne Seidlitz, "National Prison Hospice Association Facilities Deal with Inmate Deaths," *CorrectCare*, vol. 12, no. 1 (Spring 1998), p. 10; see "Appendix" in Statement of Professor Jonathan Turley before a Joint Hearing of the Senate Subcommittee on Aging and Long Term Care, Senate Committee on Public Safety, and Senate Select Committee on the California Correctional System, February 25, 2003.

60. Michael J. Osofeky, Philip J. Zimbardo, and Burl Cain, "Revolutionizing Prison Hospice: The Interdisciplinary Approach of the Louisiana State Penitentiary at Angola," *Corrections Compendium*, vol. 29, no. 4 (2004), pp. 5–7; Emma Quail, "Prisons Get Grayer, But Efforts to Release the Dying Lag," *City Limits*, August 6, 2013, www.citylimits.org (accessed August 25, 2013).

61. Tina Maschi, "The State of Aging: Prisoners and Compassionate Release Programs," *Huffington Post*, September 26, 2012, www.huffingtonpost.com (accessed September 26, 2012); Human Rights Watch, *The Answer is No: Too Little Compassionate Release in US Federal Prisons* (New York: Human Rights Watch, November 2012); and Emma Quail, "Prisons Get Grayer, But Efforts to Release the Dying Lag."

62. Tina Maschi, "The State of Aging: Prisoners and Compassionate Release Programs."

63. As quoted in Mark Johnson, "No-Risk Inmates' Release Debated: Dying, Disabled, Aged Are Eligible," *The News and Observer*, January 22, 2009, www.newsobserver.com (accessed December 19, 2013).

64. Ronald H. Aday, "Golden Years Behind Bars: Special Programs and Facilities for Elderly Inmates," *Federal Probation*, vol. 58, no. 2 (June 1994), pp. 47–54; Brie A. Williams et al., "Being Old and Doing Time: Functional Impairment and Adverse Experiences of Geriatric Female Prisoners," *Journal of the American Geriatric Society*, vol. 54, no. 2 (April 2006), pp. 702–707.

65. *Goodman & United States* v. *Georgia*, 546 U.S. 126 (2006).

66. American Civil Liberties Union, *At America's Expense: The Mass Incarceration of the Elderly*, p. ii.

67. Ibid., p. ii.

68. Karl Brown, "Managing Sexually Transmitted Diseases in Jails," *HEPP Report*, vol. 6, no. 9 (September 2003), pp. 1–3.

69. *Estelle* v. *Gamble*, 429 U.S. 97 (1976).

70. Vaughn and Carroll, "Separate and Unequal," pp. 3–40.

71. Civil Rights of Institutionalized Persons Act, 42 U.S.C. 1997 et seq. (1976 ed., Supp. IV), as modified 1980. (Current through P.L. 104-150, approved June 3, 1996.)

72. *Pennsylvania Department of Corrections* v. *Yeskey*, 524 U.S. 206 (1998).

73. Associated Press, "Supreme Court Upholds Rights of Disabled Inmates," June 15, 1998; *Goodman & United States* v. *Georgia*.

Chapter 13

1. Christopher Hope, "New Fines for Prisons If Criminals Re-offend After Release," *The Telegraph*, October 21, 2012, www.telegraph.co.uk (accessed October 24, 2012).

2. E. Ann Carson and Daniela Golinelli, *Prisoners in 2012* (Washington DC: U.S. Department of Justice, Bureau of Justice Statistics, December 2013).

3. Ibid.

4. *State Court Sentencing of Convicted Felons, 2004 Statistical Tables*. Electronic format only, www.ojp.usdoj.gov/bjs/abstract/scscfst.htm (accessed May 14, 2013).

5. Human Rights Watch, *Targeting Blacks: Drug Law Enforcement and Race in the United States* (New York: Human Rights Watch, 2008).

6. Sandi Doughton, "Seattle's Top Cop Joins Rally For Cannabis Freedom," *The Seattle Times*, May 11, 2013, www.seattletimes.com (accessed May 13, 2013).

7. United States Government Accountability Office, *Bureau of Prisons: Growing Inmate Crowding Negatively Affects Inmates, Staff, and Infrastructure* (Washington, DC: Government Accountability Office, September 2012).

8. Pew Charitable Trusts, *Public Safety, Public Spending: Forecasting America's Prison Population 2007–2011* (Philadelphia: Pew Charitable Trusts, 2007); Jennifer Warren, *One in 100: Behind Bars in America 2008* (Washington, DC: Pew Charitable Trusts 2009); and The Pew Center on the States, *One in 31: The Long Reach of American Corrections* (New York: Pew Charitable Trusts, March 2009).

9. Michael Doyle, "Ruling on Prison Overcrowding a Warning to States?" *McClatchy Newspapers*, May 24, 2011, www.mcclatchydc.com (accessed May 25, 2011).

10. United States Department of Justice, Bureau of Justice Statistics, *PREA Data Collection Activities,* 2012 (Washington, DC: United States Department of Justice, Bureau of Justice Statistics, June 2012).

11. Steven T. McFarland and Carroll Ann Ellis, *Report on Rape in Federal and State Prisons in the U.S.: Findings and Best Practices* (Washington, DC: U.S. Department of Justice, September 24, 2008).

12. James J. Stephan, *State Prison Expenditures, 1996* (Washington, DC: U.S. Department of Justice, Bureau of Justice Statistics, August 1999).

13. "The Cost of a Nation of Incarceration," *CBS NEWS Sunday Morning,* www.cbsnews.com, April 22, 2012 (accessed April 24, 2012).

14. As quoted in Marisa Lagos, "CA State Prison Projects Funded But Not Completed," *San Francisco Chronicle,* January 3, 2011, www.sfgate.com (accessed May 13, 2013).

15. J. J. Hensley, "Arizona Aims to Cut Prison Costs; In Texas, a New Approach," *The Arizona Republic,* April 18, 2010, www.azcentral.com (accessed May 13, 2013)

16. National Association of State Sentencing Commissions, www.ussc.gov/states.htm (accessed May 13, 2013).

17. David C. May, Peter B. Wood, and Amy Eades, "Lessons Learned from Punishment Exchange Rates: Implications for Theory, Research, and Correctional Policy," paper presented at the annual meeting of the American Society of Criminology, Atlanta, Georgia, November 2007.

18. Mary E. Pelz, "Gangs," in Marilyn D. McShane and Frank P. Williams III (eds.), *Encyclopedia of American Prisons* (New York: Garland, 1996), p. 213; and Marie L. Griffin and John R. Hepburn, "The Effect of Gang Affiliation on Violent Misconduct Among Inmates During the Early Years of Confinement," *Criminal Justice and Behavior,* vol. 33, no. 4 (2006), pp. 419–448.

19. Keith L. Martin, "Staying Ahead of Gangs/STGs in Corrections," Corrections.com, www.corrections.com/news/feature/index.html (accessed May 13, 2013); Melinda Rogers, "Jailed Gang Members Still a Potent Threat," *The Salt Lake Tribune,* February 15, 2009, www.sltrib.com (accessed May 13, 2013); "Gangs/Security Threat Groups," *Corrections Compendium,* vol. 34, no. 1 (Spring 2009), pp. 23–37 and "Gangs/Security Threat Groups," *Corrections Compendium,* vol. 34, no. 1 (Spring 2009), pp. 25–37.

20. Excerpted from Florida Department of Corrections, "Gang and Security Threat Group Awareness," www.dc.state.fl.us/pub/gangs/prison.html (accessed May 13, 2013).

21. Mark S. Hamm, *Terrorist Recruitment in American Correctional Institutions: An Exploratory Study of Non-Traditional Faith Groups* (Washington, DC: U.S. Department of Justice, National Institute of Justice, December 2007).

22. As quoted in Michael B. Farrell, "Are America's Prisons Incubating Radical Islamists?" *The Christian Science Monitor,* October 19, 2009, www.csmonitor.com (accessed May 13, 2013).

23. Hector Castro, "A Moment with Gabriel Morales, a Local Gang Specialist," *Seattle Post-Intelligencer,* November 27, 2008, http://seattlepi.nwsource.com (accessed May 13, 2013).

24. James Byrne and Don Hummer, "In Search of the 'Tossed Salad Man' (and Others Involved in Prison Violence): New Strategies for Predicting and Controlling Violence in Prison," *Aggression and Violent Behavior,* vol. 12 (2007), pp. 531–541.

25. Rick Ruddell and Terri-Lynne Scott, "Institutional Misconduct and Gang Membership: An Examination of Female Inmates," *Corrections Compendium,* vol. 36, no. 3 (Fall 2011), p. 1.

26. Ibid., pp. 4–9.

27. Rick Ruddell, Scott H. Decker, and Arlen Egley Jr., "Gang Intervention in Jails: A National Analysis," *Criminal Justice Review,* vol. 31, no. 1 (March 2006), pp. 33–46.

28. Burt Useem and Peter Kimball, *States of Siege: U.S. Prison Riots, 1971–1986* (New York: Oxford University Press, 1991).

29. "Prison Violence and Escapes," *Corrections Compendium,* vol. 31, no. 4 (July/August 2006); American Correctional Association, "Riots, Disturbances, Violence, Assaults and Escapes," *Corrections Compendium,* vol. 27, no. 5 (May 2002), pp. 6–19.

30. J. Lillis, "Prison Escapes and Violence Remain Down," *Corrections Compendium,* vol. 19, no. 6 (1994), pp. 6–21.

31. Vernon B. Fox, *Violence Behind Bars: An Explosive Report on Prison Riots in the United States* (New York: Vantage, 1956); Reid H. Montgomery Jr., "Bringing the Lessons of Prison Riots into Focus," *Corrections Today,* vol. 59, no. 1 (February 1997), pp. 28–33.

32. New York State Special Commission on Attica (McKay Commission), *Attica: The Official Report of the New York State Special Commission on Attica* (New York: Bantam, 1972), p. xi; for a good discussion of prison violence, see James M. Byrne, Don Hummer, and Faye S. Taxman, *The Culture of Violence* (Boston, MA: Pearson, 2008).

33. Bert Useem and Anne Morrison Piehl, *The Challenge of Mass Incarceration* (New York: Cambridge University Press, 2008); Bert Useem, Camille Camp, and George Camp, *Resolution of Prison Riots: Strategy and Policies* (New York: Oxford University Press, 1996); Bert Useem and Peter A. Kimball, *States of Siege: U.S. Prison Riots, 1971–1986* (New York: Oxford University Press, 1989); and Bert Useem and Jack A. Goldstone, "Forging Social Order and Its Breakdown: Riot and Reform in U.S. Prisons," *American Sociological Review,* vol. 67, pp. 499–525.

34. U.S. National Advisory Commission on Civil Disorders (Kerner Commission), *Report* (Washington, DC: Kerner Commission, 1968), p. 2.

35. David A. Ward and Allen F. Breed, *The U.S. Penitentiary, Marion, Illinois: Consultants' Report Submitted to the Committee on the Judiciary, U.S. House of Representatives, Ninety-Eighth Congress, Second Session* (Washington, DC: U.S. Government Printing Office, 1985), p. 1.

36. Daniel P. Mears and Jamie Watson, "Towards a Fair and Balanced Assessment of Supermax Prisons," *Justice Quarterly,* vol. 23, no. 2 (June 2006), pp. 231–270.

37. As quoted in Francis X. Clines, "A Futuristic Prison Awaits the Hard-Core 400," *The New York Times,* October 17, 1994, p. A1.

38. Daniel P. Mears, "An Assessment of Supermax Prisons Using an Evaluation Research Framework," *The Prison Journal,* vol. 88, no. 1 (March 2008), pp. 43–68.

39. Chase Riveland, *Supermax Housing: Overview and General Considerations* (Washington, DC: National Institute of Corrections, January 1999), p. 5. See also Gerald Berge, Jeffrey Geiger, and Scot Whitney, "Technology Is the Key to Security," *Corrections Today,* July 2001, pp. 105–109.

40. Chase Riveland, *Supermax Housing: Overview and General Considerations,* p. 5.

41. As quoted in Jules Verdone, "Second Thoughts About Prison Isolation," *Just 'Cause,* vol. 17, no. 3 (Fall 2010), p. 3.

42. Chase Riveland, *Supermax Housing: Overview and Considerations,* p. 4.

43. See, Hope Metcalf, Jamelia Morgan, Samuel Oliker-Friedland, Judith Resnik, Julia Spiegel, Haran Tae, Alyssa Roxanne Work, and Brian Holbrook, *Administrative Segregation, Degrees of Isolation, and Incarceration: A National Overview of State and Federal Correctional Policies,* Yale Law School, Public Law Working Paper No. 301, for an overview of state and federal policies related to long-term isolation of inmates, the commonalities and variations among jurisdictions, comparisons across jurisdictions,

and consideration of how and when administrative segregation is and should be used; Richard H. McCleery, "Authoritarianism and the Belief System of Incorrigibles," in Donald R. Cressy (ed.), *The Prison: Studies in Institutional Organization and Change* (New York: Holt, Rinehart & Winston, 1961), pp. 260–306; *Wright v. Enomoto* (July 23, 1980), pp. 5, 15; *Madrid v. Gomez*, 889 F. Supp. 1146 (N.D. Cal. 1995); Craig Haney, "Infamous Punishment: The Psychological Consequences of Isolation," *National Prison Project Journal* (Spring 1993); Craig Haney, "A Culture of Harm: Taming the Dynamics of Cruelty in Supermax Prisons," *Criminal Justice and Behavior,* vol. 35, no. 8 (August 2008), pp. 956–984; and David Lovell, "Patterns of Disturbed Behavior in a Supermax Population," *Criminal Justice and Behavior,* vol. 35, no. 8 (August 2008), pp. 985–1004.

44. Paige St. John, "Report Decries Suicides, Isolation Cells in California Prisons," *Los Angeles Times*, September 27, 2012, www.latimes.com (accessed September 29, 2012).

45. George F. Will, "When Solitude Is Torture," *The Washington Post,* February 20, 2013, www.washingtonpost.com (accessed February 27, 2013).

46. As quoted in Corey Weinstein, "Even Dogs Confined to Cages for Long Periods of Time Go Berserk," in May and Pitts, *Building Violence,* p. 122.

47. Mears and Watson, "Towards a Fair and Balanced Assessment of Supermax Prisons."

48. Ibid., p. 261.

49. Chad S. Briggs, Jody L. Sundt, and Thomas C. Castellano, "The Effect of Supermaximum Security Prisons on Aggregate Levels of Institutional Violence," *Criminology,* vol. 41, no. 4 (March 2006), pp. 1341–1376.

50. *Madrid v. Gomez,* 889 F. Supp. 1146 (N.D. Cal. 1995).

51. *Wilkinson v. Austin,* 545 U.S. (2005).

52. Maureen L. O'Keefe, Kelli J. Klebe, Alysha Stucker, Kristin Sturm, and William Leggett, *One Year Longitudinal Study of the Psychological Effects of Administrative Segregation* (Washington, DC: U.S. Department of Justice, National Institute of Justice, October 2010).

53. Susan Greene, "Questioning Study that Showed Inmates in Solitary Get Better," *Denver Post,* November 7, 2010, www.denverpost.com (accessed November 16, 2010).

54. As quoted in Nygel Lenz, "'Luxuries' in Prison: The Relationship Between Amenity Funding and Public Support," *Crime & Delinquency,* vol. 48, no. 4 (October 2002), p. 501.

55. As quoted in Garry Boulard, "What's Tough Enough?" *State Legislatures,* vol. 21, no. 10 (December 1995), p. 26.

56. Keynote speech, U.S. Attorney General's Summit on Corrections, April 27, 1998.

57. Lenz, "'Luxuries' in Prison," p. 519.

58. "Inmate Privileges and Fees for Service," *Corrections Compendium,* vol. 27, no. 8 (August 2002), pp. 4–26.

59. Ibid., pp. 8–9.

60. "5 Florida County Jails Make It Real Hard Time: No Television," *The New York Times,* August 14, 1994, p. L27; Richard Tewksbury and Elizabeth Ehrhardt Mustaine, "Insiders' Views on Prison Amenities: Beliefs and Perceptions of Correctional Staff Members," *Criminal Justice Review,* vol. 30, no. 2 (September 2005), pp. 174–188.

61. As quoted in Brett Pulley, "Always a Good Sound Bite: The 'Good Life' Behind Bars," *The New York Times,* September 22, 1996, Section 13, p. 2.

62. "5 Florida County Jails."

63. John J. Rafferty, "Prison Industry: The Next Step," *Corrections Today,* vol. 60, no. 4 (July 1998), p. 22.

64. W. Wesley Johnson, Katherine Bennett, and Timothy J. Flanagan, "Getting Tough on Prisoners: Results from the National Corrections Executive Survey, 1995," *Crime & Delinquency,* vol. 43, no. 1 (January 1997), pp. 24–41.

65. Adapted from the Web site of the American Correctional Association, www.corrections.com/aca/standards/benefits.htm (accessed June 15, 2011).

66. Malcolm M. Feeler, "The Privatization of Prisons in Historical Perspective," *Criminal Justice Research Bulletin,* vol. 6, no. 2 (1991), pp. 1–10.

67. Christopher Hartney and Caroline Glesman, *Prison Bed Profiteers: How Corporations Are Reshaping Criminal Justice in the U.S.* (Oakland, CA: National Council on Crime and Delinquency, May 2012), p. 5.

68. Cody Mason, *Too Good to Be True: Private Prisons in America* (Washington, DC: The Sentencing Project, January 2012), p. 2.

69. D. M. Sloane, D. P. Alexander, B. A. Stolz, B. I. Rabinowitz, P. V. Williams, G. R. Hamilton, D. R. Burton, S. D. Boyles, and D. B. Svoboda, *Private and Public Prisons: Studies Comparing Operational Costs and/or Quality of Service* (Washington, DC: United States General Accounting Office, General Government Division, 1996).

70. Travis C. Pratt and Jeff Maahs, "Are Private Prisons More Cost-Effective Than Public Prisons? A Meta-Analysis of Evaluation Research Studies," *Crime & Delinquency,* vol. 45, no. 3 (July 1999), pp. 358–371.

71. James Austin and Gary Coventry, *Emerging Issues on Privatized Prisons* (Washington, DC: U.S. Department of Justice, Bureau of Justice Statistics, February 2001).

72. Cody Mason, *Too Good to Be True: Private Prisons in America,* p. 8.

73. As quoted in Richard A. Oppel, "Private Prisons Found to Offer Little in Savings," *The New York Times,* May 18, 2011, www.nytimes.com (accessed May 24, 2011).

74. Adler School Institute on Public Safety and Social Justice, *The Economies of Private Detention: False Promises, Hidden Costs* (Chicago, IL: 2012).

75. Richard A. Oppel, "Private Prisons Found to Offer Little in Savings."

76. Ibid.

77. Ibid.

78. Travis C. Pratt and Jeff Maahs, "Are Private Prisons More Cost-Effective Than Public Prisons? A Meta-Analysis of Evaluation Research Studies."

79. Justice Policy Institute, *Gaming the System: How the Political Strategies of Private Prison Companies Promote Ineffective Incarceration Policies* (Washington, DC: Justice Policy Institute, June 2011).

80. Curtis Blakely and John Ortiz Smykla, "Correctional Privatization and the Myth of Inherent Efficiency" in Robert E. Bohm and Jeffrey T. Walker (eds.), *Demystifying Crime and Criminal Justice* (Los Angeles, CA: Roxbury, 2007), pp. 214–220.

81. C. S. Schloss and L. F. Alarid, "Standards in the Privatization of Probation Services: A Statutory Analysis," *Criminal Justice Review,* vol. 32, no. 3 (2007), pp. 233–245.

82. Sue Carlton, Marlene Sokol, and John Martin, "When the Salvation Army is Your Probation Officer," *St. Petersburg Times,* March 21, 2011, www.tampabay.com (accessed March 22, 2011).

83. Private Probation Association of Georgia, www.ppaonline.com (accessed May 18, 2013).

84. Southern Center for Human Rights, *Profiting from the Poor* (Atlanta, GA: Southern Center for Human Rights, 2008), p. 5.

85. Celia Perry, "Probation Profiteers," *Mother Jones,* July/August 2008, motherjones.com (accessed May 18, 2013).

86. C. S. Schloss and L. F. Alarid, "Standards in the Privatization of Probation Services: A Statutory Analysis."

87. "Federal Prisons Set Up E-mail Programs," *Corrections Compendium,* vol. 33, no. 5 (September/October 2008), p. 35.

88. Sarah Wheaton, "Inmates in Georgia Prisons Use Contraband Phones to Protest," *The New York Times,* December 12, 2010, www.nytimes.com (accessed May 19, 2013); Kim Severson and Robbie Brown, "Outlawed, Cellphones Are Thriving in Prisons," *The New York Times,* January 2, 2011, www.nytimes.com (accessed May 19, 2013); Steve Kanigher, "Prisons Face Threat of Smuggled Cell Phones," *Las Vegas Sun,* December 17, 2010, www.lasvegassun.com (accessed May 19, 2013); Brian Haas, "Dogs To Help Sniff Out TN Inmates' Cell Phones," *The Tennessean,* July 26, 2011, www.tennessean.com (accessed May 19, 2013); Jack Dolan, "Charles Manson Had a Cellphone? California Prisons Fight Inmate Cellphone Profileration," *Los Angeles Times,* December 2, 2010, www.latimes.com (accessed May 19, 2013); Therese Apel, "State's Prisons Test Technology: Cell Phones Blocked Behind Bars," *The Clarion-Ledger* (Jackson, MS), September 9, 2010, www.clarionledger.com (accessed May 19, 2013).

89. Kurt Erikson, "Officials Target Cellphones in Illinois Prisons," December 7, 2011, www.pantagraph.com (accessed December 8, 2011); Jack Dolan, "Phone Smuggling Case Costs 20 California Prison Workers Their Jobs," *Los Angeles Times,* October 14, 2012, www.latimes.com (accessed October 17, 2012).

90. Jack Dolan, "Prisons to Block Use of Smuggled Phones," *Los Angeles Times,* April 17, 2012, www.latimes.com (accessed April 17, 2012).

91. Susan Haigh, "Prisons Beef Up Teleconferencing to Save Money," *USA Today,* November 23, 2008, www.usatoday.com (accessed January 15, 2009).

92. Sadhbh Walshe, "Prison Video Visits Threaten to Put Profit Before Public Safety," *The Guardian,* October 25, 2012, www.guardian.co.uk (accessed November 28, 2012).

93. Susan D. Phillips, *Video Visits for Children Whose Parents Are Incarcerated* (Washington, DC: The Sentencing Project, October 2012).

94. Ibid., p. 5.

95. Ibid.

96. Ibid.

97. "Telemedicine Expanding in Ohio Prison System," *TECHbeat,* Spring 2002, p. 10; and "More States Turn to Videoconferencing," *Corrections Today,* vol. 71, no. 3 (June 2009), p. 14.

98. "Inmate Health Care and Communicable Diseases," *Corrections Compendium,* vol. 34, no. 4 (Winter 2009), pp. 13–35.

99. Graeme Wood, "Prison Without Walls," *The Atlantic,* September 2010, www.theatlantic.com (accessed May 20, 2013), p. 5.

100. "CORMAP It," *TECHbeat,* Summer 2002, p. 5.

101. Christopher A. Miles and Jeffrey P. Cohn, "Tracking Prisoners in Jail with Biometrics: An Experiment in a Navy Brig," *NIJ Journal,* no. 253 (January 2006), pp. 6–9.

Chapter 14

1. Details for this story come from Glen Puit, "1978 Mutilation: Family Relieved by Singleton's Death," *Las Vegas Review-Journal,* January 6, 2002.

2. Section 28(e) of Article I of the California Constitution.

3. Much of the material in this chapter is adapted from Office for Victims of Crime, *New Directions from the Field: Victims Rights and Services for the 21st Century* (Washington, DC: U.S. Department of Justice, 1998).

4. National Organization for Victim Assistance, *1988 NOVA Legislative Directory* (Washington, DC: National Organization for Victim Assistance, 1988), p. 191.

5. Victim and Witness Protection Act of 1982, Pub. L. No. 97-291.

6. Office of Justice Programs, *President's Task Force on Victims of Crime: Four Years Later* (Washington, DC: U.S. Government Printing Office, May 1986), p. 4.

7. Office for Victims of Crime, *The Crime Victim's Right to Be Present* (Washington, DC: OVC Legal Series Bulletin no. 3, November 2001).

8. Office of Justice Programs, VictimLaw, "About Victims' Rights," www.victimlaw.org/victimlaw/pages/victimsRight.jsp (accessed May 30, 2013).

9. National Victims' Constitutional Amendment Passage, www.nvcap.org (accessed January 9, 2013).

10. Victim and Witness Protection Act of 1982, Pub. L. No. 97-291, Section 2(b).

11. Crime Control Act of 1990, Pub. L. No. 101-647.

12. Ibid., Title V, Section 502–503.

13. Violent Crime Control and Law Enforcement Act of 1994, Pub. L. No. 103-322.

14. Megan's Law amendment to the Jacob Wetterling Crimes Against Children and Sexual Violent Offender Act, 42 U.S.C. Section 14071.

15. S.2329.

16. NVCAN was created following a meeting sponsored by the National Organization for Victim Assistance (NOVA) and Mothers Against Drunk Driving (MADD) in 1985.

17. See the National Victims' Constitutional Amendment Network (NVCAN), *1996 Constitutional Amendment Action Kit.*

18. National Victims' Constitutional Amendment Network, *President Bush Announces Support for Bi-partisan Victims' Rights Amendment,* www.nvcan.org/home.htm (accessed June 24, 2002).

19. National Institute of Justice, *Victim Costs and Consequences: A New Look* (Washington, DC: NIJ, January 1996).

20. Kathryn E. McCollister, Michael T French, and Hai Fang, "The Cost of Crime to Society: New Crime-specific Estimates for Policy and Program Evaluation," *Drug and Alcohol Dependence* (January, 2010).

21. Ibid.

22. Much of the material in this section comes from Office for Victims of Crime, *New Directions.*

23. Anne Seymour, "Promoting Victim Justice Through Corrections-Based Victim Services," *Corrections Today,* July 2000, pp. 140–142.

24. Office of Victims of Crime, Archive, *Corrections,* Chapter 5, https://www.ncjrs.gov/ovc_archives/directions/chap5.htm (accessed August 6, 2012).

25. A. Seymour, *National Victim Services Survey of Adult and Juvenile Correctional Agencies and Paroling Authorities, 1996* (Arlington, VA: National Victim Center, April 1997).

26. Office for Victims of Crime, *New Directions.*

27. Seymour, *National Victim Services Survey,* p. 5.

28. Megan's Law, Pub. L. No. 104-145, 110 Stat. 1345.

29. Information in this paragraph comes from the National Center for Victims of Crime Public Policy Issues page, www.ncvc.org/law/issues/community.htm (accessed November 25, 2011).

30. See Office for Victims of Crime, *New Directions.*

31. See Dorothy Mercer, R. Lord, and J. Lord, *Sharing Their Stories: What Are the Benefits? Who Is Helped?* paper presented at the Annual Meeting of the International Society for Traumatic Stress Studies, Chicago, IL, November 8, 1994.

32. Office for Victims of Crime, *New Directions.*

33. Dean G. Kilpatrick, David Beatty, and Susan Smith Howley, *The Rights of Crime Victims—Does Legal Protection Make a Difference?* (Washington, DC: NIJ, December 1998).

34. Ibid.

35. Office for Victims of Crime, *New Directions.*

36. Seymour, *National Victim Services Survey.*

37. Seymour, *Promising Practices and Strategies for Victim Services in Corrections* (Washington, DC: Office for Victims of Crime, 1999).

38. Office for Victims of Crime, *State Crime Victim Compensation and Assistance Grant Programs* (Washington, DC: OVC Fact Sheet, January 2002).

39. Office for Victims of Crime, *New Directions.*

40. President's Task Force on Victims of Crime, *Final Report* (Washington, DC: U.S. Government Printing Office, December 1982), p. 39.

41. National Association of Crime Victim Compensation Boards, *Crime Victim Compensation: An Overview* (Washington, DC: National Association of Crime Victim Compensation Boards, 1997), p. 1; Office for Victims of Crime, *State Crime Victim Compensation and Assistance Grant Programs.*

42. Office for Victims of Crime, *Nationwide Analysis, Victims of Crime Act: 1996 Victims of Crime Act Performance Report, State Compensation Program* (Washington, DC: U.S. Department of Justice, Office of Justice Programs, Office for Victims of Crime, April 14, 1997).

43. Victims of Crime Act of 1984, Pub. L. No. 104-235.

44. Office for Victims of Crime, *Victims of Crime Act Crime Victims Fund* (Washington, DC: OVC Fact Sheet, January 2002).

45. Office for Victims of Crime, *State Crime Victim Compensation and Assistance Grant Programs.*

46. President's Task Force on Victims of Crime, *Final Report.*

47. Much of the material in this section is taken from the Office for Victims of Crime fact sheet, www.ncjrs.org/ovcfs.htm (accessed September 1, 2003).

48. Victim and Witness Protection Act of 1982, Pub. L. No. 97-291, Sec. 4.

49. President's Task Force on Victims of Crime, *Final Report* (Washington, DC: U.S. Government Printing Office, December 1982), p. 72.

50. The Mandatory Victim Restitution Act, Title II of the Antiterrorism and Effective Death Penalty Act of 1996, Pub. L. No. 104-132 (1996), 18 U.S.C. Section 3663A (1996).

51. P. A. Langan and M. A. Cunniff, *Recidivism of Felons on Probation, 1986–89* (Washington, DC: U.S. Department of Justice, Bureau of Justice Statistics, February 1992).

52. R. L. Cohen, *Probation and Parole Violators in State Prison, 1991* (Washington, DC: Bureau of Justice Statistics, 1995).

53. Kilpatrick, Beatty, and Howley, *The Rights of Crime Victims,* p. 5.

54. Cohen, *Probation and Parole Violators.*

55. Office for Victims of Crime, *OVC Fact Sheet: What Is the Office for Victims of Crime?* (Washington, DC: OVC, 2004), from which much of the material in this section is taken.

56. Office for Victims of Crime, *What You Can Do If You Are a Crime Victim* (Washington, DC: OVC Fact Sheet, April 2002).

57. The National Victim Center, "INFOLINK: Victim Impact Statements," www.nvc.org/infolink/info72.htm (accessed January 2, 1999).

58. See Ellen K. Alexander and Janice Harris Lord, *Impact Statements: A Victim's Right to Speak, A Nation's Responsibility to Listen* (Washington, DC: Office for Victims of Crime, 1994).

59. *Payne* v. *Tennessee,* 501 U.S. 808, 111 S. Ct. 2597, 115 L. Ed. 2d 720.

60. National Victim Center, *1996 Victims' Rights Sourcebook.*

61. Office for Victims of Crime, *Vision 21: Transforming Victim Services,* Web available at http://ovc.ncjrs.gov/vision21 (accessed March 5, 2011).

62. Office for Victims of Crime, *New Directions.*

Chapter 15

1. www.deathpenaltyinfo.org (accessed December 31, 2013).

2. Excerpted from Susan Levine, "10 Years After Being Freed by DNA Evidence, His Life Is Still Trying," *Pittsburgh Post-Gazette,* March 2, 2003, p. A-12.

3. Details for this story come from Edward Connors et al., *Convicted by Juries, Exonerated by Science: Case Studies in the Use of DNA Evidence to Establish Innocence after Trial, Issues in Child Abuse Accusations,* vol. 10 (1998), www.ipt-forensics.com/journal/volume10/j10_3_6_2.htm (accessed February 1, 2013).

4. *U.S.* v. *Jackson,* 390 U.S. 570 (1968).

5. *Witherspoon* v. *Illinois,* 391 U.S. 510 (1968).

6. *Furman* v. *Georgia,* 408 U.S. 238 (1972).

7. Death Penalty Information Center, www.deathpenaltyinfo.org (accessed December 31, 2013).

8. Ibid.

9. Ian Simpson, "Maryland Becomes Latest U.S. State to Abolish Death Penalty," *Reuters,* May 2, 2013, www.reuters.com (accessed May 5, 2013).

10. M. Watt Espy and John Ortiz Smykla, "Executions in the U.S. 1608–2003: The Espy File" (Inter-University Consortium for Political and Social Research, 1994).

11. Tracy L. Snell, *Capital Punishment, 2011—Statistical Tables* (Washington, DC: U.S. Department of Justice, Bureau of Justice Statistics, July 2013).

12. United States Department of Justice, *The Federal Death Penalty System: A Statistical Survey* (Washington, DC: U.S. Department of Justice, September 12, 2000).

13. As cited in Marc Lacey and Raymond Bonner, "Reno Troubled by Death Penalty Statistics," *New York Times,* September 12, 2000, p. A17.

14. www.deathpenaltyinfo.org (accessed March 10, 2013).

15. Brett Barrouquere, "Lawyers Face Ethics Dilemma When Inmates Seek Death," *USA Today,* November 20, 2008, www.usatoday.com (accessed January 31, 2013). See also Death Penalty Information Center, www.deathpenaltyinfo.org (accessed December 31, 2013).

16. www.deathpenaltyinfo.org (accessed December 31, 2013). See also *The Death Penalty in 2012: Year End Report,* Death Penalty Information Center, December 2012, www.deathpenaltyinfo.org (accessed January 31, 2013).

17. Robert M. Bohm, *Deathquest III: An Introduction to the Theory and Practice of Capital Punishment in the United States,* 3rd ed. (Cincinnati, OH: Anderson, 2007); Raymond Paternoster, Robert Brame, and Sarah Bacon, *The Death Penalty: America's Experience with Capital Punishment* (New York: Oxford University Press, 2008).

18. John Boger, "Landmark North Carolina Death Penalty Study Finds Dramatic Racial Bias," www.deathpenaltyinfo.org (accessed April 1, 2011).

19. Joint Legislative Audit and Review Commission, The Virginia General Assembly, *Review of Virginia's System of Capital Punishment* (Richmond, VA: Joint Legislative Audit and Review Commission, December 2001).

20. G. Ben Cohen and Robert J. Smith, "The Racial Geography of the Federal Death Penalty," *Washington Law Review,* vol. 45 (2010), pp. 425–492.

21. *Atkins* v. *Virginia,* 536 U.S. 304, 353 (202) (Scalia, J., dissenting).

22. Jefferson E. Holcomb, Marion R. Williams, and Stephen Demuth, "White Female Victims and Death Penalty Disparity Research," *Justice Quarterly,* vol. 21, no. 7 (December 2004), pp. 877–902.

23. See, for example, Maggie Clark, *Some States Speed Up Death Penalty* (New York: Pew Charitable Trusts, June 18, 2013); Manny Fernandez, "Executions Stall as States Seek Different Drugs," *The New York Times,* November 8, 2013 www.nytimes.org (accessed November 10, 2013); Richard Dieter, "The Lethal Injection Debacle," *The Crime Report,* November 12, 2013, www.thecrimereport.org (accessed November 14, 2013); Death Penalty Information Center, www.deathpenaltyinfo.org; and J. Weisberg, "This Is Your Death," *The New Republic,* July 1, 1991.

24. George Lombardi, Richard D. Sluder, and Donald Wallace, *The Management of Death-Sentenced Inmates: Issues, Realities, and Innovative Strategies,* paper presented at the annual meeting of the Academy of Criminal Justice Sciences, Las Vegas, Nevada, March 1996.

25. Robert Johnson, "Under Sentence of Death: The Psychology of Death Row Confinement," *Law and Psychology Review,* vol. 5 (Fall 1979), pp. 141–192 and ABA Criminal Justice Standards on the Treatment of Prisoners, Standard 23-2.6.(a) (2010), available at http://www.abanet.org/crimjust/policy/midyear2010/102i.pdf.

26. As quoted in Bonnie Bartel Latino and Bob Vale, "Welcome to Death Row," *The Birmingham News,* January 16, 2000, pp. 1C, 4C.

27. Thomas J. Reidy, Mark D. Cunningham, and Jon R. Sorensen, "From Death to Life: Prison Behavior of Former Death Row Inmates in Indiana," *Criminal Justice and Behavior,* vol. 28, no. 1 (February 2001), pp. 62–82.

28. Mark Costanzo, *Just Revenge: Costs and Consequences of the Death Penalty* (New York: St. Martin's Press, 1997), p. 51.

29. As quoted in John Ortiz Smykla, "The Human Impact of Capital Punishment," *Journal of Criminal Justice,* vol. 15, no. 4 (1987), pp. 331–347.

30. "U.S. Death Penalty Support Lowest in More Than 40 Years," Gallup, October 29, 2013 and "Poll Shows Growing Support for Alternatives to the Death Penalty; Capital Punishment Ranked Lowest Among Budget Priorities," www.deathpenaltyinfo.org (accessed February 9, 2013).

31. As quoted in Rob Stein, "Group to Censure Physicians Who Play Role in Lethal Injections," *The Washington Post,* May 2, 2010, www.washingtonpost.com (accessed May 4, 2010).

32. Michael L. Radelet and Traci L. Lacock, "Do Executions Lower Homicide Rates? The Views of Leading Criminologists," *Journal of Criminal Law and Criminology,* vol. 99, no. 2 (2009), pp. 489–508.

33. "O'Connor Questions Death Penalty Fairness," ABC News, Minneapolis, July 3, 2003, abcnews.go.com (accessed February 9, 2013).

34. "Justice Backs Death Penalty Freeze," CBS News, February 11, 2009, www.cbsnews.com (accessed February 9, 2013).

35. *Callins* v. *Collins,* 510 U.S. 1141 (1994).

36. John Paul Stevens (December 23, 2010), "On the Death Sentence" [Review of the book *Peculiar Institutions: America's Death Penalty in an Age of Abolition,* by David Garland]. *The New York Review of Books.*

37. *Furman* v. *Georgia,* 408 U.S. 238 (1972).

38. *Woodson* v. *North Carolina,* 428 U.S. 280 (1976); *Roberts* v. *Louisiana,* 428 U.S. 325 (1976); *Gregg* v. *Georgia,* 428 U.S. 153 (1976); *Jurek* v. *Texas,* 428 U.S. 262 (1976); *Proffitt* v. *Florida,* 428 U.S. 242 (1976).

39. *Ring* v. *Arizona,* 122 U.S. 2428 (2002).

40. *Schriro* v. *Summerlin,* 542 U.S. 348 (2004).

41. James Liebman, Jeffrey Fagan, and Valerie West, *A Broken System: Error Rates in Capital Cases, 1973–1995* (New York: Columbia University School of Law, 2000), p. i; Barry Latzer and James N. G. Cauthen, *Justice Delayed? Time Consumption in Capital Appeals: A Multistate Study* (Washington, DC: U.S. Department of Justice, March 2007). The authors found a median of 966 days to complete direct appeals across 14 states from 1992 to 2002. Processing direct appeals was fastest in Virginia (295 days) and slowest in Ohio, Tennessee, and Kentucky (1,388, 1,350, and 1,309 days, respectively).

42. Ibid. See also Timothy G. Poveda, "Estimating Wrongful Convictions," *Justice Quarterly,* vol. 18, no. 3 (September 2001), pp. 689–708; Talia Roitberg Harmon, "Predictors of Miscarriages of Justice in Capital Cases," *Justice Quarterly,* vol. 18, no. 4 (December 2001), pp. 949–968.

43. Nancy Phillips, "In Life and Death Cases, Costly Mistakes," *The Inquirer,* October 23, 2011, www.philly.com (accessed October 24, 2011).

44. Nancy Phillips, "PA's Death Penalty Defense Pay Criminally Low, Hearing Told," *The Inquirer,* November 20, 2011, www.philly.com (accessed November 21, 2011).

45. Liebman, Fagan, and West, *A Broken System,* p. 18.

46. Steve Mills and Maurice Possley, "After Exonerations, Hunt for Killer Rare," *Chicago Tribune,* October 27, 2003, p. 1A, www.deathpenaltyinfo.org (accessed June 15, 2007).

47. Matt O'Connor, "Jury Believes Ex-Chicago Cop Framed by FBI," *Chicago Tribune,* January 25, 2005; and Shaun Hittle, "10 Years Later, Eddie Lowery's Name is Clear and the Man Accused of the Rape for Which Lowery Was Convicted Is Behind Bars," *Channel 49 News,* February 11, 2010, www.ktka.com (accessed February 9, 2013).

48. Mike Ward, "Tab for Wrongful Convictions in Texas: $65 Million and Counting," *Statesman,* February 10, 2013, www.statesman.com (accessed February 12, 2013).

49. Marie C. Baca, "Wrongly Convicted Rarely Compensated," *San Francisco Chronicle,* March 7, 2011, www.sfgate.com (accessed February 9, 2013).

50. James S. Liebman et al., *A Broken System, Part II: Why There Is So Much Error in Capital Cases, and What Can Be Done About It* (New York: Columbia University School of Law, 2002), pp. 391–428.

51. Alan Johnson, "Leave Death Penalty Up to a Panel?" *The Columbus Dispatch,* January 13, 2013, www.dispatch.com (accessed January 14, 2012).

52. John Schwartz, "Confessing to Crime, But Innocent," *The New York Times,* September 13, 2010, www.nytimes.com (accessed September 15, 2010).

53. Espy and Smykla, "Executions in the U.S."

54. Does not include Jose High, executed November 6, 2001, in Georgia. He may have been 17 years old at the time of the crime. Records concerning his age are disputed.

55. *Thompson* v. *Oklahoma,* 487 U.S. 815 (1988).

56. *Stanford* v. *Kentucky,* 492 U.S. 361 (1989).

57. Consolidated with *Stanford*.
58. *Roper* v. *Simmons*, 543 U.S. (2005).
59. James Alan Fox as cited in Meghan Mandeville, "Supreme Court Puts an End to Juvenile Death Penalty," *Juvenile Info Network* online, www.juvenilenet.org/news.html (accessed March 22, 2011).
60. *Atkins* v. *Virginia*, 536 U.S. (2002).

Chapter 16

1. "Judge: Pa. Boy, 11, Killed Dad's Pregnant Fiancee," *USA Today*, April 13, 2012, http://usatoday30.usatoday.com/news/nation/story/2012-04-13/pennsylvania-boy-kills-dads-pregnant-fiancee/54259732/1 (accessed March 11, 2013).
2. "Jordan Brown, Boy Who Killed Dad's Pregnant Financee, Moving to Father's Home," *Huffington Post*, November 30, 2012, www.huffingtonpost.com/2012/12/01/jordan-brown-killing-kenzie-brown_n_2223585.html (accessed March 11, 2013).
3. See, for example, Jeffrey A. Butts and Douglas N. Evans, Resolution, *Reinvestment and Realignment: Three Strategies for Changing Juvenile Justice* (New York: John Jay College of Criminal Justice, 2011).
4. Ken Wooden, *Weeping in the Playtime of Others* (New York: McGraw-Hill, 1976), pp. 23–24.
5. *People ex rel. O'Connell* v. *Turner*, 55 Ill.280, 8 Am. Rep. 645.
6. R. M. Mennel, *Thorns and Thistles: Juvenile Delinquency in the United States, 1825–1940* (Hanover, NH: University Press of New England, 1973), p. 131.
7. *Kent* v. *United States*, 383 U.S. 541 (1966).
8. *In re Gault*, 387 U.S. 1, 55 (1967).
9. *In re Winship*. 397 U.S. 358 (1970).
10. *McKeiver* v. *Pennsylvania*, 403 U.S. 528 (1971).
11. *Breed* v. *Jones*, 421 U.S. 519 (1975).
12. This paragraph is adapted from Howard N. Snyder and Melissa Sickmund, *Juvenile Offenders and Victims: 1999 National Report* (Washington, DC: Office of Juvenile Justice and Delinquency Prevention, 1999), p. 99.
13. Melissa Sickmund, *Juveniles in Court* (Washington, DC: Office of Juvenile Justice and Delinquency Prevention, June 2003), p. 5.
14. FBI, *Crime in the United States, 2012* (Washington, DC: U.S. Department of Justice, 2013).
15. Charles Puzzanchera et al., *Juvenile Court Statistics 2009* (Pittsburgh, PA: National Center for Juvenile Justice, May 2012).
16. Josephson Institute Press Release, "Largest Study Ever Shows Half of All High School Students were Bullies and Nearly Half Were the Victims of Bullying During Past Year," October 25, 2010, http://charactercounts.org/pdf/reportcard/2010/press-release_bullying-violence.pdf (accessed March 7, 2011).
17. U.S. Department of Education, Office for Civil Rights, "Dear Colleague Letter Harassment and Bullying: Background, Summary, and Fast Facts," (October 26, 2010), http://www2.ed.gov/about/offices/list/ocr/docs/dcl-factsheet-201010.pdf (accessed March 8, 2011).
18. Josephson Institute Press Release, op. cit.
19. Crystal Knoll and Melissa Sickmund, *Delinquency Cases in Juvenile Court, 2009* (Washington, DC: Office of Juvenile Justice and Delinquency Prevention, 2012), p. 4.
20. Ibid., p. 9.
21. Gerald Bayens, *Assessing the Impact of Judicial Waiver Laws in Kansas: Implications for Correctional Policy* (Ann Arbor, MI: University Microfilms International, 1998).

22. E. J. Loughran et al., *CJCA Yearbook 2006: A National Perspective of Juvenile Corrections* (Braintree, MA: Council of Juvenile Correctional Administrators, 2007), from which parts of this section are derived.
23. Charles Puzzanchera et al., *Juvenile Court Statistics, 2009* (Pittsburgh, PA: National Center for Juvenile Justice, 2012).
24. Howard N. Snyder and Melissa Sickmund, *Juvenile Offenders and Victims: 2006 National Report* (Washington, DC: Office of Juvenile Justice and Delinquency Prevention, 2006), from which some of the material in this section is adapted.
25. Sarah Hockenberry, Melissa Sickmund, and Anthony Sladky, *Juvenile Residential Facility Census, 2008: Selected Findings* (Washington, DC: Office of Juvenile Justice and Delinquency Prevention, 2011), p. 2.
26. Sharon Mihalic, Abigail Fagan, Katherine Irwin, Diane Ballard, and Delbert Elliott, *Blueprints for Violence Prevention* (Washington, DC: OJJDP, July 2004).
27. Ibid.
28. OJJDP, *OJJDP Model Programs Guide*, http://www.ojjdp.gov/mpg/Default.aspx (accessed March 10, 2013).
29. National Center for Youth in Custody, "About Us," http://nc4yc.org/about-us/priority-service-areas.html (accessed March 10, 2013).
30. Justice Policy Institute, *Juvenile Justice Reform in Connecticut*, (2013) p. 22, http://www.justicepolicy.org/uploads/justicepolicy/documents/jpi_juvenile_justice_reform_in_ct.pdf (accessed May 10, 2013).
31. Benjamin Adams and Sean Addie, *Delinquency Cases Waived to Criminal Court, 2009* (Washington, DC: Office of Juvenile Justice and Delinquency Prevention, 2012).
32. Tammy Hawkins (personal communication, September 21, 1998).
33. Youth Court Guidebook Advisory Committee, *Youth Cases for Youth Courts: Desktop Guide* (Chicago: American Bar Association, 2005), from which a number of the paragraphs that follow have been adapted.
34. Sarah S. Pearson and Sonia Jurich, *Youth Court: A Community Solution for Embracing At-Risk Youth—A National Update* (Washington, DC: American Youth Policy Forum, 2005).
35. Ibid., p. 13.
36. Jeffrey A. Butts and Janeen Buck, *Teen Courts: A Focus on Research* (Washington, DC: Office of Juvenile Justice and Delinquency Prevention, October 2000).
37. Tammy Hawkins (personal communication, September 21, 1998).
38. Much of the information in this section comes from the National Gang Center Web site, www.nationalgangcenter.gov. (accessed October 31, 2013).
39. Arlen Egley Jr., and James C. Howell, *Highlights of the 2010 National Youth Gang Survey* (Washington, DC: Office of Juvenile Justice and Delinquency Prevention, 2012), and other years.
40. Federal Bureau of Investigation, *Kids Crime Prevention Page*, www.fbi.gov, 2002 (accessed June 20, 2003).
41. Candice M. Kane, *Prosecutor: Technical Assistance Manual* (Washington, DC: OJJDP, 1992).
42. Ibid.
43. Office of Juvenile Justice and Delinquency Prevention, *1998 National Youth Gang Survey* (Washington, DC: U.S. Department of Justice, November 2000).
44. Jeff Ferrell, "Criminological Verstehen: Inside the Immediacy of Crime," *Justice Quarterly*, vol. 14, no. 1 (1997), pp. 3–23.

45. Janeen Buck Willison, Daniel P. Mears, Tracey Shollenberger, Colleen Owens, and Jeffrey A. Butts, *Past, Present, and Future of Juvenile Justice: Assessing the Policy Options (APO): Final Report* (The Urban Institute).

46. Reagan Daly, Tarika Kapur, and Margaret Elliott, *Capital Change: A Process Evaluation of Washington, DC's Secure Juvenile Placement Reform* (New York: The Vera Institute of Justice, 2011), p. iii.

47. Ania Dobrzanska, "ACA's Certification Program Extends to Juvenile Corrections," *Corrections Today,* June 2005, p. 20.

48. James Turpin, "Juvenile Justice in the Spotlight," *Corrections Today,* vol. 59, no. 3 (1997), p. 124.

49. Liz Watson and Peter Edelman, *Improving the Juvenile Justice System for Girls: Lessons from the States* (Washington, DC: Georgetown Center on Poverty, Inequality and Public Policy, October 2012).

50. Ibid.

GLOSSARY

Numbers in parentheses indicate the pages on which the terms are defined.

A

absconding Fleeing without permission of the jurisdiction in which the offender is required to stay. (117)

accreditation The process through which correctional facilities and agencies can measure themselves against nationally adopted standards and through which they can receive formal recognition and accredited status.

adjudication The process by which a court arrives at a final decision in a case; or the second stage of the juvenile justice process in which the court decides whether the offender is formally responsible for (guilty of) the alleged offense. (12)

administrative officers Those who control keys and weapons and sometimes oversee visitation. (308)

aggravating circumstances Factors that may increase the culpability of the offender. (510)

AIDS (acquired immunodeficiency syndrome) A disease of the human immune system that is characterized cytologically, especially by reduction in the numbers of CD4-bearing helper T cells to 20 percent or less of normal, rendering a person highly vulnerable to life-threatening conditions. The disease is caused by infection with HIV commonly transmitted in infected blood and bodily secretions (as semen), especially during sexual intercourse and intravenous drug use. (392)

Americans with Disabilities Act (ADA) Public Law 101-336, enacted July 26, 1990, which prohibits discrimination and ensures equal opportunity for people with disabilities in employment, state and local government services, public accommodations, commercial facilities, and transportation. It also mandates the establishment of TDD/telephone relay services. (408)

arraignment An appearance in court prior to trial in a criminal proceeding. (12)

Auburn system The second historical phase of prison discipline, implemented at New York's Auburn prison in 1815. It followed the Pennsylvania system and allowed inmates to work silently together during the day, but they were isolated at night. (210)

average daily population (ADP) The sum of the number of inmates in a jail or prison each day for a year, divided by the total number of days in the year. (168)

B

bail A written obligation with or without collateral security, given to a court to guarantee appearance before the court. (163)

balancing test A method the U.S. Supreme Court uses to decide prisoners' rights cases, weighing the rights claimed by inmates against the legitimate needs of prisoners. (364)

best efforts standard A requirement of the federal Victims' Rights and Restitution Act of 1990 (also known as the *Victims' Rights Act*) that mandates that federal law enforcement officers, prosecutors, and corrections officials use their best efforts to ensure that victims receive basic rights and services during their encounter with the criminal justice system. (462)

bifurcated trial Two separate hearings for different issues in a trial, one for guilt and the other for punishment. (510)

biometrics The automated identification or verification of human identity through measurable physiological and behavioral traits. (454)

blended sentencing A two-part (juvenile and adult) sentence in which the adult sentence may be waived if the offender complies with all provisions of the juvenile sentence. (538)

block officers Those responsible for supervising inmates in housing areas. (307)

boot camp A short institutional term of confinement that includes a physical regimen designed to develop self-discipline, respect for authority, responsibility, and a sense of accomplishment. (148)

bridewell A workhouse. The word came from the name of the first workhouse in England. (40)

C

capital crime A crime for which the death penalty may but need not necessarily be imposed. (494)

capital punishment Lawful imposition of the death penalty. (491)

case investigation The first major role of probation officers, consisting of interviewing the defendant and preparing the presentence report (PSR). (107)

certification A credentialing process, usually involving testing and career development assessment, through which the skills, knowledge, and abilities of correctional personnel can be formally recognized. (20)

chlamydia The most common sexually transmitted disease. Caused by the bacteria *Chlamydia trachomatis*, it can affect the eyes, lungs, or urogenital (urinary-genital) area, depending on the age of the person infected and how the infection is transmitted. (407)

chronological résumé A résumé that organizes information in reverse time sequence and emphasizes work history. (A-7)

citation A type of nonfinancial pretrial release similar to a traffic ticket. It binds the defendant to appear in court on a future date.

civil liability A legal obligation to another person to do, pay, or make good something. (357)

classification The process of subdividing the inmate population into meaningful categories to match offender needs with correctional resources. (225)

clemency Kindness, mercy, forgiveness, or leniency, usually relating to criminal acts.

cocorrections   The incarceration and interaction of female and male offenders under a single institutional administration. (348)

coed prison   A prison housing both female and male offenders. (348)

community corrections   A philosophy of correctional treatment that embraces (1) decentralization of authority, (2) citizen participation, (3) redefinition of the population of offenders for whom incarceration is most appropriate, and (4) emphasis on rehabilitation through community programs. (151)

community corrections acts (CCAs)   State laws that give economic grants to local communities to establish community corrections goals and policies and to develop and operate community corrections programs. (152)

community notification   Notification to the community of the release or pending release of convicted offenders. (474)

community service   A sentence to serve a specified number of hours working in unpaid positions with nonprofit or tax-supported agencies. (138)

commutation   A change of a legal penalty to a lesser one (e.g., from death to life imprisonment).

compensatory damages   Money a court may award as payment for actual losses suffered by a plaintiff, including out-of-pocket expenses incurred in filing the suit, other forms of monetary or material loss, and pain, suffering, and mental anguish. (358)

concurrent sentences   Sentences served together. (66)

conditional diversion   Diversion in which charges are dismissed if the defendant satisfactorily completes treatment, counseling, or other programs ordered by the justice system. (93)

conditional release   Pretrial release under minimum or moderately restrictive conditions with little monitoring or compliance. It includes ROR, supervised pretrial release, and third-party release.

consecutive sentences   Sentences served one after the other. (66)

consent decree   A written compact, sanctioned by a court, between parties in a civil case, specifying how disagreements between them are to be resolved.

constitutional rights   The personal and due process rights guaranteed to individuals by the U.S. Constitution and its amendments, especially the first 10 amendments, known as the Bill of Rights. Constitutional rights are the basis of most inmate rights. (356)

contraband   Any item that represents a serious threat to the safety and security of the institution. (451)

contract system   A system of prison industry in which the prison advertised for bids for the employment of prisoners, whose labor was sold to the highest bidder. (214)

convict lease system   A system of prison industry in which a prison temporarily relinquished supervision of its prisoners to a lessee. The lessee either employed the prisoners within the institution or transported them to work elsewhere in the state. (214)

corporal punishments   Physical punishments, or those involving the body. (30)

correctional clients   Prison inmates, probationers, parolees, offenders assigned to alternative sentencing programs, and those held in jails. (9)

correctional econometrics   The study of the cost-effectiveness of various correctional programs and related reductions in the incidence of crime. (59)

correctional officer personalities   The distinctive personal characteristics of correctional officers, including behavioral, emotional, and social traits. (305)

corrections   All the various aspects of the pretrial and post-conviction management of individuals accused or convicted of crimes. (14)

corrections professional   A dedicated person of high moral character and personal integrity who is employed in the field of corrections and takes professionalism to heart. (19)

cost-benefit analysis   A systematic process used to calculate the costs of a program relative to its benefits. Programs showing the largest benefit per unit of expenditure are seen as the most effective. (22)

counterperformance   The defendant's participation, in exchange for diversion, in a treatment, counseling, or educational program aimed at changing his or her behavior. (90)

crime   A violation of the criminal law. (3)

crime rate   The number of major crimes reported for each unit of population.

criminal justice   The process of achieving justice through the application of the criminal law and through the workings of the criminal justice system. Also, the study of the field of criminal justice. (10)

criminal justice system   The collection of all the agencies that perform criminal justice functions, whether these are operations or administration or technical support. The basic divisions of the criminal justice system are police, courts, and corrections. (10)

criminal law   (also called *penal law*) That portion of the law that defines crimes and specifies criminal punishments. (15)

cruel and unusual punishment   A penalty that is grossly disproportionate to the offense or that violates today's broad and idealistic concepts of dignity, civilized standards, humanity, and decency (*Estelle* v. *Gamble*, 1976, and *Hutto* v. *Finney*, 1978). In the area of capital punishment, cruel and unusual punishments are those that involve torture, a lingering death, or unnecessary pain. (369)

custodial staff   Those staff members most directly involved in managing the inmate population. (300)

D

day fine   A financial penalty scaled both to the defendant's ability to pay and the seriousness of the crime. (134)

day reporting center (DRC)   A community correctional center to which an offender reports every day or several days a week for supervision and treatment. (141)

death row   A prison area housing inmates who have been sentenced to death. (502)

deliberate indifference   Intentional and willful indifference. Within the field of correctional practice, the term refers to calculated inattention to unconstitutional conditions of confinement. (369)

delinquent offenses   Acts committed by juveniles that, if committed by adults, could result in criminal prosecution. (532)

deprivation theory   The belief that inmate subcultures develop in response to the deprivations in prison life. (329)

deserts   See **just deserts.**

design capacity   The number of inmates that planners or architects intend for the facility. (203, 242)

detention hearing   A judicial review of the intake officer's detention decision. (536)

determinate sentence   (also called *fixed sentence*) A sentence of a fixed term of incarceration, which can be reduced by good time. (68)

deterrence   The discouragement or prevention of crimes through the fear of punishment. (58)

direct file provisions   Provisions under which the prosecutor determines whether to initiate a case against a juvenile in juvenile court or in adult criminal court. (544)

direct-supervision jail   See **third-generation jail.** (173)

discretionary release   Early release based on the paroling authority's assessment of eligibility. (259)

disposition   The third stage of the juvenile justice process in which the court decides the disposition (sentence) for a juvenile case. (537)

disturbance   An altercation involving three or more inmates, resulting in official action beyond summary sanctions and for which there is an institutional record. (429)

diversion   The halting or suspension, before conviction, of formal criminal proceedings against a person, conditioned on some form of counterperformance by the defendant. (90)

doctrine of sovereign immunity   A historical legal doctrine that held that a governing body or its representatives could not be sued because it made the law and therefore could not be bound by it. (380)

drug court   A special court that is given responsibility to treat, sanction, and reward drug offenders with punishment more restrictive than regular probation but less severe than incarceration. (132)

due process   A right guaranteed by the Fifth, Sixth, and Fourteenth Amendments to the U.S. Constitution and generally understood, in legal contexts, to mean the expected course of legal proceedings according to the rules and forms established for the protection of persons' rights. (371)

E

equity   The sentencing principle that similar crimes and similar criminals should be treated alike. (81)

evidence-based corrections   (also called *evidence-based penology*) The application of social scientific techniques to the study of everyday corrections procedures for the purpose of increasing effectiveness and enhancing the efficient use of available resources. (21)

exchange rates   An approach to sentencing that emphasizes interchangeability of punishments; for example, three days under house arrest might be considered equal to one day of incarceration. (422)

exonerate   To clear of blame and release from death row. (489)

external classification   Interinstitutional placement of an inmate that determines an inmate's security level. (226)

F

fair sentencing   Sentencing practices that incorporate fairness for both victims and offenders. *Fairness* is said to be achieved by implementing principles of proportionality, equity, social debt, and truth in sentencing. (80)

Federal Prison Industries (FPI)   A federal, paid inmate work program and self-supporting corporation. (236)

felony   A serious criminal offense; specifically, one punishable by death or by incarceration in a prison facility for more than a year. (8)

fine   A financial penalty used as a criminal sanction. (134)

first-generation jail   Jail with multiple-occupancy cells or dormitories that line corridors arranged like spokes. Inmate supervision is intermittent; staff must patrol the corridors to observe inmates in their cells. (172)

fixed sentence   See **determinate sentence.** (68)

flat sentences   Those that specify a given amount of time to be served in custody and allow little or no variation from the time specified. (67)

folkways   Time-honored ways of doing things. Although they carry the force of tradition, their violation is unlikely to threaten the survival of the social group. (15)

frivolous lawsuits   Lawsuits with no foundation in fact. They are generally brought for publicity, political, or other reasons not related to law. (374)

functional résumé   A résumé that emphasizes abilities over work history, organizing information according to skills, results, contributions, or functions. (A-8)

G

gain time   Time taken off an inmate's sentence for participating in certain positive activities such as going to school, learning a trade, and working in prison. (302)

gang   A criminal enterprise having an organizational structure, acting as a continuing criminal conspiracy, that employs violence and any other criminal activity to sustain itself. (548)

general deterrence   The use of the example of individual punishment to dissuade others from committing crimes. (58)

genital herpes   A sexually transmitted disease caused by the herpes simplex virus or HSV. It is one of the most common STDs in the United States. (407)

gonorrhea   The second most common sexually transmitted disease. Often called *the clap*, gonorrhea is caused by the *Neisseria gonorrhea* bacteria found in moist areas of the body. Infection occurs with contact to any of these areas. (407)

good time   The number of days or months prison authorities deduct from a sentence for good behavior and for other reasons. (68)

group home   A nonsecure residential facility for juveniles. (538)

guardian *ad litem*   A person appointed by the juvenile court, often defense counsel, to serve as a special guardian for the youth being processed through the juvenile justice system. (536)

guided discretion   Decision making bounded by general guidelines, rules, or laws. (509)

H

habitual offender statute   A law that (1) allows a person's criminal history to be considered at sentencing or (2) makes it possible for a person convicted of a given offense and previously convicted of another specified offense to receive a more severe penalty than that for the current offense alone. (77)

hands-off doctrine A historical policy of the American courts not to intervene in prison management. Courts tended to follow the doctrine until the late 1960s. (354)

hedonistic calculus The idea that people are motivated by pleasure and pain and that the proper amount of punishment can deter crime. (45)

HIV (human immunodeficiency virus) Any of a group of retroviruses that infect and destroy helper T cells of the immune system, causing the marked reduction in their numbers that is diagnostic of AIDS. (392)

hospice An interdisciplinary, comfort-oriented care facility that helps seriously ill patients die with dignity and humanity in an environment that facilitates mental and spiritual preparation for the natural process of dying. (404)

I

importation theory The belief that inmate subcultures are brought into prison from the outside world. (329)

incapacitation The use of imprisonment or other means to reduce an offender's capability to commit future offenses. (59)

indeterminate sentence A sentence in which a judge specifies a maximum length and a minimum length, and an administrative agency, generally a parole board, determines the actual time of release. (68)

industrial shop and school officers Those who ensure efficient use of training and educational resources within the prison. (308)

informational interviewing Talking to people who are currently employed in a career field of interest. (A-4)

infraction A minor violation of state statute or local ordinance punishable by a fine or other penalty, or by a specified, usually very short term of incarceration. (8)

injunction A judicial order to do or refrain from doing a particular act. (358)

inmate roles Prison lifestyles; also, forms of ongoing social accommodation to prison life. (331)

inmate subculture (also called *prisoner subculture*) The habits, customs, mores, values, beliefs, or superstitions of the body of inmates incarcerated in correctional institutions; also, the inmate social world. (328)

inmates with special needs Those prisoners who exhibit unique physical, mental, social, and programmatic needs that distinguish them from other prisoners and to whom jail and prison management and staff have to respond in nontraditional and innovative. (386)

institutional corrections That aspect of the correctional enterprise that "involves the incarceration and rehabilitation of adults and juveniles convicted of offenses against the law, and the confinement of persons suspected of a crime awaiting trial and adjudication." (14)

institutional needs Prison administration interests recognized by the courts as justifying some restrictions on the constitutional rights of prisoners. Those interests are maintenance of institutional *order*, maintenance of institutional *security*, *safety* of prison inmates and staff, and *rehabilitation* of inmates. (356)

intake The first stage of the juvenile justice process. A court-appointed officer reviews the case and recommends a course of action—dismissal, informal disposition, formal disposition, or transfer to adult criminal court. (534)

intangible losses Costs such as fear, pain, suffering, and reduced quality of life that accrue to victims as a result of their victimization. (468)

integration model A combination of importation theory and deprivation theory. The belief that, in childhood, some inmates acquired, usually from peers, values that support law-violating behavior but that the norms and standards in prison also affect inmates. (329)

intensive supervision probation (ISP) Control of offenders in the community under strict conditions, by means of frequent reporting to a probation officer whose caseload is generally limited to 30 offenders. (130)

intermediate sanctions New punishment options developed to fill the gap between traditional probation and traditional jail or prison sentences and to better match the severity of punishment to the seriousness of the crime. (125)

internal classification Intrainstitutional placement that determines, through review of an inmate's background, assignment to housing units or cellblocks, work, and programming based on the inmate's risk, needs, and time to serve. (227)

J

jail accreditation Formal approval of a jail by the American Correctional Association and the Commission on Accreditation. (201)

jails Locally operated correctional facilities that confine people before or after conviction. (167)

job interview A meeting with a prospective employer in which a job applicant projects his or her most impressive qualities. (A-13)

job shadow A career exploration activity where persons observe the day-to-day activities of a professional currently working in a person's career field of interest. (A-4)

jurisdiction The power, right, or authority of a court to interpret and apply the law. (359)

just deserts Punishment deserved. A just deserts perspective on criminal sentencing holds that criminal offenders are morally blameworthy and are therefore *deserving* of punishment. (58)

justice reinvestment The practice of reducing spending on prisons and investing a portion of the savings into infrastructure and civic institutions located in high-risk neighborhoods. (246)

juvenile court Any court that has jurisdiction over matters involving juveniles. (537)

juvenile detention facility A facility for keeping juvenile offenders in secure custody, as necessary, through various stages of the juvenile justice process. (536)

L

legitimate penological objectives The realistic concerns that correctional officers and administrators have for the integrity and security of the correctional institution and the safety of staff and inmates. (364)

M

mandatory death penalty   A death sentence that the legislature has required to be imposed upon people convicted of certain offenses. (509)

mandatory minimum sentencing   The imposition of sentences required by statute for those convicted of a particular crime or a particular crime with specific circumstances, such as robbery with a firearm or selling drugs to a minor within 1,000 feet of a school, or for those with a particular type of criminal history. (75)

mandatory release   Early release after a time period specified by law. (259)

mandatory sentences   Those that are required by law under certain circumstances—such as conviction of a specified crime or of a series of offenses of a specified type. (65)

maximum- or close/high-security prison   A prison designed, organized, and staffed to confine the most dangerous offenders for long periods. It has a highly secure perimeter, barred cells, and a high staff-to-inmate ratio. It imposes strict controls on the movement of inmates and visitors, and it offers few programs, amenities, or privileges. (249)

medical model   A philosophy of prisoner reform in which criminal behavior is regarded as a disease to be treated with appropriate therapy. (216)

medium-security prison   A prison that confines offenders considered less dangerous than those in maximum security, for both short and long periods. It places fewer controls on inmates' and visitors' freedom of movement than does a maximum-security facility. It has barred cells and a fortified perimeter. The staff-to-inmate ratio is generally lower than that in a maximum-security facility, and the level of amenities and privileges is slightly higher. (249)

minimum-security prison   A prison that confines the least dangerous offenders for both short and long periods. It allows as much freedom of movement and as many privileges and amenities as are consistent with the goals of the facility. It may have dormitory housing, and the staff-to-inmate ratio is relatively low. (250)

misdemeanor   A relatively minor violation of the criminal law, such as petty theft or simple assault, punishable by confinement for one year or less. (8)

mission   That which is done to support an organization's purpose. (317)

mitigating circumstances   Factors that, although not justifying or excusing an action, may reduce the culpability of the offender. (510)

model of criminal sentencing   A strategy or system for imposing criminal sanctions. (66)

mores   A culture's behavioral restrictions that forbid serious violations—such as murder, rape, and robbery—of a group's values. (15)

N

networking   Meeting new people who can give you information about careers, the job market, and specific positions. It is often done through people you know. (A-2)

new offense violation   Arrest and prosecution for the commission of a new crime. (117)

no-frills prisons and jails   Correctional institutions that take away prisoner amenities and privileges. (439)

nolo contendere   A plea of "no contest." A no-contest plea may be used by a defendant who does not wish to contest conviction. Because the plea does not admit guilt, however, it cannot provide the basis for later civil suits. (12)

nominal damages   Small amounts of money a court may award when inmates have sustained no actual damages, but there is clear evidence that their rights have been violated. (358)

noninstitutional corrections   (also called *community corrections*) That aspect of the correctional enterprise that includes "pardon, probation, and parole activities, correctional administration not directly connectable to institutions, and miscellaneous [activities] not directly related to institutional care." (14)

nonrevocable parole   A type of unsupervised parole that cannot be revoked for technical violations; the person does not report to a parole officer. (279)

O

open institution   A minimum-security facility that has no fences or walls surrounding it. (251)

operational capacity   The number of inmates that a facility's staff, existing programs, and services can accommodate. (242)

P

pains of imprisonment   Major problems that inmates face, such as loss of liberty and personal autonomy, lack of material possessions, loss of heterosexual relationships, and reduced personal security. (329)

pardon   An executive act that removes both punishment and guilt.

parens patriae   A Latin term that refers to the state as guardian of minors and of people who are mentally incompetent. (526)

parole   The conditional release of a prisoner, prior to completion of the imposed sentence, under the supervision of a parole officer. (259)

parole eligibility date   The earliest date on which an inmate might be paroled. (268)

parolee   A person who is conditionally released from prison to community supervision. (271)

paroling authority   A person or correctional agency (often called a *parole board* or *parole commission*) that has the authority to grant parole, revoke parole, and discharge from parole. (268)

pay-to-stay jail   (also called *self-pay jails*) An alternative to serving time in a county jail. Offenders convicted of minor offenses are offered privileges for a fee from $75 to $127 per day. (188)

penal law   See **criminal law.** (15)

penitentiary   The earliest form of large-scale incarceration. It punished criminals by isolating them so that they could reflect on their misdeeds, repent, and reform. (210)

Pennsylvania system   (also called *separate system*) The first confinement in silence instead of corporal punishment;

conceived by the American Quakers in 1790 and implemented at the Walnut Street Jail. (210)

performance-based funding   A method of allocating money for programs that present reliable and valid data that they work.

perimeter security officers   Those assigned to security (or gun) towers, wall posts, and perimeter patrols. These officers are charged with preventing escapes and detecting and preventing intrusions. (308)

pleasure-pain principle   The idea that actions are motivated primarily by a desire to experience pleasure and avoid pain. (58)

precedent   A previous judicial decision that judges should consider in deciding future cases. (361)

predisposition report   A report that documents (1) a juvenile's background; (2) his or her educational history; (3) information gathered from interviews with the juvenile, family members, and others; (4) available placement options; and (5) recommended dispositions. (537)

presentence report (PSR)   A report prepared by the probation department of a court that provides a social and personal history as well as an evaluation of a defendant as an aid to the court in determining a sentence. (66)

principle of least eligibility   The requirement that prison conditions—including the delivery of health care—must be a step below those of the working class and people on welfare. (242)

prison   A state or federal confinement facility that has custodial authority over adults sentenced to confinement. (4)

prison argot   The special language of the inmate subculture. (331)

prison code   A set of norms and values among prison inmates. It is generally antagonistic to the official administration and rehabilitation programs of the prison. (330)

prisoner subculture   See **inmate subculture.** (328)

prisoners' rights   Constitutional guarantees of free speech, religious practice, due process, and other private and personal rights as well as constitutional protections against cruel and unusual punishments made applicable to prison inmates by the federal courts. (356)

prisonization   The process by which inmates adapt to prison society; the taking on of the ways, mores, customs, and general culture of the penitentiary. (329)

privatization   A contract process that shifts public functions, responsibilities, and capital assets, in whole or in part, from the public sector to the private sector. (192)

probation   The conditional release of a convicted offender into the community, under the supervision of a probation officer. It is conditional because it can be revoked if certain conditions are not met. (94)

profession   An occupation granted high social status by virtue of the personal integrity of its members. (16)

professional associations   Organized groups of like-minded individuals who work to enhance the professional status of members of their occupational group. (19)

professional development   The lifelong or career-long dedication to quality selection, training, and development of employees.

program staff   Those staff members concerned with encouraging prisoners to participate in educational, vocational, and treatment programs. (300)

property crime   Burglary, larceny-theft, motor vehicle theft, and arson as reported by the FBI's Uniform Crime Reporting Program.

proportionality   The sentencing principle that the severity of punishment should match the seriousness of the crime for which the sentence is imposed. (80)

pseudofamilies   Family-like structures, common in women's prisons, in which inmates assume roles similar to those of family members in free society. (343)

public accounts system   The earliest form of prison industry, in which the warden was responsible for purchasing materials and equipment and overseeing the manufacture, marketing, and sale of prison-made items. (214)

public works system   A system of prison industry in which prisoners were employed in the construction of public buildings, roads, and parks. (215)

punitive damages   Money a court may award to punish a wrongdoer when a wrongful act was intentional and malicious or was done with reckless disregard for the rights of the victim. (358)

purpose   The reason for an organization's existence. (317)

R

racism   Social practices that explicitly or implicitly attribute merits or allocate value to individuals solely because of their race. (24)

rated capacity   The maximum number of beds or inmates allocated to each jail facility by a state or local rating official. (185)

recidivism   The repetition of criminal behavior; generally defined as *rearrest*. It is the primary outcome measure for probation as it is for all corrections programs. (104)

reentry   The transition offenders make from prison or jail to the community. (192)

reentry court   A court that manages the return to the community of individuals released from prison. (285)

reform school   A penal institution to which especially young or first-time offenders are committed for training and reformation. (526)

rehabilitation   (also called *reformation*) The changing of criminal lifestyles into law-abiding ones by "correcting" the behavior of offenders through treatment, education, and training. (60)

reintegration   The process of making the offender a productive member of the community. (60)

release on bail   The release of a person upon that person's financial guarantee to appear in court.

release on own recognizance (ROR)   Pretrial release on the defendant's promise to appear for trial. It requires no cash guarantee.

relief officers   Experienced correctional officers who know and can perform almost any custody role within the institution, used to temporarily replace officers who are sick or on vacation or to meet staffing shortages. (308)

remote-location monitoring   Technologies, including Global Positioning System (GPS) devices and electronic monitoring (EM), that probation and parole officers use to monitor remotely the physical location of an offender. (144)

reprieve   An executive act that reduces the severity of punishment (e.g., from death to life imprisonment) but the person remains guilty.

residential reentry center (RRC)   A medium-security

correctional setting that resident offenders are permitted to leave regularly—unaccompanied by staff—for work, education or vocational programs, or treatment in the community but require them to return to a locked facility each evening. (146)

residential treatment center   A residential facility that provides intensive treatment services to juveniles. (538)

restitution   Payments made by a criminal offender to his or her victim (or to the court, which then turns them over to the victim) as compensation for the harm caused by the offense. (63)

restoration   The process of returning to their previous condition all those involved in or affected by crime—including victims, offenders, and society. (62)

restorative justice   A systemic response to wrongdoing that emphasizes healing the wounds of victims, offenders, and communities caused or revealed by crime. (62)

résumé   A list of your job and other related experiences and education. (A-6)

retribution   A sentencing goal that involves retaliation against a criminal perpetrator. (57)

revenge   Punishment as vengeance; an emotional response to real or imagined injury or insult. (56)

revocation   The formal termination of an offender's conditional freedom. (116)

revocation hearing   A due process hearing that must be conducted to determine whether the conditions of probation have been violated before probation can be revoked and the offender removed from the community. (116)

right of allocution   A statutory provision permitting crime victims to speak at the sentencing of convicted offenders. A federal right of allocution was established for victims of federal violent and sex crimes under the Violent Crime Control and Law Enforcement Act of 1994. (483)

riot   Any action by a group of inmates that constitutes a forcible attempt to gain control of a facility or area within a facility. (429)

roles   The normal patterns of behavior expected of those holding particular social positions. (299)

S

salient factor score (SFS)   A scale, developed from a risk-screening instrument, used to predict parole outcome. (270)

second-generation jail   Jail where staff remain in a secure control booth surrounded by inmate housing areas called *pods* and surveillance is remote. (172)

security threat groups (STGs)   The current term for prison gangs that describes how they negatively impact the security of prison operations. (423)

self-assessment   Learning who you are and what you can and want to do by evaluating your interests, skills, and values. (A-1)

self-pay-jails   See pay-to-stay jail.

sentence   The penalty a court imposes on a person convicted of a crime. (55)

sentencing   The imposition of a criminal sanction by a sentencing authority, such as a judge. (55)

sentencing commission   A group assigned to create a schedule of sentences that reflect the gravity of the offenses committed and the prior record of the criminal offender. (69)

sentencing enhancements   Legislatively approved provisions that mandate longer prison terms for specific criminal offenses committed under certain circumstances (such as a murder committed because of the victim's race or a drug sale near a school) or because of an offender's past criminal record. (70)

serious error   Error that substantially undermines the reliability of the guilt finding or death sentence imposed at trial. (512)

sexual victimization   All types of sexual activity, for example, oral, anal, or vaginal penetration; handjobs; touching of the inmate's buttocks, thighs, penis, breasts, or vagina in a sexual way; abusive sexual contacts.

social debt   The sentencing principle that the severity of punishment should take into account the offender's prior criminal behavior. (81)

social order   The smooth functioning of social institutions, the existence of positive and productive relations among individual members of society, and the orderly functioning of society as a whole. (55)

special master   A person appointed by the court to act as its representative to oversee remedy of a violation and provide regular progress reports. (438)

special-needs inmates   Those prisoners who exhibit unique physical, mental, social, and programmatic needs that distinguish them from other prisoners and to whom jail and prison management and staff have to respond in nontraditional and innovative ways.

specific deterrence   The deterrence of the individual being punished from committing additional crimes. (58)

staff roles   The normal patterns of behavior expected of correctional staff members in particular jobs. (299)

staff subculture   The beliefs, values, and behavior of staff. They differ greatly from those of the inmate subculture. (303)

state use system   A system of prison industry that employs prisoners to manufacture products consumed by state governments and their agencies, departments, and institutions. (215)

status offenses   Acts that are law violations only for juveniles such as running away, truancy, or ungovernability (sometimes referred to as *incorrigibility* or *being beyond parental control*). (532)

statutory exclusion provisions   Provisions under which adult criminal court jurisdiction for certain juvenile cases is established by state law. (545)

street gang   An organized group of people on the street often engaged in significant illegitimate or criminal activity. (548)

stress   Tension in a person's body or mind, resulting from physical, chemical, or emotional factors. (311)

structured conflict   The tensions between prison staff members and inmates that arise out of the correctional setting. (303)

structured sentencing   A set of guidelines for determining an offender's sentence. (422)

subculture   The beliefs, values, behavior, and material objects shared by a particular group of people within a larger society. (303)

substance-abusing inmate   An incarcerated individual suffering from dependency on one or more substances including alcohol and a wide range of drugs. (386)

supermax housing   A free standing facility, or a distinct unit within a facility, that provides for management and secure control of inmates who have been officially designated as exhibiting violent or serious and disruptive behavior while incarcerated. (434)

supervision   The second major role of probation officers, consisting of resource mediation, surveillance, and enforcement. (112)

sustainable justice   Criminal laws and criminal justice institutions, policies, and practices that achieve justice in the present without compromising the ability of future generations to have the benefits of a just society. (7)

syphilis   A sexually transmitted disease caused by the bacteria *Treponema pallidum*. If left untreated, syphilis can cause serious heart abnormalities, mental disorders, blindness, other neurological problems, and death. Syphilis is transmitted when infected lesions come in contact with the soft skin of the mucous membrane. (407)

T

tangible losses   Costs such as medical expenses, lost wages, and property losses that accrue to crime victims as a result of their victimization. (468)

technical violation   A failure to comply with the conditions of probation or parole. (117)

teen courts   Courts in which youths adjudicate and impose disposition for a juvenile offense. (545)

therapeutic community (TC)   A residential treatment program in which substance abuse inmates are housed in a separate unit within a prison or jail facility. (390)

third-generation jail   (also called *direct-supervision jail*) A jail where inmates are housed in small groups, or pods, staffed 24 hours a day by specifically trained officers. Officers interact with inmates to help change behavior. Bars and metal doors are absent, reducing noise and dehumanization. (173)

tort   A civil wrong, a wrongful act, or a wrongful breach of duty, other than a breach of contract, whether intentional or accidental, from which injury to another occurs. (358)

total admission   The total number of people admitted to jail each year. (168)

total institution   A place where the same people work, play, eat, sleep, and recreate together on a continuous basis. The term was developed by the sociologist Erving Goffman to describe prisons and other facilities. (327)

totality of conditions   A standard to be used in evaluating whether prison conditions are cruel and unusual. (369)

truth in sentencing (TIS)   The sentencing principle that requires an offender to serve a substantial portion of the sentence and reduces the discrepancy between the sentence imposed and actual time spent in prison. (82)

tuberculosis (TB)   A highly variable communicable disease that is characterized by toxic symptoms or allergic manifestations that in humans primarily affect the lungs. (402)

U

unconditional diversion   The termination of criminal processing at any point before adjudication with no threat of later prosecution. Treatment, counseling, and other services are offered and use is voluntary. (93)

UNICOR   The trade name of Federal Prison Industries. UNICOR provides such products as U.S. military uniforms, electronic cable assemblies, and modular furniture. (236)

unit management system   A method of controlling prisoners in self-contained living areas and making inmates and staff (unit manager, case manager, correctional counselor, and unit secretary) accessible to each other. (230)

utilitarianism   The principle that the highest objective of public policy is the greatest happiness for the largest number of people. (45)

V

victim   A person who suffers direct or threatened physical, psychological, or financial harm as a result of the commission or attempted commission of a crime or delinquent act. (460)

victim assistance program   An organized program that offers services to victims of crime in the areas of crisis intervention and follow-up counseling and that helps victims secure their rights under the law. (482)

victim compensation   A form of victim assistance in which state-funded payments are made to victims to help them recover financial losses due to crime. (477)

victim-impact statement   A description of the harm and suffering that a crime has caused victims and survivors. (62)

victim notification   Notification to victims of the release or pending release of convicted offenders who have harmed them. (471)

victimless crime   An offense committed against the social values and interests represented in and protected by the criminal law, and in which parties willingly participate. (92)

victims' rights   The fundamental rights of victims to be represented equitably throughout the criminal justice process. (461)

violent crime   Interpersonal crime that involves the use of force by offenders or results in injury or death to victims. In the FBI's Uniform Crime Reports, violent crimes are murder, forcible rape, robbery, and aggravated assault.

vision   The planned future direction of an organization. (317)

W

waiver provisions   Provisions under which the juvenile court orders transfer of the case to adult criminal court. (544)

work detail supervisors   Those who oversee the work of individual inmates and inmate work crews. (307)

writ of *habeas corpus*   An order that directs the person detaining a prisoner to bring him or her before a judge, who will determine the lawfulness of the imprisonment. (357)

Y

yard officers   Those who supervise inmates in the prison yard. (308)

youth gang   A gang whose membership generally comprises people between the ages of 12 and 24. (548)

PHOTO CREDITS

CASE INDEX

SUBJECT INDEX

A

Abdel-Rahman, Omar, 321, 426
absconding, 117
Abu Ghraib prison (Iraq), 213, 217
Academy of Fists, 44
accountability, 19, 56
accreditation, 17, 442–444
  defined, 201, 442
  reasons, 442–444
Achilles, Mary (career profile), 475
acquired immunodeficiency syndrome
  (AIDS), 392. *See also* AIDS/HIV
ACT (Assertive Community Treatment)
  Program, 401
Adam Walsh Child Protection and Safety
  Act of 2006, 464
Adams, Brooke, 493n
addiction theory, for female offenders, 180
adjudication, 12, 537
adjudicatory hearings, 537
administrative model of sentencing,
  66–67
administrative officers, 308
advisory sentencing guidelines, 67, 69
Affordable Care Act (ACA) of 2011,
  241–242
African Americans. *See* ethnicity/race age.
  See also juvenile justice system; juvenile
  offenders; juvenile victims
    older inmates, 402–407
    prison inmate, 79, 224, 328, 340,
      402–407
Age of Reason, 1, 42
aggravating circumstances, 510
agitator inmate role, 333
AIDS/HIV, 56, 171, 265, 297, 385, 386,
  389, 392–397
  dealing with inmates, 395
  definitions, 392
  education and prevention, 395–397
  legal issues, 408–409
  treatment, 392–395
Alabama
  citations, 167
  correctional econometrics, 246, 280
  female inmates, 338–339, 379
  jails/prisons, 219, 338–339, 379
  parole and reentry, 274, 280
  probation, 104
Ala-Pietila, Pekka, 134
Alaska
  jails/prisons, 167–168
  mental health care, 182
  parole and reentry, 274, 277
  Albin, Lisa, 308–309

Alcatraz (California), 213, 215–216,
  432–434
alcohol. *See* substance-abusing inmates
Alexander, Samantha, 471
Alexander, Travis, 14, 471
Alford, Lynch, Sr., 505
al-Qaeda, 321
Amaker, Tommy, 124
Aman, Reinhold, 332n
Amber Alert Law, 466
American Association for Community
  Psychiatrists, 401
American Bar Association (ABA)
  death penalty moratorium, 507
  disclosure of presentencing report, 111
  jails, 199
  pretrial release standard, 165
American Board of Anesthesiologists, 507
American colonies, corporal punishments,
  32–34, 36
American Correctional Association (ACA),
  1, 192
  centennial congress of 1970, 50
  certification, 20–21, 191
  classification, 226
  community corrections, 152, 153
  community service and restorative
    justice, 138, 139
  correctional health care, 239
  correctional officer characteristics, 304,
    305
  correctional officer wages, 244
  Corrections Compendium, 440–441
  ethics, 18, 21
  "guard" as term, 299
  higher education policy, 22
  hospice care, 404
  identifying inmates with special needs,
    386
  inmate education programs, 238
  intermediate sanctions, 128
  jail standards, 201
  juvenile justice, 551, 552
  mental health testing, 397
  mothers in prison, 345–346
  offenders with special needs, 387
  prison riots and disturbances, 429–430
  professional development, 19, 551
  reentry, 268, 269
  role of corrections, 15
  sentencing, 65
  standards and accreditation, 17, 442,
    443
  universal precautions, 395
  use of force, 433
  victims of crime, 467, 471, 472

women in corrections, 309
women's prison guidelines, 338
American Federation of Labor (AFL), 236
American Federation of State, County and
  Municipal Employees, 192
American Jail Association (AJA), 1, 19,
  192
  Code of Ethics for Jail Officers, 200
  intermediate sanctions, 128–129
  Jail Manager Certification Commission
    (JMCC), 21
  jail standards, 201
  mission statement, 169–170
American Medical Association (AMA),
  408, 507, 519
American Probation and Parole
  Association (APPA), 1, 19, 96, 97, 106,
  113, 128–129, 156–157, 259, 260,
  263, 283, 467
American Psychological Association, 519
American Public Health Association,
  345–346
American Revolution, 36, 42, 259
Americans with Disabilities Act (ADA) of
  1990, 403, 408
Amini, Payam, 492
Amnesty International, 492
Andrade, Leandro, 77
Anti-Drug Abuse Act of 1988, 495, 497
Antiterrorism and Effective Death Penalty
  Act (AEDPA) of 1996, 513
Aos, Steve, 225
APIC, 194
APPA. *See* American Probation and Parole
  Association (APPA)
appellate review, 13
Apprendi, Charles, 72
Aramark, 187–188
Arenas, Gilbert, 146
Arias, Jodi, 14, 471
Arizona
  community corrections/supervision,
    156
  correctional officer job satisfaction, 315
  intermediate sanctions, 137, 154, 156
  jails/prisons, 188, 220, 438
  parole and reentry, 264
  privatization movement, 447
  probation, 264
Arkansas
  intermediate sanctions, 127
  jails/prisons, 186, 355
  parole and reentry, 274, 282
  sentencing, 243
Arpaio, Joe, 188
arraignment, 12